HARDPRESS.NET
HOME OF HARD-TO-FIND BOOKS

The Eclectic Review

by Samuel Greatheed

Address:
HardPress
8345 NW 66TH ST #2561
MIAMI FL 33166-2626
USA
Email: info@hardpress.net

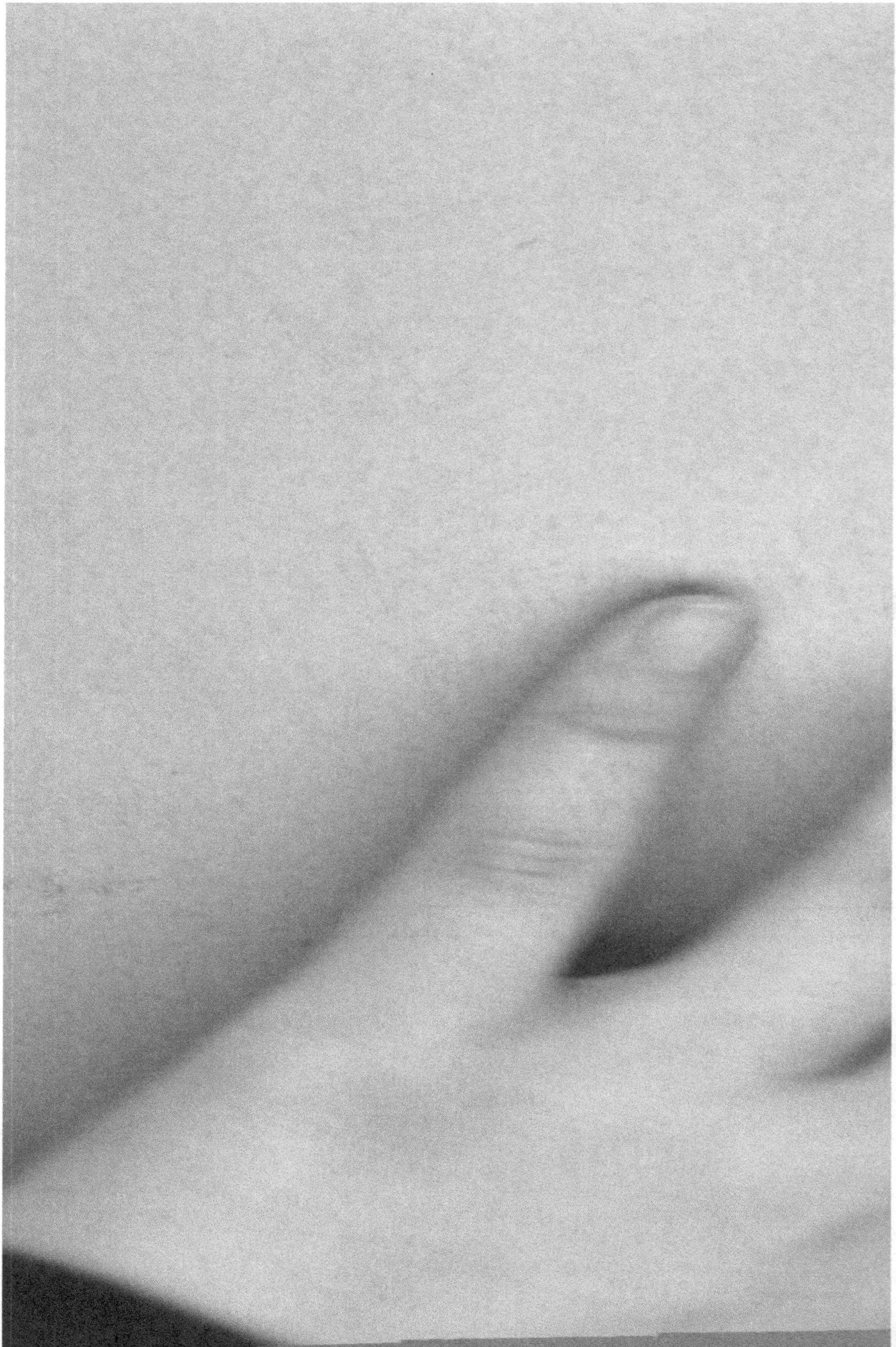

THE

ECLECTIC REVIEW.

MDCCCXLVI.

JANUARY—JUNE.

(1846)

Φιλοσοφίαν δὲ οὐ τὴν Στωικὴν λέγω, οὐδὲ τὴν Πλατωνικὴν, ἢ τὴν Ἐπικουρεῖον τε καὶ Ἀριστοτελικήν· ἀλλ' ὅσα εἴρηται παρ' ἑκάστῃ τῶν αἱρεσέων τούτων καλῶς, δικαιοσύνην μετὰ εὐσεβοῦς ἐπιστήμης ἐκδιδάσκοντα, τοῦτο σύμπαν το ἘΚΛΕΚ-ΤΙΚΟΝ φιλοσοφίαν φημι.—Clem. Alex. *Strom.* L. I.

NEW SERIES.

VOL. XIX.

LONDON:
THOMAS WARD & CO., PATERNOSTER ROW.
W. OLIPHANT AND SON, EDINBURGH;
JAMES MACLEHOSE, GLASGOW.
1846.

LONDON:
PRINTED BY G. H. WARD & CO.,
16, BEAR ALLEY.

THE

ECLECTIC REVIEW

For JANUARY, 1846.

Art. I.—*Histoire du Consulat et de l'Empire, par A. Thiers, &c. &c.* Vols. 1—5. Paulin, rue Richelieu, Paris. 1845. [History of the Consulate and the Empire.]

After his final downfall, in 1815, Napoleon was constantly appealing to posterity for a just appreciation of his character, and was incessantly expressing, to his faithful attendants, his certainty of a triumphant acquittal, *au tribunal de l'histoire*. More than thirty years have elapsed since the tornado which had so long devastated Europe, broke powerless on the rocks of St. Helena. Twenty-five years ago, the doubly imprisoned soul of the conquered chieftain was released from all earthly bondage; and, during the last quarter of a century, most of the companions and witnesses of his achievements have carried with them into their tombs, their love or their hatred, their admiration or their contempt. For more than two-thirds of the present generation, the consulate and the empire are almost as far removed into the past, as the conquests of Alexander and of Cæsar. Posterity, for Napoleon, has begun; the tribunal of history is open for the investigation and the settlement of his claims to the gratitude of France, and to the admiration of the whole world.

But it is not every one that has a right to ascend the judicial seat, in this solemn court, and to pass judgment, not on this one man only, but also upon his contemporaries of every country,—upon an epoch which, although short, if we consider its

LONDON:
PRINTED BY G. H. WARD & CO.,
16, BEAR ALLEY.

THE

ECLECTIC REVIEW

For JANUARY, 1846.

Art. I.—*Histoire du Consulat et de l'Empire, par A. Thiers, &c. &c.* Vols. 1—5. Paulin, rue Richelieu, Paris. 1845. [History of the Consulate and the Empire.]

After his final downfall, in 1815, Napoleon was constantly appealing to posterity for a just appreciation of his character, and was incessantly expressing, to his faithful attendants, his certainty of a triumphant acquittal, *au tribunal de l'histoire.* More than thirty years have elapsed since the tornado which had so long devastated Europe, broke powerless on the rocks of St. Helena. Twenty-five years ago, the doubly imprisoned soul of the conquered chieftain was released from all earthly bondage; and, during the last quarter of a century, most of the companions and witnesses of his achievements have carried with them into their tombs, their love or their hatred, their admiration or their contempt. For more than two-thirds of the present generation, the consulate and the empire are almost as far removed into the past, as the conquests of Alexander and of Cæsar. Posterity, for Napoleon, has begun; the tribunal of history is open for the investigation and the settlement of his claims to the gratitude of France, and to the admiration of the whole world.

But it is not every one that has a right to ascend the judicial seat, in this solemn court, and to pass judgment, not on this one man only, but also upon his contemporaries of every country,—upon an epoch which, although short, if we consider its

LONDON:
PRINTED BY G. H. WARD & CO.,
16, BEAR ALLEY.

THE

ECLECTIC REVIEW

For JANUARY, 1846.

Art. I.—*Histoire du Consulat et de l'Empire, par A. Thiers, &c. &c.* Vols. 1—5. Paulin, rue Richelieu, Paris. 1845. [History of the Consulate and the Empire.]

After his final downfall, in 1815, Napoleon was constantly appealing to posterity for a just appreciation of his character, and was incessantly expressing, to his faithful attendants, his certainty of a triumphant acquittal, *au tribunal de l'histoire*. More than thirty years have elapsed since the tornado which had so long devastated Europe, broke powerless on the rocks of St. Helena. Twenty-five years ago, the doubly imprisoned soul of the conquered chieftain was released from all earthly bondage; and, during the last quarter of a century, most of the companions and witnesses of his achievements have carried with them into their tombs, their love or their hatred, their admiration or their contempt. For more than two-thirds of the present generation, the consulate and the empire are almost as far removed into the past, as the conquests of Alexander and of Cæsar. Posterity, for Napoleon, has begun; the tribunal of history is open for the investigation and the settlement of his claims to the gratitude of France, and to the admiration of the whole world.

But it is not every one that has a right to ascend the judicial seat, in this solemn court, and to pass judgment, not on this one man only, but also upon his contemporaries of every country,—upon an epoch which, although short, if we consider its

duration, seems to form an age, through the multiplicity and the magnitude of the events which fill it. If, in providing for the judicial adjustment of all the differences resulting from personal rivalries and collisions, inherent in the social state, every well regulated government scrupulously attends to a proper choice of adjudicators, and takes great care that none shall be raised to the bench, but men of sound learning, of acknowledged integrity, of pure morals, in short, men of unspotted character; why should not the same good qualities be required in the men who presume to place themselves above every body and every thing; and, assuming the highest magistracy, to call to their bar, men, judges, legislators, and even governments themselves? Is it not necessary, that, before listening and giving credit to the summing up and sentence of the self-appointed lord chief justice in the court of history, we should inquire into his qualifications for the proper discharge of his duties?

M. Thiers must pass through this ordeal. To proceed methodically, we will first sketch his character. But, no! We have known him long, we know him well; and, if we were to pourtray him as we see him, as he really is, our readers would not fail to attribute to violent and inveterate hatred, that which a profound sentiment of justice alone would extort from us. Instead, therefore, of speaking our own mind, we will have recourse to the two most eminent moral and political writers of France, Lamennais and Cormenin, though both, in our opinion, have treated their subject with too much indulgence. We begin with Lamennais; and, as no translation could do justice to the style of the author, we beg to be allowed to quote the French text:—

'Un des auditeurs (in the gallery of the Chamber of Deputies) lui désigna une petite figure remuante et glassissante. Oh! que c'est drôle s'ecria-t-il. Vraiment, je te crois bien; mais n'approchez pas trop les singes mordent. Ce n'est pas que celui-ci soit, de sa nature, ou par calcul, par systême fort méchant; ce serait être quelquechose et cela oblige toujours. Il n'a ni rancune, ni pitié, ni amour, ni haine. Singe d'État, Singe á portefeuille, et, pour le portefeuille, n'hesitant jamais à livrer l' etat. Aucun autre ne gambade, ne grimace comme lui; il a des tours sans nombre, aussi comme on l'admire, comme ils sont contents, hors d'eux mêmes sitôt qu'il parait, les Ratons de ce Bertrand: celui la surtout, de ce coté, à gauche, si bien fourré, si bien léché, si grave, si profond, si plein de rien, je veux dire de lui meme.* Pour Bertrand, il rit, il se moque, il promet des marrons. Promettre est ce qui lui coute le moins. Le cynisme, en lui, n'étonne point, tant il lui est naturel,

* This short description unfortunately applies too well to Odillon Barrot.

c'est sa puissance et son orgueil, et sa séduction et sa grace. En dehors de tout ce qui a un nom dans le bien comme dans le mal, il se dérobe al'indignation et au mépris même : il passe pour dessous. Sentiments, opinions, maximes, principes, vrai, faux, juste, injuste, autant de jouets pour lui. Et la patrie, et son honneur et ses libertés, et sa gloire, quest-ce à ses yeux ? un objet de trafic ; quelque-chose qui se vond.* (Lam. Amschaspands et Darrands. Let 36, p. 166. Paris, 1843.'

Here is a subject for *Cruikshank :* a monkey sitting *in banco*, and passing judgment in the case of *Napoleon v. the whole world*. We readily admit that such a lithograph, from the pencil of the illustrious caricaturist, would be the most effective review of the History of the Consulate and the Empire. But let us now listen to Cormenin. (Livre des Orateurs, par Timon. Paris, 1842.)

'M. Thiers was not, on entering this world, dandled on the lap of a duchess. Born in poverty and obscurity, he felt the want of wealth, and *of a name*. Failing completely as a barrister, he made himself a *litterateur*, and gave himself up altogether (*se jetta à corps perdu*) to the liberal party, not from conviction, but from necessity. Then he took to admiring Danton, and the conventionals of the 'Montagne ;' and carried to the utmost exaltation the speculative fanaticism of his hyperboles. Worried with wants, like all men of quick imagination, he was indebted to Lafitte for his first comforts, and to his own peculiar talent for his reputation. Yet, had not the revolution of July occurred, M. Thiers would now probably be neither an elector, nor an eligible, nor a deputy, nor a minister, not even an academician, but would have come to old age, with only the literary esteem of some small coterie.

'But, since the revolution, M. Thiers has assumed another charac-

* 'One of the spectators, pointing at a small figure of a man, ever strutting and gobbling like a turkey cock—'Oh! how droll,' cried he. "Indeed, I believe you ; but do not go too near. Monkeys bite. This one, however, is not, naturally, speculatively, or systematically, very bad ; that would be to be something, and, to be something, always binds one ; he has neither rancour nor pity, neither love nor hatred. A state monkey, a monkey with a portfolio ; and for a portfolio never hesitating to betray the state ; no one wheels about, jumps about, and grins like him. His tricks are innumerable. Now, see how he is admired. So soon as he appears, how gratified, how transported are the Ratons of this Bertrand ! (An allusion to La Fontaine's fable of the Monkey and the Cats.) That one particularly on the left, so very neat, so well furred, so solemn, so full of nothing, I mean of himself. As to Bertrand, he laughs, he jokes, he promises chesnuts. To promise is that which costs him least. Cynicism, in him, does not surprise, it is so natural to him ; it constitutes his strength, his pride, his seductiveness, his gracefulness. Stranger to every thing that has a name in good or evil, he escapes indignation, and even contempt ; he sneaks under. Sentiments, opinions, principles, maxims, truth, falsehood, just, unjust, are all so many playthings for him ; and France, and her liberty, and her honour, and her glory, what are they to him ? Marketable articles ; something to sell.'

ter in the political drama. He has made himself the originator, promoter, and panegyrist of dynasties, the supporter of privileges and monopolies, the issuer and executor of merciless orders. He has for ever bound up his name with the martial law decreed in Paris, with the *mitraillades* (grape shooting) at Lyons, with the resplendent achievements of the Rue Transnonain, with the transportations to Mont St. Michel; with the new bastilles; with all the laws against associations, newspapers, and criminal courts of justice; with all that has fettered liberty; with all that has branded the press; with all that has corrupted juries; with all that has decimated patriots; with all that has annihilated the national guard; with all that has demoralized the nation; and, finally, with all that has prostrated in the mire, the generous and pure revolution of July.'—(pp. 553—4.)

Our readers may be inclined to think that M. Lamennais's monkey has become a tiger in the hands of M. Cormenin. This, however, is not the case. Timon himself says (p. 549), 'Taken altogether, M. Thiers, if he is not a saint, is not a bad man; he has not sufficient energy either to love or to hate. He can be led into cruel excesses, but he would not commit them from his own impulse.' This opinion, agreeing as it does with that of Lamennais, confirms the judgment which we lately found in an English newspaper. 'Guizot is the Marat of the new terrorism; Thiers is its Barrère.'

'A sceptic in religion, in morals, in politics, in literature, there is no truth which can make a deep impression on the mind of M. Thiers; there is no sincere and absolute devotion to the cause of the people, which he does not laugh at.' (Timon, p. 539.) 'M. Thiers himself declares that there are no principles; which evidently means that M. Thiers has no principles himself. (p. 554.) 'M. Thiers will speak for three hours on architecture, poetry, jurisprudence, marine, strategy, although he is neither an architect, a poet, a jurisconsult, a sailor, nor a military man;'—'fine arts, roads, railways, canals, finances, trade, history, transcendental politics, street police, theatres, war, literature, religion, pleasures, morals, everything, great, middling, or small, he is ready upon all, because he is really ready upon nothing.' (p. 545.) 'But pray, do not dissipate his illusion, when, at the tribune of the Chambers, he works himself up to heroical exaltation, and launches into strategical operations! Then, indeed, he believes himself to be not a mere general, but *a generalissimo*, and, in case of need, a high admiral. He will maintain against Soult, that, when he evacuated Genoa with his army, he passed through the gate of Italy, and not that of France. He will prove to the old marshal, and the chamber will applaud, that the bullet which wounded him at Salamanca, struck his left leg, and not the right, as Soult had hitherto thought; he will argue the point with such confidence, that the veteran general will involuntarily put his finger to his wound, to ascertain if he has not hitherto deceived himself.' (p. 538.)

Such are the moral and mental qualifications of the would-be spokesman of posterity on one of the most eventful epochs of the world, and on the men who have acted the principal parts in the political drama which closed the last, and opened the present century. Our readers, after such sketches of the character of the historian, may form a just idea of the character of his work; but, as we said before, even Lamennais and Cormenin have dealt too leniently with him, and the five volumes before us furnish abundant proofs, that Thiers is, with regard to intellectual powers, much under, and, with regard to political depravity, much above the standard given, three or four years ago, by two first-rate moral and patriotic writers.

Our task in reviewing this work is not an easy one. It has no plan, no method, no order. Like the History of the French Revolution, to which it is intended to form a sequel, it is nothing but a compilation from the *Moniteur*, and the other newspapers of the epoch, and the numerous laudatory publications written by order, and under the surveillance of the imperial censorship; a compilation made in haste, without reflection, without discrimination, nay, even without any regard for, we cannot say truth (Thiers despises truth), but even consistency in falsehood, which would, at least, show some labour and ingenuity. There is not in the volumes now published, a single new fact revealed or elicited, not a single document of any importance produced in explanation of unintelligible transactions, in justification of harsh and imprudent measures, in corroboration of the excuses preferred for the Consular and Imperial misdeeds. A few insignificant letters, on matters of no importance to the administrative and military orders, are the only documents which are given; and they prove nothing but the scribbling mania which possessed Napoleon, and his propensity to meddle with everything, and to bore every one of his subalterns. Of course, this is a proof of the all embracing genius of the great man, who issued, dated from the Kremlin in 1812, a decree to reorganize the *Théatre Français,* and to determine the number and length of the new plays which the performers were to act every month. If such be the measure of the greatness of royal or imperial minds, we are sure the Napoleon of peace beats hollow the Napoleon of war.

We cannot give our readers a more accurate idea of M. Thiers's performance, than by supposing the publication, at the present day, of those parts of the Annual Registers, entitled the History of Europe, beginning in 1799, and ending in 1815. Such a work would be as much the history of the Consulate and the Empire as the volumes now before us. There is scarcely any difference in the arrangement of the matters in point of historical composition, although there is a great difference in the appreciation of the facts; the English annals being remarkable for their impartiality and their accuracy; besides which, they always give, in support of the opinions pronounced, the numerous parliamentary and official documents referring to the matters in question. In Thiers's history, admiration for Napoleon is substituted for impartiality: garbled statements take the place of accuracy, and, instead of official documents, we have pretended extracts from pretended papers in the archives of the government; extracts which we must admit as authentic, on the good faith of our historian! The good faith of M. Thiers! *Credat Judæus Apella!*

Admitting, as we do, with every one who knows him, that Thiers *'a infiniment d'esprit,'* perhaps more than any one else, three times as much as he would want, if one third of it were turned into common sense, and the second third of it into common honesty; we could not help wondering, after reading the first five volumes of his history, that he should have compromised his reputation as a wit, by a publication which politicians of the modern school as well as true patriots, men of good taste as well as men of sound principles, must all equally condemn. Indeed, we could not believe that he was the real author of the work to which he has prefixed his name; and, in our protracted peregrinations in France, during the last six months, frequently meeting with some of our political and literary friends, who had also been the friends of Thiers, we expressed our doubts upon the subject; and the answers we received were to the following effect.

Literary industry, like all other species of industry, has, long ago, felt the advantages of the *division du travail.* Division of labour has for many years been applied to the different branches of literature; to the theatre, to philosophy, novels, poems, and history. The play writers, the philosophical writers, the historians of a certain rank in the literary, the social, or the political world, have all their journeymen, each of whom has his special task, his peculiar piece of work to prepare, so as to be easily adjusted with the parts prepared by his fellow-labourers. The whole is afterwards made up, by the chief author, who gives to it his name, receives the principal portion of the remuneration, and monopolizes all the credit of the work, when the work is creditable at all. This process, imitated from the Geneva watch makers, was first adapted to French literature by M. Guizot, who was thus enabled to acquire a renown for deep learning and extraordinary diligence. M. Cousin followed the example, and the result was the publication of his translation of Plato. It is now-a-days a general practice among the great men of France, who, having to attend to their pleasures and to their social duties, that is to say, to show themselves in all the saloons, have hardly a moment to give to literary or scientific labours. M. Thiers, who is as busy as any other man of pleasure in France, and who, besides that, though removed from the official cares of government, is nevertheless constantly absorbed in the meditation of the great things which he will have to achieve when restored to power, cannot be found fault with, for doing what every body else does. It must, on the contrary, be admitted, that no one can compete with him in ability, for regulating, coördinating, and appropriating to himself the ideas, the views, the contributions of his literary labourers, and for making them conducive to his own purpose. This is real authorship, and it cannot be denied to M. Thiers.

Without at all giving our assent to this opinion of our friend, we did not think it necessary to discuss the matter, particularly as we had another question to elucidate; so we immediately made our second observation, relating to the absolute deficiency of official documents, in support of his statements; a *lacuna* which perhaps would not be much remarked in a history published by a private individual, yet which cannot but forcibly strike every reader of a history written by an ex-president of the council, and successively minister of finance, of the home department, and of foreign affairs. Our interlocutor, a well informed and trustworthy gentleman, did not hesitate to answer our question; and his answer is not *hors d'œuvre* in our essay; therefore we give it.

It was a few months after his dismissal, and since the triumphant return of the remains of Napoleon, that Thiers announced his intention of publishing the History of the Consulate and the Empire. The King, having just witnessed the manifestation of Napoleonic enthusiasm, not unmixed with severe reflections upon his own policy, had begun to regret the attempt made to recover some popularity, by the honours so inconsistently paid to the ashes of the sovereign whom he had so long treated as a cruel usurper; whose family was still exiled from France, and whose nephew had just been sentenced to perpetual imprisonment in the fortress of Ham. He imagined, at all events, that enough had been done for Napoleon, by re-installing his statue on the top of the column in the Place Vendôme, and by granting to his remains a last resting place under the dome of the *Invalides*; and that, henceforth, M. Thiers, the promoter of the two measures, would never again awake the hateful recollections of imperial greatness, so startlingly contrasting with the politic subserviency of the new dynasty to the will of the European powers. The announcement of Thiers's intentions could not but cause great dissatisfaction; nay, even more; it was considered as a threat, and justly so; for Louis Philippe himself, during the Consulate and the Empire, had acted a part which the historian could not well overlook and suppress, and which, after his return to France, as Duke of Orleans, he had constantly endeavoured to bury in complete oblivion. The ex prime-minister had anticipated the effect likely to be produced by the publicity given to his project, and greatly enjoyed the alarms of the prince, by whom he had just been so treacherously dismissed. Negociations were entered into, and continued for more than two years, to prevent the obnoxious publication, by the restoration of the author to favour and to power; but the terms proffered by the Court, and the conditions insisted upon by Thiers, were so different, that no agreement could be come to, and the only result of the negociation was to widen the breach between the parties; when Thiers, seeing that, so far as it depended upon the King, he had no longer any chance of recovering his former situation (and he would accept of nothing less), began in earnest the compilation now before the public.

The King and his ministers, in their own defence, adopted the very best plan to baffle the designs of their enemy. They could not prevent him from throwing his projectiles, the volumes which were to cover with shame the author and abettors of the system of *peace at any price;* but they could render those volumes valueless and harmless, by withholding from the author all the official documents, which alone could, by their publication, give to the work an authority, an authenticity, which it could never derive from the character of M. Thiers. The archives of the home department were closed against him by Duchatel; those of the minister at war, by Marshal Soult; and those of the Foreign Office, by Guizot. The last, which are the most important of all, for the elucidation of the causes of so many convulsions in Europe, are under the care of a rival; M. Mignet, the author of a history of the French Revolution, published at the same time as that of Thiers, and generally considered much superior. It is, moreover, confidently said, that M. Mignet has long been engaged in writing a history of Napoleon; and that, notwithstanding his former friendship with Thiers, he keeps to himself the archives of the foreign office, of which he is the director.

Now that we have made our readers acquainted with the character of our author, that we have explained the ultimate object of his publication, that we have accounted for the want of such documentary evidence as would corroborate the statements and justify the conclusions of the writer, we must proceed to the examination of the work.

We will begin with the return from Egypt.

'General Bonaparte, owing to the news he had received from Paris, determined immediately to leave Egypt, and ordered Admiral Ganteaume to send out of the harbour of Alexandria, and to station in the roadstead of the Marabout, about five miles west of the town, the two frigates which had escaped from the destruction of the fleet, la Muiron and la Carrère. On the 22nd of August, taking with him Generals Berthier, Murat, Lannes, Andreossi and Marmont, and Messrs. Monge and Berthollet, two of the scientific men who had accompanied the expedition; he proceeded to the Marabout, went precipitately on board, and sailed immediately, from fear that the English ships would appear. The horses on which they had ridden, having been left upon the beach, galloped back to Alexandria, where their reappearance spread the utmost alarm. . . . General Menou, who had been chosen confidant, announced the departure of the general in chief, and the appointment of General Kleber as his successor.

'. . . . Kleber assumed the command. . . . . A report on the state of the colony being made by his orders, he sent it to the Directory with a letter full of errors, and with a report of M. Poussielgue, financial administrator in chief, in which the conduct of General Bonaparte was represented in the most false and incriminatory light.' . . . . 'Kleber stated in his despatch, that the general in chief was fully aware of the threatening crisis, and had no other motive for his hurried departure; and M. Poussielgue concluded his report with a calumny; saying, that General Bonaparte had taken away with him two millions of francs. To complete this picture, it ought to be known, that General Bonaparte had showered favours on M. Poussielgue.' *—vol. ii. lib. 5.

After thus relating the facts, with his usual partiality, M. Thiers devotes many pages to the refutation of the reports derogatory to the honour of Bonaparte. Of course, he knows the condition of the army, and the military and financial resources which the country could afford, much better than the general and the financial administrators. He proves that the affairs of Egypt had been left in the most favourable situation; he demonstrates it by a multitude of facts and arguments, which reflect the highest credit upon the imaginative powers of the would-be Quintus Curtius of the modern Alexander. The whole is intermingled with attacks upon the character of most of the generals, of civil officials, and even upon the army, who were loud in their execrations against the runaway general.

* In May last, M. Poussielgue, then residing in Italy, and in the ninety-second year of his age, being apprised of the calumnies contained in the second volume of M. Thiers's history, wrote to the editors of the principal newspapers in Paris a letter, in which he proves the rectitude of his own conduct and the malice of his slanderer. He died two months afterwards.

Had Bonaparte been overtaken by the English, or had the intrigue of his brothers with some generals and members of the two councils been baffled, in spite of his previous campaigns in Italy, nobody would ever have heard a word in justification of his desertion. A court martial summoned to investigate his conduct, would have cut short his glorious career, and saved France and Europe, not only from despotism and devastation, but also from the corrupting influence of the prosperity of treachery and successful ambition; but, as M. Thiers says, (vol. i. lib. 1,) 'Young Bonaparte, ever fortunate and victorious, escaping the perils of the sea as well as the perils of war, returned in a miraculous manner; and, on his appearance in France, the Directory was overthrown.' The despatches and the reports of Kleber and Poussielgue were delivered into his own hands, *en duplicate*; and probably would to this day have remained unknown, if the originals, intercepted by English cruisers, had not immediately been published in the London newspapers. The publicity thus given to the accusations compelled him and his partisans to look for a justification somewhere else than in the situation of the army of Egypt.

M. Thiers reproduces all that has been said during the last forty-five years against the directorial government; the administrative anarchy, the anxiety, the alarms of the people, the disorder of the finances, the destitution of the armies, the successes of the coalition. Then he exclaims, (lib. i.) 'Can any one wonder if France, to which the Bourbons could not be proposed in 1799, and which, after the bad result of the directorial constitution, had no longer any faith in the republican system, should throw herself into the arms of the young general who had conquered Italy and Egypt; a stranger to all parties, affecting to despise them all; a man of energetic will, equally skilful in civil and military affairs, and who, even in the excess of his ambition, instead of alarming the nation, seemed to fill her with hope? It required much less glory than he had achieved, to enable a man to seize the government. . . . All parties went to him, demanding of him order, victory, peace.' Such, according to M. Thiers, are the causes and the object of the revolution of the 18th Brumaire, and M. Thiers is but the echo of a thousand other writers, including Lacretelle.

Yet all this is false. Had the press been free, after the overthrow of the Directory, all these falsehoods would have immediately been repelled; but from 1799 to 1815, under Napoleon, the liberty of the press had given way to the censorship: and nobody was allowed to mention the Directory, except to follow in the train of its accusers, and to repeat over and over again, that Napoleon had dethroned anarchy, and was the saviour of

France. From 1815 to the accession of Charles X., in 1823, under the Bourbons and the doctrinaires, the censorship continued to stifle public opinion. Bonaparte, indeed, could not be brought forward, but to be branded as a tyrant and a usurper; but, at the same time, nobody could undertake the defence of the Directory, and vindicate the wise, mild, and patriotic conduct of most of its members. So soon, however, as the censorship was abolished, a defence of the directorial government was prepared, and published by the last president of the directors, the noble-minded Gohier, who, before and on the 18th Brumaire, resisted both the seductive entreaties of Bonaparte and Josephine, and the violence of the soldiery, obstinately refusing to abdicate an authority with which he had been invested by the people, and of which the people alone had a right to dispossess him. We cannot but recommend the perusal of the 'Memoires de Gohier' to those of our readers who have leisure, and are fond of historical truth. Gohier died in June, 1830, in the eighty-fifth year of his age. Of course, in the opinion of Thiers, he was a fool.

The revolution of the 18th Brumaire may be explained in very few words. According to the constitution of 1795, all public functions were at the disposal of the people, and subject, after a certain period of time, to re-elections, which gave the people a check upon the representative, administrative, and judicial functionaries. Many of them, afraid of losing the situations to which they had been elected, and of being reduced to the rank of simple citizens, could not but find fault with a system which made them dependent on the popular will; and they naturally thought, that it would be much better for themselves if popular will and electoral sovereignty were done away with, and if the monopoly and perpetuity of offices were secured to the occupants. This change could not be accomplished except by a revolutionary movement. It was clear that they could not reckon upon the co-operation and the strength of the people, to make a revolution against the rights of the people, and that they could not succeed, unless by a *coup de main*, executed by a military force. But to obtain the assistance of the military, it was necessary to obtain the assent, and in some sort to place themselves under the leadership, of a general known and respected by the army. This was resolved upon. General Bernadotte was first sounded; but, at the mere mention of a change in the constitution, he answered in such a manner as to leave no hope of his co-operation. An application to Augereau was equally unsuccessful. The conspirators built their last hopes on General Joubert, to whom the command of the army of Italy had been recently given; but Joubert, instead of conquering the Austrians, as was anticipated, was defeated and killed in the same battle. No one dared think of Moreau for this criminal attempt against the republic. At last Bonaparte was thought of, and every one was sure that he would readily lend himself to anything; but his already too-well known ambition, his overbearing manners, and his violent temper, did not exactly suit the views of the principal conspirators. They had some misgivings as to the probable consequences of his participation in the overthrow of the existing government; and, though his brother Lucien, with the two Fregevilles, and some other members of the Council of Five Hundred, did their utmost to calm the anxiety of their colleagues, they could not prevail upon them to require the services of the aspiring general. Lucien, in his correspondence with his brother, did not fail to inform him of what they were preparing, of the proposals already made to several generals, and of the chances of success, if, instead of being in Egypt, he were present in Paris. This news reached the general just at a time when he was fully aware of the folly of the expedition, notwithstanding the success with which it had at first been attended; and when, after the destruction of his fleet, he saw himself and his army completely separated from the mother country, without means of obtaining reinforcements, money, provisions, and ammunition, surrounded by an insurgent population, and on the eve of being attacked by the bulk of the Ottoman forces. In these circumstances, he thought his best chance was to run away to Paris; and he lost no time in doing so.

This plain and true relation of the event may one day become the real history; but we are still very far from that day. The present history runs thus. 'Providence, taking pity on France, inspired Napoleon, took him by the hand, brought him back, placed him in the consular chair, and afterwards on the imperial throne, to restore to the country order, victory, peace, and prosperity.' Ever since the 18th Brumaire, this has been the text of all the official harangues, of the declarations in the legislative assemblies, of the books published by historiographers, of the sermons of preachers, of the *mandements* (charges) of the bishops, and of the allocutions of the Pope himself.* The five volumes on our table, are but a recapitulation of these admiring ravings.

Our readers, some of them at least, may be inclined to doubt

* In 1814, a pamphlet containing the principal passages of all these compositions, was published under the following title. 'Oraison funèbre d'un grand homme, par u'ne société d' hommes d' etat, senateurs, legislateurs, évêques, préfets, magistrats, et autres.' The author, who did not put his name, is M. Peuchet, now librarian of the House of Deputies.

[illegible]

On the arrival of Bonaparte in Paris the five directors were Gohier, the President; Barras, Sièyes, [illegible] and Roger Ducos. Barras, a Marquis before the Revolution, [illegible] during the Convention. Yet when he became a Director he surrounded himself with the [illegible] in Paris. A man of pleasure and of [illegible], his house was the *rendezvous* of the elegant world [illegible], particularly of the ladies, renowned for their charms, among whom were Josephine Beauharnais, afterwards Madame Bonaparte, subsequently Empress, and Madame Cabarrus, afterwards Madame Tollien, afterwards Marchioness of Caraman and subsequently Princess of Chimay. Through the influence of the ladies, many of the emigrants were allowed to return. Their gratitude represented Barras as very different from what he had shown himself. Some old royalists, who were indebted to him for their return and the recovery of their property, sounded him upon his republican principles, and were so encouraged by his replies as to represent to him all the advantages he might obtain and secure to himself, by promoting the restoration of the Bourbons. This led to negociations in which Louis XVIII. himself took part. In short, before the 18th of Brumaire, Barras was meditating the best means of bringing back the old monarchy; and, notwithstanding his denials, his colleagues were convinced of his treachery. This was the first cause of division in the Directory.

Sièyes hated Barras with all the hatred of a Jansenist. Their ideas, their tastes, their habits, were so much in contrast, that, being unable to agree upon any one single point, they hardly spoke to each other. In the meantime, Sièyes was almost equally dissatisfied with his other colleagues, who, in his own opinion, were not impressed with the idea of his superiority, a

of conquering the Austrians, as was anticipated, was defeated and killed in the same battle. No one dared think of Moreau for this criminal attempt against the republic. At last Bonaparte was thought of, and every one was sure that he would readily lend himself to anything; but his already too-well known ambition, his overbearing manners, and his violent temper, did not exactly suit the views of the principal conspirators. They had some misgivings as to the probable consequences of his participation in the overthrow of the existing government; and, though his brother Lucien, with the two Fregevilles, and some other members of the Council of Five Hundred, did their utmost to calm the anxiety of their colleagues, they could not prevail upon them to require the services of the aspiring general. Lucien, in his correspondence with his brother, did not fail to inform him of what they were preparing, of the proposals already made to several generals, and of the chances of success, if, instead of being in Egypt, he were present in Paris. This news reached the general just at a time when he was fully aware of the folly of the expedition, notwithstanding the success with which it had at first been attended; and when, after the destruction of his fleet, he saw himself and his army completely separated from the mother country, without means of obtaining reinforcements, money, provisions, and ammunition, surrounded by an insurgent population, and on the eve of being attacked by the bulk of the Ottoman forces. In these circumstances, he thought his best chance was to run away to Paris; and he lost no time in doing so.

This plain and true relation of the event may one day become the real history; but we are still very far from that day. The present history runs thus. 'Providence, taking pity on France, inspired Napoleon, took him by the hand, brought him back, placed him in the consular chair, and afterwards on the imperial throne, to restore to the country order, victory, peace, and prosperity.' Ever since the 18th Brumaire, this has been the text of all the official harangues, of the declarations in the legislative assemblies, of the books published by historiographers, of the sermons of preachers, of the *mandements* (charges) of the bishops, and of the allocutions of the Pope himself.* The five volumes on our table, are but a recapitulation of these admiring ravings.

Our readers, some of them at least, may be inclined to doubt

* In 1814, a pamphlet containing the principal passages of all these compositions, was published under the following title. 'Oraison funèbre d'un grand homme, par u'ne société d' hommes d' etat, senateurs, legislateurs, évêques, préfets, magistrats, et autres.' The author, who did not put his name, is M. Peuchet, now librarian of the House of Deputies.

our accuracy, and to suspect our impartiality. We cannot find fault with them for their distrust, if they say, as many of our friends have done, 'These occurrences cannot be as you represent them. How could a runaway general with some few adherents and a troop of soldiers, upset the five directors and the two representative councils, if he had not been backed by the people? Supposing even that the upsetting of the government could have been easily accomplished by a small but resolute band; how could their leader not only assume, but also maintain himself in, possession of the supreme power, if the nation had been averse to him, and if the superiority of his genius had not been so universally acknowledged, that all readily submitted to him; that France, as M. Thiers says, threw herself into the arms of the hero?'—Facts shall answer.

On the arrival of Bonaparte in Paris, the five directors were, Gohier, the President; Barras, Sièyes, Letourneur, and Roger Ducos. Barras, a Marquess before the Revolution, had, like most of the revolutionists of his order, signalised himself by his violence during the Convention. Yet, when he became a director, he surrounded himself with the remnants of the nobility then in Paris. A man of pleasure and of sumptuous habits, his house was the *rendezvous* of the elegant, we do not say moral, company, particularly of the ladies, renowned for their charms, among whom were Josephine Beauharnais, afterwards Mdme. Bonaparte, subsequently Empress, and Mdme. Gabarrus, afterwards Mdme. Tollien, afterwards Marchioness of Caraman, and ultimately Princess of Chimay. Through the influence of the ladies, many of the emigrants were allowed to return. Their gratitude represented Barras as very different from what he had shown himself. Some old royalists, who were indebted to him for their liberty and the recovery of their property, sounded him upon his republican principles, and were so encouraged by his replies, as to represent to him all the advantages he might obtain and secure to himself, by promoting the restoration of the Bourbons. This led to negociations in which Louis XVIII. himself took part. In short, before the 18th of Brumaire, Barras was meditating the best means of bringing back the old monarchy; and, notwithstanding his denials, his colleagues were convinced of his treachery. This was the first cause of division in the Directory.

Sièyes hated Barras with all the hatred of a Jansenist. Their ideas, their tastes, their habits, were so much in contrast, that, being unable to agree upon any one single point, they hardly spoke to each other. In the meantime, Sièyes was almost equally dissatisfied with his other colleagues, who, in his own opinion, were not impressed with the idea of his superiority, as they ought to have been, and too frequently in the management of the government would not give way to his dictatorial utopias. In consequence of this, Sièyes was the very first to blame, even in public, the measures of the Directory, and to bring his colleagues into discredit: a second cause of division among the directors.

Gohier and Letourneur were republicans at heart; and, notwithstanding the difficulties which harassed the march of the institutions, were convinced that they were calculated to increase the freedom, the independence, the security, and the happiness of the nation. As to Roger Ducos, he was a republican, because France was a republic, and because, as one of the Directors, he was bound to uphold the Republic, without attaching much importance to the form which it had assumed, or might afterwards assume. But he, as well as his two colleagues, was a man of strict integrity, and also, like them, could boast of having passed through the revolution, without sharing in the cruelties and rapine with which Barras and Sièyes were reproached.

Bonaparte, on his return, was soon made acquainted with the disposition of the directors and with the causes of their quarrels. He owed his fortune to Barras, from whom he had received his appointment and his wife; but his love for Josephine, amounting to jealousy, had inspired him with a deadly hatred against the first protector of the widow of Beauharnais. Not only would he have nothing to do with him; but also he resolved upon his ruin. Sièyes was the man to assist him in the execution of his plans. He therefore went to Sièyes, professed the highest admiration for his political genius, expressed his regret that, owing to the anomalous organization of the executive power, that genius was in some sort fettered, checked, lost to the country; and gave it, not only as his own opinion, but also as the opinion of all the generals and of the army, that such a state of things ought to be put an end to: in short, that France, instead of five directors, wanted one powerful and experienced mind to give her laws suitable to her present situation, and one strong and victorious arm to defend her against her domestic or foreign enemies.

Sièyes clearly saw what was expected from him. His meditative and analytic mind immediately perceived two consuls instead of five directors: which was a great improvement, inasmuch as he would have to contend against but one instead of four, in carrying out his plans; and this one, too, a man still in the prime of life, who had seen nothing but the camp, was ignorant of all that relates to legislation and civil administration, and who, though illustrious by his victories, was the first to proclaim *Cedant arma togæ,* and promised to be entirely guided by the superior wisdom of the modern Solon. Sièyes could not hesitate long, and his hesitations could not withstand the constant marks of deference and respect which on all occasions the young general showed him. He resolved to upset his colleagues and with them the constitution.

An open attack against the Directory would have been hazardous. Sièyes and the best advisers of Bonaparte devised another plan, which consisted in bringing about the suicide of the Directory. Three of the directors resigning their functions and, at the same time, calling upon the councils to change the form of government, was all that was required. Roger Ducos was induced by Sièyes to resign at the same time with him, on condition of being also made a Consul, which was granted. Before giving publicity to their resignations, Sièyes and Roger Ducos, seconded by Bonaparte and a few members of the two councils, compelled Barras to set the example, by threatening him with an accusation of high treason against the Republic, for having corresponded with Louis XVIII. and his agents for the purpose of restoring the Pretender to the throne. Barras, conscious of his guilt, immediately yielded. The resignations of the three directors were sent to the two councils; in order that, in consequence of the disorganisation of the executive, they might appoint a provisional government. A member of the Council of Five Hundred, of which Lucien was president, made the motion, that General Bonaparte, Sièyes, and Roger Ducos, should be appointed provisional consuls, and that they should, with as little delay as possible, present a new constitution for the adoption of the people. The majority of the assembly rose with indignation; a scene of tumult ensued, which seemed likely to end in the discomfiture and expulsion of the conspirators, when a battalion of grenadiers entered the hall of the council and closed the session.

Now, then, let our readers say if, either in the concoction or in the execution of the plot, there is anything in which a man of only ordinary ability could possibly pride himself. In what part of this deplorable transaction do they perceive the glorious influence of genius? No doubt that the consequences for France and for the whole world are still incalculable; perhaps new catastrophes resulting from the transactions of that day are still in reserve for ourselves, or for our descendants; but the drama itself and the performers are equally contemptible. Instead of the profound and skilful combinations of a powerful mind, we have but an intrigue supported by cunning and hypocrisy; and, as to the denouement, instead of a bold and striking action, we have an irruption of cut-throats.

The further success of Bonaparte will be as easily accounted for, without supposing the intervention of anything like genius. All the military commands in Paris and in the departments were immediately given to his accomplices; so that, during the few days devoted to the settlement of the new constitution, he exercised a military dictatorship, as Narvaez does at this moment in Madrid, with two queens instead of two co-consuls. This dictatorship, however, could not have lasted long, as, with the exception of the army of Italy, all the generals and officers were hostile to despotisms, civil or military. It was necessary, therefore, to look somewhere else for support. The new constitution, which Sièyes had long meditated, with the object of founding a sort of political papacy, of which he himself was to be the sovereign pontiff, was promulgated on the 13th of December, 1799; with the modifications which the growing ambition of the military ruler had exacted, not without angry discussions, and quarrels, followed by a determination, on the part of Sièyes, now aware of his folly, to have nothing more to do with his treacherous and ungrateful colleague.

By this constitution, all the political rights of the people were confiscated. Hitherto, since the establishment of the Republic, legislative and administrative functionaries were elected by the citizens. This was done away with, and the appointment to all offices was appropriated by the government. Thus the consuls, that is to say, Bonaparte alone, had at once to dispose of eighty nominations to the senate, with an allowance of 2,500 francs to each senator; of one hundred nominations to the tribunate, with a salary to each tribune of 15,000 francs; of three hundred nominations to the legislative body, each legislator being paid at the rate of 10,000 francs a year; and, finally, of about fifty nominations to the council of state, each member receiving 25,000 francs. Such was the division of the legislative power, as regulated by this constitution.

As to the administrative organisation, it was settled upon the same principle: all the communal and departmental authorities of every kind elected by the people, were suppressed. The consul had the exclusive right of appointing the head agents of the executive, and their subordinates, the departmental and municipal councils, the prefêts and sub-prefêts (an innovation), the mayors and their substitutes; all the judges of the civil and criminal courts, and of the tribunals of appeal; all the officers of the several branches of the financial administration; in short, of all the functionaries of the state.

More than three hundred thousand places were thus at the disposal of the consul. In Paris, as well as everywhere in the departments, candidates for all these places offered themselves in numbers tenfold that of the offices to be disposed of, and to qualify themselves for them, rivalled one another in admiration for the hero of the day, and in zeal for his service. Three millions of votes were recorded in favour of the new constitution, and in acknowledgment of the authority of the first consul. Thus was the work of cunning and treachery supported by egotism and corruption. And this is what stupid or degraded beings proclaim as the triumph of an extraordinary genius! This is what blasphemers call 'the hand of Providence !'

But the majority of the French people could not be dazzled, seduced, and corrupted. The greatest part even of those who had, in the first moment, given their assent to the liberticide government, would soon have been undeceived; and, warned by the patriotic and bold denunciations of a free press, would have rallied round the flag of freedom, and made a stand against the usurpations of the ambitious upstart. The grand genius who was likely to be worsted, in the conflict between conscientious and eloquent patriotism, on one part, and overbearing tyranny, on the other, foresaw the danger, and guarded against it with his customary ability. He suppressed a great many newspapers, and allowed the publication of the rest, only on condition that they should contain nothing against the constitution, against the executive, against the army, against the foreign governments in alliance with France. Immediate suppression was the penalty awaiting those newspapers which should transgress the orders of the consul.

This last piece of dictatorial legislation was the complement of the free institutions which the revolution of Brumaire had secured for Republican France. *Order* [such appears now to be the name for irresistible tyranny] being thus reestablished in the interior, the first consul turned his attention towards the exterior. Elated by his successes in taking possession of the superior authority in his own country, he nevertheless felt, in his inmost soul, that this authority was but precarious, and that, even in France, it would never be considered as firmly established, so long as it was not, in some sort, sanctioned, by the acknowledgment of foreign governments. To obtain that sanction, principally from England and from Austria, had become the most urgent of his desires, and therefore, without any *overtures*, without complying with any of the diplomatic formalities, he wrote two letters, the one to George the Third, the other to the Emperor of Austria.

The first, which M. Thiers considers as a master-piece, is in the following terms :—

'Paris, 5th Nivose, an 8, (26 December, 1799.)

'Sire—Having been called, by the will of the French people, to the chief magistracy of the Republic, I think proper, on assuming my office, to announce the fact to your majesty, in a direct communication.

'Shall the war, which, for eight years, has ravaged the four parts of the world be eternal? Is it impossible to come to a good understanding?

'Why do the two most enlightened nations of Europe, more powerful than is necessary to their safety and independence, sacrifice the advantages of commerce, their internal prosperity, their domestic happiness, to ideas of imaginary greatness? Why do not they feel that peace is the first of blessings, the first glory?

'These sentiments cannot be alien to your Majesty, the ruler of a free nation, whose happiness is your only object.

'In this communication, your Majesty must see nothing but my sincere wish to contribute, for the second time, to a general pacification, by the adoption of prompt, and strictly confidential measures, without those formalities which may be useful to weak states, to conceal their dependency, but which, when adopted by powerful nations, only betray deceitful intentions.

'France and England may yet, for a long time, and to the distress of all nations, abuse their strength, and retard its exhaustion, but I am bound to say, that the destinies of all civilised nations are dependent upon the termination of a war which has thrown the whole world into combustion.

'The first consul of the French Republic. Bonaparte.'

M. Thiers does not give the text of the answer which Lord Grenville, in the name of the administration, sent to Talleyrand for the reason we have already explained. He only gives what he asserts to be the meaning, a sort of analysis, of the 'negative, *clumsy, uncivil, indecent note,* which was disapproved by sensible men of all countries;—reflected little honour on the character of Mr. Pitt, and betrayed in him more passion than intelligence.' The answer of the Austrian government, though expressed in milder terms, was not much more satisfactory; and the continuation of the hostilities was resolved on.

These thwartings were not the only ones Bonaparte was doomed to experience. According to the constitution, the legislative session was to be immediately open; and consequently the senate, the tribunate, and the legislative body met on the 1st of January, 1800. The tribunes and the legislators had been, for this first time, chosen by the senate, and the senators had been appointed in the following manner. Twenty-nine had been chosen by the first consul, in concert with Cambaceres and Lebrun, the new second and third consuls, and with Sièyes and Roger Ducos, the late consuls. Sièyes and Roger Ducos, dissatisfied with the treatment they had received, were intent upon placing in the senate men of energy as well as of ability, and staunch republicans, who should not allow the dictator to have all his own way. Cambaceres, warned by the fate of his friend, and having already learned how little he could depend upon the general-consul, supported most of the candidates of his predecessors. Thus it was that, among the senators who were first appointed, are found men known for their hostility to all the changes recently made in the constitution; and, as the tribunes and the legislators had been chosen by the senators, we cannot wonder if some men of the same character found their way to the tribunate and the legislative body, and prepared for resisting the encroachments of the executive.

The first act of each of the three assemblies was an act of opposition. The senate chose Sièyes for its president. The tribunes elected Daunou, and the legislators elected Perrin des Vosges. These acts were followed up by many others, in the tribunate, the only one of the three assemblies which was allowed to discuss the bills prepared by the government and the council of state; the functions of the legislators and of the senators being confined to vote by ballot on the bills introduced by the council of state or by the tribunes. Their opposition, during the first session, which lasted four months, though unsuccessful in the attempt at rejecting the bills presented, had at least the advantage of stopping the Dictator, in his march towards absolute despotism. He could not, however, dissemble his anger against the tribunes, nor refrain from threatening observations, which being reported, had no other effect than to increase the number of his opponents, and stimulate their courage to such a degree, that in their second session, though Bonaparte had recently been victorious at Marengo, they rejected the bill which had been prepared, by his order, for the establishment of extraordinary tribunals, to try cases of conspiracy against his person*; and many other measures, including his financial plans. The senators and the legislators, though far from being so spirited as the tribunes, had nevertheless given such marks of hostility, on two or three occasions, that the first consul had publicly declared to a deputation of the senate, that, 'if they chose to find fault with all the bills submitted to them, he would get rid of them, and govern by consular decrees.' Nothing daunted by this menace, the tribunes and the legislators prepared for their third session. In anticipation of the concordat, which was to be presented for their acceptation, the legislators, at their first meeting, elected for their president M. Dupuis, the author of 'L'origine de tous les cultes.' As to the tribunes, they were presented with the

* It was immediately after the explosion of the infernal machine (24th of December, 1800), that the bill was introduced; and the tribunate was aware of the use that the consul would make of it.

first part of the 'civil code, that admirable work, which alone would immortalize Napoleon;' and, after a discussion in which the real authors of the work, and the work itself, were very ill treated by the tribunes, they not only rejected the admirable code, but also caused it to be thrown out by the legislative body.

The rage of the first consul, at the news of the rejection of his chef d'œuvre, knew no bounds. M. Thiers devotes many pages to the reproduction of his invectives and of his sarcasms, against the bad faith and the insolence of the factious tribunes, and to the justification of the plan adopted by Napoleon, and which he carried into execution, to rid himself of their opposition. This plan consisted in the arbitrary exclusion of the leaders of the opposition in the two assemblies, and in the equally arbitrary appointment to the places thus vacated, of men ready to abide by the expressed will of the first consul. This new improvement in the constitution of republican France paved the way for the imperial throne.

We have frequently heard people wonder at the opposition of the legislative bodies against 'Bonaparte, at a time when his military operations, in Italy and in Germany, not only had preserved France from another invasion, but also had extended her territories, created new friendly states in the conquered countries, and compelled the belligerent powers to sue for the peace which they had so haughtily rejected when proffered by him.' Even now, many will still, with the imperialist writers reechoed by M. Thiers, accuse the tribunes and the legislators of ingratitude, and regard them as a set of incorrigible Jacobins. The names of the leaders of the opposition would be a satisfactory answer to this accusation and these false representations; whilst on the contrary, the lists of the supporters of Bonaparte present a gang of terrorists of the first water. But incriminations and recriminations are little calculated to elucidate political questions; and, for our own part, we prefer to base our judgment on the attentive consideration of all the facts.

No sooner had Bonaparte been seated in the consular chair, than, conscious of the illegitimate means by which he had risen to the first magistracy, and of the utter impossibility of long withstanding the attacks of the true republicans, supported as they were by the best generals, and the best part of the army, he looked for support, not only to those unprincipled men who have no other political creed or affection than the honour and the profits of office, but also to the royalist party, which he wished to mislead into the belief, that he was not disinclined to become a second Monk. For that purpose, he showed a great regard for the members of the old nobility; affected to give them the preference over their competitors, in the distribution of all offices; and granted to them the erasure, from the lists of the emigrants, of their relations and friends, to whom he, besides, restored their confiscated but still unsold property. He courted the good-will of the catholic clergy, by extending, in their favour, the provisions of the laws passed under the Directory, for the liberty of religious worship, and by affecting to consider the catholic religion as the only true one. With the emigrants and the priests, he was enabled to induce the leaders of the Vendeans to regard him as an ally in the royal cause, rather than as an enemy. The repeal of the law of hostages, and the release of the priests, were the preliminary measures to the negociations which were entered into, with too sanguine hopes, on the part of the royalist insurgents, to whom he offered, in the republican army, the same rank that they held in the Bourbonist bands. A suspension of hostilities was agreed upon, and was soon afterwards followed by the complete submission of *la Vendée.* So convinced were the leaders of the Vendeans of the intention of Bonaparte to bring about a restoration, that a great number of them, and, among these, George Cadoudal, repaired to Paris, to make terms with the first consul. Nay, even more, a few months later, the pretender wrote to the consul, to hasten the execution of his plans, and to tell him, '*Choisissez votre place, et fixez celles de vos amis.*' (2nd vol., book 6.)

Can any one wonder, if, under such circumstances, knowing well, by experience, the perfidious dispositions of Bonaparte, and convinced of the truth which Fox illustrated in these few words: 'The worst of revolutions is a restoration;' can any one wonder, we say, if the tribunate and the legislative body determined to resist all the measures which, by increasing the influence and the strength of the first consul, supplied him with the means of betraying the country, and of annihilating the revolution for which half a million of Frenchmen had already shed their blood? No doubt the indulgence shown to unfortunate (and many of them misled) emigrants, was an act of mercy, which all kind hearted men are bound to applaud; but to invest with the highest legislative or administrative functions, under the republic, those emigrants who, rather than assent to a limitation of the royal authority, and submit to constitutional monarchy, had fled to foreign countries, had arrayed all the absolute sovereigns against France, and had borne arms against their country:—to call those men to share in the government, was treason. No doubt the respect shown for the liberty of religious worship, the liberation of the priests, the re-opening of the churches, were sound and beneficial measures; but to rekindle religious fanaticism, to restore priestcraft, to impose a state religion, was treason. No doubt the pacification of La Vendée, was a blessing to the country at large, since it permitted the Republic to unite all the national forces against her foreign enemies; but to unite with the Vendeans in order to secure himself in power; and afterwards, with their assistance, prostrate the republic at the feet of a king: this, again, was treason. How, then, can we accuse of ingratitude, and brand as factious and Jacobins, the tribunes and the legislators who, attentive to the object and to the consequences of these too much bepraised measures, clearly perceived, and did their utmost to arrest, the march of treason.

Here again we are stopped by another objection. We are told:—'The tribunes and the legislators were wrong. Bonaparte never intended to restore, and, in fact, did not restore the Bourbons; *ergo*, all your reasonings go for nothing.' We have not said that Bonaparte intended to restore the Bourbons; we know not what he really intended to do; though we are convinced that, if he had not seen his way clear up to the throne, or if he had found out that his best chance of ever obtaining a high and permanent situation, with competent affluence, was in the restoration of the Bourbons, he would immediately have made the bargain. All we have stated is, that he made such advances to the old nobility, to the emigrants, and to the Vendeans, as to persuade them that he was *inclined* to a restoration; that they would obtain it more easily through him, and by supporting him, than by continuing to fight. They yielded, and they soon found out that they had been deceived. He did not restore the Bourbons, because he thought it would be a folly to give away a crown which, he imagined, he could keep for himself.

But if the tribunes and the legislators were justified in their opposition when they, as well as the majority of the French, suspected the Consul of preparing for a restoration; they were no less so when, in all his conduct, in the intrigues of his family, and in the frequently indiscreet manifestations of his confidential friends, they found indubitable proofs of his ambitious designs. The success of the campaign of 1800 in Italy, and the victory of Marengo, seemed, to him and to his friends, to afford a good opportunity for making a step in advance towards the sovereign power, and for preparing the public mind for the establishment of a new monarchy. An emigrant who, since his return to his native land, had exchanged his Bourbonism for the favours of Eliza Bonaparte, and who, through her influence, had been made a legislator; Fontanes (the friend of Chateaubriand) was chosen to send up the pilot balloon. He published a '*parallele entre Cesar, Cromwell, Monck, et Bonaparte*,' the object, and the conclusion of which was, the evidence of the superiority of

Bonaparte over all the three, and the necessity of bestowing upon him a power equal to his greatness.

This production of Fontanes was profusely distributed in all parts of France, by the agents of the government; but the effect produced was the reverse of that which was anticipated. Everywhere it was received with scorn and indignation, by the royalists, by the partisans of the convention, and by moderate republicans. Even the partisans of Bonaparte themselves blamed the publication of such a work, as premature, imprudent, and mischievous. To counteract, as much as possible, the dangerous impression which it had made on all minds, the Consul and the Ministers disavowed all participation in the preparation, or in the publication of the work; but the complicity was so positively proved, that the disavowal, far from mending the matter, made it worse, by proving that the haughty First Consul could be made to recoil. The legislators and the tribunes were right in taking advantage of it.

The faction, therefore, was compelled to adjourn all the plans so sanguinely elaborated. They had miscalculated the influence of the victories of Napoleon, not only upon the public mind in France, but also upon the foreign powers. Exaggerating, as they usually did, all the acts of Bonoparte, they had represented the victory of Marengo as the last blow struck at the Austrian power, and this misrepresentation seemed to be confirmed, by the armistice which followed the battle, and the consent given by Austria to meet in congress at Luneville. But another disappointment awaited them. Far from being so humbled and so helpless as to be ready to submit to any condition, as she was represented, Austria rejected the preliminaries imposed by the French plenipotentiaries, and resolved to take the chances of another campaign, in Germany as well as in Italy. The First Consul did not choose to share in the perils of this last campaign. The command of the army of Italy was given to General Brune, and the army in Germany was left under the command of Moreau, who, in the course of three weeks, swept before him the Austrian army, gained the battle of Hohenlinden, and, for the first time, led a French army to the gates of Vienna. 'He might have entered the place,' admits M. Thiers (Vol. ii. book 7), 'and secured the glory, which no French general had ever had, of conquering the capital of the Germanic empire. But the modest mind of Moreau did not allow him to be extreme in prosperity. The Archduke Charles gave him his word, that, if he granted an armistice, Austria would immediately make peace, on the conditions proposed at Luneville; and Moreau assented. Some of his lieutenants urged him to advance on Vienna. 'No,' replied Moreau, 'it is better to secure peace.' Thus, the real conqueror of the Austrians, the real pacificator, by M. Thiers's own avowal, was Moreau. Yes, to his military talents, to his bravery, to his moderation, France was indebted for the peace of Luneville; which, leaving England without allies on the continent, was soon after followed by the peace of Amiens. Yet, instead of claiming any credit for his achievements, of exhibiting himself to the public, of courting popularity, he returned to his retreat, where his young wife,* and the affection of his companions-in-arms, gave him all the happiness he wished for.

Bonaparte knew how to take advantage, not only of the victories, but also of the repose of his rival. Freed from all anxiety on the part of Austria, he disposed of the Italian principalities, the conquest of which had been secured by the last campaign. With a portion of those territories, he, a republican, the first magistrate of a republic, formed a kingdom, the kingdom of Etruria: he united Piedmont to France, and, with the rest, he formed a republic, of which, by all sorts of artifices, complacently related by M. Thiers, and eulogized as the perfection of diplomatic ability, he got himself appointed 'Président à vie.' He gave the kingdom of Etruria to the Prince of Luques, who came over to Paris, to express his gratitude to this consular protector.

Having thus shown his partiality for presidencies for life, and for royalty, is it surprising that the tribunate, and the legislative body, should have at last positively declared against him? Far from deserving reproaches for having done so, they ought to be reproached with not having done it sooner and with more spirit. Their remissness and their moderation gave to their enemy, to the enemy of freedom, the necessary time to strengthen himself, to combine and mature all his plans, to avail himself of every circumstance for turning to his own advantage, and his own glory, all the events that occurred: so that, at last, he was powerful enough to turn them out and to give their places to his own creatures.

Such was the state of the Tribunate and of the legislative body, when the conclusion of the treaty of Amiens, which gave peace to the world, was hailed with enthusiastic joy, amounting to madness; as it is too frequently the case with the French, when any grand political change occurs. They were told that henceforth, the blessings of peace, agriculture, industry, commerce,

* Moreau had recently married a young lady of large property, Mdlle. Hulot. She constantly shared in the prosperity and in the misfortunes of her husband, and died three or four years after him.

opulence, happiness were for ever secured to them. For ever? no! They were indebted, for those blessings, to the extraordinary genius which providence had sent to their assistance; but his power was limited to ten years, at the expiration of which he must resign. What then would be their lot? Was it not proper to ponder upon this matter? Was it not their interest to prolong and increase their prosperity, by prolonging, for life, the powers of the man who, in a few years, had done so much for them? Was not that a just reward of his past services, and, at the same time, the best security for the welfare of the nation?

All these questions having been reproduced, in every form, by the enslaved newspapers, were subsequently presented in a regular and official form to the nation at large, after a fruitless attempt to get a satisfactory answer from the senate, and without consulting either the tribunate, or the legislate body. The Council of state, all nominees of the First Consul, was summoned, and conformably to the orders given to them, came to the following resolution,—'The French people shall be consulted on the following questions: 1. Shall Napoleon Bonaparte be Consul for life? 2. Shall he have the right of appointing his successor? Registers, to record the votes of the citizens, shall be deposited, during three weeks, at the mayor's offices in every *commune* (parish) at the registrars of all the tribunals, and at the offices of the notaries and of all public functionaries.' About three millions of votes were for the affirmative. The senate, the tribunate, and legislative body, rather than rekindle civil war set the example of submission.

Thus it was that an illegal and unconstitutional measure, proposed by a body which was not qualified for the initiative, and approved of, by less than one-third of the citizens, (supposing, what we know to be false, that the registers were honestly kept,) raised Bonaparte to permanent power, and gave him an authority little short of that of an absolute monarch. Yet he was not satisfied; he expected more, and was determined to have both the power and the title belonging to autocratic authority: and he immedediately set to work to have his will complied with.

He rewarded the complicity of his two colleagues, by making them consuls for life too. With the exception of a few republicans, who remained faithful to their principles, the senators had generally complied with all his whims, he therefore invested it with constituent power; and, at the same time, to guard against the introduction of opponents in that body, he assumed the right of nomination to that dignity. He changed the principal provisions of the constitution; chose a body of electors for life; reduced the tribunate to the humble proportions of a mock council of state; established a privy council; organized the Catholic clergy, so as to make them subservient to his interests; altered the laws relating to public instruction, in order to better educate the people according to his own views. Doing away with the republican institution of *arms of honour*, he resolved to start a new aristocracy, by the institution of the *legion of honour*, and increased his own salary, from 500,000 francs to 6,000,000 francs, and that of his two colleagues, from 150,000 francs to 1,200,000 francs. And when he had accomplished all this, when these new institutions of the Consular Republic were promulgated, 'La France,' says M. Thiers, 'ressentit la plus profonde satisfaction.' (Vol. iii. Book 14.)

The conclusion of the peace, and the pretended conspiracy of Arena, had furnished the principal arguments for the establishment of the consulate for life; the rupture of that peace, the war with England, and the conspiracy of George Cadoudal and Pichegru, were afterwards a just motive for making the consul an emperor. This may appear rather inconsistent to our readers; but M. Thiers is of a different opinion; that is enough. The first book of the fifth volume (the 19th of the work), gives a long account of the transactions which led to this result. We need not follow our author, and prolong this already too long article, by even a short analysis of the details given. It would but be a repetition of the acts of hypocrisy, of treachery, of meanness, corruption, and apostacy, which we have already exposed, and which were the main, if not the sole instruments, of the rise, and of the extraordinary fortune of Napoleon. The only variation to be recorded, is that, in order to become an emperor, Napoleon did not again choose to consult the nation, and to open registers for recording the votes of the citizens: he was satisfied with a decree of the constituent senate; the very senate, nay, even more, the same men who, ten years later, decreed his '*deehéance,*' and hurled him from his throne into exile!

If we have expatiated to such an extent upon one part only of the work of M. Thiers, *the causes and the means of the rapid advance of Napoleon* to the highest rank that a citizen born ever reached, it is because we have considered this part the most important of all. It is in human nature to attribute, without much reflection, marvellous effects to marvellous causes; and a poor Corsican boy, reared up by royal charity, becoming the dictator of the European continent, is one of those prodigious transformations which inspire almost every mind with the idea of extraordinary genius, and of supernatural power. Courtiers, flatterers, poets, historians, have very little to do, to deepen and to perpetuate that impression; and as they are liberally paid to do this little, they rival one another in zeal for the propagation of the worship of the new demigod, protected, as they are, against all contradictions, by bills of pains and penalties. But why should we now forbear from steadfastly looking on the pretended demigod, from investigating his nature, from tracing his march, from showing him in his nakedness, we would say in his nothingness? But alas! he was something.

Not that, as a general, he is the greatest captain that ever existed. M. Thiers, indeed, constantly gives him that title in his history; but unfortunately and unconsciously proves the contrary in those parts of his work devoted to military operations, the 2nd, 3rd, 4th, 5th, 7th, and 10th books. His relation of the battle of Marengo (book 3rd, 1st vol) proves that it was brought about by faults in the movements of the army; that it was lost under the command of Bonaparte, who had been surprised by the enemy, and in spite of the intrepid defence of Ney; and that it was won by the timely arrival of Dessaix, who, without orders, nay, even more, contrary to former orders, left his positions, and, guided by the roaring of the cannon, reached the field of battle, and renewing the conflict, decided the victory which cost him his life. This accident, however, does not hinder our historian from attributing immediately after, and throughout the whole work, to Bonaparte, all the glory of Marengo*; though, at the same time, an attentive perusal of the books referring to military operations seems to establish that, there is a still greater captain than Napoleon, or any one else. It is M. Thiers himself. One is surprised, on seeing how he improves the organisation of the army; how he directs its movements; how he disposes the several corps over the vast extent of country which he will conquer; how certain his 'coup d'œil,' in cases of emergency; how he mends the blunders of the generals, of Bonaparte himself; how he follows up a success to its ultimate consequences; how, in short, he displays, in his own person, all the different qualities of the best generals.

Bonaparte was a consummate negociator, 'the sublime of diplomatic skill,' according to M. Thiers, who enters into the most minute details of all the negociations of the consul, with Spain, Prussia, and the United States of America, to maintain them in a state of neutrality, or to induce them to pass from neutrality to an alliance with France;—with the pope for the concordat, and for his coronation; and, with Russia, Sweden, and Denmark, to obtain from them a renunciation of the English alliance, in which he succeeded at last, notwithstanding the difficulties in

* 'The real conqueror at Marengo was therefore the general who had *chained* fortune, by his profound and admirable combinations, unparalleled in the history of great captains!' (1st vol., book 3.)

treating with such notorious madmen as Paul and Gustavus. But, even in the narrative of M. Thiers, the sublime of diplomatic skill appears to be low cunning, falsehood, treachery ; and, when all this fails, fits of uncontrollable passion, insults and threats, followed with a declaration of war. This system of foreign policy is praised to the skies, in every part of the books of M. Thiers, not under the unparliamentary names we give to it, but under the more decorous titles of *finesse*, caution, dissimulation, and dignity. Bonaparte was a model in all this ; yet the work insinuates that there is some one still superior, and it is M. Thiers himself, who discovers many faults in the diplomatic transactions of Bonaparte ; faults which he, Monsieur Thiers, would have avoided, by his superior knowledge of the nations of Europe, and of their governments, of their interests, their wants, their tastes, even their prejudices and their passions, which, in political affairs, must be taken into account. M. Thiers besides that, would not have been, in some circumstances, so confident and so indiscreet; or, in other circumstances, so spiteful and so irascible. He would not have insulted Lord Whitworth, the British ambassador, at a public levee. Decidedly Lord Palmerston and Louis Philippe were very wrong, five years ago, when the first would have no more diplomatic intercourse with the pattern of diplomatists, and when the second took from him the ministry of foreign affairs. We must admit, in extenuation of their fault, that M. Thiers had not yet published his history of the consulate.

'As a statesman and a legislator, nobody can be compared with Bonaparte: his organising mind (son esprit organisateur) embraced and placed all things in their proper order. France was a chaos, and Bonaparte, on his arrival from Egypt, called her into existence; and made her an object of respect and admiration to all the nations of the world.' It is in these terms that M. Thiers expresses his own unbounded admiration for the successive alterations in the institutions of the country; for the transformation of the Republic into an empire, and for the author of that wonderful metamorphosis. 'But however great as a warrior, however sublime as a negotiator with foreign powers, it is as a lawgiver, as the founder and the ruler of a mighty nation, that Napoleon stands conspicuously superior to all, and even to himself.' Yet, through these unqualified praises dispersed all over the work, one may easily discern that, in M. Thiers's opinion, there is somebody who ranks still higher, and, again, it is M. Thiers himself. With the exception of having the Duke of Enghien shot, M. Thiers would have done all that Bonaparte did; but he would have done it in a better manner. *Est modus in rebus.* M. Thiers knows the *modus in rebus.* On many occasions he would not have been so very hasty; on others, he would not have been so dilatory. Bonaparte too frequently let out his secret views, by which he gave warning to his enemies; the enemies of the country, of course; and thus afforded them the means of thwarting his vast and beneficent designs; while the consummate prudence of M. Thiers, would have kept these designs in profound secrecy, until the proper time for their manifestation. Bonaparte was too easily put out of temper, by adverse casualties, even by the least contradiction. Calm, cool, impassible, M. Thiers, no more minds being contradicted by others than he does contradicting himself. He is used to both, as everybody now knows. As to adverse casualties, they serve only to show how superior he is to Napoleon. We have an instance of it. To an untoward treaty of July, he answers by the fortifications of Paris; admirable institutions, which, thirty years ago, would have cemented public liberties, saved Napoleon, and secured his dynasty on the imperial throne!! He lost his portfolio; true! but what is that to him, when he can sing: *Exegi monumentum ære perennius.*

Let not our readers infer, from all this, that our author puts himself conspicuously forward, in competition with his hero, and asserts his claim to superiority and excellence. No; in our parallel we have proceeded by induction, and we were justified in doing so; but we must give credit, to M. Thiers, for his modesty, in this matter. He does not contend for pre-eminence over Napoleon, he is content with identifying himself with him, as much as an historian can do it, in relating the achievements of a great man. M. Thiers, in his narrative, must say Napoleon, or Bonaparte, or HE did so and so: he cannot say WE; and, doubtless, he is very sorry for it: but when an opportunity occurs of personating Napoleon he never misses it. Thus, in a great many parts of the five volumes, we find M. Thiers, meditating, reflecting, speechifying, sending despatches, and even acting for Napoleon and as Napoleon would have done. Here is one of his numerous meditations. It refers to the time when Napoleon's intervention with Switzerland, and his encroachments in Italy and Germany were found fault with by England, and when the peace of Amiens was endangered. (Vol. iv. Book 16.)

'In spite of some fits of passion excited by English malignity, in spite even of the unequalled greatness which, he sometimes felt convinced, would be the result of the war; the first consul was still intent upon remaining at peace. But by provoking him, by irritating him, his enemies compelled him to say to himself:—after all, war is my natural vocation, my origin, perhaps my destiny. I know how to govern, in a superior manner; but, before I knew how to govern, I knew how to fight. This was my profession, my art *par excellence.* If Moreau, with a French army, reached the gates of Vienna, I will certainly go much farther.' Those things he constantly repeated to himself. Extraordinary visions flirted before his mind: he beheld empires overthrown, Europe reconstructed, and his consular cap transformed into a crown, not inferior to that of Charlemagne—at any rate, continued he, sooner or later, all this greatness must be mine.'

The same epoch and the same subject will furnish us with an allocution of Thiers-Napoleon. The person spoken to is Lord Whitworth, who had been invited to the Tuilleries by the first consul.

'Every wind that blows from England brings me nothing but hatred and insults. We have now come to an emergency, from which we must retrieve ourselves one way or other. Will you or will you not execute the treaty of Amiens? On my part, it has been executed with more than punctual fidelity. The treaty obliged me to evacuate Naples, Tarentum, and the Roman States, within three months; and, in less than two months, all the French troops had left those countries. Ten months have now elapsed, since the exchange of the ratifications, and Malta and Alexandria are still in possession of the British forces. It is of no use to attempt to deceive me, on this matter. Will you have peace, or will you have war? If you are intent on war, well, do but say so, and let us have it; but a war relentless until the extinction of one of the two nations. If you are for peace, then abandon Alexandria and Malta. You object that, the Rock of Malta, with its all but inexpugnable fortifications, is of great value to you, considered under a maritime point of view; but it is of much greater value to me, considered under another point of view:—national honour. What would the world say,—would not all bring in question our bravery, if a solemn treaty was thus violated? As for me, I am determined. I had rather see you on the heights of Montmartre, than in possession of Malta.'

Thiers personating Napoleon in his acts, or to express our idea more explicitly, the acts of Thiers-Napoleon, some of them at the least, are less objectionable than either his meditations or his speeches; but, unfortunately, his acts are generally of no avail to prevent the dreadful consequences of previous acts of Napoleon alone. Thus, Thiers-Napoleon, in order to save the Duc d'Enghien, had given a written order to M. Real, Counsellor of State and Director General of the Police, to repair instantly to Vincennes, to examine the prisoner, and report to HIM who held the prince's life in his powerful hands, and who was so mercifully disposed, that, '*shut up at Malmaison,* he took a seat at a table, to play a game at chess with a lady of his new court, Madme. de Rennisat, and was heard muttering some of the best lines of the French poets, on clemency; particularly those which

Corneille and Voltaire put in the mouths of Augustus and Alzire.' (Vol. iv. Book 18.) But M. Real forgot to obey the orders; and other more ready instruments, did not fail to do as they were bid. The prince was murdered.

Again, Thiers-Napoleon wanted to save Pichegru, the conqueror of Holland; but he wished, at the same time, that he got rid of him, to make him useful to France. He said to the same M. Real. 'Go and visit Pichegru in his prison, and tell him; that I pardon him: that it is not towards him, or Moreau, or men like them, that I am inclined to be severe. Ask him how many men, and what money he wants to found a colony at Cayenne, and I will supply him.' But again M. Real* neglected the prisoner, who, some morning afterwards, was found strangled in his cell. A medical man, the gaoler of the prison, and his assistants proved that he had committed suicide, and thus disappointed the merciful intentions of the consul!

Thiers-Napoleon . . . But enough of this ludicrous personification thrown in our way, by the superlative vanity of a political dwarf, who, raised to eminence solely on account of his insignificance, presumes to set up for a political giant. Enough of ridicule. As we are approaching the termination of our task, and when, at the end of the published part of this work, we have to expose and to discuss, the foul calumnies, and the immoral arguments of the author, in his attempt to justify the darkest of the political crimes of Bonaparte, and the declaration of war;—then contempt gives way to indignation.

Two of the books, 18th and the 19th, are almost entirely devoted to the conspiracy of Georges Cadoudal and Pichegru, in which Moreau was implicated. Thiers renews, against the British government, the accusation of having organized that conspiracy, and of having supplied the conspirators with large sums of money, for the execution of their plans;—the assassination of Bonaparte and the restoration of the Bourbons. In other parts of his work, he had already accused the English ministry of the same participation in the affair of the infernal machine, and other conspiracies. A man who has lately been minister for foreign affairs,

* We were well acquainted with Count Real; and, *le petit Thiers* was present when, in 1826, we met with him for the first time, at a friend's, 121 Visille Rue du Temple, in Paris. The conspiracy of Pichegru and that of Mallet, were frequently the subject of our conversations; and I had from him many details, which are in complete opposition to the account given by Thiers. It is certain that Real knew nothing of the arrest of the prince until after his execution: as to Pichegru, he saw him but once, to interrogate him, after his arrest, as was his duty. He many times told us, speaking of the General: 'Son suicide est, pour moi, plus, incertain que son crime.'

and who looks forward, in hope of being reinstated in the office, must be a very bad man and a fool to boot, to give credit to, and to repeat such accusations. A bad man, because he, in some sort, admits that he would do it; a fool, because such an accusation, publicly made, is an insult which must for ever be resented, and disqualify its author for diplomatic relations with the government, and the nation so promiscuously insulted.

British gold was not needed, at that time, to organise a conspiracy against Napoleon Bonaparte. All the elements, not merely of a conspiracy, but of a revolution, were ready at hand, in all the departments of France, and even in Paris, the strong hold of the consular power. All the republicans in the country, the admirers of the Convention as well as the partizans of the Directory, those even who did not think the existence of a Republic incompatible with a perpetual, even with an hereditary presidency, were now fully convinced, that nothing could save the liberties of France, but the overthrow of the consul. On the other hand, the Royalists, who had been mainly instrumental in his elevation, as conducive to a restoration, were now fully sensible of their error; and, indignant at the idea of having been betrayed, they wished for nothing but an early opportunity for upsetting the treacherous usurper. The armies, with the exception of the army of Italy, had seen with indignation, their long and meritorious services passed by, and their well-earned laurels taken from them, to decorate the spoilers of Italy:—their ablest and their best generals, such as Macdonald, Gouvion St. Cyr, and Lecourbe, thrown into the back ground, to make way for such men as Soult, Augereau, Junot, and others, who had never commanded in chief, and knew much better how to plunder than how to fight. But above all, the treatment of Moreau, idolized by all, still more than he was admired, had arrayed the army against Bonaparte.

Such was the state of France, and the situation of Napoleon Bonaparte, at the beginning of the year 1803; and the measures of the government, far from improving the situation, were, without exception, calculated to increase the discontent of the bulk of the nation to such a degree, that, every one was in daily expectation of a popular, or military movement which would put an end to the dictatorship. '*Une conspiration gaterait tout*:' (a conspiracy would spoil all) said Sièyes*, to the Tribune Ginguené, who proposed some plan for hastening the manifestation of the national hostility. And to the Royalists, who, according

* We had this from M. Sieyes himself, in 1814, at Count Garat's, who was then publishing l'Eloge de Moreau.

to their old practice, based all their hopes upon foreign powers, and invoked war: '*Vous êtes fous ;*' said he: '*la guerre le sauvera.*' (You are fools: a war will save him.')

Nobody was better acquainted with this state of things, with the anticipations of public opinion, with the dangers which threatened his authority, and with the surest means of averting them, than Bonaparte himself and his confidants, Cambaceres, Fouché, Rœderer, and Regnault de St. Jean d'Angely. It seemed as certain to them as it was to Sièyes, that a war was the only thing which could, not only maintain the consul at the head of the government, but also facilitate his further progress towards a still higher rank; because a war would divert public attention from his internal administration, and would allow him to do almost anything he chose; and, besides that, the vicissitudes of the war, the anxiety with regard to its results; above all, the fears of a restoration, would rally round him all those who had had any share in the revolution, as well as those who, however opposed to his system of government, relied on his military talents to preserve France from invasion, and perhaps from partition. Therefore, war was decided upon, and the wager of battle was thrown down to England and Austria, by encroachments in Italy, in Germany, and in Switzerland, and, in the mean time, by the most insulting accusations. Thiers himself relates, with unqualified approbation, all the provoking transactions, most of which were manifest violations of the recently concluded treaties; and he maintains that the only cause of war was the refusal by England to evacuate Malta. His long and incoherent discussion upon this question, does not contain a single new argument: it is but a repetition of all that was said and printed in France forty-three years ago, and it proves nothing but the ignorance and the bad faith of the new compiler.

The declaration of war could not but produce a most unfavourable impression upon the nation, which had recently manifested its satisfaction at the conclusion of the treaty of peace, and its gratitude to the pacificator. The refusal to evacuate Malta, about which nobody in France cared, would have been considered as a paltry pretence, rather than a just cause for renewing a struggle which had already lasted too long. The reflections of the English newspapers on Napoleon, and the satires of the Ambigu, published by Peltier, a French emigrant, might be more suitably answered by the retorts of the French press than by an appeal to arms. Every one, after saying this, would add, that it was unworthy of the First Consul to notice such attacks, and to sacrifice the interests of France to his wounded vanity. Then his enemies would take advantage of this disposition of the public mind to renew their intrigues, to incriminate the whole of his conduct; to show up his insatiable ambition, and to proclaim as a contrast the true patriotism, the superior military abilities, the spotless glory, and the modesty of Moreau,—Moreau, the real conqueror of the peace, whom his soldiers loved as a father, and who was, by the citizens, considered as a model.

It was to guard against these too probable eventualities that Bonaparte and his advisers got up that conspiracy of George Cadoudal, in which Royalists, Republicans, the British Government, and Moreau himself, were involved, as having meditated and attempted the assassination of the First Consul. Conspiracies had hitherto succeeded so well that the best results were anticipated from this last one. Alas! the real authors were disappointed in their anticipations.

Most of our readers will exclaim, 'This is too horrible!' and probably will think that we are imposing upon them. They have no idea of the doings of the government of Napoleon le Grand: some avowals which our historian drops occasionally, will enlighten them, and, perhaps, will assist in restoring us to their confidence.

On the subject of the conspiracy of Caracchi, Arena, and Topino Lebrun, a conspiracy which was matured and conducted by Bonaparte himself, according to Thiers; we find the following reflection:—'In general, ignorant people, unacquainted with such affairs, accuse the police of fabricating the plots which they discover. The police had not concocted this one; but it must be admitted that they took a too great part in it. The conspirators no doubt wished the death of the First Consul, but they were unwilling to strike him with their own hands; and by providing them with what was the most difficult to find, *perpetrators,* they were led further than they would have gone, if left to themselves.' (Vol. ii. Book 6.) The three men were beheaded.

In the account given by Thiers of the infernal machine, we find that Fouché had discovered, that 'one Chevalier, a workman employed in the manufactory of arms, established in Paris, at the time of the Convention, had been found working at a dreadful machine. It was a barrel filled with powder and grapeshot, to which was attached a musket-barrel with a trigger. This machine was evidently destined to blow up the First Consul. The inventor was arrested and thrown into prison.' (Vol. ii. Book 8.) What became of the machine and of its inventor? Thiers says nothing about it; but, in the very next page, we have the account of the bursting of the infernal machine. Hundreds of republicans, described as terrorists, were arrested, as authors or accomplices. One hundred and thirty of them were transported without any trial. And afterwards *Fouché and his police discovered that it was the gold of England*, George Cadoudal, St. Rejant, and two other Royalists, who had done all the mischief. St. Rejant was arrested, tried, and beheaded.

One instance more of governmental plots, and we have done. Our author says, (Vol. v. Book 19.)

'England had committed an act which cannot easily be characterized, in providing conspirators with money, and in *ordering* or allowing three of her diplomatic agents, at Cassel, at Stutgard, and at Munich, to engage in the most criminal intrigues. *The First Consul sent a confidential and trustworthy officer, who, in disguise, and pretending to be an agent of the conspiracy, ingratiated himself with Messrs. Drake and Spencer Smith, and gained their confidence. He received from them, for the conspirators, as a first instalment, upwards of 4,000l. in gold, which he handed over to the French police.*'*

We may now be believed, when we affirm, that some of those *trustworthy gentlemen*, we beg pardon, we ought to have said noblemen, emigrants, who had, on their return, attached themselves to Bonaparte, were sent over to England; in order to rekindle the Royalist ardour of their friends; to represent to them the state of France, as the most satisfactory for the cause of legitimacy;—the whole country being ready to rise against Bonaparte; all parties agreeing to compromise their differences, and waiting only for leaders, to give the signal, and to direct the movement; a French prince, with a republican general, such as Pichegru, would immediately gather round them, the two most numerous and influential parties in France. The agents did not confine themselves to such representations; they also asserted that a conspiracy was already organised; that the

* Letter of the First Consul to the *Grand Juge*, Minister of Justice. Paris, 9th Brumaire, an 12, (1st November, 1803.) 'It is of importance to have a secret agent to watch over the proceedings of Drake at Munich, and of the French who repair to that place. . . I have read all the reports: they are interesting, but we must not be hasty in making arrests. When our man has given all necessary information, we must settle with him how to act. I wish him to write to Drake, that, while waiting for an opportunity of striking *le grand coup*, he is bold to promise that he will take from the First Consul's own table, in his private study, notes, in the First Consul's own hand-writing, concerning the Boulogne expedition, and all other papers of importance: that he will be able to do it, through a confidential person, who was formerly a member of the Jacobins, and who now, though he has the full confidence of the First Consul, and has in his charge the private study, belonged to the secret committee of the conspirators. But this will be done on two conditions: the first is, that one hundred thousand pounds sterling, shall be paid on delivery of these documents; and the second, that a French Royalist agent shall be sent over to Paris, to assist in the concealment and escape of this person.' (Vol. iv. Book 18.)

royalists who had gathered round the First Consul, and had accepted offices, had done so for the sole purpose of betraying him, and in order to be better able to serve their own cause; that even the generals to whom Bonaparte had shown the greatest partiality, Lannes, Augereau, Davoust, Junot, and others, were already tired with his tyranny, and had made up their minds not to bear with it any longer; whilst others, much better known to the army, were urging Moreau to place himself at their head, and with them and this devoted army, to crush in the bud, the usurped power of his treacherous rival. In support of these statements, the agents produced letters, written for the purpose, by most of the men they mentioned, under the dictation of Bonaparte himself, the conclusion of which uniformly was: 'Come; he has nobody to defend him but a few hundred men of the consular guard.'

As may be easily imagined, these representations, supported as they were by written documents, from such men as Vaublanc, Siméon, Jaucourt, Fontanes, and their friends, could not but induce most of the Royalist emigrants, and the French princes resident in England,* to make an attempt, which, under such favourable circumstances, could not but be attended with complete success. Some, however, more cautious, and, moreover, having cause to suspect one of the agents, Montgaillard, insisted upon sending over to France some trusty persons, to ascertain by their own observation, the state of the country, before any of the princes exposed himself to the chances of a failure. This opinion prevailed in spite of the opposition of George Cadoudal, who was intent upon acting without loss of time. He submitted, however, on condition that he should be the first to go over, with liberty to act whenever an opportunity presented itself. He was followed by Pichegru, with M. de Polignac and de Riviere. When in Paris, they soon perceived, that all that had been said as to the unpopularity of the Consul was true enough; but that very few persons, if any, thought of a restoration; and that Moreau was the man whom every one had in view. In this emergency, they resolved to sound Moreau, and, if possible, to enlist him in the cause of legitimacy. But Moreau rejected their overtures, made through Pichegru; and all of them would have gone back to England, without attempting anything, if the con-

* Thiers, in mentioning the intrigues of the French princes, names the Count d'Artois and the Duke of Berry, though he knows very well, that at that time both of them were entirely given up to the pursuit of their pleasures. It was another prince who was deeply concerned in all the projects against Napoleon, and who enlisted Pichegru in the service of legitimacy. Evidently, our author, by his voluntary blunder, gives a hint to his second Napoleon.

sular government, which were aware of all that was doing, and saw that they could not carry on their plans any further, had not arrested them, from fear of losing their victims and their conspiracy altogether.

Such was the conspiracy of Cadoudal and Pichegru, the principal, if not the sole object of which was to ruin, in the estimation of the people and of the army, and to brand as an assassin, the illustrious warrior, the modest conqueror, the virtuous citizen, who alone dared to stand erect in presence of the tyrant, whilst a crowd of degraded military and civil apostates were crouching at his feet. At the trial which took place at the end of May, 1804, all the parties incriminated, and all the witnesses, with the exception of one only—Bouvet—who had been tampered with by the government, concurred in declaring, that Moreau had from the first refused to listen to any proposal from the royalist party. His two or three interviews with Pichegru were explained so as to satisfy every unprejudiced mind: his answers to the interpellations of the court frequently drew down the applause of the assistants: but the judges had been appointed by the Consul, now an emperor, who had openly declared that he was determined to have Moreau pronounced guilty and sentenced to death. Thiers himself admits the fact; and adds, that 'when he was informed that the judges, not considering the participation of Moreau as sufficiently established, had sentenced him to only two years' imprisonment, he flew into a violent rage against the cowardice of the tribunal.'...... 'He, however, remitted to Moreau the two years' imprisonment, as he would have remitted the penalty of death, if such had been the sentence.'—(Vol. v. Book 19.) Moreau immediately after left France for the United States of America. Nineteen of the accomplices of Cadoudal were sentenced to death, and executed, with the exception of M. de Polignac and M. de Riviere. 'Henceforth,' says M. Thiers, at the end of this book, 'all resistance was conquered. In 1802, Bonaparte had vanquished civil resistance by annulling the tribunate: in 1804, he surmounted military resistance, by baffling the conspiracy of the royalist emigrants with republican generals. While he was ascending the throne, Moreau was retiring into exile.'

The last two books are filled with details on the coronation, and on the preparations for the *descente en Angleterre;* and close with the announcement of '*the immortal* campaign' of 1805. We cannot follow our author in his enumeration, in his disposition of the military and naval forces of France: we cannot enter into discussion with him upon the efficiency for an invasion of England,—of that admirable flotilla of 1200 *bateaux-plats*, which were to land on the British shores 120,000 warriors, the conquerors of Italy and Egypt. It is enough for us to have the opinion of Admiral Truguet, and even of Admiral Decrès, the minister of marine of Napoleon, who entreated his master not to venture his army upon those flat-bottomed barges. M. Thiers may be a better authority; but we are not convinced by his arguments. He has, however, overlooked one, which would go far to prove, not only that the invasion was possible, but also that it had actually taken place. Medals, apparently struck in London in 1804, to commemorate the conquest of England, exist; and we have lately seen one at a friend's, in town,* who keeps it as a proof of the sanguine genius of Napoleon. We wonder that our historian should have neglected such corroborative evidence of the greatest achievement of his hero; particularly as most of his statements are supported by far less conclusive vouchers.

We must now take leave of our readers, and at the same time apologise for the extraordinary length of this article. Indeed, the fear of trespassing on their patience, induced us to suppress the greater part of the reflections and confutations, which, whilst reading the work, were dropping from our pen at almost every page, and which would fill a volume. But, in our endeavours to confine ourselves within the narrowest limits possible, we constantly bore in mind that our duty to the public, in reviewing this History, required that we should give a true and complete account of the origin and of the establishment of the consulate, and of its transformation into imperial dignity;—that we should exhibit the intellectual and moral faculties, the designs, and the acts of the General, of the Consul, and of the Emperor, so as to enable every one to assign him his proper place among the benefactors or among the enemies of mankind: and, lastly, that we should, by studying the volumes before us, and afterwards faithfully representing the opinions, the principles, the affections, and the tendencies of the author, elucidate the character of the history, and that of the historian.

If the historian were not, at the same time, a public man,—if circumstances nearly similar to those which promoted Napoleon to the supreme authority, had not raised Thiers to ministerial power,—if he were not styled statesman, by a faction which, thanks to him, have long preyed upon the spoils of France, and who, at this very moment, are preparing his restoration to his former official superiority, by a coalition of all parties against his stern and equally unprincipled antagonist,—we would not have directed to him personally our attention, and that of the public; and very likely should not have noticed his worse

* Mr. Malton, solicitor, of Carey-street, Lincoln's Inn Fields.

than worthless performance: but knowing, as we do, the present state of France,—prepared, as we are, for events, which, before many months perhaps, may again throw the world into convulsions, is it not proper to show up the man who aspires to act a principal part in those events, and who, to qualify himself in the estimation of the degraded and corrupted oligarchy of officials, who constantly plunder and crush France, applauds all the crimes of Napoleon,—crimes of most of which he himself was guilty during his tenure of power, and all those which he will perpetrate, when once again reinstalled at the head of the ministry, either by a crafty and vindictive sovereign, or by another revolution?

Art. II.—*The Literary History of the New Testament.* 8vo. pp. 608. London: Seeley, Burnside, and Seeley. 1845.

The religion of the New Testament is to be embraced ere its literary history be investigated. Faith in that system of remedy and restoration which it developes, naturally precedes all attempts to examine the peculiar elements of its human authorship, to describe its style, or exhibit its varieties of composition. The human spirit needs the conviction that it contains a divine revelation in order to love the God it pourtrays, or confide in the Saviour it makes known, needs that assurance which miracles and other credentials of its heavenly origin impart, that it may receive its truths, trust in its promises, cherish its hopes, imbibe its spirit, and obey its commands. That belief which pardons and sanctifies, regards the fact of the oracle, while its form and mode of conveyance are but secondary considerations. It rests with implicit reliance on the declaration, THE LORD HATH SPOKEN. That voice may have been given in audible majesty as on Sinai, or have come from the stammering lips of Moses, or the eloquent tongue of Paul; the oracle may have descended into the capacious soul of Solomon the monarch, or have come down on the rustic and untutored mind of Amos the herdsman; it may have clothed itself in graceful simplicity, and taken the form of history, or have arrayed itself in gorgeous diction, and assumed the shape of poetry; it may have found utterance by the rivers of Babel, in the solitary isle of Patmos, or in the dungeons of Rome;—the date of its communication may have been in the period of the Pharaohs, or in the era of the Cesars;—faith stripping it of all such adventitious circumstances, simply inquires, what hath the Lord spoken, and on being satisfied, yields a cordial unwavering assent.

But the 'works of the Lord are great, sought out of all them that have pleasure therein.' While the great majority of Christians have neither time nor talents for profound investigation, while their hearts are sealed in the faith by the experimental evidence of Christianity, and their own consciousness of peace and joy and advancing spiritual maturity are 'the witness within themselves,' yet an intelligent mind may start many questions about the New Testament, the solution of which demands learned and lengthened scrutiny, but will amply reward those who engage in it by giving them enlarged views of the divine wisdom and goodness, increased convictions of the truth of Christianity, augmented power to illustrate scripture, or to confute those antagonists, who, seizing on its seeming contrarieties with general history or with itself, labour to destroy the authenticity of the sacred volume. But, as we have said, faith must precede such inquiries. Without faith, there is imminent danger, and the soul in the midst of its unbelieving toils, may be hurried into eternity. Safety springs from belief. The unbelieving spirit, busying itself in biblical speculation, resembles Archimedes at the siege of Syracuse, ignorant of the capture of the town which his own ingenuity had so long defended, till the fiery countenance and knife of the infuriated soldier taught him that safety should have been sought, in preference to indulgence in favourite studies. 'Add to your faith virtue, and to virtue knowledge.' We must enjoy life, ere we can penetrate into its arcana of nerve and muscle, of respiration and nutriment, of waste and repair. The fruits of the earth must yield us daily sustenance, though we be in ignorance of the process of vegetation, and ere we proceed to analyze the chemical properties of the soil and the atmosphere by which plants are reared and propagated. Let the salvation of God be embraced, and we shall possess the best preparation for examining into the age, aspect, form, and method of the books of the New Testament.

This literary investigation, no matter how it may issue, does not compromise the divine authority of the books of the New Testament. Many of the questions which it discusses may be dark and intricate, and answers entirely opposite to one another may be given, yet the genuineness, authenticity, and integrity of the sacred books remain unimpaired. We may not know where Mark wrote his gospel, or how Luke acquired his evangelical information, the length of our Lord's ministry may be disputed, and the year of Paul's conversion be variously fixed, the periods of his several journeys may remain a matter of doubt, the dates of his numerous epistles may remain unascertained, and various allusions in those compositions may be veiled in obscurity, arising from ignorance of the precise circumstances in which the churches addressed by him were placed; yet these difficulties neither impede nor modify our belief in the divine origin of the treatises which form the New Testament. Conflicting theories as to the source, nature and propagation of light, destroy not our conviction of its existence; unnumbered geological hypotheses alter not our faith in the existence and adaptations of this earthly globe. No dispute as to the time when or place where John wrote his biography of Jesus, whether he meant it to be supplemental to the other narratives, or had a polemical object in view in its composition,—no uncertainty on such points hinders us from receiving the fourth gospel as an inestimable production, and the examination of such questions leaves intact the inspiration and truthfulness of the ancient document.

The New Testament is a literary production, possessing characteristics peculiar to itself. It consists of contributions by various authors, each displaying in his composition his own temperament and mental configuration. Plenary inspiration consists with such diversity, and spiritual influence no more changes a man's modes of thought and expression than it alters his handwriting. The New Testament is formed by the union of not fewer than twenty-seven treatises, by eight different authors. Twenty-one of these treatises are epistles, fourteen of which are ascribed to Paul. We have, also, in the New Testament, narratives of pleasing simplicity, yet of distinctive character; for Matthew presents us with memorabilia occasionally grouped and classified, in order to prove that the scattered lineaments of ancient prophecy are embodied in Jesus of Nazareth; —while Mark confines his gospel especially to the actions of Christ, who went about doing good, whose days were spent in works of ceaseless and sublime benevolence. On the other hand, the biography of Luke breathes a catholic spirit, is more uniform in its progress, and more sustained in its character, exhibiting Jesus not as the Messiah of the Jews, but the Saviour-God of the world. The composition of the beloved disciple, is quite unique. The Saviour appears in it unbosoming himself as a friend, not delivering oracles as an instructor;—his eye glistens with holy ardour and pathos, while words of marvellous power, thrilling the hearts of his audience with new solace and attachment, proceed from his lips. The 'Acts of the Apostles' deals in facts, without embellishments and miracles, without exaggeration, and pourtrays with graphic ease and fidelity the toil and travel of the earliest missionary enterprize. Thus the New Testament has histories of varied form and aim;—four narratives of the life and actions of the same individual, contemplated in different points of view—as the realisation of ancient prophecy—as the untiring beneficent wonder-worker—as the Redeemer of mankind in his various functions; and as the compassionate Son of God, a type of perfect humanity, an incarnation of truth and love and sympathy, one who, uniting his friends to himself in the mystic bond of faith, ascends with them to the bosom of his Father and their Father, of his God and their God.

The concluding book of the New Testament is one of prophetic grandeur—awful in its hieroglyphics, and mystic symbols, seven seals opened, seven trumpets sounded, seven vials poured out; mighty antagonists, arrayed against Christianity,—hostile powers, full of malignity against the new religion, and, for a season, oppressing it, but at length defeated and annihilated;—the darkened heaven, tempestuous sea, and convulsed earth, fighting against them, while the issue of the long combat is the universal reign of peace and truth and righteousness—the whole scene being relieved at intervals by a choral burst of praise to God the Creator, and Christ the Redeemer and Governor.

The other portions of the New Testament consist of epistolary dissertations, the majority of them by Paul, three by John, two by Peter, one by James, and another by Jude. The last is a brief one, directed against Antinomian licentiousness. That of James, the Cato among the apostles, is an ethical discussion, a string of apothegms, not, perhaps, having a polemical reference to other apostolical treatises, but enforcing the possession of holiness as the necessary offspring of faith, and proving that Christianity is not a ceremonial institute, to be admired and observed, or an intellectual speculation, to be received with supine indifference, but a spiritual system which from its very nature governs the heart, and gives a new and lasting character to the whole life. This epistle of James the Just was written to Jews, probably before the epistles of Paul had obtained wide circulation, and may be regarded as the link between the teaching of our Lord, as contained in the gospel, and the fuller developement of Christian truth in the inspired teaching of his apostles.

Three types of Christian teaching are to be found in the writings of Paul, Peter, and John, the apostles of faith, of hope, and of love. While the system of religious truth, contained in the epistles of these inspired men, is essentially the same, the enquiring mind is gratified by observing the form it assumes as it comes in contact with their respective mental and spiritual peculiarities. This variety is a wise adaptation of the Bible to our nature. The same goodness is apparent in the physical world. Objects might have been of one colour, sounds of monotonous sameness, and the gifts of Providence meant for the satisfaction of appetite might have been of tiresome insipidity; and yet the organs of sense might have performed all the functions necessary for the support and preservation of human existence. But the benevolence of the Creator has painted objects of varied hue to refresh the eye, and modulated sound of changing tone to gratify the ear, and given the fruits of his fatherly kindness varied qualities of pungency and sweetness to please and excite the palate. So the spiritual man finds satisfaction in studying the system of divinity in the logical ratiocinations and convincing arguments of Paul, and the fervent and rapid discussions and appeals of Peter—while the heart is melted by John's seraphic delineations of experience, and his ardent incitements to the study and practice of love as the issue and embodiment of all the graces. The Pauline Gospel appears in the form of a system of lucid, compact, and orderly arrangement, and the Petrine Gospel dwells especially on the central truths of the person and work of the Redeemer—clothes them in language borrowed from the old dispensation, exhibits Christianity as the spiritual realisation of Judaism, and adapts all these elements as an encouragement and solace to the holy priesthood in the prospect of persecution. The Johannic Gospel adopts the subjective form, describes blessings not as they are in themselves, external to the believer, but as they are felt in his consciousness in the shape of life, and peace, and union with divinity.

Each of Paul's epistles has its own phasis according to the purpose he had in view in writing,—a purpose moulded according to the circumstances of the church which he intended to instruct, or warn, or reprove. Addressing those who had been adherents of the Mosaic system, and seduced by its gaudy ritual, were prone to apostatise, the apostle elaborates an argument, with extreme care and delicacy, to prove the superiority of the Lord to the angels by whom the law was given, to demonstrate the excellence of Christ the Son over Moses the servant, and to show, by a vast variety of argument, how much in dignity and value the atonement of the Son of God excelled the oblations of irrational animals made by sinful men under the Levitical statute. Or, in unfolding to the church at Rome the crowning glory of the gospel in its gratuitous justification, how wide the premises he lays down, how convincing the conclusion he deduces; the Gentiles have sinned,—their polytheism led them to ferocity and brutality; the Jew has sinned, though he possessed the law, its very possession being both the proof and the aggravation of his apostacy,—how awful then the inference, 'By the works of law can no flesh be justified, for by the law is the knowledge of sin.' But justification is of grace, and must be so, 'through the redemption that is in Christ Jesus.' Grace, however, is not the enemy of a holy life, 'Shall we continue in sin that grace may abound?' Faith and holiness are inseparably associated, 'Do we make void the law through faith? Nay, God forbid, we establish the law.' Released from the law, as a covenant of works, believers are the more bound to it as a rule of life, 'They who are in Christ Jesus walk not after the flesh but after the Spirit.' Then the apostle enters into a subject dear to his heart, the history, fates, and fortunes of the ancient people.

Again, were the question asked, to what were the successes of the gospel owing in the early times? the apostle replies, in the first chapter of his first letter to the church in Corinth, that his preaching was not with 'enticing words of man's wisdom,' that he did not assume the subtleness and rhetoric of a Grecian orator or sophist, that he did not accommodate his message to the prejudice of his audience, so as to give his gospel a philosophic covering or oratorical recommendation, but boldly, simply, and formally preached, 'Christ crucified, to the Jews a stumbling block, and to the Greeks foolishness.' If we wish to know how offenders are to be treated, how certain questions of casuistry are to be settled, how order is to be preserved in the church amidst a variety of offices and gifts, the statements of Paul in the same epistle form a clear and infallible guide. If we are desirous of beholding an unrivalled specimen of edification, comprised of an artless and happy union of doctrinal truth and practical statement, personal history, and evangelical exposition of official vindication and glowing encouragements, we have it in the second epistle to the Corinthians. The epistle to the Galatians, on the other hand, mirrors forth those strong emotions of surprise, sorrow, and anger, which agitated the breast of the apostle as he contemplated the apostacy of that church and reflected on those Judaising seductions by which it had been so easily and speedily captivated. The letter to the church of Ephesus, so polished in its style and elevated in its sentiments, resembles that temple which was the pride of their city and the boast of the world; and formed in itself a fit compensation for the loss of those magical books which had been burnt at their conversion, of which 'they counted the price, and found it fifty thousand pieces of silver.' The varied correspondence of the apostle with Colosse, Philippi, and Thessalonica, proves that all scripture is 'profitable for doctrine, for reproof, for correction, for instruction in righteousness,'—shows the fervid love of Paul for all the churches, for those he had planted and watered, and for such as 'had not seen his face in the flesh;'—how zealously he watched their best interests, how his heart rejoiced in their adherence to the truth, and grieved at any seeming defection among them. At the same time, these familiar writings furnish us with an admirable example of the manner in which all circumstances are to be improved, and all incidents turned to the best advantage—how error is to be analysed and assailed, and the truth contrasted with it and placed on a firm foundation. Where shall we find such a fatherly affection toward the younger ministry, such cordial sympathy with them in their unavoidable trials, such minute and sagacious counsels as to their personal conduct and studies, and their public relation to the church, to every class, age, sex, and office, among its members, as are treasured up in the pastoral addresses or letters to Timothy and Titus. Nor is a fugitive slave beneath the care and anxiety of the great apostle,—what condescension and sympathy, what mediating gentleness and firmness, are displayed in the brief note addressed to Philemon.

Besides, the mind of Paul was eminently suggestive. It never lost view of its object, yet it often took an excursive flight in reaching it. There is scarcely any doctrine of Christianity which is not illustrated by Paul in some portion of this inspired Cardiphonia. Morality is placed by him in its true position, as coming after faith, and as being based upon it. The doctrines of the gospel are expounded ere its ethics are enforced. His ethical code comprehends general maxims and special injunctions, and embraces individual and social duties, the relations of country as well as of family, the laws of ordinary intercourse, and those of ecclesiastical communion. What unity in variety, what multiplicity of style and address, are to be found in the New Testament. Its literary beauties are unrivalled. The precious truths conveyed to us in these fascinating compositions, are like 'apples of gold in baskets of silver.'

Now the literary history of the New Testament must be, to every intelligent Christian, an interesting study; for it comprises an examination of all these features of the external character of the books of the inspired volume. Having received it as God's revelation by Christ, we take pleasure in analysing those peculiarities which belong to it as a human production. God has written to men by men. We may therefore ask, About what year did Matthew, Mark, Luke and John, write their respective gospels?—In what country, or in what circumstances, were the authors placed? What special aim had each in view? Are the gospels four independent documents?—or did some one of the evangelists see the productions of the others, and shape his narrative accordingly, omitting what his predecessor had inserted, or amplifying what he had briefly touched, or introducing discourses, actions, or journeys, which he had left out? Again, if there be seeming discrepancies between the several accounts, as to what happened, or as to when, and how, and in whose presence, the events recorded took place, how are such apparent contradictions to be reconciled? Or we may busy ourselves with fixing when and to whom James wrote,—where Peter's epistle is dated,—who are the 'elect strangers,' to whom it is inscribed, and in what condition the churches addressed were placed. Or we may employ ourselves in forming from scattered hints a biography of the great apostle of the Gentiles, tracing his career from the day of his conversion to that of his martyrdom, noting the order of his missionary visits to various cities and districts, the reception he met with, the welcome he enjoyed, or the persecution or imprisonment he endured; and by this minute and laborious investigation throwing new light on the epistles, from the history of the Acts, and shedding light from the epistles on the brief and rapid narrative. Or we may ascertain at what place and time, and in what circumstances, those epistles were written, which form so large a portion of the canon of the New Testament. The literary history of the New Testament augments the amount of its evidences, facilitates its interpretation, and brings out new beauties and strokes of emphasis, which, by the indolent reader, are wholly unobserved. Who has not derived incalculable benefit from the accurate and laborious researches of Lardner?—or has not felt instructed and delighted at the tact and sagacity displayed in the *Horae Paulinae*?—or has not been excited to similar pursuits by studying the meritorious volumes of Greswell? The continued investigation of scripture will always bring along with it its own reward; or, as Chrysostom remarks, in a sentence prefixed as a motto to the volume before us, 'As aromatics yield their perfume so much the more, the more they are bruised, so do the scriptures give up their hid treasures of meaning, in proportion as they are constantly handled.'

The author of this 'Literary History', has come to his labour in the right spirit. 'Sympathy,' he remarks, 'is the only key that will put us in possession of the true beauties and full import of the sacred writings.' 'Let us remember, we are not to judge the scripture, but the scripture is to judge us. Woe be to him that comes to the New Testament in the spirit of an accuser, instead of a penitent, not to learn, but to impugn.' The spirit in which a man engages in biblical labour gives a tinge to the whole of his procedure. Might we not contrast, for a moment, the spirit in which some German literati come to the books of the New Testament. They earn the woe pronounced in the preceding sentence. They come to accuse the scriptures of inaccuracies and contradictions: they come to impugn the honesty and veracity of its writers. They have formed some theory to which scripture must bend; and whatever the theory be, it opposes that supranaturalism which essentially belongs to inspiration. What a contrast is this book to the far-famed *Leben Jesu*, and its eccentric theory of myths. The mind of Strauss had no sympathy with the spirit or the religion of the New Testament, but was filled with the subtleties of a philosophy anti-Christian in its tendencies. This philosophy, the irreligious portions of which are no novelty, he applied with daring consistency to the memoirs of Jesus as contained in the gospels. That anti-Christianism, which had descended through many generations and forms of philosophy to Strauss, was brought by him into immediate activity. Others had prepared the way long before him. The philosophy of Hegel, in its aspect to religion, has its germs in the writings of Spinoza, in that subtle species of Pantheism which he promulgated, for his theory that God is the identity of natura naturans and natura naturata,—that the Divine Being is infinite mind and infinite extension, (the only two modes of existence which Spinoza allowed),—was reproduced in the system of Schelling, in that *Alleinheitlehre* which is the heart of his hypothesis,—the universe being a necsssary developement of the *All-one*, which is the only existence. The *Das Ich*, the subjective entity, the germ of Fichte's system, was not very different, the personality of God and of the human mind being speciously set aside. Hegel developed those pantheistic notions still further, and verged into the absolute. The ideal with him swallowed up the real. Schelling acceded to Spinoza that the original one was a *substanz*,—that the noumenon (as Kant phrased it) lying beneath every phenomenon, was something real; but Hegel regarded ideas only as true substances. While Schelling maintained the oneness of the subjective and objective, Hegel sought this unity in absolute knowledge and absolute truth. 'Pure conception,' he says, 'in itself is existence, and real existence is nothing but pure conception.' Hegel's system is thus ideal pantheism. 'God,' he maintains, 'in himself is for himself, and so must become his second self in the universe.' Now this pantheistic Hegelian philosophy allied itself to religion, and sought to develope its religious phases in biblical phraseology, and so has become one of the 'oppositions of science falsely so called.' It explains away all that is actual in religion, all that brings peace and solace to the individual. It envelopes the great facts of Christianity in a deceitful haze, and denying the individuality of the members of the great human family, gives *no one* a blessing that *every one* is commanded to ask, and every one through faith may receive. For, to use the expressive language of Reinhard, 'in the opinion of Hegel, reason demands that the thinking individual should own the nonentity of his own individual essence, and without reluctance meet self-annihilation in prospect of being absorbed into that universal substance, which, like Chronus in the old mythology, devours all its own progeny.' No wonder that Eschenmayer should have uttered his oft-quoted philippic against this irreligious system. 'Hegel has a God without holiness, a Christ without free love, a Holy Ghost without illumination, a gospel without faith, an apostacy without sin, wickedness without conscious guilt, an atonement without remission of trespass, a death without an offering, a religious assembly without divine worship, a release without imputation, justice without a judge, grace without redemption, dogmatic theology without a revelation, a this side without a that side, an immortality without a personal existence, a Christian religion without Christianity, and, in general, a religion without religion.' Now it is this Hegelian system that Strauss has applied to the gospel histories, to destroy their authenticity, and reduce them to a series of myths. Hegelianism had attempted to reason out for itself, on principles of pure thought, some of the distinguishing doctrines of Christianity. It had invented a Trinity, and a uniting Mediator, and had declared that such tenets were instinctive matters of judgment and belief; while Strauss, advancing but a step further, affirms that such doctrines as these are found in the New Testament, and that they are but the natural expression of natural ideas,—the person of Jesus being adduced only as a background on which to paint them. Of course, on such principles no objective revelation has been given or is necessary. What constitutes the so-called revelation, is the mythical publication of truths which the human mind has always felt and yearned after, and to which by some successful intensity of struggle it gave expression in the gospels eighteen centuries ago. Therefore, also, a miracle is impossible; there being no personal God to perform it. In fine, according to Strauss, the essence of religion is a consciousness of the identity between God and man—'the consciousness which man has of himself being the consciousness which God has of himself,' and the mediatorial person of Jesus as God-man is the mythical representation of this idea, while man being but a god diffused through the universe, and emptied of his individuality, personal immortality is a mere chimera, as not the individual, but the race is immortal. Of this doctrine 'eternal life' is the appropriate symbol. Need we wonder that the impious and unwarranted application of this dark and subtle pantheism to the evangelical narratives, has produced such a book as the *Leben Jesu?*—a book false in its statement, and dogmatical in its assertions, malignant in its spirit, and daring in its scepticism, yet feeble in its learned perversions, and contemptible in its feats of critical jugglery. The possession of a very different spirit, on the part of the author of the 'Literary History,' has produced a volume of a very different character—a volume of humble piety, of industrious research, and of evangelical mould, calculated to enlighten the inquiring student in that 'wisdom which is profitable to direct.' The contrast between the two productions, which is to be traced to the spirit and purpose with which they are respectively composed, has led us into this irregular digression.

The author of the 'Literary History of the New Testament' has done a good work. The treatise he has compiled supplies a desideratum, and does honour to our popular literature. The book is designedly a popular production. It is intended for the bulk of intelligent Christian readers, and does not repel them by an awful array of critical authorities, or perplex them amidst a confusion of startling hypotheses or fanciful conjectures. A service of this nature, sanctifying our every day literature, is deserving of gratitude. We are glad, moreover, to see that Biblical literature is drawing around it public attention. Our only fear is, that being popularised, it may be presented in a superficial form, and may lose its truth by being divested of its technicality. The book that has occasioned these remarks preserves a happy medium, has enough of scientific research to give it strength and authority, and is not a mere heedless digest of ordinary materials from common sources. Almost every page of it bears witness to the independent thinking and vigourous examination of the author. He has not had the means and the leisure of ample and extended research, nor perhaps is he quite qualified to engage in such protracted scrutinies. His only acquaintanceship with the great scholars of Germany is through translations and citations. Of course, of many theories he is not cognisant. Nor does he seem at all times aware of the comparative authority of the foreign authors to whom he refers. Occasionally, too, we meet with hesitancy on points on which scholars have long ago agreed, and find decided opinions given on questions which have not yet received a definite or lasting solution. Yet we cannot but record our praise of the general caution and talent which characterise the treatise. We have, indeed, continued references to Lardner and Gresswell, and the translations of Hug and Michaelis, but the opinions taken from them are not on their mere averment at all times implicitly adopted.

The first portions of the 'Literary History' refer of course to the gospels, their age, authorship, and style. With what is said of Matthew we generally agree, though we demur to many of the opinions adduced concerning Mark. The old opinion that Mark was an abridgment of Matthew is now exploded. We wonder how it could ever be entertained. Mark's gospel is shorter than Matthew's as a whole, but relatively longer in its several parts. The incidents which it does contain, are related with more fulness of detail and more vividness of sketch. An abridgment lessens the minuteness of relation and darkens the brightness of the sketch, and judging on such grounds we should be inclined to say, that Mark's gospel has about it more features of originality than the Collectanea of the first evangelist. The author of the 'Literary History' does not indeed affirm that Mark is an epitomator of Matthew, but he considers the second gospel as entirely dependent on the first, as not merely modified by it, but virtually composed out of it, even while he fully enumerates those peculiarities of fulness, accuracy and picturesqueness of sketch which do not belong to Matthew, but which distinguish Mark. If he, also, without thorough examination rejects the hypothesis that Mark's gospel is a record of Peter's preaching—a Petrine gospel—then how does he prove its inspiration or account for its early reception. These latter questions he has overlooked in the course of his discussions. In short, the author fails to account for the many and striking coincidences of Mark and Luke where both oppose Matthew. The examination of the relationship of the first three gospels to one another, is a question involving difficulties which the author does not seem to recognise, and demanding as much time and critical examination as the whole of this goodly volume has cost in its composition. Verbal coincidences are far fewer in these gospels than is usually supposed, and are found principally and naturally in the report of Christ's discourses. The remarks on Luke and John are both excellent and in general consistent.

The next chapter is occupied with that *crux criticorum*, a harmony of the gospels—a work that has occupied the attention and industry of many learned men, and remains encumbered with many difficulties. We doubt whether it be possible to form a harmony. Those who attempt it have laboured in vain—*oleum et operam perdunt*. Not that there exist any contradictions in the evangelists which cannot be explained, but as none of them does in every instance follow the order of time, the harmonist in determining the sequency of events is left very much to the promptings of his own imagination. Neither is it easy to determine the exact duration of our Lord's ministry, though we are inclined to think that one point of calculation, the feast spoken of in John v. 1. was the passover—the other festivals mentioned by this evangelist having generally some distinctive appellation added to them, John vii. 2; and x. 22. The attempted harmony of the resurrection is not so lucid as we could have wished, nor do we think it on all points equally satisfactory. We commend to our readers one by Professor Robinson, of New York, published in a late number of the *Bibliotheca Sacra*, and though we have no great faith in the truth and success of any harmony, we rejoice that one in the original text has been advertised by this transatlantic scholar.

The chronology of Paul's life and travels is an interesting topic of investigation, and is intimately connected with all questions as to the date of the epistles, and the place whence they were despatched. It is not treated here separately, but intertwined naturally with the account of the date and place of the various apostolic letters commencing with those to the Thessalonians, Galatians, and the first to the Corinthians, proceeding to the epistle to Titus, the first to Timothy, the second to the Corinthians,and that to the church in Rome, and concluding with the five which were written from Rome, to the Ephesians, to Timothy, to the Colossians, to Philemon and to the Philippians. The anonymous epistle to the Hebrews, deserves and occupies a chapter by itself, though we conceive the loose remarks made on its authorship, are not warranted by the facts in themselves, certainly not by such of them as the author is contented to adduce. We might here apply the *argumentum ad hominem,* and compare this 'Literary History' with other works which we believe bear its author's name upon them. We might also compare the reasons why in our opinion both the epistle to the Hebrews and the book before us are published anonymously. But the many points involved in such discussions are too intricate to be satisfactorily treated in the space allotted to a review. Suffice it to say that in general every opinion adopted by the author, whether tenable or not, is surrounded by argument and has evidently not been received without due examination. After an inquiry into the time and place and design of the various epistles, we have a succinct analysis of their contents, often indeed involving exegetical opinions to which we cannot give our assent. The interpretation of the Apocalypse, for example, is delicate ground. The author of the Literary History has given a long and ingenious chapter upon it. For the most part he follows Elliott's Horae Apocalypticae, a book of uncommon cleverness and research, yet in our opinion distinguished as much by the fertility of its invention as the felicity of its discoveries. We have long had doubts as to the correctness of the methods of expounding the Apocalypse. In the hands of its expositors, it resembles a musical instrument, there being no variation or fantasia which may not be played upon it. Some authors find its fulfilment in Constantine's elevation, others in Luther's Reformation. One discerns its completion in the French Revolution, and another sees in it a portraiture of the principles and struggles of the voluntary controversy. Woodhouse and Mede, Bicheno and Croly, Faber and Elliott, Newton and Robertson, have constructed opposite systems with equal tenacity of purpose and ingenuity of conjecture. In the mean time we can only add that the year-day theory requires defence—that the purpose of the Apocalypse, needs to be more clearly defined, and that fortuitous similitude of events is not to mould our interpretation of prophetic symbols. Let us conclude by exhibiting one example of the peculiar fancies of Apocalyptic exegesis. The 'New Song' sung before the throne in heaven is interpreted by Elliott as meaning 'the new and blessed doctrines of the Reformation,' and the author of the Literary History adds, 'it might be deemed fanciful to consider the harpings as symbolical of the very remarkable rise and spread of psalmody at the time of the Reformation, and yet it is certain that this formed a very marked feature of the great protestánt revival.' We refrain from comment.

We have said that the author sometimes quietly takes things for granted which require to be proved. Thus, in speaking, page 183, of the persons addressed by Peter, in his first epistle, he styles them Christian brethren of the Hebrew stock, perhaps not aware that many and strong objections lie against such a theory. Could any of the Hebrew stock be accused in those days of 'abominable idolatries,' 1 Pet. iv. 3? We are also by no means inclined to accede so easily to the assertion, 'that the Spirit of Christ, after his crucifixion, proceeded to that region of the invisible world in which the spirits of the antediluvian transgressors were held in custody; and that to those who were disobedient to Noah, our Lord made proclamation.' We neither believe this, nor receive it as an explication of 1 Peter iii. 18—20. At least, we ask proof for the theory adduced. We are sorry to add, that the difficulties of this passage have so excited the author, that he adds, 'speaking unadvisedly,' 'in the whole compass of the apostolic writings, no other passage occurs having so much the appearance of a marginal gloss.' Page 189. We trust that this rash opinion will not be felt 'as a dead fly in the ointment of the apothecary.'

The author's assumption of Archbishop Usher's opinion, that the Epistle to the Ephesians is an encyclical letter, would probably be modified by a patient and prolonged examination of the subject. The reading 'εν Εφέσῳ in the first verse, cannot be impugned, and the quotations usually taken from Basil and Jerome, do not, when critically considered, yield any proof of the theory, that the letter was an apostolic circular.. We beg to refer the reader to the article EPHESIANS, in Dr. Kitto's *Cyclopædia of Biblical Literature*, and to a recent discussion of the same subject in the pages of this review.

Another of the author's favourite theories is that Silas and Luke are only different names for the same person. The grounds of this hypothesis are by no means very stable. For the peculiar change of name no reason is given, nor is there any traditionary hint on the subject. The two names, moreover, bear no resemblance. The author indeed adduces some changes of names as affording analogous proof to his hypothesis. But Peter and Cephas are the same term in different languages, Thomas and Didymus are similarly related, and Lebbeus and Thaddeus are synonymes. Zelotes and Canaanite are not properly names, but only the same designation, the former expressed in Greek the latter in Syro-Chaldaic. Bartholomew, if it refer to Nathaniel, is only a patronymic. The double names of Saul and Paul are distinctly recorded, and Levi, if it be the name of Matthew, has a similar signification with it according to Winer, in his *Real-Wörterbuch*, sub voce. The theorist says farther in defence of his hypothesis, 'Lucanus is derived from lucus, and Sylvanus from sylva, and *lucus* and *sylva* signify the same thing.' But so far from being related at all to Lucus, Lucanus is only the Grecised form of the Syriac Lucas and Silvanus (not Sylvanus as the author erroneously spells it) is merely the Grecised form of Silas. Neither lucus nor silva are therefore etymologically connected with the ideal Lucanus or the actual Silvanus. If the assumption of a Roman name was usual on acquiring the privilege of a Roman citizen, then Silas is easily Romanised into Silvanus, but the interchange of Lucas into Silvanus is both pedantic and unnecessary. Besides the author of the 'Acts' adheres to the short and original name Silas, between which and Lucas there is no connection. More probable than this conjecture is the theory that Silas is the same person as Tertius mentioned in Romans xvi. 22, for Silas and Tertius have in their respective tongues the same signification. The other arguments adduced on behalf of the theory which we are opposing are very precarious. They refer to the phraseology occasionally employed in the book of Acts. The author endeavours to show that the use of the term 'we,' on the part of the historian, has special reference to Silas, who by this phraseology includes himself with Paul, and proves himself to be the author of the annals. Paul chose Silas for his companion after his separation from Barnabas, and went immediately afterwards through Syria and Cilicia confirming the churches. But of this journey no account is given. It is strange, if Silas were the author, that he gives no account of this first journey with Paul. No mention is made of his progress till having gone through Syria and Cilicia he came to Derbe and Lystra. The author erroneously represents this ulterior portion of the missionary tour as the principal part of it. The progress was continued through Phrygia and the region of Galatia, and no record of the enterprise is left. Is not this a strange omission, if Silas were the author. At the same time throughout the brief account, or rather mention of the stages of this his first journey, no identification of himself as the author takes place. The 'we' never occurs. The historian first associates himself with the apostle at Troas, where he seems to have joined him—'we endeavoured to go into Macedonia,' while two verses before it is said 'they assayed to go into Bithynia.' It is added in the verse first quoted, 'assuredly gathering that the Lord had called us to preach the gospel unto them.' The author argues from this language that the only individuals divinely appointed to preach the gospel were Paul and Silas and Timotheus, who are therefore associated by Paul with himself in his epistles to the Macedonians. One of these persons therefore must have been the writer of the book. The inference is too sweeping for the premises. The use of the term *us* will not justify it. The association of the historian with his party does not prove that he put himself on an equality with them, for Paul says, '*We* shall not all die but *we* shall be changed.' The 'we' implying this association is never used when Paul and Silas are the only persons to whom it could apply. Care is taken never to use it in such circumstances. It is not used in the long account of the imprisonment of Paul and Silas at Philippi. We cannot conceive it possible, had Silas been the author, that in the narration of this interesting event he should not have for once used the terms *we* or *us*. Luke seems never to have held any official public station and so could not with propriety be associated with Silas and Timothy in the apostolic salutations. The writer in the Acts says, the Pythoness 'followed Paul and us', and the author of the theory on which we are animadverting concludes, that the *us* must be understood of Silas and Timotheus, otherwise the writer would assuredly have said Paul and Silas. But Paul was the principal personage in the scene, and his companions the historian associates with himself. Silas afterwards was absent from Paul for some time, and during this period Paul visited Athens. Now of this visit we have a full narration with a report of Paul's famous oration on Mars' Hill. Strange mode of procedure, if Silas were the author; that he is silent, or at least brief in reference to scenes in which he and Paul were the only associates, and so full and circumstantial as to other incidents, visits and addresses, when himself was absent. Does this conduct resemble nature or probability? The last account we have of Silas is his joining Paul at Corinth. His name does not occur afterwards, nor does he appear in any way to be connected with the narrative. We read afterwards of Timothy being associated with Paul, but no mention is made of Silas in the list, while Luke shows himself in the use of the first person plural. Silas does not appear again, but the author of the book of Acts identifies himself with the history, and came to Rome with Paul. There is no evidence that Silas was at Rome with the apostle, while Luke is referred to in three out of the five epistles, written from the metropolis, viz., in the epistles to Philemon, to the Colossians, and the second to Timothy. Paul's reference to Luke and Silas leaves no doubt that they were different persons. Had he used this change of name, as our author imagines, he could only have embarrassed the churches. Silvanus is associated with Paul in his opening salutation to the church in Thessalonica, both epistles being written from Corinth, while Silas was with the apostle, but if Silas were the same person with Luke, he was at Rome with Paul and is yet associated with him in no salutation, (not even in the epistle to the Philippians), while Luke is incidentally mentioned, and in such a way as his humbler station warranted. The whole history of Silas proves that he was neither Luke nor the author of the Acts of the Apostles. The theory of our author is fallacious and baseless, unnatural and unnecessary.

We cannot occupy more space. We can only say in conclusion, that we have read this volume with great pleasure. That pleasure is enhanced by the assurance that its author is a layman, to whom such studies are a pleasant occupation. He has in this instance concealed his name. The reasons of concealment are best known to himself, for his name stands on the title page of other works that occupy no mean rank in our popular and instructive literature. We believe we are not wrong in saying that we have met the author before in the field of biblical inquiry, and that we owe to him an anonymous translation and brief exposition of the epistle to the Hebrews, published in London in 1834.

Art. III. *Household Verses* By Bernard Barton. Virtue. 1845.

The reappearance of an old friend is always welcome; this neat little volume therefore, inscribed with the well-remembered name of Bernard Barton, comes before us with peculiar claims on our attention and regard. During the last ten or twelve years, death has been busy among our poets; sickness, and advancing age, too, have compelled many more to give up 'the gentle craft,' we are therefore well pleased to find a writer, whose productions have always been marked by much grace and feeling, putting forth his 'eighth volume of verse, after a silence of nine years, in trustful reliance,' as he says in his modest preface, 'on its indulgent reception by a public from whom he has never met with aught but courtesy and kindness.'

The unpretending but pleasing title given to this little volume, well describes its character. Many of the poems are addresses to living, or memorials of departed friends; many have been suggested by passing occurrences, and many are the pleasant musings of a thoughtful, pious, and grateful mind. The stanzas on page 103 are graceful, but the following poem is of a higher order; we regret our space will only allow the admission of the subjoined stanzas. They were suggested by a beautiful copy of the Madonna and child, presented to him by a friend.

'I may not change the simple faith,
In which from childhood I was bred;
Nor could I, without scorn, or scathe,
The living seek among the dead;
My soul has far too deeply fed
On what no painting can express,
To bend the knee, or bow the head,
To aught of pictured loveliness.

'And yet, Madonna! when I gaze
On charms unearthly, such as thine;
Or glances yet more reverent raise
Unto that infant, so Divine!
I marvel not that many a shrine
Hath been, and still is reared to thee,
Where mingled feelings might combine
To bow the head and bend the knee.

'And hence I marvel not at all,
That spirits, *needing outward aid,*
Should feel and own the magic thrall
In your meek loveliness displayed:

And if the objects thus portrayed
Brought comfort, hope, or joy to them,
Their error, let who will upbraid,
I rather pity—than condemn.

'For me, though not by hands of mine
May shrine or altar be upreared,
In you, the *human* and *Divine*
Have both so beautiful appeared,
That each, in turn hath been endeared,
As in you feeling has explored
Woman—with holier love revered,
And God—more gratefully adored.'—pp. 83—85,

In a similar feeling, these pretty lines were written, 'to illustrate a sketch of a ruined chapel.'

'Turn not thou in pride aloof
From this simple, lowly roof;
Still let memory's gentle spell
Save from scorn the Saint's Chapelle.

'Humble as it now appears,
Yet its floor, in by-gone years,
Has by worshippers been trod,
Gathered there to praise their God.

'Even now, though 'tis but rare,
Intervals of praise and prayer,
Which recall its former use,
Should redeem it from abuse.

'Where devotion hath been felt,
Where the devotee hath knelt,
Chance or change, which years have brought,
Should not check a serious thought.

'Where Religion's holy name
Hath preferred its sacred claim,
While a relic can be found
Count it still as hallowed ground.

'Hallowed—not by formal rite,
Framed in Superstition's night;—
Ceremonial type, or sign,
Sanctify no earthly shrine.

'But the homage of the heart,
Thoughts and feelings which impart
Trust in time, and hope in heaven,
These to hallow earth were given,—p. 91.

Many of the sonnets are worthy transcription; we give the following as a specimen :—

'And I said, 'This is my infirmity: but I will remember the years of the right hand of the Most High!'—Psalm lxxvii. 10.

'Almighty Father! in these lines, though brief,
Of thy most holy word, how sweet to find
Meet consolation for a troubled mind,
Nor for the suffering body less relief!
When pain or doubt would, as a mighty thief,
Rob me of faith and hope, in Thee enshrined,
O be there to these blessed words assigned
Balm for each wound, a cure for every grief.
Yes! I *will* think of the eternal years
Of Thy right hand! the love, the ceaseless care,
The tender sympathy *Thy works* declare,
And *Thy word* SEALS; until misgiving fears,
Mournful disquietudes, and faithless tears,
Shall pass away as things which never were!'—p. 93.

With the subjoined remarkably flowing, and graceful elegiac verses, to the memory of a young friend, we must conclude: recommending Bernard Barton's pleasant 'Household Verses' to all our readers, and assuring him that we shall always be ready to welcome a similar volume from his pen.

'Lilies, spotless in their whiteness,
Fountains, stainless in their brightness,
Suns, in cloudless lustre sinking,
Fragrant flowers, fresh breezes drinking,
Music, dying while we listen,
Dew-drops, falling as they glisten;
All things brief, and bright, and fair,
Many might with thee compare.
'Symbols these of time and earth;
Not of thy more hidden worth!
Charms, THY memory which endear,
Were not of this lower sphere;

Such we reverently trace,
Not of nature, but of grace!
By their birthright, pure and high,
Stamped with immortality.
'Brightly as these shone in thee,
THINE, we know, they could not be!
Yet we love thee not the less,
That thou couldst such gifts possess,
And, still mindful of their Donor,
Use them to advance HIS honour
Meekly, humbly, prompt to own
All their praise was HIS alone!—p. 33.

Art. IV.—*Pindari Carmina ad fidem textus Boeckhiani*. Edidit Gul. Gifford Cookesley, M. A. Etonæ, 1842 and 1844, 8vo.

There are many names of past times, renowned for genius in various branches, whose reputation rests solely on the testimony of their more immediate contemporaries, since no extant memorials enable us to judge of it for ourselves. There are others, whose remains are indeed extant, but seldom or never are read with an unprejudiced mind; since the concert of eulogies sounded forth concerning them preoccupy or abash the modern student. Among the former is Archilochus, the inventor of Iambic verse; among the latter we are disposed to reckon Pindar, the great poet of Thebes. Most of us gain our earliest opinion of him from the epithets and panegyrics of Horace; and take for granted that this 'Dircæan swan' 'borne by the copious breeze' is incapable of producing any thing tame, homely, pedantic, dry, stiff and incoherent. We conceive of him as rushing in impetuous torrent through 'dithyrambic measures, unrestrained by law,' and pouring forth nothing but the sublimest strains of a raptured bard.

Far be it from us to question that Pindar is a poet of great power, and that he has passages of vivid eloquence and delicate perception. But we do pointedly assert, that his extant poems are not at all equal to his renown; that they show rather what he might have done, than satisfy us as to what he has done; that four-fifths of them are not of what we popularly call a *Pindaric* character; that there is in them a vast deal of pedantry, of prosaic feebleness, and of trash; that, so far from being carried along in a flood of feeling, he constantly shows a painful difficulty in finding any thing at all to say. This last point is to us his most pervading fault, and may deserve to be more particularly explained.

The extant poetry of Pindar, with the exception of a few fragments, consists of songs in praise of the victors at different Greek games: chiefly horse-racing, wrestling and running on foot. To an Englishman it might seem that the great difficulty in treating such subjects would be, to give them variety. A single ode on a horse-race might be thought neither unpleasing in itself, nor alien from an epic and elevated style, however destitute of moral and intrinsic elevation: but to continue to compose ode upon ode on the same subject would appear to us utterly ruinous to the finest poetical genius. The remarkable fact is, that Pindar escapes the difficulty by cutting the knot: he never writes upon his professed subject, but carves out some byework which could never have been conjectured. In all his odes remaining to us we do not remember a single passage which sets vividly before the eyes the picture either of a horse galloping, or of two men wrestling or straining in the race. It is not difficult to cull from our own poets pictures of much beauty on these or kindred topics. Thus in Scott's Marmion :—

——— Fast as shaft can fly,
Blood-shot his eyes, his nostrils spread,
The loose rein dangling from his head,
Housing and saddle bloody red,
Lord Marmion's steed rush'd by.

In all Pindar we doubt whether any fuller description of a galloping horse can be found than the following words from his first Olympian ode: 'He rushed along the side of (the river) Alpheus, *yielding his body without spur to the race,* and advanced his lord to victory.' So far is he from being full of action and ardour in his description of the real deeds of men and horses, that we should rather call him sedate, pompous and *statuesque.* A few ornamental and common-place epithets, such as 'the flower of storm-footed steeds,' appears to him more than enough for such subjects. Having thus unceremoniously put aside his obvious materials for song, it is his business to invent new matter; and we need not wonder that he was often at a loss.

He has nevertheless a fixed system of his own for finding a topic. It is this :—to search into the family of the victor for some one whose pedigree can be traced up to a god or a nymph; in default of this, the city, or if possible, the tribe of the victor is made to yield some kindred mythological story. The foundation of the city may stand connected with some heroic tradidition, or the chief family of the tribe may have gained various other victories. In many cases, the poet brings in his personality; tells, perhaps, his peculiar reverence for a hero who has a chapel in the city of the victor, or other matter equally uninteresting to a reader. The result of all this is, that a Pindaric ode consists of several disjointed pieces. When the author has laid hold of his thread, he goes on fluently, and perhaps majestically until it is expended: he then stops suddenly short, and is embarrassed for several or many lines together, until he, as suddenly, starts on a new course. Instead of a single noble flight, like that of the eagle or the pigeon, we have a succession of minor *spurts,* like the flitting of a sparrow. The incoherence of the parts is often made still more clumsy by the prosaic remarks, moralizing or jocose and personal sallies, which are interposed between two poetical and mythological effusions. Occasionally he gives a string of half-intelligible proverbs, or wise sentiments, which, according to our ideas of poetry, are singularly out of place: or he will sing out in good dithyrambic a simple catalogue of the prizes gained by his hero at the several festivals of the Greeks. In even the most frigid of these inferior portions, the boldest or rather harshest metaphors are often intermixed, as an effort, it would seem, to rid the subject of its essentially prosaic character. Thus, instead of saying that the victor had also borne away at Pellene the prize of a 'cloak,' he tells us that he won 'a remedy (*pharmakon*, a drug?) against cold breezes.' Instead of professing to be 'incited or *whetted* to sing,' he most enigmatically declares: 'I have on my tongue an appearance of a shrill hone, which draws me on, willing as I am, to beautifully flowing breezes.' The hone, it seems, was wanted to sharpen his tongue! Even many of his better ideas lose their force by his artificial variation and intertangling of his clauses. Thus, in the opening of his first Olympian ode, he has a series of comparisons which an epic or bucolic poet would have expressed thus:—

> Water among the elements is best:
> Gold excels among metals:
> The Sun is chief among the stars:
> And the Olympian is the noblest of public games.

This indeed would have been nearly in the style of many passages in Theocritus and in Virgil's Eclogues. But Pindar is not satisfied with this simplicity, and he ambitiously enunciates his thought thus:—

> 'Water is best: and gold, as a shining fire excels in the night, eminently amid wealth which exalts a man: but if thou longest to tell of contests, O my heart, no longer regard any other star as more fostering than the Sun, through the vacant ether; nor let us proclaim any contest as superior to the Olympian.'

Here we are embarrassed by comparison within comparison. The Olympian contest is like gold among metals, and gold is like a fire in the night. The artificial structure of the whole is such, that none of the parts are impressed forcibly on the mind, and the last comparison about the sun stands in a structure so different from the two former, that these are nearly wasted; since they cannot remain on the ear until the word Olympian is named. This, however, is a most inadequate representation of the extraordinary complication and artifice which he affects, a large part of which can in no way be set forth in a translation, because his transpositions of words could not be imitated without producing mere nonsense; beside that his phraseology can have no parallel. Nothing, however, is more contrary to the fact, that to conceive of Pindar as ordinarily a gushing stream:

on the contrary, it is often a sort of elaborate mosaic work, concerning which his excellent editor Heyne has constantly to say, 'doctè extulit,' 'he has *learnedly* elevated' the expression,—exactly as in commenting on Virgil.

A really faithful translation of Pindar's extant odes would be in English quite unbearable; nor it is possible to approach to faithfulness without being thought by the English reader to *murder* the author by unskilful handling. Undoubtedly a literal translation must often of necessity drop many artifices of expression by which he sought to relieve the tameness of his thought; and in this sense does *some* injustice. But it is evident that poetry which wholly depends on artifice must be of a very inferior kind. With this preface, we venture to set before our readers a literal translation of one entire ode, which we did not select for its worthlessness, but opened on at random. There are certainly many much finer, but there are many more not at all superior.

NEMEA II.

TO TIMODEMUS, AN ATHENIAN, SON OF TIMONÖUS

α. That from which the Homeridæ, singers of constructed poems, generally begin:—Jupiter their argument. This man* also has received a foundation of victory in the sacred contests first in the much-hymned grove of Nemeæan Jupiter.

β. It is still due from him, if along his† father's road straight-escorting time has given him as an honour to mighty Athens, *often* to cull the most beautiful flower of the Isthmiads, and to gain the victory in the Pythia, son as he is of Tinonöus. And it is quite appropriate

γ. that Orion should not go far off from those mountain nymphs the Pleiades. And surely Salamis is able to rear a warrior. In Troy, Hector heard Ajax. Thee too, O Timodemus, the daring courage of the‡ tustle shall exalt.

δ. It is an old saying, that the Acharnians are brave. But in all that concerns contests, the Timodemidæ are published as eminent. At the side of high-ruling Parnassus they carried off four victories from contests, but by the Corinthians

ε. in the valley of brave Pelops, they have already been mingled with eight chaplets, and seven in Nemea: but those at home are too many to count, in the games of Jupiter. Whom, O citizens, celebrate in song, upon the glorious return of Timodemus. Lead off, with sweet tuned voice.'

* The victor.

† i.e., if time is to lead him along his father's road; if he is to take after his father.

‡ Pancratium: it united boxing, kicking, biting, &c. &c.

Here is an instance of an Athenian conqueror, concerning whose family the poet could not rake up a single legend; and in consequence, his powers are paralyzed. The only facts which he had were these;—that his father was a good boxer, his family had gained the prizes which are recounted, and his parish, Acharnæ, contained a stout militia. To hammer out of these a single poetical sentiment was no doubt arduous; but it was not requisite to vex us by all the abruptness and obscurity of the third stanza. Moreover, if Pindar had chosen, there were already many great deeds of the Athenians to celebrate; but his Theban jealousies wholly forbade expatiating in that field.

The extent to which his mind was tied down to religious legends—it mattered not how absurd, provided they were religious—is shown, when he has to write in honour of men politically great, whose own lives gave abundant subject for poetry. Such is the case with his patron and friend Hiero, the king or tyrant of Syracuse, for whom he composed numerous odes: yet in them all, we find merely meagre and generally obscure allusions to Hiero's real exploits, while the only grand poetry is about matters, some of which, he tells us, he himself suspects to be fables. Certain of these odes to Hiero, on the other hand, are overrun with *sermonizing*, as the 2nd Pythian, under which his editor and commentator, Heyne, seems to have nearly lost his patience. We could not inflict on the reader a translation of the last fifty lines, which, Heyne civilly hints, would have been better suppressed; but, fairly to illustrate the nature of his superior poetry, we perhaps cannot do better than give an analysis of the *thoughts* contained in the first Olympian, which is decidedly admired; which, also, as written for the same Hiero, will show how the poet 'runs off in a tangent,' when he has alighted, somehow or other, on a mythical name.

SUBSTANCE OF THE FIRST OLYMPIAN.

(TO HIERO, WHOSE GIG HAD WON A PRIZE.)

α. As water among the elements, gold among metals, and the sun among stars, such is the Olympian among contests; concerning which sage bards sing to Jupiter, at the blessed hearth of Hiero:

α. who sways the sceptre of justice in fruitful Sicily, culling the choicest flowers of virtue, and brilliant with the bloom of music. Come, snatch the Dorian harp from the peg, if the glory of Olympia and of (the horse) Pherenicus (i.e. *conqueror*) has inspired sweetest thoughts; when unspurred, he rushed along the side of Alpheus, and raised to distinction

A. his Syracusan master, a king who exults in horses. His glory also shines in the brave colony of Lydian Pelops; OF WHOM Neptune was enamoured, when Clotho took him out of the caldron, and he had a shoulder of ivory! Surely there are many marvels: and fables adorned with falsehood, deceive men's minds;

β. and beauty makes the incredible seem credible: but the test of truth is in time to come. It is safer for men to speak honourably of the divinities. I therefore, O son of Tantalus, contrary to former poets, assert, that when Jupiter in his turn gave a feast to the gods at the city of Sipylus, Neptune carried thee off,

β. being subdued by desire, and transported thee to the lofty halls of Jupiter. And when thou wast not to be found, one of the spiteful neighbours said that thy limbs had been cut up with a knife, and thrown into boiling water, had been distributed along the tables, and been eaten.

B. But I am at a loss to call any of the blessed gods gluttons. I shrink from it. Evil speakers meet with punishment. But if any mortal man was honoured by the gods, Tantalus was he; but he could not bear his prosperity. Therefore Jupiter, in punishment, hung a huge stone over his head, and so ruined his happiness.

γ. He is fourth with three others who endure perpetual calamity, because, when admitted to the table of the gods, he stole their nectar and ambrosia, whereby they made him immortal, and gave it to his messmates and equals in age. No one's actions can escape a god's notice. For this reason they sent his son Pelops down to take rank among common men. And when a manly beard began to darken his chin, he set his mind on a marriage ready prepared;—

γ. to get the noble Hippodamia from her father [Œnomaus] the lord of Pisa. And drawing near alone in the darkness of the hoary sea, he called upon the loud-roaring god of the trident; and he appeared to him close at his side. To him he said: 'If, O Neptune, the dear gifts of Venus count for favour, chain the brazen spear of Œnomaus: and speed me to Elis on swiftest car, and advance me to victory; since he has slain thirteen suitors, and defers the wedding

Γ of his daughter. Great peril admits not of a coward. But since die we must, why should one pine out an ignoble old age, void of glory? I therefore will undertake the risk, and do thou give me success.' So spake he; and not in vain. The god adorned him with the gift of a golden chariot, and winged horses, that knew not weariness.

δ. He conquered the mighty Œnomaus, and the maiden for his consort; and she bare him six chieftain-sons, tended by the virtues. Now funeral rites are paid at his much frequented tomb, where he lies by the channel of Alpheus, near the altar which strangers visit. And his glory has shone afar in the course of Olympia, where swiftness of foot and athletic strength contend. And the victor, for the rest of his life enjoys honied repose,

'δ. at least as far as contests are concerned. But a good which is perpetual, is the highest that man can have. I, however, must crown HIM [Hiero] with an equestrian tune in Æolic playing; nor do I expect to sing the praises of any stranger either more skilful or more powerful. God watches over thee, O Hiero; and unless he fail thee, I hope soon to celebrate a nobler victory for thee

'Δ. in the four-horse car, finding a subject of song to aid me, by coming to the sunny hill of Saturn (near Olympia). For me, at any rate, the muse keeps in store a most powerful shaft. But different persons are great in different lines; and the top of all is mounted by kings. Look not round for any thing beyond. Mayst *thou* continue to walk aloft, and may *I*, as long, associate with victors, being prominent everywhere among the Greeks for wisdom [poetical skill].'

It will be observed, that of twelve stanzas, almost the whole of eight are concerned with the legend of Peleus, upon which the poet drops bythe fortune of the word *Peloponnesus*, and from which he again disentangles himself by the fact of Pelops having a tomb near Olympia; which brings back the song to the scene of the games. Hiero had no more to do with Pelops, than had every other victor at Olympia, or, we may almost say, every one who set foot on Peloponnesus. Again, the stanzas which do refer to Hiero say absolutely no more about him than that he is king of Syracuse, and of course, very virtuous, fond of horses and fond of music. It seems wonderful that the poet could have so completely avoided anything distinctive. When he gets into the heart of a legend, he has no doubt great power of striking off much by a single touch. The appearance of Neptune to Pelops in the darkness and solitude of the sea, is majestic, by its very simplicity: and the fluency of his tale, when he feels able to tell it straight forward, is in advantageous contrast to his stumbling and arguing, while feeling after his clue. His frequent talking *to* and of himself and his muse, and even *discussing what he shall sing about*, appears slightly in this ode. His exhortations to himself are sometimes the more offensive for being clothed in enigma; as:—'Ho! charioteer, yoke the strong mules for me; for they know the road very well, since they gained prizes at Olympia; that I may drive aloft to the man and his ancestry.' This is only another mode of saying: 'Let me now sing of the man and his ancestry!'

Perhaps, on the whole, the most celebrated of all Pindar's odes, in modern times, are the first and the fourth Pythian.

The first Pythian, also to Hiero, is principally set off by a splendid description of the eruption of Mount Etna, which had recently occurred, and kindled the poet's imagination. Æschylus, also, in his Prometheus, has majestically touched on the same subject. But, beside this, the opening of the ode, concerning the power of the lyre over gods and man, and the eagle of Jupiter, is very beautiful. The elevated strain is kept up for about fifty-five short lines in all, or for less than *one-third* of the entire ode; after which he descends into talking, praying, arguing, and moralizing in proverbs, with much beside that is thoroughly prosaic. He then (v. 140) alludes to a naval victory gained by Hiero over the Carthaginians; but in the driest and most concise manner; and once more gets into 'maxim-coining' (γνωμοτυπια) which, regarded as poetry, must be judged actual trash.

The fourth Pythian is in honour of Arcesilaus, king of Cyrene, a city which, as legends told, had been founded in accordance with a prophecy of Medea, when on board the ship Argo. This leads the poet to narrate the adventures of the Argonauts. He enters upon his subject after a very short introduction, and continues it without flagging for nearly 450 lines. If he could have ended here, the ode would have been of one thread throughout: but decency to the victor obliged him, it seems, to tack on 80 more lines of very indifferent merit. There is no other instance, however, in which Pindar has laid hold of a legend which afforded him so abundant material, and allowed him so long a flight, without any of the checks and incoherences which generally disfigure his poetry.

The general conclusion to which we are brought is, that Pindar's genius was quite unsuited to the species of composition by which alone he is known to us. If he had not been embarrassed by the victor who was to be complimented—if he had been allowed to dedicate his muse directly and avowedly to the praises of some god or deceased hero—to celebrate some mythical event, and follow out his contemplations and religious musings as his feelings dictated, he would assuredly have produced poetry very superior to that which we now read, and might possibly have been admired by us now in a faithful translation. Yet, even here, we cannot forget that his religious sentiment, although it now and then rose above the common superstition, revelled in tales of extreme stupidity, and sometimes expresses them in terms of gross indecency, according to our present standard of judgment. The few fragments which remain of his Dirges for the Dead are in a noble strain; but as nothing has saved them to us but their eminent moral beauty, we are hardly at liberty to conclude that what has been lost was equally fine.

We return to the topic from which we began. Are we to take our estimate of Pindar from the suffrage of antiquity?—and how far can we trust that suffrage? A third question, indeed, may be asked: Is there any evidence that the admiration of his genius was universal among the ancients? To answer the last question satisfactorily, would belong to one who was putting forth an edition of Pindar. Here we will merely say, that in Plato he seems to be quoted, like Simonides, as a *moral* authority, and, as such, highly revered; but that purely *poetical* merit does not appear to be the ground for which poets are ever admired by Plato, who would have banished Homer from his republic. Setting Plato aside, we do not know whither next to look for any peculiar admiration of Pindar, until we come down to Horace: thus it may seem, on a superficial view, uncertain whether he was generally admired until his works became a literary study in rather late times. But dropping this as doubtful or unimportant,—for something of the kind has happened to Shakspere and Milton,—we *are* disposed to question whether the ancient judgment on such matters ought to carry with it for us a decisive weight. It is observed by Hallam, that in criticising writers of the dark ages, some historians are apt to bestow undue admiration on those few who rise above their contemporaries, forgetting, it might seem, how enormously they fall below those of other times. So, also, if the ancients ever so intensely admire some lost poet, we must not immediately infer that his merit rose high according to an absolute standard, unless we know that they had models of high excellence to compare him with. Now, in the case of Pindar, we have several warnings that he was admired with the ardour and devotion of inexperience. Horace talks, with a sort of veneration, of his impetuous dithyrambics 'free from law;' but there is strong reason for suspecting that Pindar's metres are at least as subject to law as the lyric metres of the tragedians, and that the notion of their lawlessness arose out of ignorance. Certainly, in all his extant odes, a rigid exactness prevails. They are arranged in one of two modes; some of them having but a single species of stanza, others two sorts, which recur in a fixed order. Stanzas of the same kind agree with extreme minuteness, nearly syllable to syllable; and there is no doubt whatever that all such were all made to correspond to the same piece of music. The music itself, indeed, of Pindar, (as the curious researches of some recent German critics seem to have proved) was oftenest of a quaint and wild character as regards its *time;* which, in the dialect of modern musicians, would be called *five-eighths* or *five-fours* time: that is, it had five quavers or five crotchets in a bar, like the wild tune called 'The Gypsy's Glee,' if we rightly remember the name. This circumstance is probably the true explanation of the fact which Horace dimly conceived: whether he had ever *heard* the true Pindaric music is quite uncertain.

But the rapturous praise lavished on music generally by the Greeks, is in itself a significant circumstance; when we have so much ground to believe that *their* music was of a most contemptible kind. Let not the reader start at our strong expression, but calmly consider a few facts. The legends concerning Orpheus, who was said to charm wild beasts by his music; and concerning Amphion, at the sound of whose lyre the walls of Thebes sprang up,—belong to a very early period of Greece; for in Pindar's day they were universally current and unquestioned. Yet, until the time of Terpander, about 650 B.C., the lyre had no more than four strings,—that is, it was a harp with four *notes** only! Pindar himself had a seven-stringed lyre, although an eighth string was already used, barely completing the octave. Sharps and flats could not be played, and every melody would need to be wholly in one key, or to be played out of tune. The only mode, which we can conceive, of giving variety with one instrument, would be to tune the strings at different times to a different pitch: but this would seriously injure their tone. Thus a tolerable harmonicon, and much more, the most ordinary Welsh harp, is immensely superior to Pindar's lyre. It may indeed appear, that the lyre could not be used at all to express a melody, but only to sound notes here and there, like a drum, for the sake of supporting the *voice* when singing. We must go farther. It could not play a bass accompaniment to the voice; for the learned almost unanimously teach us that the Greeks were unacquainted with the very first principles of harmony; the word 'harmony' meaning, in their language, (whence we have derived it), only what we call tune, melody, or, vaguely, music. If two persons sang together, they always sang in unison, or at an octave distance; but to give richness to the combination by a first and second part, did not occur to the greatest geniuses of Greece; and until keyed instruments of compass and power had been invented, it appears quite impossible for the modern theory of music to have had any existence. The Greeks, it is confidently stated, had not even discovered the chords which we call 'major and minor thirds;' the most useful and primary elements of musical composition. On the whole, it appears impossible to deny that under all their disabilities, the music of Pindar must have been such as we now should be unable to admire. Yet what says Pindar of his own lyre?—

* It had *no finger-board*, and must not be confounded with a guitar. One string yielded but one note. It had no bridge, and therefore could not be layed with a bow.

'Thou quenchest the warrior thunderbolt of every flowing fire; and the eagle of Jove, riveted by thy shafts, swims in slumber with his back relaxed, and drops his swift wing on each side. Marsalso leaves the rude conflict, and warms his heart with thy soporiferous influence,' &c., &c.

We will not account for this by saying,—what is quite true,—that at this day in Turkey and elsewhere, educated persons may be seen experiencing high delight at musical performances so atrociously out of tune and otherwise offending all our ideas of melody or harmony, as to seem to us unendurable. There may be something in this topic to explain the phenomenon before us, but not everything. For it is certain that the Greeks cultivated music with great care, and had a nice distinction (of their own) between good and bad. They were, no doubt, what the French would call an *amusable* people; as easily delighted as children, and capable of being thrown into raptures by that which we should receive with tranquillity or apathy: still, those of them who had studied the art of music, were by no means indiscriminate in judgment or careless in execution. The feebleness of the results attained by them was inherent in their imperfect materials. For the Pindaric* lyre, the Lydian flageolet, or the Panpipes, to rival the violin, harp, and piano, the bugle and clarionet, or the organ, was as impossible as for the laborious scribe to keep up with the steam press, or for the stargazer, unaided by a telescope, to see that which is revealed to the modern astronomer. But while we do not undervalue their talents and keenness of taste, we are forced to rate very low the absolute worth of that which they attained in music: and when we consider the unfailing stream of eulogy poured upon the early Greek music, it certainly suggests to us the danger of accepting the testimony of contemporaries as a proof of abstract excellence. That Pindar, in his lost pieces, excelled his contemporaries who essayed the same kind of composition, may be believed, in deference to the current opinion of the ancients: but this does not in itself raise him very high.

If it is not presumptuous to carry the mind on through distant ages; if we may speculate on a time, looking back from which the poets of monarchial and aristocratic England will seem to be in the grey light of antiquity; when men shall comment on Shakspere, Dryden, Scott, Byron, and Crabbe, as did later Greece on her ancient bards:—we feel assured that those remote generations will confess that the English have excelled

* Somewhat later, lyres with eleven strings were used, and some of the Asiatic instruments probably came near to our harps. But the music of these was not thought so chaste by connoisseurs.

the old Greeks in poetry, as much as in learning and science. So large an argument cannot be here opened. We must satisfy ourselves with protesting that after devoting the best years of life to the study,—having started with high admiration of the ancient classics, and under the full influence of that préstige which guards their honour,—while moreover we are still capable of finding much pleasure in their perusal,—we have a conviction, ever increasing with years and experience, that our scholars are blinded by prejudice, and singularly unjust to their native poets, when they hesitate to set them high and far above all that classical antiquity ever reached. Homer is probably the greatest name which Greece can boast: and his poetry will, in all its better parts, stand the severe test of translation into foreign prose without losing its characteristic excellences. But Shakspere is easily equal to Homer and Æschylus put together; and when those names are removed, the Greeks have none left to compare to the splendid list of English poets.

We have touched on a point which needs more elucidation. Those poets in whom *refined beauty* is the sole or chief aim, lose of necessity a large part of their merit in translations; for the *form* of their composition is an important part of the beauty. Those on the contrary whose merits are independent of the form, and who have little or nothing characteristic in that respect, admit of translation with *comparatively* little loss. Such is the case with Homer, and still more with the Hebrew prophets. Now in this very point we are disposed to be severe upon Pindar, that while he has a form of composition peculiar to himself, which often puts the greatest impediments in the way of translating him, this form does not contribute to his beauty, but quite the contrary. His mannerism is his deformity. All his really beautiful passages are simple and straight forward, and lose far less by translation than Virgil or Horace of necessity lose. The description of the Isles of the Blessed, in his second Olympian, though tinged with the puerility of ancient times, would be admired if literally turned into English prose. It is his tangled sentiments and his oracular maxims, his argumentations and his egotism, that are equally untranslateable and trashy. Nor can we defend his incoherence and most offensive abruptness by the theory, that it was in correspondence with some wildness of the music. If this were true, still, as the music cannot be recovered, the fact would not improve his odes to modern readers. But the stanzas prove to us that it cannot be true. At the parts where the same musical intonations must have recurred, there is no recurrence of continuity or transition. A sudden break in the thread of the narrative or of the feeling will be found in one stanza, and at the corresponding place of another stanza nothing of the kind. Hence his oddities must stand or fall in our judgment, by themselves; without receiving any allowance from the consideration of the music.

But while we are disposed to rate the purely poetical value of Pindar's extant odes certainly much lower than the current renown of them, they have of necessity a peculiar *historical* value as have all the remains of antiquity. Standing nearly alone of their kind, they give us a fresh insight into Greek thought and feeling; and if they were even wholly destitute of the splendid passages which are scattered through them, they would not the less need to be carefully studied by the scholar. We strongly deprecate the fashion at our public schools and universities, of teaching all youths indiscriminately as if they were to be historians, critics or professors. Unless the art of teaching shall be greatly expedited, it will always be impossible to make the study of the more obscure Greek poets an ordinary part of good education, without sacrificing what is far more valuable: it is therefore with a mixed feeling that we receive 'Editions for *schools* and colleges.' Nevertheless, as long as such authors *are* read in our schools, it is every way desirable that they should be read *well*; and the greater the difficulty, the more thankful we should be for aids to the learner. We totally repudiate the old notion of schoolmasters, that boys ought not to be allowed a 'Clavis' or book of assistance. The more assistance of this sort they have the better; it may save them the expence of 'private lessons:' and it is the master's place to find out whether they have worked the knowledge out of the book into their heads. The nature of this review does not allow of our criticising in detail Mr. Cookesley's edition of Pindar. It is sufficient to say, that though in size it is more suited to a college than to a school, it is in every respect better adapted to the wants of learners, whether at school or at college, than any other which has been published. The notes are in English; the difficulties of the author are honestly met, and are discussed with learning and good sense. The text is from Boeckh, and has frequent advantage over that of Heyne. For those who are curious of the metre, a table is prefixed to every ode, to give such help as this dark subject admits: and (whatever the success of that attempt) the new distribution of the lines in the stanzas is a great improvement on the old text.

Art. V.—*Delineation of Roman Catholicism, drawn from the acknowledged standards of the Church of Rome: namely, her Creeds, Catechisms, Decisions of Councils, Papal Bulls, Roman Catholic Writers, the Records of History, &c.; in which the peculiar Doctrines, Morals, Government, and Usages of the Church of Rome, are stated, treated at large, and confuted.* By the Rev. Charles Elliott, D.D. A new edition, corrected and revised throughout, with numerous important additions, by the Rev. John S. Stamp. Imperial 8vo. pp. xvi. 822.—London: John Mason, 1844.

The course of Christianity very much resembles that of some rivulets which travellers meet with in the Alps. These rivulets, first appearing in the higher regions of those mountains, are then pure and wholesome like the snows and rains by which they are immediately fed, but many of them afterwards find their various ways into the bowels of the mountains, where they are impregnated with metallic substances; and when they come forth to the light of day again, they show, by the sediment which marks their course, the iron or the copper which they have taken up, and which has rendered them unfit for ordinary use. So has it been with the church, its doctrines, and its practice. In the time of the apostles these were comparatively pure. Faults there were, indeed, as there ever will be in the church, while man is man; but these were not ingrained in the system, they were the result of previous habits, which, though under a process of correction, were not yet fully corrected, or of principles and tendencies which, till they thus manifested themselves, were not known to be opposed to Christianity, and the evil of which was thus revealed and remedied. The evil itself, however, was not a part of the system. It was not, so to speak, held in solution. It was something extraneous, accidentally gathered by the stream in its course, and deposited in the deeper parts of the channel as it rolled on. Very different, however, was the condition of the church in after times. Even in the age of Justin Martyr, if not before, the Gentile philosophy obtained a footing in it, and under its fostering influence many evil principles, which the apostles had successfully resisted, spread widely, and became at length very powerful. When Christianity was incorporated into the empire as the state religion, what had before been encouraged by individual fanaticism, or the evil tendencies of society, became a recognised system. To the lust of power which John had rebuked in Diotrephes, but which in the next age re-appeared in Victor's arrogant order to the Asiatic bishops, respecting the celebration of Easter, and to the will worship, against which Paul had warned the Colossians, but which was so soon practised by the Egyptian Ascetics, and afterwards by the Anchorites and Cœnobites of Syria, Mesopotamia, and Egypt, was then added the whole genius of heathenism, which, with its various deities transformed into saints, and its various orgies disguised as Christian festivals, was absorbed into the church, and became part and parcel of that monstrous system, which, for centuries, held the Roman world in bondage, and is now under the various names of Romanism, Roman Catholicism, and Popery, the great antagonist of truth and holiness wherever it is propagated.

It is beside our purpose to illustrate at length in this place the development of Roman tyranny, superstition, idolatry, and hagiolatry, just now indicated. The student of church history will find ample materials for such a purpose in the pages of Neander, and some in those of Dr. Waddington. As a popular illustration of the subject, we know of nothing better than Dr. Conyers Middleton's celebrated 'Letter from Rome,' the republication of which, in a convenient and portable form, would really be of service to the cause of Protestant Christianity.*

The general nature and object of the work before us are sufficiently explained by its long and explicit title prefixed to this article. The subject, we are informed by Dr. Elliott in the original preface, has occupied his attention for upwards of twenty years. One of his principal reasons for publishing was, he tells us, 'to disabuse the public mind respecting the deceitful character of Popery;' another, to inform Protestants concerning its true nature, tendency, and design.

Romanism is indeed disgracefully distinguished from all other systems by its deceitful character. Tyranny, cruelty, and superstition, are essential parts of it, but fraud and immorality are its peculiar blot. Here more, perhaps, than in any other features, it manifests its heathen parentage. Numerous are the details in the volume now before us, by which we are reminded of the apostle's declaration respecting the heathen mysteries:—*it is a shame even to speak of those things which are done of them in secret*. It is a remarkable, and at the same time a lamentable fact, that one of the greatest negative aids to Romanism in this country and in America, is the repugnance to the contro-

* The title of this work is 'A Letter from Rome, showing an exact conformity between Popery and Paganism; or, the Religion of the present Romanists derived from that of their Heathen Ancestors.' It was first published in 1729; and was reprinted, but at too high a price, in 1816. The work of Dr. Waddington, to which we have referred in the text, is his 'History of the Church,' published in the Library of Useful Knowledge.—See especially Part i. chap. iii. and v.; Part ii. chap. xiii.; Part iv. chap. xix.

versy, produced in minds of moral delicacy, by the impurity of some of the details, which are necessary to the thorough manifestation of the truth. But, however commendable this state of moral feeling is in itself, it is sadly out of place when it is enlisted in the service of deception. So it is no pleasant thing to see Satan as he is; but if he came to us, as an angel of light, must we not, if possible, strip him of his disguise? We fear that thousands have before now been led astray, because they had not moral courage to open their eyes in time. There are certainly details in Dr. Elliott's work which we should rather, in the abstract, that our sisters or our daughters should never see; but we had much rather that they saw and read them all, than that they should run the smallest risk of being added to the number of the victims whose ruin those details narrate.

The work is distributed into four books, headed—'On the Rule of Faith;' 'On the Seven Sacraments of the Church of Rome;' 'On the Government of the Church of Rome;' 'Miscellaneous Doctrines, Usages, &c., of the Church of Rome.' These books are again subdivided into chapters—to most or all of which the English editor has made large additions, which are distinguished from the original work by being enclosed within brackets. The discussion, with these additions, is ample even to redundancy. The continuous reader will not unfrequently find that he has more matter to deal with than he can well retain. For reference, however, this large accumulation is very valuable. This use of the treatise is also provided for by a copious general index;—no inconsiderable aid when a work extends over seven hundred and seventy-one imperial 8vo. pages printed in double columns.

As the work does not pretend to originality, and is chiefly valuable as a digested compilation of testimonies on the various branches of the Romanist controversy, it will be needless, and within our limits it would be impracticable to give an orderly view of it. We shall therefore content ourselves with a few extracts, from a single chapter, by way of specimen.

One of the most fearful engines of the Roman hierarchy is auricular confession. By this, the consciences of the timid are kept in perpetual thraldom; and what is even worse, the moral purity both of priests and people is radically corrupted. Dr. Elliott has devoted a chapter (Book ii. chap. ix.) to this rite, in which he has not only well detailed and refuted the arguments by which the practice of it is upheld, but has exposed its monstrous iniquity. We shall exhibit from his pages, as supplemented by Mr. Stamp, some passages illustrative of the course of his argument.

The following extract shows the ecclesiastical authority on which the practice of auricular confession is enforced. The italics and capitals are ours :—

'The Council of Trent decrees—

'*Canon* 6. Whoever shall deny that sacramental confession was instituted by divine command, or that it is *necessary to salvation;* or shall affirm that the practice of secretly confessing *to the priest alone*, as it has been ever observed from the beginning by the Catholic Church, and is still observed, is foreign to the institution and command of Christ, and is a human invention; LET HIM BE ACCURSED.

'*Canon* 7. Whoever shall affirm that in order to obtain forgiveness in the sacrament of penance, it is not by divine command necessary to confess all and every mortal sin which occurs to the memory after due and diligent premeditation, including secret offences, and those which have been committed against the two last precepts* of the decalogue, and those circumstances which change the species of sin; but that such confession is only useful for the instruction and consolation of the penitent, &c., &c.; LET HIM BE ACCURSED.

'*Canon* 8. Whosoever shall affirm that the confession of every sin, according to the custom of the church is impossible, and merely a human tradition which the pious should reject; or that all Christians of both sexes are not bound to observe the same once a year, according to the institution of the great council of Lateran; and therefore that the faithful in Christ are to be persuaded not to confess in Lent; LET HIM BE ACCURSED.'—p. 199.

Our next extract will give *some* idea of the extent to which confession is demanded; though we have thought it right to omit a portion of what even Mr. Stamp, in our opinion very properly, has stated in his supplementary remarks. The portion omitted relates to the seventh commandment. It will be understood that the passage inclosed in brackets contains a supplement by the English editor.

'From the catechism of the Council of Trent we take the following:—Mortal sins, as we have said, though buried in the darkest secrecy, and also sins of desire only, such as are forbidden by the ninth and tenth commandments, are all and each of them to be made matter of confession.' . . . 'With the bare enumeration of our mortal sins we should not be satisfied; that enumeration we should accompany with the relation of such circumstances as considerably aggravate or extenuate their malice.' ['Some circumstances are such as of themselves to constitute mortal guilt; on no account, or occasion whatever, therefore, are such circumstances to

*** These two precepts correspond to the tenth commandment, as the decalogue is arranged in the Reformed churches. The Romanists and Lutherans join the second, as we have it, to the first.**

be omitted. Has any one imbrued his hands in the blood of his fellow-man? He must state whether his victim was a layman or an ecclesiastic. * * * Again, theft is numbered in the catalogue of sins; but if a person has stolen a guinea, his sin is less grievous than if he had stolen one or two hundred guineas, or a considerable sum; and if the stolen money were sacred, the sin would be still aggravated. To time and place the same observation equally applies; but the instances in which these circumstances alter the complexion of an act are so familiar, and are enumerated by so many writers, as to supersede the necessity of a lengthened detail. Circumstances such as these are therefore to be mentioned; but those which do not considerably aggravate may be lawfully omitted'] After censuring those who justify or extenuate their sins, the Catechism declares—'Still more pernicious is the conduct of those who, yielding to a foolish bashfulness, cannot induce themselves to confess their sins. Such persons are to be encouraged by exhortation, and to be reminded that there is no reason whatever why they should yield to such false delicacy: that to no one can it appear surprising if persons fall into sin, the common malady of the human race, and the natural appendage of human infirmity.' If this quotation be not an apology for the commission of sin, and also for the repetition of it, it will be difficult to say what an apology for sin is.'*—p. 200.

Mr. Stamp has then supplied, from a treatise entituled the 'Garden of the Soul,' a long detail of instructions, in order to a right confession. He was obliged to mutilate them, however, for those relating to the seventh commandment were too indelicate to be inserted. He adds—

'Nevertheless, the obscene pages of Dr. Challener are purity unsullied, compared with those of Peter Dens. We cannot enter the confessional with him as our guide. The instructions with which he furnishes the priests treat of subjects which we dare not name. How agonising must be the feelings of a husband or a father, when hearing those principles of polluting obscenity with which the mind of the priest is replete for the examination of his wife and daughters in the dark and secret confessional, when the poor unprotected female, bound under terror, and constrained of necessity to eternal silence, can have no refuge or escape, no husband or father at hand, to hear and to drag from his den the monster who, under the cloak

* It is worth notice, that the catechism whence this quotation is taken, was stated by Dr. Doyle, in his examination before the Lords Commissioners on the state of Ireland, in 1825, to be the most approved and authentic summary of the Creed of the Roman Catholic Church. In this respect he even preferred it to the decrees of the Council of Trent, 'because,' as he says, 'in the Council of Trent many things are mixed up with the declarations of faith; whereas, the Catechism of the Council is confined, I believe, exclusively to matters of faith and morals.'

of religion, can put every feeling of the heart upon the rack, and, in proportion to her delicacy, her sensibility, her very reverence for what she unhappily believes to be an ordinance of God, instead of an invention of Satanic guilt and tyranny, can bow her spirit into his power, humble her into the dust beneath his feet, if she be virtuous; or drag her, if it be possible, and he be so inclined, into the paths of profligate seduction! . . . Let any parent become acquainted with the unpronounceable abominations of Dens's Theology, on this topic, and he would with pleasure exchange the horrors of the confessional for the persecutions of heresy, and prefer the stake for his wife or daughter to the racks of that moral inquisition to which she is there compelled to submit.'—p. 202.

Lest the abhorrence and fear, expressed in this citation, should appear excessive or exaggerated, we must take an extract from a subsequent part of the chapter. Under the ninth particular Dr. Elliott undertakes to show that 'auricular confession is not only useless or corrupting to him who makes it, but is extremely pernicious to him who hears it.' On this point he quotes some passages from Gavin's* 'Master Key to Popery,' passages which go to prove that confession not only has a tendency to corrupt the priest, but is a fearful engine in his hands for the corruption of others:—'especially ignorant people and young women, who, when they come to that tribunal with a sincere ignorant heart to receive advice and instruction, go home with light and knowledge, and an idea of sin unknown to them before.' But the most fearful exposure on this subject is supplied by some quotations from Da Costas's 'Narrative of the Inquisition,' referring to the priestly *solicitants* in Spain.

'The unmeasured immorality of the Spanish clergy appears in the history of sacerdotal and monkish *solicitation* in that kingdom. These *solicitants* were Spanish monks and priests, who, abusing the privacy of sacramental confession, tempted women, married and unmarried, to a violation of chastity, and in the language of Pope Gregory, administered poison instead of medicine *(pro medicina, venenum porrigunt)*. This kind of solicitation became so prevalent as to demand pontifical interposition. In Spain, the bull of Pope Paul IV., against *solicitants*, was promulgated; in which the following language is used to describe the evil which rendered such interference necessary:—'Whereas, certain ecclesiastics in the kingdom of Spain, and in the cities and dioceses thereof, having the

* This work is entitled 'A Master Key to Popery,' by D. Antonio Gavin, born and educated in Spain, nine years secular priest in the Church of Rome, and, since 1715, minister of the Church of England. Three vols. 12mo. London, 1725.

cure of souls, or exercising such cure for others, or otherwise deputed to hear the confessions of penitents, have broken out into such heinous acts of iniquity, as to abuse the sacrament of penance in the very act of hearing the confessions, not fearing to injure the same sacrament, and him who instituted it, our Lord God and Saviour Jesus Christ, by enticing and provoking, or trying to entice and provoke females to lewd actions, at the very time when they were making their confessions.'

'When this Bull was first introduced into Spain, the inquisitors published a solemn edict in all the churches belonging to the Archbishopric of Seville, that any person knowing, or having heard of any friar or clergyman having committed the crime of abusing the sacrament of confession, or in any manner having improperly conducted himself during the confession of a female penitent, should make a discovery of what he knew, within thirty days, to the holy tribunal; and very heavy censures were attached to those who should neglect or despise this injunction. When this edict was first published, such a considerable number of females went to the palace of the inquisitor, only in the city of Seville, to reveal the conduct of their infamous confessors, that twenty notaries, and as many inquisitors, were appointed to minute down their several informations against them; but these being found insufficient to receive the depositions of so many witnesses, and the inquisitors being thus overwhelmed, as it were, with the pressure of such affairs, thirty days more were allowed for taking the accusations; and this lapse of time also proving inadequate to the intended purpose, a similar period was granted, not only for a third, but a fourth time. The ladies of rank, character, and noble families, had a difficult part to act on this occasion. . . . On one side, a religious fear of incurring the threatened censures goaded their consciences so much, as to compel them to make the required accusation: on the other side, a regard to their husbands, to whom they justly feared to give offence, by affording them any motives for suspecting their private conduct, induced them to keep at home. To obviate these difficulties, they had recourse to the measure of covering their faces with a veil, according to the fashion of Spain, and thus went to the inquisitors, in the most secret manner they could adopt. Very few, however, escaped the vigilance of their husbands, who, on being informed of the discoveries and accusations made by their wives, were filled with suspicions. And yet, notwithstanding this accumulation of proof against the confessors, produced to the inquisitors, the holy tribunals, contrary to the expectations of every one, put an end to the business, by ordering that all crimes of this nature, proved by lawful evidence, should from thenceforth be consigned to perpetual silence and oblivion.'*—p. 211.

But these things, it may be said, refer to a bygone period.

*** Narrative of the Inquisition, &c., by Hippolito Joseph Da Costa Pereira Furtado de Mendonea, vol. 1., pp. 117—119.**

What then shall we say to the disclosures made by Blanco White, in reference to his own time, and of which any of our readers may satisfy himself, by turning to the 'Life' of that remarkable but unhappy man? Will it do to affirm that, though such things have been witnessed in Spain, the horrible profanation of religion was confined to that priest-ridden country? We cannot multiply details on this shameful subject. It must suffice to add, that council after council, and pope after pope, has denounced it as a general evil, as the printed records of Romanism abundantly testify. But denunciation is not punishment; and the evil being only denounced, not punished, remains under the seal and secresy of confession, rife to this very day. The present movement in catholic Germany owes the measure of success it has attained, not more to the emancipation which it promises from such frauds as the holy coat of Treves, than to the hope of a purer morality through the abolition of the Romish law of clerical celibacy.

It is remarkable that in one of the bulls which has been fulminated against the odious crime of which we have been speaking, that of Pope Benedict XIV., issued in 1745, being the second which he issued on the subject, seven enactments were made against those penitents who solicited the confessors to criminal acts. Whether this was done to stop the evil, by causing those who might be solicited by their confessors to repel their solicitations, under the influence of fear, lest they themselves should be accused, in case their guilt was discovered, of the greater crime of solicitation; or whether it was merely designed as a general shelter to the character of the priesthood, by producing the idea that they were as much sinned against as sinning, it would be difficult to decide. Dr. Elliott, indeed, says, (p. 212) thus 'the confessional has been a scene of corruption both to clergy and laity, otherwise these enactments were useless;' but we cannot persuade ourselves that priests, instructed in the art of taking confessions according to the Roman usage, ever fell victims to their *penitents*. They were corrupted *ab initio*, by the very instructions which they followed and applied. In the confessional they were led astray by their own evil imaginations; and then, like their father the devil, they beguiled Eve's daughters with their subtilty. How ineffectual all the checks have been which the papal authority has devised, may be judged of from the following statement.

'The absolution of an accomplice in guilt presents us with a very curious case in Roman catholic casuistry. It is briefly this: that a confessor cannot absolve or pardon a female penitent, who has been his accomplice in crime, *except in the article of death.** But then he can pardon at this solemn hour, though till that period he may have lived in sin.'—p. 212.

But enough on this subject. We must now briefly notice the spirit of fraud, which Rome exemplifies throughout her whole system, as it appears in reference to what is called the 'seal of confession.' The student of history will remember, that after the discovery of the fifth of November plot, the jesuit missionary Garnet was examined as to his knowledge of it. He at length confessed that he had been privy to the conspirators' design; but pleaded that the knowledge of it had been communicated to him under the 'seal of confession,' which the laws of the church did not permit him to violate. He further defended his equivocations from the charge of perjury, by asserting 'that the speech, being by equivocation, saved from a lie, the same may without perjury be affirmed by oath, or by any other usual way, though it were by receiving the sacrament, *if just necessity so require.*' Such avowals as these preventing any dependence whatever on his attempts at exculpation, he was executed as an accomplice in the treason; and even Lingard owns (vol. ix. p. 87) that 'the man who maintained such opinions could not reasonably complain if the king refused credit to his asseverations of innocence, and permitted the law to take its course.' But we must assert that, whatever Dr. Lingard may say, this distinction between the system and the man is a mere dishonest artifice, the sole object of which is to induce the readers of his history to believe that Rome discountenances such a perversion of truth. If any one is so simple as to believe this, let him turn to Dens's Theology, and he will be undeceived.

'What is the seal of sacramental confession?—It is the obligation or debt of concealing those things which are known from sacramental confession.

'Can a case be stated in which it is lawful to break the sacramental seal?—It cannot be stated: although the life or safety of a man, or even the ruin of the state, should depend upon it. Nor can the supreme pontiff dispense with it; so that, on that account, this secret of the seal is more binding than the obligation of an oath, a vow, a natural secret, &c.; *and that by the positive will of God.*

'What, therefore, ought a confessor to answer, being interrogated concerning truth, which he has known through sacramental confession alone?—He ought to answer that HE DOES NOT KNOW IT; AND IF NECESSARY CONFIRM THE SAME BY AN OATH.

* Dens's Theology, vol. vi., 'On Reserved Cases,' No. 215.

'It is objected, it is in no case lawful to tell a falsehood; but the confessor would tell a falsehood, because he does know the truth; therefore, &c. *Answer*: I deny the union, because such confessor is interrogated as a man, and replies as a man. *But now he does not know that truth as a man, though he knows it as God,* (says St. Thomas, quæd. xi. art. 1), and that sense is naturally inherent in the reply, for when he is interrogated, or replies, out of confession *(extra confessionem)*, he is considered as a man.

'What if it be directly inquired of the confessor, whether he knows that particular thing by sacramental confession? It is replied: in this case he ought to answer nothing. So think Styaert and Sylvius. But the interrogation is to be rejected as impious. Or he can say, ABSOLUTELY,—NOT IN RELATION TO THE QUESTION, *I know nothing;* because the word 'I' restricts to knowledge.'*—p. 209.

Such is the theology now taught in the Romish seminaries of Great Britain and Ireland. We could have extracted from the work before us, or supplied from other sources, numerous instances as bad as these, but have restrained our pen in deference to the modesty of genuine Protestantism. We trust that enough has been produced to guard our readers, of both sexes and all ages, from being deceived by the sanctimonious aspect, or captivated by the pomps and pageantry of Rome. It is bad enough that the money of protestant dissenters should be expended in maintaining this 'deceivableness of unrighteousness.' Let the old and young of our reformed communions stand fast in the liberty wherewith Christ has made us free, eschew the works of darkness, and beware of those 'who speak lies in hypocrisy.'

As respects the work before us, we have thought it better to select our extracts from one chapter, than to take them at random from its different parts. Our readers will thus, we believe, have a much better idea of its character, than could have been conconveyed to them in any other way. It only remains to mention, that the same principle of illustration and evidence by extracts and passages from public and private documents of the highest authority, extends to all the topics, and they are inconceivably numerous, which the treatise comprises. We say documents of the highest authority, because we are satisfied that great care has been used in selecting them. The work is necessarily somewhat bulky and complex, more so than ordinary readers may like: but to ministers, and all who desire full and well-attested information respecting Romanism, we can recommend it as a systematic, comprehensive, and popular 'Thesaurus,' on the subject.

* Dens's Theology, vol. vi., 'On the Infringement of the Sacramental Seal,' No. 160.

Art. VI.—*The Annals of the English Bible.* By Christopher Anderson. In 2 vols. 8vo. London: Pickering. 1845.

How strange it now appears, that no one should have anticipated the respected author of these valuable volumes in his present labours. History, it would seem, had a niche for each successive subject, that could be pitched upon by the imagination of man; but who ever before has laid himself out, with any adequate competency for the task, to compile the 'Annals of the English Bible?' We accept the work of Mr. Anderson with all interest and gratitude. It is beautifully got up: its pages are crowded with matter: neither time, nor care, nor expense could have been spared in bringing it before the public; and we cannot but hope that an extensive circulation will crown the enterprize. Let no modern library be considered complete without it.

Wickliffe had indeed translated the inspired page, and acquired enduring honours in doing so; but what could mere manuscripts avail for millions of common people, without the means of transcription, or purchase, or perusal? It required the revival and triumph of classical knowledge to pave the way for introducing the blessing, which the providence of the Most High had in store for these realms. Following in the rear of an awakening national intellect came the felicitous invention of printing, with all its incalculable consequences. An Archimedes might proudly say: *που στω και τον κοσμον κινησω*: but he spoke in vain. Not so has it been with that mighty machine emphatically denominated THE PRESS! This alone has furnished a fulcrum for the great levers of knowledge to rest upon. They were thus enabled to elevate the level of mind throughout Europe. England rose more or less together with the entire surface of Christendom: but the scriptures were yet 'sealed fountains,' as regarded the vast masses of her inhabitants. Let posterity, therefore, engrave upon their hearts the name of William Tyndale, born within the Hundred of Berkeley, in Gloucestershire, somewhere about the year 1484. He was brought up at Oxford, where, as Foxe says, 'by long continuance, he grew and increased as well in the knowledge of tongues and other liberal arts, as especially in the knowledge of the scriptures; inasmuch that he read privily to certain students and fellows at Magdalen College some parcel of divinity, instructing them in divine knowledge and truth.' He must have left the university before 1519; when he became tutor under the roof of Sir John Walsh, a gentleman of family and fortune, resident at Little Sudbury Manor House, not many miles from Bristol. A hospitable table naturally drew around it most of the dignified ecclesiastics in its vicinity. Abbots and priors loved ale and wine rather more than theology; although to repay the courtesy of Sir John and his lady, who were religious and intellectual persons, they often discussed the topics of the time with their host and hostess. Tyndale profited by these circumstances, for the spirit of the Lord had already began to move him at intervals; and he could not but perceive, that the established church of his country was almost wholly given to worldliness and idolatry. He even ventured to reason with, 'deans, archdeacons, doctors, and divers other great beneficed men!' Ephesus was already in arms:

"Which thing only moved me to translate the New Testament. Because I had perceived by experience, how that it was impossible to establish the lay people in any truth, except the *scriptures were plainly laid before their eyes in their mother tongue*, that they might see the process, order, and meaning of the text: for else, whatsoever truth is taught them, those enemies of all truth quench it again, partly with the smoke of their bottomless pit (whereof thou readest in the Apocalypse, chap. ix.), that is, with apparent reasons of sophistry, and traditions of their own making, and partly in juggling with the text, expounding it in such a sense as is impossible to gather out of the text itself.' These are the very words of the translator.'—vol. i. p. 33.

His boldness augmented with his years. The vast ocean of public opinion was in the process of being stirred up from its profoundest depths. We soon find the young reformer summoned before the chancellor of his diocese, 'who threatened him grievously, reviled and rated him like a dog;' and this too before all the clergy of the district. Not long after this, when in argument he had driven one of his learned opponents into a corner, the mortified disputant broke into an exclamation, that we 'were better to be without the laws of God, than those of the pope:' to which Tyndale answered: 'I defy the pope and all his laws; and if God spare my life, ere many years, I will cause a boy that driveth the plough to know more of the Word of God than you do.' His grand project was now fully in his mind,—a conception, to which that of Christopher Columbus was a trifle. His scholarship was undoubted, but he could no longer remain in Gloucestershire. An application to Tunstal, then Bishop of London, for literary employment, proved happily in vain. Alderman Monmouth, a rich metropolitan citizen, afforded him an asylum for several months, during which he preached at St. Dunstan's in the West, Fleet Street. The same gentleman befriended him when he embarked for Hamburgh; having promised to allow him ten pounds sterling to pray for the souls of sundry good people, besides obtaining him as much more from other quarters, for similar purposes. These sums, equivalent to three hundred pounds sterling at present, no doubt supported him in comfort. He was at Cologne in 1525, where was commenced his first entire edition of the New Testament in quarto; the gospels of St. Matthew and St. Mark having been printed by themselves before, although not a single copy of either is now supposed to be in existence. He thence removed to Worms. A fragment of the quarto, and one perfect specimen of the octavo publication, have survived the ravages of bigotry, persecution, and disaster; the former being found in the Grenville library, and the latter in that of the Baptist Academy at Bristol. In the year 1526 it was, that the Holy Scriptures in the vernacular tongue began to circulate in London, Oxford, Cambridge, and other places. Wolsey, Tunstal, More, Henry the Eighth, priests, lawyers, magistrates, stormed in vain. The translation was denounced by authority as swarming with errors. Wherever these bibles could be discovered, they were consigned to the flames. The entire hierarchy, with the Cardinal and the Archbishop of Canterbury at their head, contemned the genuine treasure in which the talisman of the cross was contained. Lord Chancellor More entered the lists of controversy with Tyndale. Every art of man, as well as every device of Satan, was called into requisition. The translator rose to the very height of fame and notoriety. As stolen waters are sweet, so the secresy with which the sacred writings were studied, and the fearful risk with which they were procured, endeared each page and word to the possessor. Meanwhile there prevailed an excitement throughout the civilized world almost without a parallel in any previous century. Rome was sacked by the Duke of Bourbon; the king of France was a prisoner in the custody of the emperor; the monarch of England and Ireland was eager for his divorce from the good queen Catharine; Wolsey was fast waning in power, and about to drop like an exhalation from the political firmament; myriads were hungering and thirsting for the waters of life, of which fresh supplies were filtering into the realm, through a thousand crevices of private and commercial contrivance. Neither custom-houses, nor search-warrants, nor episcopal mandates, could materially alter the case. An enormous sixth edition issued forth about the time that Wolsey died; and Tyndale, hunted and proscribed though he was, was making rapid progress in the Old Testament.

He also began his war of the pen against 'the Practice of Prelates,' from which we must transcribe a passage, in common justice both to himself and our readers, as also from its general applicability to various ecclesiastical matters and things in the present day. He delivers himself like Jotham of old, in the following graphic parable:

'To see how our Holy Father came up, mark the example of an ivy-tree. First, it springeth out of the earth, and then awhile creepeth along by the ground, till it findeth a great tree; then it joineth itself beneath unto the body of the tree, and creepeth up a little and a little, fair and softly. And at the beginning, while it is yet thin and small, that the burden is not perceived, it seemeth glorious to garnish the tree in winter, and to bear off the tempests of the weather. But, in the mean season, it thrusteth roots into the bark of the tree to hold fast withal; and ceaseth not to climb up, till it be at the top, and above all. And then it sendeth his branches along by the branches of the tree, and overgroweth all, and waxeth great, heavy, and thick; and sucketh the moisture so sore out of the tree and his branches, that it choketh and stifleth them. And then the foul ivy waxeth mighty in the stump of the tree, and becometh a nest and a seat for all unclean birds, and for blind owls, which hawk in the dark, and dare not come at the light.'—vol. i. p. 243.

It will not escape an acute observer, that all established forms of mere nominal Christianity present similar features. It is round the stump of worldly power that the ecclesiastical ivy yet continues to entwine itself within these realms; and allowing for the difference between the sixteenth and nineteenth centuries, the commencement of Bible Societies encountered the same sort of tempest as that which was so fiercely and fatally showered down, three hundred years before, upon William Tyndale and his abettors. They were not safe any where, either at home or abroad. The arrest of the translator became an incessant subject of diplomatic correspondence, particularly when he was in the Low Countries. Nevetheless, Genesis soon crossed the channel in an English dress, succeeded by Deuteronomy, and in due time by the other books of the Pentateuch. Jonah appeared in 1531, with a long prologue, endeavouring to adapt the history and character of the prophet to the state of the times. It was indeed an evil day. Even out of the multitudes thronging through what Bunyan calls the wicket gate, there were too many Pliables, and some apostates. Fryth, however, proved a splendid exception, and may be well described as the flower of protestant martyrs. He was of one heart and mind with his illustrious coadjutors, as appears from his language to Sir Thomas More:

'This hath been offered you, is offered, and shall be offered. Grant that the Word of God,—I mean the text of scripture,—*may go abroad in our English tongue*, as other nations have it in their tongues, and my brother William Tyndale and I have done, and will promise you to write no more. But if you will not grant this condition, then will we be doing *while we have breath*, and show in few words what the Scripture doth in many; and so at the least save some.'—vol. i. p. 363.

It is well known how meekly, yet steadily, he was enabled by grace to redeem his pledge; how he bore up against the bitterness of his adversaries in the spirit of Paul and Stephen; how heroically he disdained to fly, after it had become clear that flight would have compromised his evangelical testimony; how patiently he endured his incarceration in one of the filthiest and darkest dungeons of Newgate, where, 'laden with irons, as many as he could bear, and his neck made fast to a post with a collar of iron, he could neither stand upright, nor stoop down!' By candle-light he still contrived to write letters of peace and love to his friends, until, on the 3rd of July, 1533, he was led forth to the stake at Smithfield. Andrew Hewet suffered with him; and there wanted but a third to complete the parallel with the three Hebrew children; for the form of the Son of God was at least so spiritually present, that both the confessors gloried in the dissolution of an earthly tabernacle. Fryth prayed the Lord to forgive an incoherent priest who was reviling him in the fire. 'The wind made his death somewhat longer, as it bore away the flames from himself to his fellow; but his mind was established with such patience, that as though he had felt no pain, he seemed rather to rejoice for his friend than to be careful for himself.' His murderer, Henry, had now married Anne Boleyn; so that in part through her influence, there ensued a lull in the hurricane; although opposition to the truth was by no means at an end. Laws against heresy underwent some external modification. Even the Scriptures were for an interval let alone; and Tyndale availed himself of the calm, however transient, to the very utmost. He sent Anne a magnificent copy of his New Testament, imprinted on vellum, with illuminations, and bound in purple morocco. Her name, and title in Latin, were handsomely impressed upon the top, side, and bottom margins! Yet soon the scene again changed.

In 1534, the convocation had agreed that Cranmer should urge the king with regard to a translation of the whole Scriptures 'into the vulgar tongue by some honest and learned men, to be nominated by his majesty, and to be delivered to the people *according to their learning!*' We may thus judge how wonderfully the circulation of the Pentateuch and New Testament by Tyndale must have invigorated the public mind.

Their noble translator, indeed, was approaching the termination of his toils. Basely betrayed into the hands of his enemies at Antwerp, his eyes must have turned towards his native land with augmented interest. About two thirds of the old canon were finished and ready for the press. Imprisonment and peril only the more inflamed his zeal. The largest portion of Christendom appeared rocking to and fro, like a mountain in labour. Henry the Eighth had set himself up as a lay pope over the consciences of his unhappy subjects; and even Fisher and Moore had fallen before this curious 'defender of the faith.' France, and Germany, and Italy were in convulsions. The monasteries of England were being shared out amongst a tyrant and his nobles, intent alone upon plunder. The former had got weary of his consort, who was to be disposed of after the most approved fashion of Bluebeard in the fairy tale. Cromwell and Cranmer had other avocations, than to rescue their protestant fellow-subject, in his prison at Vilvorde, from the imperial decree of Augsburgh. Foxe, after the martyrdom of Tyndale, on Friday, the 6th of October, in 1536, thus beautifully portrays his character:—

'He was a man very frugal, and spare of body,—a great student, and earnest labourer in setting forth the scriptures of God. He reserved or hallowed to himself two days in the week, which he named his pastime, Monday and Saturday. On Monday he visited all such poor men and women as were fled out of England, by reason of persecution, into Antwerp, and these once well understanding their good exercises and qualities, he did very liberally comfort and relieve; and in like manner provided for sick and diseased persons. On the Saturday, he walked round about the town, seeking every corner and hole, where he suspected any poor person to dwell; and where he found any to be well occupied, and yet overburthened with children, or else were aged and weak, those also he plentifully relieved. And thus he spent his two days of pastime, as he called them. And truly his alms were very large, and so they might well be; for his exhibition, that he had yearly, from the English merchants at Antwerp, when living there, was considerable, and that for the most part he bestowed upon the poor. The rest of the days of the week *he gave wholly to his book*, wherein he most diligently travailed. When the Sunday came, then went he to some one merchant's chamber, or other, whither came many other merchants, and unto them would be read some parcel of scripture; the which proceeded so fruitfully, sweetly, and gently from him, much like to the writing of John the Evangelist, that it was a heavenly comfort and joy to the audience to hear him read the scriptures; likewise after dinner he spent an hour in the same manner. He was a man without any spot orblemish of rancour or malice, full of mercy and compassion, so that no man living was able to reprove him of any sin or crime;

although his righteousness and justification depended not thereupon before God; but only upon the blood of Christ, and his faith upon the same. In this faith he died with complacency at Vilvorde, and now resteth with the glorious company of Christ's martyrs, blessedly in the Lord. And thus much of the life and story of the true servant and martyr of God, William Tyndale, who for his notable pains and travail, may well be called the Apostle of England, in this our latter age.'—vol. i. pp. 520—521.

Meanwhile, the Word of God was not bound. Editions in duodecimo or small octavo, and quarto, multiplied on every hand; and one beautiful impression in folio had been secretly struck off in London by the royal printer. The folly of man might have as well attempted to encage sunbeams, as to arrest the spiritual illumination. Thomas Berthelot had the honour of printing the first sacred volume on British ground. An entire bible in English, prepared by Miles Coverdale, was finished before the death of Tyndale: and our author conceives it not impossible but that Sir Thomas Moore himself may have been privy to this translation. Cromwell had promoted it, and even contributed largely towards the expenses. Some of the renderings were agreeable to catholic predilections, such as *penance* for repentance, and the like. Its compilers had drawn from Dutch, Latin, and German sources. The royal license, moreover, had been already awarded to James Nycolson, of Southwark, its publisher; and perhaps down to the present moment, it might have formed the staple of the standard version, had not John Rogers, under the assumed name of Thomas Matthew, a faithful adherent to the martyred William Tyndale, entirely changed the face of affairs. This active individual, assisted by Richard Grafton and Edward Whitchurch, hastened through the press, after the tragedy at Vilvorde, all that remained of Tyndale's manuscripts, bringing his translation verbally down to the conclusion of the second Book of Chronicles. The rest of the Old Testament, Rogers, alias Matthew, probably borrowed from the printed sheets of Miles Coverdale, although he altered and arranged it according to his own notions. He inserted also the Apocrypha from the same quarter; adding, however, the New Testament, purely from the Greek, as Tyndale had translated it. Grafton lost not a moment, when all was ready, in coming over to London, and obtaining an interview with Cranmer. His grace declared to Cromwell, that he liked this last better than any bible he had ever seen; requesting of him a favour in these words:—

'I pray you, my lord, that you will exhibit the book unto the king's highness, and obtain from him, if you can, a license that the same may be sold and read of every person, without danger of any act, proclamation, or ordinance heretofore granted to the contrary, until such time, than we, the bishops, shall set forth a better version, *which I think will not be until a day after doomsday!'*—vol. i. p. 577.

The archbishop's request was speedily granted: the license previously awarded to Nycolson on behalf of Miles Coverdale was overlooked, or at least disregarded as an exclusive one: both Henry and Cromwell patronized the labours of Tyndale as they had been prepared for the public by Rogers, Grafton, and Whitchurch: and the supply of the entire Canon of Scripture, was thus doubled in a moment, when the nation most eagerly demanded it. It is not a little curious now to look back upon what was termed the 'Festival of the Third Centenary of the English Bible' celebrated in 1835. Its promoters had small recollections for the martyr of Vilvorde,—slight ideas, that the translation of Coverdale had been silently superseded,—no notion, probably, at all, that it was *never enjoined to be read* in England, or that it headed the list of interdicted publications in 1546,*—and scarcely an apprehension, that Miles Coverdale, Bishop of Exeter, sanctioned renderings which would have thrown the Record Newspaper into hysterics! Such is human fame, and the bubble of even evangelical reputation. The name of William Tyndale is happily in another record.

That the people of these realms were at the lowest ebb of spiritual knowledge, more than three hundred years ago, can be doubted by none. Subjects were scarcely better than slaves, and rulers than Neros. Great men were only tyrants upon a

* We observed the following in the Times and Evening Mail of the 14th of September last:

'Discovery of an ancient Bible.—A copy of the first complete edition of the English Bible, printed by Myles Coverdale, bearing the date 1535, was accidentally discovered a few days since in the false bottom of an old oak chest, at Holkham-hall, the seat of the Earl of Leicester. There are numerous imperfect copies of this edition of the Holy Scriptures in existence, two being deposited in the library of the British Museum, one in the Bodleian Library at Oxford, one in the Cambridge University Library, and others in most of our great libraries and public institutions, as well as many private individuals possessing the volume. The above book is the most valuable specimen of Myles Coverdale's labours hitherto brought to light, being in every respect perfect; whereas all the other volumes enumerated are deficient in many leaves both at the beginning and the end. During the religious persecution in the reign of Queen Mary the proof of the possession of the Bible subjecting the parties to the consequences of an accusation of heresy, most of the copies of the impression were buried, which accounts for the discrepancy, the humidity of the soil having destroyed a considerable portion of the leaves. The noble proprietor of Halkham has had the book appropriately bound, and enclosed in an oaken box, and it now graces the shelves of his magnificent library. Some idea may be formed of the estimation in which this bibliographical treasure is held, from the circumstance of a London bookseller having offered to purchase it for the sum of 500l.

lesser scale. The flattery, with which royal ears were addressed, may be gathered from the blasphemy with which Grafton thanked Cromwell for having secured him the royal imprimatur: 'I have sent your lordship,' he says, 'six Bibles, which gladly I would have brought myself, but because of the sickness that remaineth in the city; I, therefore, have sent them by my servant, which this day came out of Flanders. Requiring, your lordship, if I may be so bold as to desire you, to accept them as my simple gift, given to you for those most godly pains, *for which the Heavenly Father is bound, even of his justice, to reward you with the everlasting kingdom of God!*' This was the language of Protestantism, it must be remembered, nor was its writer, so far as we know, even an episcopalian. What the reformed Church of England was, after Henry had become its visible head and defender, may be inferred from such an incident as that which turns up at the commencement of the second volume now before us: it is well observed that

'Trivial matters often strongly mark the character. The very next month after the arrival of the English Bible, though the plague was still raging, Sir William Fitzwilliam, writes thus to Cromwell:—'My Lord, one thing there is, which the King's Highness, at my last resort unto your lordship, willed me to speak to you in; and at my return, his Highness asked me, whether I had remembered the same or not: which is,—*His Grace hath a priest, that yearly maketh his hawks,* and this year hath made him two, which fly and kill their game very well, *to the singlier pleasure and contentation of his Highness!* and for the pains, which the said priest taketh about the same, his Majesty would that he should have one of Mr. Bedell's benefices, if there be any ungiven, besides that which his Grace has already given! And if there be none of the said benefices ungiven, that then your lordship should have him in remembrance,—that he may have some other, when it shall fall void!—vol. xi. p. 2.

It is surely a frightful, yet significant reflection, that even the Holy Scriptures, after circulating more or less freely for ten generations, have not been able to eradicate reverend sportsmen from the sanctuary of an Established Church. We know personally a tractarian clergyman, who has daily prayers in his parish throughout the year, without any diminution of the vigour with which he hears a double barrel, manufactured perhaps by Manton. Taking his reading-desk on the way to the field, the surplice is said to be not unfrequently thrown over his clerical shooting jacket! And thus it is, and will ever be, until the grand omission of the Sixteenth century is rectified. William Tyndale, even on this complicated subject, could see much farther than his contemporaries; although, of course, it can hardly be expected, that his convictions should have reached the high level of that religious patriotism, which is destined, we trust, to illustrate modern times.

Grafton and Whitchurch supplied about 2500 Bibles for England on their own account, and a second impression was printed at Paris, in 1538, under the revision of Coverdale, and the auspices of Cromwell. By Christmas of that year it was enacted by authority that in all churches throughout the realm, there should be procured 'one book of the entire scriptures in English, and that the same should be set up in some convenient place within the said church, where the parishioners may most commodiously resort to the same and read it; the charge of which book to be rateably borne, that is to say, one half by the parson, and the other by the parishioners.' It was further ordered, that every individual should be expressly 'provoked, stirred up, and exhorted to read the same, as that which is the very lively word of God that every Christian person is bound to embrace, believe, and follow, if they look to be saved!' Two large editions of Tyndale's New Testament were also published in quarto in Southwark, and St. Dunstan's where formerly the martyred translator used to preach. Strype tells us that, 'it was wonderful to see with what joy this Book of God was received, not only among the learneder sort, but generally all England over, among all the vulgar and common people; and with what greediness it was read, and what resort to places where the reading of it was! Everybody that could, bought the Book, or busily read it, or got others to read it to them, if they could not themselves. Divers more elderly people learned to read on purpose; and even little boys flocked, among the rest, to hear portions of the Holy Scriptures read.' Four more editions issued from the press in 1539, with which the personal influence of Henry's prime minister was more or less connected. Richard Taverner and others now closed what has been termed the first series of the sacred volume, before Cromwell's fall, including above thirty impressions of the New Testament, and five at least of the entire Bible. Then came six more editions in large folio, commencing with those of Cranmer, extending to the close of the reign of Edward VI. in 1553. Mary then succeeded, whose sanguinary persecutions, however, did not commence until February 1555; which, together with political circumstances, afforded a breathing time, as well as a warning, for those to escape who could. Bibles disappeared for a season, but although many were lost, beyond all question, multitudes were preserved. The persecution too endeared its antidote and refuge as usual: more especially when pestilence stalked from city to city, in the rear of Bonner and his barbarous concremations. The summer and autumn of 1558 desolated the length and breadth of the land with sickness. Archbishop Parker used to calculate, that in those seasons, three parts out of four throughout the country suffered from severe disease. Households of thirty and forty were reduced to three or four effective domestics. Harvestmen became so scarce, that wages quadrupled. Rogers, the friend of Tyndale, ascended to his glorious reward in a chariot of fire, as the proto-martyr of the Marian enormities: but Coverdale escaped. Latimer, Ridley, and Cranmer, ascended their funereal piles, with different degrees of interest and constancy. Before, however, these were lighted up, the editions of the New Testament had augmented to sixty-five; and no less than thirty impressions of the entire Bible, in the vernacular tongue, were in secret circulation.

It is observable too, that the text had opportunities of undergoing more careful recension. The New Testament was divided into verses. At Geneva, the celebrated revisers were engaged night and day in comparing the entire translation with the original Greek and Hebrew. The accession of Queen Elizabeth, in November 1558, filled them with joy: but it was not until the last sheet having been committed to the press on the 10th of April 1560, that Whittingham, Gilby, and Sampson, returned home to London: when Bodley obtained that patent, which rendered their labours the parents of every edition of the scriptures, down to James I., and indeed much later. Archbishop Parker, ten years afterwards, launched the Bishop's Bible, as it was styled, into public notice, but not through the order of the queen, as has been generally supposed. The monopoly granted somewhat later to Christopher and Robert Barker, calls forth from Mr. Anderson the following delightful survey:

'In contemplating the long and powerful reign of Elizabeth with immediate reference to the Sacred Volume, there are three distinct points alike worthy of notice and recollection. The first is the number of editions on the whole, so very far beyond that which has ever been observed. A second peculiarity is very manifest,—of the number of impressions in what is usually styled the Geneva version, in comparison with others, or with the versions of Cranmer and Parker taken together. But the third point cannot escape notice,—the large number of Bibles, as compared with the editions of the New Testament taken separately.

'Apprehension, approaching nearly to terror, had been expressed in parliament, at the very idea of a patent for bread; but here was a commodity infinitely above it, in point of importance and value,—namely, the Bread of Life: since it had been delivered into the hands of one man to deal it out in conformity to privilege granted,—this being the first movement of the kind, every reader must be curious to observe the experiment in its first operation and consequences. Here then, he may now do so, at the distance of two hundred and forty years, and for a space of time equal to that of the entire generation first so circumstanced.' Vol. ii. p. 352.

During the forty-five years that Elizabeth swayed the sceptre of England, there were not fewer than one hundred and thirty distinct issues of Bibles and Testaments; or about eighty-five of the former, and forty-five of the latter; which furnishes an average of three editions per annum through the entire reign; and that, too, notwithstanding all the caution of the first sixteen years. 'With reference to the Geneva version, out of the gross issues now stated, the number approaches to ninety editions, thus leaving only forty for all the others. Or if we speak of Bibles alone, those of Cranmer and Parker may be stated at twenty-five, whilst those of Geneva amounted to at least sixty editions.' As our author says, justice has never been done to the period now under review, as such, nor to the people of that generation, whether in England or Scotland, who purchased all the scriptures they read, and paid for them ten times the value of the present prices. James I. professed no great relish for the Geneva translation, when at the Hampton Court Conference, a fresh version was declared to be called for. Mr. Anderson favours us with a full account of it, detailing the instruction given, the expenses incurred, the meanness of his Majesty, and the payment of the whole cost by the patentee. Its introduction into general use was gradually effected in about forty years. It had indeed one mighty advantage in its favour,—which was,—that it was encumbered with neither note nor comment. Such appendages had always attached to the Geneva edition; against which Archbishop Laud, as might naturally be expected, expressed throughout his life the most deadly antipathy. Scotland, meanwhile, had kept pace with the southern portion of the island, in its growing demand for the Word of God, which was principally imported from England and Holland, in the form of New Testaments. Our Scotch readers, at all events, will be interested in the following extract:

'From the year 1543, and for more than three successive generations, the history of the English Bible, north of the Tweed, is of a very marked and memorable character, and peculiar to Scotland, amongst all the other nations of Europe. It forms throughout a remarkable continuation of that independence of human patronage, which has been so steadily repudiated from the beginning; while no country has been more signally indebted to the gracious providence of God.

'In 1543, when it was first proclaimed to be lawful to peruse the Scriptures, although they had been reading in secret for fully sixteen years, it is to be observed that no edition of the Bible entire, or of the New Testament, separately, was ordered to be printed. Cardinal

Beaton having immediately regained his authority, such a proposal was not to be whispered for a moment. But as he was removed by death only three years after, this will not account for its being not three, nor five, but *thirty-five* years before any Bible issued from the Scotch press! This, too, was in folio, nor did a second edition follow, and of the same unwieldly character, until 1610, or about thirty years more had passed away. Nay, only the third edition, and at last in the octavo size, did not appear until the year 1633; or ninety years from the day on which, it was said to be lawful to have and to read the Bible in English! There was then also a fourth edition in 1637, and one in duodecimo next year. Thus it was,—that for more than a century, there were no more than five editions of the Bible issued from the printing presses *in the country*; not to say that two of these were in folio, no size even approaching to that which the people required having made its appearance, till so late as 1633. The first pocket Bible was not printed until 1638.

'Such then was the condition of our Scottish ancestors, so far as their own native press was concerned. No Bible, even so convenient as that of an octavo size, had been printed in Scotland for the use of the community, till one hundred and seven years after the New Testament of Tyndall had been first conveyed to Edinburgh and St. Andrews, as well as other parts! What then had become of the people at large? Had they been left destitute of the Book of Life to such an extent as this, and for an entire century, after it first reached their shores? Far—very far from it. In proportion to its population, perhaps in no other country had it been more generally possessed, if not eagerly perused; and the explanation will afford us now in review one of the most signal displays of the goodness of God to our northern ancestors. Once pointed out, it certainly will be difficult for the present generation to escape from the obligation to send the Sacred Volume over sea and land to other nations.' Vol. ii. pp. 532-3.

There is an ingenious section in our author's second volume upon the Apocrypha, in which, however, one of his assertions appears to us as standing rather upon inference, than any genuine historical foundation. He says, 'the clear and very decided views of divine truth held by Tyndale, forbid the idea, that *he* would ever have associated it (the apocrypha) with the sacred volume; and at all events, of its introduction in the vulgar tongue he stands innocent.' It may be questioned, whether the former portion of this sentence can be fairly maintained. John Rogers clearly inserted the disputed books in Matthew's Bible, and he would scarcely have done so, knowing perfectly as he did the whole mind of the Vilvorde martyr, had matters been as Mr. Anderson declares. The canon of scripture had been very little investigated at the commencement of the sixteenth century. The Anglican establishment deliberately sanctioned the use of Ecclesiasticus, Wisdom, Tobit, Judith, and Baruch, by inserting lessons from them, in her calendar for October and November. The 'Plea of the Innocent, by Josiah Nichols', in 1602,—the 'Apology from Amsterdam' in 1604,—and the denunciations of the learned Lightfoot, from thirty to forty years afterwards, all occurred long subsequent to the settlement of the Thirty-nine Articles, under Queen Elizabeth: whose divines, or at least a majority of them, concurred with Ruffinus and St. Jerom, with regard to the estimation in which the disputed books were to be held. The object, probably, which Rogers and Coverdale had in view, was similar to that entertained by the first secretaries of the British and Foreign Bible Society,—namely, the circulation of a standard version, without being over-critical, beyond the temper of the public mind. Whether such ideas were right or wrong is another question: but perhaps, by placing the pieces styled Apocryphal, by themselves altogether, between the Old and New Testaments, Tyndale, Craumer, Rogers, Cromwell, and their other contemporaries, considered that a sufficiently significant intimation was given, that the Maccabees, for example, were not in their opinion inspired, as were the pages of Isaiah, Jeremiah, the Pentateuch, the Gospels, Acts, Epistles, or the Apocalypse. Luther, moreover, with several of the Continental reformers, had given just offence, by the irreverence with which they deposed any portion of Holy Writ from the canon, which seemed to thwart favorite systems of divinity. Our deliberate judgment is that Tyndale would have done, had he been alive, precisely as John Rogers did. No bookseller, at such a cris's, would have embarked his substance in the undertaking, as Richard Grafton did, without taking care to avoid that sort of provocation, which was not absolutely necessary. Poor Coverdale even held by his darling *penance* almost to the last. He maintained that no man should be made offender for a word,—and least of all one which, as he conceived, had no connection, of necessity, with that Roman Sacrament surrendered everywhere by genuine Protestantism. In turning over, the other day, the original records of the Secundo-Nicene Council, in Father Labbe, we were struck with the use of the phrase μετανοιαν εβαλον, as merely meaning '*they knelt down.*'

From the Commonwealth to the Revolution, there was little to remark with regard to the issue of the Word of God. The Stuarts generally were no patrons to any enterprize that involved the spiritual or temporal welfare of their subjects. Their tyranny and falsehood both tended to expatriate those who were the very salt of the earth. Bankrupt treasuries, court masquerades, ruinous foreign policy, an oppressive hierarchy, persecuted puritanism, sanguinary civil wars, a restoration involving national shame and demoralization, liberty struggling for its very existence, were so many links in the long chain of disaster, which extended from the demise of Elizabeth to the accession of William the Third. Royal printers, claiming the exclusive privilege of printing Bibles, went the way of all other monopolists, and delivered to the public as bad an article, at as dear a price, as they dared. Several editions, however, by no means contemptible, illustrated even this period, through the exertions of private individuals. John Field published a correct text; and John Canne at Amsterdam, produced in 1644 the first version of the inspired volume with marginal references. In 1680, Thomas Guy contracted with Dutch pressmen, and by importing Old and New Testaments, helped to amass his then almost unparalleled fortune; so that it may be doubted whether the benefits he conferred on the souls of men were not greater than those which his celebrated hospital has afforded their bodies. After the fitful uneasy reigns of William and Anne, George the First paid some attention to the subject; and to correct the growing inaccuracies and inelegance of the current editions of the scriptures, he ordered that all future Bibles should be printed upon good paper,—that a copy of each impression should be lodged with the Archbishop of Canterbury, the Bishop of London, and with each of the secretaries of state: that only such correctors of the sheets should be employed as were approved of by these two prelates; and that the price of each book should be printed in the title-page. Under his successors, Baskerville raised the standard of scriptural typography much higher; and in 1769, Professor Blayney produced his folio and quarto Bibles. These were said to have undergone an accurate revision with respect to punctuation, a comparison of the italic interpolations with the Hebrew and Greek, a rectification and marginal translation of the proper names, the headings and running titles, the chronology and side references. Yet more than one hundred errors have been detected since. The cheering feature meanwhile was, that the good seed was being so widely sown at home and abroad, that like the harvest of Joseph in Egypt, it might be reckoned 'as the sand of the sea, very much, until he left numbering, for it was without number.' America, too, imitated the man of Macedonia. Her cry for assistance called Bibles as well as emigrants across the Atlantic ocean. The very first ever beheld by the Indians, in the deep recesses of the New World, was an English copy, in the year 1585. An American edition was not printed until 1782; for down to that date, British authority had never permitted its colonial presses to supply the bread of life; so that it was civil liberty, in its hour of triumph, which was destined to have the honour of demonstrating its intimate connection with the full and unshackled development of divine truth. Throughout, however, the long duration of our transatlantic power, in its territorial plenitude, religion had not waned. The names of Roger Williams, John Eliot, Cotton Mather, Jonathan Edwards, and David Brainerd, can never be forgotten. They were among the wise, 'who turn many to righteousness, and they shine as the stars for ever and ever.' Through their instrumentality, the Word had free course, and was glorified. The track of the English Bible accompanied their labours, like a galaxy of celestial light. When the thirteen provinces had erected themselves into independent states, results began to appear on a larger scale. America, in fact, has re-acted upon the mother country. In 1780, whilst we were at war with our own brethren, to say nothing of France, Spain, and Holland, the first Bible society was formed 'for the benefit of soldiers and sailors.' Then succeeded another and nobler era, with the aspect of which none can be unacquainted. Our respected author, in conclusion, must be admitted to speak for himself:—

'If every thing in the condition of mankind indicates the approach of some great crisis, is it not more than observable, that in this our eminently favoured land, all things else appear as though they had conspired, chiefly to render more conspicuous or glaring, and certainly far more inviting, one solitary path left open by God to British Christians as such? A path indeed, to which as far as they regard their common standard, they appear to be now nearly hedged up, just as they were above forty years ago, by the fear of infidelity. A path, however, in which they may proceed in the largest body, and by the smallest groups, or rather by both methods, in perfect harmony. That path, in which those who revere divine revelation as their common charter to the skies, or their sheet-anchor in every storm, can still meet; and meeting with success their common foe, however divided on some points, can only the more triumphantly repel the charge of sectarianism. That path, where as the asperities of discordant sentiment can have no place, so every acrimonious or noxious controversy is left to wither down to its root; and where, though they confute no heresies, they may effect what is better still, cause them all to be neglected or forgotten. In that plain path, where *diffusion* seems to be the one idea, that cometh out from the divine throne daily; dispensing with a bountiful hand the sovereign balm for every wound, through other and distant climes, the parties so engaged are in the way of being twice blessed; and there, while working in the rear of the Almighty's most determined purpose and highest end, ultimate success is no less certain, than in the course of nature: 'for as the rain cometh down, and the snow from heaven, and returneth not thither, but watereth the earth, and maketh it bring forth and bud, that it may give seed to the sower, and bread to the eater; so shall my word be, that goeth forth out of my mouth: it shall not return unto me void, but it shall accomplish that which I please, and it shall prosper in the thing whereunto I sent it.'—Vol. ii., pp. 678—679.

Such is an exceedingly imperfect sketch of a work, in our judgment highly valuable. Its style and length, however, will be probably much objected to. The former is certainly not attractive. It is often ponderous and uneven. It now and then descends to vulgarism; whilst there appears throughout an affected interchange of the present and future tenses, which strikes us as not at all agreeable. Carlyle adopts this practice in his great work on the French Revolution; but we should be sorry to see it growing into a fashion. Præter-perfects best describe past events; although of course a skilful master may ever and anon take those felicitous liberties, which bring the annals of history before our eyes, like prospect after prospect in nature. An abridgement of these volumes would doubtless be more saleable, and in every way more useful. It would condense the important matter, concentrate the lights, throw back the side objects into their proper perspective, introduce perspicuity where it is sometimes much wanted, and impart gracefulness and raciness to the whole. The subject is so noble and appropriate; the learning of our author is so various, and adapted to what he has undertaken; the almost boundless diffusion of the Bible so animates the pious mind with a sense of the goodness of God in having favoured us with a divine revelation, that we cannot help desiring to see the story of its progress in the English language narrated with such perfection, as to remind one of 'apples of gold set in pictures of silver.' Mr. Anderson, we feel persuaded, will pardon our freedom, and allow us to thank him cordially for the entertainment and edification with which his pages have furnished us. The portrait of Tyndale forms one of the most beautiful frontispieces which we have had the pleasure of seeing for a long time. May his memory never fade from the affections of British Christendom!

Art. VII. *Arrah Neil; or Times of Old.* By G. P. R. James, Esq. In 3 vols. London: Smith, Elder & Co.

We are no enemies to fiction, whether in prose or poetry. Within legitimate bounds, and under the control of sound principles, it is a fair field, which may be profitably cultivated, and out of which may be gathered some of the best and most useful lessons of which our condition admits. The wisest men have in all ages availed themselves of it, and whether under the form of fable, parable, or story, have rendered it subservient to the instruction and improvement of mankind. The abuse to which it has been subjected is no argument against the thing itself. It may be admitted to any extent without impugning the legitimacy of the province, or reflecting on the reputation of those who labour in it. If the plea of abuse be admitted in the case of fiction, it will be difficult to rebut it as urged against logic or erudition. It has existed in the latter cases, as well as in the former, and must be rejected in all, if the consistency and soundness of our conclusions be preserved.

The human mind has other faculties than those which are strictly logical. It is not merely capable of appreciating the force of a demonstration, or of tracing out the several links of a chain of reasoning, but is imaginative and keenly susceptible. A course of training, to be perfect, must have respect to all these attributes, and will be incomplete just as it fails to do so. An exclusive cultivation of any one faculty, or set of faculties, is both defective and injurious, detrimental to mental health, and productive of false judgments and a partial view of human life. This is true on the one side, as well as on the other; and an adaptation, therefore, to our whole nature should be sought in the modes of training which are devised. No states of which the human mind is capable can be neglected without injury. Some men are almost inaccessible, save through the medium of judgment; and others, except through that of imagination. To address the former with any prospect of success, the forms of reasoning and the severity of logic must be preserved; whilst the latter will remain cold and inactive, unless the warmth of passion or the bright glow of fancy be thrown around them. Hence the mathematician and the poet, as types of the two classes, are usually deficient in some essential elements of human wisdom. Their intellects—using the term in its broad and comprehensive signification—have been but partially cultivated. In the one case, judgment—in the other, imagination only has been strengthened. A wide portion of the mental domains of each has been neglected, and an unnatural and morbid state of intellect has in consequence been formed.

Now, we think that religious people have erred in this matter. They have looked to the actual, rather than to the necessary condition of things; have confounded the abuse of fiction with fiction itself; and have hence inferred that the vocation of the novelist is discreditable, and his influence uniformly pernicious. That they should have done so, we do not much wonder. There has been much in the circumstances of the case to mislead them, and the inexperience of those who are specially exposed to the evil, has awakened apprehensions adapted to precipitate their judgment. That the great mass of English novels—to say nothing of those of foreign countries—are suited to exert a very pernicious influence, is too notorious to be denied by any religious man. Not to go further back than the days of Fielding, it is impossible to peruse these productions without perceiving that, in addition to the distorted views of human life and character exhibited, they confound in many cases the primary distinctions of virtue and vice, hold up to ridicule the religion of the heart, and throw over the immoralities and profanity of the world a disguise which conceals their enormity, and weakens the moral sentiments of the young. We are not insensible to the pre-eminent talent which some of them exhibit. This talent we can appreciate at its full worth; but the more we ponder on the sagacity of Fielding, in his delineations of character, and on the skill with which the evolution of his plot is conducted, the deeper becomes our conviction of the irreligious and demoralizing tendency of 'Tom Jones.' It is the talent of the novelist which gives such power to the evil elements he wields. The empire of darkness is administered with success, in consequence of the splendid powers of the fallen archangel which rules it. If, therefore, the question to be decided respected simply the admittance or exclusion from the family circle of such publications, we could not hesitate for a moment. On no terms, and for no consideration whatever, would we consent to place in the hands of our youth a class of publications whose pervading element is immorality, and whose influence, to whatever extent exerted, is detrimental to the purest and best sentiments of our nature.

But we are not reduced to this alternative. Another and wiser course is open to us—one more suited to our mental constitution, and better adapted to the requirements and sympathies of the young. A broader and deeper philosophy teaches us to eschew whatever does violence to any part of our nature,—to look to the soundness and consistency of our reasoning, and never to reject in the one case what lies at the basis of our procedure in many others. Now, it is notorious that we do admit the legitimacy of fiction in other departments of literature. A considerable part of that which we admire as poetry, and which passes unchallenged round our family circles, is of this order; and it would therefore be as just to reject, on this account, *The Deserted Village* of Goldsmith, as to refuse admittance to his *Vicar of Wakefield*. There may be other grounds on which the latter should be excluded, but the plea of fiction cannot be maintained unless the former be banished also. Judicious selection, therefore, is that which should be attempted; and to this we are specially solicitous to direct the attention of our readers. The matter of fact is, that novels are read, and that nothing we can do—even if so disposed—would prevent their being so. The indiscriminate prohibition of the class, leads to a stealthy and most pernicious perusal of them. They are received as contraband goods, and are cautiously concealed from the parent's or tutor's eye. Habits of deceit are thus formed, a practical lie is continually told, and the benefit of a sounder judgment and a riper experience, is wholly wanting in the works selected. These evils it is possible to avoid, by the guardians of youth soliciting the confidence of their charge, and proffering to them such an admixture of light literature, including works of fiction, as may beneficially be combined with severer reading. We know parents who are in the habit of saying to their elder children, 'We do not prohibit the whole class of novels; but believing the greater part of them to be pernicious, and many shamefully immoral, we ask you to confide in our judgment, and to read only those which we approve. As a recreation, and even as a useful study, we are quite willing that you should combine a fair proportion with other courses of reading. As the body needs relaxation, so does the mind, and you may have it under our sanction, and with the benefit of our more enlarged knowledge.' We have watched this course attentively, and as it is founded on the soundest philosophy, so we are persuaded it is productive of the best results. We would willingly pursue these remarks, which have extended beyond our design, but must turn to the work which has given rise to them.

The author of *Arrah Neil* belongs to the best class of our novelists. He understands his vocation, and in the main pursues it both honestly and wisely. His pages are never defiled by the immoralities to which we have referred, neither are his delineations of character and human life adapted to corrupt the heart, or, in general, to mislead the judgments of his readers. Mr. James regards fiction as the handmaid of truth, and with such exceptions only, as his own erroneous views give rise to, employs it as the minister of virtue. There are few writers, in the department of light literature, whose productions are more unexceptionable on this ground. There are instances, indeed, and the present work supplies a signal example, to which we shall presently advert, in which his own false view of men has led him to belie the truth of history, and to administer both censure and praise in the inverse ratio in which they were merited. In such cases we regret his error, and feel required, as public journalists, to warn our readers against it. The fault, however, is shared in common with a large class of historians and controvertialists; though, in the pages of a novel,—and in this, consists one of the strongest practical objections to the class—there is most danger of its influencing the reader's judgment.

The period embraced in the present work is that of the civil war. The long parliament had met in November, 1640, and, faithful to its vocation, had employed itself in the redress of grievances, and the vindication of the subject's liberty. For some time it carried everything before it. Strafford was impeached and beheaded, Laud was imprisoned, and the Commons House protected by statute law from the arbitrary intervention of the prerogative. Division in the popular forces, however, soon ensued. The policy of Pym, Hampden, and Vane, was too radical for many of their associates, and the more moderate and timid began to rally for the crown. In 1642 it had become evident that the sword would be appealed to, and each party began preparations for its use. At this precise period the story before us opens. Charles was moving towards Nottingham, where his standard was erected in August of that year; and the popular leaders, aware of his intention, were resolved to meet force with force.

At the side of a fountain, at the foot of the lawn of Bishop's Merton, the residence of Lord Walton, sat a young girl, apparently not yet sixteen years old. Her appearance was that of poverty; 'her apparel scanty, and in some places torn, though scrupulously clean.' Her beauty was striking, and there was an air of abstraction and melancholy in her countenance, as though reason were somewhat clouded. She gazed on the fountain, as if communing with the spirit of the water, and only occasionally averted her eyes, when attracted by the notes of the lark, which brought a smile, sweet, bland, and happy, to her lips. Such is Arrah Neil, the heroine of the tale, as first introduced to the reader. The reputed grandchild of old Serjeant Neil, and now an unprotected orphan, she sat and watched for the return of Lord Walton, with whom, in her childhood, she had been on familiar terms. She was aware of some danger which threatened him on his return to the home of his fathers, and was desirous of putting him on his guard. Her watch was for a long time fruitless; but at length, catching the sounds of horses' steps.

' 'It is he!' she cried, with a smile, 'It is he! I know the pace, I know the pace!' and running into the middle of the road, she gazed down it, while a horseman, followed by three servants, came on at a rapid rate, with a loose rein and an easy seat. He was a young man of seven or eight and twenty, with long fair hair, and pointed beard, tall and well made, though somewhat slight in form, with a grave and even stern cast of features, but a broad high forehead, clear but well-marked brows, and lips full but not large. His face, as I have said, was grave, and seemed, as he rode forward, unsusceptible of any but a cold, thoughtful expression, till suddenly his eyes lighted on the poor girl who was watching him, when a bright and beaming smile broke over his whole countenance, and a complete change took place, like that which spreads over a fine country when the storm gives place to sunshine.

"Ah, Arrah Neil!' he cried, 'my poor Arrah Neil, is that you come back? Where is your grandfather, poor child, have they set him free?' And he, too, sprang from his horse, taking the young girl's hand with a look of tender compassion.

' 'No, he is not free,' replied Arrah Neil; 'he never will be free.'

' 'Oh, yes,' answered the gentleman; 'these things cannot last for ever, Arrah. Time will bring about changes, I doubt not, which will deliver him from whatever prison they have taken him to?'

' 'Not from that prison,' answered the girl, with tears rising in her eyes; 'it is a low and narrow prison, Lord Walton. I told them he would die when they took him; and he only reached Devizes. But they are happy who sleep—they are happy who sleep;' and sitting down by the side of the well, she fell into thought again.

'The stranger stood and gazed at her for a moment, without uttering a word. There are times when silence is more eloquent of sympathy than the choicest words of condolence. One of the servants, however, who had ridden up, and was holding his lord's horse, burst forth with an oath—'The roundhead rascals! I wish I had my sword in their stomachs! The good old man was worth a score of them."

' 'Hush!' said his master sternly; 'hush! no such words in my hearing, Langan!'—Vol. i. pp. 12—14.

Arrah Neil was pure as undriven snow, and the young nobleman, who had sided at first with the parliament, but was now inclining to the king, looked upon her with tenderness and sympathy. She is taken to the mansion, and placed under the care of his sister, 'Sweet Annie Walton.' The return of the young nobleman had been preceded by the arrival of the Earl of Beverley, under the assumed name of Sir Francis Clare.

Beverley was an agent of the king, and the object of his visit was, to induce his friend to take part with the monarch in the struggle now impending. His success was decided by the appearance of some parliamentary commissioners with powers to search the house of the young nobleman. Attention, however, was for a moment diverted from the political negotiation, which had brought Lord Beverley to Bishop's Merton, by the firing of the mansion, which broke out suddenly, and in a manner to awaken much suspicion. The conduct of the commissioners was unceremonious and harsh, and Lord Walton, having sent away his friend with an assurance of loyalty, seized the persons of the parliamentary officers, and prepared to join the king. His troop, which consisted of about one hundred and fifty horse, was composed of his own retainers, and of some royalist cavalry, under the command of Major Randal, with whom served Captain Barecolt, to whom a prominent part is assigned in the working out of the tale. The progress of this party was not unobserved by the parliamentarians, and it soon became evident that their advance would be opposed. Perceiving, at length, that a battle was inevitable, Lord Walton sent his sister and Arrah Neil, with their attendants, to a small copse, situated on an adjoining eminence, whence the scene of the approaching struggle could be surveyed. The forces of the parliament were too powerful for the royalists, whose destruction would have been inevitable, but for the presence of mind and courage of Arrah Neil, who forgot all personal danger in solicitude for the safety of her protector. From their elevated position, the ladies could see a small path, by the side of the bridge to which the advancing party approached, that led to a fordable part of the river, but which was concealed from the cavaliers, who essayed in vain to force the barricadoed bridge. The scene is described with spirit and brevity by Mr. James.

'With anxious eyes Annie Walton and Arrah Neil watched the advance of the larger party of horse towards the wood before them, although neither of them had heard the exact cause of alarm, or were aware of where the danger was to be apprehended, or what was its nature. All they knew was, that peril lay upon the onward road; and, notwithstanding all the assiduities of Captain Barecolt—who, riding by their side wherever the space admitted it, endeavoured to entertain them with some of the monstrous fictions in which his imagination was accustomed to indulge—they listened not to his tales, they scarcely even heard his words, but, with their eyes turned constantly to the road they had just quitted, pursued a path, forming with it an acute angle, which led round the back of a large piece of water that lay gleaming before them.

* * *

'The young lady's eyes, however, were still fixed upcnber brother's troop, as she remained half way up the little mound, with her horse turned towards the road, and her maids behind, with Arrah Neil upon her left hand, and the small party of troopers a little in advance.

'They had continued thus for some four or five minutes in breathless expectation of what was to come next, when they perceived the troop brought to a sudden halt, and an apparent consultation take place at the head of the little column. At that moment Annie Walton heard one of the troopers just before her say aloud—'They have barricaded the bridge, that's clear enough.'

' 'Good!'—she exclaimed; 'what will they do?'

'But the man, although he heard her words, only turned his head over his shoulder to give her a look, without making any reply.

' 'There is a little path, lady,' said one of the maids, who, placed higher up the hill, saw more distinctly the ground beneath—'there is a little path down from the side of the bridge into the meadows below, if they were to take that they could get out of the way of the wood, and I should think could cross the river, for it spreads out there so wide, it must be shallow.'

' 'They do not see it,' said Annie Walton; 'they do not see it for the bank.'

'Almost as she spoke, a considerable body of foot drew out from the wood; and a party of about a hundred men running forward, drew up in a line close to the bridge, and opened a fire of musketry upon the small troop of cavalry which occupied the road. Several horses at the head of the line were seen to plunge violently, and one fell with its rider. The next instant the whole were in motion, a charge was made upon the bridge; and for a few moments all was confusion and disarray, in which they could only see that the cavaliers had recourse to their pistols, and were endeavouring apparently to force the barricade.

' 'Oh! the path, the path!' cried Annie Walton. 'If any man will ride and tell them of the path, and that they can ford the river below, I will give him a hundred crowns.'

'One of the troopers was instantly dashing forward, but the man who had been left in command called him back, saying that they had been ordered to remain there, and must obey. By this time the charge had been repulsed, and the cavaliers were retreating under a heavy fire in some disarray. They formed again with great rapidity, however, behind the waggons and carriages.

'Miss Walton remonstrated against the recall of her messenger: but without waiting to hear the reply, Arrah Neil exclaimed—'I will go, dear lady, I will go;' and shaking her rein, she put the horse to its speed, and darted forward before any one could stop her.

' 'I will go, too,' cried Annie Walton; 'Why should she risk her life, and a sister fear.' And thus saying, she struck her horse with the whip and followed. In a moment, without uttering a word, the stout yeoman, Hurst, was by the lady's side; but Arrah Neil outsped them both, and rode direct for the path she had observed. Without fear, without pause, the devoted girl rode on, although, as soon as ever she was perceived from the bridge, the shots began to drop around her, for her object was instantly divined, and no consideration for her sex restrained the soldiery.

' 'This way, lady, this way,' cried Hurst, turning to the left; 'we can speak to them over the dyke, and we shall be further from the fire.'

'They were now within a few hundred yards of Lord Walton's party, and he was seen at the head of the troop gesticulating vehemently to his sister to keep back.

' 'Ride away, my dear, ride away,' cried Hurst, 'I will go on;' but at that moment a shot struck his charger, and horse and rider went down together. Miss Walton, however, rode forward, seeing the good yeoman struggling up; and Arrah Neil, too, pursued her way, reached the bridge, dashed up the path, entered the road, and, in the midst of all the fire, galloped on till, when within ten yards of the carriages, a ball struck the animal in the haunches, and he reared violently with the pain. She still kept her seat, however, till Lord Walton, spurring forward, seized the bridle and caught her in his arms, just as the horse fell, and, struggling in the agonies of death, rolled over into the dyke.

' 'Good God! what is it?' exclaimed Charles Walton, bearing her back behind the waggons. 'Annie, Annie, ride away,' he shouted to his sister; 'if you love me, ride away.'

'There is a path down by the bridge—the river is fordable below,' exclaimed Arrah Neil: 'there are no dykes beyond the stream. All is clear on that side.'

' 'Look, look! Charles,' cried Miss Walton, pointing with her hand, 'there is a body of cavalry drawing out from the village, and some one riding at full speed towards our people on the hill.'

' 'Friends, on my life!' cried Major Randal. 'Now, fair aid-de-camp, gallop round there to the right, and keep out of fire. Tell your people to charge the Roundheads in the front, while those from the village take them on the flank, and we do the best we can on the right. What was that you said, pretty maid?' he continued, addressing Arrah Neil—'a path down by the bridge—the stream fordable?'

' 'Ride away, Annie, ride away,' cried Lord Walton—'more to the right, more to the right.'

' 'We must push forward the carriages and carts,' said Major Randal; 'they will give us some shelter. Where this girl came up, there can we go down.'

' 'I saw the path quite clear,' said one of the men.'—ib. pp. 151—159.

The cavalry were those of the Earl of Beverley, and the parliamentary infantry were of course repulsed. One circumstance only shaded the victory. Arrah Neil was missing, and after the most diligent search no doubt remained that she had been carried off by a Mr. Dry, of Longsoaken, one of the commissioners whom Lord Walton had arrested at Bishop's Merton. This bad man, whose character as the representative of a class, —for as such it will be understood, and is obviously intended— is the grand defect of the work, conveys the unhappy girl to Hull, where the mystery of her early life begins to clear up. The abstraction of her countenance had arisen from confused and dreamy thoughts, which she could not reduce to definite and intelligible forms. Cloudy visions, of a beautiful and happy past, were perpetually floating before her, which she could not understand, and which it was impossible to harmonise with the destitute and cheerless character of the present. Her imagination was too much fascinated to deal with the gross outward; and the passer by, judging superficially of her character, attributed to something like mental imbecility, what really sprung from the intense though subtle activity of her spirit.

They had arrived at Hull, the beautiful Arrah Neil, and her heartless, hypocritical captor, Mr. Dry. Having obtained some clue to her parentage, his object in visiting Hull was to investigate the matter further, with the intention, if his suspicions were confirmed, of forcing her into a marriage with himself. He represented the young girl as his ward, and intimated to the landlady of the Swan that her intellect was disordered. The following throws some light on the history of Arrah Neil, and was the first clue she obtained to her real parentage:—

'The moment Mr. Dry was gone, the good woman called to the cook, and ordered a very substantial dinner for the party which had just arrived; but then putting her hand before her eyes, she stood for the space of a minute and a half in the centre of the tap-room, as if in consideration, then saying, 'I won't tell him anything about it —There is something strange in this affair; I am not a woman if I don't find it out.' She then hurried up to the room where she had left Arrah Neil, unlocked the door and went in.

'The poor girl was leaning on the sill of the open window, gazing up and down the street. Her face was clear and bright; her beautiful blue eyes were full of intellect and fire; the look of doubt and inward thought was gone; a change had come over her, complete and extraordinary. It seemed as if she had awakened from a dream.

'When the landlady entered, Arrah immediately turned from the window, and advanced towards her. Then laying her hand upon her arm, she gazed in her face for a moment so intensely that the poor woman began to be alarmed.

' 'I am sure I recollect you,' said Arrah Neil. 'Have you not been here long?'

' 'For twenty years,' replied the hostess; 'and for five and twenty before that in the house next door, from which I married into this.'

'And don't you recollect me?' asked Arrah Neil.

'No,' replied the landlady, 'I do not; though I think I have seen some one very like you before—but then it was a taller lady—much taller.'

'So she was,' cried Arrah Neil. 'What was her name?'

'Nay, I can't tell, if you can't,' replied the landlady.

'I know what I called her, but I know nothing more,' answered Arrah Neil. 'I called her mother—and perhaps she was my mother. I called her mother as I lay in that bed, with my head aching, my eyes burning, and my lips parched; and then I fell into a long deep sleep, from which I woke, forgetting all that went before; and she was gone!'

'Ay!' cried the landlady; 'and are you that poor little thing?' and she gazed upon her for a moment with a look of sad, deep interest. The next instant she cast her arms round her, and kissed her tenderly. 'Ah, poor child!' she said at length, with tears in her eyes, 'those were sad times—sad times indeed! 'T was when the fever was raging in the country. Sad work in such days for those who lodge strangers! It cost me my only one. A man came and slept in that bed, he looked ill when he came, and worse when he went. Then came a lady and a child, and an old man, their servant, and the house was full, all but this room and another; and ere they had been here long, my own dear child was taken with the fever. She was near your own age, perhaps a year older; and I told the lady over night, so she said she would go on the morrow, for she was afraid for her darling. But before the morning came, you too were shaking like a willow in the wind, and then came on the burning fit, and the third day you began to rave, and knew no one. The fifth day my poor girl died, and for a whole day I did not see you—I saw nothing but my dear child. On the next, however, they came to tell me the lady had fallen ill, and I came to watch you, for it seemed to me as if there was something between you and my poor Lucy—I knew not what—you had been sisters in sickness, and I thought you might be sisters in the grave. I cannot help crying when I think of it.—Oh, those were terrible days;' And the poor woman wiped her eyes.

'But my mother,' cried Arrah Neil—'my mother?'

'Some day I will show you where she lies,' answered the hostess; and Arrah wept bitterly, for a hope was crushed out to its last spark.

'She got worse and worse,' continued the landlady; 'and she too lost her senses, but just as you were slowly getting a little better, she suddenly regained her mind; and I was so glad, for I thought she would recover too; but the first words she spoke were to ask after you. I told her you were much better; and all she said was, 'I should wish to see her once more before I die, if it may be done without harming her;' and then I knew that she was going. I and the old servant carried you, just as you were, and laid you on her bed, and she kissed you, and prayed God to bless and keep you ; but you were weak and dozy, and she would not have you wakened, but made us take you back ; and then she spoke long with the old man in a whisper ; but all I heard was, 'You promise, Neil—you promise on your salvation.' He did promise—though I did not know what it was. Then she said, 'Recollect, you must never tell her, unless it be recovered.' Recovered or reversed, she said, I remember not well which, but from that moment she said nothing more, but to ask for some water, and so she went on till the next morning, just as day was dawning, and then she departed.'

* * *

' 'It is as strange to me as to you,' said Arrah Neil ; 'for, as I tell you, I seemed to fall into a deep sleep, and for a time I forgot all ; but since then all the things which occurred before that time have troubled me sadly. It seemed as if I had had a dream, and I recollect a castle on a hill, and riding with a tall gentleman, who was on a great black horse, while I had a tiny thing, milk white ; and I remember many servants and maids—oh ! and many things I have never seen since ; but I could not tell whether it was real or a mere fancy, till I came into this town, and I saw the street which I used to look at from the window, and the sign of the house that I used to watch as it swung to and fro in the wind. Then I was sure it was real ; and your face, too, brought a thousand things back to me ; and when I saw the room where I had been, I felt inclined to weep, I knew not why.—Well, well may I weep !'

' 'But who is this old man who is with you ?' asked the landlady, suddenly. 'He is not the old servant, who was as aged then as he is now ; and what is this tale he tells of your being his ward, and mad ?'

' 'Mad ?' cried Arrah Neil—'mad ! Oh, no ! 'Tis he that is wicked, not I that am mad. He and another dragged me away from those who protected me, and were good to me—kind Annie Walton, and that noble lord her brother, while they were fighting on the moors beyond Coventry. I, his ward ! He has no more right to keep me from my friends than the merest stranger. He is a base, bad man—a hypocrite—a cheat. What he wants, what he wishes, I know not. But he had my poor old grandfather dragged away to prison, and he died by the road.'

' 'Your grandfather !' said the widow—'what was his name ?'

' 'Neil,' answered the poor girl ; 'that was the name he always went by.'

' 'Why, that was the old servant,' said the hostess.'—*ib.* pp. 287—295.

It is not our intention to disclose the particulars of Arrah Neil's parentage, or to forestall the interest of Mr. James's volumes. Suffice it, therefore, to say, that she is released from the custody of Mr. Dry and restored to the Waltons, by whom she is regarded with increased interest, and watched over with all the tenderness of fraternal affection. In the meantime, other personages are on the stage. The plot thickens, and the skill of the narrator, as well as the interest of his story, grows upon the reader. Lord Beverley, accompanied by Captain Barecolt, proceed towards France, on a mission from the king; but, being intercepted by an English cruizer, are carried prisoners into Hull, then under the command of Sir John Hotham. They assume the character of French officers, and the part of the latter, more especially, is acted with inimitable skill. Under the name of Captain Jersval he obtains the confidence of the governor, and is employed in surveying the fortifications, the result of which, as our readers need scarcely be told, is his escape from the town. Subsequently rejoined by Lord Beverley, whose departure from Hull had been facilitated by the governor, they bore cheering intelligence to the king of his disposition to surrender the town to his majesty. The royal forces consequently moved northwards, and the Earl, with the adventurous spirit of a true cavalier, undertook to re-enter Hull, in order to facilitate the design of the governor. On the road thither he was joined by Barecolt, who, united to the boastful spirit of Falstaff, a courage and fidelity to which Shakspere's knight makes no pretensions.

A great change had, in the meantime, taken place in Hull. Suspecting the design of the king, and mistrusting Sir John Hotham, the parliament had sent thither some officers of approved fidelity, who at once acted as a check on the governor, and prepared the fortifications to resist the assault which was anticipated. The governor was further disabled by a severe attack of gout, so that when Lord Beverley, having entered the town, demanded in the foreign accent formerly assumed, to speak to him, he was introduced to his son, Colonel Hotham, a man of a different temper and far more devoted to the cause of the parliament than his father. The result was an arrest of the Earl, whose pass was torn in pieces by the Colonel as a forged instrument. What followed, on the morning when the former was arraigned before a summary court-martial, will be best described in the words of our author. The extract, which we abridge, illustrates at least one feature of the times, and so far relieves the dark shade which Mr. James throws over the adherents of the parliament.

'After pausing for a moment, while the earl stood at the end of the table as we have described, the parliamentary commander demanded, in a sharp tone,—

''What is your name?'

''Not knowing that you have any authority to ask it,' replied the earl, with perfect calmness, 'I shall, most undoubtedly, refuse to answer.'

'That will serve you little, sir,' said one of the men from London; 'for if you do refuse, the court will proceed to try you without farther ceremony.'

'"What court?' demanded the earl. 'I see five persons sitting round a table, but no court.'

'"This, sir, is summary court-martial,' replied Colonel Hotham, 'called to try a person accused of entering a garrisoned town as a spy.'

'"With a pass from the governor?' added Lord Beverly, emphatically.

'"But that pass, we have every reason to believe,' replied Colonel Hotham, 'was obtained by a false representation of your name and quality, and as such was invalid.'

'"That point will be easily established,' replied the earl, 'by calling the governor himself. I maintain that he gave it to me with full knowledge of my person; and I, therefore, require that he be called, to testify as to the validity of the pass which you, sir, most dishonourably and dishonestly tore to pieces last night.'

* * *

'"Had he a pass?' demanded the preacher officer of the train-bands, turning gloomily to Colonel Hotham.

'"He had, but under a feigned name,' replied Hotham.

'"What proof have you?' demanded the enthusiast. 'Remember, sir, 'whoso sheddeth man's blood, by man shall his blood be shed!' If you bring not your father to testify, how can we know that this safe conduct was wrongly obtained?'

'Colonel Hotham's cheek turned red, for he loved not such opposition; and he paused for a moment ere he replied, feeling that he was angry, and fearing that he might commit himself.

* * *

'"Bring in the prisoner first,' said Colonel Hotham; 'we will confront them together, gentlemen.'

'A pause ensued for the space of about two minutes, during which no one spoke, except one of the officers of the train-bands, who said a few words to the other in a low voice, and then the door opened; and turning round his head, the earl, as he had apprehended, beheld the renowned Captain Barecolt marched in amongst some soldiers. As it was not the first time that the worthy officer had found himself in such an unpleasant position, he showed himself very little disturbed by his situation, and walked up to the end of the table with a bold countenance, smoothing down his mustachios, and drawing his beard to a point between his fingers, as if he had not had time to complete his toilette ere he was brought from the inn.

'The cool self-sufficiency of his air seemed to move the wrath of Colonel Hotham, who instantly addressed him, saying,—

'"What is your name, fellow?'

'"I be not your fellow, sair,' replied Barecolt, boldly, 'and am not so call. My name were Captain Jersval, for your service, gentlemen.'

'"And now speak out, and speak the truth,' continued the colonel, while Barecolt bowed ceremoniously round the table; 'leave your mumming, sir, and answer. Who is this person, with whom you entered the town yesterday evening? Answer truly, for your life depends upon it.'

''Begar, it were one very difficult thing for me to tell,' replied Barecolt, in the same unconcerned tone. 'First, sair, it cannot alway be easy to tell who one be oneself; and much more uneasy to tell who de oder man be.'

''What does the fool mean?' demanded one of the roundhead officers; 'Not always easy to tell who you are yourself! What do you mean, man?'

''Why, sair,' replied Barecolt, with an agreeable laugh, 'one day not so very long time ago, I met wid one saucy man who to my face—to my very beard, sair—swear I was one oder man but myself. He swear I were not Jersval but Barecole—one Capitaine Barecole, a very great man in dese parts—a famous man, I hear'

'Cease this foolery, sir,' cried Colonel Hotham; 'and answer my question directly, or prepare to walk out to the water-gate, and receive a volley. Who is the person, I say, now standing beside you?'

''Pardi! how de devil should I know?' rejoined Barecolt, with some heat of manner; 'I have seen him twice, dat is all; once aboard de sheep where he was very seek, and once I meet him just half a league out of de gate. We were chase hard by a party of what you call cavalier malignant, and ride togeder for our lifes?'

''That is true, for I saw them,' said one of the officers of the train-bands.

''And do you pretend to say you do not know his name?' demanded Colonel Hotham, gazing with the fierceness of disappointment upon the worthy captain's face.

''Oh, I think I heard his name on board de sheep,' answered Barecolt; 'but I cannot be too sure. Let me see. It was de Colonel de Mery; was it not, that you told me sair?' and he turned to the earl with a low bow.'—vol. iii., pp. 159—65.

Failing in this witness, Mr. Dry, of Longsoaken, was next introduced, who speedily identified the Earl, on whom sentence of death was summarily passed, the military preacher alone protesting against the verdict. We must indulge in another brief extract, in order that our readers may be acquainted with the issue of this strange scene.

''Young man,' said the military preacher, addressing Hotham in a solemn tone, 'if you give a man in bonds a chance, it should be a fair one. Such has not been afforded the prisoner.—Why did you tear the paper?—Why do you now refuse to confront him with the witness he calls?—and if that witness be too ill, why not wait till he be well, as he requires? Why not—if not to doom him to death at your pleasure?—I will go no farther in this—I wash my hands of this blood.'

''Well, then, we will put it to the vote!' cried Colonel Hotham, fiercely, 'and look to yourself, Captain Marsh. He that puts his hand to the plough, must not turn back.—Look to yourself, I say.'

' 'I will,' replied the old officer of the trainbands; 'and I am not to be frightened from a righteous course by loud words or frowning brows. I fear not what man can do unto me.'

' 'Pshaw!' cried Colonel Hotham, turning away. 'Your verdict, sir, upon these two men—guilty, or not guilty?'

' 'Guilty,' said the Londoner to whom he spoke, without a moment's pause.

' 'Guilty,' said the other, on the colonel's left, answering a mere look.

' 'I doubt,' replied Captain Marden of the train-bands, when Hotham turned to him.

' 'But I do not,' rejoined that officer; 'and I say guilty too—so there are three voices against two. They are condemned. Take them hence to the water-gate, call out a file of men, and the rest as yesterday. I spare you the rope, Lord Beverley, in consideration of your rank. You shall die as a soldier.'

' 'And you as a murderer!' shouted Barecolt, rushing towards him so suddenly, that he caught him by the throat with both hands, before any one could interpose.

'The two parliamentary officers drew theirs words; the guards were rushing up from the door; but, under the strong pressure of Captain Barecolt's fingers, Colonel Hotham was turning black in the face, and might have been strangled before he could be delivered; when suddenly a voice was heard, exclaiming, 'Halt! Not a man stir! Guard the door!' and all was silence

'Captain Barecolt slightly relaxed his grasp; the parliamentary officers drew back; and Sir John Hotham, with an excited and angry countenance, and evidently in great pain, walked up the room, and took his place at the head of the table.

' 'What is all this?' he demanded, 'Unloose my son, sir.—What is the meaning of this, Colonel Hotham?'

' '*Pardi*, I will unloose him—now, you be come, governor,' replied Barecolt, taking away his hands, and drawing back; 'but, begar, if you had not come, he 'd be strangle.'

Colonel Hotham sank in a chair, gasping for breath, and one of the officers from London took upon him to reply. 'This is a court-martial, Sir John, summoned to try——'

' 'And by whose authority?' demanded the governor fiercely; 'who dares to summon a court martial in Hull but myself?'

' 'But you were ill, sir,' replied the officer, 'and Colonel Hotham judged it expedient to summon us.'

' 'He did! did he?' cried the governor. 'Colonel Hotham, give up your sword.—You are under arrest. Remove him, guards. Take him away. This is no court—all its proceedings are illegal, and so shall be dealt with. Gentlemen, you are dismissed. Away! We have had too much of you.'—*ib.* pp. 170—175.

The subsequent course of the narrative, and the various fortunes of the other *dramatis personæ,* must be learnt from the volumes themselves. Before parting, however, from Mr. James, we have a word or two to say on a serious blemish, which attaches to his story, taken as a whole. We do not refer to any mere literary faults, though it would not be difficult to point out such. These are trifling, compared with what we have in view, and for which, in the degree here exhibited, we were not prepared. We had thought the time was passed when men of any pretensions, in whatever department of literature they employ themselves, would venture on such a distorted representation, as Mr. James has given, of the two great parties into which the English nation was then divided. It betokens great ignorance on his part, or a degree of prejudice, still more discreditable. Either he knows not the men, whose principles and character he undertakes to sketch, or is so virulently hostile to their momory as wilfully to exhibit an exception as the rule,—a low minded, sordid, and base hypocrite as their examplar and mouthpiece. That there were hypocrites amongst the adherents of the parliament we readily admit—men whose God was self, whose paradise was earth, all whose passions were of a mean and sensual order. Periods of great excitement have always been marked by the presence of such men, and their numbers have been proportioned to its intensity, and to the circle within which it has operated. That they were found amongst the parliamentarians in greater numbers than amongst the royalists, resulted from the higher estimate of pure religion entertained by the former. Human depravity took another shape with the cavaliers. It was too wise in its generation to appear amongst them in the form of religious hypocrisy. The coin was not current, the sterling gold was not there; and we need not, consequently, wonder at the absence of the counterfeit. What we complain of in Mr. James is, not that he has admitted the fact of hypocrisy, but that he has made hypocrisy, with its concomitant vices, the characteristic of the class. That there were such men in 1642, amongst the Puritans, as Mr. Dry of Longsoaken, we are not concerned to deny; but that such a man should be introduced, and throughout an extended story should be made to act,—for this is unquestionably the case in the present instance—as a representative of the religious men who were then arrayed against the royal and prelatical power, is an offence against truth and honesty scarcely to be expected at the hands of the bitterest polemic. Mr. James may possibly allege that he has not so represented the case, and it is true he has not done so *in words.* But let the impression of his volumes on a reader not conversant with other sources of information be estimated, and what candid man will say that it does not amount to this?

There is, moreover, a meanness in the mode adopted to compass this end which aggravates the evil. Had any historical character been introduced as a type of the class, the means of detection would have been within the reach of all. Every tyro would have known that the sketch was inaccurate, or that the individual pourtrayed failed to embody the qualities of those with whom he acted. But when a fictitious personage is ushered on the stage, wearing the apparel and speaking the language of the parties to be vilified; when he is made to act alone, the darker features of his character being unrelieved by the virtues of any other member of his sect; and when, in addition to all this, as if to give greater force and virulence to the representation, such an assemblage of vices is contrasted with the bright and lovely qualities ascribed to members of the opposite sect, it is impossible to avoid the conviction that truth has been recklessly sacrificed, and the memory of the illustrious dead most foully aspersed.

Similar remarks might be made on the general impression produced by these volumes, respecting the political struggle and parties of the period in question. Lord Walton and the Earl of Beverley are the heroes of the cavalier party, and their characters are sketched in a style adapted to secure esteem and admiration. Of the parliamentarians we are left to judge from Colonels Hotham and Thiselton, and what reader, judging from these materials, can hesitate as to the verdict to be pronounced? The great actors in the solemn scene—the Pyms, the Hampdens, the Vanes and the Cromwells—are not introduced, and the reason of the omission is obvious. Sir Walter Scott, in an evil hour for his genius, attempted to pourtray the inner life of the Protector, and his failure, so complete and ridiculous, might well deter an inferior artist. But there were other men who might, if common fairness had been observed, have been allowed to mingle with the throng which at our author's bidding crowd the stage. Had they been so, however, a different impression would have been produced, one more accordant, certainly, with the truth of history, but not, as we are compelled to suspect, with the prejudices and intention of the writer.

Art. VIII.—*The Times Newspaper*. December, 1845. London.

If our readers will glance backwards at our article on the formation of the Peel ministry, four years ago, they will see that not a few of our anticipations have been fully realized. Sir Robert has been compelled, as we then predicted, to work out something like Whiggery, under the colours of Toryism. The Melbourne administration had disappointed and disheartened all classes. Notwithstanding the good which must always result from popular principles even appearing to obtain power, so much mischief intermingled itself in almost every measure,—so much heartlessness was manifested towards the rights of conscience and the claims of industry,—the lights of commercial wisdom broke on the minds of political leaders so late in the day, that Lord John Russell and his party received little pity, when the general election of 1841 drove them from Downing-street. Their clever antagonist, on the other hand, had been playing his game for some years. He had beckoned to every selfish sentiment in the land to come to his aid. He meekly bore the bitter taunts of those whom he had deserted in 1829. He had found out, indeed, that monopoly is the very first-born child of mammon; yet he kept his own counsel, and allowed stolid agriculture to imbibe and act upon the idea, that to elevate him once more to office was the surest road to protection! The established church had excommunicated him in their anathemas, for his policy towards Roman catholics; but after performing some penance in sackcloth and ashes, he so edified the bench of bishops by his bearing towards radicals and nonconformists;—he whispered such plausible, and yet alarming things, about the perils of tithes and church-rates from the wicked Whigs, that their lordships began to wonder at his white sheet, and to fancy it the spotless robe of purity and innocence. There was no end to the cajolery with which he managed to enlist hope and fear upon his own side. He soothed the prejudices, and blinded the eyes of the bigoted, the timid, and the loyal. His mouth flowed with persuasives, that the past should be forgotten, and his promises of good behaviour in future be considered as a paradise of sweets *in posse*, for all conservative followers disposed to rally once more under his standard. His advice—'register, register'—was strictly attended to both in boroughs and counties. Although his professions and pledges amounted to nothing when they were pondered and analysed,—although his reserves and explanations had secured a bridge of retreat from every position which he might find it inconvenient to maintain,—

although expediency, upon the face of it, formed the soul and essence of his political existence, yet toryism permitted its wishes to be sponsors to its confidence, and Sir Robert Peel was a second time carried by acclamation into the royal closet. In proportion to the exultation of his admirers have been their subsequent wrath and sorrow.

Yet surely the idolators were to blame, as much as the idol they had set up. He could see further, and knew more than they did. No one could be more aware than himself that there was no real love lost between them. Stern necessity alone had cemented the connexion, just as when the goat and the fox were in the well together, and reynard availed himself of the convenient long horns of his companion to effect his escape, and then wish him good morning! The premier must have long ceased to believe in the political creed of his adherents; but to get out of the pit of opposition, there was no other way than to make use of their inglorious instrumentality. They, on their part, ought to have understood their man better. Genuine patriotism would have enlightened them on the subject; but preferring, as they always have done, the purple and fine linen of this life, and casting into the shade every other interest except their own, they have only reaped an appropriate reward. Not, however, that Englishmen ever like to see any body cheated: and here lay the point of weakness in Sir Robert Peel. His majority was nearly a hundred strong. His predecessors had become bankrupt in efficiency and reputation. They worked the wheel of government like the ass at Carisbrook Castle, struggling to get forward, yet never advancing; whilst their dull routine of daily duty only brought up buckets of useless water! Circumstances, moreover, had set in against them. They were low in financial difficulties, aggravated by the expenses and disasters of two unfinished wars.. Bad harvests had embarrassed trade, through the operation of iniquitous laws; nor were the operatives quiet in our manufacturing districts. The new minister appeared with all the halo of triumph about his head, and a purse of popularity in his right hand. Yet never was failure more signal; and honest men know why. 'His speculation,' says the leading journal of our age, 'was one which could not answer, and never will answer with the British people. He thought to establish a miserable sinking fund of reserves, which might in time pay off his huge debt of promises. He did not sufficiently consider, that while he was secretly developing and cherishing the former, the latter also were fructifying and becoming due! The day of reckoning must arrive to every one at last. On the one side, the interests of the country at large demanded the repeal of the protective system, and his own ripening convictions responded to the call; on the other, the great conservative engagement must be fulfilled. The premier tried to satisfy himself and the country, and repudiate his supporters and friends. His scheme has failed; and much as we regret that any one should fail, who proposed what we really consider a blessing to the nation, we are resigned to an event, by which that blessing is dissociated from personal ingratitude and political deception. *We see in it one lesson more to do good acts by good, fair, and open means!'* In other words, honesty is the best policy, even amongst statesmen, if they would but condescend to see it so.

His position was indeed from the first a peculiar one. Cradled in that school of mediocrities, of which Lord Liverpool was so long the acknowledged head, he acquired the habit of conveying as little meaning as possible within the largest limits of verbosity. To catch and hold his auditory by the ears, and by these alone, was an early object of his ambition. With capabilities of getting through a vast amount of administrative business, the cast of his mind has always been material and utilitarian. He has calculated the effects of things, but not the hearts of men, nor the force and play of ideas. His income tax and tariff were portions of himself, prosopopæias of his natural intellect, expatiating in the calculations of a clerk rather than those of a philosophic statesman. His books for studying the wide world wear the aspect of ledgers. The laboratory of his inner soul is fitted up for being a large counting-house, and nothing more. Its tenant prefers lamp-light to the radiancy of the sun. The pen is in his hand, or behind his ear. His thoughts occasionally mount upon stilts, but they have no wings. When disturbance from without obliges him to look abroad, his survey is taken from the summits of Drayton Manor, rather than from the Alps of any lofty intellect. Hence his views of society are all flat and contracted, bounded by the park-walls of an ancestral or monied aristocracy. Not that he cares for family associations, but his notions of power assume the form of governing through an oligarchy. His sympathies, therefore, would have been identified with George III., had he lived in the eighteenth, instead of the nineteenth century. Their characteristics are essentially cold, stiff, courtly, and official. His desires seek followers, not friends. They rest exclusively on the upper parts of the graduated scale of society. He places confidence in no man. The absence of romance and imagination in his composition, is total. He may therefore be described as an enormous individualism, fit only to live in an ice-palace, such as that which was built by Catharine, empress of all the Russians. His rival possesses many more points of attractiveness than himself. Lord John Russell has frankness and courage. Nothing would have induced him, four years ago, to have retained office upon the terms of practising the shadow of deception upon the humblest of his partizans. His talents, which are highly respectable, although by no means of an order to be compared with those of Fox or Lord Gray, would disdain adventitious support, or any monopoly of applause. His notions of the premiership are essentially opposed to the *moi c'est l'etat;* upon which egotistic principle the member for Tamworth has been known to act, or rather reign, for night after night, until Mr. D'Israeli first disturbed his self-complacency. Lord John also has had more time and disposition for studying history than Sir Robert. His Whig origin and connections have taught him to watch the growth of new parties, as well as the reconstruction of old ones. Should he attempt to construct a cabinet out of those rotten materials, which have been shipwrecked again and again, he will fail to a certainty. His openly avowed recantation on the subject of the corn-laws, taken in conjunction with his general manliness of bearing, may lead us to hope, that if he can stand his ground at all, he will aim at nobler achievements. It strikes ourselves, that now will be his golden opportunity for building up a magnificent reputation. But he must be brave as well as prudent for the occasion. The wisdom of Ulysses must be blended with the genius, virtue, and energy of the first Lord Chatham.

There are phases of society, when certain words, pronounced by certain men, produce all the results of a talisman. Their sound electrifies the world. Let his lordship then contemplate some such trial, looking forward to Providence and posterity for his ultimate reward. What is more undoubted, than that the phantoms of aristocracy are waning away? Are not the schoolmaster, and common sense, teaching us lessons, which would have turned our forefathers pale with astonishment? Is not the voice of the people gradually becoming like the noise of many waters? Is it not true that abuses, which were adored by past generations, are unveiling their native hideousness to the present? Matters must come at last to king, people and Queen Victoria! We love the monarchy and the monarch; but both must rest upon a government thoroughly responsible, and essentially popular. If the Corinthian columns of the state are to stand as ornaments, or mere supporters of forms and associations, all well and good, if general opinion shall acquiesce in it. But class interests must give way to universal ones. Liberty and order must meet together, while righteousness and peace embrace each other. Let the walls of the constitution remain; but a new spirit must rule within them. Monopolies and monstrous anomalies, such as now meet the gaze, are fit for nothing but condemnation. Our institutions must be unfeudalized, as Mr. Ewart once remarked, amidst thunders of approbation from a crowded assembly, excited simply because the speaker had touched one of those mighty truths, which vibrate through the soul of millions. We trust Lord John Russell will be wise in time. Toryism he cannot fail to abhor, whether he calls to mind its cruel and fraudful opposition even to the revolution of 1688, as well as all its malversation and tyranny subsequent to that event, carried down from the days of Harley and Bolingbroke to the death of George IV. The miserable *alias* of conservatism can never cover its mountains of delinquency. It is now perhaps a departed spirit, but only in the sense of a metempsychosis, changing from one body to another, and acquiring with every successive change augmented powers of subtlety and malevolence. Whiggery also has become a *caput mortuum*, the shadow of a great name,—never a very favourite one of ours,—but at least connected with great historical passages in Hume and Hallam. To revive it would be the greatest of galvanic follies. Derision, defeat, and scandal, could be the only consequences. Like a corpse, under the influence of voltaic batteries, it would afford the most revolting mockery of life—a series of impotent contortions and ghastly grimaces! Rumour has indeed dared to say, that it was a scheme thought of for more than a few moments. But where are the living Whigs to be found—where are their supporters—where their strength, influence, talents, energies, and sinews, for the herculean attempt? They are not nearly so respectable or useful as the windmills in the annals of Don Quixote! The merest movement of their sails would be the signal for inextinguishable laughter. What, indeed, are they at all, but memorials of the wisdom of *Corn Laws!*

Meanwhile the joke would be far too serious and practical. The public mind of these realms is not now to be sported with by grandees, as in the age of the Pelhams and Newcastles. It excites deep disgust to read or hear the postprandian effusions of dukes and nobles, who had better hasten to the nearest Mechanics' Institutes in their respective neighbourhoods, to improve their knowledge, and mend their manners. Thirty years of peace have engendered apt scholars, deep thinkers, and keen observers, amongst what are termed the lower orders. High prices, and low wages have awakened, in no slight degree, their sensitiveness to ridicule, or what they consider insult, even where it is only sheer thoughtlessness. A contemptuous expression from the lips of Charles I. cost him the affections of his navy; nor will artisans easily forget, that their Graces of Richmond and

Norfolk, have gravely recommended a diet for the poor of carrots, mangelworzel, and curry-powder! The new Dean of Westminster, we believe, inserted cold peas and beans upon his bill of fare! What illustrations are all these of the gross ignorance prevalent amongst our peers and ecclesiastics, as to the real condition of their fellow subjects, and fellow creatures! In a certain sense, it cannot be concealed, that we deserve to pass through the ordeal of immense organic changes; well aware as we are of the partial yet severe misery inevitably attendant upon many of them. It is not conceivable, that men who can write as Cooper the chartist, or Ebenezer Elliot, the corn-law rhymer, can do,—types as these are of an intellectual element, augmenting in intensity and extent every day—will always submit to go on unrepresented in parliament, whilst union houses are rising in every direction, and hereditary senators are talking nonsense at public dinners. Is knowledge power; or is it not? May we imagine that ought else than mind will ultimately govern the British realms, with all their dependencies? The noble scion of the house of Bedford must therefore take Chartism into his most serious consideration. There is no help for it. The hard, yet firm hand of honest labour will touch at no distant day the ark of the constitution. To whisper such a truth in particular quarters may be like talking to stocks and stones; but the patron of the Reform Bill knows, that these are the words of sound sense and soberness. The almost living machinery, which spins cotton and wool into cloth and stockings, indirectly symbolises those various processes of civilisation, which, whilst they promote refinement, interweave also class with class, and render more perfect the beautiful fabric of society. It will soon come to be felt and understood by millions, that peers and peasants, capitalists and operatives, landlords and labourers, palaces, mansions, and cottages, are all parts of one mighty whole; that numbers have their rights as much as property has; that the entire body-politic ought to participate in that glorious Magna-Charta of the omnipotent Father, who loves all his children, and commands them to love one another. The grand omission, and cardinal transgression of government is, that it reigns for the few, and not the many. The latter are asserting their claims in the solitary path open to honest men, under their circumstances. Parliaments of their own are growing up out of the ground. Agitation is the dangerous genius of all such congresses. What is the Anti-Corn-Law League, but one of those magnificent combinations, — originated and supported indeed mainly by the middle and manufacturing classes—yet sufficiently illustrative of our position, that if rulers will persist in neglecting or maltreating their subjects, these last must take care of themselves. The member for Stockport incontestably should have a portfolio in the new cabinet. But this is merely by the way.

For there is a yet more momentous element forcing itself upwards and onwards for the benefit of mankind: we mean that of genuine religious freedom. In this country, almost more than in any other, one form of Christianity is enthroned at the right hand of the State, to the grievous detriment of all parties both for time and eternity. Our statesmen have everything to learn with regard to the true nature and magnitude of this portentous evil. It is the mastership of mammon over the slavery of souls. Nothing will undermine or overthrow it, short of the fullest development of the voluntary system: and as a general election can be at no great distance, let the friends of enfranchisement bestir themselves without further delay. Wherever there is a constituency, in which the subject can be started, we should be warned not to lose a moment. *Dimidium facti qui cœpit, habet.* Dissenters from the Established Church owe but little, it must be admitted, to secular administrations. Their heads and arms have been counted in the contest, and pretty generally forgotten at the division of the spoil. Trusting in Divine Providence, they must help themselves. At the present hour, there is no reason why every non-conformist in England should not be fined a shilling, for not attending his parish-church on the Sunday. The political—or at least the ecclesiastical brand is still upon their foreheads: do they glory in it, or are they prepared to wipe it off? There is now close at hand another of those favourable opportunities, which may be called the flowers of time. Let it be gathered with zeal, and improved with prudence to the very uttermost. We would fain circulate throughout the community such questions as the following:—How is it that the kingdom of Christ goes on to be identified with that of this world—contrary to his own clear injunction? Why should one denomination possess revenues of five millions sterling per annum—an original robbery by Act of Parliament, and a perpetual source of spiritual corruption at the very heart of society? Why should five hundred thousand pounds more per annum be raised in the shape of church-rates,—without regard to the overgrown opulence of those who receive, or the poverty, and above all, the consciences of those who pay? Why should six-and-twenty seniors of the favoured sect sit for life among the barons of the realm, with four additional ones, changed every year, from an offset of their own body, in the sister island—all Lords of Parliament—all rich in both revenues and patronage—all potent to oppress the weak, and all powerless to curb aristocratic sinners? We appeal to sentences in our ecclesiastical courts, as reported in the daily journals now upon our table, whether these queries are mere sounding figures of rhetoric. How is it, that the fornicator, and the sodomite cannot be cast out of the sanctuary, when the humbler pastor of some poor parish is ruined for life, on venturing to doubt about baptismal regeneration? These, or similar interrogatories, are the points which, as it appears to us, might now be put with advantage. Let every borough election be an echo of the late Southwark one, in every respect but its want of success. Lord John Russell found the dissenters grateful for a small modicum of relief afforded them, through the Repeal of the Test and Corporation Acts; let him now win for them an emancipation from all ecclesiastical payments—from all vestiges of humiliation,—from all the sneers of cathedral dignitaries. Let him open to them the gates of Oxford and Cambridge,—not to say of Durham, Winchester, and our other more celebrated seminaries. His cabinet would then enlist masses of religious, reflecting, and sensible men, such as would attach themselves to his person, and reverence his very name. In one word, his views must be comprehensive in range, as well as full and particular in details; or else his ministry too, if it struggle into existence at all, will pass away, like the chaff of the summer threshing-floor.

Nor would we ask more for ourselves than we demand for others. Ireland must be governed and pacified. It is a melancholy reflection, that Liberalism cannot accomplish *now*, what might easily have been achieved, when Sir Robert Peel made the Orange Societies of Lord Roden fancy him their best ally. Four years of mutual exasperation have scattered all manner of combustibles from Cape Clear to the Giant's Causeway. A single false step might at present consign the whole island to the flames of civil war. The influence of the lord-lieutenant extends little further than the battlements of Dublin castle, or the iron railings of the Phœnix park. The Times' commissioner, notwithstanding his admirable ability and intentions, has overlooked in his letters just what Sir Robert Peel always overlooks,—namely *the influence of ideas* upon social weal or woe. No doubt can exist, but that to a great extent, the Irish might advance themselves to a better state of things than that under which they at present exist: but to put that mind and wish into them, to rouse them from their political and intellectual torpor, and then guide them, when so aroused, in the right direction, is the very task to be accomplished. Certain ideas, rather than physical obstacles, stand in the way: and it is just here that the interposition of wise measures is most wanted. O'Connell, whether for good or evil, appeals to and plays with the former: and hence the influence of that magic wand which he wields. *Et mulcere fluctus et tollere vento!* The people there are under warm impressions, that for centuries they have been mis-governed; that the Anglican communion has usurped the place of their own church, and appropriated her revenues; that their country has been rendered a mere satellite and slave to England; and that the Union formed an infamous consummation to all the previous tyranny. A repeal, therefore, of that Union is the concentrated idea, embodying all these and various other analogous notions, many of them founded upon truth: and until this spell is mastered, or dissolved, it seems to us hopeless to do much for that unfortunate land. Should we, as Englishmen, be more patient than the Irish are, under similar circumstances? we much doubt it. If Mr. Macauley join the ministry, we may at least infer that the Irish church is to undergo serious modification, with a view to its ultimate surrender. The posthumous pamphlet of the late Sydney Smith should be circulated throughout the kingdom; not indeed to promote any scheme for Catholic endowment, but to exhibit the strongest illustration that can be given, as to the calamities inseparable from any Christian community encumbering itself with pelf and power. The Irish liberals have generally proved faithful to the standard of Free Trade, and are promising to be so again. Our journal has never willingly used a single expression adverse to the just demands of Ireland; and notwithstanding the atrocious grant to Maynooth,—*atrocious* being by no means too strong an epithet upon some of the principles advocated by the repealers themselves,—notwithstanding the vituperation of Wesleyanism and Nonconformity indulged in by the members for Cork and Dungarvon,—we are still prepared to concede justice to Erin, and allure her warm enthusiasm to the banner of our United Kingdom.

Hunger, meanwhile, will wait for none of us. Famine, with her pale train of ghastly spectres, fever, violence, insurrection, and death, has scared into resignation one of the strongest cabinets known since the times of Pitt and Dundas. The sincerity of Sir Robert Peel will be soon severely tested, as to whether he withdraws from office to serve his country, or aggrandize himself. If the former, he must endeavour to atone for past misconduct by present services,—by supporting his successor with all his might and main,—by giving his votes, voice, and influence, such of the last as may remain, to the glorious crusade against Protective duties. If the latter, he will then lie upon the catch for the earliest or smallest lack of judgment betrayed by the new functionaries: he will wear the demeanour of a patron, and practise the severity of a critic, towards Lord John and his colleagues: he will insiduously intimate to the peers, to the agricultural interest, and to all whom it may concern, how much more leniently he would have handled his suffering patient: in short, what a benevolent, tender-hearted physician he would still have been to his beloved country. That the Corn Laws must be sacrificed is no longer a matter open to question. The mere report of their fall has awakened a wave of emotion, of which the eddies are already circling through the markets of both hemispheres. Our commercial men, our noblest seaports and inland cities are convulsed with joy. We heartily trust, however, that the necessity for *action* will not be lost sight of amidst the universal ebullition. The sentence may be pronounced, but it will still have to be executed. We anticipate immense excitement. It has been justly observed, that 'Wherever men labour, or congregate, or converse, this coming change intrudes upon their occupations. and they lift up their heads to witness its accomplishment. Hitherto the effect of those principles of commercial freedom which have long been professed by British statesmen, in their communications with foreign governments, has been marred by the glaring inconsistency of the restrictions still imposed on the food of our own people. The repeal of the Corn Laws will therefore be an event of the utmost importance to our foreign relations. An immediate object of the measure is to promote the interchange of commodities at home and abroad, and bring the multifarious populations of the earth to one common emporium. Such a result is the greatest to which any minister can aspire, for it includes the questions of peace and war, the progress of improvement, the destruction of prejudices, the spread of civilization, and the diffusion of larger prosperity and knowledge amongst mankind.' More even than this is equally true. Important as the crisis is, there can be no delay. The stores of food are diminishing, whilst the mouths of the consumers are increasing at the rate of a thousand per diem! Shall the flocks and the herds be slain for them, to suffice them; or shall all the fish of the sea be gathered together? Such was the expostulation of an inspired legislator, some score-and-half centuries ago: but in our age, which is not one of miracles, there is but one answer:—

'Let food be free as the air of heaven,
 For labourers great or small,—
By the Father above has the boon been given,
 And there's more than enough for us all.'

We should be well pleased, if in addition to their views upon the corn question, our new ministers could present the nation with a manifesto respecting contemplated financial reforms. It would be of great service to themselves, we venture to think, could they speak out early, so as to rally large interests to their muster-roll: especially from those more numerous classes in the community who groan under the burdens of taxation. From the enthronement of King William the Third, downwards, the people have been like passive sheep at the mercy of their shearers. The aristocracy has made its own laws, and arranged its own imposts; of course taking due care to shift all conceivable pressure from the shoulders of property and rank to those of industry and commerce. Upon the whole, or at least with the fewest possible exceptions, the plans of Sir Robert Peel were true enough to their predecessors. Now will be the time to hold out some renewed prospects of realizing better systems. A fresh and honest adjustment of the sugar duties would bring into the national coffers an additional million of revenue per annum: applying the legacy duty to real property would raise two more: a fair development of the penny postage would give £250,000. a year at least under the management of its magnanimous yet ill-treated projector: and these items, with the improved customs and excise, through that moderate yet permanent and unfluctuating prosperity, which may be fairly anticipated from the removal of commercial fetters, will enable an honest Chancellor of the Exchequer to dispense with our iniquitous income tax. The shopocracy would defy conservative bribery, were good hopes held out to them of speedily reaching some such consummation. Let the noble Premier adventure upon the trial. At all events candour will be agreeable. The member for Tamworth brought his budget down to the House, very much as our old highwaymen used to carry their dark lanterns. We grant that prudence may be a feature of statesmanship: but its counterfeit, under the title of mystification, only belongs properly to mountebanks. We feel satisfied that ere long, the late Lord Congleton's investigation of our national receipts and disbursements will become a text-book amongst the middle classes. As these acquire a thorough understanding about the matter, they will coerce our rulers to reverse the present order of things. Every day adds to the number of inquirers. Every day extends the forty shilling franchise amongst those who foster no amicable relations towards coronets and mitres, towards rentals upheld by war prices, towards immunities, privileges, and exemptions, towards the preposterous claims of social caste, towards imposts bearing lightly upon the rich, and heavily upon the poor. The British people happily abhor violent revolutions: bnt they are growing more and more prepared to insist upon substantial and radical reformation. There must be an infusion of fresh life thrown into the royal councils: and this must be drawn from other sources than hereditary legislation and mouldy pedigrees. It cannot be too often repeated, that men of from ten thousand to a hundred thousand pounds per annum income, are by their very position and circumstances unfitted to enter into the genuine value of money, or fully comprehend so delicate a subject, as inflicting taxation upon the nerves of labour and industry.

Should Viscount Palmerston again take the seals of the Foreign Office, our apprehensions will in some slight degree be excited with respect to the permanent maintenance of amicable relations between Great Britain and America. The Oregon territory threatens to turn out a fire-brand: nor as impartial reviewers, can we forbear giving cordial testimony to the firmness and ability which have hitherto been manifested, in this very delicate matter, by Lord Aberdeen. The Ashburton treaty disappointed us certainly; yet a thorny discussion was terminated, and the districts surrendered are not now worth a second thought. Since that settlement, however, the tone of the United States has altered for the worse. An appeal has been made to the West, disgraceful both to its originators and supporters,—indicating two most fearful tendencies,—lust after extended dominion, and resoluteness to uphold negro slavery. The annexation of Texas, the recent negotiations with Mexico, to say nothing of sundry irate and undignified expressions uttered by President Polk, which we trust his message to Congress may explain and mollify,—all these are attracting the attention of Europe. There is also still a war party in France, who feel that Lord Palmerston touches French vanity, and who would therefore gain, rather than lose strength, by his accession to the Cabinet. As Louis Philippe advances towards the grave, it will become more and more apparent, that his wily policy is destined to reap, as it has sown. It has been essentially selfish and personal: so that although identified with the preservation of peace, it has been so for royal and private purposes. Hence the nation, with all its old propensities and all its new predilections, already like the war-horse in Job,—'smelleth the battle afar off,—the thunder of the captains,—and the shouting!' There would be joy from the Meuse to Marseilles at even the fair prospect of a quarrel, which should bring into collision the British Jack and the Twenty-seven Stars. When affairs are so sensitive as they are at present, they need a conciliatory as well as an able guidance. The eloquence and experience of the noble representative for Tiverton cannot be gainsaid: but his peculiar adaptiveness to the crisis may well be questioned. It is no wish of ours, that England should be browbeaten by a republic, who, with liberty loudly upon her lips, has repudiated many millions of just debts, and still retains an enormous population of slaves. Yet such is our horror of war, glancing at its immediate and probable consequences, that short of downright dishonour, we would submit to almost any arbitration for avoiding it. May the Prince of Peace so mercifully influence statesmen, on both sides the Atlantic, that reason and moderation may yet prevail, and the lovers of disturbance be once again baffled in their object. Our hopes, in such a direction, will hold out to the last moment.

As our last pages are passing through the press, it is announced that Lord John Russell has failed in his efforts to construct a cabinet, and that Sir Robert Peel has resumed office. Still we venture to recommend, to the most serious consideration of our readers, what we have written. As the crisis increases in complexity, so much the more simple, as it appears to us, are the duties of liberals and non-conformists. All eyes will now be turned upon two objects,—namely, the movements of Sir Robert Peel, and the election for the West Riding of Yorkshire. It affords us pleasure to reflect upon the recent course of events, more especially to learn, as we have recently done, that the noble member for London, has been constrained, though at the eleventh hour, to avow his conversion to *total and immediate repeal.* That the corn laws are to be abolished there can be no doubt; but that the struggle will be a fearful one, we also believe. In the meantime we rejoice in Sir Robert Peel's return to power, assured that the popular cause will gain more from his premiership than could have been realized from his rival.

Brief Notice.

The Congregational Calendar and Family Almanac for 1846. London: Jackson and Walford.

THIS almanac is compiled under the sanction of the Congregational Union, and contains a large mass of information specially adapted to interest the members of the congregational body. In addition to the usual intelligence of such works, it comprises an extended list of the churches of the denomination, an account of its various societies, a sketch of protestant European statistics, and a brief analysis of the condition and societies of other British sects. We should like to ask the editor, why the *British Anti-State Church Association* has been omitted, when the Orphan Working School, and the new Asylum for Infant Orphans, have been admitted.

THE

ECLECTIC REVIEW

For FEBRUARY, 1846.

Art. I.—*Lectures on the Pilgrim's Progress, and on the Life and Times of John Bunyan.* By Rev. George B. Cheever, D.D., London, 1845. *Works of the English Puritan Divines.* Vol. 1. *The Jerusalem Sinner saved: The Pharisee and Publican: The Trinity and a Christian, &c., &c.* By John Bunyan: *to which is appended an Exhortation to Peace and Unity. With Life of Bunyan.* By the Rev. James Hamilton. London, 1845.

Of no individual, whose name does not occur in the sacred writings, can it be said with more propriety than of John Bunyan, that 'being dead, he yet speaketh.' Already has he spoken to generations past, and will speak in many languages again and again, to generations to come. It is the prerogative of genius to triumph over time. Nothing can confine its influence to the transient duration of life, or even to the limitation of ages: and that this should be the case is alike honourable to human nature and profitable to mankind; honourable, as it is a proof that the petty rivalships, envyings and jealousies, which are wont to assail distinguished excellencies *can* at length be laid aside,—and profitable, as it furnishes the means of renewed instruction to posterity. If the works of men were to perish with their bodies, how would the world be impoverished; but, thanks to the press, while the *man* dies, the *author* may live for ever.

There are comparatively few, however, whose works survive them in a living and still speaking influence. The reader has only to glance at the first collection of volumes he may chance to see, in order to verify this remark. To say nothing of the vast public collections of our land, survey the shelves of any private library; and of the array of folios, octavos and duodecimos that stand in multitudinous ranks, consider the infrequency of names upon these labelled representatives of literature that for any very lengthened period command the attention of mankind. Apart from the crowds that have gone down into hopeless oblivion, some of them sufficiently notorious in their day, think only of the visible and palpable groups of authors whose names obtrude upon the searcher after the truly great and renowned; and with a sigh for humanity and for ourselves, we must acknowledge their paucity. Of course we refer only to the first-rate order of minds—the Ciceros, the Newtons, the Miltons, the Howes, and the Bunyans.

And few as they have been, the present fashion of literature has a tendency to make them fewer. Formerly our great writers both in prose and poetry elaborated all they wrote, and it must be confessed were rather prone to perplex with intricacies and weary with prolixity. Nevertheless their genius was allowed elbow room, and fair play; and though it be often toilsome, it is always instructive to follow them in their most distant wanderings. You may be led through desert paths into deep wildernesses and up painful ascents; but are infallibly guided to a noble elevation. The present is the age of compression; every thing is brought into the narrowest compass; folios, and even octavos, are almost cashiered; and science, learning, theology—all must be crammed into a book only large enough for the children's library. Woe betide the man of detail or the man of argument; the age will not endure the ramifications of the one or the exercitations of the other. It has little love for adventurers in thought. It is the age of action, not of thinking; for it demands that every thing should be ready made, and give no trouble to the wearer. Even Milton would be best liked by multitudes, if reduced to the size of a sixpenny song-book, and the History of England to a few penny numbers.

The plea is, that we want information; let the mind be stored with knowledge, and let ignorance be cured by concentrated doses of wisdom: our manhood therefore, as well as our childhood, must have the blessing in the cheapest and most condensed form. But let it not be supposed, that we would plead for extenuated and wire-drawn thought, spread out in diffusive language: we are not for ample pages with thinness of sentiment and meagreness of idea, nor are we, on the other hand, for a close shaven and curtailed expression, dry and fruitless as chopped sticks, or books stuffed with mere facts and chronologies till they are inanimate as the Guys of November. We are for great minds having their way, and their *own* way; shewing us not only what is the result of their investigations, but the manner of those investigations. We like to see the great artificers at work; to mark how they handled their implements, how they wrought their moral statuary and painting; and have very little taste for chiselling and reducing, till their giants are reduced to pigmies.

We are not aware that any attempt has been made in the present line of literary business, called compression, upon Bunyan's Pilgrim's Progress, or any of his other works. To abridge the former, indeed, is impracticable, without sacrificing the entire interest; and all the rest are full of delightful quaintnesses, epigrammatic point, and little allegorical coruscations so bright and characteristic, that it would be somewhat of a hopeless task. Yet probably his general writings being less known than his great performance, may be part of the reason; and we earnestly entreat of all the digesters and condensers of literature, that now these productions are becoming better known, they will have the kindness to allow them to stand as they do, in their Saxon and ancestral dress.

The name of Bunyan is no sooner uttered, than the Pilgrim's Progress is always and instantly associated with it; for who has not found it the entertainment of his childhood, and the frequent companion of his riper years; what religious man has not been instructed by it, or what irreligious man has not been charmed? Cottages and palaces have alike owned its power; it has carried captive the meanest and the mightiest minds; it has strengthened the weak in faith, and confirmed the strong; it has beguiled the saddest and most solitary hours, given fleetness to the dullest ones, and sunshine even to sick beds and dying moments; its wicket gate, its interpreter's house, its valley of humiliation, its vanity fair, its delectable mountains, its ill-favoured ones and shining ones, its valley of the shadow of death, the separating river, and the golden city, are vivid in the recollections of all, and may be said to have stamped indelible and visible impressions on a nation's mind, on a nation's heart.

It has been justly remarked by a contemporaneous critic, that the characteristic peculiarity of the Pilgrim's Progress is, that it is the only work of its kind which possesses a strong human interest. Other allegories only amuse the fancy; the allegory of Bunyan has been read by many thousands with tears. Perhaps it should have been said, that it is so individualising, and with such a magical skill turns abstractions into realities, and converts fictions into facts, qualities into living, breathing and speaking men and women, and even the land of enchantment itself into plain positive hills and valleys, the terra incognita of Morpheus into the terra firma of man's every day existence; that it amuses and affects at once, so that with the conviction of its visionary dreaminess, it cannot be read without an almost living consciousness of its reality. The same authority remarks, upon quoting Dr. Johnson's declaration, that the Pilgrim's Progress was one of the two or three works which he wished longer, that it was no common merit that the illiterate sectary extracted praise like this from the most pedantic of critics and the most bigotted of tories.

Allegorical writing has been practised from the earliest ages, and few persons have been able to resist its fascinations. Its simplest and most beautiful forms are to be found in the most ancient of all compositions, the books of Scripture; in which, besides parables and shorter pieces, we have a somewhat lengthened specimen in the Song of Solomon. Allegory is an appeal to the imaginative faculty which, as inherent in the human mind, is eager for employment and entertainment. All men feel that they not only need to be enlightened, but allured into knowledge, and most require that the allurement should at least accompany, if it do not precede the illumination. Allegory has, moreover, the advantage of what may be termed an innocent flattery; inducing research not only by the amusement afforded, but by leading the reader to think that he is a discoverer and self instructor. He is both surprised and pleased, so that what in a mere didactic form would become wearisome, by this method is sure to fix continued attention. The memory, too, is permanently impressed with the fanciful images which continually awaken anew into life and reality fading or obliterated truths. So strongly, indeed, has it been felt, that memory requires the stimulus of strange and fantastic combinations, that Von Feinagle and his successors have invented them in infinite variety, in order to reconcile it to the driest parts of knowledge, such as chronology, statistics, and finance.

But amusement itself becomes dull, unless the details be skilfully managed. The literal meaning must neither be too obvious, nor too remote from ordinary perception, to answer the proper purpose. If too literal it becomes insipid; if too far removed from common circumstances or conceptions, the result is indifference. There should be variety without perplexity, and probability without the sacrifice of propriety, in the fictitious colouring; though we know it we must be made to love the delusion, and extract from it both gratification and wisdom. It may thus be made to correct our follies and instruct our minds. The perfection of the art is seen when, though the subject be repulsive and the instruction disliked, we are compelled to receive it by the irresistible force and beauty of the method adopted for its communication. Then is the triumph, when we sit down to be amused, and rise up improved.

All these remarks are applicable to the Pilgrim's Progress, which almost every where displays in remarkable union a vigorous fancy and a sound judgment. Many peccadillos of incongruity might be detected by the severity of criticism, but they no more affect the general consistency of the tale, than the irregularities upon the earth's surface destroy its rotundity. This may in some measure account for its extensive and enduring popularity; but it contains many other elements of success. It is distinguished by an inimitable simplicity of language; quaint indeed, but never vulgar, possessing a plainness and perspicuity that cannot fail to make it forcible. If there were art in it, the art is according to the ancient requisition, most entirely concealed; but we take it to be nature, as if the ideas would of necessity run into the words, and in spite of effort, or in utter negligence, assume the stamp of originality. Its close resemblance to life, must also have conduced to its early influence, and its subsequently wide circulation. The moment the notion is suggested, every man perceives how true it is, with regard to his present condition, that he is on a journey; and a certain sense of reality in the representation is at once superinduced, however diverse from our individual experience the particulars may seem. Apart from whence we came or whither we are going, this comes home to every man's business and bosom; and when instead of mere abstraction, the mental or moral qualities are turned into living, walking, and talking men and women, the reader finds himself as in an actually peopled world, in company with a bonâ fide traveller. This allegorizing strain, it is true, might be utterly vapid and without impression, as it has often been in other hands, were it not for the charm of consistency, as before observed, by which the whole drama is at once converted into reality. There are, moreover, in various parts of the narrative, traces of political fitness in the representation to the times in which Bunyan lived, and the circumstances in which he was placed, which were calculated to give it an immediate currency among the people, for every one must see that many of its graphic delineations were all but literal facts, by which they possessed historic value, as well as local attraction. Supposing all the excellencies to which we have adverted, and others might have been noticed, we cannot help thinking that the sublimity of Bunyan's subject has served to impart unwonted interest and power to his production. A certain air of grandeur and mystery is thrown around the path of the pilgrim by the general relation of the whole to religion, and to the termination of his progress. His conversations and his conflicts involve questions of the deepest interest in regard to beings struggling for immortality; and principles are developed which concern the well being of man as a passenger through time, and a candidate for eternity. The tale indeed, is delightful; but the essence and staple of the volume is truth, and truth the most important. It belongs to our rational nature, our condition in this world, and our destiny in another. It possesses, therefore, a permanent interest, because it is at once sublime in its aim, and of universal application. It is not the tale of *the times*, but of *all* times and of *all* ages.

The Pilgrim's Progress was one of the most natural and spontaneous efforts of genius the world ever saw. It was not written for money, or for fame, or in consequence of the persuasive solicitations of others; but welled up from the deep fountains of the author's own mind, and, in finding an outlet, flowed on without reserve and without ceasing. He could not have written it without genius, and genius of the first order; nor *with* genius without piety. The whole of his Christian experience, which was almost—perhaps entirely—unparalleled in the breadth and profundity of it, furnished the basis of this, as well as other productions. The workings of his inmost soul are rendered visible in his 'Grace Abounding;' and we distinctly see the several elements of thought combining and condensing into compact forms of energy which supplied ample materials for the great work, and imparted a character of truth to his delectable fiction. The 'Grace Abounding' seems a kind of glass case to the 'Pilgrim's Progress,' analogous to that we employ to look through upon a busy tribe of bees, that we may trace their methods of proceeding, and their secret operations in the construction of their inimitable cells. Here we see *how* the sweet honey was made, of which we have such a delicious supply in the Pilgrim's Progress; so that we fully sympathize with Dr. Cheever's remark in the first of his valuable lectures.

'Bunyan's genius I had almost said, was *created* by his piety; the fervour and depth of his religious feelings formed its most important elements of power, and its materials to work upon. His genius also pursued a path dictated by his piety, and one that no other being in the world ever pursued before him. The light that first broke through his darkness was light from heaven. It found him, even that being who wrote the Pilgrim's Progress, coarse, profane, boisterous, and almost brutal. It shone upon him, and with a single eye he followed it, till his native City of Destruction could no longer be seen in the distance,—till his moral deformities fell from him, and his garments became purity and light. The Spirit of God was his teacher; the very discipline of his intellect was a spiritual discipline; the conflicts that his soul sustained with the powers of darkness were the very sources of his intellectual strength.'

One is apt to speak and write of Bunyan as if the Pilgrim's Progress were his only production; so great has been its celebrity in comparison with any other efforts of his mind. Yet we must not do him injustice by ascribing an unmeasureable inferiority to his other writings, as though there were little or no genius in them; for in fact most of them have the same characteristic stamp, although allegorizing was his pre-eminent talent. If, instead of giving, for instance, 'The Life and Death of Mr. Badman,' in the form of a dialogue between Mr. Wiseman and Mr. Attentive, he had pursued a similar course with that which has rendered him so illustrious in the Pilgrim's Progress, making it an allegorical representation of the progress of a sinner to perdition, we are persuaded it might have become in his hands clothed with terrific fascination, at once winning, and warning every reader. We should then have had the terrors of the Lord, as well as in the former narrative, a display of his mercies. We regret it the more that his own mind connected the two together, and by an unhappy mistake he determined on this less effective method.

'As I was considering with myself,' says he, 'what I had written concerning the Progress of the Pilgrim from this world to glory; and how it had been acceptable to many in this nation, it came again into my mind to write, as then, of him that was going to heaven, so now of the life and death of the ungodly, and of their travel from this world to hell. The which in this I have done, and have put it as thou seest, under the name and title of Mr. Badman, a name very proper for such a snbject; I have also put it in the form of a dialogue, that I might with more ease to myself, and pleasure to the reader, perform the work.'

In both he evidently erred; for nothing can bespeak a readier flow and facility in the production, than his own quaint statements.

'When at the first I took my pen in hand,
Thus for to write, I did not understand
That I at all should make a little book
In such a mode: nay, I had undertook
To make another; which, when almost done,
Before I was aware, I this began.'

* * * * *

'It came from mine own heart, so to my head,
And thence into my fingers trickled;
Thence to my pen, from whence immediately
On paper I did dribble it daintily.'

With regard to 'pleasure to the reader,' it must have been immeasurably greater had he adopted the plan of the Pilgrim's Progress. Instead of mere conversation as now, in which are many objectionable things, though accompanied with various striking and impressive representations, we might have been delighted by another series of moral paintings, graphically sketched adventures and descriptive scenery, that would have rivalled the former in grandeur and force. In the concluding speech of Mr. Wiseman, after the outwardly quiet death of Mr. Badman had been discussed, and set in its proper light, we have such a picture in prose as the pen of Dantè could not have surpassed in poetry.

'Without controversy this is a heavy judgment of God upon wicked men. One goes to hell in peace, another goes to hell in trouble; one goes to hell, being sent thither by the hand of his companion; one goes thither with his eyes shut, and another goes thither with his eyes open; one goes thither roaring, and another goes thither boasting of Heaven and happiness all the way he goes; one goes thither like Mr. Badman himself, and others go thither as did his brethren. But, above all, Mr. Badman's death, as to the manner of dying, is the fullest of snares and traps to wicked men; therefore they that die as he, are the greatest stumble to the world. They go, and go, they go on peaceably from youth to old age, and thence to the grave, and so to hell, without noise: 'They go as an ox to the slaughter, and as a fool to the correction of the stocks.' That is, both senselessly and securely. Oh! but being come at the gates of hell: Oh! but when they see those gates set open for them. Oh! but when they see that that is their home, and that they must go in thither; then their peace and quietness flies away for ever: then they roar like lions, yell like dragons, howl like dogs, and tremble at their judgment as do the devils themselves. Oh! when they see they must shoot the gulf and throat of hell! when they shall see that hell hath shut her ghastly jaws upon them; when they shall open their eyes and find themselves within the belly and bowels of hell! Then they will mourn, and weep, and hack, and gnash their teeth for pain!'

In referring to the Life of Mr. Badman, we are reminded of another of Bunyan's productions of a somewhat analogous character, less known than many of his writings, but replete with instruction and vivid painting. It is entitled, 'The World to Come; or, Visions of Heaven and Hell.' The genius of the author of the 'Pilgrim's Progress' shines through many of the representations, and produces a sense of enchantment, as if some mighty magician had waved his wand and transported us into a new and unearthly state. His description of the first appearance of the celestial messenger who was to guide him to the regions of glory is beautiful :—

'I went, and sat me down upon a bank. . . . . As I sat upon the bank, I was suddenly surrounded with a glorious light, the exceeding brightness whereof was such, as I had never seen anything like it before, this both surprised and amazed me; and whilst I was wondering from whence it came, I saw coming towards me a glorious appearance, representing the person of a man,—but circled round about with lucid beams of inexpressible light and glory, which streamed from him all the way he came; his countenance was very awful, and yet mixed with such an air of sweetness as rendered it extremely pleasing, and gave me some secret hopes he came not to me as an enemy, and yet I knew not how to bear his bright appearance; and yet, endeavouring to stand upon my feet, I soon found I had no more strength in me, and so fell flat down upon my face.' As he ascended with his glorious conductor, he said—'I would fain be informed what that dark spot so far below me is; which grew less and less as I was mounted higher and higher, and appears much darker, since I came into this region of light?'

The answer to this question will furnish an illustration of the very impressive and instructive character of the whole narrative, which contrives through the medium of dialogues admirably wrought, between himself and the spirits in heaven and hell, to suggest truths of the most important and practical nature.

'That little spot, answered my conductor, that now looks so dark and contemptible, is that world of which you were so lately an inhabitant; here you may see how little all that world appears, for a small part of which so many do unweariedly labour, and lay out all their strength, and strive to purchase it. This is that spot of earth that is cantoned and subdivided into so many kingdoms, to purchase one of which so many horrid and base villianies, so many bloody and unnatural murders have been committed; yea, this is that spot of earth, to obtain one small part thereof, so many men have run the hazard of losing; nay, have actually lost their precious and immortal souls; so precious that the Prince of Peace has told us, that though one man should gain the whole, it could not countervail so great a a loss And the great reason of their folly is, because they do not look to things above: for, as you well observed, as you ascend nearer to this region, the world appeared still less and more contemptible; and so it will do to all who can by faith once get their hearts above it. For, could the sons of men below but see the world just as it is, they would not covet it as they now do; but they, alas! are in a state of darkness; and, which is worse, they love to walk therein. For though the Prince of Light came down amongst them and plainly showed them the true light of life (which by his ministers he still continues) yet they go on in darkness, and will not bring themselves unto the light, because their deeds are evil.'

The 'Holy War,' is the longest and the best of Bunyan's allegories, with the exception of the 'Pilgrim's Progress.' Had the latter never been published, the former would undoubtedly have given celebrity to its author. It is the 'Pilgrim's Progress' alone that could eclipse the 'Holy War,' just as the beauty of 'Paradise Regained' is lost amidst the splendour of 'Paradise Lost.' In respect to these two performances of the great allegorist, children are no bad judges, for what effectually interests them is a pure impression on the imagination, apart from all theories and rules of art; and both these works possess the rare merit of equally absorbing the attention of the young and the aged, the wise and the unwise. We inquired of a little boy the other day, how he liked the 'Pilgrim's Progress,' and he at once expressed the utmost admiration. He was at the moment reading the 'Holy War;' and the question was put as to what he thought of that? His reply was highly in its favour—'Oh! it was uncommonly interesting!' But which do you prefer of the two? 'Why I like them both; but the 'Pilgrim's Progress' *best.*' The 'Holy War' is perhaps less appreciated in general than it ought to be. It is full of stirring interest. There is a consistency in the whole management of the plot, and the dramatic effect is irresistible. The same skill, with a similar simplicity and power of language is displayed throughout, as in the 'Pilgrim's Progress.' Passions are converted into persons; and amidst the hurry and confusion of the movements, the consultations and the conflicts, you feel yourself to be a witness, and, in a certain sense, an actor in a real warfare between Shaddai and Diabolus to secure possession of Mansoul, 'the metropolis of the world.' Nothing can be more appropriate and impressive than the closing address of Emmanuel.

Bunyan is too often regarded in the single character of a beautiful allegorist: the truth is, that he was an eminent theologian, and a most powerful preacher. We agree perfectly with Mr. Hamilton on this point—

'Bunyan's theological merits we rank very high. No one can turn over his pages without noticing the abundance of his scriptural quotations; and these quotations no one can examine without perceiving how minutely he had studied, and how deeply he had pondered the word of God. But it is possible to be very *textual,* and yet by no means very *scriptural.* A man may have an exact acquaintance with the literal Bible, and yet entirely miss the great Bible message. He may possess a dexterous command of detached passages and insulated sentences, and yet be entirely ignorant of that peculiar scheme which forms the great gospel revelation. But this was Bunyan's peculiar excellence. He was even better acquainted with the gospel as the scheme of God, than he was familiar with the Bible text; and the consequence is, that though he is sometimes irrelevant in his references, and fanciful in interpreting particular passages, his doctrine is almost always according to the analogy of faith. The doctrine of a free and instant justification by the imputed righteousness of Christ, none even of the Puritans could state with more Luther-like boldness, nor defend with an affection more worthy of Paul. In his last and best days, Coleridge wrote, 'I know of no book—the Bible excepted, as above all comparison, which I, according to my judgment and experience, could so safely recommend as teaching and enforcing the whole saving truth, according to the mind that was in Christ Jesus, as the 'Pilgrim's Progress.' It is in my conviction the best *Summa Theologiæ Evangelicæ* ever produced by a writer not miraculously inspired.' Without questioning this edict, we should include in the encomium some of his other writings, which possibly Coleridge never saw. Such as the Tracts contained in this volume—(these are, 'The Jerusalem Sinner Saved,' 'The Pharisee and the Publican,' 'The Trinity, and a Christian,' 'The Law and a Christian,' 'Bunyan's Last Sermon,' 'Bunyan's Dying Sayings;' and 'An Exhortation to Peace and Unity.') They exhibit gospel truths in so clear a light, and state them in such a frank and happy tone, 'that he who runs may read;' and he who reads in earnest will rejoice. The Pilgrim is a peerless guide to those who have already passed in at the wicket-gate; but those who are still seeking peace to their troubled souls, will find the best directory in 'The Jerusalem Sinner Saved.' '—p. 30.

The last work mentioned has the character of an enlarged sermon, and no doubt in chief part was delivered from the pulpit. It is solemn, pungent and effective. The plainness, raciness, and purity of the author's style are apparent throughout, and impress us with characteristic force. The very term '*biggest* sinner,' so often repeated, so quaint, yet so Saxon, though discarded in these more elegant times, works mightily upon the fancy, and wins its way to the heart. You see everywhere the peculiarities of the writer; you imagine the vehement urgency of the preacher, and observe gleaming through even the most unadorned passages—the unrivalled allegorist. We cannot forbear introducing a specimen. After adverting to the address of Peter, in which the remission of sins is promised upon repentance; he proceeds—

'This he said to them all, though he knew that they were such sinners. Yea, he said it without the least stick or stop, or pause of spirit, as to whether he had best say so or no. Nay, so far off was Peter from making an objection against one of them, that by a particular clause in his exhortation, he endeavours, that not one may escape the salvation offered.—'Repent,' saith he, 'and be baptized, every one of you.' I shut out never a one of you; for I am commanded by my Lord to deal with you, as it were one by one, by the word of his salvation. But why speaks he so particularly? Oh! there were reasons for it. The people with whom the Apostles were now to deal, as they were murderers of our Lord, and to be charged in the general with his blood; so they had their various and particular acts of villainy in the guilt thereof, now lying upon their consciences. And the guilt of these, their various and particular acts of wickedness, could not perhaps be reached to a removal thereof, but by this particular application. Repent, every one of you; be baptized every one of you, in his name, for the remission of sins; and you shall, every one of you, receive the gift of the Holy Ghost.'

'*Object.* But I was one of them that plotted to take away his life. May I be saved by him?

'*Peter.* Every one of you.

'*Object.* But I was one of them that bare false witness against him. Is there grace for me?

'*Peter.* For every one of you.

'*Object.* But I was one of them that cried out, Crucify him, crucify him; and desired that Barabbas the murderer might live, rather than him. What will become of me, think you?

'*Peter.* I am to preach repentance and remission of sins, to every one of you, says Peter.

'*Object.* But I was one of them that did spit in his face, when he stood before his accusers. I also was one that mocked him, when in anguish he hanged bleeding on the tree. Is there room for me?

'*Peter.* For every one of you, says Peter.

'*Object.* But I was one of them that in his extremity said, Give him gall and vinegar to drink. Why may I not expect the same, when anguish and guilt is upon me?

'*Peter.* Repent of these your wickednesses and here is remission of sins for every one of you.

'*Object.* But I railed on him—I reviled him—I hated him—I rejoiced to see him mocked at by others. Can there be hopes for me?

'*Peter.* There is for every one, for you—'Repent and be baptized every one of you, in the name of Jesus Christ, for the remission of sins, and ye shall receive the gift of the Holy Ghost.' Oh! what a blessed—'every one of you,' is here! How willing was Peter, and the Lord Jesus, by his ministry, to catch these murderers with the word of the gospel, that they might be made monuments of the grace of God! How unwilling, I say, was he, that any of these should escape the hand of mercy! Yea, what an amazing wonder it is to think that, above all the world, and above everybody in it, these should have the first offer of mercy! 'Beginning at Jerusalem.''

Bunyan wrote a book of poems, entitled 'Divine Emblems, or Temporal Things Spiritualized, fitted for the use of Boys and Girls.' Dr. Cheever pronounces this judgment upon them, and their author: 'Some of them are very beautiful, revealing the true poet; passages there are which would not dishonour Chaucer or Shakespere, and which show to what great excellence, as a poet, Bunyan might have attained, had he dedicated himself to the effort. What he wrote, he wrote with the utmost simplicity, and in the same pure, idiomatic language which is so delightful in the 'Pilgrim's Progress.' We have read attentively, and with all the friendly bias which accompanies admiration of the man and the allegorical writer, several of these productions, but we cannot entirely agree with this opinion. Bunyan's rudest rhymes, indeed, have a certain power that makes one forget their faults, great and manifest as they are; but we forget them not because of the poetry, but of the sentiment, the point and the amusing quaintness, which would have been better in his own prose diction. In fact, we admire them in spite of there being no poetry in them. Nevertheless we admit, with Dr. Cheever, in another place, 'In regard to those rude verses which, with such inconceivably bad spelling, and with such cramped and distorted chirography, Bunyan used to write in the margin of his old copy of 'Foxe's Book of Martyrs,' that they do not make upon the mind the impression of that word *doggerel*; the mint out of which they fall is too sacred for that, and the metal, wrought with such extreme rudeness, manifestly too precious.' Certainly, by doggerel, we mean a worthlessness, or, at best, a low commonness of sentiment, as well as a mean construction and attempt at what surpasses the writer's power; but Bunyan is not to be included in this condemnation. Had he devoted himself to the art of poetry, we cannot imagine he would have ranked with Shakespere, though we believe that the scintillations of his genius must have been occasionally conspicuous amidst his varied efforts, marking him as deserving an eminent place, but not as ranging with the first or even the second of our dramatists, or of our epic or lyrical composers. His *forte* was undoubtedly prose allegory and energetic appeal.

The times in which Bunyan lived, reckoning from his birth to his death, that is, from A.D. 1628 to A.D. 1688, were distinguished by extraordinary changes, both in the political and ecclesiastical administration of the country. During most of this period it may be said, 'darkness covered the earth, and gross darkness the people.' It resembled, in the whole extent of it, a gloomy, chilly, and miserable day in November, with but one noontide glimmer of sunshine that struggled for an hour between the clouds and amidst the murky atmosphere, rendering the traveller still more sensible of his wretched plight. The earlier part of this period was covered with the dismal despotism of the first Charles, whose Star Chamber was the star of wormwood; its concluding portion was doubly cursed and darkened by the dissoluteness and tyranny of Charles the Second, the most unprincipled of men, and the worst of kings; while, between the two, came the bright moment of the Long Parliament and the Protectorate, when downcast liberty lifted up its head, and for a brief season breathed a purer air.

Never, in the whole history of England, was a baser or more rapid succession of bad laws enacted, than in the reign of Charles II., including the Corporation Act, by which all nonconformists to the Established Church were expelled from civil rights, and precluded from serving their country in its lowest offices,—the Statute against the Society of Friends, which threw four thousand of them into prison, to suffer every indignity and barbarous usage,—the Act of Uniformity in 1662, which revived the penal laws of previous reigns, forcibly suppressing all difference of religious opinion, and imposing upon the conscience, as if of divine authority, the Book of Common Prayer,—the Conventicle Act, two years afterwards, by which, for the purpose of entirely suppressing all such unchristian things as praying and preaching out of the Established Church, it was enacted: 'That if any person should be present at any assembly, conventicle or meeting, under colour or pretence of any exercise of religion in other manner than is allowed by the liturgy or practice of the Church of England; or if any person shall suffer any such meeting in his house, barn, yard, woods or grounds, they should, for the first and second offence, be thrown into jail or fined, for the third offence be transported for seven years, or fined a hundred pounds, (no mean sum in those days,) and in case of return or escape after such transportation, death, without benefit of clergy',—the Act, by which all non-conforming ministers were banished, five miles from any city, town or borough that sent members to parliament, and five miles from any place whatsoever, where they had at any time within a number of years past preached,—and, to crown all, the renewal of the Conventicle Act in 1670, with increased severity, when the trial by jury in case of offenders was annulled, persons to be seized wherever they could be found, informers rewarded, no warrant to be reversed on account of any informality in the indictment, and justices who did not execute the law to be punished.'

But whatever detestation may be awakened by these proceedings, is there any cause for wonder at them; or can we refuse to admit that they were the natural results of ignorance, bigotry, and the love of power? It was only carrying out to its legitimate, we admit extreme,—but, nevertheless, legitimate consequences, the principle assumed in the alliance of Church and State. If it be the right of the chief magistrate to enforce or establish (which latter is a royal or parliamentary enforcement) any particular religion as the religion of a nation, it would be ridiculous to imagine that the State would not or ought not to maintain its right. But the maintenance of right or religion in a State is not its maintenance by reason but by force; the law asks a sword; it argues nothing, but enacts; demanding obedience and punishing the violation of its authority. Either a law ought not to be enacted, or it ought to be enforced. If it be proper to establish religion, it must be proper to sustain the claims of such an establishment, or the State, that is, the government, would display a weakness subversive of order and tending to anarchy. In better times, indeed, than those to which we are referring, the principle of toleration has been adopted; but this is only an additional insult, an apology, or seeming apology, for adherence to flagrant wrong. It is evidently based in the assumption that the governmental power in a nation possesses the right to constitute a religion for the people, which, when regarded in its true light, as infringing upon the sovereignty of Christ in his church, is the basest of all presumptions, and one of the foulest of all crimes; and, consequently, if it has the right to constitute religion, it has the right (and this it assumes) to punish if it please what it must deem wrong doers, as unwilling to submit to its ecclesiastical dictations. Toleration, therefore, is no other than a State proclamation of the condescending kindness of the rulers to allow persons to think and to worship God according to the dictates of their consciences, over which it thus assumes supremacy; and to do so as long as they shall see fit to continue the permission; for the permission to do any thing, necessarily implies the power to withhold it, when either an imagined state necessity, or faction, shall demand its discontinuance.

Bunyan was called into action and to suffering just in the inauspicious times to which we have adverted, when the Satanic principle of coercing the consciences of men 'exalted sat' on the 'bad eminence,' which, through a bigoted priesthood and an unprincipled court, it had attained. He was the first person who was seized upon for nonconformity, in the reign of Charles II., (November 12, 1660;) an event, which, however unwittingly on the part of the persecutor, proved of essential benefit to the Church of God, by not only furnishing a splendid example of the martyr's spirit, but occasioning the production of writings, and of one preeminently, which is already invested with the glory of innumerable conversions to the truth, and is destined to bless with its attractive teachings 'the generations to come.' The indictment against Bunyan was—'That John Bunyan, of the town of Bedford, labourer, being a person of such and such conditions, he hath, since such a time, devilishly and maliciously abstained from coming to church to hear divine service, and is a common upholder of several unlawful meetings and conventicles, to the great disturbance and distraction of the good subjects of this kingdom, contrary to the laws of Our Sovereign Lord the King.' A part of his examination before justice Keelin, we introduce as truly illustrative of his character and theological skill. After having combated the arguments of the justice about the book of Common Prayer, he added:—

'But yet they that have a mind to use it, they have their liberty; that is, I would not keep it from them, or them from it; but for our parts, we can pray to God without it, for ever blessed be his holy name. With that' says he, 'one of them said, Who is your God, Beelzebub?' Moreover, they often said I was possessed of the spirit of delusion, and of the devil. All which sayings I passed over, the Lord forgive them! And further I said, 'Blessed be the Lord for it; we are encouraged to meet together, and to pray, and exhort one another: for we have had the comfortable presence of God among us, for ever blessed be his holy name.'

'Justice Keelin called this pedlar's French, saying that I must leave off my canting. The Lord open his eyes!

'*Bunyan.* I said that we ought to exhort one another daily, while it is called to-day.

'*Keelin.* Justice Keelin said that I ought not to preach; and asked me where I had my authority?

'*Bunyan.* I said that I would prove that it was lawful for me, and such as I am, to preach the word of God

'*Keelin.* He said unto me, 'By what Scripture?'

'*Bunyan.* I said, 'By that in the first epistle of Peter, the fourth chapter, the eleventh verse; and Acts, the eighteenth, with other scriptures, which he would not suffer me to mention.'

'*Keelin* But hold, said he, not so many; which is the first?

'*Bunyan.* I said this; 'As every man hath received the gift, so let him minister the same one to another, as good stewards of the manifold grace of God: if any man speak, let him speak as the oracles of God.'

'*Keelin.* He said: 'Let me a little open that scripture to you. As every man hath received the gift; that is,' said he, 'as every man hath received a trade, so let him follow it. If any man hath received a gift of tinkering, as thou hast done, let him follow his tinkering; and so other men their trades, and the divine his calling, &c.'

'*Bunyan.* 'Nay, Sir,' said I. 'but it is most clear the apostle speaks here of preaching the word; if you do but compare both the verses together, the next verse explains this gift what it is;' 'saying, if any man speak, let him speak as the oracles of God;' so that it is plain that the Holy Ghost doth not, in this place, so much exhort to civil callings, as to the exercising of those gifts that we have received from God. I would have gone on, but he would not give me leave.

'*Keelin*. He said 'We might do it in our families, but not otherwise.'

'*Bunyan*. I said 'If it was lawful to do good to some, it was lawful to do good to more. If it was a good duty to exhort our families, it is good to exhort others; but if they hold it a sin to meet together to seek the face of God, and exhort one another to follow Christ, I should sin still, for so we should do.'

'*Keelin*. Then you confess the indictment, do you not?

'*Bunyan*. This I confess, we have had many meetings together, both to pray to God, and to exhort one another, and that we had the sweet comforting presence of the Lord among us, for our encouragement, blessed be his name therefore. I confess myself guilty ne otherwise.

'*Keelin*. Then, said he, hear your judgment. You must be had back again to prison, and there lie for three months following; and at three months' end, if you do not submit to go to Church to hear divine service, and leave your preaching, you must be banished the realm; and if, after such a day as shall be appointed you to be gone, you shall be found in this realm, or be found to come over again without special licence from the king, you must stretch by the neck for it, I tell you plainly. And so he bid my jailor have me away.

'*Bunyan*. I told him as to this matter I was at a point with him; for if I was out of prison to-day, I would preach the gospel again to-morrow, by the help of God.'

Poor Mr. Keelin; thou hast acquired most unenviable notoriety by this examination of the tinker of Elstow! Thou art doomed to everlasting fame by the labours of that day, which ranks thee with the ignorant, the bigotted, the time-serving, the mean-spirited persecutors of our race, who have gone down to the grave with the blood of souls upon them, having proudly exercised their 'little brief authority' against the servants of God!

It would not, however, be just to the memory of this examining magistrate to represent him as a man of extraordinary worthlessness and bigotry. His office rendered him prominent; but others participated fully in his sentiments and spirit. He was, in fact, but the representative of a class; it might almost be said of the whole class of the magistracy of that day. One and all were engaged in the ignoble work of suppressing the irregularities of Puritanism, that is, the teaching of religion out of the precincts of the national establishment, the daring adventurousness of men who aspired to imitate Christ and his apostles in preaching without a mitre, praying without a prayer-book,—on the shore, in the village, or by the mountain side. Nor must we cease to deplore that, though the general cultivation and advancing knowledge of the present age, which has contributed to a better conception of the rights of conscience, have thinned their ranks, yet the genus of nonconformist-hating magistrates is by no means extinct, whose petty tyrannies and exactions identify them as the true descendants of the Keelins of a former age. If they were now supported, instead of being restrained by public opinion, and had the power, none can doubt they would again cite the saints before their unrighteous tribunals, brow-beat them for their piety, and imprison them for their conscientiousness.

But the evil lies deeper than the men. Their system made them what they were, and their system has perpetuated their generation. The union of the Church and State has called them into existence, and made them what they ever have been. It is the mother and the nurse of these corruptions, and detestable malignities. In the Church of Rome, and in the Church of England, and in every other national church, men are born and bred to the dislike and denunciation of heretics. Under the worst forms of the apostacy they burn them; under its milder modifications they injuriously treat and persecute them. Those who are allied to hierarchies and sworn to their support; who are paid in pounds or in honour for giving that support, must and will be consistently wrong; true to their masters and false to their God.

The spirit which glowed in the bosoms of the apostles when they declared, 'We ought to obey God rather than man,' and which animated the zeal of Paul when before Felix, he witnessed a good confession, reasoning of righteousness and judgment to come, seems to have passed like a heavenly light along the bright succession of saints and martys, till it caught the mind of Bunyan, and elicited the memorable declaration with which he closed his examination—'If I was out of the prison to day, I would preach the gospel again to-morrow, by the help of God.' This was not surpassed by the celebrated defiance of Luther, 'If there were as many devils as there are tiles on the houses, I would go to Worms.' In times of comparative peace and freedom it is not so difficult to avow our principles, albeit no little moral courage is requisite when that avowal is met by the coldness of friends: but the great test is when suffering and death stand across the path and await their victim. It is not when nature is callous, but when its most sensitive instincts are all alive to pain, privation, and the anguish of breaking ties and violated affections that the triumph is seen; and when the hero by self-denial, brave maintenance of truth, though it be contemned and hunted from the earth, and by an assurance that all that renders life most dear is to be forfeited, conquers himself, and becomes a willing sacrifice. These are specimens of moral grandeur which the page of scriptural and ecclesiastical history alone can furnish, which time cannot destroy, and monuments cannot honour.

It remains only to say a few words on the works, whose titles are given as the heading of this article. The lectures of Dr. Cheever are an importation from the United States, and are well worthy of republication here. They are perhaps too elaborate, and too ornate; but we are much pleased with them as a whole, and consider them a very useful commentary on the chef d'œuvre of Bunyan.

The second of these publications constitutes the first volume in a projected series of the works of English Puritan Divines. The editor has rightly judged that, although the great fame of Bunyan is built on his genius as the allegorist of the Christian character and life; still, viewed more strictly as a theologian, his works place him very high even among the Puritan divines. To us it appears that the tractates are judiciously selected, and furnish a fair specimen of his merits.

The publisher intends to issue a series of Nonconformist literature; each volume being introduced by an essay from some distinguished writer. In this design we wish him success, and an ample repayment. He has begun with the right author; the author who always has, and always will interest readers of every class. Mr. J. Hamilton has given copious extracts from Bunyan's own portraiture of his religious character, and then closes with a rapid sketch of the *man*, the *theologian*, and the *author;* which is very neatly executed, but is rather too redundant in rhetorical matter. In all his writings there are many beauties of this kind, but he requires to walk with some caution in so flowery a field, lest excess should urge him into sin. His imagination collects abundant honey, but it is possible to have too much of it. We cannot however, refuse him the meed of high commendation, as an attractive and very useful writer.

Art. II. *The Tiara and the Turban; or, Impressions and Observations on Character within the dominions of the Pope and the Sultan.* By S. S. Hill, Esq. In 2 vols. London: Madden and Malcolm.

George Cruickshank, in one of the later numbers of his Table Book, has depicted an object familiar to every traveller in search of the picturesque. A burly, substantial mortal, is represented with agony stamped upon his brow—the express image of sea-sickness and despair, and at the bottom we are told the unfortunate wight is a very good man, but a very bad sailor. Mr. Hill, we are inclined to believe, is a very good sailor: for aught we know to the contrary he may be a very good man; but he certainly is a very bad writer, and has published one of the most uninteresting books that we ever remember to have read. From a most mysterious introduction, we learn that he had no vulgar end in view, that he belongs not to that class who roam gladly from land to land merely to gratify an idle curiosity, or to that other class who travel to acquire a knowledge of the arts and politics of other climes, but that his is that

'Third stage in men's lives, when not the wonders of the world abroad, nor the desire of knowledge, is able to engage us to undertake long and fatiguing journeys; and he who should at this time engage in travelling will usually be one of the exceptions, by constitutional adaptation—or through accident, which it has been above stated, are to be found in the several climates which we observe in the world. And the traveller of this class, though he might have no object that should be paramount to his own accommodation; and though he should receive less gratification, than a traveller of the first of the classes above mentioned, or acquire less knowledge than one of the other class, he should be, at least, able to exercise freer thought concerning what should seem to him to be erroneous or detestable in actions or talents, of which every corner of the world affords sufficient examples; or concerning what should be the more worthy of approval, of all that may fall under his observation.'—Vol. i. pp. 4, 5.

In this manner Mr. Hill discourses through two tedious octavos. His style is unnatural and involved. Like the weary knife-grinder, 'story he has none to tell us,'—he travels in lands of which we can never hear too much; but to narrate is not the object of his journey, and, consequently, the information communicated is of the most meagre and unsatisfactory character, and, by way of compensation for our disappointment, we have a long dissertation, the end of which is to teach how desirable the Koran is, and how great is Mahomet.

Mr. Hill leaves Paris for Strasburg, whence, after just giving himself time to visit the cathedral, he started for Basle. Of Switzerland he saw and says but little. His notions of humanity are shocked by watching some women from the mountains tearing the skins off the living frogs, that the purchaser might fry them alive. He describes the scene plainly enough, any one can understand it. The following, however, is of a different character: we give it, as our author is constantly bewildering us with similar inexplicable passages.

'But be this as it may, the feelings of this man should not surely be envied, who could stand unmoved watching one of the opposite sex, occupied in skinning the familiar animal that wakes the morning with its high-sounding and shrill notes when the day is propitious, and the elements are at rest.'—ib. p. 54.

What can be more vague and unmeaning than such language It is a style of writing however in which our author is eminently successful.

Descendiug the Alps on the Italian side, the traveller seems transported from the regions of eternal winter, into the bosom of a land of perpetual spring; but the more plentiful the bounty of heaven, the more indolent is man. There is nothing but beggary and wretchedness.

'You are presented with hovels, at the doors of ever one in three of which sit dirty women shamelessly occupied in picking the disgusting vermin, with which their persons abound, from their half-naked children's heads; while the fields present everywhere abundance of extraneous and wild vegetation, or contain half cultivated, half-wild samples of the most precious fruits of the fertile earth.'—ib. p. 60.

The first considerable town at which Mr. Hill arrives is Bergamo, the ancient Bergamono. It is fortified, and contains a population of 10,000 inhabitants. Its principal attraction is an annual fair, which lasts eight days, but which our author was too late to see. Before leaving Bergamo he meets with 'a little misadventure;' but having thus excited our curiosity, he tells us it is of 'too trivial a character to particularize,' and we are therefore left in the dark. The information succeeding, may be new to some of our readers.

'The popular method of keeping time in Italy, even in the nineteenth century, is in commencing the day at sunset, at which time the twenty-four hours begin. Thus one hour after sunset is one o'clock, two hours after sun-setting two o'clock; from which it is evident, that in order to a clock giving the correct time, it must be altered daily; seeing if we go to mathematical nicety, that two revolutions of the sun, or more properly of the earth, on its axis, within six months of each other, are never precisely equal in length. The alteration must generally too, be made at a rough guess, unless we suppose the great orb is actually seen to drop into the sea; and that every one has moreover an acquaintance with the laws which govern the refraction of the rays of light, or at least their particular effects at that time, as well as the means of making a calculation of the height at which we may happen to stand above the sea at the time of the setting; and these suppositions it would be absurd to apply to the great body of the people.'—ib. pp. 67, 8.

In the direct route between the larger towns, and at the principal hotels, this barbarous mode of measuring time has been discontinued, and the one we use ourselves, called French time, has been adopted.

Mr. Hill next proceeds to Verona. At this time it has a population of 56,000 inhabitants, and has more of gaiety and life than most of the Italian towns; but we have nothing to detain us. One traveller does little more than chronicle names with which we are familiar. As he floats in his gondola by the marble halls and deserted palaces of Venice, he involuntarily becomes interesting and eloquent, but he soon relapses, and 'Richard's himself again.' He crosses the Po, and enters the Papal States at Francolino: here he is detained, owing to some informality in his passport. In going to the inn, he passed through a court-yard full of live stock. So powerfully is Mr. Hill affected, that it reminds him of the millennium. In his own inimitable style we are told

'Oxen, hogs, sheep, horses, fowls, donkeys, goats, were all dwelling together in the utmost harmony, and yet not through necessity; for the way was open, and they all walked in and out without seeming more to regard the majestic figure of their superior in the scale of creation whom they met, than they did that of any of their brute equals. *The Millennium should scarcely exhibit a more peaceful scene.*'—ib. p. 121.

Our traveller at length reaches Rome. Here he enters rather more into detail, but it is little more than the description of the Guide Book expanded. He witnesses the ceremony of nun-making, and the fair victim is of course one of the loveliest women he has ever beheld. At the Sancta Scala, or holy steps, a few young women are doing penance. He tells us he never saw in so small a number of the younger sort of the opposite sex, so large a proportion of beauty before. Woman is decidedly Mr. Hill's weakness. When he meets one she is invariably, as Mr. Coleridge would have said, 'beautiful exceedingly.' A certain Romish priest takes him into society, not, we should imagine of the most select order, and he again meets the loveliest of all the girls he had seen in Italy. After the introduction, we were certainly not prepared for the extraordinary sensibility displayed on this point. As an illustration of the priestcraft prevalent in this city of religious imposture, Mr. Hill tells us of two criminals—one of whom was committed for murder, the other for sacrilege. The murderer dies, and eternal life is promised; but for him who committed sacrilege, there was no hope, either in this world or the next.

''But I was in want, and the evil spirit tempted me.'

''It is no extenuation, and all prayers are idle. The vessel was consecrated. It was the property of God himself.'

''But he owns the whole earth.'

''It was sacred to his worship.'

''Is one substance more precious than another, in the eyes of Him who made the whole?'

''There is no pardon here, nor hereafter.'

''The sentence is pronounced. The blood shed on Mount Calvary, hath not triumphed over the angel of darkness; his repentance is in vain.'—ib. p. 262.

At Naples, Mr. Hill seeks for a family in which he can become an inmate for the winter. He makes many inquiries after a suitable residence. Let us follow him in one of his visits. After threading his way through the difficulties and dangers of the lower floor, which, according to Neapolitan custom, is a stable, and that by no means of the cleanest description, he reached the staircase, which was perfectly dark.

'We came, however, to the proper landing of the second floor, where a little lamp gave us just light enough to observe that there was a hole at one corner of the pavement into which all the filth of that story was emptied, which it was necessary to avoid We now came to the third floor, and here there was an aperture without a window, which looked into so narrow a space, and was still so far from the top, that a very little day-light appeared; not more than enough to enable us to avoid stepping into the receptacles of filth. At the fourth floor things appeared to improve. The fifth was better still; and the sixth the best. Here, as on the landings which we saw below, there were two doors, and each had a string hanging from a hole. We rang a bell, and an old woman whom I took for a cook, put her head out of a glassless aperture, a half-story still above us, and uttered a most piercing shriek; then spoke a few words in the Neapolitan dialect, after which both my guide and the old woman broke into a fit of loud and immoderate laughing; and when I asked the binder what could be the meaning of what passed, he observed, that it was only the accustomed greeting of the country, which we had before heard was sometimes mistaken by foreigners for mere merriment, and then added, 'Perhaps, *Il Signore* has not yet been in the market square?' I had been, indeed, at the entrance of this place, for the exchange of commodities of all kinds; but the noise, the confusion, and the filth which it exhibited, arrested any further progress for the present.

'After a short parleying, the lady of the house made her appearance—

'She bore in her hand a small lamp, nearly of the form of those of the ancients now found in Pompeii; and she conducted us through a long corridor to a moderate sized apartment, which had a window through which light enough entered to enable us to dispense with that of the lamp; the room was in the utmost confusion. There was a chest of drawers with every drawer open; a round table in the middle loaded with clothes; and the walls were ornamented with a number of prints of the good saints and martyrs.

'The shrieking and laughing had somewhat subsided as we entered this apartment; and as soon as the visitors, at the command of the hostess, were seated, the lady dropped squat into a broad-armed chair, and the most gracious compliments passed between the two Neapolitans, during which I had time to make a few observations upon the person of the gentle lady. She was uncommonly fat, and had, perhaps, passed her fiftieth year, and upon a round head she wore an exuberance of black hair, which, though a large comb adorned it, did not appear to have been for many a year dressed. Her eyes were jet black and full; and her features generally not disagreeable. Several handkerchiefs of various colours were twisted and hung loosely about her neck, the yellow prevailing; but in spite of her complexion, where her skin appeared, it was visibly dirty. She wore a striped gown which hung loosely from the shoulders, and the sleeves of which were tight about her fat arms, and she had on dirty white stockings, with what had been slippers, but of which scarce enough remained to attach them to the feet.

'Compliments having ceased, a colloquy followed, the brief report of which will serve the account of this insignificant adventure.

"'And now for the business which brought us here,'' said the honest bookbinder—'' this foreign gentleman.''

'And here I confess I expected the glance of the lady, whose eye I had not yet met; but she did not favour me with a look.

''This foreign gentleman, wishes to place himself in an Italian family, for a part or the whole of the winter.

'At these words the lady raised herself upright in her seat, with her hands upon the arms of the chair, and opened her eyes to their full capacity; while her countenance expressed what might have been a feeling between consternation and curiosity.

''He is tired of hotels, and does not like the gloom of lodgings.'

'The lady's right hand was now raised, with the fingers wide spread, and the palm outwards.

''Can you accommodate him?'

'Both hands were now raised; and the head a little turned on one side; but before an instant had elapsed, she threw herself back in the chair, and opened her eyes to their full capacity, and uttered a shriek that none but a Neapolitan could have equalled, which was succeeded by a short burst of laughter in which she was now alone. The bookbinder, seemingly not in the least surprised, however, waited without adding a word for a reply to the question he had put. And now the fair Neapolitan, stretching out both arms, and throwing her body forwards, and putting out her feet to the full extent, with the heels to the ground, and the toes pointed upwards, she exclaimed, in the Neapolitan dialect, in which the discourse had commenced—

''Signore, have you taken leave of your senses; or forgotten that I have a daughter in the house—a maiden?' '

' 'Oh true:' ' said the binder, ' 'and the thought might have struck me, had not the gentleman been of a certain age, and of a tranquil disposition.'

'And here again I was greatly disappointed, that I had not so much as attracted a glance from the Neapolitan lady.

' 'All that may be true,' said she, placing her hands upon her breast; then holding out the right, and drawing the tops of the fingers and thumb to a focus; and then placing the points upon the arm of the chair, and leaning her head a little forward with her face slightly turned to the left, in which position she remained an instant still; and then, throwing open her hand as if she loosed a flock of birds from the palm, and placing her hand straight with the chin, something elongated, she added—' 'But you know I have neighbours.'—ib. 269--274.

Not deterred by this specimen of Neapolitan loveliness, Mr. Hill at length enters a family residing at a short distance from Naples, where he remains the winter, eating maccaroni to his heart's content. During his stay here, he became a witness of what he most firmly believes to be a miracle—that is, he saw the frozen or congealed blood of Saint Gennaro, the patron saint of the city, liquify, and become as quick and voluble at the presence of the head of the saint, as when it ran in the veins of the holy man during his life in the flesh. These are Mr. Hill's own words. We are rather more sceptical than our author, though he assures us, 'the miracle is beyond confutation.' We are acquainted with many substances, which would liquify when exposed to the heat of a candle, or the warm kisses of fair devotees, in much less time than did the blood of the worthy saint. Vesuvius, Herculaneum, and Pompeii, to which places our attention is next directed, we deem far more worthy of remark than this clever trick played by designing priests.

The climate of Naples is not particularly tempting, and Mr. Hill left it in the middle of February. At Palermo, on a miserable night,—for it rained in torrents, he seeks shelter, and finds it at length in a house of charity; one of the delirious inmates of which pays him a visit, more unexpected than agreeable. At Messina he meets with a priest, who proves himself a fit brother to the one at Rome, and what otherwise could be expected. At Rome, at Messina, at Oxford, at Ascott, the term denotes a man who knows little of religion, but the form.

After a month's stay in Messina, he hears of a Genoese vessel on the point of sailing for Constantinople. Mr. Hill engages a passage, notwithstanding the earnest warnings of his friend the priest, and of a Sicilian diviner, whom he had met at the coffee-house which he was in the habit of frequenting. At Syra, as the vessel makes a short stay, he disembarks, and hastily visits what remains of Athenian power and splendour. Modern Athens it seems, has little to repay or excite the curiosity of the traveller. 'Our fat contributor' in Punch, favoured the public with an account of Otho's palace, which, from Mr. Hill's sketch of that clumsy specimen of architecture, we imagine to be literally correct. However, it matters not much; the splendour of the palace is no sign of the freedom or civilization of the people. Were it so, the autocrat would no longer govern a race of serfs. Our author expatiates at some length on the famed ruins which everywhere met his view; but the information given us is not of a particularly novel character. The date of the erection of the Parthenon, its length and breadth, and such matters, have been told times without number. We needed 'no ghost from the grave to tell us that.' Of such subjects Mr. Hill gives us more than enough, whilst, of what manner of men and women they are whose sires achieved all that was noble and sublime in eloquence, in poetry, in art, we have no account whatever. For all that Mr. Hill says, he might as well have stayed in the city of the dead.

But at length our author reaches the land of the turban; and here we are rather disappointed with the dearth of information. Rambles through narrow streets where nothing is seen; and visits to coffee-houses where nothing is said, are not very interesting to the general reader. His attention, however, is attracted by an incident on which he contrives to hang a world of speculation. A dog with her puppies, is on the point of starvation, and a collection is made for her. We quote Mr. Hill's own words :—

'The collection, in a word, which the charitable old man gathered with so much ease, was for the necessities of one of the canine inhabitants of the city; and as my guide learnt as we passed along, by the remarks which were incidentally made, for an especial case of one of the females of the species, whose lately produced little litter had brought her to the verge of starvation, which would involve half-a-score, at least, of both sexes of her kind in equal perdition, without this timely interference for their preservation.'—Vol. ii.

Such is the fact—the lesson to be learnt is, the superiority of Mussulmen and their religion; but 'one swallow does not make a summer,' and this single fact does not at all incline us to believe in Mahomet. In England, from the highest to the lowest, from the gentleman to his groom, humanity towards the lower orders of creation is the rule, and not as Mr. Hill would make it the exception. But that is no test of character. Many of the blood-thirsty heroes of the French revolution were sensitive to an extreme with respect to the happiness of some favourite animal. The story of Sterne, who wept over a dead ass, and left his mother to starve, is familiar to all. The thoughtless women who are met with every day, rolling in their carriages along Regent-street, have generally a curled and scented poodle with them, over whose woes they sorrow, whilst they remain callous when they hear the tale of a victim of the world's injustice, for whom there remains nought but the workhouse, the hulks, or the grave; and the humanity our author admires, is precisely of the same maudlin character—it is the humanity of those who would fatten a dog, and enslave a man. Full of Mr. Hill's ideas, as to the superiority of the Mussulman's humanity, we turn to his next page, and find that it contains an account of the great slave bazaar! The delusion vanishes at once. If this be the humanity of the koran, let it perish for ever from the earth.

Mr. Hill devotes much of his last volume to a comparison of the religion of the bible, and that of the koran. We do not blame him for doing so. The right of private judgment which we claim for ourselves, we willingly extend to others; all we ask is, that in the discussion the truth should be fully stated. Mr. Hill takes his idea of Christianity from the mummeries and corruptions of Rome: he should have gone to the fountain head,—'to the law and to the testimony' where he would have learnt how spiritual and pure was the religion we believe and profess. It is childish to talk about sincerity. When Galileo taught the true doctrine of the earth's motion round the sun, it would have been no defence of the opposite to have said, that the believer in it was sincere. Undoubtedly in Mahomedanism there is something of the truth. No downright lie can long be a great national belief. Mr. Hill says, it teaches some truth, and therefore it would be unwise to introduce the whole truth, as contained in the Bible. He might in just the same manner argue, the moon gives some light, and therefore it would be unwise to avail ourselves of the light of the sun. Christianity, he says, would produce such a change that it would be injudicious to introduce it. A change in Turkey would raise her from her degraded position, and would be the salvation of the country. As mere politicians, we would wish to see the mosque of St. Sophia turned into a Christian house of prayer. We should deem it a bright day when the crescent gave way to the cross. We cannot think so favourably of the religion of the koran as does Mr. Hill; perhaps we have a higher opinion of that mysterious inhabitant of Mecca than he has, but we look upon the religion he propagated, with its low ideas of woman—with its sanction of polygamy and slavery—with its sensual rewards and indulgences, as infinitely beneath the religion of Jesus of Nazareth. Mr. Hill we should conjecture, is no profound theologian, but from Moore he might have learned that—

> 'A Turkish heaven 'tis easily made,
> 'Tis but black eyes and lemonade.'

And yet, professing to be a grave philosophical observer—one who has long outlived the heat and passion of young blood, he would advocate that system which teaches its followers their bliss will be an eternal round of animal indulgence; as if the Bible, with its higher and holier requirements and rewards had never been revealed to man.

We have now done with Mr. Hill. If his work reaches a second edition, we recommend him to revise his style, and to omit much of his matter. On the part of a traveller, pages of ill-reasoned speculation are perfectly gratuitous. Travels, unless notoriously ill-written, can hardly fail to be interesting.

> ''Tis hard to say if greater want of skill
> Appear in writing, or in judging ill;
> But of the two, less dangerous is the offence,
> To tire our patience, than mislead our sense!'

Mr. Hill reads Pope; at any rate he quotes him—let him bear these lines in mind, for, alas! both errors are to be laid at his door.

Art. III. *A Commentary on the Apocalypse.* By Moses Stuart, Professor of Sacred Literature in the Theological Seminary at Andover, Mass. 2 vols. 8vo. pp. 504 and 504. London: Wiley and Putman, 1845.

The oldest testimony for the canonical authority and genuineness of the Apocalypse is supposed to be that of Papias. It is only however, from other and much later writers, that we have any notice of Papias in connexion with this point, viz. from Andreas and Arethas, bishops of Caesarea in Cappadocia, in the sixth century. The words of the former are: 'But we deem it superfluous to speak at length of the divinely-inspired book, to the credibility of which, the blessed men Gregory the theologian, and Cyril, bear testimony, as also the more ancient Papias, Irenæus, Methodius, and Hippolytus.' The language of Arethas is nearly the same. In the epistle of the churches of Vienne and Lyons there is a reference to *one* passage in the book, or according to Ruinart and others to *two*. Justin Martyr, in his dialogue with Trypho, expressly attributes it to the apostle John. Eusebius informs us that Melito, bishop of Sardis, wrote a book concerning the Revelation of John, and that Theophilus, bishop of Antioch, wrote a treatise against the heresy of Hermogenes, 'in which he alleged many testimonies out of the Revelation of John. According to the same ecclesiastical historian, Apollonius 'alleged testimonies out of the Revelation, and reported how that John raised at Ephesus, by the divine power of God, one that was dead to life again.' Irenæus quotes the book as 'the Revelation of John the disciple of the Lord.' Clement of Alexandria, attributes it to the same author; and Tertullian mentions it as written by the apostle John, the same who wrote the first epistle. Hippolytus received it as the production of the same apostle, and Origen in like manner, specifies the writer as John the son of Zebedee. Dionysius of Alexandria, received the book as written by a person called John, a holy man, endued with the Holy Ghost, although he thinks that it did not proceed from the apostle. It appears to have been admitted as Scripture by Nepos, by Cyprian, Novatus, Lactantius, the latter Arnobius; and by the Manichees, the Donatists, and the Arians. In like manner it was acknowledged as canonical by Athanasius, Epiphanius, Jerome, Rufinus, the third Council of Carthage, Augustine, Didymus, Basil the Great, Cyril of Alexandria, Firmicus Maternus, Hilary of Poitiers, Philaster, Pacian, Ambrose of Milan, Prudentius, Innocent of Rome, Council of Dieppe, Andreas, Arethas, Sulpicius, Severus, Johannes, Damascenus, and Œcumenius. It is in the catalogues of Amphilochius, Dionysius the Areopagite, and in the codex Alexandrinus.

On the other side, it may be said that the opponents of Montanism generally ascribed the book to Cerinthus, thus denying its inspiration and authority. This was the opinion of Caius of Rome. Eusebius speaks in an undecided way respecting the Apocalypse, so that it is difficult to gather his own opinion regarding it. It is probable that he did not believe it to have been written by the apostle John; and besides, he has not quoted it in proof or confirmation of any doctrine, even in cases where it might readily have suggested itself to his mind. That it was not universally received may be inferred from the words: 'Concerning the Apocalypse there are, to this very day, different opinions.' According to him some rejected it, others placed it among the books universally received. Epiphanius states, that it was not universally received in his day, instancing the case of the Alogians, who rejected not only it, but all John's writings. Cyril of Jerusalem omits it in his catalogue, and his opinion appears to have been unfavourable. So also Gregory of Nazianzum. It is wanting in the catalogue of the council of Laodicea, in the canon of the Syrian church, and in the Syriac version. Amphilochius bishop of Iconium says, that the book was approved by some, though many pronounced it spurious. Jerome affirms that many Greek churches rejected the book. A passage in Augustine leads to the conclusion that it was not universally received in his time. In regard to the divines of the Antiochenian school there is some difficulty in ascertaining their opinion. Theodore of Mopsuestia, it is probable, did not receive the book. It is somewhat remarkable, that Chrysostom never quotes the Apocalypse, though he had many suitable opportunities of doing so. Wetstein and Schmid, however, refer to several passages in his homilies on Matthew, in which figures and metaphors respecting the future blessedness of Christ's kingdom have been borrowed from the Apocalypse; and Suidas states, that Chrysostom acknowledged the canonicity of John's three epistles and the Revelation. The probability therefore is, that Chrysostom received the book. Theodoret, too, does not cite the book, although he alludes to it three times in his extant works. Severian omits all mention of it. In the ninth century Nicephorus rejected it.

From the preceding summary of authorities for and against the canonical rank and genuineness of this book, it will be seen, that the weight of evidence decidedly preponderates in its favour. The stream of ecclesiastical tradition and patristic learning runs in support of it as divine. Some of the witnesses opposed it in consequence of their zeal against Montanism and Millennarianism, rather than on the ground of impartial inquiry. Hence the rejection of it by the Alogians or Antimontanists, and by Caius. Hence, too, the remarks of Dionysius, denying that the production proceeded from John the apostle, may be in part accounted for. Perhaps Eusebius was influenced by the opinion and arguments of Dionysius, as Lardner conjectures, to which doctrinal prepossessions may be added. It is no proof against the Apocalypse that it is wanting in several catalogues, because the writers may not have intended to give any books, except such as were adapted to public reading in the churches. The Syriac version wants it, but it also wants the second and third epistles of John, with the epistle of Jude. The obscurity of the work, pein comparative inutility for public reading, and the opposition to Montanism which existed, at least in spirit, in the Syrian church, combined to exclude it from the Peshito. Why Ebedjesu omitted it in his catalogue of the canonical writings, received by the Syrian church, it is not easy to explain. Perhaps he made no mention of it because the old Syrian version wanted it. The same reason may serve to account for the silence of Gregory Bar Hebraeus and James of Edessa respecting it. But the weight attaching to the testimony of these three writers is counterbalanced by the authority of Epherem, who quotes it as canonical, ascribing it to John the divine; from which circumstance, says Assemann, 'it may be seen what was the judgment of the most ancient Syrians relative to the authority of the book in question.' Besides, the inscription of the Syrian version still existing, ascribes the book to John the evangelist. The authority of Clement and Origen is by far the most considerable in the second and third centuries, in favour of the book, not only on account of the learning and critical ability of these writers, but because they took no part in the millennarian and anti-millennarian disputations. They must, therefore, be regarded in the light of impartial and competent witnesses. The millennarians would be naturally inclined to uphold the book as supporting their favourite tenet, while their opponents, for the same reason, would be disposed to reject it.

The result of our examination and comparison of the external evidence is a decision in favour of the canonical authority and genuineness of the work. *Some* doubted or denied its claims in early times; but it was always *generally* received. The current of opinion was clearly on its side. It was *usually* regarded as a part of the New Testament, and quoted as of equal value with the other portions.

II.—In regard to the time when the book was written, it is commonly assumed, that it was written or published A.D. 95 96, or 97. The reason for assuming this date is the fact of John's banishment to Patmos, which is said to have happened in the latter part of Domitian's reign. Now that emperor died in 96, and his persecution did not commence till near the close of his reign. Thus the composition of the book, or at least its publication, is assigned either to the reign of Domitian or to that of his successor Nerva. It is well attested by antiquity that the apostle was banished to Patmos, and received his revelations there. The ninth verse of the first chapter refers to his exile for the gospel's sake, and accords with the tradition. But antiquity is by no means unanimous in fixing the time of the banishment to the reign of Domitian. Eusebius (in his Chronicon and Ecclesiastical History) and Jerome, attribute it to Domitian; Epiphanius to Claudius; the Syriac version of the

Apocalypse, the younger Hippolytus, and Theophylact, assign it to Nero; while Tertullian, Clement, and Origen name no emperor. The testimony of Irenaeus is chiefly relied upon as being the earliest which favours the time of Domitian. Speaking of the Apocalypse, that father says: 'It was seen no long time ago, but almost in our own day, at the end of the reign of Domitian.' Some have conjectured that *Domitius* (Nero) and *Domitian* were early interchanged, and that even the testimony of Irenaeus may refer to Nero, by supposing that Δομετιανοῦ is an adjective, formed from Δομετιος, meaning *belonging to Domitius* or Nero. But this conjecture is utterly improbable. The language of Tertullian, Clement, and Origen, is certainly more appropriate to Nero than to Domitian. Jerome himself, though he adopts the opinion of Eusebius, says in his treatise against Jovinian: 'Tertullian relates that John being cast by Nero's order into a caldron of boiling oil, &c.' Besides, Eusebius, who follows Irenaeus in his Chronicle and Ecclesiastical History, associates the Patmos exile, in his Evangelical Demonstration, with the deaths of Peter and Paul under Nero. It would appear, too, that Arethas dissented from the tradition of Irenaeus and Eusebius, for although, in one place, he seems to follow another opinion, yet he contends that Rev. vii. 1—8, was written at Ephesus *before* the Jewish war. Thus the tradition of the early church with regard to John's banishment is neither definite nor consistent. Hence it is of little value in determining the time when the Apocalypse was written. It is very probable that the tradition was manufactured in different shapes and forms out of the statement in chap. i. 9. The passage furnishes a basis which appears not to have been overlooked. It does not, however, necessarily imply that actual persecution had assailed the apostle, but merely that he suffered for the gospel's sake. Perhaps he retired to the lonely island warned by the signs of the times of impending and fiery opposition to Christianity. Foreseeing the storm that was likely to reach the provinces in its progress from Rome, he prudently fled before it.

Abandoning the uncertain ground of external testimony, let us look if there be any indications in the book itself of the time at which it was written. In the eleventh chapter there are distinct references to the impending destruction of Jerusalem. The city is not spoken of as *already destroyed*, but as speedily to be given up to its enemies. Thus, in the first verse, the seer receives a measuring-reed, with which he is commanded to measure the temple, and the altar, and them that worship therein. This presupposes that the temple was yet standing. In the thirteenth verse of the same chapter the destruction of one part of the city is predicted, obviously implying that the holy city, i.e., Jerusalem, and the temple, were depicted in the commencement of the chapter as still standing. It is true that the writer might have borrowed a symbolic description from the temple already in ruins, especially if the measurement had been intended to denote the erection of a new temple *instead of* the former; but in the present instance it would have been incongruous to symbolize the *preservation* of the true sanctuary—all that constitutes the essence of acceptable worship—under the figure of a temple in ruins. The holy place yet undestroyed, harmonizes best with the maintenance of God's worship in the midst of opposition. On the whole, we infer from the eleventh chapter thus much, that the Apocalypse was written before the destruction of Jerusalem and of the temple. Another passage, containing a chronological allusion still more definite, is in the seventeenth chapter, tenth verse: 'And there are seven kings: five are fallen, and one is, and the other is not yet come; and when he cometh, he must continue a short space.' The whole chapter sufficiently proves that the Roman emperors are here indicated. The question is, who are the five already dead, succeeded by the one still reigning? According to Lücke and Ewald, the sixth emperor is Galba. Eichhorn and Bleek suppose him to be Vespasian, while Bertholdt and Koehler fix upon Nero. Thus, some reckon the first of the Roman emperors Julius Cæsar; others, Augustus. If we begin with the former, the five are, Julius Cæsar, Augustus, Tiberius, Caligula, and Claudius, making the sixth to be Nero, 'the one that is;' but if the series commence with Augustus, the sixth will be Galba. Eichhorn and Bleek think that Galba, Otho, and Vitellius should be omitted from the enumeration in consideration of their brief and tumultuous sovereignty; but the Roman historians uniformly insert them in the lists of Roman emperors, and there is no reason why John should depart from their accustomed method. There is some difficulty in deciding between the other two opinions, because the imperial series in a few writers begins with Augustus, while in the rest, it begins with Julius Cæsar. In support of the former, as the true commencement of the series, Lücke quotes Tacitus, Aurelius Victor, and Sextus Rufus; but the words of the first writer, which alone are of any weight, are somewhat indefinite. In support of the latter, the fourth book of Ezra, Josephus in his Antiquities, Suetonius, the Paschal Chronicle, and Georgius Syncellus, may be adduced. In the fifth book of the Sybilline writings, Julius Cæsar is the first; but in the twelfth book, Augustus. The weight of authority is in favour of Julius Cæsar. The testimony of Josephus is clear and explicit. John, being a Jew, would naturally follow the same reckoning, especially as it was agreeable to the customary Roman computation, if we may judge from Suetonius. Thus the sixth head is Nero, rather than Galba.

But the words of chap. xvii. 2, seem opposed to this view, no less than those of xvii. 8, and xiii. 3. With regard to the last passage it is far from conclusive, because in it the writer speaks of *what he saw;* and we know that things future were presented to the view of the prophets in their ecstatic state, as *present realities.* But the words of chap. xvii. 8—11, contain an explanation of the mystery relative to the woman and the beast, given to John by an angel. In this passage, therefore, chronological data are appropriately introduced. The heathen Roman empire is individualized in Nero, the first of the Roman emperors who persecuted the Christians. It was currently reported and believed among the Romans, that Nero was not actually dead, but that he was still alive in the East, and would soon return thence to subdue all his enemies, and take possession again of his own kingdom. Suetonius relates that the soothsayers (mathematici) had predicted this in the lifetime of Nero, and that the tyrant had been greatly alarmed by it. It is probable that the story was of Jewish origin. The same idea was current among the early Christians, as we learn from the fourth book of the Sybillines. It was generally believed by them that Nero would return from the East as antichrist, immediately before the advent of Christ, make war upon the kingdom of the latter, and suffer signal defeat. Agreeably to this prevalent report concerning Nero, he is represented as one of the seven heads which was apparently dead, but whose deadly wound was healed, so that he appeared alive again, to the surprise of all. He 'is the beast that was, and is not, and shall ascend out of the bottomless pit, and go into perdition.' In consequence of his supposed reappearance, he is 'an eighth, and yet is one of the seven emperors, and goeth into perdition.' Thus the Roman empire, in the person of Nero, is set forth as the representative of heathenism, the church's enemy. In the 8th and 11th verses of the seventeenth chapter, an explanation is given, couched in the language of prevalent report and belief. Nero is described agreeably to the *current tradition,* a tradition which took its rise before his death. The explanation amounts to this: 'The beast which thou sawest is the emperor, of whom it is commonly believed that he shall be assassinated, recover of the wound, go to the east, and return from it to desolate the church, and inflict terrible punishments on his enemies.' Thus xvii. 10, implies, that the visions were *received* by the prophet during the time of Nero. Whether they were *written* immediately after or not, cannot be determined from the passage.

The place at which the book was written may have been Patmos; or Ephesus, after John's return. Some of the fathers seem not to have thought of separating *the seeing* from *the writing* of the visions. Hence Jerome says: 'When Domitian raised a second persecution, fourteen years after the first which was set on foot by Nero, John was banished into the island of Patmos, where he wrote the Apocalypse.' Early tradition assigns the composition to Asia Minor. Little exactness however, need be expected from this department. Bertholdt conceives, that the command given to John to write the visions, and send them to the seven churches of Asia (verse 11), implies that he was not in Asia Minor when they were written. In connexion with this remark it may be observed, that the seven cities are mentioned in the exact order in which they would be visited by one setting out from Patmos. Thus there is a presumption in favour of the island as the spot whence the written visions were sent forth. It is true that the command to commit them to writing, given to John by the angel, may be separated from the actual writing; but it is surely implied in the narrative, that a very short interval occurred between the issuing and the execution of the injunction, during which, no good reason appears for supposing a change of abode on the part of the seer. Lücke appeals to the verb ἐγενόμην, in the ninth and tenth verses of the first chapter, for proof that the author was no longer in Patmos. But it was customary for ancient writers, both Greek and Roman, to transport themselves in idea to the time when their composition should be read, and consequently to speak of the actual period of writing as past. On the whole, we incline to think, that the visions were seen and committed to writing in Patmos.

Those who believe that the book was not written till Domitian's reign, adduce the following objections to so early a date as the time of Nero.

1. "It is evident," say L'Enfant and Beausobre, 'from divers places of the Revelation, that there had been an open persecution in the provinces. St. John himself had been banished into Patmos for the testimony of Jesus. The church of Ephesus, or its bishop, is commended for their 'labour and patience,' which seems to imply persecution. This is still more manifest in the words directed to the church of Smyrna, ch. ii. 9: 'I know thy works and tribulation.' For the original word always denotes persecution, in the scriptures of the New Testament: as it is also explained in the following verse. In the thirteenth verse of the same chapter, mention is made of a martyr named Antipas, put to death at Pergamos.—All that has been now observed concerning the persecution, of which mention is made

in the first chapters of the Revelation, cannot relate to the time of Claudius, who did not persecute the Christians, nor to the time of Nero, whose persecution did not reach the provinces. And therefore it must relate to Domitian, according to ecclesiastical tradition."

In order to account for John's banishment to Patmos, it is not necessary to believe, neither do the words of the ninth verse imply, that the spirit of persecution raged at Ephesus. When it was active at Rome, the Christians in the provinces may be supposed to have trembled for their safety. Whatever affected the capital, would naturally affect the distant parts and dependencies of the empire. The verse alluded to may imply no more than that John saw the storm lower; and, warned by the signs of the times, no less than by the Spirit of God, withdrew for a season from the scene of his labours. Or, if a banishment, properly so called, be insisted on as an unavoidable inference from the passage, we may refer to the decree of Claudius, which enjoined all Jews to leave Rome. It is natural to suppose that the prefects and presidents of provinces would act after the manner of their prince. Grotius thinks that the apostle did not suffer this punishment as a Christian, but as a Jew, or rather as the head of a new sect among the Jews, and therefore he was not only sent away, but banished to a desert island. This is certainly possible, for the heathen did not clearly distinguish between Jews and Christians till the destruction of Jerusalem by Titus. The magistrates looked upon those who worshipped so differently from themselves as disaffected towards their administration, and proceeded in some cases to extreme measures against their persons and property. Hence measures directed against Jews were extended to Christians. Besides, we may reply, in the words of Lardner, 'that the Christian writers who speak of Nero's persecution do in effect or expressly say it was general; that from Rome it spread into the provinces and was authorised by public edicts.' In proof of this, allusion is made to Tertullian, Luctantius, Sulpicius Severus, Orosius, Joseph Scaliger, and Pagi. The expressions of Suetonius, regarding the treatment of the Christians in the same reign, are general, such as, 'The Christians were punished,' including sufferings in the provinces as well as the city.

Thus much we have thought it right to say regarding that part of the argument which affects John himself.

The 'labour and patience' of the church at Ephesus are expressions of a specific character, referring to false apostles, from whom the Christians in that city had to endure much. A painful and constant opposition was required against their efforts. The words addressed to the church at Smyrna: 'Thy works and tribulation,' unquestionably involve the idea of persecution, but of persecution arising from a particular class of individuals, as the context demonstrates—from opponents of the gospel of Christ, who, professing themselves the friends of the truth, were in reality deceivers and liars. The apostle Paul encountered the frequent antagonism of such persons; they harassed him with unceasing hatred; and some at least of the churches, such as that of Smyrna, suffered from them in like manner. They disturbed the peace and marred the purity of that community. Such persecution is of a kind to harmonise with the time of *any* early Roman emperor. It is not at all necessary to refer it to the reign of Domitian; since it did not arise from heathen potentates, but from professors of religion.

In regard to Antipas, nothing is known. He suffered at Pergamos, but under whom, or in what circumstances, is uncertain. Our hypothesis does not assume as essential to it that he was put to death under Nero. Who shall deny that individual Christians suffered occasionally in the provinces even before the time of Nero?

2. 'It appears from the Revelation, that the Nicolaitans made a sect when this book was written, since they are expressly named; whereas they were only foretold and described in general terms by St. Peter, in his second epistle written after the year sixty; and in St. Jude's, about the time of the destruction of Jerusalem by Vespasian.' It is not at all certain that the Nicolaitans made a sect when this book was written, because they are mentioned. The most probable interpretation of the word is that which regards it as *symbolic*, signifying *corrupters of the people*, equivalent to Balaam, in Hebrew. Thus the same class of persons is meant whom Peter describes as 'followers of the way of Balaam.' The Nicolaitans of whom the fathers speak, were a party of Gnostics subsequently formed, whose founder was Nicholas. They were confounded with the Nicolaitans mentioned in the Apocalypse.

3. 'The condition of the seven churches as described in the Apocalypse shews, that they had been planted a considerable time. John reproves faults that do not happen except after a while. The church of Ephesus had left her first love. That of Sardis had a name to live but was dead. The community at Laodicea had fallen into lukewarmness and indifference. St. Paul writing to the church at Ephesus, from Rome, A.D. 61 or 62, instead of reproving their want of love commends their love and faith, ch. i. 15.'

An attentive examination of the language addressed to each will shew its appropriateness to the time of Nero, or soon after. The fact that the church of Ephesus were commended for their faith and love, about A.D. 61, (Ephes. i. 15), is quite consistent with Rev. ii. 2, 3, while both are in agreement with the reproof that the members had left their first love. In the lapse of a few years, amid trying and difficult circumstances, the ardour of their love had cooled. The case of Sardis and Laodicea was not very dissimilar. The patience for which some are commended, refers mainly, as we have said, to the temptations which they endured from wicked and corrupting teachers, and the difficulties attendant on the faithful exercise of discipline among them. The tribulation of the church at Smyrna had special reference to the blasphemy of Satan's synagogue. Thus there is no valid objection to the opinion, that the book was written in the reign of Nero, A.D. 67.

Pareus seems to have been the first who threw out the idea that the Apocalypse constitutes a dramatic poem. The same opinion was also expressed by Hartwig. The genius of Eichhorn afterwards expanded the suggestion into a theory pervaded by symmetry and beauty; so that the notion of its being a drama is now associated with his name alone. It is needless to enter upon a formal refutation of this sentiment. As developed by Eichhorn, it is entitled to the praise of ingenuity, but little else can be adduced in its favour. Contrary to the analogy of such Old Testament writings, as bear the greatest resemblance to this book, it resolves the greater part of it into sublime scenery and fiction. Something more is intended than a symbolic description of the triumph of Christianity over Judaism and Paganism. There is historic narrative. There are true prophecies, having their accomplishment in distinct events and individuals. The book consists of a prophetic poem. With some exceptions, its diction is the diction of poetry. When judged by the rules of rhetoric, it approaches the form of an epic poem. It is not made up of a series of disjointed visions; it is regular in structure, and highly artificial in arrangement. The parts are disposed in such a manner as to indicate unity. It is easy to see, that the book bears a close analogy to the prophetic writings of the Old Testament, especially those of Daniel. The writer has imitated the utterances of Daniel, Ezekiel, and Zechariah. Hence his language is more Hebraistic than that of the New Testament generally. And if his composition resemble in many of its features the inspired productions of a former dispensation, the interpreter of it should be qualified for his task by a familiar acquaintance with the symbols, imagery, diction, and spirit of the prophets and poets belonging to that ancient economy.

The books of the New Testament, like those of the Old, were designed to promote the instruction of men in all ages. They were adapted to teach, exhort, and reprove all mankind. They do not belong to the class of ephemeral writings that have long since fulfilled the purpose for which they were originally composed. The object of the writers was not merely a local or partial one. If this be true of all parts of the Bible, it is equally true of the Apocalypse.—'Blessed is he that readeth, and they that hear the words of this prophecy.' This characteristic is perfectly consistent with the fact, that it arose out of specific circumstances, and was primarily meant to subserve a definite end. When first written, it was destined to meet the peculiar circumstances of the primitive Christians. The times were troublous. Persecution had appeared in various forms. The followers of Christ were exposed to suffering for conscience sake. Their enemies were fierce against them. The humble disciples of the Lamb, comparatively few and feeble, seemed doomed to extinction. Amid such circumstances, the writer of the Apocalypse was prompted by a divine influence to present to them such views as were adapted to encourage them to stedfastness in the faith, to comfort them in the midst of calamity, and to arm them with resolution to endure all the assaults of their foes. Agreeably to this view, exalted honours, glorious rewards, are set before the Christian soldier, who should endure to the end. A crown of victory, the approbation of the Redeemer, everlasting felicity—these are prepared for the patient believer. In connexion with such representations, the final triumph of Christianity, and the Messiah's peaceful reigning with his saints, form topics on which the writer dwells with emphatic earnestness. The Christians of primitive times may have sorrowfully thought that they should never be able to stand the shock of their assailants, the power and policy of the world being leagued against them; but the statements of John tend to the conclusion, that truth should make progress in the earth; and the church emerging out of all struggles, become stronger and stronger. How emphatically, too, does the writer exhibit the advent of Christ, to deliver his people from their enemies. This occurrence, which he intimates, in no obscure terms, to be at hand, was peculiarly fitted to comfort the oppressed saints under their struggles. If such be the primary and principal aim of the work, we should not look in it for a history of the world's affairs. It did not comport with the writer's object to compose a civil history. The genius of Christ's kingdom is totally different from that of the kingdoms of this world. It advances steadily and silently, independently of, and frequently in opposition to them. Hence the Apocalypse cannot contain a history of the world. It exhibits a history of the church, specially of its early struggles with the powers of darkness, and the malice of superstition,

This last remark leads to another of chief importance to the interpretation of the book before us, namely, that it principally relates to events past, present, and speedily to happen in connexion with the Christian religion, as viewed from the seer's platform of observation. The glances at the past are brief; references to the circumstances of the church at the time are numerous and diversified; while rapidly coming catastrophes and triumphs are pourtrayed in full and vivid colours. Trials impending over the church, and judgments over her enemies in the age of the apostle, form the burden of the prophecy. This conclusion is fully sustained both by the prologue and epilogue; although it has been generally overlooked by interpreters. What language can be more explicit than this: 'Blessed is he that readeth, and they that hear the words of this prophecy, for the time is at hand.'—'The revelation of Jesus Christ, which God gave unto him, to show unto his servants things which must shortly come to pass.'—'He which testifieth these things saith, Surely I come quickly. Amen, even so, come Lord Jesus.'

The body of the work is contained in chapters iv.—xxii. 6, and is almost entirely a series of symbolic representations. To this is prefixed a prologue, i.—iv. A brief epilogue is appended, xxii. 6,—21.

The prologue is of considerable length, and embraces separate epistles to the seven churches in Asia Minor. John had resided and laboured for a period in the region where these churches were planted. Probably he was personally known to many of the believers of whom they are composed. Now that the other apostles were dispersed or dead, the care of these communities devolved upon himself. As their spiritual superintendent, he naturally felt the more intense and lively interest in their growing prosperity and steadfast principle. The storm of persecution had fallen upon the apostles and believers at Rome, striking fear into their brethren in the remote provinces of the empire. It is highly probable that the Christians in these regions had been already visited with trials.

After the prologue, or introduction, which is peculiarly fitted to admonish and console amid suffering, we come to the body of the work itself, commencing with the fourth chapter. This may be appropriately divided into three parts, namely, (first,) iv.—xi.; (second,) xii.—xix.; (third,) xx.—xxii. 5.

The first part narrates the fate and fortunes of Christ's followers till the destruction of Jesusalem, when *the coming* of the Redeemer took place. Here the triumph of Christianity over Judaism is exhibited, as the concluding portion evinces. The following particulars are comprehended in iv.—xi. A vision of the divine Majesty in heaven worshipped by the whole sentient creation. An account of the sealed book with seven seals, which none but the Lamb could open; and the praises presented to Him by the celestial inhabitants. The successive opening of the first six seals, in which are symbolized respectively, successful invasion, slaughter, famine, destruction, bloody persecution of the saints, great political catastrophes and revolutions. Before the opening of the seventh seal one hundred and forty-four thousand are sealed or made safe, out of the tribes of Israel; and an innumerable multitude with palms in their hands, are seen before the throne.

After the opening of the seventh seal the catastrophe is delayed by the sounding of seven trumpets, the first six announcing great plagues and disasters preparatory to the judgment. Before the last trumpet sounds, a mighty angel appears with an open book in his hand, announcing that the mystery of God should be finished when the seventh angel should begin to sound. From him the seer receives the little book and is commanded to eat it up, and to prophecy hereafter concerning many peoples, nations, tongues, and kings. After this the interior of the temple with its Jewish worshippers is measured by the prophet, while the outer court is excepted and given up to the heathen to be profaned, for the space of forty-two months. But, notwithstanding the long-suffering mercy of God, the Jews continue to persecute the faithful witnesses, so that they are punished by the fall of a tenth part of the holy city in an earthquake. Hence seven thousand men perish, while the remainder, affrighted, give glory to God. After this the seventh angel sounded; the Lord himself appearing to inflict the final blow on Jerusalem and its inhabitants. The catastrophe takes place, and the heavenly choir give thanks to God for the triumph of Christianity. The temple of God is opened in heaven, so that he is accessible to all, being disclosed to the view of the whole earth as their God, without the intervention of any priest, as in the abrogated economy. Thus the Jewish ritual is done away, the Jews who stood in the way of Christianity are destroyed, and free scope is given to the new religion.

Thus this part of the prophetic book depicts the downfall of Jerusalem, and consequent triumph of Christianity over Judaism. The Son of Man came in fearful majesty, to punish the guilty nation, as had been predicted. Some, indeed, deny the existence of a catastrophe in the eleventh chapter, supposing, that although it should naturally be there, it is procrastinated. It is, indeed, slightly touched upon; but even that may be satisfactorily accounted for. The twenty-fourth chapter of Matthew treats of the same subject, though in much briefer compass, and may be reckoned the groundwork of this portion of the book, with which it should be carefully compared.

The second division of the Apocalypse, comprehending chapters xii. — xix., depicts the sufferings inflicted on the Christians by the heathen Roman power, and the triumph of the truth over this formidable enemy. The twelfth chapter commences with a description of the Saviour's birth, who is represented as springing from the theocracy or theocratic church. Satan is malignant against him. Cast out of heaven by Michael and the good angels, Satan turns his rage upon the followers of Christ on earth. Thus far there is no account of the Romish persecuting power. It is, therefore, an appropriate inquiry, why John commences with the birth of the Saviour, and Satan's opposition to the early church, reverting to a period prior to that which had been already gone over. Why, it may be asked, does not the seer carry on the series of symbolic predictions from the destruction of the Jewish power? Why does he not commence at the point where he paused in the preceding chapter?

This question is not readily answered. The brief notice of the Saviour's birth, and of Satan's unsuccessful attempt in heaven, and against the Holy Child, is merely introductory to the proper subject. Perhaps John carries back his readers to the origin of Christianity when Satan was peculiarly active, the more naturally to connect that Spirit's malignant opposition, as embodied in the persecuting violence of heathen Rome, with his unceasing attacks on the truth even from the very birth of Christ. This might serve to keep alive in the reader's recollection the memory of Satan's past opposition to religion, and prepare, at the same time, for an easier apprehension of symbols descriptive of additional malevolence on the part of the arch-enemy. Thus the second part properly begins with the thirteenth chapter, the twelfth being simply introductory.

A beast rises out of the sea with seven heads and ten horns. Satan gives it power. The heathen power of Rome, instigated and aided by the devil, was permitted to make war with the saints, and to overcome them. Another beast appears to assist the former, having two horns like a lamb, and speaking as a dragon. The latter symbolises the heathen priests assisting the civil power to crush the Saviour's adherents. This is followed by a vision of the Lamb and the one hundred and forty-four thousand elect standing on Mount Zion. The vision is probably introduced at the present place to sustain and elevate the hopes of the struggling Christians during the dominance of this power. Such as had passed triumphant through their fiery trials sing a new song of victory in the undisturbed possession of everlasting happiness. Three angels are now introduced, proclaiming the speedy downfall of heathenism, and divine judgments on the persecuting power. The first announces that the everlasting gospel should be preached—the second, that the great city Rome is fallen—the third speaks of tremendous judgments that should befall those who apostatized to heathenism; while, on the other hand, a voice from heaven announces the blessedness of those who die in the Lord. But, although the adversaries of Christianity being impenitent must be destroyed, the crisis is not yet arrived. It is delayed. The Saviour again appears sitting on a white cloud, with a sharp sickle in his hand. Three angels also appear with the same instrument, and the harvest is reaped. The catastrophe rapidly approaches. Seven angels are seen with seven vials, which are successively poured out on the seat of the beast. The first six torment and weaken the Roman heathen power in different ways until it is ready to fall. At last the seventh angel discharges his vial of wrath and heaven resounds with the cry, *it is done!* while voices, thunders, lightnings and a mighty earthquake, conspire to heighten the terror and complete the catastrophe. Rome is divided into three parts; the cities of the heathen fall, the islands flee away, and the mountains subside. Men tormented, blaspheme God. After this, the destruction of the Romish power is described more particularly. The writer enters into detail. An angel takes the prophet to show him more closely the desolation of this enemy. The Roman power, then reigning, is indicated somewhat mysteriously, though in such a way as would be intelligible to the Christians specially addressed by the writer. The persecuting heathen power is embodied and personified in Nero, who, though not named, is yet indicated. He is 'the beast that was, and is not, and yet is.' Babylon, or Pagan Rome, being represented as fallen, the few remaining believers are exhorted to come out of her. A mighty angel casts a great stone into the sea, an emblem of the utter destruction of that antichristian power. Heaven resounds with praises. The marriage-supper of the Lamb is announced; and the church is permitted to array herself in fine linen. But the destruction is not yet completed. Another act in the great drama remains. A battle is to be fought with the combined powers of heathenism. The conqueror on the white horse appears again, and an angel calls upon the fowls to come and eat the flesh of the Lord's enemies, for the victory is certain. Accordingly, the beast and false prophet are taken captive, and cast alive into the lake of fire and brimstone. The congregated hosts are slain by the word of the Redeemer. Such is the second great catastrophe—the fall of the persecuting heathen power—the triumph of Christianity over paganism.

The third leading division of the book extends from chap. xx. to xxii. 6. This is the only portion which stretches into a period far remote from the writer's time. It was annexed apparently for the purpose of completing the delineation of Christ's kingdom, and its chief foes on earth. Though his main design was accomplished in the preceding chapters, John was reluctant, so to speak, to leave the sublime theme, without glancing at distant times, when the triumphs of righteousness should be still more marked and diffusive, when Satan's power should be remarkably restrained, and the last great onset of heathen and antichristian power terminate for ever the church's existence on earth, ushering in the general judgment, the everlasting woe of the wicked, and the glorified state of the righteous. Here the author's sketches are brief and rapid. But when we consider the place in which they are introduced, the inconceivable nature of the happiness referred to, and the tendency of minds most imbued with the spirit of Christianity to attach sensuous ideas to figures descriptive of everlasting misery and endless felicity, their brevity is amply justified. A glorious period now commences, how long after the preceding events is not affirmed. Perhaps a considerable interval may be assumed. Satan is bound, or, in other words, his influences are signally restrained, for the space of a thousand years, throughout the seat of the beast. Christianity is remarkably diffused and prevails in the Roman empire. But at the expiration of the thousand years, Satan is set free, and begins again to practise his deceptions. He incites Gog and Magog to battle. The camp of the saints and the beloved city are invaded by the assembled hosts. But fire from heaven devours the adversaries, while the devil is again taken and cast into the lake of fire. After this but at what interval we know not, comes the general resurrection, the last judgment, and the doom of the wicked. A new heaven and a new earth are prepared for the righteous, in which they shall be perfectly free from sin and corruption. Here the visions terminate, and an epilogue closes up the book.

From this outline it will be seen that the body of the work consists of three leading divisions, in which are pourtrayed the proceedings of God towards the Jews; the rise and progress of the Christian church, until, through much struggling, it possessed the Roman empire, partly by converting, and partly destroying the heathen; the millennium, succeeded by the resurrection and judgment, and the glorious felicity of the saints in the heavenly Jerusalem.

In this country little advance has been made in the interpretation of the Apocalypse, since the days of Mede. The mysterious disclosures of John have been long wrapped in obscurity. Few possessed of proper qualifications have applied the requisite labour and patience for the purpose of unfolding their meaning. It is high time that such a state of things should cease. The church of God has slumbered long enough over this portion of the Bible. Let her at length awake to its sublime utterances, and discover the lessons they were intended to convey.

The present work of professor Stuart is well adapted to excite the inquiring student to fresh investigations. It opens up a mode of interpreting the Apocalypse almost new to the reader. Few English commentators have trodden in the same exegetical path. Following out the method of investigation opened up by Herder, Eichhorn, Ewald, and Lücke, the learned author has been highly successful in the dark and difficult region through which he has passed. Henceforward this commentary must be a standard book in the estimation of impartial and independent inquirers. There is none in the compass of the English, or even of the German language, that can be compared with it in depth of learning, fundamental research, and general correctness of results. The venerable author has laboured long over it—not in vain. As the last great work which the world may expect from his pen—the legacy he bequeathes to the people of God—we accept it with thankfulness. It is the parting gift of one, who through good report and through bad, has held on his way, maintaining an honourable place among the eminent biblical expositors of the last thirty years. We pronounce no unmeaning or hasty opinion. We had arrived at the same results, as the preceding article will testify. And yet we fear that the religious world will be slow in awarding its meed of approbation to the work before us. The views developed in it are novel in this land, a circumstance sufficient with many to ensure their rejection. They are contrary to old opinions and current prejudices, and therefore by a species of logic not uncommon, they must be *neological*. Above all, they exclude Rome papal from the Apocalypse. That is 'the unkindest cut of all.' It will not be readily forgiven. The weapons drawn from the Revelation against Romanism have been wondrously serviceable to theological disputants on the protestant side; and it will be a hard struggle to give up these tried weapons for the sake of others strictly legitimate. But let not the right-minded inquirer fear to follow out truth in all its bearings, wherever he discovers it. It demands and deserves every sacrifice, for its own sake. Let him not be ashamed to adopt whatever commends itself to his best judgment, whether he find it in protestant or papal writers. For ourselves, we have been for some time convinced that the year-day theory in prophécy is wholly untenable. Setting out from this principle, we endeavoured to obtain a comprehensive view of the Apocalypse—a view, which when subsequently compared with that of the present writer, was discovered to be generally accordant. Unequivocally, therefore, do we set our seal to the correctness of the essential features belonging to the present commentary. It were to be wished, indeed, that the author had studied greater compression. Perhaps, too, he might have omitted, without detriment, the dissertations at the commencement of the first volume relative to apocryphal revelations. The remaining dissertations in the volume are valuable and masterly specimens; while the excursus at the close of the second volume satisfy our desires in regard to a more extended discussion of the difficult topics arising in the body of the commentary. On the whole, this book on the Apocalypse is incomparably the best that has yet appeared. In all the higher qualities which constitute proper commentary, it is pre-eminently abundant. The writer has entered into the spirit of the inspired composition, and shed a welcome light on its dim drapery. Future commentators, grateful for the assistance here afforded, will be stimulated to obtain a clearer insight into the meaning of the prophet, to correct what is erroneous, and to confirm the characteristic outlines of the exposition now submitted to the public.

Art. IV.—*The Fall of Napoleon: An Historical Memoir*. By Lieut.-Col. J. Mitchell, H. P. 3 Vols. London.

Whoever has attended to the process by which the counsel on opposite sides of a cause present the same facts through different media, leaving the judge and jury to pick their way to what is in most cases a kind of mean result, will easily recognize a parallel in what takes place in respect of the history of important events, as long as time has not allayed the poignancy of the feelings and interests with which both sides of the question are regarded. But even during this period, the mass of the spectators have a kind of instinct which tells them, like the rustic who attended discussions in Latin in the schools, that extremes are never right, and violence either of praise or blame is almost always in the wrong. Men and their actions are invariably of a mingled yarn. According to the saying attributed to Fox, 'They all do the best they can when they are in, and the worst they can when they are out.' Scarcely any evil springs from the pure desire of mischief; and the man must have scantily studied human nature, who is quick to ascribe the advent of good, to unmingled efforts of virtue in the actors. Men are born to interests made to their hands; and they ordinarily take the liberty to make the best of them they can. Meanwhile those whose interests happen to be the same, shout 'genius,' and 'hero,' at every instance of success; and those whose interests are opposite, look askance on everything which in their hearts they could wish to have been undone.

Unlimited by any positive boundary as are the possibilities, by which knowledge and talent may be disappointed of success, and ignorance raised to prosperity by the effects of what may be denominated chance, there are still degrees to which men will never admit the operation of these principles. It would be impossible, for instance, to induce any general belief, that Philidor won his games through the intervention of chance working in favour of a most ill-disposed head for chess; or that the mariner who guides his vessel to a hair's-breadth during a shifting storm, is a specimen of what the first landsman who should be put into his place, would do as well if he had only fortune. Men are so well known to do their best to store and acquire skill in the several arts from which they expect comfort or aggrandizement, that to imagine the director of a hundred battles so little improved by practice as that his 'dull mind' should have a difficulty in comprehending that when, for instance, he saw Moscow turning into ashes before him, affairs were going ill with him,—is a demand on the acquiescence of the company, which would not be complied with if the weapons were cricket-balls, and the stake a tavern-dinner. That millions of men should have been filled with the belief, that an individual had done for them what, whether good or evil in itself, called on them to jeopard their lives gladly in his cause; —that this faith should have survived misfortune upon misfortune, and when the object has been for twenty years removed by death, should even yet be half-disposed to rally about everything bearing the name or the appearance of connexion with the original stock;—that this should be, and be all wrong and a mistake, an effusion of reverence for talent which never existed and of gratitude for advantages which anybody else could equally have bestowed;—is what, in the naval metaphor, may be told to the amphibious marines, but will have no chance for acceptation among those whose wits have been sharpened by a more regular apprenticeship to the seamanship of life.

It would be contrary to the objects of this publication, to enter into a lengthened examination of whether Napoleon looked as might be desired of him, when calamity upon calamity was announced to him in Russia; whether the success at Marengo was owing most to his own arrangements, or to the dogged resolution of the troops and the fortunate arrival of a reinforcement; or whether a movement in *échelons* or a retreat by alternate battalions, would have been most like what would have been seen by an impartial spectator witnessing the exertions of the rugged republicans on that hard-fought day. If Napoleon was not the spring of all or any of the victories of Frenchmen, he did a vastly more difficult thing, in persuading them of it against the fact. When Austrian armies capitulated at Ulm, and Prussian fortresses opened their gates to light cavalry, in the conviction that it was 'in vain to resist Napoleon,' can anybody throw light on the means by which this reputation was compassed, except by some connexion with Xenophon's old rule, that 'as the way to be trusted as a good pilot, is to really be one,' so in politics and war the shortest road to reputation is for a man to be what he would be taken for?

What doubly strengthens the conclusion is, that the French leader had no factitious advantages to begin with, but on the contrary was thrown into the very rush and torrent of competition, when all dams and flood-gates had been just thrown down to put every man upon a footing. A born prince is sure to have credit for merits that he has not, and to find any that he has, nursed into advancement; but what would be his chance if turned out naked to the competition of the world? If any man doubt, let him try.

Now that something like a generation of men has passed between the acts and their reviewers, it is not difficult to trace out a reasonable theory of both the causes and the qualities which led to the general result. A certain mixture of what is denominated chance or fortune, there must have been; particularly in the beginning of the individual's career. An infant notoriety is as easily suppressed by what goes under the name of accident, as an infant personality; and to escape these initiatory risks, is as important in one case as in the other. But to the rise and progress of Napoleon, two things essentially contributed,—the want felt of a man, and his being felt to be the man that suited the want. The French revolution, as most know now, was the outburst of a growing dissatisfaction with the artificial inequalities of society; a phenomenon to which, if not let off by abatements competent to the effect, there is a tendency in all countries where the numerous classes are increasing in knowledge faster than their masters. In France the convulsion was exasperated by the length of time the evil had been growing, and the extent to which the dissatisfaction had been spread. The interference of foreigners acted like water upon the Greek fire, and only made its violence the greater. The want of France was, first, deliverance from foreigners; and next, security from them for the future; which last was not unnaturally, though beyond certain limits perhaps not correctly, estimated by the extent to which the tables could be turned on the invaders. When the capital of a nation has been attempted by a coalition, as the means of imposing political shackles on the community, a consequence to be calculated on by the concerned, is that if the attempt fails, the nation will go to the capitals of the others in turn if it is able. France felt this longing; and Napoleon gave token of gratifying the desire. The soldier is quick in estimating the talents of his leaders, and attaches himself to the best by a kind of natural attraction. After the death of Turenne, the French soldiers called out, '*Lachez la pie,*' ('Let loose the pied mare,') as intimating that their old commander's horse would show them the way to victory better than his successors; and their posterity in the revolutionary armies evinced equal tact in knowing who led them with effect. And for this also there was a reason; for effect of this kind comes by cause. But all great causes are simple; nothing great is ever produced by a coalition of multitudinous causes, any more than disease is cured by a mixture of the contents of all the phials of the apothecary.

The leading secret of Napoleon's war-craft, consisted in an inversion of the current rules of warfare. He did what Copernicus did with the planetary system,—made what was in the centre and in the circumference change places. The old theory was, that an army which was what was called 'turned,'—that is to say, which had got hostile bodies on its flanks or rear,—was beaten; whence it was concluded, that the good position of forces was to occupy as much as possible of the circumference of the circle, and the fatal one was to be in the centre. That this was so, is proved not only by the practice of war, and by the terms which to unprofessional ears have been made familiar by history; but by books ingeniously written, and issued as authorities for the circulation of the fact. Napoleon was the first to perceive and practically demonstrate, that in this there was a confusion between what is true of masses close at hand, and the same masses at a distance from one another;—that the mistake lay in thinking the consequences were the same, whereas they were opposite. If of two forces of equal numerical strength, one was closely attacked by the other disseminated on its flanks and rear, there was no doubt of the disadvantage to the force so attacked. But if the bodies intending to attack were at the distance of some days' marches from the force to be attacked and from each other, the latter force had always the chance of marching on one of the other bodies with superior strength, and overwhelming it before it could be succoured by the rest. To this principle, with the various modifications and extensions of which it is capable, may be traced the greatest part of the successes which at one time appeared to chain victory to the standards of the French leader. And it was in proportion as the principle became known, and was either applied in turn or means to counteract it were devised, that its efficacy began to fail. Nevertheless permanent effects were left. As war, according to General Foy's expression, 'is become plebeian by the invention of fire-arms,' so Napoleon's discovery and its consequences have established the security of an interior mass like that presented by the liberal and improved portions of the European continent, against any efforts of the less civilized populations which may tenant the circumference. What grief, that some great accession to human happiness should not have been the more direct result! What sorrow, that a military revolution which changed the face of Europe, should not have been immediately directed to the establishment of some great principle to which man might have looked with gratitude through the ages that were to come!

Not that there was an entire absence of any such principle; but there was not enough, and what there was, was allowed to dwindle and go out, till it was not sufficient to keep up the flame. He *did* establish the equality of the numerous classes in power and talent to their masters all the earth over, and broke down with a vengeance the prejudice that the *sangre azul* ('blue blood') as the Spaniards call the fluid of a different colour from other people's surmised to flow in the veins of aristocracy, was essential to success. But he carried out his principle poorly into its consequences. He sowed the seed, and then set about rooting up the harvest. To great accessory principles he was impervious. What, for instance, might have been the consequences of such a principle as the Freedom of Commerce coming into combination with the intellect of a popular world-governor? But Napoleon was talking nonsense about 'political economy destroying an empire if it were made of granite.' How was it he never talked of military tactics destroying an army if it were made of giants? Was there reason in assuming in one case more than in the other, that the application of the human understanding was to lead to absurdity, or if there was absurdity, there was any thing to do but to demonstrate it? '*Ignorance, sheer ignorance!*' as the great lexicographer said when asked how he came to give a wrong explanation of a term in farriery. The one knew as little of political economy, as the other of the pastern of a horse. The conqueror of Marengo and Austerlitz blundered like a born squire; and as the squires will do, he paid for it.

And this points to the actual sources of Napoleon's fall. He fell because no grand motives were supplied for keeping up what may be called the steam; and because such as was raised —and enormous was the quantity upon the whole—was wastefully applied. Men grew tired of expending their lives by wholesale, for no end but that France should be admitted to have the finest army in the world. While it was for homes and freedom, the case was different; but the impetus from these sources, though it went on long, could not go on for ever. In France in 1814, even the little boys were turning sulky, and vowing they would not be shot like dogs, to please '*cet homme-là.*' There had been an enormous waste, a terrible throwing away of precious material, even the blood and marrow of the citizens. It needed some notable romance to keep up the sacrifices so steadily and so long; and when the sacrifices only increased as the romance grew more distant and indistinct, there can be no wonder that the race was run out at last.

Nothing is so easy as to pick holes in a man's conduct after the event has been unfavourable. But without running much risk, two cases, one of commission and the other of omission, may be specified as having had a powerful influence upon the fall which ensued. The first was the occupation of Spain; the other, the not restoring the independence of Poland. The placing Joseph on the throne of Spain, will be called an unmixed crime by those whose interests were opposed to it; but there was a considerable party among the Spaniards themselves, though certainly not approaching to a majority, who viewed the change in something like the same manner as the English did the revolution which placed a Dutchman on the throne. It may be politic to dwell upon the romance of Spanish resistance, headed by fighting monks, and followed by the acclamations of 'the universal Spanish nation;' but everybody knows that the 'Afrancesados' were a numerous body, though not a very powerful or energetic one, consisting to a great extent of the same better-informed and middle classes, who afterwards made the resistance to Don Carlos. It is not very 'glorious,' for men to invite a foreigner to seat himself upon their country's throne; but no man can say what bad government may drive him to. The English were driven to it, and prospered. In Spain, the difference of proportions made the difference.

In addition to this it should be remembered, that the Spanish government had been taken in the act of inciting the people to arms against their nominal allies, at the time when the French armies marched against Prussia. The fact is little known or borne in mind; but Colonel Mitchell is not a dubious evidence.

'When, therefore, the French marched against Prussia, the cabinet of Madrid deemed the proper time come to throw off the dishonourable yoke which had so long pressed upon the country. A royal proclamation calling the people to arms had already been issued, when the news of the French victories of Jena and Auerstadt quickly arrested all farther efforts This attempted shield-raising was not overlooked by Napoleon; and though no enemy was mentioned in the proclamation, he easily saw that it was aimed at himself; and therefore ordered the best Spanish troops to be sent to his assistance in Germany, and imposed other heavy obligations on the government. All were submitted to by the terrified cabinet of Madrid, but this was now too late; and no sooner had the peace of Tilsit given him free hands, than he resolved on some decisiv measure respecting the Spanish monarchy.'—*Memoir*, vol. i. p 106.

'Attempted shield-raisings' of this kind, are not apt to be overlooked by anybody; and nothing is more common than for cabinets to be 'terrified,' when they are caught in the experiment and fail. The fact here commemorated by Colonel Mitchell, is sufficient to show, that the occupation of Spain was not the unprovoked piece of melodramatic mischief it may have been represented at Astley's.

The refusal to organize the kingdom of Poland, was evidence of the extent to which the man had departed from the rock whence he was hewn. It was mainly the consequence of his connexion with Austria; and that again was the consequence of his determination to 'sink into a king.' It was a grievous delict; and as fearfully was it paid for.

It is common to say, that Napoleon's ability was less marked in calamity than in success. What man's is not? Military men put small faith in the accounts of extraordinary geniuses, who turn defeat into the means of victory. A failure is always an awful thing; and there is generally very little to be done, but let the enemy tire himself, and begin again. In his operations in Germany after the retreat from Russia, and in those previous to the battle of Waterloo, Napoleon showed that his notions of defence were in making it offensive. At the latter period, he was lost again through his inability to remember his revolutionary origin. A dozen words which should have roused the old republican feeling in his behalf, might have sent fifty thousand national guards into La Vendée, and liberated thirty thousand regulars posted there; an accident capable of having given a different version of the battle. On the whole the great lesson is, that when the people fight, they conquer; and when they do not, rulers must take the consequences.

Of the technicalities scattered through the work, there are not many which can be made interesting to those who are likely to be readers here. The author's contempt for what he terms the 'button-stick' system, and the rest of the regulations which, as he says, make the life of the soldier a continual martyrdom, will carry with them general approbation. Nobody is the worse for a soldier being clean; and a uniform and facings help to keep him out of mischief. But beyond this, all is 'hay, straw, stubble.' One question of more attractive interest however, is debated. If the author of the 'Memoir' is not misunderstood, he sees a probability of the time returning, when cavalry, the aristocratic arm, shall ride down the plebeian infantry, and neutralize the effects of the invention of gunpowder on popular power. As wonders have been remarked to sink in the grasp of the computist, so also do theories. A statement of arithmetic appears a barrier in the way. An infantry soldier occupies twenty-two inches in breadth, and a horse occupies thirty-six. If the ranks of the infantry are two, as is the least they are ever intended to be, each horseman of the first rank has from three to four musquet balls directed against him, on the supposition that the infantry make only one discharge; and it does not appear that his condition is improved, if there is a second rank of horsemen behind him. And if the infantry form four or six deep against the attack, as is always supposed to be done where surprise does not enter as an element, the chances against each horseman are doubled or trebled. Military reports are uncertain, and often distorted by prejudice in the actors; and it is remarkable that the author's own facts in the aggregate tell against his theory, though he would probably say this was only because things were as they ought not. Let any man ask himself, on which side he would prefer to take his chance; and it is probable he will come to the conclusion, that there will be 'Battles of Drumclog' hereafter if anybody insists upon it, and that there is no danger of the popular arm being systematically ridden down on anything like an equal front to begin with, by all the chivalry of the past or of the future.

The retired and peaceful student may possibly ask for what then have men in all ages gone to the expense of providing cavalry at more than double the cost of the foot soldier, if these after all are not to be capable of riding down the others in equal numbers, to say nothing of doing it when they are double? Such of them as understood their work, did it not because the thing produced was to be intrinsically and universally superior, but because it was to be of increased use under certain circumstances. There was consequently a use and there was a non-use; and the business of a military statesman, was to hit if he could, the proportion which gave the maximum of result. Some, as the barbarous and nomadic nations, have never hit it; and the consequence has been that history is full of the beatings they have got from the more civilized pedestrians. The Greeks and Romans cared little for all the cavalry in the universe, considered merely as instruments of combat against infantry, though none have more scientifically noted and laid down the circumstances under which its operations were essential to an army. But they no more thought of creating cavalry with the view to riding down infantry as a general system, than of employing it against stone walls. And it is scarcely to be maintained (though this perhaps is part of the theory questioned) that the horsemen who are to move to the attack without the power of injuring their opponents until actual contact, are not placed under increased disadvantages by the invention of gunpowder. Ask the surgeons, what will be the effects of a thousand musquet balls fired into a body of cavalry, compared with the effects of a thousand *pila*, for which the horseman is probably able to return as good as he receives. But it is conceived that the current of opinion among military men does not lie with the theory of the author of the 'Memoir.' The battle of Waterloo was a crowning evidence of the consequences of underrating the defensive power of the infantry weapon. The boast of the French infantry was that there was no position they could not carry, just as it has been the boast of the English seamen that there was no line they could not break; and it had for half a century been something like an axiom among military men, that everybody that trusted to the defence of positions was beaten. The French tried it, against opponents who gave the intrinsic powers of the infantry weapon fair play; and then the physical effect of the weapon *told*. With certain limitations, the combat might be compared to that of a hundred tigers moving to attack a hundred men armed with Tower musquets. The tigers did what could be done; but they had the worst of it. They were in the main shot to pieces and disorganized, before they got into contact with their enemies; so another time the tigers will go a different way to work. If there should ever be war again on a large scale, the result of Waterloo will alter the conduct of battles. There will be fewer attacks on positions; and positions on the whole, like fortresses, will fall and not rise in military importance, because men will improve in the art of letting them alone.

And this leads to another of the theories of the author of the 'Memoir,' in which it is impossible not to agree with him. If a cat is found posted in a bee-hive, what necessity can there be for proceeding to take her out in front, if the effect of upsetting the intended combination can be produced another way? Is not all reason in favour of operating against the point where the opponent is *not* strong, rather than where he is? It may be quite true, that if the opponent is discomfited on his strong point, it will produce a marked effect upon him everywhere else. But does this prove that therefore the strong point is to be selected for attack? Is it not the error of the unfortunate political strategists among ourselves who said, 'Attack nothing but the citadel, because when it is carried the rest will fall.' The example cited by the author of the 'Memoir,' is in point; where Marlborough, though he did not escape the error of attacking the village of Blenheim because it was strong,—when foiled there, succeeded in other parts, and then twenty-seven battalions and twelve squadrons in Blenheim laid down their arms. If things could be done twice over, why was the village to be attacked at all? In like manner, why did Napoleon destroy fifteen hundred men in attacking Hougomont, because the English were loop-holed and under cover there? And why, at another period of the day, did he attack the buildings at *La Haie Sainte?* Why not try what might be done where the opponent was *not* covered, and so at all events give a version of the battle for which he was not prepared? And above all, after detaching Grouchy with a view to separate the Prussians from the English, why not make the attack upon the flank which tended to keep them separate and at the same time approximate to Grouchy, and not upon the other? These are points on which it is not easy to make answer, except that the weather was unfavourable to the party which had to move; a reason the more, it might have been thought, why the opponent should not have been attacked in his bee-hive, where he was settled to advantage. It is sometimes difficult to say, whether human design is allowed any influence on human affairs or not.

There would be little use in entering on the objections of the author of the 'Memoir,' to the *Code Napoléon*. The extent of parental authority and testamentary power, the propriety or impropriety of the equal division of property among children, and the classes of society to whom divorce shall be permitted or virtually refused, are all points on which men of strong political feelings in different directions, will interminably disagree. But on one of the author's conclusions, examination at least may be suggested. It is stated (vol. iii. p. 256) that—

> 'The free towns of Germany, on which it [the *Code Napoléon*] was forced during the period of French supremacy, returned to their ancient form of laws as soon as they were liberated from the yoke of France.'

There may be disputes on terms; but it appears to be in some degree of contradiction to the general spirit of this, that in what are called the Rhenish provinces, which formerly belonged to France and now to Prussia, the people are understood to have refused to part with the *Code Napoléon,* however disagreeable such a proof of Gallic predilections may be to their existing masters. A man may be worse off than under the *Code Napoléon;* as many a distracted Peter Peebles knows.

If those for whom these observations are meant, find any useful lessons drawn, or feel encouraged to the belief that full as human affairs are of evil, there is still provision that they shall not retrograde; the purpose intended will be fully accomplished.

Art. V *History of Our Own Times. By the Author of 'The Court and Times of Frederick the Great.'* Vol. I. and II. Colburn, London, 1834 and 1845.

This work, of which one volume was published in 1843 and a second just recently, comes down only to the year 1797, and terminates with the Battle of Camperdown. At this period the Reign of Terror in France was ended: Buonaparte had put down the insurrection of the sectionaries with cannon, and by his campaign in Italy had commenced that great and amazing career, which laid all Europe, England excepted, eventually at his feet. The volumes yet to come have, therefore, to narrate the mighty and crowding events of those unexampled years of warfare, which were terminated by the Battle of Waterloo, and the general peace in 1815, and the not less striking and eventful changes of the thirty subsequent years of peace which, especially in this country, have marked the onward progress of social reform and scientific wonder. It is evident that it must yet require a considerable number of volumes to embrace and detail all those years and their developments. Under these circumstances we shall abstain from doing more than endeavouring to give a general idea of the spirit and manner in which the work is executed.

The idea of this 'History of Our Own Times' is excellent. It is evident that for general readers, and for all who are desirous of possessing a clear and continuous narrative of those stirring times, there needs a careful and skilful gleaning of the most essential matter out of the minute details, and the many political disquisitions of the more voluminous histories. For schools, for young people, for all who would arrive at a comprehensive and well-grounded conception of the transactions of the last half century, the most remarkable period of the modern world, such a work is absolutely necessary. Well grounded in the perspicuous narrative of such a work, they are then better able to comprehend, to lay hold of, and retain the more expansive statements of larger histories; and in most of the qualities that should distinguish such work, we have no hesitation in saying that this history is in successful possession. It is written with remarkable perspicuity, and in general, judgment of the real and relative importance of the circumstances which it deals with. There is a great air of impartiality, wherever foreign facts and personages are concerned; the style is pure and good, and it has a temperate tone that pleases the reader and makes him deliver himself up willingly to the guidance of the author.

But the history has, notwithstanding, one serious defect, and this we must endeavour to make plain, not because we would have the reader to put the work itself aside, for it is well calculated, this failing being once understood, to aid his acquirement of a knowledge of the history of his own times, but to put him on his guard, and thus to enable him to read on in perfect security, having the key to the author's little foible in his hand.

That foible, and we dare say it is a most honest one, in the author, is that of a quiet conservatism which sways him, perhaps unconsciously, in his treatment of our own domestic transactions and personages. There is nothing vehement or rampant about him, he aims at no sophistical eloquence, or fiery declamation which might bring over his readers to his own views of such things, in fact, to the ideas of a political party. But the tendency to such party notions is not the less there, and so gently, and devoid of passion does it reign and run through the narrative, that young and unsuspicious readers might not soon, or perhaps not at all perceive its existence, and thus unawares might receive a distorted impression of things. In short, the author is, perhaps constitutionally, a settled conservative, quiet and amiable as he is. This we shall soon make apparent, and this once apparent, his history may be read with certain advantage, and no great danger.

This tendency is discernable in the tone in which he generally speaks of the leaders of reform. Charles Fox is styled 'the would be champion of liberal sentiments and opinions' vol. i. p. 69. George the III. is lauded in the hackneyed phrase of 'a prince indeared to his people, by his private virtues;' though it is unquestionable that he was a bigamist; and what would be thought of the private virtues of a man in private life who married one wife, and then during her lifetime married a second. If it be scandalous in private life, nay severely amenable to the laws, how much more reprehensible ought it to be in the person of the monarch on whom all eyes are fixed, and who, as the appointed guardian of the laws, should be the last to set the example of violating them, and expecially in the department of domestic morality, on the practice of which this nation so justly prides itself. There is, however, a singular ignorance in our historians on this part of the character of George III., or as singular an attempt to pass him off as much better than he was. In Knight's Pictorial History of England, we are gravely treated to this declaration. 'Though so young, healthy, and robust, and though his predecessors had been so old, he was the first prince of his house to do without a mistress. A few months after his accession he married,' &c. Vol. i. of the Reign of George III. p. 6.

Had this writer never heard of such a person as Hannah Lightfoot, the quakeress? Her history is well-known, most thoroughly authenticated; her children are still living, and well-known too, and till lately, persons were living who were in London, and witnessed the sensation created by her abduction, or her absconding with the prince. We learn from the Beckford Conversations, lately published in the New Monthly Magazine, that she was married to the prince at Kew, by Dr. Wilmot, and that Pitt, afterwards Earl of Chatham, was present at the ceremony. What is worse, George carried her off from her friends when she was on the point of marriage with a young man of her own society, and who pursued after them and entreated him in a distraction of distress to give her up, but in vain. With the characteristic obstinacy which afterwards led him to persist in the unconstitutional taxation and coercion of America, till he lost it to this country, he married Hannah Lightfoot, and when he had children by her, coolly abandoned her at the age of twenty-three, and married Charlotte of Mecclenburg Strelitz. Now this fact must be very embarrassing to the laudators of the domestic virtues of George III., and therefore they boldly slide over it. The writer of the Pictorial History must be thrown by it into a particular dilemma. If George III. was the only one of his house, at that time, who had done without a mistress, what was Hannah Lightfoot? She was, in fact, his lawful wife: for there was then no law to prohibit the members of the royal family marrying subjects; it was George himself, taught by the trouble and the crime in which he found himself involved, who, on the plea of his brother of Cumberland's vile deeds, brought forward and passed the Royal Marriage Act.

The domestic history of George III. is one of the most awful that ever befell a monarch. The consequences of his concealment of his first marriage, were terrible to his peace of mind, and to that of more than one of his children, and in this fact are we to seek for the true causes of the overthrow of his intellect. It is not common that virtuous parents bring up a whole family of licentious profligates, and yet what family ever exhibited such a troop of the most shameless and sensual ones, as that of George III.? He saw his sons seduce and abandon one woman after another, even when, as in the case of Mrs. Jordan, they too had families, and he could not reprimand them, for he knew his own story better than they who now act the historians seem to do. It is high time that history should, however, speak the truth, and the highest praise that can be allowed to George III. is that, having married two wives, and living before the nation as a bigamist, he was at least faithful to one of them; but he set a fatal example to his children, which they only too carefully followed.

As Charles Fox is styled 'the would be champion of liberal sentiments and opinions,' so also, of course, 'the immeasurably superior political sagacity of Burke' over that of Fox is loudly vaunted. This is a favourite but a shallow and untenable theme of the Tories. That Fox, like others, was carried away by a generous enthusiasm for liberty on the outbreak of the French Revolution; that, like other generous and noble-minded men, he gave credit to the fine professions of the revolutionists, and sung their praises in eloquent strains in the House of Commons, is quite true; and it is equally true that Edmund Burke, with a less enthusiastic feeling of this sort, soon saw through the tinsel patriotism of those tigers in human shape. Burke, sooner smelt the smell of blood, and raised the cry of alarm; but in a far truer sense than it can be said of Burke, did Fox, recovering from his delusion, soon demonstrate his immeasurably superior political sagacity. Burke smelt blood, but did not abhor it; he snuffed it up, and as if inspired with a Moloch thirst of it, he

Cried havoc, and let slip the dogs of war.

'Fox,' says this writer, 'lived long enough to perceive the utter fallacy of his own notions, and to witness the fulfilment of almost all the prophetic anticipations of his illustrious master.'

Fox lived long enough to feel astonished at the brutal depravity of those men from whom he had hoped so much better things, in fact, had hoped the commencement of a new and more glorious era. He wept over and deplored the dreadful wound which liberty had received from these false votaries; but with his usual nobility of character, while he fully and freely confessed his disappointment and his sorrow, like a true man he still stood by liberty itself. He did not, like Burke, like Pitt, like Southey, and a thousand others, desert liberty 'at her utmost need.' He felt that *then*, when she had been so abused, so belied, so striken to the heart by base traitors and impostors, *then* it was that she had most need that all her genuine friends should rally round her, and support her in the hour of the deepest trial that had befallen her from the foundation of the world. Numbers now were silent who had been loudest in the chaunt of the anticipated triumph of liberty; thousands turned and fled, entering the present ranks of her enemies, like Burke, Pitt, and Southey, but Fox stood firm, and in this trying hour displayed not merely 'an immeasurably superior political sagacity' to Burke, but a far nobler nature. He saw that the betrayal of liberty would be the occasion for the rising and rallying of all her enemies. The old anarchs and monarchs of all Europe would be up to tread out the very last sparks of her sacred fire. He saw that blood and horror would flow from end to end of the so-called civilized world, unless the most strenuous efforts were made by the best minds of Britain, to resist this out-break of the hell of this world in the shape of war and brutal armies. He stood, therefore, in the gap, and denounced the call to war as loudly as Burke cried—'Up England! to arms! keep no measures with the democratic horde who would overturn thrones and ancient constitutions.' Which here, as the events have proved, showed the greater sagacity? Was it he who put the dreadful wheels of war in motion, or he who strove to stay them? Was it he who to put down the bloodshed of one country would involve all the world in it; or he who saw that to interfere with the internal arrangements of another great and independent kingdom was not only an invasion of the plainest rights of man, but was to call all the furies of earth, air, ocean, and the infernal shades, in the shape of mercenary Swiss, slavish Germans, barbarous Russians, and Cossacks, to overrun the face of all the Western World, and commence a scene of destruction to which the wild-beast-quarrel of the French, amongst themselves, was but as a mole-hill to a mountain? The astounding course of the most amazing and terrible wars which ever desolated the earth, has given a fearful answer. To Burke we owe, more than to any other man, the crime and the bloodshed of the great war of upwards of twenty years, in which, so far from putting down the French democrats, *they* put down, insulted and tyrannized over every continental kingdom. To Burke we owe it, that when finding the spirit of Europe was roused to combine against the great French conqueror, but that not until God had smitten him visibly by his own hand, in the pride of his Russian campaign, to Burke, we say, we owe it, when all continental Europe had been humiliated by France in the contest which he called for, and when millions on millions of lives had been sacrificed to his troops and his 'superior political sagacity,' that we ourselves came out of the contest with the expenditure of *three thousand millions of money*, of which eight hundred millions yet remain unpaid, hanging on our commerce like a millstone, creating corn-laws and a pressure of taxation which falls with a crushing weight on those labouring millions who were not living to enjoy even the syren sound of that eloquence which fired our fathers to the thirst of French blood. Out we say on all such political sagacity as this! The time is come when we must neither sing its praises, nor allow them to be sung without a stern reproof. Reversing the language of our author, we may say that 'Burke lived long enough to have perceived, whether his pride allowed him to do so or not, the utter fallacy of his own notions, and to witness the fulfilment of almost all the prophetic anticipations of his illustrious pupil.' It was to Fox that we owed the most strenuous opposition to that fatal policy which deluged Europe with blood, and the only interval of peace that we enjoyed from 1793 to the abdication of Napoleon in 1814.

Here we come then to the further declaration on our part that the writer of this history does not confine himself to quiet terms of depreciation of the friends of liberty; he has a graver fault, he may state the truth, but he does not state the whole truth of things. Thus, he terms the Dissenters enemies to the church, and propagators of mischievous political doctrines.

'Many men, eminent for rank, talents, and understanding, extolled the French Revolution' (this was so early as 1792) 'without, however, openly disparaging the constitution of their own country. Dr. Price, who was reverenced as an apostle by the Dissenters, approved the principles of the French Revolution even in their most ruinous consequences to kings and people. Dr. Priestley, a Unitarian minister, celebrated for his chemical discoveries, lent the influence of his name to the same doctrines. A society called the Friends of the Revolution, &c.' vol. ii. p. 3.

This should be 'The Society of the Friends of the People;' not of the Revolution. But he proceeds:

'Some of the principal members, and a large proportion of the general mass of this society, were Dissenters. Dr. Price, who was a very conspicuous member, died in 1791. It included also Drs. Kippis, Rees, and Towers, men whose literary abilities and moral characters, in proportion as they added weight to the association, only gave it so much the more power of doing mischief,' &c. &c.

Who would believe that this *mischievous* society, was actually no other than that which was established merely for Parliamentary Reform in 1791—that society from which we have, as the first public moving cause, derived the ouly portion of reform we have yet gained? Who would, if he were not better acquainted with our recent history than this writer would make us, imagine that this mischievous society had at its head, as its originators, almost all those great, yet moderate men, who lived to see the desires of the English public far outgrow those ideas of necessary change which in them this author styles so dangerous? Those men, the founders of this society were—The Earl of Lauderdale, Sir James Mackintosh, Lord Kinnaird, Sir Philip Francis, General Lambton, the father of Lord Durham, Whitbread, Tierney, Dudley North, Thomas, afterwards Lord Erskine, Lord John Russell, uncle of the present Lord John, Rogers the poet, Sheridan, Lord Grey, Fox, George Byng, with those Drs. Towers and Kippis, &c. &c. Such are the bugbears of revolutionary crime, with which the writer of the 'History of our Own Times,' classes the Dissenters. They will not be much shocked at the alliance, but the truth of history resents such partial statements.

In the like strain he speaks of the proceedings of the Dissenters leading to the riots of Birmingham in 1791, and the destruction of vast property, including the house and noble library of Dr. Priestley; but he does not tell us that it was the act and instigation of the Tory magistrates and clergy themselves that brought out this brutal mob, with their savage cries of 'Church and the King.' A fact like this, than which there is none better authenticated, or notoriously established, ought not to have been omitted when the Dissenters were accused of practices and principles dangerous to the public peace. In the debates, on the disgraceful event at the time, it was fully proved before the House of Commons, that the magistrates of the town had not only connived at the atrocities which the populace had perpetrated, but had actually instigated them to their commission, and that the clergy themselves had been conspicuous in raising and leading on the ignorant and bestial mob. These charges were supported by six-and-thirty affidavits laid before the House by Whitbread.

When the Dissenters are stigmatized as enemies of the church, it becomes a fair historian, and one who desires to be a sound teacher of the people, to state *why* and *how* they are enemies to it. To do this he has only to revert to the simple fact that the church, as a state machine has, from the very day of her origin, acted the she-wolf to the Dissenters. It was the church which first created dissent by its intolerance of opinion, and then sought to crush it by fire, racks, dungeons, political exclusion, and political plunder, in the shape of tithes, church-rates, Easter dues, &c. The church at one time even prevailed to have an act passed that no Dissenter should keep a school. They were to be annihilated by abstinence of literary and intellectual food. For this reason the Dissenters are justly hostile to the church, as a *state* church, and not otherwise. This is *why* and *how* the Dissenters are enemies to the church, and this cause ought not to be overlooked by the historian. The same mode of treatment is, however, adopted by our author towards all reformers. This passage occurs in the history of the year 1793.—

'Though the political ferment was rapidly subsiding, a considerable agitation still prevailed. In Scotland, public attention was strongly excited by the prosecution of Thomas Muir, a member of the faculty of Advocates, and Fyshe Palmer, a member of the University of Cambridge, acting as Unitarian minister at Dundee. In autumn, 1792, when the political agitation was at its height, the former a man of but moderate abilities, though possessing the faculty of unpremeditated eloquence in an extraordinary degree, collected and harangued numerous assemblages of the common people on the subject of popular reform, which produced an appearance of turbulence and disorder, alarming not only the government, but even persons disposed to favour the political sentiments which he avowed. The latter was found guilty of publishing a political libel, not written by himself, but which he had corrected, and ordered to be printed. Both were sentenced to transportation, Muir for fourteen, Palmer for seven years, and accordingly sent to Botany Bay. The severity of their sentence, though conformable to the practice of the Scottish courts, was censured by many as unreasonable; but it was reserved for the sagacity of a later period to discover that these presented a just claim to the title of political martyrs, and a public monument in the metropolis of the empire.'—Vol. ii. p 50.

Now, whether they were political martyrs or not, discovered by 'the sagacity of a later period,' that is, of a period when the inflamed passions of the day, which witnessed those proceedings, have died out with the parties they agitated, not merely have the inhabitants of the 'metropolis of the empire' decided' by erecting a monument to these persecuted men, but, at a still later period, that is, at this very time, the inhabitants of the metropolis of that kingdom in which they were condemned, have confirmed that decision by also erecting a monument to their memory there. On the Calton hill, a tower-like testimony to their martyrdom in solid stone now lifts its head. These, it should be remembered, are not the products of the heated feelings of the moment, but of the after calm research and reflection of a period distinguished by a far more matured knowledge of political rights than was possessed by the last age. That they were political martyrs, let their political opinions have been what they would, is pretty well established by the fact, that neither Muir nor Palmer ever lived to reach their own country again. In fact, the whole of this statement is singularly defective in every way. Besides Muir and Palmer, there were three other persons condemned and transported at the same time, and on the same charges: Skirving, Gerald and Margarott, not one of whom survived to return to their native land except Margarott.

And for what were Muir and Palmer tried, condemned, and transported? By the account in Howell's State Trials we find that the evidence for the prosecution failed entirely to prove any intention on the part of the prisoners, or any society with which they were connected, of having recourse to insurrection, or riot, or any act of violence, much less of seeking for any French assistance.' Muir contended that he advocated only constitutional measures of reform, and had not argued for the destruction of the monarchy; and the very best witness on the part of the crown, the woman-servant that had lived in his father's house, admitted that she had heard him say that 'the constitution of this country was very good, but that many abuses had crept in which required a thorough reform—that he was for a monarchy, under proper restrictions, and a parliament that knew what they were about;—that a republican form was the best, but that a monarchy had been so long established in this country that it would be improper to alter it.'

Now is it for such opinions that men, gentlemen by birth, education, and station, or indeed any man bearing the proud name of Briton, ought to be imprisoned, brow-beaten in the foulest language by barristers and the judges set to try them? The very lord-advocate called Muir, 'that unfortunate wretch at the bar,' 'that demon of mischief,' 'that pest of Scotland,' and the lord-justice clerk on the bench said: 'Let them pack off. A government in every country should be just like a corporation; and in this country it is made up of the landed interest, *which alone has a right to be represented;* as for the rabble who have nothing but personal property, what hold has the country on them? They may pack up all their property on their backs, and leave the country in the twinkling of an eye.' Is it, we ask, for such opinions, and at such brutal hands that honourable men are to be thus treated, condemned to transportation, and thrust into the hold of transport-vessels amongst common thieves and felons; and that an historian of the present day shall sneer at them, as undeserving the name of martyrs? The writer who does this, little understands the sacred task he has undertaken, or the spirit and knowledge which now animates the mass of the people of England. On the contrary, he ought to have told his readers what was the political condition of England at that period. That the constitution was in reality destroyed by the corrupt selfishness of government. That the popular portion of the constitution was wrested out of the popular hand, and sold to borough-mongers and monopolising aristocrats. That the people were neglected, and left uneducated; and thus made, to a degree, passive under their sufferings and exactions; the hand of arbitrary power was stretched out with a brutal violence which now astonishes in the retrospect, to seize and crush the few patriotic spirits who dared to stand forth for the rights of the people. Government, venal judges, ignorant country justices, and hot high-fed clergy were then accustomed to lord it over the multitude with a reckless regard of law or humanity, which would now rouse the whole nation to a terrible state of indignation, were but an instance of it attempted. But it is to the political martyrs of the last age, that we, in a great measure, owe our present more enviable power of public opinion, the greater recognition of our inalienable rights, and we must not suffer the pen of the historic scribe to palter with the holy truth, and sneer away the honourable fame of even the humblest labourer in the great cause of political and social progress.

It may be thought that we have dealt somewhat severely with our author, when we state that after all, the portions of these volumes which contain these misrepresentations are 'few and far between.' That is true; but where great principles are concerned, and in a matter of such importance as the history of our own times, these cannot be too clearly enunciated, nor mystification of facts too earnestly set right. Moreover, these exceptions are few in these volumes, because the part which our own country plays in the drama of European action, so far as they extend, is comparatively small. The French revolution occupies far the greater portion of them. But as the author advances, this will no longer be the case. More and more, deeper and deeper, will England become implicated in the great strife, and we are therefore anxious to point out to the author the false basis on which he is building. He may make himself quite sure that it is not as he has begun, that the history of modern England is to be written. The rights of the people, their importance in the state, the factitious nature of ranks and titles and castes, all are daily becoming more truly understood, and justly appreciated, and he who will write for futurity; he who is conscientiously anxious to become a teacher of the young, must arouse himself to cast off old clinging prejudices; must look truth fully and fairly in the face, and must regard himself as writing not for this or that class, but for the nation, for whom government exists, and whose functions and deeds the general sentiment will more and more oblige it to respect, and move itself by. That public sentiment is rapidly growing into strength, because the people are better educated and better instructed in true Christian principles, and therefore more solemnly united in denouncing political profligacy, and demanding a closer conformity to the great doctrines of peace, justice, and humanity. The wretched conventionalisms which have enabled governments to represent *themselves* as the real sources of power and honour, and have taught them to wrap themselves in a proud mystery, are every day falling before the progress of knowledge, and the writer who writes to influence his age must strive to be in advance of it, and measure public acts by the eternal standard of truth, as revealed to us in the luminous philosophy of Christ.

Before closing this article we will for a moment draw the attention of the reader to a rather curious coincidence. The French Revolution was ushered in by a fearful agency of the elements. The old corrupt and tyrannic fabric of the French government, which might have gone on for years still fostering the follies and vices of the court, and grinding the faces of the poor, was brought at once to an end for ever, by as awful and manifest an act of Providence as any which is recorded in the sacred writings. It was like another Egyptian plague, when the hail, mingled with fire, smote the crops of the field.

'On Sunday, the 13th of July, 1788, about nine in the morning, an awful darkness suddenly overspread a great portion of France. It was succeeded by a tempest unexampled in the temperate climes of Europe. Wind, rain, thunder, seemed to vie in fury; but hail was the principal instrument of devastation. The rich prospect of an early harvest was changed in an hour to the dreary appearance of universal winter. The ground was converted into a morass, the standing corn beaten into a quagmire, the vines and the fruit-trees were broken in pieces, and unmelted hail lay in heaps like rocks of solid ice. The forest trees were unable to withstand the violence of the tempest. The hail consisted of solid, angular lumps of ice, some of them weighing from eight to ten ounces. The country-people, beaten down in the fields on their way to church, and terrified by this concussion of the elements, concluded that the last day had arrived, and lay despairing, half suffocated amidst the water and mud, expecting the immediate dissolution of all things. A tract of sixty square leagues had not a single ear of corn or fruit of any kind left. The Isle of France, in which Paris is situated, and the Orleannois, suffered most; the damage done there amounting, on a moderate estimate, to eighty millions of livres, or between three and four millions sterling. Such a calamity, occurring amidst a general scarcity throughout Europe, and on the eve of a great political revolution, was peculiarly unfortunate: many families found it necessary to contract their expenses, and to discharge their servants, who were thus left destitute of bread; added to the public discontents and political dissensions, it produced such an effect on the people in general, that the nation seemed to have changed its character, and, instead of that levity by which it had ever been distinguished, a settled gloom seemed to cloud every face.

'This calamity was succeeded by a winter more severe than any that had been known for nearly a century past. All the efforts of benevolence, and the extensive charities of the clergy in particular, could not keep pace with the distress prevailing in the capital, where the immense mass of indigence was swelled by numbers of vagabonds and dissolute persons, without profession and without resources, who thronged thither from all parts of France, eager to join in any tumult, and to profit by any chances.

'Nobody took such advantage of these circumstances as the Duke of Orleans, whose extraordinary wealth enabled him to confer benefits equally extraordinary on the lower classes of the people. A thousand humane acts were related of him, all of which, however, were performed with a criminal design. By this means he nevertheless made himself the man of the people; and this prince, who shortly before was an object of general contempt, was now extolled to the skies, while others, who had done as much in proportion, nay, perhaps more, were scarcely mentioned.

'The time now approached for the election of deputies to the states-general. The whole nation was in motion, and in many provinces great agitation prevailed. Men of letters, advocates, tradesmen, assembled either to procure their own election, or to influence that of others: societies, called clubs, were formed, which served to develope the talent of public speaking, but which did infinite mischief. Count Mirabeau, who was rejected by the nobles, and who had displayed eminent ability in a suit with his wife at Aix, was elected a representative of the *tiers état*, whose idol he became. He inveighed with fulminating eloquence against the nobles and the aristocracy, whom he designated as persecutors of the people, and enemies to himself. His speeches re-echoed in the remotest corners of the kingdom, and everywhere awakened a desire to imitate him. Meanwhile the deputies of each estate arrived in the capital, with totally different views of their vocation, and many with diametrically opposite intentions. Some had before their eyes Spartan, others Roman, others, again, English or American institutions—in short, the revolution had arrived.'—vol. i. pp. 61, 62, 63.

Though we fear no revolution at hand in England, who does not here see a striking coincidence of circumstances? Who does not see in the wet season that we have had, and its effect on the crops all over Europe, and especially the singular disease which has shown itself in the potatoe, as it were the hand of Providence, visibly put forth to terminate the reluctant resistance of the aristocracy of this country to allow the people of England to import and eat cheap bread? While the struggle has been from year to year going on with the selfishness of the landlords, it has become more and more impressed on the public mind that it would require some such manifestations to give a final blow to selfishness. People have said, let but a bad harvest come, and the opposition is at an end. The cry for bread will become the awful cry of a nation, which will startle the monopolists into an earnest terror. The artizan in the cellars of Manchester may get half enough, and crouch on a bag of shavings; the agricultural labourer may starve on his six shillings a week; the whole of Ireland may feed on potatoes, and nothing else; but let a real scarcity come, and the whole empire will then suffer, rich and poor, and gaunt famine will start up in such a shape, that the callous caste of landlords will shrink aghast, and let the floodgates of foreign plenty fly open. And here is the scarcity arrived, and in such a shape, and from such a quarter, as not even the deepest, and the most far-seeing of our political prophets ever for a moment dreamt of. Poor potatoe, the humble half-brother of corn, has become the unexpected agent of the mighty change. With the corn crop deficient all over Europe, and the plague in the potatoe, the rumour is gone forth, and grows daily, that ministers see that they must yield to the power of circumstances, and open the ports without delay. But once open, will the people of England permit them to shut them again? With the terrible chances that this one bad season have opened up before our eyes, are we to allow the same political machinery of injustice and starvation ever again to place us in the same or worse jeopardy? For the sake of the aristocratic rent-roll, for the luxury and the ostentation of the West-end world, shall we again see our labouring population starving, half-fed, half-clothed, cooped in Unions, or driven to the midnight woods on the deadly quest of game, at the muzzle of the gamekeepers' guns? Are we to run the risk of riot, insurrection, and general calamity, or of those fatal panics which spread atrophy and ruin through our commerce—when Providence has once sent us this emphatic warning, this dazzling hand-writing upon the wall? It is not to be believed—the ports once thrown open, must remain open.

But what is no little remarkable, is that not only the potatoe, but Ireland should be made the means of striking this salutary fear into the heart of government. Cobbett used to curse the potatoe, and say, that so far from being a blessing to Ireland, it was its greatest evil. That it enabled the Irish to live, to keep body and soul just together, and thus perpetuated the wretched condition of that country. That, had there been no potatoe there must long ago have been a famine, which would have compelled an instant change of policy towards that country.

But Ireland and the potatoe, bid fair to abolish the detestable corn-law. The potatoe crop might have failed in England, and things have gone on; but its failure in Ireland is the failure of everything. That is the sole food and resource of eight millions of people. They are on the lowest step of existence; they can fall back no further. You might as well rob a man of his skin, as an Irishman of anything, when his potatoes are gone. Thus things—the potatoe having failed in Ireland—come to a stand, and from that oppressed, and abused people, and the humble root of its maintenance, may probably come the deliverance of proud England from the greatest curse which ever befell it—the infamous corn-law.

Art. VI.—*Elements of Mental and Moral Science.* By George Payne, L.L.D. Third edition, enlarged. London: Gladding.

We are gratified to observe any symptoms of an increasing taste, in the reading public, for subjects so ominous to some who pride themselves in being practical men, as psychology and metaphysics. Whatever may be said against speculative philosophy by those who disdain the labour of thought, certain it is, that so long as the mind of man remains what it now is, no revolutions in learning and science will ever be able to divert it effectually from those inquiries which are natural to a being whose intellectual life is knowledge; and who, right or wrong, *will* form some ideas respecting the mystery of his own inward constitution. We were glad to find Sir John Herschell, at the last meeting of the British Association, sounding a note which will not die away with the progress either of the exact, or the experimental physical sciences; but will, with their advance, only tend to elicit those hidden harmonies which are latent in all branches of knowledge: for there is not one which, in its ultimate principles, does not lead us directly to the constitution of man, who forms for himself all systems, according to the laws of his own nature.

'The fact is every year becoming more broadly manifest,' says Sir John Herschell, 'by the successful application of scientific principles to subjects that had been only hitherto empirically treated, that the great work of Bacon was not the completion, but, as he himself foresaw and foretold, only the commencement of his own philosophy; and that we are even yet only at the threshold of that palace of truth, which succeeding ages will range over as their own;

a world of scientific enquiry, in which not matter only and its properties, but the far more rich and complex relations of life and thought, of passion and motive, interest and action, will come to be regarded as its legitimate objects.'

It cannot be denied, however, that, as yet, due prominence has not been given, in the higher general education, to what is usually termed *philosophy*, in distinction from exact and physico-experimental science. We have been much disappointed that so excellent an opportunity of incorporating it with other branches of knowledge, as a qualification for academical distinctions, was to so great an extent neglected, on the establishment of the University of London. Not indeed that we would demand, on the part of the *student*, an avowed adhesion to any particular form of speculative philosophy, whether empirical or transcendental. We would not ask any one to acknowledge the authority either of Plato or Aristotle, of Leibnitz, Kant, or Hegel, of the French Eclectics, or of the English or the Scottish school. But we would demand, as one of the conditions of the Bachelor's degree, a competent acquaintance with the opinions which have been most current,—a knowledge of the *History* of speculative philosophy, in its details, and in the mutual relations of the various systems. This course of training would be the best preparation for the genuine study of history, and of all the moral sciences. That speculative philosophy has been much neglected at our ancient English national seats of learning is notorious. At Dublin, in Scotland, in France, and in Germany, matters have been very different. Even the university of London, greatly as its idea of academical education is superior to that which long prevailed at Oxford and Cambridge, still makes no provision for a due acquaintance with mental philosophy, on the part of the bulk of its *alumni* in arts. It is true, indeed, that the moral sciences form one of the three roads by which the degree of master of arts may be reached, and those who choose to travel it must prepare themselves in psychology; but it is not very clear, from the present calendar, what proportion of masters have graduated on examination in the moral sciences:—we should say certainly not the majority. Indeed the number of students who have advanced to the higher degree is comparatively very small. Out of a hundred and forty-seven bachelors of arts, ninety had, according to the regulations, had time to take the master's degree up to the present year, but only *ten* had availed themselves of that distinction. We always thought it very likely that the proportion of masters to bachelors would be but small:* the greater is the necessity that a subject having so

* *Vid. 'Academical Education, and Degrees in Arts,'* 1837.

decided a bearing on the elements of all human and divine knowledge as psychology and metaphysical philosophy in general, should be provided for in the examination for the bachelor's degree. As the regulations now stand, numbers come forth every year as educated men, who may be as ignorant as they please of the subjects to which such minds as Bacon, Locke, Reid, Dugald Stewart, Kant, Jouffroi, devoted their splendid talents: nay it is not necessary even that their very *names* should be known to those who are endorsed as graduates of a university!

We are gratified, therefore, to perceive that a book on mental philosophy, no great matter of what school, has reached a third edition so comparatively soon after the publication of the second. As the work before us has already met with favorable notice in the pages of this periodical, on the publication of each of the former editions, it is unnecessary for us to dwell at length on its merits. The author has not modified any of his general principles; but still the book has undergone a careful revision, by which it has come forth in an improved state. It is also increased by notes occupying about forty pages, containing quotations from a variety of writers on mind and morals. In the portion of the volume which is devoted to pure mental philosophy, the author appears as the candid and able expositor of the philosophy of Dr. Thomas Brown. But though he chiefly follows this great Scottish metaphysician, (sometimes where we should have preferred an independent course), the work is far from being a mere compilation: every theory has passed under his own careful scrutiny. The book is well calculated to be useful to those who wish to become acquainted with the doctrines of the northern school, as they were left by the very acute, if not always very cautious, Edinburgh professor, Dr. Brown. We should have liked to see a comparison of this school with that of the most sober Germans, especially Kant; also with the French Eclecticism, as represented by Cousin and Jouffroi. We have still much to learn from the Germans, notwithstanding all their philosophical vagaries; and the modern French Eclectics have pointed out the way.

In the portion of the work which relates to ethics, the author widely differs from Brown, who lays the foundation of virtue in the arbitrary constitution of the mind. The reader cannot fail to derive advantage from the concise and enlightened criticism which is here instituted of the principal British writers on morals as a science. We are glad to find that Dr. Payne agrees so fully with ourselves on the important question relating to the existence or non-existence of *natural ethics,* as we learn by an extract which he has quoted, in his notes, from our late review of Spalding's 'Christian Morals.' In another popular work, views are maintained, which to himself, as well as to us, seem to imply that Revelation is to man the only source of the knowledge of right and wrong. We hold that this opinion is contrary to consciousness as unfolded in our moral estimate of Christianity, contrary to historic fact, contrary to the testimony of Scripture, and ultimately contrary to itself, as being incapable of being carried out with any consistency. We have not space to enter on this discussion; but we are happy to find so strenuous a testimony against the above theory from various quarters, as may be seen from the notes to Dr. Payne's volume. It is to be regretted that the views to which we allude should have been put forth under so deservedly respected a name; apparently under the sanction, too, of a large and influential religious body. The more likely, on these accounts, are those readers to be biased, who are wont to be guided by honoured names, and honoured authority: and the greater is the danger of prejudice to religious truth in a large and increasing class of minds; who may be apt to identify its modes of representation with philosophical error, and to suppose that they see an example of contradiction between religion and moral science where no such contradiction really exists.

Art. VII.—*The Life of the Rev. Joseph Blanco White, written by himself; with portions of his Correspondence.* Edited by John Hamilton Thom. 3 Vols. London: Chapman, 1845.

THE Life of Mr. Blanco White was one of the comparatively small number of lives that deserve to be published; and it is published in a manner which exhibits it fairly and fully. We do not think that three volumes were needed to present an external history, a great portion of which was without adventures—and an experience, always changing it is true, but not advancing; always in motion, but going round, not forward. Excess is, however, a small error in the present day, nor shall we quarrel much about the size of this work, when memoirs are constantly appearing, for which no sufficient reason can be adduced. It is something to find a man who has a life—who records it from a higher motive than desire for posthumous fame; who does not need to magnify it, in order to give it claims upon attention; and on whose merits, therefore, death does not act, as on his frame, producing first extension, and then corruption. Mr. White was doubtless such a man. Holding very decided convictions as to the character and tendency of his last religious sentiments, regarding them with a feeling of horror upon their own account, and pity upon his; we yet are glad that his life has been made known. It exhibits many deeply interesting phenomena, and reads many important lessons; and if it tend to promote scepticism in a few, it will as certainly act as a preservative of many from the sorrows of unbelief.

Mr. White was known to a great portion of the 'religious world,' and was an object of interest to it for some time. He appeared before Protestant England in the attractive character of a *religious proselyte.* Such persons are generally popular with the class they join. Their testimony, as to the people and things which they have left, is caught up eagerly, in strange forgetfulness, that a man may secede from a body without being able to pourtray it—that but few men can bear wise and faithful witness of *what is*—that fewer can trace its connection with its hidden causes—and that the testimony of proselytes may be as much the fruit of solicitude about self, as zeal for truth. But the spirit of sectarianism is but little anxious to note such things—a temporary party triumph is too sweet to be lost by calling them to mind. Hence, partly, the cordiality of Mr. White's reception here. With the interest of a convert, however, he united the claims of a philosopher. It was soon felt that he was an extraordinary man. His works evinced it. His associations implied it. But whatever his sagacity and acuteness as an investigater of systems, we rather value him as their mirror. The chief worth of his life consists in the view presented of the action of religious principles on a noble nature—consists in the *experience* described and traced; and therefore it is well that he himself recorded it. With the exception of a few pages respecting his last days, all is from his own pen. The first part consists of a Narrative of the events of his life to 1826, in letters addressed to Dr. Whately—the second part, of a sketch of his mind in England to 1824—and the third part, of extracts from journals and correspondence. Mr. White's design that his life should be published, may lessen the worth of some of the records, as insensibly affecting him while making them: but of the integrity of his account, there cannot be the slightest doubt. The task of Mr. Thom appears to have been discharged with judgment and good feeling. The preface has too much of the spirit of boasting, which attaches in a pre-eminent degree to writers of his school, when they have gained a convert of any mark. In this instance it has more reason than it always has. Mr. White was a great man; and those who did not regard him, speaking religiously, as a great ruin, will naturally rejoice in him as a great gain.

Mr. White's ancestors were persons of note in Ireland, where they were reduced in wealth and influence in consequence of their adherence to the Roman Catholic religion, the first spoliation taking place under Cromwell. The sufferer's son, the great grandfather of Mr. White, was obliged to follow his father from Dublin to Waterford, where they became merchants. Mr. White's grandfather was one of five children; four of whom were sent abroad to escape the oppression of the penal laws. His only sister married a Protestant. The manner in which that lady was spoken of in the family, led Mr. White to suspect that she had become a Protestant, and had thus deprived her brother of some landed property. What a story of persecution do these things belong to, and call to remembrance, in the unhappy sister island! What a miserable instance do they afford of the effects of State interference with religious opinions! And how inconsistent must they make the resistance on the ground of simple principle, of even evil measures claiming to be dictates of justice and charity, appear to a long persecuted people.

Mr. White's grandfather established himself at Seville, and an uncle, having no children, left him the whole of a large mercantile establishment. The family lived in the best style. The King of Spain granted them all the privileges of the Spanish *noblesse*, in perpetuity. The establishment failed afterwards, just enough property being saved to provide a comfortable subsistance for the family. The father of Mr. White joined in partnership with his brother-in-law, a Mr. Cahill, and, writes our author in 1830,—'carried on the mercantile concerns, which are still supporting my brother and Mr. Cahill's grand-children. It is curious enough that another Irishman (Mr. Beck), brought up as a clerk in the establishment, married my cousin, (Mr. Cahill's only child) and joined partnership with my brother after my father's death. My family, in fact, may be considered as a small Irish colony, whose members preserve the language, and many of the habits and affections which its founder brought to Spain.'

Mr. White was born in Seville, on the 11th of July, 1775. His mother, who was connected with the old Andalusian *noblesse*, had a strong dislike to his being brought up to mercantile affairs, but at first submitted, and, accordingly, at eight years of age, he commenced a severe apprenticeship in the counting house. The labour proved too fatiguing. His mother fretted lest his health and his mind should both suffer. With great difficulty she obtained permission for a private tutor to teach him Latin grammar in the evening, for which purpose he was released at an early hour from secular engagements. The Irish and the Spanish branches of his family not agreeing on the subject of his studies, though he was 'only twelve years old, and more ignorant of the world than an English child of eight,' he hit upon the expedient of declaring a strong inclination to be a clergyman. Divines decided that he had a true call. The authorities were irresistible. Still, as a few years might witness a change, the mercantile party contended that the morning should be devoted to the office, while the afternoons were given to the school. His progress was satisfactory, and when scarcely fourteen, he was hurried into the study of philosophy, for which the priests, who governed his parents' consciences, declared no great knowledge of Latin to be necessary. Accordingly, when he left school, he could hardly construe Cicero and Virgil. In other respects, his ignorance was perfect. He had read nothing but the lives of saints. At this period he obtained a copy of Don Quixote, which he read by stealth, and, says he, 'I do not recollect any enjoyment equal to that I received, when, concealing the history of Don Quixote from all the family, I devoured it in a small room which was allotted to me, that I might study my lessons undisturbed. Even Don Quixote was considered a dangerous book by my father.'

Of his parents Mr. White speaks in the highest terms, as to their excellence of heart, benevolence, and sincere piety. But nothing could exceed their submission to the clergy. In such a state of isolation was he brought up, that he looked on the poor children in the streets with envy at their happiness in being permitted to associate with their equals. Of his elementary education he says :—

'The theoretical part of that education was confined to the knowledge of the Catechism, with theological explanations in the jargon of school divinity. In such explanations of mysteries I certainly became an adept for my age. The practical part consisted in a perpetual round of devotional practices, of which I still preserve the most painful recollection. I absolutely dreaded the approach of Sunday. Early in the morning of that formidable day, when I was only eight years old, I was made to go with my father to the Dominican convent of *San Pablo*, where his confessor resided. Twice in the month I was obliged to submit to the practice of confession, which my father went through every Sunday. In the church I had to wait for nearly two hours before breakfast. A short time was then allowed for that meal; after which we went to the cathedral, where I had either to stand or kneel (as there are no seats,) a couple of hours more. Many times did I faint through exhaustion; but nothing could save me from a similar infliction on the succeeding Sunday. At twelve we returned home: dined at one; and set out at three for another church, where we spent about two hours. After prayers, if the season allowed it, we took a walk, which generally ended in visiting the wards of a crowded and pestilential hospital, where my father, for many years, spent two or three hours of the evening, in rendering to the sick every kind of service, not excluding the most menial and disgusting. He was twice at death's door, in consequence of infection. But nothing could damp his philanthropy.' Vol. i. pp 10, 11.

At the age of fourteen, Mr. White entered the school of philosophy, till which time he had not been allowed to walk out alone.

'My father's confessor was a Dominican, who naturally patronized a college of his order, founded in the sixteenth century for public instruction at Seville. The Jesuits had been its great rivals. Upon the extinction of that order, the government, then chiefly in the hands of a Minister who had a smattering of modern philosophy, had separated the university from the college, called *Mayor*, (where I afterwards obtained a fellowship,) and deprived the Dominican College of the power of granting degrees. The system pursued at the *new* university, though very imperfect, was free from the absurdities of the Aristotelic schools. It was, on this ground, charged by the Dominicans with a tendency to produce heresy. To save me from that tendency, I was sent to the Dominican College. Totally unprepared for the dry speculations of the voluminous Logic that was put into my hands, I gave up the class-book in despair, after some unsuccessful efforts to understand it. At that time, one of my father's sisters, who, I might take upon myself to say, was the only lady at Seville possessing a small collection of books, allowed me to read the works of Feyjoo, a Benedictin, who, about the beginning of the eighteenth century, made a bold attack on the scholastic system, and recommended experimental philosophy on the Baconian principles. Feyjoo had derived his knowledge from French books, and was supported by the ministers of Ferdinand VI., all of whom were trained in the anti-christian schools of France. The cautious Benedictin kept always on the safe side when he had to touch on the established religion; but, in the attack of popular errors, he gave full play to his wit, which was considerable. His principal work consists of ten or twelve closely-printed Spanish quartos. These I read with the greatest avidity; yet in spite of the rapid perusal I gave then, I fully entered into the spirit of the work, and, if my recollection does not flatter me, I understood the principle of the Baconian philosophy. Now, the very sight of the friar who lectured on logic at the Dominican College, became odious to me. One day he gave me a reprimand, before the class, for neglecting my studies. I rose from my seat, and told him plainly, those studies were not worth my attention, and never should have it I repeated a number of remarks against the Aristotelic Philosophy, which I had learned from Feyjoo. The friar was enraged . and I wonder I escaped a beating from the other students. Frightened at my own boldness, I ran home, and told my mother all that had taken place. She disliked the Dominicans, and secretly regretted that I was under their tuition. I do not know how it was, but she managed my being sent to the University. There I learnt, in less than two months, the whole of what the logical class had been employed upon during the preceding course. My removal took place about the beginning of the long vacation, during which the Professor had an *extra* class for a few weeks, to bring up those who had lagged during the regular course. I received a public compliment from the Professor on my industry and success, and at the beginning of the following course, in October, obtained a place among the foremost.'—ib. pp. 12—14.

The quarrel with the Dominican was the indication of a spirit which was never laid, and which had an important influence on his after life. 'A great love of knowledge, and an equally great hatred of *established* errors, were suddenly developed,' which, fifty years afterwards, he recognised, and rejoiced in, as identifying him with the boy of fifteen. Prior to this, however, his mind had been visited with some misgivings about Christianity, and singularly enough, the occasion of his first doubt was the reading of Fenelon's *Telemaque*. We shall give the passage describing it, as it is important in the history of his mind, and as it is not without instruction for many others :—

'My recollection of every circumstance connected with that transient doubt is quite perfect; my delight in the descriptions of the sacrifices offered to the gods was intense. I felt besides a strong sympathy with the principal personages of the story; the difference between their religion and my own struck me very powerfully, and my admiration of their wisdom and courage suggested the question, why should we feel so perfectly assured that those who worshipped in that manner were wrong? I dwelt upon this argument for some time, but when the day arrived to go to confession, and I had to look at the catalogue of sins which is contained in the book of *Preparation*, I perceived the necessity of accusing myself of doubts against the faith. At the moment I am writing, the place where the confessional stood is clearly before my mind, and I see the countenance of the Dominican who used to shrive me: his name was *Padre Baréa*, a fat, rosy, good-tempered man, who nevertheless held the office of *consulting Divine* to the inquisition, and hated heretics from his heart, as in duty bound. In accusing myself, I fairly stated my argument. The friar's astonishment made him fall back in the confessional-box: yet, using the kindest expression which the Spanish language affords for addressing a child,* he asked what kind of books I read. I answered him with great simplicity, that I read no books but *Télémaque*. On hearing this, the friar smiled, and desiring me not to trouble my foolish head with such subjects, absolved me of all my sins, and did not even interdict the book which had been the innocent cause of my scepticism. I believe he would have been inclined to twist my neck, had he possessed any prophetic spirit, so as to foresee that the time would come when even the *Heretics*, whom he

* *Angelito, qué libros lees?* Little innocent, (literally, little angel), what books do you read?

would have burnt with exultation, would find me too much a heretic for their taste.'—ib. pp. 18, 19.

From the age of fourteen, Mr. White applied himself with diligence to the acquisition of knowledge, and the performance of the varied and wearying duties of catholic devotion. The yoke laid upon him excited a desire more than once to abandon altogether the clerical profession. On one occasion, a visit to Cadiz, which was brought about by the artifice of an old lady, would probably have changed the whole course of his life, but for the seasonable occurrence of the *spiritual exercises* of St. Ignatius of Loyola, which he well terms 'a masterpiece of church machinery,' and which he describes with thrilling effect. We would fain transcribe the whole passage, but must confine ourselves to some sound and philosophical observations on *confession*:—

'This was the appointed time to begin the *General Confessions*. That name is likely to lead Protestants into a mistake; for it means, not a general acknowledgment of sinfulness, but a detailed account of the previous life of the person who is to make the *general* confession. Every thought, word, and deed, nay, every doubt, every uncertainty of conscience that can be called to remembrance, must be stated to the priest, at whose feet the self-accuser kneels during the long narrative. I say *long*, because the result ef such a process of examination, as is carried on for four or five days, by the penitent himself, under the impression that any negligence on his part must involve him in guilt far exceeding that of all his former misdeeds, produces (in the sincere and sensitive) a morbid anxiety of which none but those who have experienced it can form an adequate notion. I will not stop to urge the grounds of a conviction, on which I have enlarged elsewhere—that auricular confession is one of the most mischievous practices of the Romanist Church. To those who are not totally ignorant of the philosophy of morals, it must be clear that such minute attention to individual faults—not to trace them to their source in the heart, but in order to ascertain whether they are *venial* or *mortal* sins, according to the judgment of another man—must, in an infinite number of cases, check the development of conscience, and may totally destroy it in many. As far as my experience extends, (and I have had fair opportunities of observing the effects of Romanism in myself, and in many others,) the evils of auricular confession increase in proportion to the sincerity with which it is practised. I know that what I am going to say will sound extremely harsh and startling to many. But I will not conceal or disguise the truth. Many, indeed, were the evils of which my subsequent period of disbelief in Christianity (a disbelief full of spite for the evils inflicted upon me in its name) was the occasion; yet I firmly believe that, but for the buffetings of that perilous storm, scarcely a remnant of the quick moral perception which God had naturally given to my-mind would have escaped destruction by the emaciating poison of confession. I judge from the certain knowledge of the secret conduct of many members of the clergy, who were deemed patterns of devotion. Like those wretched slaves, I should have been permanently the worse for the custom of sinning, and washing the sin away by confession. Free, however, from that debasing practise, my conscience assumed the rule, and, independently of hopes and fears, it clearly blamed what was clearly wrong, and, as it were, learnt to act by virtue of its natural supremacy.'—ib. pp. 42, 44.

The effect of the *Spiritual Exercises* was considerable, for a time. But a coldness towards the clerical profession was renewed by every relaxation from the common tenor of life, every contact with any but the usual society. Another visit to Cadiz, at the age of twenty, had such an effect, that he openly confessed his unwillingness to enter the church. For a month he maintained his resolution, in spite of the tears of his mother, and the united influence of all around him, who seemed in a conspiracy to bind him to the church. He yielded, and, on his coming of age, received sub-deacon's orders. Marriage being now unlawful, he was less watched in his intercourse with the world. Of the law which enforces the celibacy of the clergy, who will be surprised at the following account?

'Were it consistent with delicacy to detail the effects of that horrible law, which not only enforces celibacy on the clergy, but forbids their recovering their liberty by resigning their office, it might be proved to demonstration, that wherever such a law does exist, the standard of morality must suffer a certain debasement, even in the minds of those who (as in the case in question) might be held up as patterns of purity in their own conduct. There is not, there cannot be, a Spaniard, high or low, clergyman or layman, ignorant of the fact, that the celibacy of the clergy must be kept up at a certain loss of virtue in the country. None are more conscious of this fact than the clergy, both from their own experience, and from their accurate knowledge of other people's lives, which they acquire through confession. Can all of them be supposed to abet this source of immorality, from an indifference to its evils? It would be unfair to charge so many people indiscriminately, with a deliberate feeling of that kind; but the practical result (so far as the influence of public opinion is concerned) is the same as if they fully consented to the existence of such a state of morals. I will give *one* proof of the state of feeling prevalent among the purest and most irreproachable persons in my unfortunate country: that proof is contained in the fact, that *jokes* upon the celibacy of the clergy are considered unobjectionable, provided they do not go beyond general insinuations against the supposition that the ecclesiastical law is or can be strictly observed,—provided those insinuations are expressed without alarming delicacy. My mother (must I repeat that I never knew a higher model of female conduct?)

—my own mother used to repeat the well-known saying of an old bishop to those that came to him for orders. Those who had received what are called *Minor* Orders, which do not bind to celibacy, the good-humoured prelate dismissed with this advice: 'Beware of THEM.' (You must recollect that the Spanish pronoun admits a feminine termination. The bishop's words, in Spanish, were: *Guárdate de ellas.)* When candidates had been ordained *sub-deacons*, he altered the words of the advice into '*Que ellas se guarden de ti*:' 'Let *them* beware of you.' The *holy* Roman Catholic Church practically sanctions the bishop's advice. Can, then, her *fallible* subjects pretend to improve upon her views and practice? The celibacy of the clergy (they say to themselves) must be necessary, since the church supports it. It is, indeed, the cause of a certain portion of moral evil: let every individual avoid it as well as he can. Suppose he falls, he will probably recover soon from his error: after all, the evil is accidental; the advantages to the church are permanent.'—ib. pp. 53—55.

Bound at last to the church, he became a fellow of the Collegio Mayor, took deacon's orders, was ordained a priest, elected rector of his college, successfully competed for one of the chaplaincies of the Chapel Royal of St. Ferdinand, and had a fair prospect of attaining to the highest dignities of the church, when a total disbelief of Christianity inflicted a death-blow on all his hopes in that direction.

'At length the moment arrived when, by the deliberate admission of the fact that the *Church had erred*, I came at once to the conclusion at which every sincere Roman Catholic, in similar circumstances, must arrive. I concluded that Christianity could not be true. This inference was not properly my own. The church of Rome had most assiduously prepared me to draw it.

'When I recovered from the trepidation which this violent change had produced, my thoughts were turned to the difficult circumstances of my situation. How was I to act? To be a hypocrite, Nature had put out of my power, even if it had been my wish to act in that character. To relinquish my profession was impossible: the law of the country forbids it, and construes a voluntary relinquishment of all priestly offices into a proof of heresy, punishable with death. Unless I quitted the country, my acting as a priest was inevitable. But how could I expatriate myself without giving a death-blow to my parents? Could anything justify a step which must be attended by such consequences?'—ib. pp. 111, 112.

This change from belief to unbelief was helped by two new clerical acquaintances.

'I became acquainted with a member of the Upper Clergy, a man of great reading, and secretly, a most decided disbeliever in all religion. Through him I was introduced to another dignitary—a man much older than either of us—who had for many years held an office of great influence in the Diocese; but who now lived in a very retired way. He was also a violent Anti-Christian, as I subsequently found. But I should never have known the opinions of my new friends, had not the change which took place in myself, just at that time shown to them that they might trust me with their secret. That they were not of the bigotted party was evident to me; else I should not have ventured to betray my state of mind in their presence. But as I gradually opened my views, they encouraged me to speak out. I well remember the occasion when I expressed my new views to the elder, in the presence of the younger of these two ecclesiastics. The elderly clergyman, whose manner was habitually sedate and dignified, broke out into an impassioned answer which struck me with astonishment. His language against the gospel was violent in the highest degree: he charged the religion of Christ with all the bloodshed of religious persecution; with all the vices of the clergy; with all the degradation of various countries, and especially that of our own. He concluded by telling me that, as I had just begun to emerge out of a bottomless gulf of prejudice and superstition, I could not have a correct view of things, till I had furnished my mind with historical facts, and other information which had hitherto been out of my reach. He then offered me the use of his secret library. My younger friend did the same. The latter possessed a very large collection of French prohibited works.'—vol. i. pp. 114—116.

Soon after his rejection of Christianity, having been induced to abandon an idea of emigrating to the United States, Mr. White resolved on a residence at Madrid, that he might enjoy exemption from the 'odious duties of his clerical office,' whence he was induced, by the events of the Spanish revolution, to return to Seville. After entering warmly into the political proceedings of the times, he formed and executed the plan, while the people were in a state of consternation from the advance of the French troops, to leave for ever his native country. After a detention of some weeks at Cadiz, he set sail for England, and reached Falmouth on the 3rd of March, 1810. He had not been long in England before he set vigorously to work. The first thing he did was to establish a monthly journal, called the *Espanol*, the object of which was the improvement of his native country by means of a cordial co-operation with England, and his labours in conducting which were rewarded with a pension of £250 a year. This, with what he obtained in other ways, the fruits of authorship and tuition, a noble allowance of £100 during several of the last years of his life, from Archbishop Whately, and occasional public and private grants, enabled him to live in comfort, and kept his mind free from distraction and anxiety.

Regaining his belief of Christianity, Mr. White became a member of the Church of England, and when the restoration of Ferdinand closed his labours as editor of the *Espanol*, in 1814, he subscribed the Thirty-nine Articles, and established himself at Oxford. About a year afterwards he entered Lord Holland's family as tutor to the present Hon. Col. Fox, but, after two years, bad health and worse spirits compelled him to resign the post. Visits to friends, severe courses of medicine, controversy with Roman Catholics, and other literary labours, bring us to 1826, when the Hebdomadal Board at Oxford honoured him with a degree of Master of Arts, the want of which had rendered his former residence in that city uncomfortable. His journals at this time furnish some interesting records. Who can read the following extracts with indifference? The year was 1827.

'Feb. 12th.—A walk with Dr. Whately: a long conversation about one of his sermons.

18th —Taken ill, and confined to the house the whole day. Newman drank tea with me.

28th —A great part of the morning reading the sketch of a sermon to Dr. Whately.

March 3.—Seventeenth anniversary of my arrival in England. God be praised for that most signal of his mercies to me. Walked with Whately, and heard two of his sermons, on which he wished to have my opinion. Dined with a large party at New College.

11th.—A walk with Whately and Newman.

25th. Sunday.—Preached to the university at St. Peter's.

31st.—Called on Pusey, who walked with me. Pusey, Wilberforce, and Froude came in the evening to learn the order of the R. C. Service of the Breviary.'—vol. i. pp. 438, 439.

On the elevation of Dr. Whately to be archbishop of Dublin, Mr. White became, for some time, an inmate in his family. But a change of religious opinions, which had long been going on, and indeed had long been completed, and which he felt himself constrained to publish to the world, obliged him, on the Archbishop's account, to remove from his house. This he did in 1835. For many years he had doubted respecting some of the essential principles of orthodoxy, having arrived at unitarianism as early as 1818, until at last he gave up not only 'the doctrines of the gospel,' as they are held by evangelical Christians, but the theory that Christianity was intended to teach any doctrines at all. When he determined on the publication of his 'Letters on Heresy and Orthodoxy,' in which this view is wrought out, and in the preface to which he avows, and describes his conversion from trinitarianism, he removed to Liverpool, where he died, May 20, 1841, in the sixty-sixth year of his age.

Such are some of the main facts of Mr. White's history, and, we think it is quite impossible to contemplate them without a mixture of pity and pleasure. They indicate much to admire, and much to mourn over. Mr. White possessed great abilities, and also possessed the qualities without which the greatest abilities are of little worth; industry, and application. In commencing new courses of study at an age when many give over studying at all, and in prosecuting them successfully, he showed a thirst for knowledge, and a persevering energy, the want of which would account for the failure of even greater minds, and the presence of which cause far inferior minds to 'do exploits.' His masterly knowledge and use of our language, as the editor justly describes it, 'the most perfect perhaps ever attained by a foreigner,' affords a remarkable instance of these qualities. Indeed, knowledge was the food of his mind. It was even more than his necessary meat. In the higher philosophy of mind and morals, he made glorious excursions; and had he lived longer, and been more free from bodily and mental miseries, might have attained high rank as a metaphysical thinker. It is with less pleasure we refer to him in other aspects of his character. That he was endowed with noble qualities of heart, honour, truth, and tenderness, we have no wish to deny; and that the exhibition of his moral principles and feelings is to be considered in connexion with the manifold evils of his ecclesiastical experience, and personal infirmities, and outward life, must be obvious to all. He was very proud. Self-consciousness, detracting from the force and beauty of many otherwise lovely exhibitions, frequently appears. He had a morbid zeal for his own rights. He had no idea of losing anything. His sacrifices fed his self-esteem. He brought the spirit of Diogenes to the treatment of the gay and pleasant things of orthodoxy and the church, trampling on their pride with greater pride. No man was more susceptible of harsh or uncourteous address, and yet no man could put more gall into his cup, or more thorns into his scourge. While smarting from the suspicions and indifference of former friends, he could speak of the 'whining, blubbering, sentimental tone of the confessing methodists.' Had he continued a Roman Catholic, he would have made a good one. He never got rid, amidst all his liberalism, of the spirit of infallibility. When most indignant at the imposition of *senses* of Scripture, he could say, 'I see no alternative between charging God with setting a trap for men, and my conclusion that he does not demand from them such an explicit acknowledgment: viz., That the divinity of Christ is one of the essentials of Christianity.' There is one other point in Mr. White's character to which we should not allude, but that our attention is so often turned towards it by himself. He is constantly praising his honesty and faithfulness—claiming no small share of honour on their account. That he was incapable, as he avers, of direct dissembling, there is no room to doubt, but we cannot discern much reason for self-laudation, after all, on the score of martyrdom. He confesses that he adopted every means of avoiding the opinions he came afterwards to hold—that he resisted many impulses towards them; and that he suppressed them after they received a definite form. It is plain from his narrative that he remained a Catholic priest for years after he became an infidel, or an atheist; and a Protestant clergyman for years after he became an avowed Unitarian. 'From the defects of his education, and the accidents of his position, Mr. Blanco White had, unfortunately, accustomed himself, like many of his countrymen, to disguise his sentiments; he felt it irksome to do so, but he did it; and waited until it was quite *convenient* to throw off the cloak.' In doing this he did only what many do; that he fell below the general standard of sincerity, and sacrifice, is not maintained; but a man should rise far above it to be held up as an example, or to claim special honour. The fluctuations of Mr. White's religious belief are not, we think, difficult to be accounted for. They were not so various as may at first sight appear. He went twice the same road. From Spanish popery to infidelity; and from English-churchism to ultra-rationalism, are not essentially different changes. A mind, having gone through the process once, might easily go through it again. He was of a sceptical turn; he had a morbid desire for demonstration; and this temper prevented his continuing long in one stage. But no class of circumstances could be more unfavourable to his continued belief in Christianity, than those in which he was brought up. Popery and infidelity ever play into each other's lap. We can scarcely imagine a mind like Mr. White's continuing popish. And having undergone a thorough religious revolution once, it is not surprising that change should become the order of the day. Such a revolution seldom permits the attainment of a perfect settledness afterwards. And in minds of a certain class, even when it is a change from error to truth, its consequences in instability never disappear. The man is cured, but it is by a shock, which leaves a permanent impression of its force. Mr. White was not the man to pass through an entire change of faith without receiving an increased susceptibility of change, and adding this to his natural fickleness and extravagant demand of proof, we are not at all surprised at the adoption by him of any views, and should not have been surprised if, in case of lengthened life, he had retravelled the whole way of his soul.

There was, and we cannot honestly but notice it, a serious defect in Mr. White's character—speaking religiously. We do not find proof that he ever felt the sanctifying power of Christianity. His faith was always easy. It did not gird and goad him. He had a consistent abhorrence of enthusiasts. Certainly he was calm and cool. 'The fire did not burn' so as to make him speak with his tongue, unless it was proper to do so. He had not the 'constraint' of an irresistible affection. We never behold him doing any thing as if it was impossible for him to have left it undone. Zeal to propagate what he deemed truth, he did not show. Instead of 'power,' his godliness seemed far more like a paralysis. And as to those humbling views of self which we have always associated with Christianity, he did not possess them, nor did he like them. 'Humility,' says he, 'could not be raised to the catalogue of *virtues* except in a society chiefly composed of men degraded by personal slavery, such as history exhibits the early church.' Certainly he had not this 'sanctified cloak for cowardice.' We are not complaining of a knowledge of his powers—of his rights. We have no sympathy with the degrading sentiment, that a man is proud in feeling his superiority to his fellow men. But our deep regret, in reading these Memoirs, is, that they reveal none of those estimates and feelings which every Christian must be expected to possess. Sin was a bugbear by which he was not frightened. None would suspect, but from the use of personal terms, that he was the creature of a great and holy God—that he had transgressed his laws—and that he depended on mercy for exemption from punishment. Perhaps he would smile at our mention of these things; it is very possible; but we shall only add, that if the self-complacent, defiant, temper revealed in these Memoirs be the temper of the Gospel, our views and Mr. White's differ essentially, not only as to the theoretical character, but as to the spirit, of Christianity. The truths of God never took hold of his heart. He saw things in what Bacon calls a 'dry light.'

As to his last theological views, they are soon dismissed. His only system was in having no system. He differed from all sects—Channing and Norton believing too much for him, as well as Newman and Whately. He denounced established churches. He denounced dissenting churches. They all have, according to him, the root of grave and grievous error. They hold, in different forms, the essence of despotism and persecution—a doctrinal faith. It is not orthodox opinions, but the idea of orthodoxy, that does the mischief. The only heresy is to think that there can be such a thing. The common Christian reverence for God is nothing better than idolatry—the common

Christian reverence for the Bible nothing better than bibliolatry. The Quakers are most right in their leading principle. What they call 'the spirit,' is to be taken for conscience, or practical reason; and then Blanco White agrees with Fox and Barclay. God is to be learnt from within. It is a vain attempt to seek for the knowledge of the Deity anywhere else. To define Him is to deny Him. A peculiar revelation is impossible. Christianity has nothing in the shape of critical history, but the spirit of benevolence, justice, and mercy, in the form of conscience, the ground of which is reason. The difference of right and wrong is only to be found in the conscience of each individual. Christ, and his apostles, did not mean to leave a rule for our faith and actions. The authenticity of what they left is only a probability; and even if not so, conscientious reason, God's true inspiration, must decide whether we are to receive it or not as worthy of Him. Let people give it whatever name they please, when we follow the best dictates of our conscience, we follow the Spirit of God, and of Christ. To ask by what rule we are to be guided, is the same as to ask by what rule we are to use our eyes. No historical evidence is sufficient to establish a miracle, Hume's argument against miracles being incontrovertible. The testimony of the senses, attesting a miracle, is to be rejected, if it tend to invalidate the internal idea of God; and if there could be a moral fault in such unbelief, the author of our mental constitution would be responsible for it. The Bible contains physical errors, and the supposed infallible law-giver of the Jews fell into moral mistakes. Socrates, an invalid, or valetudinarian, would have been quite another individual, and, as far as we know, the personal qualities of Jesus of Nazareth, the same may probably be asserted of him. There is nothing in Paul superior to Marcus Antoninus; the Stoic philosophy is the source of the Pauline philosophical fragments; but the philosopher's instructions have the advantage over the incompleteness, exaggeration, and rough fragmentary character of the apostle's lucubrations. Of course the main articles of popular creeds are altogether wrong. The Trinity is a bewildering and bewildered dream of African fanatics. The ultra-mundane tragedy of the atonement is a theological fable. The devil is an odious chimera. The notion of an individual eternal existence is oppressive, even when absence of evil is made one of its conditions; such existence seeming to belong only to the Infinite.

Such, in his own words, were the general sentiments of Mr. White. Our readers will have little difficulty in filling up this outline of negations. They will at once see where Mr. White was at the period of his death, and also whither he was going. There was but one thing left for him to give up—but one piece of the 'wreck' of his faith not washed away by the rolling billows of a sceptical philosophy. He still held the idea of a personal God. We cannot but think, however, that his hold even of that was giving way, and that, had he lived, it would have shared the fate of so many other things, revered through custom, though renounced in consequence of better knowledge.

It is not our design to combat the religious views of Mr. White. Such a task is incompatible with our limits. The general question relates to the deepest and most comprehensive subjects of human inquiry. It involves the profoundest speculations of philosophy. Passing this, we do not think it would be difficult to show great errors and inconsistencies in Mr. White's statements and reasonings. That he frequently caricatures the evangelical faith; that he takes advantage, as a candid man should not, of the extravagances of its adherents; that he pushes the acknowledged opinions of others to an unwarrantable extreme, and thus makes them appear ridiculous; that he erroneously represents 'saving faith' as a mere reception of theological dogmas; that he makes an absurd demand for demonstration in cases sufficiently met by moral evidence; and that he treats the views of Christianity held by others in a way that is not justified even by his own principles:—all this, we take it, might be easily proved. His great point is, that nothing exists between the concession of an infallible interpreter of Christianity, and the denial of its dogmatic character altogether. Popery and rationalism are the only things for us to choose between. Adopting the sentiment of Channing, that the supposition of an infallible church involves the supposition of infallible men in order to discover it, he maintains, that if the Gospel teach doctrines, the belief of which is necessary to salvation, there must be an absolute authority somewhere for the purpose of ascertaining what those doctrines are. This principle was at the source of both his great lapses to unbelief. Such an authority does not exist in the Romish church, for that church has erred, therefore Christianity is false, was his first conclusion; such an authority does not exist anywhere else, therefore Christianity is not a doctrinal system, was his last conclusion. But is it true that such an authority is required at all? We think not, and that something very different from calm and impartial reason led to the assertion of a principle which involves consequences of so grave a nature, violating at once the dictates of a sound philosophy, and contradicting all the analogies of life.

We have read these volumes with much interest. Apart from the personal history of Mr. White's life and mind, they contain a great deal by which the intelligent reader will be instructed and pleased. The notices and letters of such men as Hawkins and Whately, Holland and Mill, Coleridge and Southey, Channing and Norton, impart to these pages a great value. And as to matter of a different character, if it shall excite sympathy with the spiritual exercises of other minds; promote a better knowledge of some of the great principles that are coming daily into closer collision, and of the right way of dealing with them; check the excessive applications of even right theories; and, above all, teach the necessity of 'receiving the kingdom of heaven as little children,' we shall not think that 'The Life of the Rev. Joseph Blanco White' was published in vain.

Art VIII. *The Citizen of Prague.* Translated by Mary Howitt. 3 vols. 8vo. London: Colburn.

The work with which Mrs. Howitt has now presented us from the German, we have often wondered has not been translated before. In Germany, and we think justly, it has for several years been placed at the very head of all works of fiction by a female hand in that country. The writer, the Frau von Palzow, has a masculine mind, full of historic information, and creative power. Her style is clear, elevated, and vigorous. There is a truth of character about all that she does, which fills us with the deepest respect for her talents, and this respect is heightened by the exquisite purity, and moral force, of her productions. She is the author of several other works, all held in good estimation by her countrymen, but none likely to have the same attractions for us. In fact, it is evident that she is a great reader of Sir Walter Scott, and in her other subjects, whether the scene be laid in France or England, she is continually treading on his own peculiar ground, and actually dealing with some of his most prominent heroes, as Montrose, and the Pretender. In such encroachments she makes, as may be expected, strange work of it, and not the less strange is the work she makes with our titles and names of places. All these faults are sufficiently hidden from her readers at home, and therefore, do not mar to them the harmony of the general composition. In this work, the scene of which is laid in her own country, Austria, including Bohemia, of course these drawbacks do not occur. She is on ground, and among personages and events, all thoroughly familiar to her, and these happily, also, prevent any clashing with our great Scottish romancer. The subjects and the characters are entirely her own, and are finely selected, and nobly conceived. The story is laid in the time of the Empress Maria Theresa, and the interest arises out of the attempts of a patriot party to raise Bohemia., the Ireland of Austria, out of its wretchedness, or to sever it from the empire. Mrs. Howitt has briefly alluded to this fact in her preface; it is too curious to be omitted.

'I cannot let this noble work go out of my hands, without endeavouring by a few words to draw the reader's attention to the singular coincidence between the relative positions of Austria and Bohemia, as demonstated in the story, and those of England and Ireland at the present moment. Neither is this coincidence confined to the countries themselves; it extends equally to the most eminent and active personages in both cases;—a queen upon the throne,—a distinguished advocate and agitator implicated,—the public trial for high treason,—and the great national effort for a suffering people.

'It strikes me, that in these volumes there lies a profound moral lesson, which both the monarch and the subjects of these islands may read and apply to the happy advantage of the public weal. Independently, however, of this curious coincidence, which must force itself on every reader's attention, the beautiful and elevated spirit which breathes through the whole work, and animates its leading characters, makes this splendid romance an honour to human nature.'

We think these sentiments very just. In fact, the characters engaged in working out the story of these volumes are of a kind that may well be looked up to as examples, even by the monarch upon the throne. We could have wished to see this work expressly dedicated to the Queen of England. Maria Theresa, on the united throne of Austria, Bohemia, and Hungary, one of the finest women both in person and in mind that ever did sit at the head of a great empire, is an object in itself most august and attractive; but Maria Theresa sitting there, deeply and earnestly engaged in the avowed object of abolishing the serfdom, and raising to the level of the general empire the condition of one long-abused and oppressed kingdom of it, is an object befitting the glorious emulation of our own fair sovereign. What an unrivalled opportunity for winning a greater reputation than any monarch since the days of Alfred!—what a power of blessing millions, and of becoming enshrined in the heart of all posterity as the genuine mother of her people, has Providence placed within reach of the throne of Victoria! Shall it be lost? Shall the resplendent fame of such a deed die unattempted? Shall Maria Theresa stand alone as the one beautiful sovereign who roused herself to the godlike task of a nation's regeneration, and in the very exercise of the necessary energies, shone forth like a star, and became thenceforth for ever the adored memory of her nation? How easy were the task of healing and exalting here. How one firm word spoken would inspire all the best men of the age to unite with heart and intellect, to achieve that great work of redress and improvement, which in our own empire wants doing. This one word would, in fact, call out all that strength which is needed to put a check to the disunion that is going on unrestrained, and bring into proper equipoise the influence of O'Connell, the Thyrnau of Ireland. And here we would also observe how much might be learned by the Irish agitator from the noble, devoted, consistent, and self-renouncing Thomas Thyrnau, the agitator of Bohemia. In both empress and subject, even when apparently opposed, when one had called the other before her as a traitor, the truthfulness and patriotic highmindedness are so clear and mutually intelligible, that instead of anger and condemnation, there follow a unity of object, and the great work triumphs.

We have been led into these remarks by the peculiarity of one phasis of this work, forgetting that our readers are still in the dark as to the story. It is simply this. Count Lacy von Wratislaw, a nobleman of English descent, is left the heir of his uncle's vast estates in Bohemia. These estates, however, he has not seen since he was a boy, nor the guardian in whose hands they are, has he ever seen. This guardian is a Mr. Thomas Thyrnau, an advocate. Count Lacy has come of age, and has received many pressing requests from Thomas Thyrnau to go to Tein, his principle castle, in the immediate neighbourhood of which Thyrnau lives, at an old house called the Dolen-nest, or, in plain English, the Jackdaw-nest. Lacy, however, hesitates to do this, because he is assured by this Thomas Thyrnau that in his uncle's will there is a clause making the inheritance of the property contingent on Lacy's marrying the niece of this very Thomas Thyrnau, the guardian. Besides the degradation according to Austrian notions of a noble marrying a plain citizen's daughter, and besides the repugnance to be compelled into such a marriage without his wishes having been consulted, Lacy has already formed an attachment to a somewhat middle-aged Princess Morani. Thomas Thyrnau, under these circumstances, presents himself in the mysterious distance as some cunning and designing lawyer, who has managed to entrap the old Count Lacy into this scheme of self-aggrandisement. It turns out, however, that Thomas Thyrnau and old Count Lacy had been friends from youth; had been engaged in the great scheme of calling in France to assist in liberating Bohemia from Austrian despotism; that Count Lacy had actually sunk all his property in the scheme, and that it was become that of Thomas Thyrnau, who, to enable it to return to the Lacys, had consented to the plan of the marriage of young Lacy and his own niece. Lacy marries the Princess Morani, and then becomes aware of the real character of Thyrnau and his beautiful niece Magda. These revelations occur amid the charges of high treason, under which

Thomas Thyrnau is brought to Vienna, when Lacy not only discovers the noble character of the man, and the enormous sacrifices he has made both to save his uncle the old count, and his country, but that he himself and Thyrnau are equally engaged heart and soul in the same great national cause.

It may be imagined, under these circumstances, what striking incidents occur, and what a display of all the strongest and most exciting passions and sentiments is involved. The trial of Thyrnau before the empress is a masterly achievement. The scenes into which you are led, to the castles of Tein and of Karlstein, in Bohemia, the latter the royal fortress to which Thomas Thyrnau is ostensibly sent as prisoner of state, though really to form a new code of laws for his country, are extremely new, fresh, and charming. The characters of Thyrnau, Magda, his niece, and Lacy himself, are some of the finest and noblest conceptions in all fiction. There is such a beautiful self-renunciation about them, without any attempt at the superfine. They are at once natural and great.

Our limits just now will not permit us either to make extract, or to go further into the details of the work. We must not, however, omit to notice the amusing punctiliousness of the old aristocratic governor of the fortress of Karlstein, Count Podiebrad, nor the lively and witty Princess Therese.

We congratulate Mrs. Howitt on introducing to our acquaintance another foreign authoress, of such sterling pretensions. No two writers can be more unlike than Miss Bremer and Madame von Palzow. Miss Bremer is unrivalled in her scenes and characters. The spirit of love and truest human sympathies confers a peculiar charm on all she writes. Madame von Palzow, on the contrary, delights in a loftier sphere of action. There is something at once historical and dramatic in her subjects. Historic in their groundwork, they are essentially dramatic in their management. That citizen of Prague, under the name of Thomas Thyrnau, has been dramatized and brought on the stage at Vienna with great effect. There is a dignity both in the style and in the characters of Madame Palzow, which might give an air of stiffness, were not the whole alive with a glow of the tenderest and yet noblest passion. In the unity of these two qualities, the fair authoress is unrivalled.

Being familiar with the original, we have remarked with a most agreeable surprise the bold and successful manner in which Mrs. Howitt has treated this work. The fault of the original, and, in fact, of all the Frau von Palzow's works, is, that they are in places too diffuse. Any one of them would, translated, word for word, make not three such volumes as the present, but five. This is less a translation than a new casting of the story ; and we may say, without fear of contradiction, that the work in its English shape is far superior to it in the original. There your impatience outruns the progress of the narrative, here the whole is compact, lucid, and full of the eloquent interest of a finely elaborated original story.

ART. IX.—1. *An Address to Dissenters on the Religious Bearings of the State-Church Question.* By the Author of "*The Anti-State-Church Catechism.*"

2. *The Church of Christ—What is it?* (First Premium Tract.) By Brewin Grant, B.A.,

3. *The Law of Christ for Maintaining and Extending his Church.* By the Rev. D. Young, D.D., of Perth.

4. *Church Patronage; more particularly as developed in the so-called National Establishment of England and Wales; as also in Ireland.* By Matthew Bridges, Esq.

5. *State Churches, not Churches of Christ.* By Edward Smith Pryce, B.A. (Second Premium Tract.)

6. *Religious Establishments incompatible with the Rights of Citizenship.* By Edward Miall.

7. *The Separation of Church and State.* By M. Merle D'Aubigne, Author of "*The History of the Reformation.* Translated from the French, by J. M. Hare.

8 *The Anti-State-Church Catechism. Adapted for popular use.* (Third Premium Tract.) By the Rev. A. J. Morris, of Holloway, Author of "*An Address to Dissenters on the Religious Bearings of the State-Church-Question.*"

9. *The Church Principles of the New Testament.* By James Godkin, Author of "*A Guide from the Church of Rome to the Church of Christ,*" &c.

10. *A State Church not defensible on the Theory espoused by liberal Episcopalians.* By F. W. Newman, Esq., formerly fellow of Baliol College, Oxford.

11. *Organisation: Objections to it for Anti-State-Church Purposes, Considered and Refuted.* By the Rev. D. Katterns.

12. *An Address to Dissenting Sunday-School Teachers, on the Duty of Inculcating the Principles involved in a Scriptural Separation from State Churches.* By the Rev. W. Forster.

Published at the Office of the British Anti-State Church Association, 12, Warwick-square, London.

IN a former number of our Journal we gave a brief sketch of the circumstances out of which the *British Anti-State Church Association* grew, and attempted an exposition of its constitution and objects. Nearly two years have elapsed since then, and we now return to the subject, with a view of tracing the progress of the society, and of ascertaining, so far as is practicable, the character and force of the objections still urged against it. Amidst the ominous silence of some of our contemporaries, and the more than suspected hostility of others, we regard it as specially incumbent on ourselves to attempt the discharge of this duty. To neglect it would bring our fidelity into question, whilst from a fair and thorough investigation of the subject, much good may be expected to proceed, both as it pertains to the society, and as it affects the cause of truth in general. In rendering this service, we discharge simply our duty as journalists, and are concerned that no other parties should be held responsible for what we say. We speak in our own person, give utterance to our own convictions, and ask only for such a consideration of our statements and reasonings as truth and the fairness of the case require. Gross mis-apprehensions are prevalent, and we therefore owe it to our readers to disabuse them of any false impression they have received, and to convey to them the clearest and most accurate information which our own enquiries have obtained. Our position is a delicate one, and the obligations involved in it are such as, on some accounts, we should gladly be free from. Yet there are higher considerations to which we owe fealty, and we shall therefore proceed without fear to our task, endeavouring to observe the happy medium of speaking 'the truth in love.'

It might have been expected that a different course from that which we have witnessed, would have been pursued by some dissenters. Their professions appear to us to have committed them to it, while the interests of religion seem obviously to require an open and practical protest against the enormous wrongs done in her name, through the medium of a state-church. Whatever mis-conceptions therefore, attended the formation of the society, we had hoped that its calm and unobjectionable course—its enemies themselves being judges—would have served to abate hostility, and to draw within its pale all sincere adherents of scriptural Christianity. To some extent we have been disappointed. The founders of the society have indeed been confirmed in their conviction of the necessity of some such organization, new spheres of action are daily opening to it, the country is ripe for its labours, it has lived down much misconception and prejudice, and now numbers amongst its friends many, who were at first inclined to regard it with suspicion and regret. Still it is a fact, and we know not why the truth should not be spoken, that large numbers keep aloof from it; that reports to its disadvantage are industriously whispered in several circles; and that with some honourable exceptions, the more prominent members of the dissenting body throughout England, whether ministers or others, look upon it with disfavour, and systematically decline to take part in its proceedings. Whether this course be right or wrong, we are not now concerned to say. We state facts only, and shall presently examine the pleas by which they are vindicated.

The constitution of the society is at once comprehensive and simple. It is defined without equivocation or complexity in the basis originally laid down, and cannot be mistaken by any dissenter who will give himself the trouble to examine. The society is antagonistic to one principle only. It has nothing to do with doctrinal theology, or with ecclesiastical forms; but leaving its members to follow out their own conclusions on these points, it seeks to combine them against the secular relation into which Christianity has been forced. It proclaims, so far as human authority is concerned, the voluntariness of religion: and calls, therefore, on all her friends to disengage themselves from that coercive power, which has sought to render her a mere tool in the hands of earthly rulers for the promotion of their secular ends. On ecclesiastical forms it has no views, and, therefore, inculcates none. It is neither episcopal, presbyterian, nor congregational; but invites the abettors of each to confederate against the common enemy of all. It assails no man's church, it condemns no man's theology; but, asserting the right of every man to worship his Maker according to the dictates of his own conscience, it proclaims the union of things ecclesiastical with things secular to be unauthorized and pernicious, a gross violation of the law of Christ, and a fearful engine of spiritual formality and ruin. Its whole mission is directed against the civil establishment of religion, and not, be it remembered, against the episcopalianism of the endowed sect; much less against the legitimate influence of religion over the councils and measures of rulers. Dissociate the episcopal church from the state, and withdraw from other religionists all grants of public money, and the work of the society, so far as England is concerned, would be accomplished. A three-fold order of the clergy may be right or wrong, but whichever view be held by individuals, the Anti-State Church Association is in no degree, and in no sense whatever, committed to hostility to it. Its efforts are directed against the *union*, and not against either of the contracting parties. To the State it is a dutiful subject, to the Church it looks with reverence and love, but it disavows the connexion created by Act of Parliament, and in the name of the Divine founder of Christianity, and on behalf of civil liberty too, it protests against its continuance.

Recurring to the earlier proceedings of the association, it is obvious to remark, that its progress was at first somewhat impeded by the legal obstructions which lay in its way. It could not avail itself of the ordinary machinery of auxiliary societies with their local committees, on account of the laws pertaining to political associations. Like wise men entrusted with important interests, the committee felt that it became them to proceed with caution, and they therefore submitted a case to counsel in order to know what their course should be. Having ascertained the rule of law they determined to confine themselves within it, though serious difficulties were thus interposed, and their progress was rendered much slower than it would otherwise have been. If they have erred in this matter, it has been on the side of caution, and the strictness of their rule may probably be somewhat relaxed as they proceed.

Extensive publicity was given to the following suggestions, in which the machinery of the society is set forth. We commend them to the perusal of our readers, as adapted to remove some prevalent misapprehensions.

'The Executive Committee, having received many letters requesting information as to the best method of promoting the objects of the Association in the Metropolitan districts and in the Provinces, and having ascertained that local associations cannot legally hold communication with the British Anti-state-church Association, or even contribute to its funds, submit the following suggestions to their friends, as adapted to secure the greatest amount of union and practical advantage, without involving the legal liabilities which would otherwise be incurred.

'1. In order to bring the claims of the association fairly before the public, a Registrar to be appointed in each town, village, or other locality; and, where the extent of the population to be appealed to shall require it, a town or locality to be divided into well-defined districts, and a Registrar to be appointed to each of such districts.

'2. These Registrars, in every instance, to be enrolled members, and duly appointed by the Executive Committee as such officers of the Association.

'3. Except when themselves members of the Council, to be recommended, in writing to the Executive Committee by a member of the Council; or in the absence of any such person, by not less than five enrolled members of the Association.

'4. It is suggested that no individual should be recommended as eligible to become a Registrar who is not prepared to exert himself personally in promoting the objects of the Association.

'5. Each Registrar, on his appointment, to be furnished with a Registrar's book, in which he will keep a register of the names of all persons who have become members of the Association, with an account of their pecuniary subscriptions; and the Executive Committee, on receiving from individual Registrars a list of the names of members on their books, with evidence of their pecuniary qualification, will supply them with an equal number of member's cards, containing, respectively, the names of the members so reported.

'6. The pecuniary subscriptions obtained by the Registrars to be, at stated periods arranged by the Executive Committee, transmitted to the Treasurer of the Association'

'7. The Registrars of each locality to advise, from time to time, with the Executive Committee as to making arrangements for the delivery of lectures and the holding of public meetings, and for the promotion of the objects of the Association by other means; and the Executive Committee to hold themselves prepared to afford assistance, to the utmost extent of their means, opportunities, and ability, in giving efficiency to all such movements as may be adopted with their concurrence.'

With such a machinery, obviously deficient in much of the facility which characterizes the arrangements of other religious societies, the committee has been steadily and quietly at work. Its members fully appreciated the magnitude of the enterprize on which they had embarked. They were aware of the prejudices arrayed against them, and what was still more trying, had for a time to endure the sinister construction put on their views, by some whose cordial cooperation might have been anticipated. Few persons are aware of the time they have devoted, or the labours they have borne in the service of the society. Their meetings are weekly, and sub-committees commonly intervene.

Their first effort has been directed to the enlightenment of their own friends. Pledged by profession to the vindication of the spirituality of religion, the dissenters of these realms seem appointed by Providence to achieve the work of the Society. Free from the direct influences of an establishment by which the judgments of so many estimable men are warped, they are in a better condition to estimate its genuine character, and are at liberty to follow out their convictions by such modes of action as may seem to them befitting. On these therefore the earliest attention of the Society was fixed.

'The main efforts of the committee,' says the Report of May, 1845, 'have been directed, during the past year, to enlighten and to stir up professed, but apathetic Nonconformists. In the outset of their career they met with much coldness. As they proceeded, however, the number of their friends increased; and, now, the recent measure of Government has opened the eyes of thousands, dissipated their prejudices, convinced them of the perils by which their principles are threatened, and placed this Association in the proud position of having done its best, amidst much obloquy, to prepare Dissenters to weather the storm which assails them.'

Such an effort was felt to be due to the propriety of the case, and to be the appropriate vocation of the Society in the first stage of its operations. The views theoretically held by Dissenters require only to be applied to action, in order to realize the discharge of a solemn religious duty, before which all mere secular interests and political designs will be compelled to give way. The materials for effective action are thus ready; men's judgments have assented to the truth, and their religious sympathies ought to be in living and practical association with it. All that is needed is to arouse them to action, to make them so feel the weight of their obligations, as that their theoretical protest against a State Church may be converted into strenuous efforts for its overthrow. That church is either in conformity or otherwise with the mind of their Lord; its influence conduces to the spread of his religion, or is hostile to it; it is the form which Christianity appropriately takes, or a veil behind which state-craft and priestly domination have effectually concealed her pure and spiritual nature. Protestant Dissenters hold to the latter of these views, and are therefore bound, by every means which consist with their religious calling, to seek the overthrow and destruction of the irreligious system about them. To recall them to their professions, and thus to admonish them of their duty; to apprise them of the extent of their obligations, the worth of their principles, the dignity of their position; to free them from the indirect influences of the dominant hierarchy, and to make them feel that it is a distorted and misshapen caricature of the church of Christ, a thing of earthly mould and passion, a sacrifice of the inward and spiritual in Christianity at the bidding of a crafty and selfish statesmanship, is the high calling, the religious vocation undertaken by the Association before us. The operations of the Society were appropriately commenced in London.

'The Committee judged it important'—we quote again from the Report of 1845,—'to commence action in the metropolis. They wished to demonstrate to their friends in the country their readiness to grapple, at starting, with that stolid indifference to great principles which is too truly supposed to characterise London and its neighbourhood. They were able, moreover, by such an arrangement, to do the most work at the least cost; and they believed that whatever warmth they might be able to excite in the heart of the empire, would quickly find its way to the extremities. They, therefore, made arrangements for the delivery of a series of lectures, in different parts of the metropolis, during the winter months. Some difficulty was at first experienced in obtaining the use of suitable chapels for the purpose—a difficulty which lessened as time wore on. The town was divided into eight districts—a local committee was appointed for each—and several lectures were delivered in every district, not in the same place of worship, but as often as possible in different ones, in order that the audiences on every occasion might constitute fresh ground in which to scatter the seed of truth. Thirty-five lectures have been delivered, under this arrangement. The attendance upon these lectures was, of course, various; but it is gratifying to the Committee to be able to state that it steadily increased from the commencement—that, so far as facts have come to their knowledge, they have done not a little to create an interest in the proceedings of the Association—and that, at the close of each lecture, several new members were enrolled, and many copies of the Society's publications were disposed of.'

Similar lectures have been delivered in various other parts of the kingdom, and public meetings have been held at Bath, Bristol, Leicester, Northampton, Colchester, Nottingham, Derby, Sheffield, Birmingham, Coventry, and several other towns. The interest evinced has of course been various, but the general result has left no doubt of the country being fully ripe for the movement. We shall have occasion, before we close, to advert to some of the facts which have been elicited in the course of these deputations; and therefore content ourselves at present with this general statement. Were the resources of the committee equal to the invitations received, its deputations would be in every part of the country, and its stated lecturers be continually employed in setting forth the spirituality of the Christian church, and in exposing the secularity and profaneness of the counterfeit which has usurped its place. The popular mind of this kingdom has been powerfully roused during the past few years. Its inertness and indifference have been broken up, inquiry has been awakened, new convictions have been received; it is asking, and it needs some wise and healthful guidance in order to its finding rest within the province, and under the control of religion. The religious portion of the public have partaken in their full measure of this increased activity. Their principles are better understood, their obligations are felt to respect others as well as themselves, and a sense of duty to religion and of fealty to the church, is impelling many of them to adopt an aggressive policy towards that compound of things, secular and sacred, which political craft and religious error have called into being. Under these circumstances, the Anti-State Church Society wisely addresses itself, in the first place, to the religious, and especially to the dissenting, portion of the community. It seeks their enlightenment and invigoration, not simply on their own account, but as the medium through which general society must be addressed. Should it once succeed in combining the energies of an enlightened religious body in the sacred cause it has undertaken, the day of its triumph will not be distant. Before the moral force thus arrayed against the great apostacy, the powers of evil will be compelled to retire. The mists which have concealed the fair form of Christianity will be dispersed. Her rectitude and purity, her simplicity of purpose and spirituality of character, will be conspicuous to all. The faults of her professors will be manifestly their own; whilst her native dignity and freedom from all earthly passion, will command the respect and confidence of mankind. At present she is regarded as the ally of a suspected power; the mere tool of statesmen, the counterpart in England of what paganism was at Rome, or Mohammedanism is in Turkey. We are far from asserting that a separation of the church from the state will be destructive of all the evils which afflict the former. Human nature is in too vitiated a state to admit of this. There are evils inseparable from it, which will show themselves under every conceivable condition of things. We plead, therefore, for such a separation, not as a panacea for all evil, but as a means essential to the due effect of religious ministrations; as the removal of a formidable obstacle out of the path of Christianity; as that which will give free scope to her energies, and hold out the prospect of her renewing those marvellous achievements which characterized her better days.

The publications of the society constitute an important department of its operations, to which some attention must be given. As the titles placed at the head of this article shew, they are specially adapted to the same class, and are composed in a spirit, and with a degree of ability, suited to the cause they advocate. During the past year, a monthly series has been issued, in which various points involved in the church controversy have been ably discussed. These tracts have been furnished by different writers, and it is both pleasing and instructive to observe amongst their authors, episcopalians, presbyterians, independents, and baptists. This is characteristic of the constitution of the society, which is the advocate of voluntaryism rather than of dissent,—the vindicator of the church's liberty from political craft and state patronage, rather than of the forms or creed of any seceding body. The measure of ability evinced in these publications, is, of course, various; but where all are so excellent, it would be unprofitable and invidious to make selection. Two of the writers, Matthew Bridges, and Francis William Newman, Esqrs., have had opportunities, not possessed by many of us, of observing the internal working and practical effects of the state church. Both of them are Oxford men, and we should be glad to see their enlightened, deep, and earnest convictions on the whole question, more extensively prevalent amongst the nonconformists of England. We look at the church system from a distance. We treat it as a theory, discuss its principles, reason on its probable results, and are perpetually hampered by a concern to shield the inconsistencies of our fathers, or to protect from assault the weak points of our own polity. Hence the hesitation and half-heartedness, the contracted aim, the want of high and ennobling faith in their principles, so generally to be seen amongst our people. The reverse of this is observable with the gentlemen to whom we have referred. They have looked on the system itself as a living operating thing. They know its characteristics, have been reared amidst its influences, and by the simple force of fidelity to truth, have been compelled to renounce its radical principle. In the case of Mr. Newman—if we may be permitted the allusion—there is additional satisfaction derivable from his labours, on account of the contrast they furnish to those of his brother. The sale of the society's tracts has been considerable. Large impressions of each have been published, and several have reached a third, and some even a fourth edition. The sale has continued to increase up to the close of the year, and is at present, we are informed, in a more promising condition than at any former period.*

We shall not do more at present than barely allude to the publications which have been issued on the *Regium Donum* question, as we purpose, ere long, entering somewhat at length in a separate article on this subject. In the meantime, we content ourselves with remarking that, had the Anti-State Church Association done nothing more than issue the two pamphlets on this case, which bear its name, a good title to the gratitude of all consistent dissenters would have been established.

We are glad to perceive, by a recent advertisement, that the attention of the society is to be specially directed during the present year to the preparation of short tracts, written in a popular style, and adapted for gratuitous distribution. The design of the committee will be best understood from the advertisement itself, which we transfer to our pages, in the hope that beyond the information communicated, it may induce some of our readers to render literary aid to the design.

'TRACTS FOR THE MILLION.

'The Executive Committee having determined to issue, during the year 1846, in rapid succession, and in large numbers, a series of Short Tracts, adapted for popular reading, solicit the aid of persons conversant with the subject of State Churches, and able to illustrate the evils with which they are fraught in an attractive and impressive manner.

* The monthly series has been collected into a volume, and in this form should have a place in every dissenter's library.

'The Committee are prepared to pay a liberal price for such manuscripts as they may select for use, and engage to return, free of expense to the writers, those which they may not deem suited to their purpose.

'As a general rule, the Tracts must not be less than two pages, nor more than four pages, duodecimo.

'The subjects of the intended Tracts may be classed under the following general heads:

The Common Sense of Voluntaryism.
Corrupt Administration of Ecclesiastical Revenues.
Inaction of Dissenters.
Illustrations of Church Patronage.
Demoralising Influence of Church Establishments.
Anti-popular Character of State Churches.
Injustice involved in State Churches.
Impiety fostered by State Churches.
The Church-Advowson Market.
The State Church *not* the Poor Man's Church.
State Churches Political Engines.
State Churches as originating in Ecclesiastical Corruption.
Facts illustrative of Episcopal Promotions.
Ecclesiastical Nepotism.
Special Character of the Established Church of England.
&c. &c. &c.

'The Tracts may be composed in whatever form the writers prefer, whether prose or verse, essay, narrative, or dialogue.'

The Religious Tract Society has demonstrated the vast benefits attendant on a wide diffusion of brief expositions and enforcements of important truth; and the Anti-Corn-Law League, though in a different department, has acted on the same principles, with corresponding success. Now the church question is precisely the one which especially calls for such an agency, and promises the greatest result from its employment. A large proportion of our people are in the humbler walks of life. They have little leisure, and perhaps still less inclination for severe or protracted reading. The mass of our countrymen also are placed in circumstances still more unfavourable, and will remain wholly untouched, unless some such agency be employed. They never come to our places of worship; they either cannot or they will not read the more extended and formal expositions of our views; they know the minister of religion only as a state-paid functionary, and regard the church as little more than part of the machinery, by which the rich and the powerful keep the poor in a state of submission and dependence. Tracts are almost the only means of reaching such, and if the society realize its expectations of literary aid, this department of its labours will become one of the most effective in preparing the popular mind not simply to acquiesce, but imperatively to demand, that that entire religious freedom be guaranteed by politicians ceasing to trifle with conscience, or to tamper with the church.

Thus far we have glanced at what the society is doing. Our object has been to acquaint our readers with the genuine character of its measures, that they may be qualified to judge for themselves on the claims it prefers to their support. Grievous misconceptions are prevalent, which we are desirous of correcting. While indisposed to claim for the association any virtue which it does not possess, we are unwilling that its reputation should be injured by unfounded charges, or its usefulness be diminished by a prejudiced and inaccurate view of its operations. Let it be judged of as it *is*, not as its opponents—whether churchmen or dissenters—represent it to be. Let its history be examined, its procedure be narrowly watched. Let the spirit which presides over its councils be fairly scrutinised, and its publications, lectures, and public meetings, be weighed in the balance of an impartial judgment, and then let friend or enemy say whether — allowing for the infirmities inseparable from human action—there has not been, in its proceedings, a remarkable exemption from those infirmities of temper and that violence of expression, which are too commonly incident to the labours even of the good. It is not for any association of erring beings to say they are impeccable; but of this we are assured—and in it the society may well glory—that the most complete and triumphant refutation of the evil prophecies which marked its commencement, and of the charges subsequently preferred against it, is to be found in the simple narrative of its doings. Let this be read with candour, and nine tenths of the odium attached to it will instantly disappear.

It is not, of course, surprising that such an association should be regarded with disfavour by the adherents of the State Church. This is a natural result of their position, and was anticipated from the first. Whatever be the primary element in the attachment of churchmen to their system, whether it be secular or spiritual, a regard to pecuniary interests, or a conviction of the special adaptation of its machinery to promote the religious welfare of the nation, the Anti-State Church Association cannot fail to be regarded with hostility. By the one class it is bitterly assailed in the spirit which animated Demetrius and his followers at Ephesus, when they excited popular tumult against the apostles, by the cry, 'Our craft is in danger;' and by the other it is denounced as subversive of religion, and tending only to infidelity. The motives of the former are purely secular, while those of the latter, though unenlightened and erroneous, are redeemed from reproach by their religious sincerity and earnestness. The association is avowedly aggressive. There is no concealment or evasion on this point. Its constitution proclaims the fact in simple and intelligible terms, and the society itself must cease the very moment it abandons this principle, or condescends to temporize with the advocates of state churches. Believing the establishment principle to be unscriptural, it denounces it as such, calls error by its proper name, and summons the energies of religious people, to remove out of the way so fearful an obstruction to the full developement of Christian truth. It thus arrays against itself some of the most powerful influences which regulate human conduct. It is denounced by the politician as incompatible with the good order of society, by the holder of church livings as the advocate of public robbery, and by the sincerely religious, but misjudging, as the ally of infidelity and the friend of papal aggression. Now, to all this, the friends of the society had made up their minds,—they were prepared for it. It is what they looked for. It is nothing more than their predecessors had experienced, in exact proportion as they were faithful to their principles. Had it not occurred, they would have suspected themselves, and doubted the soundness of their position. The absence of such hostility would have been regarded as an omen of evil, a proof that they were not what they supposed themselves to be, a clear indication that truth had not yet been brought into close contact with error, nor the spirit of secularity and religious formalism been made to feel that it must retire, like the money-changers of old, from the temple, which its presence polluted.

To much, therefore, of the clamour which has been raised against the society amongst churchmen, we are not disposed to give heed. It will live its day, and must be suffered to die out. Truth cannot grapple with error without exciting the animosity of its adherents, and must therefore be content to endure, for a time, the hard names and passionate invectives which they utter. A steady perseverance will live down these things, and may ultimately command the gratitude of some who are now loudest in their condemnation.

There are, however, one or two misconceptions, to the correction of which a moment's attention may be given. It is supposed by some churchmen, including even the more evangelical, that our opposition to their system is incompatible with personal esteem and attachment to themselves. We are suspected of being influenced by something akin to personal hostility, or at least, of being so far under the influence of sectarian prejudice, as to be incapable of appreciating the religious worth and ministerial diligence of many clergymen. It is impossible to peruse the pages of 'The Record,' or those of 'The Christian

Observer,'—to say nothing of other journals,—without perceiving that they make the contest to bear much of a personal complexion.

From our hostility to their system, they infer, by a logic of their own, our hostility to themselves, as though no distinction could be made between systems and men, nor error be refuted without its advocates being abhorred. In the ministry of our Divine Master the sternest rebukes were associated with the tenderest compassion, and we claim for ourselves, *haud passibus æquis*, to follow his illustrious example. It requires no effort on our part to appreciate, and we feel no hesitation to avow our high estimate of, the personal worth and ministerial eminence of many clergymen of the established church. We are strangely ignorant of our own hearts, if we do not rejoice in their excellencies, recognise in them the spirit of our common Lord, and exult in their success. For that success we render thanks to the God of all grace, and humbly pray that our own spirits may partake in a larger measure of those influences which are so conspicuous in their lives. We could name men in whose presence we feel chastened and subdued, on whom the Spirit of the Lord so clearly rests, that the fact of their churchmanship has compelled us again and again to examine the grounds of our dissent. To differ from such men on points so vital, is to us matter of unaffected sorrow, and nothing could induce us to do so, but the views we entertain of the higher obligations due to truth. We believe them to be in error on the point in issue, yet we doubt not their sincerity, and love them for their Master's sake. Should the eye of a Baptist Noel, or of a Bickersteth, light on these pages, we pray them to give us credit for the sincerity with which we write. Party zealots may sneer at our profession, but the men whom we name will believe us, when we say that our strongest condemnation of their ecclesiastical system, is compatible with the fullest appreciation of their worth, and the most intimate sympathy with those common elements of Christian character, of which they so largely partake.

Another misconception prevalent amongst members of the establishment is, that the Anti-State Church Society is opposed to their church, and that its success would therefore involve the overthrow of episcopacy. To this we have already, in good measure, replied, and shall therefore content ourselves with a brief addition to what has been advanced. We distinguish between episcopacy and its incorporation with the state. The former may exist without the latter, and actually does so, in Scotland and America, to say nothing of other parts of Christendom. It is therefore possible to contend against the one, and yet to advocate the other; to believe the incorporation in question to be unscriptural and injurious, and, at the same time, to maintain the authority and advantages of a threefold order of clergy. Many episcopalians are members of the Anti-State Church Association, and amongst the authors of the tracts before us there is at least one, whose attachment to this form of ecclesiastical polity is as undoubted as his voluntaryism is earnest. It is not, therefore, against episcopacy that the society contends, and if its whole object were accomplished to-morrow, those who are friendly to the appointment of bishops would be at perfect liberty to act on their convictions, and to retain for themselves the clerical orders and forms of worship which they prefer. Every man is entitled to act for himself in this matter, and we are free to avow our conviction, that if the episcopal church were relieved from its present subjection to secular controul, its fellowship would be rendered much purer, and its ministrations far more efficient. It might lose somewhat of its splendour; the fashion which now secures it the adhesion of the affluent and worldly might pass away; the pomp of its services might cease; and the more than suspicious lustre with which its dignitaries and temples are encircled, might be withdrawn. But on the other hand, and in the stead of all this, its internal purity would be enhanced, a vast accession to its moral power would be secured, the attachment of its members would be more enlightened, and their sympathy with it more earnest and deep. It would become, in such case, what at present it cannot assume to be, an agency obviously and *exclusively* devoted to the religious culture and benefit of mankind. Let the episcopal church take its rank with sister churches, eschewing both the patronage and the controul of the state; let its own members sustain its ministrations, and its glory be made to consist in its assimilation to the only standard of Christian duty, and the Anti-state Church Society has no contest or quarrel with it. It has often been to us matter of surprise that an episcopal secession from the establishment has not taken place. We are informed that there are difficulties in the way, arising from the very nature of episcopacy, which we confess our incompetency to appreciate. Could one of the bishops, we have been told, be induced to take part in such secession, it might be accomplished, but in the absence of this,—and who is so utopian as to expect it?—the thing is impracticable. If it be so, is not episcopalianism itself brought into question? Its fiercest opponent could scarcely advance a more fatal objection to it. We know that a secession is earnestly desired by some. Many lay members of the hierarchy are prepared for it, and we cannot but suspect that some of the more reflecting and pious of the clergy would rejoice to see their way clear to such a consummation.

We must now turn to a different class of objectors, and we confess that we do so with extreme reluctance. Nothing but a stern sense of duty could overcome our hesitation, for we love many of the brethren from whom we differ, and would more gladly use the language of commendation than of censure. Necessity, however, is laid upon us. We cannot evade the conviction that the time is come when the truth should be spoken with frankness, and the grounds of continued alienation from the Anti-state Church Society, on the part of many dissenters, be subjected to a candid and thorough investigation. We are not unaware of what we hazard; but come what may, on one thing we are resolved, as we shall avoid all bitterness, so we will clear ourselves from the guilt of concealment, when the utterance of truth is matter of Christian fidelity.

Now it is the fact that the Anti-State Church Society is opposed, either covertly or in open day, by very many of the leading members of the dissenting body in England. This is the case both with ministers and laymen, and it is true in relation to the provinces, as well as to London. There are, we need scarcely say, illustrious exceptions, men of distinguished name and worth, who take pride in its membership, and readily yield it their aid. But they *are* exceptions, so far, at least, as the most prominent, and in days gone by, the most influential class is concerned. In most cases the hostility is covert. It is a quiet, stealthy, unmanly thing. It deals in whispers, it insinuates objections, it impeaches motives, it misconstrues actions. It does not come forward with an open and truthful countenance to avow its dissent, but indulges, where impunity is secured, in sneers, which the feeblest may utter, and the least principled will be most ready to repeat. Let us not be misunderstood. We are not charging these sins upon all who keep aloof from the society. Many of them are too generous and noble-minded for such things. Whatever transgressions they commit, those who know, will at once acquit them of what is mean and disingenuous. They may be hasty, they may be proud, they may resent what they deem an impertinent intrusion on their proper sphere, but they cannot be guilty of the malpractices to which others resort. Their opposition will be erect and manly. It will show itself in open day, and will speak within the hearing of those whose wisdom it questions, or whose conduct it condemns. But there are some to whom the language we have used is applicable, and we employ it here, for the purpose of acquainting them with our knowledge of their procedure.

As a general fact, however, it has come out in the course of the visits paid to several places by deputations from the society, that the leading ministers and private members of the dissenting body have kept entirely aloof. No matter how respectable the deputation might be, or how eminent its members in their respective denominations, the audiences addressed—and for the most part they have been numerous and enthusiastic—have not included those who in former days were the reputed leaders of dissent in their several localities. It is by no means an uncommon thing to forbid any announcement of the society's lectures. We have known instances in which a minister, seeing a notice bill of this kind in the hand of one of his deacons, has declared that if given out with the other notices, he should be compelled to speak against it from the pulpit. Such is by no means an exaggerated description of the state of things. The picture is far from being overcharged. It might have been made more sombre, but we have preferred to indicate merely, rather than narrate at large, what we know to have taken place in various localities.

In some instances, however, the feeling with which the society is regarded, is one of indifference simply. It is not the object of positive hostility, but is regarded with supineness and stolid neglect, as if its principles had no relation to the professions of dissenters, and its operations were as foreign from their interests as the dimensions of the remotest planet. This is not the case, we apprehend, with many of those who occupy prominent or influential positions amongst us. The views of such are more decided than the state of mind we now refer to admits of; but there are others, and, probably, a more numerous class, whose ecclesiastical training having been greatly neglected, they are indifferent to the truth, if, indeed, they understand it. It matters little to such, if their own religious quietism be respected, that the nature of Christ's kingdom is misunderstood, or his sovereignty invaded. They never trouble themselves to think seriously on the matter, but are rather surprised that others should deem the points at issue of sufficient moment to disturb their serenity, or to engage any portion of their time. The dissenterism of such is matter of accident rather than of principle. They have fallen upon it by chance, and not worked out their way to it by severe and prayerful study. There is little sympathy between them and some of the more obvious departments of religious duty. Their religion itself is defective in its range and vision, feeble in its power, and wholly inadequate to the requirements of the Christian standard. A more vigorous training of the intellect, and a profounder submission of the heart, will be the best corrective of so questionable a state of things. The points involved are too momentous, are too intimately allied with the purity of the church and the diffusion of her faith, to allow of such supineness, without serious reflection on the intelligence or piety of those who evince it. Either the one must be sadly defective, or the other be strangely indifferent to the honour of Christ, to admit of such ignorance and carelessness.

It must not be supposed that pleas are wanting by which an attempt at least is made to justify the course adopted by many Dissenters. These are various, and we shall briefly examine a few. They have been somewhat modified in the course of the society's proceedings, and the reason of the change is obvious. In the early part of 1844, we heard a good deal about the ultraism, and violence, and political designs of its originators. Some, who are morbidly sensitive to any impeachments of the wisdom or consistency of their own procedure, were sufficiently loud in impugning the motives and misrepresenting the objects of the society's earliest friends. Its machinery was represented as covert, its purpose other than was avowed. Many evil things were uttered, and some were written, over which charity would throw her mantle, and to which we should not make this passing reference, were it not needful to an accurate understanding of the case.

The society arose from the strong impulse of the many, not from the councils of the few. It did not come forth from the high places of dissent, nor was it ushered into public life with that sort of patronage which was adapted at once to secure it good standing and respectability. There was no official air about it; nothing to conciliate our secretaries and committees, who might possibly suspect in the spirit of which it was the outward and visible sign, something ominous to themselves. It arose from the people, and its whole air and complexion befitted the region of its birth. It was a thing masculine and sturdy, not eschewing the graces of life, but mainly concerned for the honest and unfettered exhibition of the truth of God in reference to the kingdom and supremacy of his Son. It had long been felt by a large body of Dissenters, that something was wanting to the discharge of duty; something less selfish and more directly religious than the objects sought by our leaders; something which should vindicate religion from reproach by working out her redemption from the political thraldom in which she had been held. There was no disposition to underrate the value of what had been done. 'Practical grievances' were felt to be evils, and the demand made for their redress was deemed righteous and befitting. But there were other and holier things which claimed attention, and the conviction had long been deepening, that to these immediate attention was due. 'These things ye ought to do,' was the language addressed to 'practical grievance' men, but 'not to leave the other undone.' The people waited long, and with deference, to see if their leaders would take this course, until at length despairing of their doing so, they met in the Conference of April 1844, in greater numbers,—and we need not hesitate to say, with more unanimity and earnestness than on any former occasion. Such was the origin of the Anti-State Church Society, and here lies the secret of much of the opposition it has had to encounter. We speak advisedly when we say this. We write in sorrow, not in anger, and our object in doing so is to put the case fairly and honestly before our friends, that they may judge between the Society and a large section of its impugners. The parties by whom it was first advocated, and the locality in which the initiatory steps to its formation were taken, had more to do, we verily believe, with the hostility it encountered, than disapprobation of its principles, or of the agency by which it proposed to work them out. Had it beeu otherwise, a much larger number of those who stood aloof from its earlier movements, whilst they avowed attachment to its principles, would now be found amongst its members. As is remarked by the author of Tract No. 11, before us—

'When this movement was merely anticipated and prospective, there might have existed some reasons for suspicion; but notwithstanding the prognostications of our opponents, from the opening of the Conference to the present hour, all has been calm—legal—religious—unimpeachable. There have been no ebullitions of a violent and intemperate bigotry; no kind of action has been taken that is not of long-established usage among Dissenters; no one among us has attempted to shake the foundations of social order by any new political doctrines; we have not laid ourselves open to state-prosecution. Our conduct ought long ago to have disarmed all the unworthy doubts of our brethren. There is not a Dissenter whose respectability of moral character or of worldly circumstances would have received the slightest shade of discredit by a connexion with us. Our proceedings are before the world, and to them we make our confident appeal. What cause, then, can be imagined, why those who hold our own acknowledged principles, and profess to be working for the same end, should deny us their co-operation? If our conduct cannot be impeached, why is it disavowed?'—p. 7.

We pass from this ungrateful topic without further comment, simply expressing our hope, that no dissenter will permit his future conduct to be regulated by a prejudice which facts prove to be unfounded, and which all candid men now shrink from avowing. It is however one of the mischiefs resulting from error induced by passion, that its influence is frequently prolonged after the error itself is renounced. May there be no ground to suspect this in the case of a single member of the nonconformist body of England!

There are other, and more honourable, grounds of exception taken to the society. Some object to it on the plea of hostility to any organization having reference to the church controversy. We are not opposed, say such, to the principles of the society, on the contrary we fully concur in them and deem them of importance. In our respective spheres we advocate them, and will yield to none in our zeal on their behalf. We are, therefore, one with the society in this respect, nor do we object to it on account of our deeming the means employed questionable, or the spirit evinced censorious or unchristian. We have heard language of this kind. It has been addressed to us in vindication of neutrality, and is obviously relied on as a valid reply to appeals on behalf of the association. The number employing it is not, we apprehend, very numerous, but in some cases with which we are acquainted, it is enforced by great personal excellencies, and the sincerely religious tone in which it is uttered.

Now we confess it has always appeared to us most strange, that the propriety of organization should be questioned in one case only. The persons who urge the objection are amongst its foremost and most zealous advocates in other instances. They admit it to be wise and incumbent in many departments of Christian duty. On the platforms of Bible, Missionary, Tract, and Sunday School Societies, they are its eloquent advocates; nay, so fully possessed are they with a sense of its importance, that they urgently enforce it as the means of raising up an effectual barrier against the encroachments of Popery, and of giving the appearance, at least, of union to a divided and contentious church. Not merely is it advocated in the more simple and obvious departments of Christian duty, but in the case of *Protestant Unions* and of *Evangelical Alliances*, it is enforced with an earnestness which betokens the fullest reliance on its soundness and utility. Now it appears to us strange that grounds so opposite should be taken by the individuals in question. We cannot reconcile the discrepancy, nor remove from ourselves the suspicion that in many instances some other and more latent cause is operating, a cause unrecognized by the individuals themselves, but not the less potent on that account.

The Divine Founder of Christianity proceeded on a different principle. The basis of his church is laid in the social sympathies of man. Of these sympathies he sought to avail himself, in order to give permanence and effect to the religious convictions of his disciples. Our churches are so many organizations, in which each member is made to contribute to the maintenance of the fidelity of all others, and the largest result is sought to be brought out by the simplest expenditure of means. Imitating his example, holy men have combined in every age, and the results of their combinations are visible in the phenomena of the moral world. What is there then, we ask, in the constitution and objects of the Anti-State Church Society, which renders improper in its case what is admitted to be wise and useful in all others? Is the evil against which it arrays itself less obvious or potent? Is its correction without the range of religious duty, or can it be effected so easily as to supersede the necessity for combination? We need scarcely reply to such enquiries. The answer is written in letters of fire, and he who runs may read. The evil assailed is of enormous magnitude, and of long duration. It has the sanction of age, and all the fearful aggravation which arises from its being confounded with the religion of the Bible. It operates directly on the religious sympathies of the nation, and does more to retard the progress of scriptural Christianity than any other cause which exists. Mr. Miall and Mr. Burnett, in their speeches at the London Tavern, on the 21st of November last, put this subject in a clear and masterly light, and we cannot do better than close our reference to it by an extract from the address of the latter.

'This Society,' said Mr. Burnet, 'is feared because of its organisation. Why should the friends of Dissent be afraid of organisation in its favour, when that organisation is both lawful and scriptural? Who ever heard of the promotion of any good principle without organisation? Are principles to be diffused by anarchy? Assuredly not. But let us see what organisation is capable of doing from what it has really done. There was an organisation of the free-traders, and what was the consequence? Many of the public prints laughed at it; many of the members of parliament sneered at it; many of the persons who professed to regard the best interests of the country, professed to be afraid of the mischief that such an organisation would be likely to effect. But that organisation went on and on, till the leading journal of the empire declared it—opening its eyes wide to its vast extent—to be 'a great fact.' When it became a great fact, even the gentlemen in the legislature who professed to be against free trade turned round upwards of 700 articles subject to duty, and made a new tariff. Does any one suppose that, but for the great fact of organisation, Sir Robert Peel would ever have gone upon the principle he has been pursuing with regard to free trade?

Organisation was got up in Ireland—it went on growing in influence and increasing in power over the people, until at last the very same politician began to veer round to it in a friendly way, and, without acknowledging it for a single moment, voted a large sum to the ecclesiastics that he thought might have the greatest influence in that organisation. If *you* do not organise, other people will. If they do, they will succeed, and you will not; and, after all their organisations have succeeded, and you have been left to pay the piper, they will laugh at your simplicity. If you go on with your organisation, increase its power, and carry with you a moral tone that will command the kind feelings of the country at large, no minister of the Crown will dare despise you, and no statesman would think of it. He will venture, while you are at your up-hill progress, to laugh at the efforts you are making; but, when you have reached the summit, and he has a full view of your numbers and strength, and sees that the spectators are surveying your array, he will begin to take measures for the purpose of meeting wishes so boldly and so manfully avowed, so peacefully and so morally and religiously sustained, so widely spread, and so deeply impressed upon the community. Let us not for a moment suppose that, without such organisation we could take any successful steps in the cause in which we have been moving.'

Another objection to the association is founded on what is deemed its ultra character. This is advanced by many who do not sympathize with the former plea. They admit the propriety of organization, but would limit it to what they call practical questions. Grievances, they say, exist; social rights are impinged, wrongs are perpetrated, and it is both reasonable and Christian-like that the legislature should be invoked to grant protection and redress. Now we have nothing to say against this, but are quite ready to join in any well-considered application for the removal of the disabilities under which, as dissenters, we labour. But the case is far different when we are called on to substitute such an application, for that exposure of the inherent viciousness of the church system to which the society in question addresses itself. Here we are compelled to pause. The course indicated is, in our judgment, more than questionable; and we should be faithless to our sense of duty, and reckless of the best interests of our fellow men, if we adopted it for a moment. The aggressive character of the association is its cardinal virtue. We love it mainly on this account, and when the mists of prejudice and the passions of the hour have passed away, it will be admitted by all true-hearted and consistent dissenters, to be its distinguishing and imperishable glory.

'I am not one of those (says Dr. Wardlaw, and we quote his words as more likely to command respectful attention than our own) who think that particular existing grievances should be disregarded, and quietly submitted to, till this great master grievance shall itself have been removed; but, while every effort is made to rid yourself as speedily as possible of the one,—*never, oh never, let the other be lost sight of. Keep it before the public mind; keep it before the minds of our legislators. Let all legitimate means, ever in the spirit of the gospel and of the spiritual kingdom of which its principles are the basis, be perseveringly employed, for imparting the light which may be necessary to both*; and especially, to that portion of the community, whom, more than all others, it ought to be our sincere and earnest desire to convince and to conciliate, our fellow-Christians of the established churches of our country,—the many 'excellent of the earth' that are to be found in them both. They are one with us in the best and most permanent bonds—the bond of Divine truth and Divine love. Let it be our aim to induce them to bring the system with which they now stand associated to the test of the only standard of principle, the only statute book of the kingdom of Christ *I feel the deepest, the most assured and settled conviction, that, if you can successfully accomplish the great object of the disseverance of the Church from the State, you will be the instruments of bestowing upon her a richer boon than any it has pleased Providence to confer since the period of the Reformation; and will have done a greater service to the interests of Divine truth, than, under the superintendence of its gracious Author, has been effected by his servants and people, since the same period. May I entreat you to commit and to pledge yourselves, individually and collectively, in the name of your common Master, the Divine 'Captain of your salvation,' to this great cause; and to go forth to the accomplishment of your end in his armour, and in his spirit, under the banner of his cross.* SUB HOC SIGNO VINCETIS. *The crisis is come. No one who holds the principles we have been advocating, can consistently stand neutral.* NEUTRALITY IS DESERTION. The voice of Him to whose authority we bow, as the only Lord of the conscience, says to us emphatically, by his word, and by all the signs of the times—'HE THAT IS NOT WITH ME IS AGAINST ME!' '

The charge of ultraism, under some form or other, has been preferred in every age against the advocates of truth. It is the common refuge of the abettors of error, and of those, also, who being themselves enlightened, are unprepared for the labours and sacrifices involved in the service of truth. It was advanced against Luther in the earlier days of the Reformation. It was charged upon Cartwright, not only by Parker and Whitgift, but by Coverdale and Fox; and when Barrowe and Greenwood advocated the polity of independency, it was equally alleged against them by the followers of Cartwright. In the Westminster Assembly, *the Dissenting Brethren* were continually exposed to the charge; and in more recent times, the founders of Methodism were reprobated on this account. To refer to other and mixed questions, it is within our own recollection, when the demand for *total and immediate emancipation,* raised in the Anti-Slavery Society by some of its more forward members, was deemed ultra and unadvised, even by our Macauleys and Buxtons. In a second and more recent case, we need scarcely say what dismay was excited, when the entire abolition of the whole system of corn laws was first advocated by Colonel Thompson.

In the charge of Ultraism, therefore, we see nothing from which to shrink; and all that is requisite to the triumphant vindication of the Society is the justification of the object at which it aims. Let that be approved, and we fearlessly challenge the whole world to deny that, within the range of Christian principle, the simplest, most direct, and speediest method of accomplishing it, is the best. If the community, as is alleged, be not prepared for the discussion of such a theme, what have dissenters been doing for the last two hundred years? But we deny the fact, and point to those signs of the times which the most cursory observer must have noticed. Events of which our fathers never dreamed, have passed before us with astonishing rapidity, and all thoughtful men are avowing the conviction that the church question is destined next to occupy the public mind. Let the bread tax monopoly be abolished, and it will instantly be seen whether the Anti-State-Church Society has been born out of due time.

Another objection urged against the Society is its alleged tendency to irritate members of the Establishment and to call forth on its behalf, more strenous exertions, than could otherwise be made. What have you accomplished say these objectors, by the outcry you have raised? Have you increased the number of dissenters, or weakened the force of the Church? Have you induced any of the clergy to secede, or won from a reluctant legislature a greater measure of respect? On the contrary, have you not driven from the ranks of dissent many of our wealthiest supporters, and induced liberal churchmen, formerly accustomed to contribute to our societies, to refuse further assistance? Is it not the fact that many of our poorer members have been seriously injured by the withdrawment of the secular patronage of churchmen, and that in small towns and villages especially, the very name of dissent has become so odious as to render it extremely difficult for many of our people to 'provide things honest in the sight of all men?' To the truth of some of the facts implied in these queries we are painfully alive, and they have served on some occasions to check us for a moment, whilst we have searched anew into the grounds of our procedure. We attach little importance to the secession of mere wealth. Not that we would drive it from us recklessly. It is not a thing to be despised, for under proper guidance, and in due subjection to religious principle, it may be auxiliary to vast and beneficial results. But we have always calculated on the secessions which have occurred. From the first agitation of the Church question, we felt assured that the mere men of wealth amongst us would seek repose in the quietism of an established faith. While things moved on tranquilly and a truce was observed between dissenterism and the State-church, old associations kept them where they were. But the moment that principle was insisted on, and conscience appealed to, our hold was weakened, and the common refuge house of the indifferent and secular received them beneath its shelter.

It is however with far other feelings that we advert to the condition of many of our poorer and more dependant members. They are emphatically sufferers for conscience sake, and are entitled to our deepest sympathy. Instances of worldly deprivation and discomfort are perpetually occurring. Shops are deserted, employment is withdrawn, and even the pittance which charity has provided, is withheld from the poor under the bidding of an intolerant bigotry. The spirit of persecution is yet rife in this land, and if it do not shew itself in the imprisonment and murder of its victims, it is in deference to the state of public feeling, and not from any amelioration of its own temper. So far however as these facts are made to bear against the Anti-State-Church Society, two things are to be noted. First, the secessions and the persecutions alluded to are not the product of the last ten years, and cannot therefore be rightfully attributed to the Society in question. They existed long before it, and are amongst the elements which led to its formation, rather than the results which have flowed from it. They may be traced clearly back to the first movements of dissenters for the redress of their practical grievances, and had become the established order of things 'ere the Anti-State-Church Society reared its head amongst the institutions of the land. Secondly, they are only analogous to what has occurred in all similar cases. This consideration does not of course diminish the evil to our suffering brethren. We do not advance it with this view. It would be idle and ungenerous to do so. But we do say, addressing ourselves to those by whom the objection is raised, why urge it in this case, when you admit it to be invalid in a hundred others? Did not our protestant fathers thus suffer in the days of Mary, the puritans in those of Elizabeth, and the nonconformists during the reigns of the second Charles and James? And if so, why, and on what fair principle, do you require us to abandon our controversy with the power which now exalteth itself against the truth of God? You retain in honour the memory of our puritan and nonconformist predecessors, though they held to truth notwithstanding the suffering which its advocacy involved, while at the same time you condemn and reprobate us, for acting on their principle. Take heed to yourselves that you are not identified with those who in ancient days built the tombs of the prophets and garnished the sepulchres of the righteous, while they filled up the measure of their fathers' iniquities.

The lesson we derive from the facts in question is the very reverse of that which these objectors inculcate. Instead of relaxing, we would increase our efforts; instead of prolonging, we would seek to abbreviate as far as possible, by the vigour and effectiveness of our labours, the regenerating process which is going on. No great evil whether in the human frame or in the body politic, has ever been corrected without much suffering, and it is the dictate of kindness, as well as of wisdom, to effect the change with the least possible delay. Instead therefore of being deterred by an apprehension of the augmented power of the hierarchy, we challenge and invite it. Let it be put forth to the utmost. Let us see its whole length and breadth. Let it summon to its aid whatever auxiliaries it may command, and embody its inherent viciousness in every form of annoyance and persecution to which its adherents can stoop. We are prepared for all, and fear not the issue. While the system reposed in tranquil possession of power, we were unapprized of its wickedness, and dreaded not its misdeeds; but now that it has come forth and challenged attention, the marks of the apostacy are visible on it, and its own spasmodic efforts, whatever suffering they may inflict for a time, will only hasten the hour of its death. Our great difficulty was to drag it into light. This once accomplished; the doom which it merits, will speedily be pronounced by the common sense and religious feeling of the people.

There is yet one more objection to which we must advert, and we regret that our limits are already so far exceeded as to prevent our doing so as fully as we desire. The society it is alleged is unfriendly to the union of Christians, is incompatible with that fellowship of the saints which is so obviously accordant with the will of our Lord. This is a grave accusation, one which we would not treat lightly, and which if substantiated would make us pause in our career. Is it then so? Let us look fairly at the facts of the case, and see how the matter stands. We believe in the spirituality of religion, and therefore repudiate state control and patronage. In our judgment, grievous wrong is done to Christianity by political men being permitted to tamper with its interests, and we, therefore, require, on its behalf, that it should be left as its Divine Founder bequeathed it, unrepressed in its energies and unsecularized in its spirit. In these views we differ from many estimable men. On the points in dispute we believe them to be in error, yet we revere their virtues, and rejoice in them as 'fellow heirs of the grace of eternal life.' Where we are agreed, there is no obstacle to fellowship on our part, and where we differ, we refer them, as they also must refer us, to our common Lord. We love them as brethren, nótwithstanding what we deem their error. The two are clearly distinguishable, and in a practical recognition of this fact lies the germ of Christian fellowship. What then is there in these views,—and they are clearly those of the Anti-State Church Society—which is subversive of Christian Union, or incompatible with the fellowship of the saints?

If our brethren of the Establishment, whom we deem in error, or others amongst ourselves speaking on their behalf, require in order to fellowship a surrender of our convictions, or even a temporary suppression of them, then we maintain that they misapprehend its nature, and though unwittingly, are in reality inviting us to the abandonment of truth and the neglect of conscience. If our views of the church system are correct, and of course their practical obligation on ourselves is as if they were so—then nothiug must intervene between them and the most strenuous efforts for its overthrow. It is matter of duty, of solemn and imperative duty, that we vindicate the supremacy of our Lord, and drive from his temple the formalism and secularity which have rendered it a charnel-house, rather than the home of purity and love.

This question has had a practical application recently given to it, in the suspension, for a time at least, of our controversy with the Establishment, which has been advocated by some members of the *Evangelical Alliance*. The professed object of this alliance is so admirable, and the views of some of its promoters are so high-toned and noble, that we have hesitated greatly to give utterance to our misgivings.

From the first, however, we have regarded the position of its clerical members as anomalous and inconsistent, and what has recently appeared in the columns of *The Patriot*, has confirmed us in the apprehension that some of our own number regarded the movement as virtually involving a surrender of the church controversy. This is obviously the view taken by its chairman, Sir Culling Smith, and though we would not hold the incipient association responsible for what individual members may advance, it is yet ominous of evil when such opinions as he advocates are broached by persons in office. The correspondence between the honourable baronet and Dr. Campbell is pregnant with instruction, and we counsel our readers to 'mark, learn, and inwardly digest' it. We thank the latter for the service he has rendered, and fully appreciate the moral courage it evinces. That his brethren will sustain him in his editorial course cannot be doubted for a moment. To fail in this would be their disgrace, not his, and the loss would be exclusively their own.

Our space compels us to close, and we do so by an earnest invitation to all our readers to give the Anti-State Church Society—its constitution, past procedure, and present prospects—their thorough and candid attention. We ask for it nothing more than this, and we can be satisfied with nothing less. Its condition is more hopeful than ever. Instead of languishing and dying out like some other societies, it is now more prosperous than at former periods. The country is awakening to its worth, and he who would not lag disgracefully behind his fellows, must speedily be found within its ranks.

Brief Notices.

A Treatise on Moral Freedom; containing Inquiries into the Operations of the Intellectual Principles in connexion generally with Moral Agency and Responsibility, but especially with Volition and Moral Freedom. By William Cairns, LL.D., Professor of Logic and Belles Lettres in Belfast College. London: Longman, 1844.

After the publication of the immortal work of Jonathan Edwards, that creature of pure intellect, there was a pause in the controversy. The literary world suspended its conflict, just as the terrific explosion of the ship L'Orient, in the bay of Aboukir, produced for a time an appalling silence among the thundering squadrons. But the contest has been renewed with energy in America: the works of Upham and Tappan, of Day and Woods, of Rauch and Schmucker, are all marked by acuteness and power. The sentiments of President Edwards are freely canvassed and boldly controverted by his recent antagonists. The question will suffer nothing by renewed discussion, in our own country, whether Reid, Stewart, Brown, Mackintosh, and Ballantyne, are to be vindicated or overthrown.

Dr. Cairns has entered on this questio vexata with a calm and unbiassed judgment, and with a good and honest heart. The tone and temper of a mere partisan are never seen in his pages. Truth is his object, and while the opinions of former authors are allowed their legitimate influence, they are neither slavishly followed, nor pertinaciously rejected. His purpose is to give an impartial verdict. Nor has he published a mere *rifaccimento* of former essayists. His style of treating the subject is somewhat novel. We scarcely expect originality on a topic which seems to have 'exhausted thought': yet we have been entertained in this volume, both with original ideas and an originality of known ideas to the solution of the grand inquiry. Professor Cairns takes a wide circuit of investigation. He has commenced with a perspicuous and able account of those mental principles and emotions, with the exercise of which moral freedom is intimately connected. The nature of volition and motive is then fully and carefully examined, and in some points these subjects are placed in a new light. Still cautiously approaching the great topic of dispute, the author enters at length into a description of the elements of moral freedom, indicating as he proceeds what side he is prepared to take. Part v. takes up the momentous theme of a self-determining power, or a power of proper origination in the will. Here the author comes into hostility with Edwards, and, in an elaborate and ingenious argumentation, decides against him. We do not intend to enter into any discussion on this most difficult of metaphysical problems, or we might attempt to show that in the wide sweep of argument and analysis which the author has taken, he has sometimes enlisted on his side intellectual processes and principles, which can be better explained and developed by the adoption of what are usually though scarcely correctly termed necessarian views. At the same time, we are bound to state that Dr. Cairns fairly meets, if he does not overthrow, every opposing argument, while he naturally concludes that his view of the subject solves many difficulties, which on any other hypothesis are all but inexplicable. Our purpose, however, in this brief notice, is principally to call attention to the publication of this important treatise. It deserves consideration. Its author is a man of matured intellect, who has long had familiar acquaintance with this and collateral topics. They have been the study and pleasure of his life. From his chastened sobriety of mind, though he can probe a theory with acute and delicate analysis, he is not bewildered in his own subtleties, nor, from constitutional sagacity, or early Scottish training, is he ever seduced by the creations of a sanguine fancy. What he writes, he writes with circumspection and clearness. His style certainly excels that of many similar works, being natural and free from involutions. We have been constrained to say much of this new treatise on an old theme, though we more than suspect that we must rank ourselves with the antagonists of Dr. Cairns, and the libertarian hypothesis.

The Nonconformist. Vol. vi. New Series.

THE dissenters of Great Britain owe much to the *Nonconformist.* It will be difficult for them to repay their obligations, and we envy not either the taste or good feeling of the man, who deems the debt discharged by any real or alleged imperfections in its conduct. Of the ability with which it has been carried on, there can be but one opinion, and on the question of its fidelity the verdict must be equally unanimous. An advertisement has just been issued, announcing the commencement of a new series, of which we gladly take advantage to urge our friends to benefit themselves by becoming its constant readers. We need not say that the principles of the journal will remained unchanged. The character of the editor is an ample guarantee for this, and we need no other; but in the general tone of the paper, a modification is announced, which will materially contribute to its circulation and usefulness.

'The spirit in which these great objects will be pursued, (says the editor) will be the same as before—a high appreciation of the ends at which it aims, and an earnest desire to compass them by peaceful and legitimate means. The pervading tone, however, of the paper, it is proposed to modify. The NONCONFORMIST has established its character both for integrity and power; and the circumstances under which this has been accomplished, imposed upon it the necessity of taking an antagonistic attitude. It has had to do battle for its present position of strength—but that position having been made good, it can henceforth wield gentleness with effect. Recognised as having a right to speak, and a claim to be listened to, it will speak in the accents of faithful friendship.'

We love the high tone and candour of this passage. It is the language of a man whose heart bears witness to his integrity, and who reverts with entire complacency to the use of a milder and more courteous style, immediately that his sense of duty permits his doing so. There is also to be a greater variety of literary talent, and a fuller adaptation of the journal to the requirements of the family circle.

We shall be glad to find that the circulation of this series is equal to its merits. Should it be so, the *Nonconformist* will become the companion and adviser of every intelligent dissenter in the kingdom.

History of the English Revolution of 1640: *from the Accession of Charles I. to his Death*. By F. Guizot. Translated by William Hazlitt. London: David Bogue.

THIS volume constitutes the second of the *European Library*, and its dimensions and style of execution have increased our astonishment at the low price of the series. M. Guizot's two octavo volumes, printed in a neat and handsome style, for three shillings and six-pence, may well suprise the old fashioned class of readers. But who can say where we shall stop in these days of railroads and steam. Unquestionably the *European Library* is the cheapest series ever yet offered to the British people, and we trust that its circulation will correspond with its merits. Nothing short of a very large sale can reimburse its publisher, and we confidently predict that this will not be wanting. The present translation has been constructed on the principle of giving the author's meaning as nearly as possible in his own words. The authorities referred to have been examined, and an ample index, which contributes materially to the value of the work, is supplied. Having formerly reviewed, at considerable length, M. Guizot's History of our noblest Revolution, we need not attempt any description of it now. Our judgment is recorded, and to that we refer our readers.

Proceedings of the Anti-Maynooth Conference of 1845. *With an Historical Introduction and an Appendix.* Compiled and Edited, (at the request of the Central Anti-Maynooth Committee,) by the Rev. A. S. Thelwall, M.A. 8vo. London. Seeley, Burnside, & Co.

There are few things which we disapprove more thoroughly than the one-sidedness which distinguishes a large portion of the periodical press, whether literary, political, or religious. The fault is chargeable on the last equally with the other two, and if needful we could specify some striking instances. We know cases in connexion with the religious and even the dissenting periodical press, in which no notice has been taken of publications regularly forwarded through an extended period, notwithstanding that such publications were devoted to the elucidation and defence of the principles professed, and were admitted on all hands to be unexceptionable in point of spirit. So far as the journals in question are concerned, the public would never learn—save through their advertising sheet—that such productions had issued from the press. Not a word is said about them. They are neither blessed nor cursed;—the one sole object appearing to be to prevent the fact of their existence from being known. There is a cause for all this, and the time may come when the interests of truth will require the mystery to be solved. This, however, we shall do with regret, and in the mean time are content to show to our contemporaries 'a more excellent way'.

The volume before us records the proceedings of a body which, from the first we deemed unsound in constitution and likely to prove injurious in its influence. Our convictions have been deepened by the result, and much labour is now entailed on our successors to remove the false impressions which have been made on the public mind. We rejoice, however, in the appearance of this report, and hasten to notify to our readers the fact of its publication. We differ, of course, from the editor in many of the views he has stated, yet we should be faithless to our convictions if we did not state that, with those views, he has executed his task with no inconsiderable measure of candour and fairness. The volume consists of an Historical Introduction, of 190 pages, and a report of the Sittings of the Conference, and a list of its Members, extending to 232 pages more. It is on the whole, a valuable record, of which the future historian of our ecclesiastical proceedings will gladly avail himself. We recommend its attentive perusal to all classes, assured that truth will ultimately gain by a calm and impartial examination of the discussions it records. When the excitement of the moment has passed, men will be in a better and more hopeful mood for separating the chaff from the wheat. We are but in the first stage of the great controversy, and much will be gained by distinguishing truth from error.

My Sonnets. pp. 72. Greenwich: Richardson.

PLEASING versification, without much power of thought or imagination.

The Pictorial Gallery of Arts. Part XII. London: Charles Knight.

THE original design of this publication is happily carried out in the parts which have appeared. They are specially adapted to interest and instruct the young. The eye is made to assist in the enlargement of knowledge and the culture of the mind, and it would be difficult to point out a work in which the *utile* and the *dulce* are more happily blended.

The Domestic Bible. By the Rev. Ingram Cobbin, M.A. London: Thomas Arnold.

MR. Cobbin must surely possess a most inventive genius, and one moreover which has been gradual in its development. There appears to be no end to his editions of the Bible, and each one in its turn is, of course, superior to all others. This may be quite true, but we are free to confess that we greatly prefer the improvement of former works, to the multiplication of new ones, by the same author. The present work has, however, distinct features, some of which are attractive and useful; and it is, moreover, issued at so low a price as nothing but an extensive circulation can justify. It is published on the 1st and 15th of every month, and is not, when completed, to exceed twenty shillings. The present part contains the Pentateuch; and, with the reservation hinted above, it has our cordial good wishes.

The Juvenile Missionary Keepsake, 1846. Edited by the writer of 'Madagascar and its Martyrs." &c. &c. 12mo. pp. 146. London: John Snow.

THIS little volume, without pretension to literary merit, is calculated to please as well as to improve the hearts of our youthful readers. Some of its contents are exceedingly interesting, and the form in which they are presented is well suited to the juvenile class addressed.

The Voluntary. No. 61. London: Ward and Co.

A SMALL monthly periodical, devoted, as its title imports, to the elucidation and defence of religious liberty. It was formerly, we believe, the organ of the *Evangelical Voluntary Church Association*, but having survived the decease of that society, is now maintained by the enterprise and public spirit of an individual. We cordially commend it to the favour of our readers, as a useful auxiliary to the cause of religious truth. We shall be glad to find that its circulation is much extended.

Forest and Game Law Tales. By Harriet Martineau. Vol. 1st and 2nd. Moxon.

THESE are two delightful little volumes. The first, containing four tales, illustrative of the earlier working of the forest and game-laws; and afford us vivid glimpses of rural life in Saxon, and in Norman times; while the third presents a noble episode in the history of the barons' struggles for the great charter; and the fourth, a spirited sketch of the times of Charles I.

In the second volume we have illustrations of the more modern period, as exemplified in three stories of the deer-stealer, the poacher, and the farmer, ruined by a game-preserving landlord; each of them most powerfully and effectively written.

As the present volumes will so shortly be followed by the remaining one, we must content ourselves for the present with this brief notice, and await the publication of the whole, to introduce more at length to our readers, a work which bids fair in interest and importance to rival the best productions of this gifted writer.

The Maxims of Francis Guicciardini. Translated by Emma Mary. With Parallel Passages from the Works of Machiavelli, Lord Bacon, Pascal, Rochefaucault, Montesquieu, Mr. Burke, Prince Talleyrand, M. Guizot, and others. London: Longman and Co.

AN elegant little volume full of noble and instructive thoughts, for which we are greatly obliged to the fair editor. As a pocket companion—or friend, to be occasionally consulted, it is surpassed by very few.

History of the Reformation in the Sixteenth Century. By J. H. Merle D'Aubigne, D.D. A new Translation, by Henry Beveridge, Esq. With a Portrait of Luther. Vol. I. 12mo. pp. 326. Glasgow: W. Collins.

D'AUBIGNE's History of the Reformation, in three neat volumes, printed with a clear type and on good paper, for four shillings and sixpence! What may we not see next? So it is, however; and the first volume of such an edition, published at one shilling and sixpence, is now before us. The emendations of the last Paris edition, revised by the author, are introduced, and another circumstance which eminently fits Mr. Collins's edition for popular use is the translation, where necessary, of the Latin notes, which brings large amount of useful reference and illustrative information within the reach of the English reader. Nothing short of a very extensive circulation can reimburse the publisher, and the reading public will fail to see their own interest if they do not secure him this.

Christian Devotedness; or Memorials of Mrs. and Miss Palmer, of Newbury. By Henry March. pp. 121. Simpkin.

A SHORT account of two amiable and intelligent Christians, written with more sense and delicacy than always mark such publications.

The Law a Rule of Life to the Christian, considered in Eleven Lectures on the Decalogue. By the Rev. Charles Smith Bird, M.A.,F.L.S. pp. 288. Cleaver.

We should not agree with Mr. Bird on the subject of his church, than which he 'believes in his heart' 'no church ever yet better deserved confidence' But we gladly allow that he has put a good deal of really sound theology into words of right nervous Saxon. We commend the style to others who may aim at more intellectuality than marks these lectures.

---

1. *The Claims of Mind.* A Lecture. By W. Leask. pp. 22. London: Jackson and Walford.
2. *Evangelical Dissenters, God's Witnesses.* By the same Author. pp. 16. Jackson and Walford.
3. *The Christian Theocracy.* A discourse delivered at the settlement of the Rev. J. S. Cuzner, Horsingsham, Wilts. By the same author. pp. 18. Houlston and Stoneman.
4. *The Character of the True Church.* By the same author. pp. 23. Houlston and Stoneman.

Mr. Leask is favourably known as the author of some poetical works, which have received the seal of public approval. But this circumstance must not be allowed to excite a prejudice against his prose productions. They are perfectly free from all traces of the sentimentalism that too many of our modern poets cultivate as a grace. The principles are sound and healthful; the question is never suggested, 'What does he mean?' and the style is correct, vigorous, and flowing. Most of the pamphlets, whose titles we have given, are occupied with different bearings of dissenting principles; and while we would not guarantee the force of every argument, nor the fitness of every illustration, we unhesitatingly avow our conviction that they embody sterling truths, in a form calculated to arrest attention, and promote faith.

One word as to the contents of these publications. 'The Claims of Mind' we judge the best of them. It is an intelligent and fervent advocacy of mental culture from *the original dignity of mind; its amazing susceptibility of improvement; the fearful consequences of leaving it uncultivated*; and *the glorious designs of its Creator respecting it*. 'Evangelical Dissenters God's Witnesses,' is a bold and well-sustained assertion of the following points, *that evangelical truth requires witnesses from among the beings to whom it is revealed; that dissenters have, from their position, peculiar facilities of distinguishing evangelical from heterodox doctrine; that facilities of discrimination involve correspondent accountability; that therefore evangelical dissenters are God's witnesses;* and *that these times summon them to declare the whole truth.* 'The Character of the True Church' treats of *its divine institution; the spirituality of the purposes* for which it is founded; and its friendly influence on *mental enlightenment*, *political justice*, and *human liberty*. 'The Christian Theocracy' is, of all the pamphlets, least to our liking. We do not think the title can be justified. There is no theocracy now. Nor is the main idea developed and sustained as fully as it might have been.

On the whole, we wish Mr. Leask good success. He is worthy of being read and heeded.

The Church, or a dream of the Past and the Future. A Poem for the Times. By Clericus, M.C.C.S. With an Address to the Clergy. pp. 55.

DREAMS are a bad sign. As physical phenomena, they are tokens of no good, often denoting disease or overfeeding; and as intellectual and moral phenomena, they are indications of similar things of an intellectual and moral nature. When men dream, they are neither asleep nor awake. It imports a state of intermediate stupefaction—absence of proper consciousness, and inability to rest. That our author's effusions may be thus accounted for, will appear from a short specimen of his poetry and his prose. The last may be fairly quoted for this purpose, as doubtless it was written soon after the 'dream,' and before the eyes were wide awake.

'There never was a time when the multiplied agencies of evil were so incalculably numerous, and so alarmingly active as they are at present. Dissent is sending forth its argus-eyed missionaries and schism-sowing teachers to the utmost ends of the earth. Socialism is convulsing society with its abominable dogmas. Infidelity, under other names and more attractive forms, is sapping the morals of our youth, and crushing in their young hearts all love for the good, the beautiful, and the true. Radicalism bids fair to become the moral lever which shall convulse the world, and shatter the last remains of the much-honoured institutions which antiquity has handed down to us, which our forefathers venerated, round which our hearts have fondly clung, and which we would fain have transmitted to our children, restored to their pristine glory, rather than deprived of that small portion of it which still lingers round them like sunshine upon graves. But alas! we are fallen on evil days.'—Address pp. xi. xii.

As to poetry—' thus he'—

'There sainted Laud
Thy venerable spirit rests sublime
Upon the peaceful bosom of thy God.
Thy earthly pilgrimage of woe exchanged
For an eternity of tranquil joy.
The martyr's anguish for the martyr's bliss—
The martyr's cross for heaven's unfading crown.
Oh! that upon this sad degenerate age
Some portion of thy spirit might descend!
Some spark of that celestial fire which burnt
With such intensity within thy breast,
Firing thy soul to deeds that merit heaven!'—(p. 35.)

After this, our readers will not wonder at the information that the Covenanter was '*the Thug* of polished life,' or that dissent is '*the abortion of the wicked one, and veriest child of hell.*' Of such 'stuff' is this dream 'made of.' Next to 'having' such 'a dream,' is the 'telling' it. Only one consolatory fact is left to us, that dreams are often more correct signs of men's real character than their waking acts. Here it is clear enough what our author really thinks and feels, and *would be at*.

Twelve Hundred Questions and Answers on the Bible; intended principally for the use of schools and young persons. By M. H. and J. H. Myers. 2 vols. pp. 98, 132. Longmans. 1845.

OUR readers must not rank this book with the mass of catechetical productions, which are worth little or nothing. The information presented is considerable. The questions are miscellaneous. Theology is avoided. It will be found useful and instructive to many, besides the young. We commend it to the attention of teachers and parents.

A Hand-Book of Devotion. By Robert Lee, D.D., Old Greyfriars, Edinburgh. pp. 295. Edinburgh: Myles Macphail, 1845.

THIS book furnishes prayers for the mornings and evenings of four weeks, four occasional family prayers, and nine prayers for individuals. The author has sought, he says, to avoid the error of making them doctrinal rather than devotional, and has made considerable use of the Psalter, and of the Book of Common Prayer. Reserving our judgment respecting the wisdom of publishing, or using forms of prayer at all, we may safely describe these as scriptural in sentiment, and simple and appropriate in thought and language. There is nothing in them controversial, or wild, or *fine*; no teaching of God, no straining after effect. They are fit expressions of the common sentiments of true religion, and may be used by any one. We should not forget to say that an Introduction of fifty-seven pages contains many very sensible observations and reasonings on the subject of prayer, in answer to objections, and in enforcement of the duty.

Sovereign Goodness the Source of Beneficial Distinctions. By W. Palmer. pp. 250. Dyer and Co., 1845.

THE writer of this treatise evidently possesses some acuteness and ingenuity, though he is sometimes fanciful, and his style would be improved by correction.

New Principles for the Poor. By Henry Hardinge, B.A., Rector of Theberton. pp. 142. Painter.

THE production of a clergyman, yet not marked by the offensiveness that belongs to many clerical effusions in the present day; and the advice tendered is more sensible, more healthy, more respectful to human beings, and therefore more likely to be useful, than the advice often given to the poor. The topics discussed are "Locality," "Education," "Manners," "Subordination," "Marriage," "Parental Obligations," "Religion," "Politics"; and though, in some things, we should speak to the poor in a different style, and of those who are not poor in a style yet more different, the "New Principles" are generally such as the poor need, and may profit by.

A Journey over the Region of Fulfilled Prophecy By the Rev. J. A Wylie, Dollar. pp. 129. Groombridge and Sons, 1845.

THE object of this little work is to present a bird's-eye view of the chief fulfilment of prophecy, for the benefit of those who have not the opportunity of perusing larger works on the subject. The plan adopted is that of an imaginary journey. It is executed with care, and is well calculated to be useful to a large class of persons.

Sea-Side Pleasures: or, a Peep at Miss Eldon's Happy Pupils. By Elizabeth Anne Allom. pp. 144. Aylott and Jones, 1845.

A VISIT to the sea-side, in the course of which some interesting information is imparted respecting shells, &c. Young persons, going to the coast, will find it an entertaining companion.

An Exposition of the Confession of Faith of the Westminster Assembly of Divines. By the Rev. Robert Shaw, Whitburn. With an Introductory Essay, by the Rev. William M. Hetherington, LL D., St. Andrew's. pp. 333. Groombridge, 1845.

IT is quite unnecessary, at this time of day, to explain or describe the Westminster Confession of Faith. We can only notice the features of this edition of it. Mr. Shaw says his object has been 'to state the truths embraced in each section, to explain the terms employed wherever it is necessary, and to illustrate and confirm the doctrines.' This he appears to have done with diligence and judgment; and those who agree with him in thinking 'that every truth set down in the Confession is 'most agreeable to the word of God,'' will be glad of his exposition. For ourselves, we do not so think, and do not think, moreover, that Mr. Shaw has, on some points, succeeded in understanding the statements which he explains. To not a little, both in the Confession and the Exposition of it, in relation to the province of the civil magistrate, we very decidedly object. We are not warm friends to confessions at all, indeed, and should not be sorry if they were entirely abolished. The good which they effect is not, in our judgment, equal to the evil.

The Village Paupers, and other Poems. By G. W. Fulcher. pp. 200. Longman, Brown, Green, and Co. 1845.

IF the poor, like some people, are satisfied with being talked about, verily they may have abundant consolation. We do not know what many authors, of both prose and poetry, would have done, had not the condition and claims of the poor happened to become a fashionable subject. We say 'happened,' for we fear that much of the present zeal respecting them is not the effect of sound principle, but rather of the laws which provide a succesion of popular national topics, operating through some particular circumstances affecting the state of the lower classes. Among those circumstances must be mentioned, beyond all question, the New Poor Law, against which much senseless sentimentality has been expended, but which nevertheless deserves, on many and grave accounts, the reprobation of a wise benevolence. The 'Union' occupies a conspicuous place in the 'Village Paupers,' as a matter of course, and its hardships and indignities are described with strong feeling, if not first-rate poetry.

The verse is correct and flowing; but we cannot place it above a great portion of modern productions of the muse. So many, now-a-days, can think with tolerable accuracy, and express themselves with propriety and even force, that a poet need be specially gifted to stand out prominently among his fellows.

Literary Intelligence.

Just Published.

Poems. By Thomas Hood. 2 vols.

History of the French, Walloon, Dutch, and other Foreign Protestant Refugees, settled in England from the Reign of Henry VIII. to the Revocation of the Edict of Nantes. By John S. Burn.

The Pryings of a Postman.

The Autobiography and Justification of Johannes Ronge, the German Reformer. Translated from the Fifth German Edition, by John Lord, A.M.

Missionary Life in Samoa, as exhibited in the Journals of the late George Archibald Lundie, during the Revival in Tutuila in 1840-41. Edited by his Mother.

Recollections of a Tour. A Summer Ramble in Belgium, Germany, and Switzerland. By J. W. Massie, D.D.

The Antiquity of the Gospels asserted on Philological Grounds, in Refutation of the Mythic Scheme of Dr. David Fred. Strauss. An Argument. By Orlando T. Dobbin, LL.D.

Salvation Certain and Complete; or, the Greatest Sinners capable of being made Holy and Happy. By John Herrick.

Agnes Moreville; or, the Victim of the Convent. By the Rev. S. Sheridan Wilson.

The Three Grand Exhibitions of Man's Enmity to God. By David Thom.

The Destination of Man. By Johann Gottlieb Fichte. Translated from the German, by Mrs. Percy Sinnett.

The English Hexapla, consisting of the Six Important Vernacular English Translations of the New Testament Scriptures. Part V.

Emmaus; or, Communion with the Saviour at Eventide. By John Waddington.

The Early French Poets. A Series of Notices and Translations, by the late Rev. Henry F. Cary, M.A. With an Introductory Sketch of the History of French Poetry, by his Son, the Rev. Henry Cary, M.A.

Lives of English Poets, from Johnson to Kirke White. Designed as a Continuation of Johnson's Lives. By the late Rev. Henry Francis Cary, M.A.

Thoughts on Finance and Colonies. By Publius.

A New Universal, Etymological, and Pronouncing Dictionary of the English Language, embracing all the Terms used in Art, Science, and Literature.

The Modern Orator. Part 13. Lord Erskine's Speeches. Part V.

Literary Florets; Poetic and Prosaic. By Thomas Cromwell, Phil. Dr. F.S.A.

British Female Biography. Being Select Memoirs of Pious Ladies in various Ranks of Public and Private Life. By the Rev. Thomas Timpson.

A Hand-Book for Lewes, Historical and Descriptive. With Notices of the Recent Discoveries at the Priory. By Mark Antony Lower.

Lays of the Sea, and other Poems. By Personne.

The Wild Huntsman. A Drama.

A Sermon, occasioned by the Death of the Rev. Wm. Knibb. By J. Aldis.

THE

ECLECTIC REVIEW

For MARCH, 1846.

Art. I.—*A Treatise on the Principles and Practical Influence of Taxation, and the Funding System. By J. R. M'Culloch, Esq., Member of the Institute of France.* 1 vol. 8vo. Longman & Co. London, 1845.

For many years, we have felt very little inclination to waste even our leisure hours, on the perusal of the works of professed political economists, either British or foreign. Indeed, our opinion of most of those works, not to say of all, that were published previous to 1839, and which we have read with scrupulous attention, was so decidedly unfavourable, we could not master enough resolution to open the many publications, on the same matter, which were afterwards put into our hands.

The principles of political economy are few, and clear; the facts, on which they rest, are known; the causes of those facts, their working, and their results, can easily be investigated and ascertained; yet, in the works which we have read, everything is darkness, uncertainty, contradiction. It seems as if the writers, and particularly those among them who are considered as authorities upon the matter, had undertaken the task of rendering political economy the most confused, unintelligible, incoherent, and unprofitable of all sciences.

We were lately expressing, in the foregoing words, our opinion concerning political economists, when an admirer of Mr

M'Culloch claimed for him an exception which we could not assent to. In the course of the conversation, the treatise on taxation and funding was frequently brought forward, in support of Mr. M'Culloch's claims to distinction. We at once confessed that we knew nothing of the book, save through the advertisements in the daily newspapers, with the customary puffings; but we no sooner had admitted so much, than we were caught in this trap:—'You admit that you have not read the last work of M'Culloch, and yet you disparage the merits of that author, whose fame is European; who is a corresponding member of the Royal Institute of France; and who, for years, has been acknowledged as the head of the economists. Either you must read all his works, before you pass judgment upon him; or you must defer to the opinion of one who knows all the labours of a meritorious man, and admit, that M'Culloch is a superior author.'

With the assistance of a bit of logic, we might have escaped the trap; but, as every one knows, logic is *mauvais ton* at evening parties. We could also assert that we know twenty *titular members*, not merely honorary *corresponding members of the Institute*, who are downright simpletons; but this, besides its proving nothing against Mr. M'Culloch, might have been considered as an infringement on the *entente cordiale*. We, therefore, in a spirit of conciliation, and submitting to his dilemma, however defective, told our opponent, that, rather than read the treatise, we would give up the contest, and even agree with him. We thought that such a concession, when we could refuse, both to read the book, and alter our opinion, would be considered as a mark of forbearance, as a proof of good breeding; and would put an end to the discussion. Quite the reverse. The reply of our adversary was a fiery provocation to a renewal of hostilities; from which, however, we were soon rescued, by the noise of another discussion, between two ladies, on another important question: viz. whether General Tom Thumb was taller or shorter than the dwarf of King Stanislas, of Poland?

When alone, we could not but reflect upon the warmth exhibited by our opponent, and we endeavoured, but without success, to discover its causes. As nothing, in the works of Mr. M'Culloch, which we knew, could, in our opinion, account for and justify the admiration of his panegyrist, we naturally inferred that the lately published treatise must be the cause of the enthusiasm evinced for its author; that it must therefore be very different from its precursors; and that we might venture to read it. These successive inductions ended in the resolution of sending for the work.

It required all the patience and the perseverance which we could muster, to persist in the resolution we had formed, and to follow our author, from the first to the last of the 504 pages in which he undertakes to correct the errors, to supply the deficiencies, and to reform the systems, of Adam Smith, of Ricardo, of Malthus, of Sir Henry Parnell, in short, of all his precursors in the field of political economy. The very first page of the introduction, the unmeaning, inaccurate, and blundering definitions of taxes and taxation, immediately convinced us, that, far from having improved since his former publications, Mr. M'Culloch had sunk deeper into the pretending, but empty abstractions, and into the misleading and mischievous theories, which characterize his former productions. We went on, however, despite of our unpleasant anticipations, which were realised at almost every page; till, at last, we had accomplished our arduous task. Now, then, we can express an opinion, and we will do it, so as to enable our readers to decide between the reviewed and his reviewer.

The work, besides the introduction, 'General Observations on Taxation,' is divided into three parts, under the titles of, direct taxes, indirect taxes, and funding system. The first and second parts are divided into as many chapters as there are different taxes, either direct or indirect. The third part contains three chapters; the first 'advantages and disadvantages, rise and progress of the funding system;' the second, 'different methods of funding;' and the third, 'reduction of the national debt.'

About two-thirds of each of the chapters are devoted to a sort of historical account of the first establishment of the tax which forms the subject of it; of the several modifications, reduction or increase, which it experienced; and of the sums produced by it, under different circumstances, and at different periods. The author might have, without any prejudice for his work, reduced this portion, which is a mere compilation from the parliamentary blue books, to much shorter dimensions; but it seems that one of the principles on which almost all professed economists agree, is book-making any how.

To these, certainly most easy 'researches, on the history and influence of the leading taxes imposed in the united kingdom,' Mr. M'Culloch adds his 'investigations on the influence of the most important taxes imposed in foreign countries:' he says so, at least, in his preface; but, with the exception of France, no European state seems to have fixed his attention; for they are hardly mentioned, and that with merely some cursory remarks, which do not exhibit any very serious 'investigation.' Not that we are going to find fault with our author, for this neglect: we think that he has acted wisely, in not speaking of that which he seems ignorant, and that he would have done better if he had been equally silent with regard to France, instead of blundering, in most of his speculations on the French system of taxation. To set him right, on this matter, would require more space than we can dispose of; and, besides that, would be without any beneficial result to our readers, as well as without interest. There is nothing, in the French system, good enough to be worth importation; and all that is bad in it, is not worse than most parts of our own system. The fact is, that in France, as well as in England, the system, the science of taxation, consists in exacting, by all sorts of indirect contrivances, from the many, the helpless, the working classes, all that can be exacted, and in making the grandees of the land, and the rich few, feel as little as possible the weight of taxation.

Mr. M'Culloch being considered, by many, as an authority on matters of political economy, our readers must be anxious to know, not what taxes exist in other countries, nor what taxes exist in England, and when and how they were established; but the opinion of Mr. M'Culloch, on the soundness or unsoundness of the principles which led to the establishment of those taxes, on the advantages or the inconveniences of their establishment; and on the policy, either of maintaining them, if they supply the administration with sufficient means for the government of the country, without being too burdensome to the people; or of substituting for them a system of taxation better and more efficient, if it is found out that the present system is equally vicious in its principles and mischievous in its effects. On opening a book, 'A Treatise on the Principles and Practical Influence of Taxation,' written, too, at a time when the whole nation demand the removal of the tottering fabric, and a more equitable and less expensive assessment of public contributions, every one naturally expects to find, at the least, something applicable to the present circumstances of the country; either a bold denial of the existing evils, and a justification of the system now in force; or an admission of the disastrous effects of that system, and the advocacy of some of the principles whose application is claimed all over the land, as the only remedy for the distress of the people; nay, even more, the only security for the stability of the government. Mr. M'Culloch has contrived to do neither the one nor the other; he seems not to see, much less to understand our present situation; or even the subject on which he writes; his object seems rather to have been to collect all the false or absurd opinions, all the captious and illogical arguments, that ever were arrayed in support of, or against every principle or mode of taxation; many of which he appropriates and reproduces as his own, however inconsistent and contradictory, however obsolete or mischievous they be.

A complete exposure of the opposite principles, of the conflicting opinions of our author, would have led to a long and tedious dissertation, which we were desirous not to inflict upon our readers; if, whilst engaged in our labour, the idea had not occurred to us, to leave to Mr. M'Culloch all the credit of confuting himself. It is, then, from Mr. M'Culloch's own words that our readers will form their opinion of his principles, of his judgments, and of his consistency.

INTRODUCTION:—INFLUENCE OF TAXATION.

'The constantly increasing pressure of taxation during the war begun in 1793, was felt by all classes, and gave a spur to industry, enterprise, and invention, and generated a spirit of economy, that we should have had in vain attempted to excite by less powerful means. . . . Without the American war and the French war, there would have been less industry, and less frugality, because there would have been less occasion for them. And we incline to think that those who inquire dispassionately into the matter, will probably see reason to conclude that the increase of industry and frugality occasioned by these contests, more than sufficed to defray their enormous expences.' (pp. 10, 11.)

'It must not, however, be supposed that, because the probability is that the capital of the country is about as great, at present, as it would have been, had the late war with France not occurred, we sustain no inconveniency from the taxes imposed to defray its expenses. Undoubtedly they form, and will most probably continue to form, for a lengthened period, a heavy drawback on the industry and prosperity of the country.' (p. 11—12.) 'The great depth of the funding system consists in its making the loss occasioned by war expenditure, seem less than it really is, which prevents an adequate stimulus being given to industry and economy.' (p. 407.)

LAND-TAX.

'Taxes on the rent of the land are extremely objectionable.' (p. 47) 'They retard, and, indeed, frequently arrest the progress of agricultural improvement.' (p. 52.) 'It is obvious that all projects for laying peculiar burdens on the land, however varnished or disguised, should no longer be looked upon as projects for the imposition of equitable taxes, but for the confiscation of the property of landlords. If such flagitious schemes be ever entertained, they will form a precedent that will justify the repudiation of the public debt, and the

'The land-tax' (of four shillings in the pound on the rental of estates, manors, and other real property,) 'has been but little burdensome, and has in no wise obstructed improvements... It was originally assessed, in most instances, on a very low valuation, and, (which is of infinitely more importance,) a limit was fixed beyond which it has never been carried.' (p. 59.) 'We may regret, perhaps, that the land-tax was not more equally assessed, and its limits considerably extended after the revolution. Whatever hard-

subversion of every right.' (p. 60.) 'The more, indeed, that their operation is inquired into, the more clearly it will appear, that taxes proportioned to the rent, or to the net produce of the land, are the bane of every country in which they exist.' (p. 61.)

ship, or even injustice might have been occasioned, in 1693, by raising the range or the limits of the assessment, supposing it had been fairly made, from two to four, five or even six millions would have been obtained, very many years ago, and the country now would have been in possession of a large revenue, raised without inconvenience or prejudice to any one.' (p. 60.)

'It is obvious, that, so far as estates may be improved by the contingencies alluded to, their proprietors would have nothing to object to the limitation of the valuation, which, on the contrary, would be highly advantageous to them. The proprietors of estates that had fallen in value, in consequence of these contingencies, would, however, have reason to complain, were they to continue to be assessed, in all time to come, on valuations made when their estates, owing to circumstances which no longer exist, bore a very high value; and therefore it would be right and proper to enact, that, though the valuation should be wholly unsusceptible of increase, it might under certain circumstances be reduced.' (p. 66.)

'It may be said, perhaps, that a tax proportioned to a permanent valuation of the land must, in the course of no very long time, become unequal, not merely from the influence of improvements, in certain districts, and not in others, but from changes of situation originating in the opening of new channels of commerce, and the shutting of the old; the growth and decay of manufactures in particular localities, and so forth. But, though these circumstances would undoubtedly alter the value of property, and vitiate the valuation, the consequences that would attend the periodical valuation of the land are such, that no policy of that sort should ever be thought of.' (p. 66.)

HOUSE-TAX.

'Taxes on houses have been, for a lengthened period, ordinary sources of revenue in this country, and we are inclined to think, that when these taxes are assessed according to the rent, they are the least objectionable that can be devised.' 'Houses used wholly as residences may, speaking generally, be taken as a pretty fair index of the incomes of their occupiers; and it may, in consequence, be presumed

'A prejudice was raised against the late house-tax, from a notion that it was unfairly assessed; and, in proof of this, it was said, that not a few of the middle class of inns and hotels paid a larger amount of house-duty than was paid by some of the most splendid baronial residences. But no one could honestly pretend that there was any unfairness in this, seeing that the house-duty was assessed, that taxes laid on them, in proportion to the rent, would be in part pretty nearly proportioned to the abilities of the parties.... At all events, there can be no solid objection to the tax, provided it be equally imposed. It is neither unfair nor unjust for the government to lay it down, that individuals using certain articles, or occupying houses of a certain value, shall be charged with certain duties..... With respect to houses used partly only as residences, and partly as shops, or places of business, the better plan would seem to be to exempt the shop or place of business from the tax, and to assess the latter on that portion only of the building that is used as a dwelling-house.' (p. 69.)

not by what a house cost, but by the rent which it fetched, or which it would have fetched had it been actually let.... Being a tax dependent on the rent, how could the house-duty be levied on houses that were worth nothing, which none would inhabit, unless enticed by a considerable bonus? This objection might, however, have been obviated, by charging the tax on superior houses, partly only in proportion to their rent, and partly also in proportion to their cost.' (p. 72.)

TAXES ON WAGES.

'A tax on any article consumed by them (the working classes), provided it be not excessive, never fails to make them more industrious. Were their powers already tasked to the utmost, such, of course, would not be the case. But though far from being so comfortable as could be wished, they are not, fortunately, reduced to this miserable state, either here or any where else; they have still ample room for the exercise of greater industry, frugality, and ingenuity; and, so long as this is the case, they will continue to contribute, in the most effectual manner, to the revenue. We have great doubts whether the taxes on tobacco, spirits, and tea, have added any thing to the wages of labour; and whether all the large sums contributed to them, by out-door labourers, be not wholly the result of the greater industry and frugality occasioned by their desire to

'It is now admitted on all hands, that when wages rise, either from being taxed, or any other cause, that rise does not raise the price of commodities, or lower rent, but forms a deduction from the profits or income of those who employ labour.' (p. 104.) Suppose that they are made to hand over ten per cent. of their earnings to collectors appointed by the government; if the produce of the tax be laid out in hiring additional troops or sailors, it is easy to see that it can be productive of no immediate injury to the labourer.... wages would be raised in exact proportion to the amount of the tax.' (p. 105.) 'We should be disposed to consider direct taxes on wages as most objectionable, unless their produce were expended on the employment of additional troops, or removing labour from the market. And even in the cases in which taxes on wages are so ex-command those gratifications.' (pp. 98, 99.) 'Without undervaluing the mischievous influence of taxes on necessaries, over the condition of the inferior classes, it may be doubted whether their depressed situation in this country is to be ascribed to them. Indeed, the taxes laid directly on necessaries amongst us are small, compared with those laid on them in most continental states.' (p. 108.) 'We apprehend, how paradoxical soever the statement may, at first sight, appear, that they have sustained still greater injury, from the late extraordinary extension of the manufacturing system.' (p. 109.)

pended, it seems very questionable whether they should be resorted to.' (p. 107.) 'Whatever may be the incidence of taxes laid directly on wages, or on necessaries, there is not much ground for supposing that the condition of the labourer would be sensibly improved by repealing such taxes.' (p. 157.) 'But whatever may be the influence of taxes on necessaries over wages, and the condition of the labourers, their repeal, after they have been imposed for a considerable period, is always of singular advantage to them.' (p. 163.)

TAXES ON RAW PRODUCE.

'It is not possible, perhaps, to form a very accurate estimate of what the countervailing duty should amount to; but it would not, we apprehend, be difficult to show, that by fixing it at 5*s*. or 6*s*. a quarter on wheat, and other grain in proportion, the justice of the case would be satisfied, and the interests of the agriculturists and those of the public conciliated, and most effectually promoted. It has been objected to a fixed duty on foreign corn, that it could not be collected in years when there was any unusual deficiency in our harvests, the prices of corn, even without any duty, being then oppressively high.' 'It appears, therefore, however much the conclusion may be at variance with popular prejudices, that a fixed duty on corn would be most onerous, when prices were about the level at which importation can take place, or but a little higher. It would then, like the generality of custom duties, fall wholly on the importers or on the consumers here. But when prices rise considerably above the level of profit-

'When a government lays a duty on the foreign commodities which enter its ports, in ordinary cases, or when there is no sudden and extraordinary demand for the articles on which it is laid, it falls entirely on its own subjects by whom they are purchased.' (p. 195.) 'For the same reason, when a government lays a duty on the commodities which its subjects are about to export, it does not fall on them, but on those by whom they are bought. If, therefore, it were possible for a country to raise a sufficient revenue by laying duties on exported commodities, such revenue would be wholly derived from others, and would itself be relieved from the burden of taxation.' (p. 196.) 'It has been demonstrated, over and over again, that, generally speaking, restraints on the freedom of commerce, or on the territorial division of labour among different nations, are adverse to the progress of real opulence, and lasting improvements; and that the advantages which they sometimes confer on parti-

able importation, the duty has no sensible influence over them, and falls wholly on the foreigner. Hence the repeal or suspension of the duties, when prices are high, would be most impolitic; it would be sacrificing revenue, not for the benefit of our own people, but for that of the growers and dealers, in Poland, and other exporting countries.' (pp 192, 193.)

cular classes of persons or businesses, is uniformly accompanied by more than a corresponding loss to the public. Providence, by giving different soils, climates, and natural products to different countries, has evidently intended that they should be mutually dependent upon, and serviceable to each other.' (p. 201).

EXCISE OR INLAND DUTIES.

'It has been objected to the excise duties that they greatly raise the cost of subsistence to the labouring class, but a glance at the foregoing tables, (of articles subject to excise duties,) 'shows that this assertion has no solid foundation.' (p. 235.) 'We do not think, notwithstanding its influence over agriculture, that the existing malt duty is open to any good objection. It is neither excessive in amount, (£4,500,000!) nor oppressive or troublesome in the mode of charge. It is needless to say, that the malt tax, like other taxes on commodities, falls wholly on the consumers.' (p. 238.) 'Its peculiar pressure on the land gives the agriculturists a legitimate claim, though all payments on accounts of tithes were abolished, to have a certain fixed duty imposed on foreign corn, in the event of the present sliding scale being abandoned.' (p. 239.)

'The oppressive extent to which the malt duty was latterly carried, coupled with the increased price of barley, and the increased amount of the beer duty, had the most powerful effect on checking the consumption of malt and beer.' (p. 237.) 'It is not easy to estimate the injury which this influence of the malt tax inflicts upon agriculture, but the fact of its inflicting an injury is indubitable.' (p. 238.) We cannot, however, afford to lose the revenue derived from it; so that it were idle to talk of its repeal. Its diminution even would be most unwise . . . . and we are disposed to regard it as one of those duties which, in case any considerable increase of revenue were required, might be advantageously raised.' (p. 239.)

'We may be assured that it is only by taxing commodities in general demand, and by identifying, as it were, the tax with the cost of the article, that the bulk of the population can ever be made to contribute largely to the support of the government.' (p. 254.)

'Whatever may be the fate of a country subject to a high rate of taxation, it seems impossible to doubt that it operates as a clog on her progress, and that, *cæteris paribus*, it is a source of impoverishment and weakness.' (p. 389.) 'The heavy taxes which the payment of

'It is further to be borne in mind, that, as the taxes required to defray the interest of the public debt are seldom very oppressive, they not unfrequently exert a beneficial influence over industry; and, through the stimulus they give to invention and economy, usually replace (and sometimes more than replace) the interest. The stupendous inventions and discoveries of Watt, Arkwright, Crompton, Wedgwood, and others, have hitherto falsified all the predictions of those who anticipated national ruin and bankruptcy from the rapid increase of the public debt; but these inventions and discoveries might have never been made, but for the stimulus given to the public energies by the increase of taxation, that grew out of the funding system.' (p. 401.)

interest (of the debt) involves, lays a country under the most serious difficulties, by reducing the rates of profits, crippling the public energies, and stimulating the transfer of capital and skill to other countries, where taxes are less oppressive.' (p. 401.) 'These statements are sufficient to demonstrate not the expediency merely, but the necessity, if we would guard against the most tremendous evils, of adopting every just and practical means for lessening the weight of taxation, and relieving the pressure on national resources.' (p. 391.)

We fear we have trespassed too long on the patience of our readers, by the multiplicity and the length of our quotations; but we beg to assure them, that, after serious cogitation, we could find no better, and, indeed, no other means of expounding, with any thing like accuracy and completeness, the principles of political economy professed by the Whig oracle in that science. We are convinced that nobody would have given the least credit to our statements, if we had confined ourselves to the customary mode of criticism, and if, after a regular controversy, on the principal points, we had expressed our honest opinion of the inconsistency of our author, instead of placing, as we have done, in juxtaposition his conflicting principles and opinions. Let not any suppose that we have taken much pains in searching for these contradictory extracts: quite the reverse; they are to be found in almost every page, and the only difficulty we experienced was in selection. We have left out ten times as many as we have inserted. Such is the work of Mr. M'Culloch, who, after approving and censuring, in turn, every kind of taxation, after advocating with the same breath, the imposition and the repeal, the reduction and the increase, of almost every duty, seeing that the day is fast approaching when the existing system must end in a dreadful convulsion, gravely tells us:—
"How unphilosophical soever it may seem, the safest course will

then probably be, to fold our arms, and to leave the *dénouement* to time and Providence." (p. 111.)

No! the people of England will not fold their arms. They trust to Providence, but they know that, to help them out of their present deplorable condition, Providence enjoins them to help themselves; and, for that purpose, has endowed them with intelligent minds, with moral feelings, and with bodily strength. At all times, and everywhere, governments who have ruled in opposition to the intelligence, and in violation of the moral feelings of the people, have succumbed under the popular arm. These are the ways of Providence, so recently exemplified by the revolutions which, during the last half century, have convulsed France and the whole European continent. That the same causes, if not prudently eradicated, by a timely return to the principles of reason and justice, will again produce the same effects, is a matter of certainty to all that are not blind to the signs of the times. What, but a painful anticipation of the disastrous consequences of the actual state of social and political economy, in this country, could have induced a prime minister, the creature of a proud and grasping oligarchy, to turn against the oligarchs, and to demand from them the sacrifice of their monopolies, to the wants and to the rights of the people? Are not the two ministerial revolutions in a fortnight, which we have witnessed, a convincing proof that the age of ruling factions is gone by, that Whiggism and Toryism are equally powerless, against the necessities of our epoch and the menaces of a futurity already dawning; and that a new order of things, of which the two factions could not prevent the growth, imperiously demands concessions which neither of them will propose, or dare refuse.

Judging of the measures which Lord John Russell would have proposed, from the nostrums of the Whig authority we have quoted, we can hardly be dissatisfied with the rëintegration of Sir Robert Peel in his office: not, however, that we expect from him the complete adoption and application in our financial system of an all-embracing reform, which alone can relieve the distress of the nation, without impairing the resources of the government. Such a reform, though indispensable, though unavoidable, though near at hand, cannot be accomplished by Sir Robert Peel. However convinced he might be of its necessity, practicability, and beneficial results, and however desirous of conferring those benefits on his country, he could not do it. He may attempt the great enterprise, and boldly take his stand on the field of civil, religious, and commercial freedom. But he will be defeated. He will open and pave the way for more fortunate conquerors. He himself, unluckily, has devoted thirty years of his public life to the strengthening of the bulwarks of universal monopoly, in the storming of which he is doomed to fall. It is twenty-three years, and it seems to us as if it were but yesterday, since the clear-sighted Canning, shaking off the fetters which had so long trammelled his nobler nature, awoke the enslaved and torpid nations, and thunderstruck all the tyrants of Europe by the toast—'Civil and Religious Liberty all over the World!' Catholic emancipation, parliamentary reform, free trade, an equitable assessment of public taxes, and the improvement of the physical and moral condition of the people of the United Kingdom, were the meaning of that toast, as much as the breaking up of the Holy Alliance. We know that all this was intended, and would have been successively attempted; had not the minister been worried to death, at the beginning of his new career. Will Sir Robert Peel be deterred by the fear of retaliation? This would not save him, now, from the distrust and hatred of his former associates, or conciliate his old opponents. His best chance is still to follow at all hazards the example of Canning: he cannot, indeed, do otherwise. There are retributions which cannot be averted. Cæsar fell at the foot of Pompey's statue.

The repeal of the corn laws is no longer the sole object of the present agitation; that question has, in some sort, melted into the question of free trade in general, and free trade means nothing but abolition of the present system of taxation, and the substitution of another, founded upon clear, equitable, and economical principles, now known to, and professed by every one who is not prejudiced by his partiality for certain classes, or by his hostility to other classes, and to the mass of the people. In opposition to the inconsistencies of Mr. M'Culloch, we are going to reproduce those principles, and show how they are to be applied; but we must first enter into some statistical details, upon the amount and division of the real and personal property, and of the population of Great Britain, taking for basis the returns of 1841.

The superficies of the soil contains, in round numbers, fifty-six million eight hundred and thirty-two thousand acres, of which thirty-four million fourteen thousand acres are cultivated, nine million nine hundred and thirty-four thousand acres are uncultivated, though susceptible of cultivation, and twelve million eight hundred and eighty-four acres are deemed unfit for any produce. The Tory economists estimate the value of the land at £3,769,500,000.

On the soil are three million six hundred and fifty thousand inhabited houses, which are valued at £1,137,800,000.

The capital of the funded debt is £774,319,913, producing to the creditors an income of £28,701,458.

The capital invested in the banks, in foreign securities, in all kinds of companies, is valued at £489,650,000.

The capital invested in manufactures, and trade, and shipping, cannot be valued, with any exactness; but it is certainly not less than £1,200,000,000. Thus the aggregate amount of the wealth of Great Britain is about £7,371,270,000.

The population of Great Britain is now, in round numbers, eighteen million nine hundred thousand inhabitants, of whom nine million seven hundred and fifteen thousand are females. Of the nine million one hundred and eighty-five thousand males, four million seven hundred and twenty thousand are under twenty years of age; so that the virile population, that is to say, the men of twenty years of age and above, number four million four hundred and sixty-five thousand. Let us now see how they are distributed.

One million thirty-eight thousand of this number form the agricultural body, composed of about one hundred and eighty-seven thousand landlords, or tenants, who employ eight hundred and fifty-one thousand labourers, ploughmen, carters, drovers, gardeners, &c., &c.

Four thousand five hundred factories employ, either at the mills or as hand-loom weavers, one million one hundred and twenty thousand workmen.

The working of the coal-pits, of the iron and copper mines, and the manufacture of the metals, employ five hundred thousand.

The trades of all kinds, wholesale and retail merchants, with their clerks and assistants, are about one million one hundred and thirty thousand.

The royal navy and commercial marine, have for their share of this part of the population, about two hundred and forty thousand men.

Persons living on their incomes, officials, capitalists, and professional men, amount to about two hundred and ten thousand, and they have in their retinue about one hundred and ten thousand male servants.

Finally, the clergy come forth with two archbishops, twenty-five bishops, seven hundred and thirty-three deans, archdeacons, prebendaries, and canons, ten thousand seven hundred and forty-two incumbents, four thousand eight hundred and thirteen curates, and the fellows of the universities; total, about seventeen thousand seven hundred. The army, the prisons, and the workhouses, provide for the rest of the virile population.

Let us now see what is the distribution of property among this population.

More than four-fiths of the cultivated lands of Great Britain, that is to say, above twenty-eight million acres of the landed property in regular course of cultivation, belong to not more than eight thousand individuals; and the remaining six millions of acres are, like the others, unequally divided among about one hundred and ninety thousand proprietors, the most part of whom, about one hundred and forty thousand, have their lands cultivated in gardens and pleasure grounds, round their residences; about two thousand only of the others are, from taste or necessity, cultivating their own small estates as gentlemen farmers.

The agricultural interest, then, is represented by the eight thousand large landowners, by two thousand gentlemen farmers, by one hundred and eighty-five thousand tenant farmers; altogether, one hundred and ninety-five thousand individuals; with a retinue of eight hundred and fifty-one thousand labourers or servants. Supposing that the interests of the labourers were identical with those of their employers, and of the landlords of their employers; and that they profited with them by the high prices of corn, in consequence of the corn laws; they altogether form but a fourth part of the virile population: they are one million and forty-six thousand producers of corn, against three million four hundred and nineteen thousand consumers, whose interest it is to have cheap bread; and, when there is such a difference in the numbers of the conflicting parties, it is madness to sacrifice the interests of the majority. But the agricultural labourers have not the same interest with their employers, with regard to the price of corn. Cheap bread will be a blessing to them, as well as to the rest of the community. Thus, then, the agricultural interest is but the interest of eight thousand landowners, and, at the utmost, of one hundred and eighty-seven thousand mistaken farmers, with ten thousand seven hundred and forty-two clerical incumbents of church livings.

With the exception, then, of two hundred thousand individuals, the people of England have no property in the soil of the country. The case is much the same, with regard to all other sorts of property. The three million six hundred and fifty thousand inhabited houses are the property of, at the utmost, four hundred and fifty thousand persons; the landowners, again, all coming in for the best share, in this sort of property. The number of the fundholders is about two hundred and eighty-three thousand. The official return of the Bank shows a striking similarity between the distribution of the public debt and that of the landed property. 'Of the two hundred and eighty-two thousand three hundred and forty-nine warrants issued to receive dividends, at the Bank of England, eighty-five thousand nine hundred and ninety-one were for sums not exceeding £5. Above forty-five thousand warrants were, at the same time, issued for sums under, and not exceeding £10.' So that about the half of the fundholders (one hundred and thirty-one thousand of them) do not take altogether £800,000, out of the £28,701,458, interest of the public debt. About one hundred thousand more receive, from the same source, from two to three millions sterling a year; but the bulk of the income derived from the funding system, £25,000,000 a year, is shared among about only fifty thousand large fundholders.

The landowners, the householders, the fundholders, are, at the same time, the possessors of the best part of the capital invested in the principal branches of manufactures and industry, in the public or private companies, and in the banks. In short, nearly the whole of the real, personal, or funded property, and the capital of the country, is possessed by about two hundred thousand individuals; one-tenth of it, at the utmost, is unequally divided amongst about three hundred thousand more; and four millions of the virile population of Great Britain do not possess an inch of their fatherland, nor a dwelling, how miserable soever, nor funds or capital of any description. Their intelligence, their hands, and their energy, are their only means of support; not for themselves only, but also, in most cases, for a wife and infant children. Such is our social economy! Can any thing be worse than this?

Yes! there can be, and there is, something worse than this social economy; it is our political economy, and especially that part of the system which regulates the assessment and the collection of the taxes. 'In most eastern countries,' says Mr. M'Culloch (p. 56), 'the government is, as it were, head landlord: the tax paid by the occupiers being, in general, equivalent to a pretty high rent. But, in European countries, the proprietors *have luckily been able to oppose a more effectual resistance to the encroachments of their rulers.'* The plain English of this Whig sentence is: Here, in England, all the lands were originally granted by the Crown, on condition of such services as should be required for its support. *Luckily*, the grantees were able to violate the agreement, to refuse the services; to substitute for them a land tax, at the rate of four shillings in the pound of the rental of their estates, which tax they subsequently reduced to less than one shilling, by the loose and dishonest valuations which they themselves made; and to throw upon the people all the burden of taxation, by enacting customs and excise duties.

The aggregate of these customs and excise duties on malt,

spirits, sugar, tea, coffee, tobacco, soap, and licences alone, amounts to above £32,000,000 a year, which, being paid by the four million four hundred and sixty-five thousand individuals of the virile population, is at the rate of £7 3s. 4d. per head. Now, if we consider that four millions of these individuals are working men, with an average salary of ten shillings per week, or twenty-six pounds a year, when constantly employed, it follows that, on the total yearly amount of their wages (£104,000,000), that part of the population who have nothing in the world which they can call their own, except their limbs, and their unparalleled industry and perseverance, pay £28,560,000, that is to say, at the rate of very nearly twenty-six per cent. of their scanty earnings, whilst the possessors of the most enormous wealth ever accumulated in any country, contribute only £3,344,000 to the two main sources of the revenue of the state.

The corn laws, as we stated before, and we must add the tithes, press almost exclusively upon the working classes, and by increasing at least twenty-five per cent. the prices of their necessaries, are but additional taxes imposed upon them, for the benefit of eleven thousand clergymen, of the eight thousand large landowners, and of their hundred and eighty-seven thousand farmers; supposing that farmers may participate, as they believe, in the profits derived from those laws; which, with other taxes and duties, such as those on cotton, wool, tallow, glass, paper, the window tax, &c., &c., pressing also, though with less inequality, on the working classes, nearly take from them another twenty-five per cent. of their hard-earned wages. About fifty per cent. of the earnings of the poor, taken from them, and the wealthy of the land scot free; such is our political economy, in praise of which Mr. M'Culloch writes in the following strain:

'It would, no doubt, be in various respects desirable that the inhabitants of a country should contribute to the support of the government, in proportion to their means. *This is obviously, however, a matter of secondary importance.* It is the business of the legislator, to look at the practical influence of different taxes, and to resort in preference to those by which the revenue may be raised with least inconvenience. Should the taxes least adverse to public interests fall on the contributors according to their respective abilities, it will be an additional recommendation in their favour. But the *salus populi* is, in this, as it should be in every similar matter, the first consideration; and the tax which is best fitted to promote, or least opposed to this great end, though it may not press equally on the different orders of society, is to be preferred to a more equal but otherwise less advantageous tax.'—p. 19.

Such were the arguments used, sixty years ago, by the aristocracy, the courtiers, and the M'Cullochs of France, who had expelled the honest and popular Turgot, and the virtuous Malesherbe from the councils of Louis XVI.; and which, seven years later, were invoked, but for a very different purpose, by Robespierre, St. Just, Couthon, Barère, and their fellow members of the Committee of *Public Safety!* Monarchy, aristocracy, clergy, seignorial and manorial privileges, tithes, immunities of taxation,—the *salus populi* had crushed and annihilated them altogether.

May Providence avert from Great Britain the calamities which overwhelmed her neighbours! But when we reflect on the distressed and unbearable condition of the people, on the one side; and when, on the other, we consider the blindness, the obstinacy, the madness of their ruling oppressors, we should almost despair of a bloodless adjustment of the national claim to a more equitable system of social and political economy, if a few men, suddenly raised to eminence, equally remarkable for their intelligence and for their energy, justly proud of, and faithful to their popular origin, did not allay our fears; and if the good sense, the forbearance, and, at the same time, the strength of the people themselves, did not give us the hope, that, under their new and trusty leaders, the struggle will not be long, nor the victory be tainted with revenge.

As to the principles which must inevitably prevail, and which alone can secure, for the future, the tranquillity and the welfare of the people, they are few and clear; and their equitable application presents no difficulty whatever to conscientious and right-minded men. They all proclaim, that, governments being instituted for the benefit of the subject, for the protection of his person, of his property, of his profession, and of his industry, the subject is bound to contribute to the maintenance of the government in proportion to the protection and other advantages which he derives from it, and also to his abilities. The necessity of taxation is admitted by all, with this restriction, however, that the amount of taxation claimed by the government shall never exceed the sum requisite to defray the expences of the state; that these expences shall be regulated with prudent economy; and that no tax, of any sort, shall be levied on certain classes, or on the whole nation, for the benefit of one or more particular classes.

As to the modes of raising the taxes, the best is evidently that which lets every tax-payer know, with the utmost accuracy, the amount of his debt to the state; and thereby protects the subject against the exactions of the tax-gatherer; that which is levied with the least possible annoyance to the parties subject to it; and, finally, that which is collected at the smallest possible cost, and, at the same time, with the least difficulty.

It results from these principles, that indirect taxation, customs duties, excise duties, corn laws, and tithes, are as bad in principle, as they are expensive in their collection and mischievous in their effects. Direct taxes are the only ones that suit a free country; the only ones susceptible of equitable assessment, and of easy and economical collection; the only ones that can prevent fraud on the part of the contributor, exaction on the part of the collector, or those combinations between the two, so prejudicial to the state, and of which we have lately seen so many instances: finally, they are the only ones whose efficacy or faults can soon and easily be ascertained, and improved or corrected. Let us now proceed to the application of our principles.

The government protects the person of the subject; all subjects are, as individuals, of equal value in the eyes of the government, and they are of equal value in their own estimation. The ploughman's and the weaver's life and security are of as much importance to them, as the life and security of the Archbishop of Canterbury or the Duke of Wellington, may be to the most reverend prelate and to the noble duke themselves. The personal tax, a head-tax, imposed upon every man of and above twenty years of age, and of the same amount for all, is a natural consequence of the natural equality of men. This tax, at the rate of five per cent. of the average wages of the working men, (10s. per week,) would produce, for the whole of the male population of Great Britain, £5,800,000 a-year.

The government protects individuals in the possession and in the enjoyment of their landed property. Individuals therefore must pay for that protection, first, in proportion to the actual value of that property, when they take possession of it, either by inheritance, or by purchase; and, secondly, in proportion to the annual rent which they derive from the land. If, as we have it from Whig and Tory economists, the value of all the landed property in Great Britain amounts to the sum of £3,769,500,000, the whole of that property passing from one to another, in the course of twenty-five years, either by the death of proprietors or by sale, it follows that, on the average, landed property to the amount of £150,780,000, passes from one to another proprietor every year. A legacy, or inheritance duty, graduated according to the degree of relationship, but the minimum of which should be three per cent., and a registration of transfer duty of six per cent. of the price of the property sold, would produce, on an average of four per cent., £6,031,200 a-year.

We have stated in a preceding page, that the land was originally granted on condition of performing some military or feudal services, but that the grantees had compounded those duties for a tax of four shillings in the pound, which, however, they contrived to reduce to one shilling. The landowners would have no reason to complain, if, instead of binding them to their former agreement, a duty of ten per cent. on their rental were demanded from them. But at the same time care should be taken to take for the basis of the assessment, the leases themselves, and the amount of fines exacted from the tenants, so that the old trick of mock valuation should not be repeated. The landlords, and their economists, in order to escape taxation, gravely tell us, that the total rental from the land in England and Wales is only £33,000,000, whilst, when they wish to prove the superiority of agriculture over manufactures, they proclaim that the annual produce of agriculture in Great Britain amounts, in value, to £280,000,000. These two valuations are rather at variance the one with the other, and prove the necessity of a more accurate assessment. But we are sure that the most rigorous researches would establish that the annual rental from land in Great Britain amounts to more than £70,000,000. A duty of ten per cent. would produce £7,000,000.

Extending to the householders that principle which we have applied to the landowners, a tax upon the transfer of houses, by inheritance or by sale, must be imposed. The total value of all the houses being £1,137,800,000, and the average value of the houses sold or inherited being £45,512,000, a duty, on an average of four per cent., will produce £1,820,480.

The total rental from houses in Great Britain amounting to from £55,000,000, to £60,000,000, a tax of ten per cent. on the minimum rental of £55,000,000, will amount to £5,500,000.

Thus the annual income of the state, arising from taxes on real property and from a tax per head, in Great Britain alone, would amount to above £26,000,000; the half of the actual expenditure for the government of the United Kingdom. Another portion of the expenditure must be supplied by taxes on personal property, which being entitled to, and obtaining the same protection from the state, as real property, must contribute in the same manner and in the same proportion, to the support of the state. We must, therefore, follow up the application of our principle.

The whole capital of the debt due by the state to some of its subjects, like real property, passes by inheritance from one proprietor to another in the course of twenty-five years. This capital amounting to £774,319,913, it follows that there are such transfers of this capital amounting, on an average, to £30,972,796. An inheritance or legacy duty, averaging four per cent., will produce during the year £1,238,911.

The interest paid to the holders of stock amounts to £28,701,458. An income-tax of ten per cent. on the interest, which is equal to that paid by the landowner on his rental, or by the working man on his wages, will annually produce £2,870,145.

Industry, manufactures, and commerce, shipping, banking, joint-stock companies of every sort; and, lastly, all professions and trades, in return for the protection which the state extends to them, are bound to provide, in proportion to the benefits derived from that protection, for the wants of the state. Here, however, there is an immense difference in the extent and efficacy of governmental protection as regards the landowner and the fundholder on the one part, and, on the other, the class which is now the subject of our observations. Government cannot secure to this class a regular and certain rate of profits for the capital invested, as in the case of the fundholder. Government cannot even guarantee the conservation of the capital ventured in pursuits which, however well combined and managed, are subject to innumerable failures from external causes. £40,000 may suddenly disappear from the banking-house of Messrs. Rogers; but nobody can steal forty thousand acres from the estates of the Duke of Sutherland. Besides risks of all kinds, there is another difference between the three classes which will justify a lower rate of taxation for the latter. The landowner and the fundholder get their incomes without giving themselves the least trouble, whilst the industrialists, agriculturists, manufacturers, and all others comprised in the latter class, must work hard indeed, and endure all sorts of anxieties, to secure profits at all commensurate with their risks. For this reason, while the landowner is taxed ten per cent. of his rent, the occupier, or tenant-farmer, ought not in fairness to be taxed more than five per cent. of his income. This income has been valued for the assessment of the income-tax at one-half of the rent, which, in Great Britain, amounting to £70,000,000, gives £35,000,000 as the profits of the one hundred and eighty-seven thousand farmers. The tax of five per cent. would therefore produce £1,750,000.

The capital invested in joint-stock banks, or companies for railways, canals, insurances, &c., &c., amounts now to above £500,000,000, which, like other property, being subject to legacy duty, would annually produce, according to the preceding computations, £800,000.

The incomes of all the joint-stock banks or companies, on an average profit of five per cent., would amount to £25,000,000; and a tax of five per cent. upon their profits, paid by the companies, would amount to £1,250,000.

The commercial marine of Great Britain numbers about forty thousand vessels of all kinds, employed in the coasting and foreign trade, the aggregate tonnage of which is above six million tons. Their value may be safely estimated at £250,000,000; on which capital, the legacy duty would annually produce £400,000.

An annual tax of two shillings and sixpence per ton on every vessel would produce £1,700,000, and the commercial marine would thus discharge its debt to the state for its protection.

The capital invested in manufactures and trades, as well as in private banks and mines, cannot be ascertained with anything like accuracy; and it is still more difficult to ascertain the profits derived from these occupations. The result of our long and laborious investigations is, that the capital invested in them, as well as by wholesale and retail merchants and dealers, cannot be less than £1,200,000,000, on which the legacy duty, as before explained, would annually produce £1,920,000.

It being utterly impossible to ascertain the exact amount of profits, we must be content with an approximate valuation, generally admitted as very fair, not only here, in England, but also everywhere on the Continent. Ten per cent. of the capital invested in trade or business is considered as the average annual return of this capital; which return is divided in halves under the two heads of interest of the money invested and profits. The annual produce of a capital of £1,200,000,000 invested in private banks, mines, manufactures, and trades, according to this computation, is therefore £120,000,000. A tax of five per cent. will amount to £6,000,000. a-year.

The adoption of a general and equitable system of licences is the most efficacious, if not the only practical mode of assessing and collecting this tax, so as to make it bear on the several classes in proportion to their respective means; that is to say, to the capital invested in, and to the income derived from, their business. To effect this, is not a matter of great difficulty. Without entering into details, which would harass our readers, we will show, in two instances, how the principle may be applied. In the case of two manufacturers, one employing one hundred persons, and the other five hundred or more, and the fixed licence duty being £50 a-year, we suppose a proportional duty should be added, such as 5*s.* a-year for every person under twelve years of age; 10*s.*, from twelve years of age to sixteen; 15*s.*, from sixteen to twenty; and, lastly, £1. for every man of twenty years of age or above. Thus both manufacturers would be taxed according to their presumed profits.

There being in Great Britain seventy thousand publicans, or inn, tavern, and hotel-keepers, a licence duty of £2. on the publicans in villages, and of £4. in towns, with a proportional duty of 2*s.* in the pound on the rent of their houses, would secure an equitable assessment of the tax. The licences of the innkeepers, subject to a duty of £6. in villages, £9. in country towns, and £12. in London, should in the same manner equally affect all persons comprised in this class, by the same addition of 2s. in the pound on the amount of the rent of their houses.

Attorneys, barristers, apothecaries, surgeons, and physicians, should be subjected to the general licensing system. Like other tradespeople, they are bound to pay for the protection which they receive, and for the professional privileges which it secures to them.

A laborious investigation of trades, professions, and occupations of all kinds, satisfies us, and would satisfy our readers, if we could enter into particulars, that £6,000,000 a year, and even more, would be produced by this tax, without harshness to the contributor, and without trouble or expense to the collector.

Of all the duties at present in existence, the only ones which should be continued are the stamp duties on deeds, bills of exchange, promissory notes, and receipts, and the duties on private carriages, servants, horses, dogs, and shooting licences, or game certificates; amounting altogether to about four millions two hundred thousand pounds. All other duties should be abolished.

The aggregate amount of the produce of this direct system of taxation would be, for Great Britain, £46,180,736, to which must be added £1,000,000, derived from the post-office and from the crown lands. Thus we have a national income, exceeding by nearly £1,500,000 that which is now raised by the unequal, oppressive, and demoralising system of customs and excise duties, and all the other taxes. The same system applied to Ireland, would yield more than the £4,000,000 which the sister country, at present, contributes to the national revenue; and the revenue of Great Britain and Ireland would amount to £51,180,736.*

To all the advantages of the proposed system of direct over indirect taxation, must be added an economy of above £2,500,000 in the collection of the revenue; the abolition of that inquisitorial espionage, frequently degenerating into regular warfare on the part of the customs and excise officers, against the people; and, last though not least, the curtailment of the corrupting patronage of the ministry, by the suppression of above fifteen thousand offices.

Such is our political economy, with regard to taxation; and

* Sir Robert Peel stated last year, that, with the reductions made in the customs duties, the revenue for the year ending April 5, 1846, would amount to £50,300,000; and it appears, from the official returns, that the income, for the year ending January 5, 1846, amounts to £50,601,988.

we feel convinced, that, before long, notwithstanding the opposition of the monopolists, in spite of the Whig and Tory economists, and without regard to the lamentations of the placeholders and of the place-hunters, something like this system must be adopted. Nothing short of it can remedy the distress and secure the lasting prosperity of the nation.

Since we wrote the foregoing article, a new publication, entitled, 'Thoughts on Finance and Colonies,' by Publius, [London: Smith, Elder, and Co., Cornhill. 1846] has come to hand. Feeling equal to any hard task, after reading Mr. M'Culloch, we did not mind wasting an hour or two in reading Publius; and, having done so, we may as well say a few words on his curious performance.

To his country, Publius dedicates 'thoughts on finance and colonies.' This dedicatory page will no doubt strike the reader, by its laconism, and impress upon his mind a due sense of the patriotism of Publius, and of the value which he attaches to his own thoughts.

In the first chapter, 'the synopsis,' Publius announces his 'plan for a slight recasting of the corn laws, and of a few items of the tariff, in 1846;' he then separates the remaining protective covering into five folds, of equal thickness, one of which he supposes removed every three years, till the fifth and last disappearance in 1861. 'There are strong financial and political reasons for fixing on the year 1861 as the limit of protection.' (p. 6.) The last twelve pages of the chapter (from 21 to 33) are devoted to a most fulsome laudation of Sir Robert Peel, whose conversion to free trade is compared to the conversion of St. Paul; and who is represented as the instrument of a watchful Providence, in forwarding the growth and progress of the church, and of the interests of the aristocracy.

In the second chapter, a very short one, on '*population—property—revenue,*'—we see how they will all prosperously increase, so that, 'in 1901, with a population of fifty-seven million inhabitants, and one hundred millions in revenue, England will go onwards, elevating her head among the nations, yet higher and higher—the chief pioneer, whom the Most High has selected out of all nations and tongues, for carrying forward his gracious designs towards the ransomed posterity of Adam.'

'*Taxation,—general principles,*' is the subject of the third chapter, in which Publius unfolds his plan of taxation, supported with scriptural texts, poetical and grandiloquent sentences, and algebraical equations, worthy of a Cambridge man; and, here and there, some hard hits at Mr. M'Culloch. In this chapter, Publius also offers a plan, 'easy and practicable,' for the redemption of the national debt, and capable of accomplishment within fixed and determined periods, (p. 99;)' 'by means of an orderly, systematised, and scientific course of life insurances.' (p. 100.)

The fourth chapter is but a short introduction to the fifth; '*Colonies: general principles stated and applied.*' Publius, however, overlooks all the colonies with the exception of Canada; and, there, the application of his general principles consists in erecting the colony into a kingdom, for Prince Alfred, who will marry a granddaughter of Louis Philippe, and, after thus conciliating the French and English populations, will keep in check the turbulent republicans of the States. It is amusing to follow the author in his speculations, in his description of the 'scene in the far-west, of the new kingdom rising up—the name New England and France: Montreal changed to New London; Quebec, to New Paris,—the prince coming with his bride to their kingdom, attended by a mighty cortege of the highest in church and state; the solemn coronation of the two at New London, &c., &c. O glorious and transporting sight!' (pp. 132, 133.)

We suppose the author to be a young man of kind and benevolent dispositions; and we regret not to be able to give to his performance any other praise than that of good intent.

Art. II.—*Sermons; Second Series. By Richard Winter Hamilton, L.L.D. D.D.* Hamilton Adams, Jackson and Walford, London.

THE author of this volume has been so frequently before the public, and some of his works have been so fully reviewed in former numbers of this journal, as to supersede the necessity of lengthened remark on his mental characteristics and style of composition.

There is no living writer, we think, who so uniformly stamps, as Dr. Hamilton does, the full impress of his powers on his various publications. Some of his subjects may be more to our liking than others, but let the theme he takes be what it may, he discovers in discussing it, the same grasp of thought, the same richness of fancy, the same affluence of illustration. If we may judge from internal evidence, most writers seem to sit down to their tasks with only a general idea of the topic they propose to handle, which, however, becomes more and more definite as they work upon it, so that many of its diversified applications are at length brought under review. Others appear as if they were able by anticipatory musings, to vision out before the mental eye the whole discussion ere they put pen to paper, and by a peculiar force of imagination to keep this picture before the understanding while it works off a description of it, as Sir Joshua Reynolds would have done of a painting by Raphael or Rubens. The author of these discourses seems to belong to this latter class. We should suppose him to be a stranger to everything like vexation or regret, over imperfect developments of his views on the subjects he lays before the public. We do not mean that he is ever flushed with a proud gladness, as if he had accomplished his task better than any other could have done it: there is every indication of his being among the humblest of men. We simply mean, that while he would be ready to assert, in all sincerity of conviction, his inferiority to many of his brethren, who yet were, in reality, far below him; he knows, we suspect, little or nothing of the distress so many endure from the impossibility they feel of doing justice to their own ideal of a subject.

Nothing can be more peculiar than the method Dr. Hamilton adopts in his treatment of a topic,—a method which has a glorious mannerism about it—but his variety under that method is inexhaustible. A chastised Calvinism is his doctrinal distinction, and activity of mind, his leading intellectual characteristic. Surprise cannot but be felt at the number of his thoughts, their easy movement, and their sure gyration round some master principle, into which he resolves his text. Whoever is familiar with his earlier books, can give a sure guess as to the way in which he will approach his theme; but beyond this general idea, can never anticipate what he will produce upon it. It is a guess which irritates instead of extinguishing curiosity. Every subject, though in one sense treated alike, has its own freshness, its own fulness, its own vastness. There is just the sameness which the reader wishes to find in a great author, with that *otherness* of thought and illustration which invests with the charm of perfect novelty each succeeding publication. The themes included in the present volume are of the loftiest order. We need only give in proof of the assertion, the titles of some of the discourses: 'The Revealed Deity,' 'The Grandeur of Redemption,' 'Moral Inability,' 'The mystery of the Incarnate God,' 'Jesus Christ the Cause and Consummator of all Things,' 'The Immediate Blessedness of Departed Saints,' 'The Ministry of Angels,' 'The Resurrection of the Just,' 'The Judgment of the Last Day,' 'The Final Heaven.'

If we were to indulge in extracts, there is scarcely a page which would not supply us with some exquisite specimens of textual exposition, or sustained argument, or vivid illustration, or piercing application; but we would rather refer our readers to the entire volume. Occasionally, expansion is, perhaps, carried to excess, and there are some figures which we wish had been expunged by the author, as he revised for the press. Yet, judging by the effect of the whole, and in the recollection of the many fine thoughts and gorgeous images, to be found in the immediate neighbourhood of what our taste would have rejected, we are in no mood to find fault. Ever and anon, also, we come to single sentences of such transcendant power, or beauty, as render us impatient of all reference to minor blemishes. They usually occur at the close of a paragraph, and are designed to exhibit its meaning in a condensed form, and yet add a something more to it. Such epitomies are made with extraordinary skill. They thrill on the understanding and heart, with magnificent effect, so that for very pleasure's sake we cannot help reading them again and again. Separated from their connection they might be given as precious texts for thought, and meditative minds would be instantly fascinated as by a spell; but their exuberant richness can only be properly appreciated, when they are read in the place where the author has put them. They plenipotise beyond the *auræ sententiæ* of any other theological writer of the day. An example of this pregnant brevity of sentence occurs in an early page of the first sermon, where, speaking of the Divine Nature, he says, 'What is congenial, what is lawful, what is susceptible for God to love fully, justly, save his own nature? For if God is love, we enquire—love of what? Say of being? He is the 'fountain of life.' Say of excellence? He is the reason, the glory, the judge of all virtue. *It is by his self-love that all the activities of his far-beaming and out-working benevolence are informed and ruled.'* A hundred others, as good, and scores of others even better, for suggestiveness than this, might be found, but we take the first which offers. It is an average instance.

It would be hardly fair, however, to omit all specimen of the manner in which subjects are discussed in this volume. The citation we shall give, will be taken from the sermon on the immediate blessedness of departed saints. It is long, but we are mistaken if it does not greatly interest our readers, by the exposition it gives of a difficult passage, at the same time rendering that passage, strikingly illustrative of the text, 'The spirits of just men made perfect.'

'These separated spirits, are represented to us, as in a state of exalted advancement, depending upon their disembodiment.

'This doctrine of immediate happiness was not entirely concealed from the ancient saints. Their language occasionally leads us to think that they had some conception of it. Yet every passage of

Scripture which has been cited, may not be found strictly to apply—'Thou will not leave my soul in the invisible world,' said David, but it was when 'in spirit' he spoke of his distant Son. 'And afterward, Thou wilt receive me to glory,' cried Asaph, but the word does not compel the strictly consecutive idea. The truth seems more clear in the following expressions: 'God will redeem my soul from the power of the grave, for he shall receive me.' 'He shall enter into peace: they shall rest in their beds, each one walking in his uprightness'. In both these passages there is an intimation of a higher nature, that which is 'redeemed,' and which can be 'received,' that which is detached from what rests in its bed and which can be actively 'upright' still. Yet, as a solacing support, it was scarcely discovered, even by 'prophets and righteous men:' feebly was it enjoyed. The grave to them was dark. Jesus had not lain in it. They shrunk from death as from a suspension of their powers and joys. Bereavement smote them as an irremediable woe. 'Lest I be like those that go down into the pit.' 'The dead praise not the Lord, neither any that go down into silence.' 'Spare me a little longer before I go hence and be no more.' 'They that go down into the pit cannot hope for thy truth. And had they known the receptacle of departed spirits, it ought not to have inspired the delightful hopes we cherish. It was doubtless a sphere of spiritual bliss. It was 'Abraham's bosom.' It was 'under the earth.' The divine presence was intimately vouchsafed. The higher advantages of the Christian economy were gladly awaited. It was a heaven, but it was not the proper heaven. It was not the dwelling of the Deity. Enoch and Elijah were not in it. They were taken to God. Christ was not then incarnate, nor offered up: consequently he was not there. We think that we but follow the light of Scripture, confessedly feeble as to this intimation, in maintaining that these spirits, held until then in a nether and unequal heaven, ascended with Christ to heaven proper and exalted, to the heaven which he now inhabits, though not necessarily the final heaven. It is fitted for materialism, because the persons of the Antediluvian saint and the Tishbite prophet have their abode in it, most of all, because the glorified humanity of Jesus distinguishes and identifies it. It is at least, all that spirits need. Who would now speak of it as Abraham's bosom? It is not the same in region, or in state, as that to which the souls of the ancient righteous were borne. It is surely reasonable to think that while all is advanced by Christianity on earth, there is corresponding advancement in all which it so entirely affects, beyond these earthly bounds. If there be more bliss here, the bliss of other worlds must be augmented. What then is the testimony of Scripture? 'Now is Christ risen from the dead, and become the first fruits of them that *slept*.' It is an action upon the past; it is a benefit to the *former* dead; *they* owe to his resurrection, a most important change—'Thou hast ascended on high: thou hast led *captivity captive*.' It is untrue, in fact, and incorrect in figure, that such language of triumph intends the dragging of *enemies*, as at his chariot wheels. How can we interpret *captivity* into the power of making *captive?* It is a subjective thing. It may be asked, in reply, How can we take captive such passive captivity? We offer the following historic illustrations: When Chedorlaomer despoiled the cities of the plain, Lot was 'taken captive.' Abraham 'armed his trained servants, pursued and smote the enemy, and brought back all the goods, and also brought again his brother Lot.' Here was recapture. Captivity was led captive, or the 'captivity was turned again.' Held of the foe, the captives seem assailed, but it is in kindness and for rescue. Though they appear to suffer a second captivity, it is at the hands of their deliverers and friends. It is not their discomfiture, but their enfranchisement.—When Ziklag was burned and sacked by the Amalekites, they 'took the women captive and carried them away.' Ahinoam and Abigail were among them. David at the bidding of the ephod pursued the robbers, 'recovered all that they had taken away, and rescued his two wives.' This was recapture. They who were torn away from home and liege, are snatched from their abductors and the 'captivity' is 'led captive.' It is a new seizure, but it is from the grasp of the foe.—When in the ode of Deborah she sings, 'Arise, Barak, and lead thy captivity captive,' the appeal supposes that he had broken the chains of his people, whom the 'Lord had *sold* into the hand of Jabin, king of Canaan.' Let these illustrations be now applied. Departed souls were in a captivity. Death had disunited them from the body. Though their captivity was made happy, it was estrangement. They were not on earth. They were not in heaven. Though their circumstances were over-ruled for their blessedness, the circumstances themselves, did not tend to it. They were children of a captivity, or a throng of spirits, over which death yet exercised a disadvantageous and fearful influence. Christ was the conqueror. 'He spoiled principalities and powers.' Of him it was declared that he should 'swallow up death in victory.' He ascends! He is 'received up into glory!' There are not only the angels and the chariots in their thousands of thousands,—there is another train! All holy spirits follow Him, who had appeared a spirit to them, in their place of keeping. They now forsake that place for 'things above.' They are led by their deliverer, as a once captive band (though made glad in spite of such bondage, by Him, who only suffered their detention with a view to their ultimate release,) and this procession, albeit 'a captivity,' is not one of prisoners, but of the enlarged and disenthralled. They rejoice in the triumph, they partake of the victory, it is their jubilee; they are the liberated, the ransomed and the redeemed. 'As he spoke by the mouth of his holy prophets, which have been since the world began, that we should be saved from our enemies, and from the hand of all that hate us'—and therefore it is said in the text; 'Ye are come to the spirits of just men made perfect.' But this is asserted as a privilege unknown before. It arises from the New Covenant, in contradistinction from the Old. It is explained: 'God having provided some better things for us,' (than for those who died before the rising of Christ,) 'that they without us' (without living until our time and under our dispensation) 'should not be *made perfect;*' but they are *now made perfect* in common with us. This perfection is bestowed upon all past, as well as for all future time, and 'ye are come to the spirits of just men made perfect.'

' 'It is thus that we shall experience the very changes which the Lord of the dead and of the living bore: He died, his spirit went from him, it sojourned in the abode where the purest spirits called from earth alone could dwell, he rose bodily, his whole manhood was completed in that event, he ascended, and when he had thus overcome the sharpness of death, he opened the kingdom of heaven for all believers.* 'Every one that is perfect, shall be as his Master.' (pp. 332—5.)

To this view of the passage we can see no valid objection. It is by no means new: with the exception of what is said of the consciousness of departed saints in the separate state before the resurrection of the Messiah, the exposition is precisely similar to that which Hallet gave in his Notes to the eleventh chapter of the epistle to the Hebrews, above a century ago, though Dr. Hamilton does not seem aware of the coincidence.

The volume is dedicated to Dr. Henry Burder, of Hackney, formerly one of Dr. Hamilton's tutors at Hoxton; and we can easily imagine the joyous satisfaction with which he will peruse the pages of his distinguished pupil.

We certainly do not expect that the work will be popular with general readers. It is too intellectual a production we fear for such a wide dispersion. The ministers of our different denominations, however, are numerous enough to purchase one or two editions, and we deliberately think that none of them ought to be without a copy. It is a book which will be pondered by many now, but which, we doubt not, will be still more read and appreciated by the generation to come.

Art. III.—*Poems*, by Thomas Hood. 2 vols. Moxon.

Although few modern writers have attained a wider celebrity than the late Thomas Hood, perhaps scarcely any one of their number has been less truly known,—we might almost say more misunderstood,—as to the true bent of his genius, than the poet, who, little more than two years since, startled the whole land, by his intensely powerful 'Song of the Shirt.' In the literary

* Quoted from that noble hymn, the 'Te Deum.'

world, indeed, Thomas Hood was always recognized as a poet of no ordinary standing; but among the mass of readers, amused from year to year, by the laughable stories, and playful verses, and whimsicalities of his 'Comic Annual,' he was known only as the humourous poet, and ludicrous prose writer, who furnished them with their Christmas-tide stock of mirth.

But it was not under this character that he wished to appear to the world, nor to have his name handed down to posterity. The publication, therefore, of these two little volumes, containing his serious poetry, affords us a suitable occasion for some remarks on the peculiar characteristics of a writer, who died ere he had half worked out the nobler purposes to which his mature genius had devoted itself, but who yet lived long enough to produce some poems, 'which the world will not willingly let die.'

The genius of Thomas Hood—strange as the assertion may appear to the majority of our readers—was essentially melancholy. We use this term rather in its elder sense, as denoting deep and solemn reflection; for with the modern melancholies superinduced by exaggerated self-importance, or by a sickly constitution, or a sickly intellect, he had no sympathy; and thus, in his earliest poems, there was a sententiousness, an intense thoughtfulness, which gave little indication of the future author of the most popular comic works of the day. In these earliest poems,—which appeared in the 'London Magazine,' when that periodical boasted the names of Charles Lamb, Barry Cornwell, De Quincy, and Thomas Carlyle, among its contributors, his noble 'Hymn to the Sun,' his wild fragment entitled 'The Sea of Death,' when—

'Sad were my thoughts that anchored silently
On the dead waters of that passionless sea,
Unstirr'd by any touch of living breath:'—

and that powerful and most pathetic tale of 'Lycus the Centaur,' as well as many shorter pieces, varied, as they were in style, were all marked by deep melancholy. His mind, indeed, seems to have been almost weighed down by the wealth of his imagination.

'All things are touched with melancholy,
Born of the secret soul's mistrust,
To feel her fair ethereal wings
Weighed down with vile degraded dust;—
O! give her then her tribute just,

Her sighs, and tears, and musings holy!
There is no music in the life
That sounds with idiot laughter solely;
There's not a string attuned to mirth,
But has its chord in melancholy."—vol. ii. p. 264.

Thus sang the future author of the 'Comic Annual.' To some, there will appear a strange contradiction in this, but the history of genius presents many similar instances. Nor is it surprising that the mind, weighed down by solemn and anxious musings, should turn with strong effort to the wildest and most playful exercises of the fancy, and find relief from deep sadness even in laughter. The great success of Mr. Hood's first comic work, 'Whims and Oddities,' encouraged him to continue; but it was still to graver poetry that his inclination turned: and in 1827 he published that graceful poem, 'The Plea of the Midsummer Fairies,' his 'Hero and Leander,'—which, in the rich quaintness of the imagery, as well as in the rythm, strongly reminds us of Shakespere's 'Venus and Adonis;' together with those poems which had originally appeared in the 'London Magazine.' From the first poem we will give a short specimen, —the picture of a Deserted Infant:—

"'His pretty pouting mouth, witless of speech,
Lay half-way open like a rose-lipped shell;
And his young cheek was softer than a peach,
Whereon his tears, for roundness, could not dwell,
But quickly rolled themselves to pearls, and fell,
Some on the grass, and some against his hand,
Or haply wandered to the dimpled well,
Which love beside his mouth had sweetly planned,
Yet not for tears, but mirth and smilings bland.

"'Pity it was to see those frequent tears
Falling regardless from his friendless eyes;
There was such beauty in those twin blue spheres,
As any mother's heart might leap to prize;
Blue were they, like the zenith of the skies
Softened betwixt two clouds, both clear and mild;—
Just touched with thought, and yet not over wise,
They showed the gentle spirit of a child,
Not yet by care or any craft defiled.

"'Pity it was to see the ardent sun
Scorching his helpless limbs—it shone so warm;
For kindly shade or shelter he had none,
Nor mother's gentle breast, come fair or storm.
Meanwhile I bade my pitying mates transform

Like grasshoppers, and then, with shrilly cries,
All round the infant noisily we swarm,
Happily some passing rustic to advise—
Whilst providential Heaven our care espies.' '—ib. pp. 89, 90.

Unfortunately, for the young poet, while his comic productions met with a favourable reception, and a rapid sale, his little volume of choice poetry was scarcely noticed, and disappointed and vexed, he turned from those higher walks, in which he so delighted, to become the humourous poet of his age.

Thomas Hood possessed great variety of talent. He drew well, and the poetry which overflowed his mind, often directed his pencil. When he commenced his series of comic works, his quick sense of the ludicrous, and bizarre, found a singular scope in his illustrative drawings, which, as some of our readers may doubtless remember, contributed full as much to the humourous interest, as his veritable 'pen and ink sketches.' This union of talent, while it increased to an incredible extent the popularity of his comic writings, was nevertheless unfortunate, inasmuch as the clever caricaturist became an object of hostility to a certain party, who never forgave the introduction of Irving into one of these pictures, just after that ludicrous presentation of the gold watch on the platform. It was certainly irritating to the admirers of that deluded man, to see the Geneva cloak in juxta-position with the ragged jackets of the placard-bearer of 'try Morrison's pills,' but the full cry of abuse and anathema, which from henceforth opened upon the caricaturist, was most unjustifiable. Unfortunately, too, these loud boasters arrogated to themselves the title of 'the religious world;' leading many, besides Mr. Hood, to take *them* as its *bona fide* representatives. Foremost among these, was Mr. Rae Wilson, to whom the caustic ode, which we regret to see here, was addressed. Such conduct produced its natural effect. Irritated beyond endurance, by abuse and insult, both in print and in anonymous letters, the satirist too indiscriminately attacked a class, although the noisy, overbearing Pharisee was the object in view; and thus gave countenance to the idea that he was hostile to Christianity itself.

We willingly pass from this subject, to trace the farther development of his singularly varied genius. Hitherto, although scorning imitation, Hood had evidently formed his style on the model of the poets of the Elizabethan age. In 1829, however, he startled the world when in the height of his fame as a comic writer, with his 'Dream of Eugene Aram.' The marvellous powers of this poem, revealed to Mr. Hood's friends the true bent of his genius, and earnestly did they wish he would again resume his serious style. The extraordinary success of his humourous writings, especially of his 'Comic Annual,' precluded this, and with the exception of a few exquisite sonnets, and short pieces, he continued to be recognized almost only as a comic writer, until his return to England, after several years absence in 1840. The stir, the restless strivings, the eager competition, which he witnessed around him, on his return, and which contrasted so powerfully with the dull monotony of German life, seem to have deeply impressed him. Although always earnest, in whatever he undertook, he now became more solemnly earnest. Even his lightest productions took a graver tone, and in many, was concealed a severe moral. 'The Schoolmistress Abroad,' and some other prose tales, which during his editorship he wrote for the 'New Monthly Magazine,' illustrate this. But unfortunately, those who avowedly read for mere amusement, care very little for profit, and the whimsical incident which was intended by the writer to awaken attention to some important point, was dismissed with an unthinking laugh. 'Ah!' said Mr. Hood, bitterly, 'they laugh at my fun, but turn aside from my moral.' One of the most striking of his compositions, about this time was, 'that wondrous piece of accumulated sarcasm and pathos,' as a contemporary has well characterised it—the story of Miss Kilmanseg's leg, with its solemn *refrain* of 'gold, gold, nothing but gold;' and its powerful painting of utter selfishness, pampered by wealthy extravagance from the cradle to the grave.

But still, utterance yet more direct, was sought for those deep thoughts, and intense feelings, that were burning stronger and stronger in his breast. At length the narrative of a poor sempstress, who appeared before the Lord Mayor, and stated that she made shirts at three half-pence a piece, appeared in the public papers. The story was read with deep commiseration, it was referred to again, and again; and after a sleepless night, Mr. Hood threw off, almost without a blot, 'The Song of the Shirt.' It is scarcely necessary to do more than refer to a poem so well known, but we think sufficient notice has scarcely been taken of its extreme simplicity. Not a word, but what a child can read; not a phrase but what the most ignorant are familiar with;—every figure, every illustration, taken from the very commonest every day life; and yet what marvellous intensity of effect! How important do even 'seam, and gussett and band,' become, when pored over until 'the brain begins to swim;' how desolate is the room, when even 'her shadow' is thanked 'for sometimes falling there;' and how desperate the misery when even of death, 'that phantom of grisly bone,' it is said—

'I hardly fear his terrible shape,
It seems so like my own,—
It seems so like my own,
Because of the fasts I keep,
Oh God! that bread should be so dear,
And flesh and blood, so cheap!'

The fame of 'The Song of the Shirt,' which originally appeared in 'Punch,' soon spread more rapidly over the land, than perhaps any other poem of modern times. But in the midst of the burst of admiration that hailed the writer, Thomas Hood, exhibited no exultation, and to the gratulations of his friends he only replied, 'I hope it will do good.'

Mr. Hood was now earnestly solicited by some of the leaders of 'the Anti-Corn Law League,' to aid that cause. As the friend of every institution devoted to the interests of humanity, or freedom, he was most willing to accede to their proposal of devoting his genius exclusively to it. But he had just commenced a magazine bearing his own name; and he thought that the advocacy of not only 'cheap bread,' but that of the various classes of sufferers through the unequal distribution of wealth, could be more efficiently, inasmuch as more indirectly, conducted there. But to the end of his life, he was an earnest advocate of that cause; and the progress, and success of the League, was always to him a subject of exceeding interest. Much about this time, his beautiful poem of 'the Elm Tree,' was written, and we regret our space will not allow us room for extracts.

Closely following on 'the Song of the Shirt,' his less known 'Lady's Dream,' appeared in the second number of his magazine, with a most forcible illustration from his pencil, entitled, 'the Modern Belinda,' in which he depicted a lady in full dress, attired by *skeleton* sylphs. As the miseries of the starved sempstress were painted in 'the Song of the Shirt,' so in this, the cause of the poor overworked young milliners was advocated. The lady starts up from a fearful dream of—

"Death, death, nothing but death,
In every sight and sound."

And then she relates it—

"'And oh! those maidens young,
Who wrought in that dreary room,
With figures drooping and spectres thin,
And cheeks without a bloom;—
And the Voice that cried, 'For the pomp of pride,
We haste to an early tomb!

"'For the pomp and pleasure of Pride,
We toil like Afric slaves,
And only to earn a home at last,
Where yonder cypress waves;'—
And then they pointed—I never saw
A ground so full of graves!

"And still the coffins came,
With their sorrowful trains and slow;
Coffin after coffin still,
A sad and sickening show;
From grief exempt, I never had dreamt
Of such a World of Woe!

"Of the hearts that daily break,
Of the tears that hourly fall,
Of the many, many troubles of life,
That grieve this earthly ball—
Disease and Hunger, and Pain, and Want,
But now I dreamt of them all!

"For the blind and the cripple were there,
And the babe that pined for bread,
And the houseless man, and the widow poor
Who begged—to bury the dead;
The naked, alas, that I might have clad,
The famished I might have fed!

"Each pleading look, that long ago
I scanned with a heedless eye,
Each face was gazing as plainly there,
As when I passed it by;
Woe, woe for me if the past should be
Thus present when I die!

"No need of sulphureous lake,
No need of fiery coal,
But only that crowd of human kind
Who wanted pity and dole—
In everlasting retrospect—
Will wring my sinful soul!

"Alas! I have walked through life
Too heedless where I trod;
Nay, helping to trample my fellow worm,
And fill the burial sod—
Forgetting that even the sparrow falls
Not unmarked of God!

"I drank the richest draughts;
And ate whatever is good—

Fish, and flesh, and fowl, and fruit,
  Supplied my hungry mood;
But I never remembered the wretched ones
  That starve for want of food!' '—vol. i. pp. 76—79.

Still intent on the object which he had now marked out for himself, Thomas Hood's next poem was a wild but forcible allegory, entitled 'the Workhouse Clock.' The conclusion is powerful—

'Oh! that the Parish Powers
Who regulate Labour's hours,
The daily amount of human trial,
Weariness, pain, and self-denial
Would turn from the artificial dial
That striketh ten or eleven,
And go, for once, by that older one
That stands in the light of Nature's sun
And takes its time from Heaven!'—ib. p. 85.

'The Bridge of Sighs,' one of the most pathetic of his poems, followed; giving the picture of an unfortunate young woman—

"Mad from life's history,
 Glad to death's mystery,
 Swift to be hurled."

and plunging—

'No matter how coldly
 The rough river ran,—
Over the brink of it,
Picture it—think of it,
Dissolute Man!
Lave in it, drink of it,
Then, if you can!

'Take her up tenderly,
Lift her with care;
Fashioned so slenderly,
Young, and so fair!

'Ere her limbs frigidly
Stiffen too rigidly,
Decently,—kindly,—
Smoothe, and compose them;
And her eyes, close them,
Staring so blindly!

'Dreadfully staring
Through muddy impurity,
As when with the daring
Last look of despairing
Fixed on futurity.

'Perishing gloomily,
Spurred by contumely,
Cold inhumanity,
Burning insanity,
Into her rest.—
Cross her hands humbly,
As if praying dumbly,
Over her breast!

'Owning her weakness,
Her evil behaviour,
And leaving, with meekness,
Her sins to her Saviour.'—pp. 68, 69.

During the whole of the time these forcible poems were being written, Mr. Hood's health was fast failing. Indeed, it was evident to his friends, that his intense feelings during their composition, had seriously injured a constitution, never robust, but which ever since an attack of ague in Flanders, had been gradually undermined. A dangerous illness followed, and during the greater part of the summer of 1844, he was wholly incapacitated for writing. This he lamented greatly, for he seemed to view himself as having a work—a great work to do, and earnestly did he desire to accomplish it. This was to have made a complete series of poems, illustrating every form of social misery, and earnestly advocating its removal. Towards the autumn, a short period of comparative convalescence, afforded him an opportunity of pointing attention to the condition of the agricultural population, and he wrote the well known 'Lay of the Labourer'—

'A spade, a rake, a hoe!
  A pick axe, or a bill!
A hook to reap or a scythe to mow,
  A flail, or what ye will—
And here's the ready hand
  To ply the needful toil,
And skilled enough, by lessons rough,
  In labour's rugged school.'

This poem, is the only one of his serious compositions which has no place in these volumes, for it originally appeared in a prose sketch, picturing a meeting of starving labourers, and concluding with the powerful appeal to Sir James Graham, on behalf of that poor young man, Gifford White, who was sentenced to transportation for life, for a threatening letter addressed to the farmers of Bluntisham. 'For months past,' says he, 'amidst trials of my own, in the intervals of acute pain, perchance, even in my delirium, and through the variegated tissue of my own interests, and affairs, that sorrowful vision has recurred to me, more or less vividly, with the intense sense of suffering cruelty and injustice, and the strong emotions of pity and indignation, which originated with its birth. It is in your power Sir James Graham, to lay the ghost that is haunting me. By due intercession with the earthly fountain of mercy, you may convert that melancholy shadow into a happier reality—a righted man.' And this apparently exaggerated picture of his feelings regarding a man whom he had never seen, was true to the letter. The description of 'the Melancholy Shadow,' was given to his friends, just as he described it to the Home Secretary, for the thought of a lad of nineteen, being driven for life from his native land—Thomas Hood was proud of his country, with all its faults—had actually severely injured his failing health.

This was his last appeal on the behalf of 'those who have no helper;' and with the exception of a few short pieces in his magazine, his career as a writer was closed. After severe and complicated sufferings endured for many months, with much patience, Thomas Hood with a humble but trustful expression of Christian hope, died on the third of May, 1845, having almost completed his 46th year. Exceedingly reserved in character, detesting not only all pretension, but even those expressions of personal feeling, which the many expect, and approve, it is scarcely surprising that he should have been greatly misunderstood. Few of these believed that there was such an abundant wellspring of feeling for the sufferings of others in his heart, until the 'Song of the Shirt' revealed it, and few, still fewer, knew the deep and solemn thoughts that passed, during his long illness, through his mind. In the midst of his family, and among his intimate friends, Thomas Hood was a delightful companion, nor can we better conclude this short sketch than by inserting the exquisite lines, now published for the first time, addressed to his daughter on her birthday.

TO MY DAUGHTER,

ON HER BIRTHDAY.

'Dear Fanny! nine long years ago,
While yet the morning sun was low,
And rosy with the eastern glow
The landscape smiled ;
Whilst lowed the newly-wakened herds—
Sweet as the early song of birds,
I heard those first, delightful words,
'Thou hast a child !'

'Along with that uprising dew
Tears glistened in my eyes, though few,
To hail a dawning quite as new
To me, as Time:
'It was not sorrow—not annoy—
But like a happy maid, though coy,
With grief-like welcome, even Joy
Forestalls its prime.

'So may'st thou live, dear! many years,
In all the bliss that life endears,
Not without smiles, nor yet from tears
Too strictly kept:
When first thy infant littleness
I folded in my fond caress,
The greatest proof of happiness
Was this—I wept.'—vol. ii. pp. 5, 6.

Art. IV.—*The Church of St. Patrick; an Historical Inquiry into the Independence of the ancient Church of Ireland.* By the Rev. William G Todd, A.B, of Trin Coll. Dublin; Curate of Kilkeedy. London: John W. Parker, West Strand.

A great deal of nonsense has been spoken and written of late on the subject of '*races.*' What race is there that has not, in its turn, been elevated by Christianity, and degraded by religious despotism and political oppression? Who does not know that the most humanizing influences that can be brought to bear on society may be fatally counteracted by political bondage? The Negro, the Esquimaux, even the Hottentot have been raised by the gospel to the dignity of manhood, and to the sanctity of Christian fellowship. We cannot doubt that the effect of a sound education and of free institutions, with a favourable soil and climate, would be, in the course of a few generations, to obliterate every trace of their aboriginal inferiority. Physiology teaches us that proper regimen and exercise, combined with a right moral education, tend to enlarge the volume of the brain, to give power to the intellectual faculties, health and purity to the moral feelings, and so to develope a noble character, which, being influenced by hereditary causes, goes on improving from age to age. Of course, semi-starvation, ignorance and slavery will have an effect quite opposite.

Some Irish repealers, through ignorance, bigotry or policy, revile the Saxon, as if his blood generated tyranny. But if Celtic-France ruled the destinies of Ireland instead of Saxon-England, would the lot of that afflicted land have been better? The worst evils perpetrated by its conquerors amidst the barbarism of a dark age have been surpassed in infamy by the French in Tahiti and in Africa. Will the loyal South-Sea Islanders, who nobly struggle for independence in their mountain fastnesses, or the devoted Africans who moisten their burning desert with the blood of the *soi-disant* 'civilizers,' receive a better character from the invaders than the wild Irish did from theirs?

The boast of superior blood is one of the silliest forms of pride, and betrays no great consciousness of moral worth. Those who are prone to generalise rashly in favour of their prejudices, readily ascribe every virtue under heaven to their own happy temperament, to the credit of which they place the fruits of all other advantages. Surely the English people, to whom Providence has given, for its own gracious purposes, a predominant power in the earth, arising chiefly from their free institutions and scriptural religion, with their concomitants,—industrial habits and commercial prosperity— may well despise such childish vaunting. They are now a great and glorious people; but what were they once? It is wise for us occasionally to look back. Sir James Macintosh thus describes our ancestors in the eleventh century:—

"'We gather a few particulars of the sufferings and degradation of the Saxons from a sermon by Lupus, a Saxon bishop. Such is their (the Danes) valour, that one of them will put ten of us to flight; two or three will drive a troop of captive Christians from sea to sea. They seize the wives and daughters of our thanes, and violate them before the chieftain's face. The slave of yesterday becomes the master of his lord to-day. Soldiers, famine, flames, and blood surround us. The poor are sold far out of their land for foreign slavery. Children in their cradle are sold for slaves by an atrocious violation of the law.'—We should more pity these miseries, if we did not bear in mind the previous massacre of the Scandinavians. . . . . But in contests between beasts of prey, it is hard to select an object of compassion. Let those who consider *any tribes of men as irreclaimable barbarians*, call to mind that the Danes and Saxons, of whose cruelties a small specimen has been given, were the progenitors of those who, in Scandinavia, in Normandy, in Britain, and in America, are now among the most industrious, intelligent, orderly and humane of the dwellers upon earth.' (History of England, vol. i. p. 60.)

Certainly the blood which, 800 years ago, tamely endured

the basest bonds and the most maddening indignities, cannot be the cause of that superiority about which '*The Times*' commissioner' has been lately venting such impertinent puerilities.

Among the circumstances which modify national character, *climate* is too much overlooked. Mountaineers have always clung heroically to liberty and independence; while in flat countries—where man's blood stagnates like their rivers—little has been done to win human rights or maintain them, except by commercial cities, where trade, flourishing only in freedom, naturally generates self-reliance. Take the most unresisting and phlegmatic Saxon population, who merely vegetate in a dull atmosphere on rich lowlands, and place them among the Alpine, Caledonian, or Cambrian mountains, and think what the temperament of their grandchildren will become! Cold, wet and hunger, may, in many cases, harden their features, and stunt their figures; plodding industry and the mechanical skill which results from always doing one thing, and thinking of nothing else, will undoubtedly give place to irregular exertions, impulsive movements, impetuous efforts, a love of boisterous pleasure and wild excitement, and the lazy habit of living for the hour, without pondering much on the rainy day. But then there will be the bold spirit of independent individuality, a temperament, poetic, mystic, enthusiastic, courageous, combined with that strong attachment to places, and to all the names, that, in past ages, made those places holy and renowned, which characterise the *highlander* of every country, and of every race.

'All the northern French,' says Michelet, 'are the offspring of the Germans, although the language contains so little German, and Gaul has perished utterly, like the Atlantides. All the Celts are gone; and if any remain, they will not escape the arrows of modern criticism. Pinkerton does not suffer them to rest in the tomb, but fastens furiously upon them like a true Saxon, as England does on Ireland. He contends that they had nothing of their own, not a particle of original genius; that all the *gentlemen* are descended from the Goths, (or Saxons, or Scythians, it is all the same to him;) and in his whimsical furor desires the establishment of professors of Celtic, to teach us to laugh at the Celts.'

Yet, the French historian remarks—

'The old Celtic races, seated on their native rocks, and in the solitude of their isles, will remain faithful to the poetic independence of barbarous life, until surprised in their fastnesses by the tyranny of the stranger. Centuries have elapsed since England surprised and struck them down; and her blows incessantly rain upon them, as the wave dashes on the promontory of Brittany, or of Cornwall. The sad and patient Judea, who counted her years by her *captivities*, was not more rudely stricken by Asia. But there is such a virtue in the Celtic genius, such a tenacity of life in this people, that they subsist under outrage, and preserve their manners and their language.

'Whatever has been the result (of the law of gavel-kind) it is honourable to our Celts to have established in the west the law of *equality*. The feeling of personal right, the vigorous assumption of the I, which we have already remarked in Pelagius and in religious philosophy, is still more apparent here; and, in great part, lets us into the secret of the destiny of the Celtic races. While the German families converted moveable into immoveable property, handed it down in perpetuity, and successively added to it by inheritance, the Celtic families went on dividing and subdividing, and weakening themselves,—a weakness chiefly owing to the law of equality and equitable division. As this law of precocious equality has been the ruin of these races, let it be their glory also, and secure to them at least the pity and respect of the nations to whom they so early showed so fine an ideal."—(*Hist. France*. b. i. c. 4.)

How much the fortunes of a people depend on institutions! The same system of dividing and subdividing would have equally impoverished and ruined any other people, no matter what their blood. However, this characteristic of the Helleno-Celtic genius was not confined to civil society 'The independent I, the free personality,' passed into religion also, as well as the Celtic tenacity of the past. So unresisting, we are told, is the German nature, that Franks, established in Gaul, were subdued and thoroughly changed in the second generation, by the ecclesiastical influence. It is indeed a remarkable fact, that the nation which of all others is now most devoted to Rome, fought longest against her power, and stuck to its religious independence with most desperate fidelity. How this fidelity of the church of St. Patrick came ultimately to be transferred to the great usurper of Christendom,—how that deadly foe of nationality planted her foot on the free sanctuaries of Ireland, is a question of deep interest to the protestant people of Great Britain.

We are glad that the 'furor' of contempt for Irish Antiquities is fast departing from among us. The most enthusiastic Irishman can desire nothing better than the spirit of the eloquent and generous article on '*Petrie's Round Towers*,' in a recent Number of the '*Quarterly Review*.' Indeed, 'the Ancient church of Ireland' seems to have become quite a favourite of late. As it is acknowledged on all hands that 'St. Patrick was a *gentleman*,' various bodies are anxious to claim kindred with so respectable a personage. Irish episcopalians are anxious to derive through him their apostolical succession. The General Assembly has no doubt that the patron saint of the Green Isle was a staunch presbyterian; and the independents maintain that the churches he planted were clearly of the 'congregational order;' and that his three hundred bishops were nothing but pastors of particular churches, like their own :—while the Roman catholics can no more believe that their old Celtic church, which said its prayers in Irish, was a *protestant* institution, contending against the pope with even bigotted pertinacity for seven centuries, than they can believe that the said Irish-speaking church still exists by a mysterious transmigration in the present establishment.

Yet these two propositions are firmly maintained by the Rev. Mr. Todd, whose work is now before us.—The first, namely, that the Celtic church of Ireland was, from its foundation, by Patrick, to its fall in the twelfth century, strictly independent of Rome, and decidedly opposed to the claims of the pope, he has established in the most satisfactory manner. Seldom has historical argument been conducted with more fairness, so far as Rome is concerned, or brought to a more triumphant conclusion. It is creditable to the author's candour, learning, and talent. We cannot but wonder that so clear a mind should be to any extent mystified by the absurdities and inconsistences of Puseyism.—As, however, this is a vital point with the Irish priests, one on which they are ready to stake the whole authority of their church, we consider it a matter of no small importance that protestants in general should be familiar with the main facts of the case. The question at issue is this :—Did the early Irish churches regard the bishop of Rome as supreme head of the universal church of Christ on earth, not merely paying respect to him as patriarch of the west, and bishop of the imperial city, but acknowledging his *jurisdiction* over themselves, so that their own bishops were only his delegates, or vicars, exercising their functions by his commission, and subject at any time to his absolute interdict, just as the Roman catholic prelates are now? To answer this, we must appeal to facts :—

Previous to the year 430, we read of Christian churches in Ireland, and bishops labouring among them. When the Gospel was first introduced into that country, or how far it had extended before the arrival of Patrick, we are not satisfactorily informed. But of the fact that Christianity had made considerable progress there before him, there can be no doubt; for in the year 431, Palladius, once a deacon in the church of Rome, was sent 'to the Scots believing in Christ.' (Ad Scotos in Christum credentes ordinatur a papa Celestino, Palladius, et primus episcopus mittitur. Prosper Chron. ad Ann. 431.] Palladius was not sent to the heathens, but to the *Christians* in Ireland, with a view, probably, to bring them under the Roman jurisdiction. Whatever was his object, his mission was an utter failure; and in less than a year he was obliged to fly from the country, and he died soon after in Scotland. Some ascribe his want of success to the hostility of an Irish chief; some to the opposition of the Christian pastors, and some to his ignorance of the Irish language, supposing that he attempted something among the heathen.

By the way, it is a curious fact, that the gift of tongues—the necessity of which, to missionaries, is alleged by Romanists and Puseyites, as the most conclusive reason why miraculous powers were designed to remain for ever in the church—has never been available to any since the days of the apostles. Even the jesuit Francis Xavier, whose other alleged miracles were as plenty as blackberries, and equally useless, complains strongly of his want of success in India, owing to his ignorance of the languages of the tribes whom he sought to convert. If a Roman deacon could not bring this gift with him to Ireland, or was not content to sit down and learn the language, it is evident he had no business there. Patrick owed this indispensable qualification to his former residence in it as a shepherd on the plains of Antrim. As, then, the precise miracle which was most wanted, and most easily tested, and the alleged necessity for which is supposed to furnish a *prima facie* reason for the perpetuity of apostolic power, is just the one that has *never* been forthcoming, however urgent the demand for it, the conclusion is inevitable, that all *post*-apostolic 'miracles' have been impostures and delusions.

It is doubtful whether Patrick was ever at Rome. But Drs. Lanigan and Colgan both admit that he was *not* ordained by the Pope. In the ancient life, preserved in a MS. called Leabhar Breac, the following account is given of his ordination and subsequent reception at Rome:—'Afterwards he went to a certain noble personage, who conferred upon him the order of Bishop. After this he went to Rome, and found honour and respect from the Romans, and from their *Abbot,* whose name was Celestinus.' This is not the style in which an Irish Catholic would now speak of the 'vicar of Christ.' It is only in the modern, interpolated and legendary lives of Patrick,—rejected by the eminent catholic historian, Dr. Lanigan,—that we hear of his being ordained by the Bishop of Rome; but 'the more *ancient* as well as the more *Irish* the authority, the more distinct is its testimony that Patrick did *not* receive his orders from Rome.' All that is certainly known about his ordination is, that 'he appears to have been consecrated by *some Gallican prelate.*' (Todd, p. 24.)

Now did it not occur to Mr. Todd, that had Patrick laid as much stress on 'the succession' as the Anglo-Catholics, he would have said something of his mission in the *Confession,* or in some authentic document? This party in Ireland is anxious to rest its authority on this saint, and to come at the apostles without going to Rome. But how far, on their own showing, can they trace the chain, even if it be admitted that the Protestant Episcopal church really succeeds to that of Patrick? Just to '*some* Gallican prelate' in the fifth century, who '*appears*' to have consecrated the Irish missionary! Is this an authority on which any honest Christian should stake the credit of his religion?

Patrick founded churches and ordained bishops in Ireland, without seeking the sanction of the Pope for any of his acts, No report of his labours was ever sent by him to Rome; no rescript from 'the successor of Peter' ever reached him. About a century and a half later, Austen of Canterbury maintained a constant correspondence with his master, Gregory; and some centuries later still, when the Pope really *had* jurisdiction in Ireland, there are ample documentary proofs of the fact. But though the history of the early Irish churches is much fuller and more satisfactory, it does not contain the least trace of Roman power in the government of the church.

According to the papal theory, Patrick's successor, Benignus or Binen, being regarded as 'primate,' must have received the Pope's confirmation of his appointment. But it was neither sought nor given. Nor is there an instance of an Archbishop of Armagh, invested with office by the court of Rome, till the twelfth century.* From that time, till the sixteenth century, the interference of that court at the consecration of bishops is manifest enough, but never before. Indeed this fact is admitted by a learned Roman catholic antiquarian, who expressly says:—'Our episcopal clergy *never* applied to that see for bulls of ratification, provisions or exemption,' (O'Conor's Diss. on the Hist. of Ireland, p. 205.) One David, Archbishop of Armagh, between 548—551, is said to have exercised the office of legate-apostolic in Ireland. 'But,' writes Dr. Lanigan, 'this opinion is founded on a mistake, whereas there did not appear any person invested with that title in Ireland, until the end of the eleventh century.' (Todd, p. 35.)

For several generations the see of Armagh was the hereditary possession of one powerful family; and this usurpation lasted, without any interference of the Pope, or appeal to him, till the appointment of Mallachi, about the year 1134, whom Archbishop Celsus, on his deathbed, nominated to the see, enjoining the

* Moore admits that the title 'archbishop' was not known in Ireland till the eighth century.

Kings of Munster, 'by the authority of St. Patrick,' to see Mallachi seated on the desecrated throne, never hinting that the Roman bishop had anything to do with the matter. And do we not well know that the good father would not be slow to exercise his right, if he had any? We shall see, soon, that this is the very thing he was longing for.

The Danish pirates, sailing up the Liffey, the Suir and the Shannon, eventually settled in Dublin, Waterford, and Limerick, whence they could maintain a communication with their friends by sea, and escape from their enemies when necessary. Between such invaders and the natives there could be no friendly feelings for a long time. Accordingly, when the Danes were converted to Christianity, they chose in these three cities bishops of their own, who were sent to Canterbury for consecration, and declined the jurisdiction of Armagh. In 1073, Gotheric, the Danish king, with the consent of the clergy and *people* of Dublin, chose one Patrick for their bishop, and sent him for consecration to Lanfranc, Archbishop of Canterbury. In 1122, Gregory was sent in like manner, with a letter from the burgesses and clergy of Dublin, 'To the most reverend and most religious Lord Raph, Archbishop of Canterbury,' in which they say—' Know you truly that the *bishops of Ireland* have great indignation against us, and that bishop especially who dwells at Armagh, because we are unwilling to obey their ordination, but always wish to be under your dominion.'

It is plain from this, that even at this late period, the papal supremacy was not acknowledged, *directly*, even by these three Danish cities; and that the rest of the Irish bishops- *all* the Celtic bishops,—had no fellowship with the see of Canterbury, which was closely connected with Rome. Besides, if the Irish primate were then subject to the Pope, the Danish bishops could not have declined the legitimate jurisdiction of their own primate, whose just 'indignation' would have found a voice at Rome; nor could the Archbishop of Canterbury have presumed to consecrate the suffragans of Armagh, without the grossest breach of order: what would be thought of a vicar apostolic, in England, thus interfering with the rights of primate Crolly? Would not the intruding prelate be at once summoned to Rome and punished? There is but one fact that can account for these anomalies—the Pope's supremacy did not extend to Ireland.

'But again,' says Mr. Todd, 'let us observe the mode in which the bishops of those three cities were elected. They were chosen by the clergy, people, and provincial chieftains of their respective towns, and then sent to Canterbury to be ordained Undoubtedly this was the ancient and catholic mode of electing bishops; but, let me ask, was it the mode approved of in the eleventh century, when the power of Rome was at its highest, and when Gregory VII. sat upon the chair of St. Peter? Was the interference of the laity in episcopal appointments a practice of which that pontiff would have approved?'—p. 47.

Certainly not; and this is another decisive proof against the papal supremacy. But we respectfully ask Mr. Todd, is it not a proof equally strong against the Anglican hierarchy? Are the English Bishops chosen by the *clergy* and PEOPLE? And if this was undoubtedly 'the ancient and catholic mode of electing bishops,' (and which continued universally in Ireland, till the twelfth century) does it not follow irresistibly that the Anglican system is neither ancient nor catholic? So far as ecclesiastical organization is concerned, it differs *essentially* from the ancient Irish church, and from every other church in Christendom, during the Nicene period to which its advocates are so fond of appealing. Why not go back to the primitive practice? Because you are bound by the State, which mocks you with a *congé d'elire*.

It may be as well to add a few sentences here on the *constitution** of the early churches of Ireland. In an ancient MS. quoted by Ussher, (Primord. Eccles. Brit. Cap. 17,) and accepted as authentic by Roman Catholic writers, the Irish clergy, during the two centuries after Patrick, are divided into three classes. The first, amounting to 350, who were all founders of churches, and acknowledged Patrick as their head, after Christ. Whatever was excommunicated in one church was excommunicated in all. They did not shun the society of women. The second class acknowledged *but one head,* namely JESUS CHRIST. They had *different liturgies* and different masses. The third class were anchorites, or hermits. They too had different rules and different liturgies. These diversities in the forms of worship continued till the end of the eleventh century, when Gilbert, bishop of Limerick, the Pope's legate, was appointed to draw up one, in order, as he says, 'that the different and *schismatical communities*, with whom almost the *whole of Ireland abounds,* may submit to the Roman Catholic discipline.'

There was no act of uniformity in force in Ireland—they had not bowed to the yoke; but, may we ask, which of these 'schismatical communities,' will our Anglican friends select as the only true church in that realm, to which they are pleased to be the successors, and out of whose orthodox pale, there is no ordinary means of salvation?

* For an account of their substantially Protestant *doctrines*, see the admirable strictures on Moore's History, by Dr. H. Monk Mason.

'The men of Erin,' says Thierry, 'like the Britons of Cambria and Gaul, having organized Christianity in their country spontaneously, without conforming in any way to the official organization decreed by the emperors, had among them no fixed episcopal sees; their bishops were simply priests (presbyters, or bishops,) to whom had been confided by election, the office, purely honorary, of visitors or supervisors of the several churches. They did not constitute a body superior to the rest of the clergy, nor were there among them different degrees of hierarchy. The church of Ireland, in short, had not a single archbishop; none of its members had occasion to go to Rome to solicit or buy the pontifical pallium. So that this church, enjoying full independence with regard to all foreign churches, and its administration, like that of every free society, being in the hands of dignitaries elected and recalled by itself alone, was at an early period regarded as schismatic by the conclave of St. John's of Lateran; and a long system of attacks was made against it, with the perseverance innate in the successors of the old senate, who, by dint of willing one and the same thing, had subjugated the universe. It sedulously watched the first ambitious thoughts of *invading Kings*, to enter into co-partnership with them, and in default of foreign conquests, it, with crafty policy, ever admired and fostered the principle of despotism.' (Thierry's *Norman Conquest*, p. 193 of Whittaker's edition.)

Another eminent French historian speaks to the same effect:—

'The *Culdees* of Ireland and Scotland . . . . were independent, even while living under the rule of their order, which associated them in small ecclesiastical clans of twelve members each. . . . . The Cymry of Britain and Wales—Rationalists, and the Gaël of Ireland—Poets and Mystics, nevertheless exhibit throughout their entire ecclesiastical history one common character—the *spirit of independence and opposition to Rome*. They enjoyed a better understanding with the Greeks; and notwithstanding distance, revolutions, and manifold misfortunes, they long preserved relations with the churches of Constantinople and Alexandria . . . . Their monks, called Culdees, recognized hardly more of the ecclesiastical state than the modern Scottish Presbyterians. They lived in societies of twelve, under an abbot of their own election. Their bishop, according to the strict etymological sense of the word, was only their overseer.' (Michelet, *Hist. France*, b. ii. c. 1.)

We have adduced these authorities from learned writers, who know and care nothing about our ecclesiastical controversies, in order to let our episcopalian readers see how the case stands as to the apostolical succession through the Irish channel; and we ask them to say, candidly, can they discover their own system of diocesan episcopacy in the Celtic church? Mr. Todd, indeed, admits the glaring contrariety between the two institutions. He grants, for it cannot be denied, that there were in Ireland as many bishops as *congregations*—but will the reader guess how he gets over this difficulty? With the greatest ease, he escapes from it by modestly affirming that Patrick and his saintly followers 'fell into error!'

'The very errors,' says he, into 'which St. Patrick fell, in his organization of the Irish church, are an additional and to my mind a very striking proof that he maintained no official connexion with Rome. The chief defect in the discipline of the ancient church in Ireland was this, that the *dioceses* were not marked out with any care or precision. Bishops were allowed to *wander about* from one place of residence to another, and *many* bishops were consecrated to whom no episcopal duties were assigned. St. Bernard in the twelfth century, complained that the Irish bishops were changed and multiplied without order or reason, at the caprice of the metropolitan, so that *almost every church was provided with a separate bishop.* (' *Sed singulæ pene ecclesiæ singulos haberent episcopos,*' Opp. S. Bernard. ed. Benedict. tom. i. p. 667. This *mistake* (!) there is reason to apprehend, originated in some degree as early as the times of St Patrick. It was an *error* into which a very zealous man, who thought he could not have enough of *chief* pastors (!) and shepherds of Christ's flock was likely to fall; but it was one that could not for a moment have been tolerated by Rome. Had she known it, she would have immediately put a stop to such an irregularity.' (p. 31.)

Is it not strange to find the very men who claim Patrick as the apostle and founder of their church, charging him with fundamental error in its very organization! Their argument is this:—You Romanists and Ultra Protsetants ought to submit to our church, because it agrees with the church of St. Patrick,—with this slight difference, that the Irish apostle 'fell into error,' and committed a grave 'mistake,' in making his bishops *congregational* instead of *diocesan.* We implore you, therefore, by *his* authority, to follow us as we do *not* follow him!

Truly, facts are stubborn things. It is quite clear, that, whether Patrick, Columba, and Columbanus, with all the Irish churches and colleges down to the twelfth century, were in error or not, they were as far removed from modern prelacy as from Romanism. And for the church that refuses to recognize the orders of Presbyterians and Independents to claim exclusive kindred with those irregular and 'schismatic' commuuities, is almost as absurd as the doctrine of consubstantiation. In stating that the Pope would not tolerate such a number of chief pastors'—(a singular title for the bishops of separate congregations, or ministers with no congregations at all,)—Mr. Todd, and his brother, the Fellow of Trinity College, Dublin, (a learned antiquarian, and zealous Puseyite, who corrected the sheets of the present work while going to the press,) strangely forget the condition of the Roman and Italian churches in the fifth century. There was little or no difference *then* between the Irish churches and the churches of other countries, whose founders were apostles. Even the *Tracts for the Times* would have instructed our author on this point.

'Few persons who have not expressly examined the subject, are aware of the minuteness of the dioceses into which many parts of Christendom were divided in the first ages. Some churches in Italy were more like our rural deaneries, than what we now consider dioceses, being not above ten or twelve miles in extent, and their sees not above five or six miles from each other. Even now, (or at least in Bingham's time,) the kingdom of Naples contains one hundred and forty-seven sees, of which twenty are archbishoprics. Asia Minor is six hundred and thirty miles long and two hundred and ten broad; yet, in this country, there were almost four hundred dioceses!' (*Tracts for the Times*, No. 33.)

'When Bingham says there were four hundred bishops in Asia Minor,' remarks Professor Killen, 'he refers to the condition of the church in the latter end of the fourth century. At that period, most of the village and rural bishops were extinguished, so that his statement cannot be considered as a fair exhibition of primitive arrangements . . . . How different must a bishop, even of the fourth cencentury, have been, from a prelate of the present day, when, after the suppression of so many rural and village bishops, there were still four hundred remaining in a tract of land which is not much larger than Great Britain, and in which *only a fifth part* of the people were evangelized.' (*Plea of Presbytery*, 2nd edit. pp. 31—33.)

Thus, as we go back to antiquity, dioceses became small by degrees and scripturally less, till at last they dwindle into mere parishes, and their bishops into mere pastors, as it was in the beginning. Unless, therefore, Mr. Todd can bring forward some proofs that Patrick fell into error, and made a mistake in his church polity, which will not implicate the twelve Apostles in the same irregularity, we respectfully submit that he should be bound over to keep the peace towards the memory of that venerable personage. Such is the influence of this author's church theory, that, rather than admit its errors and evils, and its corrupt departure from the primitive model, he presumes to charge the whole galaxy of Irish saints with having, as regards church order, wandered universally into fundamental error, for the space of seven hundred years! Surely this is not the way in which a good Catholic should treat antiquity, nor is it the way in which a good logician, like our author, should treat facts.

As the Pope has been completely non-suited on the questions of organization and jurisdiction, let us see whether he had any thing to do with Irish missions to Britain and the Continent.

Columba, or Columb-Kille, was born in the county of Donegall, about the year 521. When he was only twenty-five years of age, he had founded a monastery in Derry. He then proceeded to Iona, where he established an Irish monastery, or college, which became afterwards so famous as a nursery of missionaries, who went forth to educate, evangelize, and civilize the barbarous nations of Europe. But when the Venerable Bede records the achievements of this 'college of monks,' he does not give us the slightest intimation that they sought, or obtained, the Pope's sanction for any of their acts, though these acts included the founding of monasteries, the appointment of abbots, and other things which could not be done without the concurrence of Rome, by any within the pale of that church.

Virgilius, so celebrated as the first who taught the rotundity of the earth and the existence of antipodes,—a doctrine denounced by the pope of that day (Zachary) as 'corrupt and impious,' went to France as a missionary in the eighth century, and was made bishop of Saltzberg by King Pepin, without the sanction of the pontiff. In fact, not one of the Irish missionaries was ever known to seek the Pope's appointment to any sphere of labour. When moved by their zeal to go abroad in their Master's service, they were separated to the work whereunto He had called them by their own ministers at home precisely as missionaries are sent out now by the Dissenters.

And yet Dr. Rock, an English priest, in a letter to Lord John Manners, ventures to assert that 'the early missioners from Ireland used to go to Rome to do homage to the pope, and crave the apostolic leave and blessing *before* they went and preached to pagan nations.' But he has been able to produce but three instances, none of which is to the point. The first is the case of Dichuill, who went not forth as a missionary at all, but to enjoy the perfection of an ascetic life in solitude; and having founded a monastery at Lure, he is said to have laid all right over it at the feet of the 'chief bishop.' The argument is well put by Mr. Todd thus:—

'Dichuill founded a monastery, and obtained for it a rich endowment; and *after* having done so, he went and laid it at the pope's feet: therefore Irish missionaries used to do homage to the pope *before* they went and preached to Pagan nations.'—p. 69.

But the learned Catholic historian, Dr. Lanigan, rejects this as a 'foolish story.' 'Such deeds of vassalage, for monastic privileges, &c., were not known in the days of Deicolus (Dichuill). The author imagined that because they existed in the tenth century, in which he appears to have lived, that the same practices prevailed at all times.'—Eccl. Hist. Ireland, vol. ii. p. 441.

Willibrord is another of Dr. Rock's best instances; but he was a Saxon monk, though he had lived twelve years in Ireland with the Saxon saints, Egbert and Wigbert, where he is said by Alcuin to have gone in search of *scholastic,* not ecclesiastical learning. He was not a missionary from the Irish churches at all. Kilian's is the only other case which the records of centuries could afford to sustain the assertion of Dr. Rock as to the *usage* of Irish missionaries. He was one of those who, interpreting literally our Lord's words, believed that, whosoever followed him, must forsake father and mother, houses and lands, and country. Therefore, he went to the continent, not as a missionary, but as a hermit. Having afterwards resolved to preach the gospel to the heathen in Franconia, he naturally sought the pope's sanction in this work, as he was far away from the church of his fathers; and as the Church of Rome was acknowledged as true, and had not then to any great extent betrayed the corrupt and ambitious spirit which afterwards prompted its encroachments on the liberties of other bodies. This occurred in the seventh century, when all churches still reverenced the bishop of Rome as one of the four patriarchs. But respect is not obedience; and if an Irishman on the Continent happened to place himself under papal jurisdiction, that is not any proof that the churches of his native land did so, especially when it is known that the authority of the Roman see was always strenuously resisted whenever a point of difference arose, as in the question regarding the time of observing Easter.

It would appear—though this is by no means certain—that sometime between the fifth and the eighth century, certain canons were enacted by a synod in Ireland, to the effect, that when a doubtful question should arise, which could not be decided at home, reference should be had to 'the chair of St. Peter;' but no instance occurred in which they were acted upon, till the fourteenth century. They were, therefore, if genuine, a dead letter, quite at variance with the spirit of the church. (Ussher's Religion of the Ancient Irish, chap. viii.) Something like an *appeal* to the pope occurred once, and it arose in this way:—The Irish computation, as to the time of holding Easter, differed from that of all other churches, erroneously, although Columbanus said that the Irish knew astronomy better than the

Romans. But while other nations corrected their calendars, the Irish were so firmly attached to their own national customs, that they would not yield, even when some of their learned men had proved them in the wrong. The attention of the Irish church was first called to this subject by Laurence, Archbishop of Canterbury, in a letter addressed to the bishops and abbots of that country, about the year 609, urging upon them concurrence with the rest of the Catholic church. A few years later, a similar letter was addressed to them by Pope Honorius I., exhorting them, a small body living at the ends of the earth *(in extremis terræ finibus)*, not to set themselves against the decrees of all the bishops of Christendom. (*totius orbis pontificum*.)

Soon after the receipt of this letter, which was not an authoritative decision, but an argument *ad verecundiam*, precisely such as Laurence had addressed to them, and implying supremacy in the one case no more than in the other, a synod was held near Old Leighlin, to consider the matter, when plans were recommended to bring about the desirable uniformity. The result is thus related by Dr. Lanigan :—

'This was agreed to, and the thing appeared to be quite settled, when, not long after, a troublesome person started up, and, by his intrigues, rendered abortive part of what had been decreed. To put an end to this opposition, it was resolved by the *Elders* that, where, as according to a synodical canon, every important question should be referred to the head of cities, some wise and humble persons should be sent to Rome as children to their mother. These deputies being arrived there, *saw with their own eyes* Easter celebrated at one and the same time by people from various countries; and having returned to Ireland, in the third year from their departure, solemnly declared to those that had deputed them, that the Roman method was that of the whole world.'—*Lanigan*, vol. ii , p. 389.

This is the only thing bearing the semblance of an appeal to Rome to be found in the whole history of the Celtic church in Ireland before the Conquest ; yet there is nothing in it about the pope or his judgment. To the messengers he seemed to have nothing to do with the question. Those who sent them would not receive even his *testimony* as to the matter of fact, not to speak of his authority ; for if so, why were the deputies sent? Must not the pope's letter have settled the question? No,— they went to witness the fact with their own eyes ; and when they arrived at the 'head of cities,' *i. e.* the western capital, where streams of population from all nations converged, and saw Greeks, Egyptians, Hebrews, and Romans, the representatives of all the *four patriarchates*, agreeing as to the time of Easter, they took this accordance as a plain proof of the Catholicity of practice, and reported accordingly. But, so strong was the Celtic feeling against foreign influence, that, after all, their report did not settle the question; for Bede states that it was only in the south of the island that the decree of the synod, to observe the Roman computation, was received and obeyed. (Lib. iii. c. 3.) Does not this appeal to *Catholicity* furnish the strongest argument against *popery?*

Such, however, was the excitement and agitation that arose on this subject, that all who sided with Rome were branded by the popular party with error and 'heresy.' O'Conor says, 'a schism ensued.' (Diss. on Irish Hist., p. 205.) The spirit of Dagan, an Irish bishop, who, in 609, refused to eat or drink with the Archbishop of Canterbury on this very account, animated the Anti-Roman party for many a year. At length a synod was convened, to consider these differences, in Whitley, Yorkshire, when Colman, Bishop of Landisfarne, argued in defence of the system prevailing in his own country; but as he was out-argued and out-voted, he resigned his bishoprick, and returned to Ireland, Wilfrid, his principal opponent, being chosen in his stead; who at first refused, lest he should be ordained by the Irish bishops, 'whose communion,' says William of Malmesbury, 'the apostolic see had rejected.' (Ussher's Religion Anc. Irish, cap. x.)

Is it not marvellous that men who felt themselves so bound by the traditions of their own elders, as to resign the most important offices in the church, and to refuse to eat even with an Archbishop of Canterbury, rather than comply with the customs of Rome, should be represented by modern writers as considering the very conduct which they themselves adopted heretical and worthy of excommunication,—as yielding to the pope, in Mr. Moore's phrase, 'profound and implicit reverence?' Whereas the whole body of the people, clergy and monks, were so passionately opposed to the pope on this question, that the few who agreed with him incurred the greatest odium; and even these, with the learned Cummian, of Durrow, differed with their brethren, not because the pope had spoken, but because they 'found it written that they were to be excommunicated and expelled the church, who contravene the canonical decrees of the FOURFOLD APOSTOLIC SEE (to wit, Rome, Jerusalem, Antioch, Alexandria), all agreeing in the unity of the Pasch.' (Ussher's Sylloge, Ep. xi.)

As to the force of the expression, 'Going like children to a *mother*,' that it implies no sovereign authority in Rome, is plain, from the following words of Cummian :—'He that curseth his father or his mother, let him die the death.' 'But what can be thought more evil of mother church, than if we say Rome errs,

Jerusalem errs, Alexandria errs, Antioch errs, the whole world errs, the Scots (Irish) and Britons alone think right.' Here we see how comprehensive are the terms 'mother church,' not restricted to one community, but embracing the whole catholic body. *This* was the mother the Irish deputies were sent to consult, though they owed no more allegiance to the 'head of cities' than the holders of scrip do to 'the railway king.'

We must now briefly notice the case of Columbanus, founder and superior of the monastries of Luxeuil and Bobbio, in the sixth century. Catholic writers claim him as an unexceptionable witness of the prevailing faith of his country and his age, on the question of papal supremacy. Yet there are few names in ecclesiastical history more closely associated with bold and persevering dissent. 'St. Columbanus passes into Italy,' says Michelet, 'but it is to give battle to the pope! The Celtic church separates from the church universal, rejects unity and co-operation, and refuses to lose herself humbly in European catholicity.'—(Hist. France, b. i., c. 4.)

The condemnation and expulsion from France of Columbanus are thus referred to by Thierry:—

'Columbanus, unused to address potentates, or to the employment of respectful discourse, remonstrated severely with his visitor on his morals and the licentious life he led with depraved women. These reproaches were less displeasing to the king than to his grandmother, that same Brunehilde whose piety Pope Gregory had so complacently lauded, and who, to maintain her influence over her grandson, dissuaded him from marriage, and was careful to furnish him with women of pleasure and beautiful slaves. *At the instigation of this queen*, an accusation of heresy in the first degree was preferred in a council of bishops, against the man who dared to show himself more nice than the Roman church, respecting the morality of princes. He was condemned by an unanimous sentence, and banished from Gaul. . . . . . The same church which expelled from Gaul those who censured the vices of the Frank monarchs, gave holy crosses for standards to the Anglo-Saxon kings, when they went forth to exterminate the old Christians of Britain. The latter, in their national poems, charge a part of their disasters on a foreign conspiracy, and on monks whom they call unjust. (Horæ Britt. ii. 290.) In their conviction of this malevolence of the Roman church towards them, they became strengthened in the resolution of rejecting her tenets and her empire; they chose rather to apply, and did actually apply several times, to the church of Constantinople, for counsel in their theological difficulties. The most renowned of their ancient sages, who was both a bard and a Christian priest, cursed, by a sentence clothed in poetry, the negligent shepherd who kept not God's flock from the wolves of Rome.' (*Norman Conquest*, Whittaker's edition, p. 18.)

The superscription of the Irish letter, on which so much stress is laid, is certainly fantastical enough. In this very letter, however, the Irish monk deals with the pope very much in the style of Luther. He urges upon him the necessity of convening a council—tells him he was suspected of receiving heretics, and exhorts him in the following language:—

'That thou mayest not lack apostolic honour, preserve the apostolic faith: confirm it by testimony, strengthen it by writing, fortify it by synod, *that none may justly resist thee.'* . . . . 'Lest, therefore, the old robber bind men with this very long cord of error, let the cause of the schism, I pray, be immediately cut off from thee, as with the sword of St. Peter; *that is*, by a *true confession of faith*, in a synod, and by an abhorrence and anathematizing of every heretic, *that thou mayest cleanse the chair of Peter from all error*, or rather horror, if any (as *is reported) have gained admission*; if not, that its purity may be known to all. For one must grieve and mourn, if, in the apostolic see, *the catholic faith be not maintained*.'

Is this the language of a Roman catholic—of one whose faith may be comprised in the single sentence, 'the chair of Peter can never be defiled with error?' Columbanus expounds his protestantism still farther; and when we recollect that he is writing in Italy, in the sixth century, when the mystery of iniquity had not yet fully developed itself, we must admit that his protestantism is not the weakest.

'Now it is your fault if you have deviated from the true trust, and have made void the first faith: *deservedly your juniors withstand you*; and *deservedly they do not communicate with you*, until the memory of the wicked be taken away and delivered over to oblivion For if these things are more sure than false, the tables being turned, your sons are changed into the head, *and you into the tail*, which is sad even to be mentioned; therefore, also, *they* shall be your *judges*, who have always preserved the *orthodox faith, whosoever they may be*, even though they appear to be your juniors. . . . . We (the Irish) are bound to the chair of St. Peter; for although Rome is great and renowned, on account of that chair only is it great and illustrious with us. . . . . Rome is the head of the churches of the world, *saving the singular prerogative of the place of our Lord's resurrection*.'

Rome is thus spoken of 'on account of the *two* apostles of Christ,' and its pre-eminence as the imperial capital; but the Irish churches allowed *a greater deference* still to the real mother church at Jerusalem; which, however, never claimed or received any jurisdiction over them.

He proceeds, in a truly protestant strain:—

'And therefore, as your honour is great in proportion to the dignity of the chair, so have you need of great care that you lose not your dignity through any perversity. ***For so long shall power remain with you, as right reason shall remain***; for he is the true porter of the kingdom of heaven, ***who, through true knowledge, opens to the worthy and shuts against the unworthy.*** . . . . . And you by this, I know not what arrogance, claim to yourselves greater authority and power in spiritual matters than the rest. You should know that your power will be less with the Lord, ***if you even think this in your hearts***; because ***unity of faith*** has made ***unity of power and prerogative in the whole world,*** so that liberty is given to the truth every where, and by all, ... because a ***right confession*** gave the privilege to the holy possessor of the keys, the common Father of all, it is lawful even for your juniors to stir you up for the zeal of the faith, for the love of peace, for the unity of the church.' *

These extracts show, that we should take his complimentary titles with a grain of salt, and remember that the words (if serious) come from the fervid and poetical genius of an eloquent Irishman. When Dr. Smiles's History of Ireland was published, some of the Irish priests were thrown into a panic, because he gave prominence to the fact of the independence of the ancient church of Ireland. Dr. Miley wrote two long and elaborate letters, to show that the Irish were always most submissive to the Pope, relying principally on the testimony of this same Columbanus. The awkward fact, however, that there are no records of Roman government in Ireland during all those ages, when she was the Island of Saints, troubled him a good deal. This he accounted for by saying, that in those lawless times travelling was impossible, and they had no means of communication. But he forgot the other contradictory fact, that the Irish missionaries were in the habit of travelling over Europe in such numbers, that historians compare their imigrations to 'swarms,' and 'shoals;'—and another fact, equally decisive, that no such difficulties prevented the Pope's bulls from reaching Canterbury. It is interesting to think, that this great historical fiction is the chief support of papal influence in Ireland at this moment. Prove to the people of that country that Rome was the unwearied antagonist of their nationality, their religion, and their liberties, in the days of their glory, and you go far to break the foreign yoke. On this point, therefore, their clergy are extremely sensitive.

We have seen how the Danish bishops paved the way for connexion with Rome *viâ* Canterbury. But they could never have thus subjugated the Celtic church, if their countrymen had not,

* Epistola S. Columbani ad Bonafacium Bibliotheca Patrum, Tom. xii. p. 30. Apud Todd, chap. vi. and App. Note 6. Cardinal Barronius says, that in this controversy, '*all* the bishops that were in Ireland, with most earnest study, rose up' to join Columbanus.

by their invasions, plunderings, burnings and desolations, demolished the schools and monasteries, and banished their inmates, entailing on the country anarchy, insecurity, ignorance, and degeneracy of manners. These things afforded a colourable pretext to the Royal Commission, appointed by Henry II., called the council of Cashel, who gave such a bad report of the country, that the Pope might have an excuse for selling it; and that the bishops might better their own condition. The English sovereign certainly rewarded *them* well for their sevices; for thenceforward, in style, title and power, they ranked before the princes and nobles of the land, and sometimes before the lord deputy.

It took four years of hard labour and intriguing from Christian, bishop of Lismore, and Paparo, the cardinal, to bring the principal Irish bishops under the Roman yoke, by erecting Dublin, Cashel, and Tuam into archbishoprics, and inducing their prelates, with the primate, to receive the palls, A. D. 1152.

'But, notwithstanding,' says Thierry, 'the appearance of national consent given to these measures, the old spirit of independence yet prevailed. The clergy of Ireland showed little docility in their submission to the new hierarchical order; and the people had a repugnance for the foreign practices, and especially for the tributes in money which were attempted to be levied under various specious names for the benefit of the ultra-Montane church. The court of Rome, still dissatisfied with the Irish, in spite of their concessions, continued to give them the epithets of 'bad Christians,' and 'lukewarm Christians, rebellious to the apostolic discipline;' it watched as attentively as ever for an opportunity of obtaining a stronger hold of them, by associating its own ambition with some temporal ambition; nor was it long before such an opportunity presented itself.'—(Norman Conquest, p. 193)

Such was the state of things when Henry obtained the '*apostolic*' bull and blessing for the conquest of Christian Ireland.—Thenceforth Irish Catholicity was thoroughly Romanized, so far as the English power extended. The invaders imported, not the church system against which the patriot saints of Ireland had in better times, so vigourously contended, but worse and more obnoxious still, the hierarchy of Hildebrand, with an infusion of Norman pride, and pomp, and secularity. But this new system spread very little beyond the colony. The Celts were still in spirit true to 'the traditions of their own elders,'—which they did not love the less because the objects of Anglo-Popish persecution. They could not reverently kiss palls sprinkled with Celtic blood, and placed by the conqueror on the shoulders of enemies, or traitors, who were sworn on the host 'to curse the king's enemies,' i. e. the Irish, whenever he might call for their services in that line.

Thus matters remained till the Reformation. There were in fact *two* churches in Ireland, quite as alien to one another then, 'in blood, language and religion,' as when Lord Lyndhurst uttered his pregnant sentence.

The one was English, and the other Irish. The English church would not receive an Irishman into any of its offices; nor even admit a native into its monasteries or nunneries. How, then, did this intensely national and obstinately independent church (though greatly fallen from its original purity) come to be so enthusiastically attached to Rome, as it has been for the last two centuries? This is a deeply interesting question, which has never received the consideration it deserves. By one of those strange reverses in the history of nations, the relations of the Celtic church to Rome were wholly changed by the Reformation. If Henry VIII. had only thrown off his allegiance to the pope, and allowed the Irish church to enjoy independence, celebrating its rites in its own language and in connexion with its own national customs, the Reformation would have been popular and triumphant in every part of the country. But when the still-hated English power began to wage a war of extermination against everything *Irish*—when all Celtic blood was pronounced vile, all Celtic manners vulgar, all Celtic customs barbarous, the very language outlawed—when this degrading proscription was decreed in the name of the new faith, and enforced by fire and sword, popular sympathy with the English Anti-Roman movement was impossible. Hitherto the old Celtic church had been the sanctuary of nationality against the pope; henceforth popery became the bulwark of the same nationality against England. During two centuries of strife, Rome, for her own purposes, has sympathised with Irish patriotism; and for this cause has been devotedly obeyed and loved. England first forced the pope upon the Anglo-Irish church; and then, by a most infatuated and criminal policy, obliged his old enemy, the Celtic church, to fly into his arms for refuge from the fury of the exterminator! The steadfast and genial support of nationality being smitten down and torn away from the Irish vine, its trampled tendrils clung, of necessity, to Rome, and it has ever since brought forth 'wild grapes.'

Mr. Todd dedicates his work to the 'Warden and Fellows of the College of St. Columba' (a Puseyite institution), 'an *undertaking*, the first that has ever been *made*, to recommend the Irish church to the Irish people, by asserting its connexion with the ancient church of their fathers.' What a pity so admirable a thought was so late in coming into the world! How did it happen that 'the Irish church did not *make* this *undertaking* sooner?' For centuries this mysterious connexion between the church of Patrick and the church of Primate Beresford was never once '*asserted!*' We have seen that there were *two* churches in Ireland before the Reformation. The Dean of Ardagh most accurately distinguishes them thus:—'The one was the church of the *anglo-popish aristocracy, and of the ascendancy party*; the other was the church of the Irish clergy and people.'—(*Ireland and her Church*, p. 112, 113.) Strange to say, the Dean also dreams of an identity between the *latter* and the Protestant establishment.

But we would seriously ask these gentlemen, which of these 'sisters' was reformed by Henry and Elizabeth, and converted into *their* Irish church? Was it the Celtic, the Gaelic, the native, the national, the popular, the anti-Roman? or was it 'the anglo-popish church of the aristocracy and of the ascendancy party,' of the colony and the pale? Is there a child who has read even a primer of Irish history, but will answer,—Certainly the Reformation took effect among the English-speaking people of the pale, and not among the 'mere Irish'—not among 'the Irish clergy and people?'

Yet there are learned antiquarians and very reverend divines, who insist on the very reverse of this; and who can doubt it now, since it is '*asserted*' in the College of St. Columba!

At this moment, there seems to be another leaf turned in Ireland's destiny. For more than two centuries, England has been labouring to tread out her national life, in spite of the pope. She has not succeeded; and now she is trying another process with *his* assistance. The re-union of the British crown and the Roman tiara, to repress political agitation in the sister island, is a fact which seems to indicate a new era, and a very unlooked-for revolution in its history. But the present working of this alliance, and its probable consequences, must be reserved for a future article.

Art. V.—*A Memoir of the Rev. John Elias*. By the Rev. E. Morgan, A.M., Vicar of Syston, &c. With an Introductory Essay, by the Rev. J. K. Foster, &c. Jones, Liverpool; and Hughes, London.

Never did reviewer sit down to read a work influenced by kindlier feelings than we did the one now before us. We knew the great man whose life it records, and had heard him preach in the strength and glory of his days. The reminiscence is one of the imperishable treasures left us by the past. The fact of Mr. Morgan's having written this book prepossessed us much in his favour. We were sensibly affected by the gracefulness of the act, and the noble candour of the man's spirit, who, being himself a clergyman of the established church, becomes the biographer and eulogist of a celebrated dissenting minister. Besides, we happen to have a profound interest in the subject of this volume—his life, his times, and his ministry. We have from earliest recollection been deeply curious in the ecclesiastical affairs of the Principality, and have studied somewhat carefully the constitution and history of all its sects. The portraiture of a life so intimately connected with these matters, had therefore to us no common attraction. There was another cause of our predilection for the volume before us. We had read some very flattering notices of it in one or two periodicals; in one especially, whose editor we would have willingly trusted in such a case. Thus disposed, we read the book—aye, we actually read it through; and now we make our report. It must be an honest one; and, however much we regret the necessity laid upon us, we must say nothing but the truth. We have, then, put down this volume with feelings of intense mortification. In all the necessary characteristics of such a work, it is a most signal, a most pitiful failure; in its style, or rather its no-style, it is excessively puerile and powerless, with scarcely a tolerably constructed sentence, excepting in some of the quotations from other writers, throughout its two hundred and sixteen pages: and this from a clergyman, and M. A. of Cambridge! Nothing can be more feeble, more pointless, more jejune than the composition. The book mainly consists of exclamations of wonder, iteration and reiteration of unmeaning and common-place eulogy, interwoven with the baldest and most indiscriminating detail of John Elias's personal, domestic, and public history. We have again and again wondered that Mr. Morgan did not catch some of the spirit of his hero, some little of that vivacity and vigour which distinguished the remarkable man commemorated in his pages. On the contrary, he transfers his own dulness to the great subject itself.

The 'Elias' of this book (for, with wretched taste, Mr. Morgan calls him 'Elias,' without any prefix whatever) is not *the John Elias* whom formerly we heard with wonder, with tears, and with joy. Had we not previously the means of forming our own estimate of the great preacher, we are bound in truth to say this production would have been of no real use to us. He was a good man, we might have said, perhaps, he was a great man; for Mr. Morgan says so, but he does not give us any materials by which we may ourselves come to that conclusion. Had it not been for some quotations from letters of friends, especially Mr. Thomas's graphic and vigorous sketch, the reader would not have, in the whole volume, a single datum upon which to form his opinions of John Elias. Mr. Morgan does not in one instance bring before us a concise, or even intelligible account, of one of the sources of his eloquence. Epithets there are enough, but discrimination there is none. In the very first paragraph we find him saying, 'Very few have been so gifted as Elias.' He might have left this unsaid until we had heard something of his personal history. It is just saying nothing, that is, nothing to the purpose, because at no proper time and in no proper place. He quotes largely from John Elias's autobiography, but very much mars the effect of these sketches, by frequently interrupting the narrative to interpose remarks of his own, in which he sometimes repeats, *in less forcible language*, what the writer has been saying; and in other instances he indulges in pious reflections, the obviousness of which, and their tameness of style, make them superfluous, and sometimes worse than useless. For instance, in page 4:—

'As soon as I was able,' he is quoting from the autobiography, 'to walk with my grandfather to the parish church, I was obliged to go with him that very sabbath. He was a true churchman. There were at that time no Methodists, to the best of my knowledge, in that neighbourhood. There was, however, a small chapel, that belonged to a few people of that denomination, within about two miles of us, in a place called *Pentref uchaf*. My grandfather used to have family prayer morning and evening. He would read a chapter in the Bible with Mr. P. Williams's exposition; then he would pray in one of those excellent forms of Mr. G. Jones, of Llanddowror, in a very devout and serious manner. My grandfather endeavoured to teach me to read the Welsh language, when I was about four or five old. I had even read from the beginning of Genesis to the middle of Jeremiah, when I was at the age of seven years.'

Let the reader remember this is a translation by Mr. Morgan. At this point he stops for a moment, and gives the following *profound* and *striking* reflections :—

'We cannot but perceive that there was something remarkable and promising in such a child as this. We are reminded of young Timothy, by his love of the Scriptures and diligence in perusing them. *Not many had read the Bible* (the italics are our own) *so far as he had, even at a more advanced age*. We find by the account Elias has given of himself, that his grandfather's pious attention towards him, particularly in training him up in the ways of the Lord, was not in vain,' &c.

Again, in page 6 :—

'Once,' he says, 'I heard a lad swearing: it was new to me, for I was not allowed to be in the company of immoral characters. However, I thought the boy was clever and masterly in uttering the words, and I was tempted to follow his example: and I went far from all people, even into the middle of a field, to try to utter the oath! Alas! I was so unfortunate as to speak the awful word, upon which I was immediately seized with such fears and terrors, that I apprehended I should be swallowed up instantly alive on the spot into hell.'

Here the biographer interferes, and says—'How remarkably tender was Elias's conscience, and how carefully he must have been brought up in the fear of God and his holy ways.' To this he adds, *in a note at the foot the page*, 'Young Elias might be fearful some person should hear him from the hedges, or that some judgment might befall him from thence: he consequently went as far as possible in his apprehension from all danger, on the painful occasion of taking the oath,' &c. We are, indeed, quite puzzled as to the principle upon which our author arranges his notes. In the above instance the note might have been incorporated in the text, without impairing its continuity or disturbing its coherence. Sometimes he seems to insert a note to fetch up what he appears to feel has not been said in the text; and we are sorry to add, the failure is equally certain at the foot of the page. Again, he puts part of a letter in the text, and the other portion in a note. In one instance, p. 209, he inserts a letter in the text, which the writer refers to a former letter to the author; and when you have read the second letter, an asterisk sends you to the first in a note below! The reader may indeed be amused by such introversion; but if he expects by inserting in the text the matter in the notes, to deduce from the whole some intelligible and consistent outline of biographic incident, some definite and marked description of private and public character, his amusement will soon give place to utter disappointment and mortification.

In what Mr. Morgan endeavours to say, he offends greatly against right feeling and good taste, by omitting all reference to the *weak points* in John Elias's character. Such there are in all men, and in men of strong minds they are frequently very apparent. If Mr. Elias were indeed the good man which Mr. Morgan attempts to describe him, and had no neutralizing qualities, in addition to and dissimilarity from those attributed to him in this book, he was the 'faultless monster' so often described as existing only in imagination amongst the sons of men. There is in these pages no hint of any defect in temper, in discretion, or in spirit. The fair inference from these premises would be, that as far as human cognizance went, there actually was no blemish in him. Now we would not record with invidious care a long catalogue of the weaknesses of good men, who are departed, and are now faultless before the throne; but we would, if there be any biographical delineation of a departed servant of God, have briefly indicated the leading features of his *entire* character; and therefore the respects in which he was most liable to failure should have their place—not a prominent one, indeed, but an actual place. We would have it so for the truth's sake, and for the sake of the real and abiding utility of biographic writings. In the present instance, it is not in the spirit of depreciation we say that we are sorry Mr. Morgan did not, even in his way, tell us more than he has, and did not give us some few things of a different character to those he has communicated. John Elias was a Welsh Calvinistic Methodist, formed by their system of church government into a most devoted admirer of his own connexion, and a most determined opponent of every change or innovation. He did not (and no Welsh Methodist in existence who is forty years of age will say he did) always conduct himself in matters coming into this department with any very eminent exemplification of the milder and more benignant qualities. His opposition to the Catholic Relief Bill was, we doubt not, quite honest, but it was very vehement and denunciatory; and woe to the wight in his denomination who dared to avow any friendship to it. Some members of the Welsh church at Jewin Crescent petitioning parliament in favour of the measure; were most unceremoniously, not to say *cruelly*, excluded from membership; and this extreme step John Elias afterwards elaborately defended. His fear of *Fullerism* was very great, and his attacks on those whom he suspected of favouring it amongst his brethren, at the B—— and other associations, were not eminent for candour or kindness.* We are far from wondering at these things; we can revere the good man's memory, while we distinctly remember them; we can, in our own way and to our own satisfaction, account for them. We only tell Mr. Morgan he ought to have let us know something of them.

We are sorry to have another objection to make. There is no proportionate place given in this volume to John Elias's contemporaries. Has Mr. Morgan never read Orme's Life of Dr. Owen, or Milner's Life of Watts? How adroitly these biographers bring in as a fitting and coherent part of the narrative, so

* 'People now say, yes, Welsh Methodist preachers say, *that man can believe the Gospel*,' was his indignant complaint at the Bala Association not many years before his death. An excellent minister still living, observed, that probably such a statement might *not* be altogether erroneous. 'I say he cannot, *as a sinner*,' thundered out the mighty orator. 'I beg to say,' was the shrewd rejoiner, 'that God *did not* make man a sinner, and man is answerable to him as a creature, irrespective of his self-acquired sinfulness.'

many bewitching sketches of contemporary biography! How necessary this seems to be to the completeness of these works and how commandingly interesting it makes them! It escapes, our ingenuity to devise how Mr. Morgan has avoided all reference to John Elias's contemporaries in and out of his own denomination. In a country like Wales, so isolated, in consequence of its language, so united in religious creed, and so unsophisticated as to the general character of its people; a preacher, of Elias's celebrity, must in the course of his long life, have had much acquaintance and intercourse with other eminent men, engaged in similar pursuits. With the exception of some utterly uninteresting references to a few ministers who aided him in his youth, and a few allusions to Mr. CHARLES, we have nothing of the kind in the whole book. Out of his own connexion, a considerable number of names occurs to us with whom he was more or less, directly, or indirectly acquainted. JOSEPH HARRIS amongst the Welsh Baptists, the reviver of Welsh literature, and the first editor of *Seren Gomer*, a periodical in which some of John Elias's most characteristic productions appeared :—CHRISTMAS EVANS, the Welsh Demosthenes, in the same denomination, and for many years resident contemporaneously with John Elias, in the island of Anglesea; WILLIAM WILLIAMS, that profoundly metaphysical preacher, one of the noblest men of our day, and one of the principal ornaments of the Welsh Independents. JOHN ROBERTS labouring in the same ranks, once engaged in friendly controversy with the subject of these Memoirs, 'pure as a seraph, and gentle as a lamb;'—these must have come so often in his way, and he in theirs, that we incline to think the biographer has designedly avoided all allusion to them. This, however, astonishes us less than his silence, with regard to Elias's excellent contemporaries in his own religious body. According to Mr. Morgan's account almost every thing great and good amongst the Welsh Calvinistic Methodists, is to be attributed to his hero. How little must he have really known of them, or how *unthinkingly* has he written this work! That John Elias was their greatest preacher, as far as mere popular effect was concerned, we readily admit; but as to the actual management of their affairs, and thorough and pervading influence on their general mind, he was by no means predominant. We certainly expected in this connexion some reference to EBENEZER MORRIS, that man of apostolic energy of character, of personal presence and power, and of such severe taste in the composition of his sermons, that we once heard a masterly Welsh scholar say of him, 'I never heard him use a word which did not seem to me to be *the* *only* proper one.'* EBENEZER RICHARD, that cool, self-possessed, and sagacious mind, made to govern without exciting envy, and to warn without inspiring anger. DAVID CHARLES, whose sermons were a series of apothegms, and from whose lips in dry language, and with dryer manner, concentrated wisdom fell; these, (we refer not to those still living) were inferior to John Elias only in the article of popular oratory, while in other respects they were his equals, and in the actual controul of connexional matters his superiors. They arrogated less power and had more, they were less dogmatic, but not less apostolic.

With regard to the peculiar character of John Elias's preaching, we look in vain for information in these pages. What was the source of his power? Was it principally natural or artificial? What was the distinctive modification of his mind? Was it strength of faculty, clearness of apprehension, or vividness and variety of fancy? Read the book again and again, and you cannot answer these inquiries. How did he deport himself in the pulpit? Was he quiet or animated? Had he any remarkable intonations of voice, or emphasis? On all these matters 'this deponent sayeth *nought*.'

We are sorry for this, for Mr. Morgan's own sake. We regret that a man so evidently Christian-minded, and so catholic in spirit, should do himself so little credit. We are still more sorry for it on public grounds. A great occasion has been thrown away, and an opportunity for extensive usefulness has been lost. 'The Life and Times of John Elias,' present a rich and inviting theme, to an ordinarily practised pen. They supply much, very much of most interesting detail, connected with the man, his connexions, and the history of religion in his country, and might have been made the medium of conveying to the English public a more accurate view of Welsh ecclesiastical affairs, than is commonly possessed. But this opportunity has been lost, and we part with Mr. Morgan, thanking him for his intentions; while we regret we can thank him for nothing else. We must add, that *the Life* of John Elias is unwritten; and let us also add, that we shall anxiously look to Bala, or Trevecca for it. We earnestly hope we shall not look in vain.†

* Ebenezer Morris's voice was stentorian, yet perfectly manageable. An English traveller hearing him at Bridgend, in Glamorganshire, as he passed through the town, inserted in a small book he afterwards published, this remark, "*It was as though he had received the rudiments of his elocutionary education at the mouth of a speaking trumpet.*"

† A subject to which this volume strongly tempts us to refer, is the relation between the Welsh Methodists and the Established Church. It contains some strange statements, which we should much like to dwell

We subjoin a hurried sketch of John Elias; relying for dates, and biographical incidents, on Mr. Morgan's authority.

He was born on the 6th of May, 1774, at Brynllwynbach, in the parish of Awerch, near Pwllheli, Caernarvonshire. His father was a weaver, and had some share in the advantage of a small farm, which he jointly cultivated with his father. This grandfather of John Elias took an early liking to his grandson, and with exemplary assiduity sought to direct his footsteps aright. He taught him to read, took him regularly to church, frequently conversed with him on questions of morality and religion, and especially succeeded in fastening his attention on the Bible. In the seventh year of his age, he was afflicted with the small-pox, and its effects debilitated him for some years; during which, many interesting conferences occurred between him and his devoted grandfather. On his recovering strength sufficient to move about, he accompanied the old man to church, and to hear celebrated Dissenting ministers, who, principally from South Wales, from time to time visit the north. Sometimes the preacher was late, and then John Elias was put to read the scriptures to the expectant people. On one such occasion, before he was twelve years of age, he was thrust into the pulpit to do so, and with trembling, read part of the Sermon on the Mount. 'At length,' he says, 'I looked sideways, and observed the preacher standing by the door of the pulpit; I was greatly alarmed, I closed the Bible immediately, and came down as fast as I could.' The history of his boyhood, is the history of the constant struggles of his mind, under a conviction of sin, a desire towards God and his cause, and the corrupt propensities of his nature. At length it pleased Him who had separated him to His work and service, to give him liberty and peace by means of 2 Cor. v. 18, 19.

'About this time,' he says, 'the Lord was pleased to favour me with strong and clear manifestations of his mind by his Spirit in my soul, respecting the gospel, and his gracious method of saving sinners. A passage from the Scriptures struck me one day in a remarkable manner, and on a certain spot on my way to Pwllheli, which I well remember. It is 2 Cor. v. 18, 19,—*the ministry of reconciliation*: the expression came into my mind with new light and power. Oh! the enjoyment of my soul! God in Christ reconciling the world unto himself. I beheld the wondrous excellence and glory of the plan, which reconciles *without imputing trespasses!* I then perceived how that God

upon at large, but our limits forbid it at the present moment. It will come in our way in an article we contemplate on the History and Character of Welsh Nonconformity.

effected this, by imputing our sins to Christ, and counting his righteousness to us. The doctrine of justification has ever since been of infinite importance in my esteem.'

Young John Elias soon felt a desire to preach the gospel to his fellowmen, but 'perceived,' (he says) the desire was not reasonable in him, who had not yet been received as a member of the church.' In September, 1793, he united in church-fellowship with a small Methodist society, at *Hendre Howel*. The good man at whose house he stayed, and with whom he worked, as a weaver, put him to engage in family prayer alternately with himself, and his devotional spirit soon became very eminent. He attended a night school, (Sunday-schools then 'were not,') which circulated through the hamlet. These schools were very religiously conducted, and it frequently devolved on John Elias to perform every service that was observed. He read Welsh well, and this he was often called upon to do, as well as to catechise and engage in prayer. On some of these occasions he delivered a brief exhortation. 'Prayer meetings he also attended with great industry and earnestness.' Some old disciple, in his simplicity, (he says), urged me to speak a few words as an exhortation whilst reading the chapter. I soon felt a desire in my own mind for that work. Some passages of Scripture came to my thoughts, and some matter of warning or admonition would occur to me. When a preacher failed to keep his appointment I was occasionally requested to speak to the congregation. It was soon noised abroad, that the lad with Griffith Jones preached, and this caused much talk in the country.' He was at length admitted by the Welsh Methodist monthly meeting, a regular preacher in the country. This took place on Christmas-day, 1794. This day he always afterwards re-remembered with devout gratitude. He soon became anxious for education and mental improvement, and it is curiously interesting, at this time, to find that his elder brethren, so far from stimulating the desire, gave him every discouragement. Some Welsh people at Manchester, invited him there, that he might go to a school, and preach to them on the Sabbath. They generously offered to defray the expences of his education. He applied to his brethren at the next monthly meeting, for permission to go to Manchester for six months' education. He was sharply rebuked by the meeting, and told that it arose from nothing but the pride of his heart, and that it was the thirst of becoming a great preacher that made him now think of going to school. He then courageously determined, that congregations should not lose on account of his not having learning when young. 'I determined, (he adds), if the Lord would please to support and help me, to make up the deficiency by study and hard labour.'

He afterwards succeeded to have a few month's (*only a few month's !*) education at the school of the Rev. E. Richardson, Caernarvon. He here learnt so much English, he says, as led him to understand the subject matter of a book. However, he confesses, 'I did not learn anything to perfection, for I was but a short time under the care of that good friend; but I was put into the way of acquiring many things by industry and hard labour. I was enabled to persevere day and night in my studies without fatigue or delay, and continued unceasingly in this work, until I had, in some measure, acquired a general knowledge of the things most necessary for me. *But I am now, even in my 67th year, learning, and see greater need of knowledge every day.*'

In the year, 1799, Mr. Elias removed to the island of Anglesea, where he resided during the remainder of his days. He henceforth took an active and distinguished part in all the affairs of his denomination, and soon achieved as a preacher the highest eminence among them. His preaching was early of great promise. The seriousness of his spirit, and the earnestness of his purpose gave him weight with the truly religious; while the rapid flow of his elocution, combined with entire self-possession, commanded general admiration. The circumstances in which he was placed, contributed much to call forth the prominent characteristics of his mind and ministry. Preaching is eminently popular in Wales. It was then, and to a great extent, is still almost the only occasion of public assembling. The people are eminently theological. Stand and listen to two peasants on the mountain side, go to the field at harvest, to the mill, or the smithy, or mingle with Welshmen among the iron and copper, and coal works, aye, go the public house, and in a majority of instances you will find them discussing theology. Points of the most abstruse description, and difficult passages of Scripture, form the staple of their talk, in fair, in market, by the way, throughout the day's labour, and at evening's rest. Thus, we can easily account for that, which so much astonishes strangers visiting the principality in the spring and summer. When during such visits they attend the meeting of a Welsh association, they are astonished to find the most intense sympathy between a mass of four or even ten thousand people of all ages and conditions, and every word the preacher utters; and this when the discourse is so thoroughly doctrinal, that its principal portions would be utterly unintelligible to a congregation of English peasants. John Elias began to preach to such people in their own tongue. His qualification was then rather of the heart than of the intellect. The latter was but scantily furnished, while the former was swelling with love to God and to man. In youth he was mighty in the Scriptures. This gave him great power with a people who refer to the Bible to settle every kind of dispute. His connexional relations were also in his favour. He was engaged in an itinerating ministry. In the comparatively uncultivated state of his mind this circumstance aided him materially, as fewer sermons were necessary, and he had more time to give them completeness, while his repeated delivery of a discourse furnished opportunities for alteration and emendation; which advantages are virtually lost in a stated ministry. We trust we shall not be misunderstood, when we add that a narrower range of intellectual qualifications sufficed for the Calvinistic Methodists in Wales, during the greater portion of John Elias's life, than had been enjoyed by them during the life time of their founders, and than they must have, and are endeavouring to secure for themselves, henceforth. The founders of this denomination were almost to a man clergymen and scholars. When they were dying off, THOMAS CHARLES left the Establishment and cast in his lot among them. As far as he had gone in the walks of literature, he was a ripe scholar. With the original languages of the Bible, and the English tongue, he was exactly and critically acquainted. Of the language of his native mountains he was a perfect master; and there is not in the principality any work to surpass, few to compare, with his GEIRIADUR as to purity and chasteness of style, apart from its other and manifold excellencies. These great men died and left behind them a large number of preachers, but not, with very inconsiderable exceptions, men of early mental culture. Their ministry has therefore of necessity, been destitute of the many nameless advantages which result from such culture, and this has habituated the people to *a less varied* kind of preaching than the two congregational denominations have enjoyed. Indeed, and they must not be offended by our plainness of speech, the Welsh Methodists have been most unfaithful to themselves in respect to their ministry. For many years they did nothing towards educating their preachers, beyond sending one now and then to Glasgow, and more often to Cheshunt, and latterly to Highbury. Some of these became congregationalists and settled in England, others settled over Countess of Huntingdon congregations, and with some two or three exceptions only the feeble returned home; latterly they have seen this subject in the same light with Independents and Baptists, and have now promising institutions at Bala and Trevecca.

John Elias as a preacher was created by and for this state of things. His popularity was not confined to Anglesea, or to North Wales—indeed, in this body popularity in one part of Wales is popularity every where. A minister ordained at the Bala association, and residing at Holyhead, is, during his visit, as much the pastor of the Methodist church at Cardiff, as he is of that in the town of his residence. The following is a brief account of one of John Elias's preaching tours. He leaves Anglesea for the association at Llangeitho. He preaches twice or thrice a day during his whole journey, and is followed by crowds from village to village. At length he arrives at the great rendezvous of Welsh Methodism. He preaches the evening before the association. Two strange brethren had been announced the preceding Sabbath, names not given. The principal part of the available population attends. A few strangers have arrived, ten or twelve *balaenoriaid* from Carmarthen and Pembrokeshires, some of them came last Saturday that they might spend one Lord's-day at Llangeitho before they die! Much have they spoken on the Monday about the olden men (*yr hen ych*). They have been anxious to know whether any body lives who remembers Daniel Rowland, and not taking into account the lapse of time, are disappointed to find that there lives in the neighbourhood but one woman who heard him preach, and that she is bed-ridden; and that the old man who heard his last sermon, and whom he shook hands with the last time he was out, died three weeks ago. Time for commencing divine service arrives—the capacious chapel is crowded—a stranger, in slow and measured accents reads a psalm, gives out one of William William's hymns, and engages in prayer. Another stranger ascends the pulpit, he is sad-looking, his hair straight over his forehead, clad in a blue single breasted coat, a black double breasted waistcoat, buttoned up under his chin, with his legs encased in patent cords and top-boots. He reads his text in a low tone of voice, with somewhat of a drawl;—the people know him not, but he is from the north, and of the connexion, and that is enough. He dwells at some length on the context, then gives his discourse: there is nothing great; but it is sound orthodox matter; besides, he quotes Dr. Owen, and perhaps Manton, or Flavel. A flash of light gleams, and then another, but he does not allow himself to get excited; and having succeeded in awakening and fixing the people's attention, he closes, invoking the Divine benediction on what they have heard, and, with emphasis, '*on what they shall hear.*' John Elias then stands up—his face is strongly marked with clear and distiuct expressions of real and personal character, somewhat 'sicklied o'er with the pale cast of thought;' he is calm, self-possessed, and firm, and with a gravity so profound, that every approach or tendency to levity dies at once in his presence. He is a somewhat tall, slender man, his whole personal make and appearance denoting habits of untiring activity. 'Whoever this is (the observant hearer will say to himself), *I feel I shall be bound to listen to him.*' He gives out a single verse of Edmund Prys's translation of the Psalms, and then proceeds with his text—read with quiet, but most effective emphasis. He makes some interesting remarks of an obvious, but very appropriate character. Probably he takes some pains to settle the exact force of its principal terms, quoting some critical authority, but in the simplest and most unaffected manner. He divides the subject naturally, and becomes somewhat animated. The first head of discourse has been discussed, every body feeling that no more can be said upon it, so completely has he opened and laid it bare before their eyes. He approaches the salient point of the sermon, and his vivacity increases, the right hand seems a thing inspired, its motions are an integral part of the matter, deeper and deeper grow the intonations of the voice, while the animation increases mightily. Nothing can be more measured than its cadences—and still they are instinct with living fire: they blaze, they burn, they scorch: the preacher pauses—look, now, at that right hand aloft in the air—look at the poising of that fore finger, once, twice, thrice; look at that face, the firmly compressed lips, the distended nostrils, the sparkling and brilliant eyes reposing themselves for a moment; the expansive forehead, bright and fair in all its manly beauty; a thousand human beings before him, with slightly opened mouths, suspended breath, and rapt attention, all hang on the lips of this once poor weaver boy; yes, he has got it; he has been looking at and into the people—he has been catching a thought, and reimpressing his memory and his conscience with it, out it comes with all the splendour and energy and sublimity of the most finished, sustained and impassioned sacred oratory. The people tremble, weep, and are possessed—the charm is upon them—he sways them at his will—they move before him as shocks of corn before the breeze. He closes his discourse in a short prayer. Two men walk home together. The youngest asks, 'Who could that preacher be?' The other, somewhat contemptuously, replies, 'Who? John Elias, to be sure. Who else could preach such a sermon?'

When the whole scene has passed away, and the recollection of it remains, an unimpassioned analysis of the preacher's peculiar qualifications will perhaps produce some such result as this. It is not his personal godliness that distinguishes him; though that be eminent, other men are, in this respect, as eminent as he, and are immeasurably his inferiors in the pulpit. It is not the depth and closeness of his reasoning—many preachers in his own day, and country, and denomination, have been abler logicians, and far less prone to false reasoning—while they are dwarfs beside him before the public. It was not the power and excursiveness of his fancy, for he never excelled in metaphors, and those he employed were never original or striking. It is, firstly, the continued presence and influence of good common sense, and of a sober, if not always a sound judgment, in the selection of his subjects, and the manner of discussing them; secondly, a subtlety, though not a depth of intellectual power, which invested whatever he treated with an interest that freshened and brightened it up for the time, and smote the hearer with admiration and delight; and, above all, a well conceived, and consummately elaborated elocution. His greatness, his one greatness, was, we do not say matchless, but we do say, UNSURPASSED ORATORY. We think we have read all that has appeared in this country in the shape of accounts of Whitefield's eloquence, and we have no inclination to yield even him the palm; we have no idea that in mere oratory he was at all superior to John Elias. William Williams was eloquent, but it was the eloquence of his conceptions, while he was utterly careless of manner, and even of words. Christmas Evans was, on some occasions, mightier in his eloquence than John Elias, but it was when his imperial fancy led him aloft, and his hearers with him, and no more the result of previous elaborate study than are the complaints of a child But John Elias was THE ORATOR. Inconclusive, and common-place, he might occasionally be, but otherwise than eloquent he could not be. He was THE SACRED ORATOR, who devoted his long and godly life to the best interests of his country and of mankind. His career has closed, his remains lie at peace at Llânfaes, until the morning of the great and awful day, when the Son of God will come with the clouds to ransom 'the purchased possession,' to restore to the souls of his redeemed their glorified bodies, and "to deliver up the kingdom to God and his Father, that GOD MAY BE ALL IN ALL."

Art. VI. *Margaret: or the Gold Mine.* From the French of Elie Berthet. London: Robert Weir.

THIS is a very interesting tale, written—as the translator remarks, in her modest preface, 'in a spirit so different to that which generally pervades the writings of our lively neighbours, that no apology need be offered for its production in an English form, even to that class of readers who are the most rigid condemners of the present French school of romance.' The story is, indeed, characterized by a unity of design, an earnestness, a severity of thought and style, which contrasts most favourably with the extravagancies of Dumas, Soulié, Jules Janin, and that leader in all that is unnatural and revolting, Eugene Sue, while the lofty morality which breathes throughout, separates it still more widely from a class of works with which it has nothing in common, save the name.

Although the translator has not remarked it, we believe the main incidents of the tale to be founded in fact. Indeed, from the truthfulness of each incident, and the dramatic character of the whole, it is difficult to persuade ourselves that we are not reading a narrative of what actually occurred, instead of a skillfully constructed fiction based only on an historical anecdote.

The scene is laid in the French Alps, toward the close of the last century, but previous to the Revolution, among those almost inaccessible mountains where 'Mount Pelvoux, monarch of all, shoots up to the elevation of fourteen thousand feet, (almost the height of Mont Blanc,) and appears to shake the snow from his own head on those of his rivals, Mounts Olan and Genèvre, although separated from them by several leagues.' At the foot of Mount Pelvoux, a small monastery, called Lautaret, stands, and here, one summer evening, two young men and a stranger sought refuge from a violent storm.

'The stranger who had thus coolly introduced himself into the hospice, and who, when there, conducted himself as if in a common inn, was a mountaineer of some forty-five years, of a frank open countenance and robust frame, whose whole exterior bespoke a man in easy circumstances, and whose home was probably in some adjoining valley. He wore a large square coat of thick cloth; his striped waistcoat, descending very low, almost covered trousers of the same materials as his coat; and these were met by large stockings drawn above the knee, where they were confined by red ribbon garters. His long light hair flowed upon his shoulders, from beneath a large slouched hat, placed carelessly on his head. The ample *sombrero* cast a shade over a countenance bronzed by exposure to the inclemency of the weather; but, by the fire's fitful blaze, much of the steady intelligence and somewhat rough goodnature, which characterises the inhabitants of the Upper Alps, might be read in the traveller's features. To sum up all, the stranger's exterior was certainly prepossessing, and in any other than this canton, so unfavourable to agriculturists, he would have been set down as one of that body, returning from an excursion to some neighbouring farm.'—p. 89.

The kind enquiries addressed by this mountaineer to the two young men, are parried by the elder with an anxiety which excites his suspicions. These are increased by the subsequent appearance of two officers of the mounted patrol, in attendance on a magistrate, which, it soon appears, is charged with the arrest of two fugitives from Lyons. The extreme terror of the younger of the two at the sight of these new comers, and his whispered prayer to the mountaineer to save them, proves that they are the very persons the officers are in pursuit of. Martin Simon, the mountaineer, struck with the sickly appearance of the younger, interposes, and by pretending they are his nephews, lulls the suspicions of the magistrate who is worn out with fatigue, and then conducts them to their chamber. He now closely, but kindly questions them; and learning that the elder is the Chevalier de Peyras, and his companion, no brother, but Ernestine de Blanchefort, a young lady of family, who has fled with him as his affianced bride, he lectures them severely; but, on finding that the poor girl has fled from a harsh, unloving father, finally assures them of his protection. The mystery which seems to shroud this Martin Simon, is increased, when, on taking their departure the following morning, they observe him throwing a handful of gold into the alms box!

It has been arranged that the two young people should accompany Martin Simon, as brother and sister, until the danger was passed. They now proceed, and meet an old man, who has been sent with a message to their protector, who leaves them under escort. He was the village schoolmaster, and from him, after much questioning, they learn that their protector is 'the present proprietor of the village Bout du Monde, and he whom men have named the 'king of Pelvoux.'

''The king of Pelvoux!' repeated the Chevalier, in astonishment; 'do you mean to say that the person to whom we have been talking as Martin Simon, is the king of Pelvoux?'

''It is he himself. Have you ever heard him mentioned?'

''Yes,' said Marcellin, trying to recall the circumstances to his recollection. 'It is reported that he is a rich nobleman, who has established a kind of little kingdom in this inaccessible country, and has the credit of being enormously rich. Many persons most firmly believe that he is in communication with the Evil One; and I am not sure, but I think, that the parliament considered it their duty, to investigate some charge of sorcery in which he was concerned.'

''No, no!' said the schoolmaster, with much gravity; 'things were not quite so bad as all that. The parliament certainly did send commissioners into our valley, to search for an imaginary gold mine, but M. Martin Simon suffered no more molestation than any other inhabitant of the village. I can fully comprehend, however, that those who charged him with sorcery, fancied that they had substantial grounds for the accusation. His father, the Spirit of the Mountain, though a better character towards the close of his life, was at best but a singular being. Certainly, M. Martin Simon is the Bailli, and the person of greatest consequence in our valley; but he bears no lordly title.''—pp.82—83.

After encountering many difficulties, not the least of which was, the appearance of the magistrate, M. Michelot, who, although charged with their apprehension, now to their surprise accompanies them as a friend, they reach—

'Two rocks, steep and close to each other, which served as posts to a gigantic doorway; whence arose the idea of uniting them at their base by trunks of almost unhewn trees placed crossways. Enormous stakes, driven into the ground, completed this rough enclosure, to which were fastened folding gates, large enough to admit two chariots abreast.

'This was the entrance into the little valley of Bout du Monde: and such was this disposition of the ground, that this door, as in the Grande Chartreuse, was the only means of access into an enclosure, protected on every other side by inaccessible mountains.

'But it was after passing this portico, nature's unassisted work, that the majesty and beauty of the scene engrossed the travellers' entire attention. Although the defile was neither so long, nor so dark, as that of the Lautaret, an obscurity reigned in it, that enhanced the gleaming brightness of the valley thus viewed in perspective.

'It was an enchanting English garden, among granite rocks; a terrestrial paradise, where every thing appeared good, pleasant, and harmonious. Orchards filled with fruit-trees, fields of corn and rye, and green pastures, trenched on the dark barren sides and dazzling snows of the mountains. In the centre stood the village, where each house, white and gay, with its little garden and hedge-rows of fruit trees, seemed a palace, compared with the miserable hovels of the adjoining valleys. The church raised its tapering slated spire at the foot of an enormous rock, which, overhanging the other buildings, defended them from the fall of the avalanches. But all were partially concealed by the thick foliage, now gilded by the sun's rays, and the whole valley might not inaptly have been compared to a basket filled with evergreens and flowers.

'Martin Simon, for one moment, enjoyed the astonishment and enthusiasm of his visitors.

'' It is I who have created the little world that is before you,' said he, with the greatest satisfaction in his voice; 'it is I that have made these sterile rocks productive, that have peopled this dreary wilderness, that have rendered it a sure asylum for man, in this inhospitable climate. . . . . The day that my father first put his foot on this desolate corner of the world, a ragged shepherd, and the chamois were its sole inhabitants.'

'He paused, as if fearful of having said too much; the two strangers gazed on him in admiration.

''You must have been very rich to have accomplished such wonders!' exclaimed the Procureur.

'' And most courageous to dare the undertaking!' said the Chevalier de Peyras.

'The king of Pelvoux thoughtfully shook his head.

''Both riches and courage, were, perhaps, requisite,' said he, 'and perhaps, something more. . . . . I have often been accused of sorcery, and truly I know not, if there be not some foundation for the charge, in the history of this country! . . . . But come, gentlemen; you will have time hereafter to examine the wonders of this valley,''—pp.107—109.

Martin Simon conducts the party to his house, and introduces them to his only daughter, the heroine.

'Margaret Simon's features, though tanned by the air and sun, were regular and faultless. Her figure was majestic, and her whole person attested that purity of blood and strength of constitution so admired in the women of Piedmont and Savoy; a serious and reflecting air characterized her demeanour, and well became the style of her countenance; her carriage was dignified, almost noble; and the villagers remarked that her deportment was an index to her mind. They said that she was tolerant and lenient to the opinions of others, but rigid and inflexible in her own. She spoke little, but that little was always marked by good sense, and the strictest adherence to truth: whilst from her father, Margaret, or Margot, as he familiarly called her, inherited a discerning and active mind, which had been cultivated and strengthened by the sound and useful education imparted by Eusèbe Nöel, the poor enthusiastic admirer of Virgil. Her costume, simple, unpretending, and without ornament, consisted of a red and black striped apron over a brown cloth dress, so short that it fully displayed her neatly embroidered stockings. On her head she wore one of those straw hats, so fantastically embellished at the opera; but which in their simplicity are not devoid of elegance. Nothing in her person revealed that spirit of coquetry that we almost admiringly pardon in young girls. Margaret was either unconscious of her beauty, or judged that 'beauty unadorned, was adorned the most;' perhaps she was perfectly devoid of woman's vanity, perhaps too proud to allow any indications of such feminine weakness to become visible. In short, dignity, rather than naïvetè or elegance, was the general character of her person.'—pp. 114—115.

Margaret is presented to the pretended brother and sister, and, with this deception, the tale of her sorrow begins.

Martin Simon feasts his friends pleasantly, but they are disturbed in the midst by the entry of an old man—a mere drunken knife-grinder, but who, nevertheless, appears to have the power of irritating the King of Pelvoux almost to madness. The subsequent scenes draw out Margaret's character very finely, and deepen the mystery that hangs about her father, who not only converts the *procureur* Michelot into an active assistant on behalf of the lovers, but assures them that within a few days he will obtain even the consent of Ernestine's father to their marriage.

The mystery that shrouds his benefactor, makes a deep impression on the Chevalier de Peyras, and scarcely less deep is the influence of the noble beauty, and still more noble character of the unconscious Margaret, on his wayward heart. Ernestine quickly perceives the change, and awaits, with sorrowful forebodings, the return of M. Michelot, while her lover wearies himself with enquiries and conjectures, as to whom his host really is, and whether he is indeed the possessor, as is whispered, of a gold mine. After some days Michelot returns, charged with a kind message from Ernestine's stern father, consenting to the marriage, and Margaret, who is now for the first time made acquainted that her guests are not brother and sister, is sent to summon them home.

'At this instant, Margaret reached the small kind of platform on which Ernestine and the Chevalier rested. The expression of her countenance was even greater than usual, and when she was near the young people, she said coldly:

''You are expected in the village, come! the lawyer, who accompanied you, is returned, and brings you some important news.'

''Michelot!' exclaimed Marcellin, eagerly.

'Martin Simon's daughter assented, and turned to descend the mountain; Ernestine gently detained her.

''Pray, Margaret,' asked she, 'tell me if the news of which you speak, be good or bad; has my father at length consented to——'

'She checked herself abruptly.

''To your marriage with the Chevalier de Peyras?' replied the young girl, with a cruel intention, of which no one would have judged her capable, 'I cannot tell you.'

'Ernestine blushed, and bent down her head.

''Who has told you? who has made you believe that——'

''Seek no longer to deceive me,' drily answered Margaret; 'this young man is not your brother.'

''Believe me,' stammered Mademoiselle de Blanchefort, 'the necessity alone could——'

''He is not your brother,' repeated the young mountaineer, with cold dignity; 'you have uttered a falsehood, and take care that God does not punish you for it?'

'Ernestine bent her head at this unexpected humiliation, and hiding her face in her hands, sobbed aloud.

''Yes, yes?' she exclaimed, 'you are right; God will punish me, he already punishes me! Marcellin, can you now say I have not made sacrifices sufficiently great for you?'

They return together to the house; but on their road meet a party of villagers carrying a dead body, which proved to be that of the old knife-grinder. 'All Margaret's presence of mind gave way, she turned horribly pale, staggered, and wildly shrieked, 'Raboisson—dead! at the foot of a precipice! who has commanded this crime, who has murdered him?'' The peasants are astonished at her violence, but can only say that he probably fell into the gulf on the side of the road, where he must have lain for some days.

Margaret is led home; and the lovers are summoned to the presence of Martin Simon and the lawyer. Here they find their marriage contract, bearing the signature of Ernestine's father, and giving her a handsome portion, and papers, restoring to the Chevalier de Peyras the family chateau, and its dépendencies, which he had mortgaged in his extravagant career. The kind, yet commanding manner of their benefactor, together with the extent of his gifts, excite their utmost astonishment.

'Marcellin and Ernestine seemed petrified: the king of Pelvoux observed them with profound satisfaction, from out of the corner of his eye.

'Suddenly the Chavalier rose.

''I cannot accept so many benefits, without knowing my benefactor!'

'The mountaineer seized de Peyras' delicate hand in his strong grasp.

''Young man,' said he, 'have you then no relative who might be anxious to redeem the honour of his house, by repairing your faults?'

''A relative,' repeated Marcellin, in a thoughtful tone; 'I have none.'

''Are you sure?' said the mountaineer, sadly; 'are you sure that you know all who still bear your name?'

''Too sure . . . . at least——'

'He paused, and gazed fixedly on his interrogator, who rising in his turn, said gravely—

''You have one, Chevalier—you have one; although in the humble condition in which he now lives, he bears not his own illustrious name: that relative is Martin Simon, baron of Peyras, the actual head of your family—for I am the eldest branch.''—pp. 176—177.

He now proceeds to relate, how his father, in consequence of a quarrel with his younger brother, retired to these inhospitable mountains, and after long wandering about, married a goatherd's daughter. The relator was their only child; and, brought up at a distance from the world, he felt no wish to enter it, and resume his title. He, therefore, also took a wife from among the peasantry. 'Thus, let not the brilliant title of Baron de Peyras, still mine, cause you any illusion;—I have made for myself another title, in which I glory.'

The secret of his immense wealth is, however,, still unrevealed; and the thoughts and wishes which had been brooding in his young cousin's breast, now break forth beyond controul. This mysterious possessor of untold gold—perhaps of a *gold mine,* is his own cousin, still attached to his family, still anxious for the honour of his house. And Margaret, that noble girl, is no Alpine peasant, but the bearer of his very name, the sharer of his lordly blood—what a bride would Margaret be for him! He now prays his cousin to postpone his signing the marriage contract, much to the surprise of Martin and dismay of Ernestine; but his benefactor is determined, and the contract is signed.

More unpleasant duties now occupy the king of Pelvoux; he has to draw up the verbal process, detailing the discovery of the body of the knife-grinder, at whose death he seems greatly surprised, and he asks the help of *procureur* Michelot, which is eagerly given. Still a cloud of anxiety seems to rest on them all; and the following morning being appointed for the marriage, they retire early to rest.

Unable to sleep, Marcellin rises ere dawn, and being on the balcony of his chamber, sees Margaret 'gliding along like a shadow,' and completely shrouded in her mantle. What could she do at so early an hour? Surely she was going to the gold mine! He leaps from the low window, and follows her. But her footsteps are not bent toward the mountains; she hurries to a house at the end of the village, and is admitted by two old men—the schoolmaster, whose house it was, and the Prior of Lautaret. He waits anxiously to learn her errand, and listens to some preparatory conversation. At length—

'"You know of Raboisson's death?' said she at length, in a hoarse tone, and in one long breath, without raising her eyes.

'The schoolmaster turned pale.

'"I know it, I know it,' he answered. 'Did they not, in the presence of the dead body, make me act as scribe, when the verbal process was drawn out? The horrible figure follows me yet! I think I still see the unhappy wretch as he——'

'He paused suddenly, and placed his hands before his eyes, as if to exclude some horrible sight.

'"It is about that writing that I wish to question you,' replied Margaret, very sorrowfully. 'I wish to know if it said that Raboisson died from accident, or . . . . in any other manner.'

'Eusèbe and the monk exchanged rapid glances.

'"Who can say?' was the schoolmaster's feebly muttered answer.

'"Thus, then, nobody has exprèssed a suspicion that the death of this miserable man was the result of . . . . of . . . . of crime? Answer,' said she, vehemently, 'has nobody entertained such a suspicion?'

'Eusèbe became fearfully agitated.

'"I must confess,' said he, in broken accents, 'that this lawyer . . . . this . . . . Procureur Michelot——'

'"I knew it!' said Margaret, as if speaking to herself. 'That man scents out wickedness, like as the vulture of our mountains scents his prey in the air. In what manner think you did Raboisson meet with his death? Was he murdered? Was he assassinated?'

'She pronounced these words with savage energy.

''Pray, Margaret,' cried the schoolmaster, drops of agony running down his face, 'do not question me; do not force me to tell you——'

''He dares not speak! He fears to lacerate my heart with the horrible suspicions thet we have mutually conceived!' said the young girl, with bitter irony. 'Very well! then you, my reverend father,' she continued, suddenly turning to the monk, who had testified the keenest interest in this conversation, 'you will not hide from me the impression that has been made upon you by this horrible event, of which all the circumstances are familiar to you; you are God's minister, and you *dare* not lie. Answer—answer me then! has not this man perished by the hand of some murderer?'

'The old monk fixed upon her his calm piercing eye.

''There are some reasons for thinking such to be the case,' said he, in a solemn tone; 'but you—you, my daughter, what interest can you have——'

''It is true, then,' screamed Margaret, in a heart-rending accent, 'both of them think it—both of them! And I—I thought that to me alone had this mystery of shame and crime been revealed! They suspect who the guilty man is; they accuse, and have even judged him in their hearts, although in my presence they have not dared to call *my father a murderer!*'

'At the same time, Margaret fell back in her seat, evincing every symptom of the most dreadful despair.'—pp. 215—218.

The old men hasten to console her, and to assert their conviction of her father's innocence; although they both acknowledge that they knew Raboisson was master of the secret from whence he obtained his wealth. The whole of this long scene is written with a power, which forcibly reminds us of our early dramatists; and the struggle of the two old men, between sympathy for the distracted girl who believes her father a murderer, and their anxiety to be partakers of her secret, is most skilfully brought out. Poor Margaret learns that the belief in her father's possession of a gold mine is becoming stronger and stronger every day; and carried away by this dream of gold, both the old men urge her to confess it to them, promising to save her father from the danger, to which the suspicious circumstances, of Raboisson's death, exposes him. She parries their entreaties, and sadly turns homeward. On her road she is met by her cousin; who now convinced of the reality of this gold mine, determines on breaking off with Ernestine, and he offers himself to Margaret; but on receiving her decided, though faltering refusal, he in his turn, discloses his suspicions respecting the gold mine, and threatens vengeance, unless she points out its site.

'Nothing that Peyras had hitherto said, appeared to touch Margaret so deeply as this threat: the frigid manner, which at all times concealed her feelings, suddenly disappeared. She looked at Marcellin in deep anguish, and a full tear trickled from her dark eye.

' 'Thus then,' she said, in a tone of uncontrollable grief, 'even the love that you feigned for me was not sincere! It was not I whom you loved, it was my father's gold mine—Marcellin, Marcellin! why not have left me a little longer in the belief, that it was your passion for me which made you trample under foot such sacred duties.'

'A malignant joy was stamped on Peyras's features; he was too skilful to be mistaken in the nature of such sentiments—'Margaret,' cried he, 'you have betrayed yourself; Margaret, you love me; I *know* it!'

'But short-lived and rare were the weakness of this sternly constituted mind.

'When Margaret heard this exulting exclamation, she turned haughtily, and with striking dignity replied—

' 'I despise you!' '—p. 244, 245.

They return to the village, where all is confusion. Michelot has accused the king of Pelvoux of the murder of the old knife-grinder, and some very powerful scenes follow. At length on the confession of the schoolmaster, that he was by accident the cause of Roboisson's death, Martin Simon is acquitted. Margaret now seeks her father alone, and reminds him that he vowed to his father on his death-bed, to give up this hidden treasure, when it should begin to prove a curse instead of a blessing.

' 'Margaret, Margaret,' interrupted Martin Simon, brushing away a tear, 'why recall these sorrowful recollections?'

' 'Because, my father, the warning signs foretold by Bernard, have been fulfilled; because, now that your secret is known, crime and treason enclose you in a circle which daily narrows around you; because, already by your side the old man dishonours his grey hairs, the husband deserts his wife, the priest blasphemes his God, and even your own daughter has cursed you in her heart. Yes, yes, the appointed time is come! that fatal power which every moment threatens destruction to this humble corner of the earth, must be destroyed. Besides, have you not found the distribution of this gold too heavy a charge for a good and simple man like you? This gold that produces so much good and evil on the earth, from which you only reap ingratitude! Father, you have done much good with this treasure, take heed lest you now only do evil.'

'Martin Simon mused.

' 'I have forgotten nothing, Margaret,' said he, at length; 'and I am ready to keep the oath exacted from me, and which thou must also have exacted from thy children. This promise is always in my mind.'—p. 282.

It was not, however, without a long struggle that he finally consented.

We must now pass on to the winding up of this solemn drama. Martin Simon gives a promise to each of his four guests, that that very evening he will show them the source of his wealth; and each, unconscious that the promise has been made to another, repairs to a solitary cave, opposite the inaccessible heights of Mount Pelvoux. The rage, and disappointment of the four when they meet in this cave, are powerfully painted, and on Martin Simon's arrival, they all tax him with duplicity. 'I have not deceived one of you. I promised to show each this precious mine, but I did not pledge myself to show it *only* to him,' is the reply. A number of mountaineers appear with Margaret, at the cave's mouth, and Martin Simon bids them all follow him to the Follet, a steep mountain on the other side of the valley. After a long and toilsome journey, the wearied company at length arrived at the foot of the peak. They mount with great difficulty, and at length find themselves on an immense cone, only surpassed by its neighbour Pelvoux.

' 'The gold mine! Shew us the gold mine!'

' 'Willingly, my friends,' said Martin Simon, with much composure, proceeding to the spot where Mount Follet joined Pelvoux; 'we have now arrived at the end of our journey.'

' 'What?' querulously asked the Chevalier, who was closely following on his footsteps, 'is the treasure buried in this inaccessible place? I hoped——'

' 'You hoped that it could be more easily worked, did you not?' said Martin Simon, bitterly; 'but what can be done, my dear cousin? Those who come after us, may work it, *if they can*, in the same manner that we have done. . . . . I filled large bags full of the metal, which I left carefully concealed upon the mountain's sides; in the night I came for these sacks, and took them to the village, where, acting upon some chemical knowledge, imparted by my father, I separated the gold from its dross; a cave in my own house, where that miserable Raboisson discovered my secret, served as my laboratory, and from time to time I sent large ingots to Durand, my banker at Grenoble, whose interest in the transaction guaranteed his discretion; from him I received them back in money. By these means, my father and I managed to enjoy our riches, without arousing suspicion.'

'The king of Pelvoux gave these details, as calmly and cheerfully as if he were not going to resign the treasure, of which he had enjoyed exclusive possession for so many years.

'Martin Simon removed some stones, so skilfully arranged that they formed a shifting wall, and discovered a grotto of about five or six feet high, and ten or twelve deep. *It was the Gold Mine!*

'A silence, expressive of unbounded admiration, reigned among all present. Heads were curiously thrust forward to examine the precious metal in its primitive state. The vein was narrow, and appeared as if crushed in its bed, but it likewise looked perfectly pure, and the crystals of the copper ore, with which it was but slightly mixed, added apparently to its richness. Avaricious nature, reluctantly compelled to yield her riches to man, seemed to delight in previously dazzling his eyes and exciting his cupidity even to madness; for the sun, just sinking in the west, now darted his brilliant rays full into the cave, as if freely to expose to their longing eyes the gold dust that glittered in the vaulted roof, sides, and floor of the precious mine.'—pp. 314—316.

Martin Simon at length bids them descend, lest night should overtake them. They reluctantly withdraw, and return to the cave, leaving him to follow.

'At last quick steps were heard, and Martin Simon, breathless, threw himself rather than walked, into the cave, saying in a commanding voice—

'"Let no one stir, unless he wish to perish!"

'They were about to demand an explanation of the father's and daughter's extraordinary conduct, when a fearful sound shook the valley; the air was violently agitated, the earth trembled, and at the same instant a shower of stones and masses of rock fell heavily on the ground. All rushed to the cavern's entrance, to see what could have caused this strange occurrence.

'"Take care," said Martin Simon, trying to keep them back; "If my apprehensions be correct, the greater danger is not yet passed."

'But curiosity prevailed over the good man's warning. All rushed to the flat ground before the grotto, and all eyes were turned towards the Follet, whence the noise seemed to proceed. Then a grand spectacle met their eyes. A train formed of several barrels of gunpowder, had been secretly laid under the enormous granite mass that formed the basis of that chain of rocks already mentioned, by which alone the Follet could be reached. It was to this train that Martin Simon set fire when he lingered behind his party. An enormous cloud of smoke was slowly rising to the heavens, and large quantities of still falling stones proved how tremendous had been the explosion.'—pp. 320, 321.

A second follows, and the gold mine is placed for ever beyond the reach of man!

The story ends mournfully, and this is, we think, a great defect; for the generous Martin Simon, and his high-minded Margaret, in justice, deserved a better fate than overtakes them. The beautiful village rapidly sinks into decay, and ruin overtakes every one. Martin dies of grief; the land becomes barren as of yore, and poor Margaret sits like the wailing Banshee, of Irish superstition, contemplating the ruined scenes of her childhood. Such is an outline of the powerful tale of this gold mine. It is some time since we have read so admirable a story—as the production of a French writer, it almost stands alone. We must also award a just meed of praise to the translator. She has performed her task with great skill, indeed we have scarcely ever seen a translation, in which the very spirit of the original has been more closely preserved.

Art. VII.—*History of the Reformation in Germany.* By Leopold Ranke. Translated by Sarah Austin. 8vo. Vols. I. and II. London: Longman and Co.

THE real character of the reformation from popery has been greatly misunderstood. Both friends and enemies have misconceived its nature, and have spoken and written about it in a style which the calmer judgment, more extended investigation, and sounder views of the present age, cannot sustain. To the one class, it has been a theme of unmingled praise. Its agents and its history, the virtues of the former, and the critical and varying fortunes of the latter, have been dwelt on in a style of simple eulogism. To the other class, it has presented an aspect the reverse of all this. With an origin traceable to personal vanity, or class rivalship, it is supposed to have betokened an irreligious temper, and to have been patronized with a view to secular ends. Identified in spirit with the rebellion of Lucifer, it has been regarded as a personification of the worst qualities which our nature can assume. An impartial judgment will fail to sympathize with either of these views. They are both extremes, though the latter is specially destitute of support. Few of our readers are in danger of adopting it, and even catholic writers must be strangely destitute of candour, and regardless of historic evidence, who should now attempt its defence. We may be content, therefore, to leave it amongst the exploded errors of a former age. It stands on record as a warning to the excited polemic, enforcing the necessity of caution and self-controul in the judgments formed on passing events.

The other, or protestant view of the reformation, though containing a large portion of truth, is destitute of discrimination and largeness of view. It fails to do justice to the real character of the movement, or to place its distinctive merits fairly before the mind. It attributes to it virtues which it did not possess, and shades its glory by an admixture of earthly passion, which only serves to weaken its power, and check its triumphant course. The interests of truth will be best advanced by an intelligent discrimination of its qualities; praise being awarded when due, and censure pronounced when human infirmity intervened to mar the benefits, or to restrain the inherent energies of Christianity. There was so much in the personal character of Luther to command admiration, and so much in his public life to constitute him a benefactor of his species, that the most ardent of his disciples need not scruple to make the admissions which truth requires. After all the deductions which a rigid investigation can demand, the German reformer will still possess claims on the admiration and gratitude of mankind, to which few parallels can be found.

The character of his achievement is visible in its progress. It is written on the surface of his history, and is only lost sight of, when that history is made to give place to the theories of philosophical speculatists, or to the passions of party zealots. The earlier movements of Luther were in perfect keeping with a dutiful submission to the papacy. He himself had no idea of the rupture to which they would lead, nor, indeed, of any other issue than the correction of some notorious abuses, which he verily believed to be as distasteful to St. Peter, as they were repugnant to his own views of religion. He was led on step by step, without perceiving whither things tended. A sense of duty, a conviction of spiritual necessity, the earnest yearning of a soul partially enlightened, impelled him onward. He could not stop, and yet he trembled to proceed. The 'powers of the world to come' were upon him, and he felt that to pause in his career would be to renounce his hope, and to abandon the church to pollution. When we read the fine spun theories of some protestant writers, we are led to imagine that Luther acted throughout on one uniform system. They appear to conclude that his views were matured from the first; that his whole movements were adjusted; and every part so fitted to all others, as that a complete and perfect whole should be secured. The illusion may be pleasing, but it is illusion still;—a mere fiction, which fancy creates, but which facts instantly disprove. The monk of Wittenberg was led on in a way which he did not know. Had he done so, he would probably have been scared from the great undertaking, so little prepared was he, at first, for the struggle into which he was subsequently precipitated.

Hence then the excellences and the defects of his reformation. It was the protest of the spiritual against the sensual; the revolt of the inner religious man against the forms which had been substituted for faith, and the corruptions which threatened to overwhelm the church. The spiritual nature of man had been lost sight of for ages, and a system of ritual observances, and of mere childish mummeries had been erected on its ruins. This system was enforced by power, and sanctioned by long standing. It was interwoven with political institutions, and social sympathies; had overshadowed the relations of public and private life, and was obviously tending to the obliteration from human memory of the future and the eternal. Against this all the better elements of Luther's mind revolted. He felt that religion was insulted and depraved; that men were in danger from perilous errors; that the church had lost its distinctive character; and that the hope of the world would be extinguished, unless some brave soul were found to rebuke popular corruptions, and to re-erect the standard of truth. He therefore did, at any one time only so much as was, in his judgment, absolutely requisite to meet the necessities of the case. He sought to discharge present duty, and at every successive stage of his early career, anticipated repose and satisfaction. Hence it happened, that while his reformation betokened the earnest yearning of a religious mind after emancipation from gross and destructive error, it failed to realize, or even to attempt, the complete deliverance of the Church. He was content to meet the exigency of the hour, and his work was consequently left unfinished and incomplete. Another example was furnished of fidelity to truth, so far as it was apprehended; but the constitution of the Christian Church and the means of its extension were but imperfectly understood. A particular case was met in a spirit of moral heroism never surpassed; but the interests of the Church were not provided for by a recognition and enforcement of those general principles which lie at her basis, and are essential to her triumphs. Branches were lopped off, but the trunk remained untouched. Luther's own liberty was claimed, but the human mind was permitted to remain in bondage. The indirect influences of the Reformation on the progress of religious liberty were most powerful. They have not yet worked themselves out. They are to be traced through the successive stages of puritanism and independency, and are now moulding the sentiments of our age in the shape of Anti-State-Church principles. But the earlier Reformers were far from contemplating this. They demanded liberty for themselves, but refused it to all others. They claimed to worship God according to their own convictions; but when others pleaded conscience, and requested a similar license, they were refused with a dogmatism as assumptive as the infallibility of the pope.

Nor was there anything very marvellous in this. It might have been anticipated. It was only what an intelligent estimate of the human mind would have led us to expect. Luther and his associates were but one stage removed from spiritual serfdom, and they saw only the most simple and obvious forms of truth. It required long experience, a dark night of trial, in order to bring out those universal laws, on which the right of private judgment, and the voluntariness of religious service are based. The best minds of that age recoiled with pious horror from the principles in which we glory. The generations immediately preceding them had furnished no precedents. The lights of experience were wanting, and the evils incident to their movements, and the misconstructions to which their best actions were subjected, rendered them timid, and warned them to be cautious. Like unpractised mariners they skirted along the shore, and feared to launch out into the mighty deep. In what they did, however, they contributed mightily to what we are. They laboured, and we have entered into their labours; and shall prove ourselves both ungrateful and unreflecting, if we permit their imperfections to render us insensible of their merits, or thankless for the testimony they bore. An enlightened appreciation of their worth is the best preparation for a successful carrying out of their undertaking. Let us do justice to the men and their work; let us estimate at its true value their approximations to truth, whilst we regret their short-comings and errors; and the Church may then hope to receive, at our hands, the boon for which she yet waits.

The story of the Reformation is on this account eminently instructive. We regard it with deep interest, and counsel all classes of Protestant Dissenters to give it more continuous and profound attention. It is intimately connected with our own times and struggles, and holds out both encouragements and warnings in the service on which we have entered. That it should now engage a greater measure of attention, is the natural result of our position, and constitutes a propitious sign of these times. It would be ominous of evil, if the lights of past ages were disregarded. That philosophy is both shallow and delusive, which, under pretence of honouring revelation, or of any other plea whatsoever, refuses to learn wisdom from the records of a former age. It is by communing with the best of men, the emissaries of truth in former times, that we are enabled to advance on the positions they maintained; or to render more effective service than their imperfect views, or unfavourable circumstances, permitted.

With such convictions we have been much gratified by many publications which have recently been issued. The literature of the Reformation has been greatly enriched, and we mistake much, if important advantages will not thence accrue. Its previous state was disgraceful both to our historical research and to our protestant zeal, and can with difficulty be accounted for, when the interest of the narrative and the direct relation of its incidents to ourselves are borne in mind. A combination of rare talents was, however, required, for the successful preparation of such a history, and hence, probably, the cause of its being so long unsupplied. This reproach is now in the course of being wiped away. The publication of De Wette's edition of Luther's Letters, extending to five thick and closely printed volumes, has supplied the learned with the best diary of the reformer's life, whilst the works of D'Aubigné and Waddington have condensed the scattered lights which were needed to illustrate his character and achievements, as well as those of his contemporaries.* The brilliant fancy, and discriminating judgment of the former of these writers, combined in a rare degree with the faculty of minute and dry research, have invested his volumes with the attraction of a romance, and the sterling value of a veritable history. The result has been an almost unprecedented circulation, extending, as we are informed by the author, in his preface to the volume just issued, from 150,000 to 200,000 copies in the English language. Dr. Waddington's work, though less brilliant, is not inferior in any of the more sterling qualities of history, and, as a contemporary journal justly remarks, 'in severe fidelity, is perhaps even superior.' †

The work now before us, and which has given occasion to these remarks, is worthy to sustain an honourable comparison with those we have named. The author, Leopold Ranke, is well known to English readers, through the medium of Mrs. Austin's admirable translation of his *History of the Popes;* and his high reputation will suffer no abatement from the manner in which he has excuted his present undertaking. With indefatigable diligence he has explored all the public archives which promised to furnish materials for his work, and with truly German drudgery has sifted the several publications connected with the period embraced, which for many years past have been issued on the Continent. Few minds can appreciate the force of the impulse under which his researches were prosecuted. What would have been toil to others was recreation to him, and the solitude which the light-hearted and the frivolous would shun, was peopled with the forms of an ever-varying and most instructive life. 'Let no one,' he remarks in his preface, 'pity a man who devotes himself to studies apparently so dry, and neglects for them the delights of many a joyous day. It is true the companions of his solitary hours are but lifeless paper, but they are the remnants of the life of past ages, which gradually assume form and substance to the eye occupied in the study of them. For me they had a peculiar interest.'

It must not be supposed that the faculty of continuous research coustitutes the only, or even the prominent, quality of Ranke. He possesses in an eminent degree the power of imaginative

* Whilst writing the foregoing, we have received from Messrs. Oliver and Boyd the fourth volume of D'Aubigné's History, which is first published in English by the author. Its appearance will be welcomed by a large class, and we heartily join in the hope expressed, that no attempt will be made, through the medium of a translation from the French, to deprive a learned stranger of the legitimate reward of his labour. 'To English honour,' he emphatically remarks, 'I confide this work.'

† Edinburgh Review, No. 165, p. 95.

combination, paints his scenes with a force and reality which betoken the vividness of his own conceptions, cautiously traces out the influences which concur in the production of events, and keeps before his reader the connexion and mutual operation on each other of the political and the religious. It is not so much the inner as the outer life of the Reformation which he depicts. Other works render us more familiar with the spiritual conflicts and theological discussions of the German and Swiss reformers; their intense love of truth, their earnest reaching after the invisible, their deep humiliation and penitence, their confiding trust in the great atonement,—all, in a word, which constitutes the spiritual ordeal or experience of the renewed mind. Ranke's volumes supply little of this. He did not aim at it. The province appropriated was distinct, and though less captivating to the religious mind, is equally needful to the full elucidation of the truth. His work, therefore, should be read in connexion with that of D'Aubigné, and not as a substitute for it. It is not a rival, but an auxiliary; and he will be best versed in the narrative of the Reformation, who has made himself master of both.

The work opens with a sketch of the early history of Germany, in which the progress of the papacy, and the struggles which occurred between the civil and the ecclesiastical authorities, are ably developed. The humiliation at Canossa of Henry IV. before Gregory, marked the fearful strides which the spiritual power was making, but was itself outdone by what subsequently occurred at Venice, when Frederic I. succumbed before the terrors of the church.

'At Canossa, a young and passionate prince sought only to hurry through the penance enjoined upon him: at Venice, it was a mature man who renounced the ideas which he had earnestly and strenuously maintained for a quarter of a century; he was compelled to acknowledge that his conduct towards the Church had been dictated rather by love of power than of justice. Canossa was the spot on which the combat began; Venice beheld the triumph of the church fully established.' (Vol. i. p. 38.)

From the ninth to the thirteenth century, the papacy worked out its policy with a resoluteness and skill of which history furnishes few examples. Its aggressive spirit was steadily maintained, and the various orders of the empire were so adroitly balanced against each other, as to help forward its ambitious scheme. Intellect was then in the service of the church, and gave to her proceedings a mighty advantage. The secular was in this respect wholly unfitted to grapple with the spiritual. In the arena of arms it might prove victorious, but, as our author observes, 'the result of a contest is not always decided on a field of battle.' The public sentiment of Europe, at once unenlightened and superstitious, was moreover with the papacy, and the empire was consequently reduced to a state of disgraceful vassalage. The state of things which resulted is thus sketched by Ranke:—

'The pretensions of the clergy to govern Europe according to their hierarchical views—pretensions which arose directly out of the ecclesiastical institutions of Charlemagne—were encountered and resisted by the united body of the German people, still thoroughly imbued with the national ideas of ancient Germania. On this combined resistance the imperial throne was founded. Unfortunately, however, it failed to acquire perfect security and stability; and the divisions which soon broke out between the domineering chief and his refractory vassals, had the effect of making both parties contribute to the aggrandisement of that spiritual power which they had previously sought to depress. At first the emperors beheld in a powerful clergy a means of holding their great vassals in check, and endowed the Church with liberal grants of lands and lordships; but afterwards, when ideas of emancipation began to prevail, not only in the papacy but in all spiritual corporations, the temporal aristocracy thought it not inexpedient that the emperor should be stripped of the resource and assistance such a body afforded him: the enfeebling of the imperial authority was of great advantage, not only to the Church, but to them. Thus it came to pass that the ecclesiastical element, strengthened by the divisions of its opponents, at length obtained a decided preponderance.

'Unquestionably the result was far different in the twelfth and thirteenth centuries, from what it would have been in the ninth. The secular power might be humbled but could not be annihilated; a purely hierarchical government, such as might have been established at the earlier period, was now no longer within the region of possibility. The national development of Germany had been too deep and extensive to be stifled by the ecclesiastical spirit; while, on the other hand, the influence of ecclesiastical ideas and institutions unquestionably contributed largely to its extension. The period in question displayed a fulness of life and intelligence and activity in every branch of human industry, a creative vigour, which we can hardly imagine to have arisen under any other course of events. Nevertheless, this was not a state which ought to satisfy a great nation. There could be no true political freedom, so long as the most powerful impulse to all public activity emanated from a foreign head. The domain of mind, too, was enclosed within rigid and narrow boundaries. The immediate relation in which every intellectual being stands to the Divine Intelligence was veiled from the people in deep and abiding obscurity.' (Ib. pp. 43—45.)

Efforts were not wanting to check the exorbitant power of the clergy. Men of capacious minds and of profound reflection occasionally arose to protest against the existing order of things, and the seed which they scattered, though unproductive for a time, was not lost. Amongst these, Nicholas von Kus, and Berthold, Elector of Mainz, are entitled to a foremost rank, and we are tempted by the high qualities and important services of the latter, to present our readers with Ranke's brief sketch of his character.

'Nobody, so far as I have been able to discover, has thought it worth while to give to posterity a description of his personal appearance or characteristics: but we see him distinctly and vividly in the administration of his diocese. At first people feared his severity; for his administration of justice was as inexorable as it was impartial, and his economy was rigorous; but in a short time every body was convinced that his austere demeanour was not the result of temper or of caprice, but of profound necessity: it was tempered by genuine benevolence; he lent a ready ear to the complaints of the poorest and the meanest. He was peculiarly active in the affairs of the empire. He was one of the venerable men of that age, who earnestly strove to give to ancient institutions, which had lost their original spirit and their connection with higher things, the new form adapted to the necessities of the times. He had already conducted the negociations of 1486; he next procured for the towns the right of sitting in the committees; it was mainly to him that Germany owed the promises made by Maximilian in the year 1489, and the projects of Worms were chiefly his work. In every circumstance he evinced that serene and manly spirit, which, while it keeps its end steadily in view, is not self-willed as to the means or manner of accomplishing it, or pertinacious on merely incidental points; he was wearied or discouraged by no obstacles, and a stranger to any personal views: if ever a man bore his country in his inmost heart, it was he.' (Ib. pp. 131—132.)

The state of affairs, down to the period of the Reformation, foreshadowed coming events. Dissatisfaction was universal. The Emperor and the Pope, the princes and the minor nobles, the feudal lords and the peasantry, were in deadly hostility with each other. All had interests of their own, which were promoted by craft, and in a spirit of relentless cruelty of which modern times are happily ignorant. 'It is evident,' says our author, 'that the peaceful security, the undisturbed prosperity, which are often ascribed to those times, had no existence but in imagination. The cities kept their ground only by dint of combination, and of unwearied activity, both in arms and in negotiation.'

This state of things prepared the way for Luther, by loosening the foundations of ancient institutions, and by destroying the respect and confidence with which the national mind might otherwise have regarded what he assailed. Events waited their time, until, in combination with universal discontent, a new power was elicited in the shape of a revived literature. The materials for effective action were then prepared, and the voice of Luther sounded with a potency which struck dismay into the heart of Rome.

The great reformer was a peasant's son, born at Eisleben, in November, 1483, and grew up in the mountain air of Mansfeld. His education was harsh and rude, and his bread was early earned 'by singing hymns before the doors of houses, and new year's carols in the villages.' This was a training well fitted for his subsequent missions. It inured him to privation and hardness, though it probably stunted the milder qualities, whose absence from his character was matter of regret. A new impulse was given to his young heart in the month of July, 1505. Depressed by the unexpected death of an intimate friend, he was returning from his father's house to the University of Erfurt, when he was suddenly overtaken by a fearful tempest, in which his excited imagination saw the wrath and vengeance of God. In his terror, he vowed, that if permitted to escape, he would enter a convent, and, true to his pledge, he passed only one more evening with his friends. The following day saw him enter the Augustine convent at Erfurt. The determination of his character was apparent from the first. 'If ever,' he afterwards remarked, 'a monk got to heaven by monkish life and practises, I resolved that I would enter there.' To the duties of his new station he applied himself with unwonted vigour, but contrary to his hopes, he found no rest. There was a mysterious process going on within. The eye of Omniscience was on him. He was a selected man, the ordained of heaven for a mighty work. His preparation involved much suffering, a tempest of the soul even more fearful than the raging elements which had burst on his solitary path in the field near Stotteruheim.

'In the course of his study of the Scriptures, he fell upon texts which struck terror into his soul; one of these was, 'Save me in thy righteousness and thy truth.' 'I thought,' said he, 'that righteousness was the fierce wrath of God, wherewith he punishes sinners.' Certain passages in the Epistles of St. Paul haunted him for days. The doctrine of grace was not indeed unknown to him, but the dogma that sin was at once taken away by it, produced upon him, who was but too conscious of his sins, rather a sense of rejection—a feeling of deep depression, than of hope. He says, it made his heart bleed—it made him despair of God. 'Oh, my sins, my sins, my sins!' he writes to Staupitz, who was not a little astonished when he received the confession of so sorrowful a penitent, and found that he had no sinful acts to acknowledge. His anguish was the longing of the creature after the purity of the Creator, to whom it feels itself profoundly and intimately allied, yet from whom it is severed by an immeasurable gulph: a feeling which Luther nourished by incessant solitary brooding, and which had taken the more painful and complete possession of him because no penance had power to appease it; no doctrine truly touched it, no confessor would hear of it. There were moments when this anxious melancholy arose with fearful might from the mysterious abysses of his soul, waved its dusky pinions over his head, and felled him to the earth. On one occasion when he had been invisible for several days, some friends broke into his cell and found him lying senseless on the ground. They knew their friend; with tender precaution they struck some chords on a stringed instrument they had brought with them; the inward strife of the perplexed spirit was allayed by the well-known remedy; it was restored to harmony, and awakened to healthful consciousness.' (Ib. pp. 320—321.)

So deep and earnest a longing of the soul after God was at length satisfied. An old Augustine monk—pleasing proof that the fellowship of saints is wider than party zeal admits—saw his anguish, and. with fatherly tenderness, pointed him to the Christian doctrine of justification by faith.

'Then was I glad,' says he, 'for I learned and saw that God's righteousness is his mercy, by which he accounts and holds us justified; thus I reconciled justice with justification, and felt assured that I was in the true faith.' This was exactly the conviction of which his mind stood in need: it was manifest to him that the same eternal grace whence the whole race of man is sprung, mercifully brings back erring souls to itself and enlightens them with the fulness of its own light; that an example and irrefragable assurance of this is given us in the person of Christ: he gradually emerged from the gloomy idea of a divine justice only to be propitiated by the rigours of penance. He was like a man who after long wanderings has at length found the right path, and feeling more certain of it at every step, walks boldly and hopefully onward.' (Ib. p. 322.)

At this time, however, Luther was a faithful son of the church, and vied with the most devoted of his associates in a scrupulous observance of her institutes. A few years later, he visited Rome on the affairs of his order, and his joy on beholding the imperial city was unbounded. Still, however, he was not satisfied. The monk and the Christian struggled with each other. The convictions and sympathies of the inner and spiritual, were repugnant to the outward and ritual. There was an obvious incongruity, a want of harmony and cohesion between his practices as a devotee and his faith as a disciple of the Son of man. He saw and felt this, and all his visions of mental peace faded away. He himself tells us that whilst climbing the Scala Santa on his knees, in order to obtain the plenary indulgence, a reproving voice continually sounded within him, 'The just shall live by faith!' His views, however, gradually cleared up, and became more decidedly Augustinian: while his piety assumed a deeper and more enlightened tone. This was his salient point, the importance of which to his future course cannot be too highly estimated. His own mind was first imbued with the evangelic spirit, and all his subsequent labours were actuated by it. Had it been otherwise, his earlier efforts would have betokened more of pride and less of self mistrust than was visible. The heat of passion, and the selfishness of earthly policy would have taken the place of that earnest devotion to the welfare of the church which was so conspicuous throughout his career.

It was not long before an opportunity occurred for the commencement of his great mission. God's providence had prepared the theatre on which he was to act, and the spiritual discipline, under which he had passed, well qualified him for his work. At length the fulness of time came, and the impiety of the papacy roused him to action. The Lateran council, immediately prior to its dissolution, in March, 1517, granted the pope a tenth part of all church property throughout Christendom. Three commissioners for the sale of indulgences immediately traversed Germany, the proceeds of which were professedly to be applied to the building of St. Peter's Church. The impiety of this procedure need not be pointed out, and its folly was equally glaring. It was a foul and monstrous insult both to religion and to common sense, and Luther, in the opposition which he offered, was sustained by the sympathy and expressed approval of all candid men. John Tetzel, one of the pope's commissioners, appeared in the neighbourhood of Wittenberg, and Luther, jealous for the safety of the people, whom he saw to be in danger of delusion, on the 31st of October, 1517, nailed on the gates of the parochial church ninety-five propositions; in which he undertook to explain the power of indulgence. His views had not then attained the clearness by which they were subsequently distinguished. The truth was only partially apprehended; but so far as it was known, its advocacy was followed up with an honesty and fearlessness characteristic of his mind. The ground on which the sale of indulgences was contested, is thus briefly stated by our author—

'Not that he altogether denied the treasures of the church; but he declared that this doctrine was not sufficiently clear, and, above all, he contested the right of the pope to dispense them. For he ascribed only an inward efficacy to this mysterious community of the Church. He maintained that all her members had a share in her good works, even without a pope's brief; that his power extended over purgatory only in so far as the intercessions of the Church were in his hand; but the question must first be determined, whether God would hear these intercessions: he held that the granting indulgences of any kind whatsoever, without repentance, was directly contrary to the Christian doctrine. He denied, article by article, the authority given to the dealers in indulgences in their instructions. On the other hand, he traced the doctrine of absolution to that of the authority of the keys. In this authority, which Christ delegated to St. Peter, lay the power of the pope to remit sin. It also extended to all penances and cases of conscience; but of course to no punishments but those imposed for the purpose of satisfaction; and even then, their whole efficacy depended on whether the sinner felt contrition, which he himself was not able to determine, much less another for him. If he had true contrition, complete forgiveness was granted him; if he had it not, no brief of indulgence could avail him: for the pope's absolution had no value in and for itself, but only in so far as it was a mark of Divine favour.'

'It is evident that this attack did not originate in a scheme of faith new to the Church, but in the very centre of the scholastic notions; according to which the fundamental idea of the papacy—viz. that the priesthood, and more especially the successors of St. Peter, were representatives and vicegerents of Christ—was still firmly adhered to, though the doctrine of the union of all the powers of the Church in the person of the pope was just as decidedly controverted. It is impossible to read these propositions without seeing by what a daring, magnanimous, and constant spirit Luther was actuated. The thoughts fly out from his mind like sparks from the iron under the stroke of the hammer.' (Ib. pp. 339—340.)

Such were the circumstances of Luther's early life, and the events by which he was summoned forth to his appointed work. They are worthy of attentive study, and in the lessons they inculcate will amply recompense for any time or labour which may be expended on them. Other opportunities will occur for tracing his subsequent career; and we therefore take leave of the volumes before us, with a sincere and earnest recommendation of them to our readers. The original work consists of five volumes, of which the first epoch only is here given to the English public. We trust that the more popular character of D'Aubigné's volumes will not prevent the cordial reception of Leopold Ranke's, which, as already remarked, have qualities of their own that entitle them to a high rank in in the literature of the Reformation. We need scarcely add, that Mrs. Austin's translation has all the force, clearness, and flexibility of an original work.

Art. VIII.—*The History and Literature of Flanders, Old Flanders, or Popular Traditions and Legends of Belgium.* By Octave Dele Pierre, Attaché to the Belgian Embassy; Member of the Society of Antiquaries in London; of the Historical Comity in Paris; of the Royal Archeological Society in Belgium, &c., &c., &c. 2 vols. 12mo. London, 1845.

These pleasant, and useful volumes, written a little rashly perhaps *in English,* by a foreigner; may appear to be but a slender peg, whereon to hang a heavy dissertation upon Belgian history, and Flemish literature;—subjects too long treated with no small disdain by the savans and the statesmen of Paris, when deluding themselves with the hope of being able to substitute modern French for the oldest language of Western Europe, still spoken by a large body* of French subjects, to whom the attempt is a serious grievance.

In that point, indeed, the work before us opens views of high interest; and although the time is certainly much more remote than its author is sanguine enough to anticipate, for uufurling *'the flag of universal concord;'* (vol. ii. p. 285), few persons will refuse assent to his further remark, that foreign governments commit a grievous 'error in forcing new laws upon nations already mortified by subjection.' (*ib.*) The passage here alluded to, concludes with the expectation of a speedy and universal peace, for the coming of which all good men must give their hearty wishes, even if less hopeful than M. Dele Pierre, of its early arrival. 'The wide propagation of knowledge,' says he, 'promises fair a time, when the enlightened world shall struggle no more for any ascendency but that of knowledge and wisdom; and when the trumpet of war, and the cry of the wounded, shall cease among Christians.' (*ib.*)

The tinge of foreign idiom here perceptible, and of which we shall have occasion to notice other instances in the work, does not take from it great beauty of style, and occasionally pure eloquence. A hope may, therefore, be reasonably expressed, that some additional stores, spoken of in the preface, will be soon published to complete the vindication so worthily begun by M. Dele Pierre, of his country's just station among the nations of Europe.

Her independance so difficult to be established, is held to be indispensable to the general peace; and the great powers have even guaranteed neutrality to Belgium in order to establish a new assurance in favour of this momentous object. But to turn

* Upwards of 200,000 Frenchmen in the departments of the North, and of the Pas de Calais, speak Flemish.

neutrality to the best account; and to place this rich country more and more in a condition to defend its own complex rights, the *antient language* of the people as well as their history, should be cultivated with so much the greater care, that it is the principal link by which their dearest interests and feelings are connected with both the present, and the past. This may be accomplished without sacrificing other indispensable languages, such as English, and more especially French, which has incontestable political claims upon the attention of the inhabitants of French Flanders, and claims of science which neither Belgians, nor even Hollanders are disposed to overlook. One of the ablest writers upon the Low Countries, says, that he employs French, notwithstanding the incorrectness of his style, because Belgium is *half* French, and because he is glad to use a language so admirably adapted to scientific discussion.* Perhaps the greatest evil consequent upon the forced dissemination of this language is, that a spirit of resistance is thus roused, fatal to its suitable adoption.

In another province a million of Bretons struggle now, as they have struggled successfully for two centuries, against the loss of their Celtic tongue: and they continue to cling to Celtic customs which have survived the influence of Christianity, as well as that of Roman law.

But not France alone has sinned, and is still sinning by attempts to extinguish the customs, and the languages of conquered races. Britain has made such attempts upon an enormous scale. In vain did the Berkeleys and the Chesterfields of former days urge the cultivation of the native speech of Ireland, and the preservation of her records, in order to the conciliation of her people. In our madness we preferred absolute domination to a friendly union; and thence we have naturally reaped the hatred of millions. So Russia is preparing the same way for revolutions which must break up a barbarous unity of despotism built upon the ruins of an hundred people. *More books are published in Polish now, than before the language was prohibited by Ukase!*

Old Flanders is a series of stories upon Belgian subjects of early and late dates. The first is a romantic tale of the exemplary vengeance wreaked by a young girl upon a monster of cruelty who had put her lover to death. It commemorates the founding of Antwerp in the days of Julius Cæsar—'the *Antwerpen* of the ancient Flemish language which still preserves its original strength, and richness, and its Saxon garb.' (p. 11).

* Historical Analysis of the laws of the Belgians and Gauls. Œuvres de J. J. Rapsaet, 1838, tom. iii. p. 5.

Overleaping more than eleven hundred years of Flemish history, and the inviting period of Charlemagne, the author then tells a famous tale of Count Baldwin's summary and personal execution of justice against a party of young knights for an act of signal oppression done by them upon some peasants.

A pathetic tale follows of the period of Count Charles the Good, murdered by the party of the *Provost of Bruges*, known to the English readers of historical romance, by the novel of Mr. Grattan. This brief sea-side tragedy is exceedingly touching; and if not written with all the power of Sir Walter Scott's description of the Fisherman's death in the Antiquary, it may be fairly placed high in the same class of productions. Late in a stormy night, a young fisherman on the Flemish coast, with his wife, and two young children, are alarmed by a violent knocking at their door. A follower of the count who had witnessed the murder, is fleeing for his life; and offers a large reward for a passage to England in the midst of the storm. The offer is boldly accepted, and the perilous voyage undertaken in an open boat. After four days passed in deepest anxiety, whilst the storm is unabated, the poor wife discovers the body of her husband entangled in the sail of his own boat, wrecked on the shore. The children are present at the frightful discovery, which ends in the destruction of the whole unhappy family, whilst attempting to drag the poor fisherman from the wreck.

The next tale is also a deep tragedy, strongly depicting the precarious tenure on which the lives of the nearest relatives, and the prospects of domestic happiness were held in the middle ages.

One of the most surprising events of those ages comes next,—the mysterious fate of Baldwin, Emperor of Constantinople. This enterprising Count of Flanders, elected chief of the victorious Crusaders in the East, was at length defeated by the infidels; and after the conflict, he was never more seen. His misfortunes were attributed in a superstitious age, to a rash marriage with a beautiful Saracen. Among the consequences the most extraordinary was the appearance of an impostor, who many years afterwards pretended to be the lost emperor. His daughter, Jeanne, then the reigning countess of Flanders, resisted these pretensions; but a numerous party of all ranks, countenanced them. A ridiculous denouement occurred at Peronne in France, where this great cause was adjudicated before the King of France, as the suzerain of the Flemish Counts. In its course, the Bishop of Beauvais, in support of the countess, asked the pretender, where, and on what day he married 'Madam Marie de Champagne, whom he called his wife?—where, and from whom he received his order of knighthood?—in what year he did homage for the Dukedom of Flanders to Philip, the King of France? and what he received from the King on that occasion."

These simple questions confounded the Pretender, who had not learned his lesson well; and he asked till next morning, to reflect upon his answers.

The next day came; but the false count had fled; and he was ultimately put to death for this treasonable imposture.*

Short narratives of private feuds, and of high festivities follow in the first volume, with two more frightful tragedies,—one upon a career of violence, and the destruction of a band of robbers;—the other respecting perhaps more horrible acts of voluptuous brutality on the part of a young Venetian merchant at Antwerp, ending in his utter ruin, in a way consistent with the popular belief of the time—the fifteenth century.

The second volume pursues Belgian history in similar tales through the periods of the German and Spanish possession of the country; returning in the last pages somewhat unnecessarily to the middle ages, for fresh matter.

In both volumes, the subjects are taken from all ranks of society, the author having correctly remarked, that in Flanders, the people have always acted a distinguished part, along with the princes of the land; so that its heroes are to be sought among its artists, its merchants, and even its artisans no less than among its nobility. The two stories from which extracts will be made as specimens of the author's style, belong to the humbler ranks. The first is that of Herman the Tiler; whose unhappy death with those of his intended wife and his own father, are commemorated by a blue stone on the pavement of the Church of Notre Dâme at Antwerp. It is on the eastern side, facing the tomb of Quinten Metsys, the celebrated smith, who became a painter to gain the object of his affection, and whose famous picture is well-known to every visitor of the collection in Windsor Castle. A thousand little pieces of copper, placed without order, are incrusted on this stone; but no explanation has been preserved of so strange an inscription. The deaths of the three persons buried under it, took place thus. On the 20th of October, 1520, the day of the coronation of Charles v., the citizens of Antwerp celebrated the event by a general fête. A storm of unusual violence, furious wind, and floods of rain with thunder and lightning, put a sudden end to the rejoicing; and destroyed every vestige of the gay preparations with which the streets, and quays had been covered.

* The same story has been lately better told by M. Leblay of Lille in a valuable History of the Counts of Flanders.

Among other damage done by this storm, it was soon perceived that the iron cross on the pinnacle of the cathedral was bent by the lightning. The omen was in the highest degree alarming in that superstitious age; but the boldest workmen refused to hazard their lives in the dangerous task of repairing the damage. At length *Herman the Tiler* undertook it under very peculiar circumstances. He was a young lover; but not wealthy; and the avaricious father of the object of his love had refused to consent to their marriage if, within a certain time, he could not command a sum of money, which happened to be then proclaimed by the authorities of Antwerp as the reward of the successful repairer of their dizzy cross. Herman therefore engaged to straighten it. The engagement when formally published to the people, excited the deepest interest, expressed in almost tumultuous agitation upon the feat of the daring youth. His motive was not known; but the extreme danger of the attempt was felt by all, and produced a feverish curiosity in the people to see him, with the most absurd conjectures as to what had led him to risk it. The remainder of the story is thus told by our author.

'Whilst this scene of tumult was going on in the street, a more serious tragedy was acting in the house of Herman. Three actors were here deeply affected; Herman, his father, and the young girl, Ciska. The youth was glowing with hope and resolution! every feature swelled by the violence of his emotion, though *one deep* wrinkle on his brow showed an internal struggle. The maiden and his father were so wholly wrapped up in sorrow as to be almost deaf and blind to what passed around them. Their eyes were fixed! their lips firmly closed! their hands clasped as in death agonies! for to them all seemed an awful and hopeless wonder!

'The father first moved, and, clasping his hands together, approached his son.

''Oh, Herman! is your rash scheme so irrevocably fixed in your mind, that neither the prayers of your fond old father, nor the affecting tears of that loving creature, can move you. Think only upon our wretched and forlorn state, should you perish.'

''If you have no pity for yourself,' said Ciska, 'have pity on me, who love you beyond all things in life. And think, oh! think, Herman, what my fate will be if you find your death, where you seek our happiness.'

''To-morrow, Ciska,' replied Herman, 'I shall be thy affianced husband; and what you suffer to-day, will be amply repaid to-morrow by our mutual congratulations. To-morrow you shall be proud and happy,' he added, as he clasped the weeping girl to his breast.

'She appeared more gracefully touching than ever before, and Herman thus beholding her, felt his fearful purpose almost shaken. But, when his father spoke to him and said,—

''*Go my son, to the town-hall, and tell them to choose another to fulfil this imprudent engagement*;'—the courageous youth dashed off the tears which swam in his bright black eyes; and collected himself, more firmly determined than ever, ere this incautious sentence had met his ear.

''When I accepted the enterprise, my dear father, it was prompted by my love to Ciska; and through love and duty to you, whom I saw labouring daily, when you require repose. These reasons would still urge me, even though I did not hear a thousand voices proclaiming my cowardice, should I retract my promise; even though the whole populace were not waiting for me in the streets—listen to their voices calling for me!'

'The father bowed his face! But Ciska made one last effort to shake her lover from his desperate purpose.

'That effort was vain, although Herman felt that if he would not yield, he must tear himself away. He wept, and hardly could his fixed resolve carry him on against his love and his pity. He wished to give some consolation, but was only able to say—'*It is noon*, Ciska! My duty calls me.'

'Then placing his lips on the young girl's forehead, he imprinted a parting kiss, and tore himself away. She sunk fainting in the arms of the old man, whose tender care soon revived her; more happy had she never recovered her sense of misery. Soon both followed the venturous youth; a vague and indistinct feeling of hope, and triumph, of terror and despair, urging them on to be witnesses of the act of their ruin, or happiness!

'When Herman appeared in the street, loud acclamations greeted him, for few had believed that he would actually dare attempt what he had engaged to do. When he had a little got rid of the crowd, and found himself more unmolested, he began to consider what he had so hastily engaged to perform. The weeping scene he had quitted within his own house came before him, but not with any doubt, or despair; on the contrary, with a confidence of success. Then, on a sudden, a burst of shouts from behind seemed like welcome heralds of success. His courage and his strength of nerve returned; he walked quickly on; passed over the grand square; and arrived at the church yard of the cathedral. There he found the city authorities awaiting his arrival, which was hailed by one unanimous hurrah from an immense crowd.

'The gate of the tower was opened for him, and he soon appeared at the first gallery. He looked around, but did not see his father, and his beloved Ciska, who, pale and trembling, were in the crowd. He passed rapidly as a vision from gallery to gallery, nor stopped, till, panting and breathless, he reached the top of the last stairs, where his arduous task was to begin. Here he rested to take breath; to rid himself of his coat; and to fasten one end of a strong cord to two large iron plates hollow in the middle, a light pair of bellows, a forge hammer, and some charcoal; the other end of the cord be tied firmly round his waist. The people, with every eye fixed upon him, then beheld him seize hold of one of the many projections of the carved work of the tower, cling firmly to it, and raising himself as gently as he could, fix one foot after the other on some head of a sphinx, or out-standing cornice, or in the centre of a hollow rosette of the ornamental work. Every eye was fixed, every tongue mute, every heart beat with terror and anxiety whilst watching the perilous climbing of the intrepid Tiler. But he reached the pinnacle of the tower; he stood on that platform of six feet square,—two of which the cross filled.

'"*Then he is safe!*" cried out with one voice the almost breathless spectators.

'But the father, and the maiden, unseen by Herman, spoke not! they scarcely breathed, their blood freezing in their veins. Their eyes were still fixed, watching every movement;—their tongues cleaved to their mouths, for they did not think the danger over.

'Herman had now drawn up his tools, and was perched upon one of the bars of the cross, looking like one of those large eagles which are driven by the wintry storms for refuge to our high buildings. His eye measured, without giddiness or fear, the immense distance between himself, and the abode of men. Having so far succeeded, all doubt, all fear, was at an end. He looked for his father, and his mistress. He did not however distinguish them.

'Soon red-hot coals were seen at the foot of the cross, whilst a figure like a spirit of the upper regions kept close to the fire, which he continually brightened till the stem of the cross became red-hot. Then strong, steady, loud strokes of the forge hammer were distinctly heard, and fearfully repeated by the echoing vaults. It might have formed a picture of some evil spirit warring against the emblem of Christianity! At every blow the cross moved a little, and the crowd applauded These plaudits came like the dashing of a tide, to the ears of the adventurer; but did he know how every blow throbbed on the hearts of his beloved friends? Full of joyous hope he laboured, still cautiously, judiciously, vigorously. Surely the soul of Quinten Metsys, the artist who framed the cross, was assisting at this stupendous task, to restore to his native city his grand work.

'One more, only one more stroke; and the cross stood erect! the proud summit was in its due place and proportion. A shout of admiration filled the place, and reached the ears of the half-stunned workman. Then did the father, for the first time, turn his eyes towards those of Ciska; both were full of tears, but tears of joy, which relieved their agitated hearts, whilst the continued plaudits of the gathered multitude were now welcome, for they were consolation for the past, horrible suspense.

'Before he began to descend, Herman stretched forward to look if his father and his beloved were witnesses of his success. Oh, horror! his foot slipped upon the iron plate, and over the hot burning charcoal; he fell from the platform, and bounded violently against the angles of the building. The cord which was fixed round his waist, and the other end of which he had fastened to a ledge of the tower, held him up for a moment, over the dreadful height.

'*What a moment!* Numbers of active spectators rushed up the stairs, and thence to the first gallery, with a blind hope of being of some use; but ere the swiftest, the most active, the most zealous foot reached even the first gallery, the red-hot cinders had caught the cord; and it quickly blazed, and crackled, and gave way! Herman bounded off from angle to angle, now his head struck one sharp point, now another, now balanced an instant on some broad ledge, then plunged downwards, broken, twisted, crushed, till over and over he fell head-foremost on the stone pavement, and was dashed to a thousand pieces.

'When men, all trembling, gave way to those who dared pick up the body, and examine the fractured head, two other dead bodies were stretched near it. Herman's father, Herman's beloved, expired on the spot.

'They were all three buried there; and over their tomb was placed a blue slab, on which was beaten in as many pieces of copper as there had been found fragments of the skull of Herman.' (Vol. xi. p. 43—55.

The next tale, from which we shall make a very short quotation, is that of an artist of Bruges, named Andrè, whom an envious rival exposed to a false charge of murder. By a rash judgment of the authorities of his native city, the poor victim was sentenced to death, but with a year's respite to prove his innocence. He was at the same time allowed the usual indulgence of working whilst in prison, at his art of carving in wood; and he accepted it, in the hope of procuring some resource for his only child, a little girl, soon to be left the pennyless orphan of a disgraced father. It was the period when the fine arts in every branch were at a high pinnacle of excellence in Flanders. He began his task under extremely disadvantageous circumstances; and sacrificed his life in completing it.

The progress of the work, and its unhappy ending, are told in these words:—

'The wainscotting of the Hall of Judgment in Bruges, is only lit by windows from the further end, and would not admit of any fine carving. The artist began then to carve rosettes on a part of the ceiling above the enormous chimney-piece of that hall. Then with a natural taste which the ancient productions more frequently exhibit, than those of the present day, he united those festoons with others round the chimney-piece, so as to become one fine picture. Many tasteful ornaments united the carved panels together, so as to make a beautiful whole, when the most minute trifle was finished with perfect skill.

'The elaborate work in an imperfectly lighted room, so fatigued his eyes, that there were moments when he was compelled to desist.'

After further details respecting this arduous work of art,

which Andrè, comforted by the society of his hapless child, persevered in, the story concludes with a touching account of his rapid and deep change of features. He was like a spectre; and when his rash judges, struck with admiration at the elaborate perfection of the carving, ordered Andrè's release, upon a reconsideration of the insufficiency of the proofs of his guilt, he was found to have sunk into a premature grave in his prison.—(vol. ii. p. 57—73.)

The Castle of Maldeghen, 'one of the most beautiful hamlets in Flanders,' where beautiful hamlets abound, is given from one of the Flemish ballads, a class of popular productions well worth an English student's attention. The almost identity of the Flemish language with ours in its *tones*, as well as in numerous original words, is shown in the singing of these ballads. Not many weeks ago, the writer of this article was walking with some friends near Cassel in French Flanders, when one of the party insisted upon speaking to some children who were singing as they gathered nuts in an adjoining wood. From their voices, he thought they must be English children. After no small difficulty, he made out from their Flemish, for, although belonging to a village which had been French for one hundred and seventy years, not one word of French could they utter or understand, that these genuine children of the soil were carolling stanzas far older, perhaps, than *Chevy Chase*, or *Childe Waters*. Ignorance of their kindred tongue found its suitable punishment in the mortification attendant upon perceiving, that a great treat was lost by an imperfect apprehension of the subject of the ballad; but the tones of the young songsters could not be mistaken. They were thorough Sussex-English.

The incident occurred within five hours and a half of London by rail-road, and steam boats, at a spot where the true Flemish tongue is spoken by the people of all classes; and where a line of little hills beginning fifteen miles east of Calais, presents for as many miles more as perfect a series of picturesque views, hills and dells, shady lawns, meadow paths, and sheltered cottages, as can be found in the whole world, not excepting Devonshire, or Wales.

Our Belgian author appreciates the picturesque at its true value; and he seizes eagerly upon every opportunity of introducing brief notices of scenery, such as that which closes the strange and terrible story of the *Iron Lady of Maestricht*, told rather obscurely; and to our great surprise ranging in date from the Middle Ages to 1790 and 1826.

Little room is left for our intended catalogue of curious errors of *style*, not of the *press*, which betray the foreign pen in this creditable production. Credit will be given us for not having overlooked them; and rather too abundant a sprinkling of press errors besides. As general advice, we will venture to recommend M. Dele Pierre to study Sir Walter Scott with the greatest diligence as a help in his promised future labours.

Still less room is left us for a contemplated examination of the history and language of Flanders. Materials for both are most abundant; and those materials are of great value. No English library should be without an ample collection of the Flemish, Latin, and French books which mainly constitute them; and of which considerable catalogues have been published. Studied with discrimination, this history in its successive periods, Celtic, Roman, Middle Age, and Modern, and that language in its simple form, will resolve more than one problem in human affairs; and in science. To English students both have peculiar attractions. There can be little doubt of the fact, that the Flemish and our Saxon speech had a common origin, and a very extensive similarity exists to this day, more especially among the common people—the millions; and in old books. And from the earliest periods of time of which records exist, our mutual intercourse has been frequent and important; and the changes which the wonders of modern powers of locomotion have already begun to work, promise to bring the fine land of Flanders, with all its ancient associations of so many kinds, and the multitudinous resources of its present population, remarkable for their industry and denseness even in a state of long comparative decline, to our very thresholds. An eager desire prevails in Belgium for the revival of the better times when its trade, its arts, and its science, were honoured in Europe. Our author shares this desire; and we join him heartily in his hope, that the past peaceful glories of his country may be profitable stimulants to greater actions than even those which once created what has been so deplorably lost by the influence of wars and foreign domination. Belgium is now independent, and through the extraordinary events of latter days, she enjoys a declared neutrality. In the new conflicts of industry, which we trust will long be the only ones to occupy mens minds in Europe, may wisdom guide her public councils, and the right intelligence, which M. Dele Pierre is anxious to propagate, bless her people.

ART. IX.—*Cobden et la Ligue, ou L'agitation Anglaise, pour la Liberté du Commerce.* Par M. Fred. Bastiat, Membre Correspondant de l'Institut, et Membre du Conseil Géneral des Landes. 8vo. Paris, 1845. [*Cobden and the League, or the English Agitation for Commercial Freedom.*]

THE appearance and reception of this volume, are among the good signs of the times. Since its publication, the author has been chosen a member of the Institute of France, a body of men, as far removed from the influence of mere agitation as any scientific society in the world; and at this moment, the walls of Paris are covered with its advertisement. There is even a fair prospect of this grave book of political economy becoming as popular as a new novel from any well known pen.

This successful result of M. Bastiat's labours, only requires a little nursing by the League, and by its French friends, to make millions of converts to free trade abroad, by simply telling the story of the free traders in England.

Before stating what this echo to the League is, we will add, one or two more proofs of our active neighbours being alive to the importance of the free trade question.

The general councils of agriculture, manufactures, and commerce, assembled last December, after an interval of four years, have just closed their meetings in the best possible spirit. They have recommended, *by a great majority,* that foreign iron should be admitted into France free of duty for ship building. This is not a day too soon; as the high price of iron made by the French themselves, has already driven their large ships entirely out of use; and extensively reduced all their merchant shipping.

The same important bodies have recommended in January, 1846, analogous changes in other fabrics.

Again, in the Chamber of Peers, a zealous, and eloquent appeal has just gone forth from one of the oldest Dukes in France, in favour of unconditional free trade. And again, in the Chamber of Deputies, a strong disposition has lately been expressed in favour of the same objects.*

This is sudden—so sudden, that the author of the French history of the *League,* opens his book with the extremest apprehension, that it will be utterly neglected, inasmuch as 'free trade,' says he 'is looked upon in France as utopian, or worse.'

Yes, M. Bastiat,—who last autumn was a very prophet, when

* These evidences of opinion in France, upon free trade, are to be seen in the first part of *La Liberte des Commerce,* published at Mr. Eff. Wilson, Royal Exchange.

he sagaciously conjectured what Sir R. Peel must have been about in November, in regard to the prodigious changes now in progress, modestly doubts whether his work will be read at all.

Nevertheless, we repeat, it has procured him a most honourable, unsolicited admission into the most cautious society in France; and the earnest language of his introduction, with his curious collection of our leaguers' speeches at Manchester, in London, Norwich, Plymouth, Perth, Carlisle, and elsewhere from 1842 to 1844, are likely to make the names of Cobden and Bright, Hume and Thompson, Fox and Wilson, and those of a host of other men, as familiar over all France as household words; and their purposes as acceptable as they are beginning to be intelligible there.

Our readers know the originals too well to need French translations of their speeches; and they do not want M. Bastiat's doctrines for their instruction. But this book is well worth buying as a curiosity; and it will be useful hereafter, when the present barriers of monopoly between us and France shall be broken down, to remind us of what may be accomplished by resolution in a good cause.

ART. X.—1. *Voices of the Church, in Reply to Dr. D. F. Strauss, author of "Das Leben Jesu"; comprising Essays in Defence of Christianity, by Divines of Different Communions. Collected and Composed by the Rev. J. R. Beard,* D.D. London: Simpkin and Marshall, 1845. Pp. xv. 437.

2. *Tentamen Anti-Straussianum. The Antiquity of the Gospels asserted, on Philological grounds, in refutation of the Mythic Scheme of Dr. D. F. Strauss.* An Argument. By Orlando T. Dobbin, L.L.D. London: Ward. 1845. pp. xvii. 113.

THE first of these works embodies eight very valuable essays which have been published separately in the course of the years 1844 and 1845, by Dr. Beard. Two of them are original; four are translated or compiled from the German, and two from the French. The one object to which the whole are addressed, is—

'To furnish the English reader with some means of becoming acquainted with the aims and tendencies of the work by Dr. Strauss, entitled, *Das Leben Jesu, kritisch.bearbeitet von Dr. David Freiderich Strauss;* as well as of forming a calm estimate of the justness of its principle, the accuracy of its arguments, the soundness of its views, and its general bearing on the historical verity, of the gospel. This reply was undertaken in consequence of the wide diffusion in this country — not least among the labouring classes — of opinions and impressions adverse to Christianity, derived more or less immediately from the publications of Dr. Strauss. Even where the *Leben Jesu* was not known, and could not be read, a conviction has prevailed, that some great work had been put forth in Germany, which as being destructive of the Christian religion, its ministers wished to keep from the knowledge of the people, and were afraid even to study themselves. So untrue and unsound a state of feeling may well be regarded with regret, if not alarm, by every enlightened disciple of Christ. The present work will enable the reader to judge how far the attack made by Strauss on the historical foundations of our common faith, is of so deadly a character as many have supposed.'—p. v.

As this is almost the first work in the English language that has addressed itself to the great Straussian controversy, which has deluged the continent with books, the editor very properly employs his first essay in setting forth the views which Strauss has advanced. This is entitled '*Strauss, Hegel and their Opinions.*' And is a most able, luminous, and candid exposition. We know not where else the English reader, desiring to acquaint himself with the bearings of controversy by which so many active minds have been agitated, and in which so many able pens have been employed, can so readily obtain the information he requires. The writer's dread of being unfair has occasionally led him into greater concessions than some of his readers will admit: but this is so rare a fault among controversialists, that it may easily be pardoned. Thus he gives Strauss credit for 'candour,' although presently after he gives us many instances from the *Leben Jesu* of gross 'unfairness,' (his own word) in argument. Candour and unfairness are not very compatible qualities.

Having thus laid his foundation in the first Essay, Dr. Beard proceeds in the second to furnish *A Review of Strauss's Life of Jesus*, from the French of M. Quinet, the Professor of Modern Literature in the University of Paris. This is a clever and informing paper, exhibiting uncommon intimacy with German theological literature; as does also the one that follows, entitled a *Reply to Dr. Strauss's Book—the Life of Jesus*; from the French of the well known Rev. Athanase Coquerel, which however is more solid and argumentative, as becomes the station and character of the writer. Next, in the fourth Essay, comes Dr. Tholuck on *the Credibility of the Evangelical History, illustrated with reference to the 'Leben Jesu' of Dr. Strauss.* These illustrations are drawn from the gospel of Luke and his Acts of the Apostles; and the gist of the argument, which is handled with great ability and research, is to prove the incidental exactness and accuracy of the writer of the Acts of the Apostles, who is there constantly on ground where we are able to check his statements, and to test their accuracy, from the information of contemporary writers: and on the strength of the fidelity and exact information thus evinced, to claim the same qualities for the gospel which even Strauss admits to be the work of the same author, and which does not afford the same ample materials for collateral verification, although such as it does furnish manifest the same characteristics. There is less perhaps that is absolutely new to the English reader in this tract, than in most of the others; as the greater part of the illustrations are such as may be found in Lardner and in good commentaries on the New Testament. The fifth Essay is '*the Theory of Myths in its Application to the Gospel History, Examined and Confuted,* by Dr. Julius Müller. The following passage exhibits the application of the Mythical theory, against which Dr. Müller contends, and also displays the process usually followed by Strauss in forcing this application:—

'The plan of the author is, in general, this:—

'First, he endeavours to point out in the gospel narratives, partly internal improbabilities—partly contradictions, either with what the same evangelist has elsewhere stated, or with the accounts of other evangelists and New Testament writers, concerning the same events, or with the historical statements of Josephus, so far as they relate to events within the gospel history. When he thinks the negative part of his work to be thus completed, and the historical character of the particular narrative to have been rendered sufficiently suspicious, he proceeds to the more positive side of his work. He searches throughout the Old Testament to see if he cannot find in the history of the patriarchs—of Moses, David, of the prophets, especially Elijah and Elisha, or of other eminent men—traits which correspond to the accounts of Christ, and thus render it intelligible how, out of their legendary poetry, the most ancient church (which so gladly recognized in the deeds and destiny of their founder; i. e. of their supposed Messiah, every thing great and noble that is preserved to us of those men) could manage to fabricate the narrative. Just as easily is this explained, when a kindred passage of the Old Testament is at hand, which was considered by the Jews, at the time of Christ, and by the Apostles as a Messianic prophecy. Since, according to the notion of the primitive Christians, the life of Jesus must correspond accurately with those prophecies (which is the reason for the formula ινα πληρωθη το ῥηθεν, *in order that what was said might be fulfilled*, so often recorded in the gospel), the author has no scruple in directly reversing the mode in which the Biblical church views this connection, according to which the prophecy arose directly out of the prophet's vision; and in considering one portion of the gospel records as a free invention, in accordance with the type of these prophecies. For this purpose he makes use of particular declarations of Jesus, which bear a relation to the recorded events.'

We next come to a vigorous and well-written essay by Dr. Beard himself, under the title, '*Illustrations of the Moral Argument for the Credibility of the Gospels.*' This is more original, and in most respects equal, if not superior, to the best of the translated essays of the book. The writer shews that the German authors have no right to regard the gospels as regular historical narratives. They are not history, in the proper sense of the term, although they contain history. Neither are they biographies, seeing that they describe but a short portion of the life of Christ; but are rather to be regarded as approaching to what the French call *Memoires pour servir à l'histoire de*—. The idea, therefore, of dealing with them as philosophical histories, is unfounded; and it is also modern—'an offspring of the nineteenth century, and from the features which it has, could obviously not have come into existence till after Voltaire had scoffed, and Gibbon generalized, and Niebuhr upturned the foundations of Rome.'

Yet, although no one could be justified in applying the tests of philosophical history, to books which are less histories than arguments, there is no history which admits of better and fuller proof than that the writings of the New Testament present to us a true picture of Christian doctrine, and a true portrait of their great subject, Jesus Christ. After alluding briefly to the nature of this proof, and to the historical corroborations from Josephus, and other writers, Dr. Beard gives a home thrust at those who are not satisfied without such coroborations:

'Some of the departures from historical verity which are attributed to the writers of the New Testament, are sought to be established by an appeal to Josephus, and other historians. We have sometimes had a smile forced from us by the curious union which this appeal presents of credulity and incredulity; for, in order to invalidate Luke, Josephus, and older ancient writers are allowed, and assumed to be immaculate. Unbelief has sometimes a short memory. The writer of the 'Philosophical Dictionary' denied that Josephus—this now unquestioned authority—was worthy of belief. Other far greater names than that of Voltaire might be adduced, as more or less impeaching the credulity of the Jewish historians; and who can say, that, should a German divine find a dearth of novelty, or fail in a subject by which to gain distinction,—the only way to get his daily bread—he may not, after the manner of Strauss, ere long rake together all the objections which have been taken to Josephus, and, writing his life, do his best to undermine the authority, and destroy his fame. For ourselves, we do not believe that the charges adduced against the Jewish historian can, in all their breadth, be sustained. Yet is he by no means a faultless writer; and we are very far from thinking, that, in any case in which his statements may appear to contradict or qualify the statements of an evangelist, the presumption is necessarily in favour of the first, and against the second. And, if the general tenor of the narrative—say of John and a book of Josephus—is to be taken into account, we have no hesitation in giving the preference to the former.'—pp. 229, 230.

The arguments built upon the minute apparent discrepancies of the evangelical records, might be met, even were they admitted, by this playful illustration :—

'John Milton has not been yet two centuries in his tomb. His life has been repeatedly written: first, a short period after his death; recently by Sir Egerton Brydges. Our eye has fallen on discrepancies of no ordinary kind. The register of his birth, and his biographer Todd, fix the time when he was born as the 9th of December, 1608. Another biographer, Toland, who wrote near Milton's own day, says he was born in the year 1606; while Hallam declares 'John Milton was born in 1609.' His biographer Simmons states, that he died on the 8th of November, 1674; Wood gives the 9th or the 10th as the day of his decease; while the register shows that the interment took place on the 12th of the same month. Wood affirms 'his eyes were none of the quickest;' Symmons—'their lustre, which was peculiarly vivid, did not even fade even when their vision was extinguished.' Todd reports that Milton married a daughter of Justice Powell, of Sandford, in the vicinity of Oxford, and lived in a house at Forrest-hill, about three miles from Oxford. Brydges states, in opposition, that the family of Powell, of Sandford, and that of Powell, of Forest-hill, were not in the remotest degree connected. Hallam gives it as his opinion, that none of Milton's extant poetry reaches back beyond the sonnet which he composed on arriving at his twenty-third year. Brydges speaks without hesitation of other poems, written at earlier periods; fixing, for instance, his poetical versions of the 114th and 136th Psalms in his sixteenth year.

'Now these discrepancies afford good materials for critical ingenuity to work with. Surely there could be no difficulty in ascertaining the true day of Milton's birth. He could not be born in the years 1606, 1608, and 1609. Who can say that he was born at all? These discrepancies look very suspicious. Was Milton any thing more than a poetical impersonation of the republican spirit which produced the Commonwealth? Then, in regard to his eyes, were they lustrous or were they not? This, in the contradictory state of our evidence, cannot be determined. One thing is clear: both accounts cannot be true.—Is either true? Had Milton any eyes at all? In other words, was he anything but a free invention of the myth-forming tendency of the days of the first Charles?'—pp. 20, 21.

But Dr. Beard argues that the variations in the Gospel accounts are less in number and magnitude than even some friends may think. It is not merely by an unfriendly, but an unjust, method of proceeding, that Strauss often gains the appearance of succeeding to display variations and discrepancies between the Evangelists.

'The extent to which this method is unjust, can be measured only by a systematic study of the Gospels, in connection with his perverted comments. We may, however, give a specimen:—suppose that one narrator, A., states that Fenelon, in the thirtieth year of his age, visited Rome, and saw St. Peter's church. Another narrator, B., records that Fenelon, in his fortieth year, came to London, and saw Westminster Hall. These two accounts are first considered different versions of the same journey. Here, then, are contradictions. A. declares that Fenelon went to Rome; B. that he went to England: both cannot be right; one must be, and both may be, in error. At any rate, here is contradiction the first. The second contradiction is found in the divergent statements, that Fenelon inspected St. Peter's Church and Westminster Abbey. But there is a third contradiction,—one in regard to time: A. fixes on the age of thirty; B. prefers the later period of forty years; both, doubtless, with reasons quite satisfactory to themselves. But what is the value of two writers that thus contradict each other? Now let the reader observe, that this heap of cloud is built on pure assumption; namely, that there was but one journey, and that the time specified, which explains every thing, is adroitly turned into an objection, and even made to appear as an additional contradiction.'—(pp. 22, 23.)

After some further description of these alleged discrepancies, the writer proceeds to argue the truth of the Gospels from their undoubted concurrence in the doctrines which they exhibit, and from 'the unity of the image of Jesus, as presented in the New Testament.' He then urges that Christianity presents itself to us as an essentially miraculous system; and that those who reject or attempt to separate the miraculous from it, are constantly baffled by the intricate incorporation of the miraculous even in the minor details, and might quite as well and as wisely reject the whole.

After instancing this from Scripture, the author proceeds to produce the testimonies of Jews, Greeks and Romans, who did not hold the faith of Jesus, but who confess against their will that miracles were alleged to be wrought by Christ; and indirectly admit their inability to show that the pretension was groundless. By this we see what the impression was that our Lord made on his contemporaries; what impression he left behind in the world; what impression of him was received, not only by his apostles, and immediate successors, but also by enemies. This impression was, that he at least assumed to work miracles. He even appears on the page of history as the worker of miracles. 'Is all this, delusion?' asks the author; 'were his enemies deceived as well as his friends; did they, too, readily admit a pretension with which it is clear they knew not well how to deal. Must not the stamp of the miraculous in this system have been deep and broad, which Josephus could not disown, which compelled a record from the pen of Suetonius, and which neither the philosopher Celsus, nor the Emperor Julian, could assail except with sarcasm and invective.' The writer then proceeds to a minute and highly interesting examination of the circumstances attending the resurrection of our Lord as 'the actual miracle of the Christian religion;' and after laying bare the clumsy fallacies by which Strauss has sought to explain away that great fact, and the belief in it, so earnestly and frequently declared by the apostles, he favours us with a truly impressive account of the influence of that belief upon the life and conduct of Paul, contrasted with a view of the life and conduct of Seneca, under the influence of that stoical philosophy, of which he was, in his day, one of the first teachers. The beautiful consistency of the apostle's course under the influence of his persuasion of a fact, without which he believed his teaching and sufferings vain, (1 Cor. xv. 14,) stands out in high relief beside the inconsistent and weak conduct of the luxurious and greedy teacher of self-denial and submission to fate.

Dr. Beard concludes this masterly treatise by urging, that were all the miracles of the New Testament explained away, or exploded, or denied, one great miracle still remains—the character of Christ. Of that character he draws, in eloquent words, a discriminating and lovely picture, shewing that it forms a great and irrefragable miracle in itself, seeing that it could not have been formed by, or have grown out of the conditions of the time in which he appeared; or out of the circumstances of the people among whom he sojourned.

After this grave, yet any thing but dull discussion, we are entertained in the next Essay by '*The Fallacy of the Mythical Theory of Dr. Strauss, illustrated from the History of Martin Luther, and from actual Mohammedan Myths of the Life of Jesus*. This consists of two papers, the first of which, by J. F. Warne, is a clever and amusing application of Strauss's mode of investigation to the History of Luther. The pamphlet professes to be written in the year 2836, by a Mexican disciple of the Hegelian philosophy. At that date, it is not difficult to believe, much of the multifarious literature on Luther's history will no longer be in existence; there will be doubts and difficulties in connection with the German reformer, for the removal of which, materials are not to be found. In the supposed circumstances, the author shows with what destructive effect the theory and reasonings of Strauss may be applied to the history of Luther,

—well known, authentic and credible as it now is, in all its great leading features. After the manner in which the German critic of the nineteenth century resolves the gospel records of the life of Christ into mere fictions, so does the Mexican of the twenty-ninth century easily prove, that much in Luther's history is mythical and unworthy of credit; arguing himself, while so doing, into many an absurd and false conclusion, on what, to us, in this earlier age, is plain and substantive matter of fact. This ingenious paper is obviously founded on Dr. Whately's *Historic Doubts relative to Napoleon Bonaparte,* which is known in Germany, having indeed been translated with special reference to the work of Strauss.

This is followed by a piece containing extracts from real Mohammedan myths concerning Jesus, the object of which is, to shew how perfectly sober and rational is the evangelical history, in comparison with the genuine myth: this is the work of M. C G. Bark, a clergyman of Möttlingen.

The eighth and last of these collected pamphlets, consists of a series of translated extracts from Neander's *Leben Jesu,* of those passages which bear the most strongly on the points which Strauss has endeavoured to impugn. This needs no recommendation of ours.

We have thought it right thus to describe the contents of a book which appears to us very important, and which is certainly very interesting. The Christian public is not less indebted to Dr. Beard, for the care and judgment which have dictated his choice of pieces for translation, than for the very able and effective manner in which he has conducted his own share of the statement and argument. This share is larger than may at first appear, as the two essays by him occupy nearly one-third of the volume.

We do not ourselves apprehend much danger to our educated youth, from the diffusion in this country of the views and principles of interpretation of which the name of Strauss affords the most convenient designation. The danger is to our manufacturing population in large towns, where we find a good deal of rude, uncultivated talent, and a smattering of knowledge, which, unhappily, the possessors are but too prone to think it most clever and most original to display in carping at established truths. To such minds, and to the publications which feed them, a bad translation of Strauss, sold cheaply, affords rare materials, greedily received, and unsparingly applied. To this class, most exposed to the danger, the present work is not likely to find much access: but it is of the utmost importance that ministers and others who dwell among them, should be qualified to meet them, as occasion arises, upon their own ground. The want of a readiness, on the part of those who are the recognised champions of the Christian verity, in meeting the fallacy on the spot, by such forcible arguments as can only arise out of a clear understanding of the whole matter, is highly injurious to the cause of truth. To such persons little allowance is made for unpreparedness; and they are supposed to give the best answer that the subject admits. The damage of a feeble answer in such cases is incalculable; and it seems to us the bounden duty of every minister and educated person, who has any access to those whose minds have been tainted by the influence of such opinions, to stand prepared for all occasions, small or great, of offence or defence, by that mastery of the subject, and thorough knowledge of the question, which the work under notice is admirably calculated to afford.

The very interesting and valuable production of Dr. Dobbin, the title of which we have placed at the head of this article, might very well have formed one of the series of treatises to which our attention has been given. It is perhaps more curious, and certainly more elaborate than any single tract in that series; but the object is the same, and the mode of handling is not materially different from that which some of them exhibit. It is well, therefore, to notice it in this connection.

The work is well called by Dr. Dobbin, 'an argument.' It is as close and well reasoned an argument as our day has produced, and yet withal, rendered attractive and readable by a pleasant style and by much felicity of illustration. The writer has, with great self-command, restrained himself from wandering to the right hand or to the left from the high road of his great argument, into any of the tempting side-paths which his course must have offered; and the result is visible in a degree of singleness and completeness of effect not often met with in our discursive days.

The object of the work is to show by a single philological fact, and by an argument founded thereon that, contrary to the assertion of Strauss, the gospels were of very early composition —that they were written before the epistles, and could not by any possibility have been put forth at the same time with the epistles, or at any time after them down to the end of the fourth century. The importance of this matter can only be fully estimated by those who have had occasion to become acquainted with the tendencies of the recent neological literature of Germany, which has made the historical authority of the gospels the special object of its assaults.

The proof or fact, is found in the peculiar and distinctive usage in the gospels and epistles respectively, with regard to the designation of the Saviour of men.

Dr. Dobbin shews, by actually producing the examples to the eye, that in the Gospels and the Acts, the name *'ΙΗΣΟΥΣ*, Jesus, is that by which our Lord is known to the exclusion almost of every other. In these books it is found nearly seven hundred times, whereas, in the epistles it occurs less than seventy times, although the mention of the Saviour by other names is frequent.

It is then further shewn, that the word, *ΧΡΙΣΤΟΣ*, Christ, alone, as a designation of our Lord, occurs but sixty times in the Gospels and Acts, whereas in the epistles and Revelation it is found not less than two hundred and forty times; and that in the former it occurs with the article as an official designation, whilst in the latter it stands without the article, as a proper name.

Our attention is next directed to the form *'ΙΗΣΟΥΣ ΧΡΙΣΤΟΣ*, Jesus Christ, which occurs only five times in the Gospel and Acts, but is met with one hundred and sixty times in the Epistles and Revelation.

The form *ΧΡΙΣΤΟΣ 'ΙΗΣΟΥΣ*, Christ Jesus, never occurs in the Gospels, and only twice or thrice in the Acts, while in the Epistles it is very common.

Dr. Dobbin then states these further results:—

'That while the epistle writers use the same terms by which he is designated in the Gospels 'ΙΗΣΟΥΣ and ΧΡΙΣΤΟΣ, separately about two hundred times, (that is supposing—what we are not prepared to grant, that the 'Ο ΧΡΙΣΤΟΣ of the Gospels, and the ΧΡΙΣΤΟΣ of the epistles are the same,) in three hundred cases besides, they use an appellation altogether unknown, or scarcely known to the Evangelists.

'That 'ΙΗΣΟΥΣ in the Gospels occurs in the proportion of *fourteen* to *one* to ΧΡΙΣΤΟΣ in the Gospels; and that ΧΡΙΣΤΟΣ in the epistles occurs in the proportion of *ten* to *one* of 'ΙΗΣΟΥΣ in the epistles. That thus the immense predominence of 'ΙΣΗΟΥΣ is the characteristic of the one, as that of ΧΡΙΣΤΟΣ is of the other.

Lastly, a comparison of an equal number of chapters, in each class of writings, presents the following curious proportions. We take Mark as the representative of the Evangelists, because containing the same number of chapters as Paul to the Romans, and his first epistle to the Corinthians.

'ΙΗΣΟΥΣ, the Gospel designation, occurs

in Mark,	95	times
in Romans,	38	,,
in 1 Corinthians,	28	,,

ΧΡΙΣΤΟΣ, the Epistolary designation, occurs

	in Mark,	7	times
	in Romans,	68	,,
	in 1 Corinthians,	68	,,
'ΙΗΣΟΥΣ alone,	in Mark,	94	times
	in Romans,	1	,,
	in 1 Corinthians,	1	,,
ΧΡΙΣΤΟΣ alone,	in Mark,	6	times
	in Romans,	36	,,
	in 1 Corinthians	46	,,

Such are, in substance, the facts by which Dr. Dobbin establishes the remarkable difference of usage in respect of the names applied to our Lord between the writers of the Gospels and of the epistles. The facts are not open to criticism. They are obvious and undeniable, and the striking effect which they here produce, is accomplished chiefly through the juxta-position in which they are now placed by Dr. Dobbin, and through the inferences deducible from them.

The solution of the fact thus established is cleverly and satisfactorily wrought out by the author; and it is in substance this:—

'That the name 'ΙΗΣΟΥΣ, as the designation of the Jesus of Galilee, was the prevailing one at the time the sacred historians wrote. That the lives of Christ which they compiled were drawn up before the simple appellation, 'ΙΗΣΟΥΣ, had given place among his enemies to the opprobrious name 'Son of Mary,' 'the Nazarene;' and before the familiar appellation of friendship among his followers, had been superseded by the titles of veneration, the Lord, the Lord Jesus, the Christ of God.'—p. 54.

From this, results the necessity of an earlier date for the Gospels than for the Epistles, seeing that the usage embodied in the latter, is, from its very nature posterior to that which the former exhibits. It is also shewn that the usage of the early fathers in this matter, is the same with that of the Epistles, as they doubtless took up and followed their immediate antecedent, this shews that the Gospels were produced before the Epistles, for had they been later, the fathers would have been disposed to follow the nomenclature established in them. The early origin of the Gospels being established by these facts and arguments, it follows that the system of Dr. Strauss, which is built upon the hypothesis of their much later compositions, must necessarily fall to the ground; the mythic dress which historic events assume under this system, being utterly at variance with the supposition of their recent occurrence. Apart from this, its application as a weapon from the armoury of God's word against the daring speculation of unblessed learning, this tractate of Dr. Dobbin's is useful and interesting as a contribution to the literary history of the New Testament; which cannot hereafter be discussed without a careful consideration of the facts and arguments which he has with so much ability produced.

It is probable, that the idea of the work was suggested by the use which the German divines have made of the names JEHOVAH and ELOHIM, in attempting to distinguish the parts or portions of which they suppose the book of Genesis to be composed. There is much in the discussions connected with this subject—and particularly Hengstenberg's acute and able treatise *Die Gottesnamen in Pentateuch,* contained in his *Authentie des Pentateuches,* from which a hint for the enquiry which has engaged Dr. Dobbin's attention might be drawn.

Art. XI.—*Selections from the Kur-an, commonly called in England, the Koran; with an interwoven Commentary; translated from the Arabic, methodically arranged, and illustrated by Notes, chiefly from Sale's edition; to which is prefixed an Introduction, taken from Sale's Preliminary Discourse, with Corrections and Additions.* By E. W. Lane, &c. &c. London: Madden and Co 8vo. pp. 318.

THERE certainly has existed for many years past little curiosity among either the learned or the unlearned respecting the history and character of the Mohammedan imposture. This indifference, which has been all but universal, to the mortification of some gentlemen, who occasionally hint that they would not object to fraternize with *good* Mohammedans, is, we suspect, attributable to reasons widely different from those which Mr. Lane assigns for it. To inquisitive men, it must always be a chapter of deep and thrilling interest in the history of human nature; but in any religious sense, it has scarcely the slightest attraction even for speculators. It is an effete imposture which, though once exercising a terrific sweep of physical power, when the Christian body was paralysed by superstition, never had, and never could have, any moral or intellectual force in the presence of that civilization which Christianity has originated and sustained, and which, at the present moment, it is advancing beyond all former precedent. The Kur-an will no doubt remain in the libraries of the curious, as mummies will in their museums, and as the instrument of sustaining the faith of the Moslem through many centuries, as well as of keeping them in a semi-civilized state, it will always be a remarkable and interesting piece of antiquity; but, excepting the high literary interest which attaches to it as a specimen of Arabic composition, it can never be otherwise than contemptible. What share the prophet himself had in the fabrication, appears involved in an obscurity that is never likely to be dissipated; but it seems pretty certain that his scribes and assistants are entitled to a full share of the praise or blame. Without the assistance of better heads than his own, he never could have bequeathed to the world the Kur-an, even such as it is. Every thing that is good in it is borrowed, and for every thing bad, credit may be given to the fabricators in general. The great feature of its theology, if such we may be allowed to call it, is undoubtedly a pure or simple theism vindicated against polytheism by the wrath of man. But it is the bare principle, borrowed from that revelation, with which the fabricators were undoubtedly well acquainted, yet without those necessary and beautiful accompaniments which, in the genuine revelation, cause the pure ray of divine light to fall upon us rather in its prismatic colours than as an abstract and independent element. Mohammed and his coadjutors caught a glimpse of the glorious truth, but it was merely partial. The sight dazzled and blinded them. Reason lost its sway, and ceased to be a pupil; but under the guidance of a fanatical and voluptuous imagination, commenced teacher. The step thence to the assumption of prophecy and a divine commission, was short and easy. Among a semi-barbarous people, it seemed necessary to give success to the grand truth acquired, and the shortest way to it. Some authors have pretended to admire the Mohammedan system, as better adapted for that semi-barbarous age in which it arose, than Christianity, and have congratulated the world upon its rise as an important step towards higher attainments—something better than heathenism, though not quite so good as the gospel of Jesus Christ. For our own parts, we can view it as nothing better than an infernal machination to impede the progress of Christianity, and keep the nations still under the domination of those passions which work in perpetual antagonism to divine love. In the light of that principle, the difference is immaterial between stupid, degrading idolatry, and savage, proud, exterminating, voluptuous Mohammedanism, under the name of the one true God. Certain we are that the heathens have proved more accessible to the truth of Christianity than the Moslem; and who can pretend to say that the rise of the Arabian imposture has not impeded the spread both of civilization and Christianity? True it is that at the period of its rise, Christianity had become nearly as corrupt and useless as heathenism. It had undergone a similar decay with Judaism in its later ages. The truth was so encrusted with traditions, that scarcely a feature was to be seen. Yet the living principle was concealed within, which was destined one day to burst through the incrustations, and cast off the cerements. Mohammedanism contributed nothing towards this change. It has never possessed a piercing and comprehensive vision. It is at this day as proud and self-complacent in its isolation as it ever was. Against Christianity its hostility is as implacable as against idolatry, if not more so. But its doom is sealed, and its day is approaching. Progress it has made none for a long season, and apprehensions are becoming rife, even in the imaginations of its votaries, that its glory must wane. The spreading triumphs of Christianity will, ere long, extinguish the hopes of the crescent.

Yet the history of the Arabian prophet, and of the nations that once owned his religion, as well as of those that felt the keen edge of his scimitar, will form one of the most remarkable and interesting episodes in this world's history. The system itself, which has prevailed so long, and extended so far, cannot be understood without the study of the Kur-an. Since Sale's translation and dissertation appeared, little has been attempted further to illustrate the system; but the entire translation is no doubt unfit for general perusal. This fact, which is commonly acknowledged, sufficiently condemns the system, and justifies the Christian public in neglecting it. Mr. Lane hopes, by a selection and a more intelligible version, to revive attention. But a selection of the best passages has the effect of concealing the deformities, and thereby of conveying a wrong impression. No one can form an opinion of the Mohammedan imposture by a translation of those passages which are mostly derived from the Jewish and Christian scriptures, mixed up with some foolish and trifling tales. It may, however, be sufficient for the reader of these choice selections to form the conclusion, that '*what is true is not new—and what is new is not true;*' and as to all the rest, it is quite as well to leave it in its native Arabic.

Mr. Lane, by means of explanatory words, has thrown light upon some obscure passages; but others he leaves wholly incomprehensible by English readers. The fault no doubt lies in the impenetrable obscurity of the text, and not in the translator. The introduction, which treats of the Arabs before Mohammed, of the establishment of El-Islam, and of the Kur-an itself, is mostly taken from Sale, occasionally corrected by useful notes. Readers who may wish to acquire a knowledge of the rise of Mohammedanism, with some insight into the contents of the Kur-an, will find this a useful volume, especially if read in connexion with Dr. W. C. Taylor's 'History of Mohammedanism and its Sects.'

The volume is handsomely 'got up,' but in a few instances errors have escaped correction. The translation is upon the whole very respectable, though in some points susceptible of

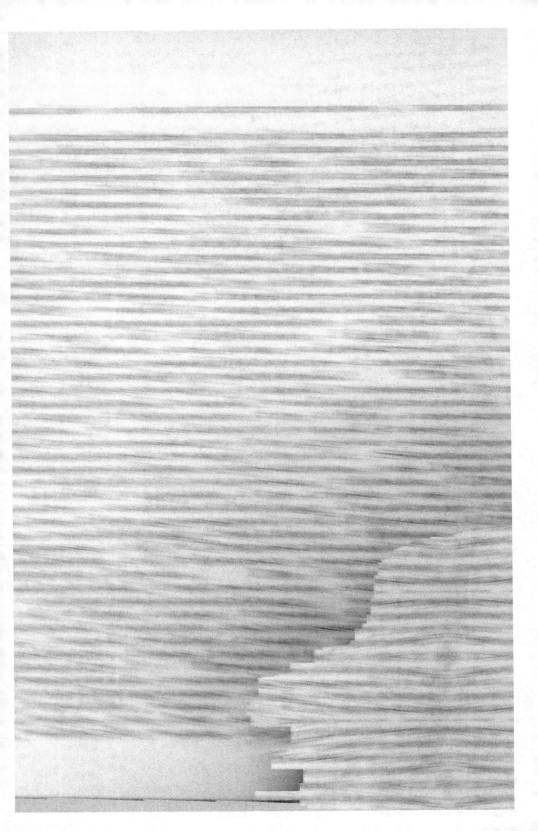

[illegible]

...astors, even if the state should ...ns, by taking their clergy again

...e seems to be a devoted and ...ommunities, though no friend to ...s written ably on many points, ...lially concur. But we fear he is ... speedy overthrow of the Romish ...e protestant churches. The be-...een, but its end will not be 'by-...out the protestant world, is in too ... the effort of faith, and hope, and ...adulterous alliance would demand. ...ely at the movements, whether in ...d, will find still a great deficiency ...e truth is not yet felt, and the pure ...t yet dissipated the darkness which ...ment men. We are quite aware ...be made for previous habits; but ... a large discount be taken from the ...ted. The emancipation and purifi-...stantism, which the author so glow-... to the fall of Babylon, is doubtless ... by the 'Crisis' which he says is ...s given only 'an uncertain sound.' ...ough it calls rather to celebrate the ...; because we know both will come ...el an interest in the Free Church, ...ulation.

...e Church of Rome truly represented: ...Papist Misrepresented and Represented.' ..., Bishop of Worcester. With a ...nningham, D.D., Prof. of Divinity ...ge, Edinburgh. A new edition

...rint of one of the best small pieces ...hich prevailed towards the close

...ery particular though succinct ...ted and Represented, or a two-... in 1685. The object of this ...rities of Romanism, to remove ...ccasioned to the bulk of the ...ewn in the preface, ...an church. It is ... but for the learning ...o frequently exposed.

improvement. A preliminary essay, or even occasional notes, pointing out the attempts at imposture, and contrasting these pretended revelations with the true ones, would have been a valuable addition; yet possibly the author deemed all this so obvious as to be needless, or beyond a translator's province. We think, however, that justice to Christianity demanded, and would have justified it.

Brief Notices.

The Crisis is Come: or, the Crisis of the Church of Scotland; the Apostasy of the Church of England; and the Fall of the Church of Rome. With an Appendix, containing the Speeches and Decision of the House of Commons on the Petition of the Church of Scotland. By the Rev. B.D. Bogie, Rector of Lusby, &c.

THIS is a spirited exhibition of the effect which recent events are producing upon the stability and prospects of civil establishments of Christianity, and coming, as it seems, from the hand of a clergyman, is one of the strangest signs of these strange times. The author rejoices, indeed exults and revels, in the anticipation that the Protestant churches must all be thrown upon the voluntary principle. But he seems to forget that the adoption of the voluntary practice by the Free Church is a widely different thing from the adoption of the voluntary principle. It may be necessary, ere long, to adjust the discrepancy under which the friends of the Free Church at present appear: it may be impossible long to sustain a practice that is not upheld by principle: and it is not unlikely that the coming generation may look more favourably upon the principle, which, to say the least, is the only one sanctioned by Christ and his apostles; and may not feel it any shame, nor be conscious of any recantation, in defending their practice by New Testament authority; but it ought not to be overlooked, that no change of principle has been avowed by the Free Church; and that, in all probability, they would become again an established church, if the state would either pay them out of the taxes, or allot to them a portion of the tiends, unencumbered by restriction upon ecclesiastical proceedings. Efforts have been made, and are still making, to keep alive in the breasts of the people a love of the state alliance. Neither is it yet perceived that an independent establishment is an anomaly which no government ought to encourage, and a peril to liberty which no people ought to endure. An independent hierarchy, even partially so, for none have been absolutely free, has always proved, whether papist or protestant, heterodox or orthodox, an intolerable tyranny—a curse, rather than a blessing: and if the laity of the free church are awake to the lessons of history, they will never consent to have that healthy tie severed which now connects them with their pastors, even if the state should consent to relieve them of their burdens, by taking their clergy again under its fostering wing.

The author of the present volume seems to be a devoted and zealous friend to all the protestant communities, though no friend to the establishment principle. He has written ably on many points, and in most of his opinions we cordially concur. But we fear he is much too sanguine in expecting the speedy overthrow of the Romish apostasy, and the rectification of the protestant churches. The beginning of the struggle we have seen, but its end will not be 'by-and-bye.' Religion itself, throughout the protestant world, is in too feeble and sickly a state to sustain the effort of faith, and hope, and love, which a severance of the adulterous alliance would demand. Those who look calmly but closely at the movements, whether in Scotland, Germany, or Switzerland, will find still a great deficiency of the right principle. The simple truth is not yet felt, and the pure light of the New Testament has not yet dissipated the darkness which hangs about the ideas of establishment men. We are quite aware that a large allowance ought to be made for previous habits; but just in the same proportion must a large discount be taken from the calculation of good already effected. The emancipation and purification of the churches of protestantism, which the author so glowingly anticipates, as the prelude to the fall of Babylon, is doubtless *nearer*, and may be accelerated by the 'Crisis' which he says is come; but as yet the trumpet has given only 'an uncertain sound.' We hail, however, the sound, though it calls rather to celebrate the victory than prepare for the battle; because we know both will come in their due order. To all who feel an interest in the Free Church, this will prove an acceptable gratulation.

The Doctrines and Practices of the Church of Rome truly represented; in answer to a book, entitled 'A Papist Misrepresented and Represented.' By Edward Stillingfleet, D.D., Bishop of Worcester. With a Preface and Notes, by W. Cunningham, D.D., Prof. of Divinity and Church Hist. New College, Edinburgh. A new edition revised. Edinburgh, 1845

THIS is a cheap and very useful reprint of one of the best small pieces produced during the controversy, which prevailed towards the close of the Stuart Dynasty.

The original work consists of a very particular though succinct reply to Gother's 'Papist Misrepresented and Represented, or a two-fold character of Popery,' published in 1685. The object of this book was, by softening down the peculiarities of Romanism, to remove or diminish the offence which they occasioned to the bulk of the English nation. This, as Dr. Cunningham has shewn in the preface, is no unusual device of the adherents of the Roman church. It is one which would have been long ago successful, but for the learning skill, and diligence with which it has been so frequently exposed.

We know of no exposure among the smaller treatises superior to the one now for the second time reprinted. It is a manual of about 380 pages, well laid out, treats of none but really useful matters; and with the introduction and notes, is as seasonable at the present hour, as when it originally issued from the press

To each of Stillingfleet's thirty-seven chapters, Dr. Cunningham has attached notes, sometimes short, at other times of equal and even superior length to the chapter itself. The subjects of the chapters are too multifarious to be here enumerated, even if the work were entirely new They comprise together a considerable portion of the Romish controversy. The notes not only impart details, and explanations derived from the treatises and pamphlets by which the works of Gother and Stillingfleet were followed up until the controversy closed for the time, but afford much collateral information, and notice the most useful books on the several subjects of the chapters which have appeared down to our own times. We suppose that the length to which several of them extend was the reason why they were not distinguished from Stillingfleet's text by a different type,—which is the chief thing we regret in the book.

Dr. Cunningham's preface, which occupies fifty-seven pages, is highly interesting and instructive. It commences with a comparative draught of the three leading forms in which the true religion has been corrupted, Paganism, Pharisaism, and Popery. The points of resemblance between Paganism, the corruption of patriarchal religion, and popery, the corruption of Christianity, are then briefly indicated. After this we have a few clear, though summary, illustrations of the '*deceivableness of unrighteousness*,' which has been exhibited by the papists in order to secure the subjection of the Christian world to the bishop of Rome. These illustrations are derived from the priest's oaths, and from the canons and legends of the church. Then follows a brief notice of the craft by which the Council of Trent was packed, and of the fraudulent suppressions and evasions by which its mere decisions have been prevented from exploding into open dissensions. The remainder of the preface characterises in a very just and striking manner, the fraudulent principle on which Bossuet's 'Exposition of the Doctrine of the Catholic Church in matters of Controversy,' and Gother's 'Papist Misrepresented and Represented,' were written, and shews that the same principle has been continually acted upon either in printed books, or in the examinations of Popish prelates before Parliament until our own days. The work is eminently seasonable, and we earnestly recommend our readers to purchase and peruse it.

Two Discourses, delivered at Sion Chapel, Whitechapel. On Sunday Evenings, Dec. 7th and 14th, 1845. By the Rev. R. S. Bayley, F.S.A. 8vo. pp. 31. London: Justin and Son.

There are few men amongst us competent to the production of such sermons as these, for which the author apologizes as having been 'purely extemporaneous, and only partially corrected by him, because not seen till they were in print.' If the undress of Mr. Bayley be so attractive, what would his appearance be, if he expended on his composition the labour of which it is so worthy. We would gladly give the polish and the elegance on which some men pique themselves for a tenth of the mental vigour and affluence which his productions indicate. We know not what may be his purpose, but if he can abstract from the 'People's College,' to which, with such self-denying heroism he has consecrated himself,—sufficient time and energy for the work, we would earnestly and respectfully counsel his devoting himself to some literary achievement worthy of his powers. Where is 'The Life of Strafford,' of which we heard some promise in days gone by?

The subjects of the present discourses are, 'The Conversion of Saul,' and 'The Offence of the Gospel;' and we pity both the intellect and the piety of that man, who is not gratified and benefited by their perusal.

Bohn's Standard Library.

1. *The Miscellaneous Works and Remains of the Rev. Robert Hall, with a Memoir of his Life.* By Olinthus Gregory, L.L.D. *And a Critical Estimate of his Character and Writings.* By John Foster.
2. *The Life and Pontificate of Leo the Tenth.* By William Roscoe. Fifth edition. Revised by his son, Thomas Roscoe. In two volumes. London: Henry G. Bohn.
3. *The Life and Pontificate of Leo the Tenth.* By William Roscoe. In two volumes. Vol. I. London: David Bogue.

We are not concerned to enter into the merits of the controversy between Mr. Bogue and Mr. Bohn, the publishers of the European and of the Standard Libraries. In substance, we believe it stands thus. The former gentleman having announced a collection of Mr. Hall's miscellaneous pieces, as being intended to form one of the volumes of the European library, Mr. Bohn, the proprietor of the uniform edition of Mr. Hall's works, feels himself aggrieved, and, in self defence, has produced the volume before us. Its appearance is a perfect marvel in book-making, and unless Mr. Bogue has already printed his projected volume, he will be wise in foregoing his intention. No sale, we imagine, can reimburse Mr. Bohn, as the volume, which is handsomely 'got up' in post 8vo., consists of five hundred and seventy-two pages, and is sold at the incredibly low price of three shillings and sixpence. It contains, besides minor pieces, 'Christianity consistent with a love of Freedom,' 'An Apology for the Freedom of the Press,' 'Modern Infidelity,' 'Reflections on War,'' 'Sentiments proper to the Present Crisis,' 'The Advantages of Knowledge,' 'The Funeral Sermon for the Princess Charlotte,' and various reviews. 'Dr. Gregory's Life of Mr. Hall, and John Foster's Critique are also included, together with a large body of editorial notes. These latter are Mr. Bohn's copyright, and must give his volume an advantage over every competitor. A more valuable and bewitching companion we know not in the whole range of English literature, and we strongly recommend every young man immediately to possess himself of it.

Mr. Bohn's edition of the 'Life and Pontificate of Leo the Tenth,' is printed from that of 1827, which underwent the immediate revision of the author, of which Mr. Bohn holds the copyright. This is an advantage not possessed by Mr. Bogue's, of which only one volume has yet been published. We regret the collision which has arisen, not merely as it threatens the commercial interests of the gentlemen concerned, but as it tends to prevent the public from realizing the expectations awakened by the original prospectus of the European Library. Nothing short of a very extensive sale can induce either Mr. Bohn or Mr. Bogue to prosecute his design, and we fear this will be prevented by the clashing interests of their series. As the first projector, our sympathies are with the latter, but justice requires us to say that Mr. Bohn's edition of the work now before us, has indisputable claims to preference.

We shall be glad to hear of some amicable arrangement having been made which shall reconcile the interests of the litigant publishers with that of the public.

The History of Greece. By Connop Thirlwall, D.D. Vol. II. London: Longman and Co.

THE second volume of a handsome library edition of the only work in our language which is entitled to be called a *History of Greece.* Having recently expressed, at some length, our high estimate of Bishop Thirlwall's work, we need do nothing more at present than announce the appearance of the volume before us, which is alike creditable to its author and its publishers.

Knight's Book of Reference. Political Dictionary: forming a Work of Universal Reference, both Constitutional and Legal, &c. Part XI. First Half. London: Charles Knight.

THIS work proceeds in a manner highly satisfactory, and will unquestionably, when completed, form one of the most useful books of reference which any library can contain. Such a publication has long been needed, and we are obliged to Mr. Knight for supplying it. It contains the results of very extended and accurate research, throws light on innumerable points of general as well as of political knowledge, and is moreover printed in a portable form, well suited to promote its extensive circulation.

The History of England during the Thirty Years' Peace, 1815—1845. By Charles Knight. Imperial 8vo. Part I., pp. 56. London: Charles Knight.

THIS is a somewhat hazardous, but most attractive undertaking. If executed with competent skill, labour, and impartiality, it will prove one of the best books published in our day, and cannot fail to secure a large class of readers. The period embraced is sufficiently recent to be interwoven with the interests and passions of the present day, whilst its earlier portion is already beginning to rank with the past, in the view of a large class of readers. We shall watch the progress of the work with interest, and take an early opportunity of recording our judgment on its execution. At present we simply say that it promises well. Mr. Knight enters on his undertaking with a full knowledge of its difficulties, a clear perception of the real points of the history, and an honest purpose—as we verily believe—of making it subserve the social welfare of the people. The work is uniform in size with *The Pictorial History of England*, and is to be completed in twenty-four monthly parts, price two shillings each.

The Year Book of Facts in Science and Art, exhibiting the most important Discoveries and Improvements of the Past Year. By the Editor of 'The Arcana of Science.' London: David Bogue.

A VERY useful book of reference, well adapted to stimulate a reader to enlarge his acquaintance with the various branches of useful knowledge. Its contents are classified under the following divisions: Mechanical and Useful Arts, Natural Philosophy, Electrical Science, Chemical Science, Natural History, Geology and Physical Geography, Astronomical and Meteorological Phenomena, and Obituary. Great labour has been expended on the preparation of the volume, and we shall be glad to find that its circulation is equal to its merits.

Literary Intelligence.

Just Published.

Memoirs and Correspondence of the Most Noble Richard, Marquess Wellesley, comprising numerous Letters and Documents, now first published from original MSS. By Robert R. Pearce, Esq. 3 vols. 8vo.

The History of Greece. By Connop Thirlwall, D.D., Bishop of St. David's. 8vo. Vol. II.

The Three Kingdoms, a Book for the Young.

Palestrina, a Metrical Romance, by Robert M. Heron, Esq.

Forest and Game Law Tales, by Harriet Martineau. Vol. III.

The Native Irish, and their Descendants, by Christopher Anderson, 3rd edition, improved.

The Voluntary, or Advocate of the Voluntary Principle in Religion, including the separation of Church and State, and the perfect Freedom of the Church. Vol. V. 1845.

Sermons in Proof, Development, and Illustration of the Evangelical Doctrines of the Church, Holy, Catholic, and Apostolic, with an Appendix and Notes on the Evangelical and Apostolic Characteristics of the United Church of England and Ireland. By the Rev. Tresham Dames Gregg, M.A.

Hogg's Weekly Instructor, Part XI.

North British Review, No. VIII.

The History of England during the Thirty Years' Peace, 1815 to 1845. By Charles Knight.

Knight's Penny Magazine, Part I.

Knight's Books of Reference, Political Dictionary, Part XI., first half.

Sketches from Life, by the late Laman Blanchard, with a Memoir of the Author, by Sir Edward Buller Lytton, Bart. 3 vols.

Bohn's Standard Library. The Miscellaneous Works and Remains of the Rev. Robert Hall, with a Memoir of his Life, by Olinthus Gregory, L.L.D., F.R.A.S., and a Critical estimate of His Character and Writings, by John Foster, author of the "Essays on Decision of Character," &c.

The Life and Pontificate of Leo the Tenth, by William Roscoe, fifth edition, revised by his son, Thomas Roscoe. Two vols.

Every Man his own Landlord; or, How to buy a House with its own Rent.

Antonio Peres and Philip II., by M. Mignet, Member of the Institute of France. Translated with the approbation of the Author, by C. Cocks.

The Year Book of Facts in Science and Art, exhibiting the most Important Discoveries and Improvements of the Past Year, by the Editor of the Arcana of Science.

Fasting; an Essay occasioned by the Increased Importance attached to its Observance, by John Collyer Knight.

A brief Commentary on the First Epistle of St. Paul to the Thessalonians, by the Rev. Alex. S. Patterson.

Instructions about Heartwork, and a Companion for Prayer, by the Rev. Richard Alleine, revised and corrected, with a Biographical Sketch of the Author, by the Rev. John S. Stamp.

History of the Reformation of the Sixteenth Century. Vol. IV. By J. H. Merle D'Aubigne, D.D., Assisted in the Preparation of the English Original, by H. White.

Anastasis; or the Doctrine of the Resurrection of the Body, Rationally and Scripturally considered, by George Bush. 2nd Edition.

A Harmony of the Four Gospels in Greek, according to the Text of Hahn, newly arranged, with Explanatory Notes, by Edward Robinson, D.D.

Original Sketches in Poetry, designed to Illustrate various Subjects and Characters selected from the Holy Scriptures. By C. L. B.

A Manual of Natural Philosophy, with Recapitulatory Questions on each Chapter, and a Dictionary of Philosophical Terms, by John L. Comstock, M.D., and Richard D. Hoblyn, A.M., Oxon.

A Proposal for an Agrarian Endowment of the Population, in lieu of the existing Poor Law and Corn Law, in a Letter to His Grace the Duke of Richmond, K.G. By David Owen Edwards, a Freeholder of South Lincolnshire.

The Appeal of the Congregation of the West London Synagogue of British Jews, to their Brother Israelites throughout the United Kingdom.

The Blessedness of Departed Spirits: a Discourse preached on occasion of the lamented death of the late Mrs. Elizabeth Fry. By the Rev. Robert Ferguson, L.L.D.

The Oregon Question as it Stands. By M. B. Sampson, with a Map.

A Discourse on the Personal Presence of the Spirit with the Church, and in all Believers, as the Peculiar Privilege of the Gospel Age. By George Hall.

Two Discourses, delivered at Sion Chapel, Whitechapel, on Sunday Evenings, Dec. 7, and 14, 1845. By the Rev. R. S. Bayley, F.S.A. of Sheffield. 1st, The Conversion of Saint Paul; 2nd, The Offence of the Gospel.

THE

ECCLECTIC REVIEW

For APRIL, 1846.

Art. I.—1. *The History of the Presbyterian Church in Ireland.* By James Leaton Reid, D.D., M.R.S.A. Vol. I. and Vol. II.

2. *An Account of the Regium Donum issued to the Presbyterian Church of Ireland.* By George Mathews, Esq.

3. *The Eastern Reformed Presbyterian Synod's Protest against the Endowment of Maynooth College.*

No one who looks at the character of the times in which we live with the eye of a philosopher, not to mention that of a Christian, will pronounce them devoid of interest. Opinion is no longer stagnant. Sentiment clashes with sentiment. The present is the age of moral forces. Some thinkers are striving to force back the human mind, and adopt, as the type of all that is great and good, the days of monkish superstition and priestly rule; others, the enemies of social and religious reform, would keep it stationary; while a considerable body of energetic and high-minded men are resolved, by God's help, to extend to all nations the blessings of civilization, social reforms, and religious freedom.

Among the mightiest obstacles which impede the progress of the human mind, must ever be classed the system of civil ecclesiastical establishments. This gigantic power stands as a hoary monument of the selfish and slumbering spirit of days gone by. It frowns on the genius of all advance. Civil endowments of religion, under every form, are unfavourable to the march of improvement. We must class in the same category, both the head of an archiepiscopal see, and the modest, though no less culpable, recipient of a *regium donum*. Evangelical truth owes but little to either, civil liberty next to nothing.

The recent conduct of the endowed Presbyterians of Ireland, in regard to the Maynooth question, supplies volumes of instruction on this point. It has forcibly attracted the attention of thoughtful men to their position. While other religious bodies were arousing every energy to defeat the unprincipled measure, the movements of this body were tardy, creeping, and ineffective; and even when public opinion had forced a portion of it into something like resistance, that opposition was but feeble and spiritless. It was easy to see that there was a drag on the wheel, something, no matter what, which kept 'tongue-tied,' and in a state of comparative quiescence, the most excitable men on some questions in the world.

It would be tedious to investigate every circumstance of sad, but stirring interest in the history of endowed Presbyterianism in Ireland. Our remarks for the present we must confine to a few general observations, on its early history, its present position, and its prospective influence; and in these observations, we do not mean to touch upon the Unitarian body, who call themselves Presbyterians, and as such receive the *regium donum*, but may have a word perhaps to say in reference to them, on some future occasion.

Presbyterianism in Ireland, owes its origin to a political scheme of no small note,—the colonization of Ulster. This province was remarkable in early times for the rebellious spirit of its chiefs. The Earls of Tyrone and Tyrconnell, gave almost unceasing annoyance to the English government, by the turbulent risings which they headed. The suppression of these outbreaks was followed of course, by the forfeiture of the lands in the possession of the insurgents. It occurred to the statesmen of those times, that one effectual way to repress the turbulence of the Irish, would be to place on the forfeited lands, a colony of English and Scotch settlers. Such a line of policy seems to have been projected, and partially acted upon even so far back as the times of Elizabeth. Shortly after the accession of James, this scheme was adopted anew, and carried out with considerable success. A large majority of the settlers were natives of Scotland. This circumstance is accounted for by Dr. Reid, in the following extract from an unpublished manuscript, by a Presbyterian minister, whose father accompanied the first settlers.—'The king (James) had a natural love to have Ireland planted with Scotch, as being beside their loyalty of a middle temper, between the English tender and the Irish rude breeding, and a great deal more like to adventure to plant Ulster than the English, it lying far from the English native land, and more from their humour, while it lies nigh to Scotland, and the inhabitants not so far from the ancient Scots manners : so that it might be hoped, that the Irish untoward living, would be met both with equal firmness, if need be, and be especially allayed by the example of more civility, and Protestant profession, than in any former times had been among them.' The Scotch settlers retaining their predilections for the religion of their fathers, brought their Presbyterianism with them. Several ministers accompanied them from Scotland ; and it is but justice to add, that all of them seem to have been men of much simplicity of character and apostolic manners, much zeal, and possessed of considerable mental ability. If we may credit the testimony of contemporary writers, the character of the colonists was generally such as required the labours of such men.

The presbyterians and prelatists lived together at first in great harmony. This was no doubt mainly owing to the mild and charitable spirit of the pious and learned Usher, Archbishop of Armagh. In some places presbyterian ministers seem to have been allowed even to participate in the ecclesiastical revenues. But jealousy soon began to display itself, which in a short time issued in open persecution on the part of the hierarchy. The presbyterians were greatly harassed during the reign of the first Charles, nor did they obtain permanent relief till the Long Parliament. Under the government of Cromwell, they obtained, along with other religious bodies, a share of public endowments. Some have attempted to throw dubiety on this circumstance, but the researches of Dr. Reid place it beyond a doubt. It must be acknowledged that by no party were the secularising effects of state endowments then apprehended. The Presbyterians received their salaries under the Protectorate in lieu of the tithes to which they conceived themselves as having a right. It may be owing to our obtuseness, but to us the arguments employed to make out a right to the one, seem equally good with those that would prove a right to the other, and both equally worthless.

The Presbyterians of Ireland took an active part in the restoration of Charles II. in the hope of getting their own system established ; but when they found him bent on the establishment of episcopacy, they were grievously disappointed. In the earlier part of his reign, they were exposed to much persecution, and the arbitrary measures adopted by Jeremy Taylor, who had been made Bishop of Down and Connor, reflect but little honour on his character, and are sadly out of keeping with the enlightened spirit of 'the Liberty of Prophecying.' But the policy of Charles underwent subsequently a great change, as regarded the Irish Presbyterians. This circumstance is thus related by Mr. Hutcheson, a Presbyterian minister, in the county of Down, who died in 1711:—

'The truly honourable Sir Arthur Forbes, the steadfast and real friend of the ministers and people in that part of the country, wrote for four ministers to come to him to Dublin, that he might communicate a matter to them wherein they were highly concerned. The matter was, as he related it himself, as followeth:—He being a little before in London, and being in conference with the king, who had a great kindness for him (and deservedly), the king, among other things relating to this kingdom, inquired at him concerning the Presbyterian ministers and people in the north; how the ministers lived, and that he had always been informed that they were loyal, and had been sufferers on that account, and were peaceable in their way and carriage, notwithstanding the hardships they were under.

'Sir Arthur replied, ''twas a true account his majesty had heard of them; and as to their present condition, they lived in no great plenty, though they had the affection of the people where they did reside, but that they were not in a capacity to afford them a comfortable subsistence, being under many heavy burdens. The king, of his own mere notion, told Sir Arthur that there was twelve hundred pounds a year in the settlement of the revenue of Ireland, which he had not yet disposed of, and designed it for a charitable use, and he knew not how to dispose of it better than by giving it to these ministers; and told him that he would forthwith give order, and desired Sir Arthur to bring the secretary to him to-morrow, that the order might be passed under the king's privy seal, and the money to be paid to Sir Arthur quarterly for secret service, as the order ran; but when the secretary came to the king, it was found there was only six hundred pounds to be disposed of, which he ordered to be paid, as is formerly related.'

The circumstances connected with the parliamentary grant, usually designated *regium donum*, form a painfully interesting chapter in the history of Irish Presbyterianism, and it is a somewhat noticeable fact, that it should have had its origin under the corrupt administration of the profligate monarch Charles II. But so it is. In consequence of the exhausted condition of the treasury, the grant was discontinued, towards the latter part of his reign, and the troubles in which his successor was speedily involved, prevented him from attempting its renewal.

The revolution of 1688 brought the Presbyterians of Ireland once more into favour with the ruling powers. They were among the first to hail the arrival of the prince of Orange. Before the end of the month in which he landed, they appointed a deputation to proceed to London, tendering their allegiance; and no sooner had William erected his standard on Irish ground, than he found himself surrounded by the sturdy Presbyterians of the north. They hailed his arrival with enthusiasm, and marched to the field with alacrity under his banner. Their fidelity did not pass unnoticed or unrewarded. On the 19th of June, 1690, he was pleased to express his royal approbation, by an order issued from the camp at Hillsborough, for the sum of £1200 to be paid annually to the Presbyterian ministers of Ulster. This grant was made payable by the collector of customs at the port of Belfast; but so trifling was the trade of that port at the time, that the revenue was found insufficient to meet it; and it was eventually placed on the civil list to be paid out of the Irish treasury.

This grant ceased with the demise of king William; but the trustees lost no time in forwarding a memorial to queen Anne, reminding her majesty of the kindness of her predecessor, and entreating the continuation of the royal favour. To refuse the prayer of the petitioners would have been impolitic. It was, therefore, readily assented to, but with certain limitations. The grant bestowed by king William, was given as a reward for past services, and does not seem to have been accompanied with any terms implying royal control. But this arrangement was only temporary; and accordingly we find when the grant ceased and was renewed by queen Anne, that it was accompanied by the following conditions:—'Upon trust, nevertheless, that the money which shall be received thereupon from time to time shall be distributed to and among the said Presbyterian ministers, *or such of them*, and in such proportions as shall be appointed from time to time, in lists to be approved of and signed by our lieutenant-deputy, or other chief governor, or governors of our said kingdom of Ireland for the time being.' The statesmen of those days were not ignorant of the arts of statecraft, and clearly saw the mighty influence which endowments of religion were capable of affording to the ruling authorities over the conduct of their recipients.

Meanwhile a number of English Presbyterians had settled in the south of Ireland. These had come over during the government of Cromwell, or had fled to Ireland after the act of uniformity. It was found inconvenient to withhold from them a share of the royal favour enjoyed by their brethren in the north. Queen Anne, therefore, with advice of her council, was induced to allow their ministers a pension of £800 per annum. This was called the Queen's bounty, as being given out of the privy purse, and remitted from London to the Irish treasury.

The grant now became in the full sense of the word an instrument of State policy; and the avidity with which the subsequent augmentations were seized upon by the Presbyterian clergy, but too plainly shows that 'increase of appetite had grown by what it fed upon.'

During the reign of Anne, this endowment remained as we have stated, unchanged in amount or in the terms of its bestowment; but in the reign of George I., an addition was made to it of £800 per annum, as an acknowledgment of the services of the ministers in promoting the Hanoverian succession. This sum was equally divided between the ministers composing the synod of Ulster, and those belonging to the southern association, known by the name of the Synod of Munster.

The pernicious fruits of state-pay were now everywhere to be seen throughout the presbyterian body. The life-blood of the system had become tainted with the virus of Arianism; and even where its principles had not found 'a local habitation and a name,' there was little to be seen but the cold, barren wastes of religious formalism. The form indeed remained, but the spirit had departed.

The state of religion in Ireland did not escape the observation of the Scottish secession, which had recently sprung into existence. Some of their ablest men visited Ireland, and were eminently useful in their efforts to do good. Whilst free from state-connexion, their labours proved a signal blessing to the country. But the policy of government watched for an opportunity of binding them to the state-chariot, and at length found it. The demon of state-craft slumbers not. By king's letter, bearing date the 7th Jan. 1784, the sum of £1000 per annum was added to the original grant to the synod of Ulster, and a bait of £500 per annum was thrown out to the seceders. As this grant seemed accompanied with no conditions, it was joyfully accepted. Lord Castlereagh, however, in 1804, thought proper to present it under a different form, and accompanied with such conditions as placed the body entirely under government control. There was then, at first, considerable hesitation as to its acceptance. But, alas for human infirmity! After a little toying and shying, *interloquiturs*, and synodical deliverances, it was again eagerly swallowed. The only exception was, in the case of the Rev. James Bryce, of Killeng, a stubborn Scotchman, who,—

> Faithful found
> Among the faithless, faithful only he,—

resolutely resisted the temptation, and is now a hoary witness of nearly half a century's standing, to the corrupting influence of this grant. Mr. Bryce published a pamphlet on the subject, in which he exposed with merciless fidelity the weakness of his brethren. The terms on which the seceders obtained the regium donum indicate with equal clearness the policy of government. The link which bound them to the civil power is undisguised in the following language, which formed part of the terms of arrangement: 'The present ministers of the fore-named congregations shall be entitled to receive the said sums according to the above arrangement, until the death or removal of each respectively; and after such death or removal, the same sum shall be paid in like manner to their successors; provided always that such successors shall have been first certified to his Grace the Lord Lieutenant, *and approved of by him.*'

It were perhaps impossible to obtain a more striking illustration of the baneful effects of ecclesiastical endowments, than in the history of this body. While the Scotch secession grew in strength, and walked abroad with manly and firm step, under the bracing influence of voluntaryism, the Irish secession in the frigid atmosphere of state patronage, became nerveless in its movements, and shrivelled in every limb, till it was fain, in order to preserve an existence, to rush into the embrace of a body, it had frequently denounced, in the strongest terms, as Arian and heterodox. But of this anon.

Another increase to the *Regium donum* took place in the year 1792. By King's letter of the 21st June of that year, the sum of £5,000 was placed on the Irish Civil List to be divided among the Presbyterian ministers in the following proportions:—The Synod of Ulster, £3,750; Seceders, £927 8*s.* 5*d.*; Synod of Munster, £332 11*s.* 7*d.* Since that time the grant has received various augmentations, and undergone several modifications. It was a mighty instrument of political cunning in the hands of that unprincipled minister, Lord Castlereagh. The conduct of the Government of that day, and even that of some leading Presbyterian ministers, who negotiated the affair, was such as most Presbyterians would now reprobate. One arrangement was curious enough, but clearly developed the mercenary ideas of the minister. The State payments were graduated by a scale, the ministers of the larger congregations receiving the larger bounty. The Synod of Ulster had three classes, those in the first receiving £100; those in the second £75 per annum; those in the third only £50 per annum, while the Secession Synod had only two classes, including ministers who received £70 and £40 per annum. This arrangement was founded on the principle, that the ministers of the larger congregations had the greater influence, and as influence was the *quid pro quo* in the eyes of the Government, it was meet and seemly the men who had the most of it should obtain the larger *donum*. Lord Castlereagh, the author of this arrangment, was in heart an enemy to the Presbyterians, and is thought by some to have designed it as a bone of contention, in the hope of dividing and distracting the body, by exciting feelings of jealousy through the unequal measure of State favour bestowed.

It is impossible to contemplate the whole affair without a thorough conviction of its entire political bearing. This is freely admitted by Mr. Mathews, in a pamphlet before us. Mr. Mathews is a gentleman of high respectability, filling an official situation in Dublin Castle, and having access to the best means of information; he is, moreover, a Presbyterian, and a friend of endowments. His testimony is therefore free from all suspicion of partiality.

'The several grants,' he says, 'out of the Civil List appearing to have been made at times of great public emergency, give in some degree a particular character to the transaction. The first patent for £1,200 was executed ten days before the battle of the Boyne, while King William was advancing through Downshire, surrounded and supported by the Presbyterians of Ulster; the grants of £1,000 and £500 in 1784, arose out of the memorable struggles of 1782, and the Irish Volunteers; the grant of £5,000 in 1792 was connected with certain electioneering contests in two northern counties, of much importance to the Government of the day; while the increase in 1804 was promised immediately after the rebellion of 1798, and held out as in contemplation during the discussion on the Union; but various obstacles retarded the fulfilment of the promise for three years afterwards.'

It might seem invidious, and it is certainly painful, to touch upon the abuses connected with this grant; but we should not do justice to our subject, nor fairly exhibit the influence of this endowment on the body which receives it, were we to pass these over without remark; more especially as we greatly fear there are some of these abuses still in existence, or others of a similar character. This painful task, we shall chiefly perform in the words of Mr. Mathews, with merely one line of explanation. By an old arrangement the Government allows the portion of *Regium donum,* which falls due to a congregation during a vacancy (the time intervening between the removal or death of one minister, and the settlement of another) to be appropriated to a fund for the support of the widows and families of deceased ministers. This, however, has led to the abuse of returning to government as *vacant,* congregations which have ceased to exist, or whose ministers may have separated from the body, and refused the grant. Hear Mr. Mathews on this point—

'Two very small congregations once existed in Dublin, belonging to Scots Burghers and Anti-Burghers, the one meeting in Back Lane and the other in Mass Lane; £70. a-year were assigned to the latter, and £50. to the former. A third congregation afterwards sprung up to which £70. were also assigned, and the handful of people attached to the former two gradually merged into the third; the two old congregations were extinguished, the meeting-houses disappeared, and of course no clergyman was ever appointed to either. But the *regium donum* has been, nevertheless, punctually drawn every quarter for these two fictitious congregations, and, of course, is intended to be drawn until what are gravely called the *vacancies* are filled up. In all the synodical returns to government these congregations are described as only 'vacant,' nor was the slightest intimation ever given when asking for increase or equalization of bounty, that money was already obtained under such unusual circumstances.'

Another flagrant abuse connected with this endowment is that of its continuance with ministers suspended from the ministerial office, and pronounced by ecclesiastical authority disqualified for the discharge of official duty. Such charitable laxity of principle deserves the severest reprehension.

'We know a town in Ulster,' says a writer in an able article on this subject in the 'Congregational Magazine' for May 1838, 'in which are two ministers, each separated by the discipline of his synod from his former congregation, and each *drunk* every day in the week, sabbath included, and each supported by *regium donum!* A list of the ministers who have been suspended or degraded—a catalogue of the crimes for which the sentence was passed—the amount of the sums of *regium donum* they were permitted to retain—would astonish and even astound British Christians. Yea more; a list of the ministers now living, and though not exercising the ministry, yet receiving the whole or part of this parliamentary grant, would excite very painful emotions in the breasts of the Christian and the patriot.'

We may have occasion to advert to other abuses before closing this paper, but the subject is too heart-sickening to be dwelt upon.

In 1840, a union took place between the Synod of Ulster and the Secession Synod. The two bodies had, indeed, become so assimilated in spirit, that this event was nothing more than the natural result of existing tendencies. A small party stood opposed to it, but being men of feeble minds, and generally of no great moral influence, their opposition had but little effect; and more especially while denouncing the general body from which they stood apart, they still clung to the great source of corruption, the *regium donum.*

As these bodies appeared now under a united form, it was necessary to obtain the approval of the ruling powers, which was tantamount to an assurance of the continuance of the parliamentary grant. Intimation was previously conveyed to the Lord-Lieutenant, informing his Grace of what was about to take place. His Excellency signified his approval by transmitting a batch of rules for the endowment of the new congregations, for which he had the thanks of the body in an humble address. The Presbyterians of Ireland have often boasted of their freedom from state control. What sort of independence that is, in which they so much rejoice, the following extract from this address will serve to show.

'We desire,' say they, 'to return our humble and respectful thanks for the special interest your Excellency has taken in organising a system of rules for the endowment of our new congregations; and though the rules transmitted have not fully met the hopes of the Assembly, yet relying on your Excellency's experienced kindness, we trust they may be so modified as to afford unmixed satisfaction.'

The Lord-Lieutenant replied:—

'In the regulations which after much consideration have been finally laid down for the endowment of your new congregations, I cannot hold out any prospect of change.'

Such was the language of the state.

Since then an arrangement, however, has been effected with the government, not quite, perhaps, to 'meet fully the hopes of the assembly,' but such as is likely to prove permanent. It was the wish of the endowed that the individual payments should be equalized, by raising them to the highest point on the scale, namely £100. to each minister. The government did not accede to this, but so far agreed that each minister should have £75. per annum, continuing £100. per annum, however, with those who enjoyed it, till their death or removal.

The *regium donum*, on its present footing, may be obtained by any Presbyterian minister on complying with the following preliminaries. On his induction to a vacant charge, he must transmit a memorial to the Lord-Lieutenant stating the fact of his settlement, and that his congregation have agreed to raise £35. per annum for his support, and praying that his Excellency may be pleased to order the payment to him of the portion of royal bounty allotted to such congregation. The accuracy of the memorial must be certified by the moderator of the presbytery. Formerly it was necessary for the minister to take the oath of allegiance, but this has been dispensed with. The Lord-Lieutenant, looking at the matter politically, if there is no civil obstacle, assents to the petition. But in order to the continuance of the endowment, it is necessary that an annual report be transmitted to the castle, to the effect that the sum of £35. has been raised during the year for the minister's support. This is an important link in the arrangement as connecting the body closely with the government. Those ministers ordained before 1839 are not subjected to this regulation, but obtain their endowments irrespective of the amount raised for their support.

A new congregation must have been established for three years before it can obtain the endowment, and any congregation remaining vacant for more than twelve months loses the donum, and comes under a similar regulation. There are two distributors of the grant, Dr. Henry, of Armagh, who has been recently appointed president of the new college at Belfast, and a gentleman of the name of Hutcheson, residing in Tandragee, both of whom receive handsome salaries from government.

There are somewhere about 400 orthodox Presbyterian ministers in Ireland who participate in the parliamentary grant, and the Presbyterian population with which they stand connected has been generally reckoned about 624,000.

A good deal of missionary zeal has of late years been awakened in the body. An Irish Presbyterian orator recently adverting in Exeter Hall to this fact, gave the credit of it to the stimulus imparted by the London Missionary Society, and stated that a few years back his church had been like the Dead Sea. It must not be forgotten, however, that every one who contributes to the Home Mission fund, is thereby helping indirectly to increase the burdens of his country. An effort is made in the south and west to collect a few Presbyterians and straggling Scotchmen, who have a predilection for the system, and a minister is sent to them, and supported out of the Mission fund till such time as he can obtain the government endowment.

We have known the prospect of founding congregations which might obtain in a short time the donum, held forth as an inducement to contributors for continued and increased support. Besides, we have reason to believe, there are some congregations who receive so much from this fund, as enables them to make up the sum for the support of their minister, which must be returned to government, in order to the continuance of the endowment.

From our brief view of the character of this form of ecclesiastical endowment, it is obvious what immense influence it must give the government over its recipients. A regular ecclesiastical establishment, is, in some respects, less to be deprecated than a *regium donum*. The incumbent of a parish, may oppose the measures of the ruling powers with impunity, but the recipient of a *regium donum* never can. The truth of this remark, is abundantly manifested in the case before us. The lord lieutenant may withhold the *regium donum* from any Presbyterian minister in Ireland, without assigning any reason whatever. Such a stretch of authority has, we believe, seldom been resorted to, for there has been no occasion for it, but let any one in the receipt of the *regium donum* fall into the extreme class of political opinion, and he will soon experience to his cost, the full verity of our statement. Besides, should the ministry be dissatisfied with the conduct of the receivers of this grant, they can very easily leave it out of the estimates to be voted for the next year. After all, it is in the power of Parliament to reject it when it comes to the annual vote. It has in every view of it, very much the appearance of a reward held out to obedient children, but altogether dependent on their good conduct. Apart, therefore, from the secularising influence of such a grant, it must necessarily engender a spirit of sycophancy, foreign to the free and dignified bearing of independent minds.

But the worst effects of this endowment appear in the spiritual condition of the body. Its pernicious influence on both pastors and people, is almost everywhere apparent. A cold formal profession has, in very many instances, assumed the name, and usurped the place of vital godliness. The springs of Christian liberality among the people have been dried up. We can affirm of some considerable congregations that for years the sum raised for the support of their ministers has been perfectly trifling, not perhaps amounting to £5 per annum. This state of things is candidly admitted by Mr. Mathews, in the pamphlet before us:—

'The seat-holders in many congregations do not by any means pay their fair proportion towards paying the minister; and, in fact, the ministers of other dissenting congregations have, in certain stations, better salaries without any *regium donum*, than the Presbyterian clergy in the same parts, and with wealthier followers, have with it. A people who are well able to support their minister, but who find the government ready to bear a large proportion of the expense, very naturally save up their own money, and give little to the minister or to missionary claims.'

Some large congregations have not for several years contributed £35 per annum for their minister's support, and would of course have lost the endowment, had not the government arrangements been prospective, and only applicable therefore to congregations over which pastors had been settled after the period fixed upon for the commencement of its operation. There are cases, however, which would be effected by the arrangement referred to, where indeed its operation is avoided by shifts which it would take much logic to reconcile with any system of Christian ethics. These shifts we need not enumerate, but the result is, that a return is transmitted to the castle, which is received as *bona fide*, to the effect that the congregation has raised the sum requisite to entitle it to the royal bounty, while perhaps a considerable proportion of that sum has been contributed from the pocket of the minister himself, or by some wealthy relative, a father, it may be, or a father-in-law, who gives a sum sufficient to enable his clerical relative to secure the allowance of the State. Many seem to think that the government of the country, having made a provision for their ministers, they are bound in duty to contribute little or nothing at all. This feeling of unwillingness, occasioned by the circumstances of the case, has unhappily engendered a sense of inability. It were indeed a hopeless task to persuade some Presbyterian congregations, that they have the ability, had they only the will, to support their pastors. In the face of the plainest facts, they stare at the affirmation as implying an impossibility. Though pointed to their poor Roman catholic countrymen, on the one hand, supporting a system of error by their own contributions; and on the other hand, to a portion, resolute though not large, of their Presbyterian brethren, together with the whole of the Wesleyans, Independents, and Baptists, supporting their teachers entirely by their free-will offerings, and the help of their wealthier brethren, they refuse to be instructed, and wrap themselves up in blindness.

One way in which the secularizing influence of this endowment operates, appears clearly in the practice of some of the most worldly men in the body, training up their sons from their boyhood for the Christian ministry. This fact is sufficiently notorious. The habit of placing young men under a process of preparation for filling the most important office in the church, before they have even been admitted into its fellowship, is so decidedly anti-scriptural, that we lack terms sufficiently emphatic to denounce its sinfulness and utter incongruity. In some particular places, a great disposition prevails among the ministers themselves, to bring up their sons for the ministry; and in certain localities, which we could name, the office has become nearly hereditary. No wonder that the love of government pay, inspired in the nursery, cherished in the school, and fostered in the college, should appear so strong in after-life. We once had an opportunity of looking at the raw materials in an early stage of preparation for the sacred office, and the impression has not yet left our minds.

While this endowment has had the effect of drying up the liberality of the people, it has greatly contributed to foster a secular spirit among its recipients, the natural effect, no doubt, of their peculiar position. One devotes himself to his farm, another to his merchandise, whilst a third is engaged in the laborious work perhaps of teaching. On a summer afternoon, one might with little trouble, obtain the spectacle, in certain localities, of some worthy ecclesiastic, with his umbrella over his head to protect him from the sun, with all becoming gravity, taking the oversight, not by constraint, but willingly, of some dozen-and-half of females employed in weeding his flax crop. It would not be difficult to refer to various cases where the village pastor sustains, in his own person also, the character of the village schoolmaster. In a case or two we suspect a visit might reveal his reverence, in conjunction with his worthy spouse, taking stock, or perhaps balancing the books. A memorial was presented a short time ago to his excellency the Lord-lieutenant, by a number of the inhabitants of a certain country town, praying his excellency to withdraw the bounty from a certain Presbyterian minister in the place, on the ground that being engaged in trade, it was impossible he could devote the whole of his energies to the duties of his sacred calling. The memorialists stated, moreover, that they felt it a grievance, that one having an endowment from the State as a Christian minister, should be allowed to employ the capital thence obtained in competing in trade with his fellow-citizens and neighbours. The memorial was remitted to the moderator of the general assembly for investigation; how the matter ended we did not hear.

But the evil effects of this endowment are not confined to the body who receives it. It has created prejudice in the Roman catholic mind, which has almost totally barricaded every avenue against the missionary efforts of Presbyterians, thus shutting their darkened countrymen out from the means of enlightenment around them. No ray of truth can, in the view of the Romanist, possibly descend through the selfish and political medium of a *regium donum*. Several worthy men, it is true, among the endowed Presbyterians, are labouring hard for the conversion of the Romanists against this mighty disadvantage, among whom may be classed the present moderator, a most excellent man: but their success has been extremely limited, and this is owing, in no small degree, to their peculiar position. Paddy is too clear-sighted not to perceive that the State-paid Presbyterian minister is partaker of the fruit of his toil, as well as the more richly endowed parish parson. Appeal to the Irishman's generosity, and there is not a more warm-hearted being in the world; but subject his little property, his potatoes, and his pig, to the crushing weight of an impost, to sustain a religious system which he hates, and you array against you all the worst passions of his nature. His very generosity is turned into gall, and he looks upon you as the enslaver of his country, and the would-be enslaver of his mind. Had Presbyterianism been proof against the lure of state patronage, it might have been the instrument under God of immense good to the Roman catholics of Ireland. The Presbyterian church might have taken its place in the very front ranks in a grand spiritual expedition against the darkness of popery, diffusing blessings in every stage of its progress, till the empire of the pope in the sister isle had been subverted, and its millions of generous children brought into the light and liberty of Bible Christianity. This honour, we believe, is now reserved for other parties. Let unendowed bodies see to it, that they lose it not.

It is obvious to common observation that endowed Presbyterianism in Ireland has been, and still is, a grand prop of the Irish ecclesiastical establishment. Had the Presbyterian body been true to themselves, to their country, or to the cause of God, that monstrous anomaly had long, ere now, been removed. The Irish regium donum is a mere outwork, raised by state policy in defence of 'the monster grievance,' the Irish church. 'The powers that be' have never manifested much love for Presbyterianism, as such. The caresses of the state have not been the fruits of pure affection, but the corrupt blandishments of a sinister policy. Maintain the protestant ascendancy, fortify the ecclesiastical establishment, protect it from the hatred of the Romanist, and the worldly politician cares not a straw about presbytery. The present ministry gave abundant proof of this. Sir Robert Peel has shown very little disposition to augment the favours of the state so far as the evangelical Presbyterians are concerned. The unitarian party has had a much greater share of his sympathies. The golden cord which connects them with government, he feels to be strong enough for state purposes, and this is all he cares about. The game played by successive governments has always been to conciliate the Presbyterians, and disarm their opposition to the state church by means of endowments. With a body so numerous and influential, resolutely opposed to it, the ecclesiastical establishment could not have been maintained. English bayonets would have been unequal to such an end. On this point the policy of the Presbyterian body has been exceeding narrow and short-sighted. The withdrawment of the endowments of the episcopal church would have been worth fifty times the regium donum to them. Free episcopacy could not maintain its ground in a poor country like Ireland against free Presbyterianism. Instead of drawing over, by its wealth, ecclesiastical emoluments and polished society, as it does at present from the ranks of Presbyterianism, the more wealthy and refined in that connexion, we feel persuaded that the volume would have been altogether in favour of the latter—the tables would have been quite turned. But the gift blinds the eye. How often a little present advantage appears in the eyes of weak and erring man, to outweigh a great prospective good!

The future influence of endowed Presbyterianism in Ireland on the interests of religion and that of the empire, must be great, much greater than many seem to think. Viewing the *regium donum* as a corner-stone in the structure of ecclesiastical establishments, we should regard its detachment or destruction as the precursor of mighty changes, and much-needed reforms. The influence of the body must also be great in retarding the advent of these, by clinging to their endowments. We confess we are not very sanguine as regards the 'consummation so devoutly to be wished for.' We are not ignorant of the power of habit in dimming the perceptive faculty, and blunting the sensibilities of conscience. That the eyes of the Presbyterian clergy generally, are therefore likely soon to be opened to the evils of the parliamentary grant which bows down their strength, we have but little hopes; and that impressed with the sense of its unscriptural character and secularising tendency, they will be speedily brought to evince the moral heroism requisite for its renunciation, we have no faith. We speak *generally*, however, of their blindness to the true character of the grant, for there are several who see its baneful tendency, but have not sufficient strength of principle to cast it to the winds. There are several whom we could name, each of whom might in truth say—

'Video meliora proboque sed deteriora sequor.'

We ourselves have heard from the lips of some, rather curious principles of casuistry given out to justify their acceptance of it. We are glad, however, to perceive that the people are beginning to wake up to a perception of its unhappy effects. The example of the Free Church in Scotland has not been altogether lost upon them. We have reason to know, that a pretty general feeling against the government grant begins to prevail among the best-informed and religious portion of the Presbyterian population. Few, except perhaps the mere creatures of the clergy, would have the courage to enter on a formal defence of it. An indication of this state of feeling has come recently before the public. During the sittings of the last annual meeting of the General Assembly of the Presbyterian church in

Ireland, held in Dublin, two memorials, one from Belfast, and another from Londonderry, were presented, urging on the members the duty of immediately giving up the *regium donum*, and suggesting a plan for a sustentation fund, like that of the Free Church. The memorials met with but little favour, but it is to be hoped the public discussion of the subject will not be without beneficial results. The people have much in their power. May they have strength of principle and boldness worthy of their lineage! They can if they will, burst the golden fetters of their spiritual instructors, and thereby invest themselves with immortal honour. In the Free Church movement the ministers led the people; but in the emancipation of endowed Irish Presbyterianism, the honour of leading the ministers seems reserved for the people. We should be delighted to behold the expression of popular feeling in the shape of a sustentation fund. This would tell powerfully on the endowed ministers. It would show them the people were in earnest, and that they were prepared to act as well as think. Why not begin it? We feel assured it would not prove a failure. The Irish are naturally generous, only there must be a channel for their generosity to flow in. Open such a channel, and the golden stream would soon convince the most incorrigible of the inutility of a *regium donum*.

If we may judge from the signs of the times, the period is not distant, (indeed, we may say it now is), when the Presbyterians of Ireland will be called to give up their endowments on other grounds than those on which they have been generally appealed to—from love to their country, to avert a great national calamity—the civil endowment of Romanism. We are fast approaching a mighty crisis in the history of Ireland, perhaps in that of the empire. A storm threatens. The cloud already thickens, and the thunder is heard in the distance. The question of the endowment of the Roman-catholic priesthood of Ireland will prove one of the most stirring, which have agitated the minds of men since the revolution. That the priests will accept of endowments, provided they are offered sufficient in amount and in their own way, we have no doubt. But should this event take place, on whom will the blame rest? We answer emphatically, on the endowed Presbyterians of Ireland. Their regium donum has furnished the type of the endowment of the priests, and it is in their power, by the timely rejection of their own endowment, to prevent the endowment of the latter now, and for ever. The following passage in the 'Protest' now before us of the Eastern Reformed Presbyterian Synod against the endowment of Maynooth College, is so much in point, that we cannot forbear quoting it.

'The General Assembly of the Presbyterian church occupy a most important post. In our estimation, the balance of power is in their hands On them it depends, under Providence, whether the Roman-catholic religion shall be the established religion of Ireland or not. If they give up their royal bounty, it *cannot* be established. If they do not give up that grant, *it will* be established. This opinion we expressed ten years ago in our 'Signs of the Times.' In this opinion we are now confirmed. The Assembly themselves have confirmed us. Their most talented members have, in public meetings, declared that the smallest movement of their little finger would suffice to overturn the tythe system. Now, if the tythe system were overturned, and the regium donum given up, the ladder would be removed, by which Roman-catholics can climb to power and ascendency.'

Will the Presbyterians be persuaded to break down 'the ladder,' and save their country? In their present position, their opposition to the endowment of Romanism must of necessity be feeble. Though their recent apathy in the Maynooth affair may, in some degree, be referred to the prospect of obtaining an endowment for a newly-projected Presbyterian college, which occupied the minds of some of their leading ministers at the time, yet many of the more intelligent classes felt their hands tied up by the regium donum. Holding this grant, they cannot move with effect against the project referred to. Will they give it up? We pause for a reply. Deeply should we grieve to behold (what we are free to confess we fear may be the case) this large body wheedled into quiescent compliance by the cajolery of an unprincipled cabinet, and their moral energy annihilated by the addition of a few thousand pounds to the annual parliamentary grant—the endowment of a college, perhaps, and the establishment of the grant on a permanent footing, like that of Maynooth. The British lion in such a case might roar, the voice of the people be heard from Land's End to John o'Groat's, but the crafty minister would probably chuckle in his sleeve, and say, with a significant shrug, like Sir Robert Peel, during the Maynooth agitation, that he would be prepared to pause in his policy only when the protestants of Ireland had pronounced against the measure.

The dissolution of the connexion of the Presbyterians of Ireland with 'the powers that be,' would be an event of the highest importance to religion, and the interests of civil and religious liberty. We know the body, and though enervated by their present connexion with the state, we can confidently affirm that the elements of greatness are in their nature. They are the descendants of Knox and Melville. The spirit of freedom slumbers in their breasts. Their emancipation would be, in the full sense of the terms, the grand prelude to the emancipation of the sister isle. It would speedily elevate the standard of piety among themselves, open the founts of Christian liberality, and prepare them for uniting with other bodies of Christians, in giving to their country the blessings of a pure Christianity. They would at once become resolute and bold asserters of anti-state church principles, and before the mighty onset of their combined energies, the Irish state church, that source of everlasting irritation, would be subverted. This would be the death-blow of the establishment principle. Romanism would not, could not, dare not attempt to revive it.

The dissenters of England have not discharged the duty they owe to their endowed brethren in Ireland—that of faithful remonstrance. The conduct of some leading ministers in the ranks of English dissent, in regard to that paltry affair the English *regium donum*, has, on the contrary, tended to justify the Irish Presbyterians in the acceptance of theirs; and one honoured name in the theological world, has, we know, been frequently appealed to as affording a complete sanction for their conduct. By this means the hands of the little band of men in the sister island, who are striving by word and deed to vindicate the scripturality and justice of the voluntary principle, have been greatly weakened. The dissenters of Britain will only have discharged their responsibilities to Irish Presbyterians, when they have scattered over the length and breadth of the land addresses and faithful remonstrances, exposing the evil of this grant,

> 'Thick as autumnal leaves that strew the brooks
> In Vallombrosa.—'

We have said nothing of the publications heading this article. 'The history of Dr. Reid,' though savouring considerably of the spirit of his party, is a work of considerable research, and will amply repay a careful perusal. Mr. Mathew's pamphlet is the production of a thorough-paced opponent of voluntaryism, and its testimony therefore to the corrupting influence of the *regium donum*, becomes the more valuable. We almost wonder it has not been suppressed, or bought up and destroyed by the parties it so seriously affects. The protest of the Eastern Reformed Synod against the endowment of Maynooth, is a liberal and enlightened declaration of great principles, which ought, and will yet prevail. This body are generally known in Ireland by the name of Covenanters, and though for the most part poor, have never yet been lured to the acceptance of a *regium donum*. The document referred to, has, we believe, done good.

Art. II.—*Anastasis; or the Doctrine of the Resurrection of the Body Rationally and Scripturally considered.* By George Bush, Professor of Hebrew, New York City University. London: Wiley and Putnam.

Three-and-forty years after the death of John Wycliffe, in pursuance of a decree of the council of Constance, the mortal remains of that noble servant of God were dragged forth from their resting place, burned, and the ashes scattered on the waters of a neighbouring brook. 'The brook,' says Fuller, 'did convey his ashes into Avon, Avon into Severn, Severn into the narrow seas, they into the ocean.' Those remains had been committed to the dust by plain men, who believed, in their simplicity, that 'the self-same bodies of the saints' that were laid in the grave, would be raised at the coming of Christ, and 'made like unto his glorious body.' And even in this enlightened and philosophic age, such, we presume, is still the current belief of the Christian church. Nor is it imagined that their disinterment, dispersion, and the countless transformations to which they may have been subject, perhaps on every shore, shall avail to rob those sacred ashes of their exalted destiny. At the same time, it must be admitted, that such an expectation is not unattended with considerable difficulties. The kind and degree of identity between the buried and the raised body have been reckoned open questions, and discussed with much acumen, if not with much success. The point is one on which it is very easy to ask perplexing questions, and not at all easy to answer them; except by the general reply, that the doctrine of the resurrection must be received implicitly as matter of faith, upon the divine testimony, and that God is able to accomplish his declarations, whether we are able to understand them or not.

Philosophical scruples and sceptical arguments on this subject are by no means of recent origin in the Christian church. Not only did the philosophers of the Garden and of the Porch scout the doctrine of the Resurrection as an absurdity, when alluded to by Paul on Mars' Hill; but among the apostle's own converts, there were some who asked, '*How* are the dead raised, and with what body do they come?' The apostle's answer, it must be confessed, is more pithy than complimentary:—'Thou fool!—God giveth it a body, as it hath pleased him.' But had Paul lived in the nineteenth century, and been an inductive philosopher, no doubt he would have replied differently. And as Professor Bush is an inductive philosopher, and does live in the nineteenth century, we are not to wonder that he feels dissatisfied with the apostle's mode of treating the question. Indeed, if the apostle really was acquainted with 'the true doctrine of the resurrection,' 'as inferred by reason' and set forth in the volume before us, it is to us perfectly unaccountable how he came to give such an answer, even as it was. He was writing not to Jewish converts, but to Greeks. He could therefore have no inducement to adhere to a mode of representation founded on a popular misinterpretation of the Hebrew Scriptures. Nothing could have been easier than at once to dispel all doubts, by explaining that the resurrection of the dead did not mean the resurrection of the body, but simply the immortality of the soul, as taught by some of their own philosophers, and even poets. For, according to Professor Bush, the 'view' of the future state contained in the poetry of Homer approaches much nearer to the truth than those derived from a *literal* interpretation of the Christian Scriptures.* This assertion from a Christian divine may possibly startle some of our more simple-minded readers. We may as well, therefore, state at once the leading views of Professor Bush, as unfolded in this volume. After a general discussion of the question (Pt. i.), and an elaborate examination of particular passages of Scripture bearing on the point, he sums up the result, so far, to which his logic and exegesis lead, in these words :—'*that the resurrection of the body is not a doctrine sanctioned either by reason or revelation, so far as we have hitherto interrogated the testimony of each.*' (p. 274.) With this conclusion, several others, equally or even more important, are closely connected. The resurrection takes place at death. The 'general resurrection,' therefore, is not a future event, but a process that has being going on ever since the death of Adam. The second advent of Christ is not personal, but providential: the 'last day' has long since commenced; the 'great white throne' long been set; and the 'last trumpet' long begun to sound: and 'that blessed hope, and the glorious appearing of the great God and our Saviour,' is a chimera, the mongrel offspring of Jewish metaphors and bad exegesis! Those who have any acquaintance with the system of Emmanuel Swedenborg, will recognise the coincidence between these positions, and the tenets of the New Jerusalem apostle. And had the author of 'Anastasis' come forward as a professed disciple of Swedenborg, we should scarcely have deemed it necessary to occupy our pages with an examination of his book. But Mr. Bush takes other ground. He admits the agreement between his views and those of that northern light, but states that he has arrived at them by an independent process, and claims to establish them, not on the inspired disclosures of the Swedish assessor, but by a 'fair

* See pp. 72, 73.

and uncensurable exegesis' of those Scriptures, with which ordinary Christians rest content. True, the popular errors which he aims to explode, are countenanced by 'the *letter* of Scripture,' were connived at as harmless, or even useful, by the Great Teacher, and probably participated in by the apostles themselves. But then, 'the knowledge of revelation is progressive.' At the approach of sound philosophy, as if touched by Ithuriel's spear, these errors vanish; while (as necessity is the parent of invention) 'a refined exegesis' discloses unsuspected resources and unheard-of expedients, by which the plain but inconvenient meaning of Scripture may be got rid of in the most satisfactory manner, and the philosophical sense be substituted. The only consolation (if it be one) is, that it is still '*safe*' for the preacher, in his 'pulpit references' to the subject of the resurrection, to adopt 'the scriptural mode of presentation,' 'whatever *esoteric* interpretation may be embraced.' The time will come when 'it will be at length everywhere conceded, that the destinies of our being are to be evolved according to established laws, and not in violation of them. These laws will be developed by the progress of scientific research, the conclusions of which will carry with them a force of authority as irresistible as the literal announcements of the sacred text.' When that time does come, we presume the human race will so far have outgrown the Bible as to dispense with the use of it altogether.

A brief examination of this volume is all that our limits allow, and some may think more than the importance of the work would claim, but for the confident pretensions with which it has been advertised, and the ruinous tendency of the principles on which the inquiry is conducted.

The introductory chapter, on the progressive character of our knowledge of revelation, contains some excellent remarks. We fully believe that the words uttered by Robinson two centuries ago were true, and are true still: 'the Lord hath yet more truth to break forth from his holy word.' But we utterly dissent from Mr. Bush's application of this principle. The profoundest student of the Bible has something yet to learn. But the great outline of truth may be understood by a child. And could any one fundamental doctrine (and such the resurrection has ever been deemed) be shown to be so stated in the Scriptures, as to be *inevitably misunderstood* by the mass of readers, this would go far to destroy all confidence in the Bible as the rule of faith. We freely confess, could we be convinced of the truth of Mr. Bush's philosophy, we would sooner abandon the inspiration of the New Testament than adopt his exegesis.

Part I. is occupied with the argument from reason. We must be pardoned for saying, that the writer appears to us possessed of an essentially illogical mind. He adduces the most fanciful analogies to prove what the strongest could not. He interweaves different lines of argument, and shifts his ground, in the most perplexing manner. He is far more abundant of interrogations than becomes a sound or calm reasoner. Repeatedly we have been tempted to lay down the volume in that sort of quiet despair that is apt to be produced when an opponent overwhelms you with a host of questions, relevant and irrelevant, without giving you opportunity to answer one. The learned Professor falls into that common yet obvious error of shallow reasoners, which regards a position or doctrine as disproved, merely by a statement of the objections or difficulties it involves. His notion of 'interrogating reason' seems to be, asking a reason for everything; while his mode of 'interrogating revelation' not a little resembles some methods of interrogation used (with similar success) in the Inquisition.

With some difficulty, we have succeeded in extricating and arranging the leading arguments advanced by the author against the resurrection of the body. They will be found, we believe, to be the following. First. The common doctrine does not explain *what* body is to be raised; for, from the constant change taking place in our frames, the soul really inhabits a succession of bodies in a long life; and no reason can be given why the preference should be awarded to the *last* of these (i. e. that which existed at death). Secondly. The resurrection body is to be 'a spiritual body,' and therefore cannot be the body that was buried. Thirdly. Difficulties 'absolutely insuperable' are thrown in the way of the common theory by the changes which the particles of the dead body undergo, dispersed by the operation of natural causes through air, earth, and ocean, and often becoming component parts of other human bodies. Fourthly. No conceivable *relation* can be made out between the buried and the raised body, in virtue of which the latter could be pronounced the *same* with the former. Fifthly. Multitudes of bodies either were never buried at all, or have long since vanished, every atom of them, from their place of sepulture; and how can they be raised from the grave if they are not there? Sixthly. It is very strange to suppose that the resurrection of bodies will be going on while the world is burning. Seventhly. No superior adaptedness can be imagined in any particular atoms of matter to become the abode of the glorified spirit. Perhaps we should add an eighth, which is the last in a more general form; namely, that no *end* can be answered by the resurrection of the body.

Those who are at all familiar with the subject, will not, we think, discover any thing particularly new in this vaunted 'argument from reason.' It is, as we have already observed, a mere statement of difficulties. The substance of the most important points may be found in Locke's famous controversy with the Bishop of Worcester. And it would not be easy, perhaps, to state them more forcibly than Locke, with his quiet humour, and racy, vigorous English, has done. Mr. Bush constantly speaks, indeed, as if the progress of modern physiological science had thrown some new and suprising light on the question. But, though modern science may have presented many points of the discussion under new aspects, or, at all events, altered the language in which we speak of them, we are not aware that it has really disclosed a single objection to the popular view, which might not have occurred, in substance, to any acute and reflective mind in the age of the apostles. A reasoner of that age could not tell, indeed, into how many gases, metals, and other ultimate elements the human frame was resolvable. He did not know that the putrefaction of animal substances furnished azote in the form of ammonia, as the food of plants. He might have very confused and erroneous notions of the nature and rapidity of the changes effected in the body by nutrition and other vital processes. But he knew perfectly well why corn flourished rankly on the recent battle-field. He did not suppose a man to have the same body when he is eighty that he had when he was born. He was quite aware that if a body, is burnt, it cannot be buried. And he might have a shrewd guess that, if one of the ancient Massagetæ had chanced to die soon after having paid the last pious honours to his respected grandsire by dining or supping off him, a question of ownership might be raised, touching the particles so disposed of. In other words, our antique sceptic might see all the real difficulties of the subject, without being prepared to rival Mr. Bush in acquaintance with modern physiology. Though, if the truth must be said, from the remarkable manner in which the Professor analyses the human body into 'gases, *earths*, metals, and *salts*,' we suspect his own chemistry to be of a very unsophisticated character. It might be ill-natured to judge of his botanical lore by the repeated use of the word 'stamen' as if it were the same with *semen*, or *germen*. Possibly that is the fault of an unscientific printer. But possibly, also, if our author knew more of physical science, he might expect less from it. The question is, in short, one of those which the progress of modern discoveries has left pretty much where it was. All this high-sounding verbiage about the 'demonstrations of physical science,' and the 'progress of scientific research,' and the parallels drawn with the discoveries of astronomy and geology, are mere rhetorical flourish, when applied to a topic like this.

We must be content to discuss the question on grounds often debated, and little aided by the lights of the Baconian philosophy. Some of the foregoing objections strike us as trivial; others, as presumptuous; and the most forcible, as inconclusive, because a mere statement of difficulties cannot weigh an atom against clear positive evidence, if we have it. Every one knows Dr. Johnson's remark about a *plenum* and a *vacuum*. And this is one of those simple but fundamental lessons in reasoning, which a writer ought not still to have to learn, who aspires to dispel the errors of eighteen centuries, and reform the faith of Christendom. Yet a large part of the reasoning in this volume might be resolved into two sentences: 'I do not understand *how* it can be;' and, 'I do not see what use it would be.' Possibly, most conclusive logician! but it may be true, for all that. These remarks apply to the first, sixth, seventh, and eighth objections. The second objection is supported by the assertion (p. 40), that 'a material body is a body of flesh and blood,' which St. Paul declares cannot inherit the kingdom of heaven. What is the ground for this singular assertion, we must leave our readers to divine. The professor has already showed himself chemist enough to analyse the body into 'gases, earths, metals, and salts.' And we venture to think it perfectly possible for these materials to be re-moulded in some form as different from flesh and blood as diamond is from charcoal, or oxygen and azote from nitric acid. But, what is still more singular, at p. 72, we find the professor actually identifying *matter* with *substance*. At least, since 'body' certainly implies matter, we do not see what else can be made of that extraordinary passage. Whereupon the conclusion would seem to follow, by this author's logic, that the resurrection body must be a body of flesh and blood! This argument is introduced as though considerable importance were attached to it, thus: 'The truth is, the whole theory proceeds upon a fundamental fallacy, which a single glance of the mental eye detects.' Having prepared our minds to see this 'fundamental fallacy' fully exposed and put *hors de combat*, we were a little surprised to find it dismissed within a dozen lines, and the next paragraph commencing thus: 'But, waiving all objection on this score, the doctrine of the resurrection of the same body, *in any sense whatever*, encounters difficulties in our view absolutely insuperable, arising from the changes and new combinations which the particles of the dead body undergo in the interval between death and the resurrection.' (p. 40.)

This objection is the third in our foregoing enumeration. The fifth is closely connected with it. It is urged, that bodies which have been burnt, devoured, washed away in the lapse of ages by filtering rain or rushing torrents, scattered in the dust of the desert, or exhaled in the vapours of the ocean, cannot be raised from the tomb, because they either never were there, or have long ceased to be. A very simple answer may be given to all this. The doctrine of the New Testament, as commonly understood, is, that those bodies which are in the graves at the time of the resurrection, will come forth. The objection is, that many bodies will not then be in the graves. Every one sees there is no inconsistency between these propositions. The latter is true, but it does not imply that the former is false. But it is urged, further, that it is inconceivable that those dispersed and transformed materials should be re-united into a body. Why so? There is nothing in this physically impossible. It is a simple question of fact, to be determined by the divine testimony, or, if that be not explicit, by the event itself. But it is especially urged, that some of these scattered particles may belong to different bodies, and who shall then decide the conflicting claims? The author has himself supplied an illustration most unfortunate in the application it suggests, by alluding to the famous question of the Sadducees—'In the resurrection, whose wife shall she be of the seven?' And we are forcibly tempted to remind the learned Professor of our Saviour's reply. But as he has himself furnished what may be regarded as a sort of *reductio ad absurdum* of this puissant objection, and at the same time a charming specimen of his logic, we cannot resist the inclination to transcribe it. After a strange passage about dancing dervishes, Alexander's horse, and Goliath of Gath, he proceeds :—

'Suppose an individual body of the present day to consist of a million of particles, *what is easier than to conceive* than that each of these particles was derived from one of a million of bodies that have lived in former ages? If these bodies were each to claim its own on the ground of the same right which the present possessor has to them (?), what would be left to *him*, from whence to form a resurrection body? But each one of this million of bodies might, perhaps, owe its component particles in like manner to as many predecessors; *and we think it a fair question, whether, if we were to follow out the supposition to its legitimate results, it would not compel the conclusion that the whole human race must be resolved back into Adam; and every animal and every vegetable back into the first animal, and the first plant ever created.*'

The italics are ours. We leave this astonishing piece of logic to our readers, only fearing that they will blame us for occupying our pages at all, with a writer of whose reasoning capacity this extract is a specimen.

No doubt many equally absurd things have been said on the

opposite side. We do not draw our notions of the resurrection from Young's 'Night Thoughts,' nor do we pretend to justify the eloquent extravagancies of President Davies's sermons. But as to the general question, we repeat, it is simply a question of fact. If there be any sufficient end to be answered (of which we are not the judges) in re-assembling the identical atoms which formed the earthly dwelling of the glorified spirit, who dares affirm that Omniscience cannot trace every atom of that fabric through all its transformations, and Omnipotence guide its course, and prepare it for its destined employment, as easily as if it had been sealed in some inviolable coffer till the day of doom? Nothing perishes, or is lost. There is not an idle or supernumerary atom in the universe. The ultimate particles, 'the highest part of the dust of the world,' are as much the objects of divine knowledge as suns and systems. And unless any one will affirm that God does not know what is become of Wycliffe's dust, or is unable to collect it again, there is clearly nothing contrary to reason in the supposition, that the actual particles of his dishonoured clay shall be inwoven in the imperishable vestment with which he shall be clad at the day of the manifestation of the sons of God.'

The only really perplexing objection in the foregoing formidable array, is, we think, the fourth. It is difficult, perhaps impossible, to say, what it is in virtue of which the resurrection body can be pronounced the *same* as the body which was buried. That which constitutes the identity of the human body, in infancy, childhood, manhood, and age, is not the identity of its particles, for these are constantly changing, but the continuance and oneness of that living power which unites them. That mysterious power which we call *life*, forms the invisible centre round which the material particles ceaselessly move, coming and going, never two hours numerically the same, but still bound together in one system, which has its growth, maturity, and decay. But, life being withdrawn, we seem compelled to resort to a new principle of identity, and know of none but the numerical sameness of the component atoms. This, we admit, is a difficult point. Science can tell us nothing, and Scripture is silent. But the essence of the doctrine of the resurrection is not involved in its determination either way. That *the same body* shall be raised, is nowhere stated as a universal fact in Scripture, but only that the dead shall be raised. All the declarations of Scripture would be literally fulfilled, if those bodies which at the time of the 'last trump' are still undissolved in the tombs, should be raised, and the rest produced, as Adam's was at first, from the dust of the earth; such transforming process passing upon both as is represented in the words, 'we shall be changed.' Be it remembered, we are not stating any theory or opinion of our own. We are merely aiming to show the utter inadequacy of the reasoning of 'Anastasis.' The writer, after all, has but busied himself with some of the outworks of the doctrine he attacks, and without even dismantling these, flatters himself that he has overthrown the citadel. Admitting all his objections to be as forcible as we think them the reverse, they would not affect the substance of the Catholic faith on this point, nor advance him one step towards what is really his main theorem, that the resurrection takes place at death, without an intermediate and disembodied state. There is the vital point of the controversy.

We have not space, and our readers would probably not have patience, to follow Mr. Bush into his exposition of 'The True Body of the Resurrection, as inferred by Reason.' It is sheer conjecture, not only with no real foundation, but with hardly the semblance of one: for the fanciful analogies adduced scarcely deserve that name. Because 'a vital principle, pervading the whole frame, co-exists with the intellectual principle *in* the body, is not the presumption perfectly legitimate,' naively asks the Professor, 'that they coexist also *out* of the body? In other words, that we go into the spiritual world with a *psychical body?*' The fact is, our author theorizes, not on what science has discovered, but on what he has a shrewd guess it *will* discover some day. A most un-Baconian method, it must be confessed. The vital principle is a matter on which we are almost utterly in the dark. The view to which physiologists now incline, if we are not mistaken, is, that it is *a force*. If so, the Professor's airy hypothesis is blown away at once. It is much the same as if one should say, because a principle of motion, pervading the whole mass, exists *in* a flying cricket-ball, the presumption is 'perfectly legitimate,' that it may also exist *out* of it. And this would be, we presume, a 'psychical' cricket-ball!

We have already exceeded the limits we intended to occupy; otherwise we might have said a word or two on that portion of the volume which, out of courtesy, we must call exegetical. Every passage of the Old and New Testament bearing on the subject, is submitted to elaborate examination. The Professor has not studied the German craft of exegesis in vain. Accommodation, Jewish prejudice, the imperfect ideas of the apostles, all stand him in good stead. When other resources fail, he resorts to the 'general drift' of Scripture, or sets text against text, and throws the responsibility of reconciling them on his reader. One singular method of disposing of a New Testament passage, is by showing that it is only a 'development' of some passage in the Old Testament; and as the latter has been shown not to teach the resurrection, of course the former cannot! This is on the 'principle' (p. 279) 'that the New Testament teachings on this theme are but the expansion of the Old.' But the most daring length, perhaps, to which the author is led in support of his views, is his explanation of the express declaration of our Saviour, recorded Luke xxiv. 39, as a sort of pious fraud—a kind deception practised on his disciples for their consolation. 'And when we consider,' says Mr. Bush, 'the object to be attained by such an illusion, we see nothing inconsistent or unworthy the Divine Impersonation of Truth in having recourse to it.' Comment on this is needless.

The truth is, this writer does not come to the page of Scripture in the attitude of a learner—the only one in which divine Truth condescends to unveil herself to us. He comes to it with his foregone conclusion: the doctrine of the resurrection is contrary to reason; therefore, this and that, and the other text, cannot teach it, but must be shown capable of another meaning. Whereupon he proceeds to 'interrogate' accordingly.

The apostle Paul warns Timothy against some speculators, 'who concerning the truth have erred, saying that the resurrection is passed already, and overthrow the faith of some.' If our remarks shall serve to convince our readers, that the confident pretensions of this volume are unfounded, that its philosophy is shallow, its logic unsound, its exegesis based on false and fatal principles; and to indicate at the same time the manner in which objections may be met, and the spirit in which the whole subject should be studied, our object will be attained.

Art. III.—1. *Oliver Newman: A New-England Tale.* By the late Robert Southey. Longman, & Co.

2. *The New Timon: A Romance of London.* In four parts. Colburn.

3. *Bells and Pomegranates.* By Robert Browning, Author of Paracelsus; Nos. 7. Moxon.

4. *Ballad Romances.* By R. H. Horne, Author of Orion, etc.; London. Ollier.

Oliver Newman, by the late Laureate, is only a fragment amounting to eighty pages of a small octavo. It forms no exception to the great fact, that those poems which the authors wrote in the latter days of a hard-writing life, and which they, themselves, never found sufficient interest in to finish, are not likely to interest the reader much more than they did the writer. Southey proposed to make a regular epic of it. Let us be thankful that he did not. Authors of late years, warned by the fate of their predecessors, have frequently during their life-time made an *auto-da-fè* of their loose papers, and unfinished productions. It is a very salutary practice; for those literary rag-gatherers, relatives, and trustees, generally bring forth and publish the very things which the unlucky deceased meant to die with him. It is exactly the case here. It is a mere study sweeping. Poetry, which in many men is very much a matter of temperament, and is only produced in its best state in the earlier periods of life, like the flower of that life, was of this kind pre-eminently in Southey. His poetic genius was not of that intense kind which absorbed and carried away the whole man; it was of an easy, though sufficiently seducing character, to engage him from time to time in long efforts. But it did not master him. He could take up his daily prose work, or his daily poetic work, as it best suited his humour. It was not likely, therefore, that as time advanced, and the zest for labour diminished, and the roseate hues of the young imagination faded, that the charm of poetry would continue to exist in him with sufficient force to make its production a luxury to himself, far less a necessity. Perhaps never did the poetry of any man depend more for its power of pleasing on those evaenscent lights, and as it were vernal odours of a delicate fancy, than Southey. With the exception of some parts of the Curse of Kehama and of Roderick, it is seldom that his soul is sufficiently fired with passion and zeal to make that fire and passion the very substance of his production. In most cases, the attractive quality of his verse is that peach-bloom of the fancy which is easily separable from the solid fruit, the dew and glitter on the dawn of a spring morning, which in the heat of the day disappear; in a word, the champagne spirit of the poetic feeling which gone, leaves a sweetish insipid liquor. The present poem is a striking example of this. There is no lack of good sound sense and right and wise sentiment in it, but we feel that the spirit has evaporated. It is mere prose in metre. As the first work of an unknown writer it must have ranked with those hundreds of poems, so-called, which are daily issued to the day-light that does not heed them. We should have said, this is only another of the manufactures of that vast class of people, who will not learn that any body can put words into metre, though few can put real poetry into the words. The few other fragments which fill up the volume are principally passages of the prophets arranged in rhythmical order, evidently rather for the author's own private pleasure, than with any idea of their ever being published.

In an appendix we are furnished with Southey's own prose caste of the work, from which we may see that the idea of such a subject worked into a regular poem, and that in Thalaba-verse, betrays at least a strong symptom of the giving way of that clear judgment of the fitness of things which was but the premonition of the total prostration of mind which made awfully melancholy the latter days of Southey. Nothing but the utmost vigour of genius and original life in the dialogue and general working out could have made such a thing tolerable. Southey would seem most totally to forget how fully and completely the ground was already occupied by Washington Irving and Cooper. There is not a piece of colonial or Indian history here to be introduced which was not already made use of, and made familiar to all readers; we mean which had not become so before Southey had made much progress with his poem, for the idea of it, it seems, was conceived so early as 1811. Its present advance, however, was not reached till 1829, by which time a moment's reflection must have shown that the whole subject was rifled by the popular writers just named. Perhaps this idea *did* occur to Southey, and determined him to lay the unfinished composition aside. In that case the fault of publication lies with the present editor. That we may show clearly the complete pre-occupation of the ground, we will give as concisely as we can the author's own detail of his plan.

'In reviewing Holmes's American Annals, I pointed out Philip's War as the proper subject of an Anglo-American Iliad. I have now fallen in love with it myself, and am brooding over it with the full intention of falling to work as soon as Pelayo is completed. The main interest will fix upon Goffe, the regicide, for whom I invent a Quaker son, a new character you will allow for heroic poetry. This Oliver Goffe, however, is to be the hero.'

The poem itself is in the first draught called Oliver Goffe.

The facts relating to those regicides whose fate is alluded to in the poem are as follows:—

'When the restoration appeared inevitable, Colonel Goffe, with his father-in-law, Colonel Whalley, seeing that their life was in danger, left the kingdom, and arrived in America on the 27th of July, 1660. For some time they resided at Cambridge, four miles from Boston, attending public service, and being received with respect and hospitality by the inhabitants. But when the Act of Indemnity, out of which they were expressly excepted, arrived at Boston in November, the magistrates withdrew their protection, and Whalley and Goffe retired to Newhaven. Here they were forced to conceal themselves, and eventually to fly to a retirement called Hatchet's Harbour, in the woods, where they remained two nights, till a cave in the side of a hill was prepared to conceal them. To this hill they gave the name of Providence, and remained some weeks in their hiding-place, sleeping when the weather was tempestuous, in a house near it. They behaved with great honour to their friends; and when Mr. Davenport, the minister of Newhaven, was suspected by the magistrates of concealing them, they went publicly to the deputy-governor of Newhaven to offer themselves up; but he refused to take any notice of them, suffering them to return again to the woods. The pursuit of them afterwards relaxing, they remained two years in a house near Milford, where they frequently prayed and preached at private meetings in their chamber; till the king's commissioners coming to Boston, they were again driven to their cave in the woods. Here some Indians discovered their beds, which obliged them to seek a fresh refuge; and they went to Hadley, one hundred miles distant, where they were received by Mr. Russell, the minister, and remained as long as they lived; very few persons knowing who they were. Whalley's death took place about 1678. They confessed their lives were 'miserable and constant burdens to them;' especially when their fanatical hopes of some divine vengeance on Charles II. and his adherents were perpetually disappointed. The fidelity and affection of Goffe's wife to her husband, were remarkably displayed in her letters.'—p. 85.

Here is given the well known anecdote of Goffe, in his old age, suddenly appearing, when the people of Hadley were surprised by a band of Indians while in church, and putting himself at the head of the worshippers, and routing the Indians. It has been made good use of in Cooper's 'Wept of Wishton Wish.'

In his Oliver Newman, Oliver is, somehow, a son of Goffe; and, what is still more strange, a quaker, and is gone, after his mother's death, to seek his father. He, by converting one of the principal Sachems, weakens Metacom's party so materially, as to decide the contest; and with that Sachem he retires into the interior. In the course of his wanderings Oliver meets with Pamya, an Indian woman, who has been cruelly treated by the whites. He purchases the freedom of herself and her two children, and she becomes his guide and safeguard amongst the Indians. He finds his father. They discover the body of Whalley on its way to be interred. Pamya is restored to her friends, the Narhagansets. Oliver and his father are surprised and taken by Randolph, the royalist. There is now a surprise by the Sakonet Indians, and Oliver and Randolph are taken, while Goffe escapes, and collecting some stragglers, attacks the Sakonets, and rescues his son and Randolph. In a dispute, Oliver being insulted by a renegade, forgets his quaker meekness, and kills him. Eventually, through Oliver's means, Randolph is restored to safety; Oliver marries the daughter of Willoby, an

English officer; has a grant of land procured through Randolph's interest; and Pamya's children coming to him, are baptized. Such is an outline of what this great American Iliad was to have been. Of the quality of the small portion presented to us, we must give a specimen, and the following is perhaps as favourable an one, as can be selected. Annabel, the daughter of Willoby, the cavalier, who, we should before have stated, went over in the same ship as Oliver to America, and afterwards became his wife,—as they lay under stress of weather at Cape Cod, suddenly introduces him to the suffering Indian woman Pamya, whom Oliver frees:—

'With hurried pace she comes, and flushed in face,
And with a look, half pity, half affright,
Which, while she spake, enlarged her timid eyes:
'O sir! I have seen a piteous sight!'
The shuddering maiden cries;
A poor wild woman. Woe is me! Among
What worse than heathen people are we thrown?
Beasts in our England are not treated thus,—
Our very stones would rise
Against such cruelties!
But you, perhaps, can reach the stony heart,—
Oh come, then, and perform your Christian part.'

'She led him hastily towards a shed,
Where, fettered to the door-post, on the ground
An Indian woman sate. Her hands were bound,
Her shoulders and her back were waled and scored
With recent stripes. A boy stood by,
Some seven years old, who, with a piteous eye,
Beheld his suffering mother, and deplored
Her injuries with a cry,
Deep, but not loud,—an utterance which expressed
The mingled feelings swelling in his breast,—
Instinctive love intense, the burning sense
Of wrong, intolerable grief of heart,
And rage, to think his arm could not fulfil
The pious vengeance of his passionate will.
His sister by the door
Lay basking in the sun: too young was she
To feel the burden of their misery;
Reckless of all that passed, her little hand
Played idly with the soft and glittering sand.

'At this abhorred sight
Had there been place for aught
But pity, half relieved by indignation,
They would have seen that Indian woman's face
Not with surprise alone, but admiration:

With such severe composure, such an air
Of stern endurance did she bear
Her lot of absolute despair.
You rather might have deemed,
So fixed and hard the strong bronze features seemed,
That they were of some molten statue part,
Than the live sentient index of a heart
Suffering and struggling with extremest wrong.
But that the coarse jet hair upon her back
Hung loose, and lank, and long,
And that sometimes she moved her large black eye,
And looked upon the boy who there stood weeping by.

'Oliver in vain attempted to assuage,
With gentle tones and looks compassionate,
The bitterness of that young Indian's rage.
The boy drew back abhorrent from his hand,
Eyed him with fierce disdain, and breathed
In inarticulate sounds his deadly hate.
Not so the mother: she could understand
His thoughtful pity, and the tears which fell
Copiously down the cheeks of Annabel.
Touched by that unaccustomed sympathy
Her countenance relaxed: she moved her head
As if to thank them both;
Then frowning, as she raised her mournful eye,—
'Bad Christian-man! bad Eglishman!' she said:
And Oliver a sudden sense of shame
Felt for the English and the Christian name.'—p. 25.

The New Timon is a novel in verse, which issuing from Mr. Colburn's shop anonymously, yet with certain mysterious hints, has been eagerly seized upon by our contemporaries, and ascribed to Sir Edward Bulwer Lytton, or to Mr. D' Israeli. The balance of opinion leans towards its being Sir Edward Bulwer Lytton's, but be it whose it may, we cannot rate it by any means so highly as we have seen it rated. There is great talent in it, but still not great poetry. There is a certain practical flow, or rather march of style about it, but there is at the same time a great monotony. At times it almost mounts into genuine harmony, at times it seems ready to warm into poetry, but it as certainly disappoints us. There is a parade of a superior morality, of a nobler sentiment than common, but at the moment that these seem about to pass the bounds of conventionalism, the invisible chain of the world's teaching drags it back, and we find ourselves sighing over the disappointment of something really great and good. If there wanted, however, one proof that the writer is not a true son of the muses, it is that he cannot, or will not, recognise those who are.

He steps abruptly, needlessly, disgracefully, out of his way to vent his spleen on tha ttrue poet and true man, Alfred Tennyson. Having first in no feeble fit of gasconade puffed himself:—

'Me life hath skilled!— to me from woe and wrong
By passion's tomb leapt forth the source of song.
The '*Quidquid agunt Homines,*'—whate'er
Our actions teach us, and our natures share,
Life and the world, our city and our age,
Have tried my spirit to inform my page;—p. 50.

he then launches this vaunting bolt of critical thunder at Tennyson.

'Not mine, not mine, O muse forbid!—the boon
Of borrowed notes, the mock-bird's modish tune,
The gingling medley of purloined conceits,
Outbabying Wordsworth, and outglittering Keats.
Where all the airs of patchwork-pastoral chime
To drowsy ears in Tennysonian rhyme!
Am I enthralled but by the sterile rule,
The formal pupil of a frigid school,
If to old laws my Spartan tastes adhere,
If the old vigorous music charms my ear,
Where sense with sound, and ease with weight combine,
In the pure silver of Pope's ringing line;
Or where the pulse of man beats loud and strong
In the frank flow of Dryden's lusty song?
Let school-miss Alfred vent her chaste delight
On 'darling little rooms so warm and bright!'
Chaunt 'I'm a-weary,' in infectious strain
And catch her 'blue fly singing i' the pane.'
Though praised by critics, though adored by Blues,
Though Peel with pudding plump the puling muse,
Though Theban taste the Saxon's purse controls,
And pensions Tennyson while starves a Knowles,
Rather be thou my poor Pierian maid
Decent at least, in Hayley's weeds arrayed,
Than patch with frippery every tinsel line,
And flaunt admired, the Rag Fair of the Nine.'—pp. 51-2-3.

Little dogs at the foot of Mount Parnassus, as here manifest, will still bark at the moon. This writer before venting his bile at Tennyson or bragging of himself, should first have presented us two poems, we ask no more, equal to 'The Two Voices,' and 'Locksley Hall.' If Alfred Tennyson needed a revenge, it would be found in the dullness of the poem which attacks him. There is just one little difference between his poetry and the New Timon, one is for all time, the other for a day.

The story of the New Timon is this. A gentleman, extremely rich, but with Indian blood in his veins, is taking an early morning walk in the streets of London, and finds a young girl, sitting in deep wretchedness on a door-step. She is handsome, and says she has not a friend in the world. Morvale, the Anglo-Indian, or in other words the New Timon, invites her to make his house her asylum, under the care of his sister. She does so, this sister Calantha, wholly English, being by a second marriage of Morvale's mother, with an English gentleman, becomes much attached to Lucy, the poor girl; and very soon Morvale falls in love with her. It turns out, as usual in such stories, that Morvale's sister, Calantha, is dying under unrequited or slighted love, and it is soon developed that the object of this is Lord Arden, the richest man in England, and the most handsome and accomplished and fashionable, of course. Still further, this Lord Arden has formerly made a sham marriage with and broken the heart of a country clergyman's daughter, and actually is the father of Lucy, Morvale's protegé and affianced bride. Well Calantha dying, Lucy coming to know her real father, Morvale coming to know all these sins of Lord Arden, and imagining that his Lordship may object to his Indian blood as a son-in-law, makes a grand Timon-like resolve—does not shoot Lord Arden, but shoots off into the country and wanders about in a sort of Werter-like, sentimental mock-heroic of self-renunciation, and he does not know what. Lord Arden, in the mean time, turns very pious, takes his daughter home to his splendid mansion, where she is at once a worshipped beauty and heiress, and very miserable in her loss of Morvale; and then Lord Arden digs up the remains of his long-deceased wife, conveys them to his estate, and raises over them a fine monument in the churchyard, to which he has access by a little wooden bridge, over a *very, very* deep stream.

The reader sees, of course, what happens. Morvale, in his *aimless* wanderings, wanders *directly* down to this spot. He goes by night, also, to this solitary churchyard—where, of course, Lord Arden comes to mourn over the tomb of one whom he had years ago abandoned, and—what?—of course, tumbles into the *very, very* deep stream from off the little wooden bridge. Of course he could not swim, or there could not be much harm done. He would merely have got out, shaken himself, and gone off to lecture the carpenter for not putting a safer hand-rail over the stream. Morvale *can* swim, and though he sees it is his foe who has killed his sister, and spoiled his match with Lucy, *he*, of course, plunges in, and carries Lord Arden to shore. This is very magnanimous, and, Providence, to reward such magnanimity, carries Lord Arden out of the world, and out of Morvale's way. Morvale goes haunting this churchyard again, and Lucy, being so amiable and pious a daughter, goes also to visit her mother's tomb. The lovers meet, they rush into each others' arms—and there is an end of the matter.

Such is the staple stuff of 'The New Timon.' It may be safely said, that 'The *New* Timon' is a *very old* novel put into verse. There is no doubt in our minds of its parentage. It is Young England all over. The affectation of a high moral tone with the ingrained actuality of fashionable conventionalism. The assumption of such a knowledge of real life, with the employment of such outrageously hackneyed and impossible incidents. What fashionable young men go wandering about the streets of London in early mornings, and pick up young deserted maidens from door steps, and take them home to their sisters? And what young maidens, if they were thus picked up, would, as a matter of course, turn out lord's daughters? And when do the richest and most dissipated lords of England go on pilgrimages at midnight down in the country to the tombs of their wives, and tumble over wooden bridges, and have their magnanimous enemies there ready to save them. Surely this is trash too sad to create a sensation even in the silly brains of the most silly daughters of the idlest aristocracy. How Lord Arden can contrive to be the youthful lover of Calantha, while he is the well-advanced father of Lucy, we leave to Mr. D'Israeli to clear up, for by many indubitable signs we believe him to be the author.

The 'Bells and Pomegranates' of Mr. Robert Browning, are poems chiefly in a dramatic form, published in numbers. They possess all the beauties and the blemishes of the writer, and these are many and great. Mr. Browning would be a poet of a high order, if he could free himself from his affectations, and set before himself a great aim in poetry. That aim should be the advocacy of great principles, and inculcation of great sentiments. As it is, with powers capable of all this, he makes himself merely a puzzle to those that see here and there really brilliant passages in him, and to the general reader—caviare. For a long time we were inclined to believe him really insane. We could not bring ourselves to believe that any man who possessed the power evidenced in his writings would voluntarily assume a form of confused and crazy eccentricity, merely for the poor pleasure of making people wonder. But we came at length to his drama of 'The Blot in the 'Scutcheon,' written for representation at Drury-Lane, and then the conviction was forced on us. Here all is as clear and rational in language as any plain understanding can desire. Mr. Browning, then, *can* be intelligible, if he will. He *can* be sane at his pleasure, and we beg of him that if he must indulge in mystification, he will do it in some private circle, and not before the public. If he really understands his own powers, he ought to know that the lasting reputation of a poet cannot spring out of the buffoonery of a barbarous style, but out of great truths, truthfully and clearly enunciated. We see in the progress of these 'Bells and Pomegranates' symptoms, hopeful symptoms, of this knowledge dawning upon him. In the first, 'Pippa Passes,' the craziness is outrageous; in the second, 'King Victor and King Charles,' there is scarcely less of it; in the third, 'Dramatic Lyrics,' there is enough; in the fourth, 'The Return of the Druses,' pretty well; in the fifth, the 'Blot in the 'Scutcheon,' all is clear; in the sixth, 'Columbus's Birth-Day,' there is not much to complain of; and in the last, there is not only clearness but higher purpose.

But besides muddiness of style, Mr. Browning has also much muddiness of matter to get rid of. There is a sensual taint about his writings which will bring him one day a bitterness that no amount of reputation will be found an antidote for. Let him purify his style and his spirit, and we shall hope to meet him again on a future day in a far higher and nobler position. Let us take a specimen of the cloudy and the clear, leaving the licentious for the author to purge it out of his next edition. The title of 'Pippa Passes,' is derived from an Italian girl, Pippa, who, during the progress of a dramatic sketch, which actually comes to no conclusion, though there is murder in it, is constantly passing and saying something. She jumps out of bed in the morning, uttering a very incoherent soliloquy, and goes to bed with another as incoherent, of which the following is an extract:—

PIPPA's *chamber again. She enters it.*

The bee with his comb,
The mouse at her tray,
The grub in its tomb,
Wile winter away:
But the fire-fly, and hedge-shrew, and lob-worm, I pray,
Where be they?
Ha, ha, thanks my Zanze—
'Feed on Lampreys, quaff Breganze'—
The summer of life's so easy to spend!
But winter hastens at summer's end,
And fire-fly, hedge-shrew, lob-worm, pray,
Where be they?
No bidding you then to . . . what did Zanze say?
Pare your nails, pearlwise, get your small feet shoes,
And like . . . , what said she? . . . and less like canoes.'

Pert as a sparrow . . . . would I be those pert
Impudent staring wretches! it had done me,
However, surely no such mighty hurt
To learn his name who passed that jest upon me.
No foreigner, that I can recollect,
Came, as she says, a month since, to inspect
Our silk-mills—none with blue eyes, and thick rings
Of English-coloured hair, at all events.
Well, if old Lucca keeps his good intent,
We shall do better—see what next year brings—
I may buy shoes, my Zanze, not appear
So destitute, perhaps, next year!
Bluf—something—I had caught the uncouth name
But for Monsignor's people's sudden clatter
Above us—bound to spoil such idle chatter,
The pious man, the man devoid of blame,
The . . . . ah, but . . . ah, but, all the same—
No mere mortal has a right
To carry that exalted air:
Best people are not angels quite—
While not worse people's doings scare
The devils; so there's that regard to spare,' etc. etc.—p. 15.

If this were meant for the mental ramblings of a crazy girl, it were admirable, but three-fourths of the people in the drama talk more confusedly. Who would believe that these ravings and 'The Flight of the Duchess,' 'The Lost Leader,' 'Italy in England,' and 'England in Italy,' with many smaller poems, rich with descriptive power and brilliant thought, were the product of the same mind? Let us take a portion of 'Italy in England,' as our second specimen:—

'ITALY IN ENGLAND.

'That second time they hunted me
From hill to plain, from shore to sea,
And Austria, hounding far and wide
Her bloodhounds through the country side,
Breathed hot and instant on my trace,
I made six days a hiding-place
Of that dry, green old aqueduct
Where I and Charles, when boys, have plucked
The fire-flies from the roof above
Bright creeping through the moss they love.
— How long it seems since Charles was lost,
Six days the soldiers crossed and crossed
The country in my very sight;
And when that peril ceased at night,
The sky broke out with red dismay
Of signal fires; well there I lay

Close covered o'er in my recess,
Up to the neck in ferns and cress,
Thinking on Metternich our friend,
And Charles's miserable end,
And much beside, two days; the third
Hunger o'ercame me when I heard
The peasants from the village go
To work among the maize; you know
With us, in Lombardy, they bring
Provisions packed on mules, a string
With little bells that cheer their task,
And casks, and boughs on every cask,
To keep the sun's heat from the wine.
These I let pass, in gingling line,
And, close on them, dear noisy crew,
The peasants from the village too;
For at the very rear would troop
Their wives and children in a group
To help, I knew; when these had passed,
I threw my glove to strike the last
Taking the chance. She did not start,
Much less cry out, but stooped apart
One instant, rapidly glanced round,
And saw me beckon from the ground.
A wild bush grows and hides my crypt;
She picked my glove up while she stripped
A branch off, then rejoined the rest
With that; my glove lay in her breast:
Then I drew breath: they disappeared:
It was for Italy I feared.

An hour, and she returned alone
Exactly where my glove was thrown.
Meanwhile came many thoughts; on me
Rested the hope of Italy;
I had devised a certain tale
Which, when 'twas told her could not fail
Persuade a peasant of its truth;
This hiding was a freak of youth;
I meant to give her hopes of pay
And no temptation to betray.
But when I saw that woman's face
Its calm simplicity of grace,
Our Italy's own attitude
In which she walked thus far, and stood,
Planting each naked foot so firm
To crush the snake and spare the worm—
At first sight of her eyes, I said,—
'I am that person on whose head

They fix the price because I hate
The Austrians over us; the State
Will give you gold—oh, gold so much,
If you betray me to their clutch!
And be your death for aught I know,
If once they find you saved their foe:
Now, you must bring me food and drink,
And also paper, pen, and ink,
And carry safe what I shall write
To Padua, which you'll reach at night
Before the duomo shut; go in,
And wait till Tenebrae begin:
Walk to the Third Confessional,
Between the pillar and the wall,
And kneeling, whisper *whence comes peace?*
Say it a second time; then cease;
And if the voice inside returns,
From Christ and Freedom: what concerns
The cause of Peace?—for answer, slip
My letter where you placed your lip;
Then come back happy, we have done.
Our mother service—I, the son,
As you the daughter of our land!'
Three mornings more she took her stand
In the same place, with the same eyes:
I was no surer of the sun-rise
Than of her coming: we conferred
Of her own prospects, and I heard
She had a lover—stout and tall,
She said, then let her eye-lids fall,
'He could do much'—as if some doubt
Entered her heart,—then, passing out,
'She could not speak for others—who
Had other thoughts; herself she knew:'
And so she brought me drink and food,
After four days the scouts pursued
Another path; at length arrived
The help my Paduan friends contrived
To furnish me; she brought me news:
For the first time I could not choose
But kiss her hand, and lay my own
Upon her head—'This faith was shown
To Italy, our mother;—she
Uses my hand, and blesses thee!'
She followed down to the sea-shore;
I left, and never saw her more.'—pp. 4—5.

That is the mode of writing; let Robert Browning pursue that, and he will not only be well understood, but justly esteemed.

There is a sense of what is noble in these lines, which, if followed, will lead on to a fame far beyond all the wonder to be excited by eccentricity and strange phrases. Perhaps, however, there is nothing in these numbers fuller of the evidences of great poetical power than the small piece, 'Pictor Ignotus.'

We have left ourselves little space to speak of Mr. Horne's ballad romances, and less for extract. The principal one is—'The Noble Heart, a Bohemian Legend;' but in our opinion 'The Monk of Swineshead Abbey;' a 'Ballad of the Death of King John;' 'Bedd Gelert;' and 'The Elf of the Woodlands,' are much the finest things in the book. In the ballad of 'The Death of King John,' the farmer who contends with the monks that—

> The worth of corn
> Is highest of all things on the earth ;

the patient monk, Father Luke, who contends on the contrary, that the church and the soul are the highest things on earth,

> Therefore, before the church or soul
> A corn-field stands, and bows its head ;

the tyrant king who will lay waste the whole country to find out who is loyal only out of gluttony; and again Father Luke who poisons the tyrant to prevent the mischief, and is compelled to drink of the poisoned cup, and dies too, confessing the error of doing evil that good may come of it—all are fairly conceived and beautifully worked out. Bedd Gelert is from the old Welsh legend to which, however, Mr. Horne has given a new and admirable term; but 'The Elf of the Woodlands,' a child's story, is one of the most charming, playful, and spirited things we have for a long time seen. The whole volume is well worthy of the author of them, and is indeed a very delightful book to read.

In casting a parting glance at the last two poets we have here noticed, we cannot help feeling that there is great poetical power yet amongst us, could it but resolutely free itself from the false taste of attempting surprise by quaintness or mystery; and aim only at the teaching of noble truths in a nobler simplicity of style. Of the three living writers here reviewed we look upon Mr. Horne as nearest to the right track. His muse is pure, genial, and generous; perhaps a little more earnestness of purpose, and he would rise into that lofty region of song towards which nature, and his heart direct him.

Art. IV.—*The Reformation and Anti-Reformation in Bohemia, from the German.* In two volumes, 8vo. London: Houlston and Co. 1845.

Bohemia has always appeared to us a country far less known than it ought to be, with its magnificent basin at the foot of the Carpathian mountains,—its interesting rivers,—and its noble capital. Beneath the blighting influences of Austrian absolutism, its inhabitants, if they have not altogether lost their spirit,—yet are no longer what their gallant forefathers were, when they listened to the voice of Huss, or Jerome of Prague; or when, two hundred years later, they hurled out of window the tools and ministers of national degradation. Whatever arrests thought, arrests power. A people, deprived of their political institutions, make perhaps desperate efforts to regain them: but if despotism prove successful in resisting those efforts, there then sometimes ensues the stillness of death. Liberty lays her forehead in the dust, and utters not even a sigh! Meanwhile ages roll along, and generations pass away. Those who could remember heroes, become themselves only the subjects of remembrance. Their children grow up as slaves, and so the iron rust of bondage eats into the soul of a nation. The memories of men, who unfurled the banners of freedom, are exhibited, or pointed to, as so many Egyptian mummies—great curiosities of antiquity, yet without associations sufficiently palpable and distinct to rouse recollections into energy, or resentment into action. The sceptre of autocracy thus perpetuates its leaden reign. There is no dust of slumbering genius to be wakeful when the trumpet sounds. The idea of any social resurrection subsides into a dream, like one of the Arabian Nights Entertainments. Alas! that it should be so; for no one can calculate the vast amount of human wretchedness thereby developed. Spiritual intelligences, who doubtless watch this lower world, as one of the fields in which the processes of Divine Providence are wrought out, alone are able to estimate such catastrophes aright. We may also learn our own humble lesson from these affairs, by guarding the constitutional privileges, which have been vouchsafed us, with a vigilance of attachment in some degree proportioned to their value.

It was in an evil hour, that the Bohemian crown descended upon the brows of German Cæsars. They treated its provinces just as Great Britain was once in the habit of treating Ireland or Canada. Instead of remaining an elective sovereignty, as in former times, emperors dictated, and officials obeyed. The inhabitants, moreover, were always furnishing excuses for imperial controul and interference; inasmuch as they were rough in their manners, rude in their notions, blind in their national prejudices, and fiercely precipitate in their actions. Even the introduction of Christianity had not occurred without scenes of most revolting cruelty. Methodius and Cyril were the means of baptizing the first chieftain and his retinue, as well as of preaching the gospel in Moravia. These worthy missionaries flourished about the middle of the ninth century. Both were Greek monks,—the former an ingenious painter,—the latter the inventor of the Sclavonian alphabet. In the tenth century, under the Othos or Saxon emperors, Romanism, to which those potentates were devoted, attempted to enforce her peculiar customs,—the use of the Latin language in religious worship,—celibacy for the clergy,—and the withdrawal of the cup in the sacrament from the laity. Resistance brought about interminable confusion and bloodshed; but the last peculiarity it was, which seems, from the earliest periods of Bohemian history, to have come out as the grand bone of contention. Doctrines, in those dark days, were unhappily lost sight of in forms and ceremonies. Most men had a mere name to live. Religion itself indurated into a hard, though externally gorgeous system. When the House of Luxembourg got possession of the country, in the fourteenth century, matters had become worse, rather than better. Charles IV., in 1376, issued a mandate enjoining strict adherence to the popedom, under pain of death; whilst to all official appointments, foreigners, instead of natives, were nominated. The Waldenses had here and there scattered some seeds of evangelical truth; and not a few writings of Wiclif, now forced an entrance through the instrumentality of an individual named John Payne. Our King Richard II. married Anne, daughter of Charles IV. Jerome of Prague also came over to our shores, and returned home laden with the treatises of the Rector of Lutterworth. Huss translated many of them; and soon the stagnant waters were again stirred.

'In the year 1404, two learned Englishmen, James and Conrad of Canterbury, came to Prague, and spoke much against the Pope. But when this was prohibited, they by consent of their host, Luke Welenskey, caused to be painted in a room of the house where they lodged, in the suburb of Prague, the history of Christ's Passion on the one side, and on the other, the Pomp of the Papal Court. Huss mentioned these representations publicly, as a true antithesis between Christ and Anti-Christ:—and all ran to see them!' (Vol i. pp. 7, 8.)

Mother Church, established as she then was, and is now in Bohemia, of course took prodigious umbrage. Articles, extracted from the works of Wiclif, were formally condemned by forty masters and a great number of bachelors in the University; and it was forbidden, under penalty of banishment, for any to teach them. Indulgences came from Rome about A. D. 1411, that the Pope might obtain money to wage war against Lewis, King of Naples; a sad pretext this for the vicegerent of the Prince of Peace! Even monks began to mutter and peep. Huss and Jerome waxed bolder and bolder. The bulls of his holiness were committed to the flames in the central market-place of Prague; and because John Huss refused to obey a summons to the Seven Hills, to answer for his heresy, the capital of the kingdom was laid under an interdict. This brave reformer, to relieve his fellow citizens from inconvenience, at length withdrew, and after being hunted like a partridge on the mountains, enjoyed some temporary shelter in the castle of Cracow. Thence, confiding in the treacherous safe-conduct of Sigismund, he ventured to appear before the council of Constance. The rest is well known; and we are persuaded that all candid minds, whatever may be their religious idiosyncrasy as to externals, will number John Huss and Jerome of Prague amongst the martyrs of genuine Reformation.

Their followers unfortunately resorted for revenge to the civil sword. They soon, however, came to reap the bitter fruits of their folly. The spirit of real religion took flight amidst the din of arms. On the 30th of July, 1419, ensued that terrible tumult at Prague, when twelve senators, with the chief magistrate of the old town, were thrown out of the senate-house windows, and cruelly caught upon the points of lances below. This savage impalement was quite a distinct event, from the more justifiable and comparatively harmless *defenestration* (as our historian politely calls it) which commenced the Thirty Years War. The Hussites had indeed received terrible provocation both at, and after the Council of Constance. Martin v. adjured the cities and potentates of Germany by the wounds of Christ, and their own salvation, to attack his disobedient children, promising universal remission of temporal penance, even to the most wicked, who should be happy enough to slay but one heretic. Sigismund collected an army, and slaughtered thousands; yet for thirteen years Ziska, at the head of his enthusiastic Taborites, kept at bay the imperial forces, and was himself never conquered. Before his death, it is said, he bequeathed his skin to his comrades, that it might be made into a large drum for animating the revival of fanaticism, if it should ever flag through the absence of its repeatedly victorious leader. The public misery, on the other hand, stood in need of no excitement. Fire and water were called into requisition for the innumerable massacres and executions: and as if comburation and drowning were not horrible enough,—the poor prisoners of all ranks and both sexes were cast headlong down the old pits and mines of Kuttenberg. In one shaft alone 1,700 found a dreadful grave: in another 1,308 were ruthlessly destroyed. A third of these terrible abysses swallowed up 1,321 persons; and every year on the 18th of April, solemn meetings were afterwards held in a chapel built over the spot, to commemorate such a multitude of martyrs. Not that we can allow them all to have been literally such, in an ecclesiastical sense, as there were many, or most of them, who were captives taken in warfare, with arms in their hands. But Christianity and philanthropy, on the other hand, can never restrain their execrations as to deeds so opposed to the laws of God and society.

'However the greater portion of those, who took upon themselves the name of Huss, had by this time greatly degenerated, which not only produced separation, but many of them even persecuted the faithful Hussites. All, indeed, agreed in this one thing, to attack whatever was anti-Christian, after the example of John Huss. But there was wanting an able, wise, and upright leader to keep the excited populace within the bounds of order. The lower classes of the people, and the priests, sought for nothing, but the *participation of the cup*, from whence they were called *Calixtines*, and paid no regard to the other doctrines of their reformer. They confessed, that in all other rites they agreed with the Romish church. To this party belonged at that time the greatest part of the nobility, the council of Prague, the councillors of other cities, and many of the people. The cup had become the object upon which their minds were fixed, and every contention was based upon the point, whether one was for the communion *sub unâ*, or *sub utrâque specie*. The papal permission of the cup finally obtained in 1437, almost by force, was published at Prague, in the Latin, German, and Hungarian languages; was written in the churches in golden letters; and large cups were even placed upon the steeples, as may be seen at Leitmeritz to this day. The most remarkable cup, with a gilt sword, was fixed to the gable-end of the Tein church of the capital.'—Vol. i. pp. 21, 22.

Meanwhile, however, another community arose out of the ashes of the martyr of Constance, more than worth all the Utraquists and Unaquists put together: we mean the church of the United Brethren, in this country, commonly called Moravians. They formed a remnant of faithful souls, who sought to live above the world, and glory in the cross of Christ. Notwithstanding their oppressions from nearly every quarter, they still increased in numbers, and extorted praise even from persecutors, for their constancy and consistency in faith and morals. Before the Lutheran Reformation, they possessed several hundred houses of prayer: although at no period was their general characteristic aught else, than that of 'a little sanctuary in the wilderness.' Each pitiless storm seemed to cement their union; whilst the furnace of affliction, which they bore with invincible fortitude, marked them out as the very children of God. Reviled as Waldenses and Picards, (nicknames answering to our own Methodists of the last generation,) they clung to episcopacy as their form of external organization, and to the use of the Scriptures in the spirit of the noble Beræans. Many of them were mutilated, quartered, burned, imprisoned, and exiled by the bishop of Olmütz. Some assayed to find refuge in forests, caverns, and dens of the earth; whence they earned from their enemies the appellation of grubenheimer or pit-dwellers! 'In the daytime they dared not kindle a fire for fear of being betrayed by the smoke; but during the night, being under no apprehension, they studied the word of God by its light. That their traces might not be perceived in the snow, they all trod in the same line; the last of the party obliterating their footsteps with the branch of a tree, to give to their track the appearance of a peasant having dragged a bush behind him. Under these circumstances they taught, strengthened, and comforted each other, and exercised themselves in the pure confession of the gospel.' They remind us of the vision which solemnized Moses in Horeb—a bush burning, but not consumed.

The dawn of the sixteenth century shed varied lights and shadows upon Bohemia. The Brethren, whom we have just described, were expelled almost altogether from the kingdom, under the malignant auspices of Ferdinand the First. But this was only half the mischief; for the protestants, remaining behind, fell into fearful and exasperating jealousies amongst themselves. Here and there the deep principles of Calvin struck their roots into the soil; yet, strange to say, those who espoused them, were abhorred by the Lutherans much more than the Romanists. *Tantæne animis cælestibus iræ!* Maximilian the Second, successor to Ferdinand, had imbibed from Wolfgang Sever his companion, and John Sebastian Pfauser the court chaplain, not a few notions of equity and toleration. His catholic instructors also are recorded as having deserved 'a share of praise' in this respect, since they imbued their imperial pupil 'with such peaceable and scriptural sentiments, that even when regent, he would not have any one vexed or persecuted on account of matters of faith.' His furious father had once well nigh murdered Pfauser, 'seizing him by the throat, and drawing his sword,' so that the worthy clergyman had to be forcibly rescued by the attendants. His only crime was instilling the moderation of Philip Melancthon into the youthful Maximilian.

The latter, after assuming the diadem, was riding out with his favorite physician, John Crato, when his majesty 'lamenting the religious dissensions which existed among Christians, asked him who, of all the various sects, approached the nearest to apostolic simplicity.' Crato answered, that he thought 'the Brethren under the name of Picards, might bear away the palm.' The emperor replied, 'I think so too!' He liked the Jesuits indeed, but could never give into their views of coercing conscience; which he sagaciously considered as neither more nor less, to use his own words, 'than assailing heaven.' It would have been happy, had those who came after him been of his opinion. The calm was only destined to be of brief duration; yet, during its continuance, the Moravian brethren translated the Scriptures, and made their famous confession in 1575, which united the Hussites, Utraquists, and Calixtines, into one body for the time being, under the general denomination of Evangelicals.

We pass over the reigns of Rudolph II. and Matthias, to reach that of the Second Ferdinand, whose cardinal notion was that 'he ought to have no heretics among his subjects.' In other words; however the worshippers of Hooker may admire it, the State and the Church were to be identical. It is remarkable, as our author observes, that about this era, 'Lutheran rulers made similar demands on *their* subjects; for the calvinists in Saxony, as well as the catholics and puritans in England, were expelled with equal rigour.' Augustus, from his capital at Dresden, openly declared in broad terms, 'I will, that my people shall think in religion as I myself think!' So also spoke our James the First, and so in effect must every head of any established church say! Here, then, is the core of that question of questions, which is destined to revolutionize the religious world. Select any form of Christianity we may please—array it with rank, choke it with wealth, and encumber it with secular power, —and it will turn into a very respectable persecutor—do whatever else we will! This is the grand axiom, which we want to impress as an eternal truth upon the public mind. Ferdinand the Second did no more than act in his vocation; as any one of our own Stuarts would have done, with the prodigious applause, and apostolic benediction, of archbishop Laud and his whole college of prelates. Anglican principles are far worse than Roman ones, in relation to their present bearing upon social politics. The former are pledged irremediably to the unholy alliance: the latter have conceded much already, and are promising to yield yet more upon at least this most important point. The Maynooth affair was an exception certainly: but, notwithstanding the hollow clamours of Exeter Hall, and the honest simplicity of the Hon. and Rev. Baptist Noel's pamphlet, we feel persuaded, that the Church of England as a body, and as a system, will sooner consent, after a due allowance of groans and grimaces, to endow its Mother of Rome in Ireland, than surrender its ecclesiastical position and emoluments for the welfare of protestantism in general. Our readers must kindly pardon this short digression, which has naturally arisen out of the volumes before us, and which respects a topic lying nearer to our hearts than we sometimes well know how to acknowledge.

With Ferdinand II., commenced what is styled the Anti-Reformation in Bohemia. He was a bigot on the most magnificent and malignant scale. His ablest instruments were a couple of commissioners or governors, who as colleagues in mischief, had manifested at Prague, the strongest hostility against religious liberty. Their names were Slawata and Martinitz. The kingdom was already in an attitude of revolt, for the emperor had trampled under foot every relic of the national constitution. Those who still loved it, and had been chosen by the people to rescue it, if possible, from ultimate destruction, were Matthias the Count of Thurn, and Kolon Fels, together with William Lobkowitz, Count Schlik, Wenzel Raupowa, Albert Smirckzizky, Paul Rziczan, Ulric Kinsky, Paul Kaplirz, and some others. Popular ebullition had elevated them to the crest of the billow about to burst upon the two imperial officers. On the memorable 23rd of May, 1618, when the people with muskets and sabres, had occupied all the avenues to the castle of Prague,—their leaders, wearing no other weapons than pistols at their girdles, passed into the government-hall, where Paul von Rziczan courageously charged Slawata and Martinitz with being the real disturbers of the public peace, and as having endeavoured to deprive the Utraquists of their charter: the chief burgrave and grand prior were both present with the two obnoxious governors:—

'Each of the latter was now requested separately to acknowledge whether he had any hand in the imperial mandates. The chief burgrave addressed the insurgents seriously, yet calmly and mildly, entreating them not to act rashly, or with violence. Fels replied, that they had nothing to say against him,—but that it was Slawata, and Martinitz, (who now put them to defiance,) who on every occasion oppressed the Utraquists. Here Wenzel Raupowa called out, —'The best way is, *straight out of the window*, after the old Bohemian fashion!' Some now stepped nearer to the chief burgrave, and the grand prior, who was less noted, but more feared, took them by the arm to lead them out of the room. But Martinitz and Slawata, asserted their innocence, and prayed that they would judge them according to the laws, if they were guilty of anything: but the popular leaders were by this time so embittered, that they would not be softened down. Lobkowitz finally caught Martinitz by both hands. Smirkzižky, Rziczan, Kinsky, and Kaplirz, in their fury, also laid hands upon him, dragged him to the next window, and actually threw him down sixty feet into the moat. They all stood terrified and speechless. Thurn then interrupted the silence, and cried, 'Noble lords, here is the other:' upon which, Slawata was seized in a moment, and likewise thrown from the window. After them was also cast their secretary, Philip Fabricius Platter, who had been much implicated in the scheme for destroying the Protestants.

'Those, who had been thrown down, though they had fallen so many feet, alighted upon a heap of mire, where stone monuments with inscriptions were afterwards set up. None of them had broken a limb. Platter was the first who could rise: he went back to his house in the old town, and afterwards proceeded hastily to Vienna, and acquainted the emperor with what had happened. The servants of Martinitz and Slawata, ran to their help; and notwithstanding they were fired at, brought them over a ladder into the adjoining house of the chancellor, whose lady used every means to restore them. Count Thurn came thither, and demanded them. But the prudent and bold Polyrena, (that was her name) softened down his fury by kind words, assuring him, that both were in bed, in a pitiable state, and thus sent him back. Martinitz afterwards disguised himself, cutting off his beard, and blackening his face with gunpowder, by which means he escaped from Prague, without being recognised, until he reached the White-hill, whence he went to Munich, and resided with the Duke of Bavaria. Slawata could not follow on account of a wound in his head. The insurgents finally granted him a physician, and had him closely guarded. Out of gratitude for their wonderful escape, the three united in a present to Maria of Loretto, consisting of a diadem of gold, with precious stones. There is extant an account of a scene between the ladies of Slawata and Thurn. The former is said to have interceded with the latter for her husband; when the reply was, that if she complied, she would soon herself require intercession.'—Vol i. pp. 292—4.

Amidst such scenes as these, was ushered in the Thirty Years war. Ferdinand conceived an excuse was now afforded him for any excesses: as if he had not been the aggressor from the very commencement. As might be anticipated, the protestants fiercely retaliated. John Ernest Schosser, burgomaster of Aussig, celebrated as an elegant poet, a learned judge, and a zealous catholic, was first thrown from the roof of his own house, and then horribly pierced with two hundred and seventy wounds, before he expired! John Sarkander, the catholic dean of Holeschau, was tortured to death, amidst unexampled torments. Men degenerated into demons. The revolt had become general, although respectful language was still held towards the emperor. Troops were levied throughout the country, of which Count Thurn took the command. Lutherans, Calvinists, and Utraquists drew up articles of defence, as three grand ecclesiastical states, standing out for the rights of man, and more especially the claims of conscience. When his imperial majesty began also to move, on his part, the insurrection only glowed with greater fervour. The Evangelicals then threw off all disguise. They seized the entire administration of government, as well as all the public revenues. Bohemia was summoned, from one end to the other, to rally round the common cause. Assistance was invoked from Hungary, Moravia, Silesia, and Lusatia. Ferdinand the Second possessed little more than an empty title, until the demise of his predecessor the emperor Matthias, which occurred on the 20th of March, 1619; but from that moment, matters grew into one universal contest against the house of Austria. The latter had resolved to obliterate every vestige of regal election, and re-catholicise its dominions. We may now look back with wonder to the extent of success attendant upon its efforts. Meanwhile, the protestant states were no better than a mere rope of sand, without a king of their own; and so they determined to choose one. The election fell, as is well known, upon Frederick, the Elector Palatine—a prince, of lively spirit and benevolent heart,—but by no means adapted to his position. He contrived to ruin himself, and many of those who supported him; although such was the joy expressed at his coronation, that superficial observers imagined he would have nothing else to do than revel in the loyalty of a gallant and united people. Those, however, who saw further, ventured to predict the most melancholy consequences. In the capital, there appeared much unwise precipitation, in surrendering the cathedral to the Calvinists, rather than the Lutherans. Disorders ensued in rapid succession. The new sovereign had more about him of the popinjay than the potentate. He fluttered from one palace to another 'in a furred coat of red silk, and a white hat with yellow feathers. He showed himself affable to the nobility, but more condescending than became royalty.' It seemed scarcely to pass through his mind that he had any duties to perform beyond those of the parade, or the ball-room,—in which last, the graver classes considered him too free in dancing; whilst he complained, 'that he knew not what to think of the Bohemian young ladies refusing to kiss him!' He foolishly attempted to combine the severity of religious reformation with gaiety of manners, and some profligacy in morals. This was not the way to baffle either the armies of Ferdinand, or the sagacious disciples of Ignatius Loyola. Elective royalty is no bed of roses!

The Jesuits, who had been despoiled and insulted, only waited for their victory. It was achieved for them on the 8th of November, 1620, at the battle of the White Hill, near Prague. Prince Christian, of Anhalt, had now superseded Count Thurn; and, with twenty thousand evangelicals, marched out that day against the approaching imperialists. Never was defeat more total or more disastrous. Protestantism waned in Germany from that day. Frederick, during the engagement, was entertaining himself with a number of ladies, at the table of the English ambassador. His few troops, which escaped massacre, dispersed to their homes. The crown jewels, and archives of the kingdom were packed up for immediate removal; but the king, leaving them at last behind, fled with his consort and children, first into Breslau, and afterwards into Holland. Prague was surrendered to an enemy, whose rage was as cruel as death, and whose appetite was as greedy as the grave. Millions of florins were extorted from the unhappy citizens. Italian, Spanish, French, Polish, and Croatian soldiers, plundered and pillaged at pleasure, 'burning the houses, and murdering the people.' Let us hear the touching exclamation of the honest historian Jacobus:—

'Oh! to what torments many honest promoters of the gospel were exposed! How were they tortured and massacred! How many virgins were violated to death; how many respectable women were abused; how many children were torn from their mothers' breasts, and cut in pieces before their eyes; how many were mutilated; how many dragged out naked from their beds, and thrown from the windows! What cries of woe we were forced to hear from those who lay upon the rack, and what terrible groans from those who besought the robbers to spare them, for God's sake! How were we everywhere hindered in our church services! The innocent blood which was shed, still cries, waiting for the vengeance of righteous heaven! Yet, oh God, spare our enemies and persecutors,—comfort the afflicted,—the widows and the widowers,—the orphans, and bereaved parents. Grant again joy and blessing to the good and righteous, for thine own ever-praiseworthy name's sake, Amen!'—vol. i. p. 382.

We have no space to particularize the affecting executions of individual leaders, who shed their blood upon scaffolds at Prague, with an heroism rarely paralleled since the days of primitive Christianity, and with a firm confidence in their principles, which certainly conferred honour upon their cause. That cause, however, was now to all appearance ruined in Bohemia. Property changed hands, through imperial confiscations, upon the largest scale. Many names of very ancient families passed altogether away. The emperor sent for all municipal charters to Vienna, and there consigned them with his own hand to the flames, amidst sundry expressions of contempt at the folly of his ancestors. The churches were restored to the catholics; and all the enginry of the most skilful organization was set successfully in motion to weed out protestantism from the kingdom. Troops overspread the land. Fire and sword wasted it, from the domains of the noble to the cottage-garden of the humblest peasant: nor did adjacent realms escape. The evangelical clergy gradually disappeared. Schoolmasters and tutors were expelled, unless they conformed; in which case they were patronised, or otherwise kindly treated. The famous Caroline College fell into the hands of the Jesuits, who turned, with an ingenuity truly marvellous, every faculty of theology, philosophy, literature, and science, towards the single purpose already mentioned. Even books and protestant documents of all descriptions seemed to pass into annihilation, as though they had never existed. Father Adam Krawarsky alone, by his zeal and labour, brought over to Rome 33,140 persons; and others from 10,000 to 16,000 each! It must be, however, remembered, that they followed in the train of military conquest. The course of procedure, in general, was,—that commissioners of high rank travelled from town to town, proclaiming the emperor's will and pleasure. Companies of clergymen followed in the rear, with allurements for the pliable, and punishments for the obstinate. The Dominicans joined their brethren of the Society of Jesus in this task. Members of other religious orders were also engaged in a similar manner; especially in places where the work of catholic conversion promised well. What eloquent persuasion failed to do, violent and horrible means effected. Not that we at all charge all the abominations detailed in these volumes upon pure Romanism. The most rabid readers of the 'Record' newspaper would not do that. In those days of terror and confusion, a protracted war raged throughout an entire generation! Atrocities generated atrocities on both sides. But the emperor, at the same time, was a modern Nero: there is no denying that, as will appear from only one of his more moderate edicts in July, 1627. 'We cannot conscientiously permit,' says this blasphemous autocrat, in usurping the prerogatives of God, 'that there should be found, within six months, any one in the lower, much less in the higher classes, who shall not have embraced the very holy and only saving Roman catholic faith. And that there may be no lack of such people, who can instruct in so salutary a work, we have, from a godly determination, appointed and provided for that purpose certain governors and commissioners from the clergy as well as the laity. Wherefore we, in our paternal care for the welfare of this realm, inform and exhort every one by this our royal mandate, that all and every one should, for their temporal and spiritual welfare, be diligent in taking instructions *from the above-named commissioners of the Reformation,* and thus be obedient to our gracious will. Whosoever shall not have complied with our will, within six months, *and not be of one faith with us,* the same shall not be permitted to remain in the country, much less enjoy his property. For we are entirely resolved, that all rebellious and obstinate people *shall sell their property to the catholics,* and quit this country at the expiration of the specified time, and never again be permitted to return, unless they become catholics!'

We are well aware, that throughout large portions of this very century, and in our own island, acts of the British legislature, about as atrocious as the above, consigned to expulsion, loss of income and property, degradation, imprisonment, and death, many thousands of nonconformists and catholics, on no other ground than that they were not, and would not, become *of one faith* with the dominant established church. Nor had Anglican episcopacy the apology of the popedom on its side: it laid no open claims to infallibility, however pregnant with inconsistencies might be both its practices and professions. Let our readers then beware of all approaches to similar perils. Every blow honestly aimed at so enormous an abuse as the grand ecclesiastical upas-tree of these kingdoms, is an arm lifted up for God! Let the countrymen of John Huss neither have lived nor died in vain. Between 1623 and 1628, no less than 36,000 exiled families fled into Lusatia alone, to say nothing of Prussia, Lithuania, and Hungary. Amongst these emigrants were the flower of Bohemian literature, the most industrious of the cloth and linen weavers, tin-workers, and blue-dye manufacturers, besides one hundred and eighty-five of the prime nobility. The confiscations of 1621, poured forty-three millions of guilders into the imperial exchequer. In order to restore and increase the impaired and exhausted condition of his kingdom, the Emperor filled up the vacancies, with an eye to Rome and her objects. In 1626, he created sixty new earldoms and twice that number of fresh baronies. He moreover abolished all the old laws of the country, and enacted quite a novel code, after the much approved fashions of Vienna. Ferdinand must have been the model to our modern Nicholas in Poland, —exhibiting analogous energy, and perseverance, with the same cruel mockery of righteousness. He declared his gracious and paternal willingness 'to confirm all the national privileges, with the exception of those concerning religion, the free election of a king, and the exclusive use of the Bohemian language in the public courts;' besides which, the customs of law and equity were to undergo an entire change. This was the Muscovite all over,—being tantamount to saying, 'That he would respect all rights except those of liberty, property, and conscience!' The circumspect Pelzel declares, that 'History scarcely presents an instance, where a whole nation was so much altered in the short space of fifteen years, as was that of Bohemia, during the reign of Ferdinand II. In 1620 all the Bohemians were Protestants, (a few of the nobility, and some monks excepted); at the death of Ferdinand, they were externally at least all Catholics.' Freedom, independence, prosperity, and even personal valour, appeared to have found a melancholy sepulchre! 'All bravery was buried,' says the same historian, 'on the White-Hill.' They fled, like sheep before the Swedes, in subsequent actions, or suffered themselves to be trodden under foot. In fact, what have men to struggle for, when their souls are not roused at the most distant clank of chains?

The last chapter of this work presents us with the exile of the remnants of the Bohemian Brethren, and their final settlement at Herrnhut, on the estates of Count Zinzendorf. There they have attained a happy resting-place; from whence have emanated those Moravian congregations and missions, with which our own religious public can scarcely be too well acquainted. We are much gratified in the main, with the two volumes before us: whilst we are also of opinion, that they might easily have been made much more interesting by a compression, and quite a different arrangement of their contents. There is an absence of perspicuity and variety in the narrative, a want of clearness and fulness as to dates of events, a needless repetition of details and circumstances. It strikes us that the translator might very well have recast the affair from beginning to end. The general tone of the author we think admirable, as regards his attachment to evangelical truth, and constitutional liberty. Some of the more picturesque scenes from the career of Ziska, Procopius, and the Taborites, or from the tragedy of the Thirty Years War, might have been introduced with advantage, so as to have given a back-ground to the general religious picture. We should like to have seen the genius of Schiller, in connection with the consecrated abilities of Professor Tholock, employed upon such subjects, as those we have been rapidly contemplating. At the same time, we are perhaps bound to transcribe the concluding lines of the writer's very modest and beautiful preface:—'No attempt,' he says, 'has been made to improve the narrative by studied eloquence. The pages are filled with documents and facts only; and the author aspires to no higher merit, than that of collecting, examining, arranging, and communicating those materials of history. He has at least preserved the memory of many warriors and sufferers,—of many fearless confessors of scriptural truth,—and of many undaunted martyrs who cheerfully preferred death to the defilement of their conscience.' We doubt whether the latin work *De Persecutione Bohemicâ*, is quite so rare as he supposes; although Mr. James Montgomery would, as we should imagine, have been very glad to have fallen in with it, in the original language, (instead of a mere imperfect translation,) in his recent Memoir of the late Bishop Holmes, of Fulneck.

Art. V. *Proceedings before the French General Council of Agriculture, of Manufacture, and of Trade, opened in Paris the* 15*th December*, 1845; *and their Reports*, 15*th January*, 1846.

It is too much the fashion on both sides the channel, to trumpet forth topics of hostility between England and France. It is a wiser, a better, a more truly Christian, and, we add with confidence, a more patriotic course, to discuss other topics of a steady peaceward aspect. Among the more important of them, are such as tend to open a wider intercourse of trade between us, and our neighbours. In these cases, the profits of trade, like acts of charity, confer a double blessing; and increasing wealth on both sides, purchases a new security, and increasing international good-will. It is in this point of view, that we hail with extreme satisfaction, a movement *now decidedly begun in France in favour of Free Trade*.

This first arose from the alarming decline of the French Merchant Navy; which has produced a strong call for the admission of British iron, for ship building; to which is added a call for the admission of Swedish iron, for the manufacture of steel in France.

The latter topic we dismiss in a very few words. France possesses within itself abundant materials for an increasing steel manufactory; and new mines have just been discovered in Algeria, fit for the same purpose. Therefore France is not compelled, as England is, to get steel-iron from Sweden. Besides, in consequence of certain contracts made between the English and Swedes, the whole of the produce of Sweden fit for steel, is bought up for England. So that if France would have it, she cannot. Whether facts support this reasoning, we do not mean to discuss, inasmuch as it is secondary in importance to the first topic, involving as that does, a grand question, upon which we shall present our readers with the whole case, as now opened in France; and which concerns, in the first place, the free supply of iron for building French merchant ships, and then, perhaps, it may be introductory to a new system of commercial intercourse between the two people.

Unfortunately the question is far deeper than at first sight it appears to be; it must therefore be examined briefly, at least, in all its great bearings.

As stated in the French documents, this question stands thus:—

The French merchant service, is undoubtedly in a deplorable condition in itself, and as compared with the English and American mercantile navies, its decline excites the extremest anxiety in France, among the reflecting portion of the community.

The test of figures selected to establish this capital point, is the amount of the merchant tonnage of the three countries in 1830 and in 1843; and the comparison deserves to be set up in large character for the daily and hourly contemplation of the Prince de Joinville. His illustrious parent, Louis Phillippe, has had deserved credit for turning his own early years of misfortune to a good account, as a teacher of youth; but in his old age, he has sadly forgotten the lessons of moderation, which belong to adversity. These fatal figures would form a better A B C for his sons, than the scenes of slaughter he has so diligently made them familiar with in northern Africa.

These merchant tonnage figures exhibit in a striking light, the decline of French shipping, at the very same time that English and American shipping has made a great advance.

		Tons.		Tons
In 1830, the French merchant tonnage	was	689,588;	in 1843;	599,707.
But in 1830, the English do.	was	2,531,819;	and in 1843;	3,588,387.
But in 1830, the American do	was	1,191,776;	and in 1843;	2,158,602.

(Document laid by the French minister of trade, before the General Councils of agriculture, manufactures, and of trade, assembled in December, 1845. *p.* 20.*)*

Another comparison is also disadvantageous to France, under the very peculiar circumstance of the superiority of the foreign shipping, which it establishes, over that of France, taking place in French ports.

		Tons.		Tons.
In 1830, the arrivals and departures of *French shipping* in French ports.	were	704,797;	in 1843,	1,204,919.

In 1830, the arrivals and departures of Foreign shipping in French ports } were 1,039,801; in 1843, 2,041,714.

—ib. p. 19.

It is true that the returns of 1844, are a little more favourable to French shipping; but this slight improvement does not satisfy the public mind, that something is not radically wrong in the system which produces such results; and after an earnest discussion of the subject in the legislature, and in the newspapers, the government has resorted to the extraordinary measure of laying the whole matter before the General Councils of Agriculture, Manufactures, and Commerce, lately assembled in Paris after an interval of four years. This is a body to which we have nothing analogous, except perhaps, our occasional unpaid commissions of inquiry, issued by the crown, which, however, do not usually combine the several heads examined by respective sections of the French Councils, and reported upon by the united body.* It completed its labours in Paris. Among them was the question respecting foreign iron for ships; which was presented to the body by the Minister of Commerce on the 15th of December in the following terms:—

'The first subject to be submitted by us, is the admission of foreign iron for ship-building, upon which both branches of the legislature have called upon the government to propose an alteration of the duty. Our laws strictly tend to protect our shipping and our trade against foreign competition, by means of differential duties, making up to our ship-owners the great disadvantages they are exposed to in the high price of everything that is wanted in our shipping. We are compelled to admit foreign ships to a considerable share in the

* The composition of this body, and the character of its enquiries will be well understood from the following table of its sections:—

1. Committee upon irrigation and draining. President, the Count de Gasparin: Secretary, M. de Mornay.
2. Agricultural loans. President M. Darblay: Secretary, M. Pommier.
3. Improvement in the breed of cattle. President M. de Vaitry, a member of the Chamber of Deputies; Vice-president, M. Tourette.
4. Wool. President, M. Lemaire, a deputy: Secretary, M. Pommier.
5. Linen. President, M. Leroy de Bethune: Secretary, M. Rendu.
6. Wine. President, M. le Duc de Liancourt: Secretary, M. Rendu.
7. Instruction in Farming. President, M. Tourette: Secretary, not named.
8. *Iron and Steel. President, M. le Baron Dupin: Secretary, M. le Baron Busch.*
9. Savings Banks. President and Secretary not named.
10. Miscellaneous Topics. President, M. Saunai: deputy.
11. Waste Lands. President, M. Saunai, deputy: Secretary, M. le Baron Busch.

export of our own produce, for example to India, where we have little trade; and the English ships take our produce cheaper than we can ourselves afford to send it in our own. But we seek diligently to reestablish our means of making such exports in French bottoms. In some instances we have succeeded, as in Algiers, where in 1843, we sold cotton goods only, to the value of £250,000; but by raising the Tariff, we carried their value to £1,500,000, in 1844; and in cotton goods generally, in woollen goods, in silks, in linen, hemp goods, in wines, and in the manufactures of Paris, the increase of exports has been from fifteen to thirty per cent., since 1843. *On all other heads there is improvement.*

'If, notwithstanding this increase, our shipping does not possess the share in exports which it had in 1830, and if foreign shipping increases more than ours, the causes may be easily stated. They depend on the nature of our country and its products; and upon the character and habits of our people. France does not possess, like the people of the North of Europe, bulky articles such as timber for building, tallow, hemp, and flax, nor coals, iron, copper, like England; nor cotton, dye-woods, and skins, like the United States of America. Our exports generally take up little room.

'Again, our population is essentially agricultural, with little taste for or habit of foreign adventure, and the sea. Our merchants are not disposed to employ agents abroad; and thus we lose both the advantage of disposing of our own produce beyond sea, and also of collecting return cargoes.

'Besides, all the materials for ship-building are dearer in France than in other countries; and the crews of our ships being more numerous, and better fed than those of our rivals, add to the greater cost of our shipping.

'These are steady causes of our inferiority. Its consequences are of a nature to call for earnest consideration; and the government is anxious to have your opinions upon all branches of the case; and especially upon the subject of a change of the duty upon iron imported for ship building.'

A document distributed among the members of the Council states the arguments on both sides of this subject. Amongst other things the motive of the establishment founded of late years in the South Seas, with such disastrous consequences, is asserted to have been, the wish long felt by the French government, to raise the French Mercantile Navy, from its admitted and alarming inferiority. We suspect that this scheme has not answered; and we are sure, that the dreadful outrages committed against the rights of humanity, on the persons of the people of the South Seas, in carrying it into effect, could not be compensated by any possible advantage to all the navies of the civilised world. The neglect of those rights, by the do-nothing system of the British government, encouraged by the philanthropists; and the violation of them by the government of

France, open an account, which it will require new and long efforts on the part of the wise and good to settle.

The reasons assigned for the admission of foreign iron for ship building into France, are, that iron-built ships are superior to timber built. They are lighter, stronger, make better way, are more lasting, and require fewer repairs, consequently, they are much more economical. The stowage is easier, because of the divisions in the hold. With equal draught of water, the iron ships carry from twenty to thirty per cent. more cargo. They are less easily sunk; less exposed to fire, and all accidents. They are healthier for the crew; and safer for the goods. These advantages have settled the question among the English, who are adopting iron ships as fast as possible. Especially are the India ships, of great bulk, built more and more of iron. France may by following this example, recover her place among mercantile states.

It is denied on the other hand, that men's minds are made up in England to adopt iron generally in building ships. Besides, its positive advantages, in so far as they can be said to be yet ascertained by a short experience, the English favour it, because they have less *crooked* timber than formerly. Even if the advantages of iron be admitted, France will act wisely in securing the supply of it from her own forges; and a sacrifice of about £400,000 a year as a sort of premium in their favour, will enable the iron masters, to produce all that is wanted for this purpose;—as the experience of many years has proved, that the protection of iron for general purposes has succeeded.

In support of the argument in favour of the French monopoly, the gradual reduction of the price of iron, at the forges, from about fourteen shillings, in 1834, to about twelve shillings and sixpence, the hundred pounds, English; it is urged that the quantity wanted for the shipping, amounts only to one tenth of the whole present produce, so that with encouragement there will be no difficulty in securing the supply.

The point which seems to have determined the government is the urgent need of relief to the merchant service, which can be afforded by obtaining iron of at least an equal quality, from England, at prices, varying from fifty to seventy per cent. cheaper than the iron of France is now sold at.

The councils, after stating the case in far stronger language, resolved, *with a large majority*, that foreign iron ought to be admitted into France, free of duty, for building merchant ships.

Pending these official inquiries, the crisis among us had begun to excite the liveliest interest in that country; and in a speech on the 12th of January last, in the chamber of peers, the Duc d'Harcourt, an old advocate of free trade, expressed opinions respecting its beneficial influence, which deserve to be written in letters of gold in every chamber of commerce from Canada to Canton. This speech has been reprinted twice,* in separate publications; and it has been copied into half the newspapers of France.

After shewing that the present French ministers taught free trade principles readily enough before taking office, but that they coolly laid that 'baggage' aside when called into the public councils, the Duc d'Harcourt proceeds thus:—

'How can the nation confide in men who turn about in this manner? What the people really want is, a minister capable of declaring boldly his resolution to aim at the public good alone. This would rouse the enthusiasm of the people. There is deep suffering in the land. The combinations of the workmen, and the dreadful excess of toil exacted by parents from the little children sent by them to the factories, settle the point of their extreme want. And for this misery there is a remedy at our command—a remedy that will give the people cheaper food, cheaper clothing, and cheaper comforts, in spite of every difficulty. If a minister should address the nation upon this theme, he would soon find friendly echoes in all quarters, and posterity would bless his name. I mean *free trade* with all the world; and could the government but summon spirit to proclaim it, success is certain.

'Private interests have hitherto prevailed against free trade; but the nation is ready to adopt it. It is the grand question of modern times. The ancients were our superiors in letters, and the fine arts. But a privileged few only shared that superiority, whilst the millions were ignorant slaves. Christianity has rescued them from their degradation; and it remains for us to carry out the doctrines of Christianity, by making our laws conform to them. These doctrines are as yet to be better than mere theories with us. Religious liberty, civil liberty, commercial liberty, are all refused with disdain by the monopolizers of every degree. They know well that the best means of getting the most money out of the nation is to set class against class. They do not know that the true germ of civilization, perhaps the only universal one, is *free trade*. There is no mistake in the arguments establishing the triumph of free trade. They are these: first, mutual wants must lead to communication between man and man; and, secondly, without mutual wants, the earth would become a silent solitude. The more wants men have, the greater must be their intercourse, and the steadier their progress. Providence, in its wonderful plan, has infinitely varied the productions of

* It is the first article in a book published by Mr. Wilson, Royal Exchange, entitled '*Liberté du Commerce*.' Price 1s. 6d. The Duc d'Harcourt is a rich landed proprietor. Upon a similar topic, in 1845, he said that he was 'an owner of iron forges and of forests; and not at all disposed to ruin himself by way of experiment. At least, he was *disinterested* when he wished the tariff to be changed.' (10th June, 1845.)

different countries, in order to compel their inhabitants to seek each other out. To put obstacles in the way of that intercourse, is to oppose the course of Providence. Savages are savages only because they live apart from us, and have no wants. Free trade, then, is civilization; and prohibitions are real barbarism. Archimedes said, that with a *fulcrum* he would move the earth. I venture to assert, that with free trade at my command, I could defy religious animosities, war, famine, poverty—too often the sad lot of man.

'Nor will free trade only make food and clothing the cheaper; it will improve men's morals, and increase their intelligence, because it will give them time for the one, and incline them to the other. It is in vain to open schools if the scholars are starving. But feed them well, and they will rapidly acquire all the knowledge you can offer them.

'The industry of man is in an eternal ferment. Its last result is, *over abundant production*. Consumption has its natural limit; production has no bounds. England and Belgium and France have all reached the last point of consumption in several articles. Our two neighbours admit this fact; and half France does the same thing, when year after year complaining bitterly of the tariff, which cuts them off from the proper remedy—*access to foreign markets*. The whole civilized world, with its natural, instinctive view of the truth, perceive this to be the case; and therefore it is now eagerly seeking an outlet in all quarters for its overflowing abundance. Unhappily the government of France, well as it knows all this, is bound hand and foot by our monopolists.

'There is, however, one example near us, which we ought to follow. What is passing in England surpasses in grandeur all that is recorded in history—*the struggle of the League to emancipate industry*. The British free trade League is making prodigious strides. And when we reflect upon the obstacles in its way,—upon the private interests opposed to it, and upon the power of a once resisting government, we are bound to do justice to a nation capable of such an effort. Mr. Cobden deserves to be enrolled among the benefactors of mankind for his share in this prodigious success. On our parts, instead of fostering a blind, unprofitable hate towards our neighbours, let us imitate their great deeds—let us become free, like them—above all, let us become free traders. All the rest will follow.'

This is a faithful translation of a small part of the speech of a French duke, on the 12th of January last.

An equally strong testimony in favour of our proceedings has just been given in a very different quarter. *The Populaire* is the organ of a zealous, numerous, and very honest body of labouring people in France, who, despairing of better reforms, would EXTINGUISH POVERTY by the voluntary establishment of *a common purse*. In professing a reformed pure Christianity and *communism*,—a voluntary, equal division of property, they forget that the poor are to be 'always with us.'

They are strenuous opponents of monopoly and privilege in all shapes; and their leader in the *Populaire* of the 26th of February, responded to the free trade movement in England in a way that shews that he and his friends comprehend all its value as a practical means of doing good.

We hail this sign of returning good-will between us and our neighbours across the channel.

The movement is fast spreading in other directions. The wine growers of Bordeaux are naturally among the first to form a free trade society. The political economists of Paris have formed another, which includes some of the ablest men in France. In the north, the strong hold of protection, a spirit is shewing itself that cannot be mistaken—*a spirit of inquiry*, which must lead to a great change of opinion. The form this has taken is interesting to us. It is in the foundation of a permanent society in Paris, to represent the department of the north (from Dunkirk to Lille), having for its object *the collection and dissemination of correct intelligence* respecting all that concerns that most populous, and most industrious district. This society combines agriculture, manufactures, and commerce. Our *county-clubs* might take it for a model.

Great good must come of this change in France. A fearful spirit of hostility against England has of late years prevailed in that country; the numerous proofs of which, it will be interesting to put in contrast with the signs now every day shewing themselves, of friendly dispositions such as those in the speech of the Duc d'Harcourt, and in the columns of the *Populaire*. We promise our readers to make a careful collection of such signs of the times; and we hope to see the good feelings which founded our British and *Foreign* Bible Society, and our British and *Foreign* Anti-Slavery Society, and the like, prompt the formation of an *universal free trade league*. We are convinced that not only France, but every country on earth, barbarian* as well as civilized, will furnish zealous members of such a body.

* It was a savage chief who remonstrated against the old law of the Cape of Good Hope, prohibiting trade between the colonists and his people. 'Where there is no intercourse,' said the savage, 'there can be no peace.'

Art. VI.—*Narrative of a Four Months' Residence among the Natives of a Valley of the Marquesas Islands; or a Peep at Polynesian Life.* By Herman Melville. London: John Murray.

The Marquesas Islands are situated in the South Pacific Ocean, extending from one hundred and thirty-eight to one hundred and forty degrees of west longitude, and from eight and a half to ten and a half south latitude. They were discovered in 1525 by Mendana, a Spanish navigator, and were named after his patron, the Viceroy of Peru. Captain Cook visited the group in 1774, and the slight accounts furnished by subsequent voyagers have, till recently, done little towards removing the mystery in which they were enwrapped. The islands are five in number, presenting an aspect bold and rugged, with high lands and a shore marked by volcanic eruptions. The most authentic information yet received has been through the medium of religious missionaries, who in this, as in many other cases, have been the link between savage and civilized man. So much respecting the region to which Mr. Melville's 'Narrative' pertains. It is a fitting theatre for the adventures which his volume describes, and we commenced its perusal in the expectation of meeting with strange and stirring incidents.

'Sailors,' he remarks, 'are the only class of men who now-a-days see anything like stirring adventure.' There is much truth in this, though not probably to the extent alleged. In the present case, there is no lack of incident or novelty, and he who commences the perusal of Mr. Melville's narrative will scarcely fail to complete it. Some misgivings will probably occur to an intelligent reader, but the scenes described are so novel, the habits so unique, the adventures so hazardous, that the attraction of the volume necessitates a perusal of the whole, which leaves the impression of increased knowledge arising from introduction to a new and singularly interesting race. The author apologizes for the absence of dates by his having lost all knowledge of the days of the week during the occurrence of the events recited. To a certain extent this plea must be admitted, yet we should be better satisfied had the notations of time been more distinctly marked. It was in the summer of 1842, that our author arrived at the Marquesas, the French expedition for the occupation of the group having sailed from Brest in the previous spring.

Mr. Melville belonged to the crew of an American whaler which had been 'six months out of sight of land, cruising after the sperm whale beneath the scorching sun of the line.' At the period his narrative commences, the sailors were thoroughly weary and anticipated the death of the last tenant of the poultry coop, as what would furnish to the captain an intelligible hint that it was time to make for land. The 'Dolly' was at length put under weigh for the Marquesas, and the sailors looked forward with more than boyish excitement, to the indulgences which awaited them there. Nearly three weeks were consumed in the passage from their cruising ground to Nukuheva, during which the crew had little to do, the light tradewinds silently sweeping them towards their desired haven. 'Every one seemed to be under the influence of some narcotic.' The beauty of the scenery, however, did not escape our author, whose vivid description may well serve to stimulate the languid appetite of European tourists.

'The sky presented a clear expanse of the most delicate blue, except along the skirts of the horizon, where you might see a thin drapery of pale clouds which never varied their form or colour. The long, measured dirge-like swell of the Pacific came rolling along, with its surface broken by little tiny waves, sparkling in the sunshine. Every now and then a shoal of flying fish, scared from the water under the bows, would leap into the air, and fall the next moment like a shower of silver into the sea. Then you would see the superb albicore, with his glittering sides, sailing aloft, and often describing an arc in his descent, disappear on the surface of the water. Far off, the lofty jet of the whale might be seen, and nearer at hand the prowling shark, that villainous footpad of the seas would come skulking along, and, at a wary distance, regard us with his evil eye. At times, some shapeless monster of the deep, floating on the surface, would, as we approached, sink slowly into the blue waters, and fade away from the sight. But the most impressive feature of the scene, was the almost unbroken silence that reigned over sky and water. Scarcely a sound could be heard but the occasional breathing of the grampus, and the rippling at the cut-water.'—p. 9.

At length the joyful announcement of land was heard from aloft, and the 'Dolly' entered the bay of Nukuheva, to the beauty of which our author informs us no description can do justice. Six French men of war were riding in the bay, the whole group of islands having recently been taken possession of by Rear-Admiral Du Petit Thouars. We pass over the account given of the reception met with from the natives, simply remarking that it affords an apt, but most humiliating illustration, of the unblushing profligacy practised on such occasions. There are grounds on which we demur to the desirableness of such facts, as are here referred to in general terms, being communicated to the public. But other considerations more than reconcile us to the disclosure, and render it matter of duty to notify to our countrymen the whole facts of the case. The character and operations of Christian missionaries are perpetually assailed by visitors to these remote regions, and it is, therefore, needful the public should know, how far the practices of such visitors are likely to disincline them to a candid construction and fair report, of the proceedings of Christian missionaries. The worth of the testimony borne must, in all cases, be greatly diminished, when the witness is proved to have an interest in disparaging the party accused. The narrative before us furnishes painful evidence on this point, and we would have our readers ponder its statements well, in order that they may duly appreciate some of the opinions expressed. We must not permit a false delicacy to disqualify us for vindicating the character of our brethren from the misconstructions of men, whose anger has been aroused by the obstacles interposed to their criminal indulgences.

Mr. Melville is no admirer of the French, whose unprincipled and piratical aggressions he denounces in indignant terms. Referring to Tahiti, he records an anecdote highly creditable to the self-possession and firmness of Mrs. Pritchard, and on which senators and poets would exultingly have dilated, had it occurred in any other case than that of the wife of a missionary. We give it in his own words:

'In the grounds of the famous missionary consul, Pritchard, then absent in London, the consular flag of Britain waved as usual during the day, from a lofty staff planted within a few yards of the beach, and in full view of the frigate. One morning an officer, at the head of a party of men, presented himself at the verandah of Mr. Pritchard's house, and inquired, in broken English, for the lady his wife. The matron soon made her appearance; and the polite Frenchman, making one of his best bows, and playing gracefully with the aguilettes that danced upon his breast, proceeded, in courteous accents, to deliver his mission. 'The admiral desired the flag to be hauled down—hoped it would be perfectly agreeable,—and his men stood ready to perform the duty.' 'Tell the pirate your master,' replied the spirited Englishwoman, pointing to the staff, 'that if he wishes to strike those colours, he must come and perform the act himself; I will suffer no one else to do it.' The lady then bowed haughtily and withdrew into the house. As the discomfited officer slowly walked away, he looked up to the flag, and perceived that the cord by which it was elevated to its place, led from the top of the staff, across the lawn, to an open upper window of the mansion, where sat the lady from whom he had just parted, tranquilly engaged in knitting. Was that flag hauled down? Mrs. Pritchard thinks not; and Rear Admiral Du Petit Thouars is believed to be of the same opinion.'—p. 19.

Captain Vangs, who commanded the 'Dolly,' was a hard taskmaster, hated and feared by the crew. Our author was disgusted with the service; and soon after his arrival at Nukuheva determined to risk himself amongst the savages of the island rather than continue under his power. In this resolution he was joined by a shipmate, named Toby, a light-hearted, adventurous youth, who felt only the sorrow of the hour, and was ready to hazard a thousand dangers in order to escape it. Having concerted their plans, they waited till 'the starboard watch,' to which they both belonged, was sent on shore, for a holiday. This speedily occurred; and they watched their opportunity to escape from their companions, and fly into the woods. Knowing that the valleys were inhabited by hostile tribes, of some of whom they had heard alarming accounts, they resolved to make for the high land, on which it was supposed the savages rarely ventured. Their object was to lie concealed till the 'Dolly' had sailed, and they calculated on the bread-fruit tree to furnish them with the means of subsistence. In this calculation they were disappointed; and the difficulties early experienced, would have induced less adventurous youths to retrace their steps. Their course is thus graphically described :—

'Since leaving the canoe-house we had scarcely exchanged a single syllable with one another; but when we entered a second narrow opening in the wood, and again caught sight of the ridge before us, I took Toby by the arm, and pointing along its sloping outline to the lofty heights at its extremity, said in a low tone, 'Now Toby, not a word, nor a glance backward, till we stand on the summit of yonder mountain, so no more lingering, but let us shove ahead while we can, and in a few hours' time we may laugh aloud. You are the lightest and the nimblest, so lead on, and I will follow.'

''All right, brother,' said Toby, 'quick's our play; only let's keep close together, that's all;' and so saying, with a bound like a young roe, he cleared a brook which ran across our path, and rushed forward with a quick step.

'When we arrived within a short distance of the ridge, we were stopped by a mass of tall yellow reeds, growing together as thickly as they could stand, and as tough and stubborn as so many rods of steel; and we perceived, to our chagrin, that they extended midway up the elevation we purposed to ascend. For a moment we gazed about us in quest of a more practicable route; it was, however, at once apparent that there was no resource but to pierce this thicket of canes at all hazards. We now reversed our order of march, I, being the heaviest, taking the lead, with a view of breaking a path through the obstruction, while Toby fell into the rear. Two or three times I endeavoured to insinuate myself between the canes, and by dint of coaxing and bending them to make some progress; but a bull-frog might as well have tried to work a passage through the teeth of a comb, and I gave up the attempt in despair. Half wild with meeting an obstacle we had so little anticipated, I threw myself desperately against it, crushing to the ground the canes with which I came in contact; and rising to my feet again, repeated the action with like effect. Twenty minutes of this violent exercise almost exhausted me, but it carried us some way into the thicket; when Toby, who had been reaping the benefit of my labours by following close to my heels, proposed to become pioneer in turn, and accordingly passed ahead with a view of affording me a respite from my exertions. As, however, with his slight frame he made but bad work of it, I was soon obliged to resume my old place again.

'On we toiled, the perspiration starting from our bodies in floods, our limbs torn and lacerated with the splintered fragments of the broken canes, until we had proceeded perhaps as far as the middle of the brake, when suddenly it ceased raining, and the atmosphere around us became close and sultry beyond expression. The elasticity of the reeds, quickly recovering from the temporary pressure of our bodies, caused them to spring back to their original position; so that they closed in upon us as we advanced, and prevented the circulation of the little air which might otherwise have reached us. Besides this, their great height completely shut us out from the view of surrounding objects, and we were not certain but that we might have been going all the time in a wrong direction.

'Fatigued with my long-continued efforts, and panting for breath, I felt myself completely incapacitated for any further exertion. I rolled up the sleeve of my frock, and squeezed the moisture it contained into my parched mouth. But the few drops I managed to obtain gave me little relief, and I sunk down for a moment with a sort of dogged apathy, from which I was aroused by Toby, who had devised a plan to free us from the net in which we had become entangled. He was laying about him lustily with his sheath-knife, lopping the canes right and left, like a reaper, and soon made quite a clearing around us. This sight reanimated me, and seizing my own knife, I hacked and hewed away without mercy. But alas! the farther we advanced, the thicker and taller, and apparently the more interminable, the reeds became. I began to think we were fairly snared, and had almost made up my mind that without a pair of wings we should never be able to escape from the toils; when all at once I discerned a peep of daylight through the canes on my right, and communicating the joyful tidings to Toby, we both fell to with fresh spirit, and speedily opening a passage towards it, we found ourselves clear of perplexities, and in the near vicinity of the ridge.'—pp. 39—41.

This was surely enough, but it formed only a small item in their adventures. Having gained the ridge, they found no bread-fruit trees, or other natural provisions, and were compelled to keep themselves as concealed as possible, in order to avoid detection either by the natives, or by the crew of the ship they had left. The ground, moreover, was broken by deep and precipitous ravines, at the bottom of which flowed mountain torrents. Ultimately, compelled to follow the course of one of these, they met with a new danger which, under ordinary circumstances, would effectually have arrested their progress. A precipice of nearly a hundred feet in depth, extended across the ravine, over which the wild stream poured in tumultuous fury.

'What's to be done now?' said our author to his companion; who replied, with the light-heartedness characteristic of his class, 'Why, as we cannot retreat, I suppose we must keep shoving along.' In truth, retreat was impossible, and they were threatened with starvation. What followed, will be best described in our author's own words.—

'With this he conducted me to the verge of the cataract, and pointed along the side of the ravine to a number of curious looking roots, some three or four inches in thickness, and several feet long, which after twisting among the fissures of the rock, shot perpendicularly from it and ran tapering to a point in the air, hanging over the gulf like so many dark icicles. They covered nearly the entire surface of one side of the gorge, the lowest of them reaching even to the water. Many were moss-grown and decayed, with their extremities snapped short off, and those in the immediate vicinity of the fall were slippery with moisture.

'Toby's scheme, and it was a desperate one, was to intrust ourselves to these treacherous-looking roots, and by slipping down from one to another to gain the bottom.

''Are you ready to venture it?' asked Toby, looking at me earnestly, but without saying a word as to the practicability of the plan.

''I am,' was my reply; for I saw it was our only resource if we wished to advance, and as for retreating, all thoughts of that sort had been long abandoned.

'After I had signified my assent, Toby, without uttering a single word, crawled along the dripping ledge until he gained a point from whence he could just reach one of the largest of the pendant roots; he shook it —it quivered in his grasp, and when he let it go it twanged in the air like a strong wire sharply struck. Satisfied by his scrutiny, my light-limbed companion swung himself nimbly upon it, and twisting his legs round it in sailor fashion, slipped down eight or ten feet, where his weight gave it a motion not unlike that of a pendulum. He could not venture to descend any further: so holding on with one hand, he with the other shook one by one all the slender roots around him, and at last, finding one which he thought trustworthy, shifted himself to it and continued his downward progress.

'So far so well; but I could not avoid comparing my heavier frame and disabled condition with his light figure and remarkable activity; but there was no help for it, and in less than a minute's time I was swinging directly over his head. As soon as his upturned eyes caught a glimpse of me, he exclaimed in his usual dry tone, for the danger did not seem to daunt him in the least, 'Mate, do me the kindness not to fall until I get out of your way;' and then swinging himself more on one side, he continued his descent. In the mean time I cautiously transferred myself from the limb down which I had been slipping to a couple of others that were near it, deeming two strings to my bow better than one, and taking care to test their strength before I trusted my weight to them.

'On arriving towards the end of the second stage in this vertical journey, and shaking the long roots which were round me, to my consternation they snapped off one after another like so many pipe stems, and fell in fragments against the side of the gulf, splashing at last into the waters beneath. As one after another the treacherous roots yielded to my grasp, and fell into the torrent, my heart sunk within me. The branches on which I was suspended over the yawning chasm swang to and fro in the air, and I expected them every moment to snap in twain. Appalled at the dreadful fate that menaced me, I clutched frantically at the only large root which remained near me, but in vain; I could not reach it, though my fingers were within a few inches of it. Again and again I tried to reach it, until at length, maddened with the thought of my situation, I swayed myself violently by striking my foot against the side of the rock, and the instant that I approached the large root caught desperately at it, and transferred myself to it. It vibrated violently under the sudden weight, but fortunately did not give way.

'My brain grew dizzy with the idea of the frightful risk I had just run, and I involuntarily closed my eyes to shut out the view of the depth beneath me. For the instant I was safe, and I uttered a devout ejaculation of thanksgiving for my escape.

'' Pretty well done,' shouted Toby underneath me; 'you are nimbler than I thought you to be—hopping about up there from root to root like any young squirrel. As soon as you have diverted yourself sufficiently, I would advise you to proceed.'

'' Aye aye, Toby, all in good time: two or three more such famous roots as this, and I shall be with you.'

'The residue of my downward progress was comparatively easy; the roots were in greater abundance, and in one or two places jutting out points of rock assisted me greatly. In a few moments I was standing by the side of my companion.'—(pp. 65—67.)

Their hope, in following the mountain stream, was to find an opening into one of the valleys. From what they had heard, they concluded that two hostile tribes were in their neighbourhood, the one named Happar, a peaceful and humane race; the other Typee, a set of cannibals. Their desire was to reach the former, but their uncertainty awakened a thousand apprehensions which they in vain essayed to conceal. At last they came upon the signs of habitation, and their movements were more cautious and slow. Their introduction to the Typees,—for into the valley of this dreaded tribe they had entered—was sufficiently picturesque.

'It was too late to recede, so we moved on slowly, my companion in advance casting eager glances under the trees on either side, until all at once I saw him recoil as if stung by an adder. Sinking on his knee, he waved me off with one hand, while with the other he held aside some intervening leaves and gazed intently at some object.

'Disregarding his injunction, I quickly approached him and caught a glimpse of two figures partly hidden by the dense foilage; they were standing close together, and were perfectly motionless. They must have previously perceived us, and withdrawn into the depths of the wood to elude our observation.

'My mind was at once made up. Dropping my staff, and tearing open the package of things we had brought from the ship, I unrolled the cotton cloth, and holding it in one hand, plucked with the other a twig from the bushes beside me, and telling Toby to follow my example, I broke through the covert and advanced, waving the branch in token of peace towards the shrinking forms before me.

'They were a boy and girl, slender and graceful, and completely naked, with the exception of a slight girdle of bark, from which depended at opposite points two of the russet leaves of the bread-fruit tree. An arm of the boy, half screened from sight by her wild tresses, was thrown about the neck of the girl, while with the other he held one of her hands in his; and thus they stood together, their heads inclined forward, catching the faint noise we made in our progress, and with one foot in advance, as if half inclined to fly from our presence.'—p. 74.

Their reception, however, was far kinder than could have been anticipated; though their serenity was sadly disturbed by the suspected cannibal propensities of the natives. Nothing was denied them but liberty, and that only beyond the limits of the valley. It was evidently the desire and aim of the savages to retain them, though with what design it was difficult to imagine. The appearances of restraint were avoided to the utmost possible extent, yet they painfully felt that their movements were not free, and that their return to Nukuheva was strictly prohibited. They grew at length into familiarity with the people, and were fortunate enough to secure the favour of Mehevi, their chief. Their days passed in dreamy slothfulness, the habits of the valley affording little to vary the monotony of their life. It was little more than an animal existence which they spent. Their hope of escape gradually diminished, and their only strong excitement sprung from the fear of the fickleness and savage propensities of the tribe. A dark and cruel superstition prevailed in this earthly paradise, of which a faint notion may be found from the following description of the spot consecrated to its rites.

'Here were situated the Taboo groves of the valley—the scene of many a prolonged feast, of many a horrid rite. Beneath the dark shadows of the consecrated bread-fruit trees there reigned a solemn twilight—a cathedral-like gloom. The frightful genius of pagan worship seemed to brood in silence over the place, breathing its spell upon every object around. Here and there, in the depths of these awful shades, half screened from sight by masses of overhanging foilage, rose the idolatrous altars of the savages, built of enormous blocks of black and polished stone, placed one upon another, without cement, to the height of twelve or fifteen feet, and surmounted by a rustic open temple enclosed with a low thicket of canes, within which might be seen, in various stages of decay, offerings of bread-fruit and cocoa-nuts, and the putrefying relics of some recent sacrifice.

'In the midst of the wood was the the hallowed 'hoolah hoolah,' ground--set apart for the celebration of the fantastic religious ritual of these people—comprising an extensive oblong pi-pi, terminating at either end in a lofty terraced altar, guarded by ranks of hideous wooden idols, and with the two remaining sides flanked by ranges of bamboo sheds, opening towards the interior of the quadrangle thus formed. Vast trees, standing in the middle of this space, and throwing over it an umbrageous shade, had their massive trunks built round with slight stages, elevated a few feet above the ground, and railed in with canes, forming so many rustic pulpits, from which the priests harangued their devotees.

'This holiest of spots was defended from profanation by the strictest edicts of the all-pervading 'taboo,' which condemned to instant death the sacrilegious female who should enter or touch its sacred precincts, or even so much as press with her feet the ground made holy by the shadows that it cast.'—p. 100.

In this spot they fell asleep, and the scene which presented itself on their awakening, was well adapted to stimulate their terror to the utmost. We will give it in Mr. Melville's own words, simply remarking, that the overdone levity of his companion shakes our confidence in its authenticity :—

'I awoke from an uneasy nap, about midnight, as I supposed; and, raising myself partly from the mat, became sensible that we were enveloped in utter darkness. Toby lay still asleep, but our late companions had disappeared. The only sound that interrupted the silence of the place was the asthmatic breathing of the old men I have mentioned, who reposed at a little distance from us. Beside them, as well as I could judge, there was no one else in the house.

'Apprehensive of some evil, I roused my comrade, and we were engaged in a whispered conference concerning the unexpected withdrawal of the natives, when all at once, from the depths of the grove, in full view of us where we lay, shoots of flame were seen to rise, and in a few moments illuminated the surrounding trees, casting, by contrast, into still deeper gloom the darkness around us.

'While we continued gazing at this sight, dark figures appeared moving to and fro before the flames; while others, dancing and capering about, looked like so many demons.

'Regarding this new phenomenon with no small degree of trepidation, I said to my companion, 'What can all this mean, Toby?'

''Oh, nothing,' replied he; 'getting the fire ready, I suppose.'

''Fire!' exclaimed I, while my heart took to beating like a trip-hammer, 'what fire?'

''Why, the fire to cook us, to be sure; what else would the cannibals be kicking up such a row about if it were not for that?'

''Oh, Toby! you have done with your jokes; this is no time for them; something is about to happen, I feel confident.'

' 'Jokes, indeed!' exclaimed Toby, indignantly. 'Did you ever hear me joke? Why, for what do you suppose the devils have been feeding us up in this kind of style during the last three days, unless it were for something that you are too much frightened at to talk about? Look at that Kory-Kory there!—has he not been stuffing you with his confounded mushes, just in the way they treat swine before they kill them? Depend upon it, we will be eaten this blessed night, and there is the fire we shall be roasted by.'

'This view of the matter was not at all calculated to allay my apprehensions, and I shuddered when I reflected that we were indeed at the mercy of a tribe of cannibals, and that the dreadful contingency to which Toby had alluded was by no means removed beyond the bounds of possibility.

' 'There! I told you so! they are coming for us!' exclaimed my companion the next moment, as the forms of four of the islanders were seen in bold relief against the illuminated back-ground, mounting the pi-pi and approaching towards us.

'They came on noiselessly, nay stealthily, and glided along through the gloom that surrounded us as if about to spring upon some object they were fearful of disturbing before they should make sure of it.—Gracious heaven! the horrible reflections which crowded upon me that moment.—A cold sweat stood upon my brow, and spell-bound with terror I awaited my fate!

'Suddenly the silence was broken by the well-remembered tones of Mehevi, and at the kindly accents of his voice my fears were immediately dissipated. 'Tommo, Toby, ki ki!' (eat) —He had awaited to address us until he had assured himself that we were both awake, at which he seemed somewhat surprised.'—p. 102—104.

A large trencher, containing portions of a roasted pig, soon attested the kindly purposes of their visitors, and restored them to their equanimity. Yet the fear of being themselves subjected in turn to the same process as the pig, continued to haunt them, and especially disturbed the excitable imagination of Toby. Our author acknowledges his 'almost entire inability to gratify any curiosity that may be felt with regard to the theology of the valley,' and alleges that there is 'a vast deal of unintentional humbug' in the accounts received from scientific men of the theological institutions of Polynesia. To this sweeping censure we more than demur, and adduce the following in proof of the senseless character, at least, of the prevalent superstition.

'In one of the most secluded portions of the valley, within a stone's cast of Fayaway's lake, for so I christened the scene of our island yachting, and hard by a growth of palms, which stood ranged in order along both banks of the stream, waving their green arms as if to do honour to its passage, was the mausoleum of a deceased warrior chief. Like all the other edifices of any note, it was raised upon a small pi-pi of stones, which being of unusual height, was a conspicuous object from a distance. A light thatching of bleached palmetto leaves hung over it like a self-supported canopy; for it was not until you came very near that you saw it was supported by four slender columns of bamboo rising at each corner to a little more than the height of a man. A clear area of a few yards surrounded the pi-pi, and was enclosed by four trunks of cocoa-nut trees resting at the angles on massive blocks of stone. The place was sacred. The sign of the inscrutable taboo was seen in the shape of a mystic roll of white tappa, suspended by a twisted cord of the same material from the top of a slight pole planted within the enclosure. The sanctity of the spot appeared never to have been violated. The stillness of the grave was there, and the calm solitude around was beautiful and touching. The soft shadows of those lofty palm-trees!—I can see them now, hanging over the little temple, as if to keep out the intrusive sun.

'On all sides as you approached this silent spot, you caught sight of the dead chief's effigy, seated in the stern of a canoe, which was raised on a light frame a few inches above the level of the pi-pi. The canoe was about seven feet in length; of a rich, dark coloured wood, handsomely carved and adorned in many places with variegated bindings of stained sinnet, into which were ingeniously wrought a number of sparkling sea-shells, and a belt of the same shells ran all round it. The body of the figure, of whatever material it might have been made, was effectually concealed in a heavy robe of brown tappa, revealing only the hands and head; the latter skilfully carved in wood, and surmounted by a superb arch of plumes. These plumes, in the subdued and gentle gales which found access to this sequestered spot, were never for one moment at rest, but kept nodding and waving over the chief's brow. The long leaves of the palmetto dropped over the eaves, and through them you saw the warrior holding his paddle with both hands in the act of rowing, leaning forward and inclining his head, as if eager to hurry on his voyage. Glaring at him for ever, and face to face, was a polished human skull, which crowned the prow of the canoe. The spectral figure-head, reversed in its position, glancing backwards, seemed to mock the impatient attitude of the warrior.

'When I first visited this singular place with Kory-Kory, he told me, or at least I so understood him, that the chief was paddling his way to the realms of bliss, and bread-fruit, the Polynesian heaven, where every moment the bread fruit trees dropped their ripened spheres to the ground, and where there was no end to the cocoa-nuts and bananas: there they reposed through the livelong eternity upon mats much finer than those of Typee; and every day bathed their glowing limbs in rivers of cocoa-nut oil. In that happy land there were plenty of plumes and feathers, and boars' tusks and sperm-whale teeth, far preferable to all the shining trinkets and gay tappa of the white men; and, best of all, women far lovelier than the daughters of earth were there in abundance. 'A very pleasant place,' Kory-Kory said it was; 'but after all, not much pleasanter, he thought, than Typee.' 'Did he not then,' I asked him, 'wish to accompany the warrior?' 'Oh, no: he was very happy where he was; but supposed that some time or other he would go in his own canoe.'

—

'Whenever in the course of my rambles through the valley I happened to be near the chief's mausoleum, I always turned aside to visit it. The place had a peculiar charm for me; I hardly know why; but so it was. As I leaned over the railing and gazed upon the strange effigy and watched the play of the feathery head-dress, stirred by the same breeze which in low tones breathed amidst the lofty palm-trees, I loved to yield myself up to the fanciful superstition of the islanders, and could almost believe that the grim warrior was bound heavenward. In this mood when I turned to depart, I bade him 'God speed, and a pleasant voyage.' Aye, paddle away, brave chieftain, to the land of spirits! To the material eye thou makest but little progress; but with the eye of faith, I see thy canoe cleaving the bright waves, which die away on those dimly looming shores of Paradise.'—pp. 190—193.

The view given of the moral and social condition of the Marquesans, is strikingly opposed to all, which our knowledge of human nature and experience of its state in other regions, would lead us to expect. We demur on this account to the accuracy of the narrative; and smile, if a deeper feeling be not enkindled, at the favourable light in which our author contrasts savage with civilized man. That there are grievous evils attendant on civilization, we readily admit; but it is now too late gravely to argue its preference. The common sense of mankind has long since decided this question, and laughs down, in very scorn, the effort to open it afresh.

Equally impotent is his obvious aim, to connect the Christian missionary with the atrocities practised on savage tribes. This, we admit, is not done directly and in explicit terms, but it is clearly his design. That such atrocities are perpetrated we cannot deny. They are attested by too many witnesses to admit of doubt, but they do not lie, they are not chargeable on religious men. The refuse of Europe and of America will come in contact with savage tribes whether missionaries be sent to the heathen or not. The progress of commerce has determined this; and the only hope of uncivilized man, his only chance for life itself, is in the presence and undaunted courage of the religious teacher. The missionary of the gospel has been the friend, the advocate, and the defender alike of the Polynesian islander, the Caffree, the Hottentot, the Bushman of Africa, and the Negro Slave of our western colonies. Whilst humanity survives, who will cease to hold in grateful reverence the names of Williams, Philip, and Knibb. We doubt not that our American brethren, to some of whose agents Mr. Melville disparagingly refers, will be able to rebut his ungenerous insinuations. Let him learn the worth of the morality taught by the Christian missionary, before he ventures to criticise his motives, or to disparage his work. The world is too full of testimonies in favour of our brethren to permit us lightly to credit an unknown witness against them.

Art. VII.—*Memoir of the late Rev. John Reid, M. A., of Bellary, East Indies: Comprising Incidents of the Bellary Mission for a period of Eleven Years, from* 1830 *to* 1840. By Ralph Wardlaw, D D. p.p. 468. Glasgow: James Maclehose. 1845.

Dr. Wardlaw does many things well, but we think he does nothing better than biography. His mental and moral qualities peculiarly fit him for this kind of composition. His care in collecting and fairly representing facts; his cool and conscientious judgment; his nice perception of moral excellencies; his sagacity in eliciting the meaning and lessons of events and experiences; the delicacy and warmth of his affections; and the easy elegance of his style, all qualify him, in no ordinary degree, to be the chronicler of good men's lives. In the present instance, he possessed, in addition to these qualifications for his task, peculiar advantages. He knew and loved his subject, was intimately related to him, and had access to all the information which could be of any service in the fulfilment of his work. It is quite needless to say, after this, that he has produced a beautiful specimen of Christian biography.

Mr. Reid appears to have been entitled, upon many accounts, to such a record. Without what are termed sparkling gifts, he possessed a good measure of most of the intellectual powers, with that aptitude and diligence in their application, which are far better than brilliant parts. But the great charm and usefulness of his life are doubtless to be found in his earnest Christian devotedness. He not only had Christian principle, but had it 'more abundantly.' His choice of the missionary's office arose from a deep spiritual compassion for the heathen; and his discharge of its duties was not, therefore, merely decent and respectable, but was marked by a fervour and self-denial and laboriousness, which must compel the admiration of every religious mind. He was cut off in the midst of his days, but few in modern times have left upon the world deeper spiritual traces of their having lived and laboured in it. We can hardly conceive the perusal of his memoirs, by either minister or private Christian, not producing a very vivid impression of both the claims and privileges of the Divine service—not exciting an earnest sense of its solemnity, and an earnest solicitude for its honour.

There can be no doubt that biography is a most important species of literature, and might be rendered immensely serviceable to the church and the world. History, in one form or other, occupies a great portion of the Bible; it is the shape in which the God of souls has revealed his truth to men, and the reasons of its selection by him are not far or hard to seek. The embodiment of truth in events and actions, has charms to the vast majority of minds which no abstract teaching will ever possess. It is more plain and palpable, it addresses more powers and sentiments, it possesses more variety and force. It is therefore a subject of sincere lamentation, that this kind of composition should not be rendered more fruitful for the highest purposes — the instruction and sanctification of the mind. There is no lack of lives. Memoirs abound. So numerous are the records of modern men, obscure as well as of note, that Foster's essay 'on a man's writing memoirs on himself,' which was once thought strangely destitute of practical utility, is likely to be as popular and useful as the books that figure with the titles, 'Every man his own Gardener,' 'his own Lawyer, &c.' The privacy of individual life is recklessly invaded. People dwell in glass houses. There is no need of mesmerism to reveal secrets. Every man who would live aright, must live with a view to publication. How then is it that so few memoirs are of any worth? The answer seems to be that the true end of biography, is not 'the writer's end.' It is not the public good, but the gratification of vanity or of affection, that is sought. Hence appear lives of men, without number, who have possessed no particular characteristics, passed through no particular experiences, pursued no particular end, and exemplified no particular law, mental, moral, or social. And hence, even in the case of men who have a right to be remembered, parts of their character and history are dwelt upon because of their interest to a small circle of friends or relatives, while other parts are omitted, or but slightly touched upon, which, nevertheless, though imparting less private pleasure, would confer a greater public benefit. The personal is allowed to occupy too prominent a position. The man is remembered, but his age is forgotten. What he thought, felt, and did, is clearly recorded — that is, all that has but a passing worth and being is made much of — but his relations to his kind and to futurity, how he received the influences of the past, and how he helped to transmit them to the coming generation — the specific principles which his history was designed to illustrate, and the great events and problems with which that history was connected, and to the knowledge and impression of which the record of it ought to be a means — these are matters that seldom trouble the minds of biographers, and that would trouble the most of them to very little purpose. This omission is the more marked, and the more miserable, when the person whose life is written, was, in some sense, a public person, discharging a special office, representing important truths, and engaged in dispensing important blessings. Few things are more unsatisfactory to our minds, than to take up a mere list of facts and feelings in the life of one who we were prepared to expect would be treated more as a sign than a substance, a glass through which we might see his 'times,' a connecting link with the mental and spiritual state and progress of our common nature.

Now it is here, if we were to object at all, that we deem Dr. Wardlaw not to have magnified the office of a biographer. He has not realised such portion of our remarks as are applicable to his theme, for he has not attempted it, and in not attempting it he has only followed nearly all of those that have gone before him. He has certainly done full justice to the amiable and excellent qualities of Mr. Reid. He has given a full view of his life and labours. But we confess that the book would have had a much larger value to us, had there been less of minute detail, less of personal and domestic incident, less of reflection, and more of the scenes and subjects with which the life of a missionary, and especially a missionary in India, must of necessity be familiar. We cannot but think that, without increasing the size of the volume, and without omitting anything, the retention of which is of much importance, a fine opportunity might have been embraced of promoting the knowledge of some of the most momentous spiritual principles, and deepening by enlightening the interest of Christians in the heathen world. It is comparatively easy to represent the vast systems of paganism in one point of view, as a mere manifestation of depravity, but we suggest that this is, alone, a very superficial and unsatisfactory mode of representation. Even as thus represented, we imagine that readers of Mr. Reid's memoirs must look elsewhere for much that they may wish to know. Visits to heathen festivals, and labours at them, are certainly described, but what those festivals are, and what is the real nature of the systems to which they belong, they will form but a poor conception of, from this volume. Even the *Thugs*, an association which, it is said, 'is now known to have existed to a great extent, and for a length of time in India, but of which anything like accurate and consistent accounts in this country are but of singularly recent date,' even this 'extensive and organised fraternity of robbers and murderers,' described, and justly described, as an exemplification than which few can be more 'striking of the hardening and ruthless influence of idolatrous superstition,' and some description of which might, therefore, be naturally expected in a work designed to record 'missionary facts,' and to teach 'instructive lessons,' is dismissed in a page, although Mr. Reid had forwarded a statement respecting them in the form of an abstract from the work of Captain Sleeman, 'whose accuracy,' he says, 'may be fully relied upon.' We cannot understand why this abstract, 'how interesting soever, would be out of place,' in this volume, and regret that Dr. Wardlaw should have formed a plan that, in his view, required its exclusion, a plan, which, to some extent, sacrifices the worth of the memoir to the many, by increasing its worth to the few. With the exceptions now mentioned, the book is just what such a book ought to be. Some of the observations called forth by the experience and sentiments of Mr. Reid are exceedingly judicious and appropriate, and not a few are worthy the most careful consideration of all engaged in plans of spiritual labour, especially in connection with Christian missions, an enterprise which deserves and requires, in order to its successful conduct, very much besides the purest suggestions of Christian piety, and the warmest impulses of Christian zeal.

The Bellary mission, in connection with the London Missionary Society, was commenced in 1810, by the Rev. J. Hands, who, having found it impracticable to fulfil the purpose for which he was sent out in the establishment of a Canarese mission at Seringapatam, obtained permission from the government to settle at Bellary. He immediately set himself to acquire a knowledge of the Canarese, the vernacular language, in which, 'without a dictionary, without a grammar, and with very incompetent native aid, he soon made great progress and was able to commence the work of conversing with, and preaching to the people, and the more arduous duties of a translation of the word of God.' In 1812, a version of the gospels of Matthew, Mark, and John was completed, a grammar and vocabulary commenced, and a church formed of twenty-seven Europeans and Indo-Britons, among whom the labours of Mr. Hands were very useful. Two schools, one of natives, and the other for Europeans and Indo-Britons, were likewise established, the existence of the first being soon after endangered by an attempt to introduce direct Christian instruction. Although most of the children were withdrawn, the alarm and prejudice gradually subsided, and in the following year the school was enlarged, and another school established for the instruction, in English, of the more respectable classes of the natives, which was afterwards abandoned on account of its occupying more time than it was thought right to devote to a merely secondary object. In 1819, the first native member was received into the church—a native of Vizagapatam—a Brahman—who, it was feared, subsequently apostatized. In the year following, the Gospels and Acts were printed at Madras in Canarese. The establishment of a printing-press in

1826, greatly increased the efficiency of the mission, as may be inferred from the fact, that from it have proceeded one thousand copies of the whole Canarese scriptures, a second edition of five thousand copies of the Gospels, Acts, the Psalms, and Genesis, and twenty-five thousand copies of Matthew, and five thousand of Genesis in Teloogoo, besides some hundreds of thousands of tracts and other books in both languages. In 1828, Mr. Hands left India for England to recruit his energies, having been an active missionary eighteen years, during which time he completed a translation of great excellency as a first version of the whole scriptures, with the exception of three or four books by Mr. Reeve. Mr. Reid arrived at the scene of his labours in the beginning of 1830, and presented the following melancholy picture of its moral condition to his friends at home.

'The more I see and hear of Belary, the more wretched its condition appears. It is a sink of pollution and iniquity, and the horde of every unclean thing. The state of European society is most shocking. Four or five European families, and three or four country-born, is the extent of our religious society, in addition to our mission families. Some few are moral people; but the bulk are the most dissipated, profane, worthless characters, living in every vice, the very lowest you can possibly conceive. The influence of such characters is very extensive. All the most respectable natives are in some way or another connected with them; they are affected by their example, and are glad to find a plea for their own crimes in the vices of their superiors; and it is an argument in every one's mouth—'We live as morally as you Christians do—look at such and such an individual: how does he act?' They will not understand the difference between nominal and spiritual Christianity. The very last time that Mr. Beynon was preaching in Pettah, (a village of Bellary,) a Bruhmin passed by, and with a crack of the finger, called out—'Oh! it is only these missionaries who care about their religion;—all their other countrymen live as we do.' This man is under a person who is almost an idolator, and holds one of the first stations in the Civil Department at Bellary. I could tell you of things that would confound you, of the dreadful lives these people lead. But they are unmentionable. It would be a shame to speak of them. The next class of people at Bellary, are merchants and shopkeepers, who are come hither with the sole intent of becoming rich; and it is next to impossible to get any access to them, they are so thoroughly engrossed in business, without, alas! even the intermission of a sabbath. The lower classes of Canarese are very much under Brahminical and priestly influence; they do, however, in considerable numbers, attend the preaching of the word; but generally, being very poor, are obliged to toil from morning to night at their daily occupations and are thus prevented from receiving the tidings of the gospel. The Tamil population, which is very considerable, consisting of servants, camp-followers, &c., are a very indifferent race. They will profess any religion, or none, as their interest in a worldly sense may chance to direct them. I could, if I liked, make a grand show-off, and cause the religious world to marvel at the number of converts made under my instrumentality, if I felt disposed to encourage these people to make a profession. Schwartz made five thousand Christians from among them. How many may stand at the judgment-seat of Christ, on his right hand, God only knows; but I should be glad to hear if fifty had lived consistent lives. I could venture to say, that if I were to make it known that I would baptize those who would come forward and make a profession, even without any worldly inducement held out by me, but merely from the desire of becoming, like Europeans, Christians, I could baptize twenty a month. This would look very fine. It might bring a good deal of *éclat* in association with my name from a well-meaning but ill-informed public; but how would it stand before God? No. Let me only be the instrument of one real conversion to God: my heart will rejoice, and my labours, if at the expense of my life, will be abundantly remunerated, but away with these professional . . . !'—pp. 136—138.

Let it not be inferred from these ominous dots, that something very shocking has been suppressed. The last word 'is torn away,' from the letter—that is all. The closing sentences of extract now given, intimate the real spirit and aim of Mr. Reid's missionary life. Few men have been more anxious about the reality, or more careless of the show, of success. One of the objects to which he soon directed his attention was, the formation of an orphan school. The design of this school was to clothe, and board, and teach the elements of education, and the principles of Christianity, not only to children who were orphans, but children who might be willingly given up by their parents, from the difficulty of maintaining them, or any other motive. Each child, it was found, could be supported for 4*l.* sterling. A separate fund was raised for this purpose. The following relates to this institution:

'I received,' says Mr. Reid, 'a most kind and encouraging letter from the Directors on the subject; expressing their regret that so much time and money had been expended on the old system of educating by heathen schoolmasters,* and giving their full sanction

* The following may serve as an example of the pernicious consequences of that system. The circumstances related took place soon after Mr. Reid's arrival at Bellary. 'From particular symptoms which had chanced to come under his notice, he began to entertain suspicions of a practice prevailing in the

to my plan. I set to work immediately and in earnest. A Christian friend here, who had been previously anxious for such a school, generously and kindly came forward, and offered to support six children. Each child will cost *four rupees a month.* Two other gentlemen, pious friends, who had found children, brought them to me, and promised to support them. So I have eight provided for. The building cost one hundred and thirty rupees, and is attached to my house. (Reckon ten rupees to 1*l.*) I soon expect to get several more children; and, oh! if you can aid me, God will reward your endeavours, and bless the givers. I will promise to do my duty, as far as I can, to the children; and then, is there not a promise in which success is ensured? 'Train up a child,' etc. *Pray for me, too.* The work is difficult and arduous. The poor little dears are very happy; they have never been so happy in their lives. They are very good, and very easy to manage. It would give you at once a deep interest in them, to see them. They call us *father* and *mother,* and love us more than they ever did their parents.'—p. 203.

This institution seems to have worked admirably. It secured the support, a great matter, of intelligent Christians *on the spot*—it exercised a sound moral influence in the formation of mind and character—and several of the scholars became, in Mr. Reid's lifetime, the subjects of a spiritual conversion.

Our limits will not allow us to dwell, as we should like, on the labours of Mr. Reid in translating the Scriptures, and similar works, in preaching and pastorating among his own people, or in visiting the festivals of heathen idolatry. And we the less regret this, as the profits of the publication are to be devoted to an object possessing very strong and tender claims. But we would just present one or two views of public and general interest, and which modern discussions and movements render peculiarly appropriate for citation.

'ACCOUNT OF CHOUROO MOOTOO, LATELY ADMITTED MEMBER INTO THE BELLARY CHURCH.

'I was born of Roman-catholic parents, and trained up in this religion, which I professed till about eleven months ago. When I arrived at Bellary, I was told by several persons that the religion which I had received from my forefathers was no better than hea-

schools under the sanction, or with the privity, of native teachers, the practice of substituting heathen books for Christian, when he himself was out of the way. He said nothing; but determined to ascertain the truth, without putting any such questions as would only, he well knew, lead to falsehood or prevarication. He went out on horseback to his customary ride, which was just the time when he suspected the practice to exist; and, returning suddenly, ere they were aware, and entering the school before they could have time to make any change, he satisfied himself of the fact.'—pp. 127, 128.

thenism.* I felt anxious to know the truth of this bold assertion; and, through the instrumentality of a member of the mission church, who read to me frequently the Word of God, and pointed out from it the errors of the Romish church, and how contrary their practices and ceremonies were to what was appointed in it, I was much shaken in my former belief. This person also advised me to attend the preaching of Mr. S. Flavel, which I did. After hearing him several times, my mind became more convinced that I had been led astray, and that my soul was in danger of perishing, if I did not forsake the worshipping of images, and take refuge in Jesus. From that time I became more anxious than I had ever been in my life before, about my soul, and went frequently to speak to Mr. Flavel, who showed to me very clearly what to do to obtain salvation, and removed every objection I had in my mind against the Christian religion, of which, indeed, I was very ignorant. I immediately determined to renounce popery, and spoke to my relations of the discoveries I had made of the errors of the Romish church, and of the true way of salvation through Jesus Christ. As soon as they heard the confession I made, they were very angry with me; and, finding me continue in the same mind, they did all they could to persecute and annoy me, and at last they took me to the Roman priest, who publicly examined me. The substance of the examination was as follows:—

'*Roman Priest* —Why have you left us?

'*Chouroo Mootoo.*—Because I have found out that you do not walk according to the word of God, and do not teach the true way to obtain salvation.

'*R. P.*—From your youth up, to this your old age, you have remained in the church: why are you now going to leave?

'*C. M.*—The reason of my remaining so long is, that I did not know better; but now, having heard the word of God, I am determined no longer to endanger my soul by following those who can only lead me in the dark

'*R. P.*—What! have we not the word of God with us, as well as your present teachers? Listen to it now, for the clerk will read a portion to you.

'*C. M.*—I do not wish to hear it, for I know that it is not the true word of God; for one thing, it has not got the second commandment in it, which forbids image worship.

'*R. P.*—Then are we all fools, and you only a wise man? Go; go out of this place.

'Many other questions he asked me, but I do not remember them well. I thank the Lord, that he enabled me to speak plainly, as far

* The similarity of popery and heathenism appears in many things. In the account of the conversion of *Nargum*, one of the native teachers, occur these striking expressions: 'I could not find in the Roman-catholic religion any proper way of salvation; no one could or would teach me how to get pardon; and I did not see any way in which the people who went to the chapel differed from the heathen; for they were all worshippers of idols, and lived in sinful ways.'—pp. 257, 258.

as I knew. As I retired, I told him that I had been too long led by him and others of his persuasion, but that I was thankful to God that I had become acquainted with the true religion of Christ, which alone can lead a sinner to heaven. The priest then set the example of deriding me; and I went out of the chapel under his curse of excommunication, and under the scoffs and ridicule of the people. I returned home joyful that I was delivered out of their hands. I have since found more delight in attending the means of grace. I do not know how to tell how thankful I am that the Lord has had mercy upon me in my old age, bringing me to know my own lost condition, and leading me to Christ's atoning blood for the pardon of the sins of my past life. I trust in Him alone for the salvation of my soul, and I hope he will give me grace to serve him the rest of my life.'—pp. 285—287.

Our next extract relates to the hindrance to real spiritual usefulness which arises from the prevalence of nominal religion, in connexion with church-of-Englandism.

'We have had,' writes Mr. Reid, 'during the last week, a visit from the Bishop and Archdeacon of Madras. The bishop, Dr. C——, is a very excellent, liberal-minded man, and well fitted for the exercise of the episcopal duties of his church, in this land of liberty, as it regards ecclesiastical matters among Christians. He was very very kind and complaisant towards me, when I was in his company. He presided at our Bible meeting, and tried to do all the good he could; but he is very feeble, and will not, I fear, long continue his labours in India. I fear, however, that their visit will not do much good, but may do much harm, among the most interesting part of the little community here—the young, and some who were inquiring after the truth, but had not reached anything like satisfactory acquaintance with it, or felt its sanctifying power. These persons have been *confirmed*, and now think all is well with them: that the bishop, who is an acknowledged good man, has blessed God on their account; that they are *regenerate*, and that their *sins are pardoned*; and what can they now want for peace towards God, or confidence regarding their eternal safety! Miserable delusion! Woe to the church which thus leads blindfold its disciples, from an attachment to the forms, and a disregard to the vitals of religion! Six years of plain practical preaching is now become a thing of no efficacy; an easier way to peace is found than penitence toward God, and faith in the Lord Jesus; and it is eagerly embraced. In vain do I now stand up to illustrate and enforce the plain requisitions of the Gospel.—Well, this is my duty, nevertheless,—'Whether men will hear, or whether they will forbear;' and thus only shall I 'deliver *my* soul' from the guilt of blood. Pray for me, that I may be found faithful.'—pp. 293, 299.

Thus strongly does a meek-spirited labourer, far enough removed from any suspicion of bigotry or violence, complain of the operation of a system which is daily working in precisely the same way at home, but which many, who profess to perceive its erroneousness, deem it right and prudent to let alone, if not indeed, to compliment.

Art. VIII.—*Oliver Cromwell's Letters and Speeches: with Elucidations.* By Thomas Carlyle. 2 vols. 8vo. pp. 522 and 669. London: Chapman & Hall.

So hard is the lot of those who undertake the task of leading mankind away from the flesh-pots of some half-cherished slavery, that the wonder only is that human nature should furnish from time to time the stimulus required to prevent the world's stagnation. Compare what is to be obtained by any individual, combined with the chances of obtaining it, in a course of subservience to dominant evils, with the prospects from resistance; calculate the certainty with which present rewards and pleasures drop into the mouth of him who follows a multitude to do evil and can make even the most moderate contribution to the success of the general concern, and then place it by the side of the doubtful, or perhaps never-arriving returns, in the shape of anything externally inviting, which may be reckoned on by the servant of the right; and wonder at the idiosyncrasy which pushes any man forward to take the risk, and quit his bed for the sake of struggling for anything that is true in theory or equitable in practice.

There is a meanness also in mankind, which makes them ever ready to clinch and secure the advantages they have received from others, by the sacrifice, if it will gain the end, and disavowal of those to whom they are conscious they owe the good. There is not a man that would shrink from the worst of continental despotisms if it were proposed to him, who is not aware that to the tough Saxon greatness of Cromwell and his followers, he owes all of exemption which himself can boast; and yet the House of Commons has not produced a member who has dared to record his personal reprobation of the ceremony, by which that House presents itself annually by its sureties, to perform the *fico* as in Italian story. Of the numerous individuals, too, who profess a sweating loyalty to the existing dynasty, not one shall find out that this dynasty is rudely kicked by every insult offered to those who were in point of fact the nursing-fathers of its establishment, however far their views may have been from being directed to such a termination. When a Stuart was last at Derby, it is on record that Cromwell and his supporters could be civilly talked of by the loyal. It is the proverbial story, of the improvement made on the fiend when he was sick, and the sad relapse which attended upon convalescence.

It would be an interesting scene, if the palterers and time-servers, and these who wait for the opinion of the powerful to follow it, could be made to declare distinctly what it is they would have desired to be the result of the struggle of our ancestors. Would they have wished, for instance, that the fate of Prynne should have been extended at the discretion of the ruling powers, to all ears, their own included? Would they have coveted the portion of security and wealth which might have befallen ordinary members of the community, if all men had agreed, like brother Neile, to invite "the breath of our nostrils" to be familiar at pleasure with our pockets? Was the church, too, to be saddled on us after Laud's approved model,—and should we all by this time have been fashioned, to watch and follow a licensed mummer playing at bo-peep with his idol in a sauce-boat? On this last point, it is not needful to go far for company. One of the most marked analogies between the present and the æra which produced our 'chief of men,' consists in the effort making to go back to the ancient darkness, except as regards the division of the spoil. A Church bearing much resemblance to a wild animal half-reclaimed, and wanting only temptation to prove identity of race, is leaning, not only by the acts of individual members, but by the tendency of what is both done and *not* done by its official leaders, to a return to the ancient folly which the stomachs of our ancestors could not endure. The creature that was imperfectly washed at the Reformation, has her natural leanings towards 'the element from which she rose,' and has borne away sufficient patches indicative of origin, to direct her instincts to discovery of the way back. What at the time might only be the results of the difficulty of riddance, now start up into authorities and guides; and Oxford hears the wail, significant of longing for recumbency in the forsaken mire. The crisis is the same in kind, though not in degree. When one side is moving forward, the other must either advance or give way; for to be stationary is not in human things. Ears may not be in danger; but there are those who know the flavour of four walls administered in support of church-rates. And it is only the certainty that the movement would be met with corresponding energy, which keeps the ears in safety. We shall do without a drill of Ironsides in the flesh; but there must be many Cromwells in spirit. The sturdy Saxon vigour of the commonwealth leader, is one of the legacies of many martyrs, some in death and some afterwards, to which we owe "our portion of the good which heaven bestows." If Milton is evidence, Cromwell's martyrdom began, before the day when 'hyæna' royalists tore up his bones*. Few names have been followed with such a perseverance of detraction since. The accidental raising of the question of a statue, will probably be the little shake which will end in restoring the memory of Cromwell to its righteous level.

The author of the 'Letters and Speeches,' has done much towards this by his 'Elucidations.' Everything which was obscure either through antiquated dialect or personal peculiarity, was to be set down to evil. A Puritan must be hypocritical, because he was occasionally long-winded; and if he lost the thread of his argument, or his reader did, it could be only because there was something it was necessary to conceal At the same time it may not be certain that Cromwell did not sometimes fall into the temptations which beset men who insist on habitually stretching their proceedings upon the measure of the Jewish dispensation. He was clearly not insensible to the inference, that he who spake the language of the prophets, had something of the prophetic about him in return. It is a dangerous assumption for man to make, that because he wishes to be God's special instrument, he is so. Nevertheless, to a great extent, he was; and so far was right. But the undoubtingness of his credence upon this point may sometimes excite a smile; as for instance where he is found endeavouring to raise a horror in Speaker Lenthall, by reporting the very indefensible language of a royalist while being burnt in St. Peter's steeple; —without the smallest suspicion that some of the blame might lie on those who burnt him without his consent†. But what was to be done with men who 'refused to yield to mercy.' True enough, that some of them got small mercy by yielding; but Cromwell appears to have been particularly conscientious in all his doings in that way, according to the ideas of his age and country. He never stormed without giving full warning of the consequences; and this he plainly considered as satisfying all demands. This is not necessarily to be a precedent two centuries afterwards; but it may be reason why Cromwell should not be held up to execration for conquering as men in his time were wont to do. He could be zealous to the death, for what he

* ——— ———who through a cloud
Not of war only, but detractions rude,
Guided by faith and matchless fortitude,
To peace and truth thy glorious way hast ploughed.

† I. 462.

considered the rights of belligerents, on one side as well as on the other; witness his conduct at the surrender of Winchester, where of six soldiers convicted of plundering the captives contrary to the articles of surrender, 'one of them by lot was hanged, and the other five were marched off to Oxford, to be there disposed of as the' enemy's 'Governor saw fit.' This was manifestly a man conscientious after his way.

The great merit of the author of the present work, is, that he has thrown the light of his genius, like a lantern into an owlet's nest, to the dispelling of the vague and undefined apprehensions of the disagreeable, attaching to the individual who is his subject. Instead of a man morose, deceptive, hypocritical, wishing to be taken for anything but the reality, he is discovered to be a hale, hearty composition of something between the yeoman and the squire, full of all wholesome domestic feelings and propensities, as earnest at his prayers as with his broad-sword, a man that can be as gallant 'from Aboard the John' to his daughter-in-law as might have done for a lover; his affection indeed for 'dear Doll' seems always to have been eminent; irresistibly conscious of the humorous and the odd, and given in consequence to inextinguishable laughter at the sight of soldiers with their heads under a churn. On some occasions these dispositions may have been dangerous; and it is clear, as the author indeed intimates, that the Protector did somewhat quiz George Fox, when he sat down on a table, and even 'spake light things to him*.' Oliver and George, were both of them men whose works follow them; and the Protector seems, after all, to have been really kind to his comrade, considering the difference of their humours. A sample of his free and kindly spirit, is given in his accidental visit, on a reconnoitring party in an enemy's country, to Allertoun House; where he won the heart of a royalist lady, by stroking the head of her sickly boy, and calling him 'his little Captain†.' His guests at the Cockpit he 'entertained with rare music, both of voices and instruments;' and 'by way of diversion would make verses'—*bouts-rimés*—with his privy councillors. On which latter occasions, 'he commonly called for tobacco, pipes and a candle'—a very gay thing in those days—'and would now and then take tobacco himself.' It is clear His Highness on the whole, was a right worthy gentleman. Considering what palaces have seen, before and after, the bricks and mortar must have felt a sort of holyday.

There can be no doubt upon scrutiny, that Oliver was an honest man and a true; warped sometimes, perhaps, to a certain extent, by temptations which nobody else was exposed to, and

* II, 661. † II, 122.

rather inclined to make the most of his resemblance to a judge and mighty man in Israel of the early day. But where should we all have been, if it had not been for him and his? In what particular attitude of prostration, should we have been worshipping the Baal of civil and religious tyranny, or else gracing the pillory, and the place of ears if not of skulls? When, therefore, after the exhortation of the Apocryphal rhapsodist, we 'praise famous men and the fathers that begat us,' let us never forget the fathers of England's and the world's freedom, such as it is and shall be, without whom we had been left in outer darkness, and been groping our way to this hour about the fences of our prison-house.

When Oliver is called to mind as chief, it always includes the valiant men and good at need, who were his help and stay. Miserable was the conclusion to many or most of them; as is the general ending to those who are hot in the good work. If Thomas Carlyle goes to Vevay as he intimates, there are monuments there to be read with more 'emotion' than Ludlow's. His inscription is lengthy and guarded, as having been written in 1692 or later, by friends apparently anxious to introduce nothing unpleasant to any of the supporters of 'the present happy settlement.' The gem of the inscriptions at Vevay, is in the flash of republican and puritanic feeling, such as neither friend nor enemy can refuse to admire, sent forth by the man on the floor, who being dead yet speaketh, 'Andreas Broughton, of Maidstone in the county of Kent, twice mayor,' who 'was found worthy to utter *the Sentence of the King of Kings*; for the which being banished from his own land, when his pilgrimage was finished, and stricken by no disease but old age, resting from his labours he died in the Lord, 23 February, 1687, in the eighty-fourth year of his age*.' And, true enough, he was the man who read the sentence of the High Court of Justice to the criminal, and there he lies, glorying that he was smitten with no judgment and cut off by no vengeance, but lived to the extremity of what is allowed to man, and left to posterity the record of his intrepidity.

* Depositorivm | Andreæ Brovghton Armigeri | Anglicani Maydstonensis | In Comitatv Cantv | Vbi bis Prætor Vrbanvs | Dignatvsqve Etiam Fvit Sen | tentiam Regis Regvm Profari | Qvam Ob Cavsam Expvlsvs Patriâ svâ | Peregrinatione eivs finitâ | Solo Senectvtis Morbo Affectvs | Reqviescens a Laboribvs svis | In Domino Obdormivit. | 23° Die Feb an° Domini 1687 | Ætatis suæ 84.

In the church of St. Martin at Vevay. The perpendicular marks indicate the termination of the lines. The grave-stone is on the floor, not far from Ludlow's monument; and there are two more near it, in which one half of all the lines is covered, but enough is visible to show that they are upon others of the exiles, and that the Christian name of one was Nicolas and the other William.

In studying the history of these times, there is no need to limit the application to the recurrence of a precisely similar state of things, any more than to confine the improvement of a martyrdom to the contingency of a return of fire and faggot, or to draw no lesson from the combat in the Valley of Humiliation except to the piercing of the substance of an actual Apollyon. Valour and a single eye, are everywhere the same; and the use of them is not restrained to the repetition of the case which brought them into play. There may have been great changes in public opinion, as to the propriety of using certain means and instruments; and still the debate on the main question remain, with this exception, where it was. The question tried by our ancestors and gallantly carried out, was whether an individual holding the rank of sovereign prince, was amenable in any case, to judgment for high crimes and misdemeanours committed against the community at large; for treason in short, and violent and sanguinary infraction of the compact which bound the community to him, and him to them. They settled it in their own way; and so did the government which followed, after the Revolution of 1688, when it set a price upon the head of the heir and representative of the beheaded one. Whether heading be or be not the proper punishment for political offences or for any offences, is a nicety of more modern origin than either. What is clear is, that the later government, like the earlier, maintained and acted on the principle that royal blood might be shed by law in the extreme case; and it would be mere paltering, for men upholding the right of what was attempted in the spirit this day hundred years, to be mealy-mouthed about what was executed in the flesh a hundred years before. Let the question of whether death be the fit punishment, be debated by itself; but let no cloud be raised about the question of responsibility, which has since been settled so often, as to have become among the commonest of the common law of Europe. It may not have been engrossed upon calf-skins, nor graven upon stones; but at least seven of the present regnant families of Europe, our own included, are living and tangible witnesses, which it were high treason within their several borders to dispute. No Englishman, no Frenchman, no Belgian, no Swede, no Spaniard, no Portuguese, no Brunswicker, can refuse to support the principle of our ancestors, without in various degrees and proportions running amuck against the constituted government of his country. Let there be an end then of drivelling hair-splittings and sheepish treason; and claim for England the right which facts and history assign her, of having been the first mover in this branch of legislation. Time and alteration of manners may have softened down the penalty, from the dividing of the head from the body, to being wheeled out of the country in a coach and six. And the next thing to be expected is, that as the public appears to have given up its claim to the heads, hearts, bowels, or other fractions of the anatomy of sovereigns proved to be in the wrong, so governors will see it to be but a fair return, a simple reciprocity under the ignorance of which way the die may fall, to give up the delights of blood when a popular opponent is found guilty by failure of success. The people have perhaps been hasty on their part; though it is well to be hasty the right way. But truly a disgusting thing it is. to see a minister who has perhaps seized on the supplies by military force in his own country or in a colony, and put to death his prisoners of war who made defence, standing up to protest against the inclusion of what are called political offences, in the abolition of death punishment; when if himself were brought before the High Court of a just public for what he has done and meditated, his first proceeding would be to whine about his wife and children as Strafford did, and claim the amnesty the people has too generously granted without taking fair precautions in return. The last debate on the transported Chartists, contained the gloating of exulting hangmen,—'We hanged' was their own phrase, it was not forced upon them,—over the deaths of men who, if the nation had been wise, would have changed places with their judges. Not that the Chartists were not guilty, and fortunate to escape with life. The more the folly, that could not let the subject pass, without calling up the memory of the olden crime.

Since the subject of death punishment at large, is one which takes continually-increasing hold upon the public mind, it can be no unwarrantable digression that should enter into the baseness and injustice of the distinction, which would claim exemption from capital punishment for the defeated tyrant, and preserve the infliction for his unsuccessful opponent. Compare the temptations, and the opportunities, of the two men; supposing it admitted, that in either case taken, there has been error. The governor, with no individual suffering, no family's hopes destroyed, no industry ruined, no religious opinions insulted, or personal happiness invaded,—in the full blow of pampered existence, and the enjoyment of the great prizes of society, has been unable to restrain his feet within the bounds of law, and keep his hands off the ewe lambs of his neighbours' low estate. The governed, with little prospect but changing one suffering for another, has through great unwillingness, and the gnawing of strong necessities, resisted what he could not find patience to endure. Granted, that he may have been in some degree in the wrong; that he may in particular have been in error in thinking he could remedy his evils; that he may to some extent or to any extent have been the dupe of evil counsels, or perhaps even have been the victim of men wishing to damage the cause they professed to set him on supporting. What comparison is there in the guilt of the two? what shadow of approximation in the probability of occurrence, or the consequent necessity for prevention by severity? No fact connected with mankind is more certain, than that the numerous classes do not incur the danger and trouble of resistance for nothing. They never make *battues* of the rich and powerful for mere amusement. Nothing but the conviction of a grinding necessity, can ever bring them into the field. They are too much disposed, instead of too little, to court power and woo abuse. The argument that if resistance were not punished with death, resistance would be perpetual, is at least fairly balanced by the argument, that if tyranny were not punished with death, tyranny would be perpetual. The danger is all on the side of tyranny; and the endeavour to assign sanguinary punishment to one side, and let the other go free, is only a plausible effort at increasing the chances of tyranny's success. If the death punishment is to be continued, let there at least be equality. Or if justice cannot at this moment have its way, let the minister who shall have politically offended, be made sensible of the peril he determines to incur. Beard him, point to him in the House of Commons and out of it, make him conscious of the halter he keeps suspended over himself, and to this end convince him there is a feeling out of doors, which will not see death punishment awarded all on one side. Do this substantially and energetically, and there will be no more of a minister coming forward to except political offences from the abolition of death punishment, with the virtual reservation always of the offences of a governor.

On another point the knowledge of the age has increased, and with the effect of throwing unmingled light on the absurdity of the enemies of our forefathers of the Civil War. It is little else than ludicrous, now, to look upon the doctrine, that because the 'Nell-Gwynn defender' and his myrmidons had not found their way back to Whitehall, the legislative faculty in England was for long years in abeyance, a knife without a blade, a lock without a key, or any other of the similes by which the comic stage portrays the absence of what is essential to fecundity or to effectiveness. Men there were of iron minds and bodies too; but the man Charles Stuart, who merely escaped by his laziness being sent on his travels as his successor was, was not yet there, and consequently government was not. Men slipped through life after some rude fashion of their own;

children were born, and thieves hanged, in an imperfect imitation of what such processes are under a legal government; but the king of misrule was absent, the fraction of humanity whom his own followers saluted under the table with rhymes upon his utter incapacity for truth or wisdom, and for whom their current appellation was a reminiscence of the stable's heraldry, as complimentary perhaps as anything else that could have been said of him; this king-bee and nursing-father of the state (a nursing-father he verily was to his own, and his own abide among us to this day), was not yet returned to vivify and to create, and twelve millions of Christian people sat inert, incapable to either do without him, or make another in his stead. The very bees, it has been discovered, can in their extreme necessity take an ordinary *pupa*, and feeding it upon some æthereal diet unknown to vulgar maggots, can furnish it with all the attributes of sovereignty, including that strange one which it appears exists in Bee-land, of being the literal parent of all its future subjects. Honour then to the Revolution of 1688, which took a Dutchman, and with a few doses of ambrosial bee-bread, cockered him up into as good a finisher of acts of parliament as the best, and kept him and his successors of the same leaven on the throne, in perpetual remembrance of the miracle performed. Thus do men live and learn; and thus the babblements of society's infant years, give way before the discoveries of experience and riper knowledge.

Of the most vulgar of the charges against Cromwell, that of religious hypocrisy, there is absolutely no evidence at all. Religious hypocrisy means, that he simulated religious feelings, for interested purposes. But the religious feelings of Cromwell are just as distinctly expressed, when he had no purposes to gain by them; it would be as wise, therefore, to say that the royalists simulated profligacy. Each did after his kind and his breeding; the profligates were profligates throughout, and the religious man carried the religion which began with him on the banks of the Ouse, into the battle-field and the palace. That his religion was of the sort which has the promise of this life as well as of the life to come,—that it steadied him in the hour of conflict and cheered him in the day of ill success,—that he did all things through One that strengthened him, and was thereby raised above earthly fears and misgivings, —were causes of his success because they were real, and not because they were simulated. The man who can maintain these hopes and confidences, may in one sense be said to have small credit for succeeding; like Achilles, who was understood to be invulnerable all save the heel. But however that may be, the thing cannot in either case be done by simulation. There may be a closet hypocrisy, and a House of Commons cant; but the religious feeling which runs through a man's whole life and conversation, is not a thing simulated, any more than the breath that is in his nostrils.

On the religious character of Cromwell we are tempted by Mr. Carlyle's volumes to dwell somewhat more fully. It has interested large classes of his countrymen, and has been represented in very different lights. Our readers will probably expect something of the kind from us, and our own conviction of the fitness of the occasion and the ample materials furnished prompt us to the task. Now it is impossible to understand Cromwell without understanding his times. We must know the character of his age, its imprint and spirit, if we would rightly estimate the lord protector. He was the embodiment of the elements then afloat, a more exact and living portraiture than is commonly seen, of the inner spirit which animated our section of the human family. He was created by his times. They called him forth and rendered him visible to himself and to others. There was harmony between them and him; the rough influences without, and the susceptibilities within. Continuous music was the result, sometimes harsh and terrific, but always such as is produced by skilful execution on a fine-toned instrument. We must look therefore to his age, if we would read aright the character of the man. Neglecting this, we want the key to the lock, the solution to the enigma; and shall only do what many others have done, sketch a caricature rather than a likeness.

Now the age of Cromwell was emphatically the age of religious excitement. This was the element of men's being, their very life and soul. It prevailed to a much greater extent than at any other period of our history. It had been gradually attaining strength from the time of the Reformation. The iron rule of Elizabeth and her bishops kept it in check during the early part of her reign. They endeavoured to tread it out, but without success. It lived, and thrived, and grew strong. The senate and the pulpit, the forum and the market-place bore witness to its rising power. Sagacious men read its character, and saw in its earlier movements the shadow of coming events. Tyranny, both in church and state, trembled before it: and in the violence of the measures adopted for its extinction, recorded their dread of its might. It was present everywhere, and on all occasions, and during the imbecile tyranny of James, rapidly advanced to maturity. The hold which it had on the national mind is strikingly evidenced in the parliamentary discussions of that period. Patriotism appeared in the garb of puritanism, and the language of the Bible was transferred to the debates of St. Stephen's. That cold and frigid region from which everything but the name of Christianity has long been banished, was then warmed by the presence and animated by the appeals of a religious fervour, now deemed ungentlemanly and bigoted. No inconsiderable measure of scriptural knowledge, is needful to an intelligent perusal of the debates of that day. Senators spoke the language of divines, and invoked in aid of their arguments the authority of Moses, the predictions of Daniel, and the more comprehensive and spiritual laws of the Founder of Christianity. Different opinions may be entertained on the propriety of all this, but of the fact itself there can be no doubt. Now that fact was symptomatic, an outward and visible sign which all men could understand. Mr. Carlyle has put this matter strongly, but not too strongly, in his *Introduction*, when he advises the reader of our history,—

'Not to imagine that it was constitution, 'liberty of the people to tax themselves,' privilege of parliament, triennial or annual parliaments, or any modification of these sublime privileges, now waxing somewhat faint in our admirations, that mainly animated our Cromwells, Pyms, and Hampdens, to the heroic efforts we still admire in retrospect. Not these very measurable 'Privileges,' but a far other and deeper, which could not be measured; of which these, and all grand social improvements whatsoever, are the corollary. Our ancient Puritan reformers were, as all reformers that will ever much benefit this earth are always, inspired by a heavenly purpose. To see God's own law, then universally acknowledged for complete as it stood in the holy written book, made good in this world; to see this, or the true, unwearied aim and struggle towards this: it was a thing worth living for and dying for! Eternal Justice; that God's will be done on earth as it is in heaven; corollaries enough will flow from that, if that be there; if that be not there, no corollary good for much will flow. It was the general spirit of England in the 17th century.'—vol. i. p. 120.

Such, then, was the spirit of the age in which Cromwell lived and acted; such the atmosphere he breathed, the principles and the aims of the men with whom he associated. Bearing this along with us, we shall have a clue to much which is otherwise incomprehensible. Our historians generally have overlooked it, and hence the blunders they have made. Judging of appearances by their own shallow and sceptical notions of religion, they have condemned as cant, or ridiculed as mere hypocrisy, what arose from the deepest and most intense emotions of the human heart. It would have been so in their own case, and in men like them, but their blunder consisted in supposing there were no other things in heaven and earth than were dreamt of in their philosophy.

And now let us see what Cromwell was. His whole correspondence is here supplied. His written and spoken life are before us. We see the man as he appeared in daily intercourse with his fellows. We meet with the husband, the father, the friend, the general, and the Protector. We read his letters, we listen to his talk, under all the relations, and in all the circumstances, of his eventful life. There is no mutilation practised, no selection made. We are not supplied with extracts merely, the 'beauties' which indulgent friendship might cull from a mass of impertinent, useless, or even mischievous writings. All that time has preserved, or at least all which the most laborious research has discovered is laid before us, and Cromwell, for the first time, now claims to be judged of by a comprehensive survey of his whole life. This to us is the great charm and value of Mr. Carlyle's work. It presents the man himself, the actual living man, and as we gaze upon his countenance and listen to his words, we obtain an insight into his character which deepens every favourable impression, and satisfactorily explains much that had previously appeared questionable. We feel the charm that was about him to his contemporaries, and no longer marvel at his triumph. Would it be so with his detractors, the poets, divines, and court sycophants, who worshipped the restored Stuart, by retailing slander and heaping invective on the illustrious dead. We judge not, but let this pass.

From Cromwell's first appearance on the page of history, he wears the semblance and talks the language of a man fervidly religious. Before he was known to fame, when he lived a quiet and unobtrusive life at Huntingdon and afterwards at St. Ives, he was deeply pervaded by the religious spirit. His mental conflicts were fearfully severe, threatening apparently his sanity, and calling for medical aid. Dr. Simcott was often sent for at midnight, and reported to Sir Philip Warwick that he was 'splenetic,' and had 'fancies about the Town Cross.'

The solution of all this is not difficult to the religious man. Practical Christianity explains it. The dark, the tempestuous, and the despairing, often precede the calm of settled conviction and of Christian hope. With strong minds this is specially the case, and where the temperament is somewhat melancholy, it often tinges, for a time, with a sombre and repulsive colouring every view of men and things. In proportion to the manhood of the sufferer is the severity of the conflict. But when light does come, when the troubled spirit apprehends the import of God's communication, and reposes in the confidence it inspires, there is a masculine strength and true-hearted devotion in the religious character developed, not otherwise to be attained. It was so with Cromwell. From the dark tempest he emerged a well formed, a fairly proportioned Christian man, the earnestness of whose religion continued undiminished to the close of life. In proof of this we appeal to the Letters and Speeches before us, by the aid of which we are enabled to supply what was needed, to elucidate some portions of his otherwise unintelligible biography. From the time of what Mr. Carlyle, in the language of the age, denominates 'his deliverance from the jaws of eternal death,' his associates and friends were amongst the most religious men of his day. His house was the refuge of the puritan clergy, and by his fireside there sat and talked men of the noblest mould, whom England has ever known.

'Oliver naturally consorted henceforth with the puritan clergy, in preference to the other kind; zealously attended their ministry, when possible; consorted with puritans in general, many of whom were gentry of his own rank, some of them nobility of much higher rank. A modest, devout man, solemnly intent 'to make his calling and his election sure'—to whom, in credible dialect, the voice of the Highest had spoken. Whose earnestness, sagacity, and manful worth, gradually made him conspicuous in his circle among such. The puritans were already numerous. John Hampden, Oliver's cousin, was a devout puritan, John Pym, the like; Lord Brook, Lord Say, Lord Montague,—puritans in the better ranks, and in every rank, abounded. Already either in conscious act, or in clear tendency, the far greater part of the serious thought and manhood of England had declared itself puritan.'—*ib.* p. 79.

The first letter in this collection, addressed to his 'loving friend Mr. Storie,' under date of January 11th, 1635, is nobly expressive of Cromwell's solicitude for the maintenance of 'a pure gospel;' but we pass it over to make room for the second, written two years before the meeting of the Long Parliament, dated October 13th, 1638, and addressed to his 'beloved cousin Mrs. St. John.' It is the beautiful expression of a devout mind, and was written under circumstances which preclude the supposition of sinister design.

'I thankfully acknowledge your love in your kind remembrance of me upon this opportunity. Alas, you do too highly prize my lines and my company. I may be ashamed to own your expressions, considering how unprofitable I am, and the mean improvement of my talent. Yet, to know my God by declaring what he hath done for my soul, in this I am confident, and I will be so. Truly, then, this I find, that he giveth springs in a dry barren wilderness where no water is. I live, you know where,—in Meshec, which, they say, signifies Prolonging; in Keder, which signifies Blackness; yet the Lord forsaketh me not. Though he do prolong, yet he will, I trust, bring me to his tabernacle, to his resting-place. My soul is with the congregation of the firstborn, my body rests in hope; and if here

I may honour my God either by doing or by suffering, I shall be most glad.

'Truly, no poor creature hath more cause to put himself forth in the cause of his God than I. I have had plentiful wages before; and I am sure I shall never earn the least mite. The Lord accept me in his Son, and give me to walk in the light, and give us to walk in the light, as he is in the light! He it is that enlighteneth our blackness, our darkness. I dare not say. He hideth his face from me. He giveth me to see light in his light. One beam in a dark place hath exceeding much refreshment in it. Blessed be his name for shining upon so dark a heart as mine! You know what my manner of life hath been. Oh, I lived in and loved darkness, and hated light. I was a chief, the chief of sinners. This is true: I hated godliness, yet God had mercy on me. O the riches of his mercy! Praise him for me; pray for me, that he who hath begun a good work would perfect it in the day of Christ.'—*ib*. p. 141.

We pity the man, whether sceptic or believer, who can read this letter without an impression of the true-heartedness of the writer. Its tone is in perfect keeping with what follows, and gives, we are persuaded, the clue to Cromwell's character and life. It will not do to turn aside with a sneer, or to reject as mere cant, what was so inseparable from the man himself, as to appear wherever he was seen, and to gush forth with a spontaneity which renders the very supposition of artifice ridiculous. To do this, is mere trifling, the refuge of a shallow and sceptical philosophy. That Christian men should lend their countenance to anything of the kind, might well awaken surprise, did we not know the corrupting influence of prejudice.

The public despatches and private letters of Cromwell are full of the same. Whether he notes the ways of Providence, or gives utterance to the innermost thoughts of his heart; whether he counsels parliament, or exhorts his troops; whether he reports a victory, or stimulates to renewed effort in the event of anticipated defeat; whether he writes respecting his son, or to his wife, no matter to whom, or on what occasion, his letters are alike expressive of a simple-minded and earnest piety; a soul honestly concerned to regulate itself by the divine will, and unconsciously giving utterance to the devoutest thoughts and sympathies. It were endless to quote evidence on this point. All his letters are full of it, and they must be read entire, if its conclusiveness would be appreciated. We select the following as a brief sample, on account of its referring, in connection with our present topic, to the great question which was soon to separate between the parliament and army. It is dated June 14th, 1645, and forms part of a letter to Speaker Lenthall, announcing the victory of Naseby:—

'Sir,—This is none other but the hand of God; and to Him alone belongs the glory, wherein none are to share with Him. The general served you with all faithfulness and honour; and the best commendation I can give him is, that I dare say he attributes all to God, and would rather perish than assume to himself. Which is an honest and a thriving way; and yet, as much for bravery may be given to him, in this action, as to a man. Honest men served you faithfully in this action. Sir, they are trusty; I beseech you, in the name of God, not to discourage them I wish this action may beget thankfulness and humility in all that are concerned in it. He that ventures his life for the liberty of his country, I wish he trust God for the liberty of his conscience; and you for the liberty he fights for.—*ib.* p. 215.

The following, addressed to 'My beloved Daughter Dorothy,' the wife of his son Richard, is still more to our purpose, and is only a fair sample of his private correspondence. It is dated, August 13th, 1649.

'I desire you both to make it above all things your business to seek the Lord; to be frequently calling upon Him, that He would manifest himself to you in his Son; and be listening what returns He makes to you, for He will be speaking in your ear and in your heart, if you attend thereunto. I desire you to provoke your husband likewise thereunto. As for the pleasures of this life, and outward business, let that be upon the bye. Be above all these things, by faith in Christ; and then you shall have the true use and comfort of them, and not otherwise. I have much satisfaction in hope your spirit is this way set; and I desire you may grow in grace, and in the knowledge of our Lord and Saviour Jesus Christ; and that I may hear thereof. The Lord is very near; which we see by His wonderful works; and therefore He looks that we of this generation draw near to Him.'—*ib.* p. 448.

We shall indulge only in one more brief extract, which is amongst the most beautiful in these volumes. It is addressed from Dunbar, Sept. 4th, 1650, to 'My beloved wife, Elizabeth Cromwell,' and does equal honour to the piety and to the conjugal tenderness of the writer.

'My dearest,—I have not leisure to write much. But I could chide thee that in many of thy letters thou writest to me, That I should not be unmindful of thee and thy little ones. Truly, if I love you not too well, I think I err not on the other hand much. Thou art dearer to me than any creature; let that suffice.

'The Lord hath shewed us an exceeding mercy:—who can tell how great it is? My weak faith hath been upheld. I have been in my inward man marvellously supported; though I assure thee, I grow an old man, and feel infirmities of age marvellously stealing upon me. Would my corruptions did as fast decrease! Pray on my behalf in the latter respect.'—vol. ii. p. 52.

Here we must reluctantly stop. The theme is inviting and we would fain pursue it, but our limits are exceeded, and we hasten to other topics. Let us not be understood to plead for the impeccability of Cromwell. We do no such thing. It is enough to assert—*and this we do*—that he was honestly and intensely religious, and that it requires only a full knowledge of his circumstances, and an ordinary measure of candour, to reconcile his conduct—with such occasional deviation only as the infirmities of our nature involve—with the highest and strictest rules of integrity. In common with the best men of his day, he appealed to and relied on the use of physical force. The conflict of arms he regarded as an appeal to God, and the victory vouchsafed as his favourable response. He wears, in consequence, much of the aspect of Old Testament saints; and however incongruous the character, was yet, in reality, an embodiment—in its noblest and most exalted form—of the military religious spirit. From his countrymen he has little to ask beyond a faithful application of the rule—

'Nothing extenuate
Nor set down aught in malice.'

And when Cromwell came to the last hour, when fiction, if it had been there, was vain, and he saw himself on the point of appearing face to face before the Power he had professed to trust in, there was nothing to shake the opinion of his sincerity, or suggest the suspicion that he had been playing a part. His religion proved to be as good for dying, as it had been for living. If imagination were set at work to compose fit language for a spirit returning to God who gave it, nothing worthier could be framed, than the last breathings of England's judge and warrior, while the prince of the power of the air made unseemly racket overhead, and held wild jubilee in prospect of the coming change.

The greatest defect in Cromwell's conduct, is clearly his neglect of measures for securing the continuance of the government after his life-time. By what perversion of thought, he could have dreamed of leaving it to be imagined that the office of Protector was either hereditary or at his own disposal, and still more that so thinking he should have left it to fall on the head of the lack-lustre Richard, who seems to have been the very image of a son born with an incapacity for carrying on the firm after his father's death,—is only to be explained by supposing that he counted too much on the threescore years and ten, which, as his biographer notices, might have produced such great effects had they been granted. In this view, Washington was the wise and able man, who placed the reins in other hands during his own life-time, and while there was the prospect of his own assistance in reserve, in the event of circumstances calling for the old pilot at the helm.

In Cromwell's military conduct, the leading features appear to have been decision and activity, but under no very peculiar forms. Tactics were in a kind of transition state, between the use of the pike and the musquet. Artillery seems to have been well understood, and to have approached very nearly to the modern practice, as regards foot and siege service. Cavalry, from the active nature of the war, played an important part. By 'horse' in that day was meant the picked and well-mounted cavalry, armed and equipped for the particular purpose of service on horseback; while the 'dragooners' were a body of musqueteers inferiorly mounted, whose object seems to have been to dismount and take possession of a hedge, or else to fire on the enemy's horse as it approached. In the present day, the name of 'Dragoons' has eaten up the other; and the 'Horse-Guards Blue' are the only British regiment that claim the title of 'Horse,' and where the privates rejoice in being addressed as 'troopers.*'

* In Cromwell's letter to Speaker Lenthall from Cork, dated 19th December 1649. mention is made of the capture of 'the renegado Wogan with twenty-four of Ormond's *kurisees*.' Nothing further is there found to throw light on what these were; and Mr. Carlyle appears to give it up.

The word that will suggest itself, is *cuirassiers* or *cuirasses*, either of which was the term in common use on the continent, both before and after, to express the heavy cavalry of the time, as distinguished from the light. For example, the term (in Italian *corazze*) is used in the *Carichi Militari* forty years before, and by Montecuculi within fifteen years after (*Mémoires*). The probability therefore is, that the prisoners in question were some cavalry of Ormond's force, armed after the continental model. The English horse appear to have preferred the buff coat to the steel cuirass.

On consulting Carte (*Life of Duke of Ormond*, I. 68, 81.) the matter is explained. The Earl of Brentford had sent to the Duke of Ormond's force '1000 *back, breast and head pieces*,' from Sweden; and the men were English, of those to wit who had deserted with Wogan the year before, which accounts for their desperate defence. Cromwell's first movement clearly was to hang them; but on his finding that somebody had promised their lives, they were saved, which accounts for Wogan's appearance afterwards. Compare this with Nelson's conduct at Castel d'Ovo. But Cromwell was not a man to break a capitulation on a quibble about powers.

In one of Cromwell's extraordinary *King's Speeches* (II. 439.), he is speaking of the measures taken to make the defeated royalists bear their share in the expense of keeping the country in order; and says, 'And truly if any man be angry at it,—I am plain, and shall use an homely expression: *Let him turn the buckle of his girdle behind him!*' The author notes, that 'the proverb is in *Ray*; but without commentary.'

In *Much Ado about Nothing* (Act v. sc. 1.) 'If he be [angry], he knows how to turn his girdle,' is used in a way which pretty evidently means

What should induce any man to prefer the political position of Great Britain, as it existed under the two successors of Cromwell, to the condition in which it was left at his death, is among things inexplicable, except upon the principle that like is attracted to like. If it was necessary there should be a personal chief of the state, to extract and pump up honour and wealth from the community and dispense it to the favoured few, it did not seem worth while to introduce the pensioner of the French King, for the sake of the difference between his performance of the part of pump, and a Protector's. Nobody, in fact, is deceived now, upon the merits of the case; and the worst compliment that can be paid to the engrafted branch which has succeeded to the intolerableness of our wild stock of original royalty, is to put slight upon the great man of the English people, who was in reality the leading instrument of the happy change.

The great lesson from Cromwell's history appears to be, that wants make men. Or more strictly, perhaps, there are men always, and wants make way for them. When the effectual majority of a nation is convinced of its wants, and bent on their attainment, it has not to wait for the appearance of some great one, sung by poets and foretold by seers. The 'coming man' is always in time. When the people are ready for the leader, a barley-cake of a fen esquire shall be found able to roll into the enemy's host and overthrow it. Such is one of the compensations, in the coarse struggle of which the world is the scene, for the many disadvantages under which the people's party lies. With change of times may come changes of means; but the warning is always there, if the enemies of the right can only interpret the tokens.

'He knows how to draw his sword and fight;' turning the girdle, it is presumable, being an action connected with bringing the sword attached to it, into a position for drawing. Does not Cromwell, therefore, mean, 'If the Royalists are angry at being made to pay, let them draw their swords and try their luck again.' It is not impossible, that the passage in Shakspeare may have been at the bottom of the proverbial expression. As an instance of something like it, sailors have a proverbial phrase, of a thing being 'worth a Jew's eye,' of which no account can be rendered, unless it has originated in a misreading by some nautical student, of the line in the *Merchant of Venice*, (Act ii. sc. 5.) 'Will be worth a Jewess' eye.' The two favourite plays of Shakspeare, with sailors, are the *Merchant of Venice* and *Macbeth*.

Art. IX. 1.—*Conference on Christian Union. Narrative of the Proceedings of the Meetings held at Liverpool, October,* 1845. London: Nisbet and Co.

2. *Proposed Evangelical Alliance. Provisional Committee. Minutes of the Meetings of the Aggregate Committee, held in Liverpool, October,* 1845, *and January,* 1846. Liverpool: Kaye, Castle-street.

3. *Proposed Evangelical Alliance, Report of the Speeches delivered at Public Meetings held in the Royal Amphitheatre, and the Commercial Hall, Liverpool, on Tuesday Evening, December* 16*th,* 1845. Liverpool: Kaye.

4. *Proposed Evangelical Alliance. Report of the Speeches delivered at the Public Meeting held in the Free Trade Hall, Manchester, on Friday Evening, January* 16*th,* 1840. Manchester. 51, Piccadilly.

These pamphlets, and others now before us, introduce a subject which we approach with strong reluctance. Yet in the position we occupy, we have been silent long enough. Our readers have a right to claim what assistance we can give them in the formation of their estimates of all great public movements: at least, if any movements be excepted, such as are distinctly evangelical could hardly be so. Were our work a chronicle, we should be bound to put on record whatever might contribute to the future history of the proposed 'Alliance.' We feel, however, no such obligation; especially as we have no doubt, that all our readers are as well acquainted as ourselves with the public measures that have been adopted in reference to this 'Alliance.' With the private memorabilia we have no wish to meddle; and, in truth, we believe they are but few, and, in general, very unimportant. Our remarks will, therefore, be confined to the character and tendency of the proceedings, of which, if they be not already known, an authenticated report may easily be found in the pamphlets whose titles we have given.

We deem it an unfortunate circumstance for the 'Alliance,' that its objects are not presented in the proceedings of the conference and the committees, just as they appear in the speeches delivered at the public meetings. In the circular which occasioned the conference it is proposed 'to associate and concentrate the strength of an enlightened Protestantism against the encroachments of Popery and Puseyism, and to promote the interests of a scriptural Christianity.' The requisitionists who signed the circular, also presented to the conference a paper more fully exhibiting 'the grounds on which they had been led to convene the brethren in Liverpool,' and 'the nature, terms, and objects of Christian union, which had been unanimously adopted by themselves.' This paper was not adopted by the conference; but care enough is taken in the first pamphlet at the head of our article to produce the feeling, that it was substantially approved of, and was regarded as nothing but a fuller development of what the circular invitation, accepted by all present, had proposed already. It is true, that this 'statement' says distinctly, page 73: 'If we simply united, and did nothing more, immense good would be accomplished.' But it adds directly afterwards, 'but if unity be in one view an end, it is in another light a means.' And it then proposes, (pp. 74—76,) to unite because of 'the prevalence of popery, the inroads of infidelity, the condition of the heathen world, and the condition of Protestant churches themselves.' We find farther on, p. 35, that the committee appointed by the conference to prepare the basis of union, 'had unanimously agreed to reserve the promotion of sabbath observance among the practical *objects* of the Alliance.' 'Long and earnest conversation followed the presentation of a report to this effect: but the result was an approval of the conduct of the committee on the point in question; with the understanding, that the promotion of the better observance of the Lord's day should have a leading place among the objects of the proposed Alliance.' And on p. 10 of pamphlet No. 2, we find that a select sub-committee was appointed to consider among other points, 'the practicability of specifying distinctly the objects at which the Alliance should aim.'

Such passages as these put it beyond all question, that the conference and the provisional committee aim at other objects than an exhibition of Christian union, and, in fact, regard an organized form of union chiefly as a means to something yet ulterior.

The chairman of the Manchester meeting, however, is reported to have said, 'The direct object of the union is to give an opening to brotherly recognition and conference among sincere Christians holding the Head, notwithstanding minor differences in doctrine and discipline. The *great* end,' (the italics are ours) 'proposed by the alliance is, a manifestation to the world of that real unity of believers which already exists, but which is obscured by the present divisions of the church.' (Pamphlet No. 4, p. 5). 'Our object,' too, says Dr. Urwick, (No. 4, p. 13) 'in this movement, is to bring out the manifestation, the practical display of that love which already exists.' Mr. James, also, (p. 16,) declares, 'What we want, and what we are seeking, by this alliance, is a fair field for truth, as a conflict in which charity shall not be wounded in the strife. . . . .
Do they ask us what we shall do? Do! Meet,—pray,—love,—sing together,—and what they do in heaven, with the exception of praying. Do! Conquer ourselves; subdue our prejudices.

Do! Ameliorate controversy; soften the asperities of discordant sentiment. Do! Grow in grace.' We are bound to add that we find on the next page:—'Do! We shall prepare for future action, whatever it may be; and we do not pretend, as yet, to see the way clearly before us; we are waiting to see where and how God will lead us.' Mr. Noel, also, in submitting the propositions of the Liverpool conference, quotes, as among the designs of the alliance—'and, by the press, and by such scriptural means as, in the progress of this alliance, may be deemed expedient, to resist not only the efforts of popery, but every form of anti-christian superstition and infidelity, and to promote our common Protestant faith in our own and other countries.' (No. 4, p. 19.) But except such a vague intimation as that already given by Mr. James, we do not find that Mr. Noel spoke a word in recognition of any objects ulterior to 'a manifestation to the world of the real unity of believers.' Nor, unless from a hint or two of the same kind from other speakers, could any person present at the meeting have conjectured that ulterior objects had been either thought of or desired.

The two meetings in Liverpool were of a similar character. Neither of the chairmen referred at all to ulterior objects; though Mr. Stewart, one of them, professedly enumerated 'the purposes for which the evangelical alliance is proposed to be formed.' Other speakers, indeed, particularly Mr. Ewbank and Mr. Cordeaux, did not altogether lose sight of what had been projected at the conference. Still, whereas union, as a means, was the distinctive object aimed at in the conference and the committees, union, as its own end, was the most conspicuous object placed before the public meetings.

We do not refer, now, to this circumstance, in the spirit of complaint; still less with the design to attribute anything unworthy to the leaders in the movement. We are struck, however, by the fact; for such we deem it: and though we may not think the public injured by it, we apprehend that the 'Alliance' is. For the impression, and we believe a just one, is produced, that the committee find a scheme for co-operation, a much more difficult undertaking than they had expected. Assuredly it should have been forthcoming together with the calls upon the Christian public for an evangelical alliance. Should, no cooperation be, after all, proposed, the manifested 'unity' will become the world's derision. Without a doubt the apprehension is prevalent with thousands, that this result may be expected. Those parties might have joined an evangelical alliance, whose final object was to manifest how many common bonds of union comprised some twenty sects, or more, of Christians; and, had ulterior objects been at once presented, they would, possibly, have joined it still. And if a practicable scheme for united operation should be laid before them at the promised conference in August; a scheme, we mean, such as on general considerations would commend itself, and such, as by its grandeur, fairness, and well-digested details, should attest that its promoters had enlarged and not contracted, had added to, not taken from, their primary desires and designs; the candid observants whom we speak of, will, doubtless, yet identify themselves with the 'alliance.' But, at the present, the postponement till August of the practical, coupled with the strenuous effort, in the mean time, to enlist the Christian public so in favour of the sentimental as almost to necessitate their subsequent adoption of the practical, let this prove what it may; this course, we say, necessarily produces distrust of the leaders; and though the distrust may not be perpetuated, it certainly is not without foundation. Mr. Bevan, indeed, (No. 3. p. 25.) contends 'that the indefiniteness in which our plans now appear, is one of the most auspicious circumstances which could have attended us. It shows that wise men are taking time, wisely, anxiously, and prayerfully to consider; that they are pondering deeply and long on a momentous subject, which they desire should command a great influence through all departments of the church, and to the end of the world. They, therefore, approach it with a feeling of solemn responsibility; a feeling that has restrained, and, I feel assured, will yet retrain them from precipitate measures.' We, too, think that the brethren alluded to, are wise; all that we mean, is, they would certainly have been esteemed much wiser, had they taken time to form and to mature their ultimate designs, before exciting the public to embrace their nearer and preliminary. We dare not, and we cannot, charge them with a guileful effort to amuse their Christian brethren with a little pleasant poetry concerning love and gentleness, and then to induce them, while enchanted, to uphold an agency which, in their cooler moments, they would have scrupled to employ. If they need additional defence to what their general characters supply, from malignant charges such as this, we tender them our championship with all devotedness and faith. Still, we cannot regard the present indefiniteness of their plans as an *auspicious* circumstance. Whatever time, anxiety, and prayer, had distinguished their deliberations before appealing to the public, or proposing to appeal, might certainly have been referred to as proportionally indicative of wisdom and of solemn desire to be restrained from precipitate measures. Their present delay is indicative of nothing more than this: that finding their engagements more arduous than they had looked for, they desire to avoid the error of fulfilling them amiss. A higher wisdom would, perhaps, have refrained from making the engagement, until it had investigated fully all the difficulties involved, and by simple subjugation of them, had precluded the necessity of self-laudation; nor would it need the *highest* wisdom to act thus, when, as was here the case, the difficulties were already pointed out, and former vain experiments to reduce them were recorded. Scarcely a leader in this movement can, however, be referred to, who has *given proof* of having thought out thoroughly the first principles of Christian fellowship, or who has seemed to do justice even to fraternal efforts made by others to instruct him, or, at least, to interest him, in the matter. Our brethren's projected Evangelical alliance may be formed; and their plans for practical co-operation may be such as will ensure the enthusiastic support of those even of their friends who see no need of an association to manifest believers' unity; and, whatever be our fears, or the tendency of this article, none would more rejoice than we should, if such co-operation be found practicable. But we think it no auspicious circumstance for such a project, that as soon as its promoters take it duly into consideration, they find themselves confronted with the very difficulties we, among others, had in vain endeavoured to prepare them for; and, instead of experiencing the expected facility of working in fellowship, provided only that the heart be right, they are obliged to spend an additional half-year in thought, and meanwhile to occupy the public, made anxious by their busy movements, with addresses on what the public never doubted, the propriety and practicability of Christian love, and with appeals for that for which the public are quite ready, more extensive Christian co-operation, if only the appellants would show them how it can be brought about. This 'auspicious circumstance,' we repeat, has forced the most thoughtful and observant minds in all denominations to distrust the originators of the movement; and though the distrust be, as we believe and feel, of the most generous and candid character, it is necessarily, as such, the more profound and vigilant.

At present, then, it is designed to make the Evangelical Alliance an active organization of all who agree to a so-called doctrinal basis, for the diffusion of certain truths, and for aggression upon certain errors and mal-practices. Should this be found impracticable, an alliance, notwithstanding, it is expected, may be formed of the same parties, for the sake of showing to the world the points in which Christians, who differ otherwise, agree, and of inspiring such Christians with mutual respect and love on the ground of this agreement. Should the first described society be formed, it will of course, aim also at the objects specified as *peculiarly* distinctive of the second. Whoever, then, would join the second, is almost sure to join the first, if well constructed; though many who would support the first for the sake of its more practical objects, might feel no interest at all in the second, regarding it as superfluous.

We now proceed to offer some remarks concerning the first project, fixing our mind on those ultimate objects which give it its specific character. Afterwards, supposing all these objects withdrawn, and nothing but the second and diminished form of association to remain, we shall tender a few observations on that also.

The Evangelical Alliance is at present, then, designed to be a society composed of persons holding 'what are usually understood to be evangelical views in regard to' eight specified 'important matters of doctrine,' and associating, while for the manifestation and the increase of brotherly affection, especially to 'concentrate the strength of an enlightened Protestantism against the encroachments of Popery, and Puseyism,' and 'the inroads of Infidelity,' to extend the gospel in the heathen world, and to promote the better observance of the sabbath. What modification of these objects has already taken place in committee, it is not for us, of course, to say. If ultimate objects be designed at all, they must be substantially such as those we have enumerated: unless, indeed, the alliance, like some other unions, finding these impracticable, yet ashamed to confess that it is able to accomplish nothing, forms some new specific employment for itself, and directs the concentrated strength of Protestantism to the preparation of a Protestant calendar, or the reformation of Protestant psalmody. Were the alliance to be confined to the United Kingdom, and its dependencies, there might be more hope of its efficient operation. But it is to be European, Catholic; a unity as comprehensive and distinct as Rome's, but not, like Rome's, 'unreal and hollow;' (No. 3, p. 10;) one visible, Protestant, evangelical, free church, not of England, nor of Europe, but of the entire world, seeking to accomplish as a church more than the various sects, whose members may compose it, are at the present fitted to accomplish. We have determined to employ no irony, nor any mode of ridicule, in handling this grave matter: we respect too much our brethren's godliness; we believe too confidently that they soon will be self-taught. We do not mean that they would like to use such terms as we have used above, in describing their project: but we believe our terms as denoters of *principles,* to be the fair equivalents to theirs; and we have chosen them in hope that their more suggestive power, in regard to *tendencies,* may supersede the necessity of much dry logical discussion, and prove more serviceable than shrewd pleasantries, which, however good-naturedly intended, might not be so good-naturedly received. We say not that our brethren *cannot* form the association they design; nor even that if formed it *cannot* be scriptural in its principles, simple and facile in its operations, or in its results productive of what, but for it, must be permanent desiderata. But we frankly tell them, that we know of no such institution; nor can we conceive of any: and we affectionately and in all good faith declare, that if they prosper, theirs, as to man, shall be all the honour of success, and ours, the much humbler honour of confession. The only powerful plea for such an institution would be, in our esteem, that it is designed for a brief and well defined service; and, while preparing a more purely scriptural instrumentality, is ready to give way to such when formed. Even then, though supporting it, we should view it with misgiving; constrained to do so by the history of every religious society we know, except alone a Christian church. But the Alliance from its very nature is designed to be perpetual; nor can we doubt, that as long as it shall last, it will be marked by the 'auspicious circumstance' of 'indefiniteness.' We turn, then, to the scriptures; and find nothing there whose expansion necessarily leads to any such association; while the Divine ordinance of Christian churches cannot, it seems to us, but suffer an eclipse, and be virtually abridged of some of its important obligations, if such an association be established. The social tendency, and the weakness of isolation, and all the favourite topics of the promoters of centralization, may be adduced against us. We regard it, however, as an axiom, that society is good and useful only where individuality is altogether or comparatively powerless. We hold, too, that a society becomes injurious, when, instead of promoting, it represses the sense of individual responsibility. And when a more comprehensive society proposes to perform what already falls within the province and the means of other societies, and numerous too, though less comprehensive, we unhesitatingly declare the new society an evil, great in proportion to its comprehensiveness and to the number of small societies it would supersede and consign to inefficiency. How great it *may* become, and how devoid of all importance they, is not the question. We, too, might speculate on the probable efficiency of scripturally formed churches, if only a portion of the care were spent in working them that must be spent in rendering the Evangelical Alliance worthy of its first idea. All that as Christian philosophers we now maintain is, the duty and the policy, if operative organizations in addition to Christian churches are required, of preferring those which most of all bring Christian churches into view, give demonstration of their aptitude, tend to augment their effective power, and thus at once do honour to the Divine idea as embodied in them, and deepen the sense of individual responsibility, and promote the general edification, of the several members they contain. While waiting with all candour to do justice to the 'Alliance' when in being, we fraternally express our present judgment; that neither is any additional society required to accomplish what it proposes, nor is its general constitution, as sketched by the provisional committee, in harmony with the principles of Christian co-operation as stated in the Scriptures, and as embodied in New Testament churches. The history of the Bible Society will amply illustrate *to those who know it*, much of the negative that we maintain in regard to honouring God's ordinance of churches. The history of the London and the Baptist Missionary Societies will equally illustrate the positive that is implied. Continental Societies, Reformation Societies, Sabbath Observance Societies, and a host besides, have their lesson for those who wish to learn; but not one of them encourages a scheme like that for the Evangelical Alliance. The scheme, however, may be essentially improved by August. We should have awaited its maturity before offering a remark upon its nature and its first apparent tendencies, had we more trust in the judgment of its chief promoters, or been content, without giving them a caution, to see much-honoured brethren persevere in what appeared to us a course of mis-spent labour and of disappointment.

We have not adverted to such difficulties in the way of a comprehensive co-operation, as arise from the different views entertained by various promoters of the Alliance respecting the nature of the ulterior objects to be sought. The promotion of sabbath observance, for example, one of the first objects to occupy the new association, is likely by itself to divide the association into almost as many sections as there shall be members. But on matters of this kind it would be premature for us to dwell. Having referred to the cumbrousness, the centralizing tendency, and the want of harmony with the divine ideas, which, we think, must characterize the 'Alliance' as an operative association, we leave inferior things to the spontaneous suggestion of the provisional committee; and the more, when August comes, these shall be found to have been thoroughly investigated and handled with a careful justice, the less unpleasant shall we feel our future task.

The remaining observations we now wish to offer, will more appropriately refer to the 'Alliance' as intended chiefly to manifest 'to the world that real unity of believers which already exists, but which is obscured by the present divisions of the church.' And at once we must entreat our brethren to assume another name than that proposed. AN evangelical alliance they may prove; and were there a prospect of their becoming at any time such a comprehensive and an impressive unity as might emulate the Roman, we should not think it particularly immodest were they to employ the more imposing and significant '*The*.' We allow a society's right to assume whatever unappropriated name it pleases. It is not right we speak of, but propriety. And with our expectations of the expansion the 'Alliance' will enjoy, we feel the sense of contrast almost ludicrously roused when we look on the catholicism of its name. Doubtless it will manifest to the world, that the particular individuals who compose it, hold eight important points in common, and regard themselves as bound, in consequence, to walk in love: but it will neither show that others do not hold the points, and walk in love, as well as they; nor render the propriety of this particular mode of manifestation, self-evident and unquestionable. In our esteem, it is a marvellous confession that our brethren of the Alliance virtually make. For if they mean any thing *particular*, of course it is the following; that all *their* private and all *their* social efforts to preserve a brotherly spirit, and to express it in ways conformed to the dictates of integrity, are signal failures in both their personal consciousness and the apprehension of the world. If this, truly, were the fact, we would join our brethren in bewailing their weakness and acts of inconsistency; but we think *them* of an eminently fraternal spirit towards each other, and we believe that want of mutual kindness is not the weighty element in the charges that the world would bring against *them*. If our brethren, however, design to accuse others, not themselves, it would be well to point their accusations. General charges are worth nothing; and if personal charges are devised within the breast, our brethren need no monitor to urge them to a private dealing, not a public, to a personal and direct, not a social and indirect, with the supposed offenders and their faults. To this private, pointed, frank, and affectionate expostulation with each other, in cases of alleged unbrotherliness, as well as in cases involving the integrity of character, must Christians, we maintain, whether of the same church or of different churches, and whether or not of the same denomination, come, if ever the supposed evils shall be rectified. Such evils, we admit, abound; and especially, we think, in the conduct of all the bodies of the Wesleyan Methodists towards the younger and more ignorant members of Independent and Baptist congregations; in that of almost all evangelical churchmen, both clerical and lay, towards as many dissenters and methodists as come within their reach, and do not overawe them; in that of almost all protestants, particularly church-of-England-men, presbyterians, and methodists, towards the catholics; (Mr. Ewbank half suspects this, we think; see No 3, p. 10); in that of almost all evangelicals towards unitarians; and in that of a large number of dissenters towards their brethren who constitute the Anti-State-Church Association, and others who think with them, though not joined to the Association. The evils, then, deplored, we do not think imaginary. But we see no need of a new association expressly established to correct them; neither can such an association effect the least real spiritual good, unless by prevailing on individual men to use their individual influence against falsehood, meanness, slander, priestly assumption, and all dogmatism. Should it be replied that this would be the explicit object of the Alliance, we have only to answer with all simplicity, but grave significance, that if God's Word and ordinances, as administered in Christian churches, are ineffective to attain these ends, we have no hope of their attainment by means of a human institution established in the nineteenth century. Truth in their statements of what other men believe, love in the imputation of motives and the construction of conduct, integrity in proselyting, or in refraining from it altogether, fairness in the reciprocation of kind offices; and general humanity without respect of persons or of creeds; let pastors and all men of social influence in their respective congregations, observe these for themselves, and see that all around them do the same, *or hear of it;* and the world no longer will complain that Christians do not love. But if no sense of social decency, no care for a respectable manliness, no dread of God, no love to Christ, no profession of religion, no special obligation as a teacher and a chosen pattern, can bring a man to put away lying, and to follow whatever is lovely and of good report; and if no motives, whether these or others cognate to them, can induce his neighbour when witnessing his fault to use his influence to reclaim him; it is not to an evangelical alliance we, at all events, can look with hope of rescue. As a promoter of love, where love does not exist, we think it altogether powerless: as a manifestation of love where love is actually existent, we deem it superfluous and uncalled for.

But the alliance is designed to manifest unity as well as love; and in this light, therefore, we are bound to view it. Now, without a doubt, it must manifest a kind of unity in faith among its various members: that is, it will show that the persons constituting the alliance, though belonging to some twenty different denominations, wish to be understood as holding eight great points of doctrine substantially in common. Perhaps, now, there is not a person in the country at all curious about such matters, but is already well aware, that these different denominations comprise individuals who heartily believe in all these points. The alliance, then, will teach us nothing. Could it form a tabular account of all professed believers in these points, something, indeed, would then be done; but it would be only worse than nothing. For statistical purposes, the alliance would be most deceptive and mischievous. No calculation, but what would certainly be false in many ways, could be made from the number of its adherents, respecting the aggregate of the hearty receivers of these eight important points. Meanwhile we have a most serious apprehension to suggest respecting the acknowledged recognition of 'The Points,' by the promoters of an alliance on their basis. For the doctrine of Tract 90, appears to us exemplified, unwittingly it may be, but still most thoroughly, by the adherents to these points. We hold, indeed, with the bishop of Norwich, and with every man, as we suppose, of truth and common sense, that no subscribers in common to a creed or to articles, and no acknowledged supporters, though without subscription, of what they deem a form of sound words, believe each other to attach precisely the same shades of thought to the symbols they agree together to uphold. A generous latitudinarianism, though not logically defined, is morally perceived and ingenuously confessed. No party is deceived. The joint assenters and their auditors have a common understanding of the matter. The witnesses and the jury alike attach the same signifying power to the symbols. Dr. Pusey and his party, we *believe*, transgressed, in the conviction of all honest men, the indefinite but, because indefinite, *most easily* cognizable limits. Their avowed opponents, the promoters of the evangelical alliance, are, we *fear*, pursuing a like course. If Congregationalists and Baptists agree to declare together their common faith in the authority and perpetuity of baptism, they observe, we think, the necessary limits; for they neither deceive each other, nor mislead the world. Everybody knows, or may know, all that is required for a clear understanding of the value of the symbols. But, we maintain, there are pledged members, and active members too, of this alliance, who, if they knew the reserve, the qualifications, and the supplementary additions, with which they severally give their assent to the first, the third, the sixth, the seventh, and the eighth, of these important points; still more if they thought the world around them were aware of all; would calmly, hand in hand, expire together at the stake or on the scaffold, ere they would concert a set of symbols to indicate their substantial unity of faith. Our brethren cannot think us upbraiding them as Jesuitical; let them not meet us, therefore, with a declaration of their honesty. *We* uphold their honesty; and the support is seemly as thus tendered. But as surely as we reverence their honesty, we are as thoroughly convinced that from certain strong and ill-regulated impulses to a manifestation of unity, they have become blind to the wide, and, unless to transcendental philosophers, irreconcileable differences, which in innumerable instances may be, and in some actually are, latent behind the symbols they have thought proper to employ. Were we responsible for this movement, we should say with Mr. Kelly, (No. 3, p. 20,) that the first article 'contains, by necessary implication, another important truth relating to the supremacy and headship of our Lord Jesus Christ.' Mr. Kelly's sagacity evidently requires the recognition of this truth, in order to complete his creed. Not finding it distinctly asserted in the Points, (most marvellous, yet significant omission,) his logic infers it from the first. His desire for 'visible unity,' content with its involvement there, his conscientiousness constrains him, notwithstanding, to declare what he considers necessarily involved; while with honest boldness he expounds his meaning, adding, 'I can form no other conception of that headship, than as consisting in the *supremacy* of Christ's *laws*, and the willing submission of his people to them; and of these laws *the word of God alone* is the depository.'' The italics are our own, though we have little doubt that the speaker's voice must have remarkably intoned the words. All this, now, we admire, on the supposition that we substantially approve of the preliminary proceedings. Once at that meeting, as its understood supporters, we too should have done what Mr. Kelly did. But that the church-of-England promoters of the Alliance believe or recognize this 'necessary implication,' or, though Mr. Noel and his personal friends may perceive it, and exalt it too, that by works, the only criterion, they indicate their faith; or, that constitutional church-of-Englandism is, or is commonly believed to be, in harmony with the doctrine thus implied, and, therefore, that Mr. Noel and his friends can consistently adhere to both; all this is simply and utterly incredible; nor do we know a position taken by Dr. Pusey and his clique more startling to the understanding, and more offensive to the moral feeling of the British public, than would this position be if taken. That the most influential Wesleyan Methodists, if acquainted with the present state of popular Methodism, (and as they have helped to make it what it is, can they possibly be ignorant?) could assent to the third and the sixth points; all that Calvinists hold relating to God's sovereignty and gracious election being, we think, as necessarily implied in those points viewed together, as Christ's headship is implied in point the first; this, we say, arousing as the deeds of great men have recently been felt, is surely one of the most awakening, and sobering too. Generalization has done much for physical science; but its loftiest triumphs were reserved, it seems, for its management of theological. Reserved, we have not a doubt they were; but we apprehend they are not forthcoming yet. Neither the Methodists nor the churchmen, at all events, appear to us to have displayed them, while aiding in the preparation of 'the Basis of Union.' The churchmen, most of all, have failed: and when the future historian of the present times shall point to the occasions on which the schismatical nature of the state-church principle was most apparent, and efforts to unite state churchmen and dissenters in either general evangelical co-operation, or a full and unequivocal profession of evangelical faith, were defeated entirely and hopelessly, and solely through the unalterably and untamably schismatic force peculiar to that principle, and identified with its vitality; among the first, if not as first of all, he will refer, we doubt not, to the movement we are now considering. Already is the movement charged with illustrations of what we now assert in relation to the state-church-principle. Want of space, however, forbids us to record them: and we must be content with having taken the opportunity afforded us above, of showing that churchmen and dissenters can unite in putting forth a creed, only when their perceptions are perturbed through the agitating power of temporary and peculiar motives, or by appearing to their countrymen, whose contemplation of their common faith they court, to use a set of words in one sense when they use them in another, and neither use them in the same. Rome's union is far more sound and real than such as this.

We have eschewed, as much as possible, all mere matters of detail, and confined our observations to great principles. In the same earnest and uncensorious spirit we would now direct our readers' minds to another grave consideration. Some of the quotations we have already made, manifest the deep importance attached by the friends of the Alliance to the visibility of the unity existent among evangelical believers. Two extracts more, purposely selected from the remarks of men of very different sentiments on many points, will set this yet more strikingly before our readers. Mr. Ewbank, (No. 3, p. 10,) declares,—

'I must always feel that the greatest hindrance in our controversy with Romanism is our want of manifested union . . . . . The unity of Rome has a most magnificent appearance, and is most captivating to the imagination. I know some young friends of ours have joined that apostate church on account of this captivation; . . . . . not satisfied with its purity, but feeling sure that we cannot be the true church, because we have not that manifested union for which our Saviour prayed.'

Mr. Kelly, too, (No. iii. p. 19), proceeds as follows:—

I take it for granted, that open, visible union, amongst the true disciples of Christ, is not only desirable, but an imperative duty, from the obligations of which, on every favourable opportunity, nothing can release us. To affirm that it is an impracticable thing is either to libel the word of God, to impeach the wisdom of our Divine Master, who, foreseeing, with infinite precision, all the differences which should prevail amongst His redeemed people, nevertheless imposed on them a duty which these very differences render it impossible for them to fulfil; or it is to pronounce the severest condemnation imaginable on the whole church of God. For myself I repudiate both. I firmly believe that the duty is as practicable as it is imperative and beneficial.'

And so do we; but not in the way proposed in the Evangelical Alliance. If Mr. Kelly's observations mean anything, they must mean, time and circumstances considered, that in the Alliance a 'favourable opportunity' will be afforded for fulfilling a duty at present not fulfilled, and not likely to be fulfilled unless by some such institution as the Alliance. Mr. Kelly, of course, is not responsible for Mr. Ewbank's statements; and, indeed, in this matter, we would rather lose sight altogether of our two brethren as individuals; and, regarding their quoted words, as we think we fairly may, as substantially denoting some of the principles and views that have instigated to the movement, we would make our strictures correspond. We believe, then, that the visible unity of believers is practicable, imperative, and beneficial: and we have not a doubt, that if evangelical men of every denomination would cease from the evil speaking and the indescribably base practices we have already reprobated, the visibility of their union in faith would be at once in exactly equal ratio to the reality. We have already declared our conviction, that the Alliance will be powerless to reform the mal-practices of which we speak; and, also, that it will profess a unity much more comprehensive than will actually exist. We add, that to multiply our declarations of unity while such conduct is prolonged, will deepen what impression the world already has of our wordiness and cant; and that whoever, by means of the alliance, might be favourably persuaded of our unity, would be still more so, if, without the alliance, they perceived our mutual bearing to be such as we would have it. Our readers will, of course, apply these observations to an alliance comprising no member whatever of a State-Church. To admit State-Churchmen degrades the whole into a farce. What might at first impose, becomes burlesque: or if consideration of the general character of the actors should repress the ludicrous, their self-delusion, approaching to a monomania, would excite the pitiful within us till pain, in our inability to help them, would constrain us to avert our gaze. Declaring his brotherly equality, yet buttressing a system which declares his vast superiority; invoking public investigation of his union with others in a spiritual faith, while taking a part in excluding the same brethren from joining in his spiritual worship; trumpeting his candour, his forbearance, his joy in our prosperity, yet openly or tacitly assisting those whose theory, exemplified as often as opportunity is given, dishonours us, annoys us, persecutes us, or in its best displays, but tolerates us; a State Churchman acting thus—and thus acts each State Church-pleader for the Evangelical Alliance,—presents, in our esteem, a spectacle, we say not so unmanly, for we wish not to excite mere human feelings, but so totally unchristian, that we can find one more type only of the Christian character, where cognate faults assume a still worse aspect. That type, we hardly need to specify it, is the man, who, dissenting from the State-Church principle, abhorring its tendency and policy, and more willing, infinitely, to endure its persecutions than to take its pay, yet listens with admiring and greedy ears to all his allied brother of the State-Church says, extols him for his liberality and candour, deems him an eminent exemplar of all Christian graces, and, that we may quickly know the worst, is pleased with, and feels honoured by, his commendations.

Such a visible unity, however, as the Alliance will present, will be serviceable, we are taught, as a rival, or an antagonist, of Rome. Our spiritual predecessors took another way of humbling Rome. They denied the Roman church to be a Christian church at all; still more, that it presented a visible unity of faith as experienced among all believers. Declaring their own faith as good as any found in Romish churchmen, they dared Rome to the scrutiny; and when pressed with declamation concerning their disorganized condition, they were beginning to allow the fact and glory in it, and to intimate that such a state would, possibly, be found more Christian and more godly, than any organized union of all believers ever could become. State-churchmen and dissenters now agree to try a different course; and magnanimously adopting the broken weapon of their foe, having beaten her with the sword of the Spirit, now essay to show how easily they can beat her with her own. We earnestly protest against a passage of spiritual arms like this. We deny the practicability of such an Evangelical Alliance, as shall, even when first formed, still less in the course of years, comprise a fair representation even of the Evangelical believers. We take this position, and care not to protect it. We have no time to fortify it now; and, besides, no one will attack it but from far. Denying the practicability of the Alliance, we are reminded that Christ orders it, or something like it. This, too, we still more earnestly deny. Had He when 'forseeing, with infinite precision, all our differences,' imposed on all his redeemed people the duty of an *organized union*, we, too, should have felt obliged to try through life to form one, and when dying, to encourage our successors to persevere for ever. Christ did nothing of the kind, however; nor gave a hint of the need of any more extensive organization of his people than such as is found in independent churches. We allow that 'open, visible union amongst Christ's true disciples is an imperative duty, from the obligations of which, on every favourable opportunity, nothing can release us.' But we deny that any call exists for an alliance now, which did not equally exist in apostolic times. We deem ourselves warranted to be content with such 'favourable opportunities' for manifesting what unity of faith there is, as were embraced by members of apostolic churches when they, too, differed, as we know they occasionally, for a season, did, in some matters of opinion, and still more in divers practices. We maintain, too, most distinctly, that, if there be, though we believe that there are not, such peculiarities in our mutual differences, as require for their extinction, or for the manifestation of the faith we hold in common, a new catholic union of evangelical believers, it is inconceivable that Christ should have given no instructions for the formation of such union, or should, at least, have enacted no principle of union susceptible of the expansion now desired. We deny, moreover, the expediency of the Alliance; and we mean thereby to assert its inexpediency. We have already indicated not a few objections to it on this ground. We add, that only those of its members who occasionally meet, can increase their mutual confidence; for there is not, and there cannot be, a sufficient test of spiritual character. The Alliance, we must repeat, too, will tend to exclude from general view Christ's ordinance of independent churches; and thus a profession of faith, subject to no brotherly and mutual oversight, and made apart from the practical observance of church ordinances, may be substituted for the deeply-felt profession enjoined on believers by the Word of God. Nor can we doubt that membership in such an an alliance, inducing the feeling that our personal share in promoting real unity and concord among Christians, is virtually deputed to representative committees, will tend decidedly to deaden the sense of individual responsibility, and to be a cloak to such unholy conduct as we have more than once exposed in previous pages. With grief, too, such as we have rarely felt when animadverting upon public men, we are, finally, compelled by the recent letters, as published in the 'Patriot,' of Mr. Thirlwall and Sir C. E. Smith, to speak of the Alliance as tending, whatever be its documentary professions, to suppress, and to cast into oblivion, some among the grandest discoveries of revelation, the most stirring, potent, liberating, and sanctifying elements of the truth called evangelical. The correspondence between Sir C. E. Smith and Dr. Campbell has confirmed our worst fears, especially when we are informed by Sir Culling, writing from Liverpool, where he was presiding over the aggregate committee, that he had not spoken to a dissenter who did not blame his correspondent's tone towards the Church of England. 'Already?' we exclaim. 'Are words spoken in committee so soon opposed by words without? After all our charitable hope, then, was a snare, indeed, intended for the truthful but unwary?' But we forbear. The peculiar motives that have prompted many men to join the movement; its probable results; numerous facts, too, illustrative of all the tendencies we have ascribed to the Alliance; these, and other matters like them, call for enumeration and remark. But we approached the whole subject with reluctance; and we leave it as quickly as with honesty we can. We await the future in the spirit we have manifested towards the past; and we should be relieved, if assured that we need concern ourselves no more about the Evangelical Alliance.

Brief Notices.

Life of Julius Cæsar. Religious Tract Society.

THE purpose of this brief biography is to place before a class of readers who otherwise are not likely to know much more of Cæsar than the name, an outline of the events of his life, and to state them apart from that homage to military genius and glory with which they have usually been associated. We could have wished that instead of following Suetonius so closely, the compiler had given to his narrative the freshness and unity of an independent biography. By going less into detail in other parts, the chief occurrences might have been placed in greater prominence and relief, and room might have been found for that preliminary sketch of Roman customs and laws which the readers for whom the Life is specially adapted, will need, and for those incidents, in greater variety, which mark the social condition of the people at the epoch selected. But we shall be glad to see the publication of such a series as that of which this appears to be the first, believing that whatever gives enlargement and variety to the knowledge of those who have little time and money, and whose predilections are happily of a religious order, is a good.

We do not like, in such works, a running commentary of devout reflections—a determination to *improve* any and every thing, and think that a supplementary chapter embodying and enforcing them, has been judiciously preferred.

The Women of England, their Social Duties and Domestic Habits. By Mrs. Ellis. London: Fisher and Co.

THIS volume forms the commencement of a uniform series of Mrs. Ellis's popular works, under the title of *The Englishwoman's Family Library*. The size is foolscap octavo; the price five shillings; and the whole are to appear in monthly volumes. We need not recommend a work which is already known, and highly appreciated throughout the British empire. The attentive perusal of such volumes cannot fail to be productive of great social improvement.

The Bible, the Koran, and the Talmud; or Biblical Legends of the Mussulmans. Compiled from Arabic sources, and compared with Jewish traditions. By Dr. G. Weil. Translated from the German, with occasional Notes. 12mo. London: Longman and Co.

AN interesting and instructive volume which ought to be extensively circulated amongst biblical students, and from which general readers may derive much attractive information The strange mixture of truth and error, fact and fable, which it unfolds, is not without its value in relation to the Christian evidences, at the same time, that it may well render us grateful for a purer and more veritable faith than the Koran or the Talmud furnishes. Should the public patronize the work, the translator purposes, 'in a future volume, to discuss the legendary principle, at some length, and to show the analogy of its practical working in the Jewish, the Mohammedan, and Roman catholic systems of religion.'

The English Hexapla, consisting of the Six important vernacular English Translations of the New Testament Scriptures. Part VI. London: Bagster and Sons.

WE are glad to report the satisfactory progress of this work, which ought speedily to be in the hands of every intelligent Englishman. Amongst the many services rendered by the Messrs. Bagster to the cause of sacred literature, the publication of this volume is by no means the least. It is to be completed within twelve parts, of which one half has now appeared, and the character of the publishers is a sufficient pledge for the honourable fulfilment of their contract.

We are specially concerned to prevent the supposition of this work being suited only to the learned. So far from this being the case, it is peculiarly adapted to the English reader, and will probably do more than any other single volume, to render him accurately versed in the precise significancy and force of the New Testament

Scriptures. To such, therefore, we strongly recommend it, whilst to the more erudite it is scarcely necessary to add, that it presents points of interest which they only can fully appreciate, and for which they will vainly look to any other single publication.

History of the Reformation in the Sixteenth Century. By J. H. Merle D'Aubignè, D. D. *A New Translation (Containing the Author's last Improvements).* By Henry Beveridge, Esq. Vol. III. Glasgow: W. Collins.

In our notice of the first volume of this edition—the only one we have seen prior to this—we intimated our intention to waive, in its favour, our strong objection to the multiplication of translations of popular foreign works. Mr. Beveridge has much to plead in his favour, and the unprecedently low price at which the edition is issued, is unquestionably a great boon to a large class. The present volume containing 377 pages 12mo., printed in a good and clear type, is issued at eighteen pence, and may, therefore, be procured, with its predecessors, by almost every reader in the kingdom. There are comparatively few whose means place it beyond their reach, and we hope that the enterprizing publisher will find such a sale as will encourage him to furnish other works of standard value at an equally low price.

Select Devotional Works of Joseph Hall, D. D. Bishop of Norwich. London. Religious Tract Society.

This volume belongs to a series of publications entitled 'The Doctrinal Puritans,' now in the course of being issued by the Tract Society. The series is intended to combine some of the best works of the seventeenth century, and will 'be arranged in pocket volumes, containing on the average, three hundred and sixty pages each, in neat cloth boards; the price to subscribers and booksellers, being one shilling the volume, and one shilling and fourpence to non-subscribers. It is proposed to issue them to subscribers to this series at the rate of a volume every alternate month, or six volumes in the year, for the subscription of six shillings annually, paid in advance.'

We are no great friends to this plan of selection. It has many, and some of them serious, evils, yet we apprehend on the whole, that good preponderates. The circumstantial and mental training of many disqualify them for the perusal of extended treatises, while the religious feelings of all may be awakened by a casual recurrence to such pocket companions as the present.

---

is from day to day dispensed to the hungry intellects
d scandal, and in which, as a learned bishop lately
es find their living pictures (*tableau vivants*) and all
ful its apology. Those deplorable fictions of delirious
every sentiment of honour and modesty, derive their
ing but corruption itself, like the sickly rays, which,
escape from putrifying carcases. They are the cor-
e tomb. We may say, with a German poet, that the
, like that of decaying wood, has no flame, and that
t of a fever, is without light. It is therefore a deadly
us and destructive heat.

tely heard these voices, so full of mockery, contempt,
sacrilege, exalting themselves like a tempest against
ion, which they have cited to the bar of the public.
, no new fact. A stranger in the world, the church
been exposed to all sorts of insults and outrages.
—what is strange among all the strange things of the
with men who have lost the sense of modesty, and yet
s out as guardians of catholic chastity. They live
ce, and in the depths of the sensual slime; their
d to a mere materialism; and—who would believe
dare to accuse the French bishops of stifling, by
their higher seminaries, what has been called 'vir-
ent,' in the hearts of their young pupils!

ing the virtue of these young Levites to reveal to
ral debasement, all the infamous secrets which exist
orld which they are called to reclaim to the reign of
?

hen regard as a withering of the intelligence and
ose young men who have devoted themselves to the
naladies, their initiation for several years into the sad
spectacle of human infirmities. For have not the
physician also their danger? Certainly they have;
is incontestably more certain, more real, and more
n medical studies, the pupil is not exercised upon
iples which are merely speculative; he works upon
ing realities. Everything, then, may become a trap,
r in medical education; yet against this no reproach
hose who are hostile to clerical education.

d ask, to which class in general, may the memorable
aul, *omnia munda mundis,* be with the greatest pro-
he pupils of the sanctuary, or students of medicine?
he physician sees only material facts, and that he
neans of prolonging this transitory life a few days;
candidate of the sanctuary investigates facts with a
hat is to say, having in view the true and perfect
ion of man. He labours therefore, in order to the
d over matter, that is to say, for the conquest of the
man, while the physician aspires to save only his
nal covering.

Correspondence.

We have just received from a friend a communication on the subject of 'Auricular Confession,' to which we referred in our January number, on which we think it desirable to make a few observations. The communication enclosed a prospectus (in *French,* we are happy to say) relating to a number of treatises on subjects of moral theology, physiology, etc., written by a priest and religious of La Grande Trappe, who is also M.D. of the university of Paris, and private professor of practical medicine. We are unwilling to be more explicit, as it is not our object to draw attention to these treatises, but in connection with one of them (a work whose title we should not venture to translate), some statements are made which it may be useful to expose. The object of the prospectus is to justify the initiation of the young seminarists of France into all the mysteries attending the violation of the seventh and tenth commandments, together with others (hinted at in the title to the work in question), of which we cannot speak. The following are extracts:—

'It is then necessary to study with care the moral deviations and aberrations of human nature, in order that this analytical study may contribute to restore it, and cause it to return into the path of truth and order, that is to say, of virtue.

'The object of this labour is to lay hold of man only by his carnal and animal nature; to view him in the state of abject servitude in which he is inexorably enchained by the tyrannical empire of his senses; lastly, to contemplate him with a sentiment of mournful compassion in the state of moral degradation to which his brutal and vilifying passions have reduced him.

'We shall therefore follow humanity in the polluted career of the shameful vices of the flesh, holding always before us the torch of physiological and medical science.

* * * * *

'As for those who shall dispute the necessity of the publication, or who shall pretend that we have no title, credentials, or mission to undertake the work, we shall say to them, we allow you no other right than that of reading and refuting us. Refute us, and we shall reply. There is the whole question.

* * * * *

'If any Voltarian critics, faithful to the maxims of their master, should calumniate us, we, also, faithful to the word of our master, shall pity, without fearing, and shall pray for them. *Orate pro calumniantibus vos.* No—we shall not fear calumny: we shall disdain the attacks of impiety, rationalism, and pantheistic materialism. We shall despise those pitiful literary productions, that filthy provender which is from day to day dispensed to the hungry intellects of cynicism and scandal, and in which, as a learned bishop lately said, all the vices find their living pictures (*tableau vivants*) and all that is disgraceful its apology. Those deplorable fictions of delirious talent, braving every sentiment of honour and modesty, derive their light from nothing but corruption itself, like the sickly rays, which, in a dark night, escape from putrifying carcases. They are the coruscations of the tomb. We may say, with a German poet, that the light of impiety, like that of decaying wood, has no flame, and that its heat, like that of a fever, is without light. It is therefore a deadly light, a troublous and destructive heat.

'You have lately heard these voices, so full of mockery, contempt, blasphemy, and sacrilege, exalting themselves like a tempest against catholic education, which they have cited to the bar of the public. This is, indeed, no new fact. A stranger in the world, the church has in all ages been exposed to all sorts of insults and outrages. But what is new—what is strange among all the strange things of the age, is to meet with men who have lost the sense of modesty, and yet give themselves out as guardians of catholic chastity. They live below the surface, and in the depths of the sensual slime; their views are limited to a mere materialism; and—who would believe it?—these men dare to accuse the French bishops of stifling, by the training in their higher seminaries, what has been called 'virginity of sentiment,' in the hearts of their young pupils!

'Is it destroying the virtue of these young Levites to reveal to them all the moral debasement, all the infamous secrets which exist in the impure world which they are called to reclaim to the reign of truth and virtue?

'You must then regard as a withering of the intelligence and virtue of all those young men who have devoted themselves to the cure of bodily maladies, their initiation for several years into the sad and disgusting spectacle of human infirmities. For have not the studies of the physician also their danger? Certainly they have; and this danger is incontestably more certain, more real, and more pressing; for in medical studies, the pupil is not exercised upon ideas and principles which are merely speculative; he works upon material and living realities. Everything, then, may become a trap, a snare, a danger in medical education; yet against this no reproach is directed by those who are hostile to clerical education.

'But we would ask, to which class in general, may the memorable saying of St. Paul, *omnia munda mundis*, be with the greatest propriety applied, the pupils of the sanctuary, or students of medicine? We know that the physician sees only material facts, and that he seeks only the means of prolonging this transitory life a few days; while the young candidate of the sanctuary investigates facts with a moral object, that is to say, having in view the true and perfect moral amelioration of man. He labours therefore, in order to the triumph of mind over matter, that is to say, for the conquest of the noblest part of man, while the physician aspires to save only his earthly and animal covering.

· Instead therefore, of finding fault with the studies of the clergy, and calumniating the theological instructions of the seminaries, all these new Aristarchuses who all at once have fallen upon the books of [our] theologians to distort and misrepresent them, without understanding either the doctrines or the spirit, or even the language of them, since they confound thoughts with material actions, or sins of intention with actual sins; these writers we say, whether ignorant or ill-intentioned, instead of calumniating what they know, or blaspheming what they do not know, would better prove their love for truth, humanity and the happiness of society, if they rose up against the vice and corruption of morals which have created a sad and deplorable necessity to studies of this kind.

* * * * * * *

So far the prospectus forwarded to us; whence our readers will perceive the nature of the moral training by which candidates are prepared for the Romish priesthood; the arguments by which this species of training is vindicated, and the spirit in which all objections to it are received. We presume, from the communication of the prospectus to ourselves, that it is considered to detail arguments adapted to convince us, and representations of conduct and character calculated to arouse in us some sense of shame.

For the latter purpose this document is entirely powerless. Among the countless adversaries of Rome, there may be many who deserve the character this prospectus ascribes to all of them. We do not doubt that Romanism, like Anglicanism, invading not only the religious, but the civil rights of men, evokes the hostility not only of the virtuous but the vicious, not only of the pious but the profane. These enemies, however, have their well ascertained, distinct, and separate grounds; and while the principles and motives of the latter class are not transmuted or ennobled by those of the former, those of the former are not debased or compromised by those of the latter. For our own part, we disapprove of impiety, rationalism, and material pantheism as strongly as Rome can do, much more so than Rome can do, if there be any truth in history. Our hostility to Rome is incalculably deepened by our conviction that the progress of all these evils is greatly promoted by her. We are therefore by no means anxious to excuse our opposition. We reiterate every assertion contained or implied in our article, that the cause of Rome is that of immorality and fraud; a cause which every friend of scripture and religion, every advocate of truth, virtue and decency must oppose.

Neither are the arguments by which the Romish system of priestly education is supported in our judgment, a whit more convincing. Because students of medicine are instructed in physiology,—because they are made acquainted with the natural functions of man, and the physical consequences of their use or abuse; are young students of divinity therefore to have revealed to them—we quote the terms of the prospectus—'all the moral debasement, all the infamous secrets which exist in the impure world?' Who would admit the deduction for a moment? There is no parallel between the cases, either as to the degree of danger incurred, or the necessity of incurring it.

There is no parallel as to the degree of danger incurred. Here we shall not deny that the medical student runs considerable moral risk. This risk, however, though in the first instance, occasioned by the senses, is chiefly fostered by the imagination; and we believe, that, after a time, the irregular exercise of the imagination is usefully controlled and checked by the way in which the senses are exercised in medical studies. The senses and imagination are captivated universally by external and perspective view of things: nearer and more analytic views, (as in the proverbial instance of the city of Constantinople) supersede passion by consideration, and enthusiasm by reflection. But how stands the case with the *élève* of the seminary in France, in Ireland, or in England, under the system of Rome? He is initiated into the knowledge, not of diseases but of vices; not of the penalties only, but of the allurements of vice. It is his duty to understand sensuality in every form. This he can do only by the commission or imagination of sin. The most favourable account then that can be given of this initiation is, that his imagination is filled with sensual images. The object of this initiation is that he may examine, cross-examine, and convict supposed offenders at confession. Must it not then be his duty to exercise his imagination in devising sins and circumstances, and proofs of sin of a most seductive and ensnaring character to youth?

In our January article we dwelt chiefly, as respects the priest, upon the mischievous influence on his mind of *receiving* confessions. We made but one remark (p. 79 line 10 from the foot) concerning the corrupting effect of the instructions he receives in the seminary. This corrupting influence has been denied. It is so emphatically by a French catholic priest, whose confessions were edited by the Rev. F. B. Morse, A.M., who asserts that the corruption of the clergy begins after they leave the seminary. We can very well understand this denial. We believe it to be veracious. But it is incorrect, nevertheless. It is morally but not physically true. How, we would ask, was the contrary to be discovered in the isolation of the seminary? The spark must be applied to the tinder before it will catch. This is done at confession. Even then temptation would, in many cases, be long resisted by earlier good principles, by the warnings which accompanied their instructions in the seminary —for we are not pretending that it is the *object* of the seminary to make the pupils vicious—or by a sense of shame, or other difficulties in the way of sinful indulgence. But the fact is glaring, that the great majority of confessors fall victims when temptation has reiterated its attacks for a shorter or longer period; and who can doubt, with the evidence (relating to two different countries) supplied in our foot note,* that the foundation of this

* 'The intimacy of friendship, the undisguised converse of sacramental confession, opened to me the hearts of many whose exterior conduct might have deceived a common observer. * * * A more blameless, ingenuous, religious set of youths than that in the enjoyment of whose friendship I passed the best years of my life, the world cannot boast of. Eight of us, all nearly of the same age, lived in the closest bond of affection, from sixteen till one-and-twenty; and four, at least, continued in the same intimacy till thirty-five. Of this knot of friends not one was tainted by the breath of gross vice till the church had doomed them to a life of celibacy, and turned the best affections of their hearts into crime. * * * I cannot think on the wanderings of the friends of my youth without heart-rending pain. One, now no more, whose talents raised him to one of the highest dignities of the church of Spain, was for many years a model of Christian purity. When by the powerful influence of his mind, and the warmth of his devotion, this man had drawn many into the clerical and the religious life, (my youngest sister amongst the latter,) he sunk at once into the grossest and most daring profligacy. * * * Such, more or less, has been the fate of my early friends, whose minds and hearts were much above the common standard of the Spanish clergy. What, then, need I say of the vulgar crowd of priests? . . I have known the best among them; I have heard their confessions; I have heard the confessions of young persons of both sexes, who fell under the influence of their suggestions and example; and I do declare that nothing can be more dangerous to youthful virtue than their company.'—*Blancho White's Practical and Interesting Evidence against Catholicism.* pp. 132—137. 2nd edition.

'The young man, previous to his profession, had anticipated a pleasant existence in the ecclesiastical state, and he finds but privation, ennui and disgust. His passions are raised; the demon of evil thoughts takes possession of him. His ministry also places him in many circumstances with ignorant young women, into whose most secret thoughts he is obliged to enter, and his virtue is shaken. And can it be otherwise where the cleric has those intimate associations with females which the papacy requires? . . . I do not say this to veil or excuse the crime, the natural result of the institution; but I think I am bound to state the fact as it is. Sometimes the resistance is firm and the struggle long; but, at length, this martyr of fanaticism, this victim of his system, and of his superiors, abandons his vow, through despair, and shuts his eyes, and throws himself into the slough of passion. This is the end of almost all the priests.'—*Confessions of a French Catholic Priest. Edited by the Rev. S. F. B. Morse,* M.A., *New York,* 1837. pp. 132, 133. These extracts testify to the universal extent of priestly immorality, but ascribe it to the law of celibacy. There is no doubt that the abolition of this would work a favourable change. But the existence of this law is one of the very things which makes the instructions of the seminary so dangerous. What real Christian discipline would suffer the imagination to be stimulated by such studies, when the only safety valve, marriage, was forcibly closed upon them.

all but universal immorality is laid in the corrupt imaginations first suggested at the seminary? This is we know a very general conviction in France; and we do not believe that there is one protestant in fifty in this country who could read Peter Dens, or any other Romish moral theologian on this subject, without arriving at the same conclusion.

Neither is there any parallel as to the necessity of incurring this risk. The medical student, if he is to heal diseases, must know their nature, symptoms, tendencies, and remedies. He must also know, in general, their causes; but even he need not inquire into the circumstances of their origin. To the guide of souls, however, the one great point when the fact of sin is avowed, is to ascertain the genuineness of the confessing spirit, and to apply the one great remedy, the gospel method of reconciliation and forgiveness in the blood of Christ. Here, of course, we touch upon another branch of our extensive quarrel with Rome—the efficacy of confession, and priestly absolution, as practised in her communion. We shall not reopen this question, on which it will be sufficient to refer to our January number, where its actual efficacy is sufficiently developed. It is sufficient for our purpose to show that, according to God's plan, the minister of righteousness is not required to have this intimacy with the 'unfruitful works of darkness.' *'It is a shame even to speak of those things which are done of them in secret.'*

Our readers will not imagine that we have noticed this prospectus under any apprehension that our article needed defence. Far from it. But we could not shut our eyes to the monstrous delusion which pervades the document, or forbear to disclose the 'mystery of iniquity,' which is hatched in the seminaries of Rome. Our object in this, as in our former paper, is to put our readers on their guard against the sanctimonious pretensions, and sensual attractions of Romanism. And who, we would ask, would, after the facts which we have disclosed, leave a stone unturned to save his female relations from the influence of confessors, familiar in the entire theory of vice, or to preserve his sons from the stupendous moral risk which attends so infamous a system of theological training?

Literary Intelligence.

Just Published.

The Talents; or Man's Nature, Power, and Responsibility. By Robert William Dale.

Englishwoman's Family Library. The Women of England, their Social Duties and Domestic Habits. By Mrs. Ellis.

The People's Dictionary of the Bible. Part VII.

Temper and Temperament. By Mrs. Ellis. Vol. I.

Knight's Penny Magazine. Part II.

Simple Sketches. By the Rev. John Todd.

The Physical Atlas; a Series of Maps illustrating the Geographical Distribution of Natural Phœnomena. By Henry Berghaus and Alexander Keith Johnston.

The Bible, the Koran, and the Talmud; or Biblical Legends of the Mussulmans. Compiled from Arabic Sources, and compared with Jewish Traditions. Dy Dr. G. Weil. Translated from the German with original Notes.

Essays on Subjects connected with the Literature, Popular Superstitions, and History of England in the Middle Ages. By Thomas Wright. 2 vols.

Scotland, its Faith and its Features; or a Visit to Blair Athol. By the Rev. Francis Trench. 2 vols. 12mo.

The Age of Pitt and Fox. By the Author of 'Ireland and its Rulers.' 3 vols. Vol. I.

The Miscellaneous Works of the Right Honourable Sir James Mackintosh. 3 vols. Vol. I.

Bohn's Standard Library. The Philosophy of History, in a Course of Lectures delivered at Vienna. By Frederick Von Schlegel. Translated from the German, with a Memoir of the Author. By James Baron Robertson, Esq. 2nd Edition, revised.

The Philosophy of Trade; or Outlines of a Theory of Profits and Prices, including an Examination of the Principles which determine the relative value of Corn, Labour, and Currency. By Patrick James Stirling.

The Novitiate; or a Year among the English Jesuits. A Personal Narrative; with an Essay on the Constitutions, the Confessional Morality, and History of the Jesuits. By Andrew Steinmetz.

Characters. By the Rev. Denis Kelly, M.A.

History of the Reformation in the Sixteenth Century. By J. H. Merle D'Aubignè, D.D. A new Translation, (containing the Author's last improvements). By Henry Beveridge, Esq., Advocate. Vol. III.

Curæ Romanæ. Notes on the Epistles to the Romans, with a revised translation. By W. Walford.

Select Devotional Works of Joseph Hall, D.D., Bishop of Norwich.

The People. By M. Michelet. Translated with the Author's approbation, by C. Cocks, B.L.

Life and Correspondence of David Hume, from the Papers bequeathed by his Nephew to the Royal Society of Edinburgh, and other original sources. By John Hill Burton, Esq., Advocate. Vol. I.

In one volume 8vo, (nearly ready,) The Scripture Doctrine of Future Punishment. An Argument in Two Parts. By Rev. H. H. Dobney. Being a second Edition of 'Notes of Lectures,' revised and greatly enlarged, &c.

THE

ECLECTIC REVIEW

For MAY, 1846.

Art. I.—1. *Die Briefe Pauli an die Korinther bearbeitet.* Von L. J. Rückert. Leipzig, 1836, 7. 2 Theile, 8vo.

2. *Kurze Erklärung der Briefe an die Korinther.* Von Dr. W. M. L. de Wette. Zweite verbesserte Ausgabe. Leipzig, 1845, 8vo.

3. *Paulus, der Apostel Jesu Christi, sein Leben und Wirken, seine Briefe und seine Lehre.* Von Dr. F. C. Baur. Stuttgart: 1845, 8vo.

4. *Die Parteiungen in der Gemeinde zu Korinth.* Von F. Becker. Altona, 1842, 8vo.

5. *De ecclesia Corinthiaca primaeva factionibus turbata. Disquisitio critico-historia, &c.* Dan. Schenkel. Basel, 1838, 8vo.

6. *Theologische Studien und Kritiken.* Jahrgang, 1830, drittes Heft, pp. 614—632. Von Dr. Bleek.

Corinth, as is well known, was situated on the isthmus between the Ægean and Ionian seas. It was the capital of Achaia, distinguished by the celebration of the Isthmian games in its vicinity, and equally noted for its arts, wealth, and luxury. Hence Cicero styled it the 'Light of Greece.' About the year 146 B.C., it was destroyed by Mummius; but Julius Cæsar caused it to be rebuilt and peopled with a Roman colony. Its favourable situation in relation to commerce soon secured a flourishing trade. Hence it rapidly regained its former splendor, in connexion with its former vice and licentiousness. The testimony of heathen writers is unanimous not only with respect to the learning and culture of the inhabitants, but also their wealth, effeminacy, and impurity. The gross worship of Venus, who had a renowned temple in the place, furnishes melancholy proof of debasement and degradation, notwithstanding the schools of learning and the philosophers on which, as Aristides says, a person stumbled at every step. Hence Dio Chrysostom calls it a city 'the most licentious of all that are or have been;' so that the verb κορινθιάζειν was synonymous with *to be lewd*. This city, the centre of eastern and western commerce, was selected by the apostle Paul as the scene of his labours for a considerable period. The number and character of the inhabitants, added to the importance of its situation and the conflux of so many strangers into it, rendered a permanent lodgment for Christianity within it highly desirable, that the truth might pervade neighbouring not less than distant nations. No station could have been selected more favourable to the diffusion of the new religion through the Roman empire. The circumstances belonging to it were such as none other city presented. Hence the great apostle chose it as the sphere of his unwearied activity for eighteen months. Here he laboured in company with several associates, amid the opulence, the luxury, the licentiousness, and the learning of the idolatrous inhabitants. Nor were his efforts without success. It may be readily imagined that many Jews had settled in it for the purposes of traffic, from whom the apostle received, as in other places, much opposition. Yet some chief men among them believed, such as Crispus and Sosthenes, although there is no reason for supposing that many such had become converts. The Christian church collected by Paul consisted chiefly of the poorer class :—Not many wise men after the flesh, not many mighty, not many noble were called.

On his second missionary journey, the apostle Paul came from Athens to Corinth, where he remained eighteen months. Here he found Aquila and his wife Priscilla, who had lately come from Italy, because Claudius the emperor had expelled the Jews from Rome. The Romans did not distinguish Christians from Jews; and therefore the former no less than the latter were included in the edict. (Suet. vit. Claud. cap. 25.) In Aquila's house he took up his abode, and wrought at the same manual employment, both being tent-makers. It is not clear whether Aquila was converted to Christianity *at* Corinth, or *before his arrival*. It cannot certainly be inferred from the expression τίνα Ἰουδαῖον in Acts xviii 2, that he was not then a Christian; for the phrase merely marks *the nation* to which he belonged. The probability is, that he had been already converted at Rome along with his wife Priscilla. Still his Christian knowledge could not have been other than imperfect and limited. It must have been greatly enlarged by the closeness of relation in which it was his happiness to stand towards Paul at Ephesus.

In consequence of his association with the apostle, he became acquainted with the doctrines of Christianity so as to be able to instruct Apollos, explaining to him the way of God more perfectly.

According to Paul's custom, he addressed himself in the first instance to the Jews, who had a synagogue in the city. Thither he repaired on the Sabbath-day and preached Christ. His discourses appear to have made a saving impression on the minds of several Jews and proselytes, especially Crispus, chief ruler of the synagogue, who believed in the Lord, with all his house. After Timothy and Silas had come from Macedonia, he became bolder, and testified more plainly that Jesus was the Christ. High offence was now taken to his doctrine by the unbelieving Jews, who contradicted and blasphemed. He therefore turned to the Gentiles, and ceased to frequent the synagogue. But the great success of his labours among the Gentile inhabitants exasperated the Jews so much, that they seized and dragged him before the tribunal of Gallio the Roman proconsul, accusing him of opposition to the law of Moses. The governor wisely and properly refused to interfere in ecclesiastical matters as lying beyond his province. Even after this insurrection we are informed that he remained still a *good many days;* at the expiration of which he sailed to Syria, in company with Aquila and Priscilla, (Acts xviii. 18.) leaving, perhaps, his faithful assistants Timothy and Silas in Corinth, together with a numerous church chiefly composed of Gentile converts of the poorer class. While the apostle was passing through Galatia and Phrygia, Apollos, an Alexandrian Jew, removed to Corinth, and mightily contributed to the advancement of Christianity in that city. This eloquent preacher had been instructed in the gospel previously to his coming thither, by Aquila and Priscilla. (xviii. 24—28.) After the apostle had come from Galatia to Ephesus, the second time, he received unfavourable reports of the Corinthian church from some members belonging to the household of Chloe. (1 Cor. i. 11.) Perhaps also Apollos, who appears to have come to Ephesus while the apostle resided there, gave him information respecting the distractions at Corinth. In consequence of these representations Paul had resolved to take a journey through Macedonia and Achaia to Jerusalem, and sent Timothy and Erastus into these parts both to forward the collection among the Gentile churches, for the relief of the poor Hebrew Christians at Jerusalem, and also to rectify the irregularities of the Corinthian Church; when messengers arrived, viz, Stephanas, Fortunatus, and Achaicus, bringing a letter concerning several doctrines and practices, and requesting a solution to various questions. By this means he obtained a knowledge of the contentions in the church at Corinth, the viciousness of the members, and the great disorder into which it had fallen. Such was the occasion of writing the first letter, which he sent by the hands of Stephanas, Fortunatus, and Achaicus. It was Paul's wish that Apollos should accompany the bearers, and use his endeavours to heal the distractions that had arisen; but the latter decidedly refused, conscious perhaps that his presence might rather foment than allay dissension.

Some have thought that Timothy was the bearer of the letter, but this opinion appears to be incorrect. He is mentioned in 1 Cor. xvi. 10, and iv. 17, in such a way as to intimate, that he was *not* the bearer, and that Paul did not expect him to arrive at Corinth till after the Epistle, ἐὰν ἔλθῃ Τιμόθεος. Timothy had been dispatched before the writing of the Epistle, for, had he been with the apostle at that time, he would most probably have been specified in the salutation at the commencement. His going into Macedonia could naturally lead the apostle to conclude that he would not arrive at Corinth till after the letter's reception.

It is matter of debate, whether Timothy actually visited Corinth after collecting the contributions in Macedonia. Certainly it was the apostle's intention that he should go to the city. We know, however, that he had returned during the writing of the second Epistle to the Corinthians and was then with Paul; for he is mentioned in the salutation. According to Bleek, Timothy had been in Corinth; and on his return to Ephesus, communicated to Paul important information relative to the church, to what he himself had done, and the effects of the letter already sent. He supposes that Timothy himself was probably the bearer. It appears to us, however, that Timothy had been sent away previously to the first letter, and that he was also prevented from going to Corinth. In Acts xix. 22, he is said to have been dispatched into Macedonia, without any allusion to Achaia; and in the second Epistle to the Corinthians, no reference is made to Timothy's visit, to the manner in which he had been received, or the information which had been communicated to the writer founded on the personal observation of his friend. It is more probable, therefore, that Timothy, owing to some unknown circumstances, did not go as far as Corinth.

It has also been debated, whether the apostle had visited Corinth *once* or *twice* before he wrote to the inhabitants; and whether there be any reason to conclude that he sent them a letter antecedently to the two extant epistles. We shall attend to both points in order.

I. Did the apostle undertake a second journey to Corinth before writing to the Corinthians? This question has been answered in the affirmative by Chrysostom, Œcumenius, Theophylact, Erasmus, Baronius, Mill, Tillemont, Schulz, Michaelis, Schmidt, Leun, Schrader, Koehler, Bleek, J. G. Müller, Lücke, Schott, Scheckenburger, Neander, Anger, Billroth, and Olshausen. The Acts of the Apostles do not notice such a visit. A knowledge of it is derived from certain passages in the epistles to the Corinthians, such as 2 Cor. xiii. 1, 2; xii. 14; ii. 1; xii. 21; 1 Cor. xvi. 7. The first two are mainly relied on. The second two are adduced by *some* advocates of the hypothesis. The last text is mentioned by a very few writers with the same view. The places in question must be examined separately. But before proceeding to their investigation it may be necessary to state, that the supposed second visit could not have happened between the composition of the two extant epistles, because the first was written near the close of the apostle's abode at Ephesus, and the second in his journey through Macedonia, probably at Philippi, a journey which he undertook after leaving Ephesus. The two visits must both have been antecedent to the *first* epistle addressed to the Corinthians.

2 Cor. xiii. 1, 2. 'This is the third time I am coming to you. In the mouth of two or three witnesses shall every word be established. I told you before, and foretell you, as if I were present, the second time; and being absent, now I write to them which heretofore have sinned, and to all other, that if I come again, I will not spare.' These words, considered by themselves, are sufficiently obvious. They express the idea that the apostle purposed to pay a *third* visit.

2 Cor. xii. 14. 'Behold, the third time I am ready to come to you, and I will not be burdensome to you: for I seek yours, not you, &c.' Here τρίτον refers to ἐλθεῖν, as the connexion evinces.

2 Cor. ii. 1. 'But I determined this with myself, that I would not come again to you in heaviness.' Paul had not come to them in sorrow, as we learn from Acts xviii. 1. Some subsequent visit therefore of a sorrowful character must be referred to. Neither can it be said that he was humbled on the occasion of his first visit (xii. 21).

1 Cor. xvi. 7. 'For I will not see you now by the way; but I trust to tarry awhile with you, if the Lord permit.' These words seem to intimate, that his future visit to the Corinthians would be of some continuance, as opposed to *the passing visit* he had previously paid. But when first at Corinth, he staid nearly two years, and therefore he must have been with them afterwards for a very short time, before these words were written.

Such are the passages which have been thought to imply a second visit previously to the writing of the first epistle. We shall show in the first place, that the last three texts do not support the prevailing hypothesis; and secondly, we intend to subject the first two to a rigorous examination, so as to render it apparent that they also are not a secure foundation on which to build it.

In regard to 2 Cor. ii. 1, it has been disputed, whether πάλιν belongs to ἐλθεῖν singly, or to ἐν λύπῃ πρὸς ὑμᾶς ἐλθεῖν. The received reading πάλιν ἐλθεῖν ἐν λύπῃ πρὸς ὑμᾶς favours the former; the more approved reading πάλιν ἐν λύπῃ πρὸς ὑμᾶς ἐλθεῖν, harmonizes better with the latter. It is a matter of little consequence whether the one or the other be adopted. Paul's coming again to them in sorrow is contrasted with his leaving them in sorrow. He could not have been with them so long as not to perceive elements at work which threatened to disturb and rend the church. Hence arose his comparative regret.

2 Cor. xii. 21. Here it is undoubtedly more natural to join πάλιν with ἐλθόντα than with the verb ταπεινώσῃ. In this way no previous humbling is alluded to. There is simply a reference to the possibility of his being humbled at the time of his coming again to the Corinthians. Admitting, however, that πάλιν belongs to ταπεινώσῃ, the passage does not prove a second visit to Corinth. The humiliation in question was that which he had felt at some part of his first stay which lasted more than a year and a half. Every thing which he saw in the Corinthian church did not please him. It would be unreasonable to suppose, that he had not occasionally perceived cause for self-abasement and sorrow.

1 Cor. xvi. 7. These words do not imply that the apostle had really paid a passing visit to Corinth. The sense is: 'I do not wish to see you now merely as I am passing on to some other place; I am rather hoping that I shall be able to spend some time with you.' In the preceding verse he says, '*perhaps* I shall continue with you or even pass the winter at Corinth.' In the present passage, he expresses his *desire* and *intention* to abide with them for a considerable period, although the accomplishment of his purpose was greatly dependent on external circumstances.

The passing visit may be referred to the short period which *he purposed* to spend with the Corinthians. On comparing 2 Cor. i. 15, 16, we learn, that Paul had formerly purposed to go first to Corinth, then to Macedonia, and then to return to Corinth; but it appears from 1 Cor. xvi. 5, that his determination was changed. To this short period, which, if his purpose had been carried out, he would have spent with them, he opposes his present intended visit of some length, (1 Cor. xvi. 7). The adverb ἄρτι belongs to ἰδεῖν not to θέλω.

2 Cor. xiii. 1, 2. The first verse of this passage we explain by

the aid of 2 Cor. xii. 14. 'This is the third time I am coming to you,' *i. e.* this is the third time I am *ready*, or *prepared to come.* The τρίτον τοῦτο ἔρχομαι of the one passage, is explained by the τρίτον ἑτοίμως ἔχω of the other. If the journey in which he had been disappointed was reckoned one of the times, then the present would be *the third time* at which *he was ready* to come, although he had actually been at Corinth but once. It cannot be denied, that ἔρχομαι may signify, I *am purposing*, or *prepared to come*; and certainly the parallel passage (xii. 14.) favours this sense. 'In the mouth of two or three witnesses shall every word be established,' *i. e.* 'every threatening word will be fulfilled as surely as what is supported by two or three witnesses is true.' The second verse has been differently punctuated by different interpreters. All, however, agree, that γράφω should be expunged. Bleek and Schrader divide the words thus: προείρηκα καὶ προλέγω, ὡς παρὼν τὸ δεύτερον, καὶ ἀπὼν νῦν, τοῖς προημαρτηκόσι καὶ τοῖς κ. τ. λ. The explanation given is this: 'I have told you before, when I was present with you a second time, and foretell as I did when present the second time, though now absent, to those who had sinned and to all the rest, that if I come again I will not spare.' The τοῖς προημαρτηκόσι is referred to προείρηκα; the τοῖς λοιποῖς πᾶσιν to προλέγω—those who had sinned at the time of his second visit; all others who have since erred.

But the interpunction in question does not necessarily lead to the interpretation given. The context implies that Paul had seen several things in the Corinthian church during his last residence among them with which he had not been pleased—that some persons had fallen into sin, and that he had been sparing in his rebukes, not proceeding to extremities, but threatening that unless certain vices were remedied, he should not spare at the time of his next coming. The verb προείρηκα need not be referred exclusively or chiefly to the apostle's last visit to Corinth. Some particulars in this very letter will serve to make it probable that the word in question alludes to these indirect reproofs more than to what had been spoken by word of mouth. Perhaps there is an especial allusion to 2 Cor. xii. 20, 21; or should the allusion be referred to the *first* epistle, as some think, then will 1 Cor. x. 2, be mainly intended. The clause ὡς παρὼν τὸ δεύτερον, which immediately belongs to προλέγω, seems to favour the opinion that the writer had only been once at Corinth. The preposition of the compound verb προλέγω and the ὡς prefixed to παρὼν indicate, if we are not mistaken, that Paul had not been among his readers a second time. He *tells beforehand, as if* he were present the second time—such is his language—instead of, 'I tell you *again* what I stated already, when with you a second time.' Τοῖς προημαρτηκόσι καὶ τοῖς λοιποῖς πᾶσιν should be joined to προείρηκα καὶ προλέγω. The particle ὡς should be rendered *as if*, not *as*. It has the same signification in 1 Cor. v. 3. It is too artificial to refer, with Olshausen, the phrase ὡς παρὼν τὸ δεύτερον to προείρηκα alone, or to προλέγω alone. It belongs to both verbs. It is also too artificial to refer προημαρτηκόσι to προείρηκα alone, and τοῖς λοιποῖς πᾶσιν to προλέγω alone. They belong equally to both verbs.

Griesbach puts ὡς παρὼν τὸ δεύτερον καὶ ἀπὼν νῦν in a parenthesis. This mode of division is neither favourable nor otherwise to the hypothesis of Bleek. The parenthesis should probably be removed, as the later editors have done. Both Lachmann and Tischendorf have expunged it.

But it is said that the context of 2 Cor. xii. 14, suggests a different acceptation both of the present passage and of itself. In the thirteenth verse Paul writes: 'For what is it wherein ye were inferior to other churches, except it be that I myself was not burdensome to you? forgive me this wrong.' Here the keen irony of the apostle is strongly expressed. He declares that he had not been burdensome to them when he was with them before. In the fourteenth verse he affirms, 'and I will not be burdensome to you,' at my next visit. Hence it is said, that there is a want of appropriateness attaching to the statement of his determination to go twice to the Corinthians. Whether he had resolved to go once or twice was of no moment. But if we suppose that *he had really been twice* at Corinth, the argumentation is thought to be apposite. The greater the number of his visits during which he had received no maintenance from the people, the more severe his irony. It would have been superfluous to state how often he had purposed to be among them; while it is quite consistent to mention *all* the visits on the supposition that his intention of visiting Corinth had not been disappointed, but that he *had been twice* in the city.

This reasoning is plausible, but not, perhaps, so forcible as has been assumed. The apostle in speaking of his visits to them, usually mentions his purposed visit; for though he was disappointed in performing it, it must be reckoned as great a proof of his interest in their welfare as if it had been really paid. He speaks of *it*, and of his first actual visit together, as evidences of his affection for them, and of zeal for their true benefit. His connecting the two shews that he *would have* taken no support from the Corinthians the second time any more than the first; and therefore the expression οὐ καταναρκήσω is equally applicable to both. 'I will not be burdensome to you any more than I was on my first visit, or *would have been* on my second.'

In this manner the appropriateness of mentioning his previously intended second visit along with the first which he really paid, may be clearly perceived. Thus the context is consistent with the supposition of but one visit. Hence τρίτον must be connected with ἑτοίμως ἔχω, not with ἐλθεῖν as the adherents of Bleek's hypothesis maintain.

The words of 2 Cor. i. 15, 16, present a serious obstacle to the hypothesis of a second visit: 'And in this confidence I was minded to come unto you before, that ye might have a second benefit; and to pass by you into Macedonia, and to come again out of Macedonia unto you, and of you to be brought on my way toward Judea.' Why should not the apostle speak uniformly and consistently in relation to the same subject? If his language presuppose two visits to Corinth, why should he speak of *one* benefit conferred by his personal presence during these *two visits?* Why not mention *two benefits*, and so have τρίτην χάριν in 2 Cor. i. 15?

Bleek, after Chrysostom, takes χάρις to be the same as χαρὰ, and δεύτερος as equivalent to διπλοῦς—'that ye might have a twofold joy,'—the joy of seeing Paul twice, first on his way to Macedonia, then again on his return, as we learn from the sixteenth verse. But χάρις is not equivalent to χαρὰ, neither can δεύτερος be taken for διπλοῦς. The *usus loquendi* of the Greek language will not permit such a sense. It is easy to see that the proposed interpretation sets the passage aside as evidence either for *one* previous visit paid by Paul to Corinth, or for *two* previous visits, so reducing it to neutrality; but the exegesis is unnatural and arbitrary.

It will be observed, that the words ἵνα δευτέραν χάριν ἔχητε succeed ἐβουλόμην πρὸς ὑμᾶς ἐλθεῖν πρότερον, and *precede* the sixteenth verse by which they are partly explained. They ought, therefore, to be brought into harmony with the *preceding* context. It is improbable that δευτέραν χάριν should not be understood till after the sixteenth verse. The phrase manifestly alludes to the apostle's *first* presence at Corinth when he planted the church in that city. In speaking of the journey which he had purposed taking but was prevented, he speaks of his conferring a *second* benefit, whereas had he been twice present, he would naturally have spoken of a *third*. When he first lived among the Corinthians nearly two years, he had given them a first benefit; and the journey by which he had intended to bestow upon them a second benefit had not yet been made when he wrote the second letter. This is the obvious sense of the passage. It is contradictory to the interpretations assigned to 2 Cor. xiii. 1, 2, and xii. 14, by such as assume that Paul had been twice at Corinth before he wrote his epistles to the church at that place.

Many continental writers rejecting Bleek's mode of reconciling 2 Cor. i. 5, 6, with their favourite hypothesis, divide the one-and-half-year, during which Paul was first at Corinth, into two parts, supposing that he took a short excursion during it into the neighbouring parts. In this way he may be said to have come twice to Corinth, and so promises, in his second epistle, that he should come a *third* time. The apostle speaks of a *second* benefit, because during the greater part of the year-and-half he had taught at Corinth. Such is the interpretation of Baronius, Michaelis, Schulz, Leun, Schmidt, Schott, Anger, and others. To us, however, it seems unsatisfactory, because it makes the apostle speak *inconsistently*. At one time he mentions a *third* coming, or a *purpose* of coming a *third* time; whereas according to this exposition, he speaks of a *second* coming as a *second* benefit. This is not consistent in reference to the *same* visit.

The visit in question, i.e. the second, is assumed to be one of an unpleasant nature. Is it not strange then, that he never alludes in the first epistle to the admonitions and warnings which he had employed on that occasion. He must have acted as a reformer of abuses, and have spoken much of the disorder and dissensions he witnessed. And yet there is no reference to such conduct on his part, when he was last with the Corinthians. We say nothing of the difficulty which has been felt in finding a suitable place for inserting this second visit in the narrative of the Acts, nor of the arbitrariness of imagining that Luke did not speak of it because he was unacquainted with its existence. At whatever place it is inserted, whether at Acts xix. 1, as Neander conjectures, or in the three months stay in Hellas, (Acts xx. 2, 3,) as Koehler supposes:—whether we assume with Schrader, that Paul, after he had come to Ephesus where he remained three years, had made this second journey to Corinth, and returned before he wrote any letter to the Corinthians,—or agree with those who think that the second visit to Corinth took place immediately before he came a second time to Ephesus,—we say, at whatever place it is inserted, it must have the appearance of being *forcibly* put into the text of the Acts; although we readily concede that Luke omits various particulars which we learn from the epistles alone.

Thus the passages on which a second visit has been based, do not appear to us to prove its existence. One thing they *do* suggest, viz. that the apostle had discovered, during his long residence at Corinth, symptoms of ominous tendency, which awakened within his mind a deep solicitude. This circumstance shaded with melancholy his departure from the church.

II. It is an ancient opinion that a letter of Paul addressed to the Corinthians has been lost. A passage in the first epistle has given rise to the sentiment ἔγραψα ὑμῖν ἐν τῇ ἐπιστολῇ, μὴ κ.τ.λ., translated in our version, 'I wrote to you in an epistle, not to company,' &c. The words just quoted form in the opinion of many, a basis too slender on which to build the hypothesis. There is no other passage containing a similar reference, for ἐπιστολαὶ in 2 Cor. x. 10, to which some have pointed, may refer to Paul's epistles generally, of whose character the Corinthians judged by the specimen they had received in the first. It is well known also, that the plural might be taken for the singular. We should not therefore *hastily* adopt the hypothesis on the sole ground of a single passage, or rather a single expression.

In regard to ἔγραψα we demur to the opinion that the aorist is ever equivalent strictly to the perfect. The verb γράφω indeed is used in a peculiar manner both in the Greek and Latin languages, a past tense of it being employed as a present. This however, does not apply to verbs in general. The instances adduced by Lardner, and others, of the aorist being employed for the present, fail to establish the point. Γράφω is an apparent exception to the general rule. So in latin *scripsi*. And yet, strictly speaking, a past tense of γράφω refers to past time, for when it is put at the termination of a letter it alludes to the *writing finished*. Thus the exception is *apparent* rather than *real;* and the position that a *past tense* is employed to designate *present time,* must be rejected in every case, as unphilosophical. Equally incorrect is the assertion that the aorist stands for the perfect. Ἔγραψα must be translated *I wrote,* not *I do write,* or *I have written.*

If the apostle refers to the letter he was then writing, it may be asked, to what part of it does he allude. Lardner regards the allusion as anticipative, and fixes upon the tenth chapter. This position is utterly untenable. Others think, that the second verse of the fifth chapter is meant, although no precept prohibiting associating with a fornicator is there given. Others again point to the fifth, sixth, and seventh verses, which are not appropriate, because they do not expressly enjoin upon the Corinthians for the first time, to excommunicate the incestuous person; but speak of *Paul himself as having already determined* to deliver such an one to Satan, as though he were present in spirit, and presiding over the meeting of the church at which this should take place. Here there is certainly an intimation to the Corinthian Christians that they should proceed to excommunicate the offender. Yet it is not such a direct injunction as would have been addressed to them *at first* on the subject; and besides, they are regarded merely as consenting; while Paul himself *virtually* excommunicates. The verb παραδοῦναι is connected with κέκρικα. The antecedent context therefore does not seem appropriate, as that to which ἔγραψα refers. No part of it exhibits a prohibition to company with fornicators; but the whole contains a general exhortation to purity, and an assumption on the part of the writer that his readers should not delay to deliver, on his authority, the notorious offender to Satan. The expression τῇ ἐπιστολῇ must always appear strange to those who find the allusion in the context immediately preceding. What is the use of τῇ ἐπιστολῇ on the supposition that the second verse, or that the fifth, sixth or seventh verses are meant? It is utterly inexplicable.

But the eleventh verse is appealed to, in which ἔγραψα, the same tense as in the ninth, is found along with νυνὶ; the adverb being explanatory of ἐν τῇ ἐπιστολῇ and synonymous with it. Here, however, it is assumed, that νυνὶ is an adverb of time, as Morus, Pott, and Heydenreich, take it. But it is a transition-particle. If it were a particle of time, the association of it with ἔγραψα would be incongruous.

The article should certainly be translated *the* epistle. But this is still indefinite. Is it agreeable to the usus loquendi to understand it of the present epistle? In proof of the affirmative, Middleton refers to Romans xvi. 22, where τὴν ἐπιστολὴν means *the epistle to the Romans*. In like manner ἡ ἐπιστολὴ in Coloss. iv. 16, signifies, *the Colossian epistle*; τὴν ἐπιστολὴν in 1 Thessal. v. 27, *the first Thessalonian epistle*, and τῆς ἐπιστολῆς in 2 Thessal. iii. 14, *the second Thessalonian epistle*. These examples are not apposite. The expression ἡ ἐπιστολὴ occurs in them at *the end* of the writing. The letters in which the phrase appears are virtually finished. It means *the letter which I am now concluding*. This is quite different from the present instance, in which the same expression ἡ ἐπιστολὴ, so far from referring to a letter the composition of which is all but completed, is supposed to allude to the verses immediately preceding. *Parallelism* of examples is wanting. One important circumstance creates a distinction which sets aside the similarity. Ἡ ἐπιστολὴ can only denote *the present epistle*, when it is *virtually written*, not when it is towards the commencement. That it may denote *the former epistle*, is shewn by 2 Cor. vii. 8, where ἐν τῇ ἐπιστολῇ means what is now the first epistle to the Corinthians. The article prefixed to the noun signifies *the well-known* letter — the letter with which the readers were acquainted. Some affirm, that if the apostle had really meant to refer to a former letter he would have written ἐν τῇ προτέρᾳ ἐπιστολῇ, and not simply ἐν τῇ ἐπιστολῇ, but the assertion is refuted by 2 Cor. vii. 8.

Other arguments are adduced against the supposition of a lost epistle. It is thought unaccountable, for example, that the apostle should never notice in any other place the fact of his having written a letter to the Corinthians, or refer to its contents, in the same manner as he does in the second to the first. Why does not the writer allude to admonitions in this lost epistle, and charge his readers with direct disobedience to his injunctions?

Jones insists much on the improbability of a canonical book being lost. Lardner has also adduced various considerations affording presumptive evidence that 'no sacred writings of apostles composed for the instruction and edification of Christian people, their friends, and converts, could be easily lost.' But these writers reason on the ground that whatever apostles and evangelists wrote, was inspired and canonical. And yet apostles may have written at times when they were not under the peculiar influence of inspiration. An apostle's *conduct* was not always right, as we learn from that of Peter, who was reprimanded by Paul for hypocrisy. So also *every thing* that an apostle *wrote* may not have been dictated by the Holy Spirit or guided by his superintendence. It may *appear* inconsistent with the wisdom of the Deity, who employs no superfluous expenditure of means, that any epistle composed under his direction should soon be lost and forgotten. Still we may separate the canonical and inspired compositions of an apostle from occasional and uninspired writings proceeding from the same source.

The opinion that a lost epistle is alluded to, gave rise to one purporting to proceed from the Corinthians, and a reply to it from Paul. Both are spurious documents preserved in the Armenian language. They were first published in Armenian, by Masson, with a Latin translation by Wilkins, at Amsterdam, 1715; and reprinted by Fabricius, in his Cod. Apocryphus N. T. with La Croze's arguments to shew their spuriousness. Whiston defended their authenticity. Carpzov afterwards published them in Greek and Latin, with the notes of Whiston's two sons, William and George. Recently their authenticity has been defended by Rinck. But Ullmann has refuted his arguments. The epistles in question are evident forgeries; and it is strange that their authenticity should have found an advocate.

State of the Corinthian church.—A church gathered from among the inhabitants of Corinth may be supposed to have contained elements demanding special care and culture. Surrounded by immorality and prevailing licentiousness, it was difficult to preserve that purity which true Christianity requires. Established amid excessive corruption, the society soon fell into disorder. The seeds of former vice had not been wholly eradicated from the hearts of the converts. Former habits had left behind them a lingering influence, which it was very difficult fully to subdue. Their piety was of a less steady and consistent character than it would probably have been, had their state before conversion been different. The depravity in which they once lived and moved, exerted a considerable power on their conduct, even after regeneration. In consequence of the prevailing degeneracy of their city, they were in greater danger of relapsing into the practices from which they had been saved. Rescued from abounding vice, they found it exceedingly difficult to maintain a high standard of moral excellence, because of the corrupt atmosphere in which their spiritual breath was drawn. Thus it has always been. Christianity does not at once and entirely deliver the soul from the sinful excesses in which that soul has indulged. It lays indeed the axe to the root of the tree; but repeated strokes are necessary to prostrate the deep-rooted plant which has grown up large and luxuriant. There is no magic in regeneration. It does not act in the way of a sudden spell. The power of Divine grace employed in effecting that great change, acts in accordance with the laws of our moral nature. The process is not perfected at once. Continued efforts on the part of man, and the continued effusion of Divine influences are necessary to carry forward and to consummate the life begun. There is *progress* in virtue and holiness. We need not, therefore, be surprised, that the Corinthian church should have exhibited, after Paul's departure, various disorders. The irregularities and improprieties that began to prevail may be accounted for in a great degree, by the previous life of the members, and the extraordinary wickedness of the inhabitants generally. Some, unable to resist seductive temptations, relapsed into excesses similar to those which were too common in the world around; one had even married his step-mother; others declined in holiness; while the majority manifested a spirit of dissension arising out of personal preferences for individuals. The gifts which many possessed were abused and made a ground of ostentation. Humility disappeared in consequence. The members were puffed up one against another. In the midst of these disagreeable circumstances, the church wrote to their founder, imforming him of their condition, and requesting his opinion on several points. The apostle had also heard from other quarters of the prevailing disorders; and we may well imagine the great solicitude which such intelligence must have stirred up within him.

In regard to the parties by which the church was distracted, it is impossible to arrive at certain and satisfactory conclusions. Where there is so much uncertainty, there are numerous hypotheses. Nor is it matter of surprise that the topic should have given rise to speculation, when the data furnished by the two epistles for determining the nature and number of the parties in the church, are so slight and fragile. It is sufficiently obvious, that there were such parties, ranged under different leaders, whose names were employed as symbols of peculiar views; but it is exceedingly difficult to ascertain and to develop the position in which they stood to one another, and the characteristics that marked them out in their associated relations. The epistles contain little more than *an indication* of their existence. Their number and tendencies are obscure and undefined. Hence arises the danger of constructing hypotheses respecting them, not out of materials furnished by revelation, but from our own conceptions. There has been a manifest desire of knowing far more concerning them than what is written—of supplying, by the aid of ingenuity, what the apostle has omitted to record. And yet it is impossible to do justice to the theme, without *endeavouring*, at least, to present something definite in relation to it, although probable conjecture must necessarily be summoned to aid the inquiry. To arrive at certainty is a result that cannot be expected. None need hope to be able to construct such an account as will be tolerably satisfactory without the assistance of slight *presumptions*, or minute probabilities. Where the historical circumstances are so few, it is necessary to carry out their intimations as far as they will consistently warrant. Perhaps hypotheses of too subtle and arbitrary a nature have been already framed in connexion with the Corinthian letters. The peculiar complexion of many minds when turned towards such a topic, may easily lead them beyond the limit of safe speculation, into the region of pure theorising. The tendency of the German mind, in particular, may have originated various accounts of the parties in the Corinthian church, more fanciful in their fullness than most should be inclined to allow. Still, however, the Germans have done good service in this department. They have explored it with wondrous diligence. Instead of shrinking from the tenuous difficulties with which it is beset, they have dived into the region of its shadowy dimness, with all the searching subtleties of which they are pre-eminent masters. But it is likely that they have gone too far. In their intense eagerness to learn much, they have developed much of the fanciful. It is possible to be wise above what is written; but *such* wisdom is available for no practical or useful purpose.

Four parties in the Corinthian church appear to be mentioned in 1 Cor. i. 12.: 'Now this I say, that every one of you saith, I am of Paul; and I of Apollos; and I of Cephas; and I of Christ.' It is also thought that notices of them, more or less distinct, are contained in iii., 4, 22, and in 2 Epist. x. 7.

According to the hypothesis of Eichhorn, the Christ-party

consisted of the *neutrals*—of those who ranged themselves under no human leader, but adhered to the simple doctrine of Christ, following him alone as their master. Pott and Schott adopt the same view. In this way a world of inquiry is saved. Those simple-minded Christians who continued stedfast in their attachment to the apostolic doctrine, looking to the great master from whom it proceeded through the instrumentality of human agents, stand apart, in this way, from the less pure members of the Corinthian church. It is natural that doubts should rest in the minds of many relative to the existence of a distinct party calling themselves *the adherents of Christ,* in a bigoted and exclusive spirit. The apostle certainly mentions the others in the way of censure. But is it not possible, that the expression οἱ Χριστοῦ might simply denote those who followed Christ alone and his doctrine as taught by Paul, acknowledging no other master, and keeping themselves at a distance from party-contentions? The terms will bear such an interpretation. It may be supposed that the apostle mentions them along with the others because he could not clearly explain the different factions that had arisen, unless in such a way as to state that some preferred one teacher, others, a different one; while others called themselves simply the followers of Christ. The passage thus exhibits a historical enumeration of the different parties in the church, without implying that all who are characterized in it incurred the apostle's censure. But this view is, as appears to us, untenable. The others mentioned in the verse are noticed, in the way of disapproval; and since the Christ-party is classed along with them, *it* must be involved in the general condemnation. The subsequent words, 'Is Christ divided?' refer equally to all the preceding parties—to the Christ-party as well as the rest—as if *the former* were guilty of attempting to divide Christ. This they could not have been, had they assumed the title in a good sense. They must have claimed the appellation for themselves in a narrow and selfish spirit, as though they alone truly belonged to the Saviour. The form of the expression μεμέρισται ὁ Χριστός, derived, as is most probable, from ἐγὼ δὲ Χριστοῦ, obviously leads to the conclusion that *all* the preceding factions were exposed to the charge of rending Christ asunder. If the view of Pott be correct, the persons calling themselves οἱ Χριστοῦ must have met with the approbation of Paul; and he would not have failed to state his approval even of a few, while censuring the many. The apostle was not prone to censure. He spared the Corinthians as long as he could; and was careful to speak favourably of those who continued stedfast in the pure faith, as he had instructed them. In 1 Cor. iii. 22, 23, on which Pott chiefly rests, there is no reason for believing that the

Christ-party are mentioned or referred to. The writer speaks of *Christians*.

Another hypothesis was proposed by Storr, according to which the Christ-party took for their leader James the apostle, our Lord's brother (Gal. i. 19). In support of it such passages as 1 Cor. ix. 5; xv. 7; 2 Cor. v. 16, are quoted. But it is easy to see, that they afford no countenance to the hypothesis. The brethren of the Lord and James are indeed mentioned in them; but not as leaders of a party in the church. The expression 'to know Christ after the flesh,' does not indicate *family relationship*, but intimacy with Christ in the days of his flesh. It is impossible to account in any satisfactory way for the Christ-party being named after Christ, instead of James their head; and besides, κύριος should have been used, not Χριστὸς; ἐγὼ εἰμι τοῦ ἀδελφοῦ τοῦ κυρίου, or, οἱ κυρίου in an abbreviated form, would have been the distinguishing appellation. In this case, also, the party of James would have been identical with that of Peter, both consisting of Jewish Christians. Bertholdt slightly modifies the hypothesis, by supposing that this party assumed as their leaders several *brethren of the Lord*, and not James alone; but the conjecture is improbable. We reject the opinion, although adopted by Hug and Heydenreich.

Another hypothesis is that of Baur, who is followed by Billroth. According to it there were, properly speaking, but two parties in the Corinthian church, *the Pauline and the Petrine*. The latter and the Christ-party were substantially the same, although they adopted different names. They were Jewish Christians, whose object was to undermine the apostle Paul by impugning his apostolic authority, and so to engraft Judaism on Christianity. They called themselves οἱ Κηφᾶ, because Peter was the chief among the Jewish apostles. But in order to shew that they were also intimately connected with Christ, through their teachers, they assumed the name οἱ Χριστοῦ, indicating that they were the followers of Christ's genuine apostles, and consequently that they alone were possessed of the genuine gospel. In this way they cast indirect reproach on Paul, as if he was not a true apostle, because he was not called in the same way and at the same time as the others; and also on his adherents, as if they were not the true followers of Christ, because they attached themselves to one who was not a genuine apostle, but corrupted the gospel by views of his own. They singled themselves out from all the other members of the Corinthian church, as though they alone were Christians, in the proper sense of the term. They alone were converted by genuine apostles selected by Christ himself. Thus the Cephas-party and the Christ-party were identical; although the state of affairs at Corinth caused the Judaisers to keep their legal notions and practices in the back-ground, and to render prominent that aspect of them which combated Paul's authority. But if, as Baur believes, they had not gone so far as to broach their Judaising opinions plainly—if they subordinated their legalising tendencies to the undermining of Paul's apostleship, that they might the more effectually promote their ultimate object, we ask, what was the use of the two appellations? Would not the one have been sufficient? Would not the title *οἱ Κηφᾶ* have been superfluous in that case, not to say injurious to their chief design? For if an *immediate* introduction of their Jewish principles would have probably defeated their object, and therefore they proceeded more cautiously; might not the appellation, *Cephas-party*, have prematurely betrayed their leading purpose in impugning the apostolic authority of Paul? Besides, as Neander remarks, 'by the position of the phrase *οἱ τοῦ Χριστοῦ*, we are led to expect the designation of a party in some way differing from the Petrine, though belonging to the same general division; but, according to this view, the Christ-party would differ from the Petrine only in name, which would be quite contradictory to the relation of this party-name to those that preceded it. Accordingly, this view can only be tenable, if not a merely formal, but a material difference can be found between the last two parties.' If this view be correct, it is very strange that the first epistle should contain no arguments against the Cephas-party. The writer does not defend his apostleship in it. He mentions the divisions in the church in such a way as to censure them, and copiously treats of the various questions which the Corinthians had submitted to him in a letter; but he does not combat the party opposed to himself, who must have chiefly given rise to the disorders by which the church was weakened. In this omission there is something so unaccountable as to suggest strong doubts of the correctness of the hypothesis. Paul's usual mode of combating error was to seize upon it by the roots; to supplant its foundation, and not merely to lop off a few of its externalities. If, then, his opponents in the Corinthian church, who, as secret Judaisers, sought to represent him as no apostle, had caused the agitations within the church, as is most probable, why does he not directly combat them, and defend his apostolic authority. It is improbable that *all* the errors and disorders which the apostle condemns throughout the epistle had no connection with the contention of the parties mentioned in chapter i. 12. If they stood in close relationship to such factions, as we must believe, then is it unaccountable that Paul should not combat the hostile party who employed themselves in the unhallowed work of subverting his true apostleship. Baur himself appeals to no passage in the first epistle, except to ix, 1, where Paul says of himself, 'Have I not seen Jesus Christ our Lord,' in opposition to those who asserted that he had not seen Him. The proofs of Baur's hypothesis are derived from the second epistle to the Corinthians, particularly the third chapter, verse 16; x. 7, 11, 13, etc; xii. 2. It is unnecessary to examine the peculiar interpretations assigned to these passages, or the peculiar views against which Baur thinks they were directed, since even Billroth acknowledges, that, with one exception, they do not decidedly favour what they have been adduced to support. They have nothing more than *the appearance* of countenancing it; and that too, not to a common reader, but after they have been set forth in the ingenious light which the framer of the hypothesis himself has thrown around them. The only passage which Billroth thinks decidedly favourable, is 2 Cor. x., 7, etc., where he affirms the Christ-party is manifestly intended; but even if it be alluded to in the words, and a comparison of them with xi. 12, instituted, the conclusion that they were *Jewish* errorists cannot be made out. Billroth has attempted to make a slight modification of Baur's view (in relation to the Christ-party) by drawing a kind of distinction between the Petrine and the Christ-party. 'Perhaps,' says he, 'they had assumed the title Χριστοῦ at first, in their presumptuous pride. Those of their followers who came nearest to them, and who were most assuming, probably took the same appellation; while others contented themselves with the name Κηφᾶ after them (in a manner analogous to the parties of Paul and Apollos), having no other object in so doing than the desire of having for their voucher one who had been really, and by actual personal intercourse with Christ, constituted an apostle. We thus arrive at a distinction (though not a very important one), between the Petrine and the Christ-party, to the necessity of which Neander very carefully draws the attention of his readers, and the omission of which he justly regards as a defect in the theory of Baur. The same individuals did not call themselves at one time of Cephas, and at another of Christ, but each one of those who had been led astray by the false teachers, in speaking of his party, applied to it that name which most suited his own views. It thus appears, that the Petrine division of this party, or that of Peter, strictly so called, was the better disposed of the two.' It is easy to see, that all this is pure conjecture; and that the objections already urged against the hypothesis are not removed. Indeed, it remains *essentially* the same, notwithstanding the modification introduced into it.

The most plausible circumstance in favour of this view is *the position* in which the *οἱ Χριστοῦ* are named, from which it might be inferred that they bore the same relation to the Petrine, as the Apollos party to the Pauline. In this way there would be no material difference between the last two parties, just as there is no essential distinction between the first two. But the mere connexion of members in the sentence must not be pressed in opposition to stronger considerations. If the Judaisers formed but one party, it is improbable that they assumed more than one name. Besides, the apostle was not intent on the nice adjustment of clauses, such as a logician might be solicitous to present. 'Paul does not,' says Neander, 'as in other cases, form the members of the antithesis merely from the thoughts; but the manner in which he selected his terms was determined by matters of fact.'

Becker supposes, that the Petrine party were strangers who came to Corinth, who on setting up as preachers of the gospel, claimed support from the community, which was refused. Their adherents in the Corinthian church became the Christ-party. There are many considerations adverse to such an hypothesis, which it is unnecessary to mention.

According to Neander, the Christ-party consisted of philosophical Christians who constructed for themselves a peculiar form of Christian doctrine, modelled according to their Grecian subjectivity. They probably belonged to the class of the wisdom-seeking Greeks. These persons professed to adhere to Christ alone, yet with an arrogant self-will which set aside all human instrumentality ordained by God. Olshausen holds the same opinion, but states it more strongly, asserting even that the first epistle was wholly directed against the Christ-party, in whom the essence of the Greek philosophy was concentrated.

The number, however, of philosophic Christians must have been small—too small to form such a party. There is nothing to warrant the idea that the gospel had made converts of many cultivated heathen at Corinth. The wise and the noble had not obeyed its call. The apostle Paul presented it in its naked simplicity, and it was not adapted to arrest the attention of those who boasted of their wisdom.

That the first epistle has a polemic reference throughout to the Christ-party, is an assertion not accordant with the character of it. On the contrary, it has little of a polemic tone and tendency. The greater part of it is didactic, occupied with topics about which Paul had been consulted, although they appear to have been unconnected with the different parties in the church.

The hypothesis of Schenkel which De Wette adopts, is more plausible than any yet proposed, although it is constructed in part of several arbitrary assumptions, and is made to embrace too many particulars. Hence many of Neander's objections to it are not without weight, while others are irrelevant or feeble.

According to it, the distinguishing peculiarity of those calling themselves the adherents of Christ was *mysticism*. They appealed to an inward revelation as Paul appealed to the immediate revelation of Christ to himself, and thus, placing themselves on the same level, assailed his apostolic authority. Such a tendency was highly pernicious, inasmuch as it would soon lead the advocates of it to set aside the reality of Christ's person and work by substituting an ideal person. *The historical* would be forced to give place to the ideal Christ, *the objective* merging into *the subjective*.

In taking a survey of the parties belonging to the Corinthian church, it will perhaps occur, to the careful reader of the epistles, that there is little real ground for believing them to have been so definite or distinctly marked as most German writers suppose. There is not sufficient reason for concluding that they were well defined factions, with wide boundary-lines of doctrine isolating them the one from the other. That there were *broad marks* of separation between them, can scarcely be made out from the epistles themselves. It cannot be shown that they were so peculiarly divided by *doctrinal features*, as has been assumed. That there were distinctions between them in a theological view may be allowed; but that these theological peculiarities were so great as *to characterise* the parties, is a questionable position. Who can tell how far personal attachments and antipathies may have influenced the divisions in question? Who shall affirm how much human passions and prejudices had to do with these unhappy dissensions? Perhaps the latter causes were equally active as the former. In the many attempts which have been made to ascertain the principal features that distinguished the Christ-party, the attention has been directed too exclusively to *doctrinal belief*. Other considerations have not been sufficiently brought forward. An excess of importance has been attached to *the tenets* they are supposed to have held.

After all the investigations which have been instituted, and the various hypotheses that have been framed in regard to the Christ-party, their sentiments will always remain in obscurity. They may have entertained dangerous notions. On the contrary, they may have indulged in speculations comparatively innocuous. Most of their opinions respecting the nature of Christianity may have been curious and unprofitable; or they may have been detrimental to the truth of that holy religion. It is impossible to affirm with certainty one or other of these opposite views. Various errors in doctrine and practice are combated in the epistles: but there is great difficulty in assigning such aberrations to one individual party rather than another.

There are no good data on which the inquirer can proceed in apportioning the incorrect opinions condemned by the apostle to their proper advocates. Some of them may have been entertained by more than one of the parties; while it is possible that others were peculiar to a single faction. They may have belonged to a very few persons, who endeavoured to propagate them in the church; or they may have infected the minds of the majority. The subject is fitted, from its very nature, to give rise to innumerable inquiries; but the means of arriving at a satisfactory result are scarcely at our disposal. One hypothesis after another may be framed with a degree of plausibility; while no real light is thrown on the state of the church at the time when the apostle wrote. The epistles themselves scarcely warrant a definite conclusion. The hints which they afford are too ambiguous to form the groundwork of a well-adjusted theory. They merely excite inquiry without leading it onward to a legitimate termination. Curiosity is awakened, and again painfully repressed.

It is natural to suppose, that such of the Corinthians as had been converted by Paul, were most attached to *his* person. They asserted his apostolic authority, and insisted on his pre-eminence. On the other hand, such as had been converted by Apollos looked up to *him* as *their* apostle, with similar reverence and respect. The idea cannot be entertained that the doctrinal sentiments of the Pauline and Apollos-Christians really differed, since Paul and Apollos preached the same doctrine. The one had planted, the other had watered the church. The Pauline and Apollos-parties therefore were one in creed and in all important particulars. They had received the same lessons; the form and dress in which these lessons were presented varying according to the mental peculiarities of the instructors. Apollos was perhaps the more eloquent; but Paul was the more learned, at least in Jewish literature. It does not appear probable that the two parties contended about the superior wisdom and science attributed to Apollos by the one; for it is difficult to see how Paul could have been justly represented as inferior to Apollos in these qualities. It is true that the writer condemns a false science—a worldly wisdom—but it is unlikely that Apollos would have propounded the gospel in such a way as to mix up with it, either in matter or in form, a science that could be so denominated. The relations in which he stood to Paul were too intimate, and the notices of him are too commendatory, to allow of the supposition that a wisdom stigmatised by the apostle as worldly and false, could have formed a ground for Apollos' preference in the eyes of his adherents. The two parties, therefore, personally attached as they were to their respective leaders, came into collision about the degree of apostolic authority due to *the founder*, as compared with *the builder up* of the church. Members of the church foolishly disputed which of the two was superior in dignity—which was *the greater* apostle entitled *to the preeminence*.

Thus the Pauline Christians—those who adhered to the doctrines of this great apostle in the Corinthian community—were divided into two parties. One in faith, they chose to designate themselves after two different leaders, respecting whose authority they did not agree. Whatever may have been the mode in which Apollos set forth the doctrines of Christianity, it cannot be inferred that he cast them in a theosophic Alexandrian mould, or presented them in such a dress as a cultivated philosopher of Egypt would naturally do, without attributing to him a culpability for which there is no warrant in the epistles themselves.

The Jewish Christians belonging to the Corinthian church, still entangled with prejudices and national prepossessions, tood in some degree distinct from the Pauline. Their modes f thought were opposed in a certain sense to those which haracterised the Pauline and Apollos-parties. They were not ble to sympathise in the *free* views of those who had been conerted from heathenism. They could not bring themselves to iink and act as Christians released from the obligations of the Iosaic law, without considerable difficulty. They felt a lingering attachment to former practices which they were unable at once to eradicate. The difference between them and the Pauline Christians manifested itself mainly in regard to the use of flesh which had been offered in sacrifice to idols; as may be seen in the eighth, ninth, and tenth chapters of the first epistle, where they are called *weak brethren*, and where such as possessed greater knowledge are exhorted not to offend less enlightened consciences by doing things which would cause them to stumble. These Jewish Christians naturally chose Peter for their head; notwithstanding Peter's doctrine in regard to the law did not differ from Paul's. They ranged themselves beneath the banner of the apostle of the circumcision, although there is no probability that he had been personally at Corinth. But they were not actuated by hostile feelings towards Paul. Their creed agreed substantially with his; yet it was restrained from exercising its full power over them. They did not undermine his authority, or call his apostleship in question. But when they saw the other members manifesting their personal preferences by calling themselves the special adherents of Paul and Apollos, they began to look about for an apostle or apostolic man as *their* authority, in order that they, too, might have some distinctive appellation. There is no ground for believing that they were enemies to Paul's doctrine and person, or that they undermined his apostolic character.

It should be noticed, that they were *Jewish Christians*, not *Judaisers*. They were not teachers, but private members of the church, manifesting no intention of returning to Judaism, or of mixing up the observances of the Mosaic law generally, with the doctrines of Christianity. It is arbitrary to impute to them any such designs as those by which the Judaising teachers were commonly prompted. They were not persons of the same influence or proselytising activity as the *Judaisers* whom Paul had so frequently to combat. They had passed from the religion of one dispensation to that of another, but were still partially unenlightened as to the genuine freedom of the gospel. Their consciences were greatly offended at the conduct of those Gentile converts who were not sufficiently circumspect or guarded in their actions before their weaker brethren. It is true that their scrupulousness was excessive; but yet, they could not at once lay aside their prejudices. They thought that they were guilty of idolatry if they ate of the food which had been offered to idols, even though they did not know that it had been so used. In this respect their consciences were certainly weak; but yet their more enlightened Gentile brethren should have abstained from doing any thing that might offer violence to conscientious feelings and even to prejudices.

While these three parties were thus divided, they all agreed in acknowledging apostolic authority. But there were others in the same church who disdained to follow or to acknowledge the divinely ordained instrumentality of any apostle. This party looked upon themselves as more enlightened than the rest, and styled themselves after Christ alone. They were particularly opposed to Paul, whose reputation they sought to lessen in various ways. They must be regarded as the most dangerous of all, whatever may have been the complexion of their sentiments.

It is impossible to ascertain what peculiar theological opinions were held by the Christ-party, if it be supposed that they *did* disseminate definite characteristic notions. It is apparent that in both Epistles, especially the second, the apostle refers to persons who questioned his apostleship, and in so doing enters into a lengthened vindication of his own claims. It is probable that the individuals alluded to belonged to the Christ-party. There were also, in the Corinthian church, some who preferred celibacy to married life, attaching a virtue to the former in preference to the latter state. Perhaps the question of marriage was not mixed up with the parties, as though celibacy were a peculiar tenet belonging either to the Pauline or the Christ-party. The disposition to celibacy shewed itself very early in the Christian church, and it seems unnecessary, in the present instance, to confine it to one particular section of the community at Corinth. Paul, indeed, was unmarried; but it need not thence be assumed that his adherents seized on this feature of his life, and elevated it into general prominence in their doctrinal sentiment.

The fifteenth chapter of the first epistle also shews that *some* (τινὲς) of the Corinthians denied or doubted the resurrection. Whether *they* should be assigned to the Christ-party, is matter of uncertainty. Rather do they seem not to have belonged to it; although Neander, Olshausen, and Jäger, assume that they did so; while Meyer, on the other hand, imagines that they pertained to the Apollos-party. The manner in which they are introduced (τινὲς ἐν ὑμῖν λέγουσι) shows that the error in question had not yet taken deep root, or developed itself so extensively as to be maintained by a whole party. Besides, the words of the apostle relative to the persons who speculated about the mode of the resurrection, seem to imply that the error had not spread widely, because he employs mild language, and abstains from severe reproof.

Let us now look at the conduct and principles of those who set themselves in opposition to the apostle, for by them alone can the Christ-party be discovered. It was after Apollos's departure, that certain persons of Jewish descent came to Corinth, furnished with letters of recommendation, probably from some part of Asia Minor, who set themselves forward as apostles, and commenced building on Paul's foundation. But their spirit and aims were different from those of the disinterested labourer into whose field they intruded. Puffed up with notions of their own importance, they used the appliance of a worldly wisdom in preaching the gospel, surrounding the simple story of the Saviour's teachings and death with the garb of human philosophy and eloquence. In consequence of the undue stress which they laid upon *their science*, the contrast between them and Paul became all the more apparent. *He* had insisted on the great fact that Christ died for sinners, without employing the aids of learning or the artificial ornaments of rhetoric. *He* had determined not to know anything among them, save Jesus Christ and him crucified. Hence *they* began to lessen the apostle in the eyes of the Corinthians, on account of his pretended deficiency in the very qualifications in which *they* boasted, and to inspire their followers with a pride similar to that which they themselves exhibited. *They* were the men who possessed a high degree of wisdom which raised them far above the ordinary apostles. In consequence of their conduct in impugning his apostleship, and teaching others to disobey his precepts, they are deservedly branded as 'false apostles, deceitful workers,' who transformed themselves into the apostles of Christ. Most of the allusions to them are found in the second epistle. Perhaps they had become more open and determined in their proceedings in the interval between the first and second letters.

Now it is to the adherents of these false apostles that we should probably look for the Christ-party. The errors that appeared in the church at Colosse, and which are traceable to a Jewish source, may serve to show that the wisdom of which the teachers boasted was allied to Alexandrian theosophy. They were spiritualizing or Gnostic Christians, who pretended to have attained a deep insight into the mysteries of revelation. Schenkel, followed by De Wette, conjectures, that they pretended to stand in an intimate connection with Christ by *visions* and *revelations*. They gave out that they enjoyed a mysterious and immediate communion with Jesus, such as Paul himself never had. In this manner he supposes that the appellation by which they were distinguished is best accounted for. Accordingly Paul reluctantly introduces visions and revelations, relating how he was caught up into Paradise and heard wondrous things. Perhaps it is unnecessary to resort to this conjecture. The passages in which the apostle of the Gentiles dwells upon the historic Christ and Him crucified, as the essence of the gospel, those which affirm that he *saw* the Lord, and such as speak of extraordinary revelations communicated to him, may have been introduced simply to vindicate his apostleship, to uphold his official character so unjustly depreciated, and to show how he relied on the simple presentation of the great fact that Christ died for sinners. It is not very probable that the distinguishing peculiarity of those calling themselves the adherents of Christ was the *mystical*. Perhaps, they did appeal to an inward revelation as Paul appealed to the immediate revelation of Christ to himself, and thus placed themselves on the same level to assail his apostolic authority. That the prevailing tendency of their belief was to set aside the reality of Christ's person and work by substituting an ideal person can hardly be allowed. It is pure conjecture of an improbable kind to affirm, that their creed forced the *historical* to give way to the *ideal* Christ, the *objective* merging into the *subjective*. We assume that the Christ-party was composed of such as had listened to the false teachers who had come to Corinth, that they exalted human wisdom and human eloquence, laid claim to a deeper γνῶσις by which they were specially united to Christ, and moulded Christianity into a theosophic, spiritualizing form, endangering thereby its simplicity, essence, and beauty. Following the example of their instructors, the adherents of these selfish errorists had become inflated with self-conceit, and depreciated Paul, as though he were no apostle. They rejected, indeed, the authority of *all* the apostles. They scorned to be considered the adherents of any man; and named themselves accordingly, after Christ himself, as if they were more closely related to him than their brethren. Their great bane was the science and philosophy of the world, inspiring them with extravagant notions of spiritual freedom.

In addition to the four parties in the church, there were various disorders, as has been already intimated. We shall particularize and consider them separately, in the same manner as has been followed with regard to the topic just treated.

2. Some of the converts had fallen into sins of uncleanness, in consequence of the prevailing immorality around them. Various individuals in the church had yielded more or less to lasciviousness. Lewdness in different forms seems even to have become general, as may be inferred from the words ὅλως ἀκούεται ἐν ὑμῖν πορνεία (v. 1.), where ὅλως must be referred not to πορνεία exclusively, or to ἀκούεται alone, but to the whole clause, intimating that varieties of uncleanness, included in the generic term πορνεία, were common among the Corinthians. This conclusion is confirmed, if not by chapter x. 8, at least by 2 Cor. xii. 21. Πορνεία does not here signify a *case* of fornication first stated generally and then more definitely noticed in the terms καὶ τοιαύτη πορνεία. The apostle speaks of the intelligence he had received that lewdness commonly prevailed among them, and proceeds to notice an extreme case of it, viz. unnatural intercourse between a step-son and step-mother. Notwithstanding the scandalous nature of the deed, it would appear that the members of the church had not withdrawn from intercourse with the incestuous person. The writer, after expressing his astonishment that they had allowed the man to remain in connexion with them, enjoins his immediate exclusion from the church. At the same time he takes advantage of the opportunity to speak of other vicious persons, the covetous, the idolater, the railer, the drunkard, the extortioner, who were to be dealt with in a similar manner. He exhorts them to hold no intercourse with the fornicator, or those guilty of notorious vices, to disavow their doings entirely, lest Christians should seem to countenance their sins, and so disfigure the purity of religion in the eyes of the heathen. At the same time he wishes his readers not to understand him as saying that he meant to exclude them from all communication with wicked men not belonging to the church, for that were impossible. He refers only to the vicious *in the church*. They are enjoined to expel from their society incestuous and immoral characters, to

keep no company with them, lest infection should pervade the whole body, and they themselves should be encouraged in a course contrary to the genius of Christianity.

3. Another impropriety into which the Corinthian Christians fell, was that of their appealing to heathen tribunals. They had lost the primitive spirit which distinguished the earliest adherents of Christianity. Hence they disputed about property. They were not of one heart and one soul. They had not all things in common. Brotherly love had become cold. Mutual distrust had taken possession of their minds. A generous confidence in the honesty and fidelity of their brethren had given place to selfishness and envy. It was customary among the Jews to decide their disputes by men chosen from among themselves, a practice which they founded on Exodus xxi. 1; and, in the opinion of some, it was transferred from the synagogue to the Christian church. Christ, however, gave no express command on the subject, and therefore Paul could appeal to none. In order to correct such unseemly conduct, he reasons with them in another manner: 'if the saints are destined to judge the world and angels themselves, they are much more competent to decide the small affairs of the present life.' He informs them that they should not go to law with one another on any occasion, much less appeal to heathen tribunals. All legal disputes between Christians are censured, as contrary to the love they ought to cherish towards one another. How absurd was the course which these Gentile Christians pursued in this matter, when the dignity and future elevation of the believer are considered. And what a low standard of moral excellence did the Corinthian church present, notwithstanding the multitude of spiritual gifts possessed by the members.

4. In their observance of the Lord's supper, the Corinthians had committed various abuses. In order to bring the institution as near as possible to the form in which it was observed by Christ, a feast or evening meal preceded the supper among the Corinthians, just as the paschal feast preceded the Last Supper properly so called. Both were considered as *one* solemn transaction in commemoration of the Redeemer's death, and designated by the *one* appellation δεῖπνον κυριακόν. At the preparatory meal, or *agape*, all the members assembled, and partook on an equal footing, without distinction of age, sex, or rank; to show that *all* the brethren stood in the same relation to their common Master, and to evidence their mutual love. Each according to his circumstances brought meat and drink with him, to be shared in common by all. The poor man partook of the bounty of the rich, as if he had contributed his share of the meal; and the brethren rich and poor, masters and slaves, in one holy fellow-

ship, exhibited a beautiful spectacle of unity to the world. Such were the *agapæ*, or love-feasts, of these early Christians—meals preceding the symbolic ordinance specifically styled the Lord's Supper. But when Christian love declined, these *agapæ* lost their true character and object. They ceased to be meals of which all the members partook alike and indiscriminately. Those who brought food with them ate and drank by themselves, apart from the members who had been prevented by poverty from contributing. In consequence of this distinction, the poor in their hunger were compelled to look on; while their rich brethren, having more than was necessary, sometimes indulged in excess. The one was hungry, and the other was drunken. The meal degenerated into a private feast, losing all its significance and beautiful propriety. Better had it been to eat and drink in their own houses, than thus to despise the church of God, and to put to shame such as had no houses of their own, when the poor saw their wealthy brethren revelling in abundance, without being invited or allowed to partake. By that conduct the rich rendered themselves unfit to join in the essential and more solemn part of the ordinance, with reverence and spiritual discernment. These irregularities and excesses the apostle strongly censures. In many countries there existed an ancient custom of holding general entertainments, to which each family brought its own contribution, and where each family also consumed its own quota apart, without sharing in the viands of the rest. In this manner the *agapæ* were conducted, although the spirit of the institution was so different. From whatever source the Gentile Christians borrowed their love-feasts, similar meals do not appear to have prevailed in other apostolic churches. They did not therefore constitute an essential or necessary part of the Last Supper. The Corinthians associated the meal with the solemn ordinance instituted by Christ to commemorate his death; and the apostle did not forbid it. He wrote against its abuse, without condemning it altogether; because there was something in the custom appropriate to the occasion.

5. Some of the Corinthians doubted or denied the truth of the resurrection. It is difficult to ascertain the precise form which their scepticism assumed, or the connexion in which it stood to other and kindred doctrines. They do not appear to have denied the fact of Christ's resurrection; neither is it necessary to assume that they rejected the immortality of the soul; for although the reasoning of the apostle asserts these truths as well as the resurrection of the body, he may have adduced them, not because they were rejected, but because he would show that they were inseparably connected with the tenet impugned. It is agreeable to Paul's mode of developing doctrines and refuting

opponents, to point out the necessary bearings and consequences which the denial of an important truth must have on other parts of the Christian system. It is not probable that such doubts sprang from *Sadduceeism*, as Michaelis and others supposed; or from *Essenism*, as Mosheim conjectured. According to either view, the impugners of the resurrection belonged to the Jewish party in the Corinthian church. The manner in which the apostle combats the error, is not such as he would have employed against these Jewish sects. Rather do the doubts in question seem to have sprung up in Gentile soil, and to have been entertained by Gentile Christians. But it cannot well be maintained that they were the product of Epicurean philosophy, since Epicureanism presents a marked opposition to Christianity in almost all its features. It has no points of contact by which it could be united in part or whole, with the principles of the gospel. Besides, the epicurean maxims of life referred to in chapter xv. 32—34, are represented as *the consequence* not *the source* of the particular scepticism combated by Paul. A denial of the resurrection and immortality is set forth as *naturally leading to* a course of life practically godless, and sinful in all its manifestations. Neander and others suppose, that the impugners of the doctrine in question were cultivated Gentile Christians—men who had exhibited a philosophic tendency before conversion. It may be doubted, however, whether there were many belonging to that class in the Corinthian church. *Very few* of the Grecian philosophers had turned to the new religion. Those who had received a philosophical training, stood aloof from the simple preaching of the cross. Hence Olshausen thinks, that these deniers of the resurrection were *allegorists*, such as Hymeneus and Philetus, who taught that the resurrection was past already, setting aside *the historic reality* of the doctrine by a spiritualising process. But the apostle's argumentation does not suit these doubters. His polemics are too mild in relation to such dangerous and daring sceptics. To whatever class the persons under consideration belonged, they speculated about the resurrection in a manner which led to a denial of the fact, probably because they could not see how a body which has mouldered away into corruption could be raised again from the dust; or how a material structure, such as it is in the present state, could be intimately associated with the soul in a higher condition of being.

In refuting their notions, the apostle begins with the fact of Christ's resurrection as a cardinal point in the gospel. Having proved *its* reality, he assumes it as the basis of his reasoning. He grounds the fact of the general resurrection on it. After shewing that there will be a resurrection of the dead, he adverts to the *how* of the question, and lessens the difficulty by stating that the resurrection-body will be a *spiritual* body, different from the *natural* body of the present life.

Paul seems to have *heard* of the preceding improprieties, without perhaps being consulted about them by the Corinthians in their letter. Let us now advert to other topics, regarding which he had been *asked* for instruction.

1. The subject of marriage was one that gave rise to perplexity in the Corinthian church. Hence Paul's opinion of it was sought. It is not easy, however, to discover *the precise point* to which the question of the Corinthians referred; or the particulars respecting which they were unable to come to a definite conclusion; because the writer touches upon several things in the seventh chapter. In the first place, he speaks of marriage generally, and enjoins the married state on all, as one tending to prevent fornication. On this account the parties joined in wedlock should not defraud one another in respect to the obligations of the married state. At the same time, he expresses his preference of a single life in the case of those for whom such a life was safe. In the next place, he condemns separations and divorces, even though one of the parties was a heathen, as long as the unbelieving party chose to continue with the other. After a short digression, the apostle turns to the unmarried, recommending them to remain single because of impending calamities; and lastly, he touches upon the second marriage of women, but so cursorily as to intimate that it had not been included among the interrogatories addressed to him. *The ascetic spirit* had manifested itself among the Corinthians, leading some of them to argue for celibacy, as though it were not only preferable to marriage, but had a peculiar virtue in itself. An extreme view was taken of the single life as essential to Christian perfection, or at least as far superior in every instance to the married state. Here, then, was the particular point of inquiry—Was celibacy in all cases to be recommended as preferable to a wedded life? It is *possible* that the inquiry extended to the subject of separation between married parties, especially when one of them was an unbeliever; because Paul treats of this also in his answer; but it is not *certain*. It need not be supposed that the apostle confined himself to the single thing about which he was specially consulted. Rather should we expect from him a comprehensive view of the question in its collateral aspects and bearings. Celibacy, and the absolute preference due to it, is *the great*, perhaps *the only point* of which his opinion was asked.

It is difficult to discover the party from which this ascetic propensity proceeded. It is improbable that it originated with the *Jewish* Christians, because in the eyes of the Jews, marriage was a most honourable and blessed institution, while celibacy was reckoned a disgrace. Neander appears to think that it took its rise with the Pauline Christians, who overvalued celibacy because their leader was unmarried. This is improbable. The adherents of Paul in after times never insist on a single life. Olshausen again traces it to the Christ-party, whose *idealistic propensities* as developed by the Gnostics, accorded with the erroneous tenet. All this is mere conjecture without the shadow of a basis. Perhaps the ascetic disposition which manifested itself very early in the churches, was not confined to the adherents of one party among the Corinthians. It may have been adopted even by some Jewish converts who borrowed it from the Gentile Christians. It depended in a great degree on the temperament of individuals.

When treating of the marriage relation, the apostle lays down a general maxim deserving of particular notice from the important applications of which it is capable. In whatever situation or position conversion found an individual, it did not command him to start away abruptly from the externalities of former associations and pursuits. Christianity did not interfere with the relations of his outward life. They remained unaffected by its reception. The existing order of society was externally undisturbed by the new religion of the Redeemer. Such were the wisdom and moderation of its principles, that their tendency was to introduce outward reforms gradually and surely, apart from premature and revolutionary measures. This is applied by Paul to the case of slaves. The institute of slavery entered extensively into all the relations of the ancient world. Society in its manifold connexions was pervaded by its influence. Hence it comes under the notice of the New Testament writers, especially as many slaves were converted to Christianity and incorporated into newly-formed churches. It is obvious that the principle on which it is founded, is expressly condemned by *the spirit of the Christian religion.* It cannot be sanctioned by a system which enforces the comprehensive rule, 'Do unto others, as you would wish to be done to by them.' Had the attempt been made to introduce compulsory servitude as a new thing, in the time of our Lord and his apostles, it would have been denounced and resisted as a measure of unmitigated evil. But it was then an old system. It had taken root and grown up as one of the prevailing vices which characterised the ages antecedent to the Lord's advent. Accordingly the apostles did not enjoin masters to set their slaves at liberty. By moulding the dispositions of the masters, Christianity prepared them to be kind and benevolent, and to regard such as were placed under them in the light of brethren. In like manner the latter are exhorted to submit cheerfully and patiently to the yoke, recollecting the true freedom conferred on them, and consoling themselves with the assurance that inward and spiritual liberty raises them far above the boasters of mere outward freedom. Yet Paul does not undervalue civil liberty, although it was not the direct object of the religion which he inculcated to interfere with civil arrangements. On the contrary, he exhorts every slave to avail himself of a legitimate opportunity to obtain his emancipation. He prefers freedom to slavery when it could be procured without doing violence to the principles of justice, or the established relations of social life. From this it is sufficiently apparent, that the apostle looked upon slavery as uncongenial with the genuine spirit of Christianity. He anticipated the time when it should be done away by the regenerating influence of that new religion which was destined to effect an entire revolution in the state of society. Since all of us are ransomed by the blood of Christ, it does not become our proper dignity to be the compulsory servants of human beings like ourselves.

The second question relates to the duties of Christians, respecting the eating of flesh previously offered to idols. Some of the Gentile converts, presuming on their freedom under the gospel, not only ate without scruple the meat that was sold in the market, after it had been dedicated to idols, but went so far as to partake of the feasts held in heathen temples where such flesh was set before the guests. This gave offence to the Jewish Christians, whose weak consciences naturally revolted at the conduct in question. There are three points of the subject which the writer takes up, as if there had been three questions put to him concerning it.

(*a*) Should a Christian eat the flesh of an animal offered in sacrifice to idols, after that flesh has been exposed in the market for sale and purchased as food?

(*b*) Should a Christian accept the invitation of a friend to partake of a feast held in a heathen temple, and eat the flesh there presented?

(*c*) Should a Christian go to a private entertainment and partake of the flesh of animals that has been dedicated to idols?

To the first the apostle replies in the affirmative. One might lawfully partake of meats offered to idols if he were established in knowledge and faith, being fully convinced that idols are nothing. The apostle, however, proposes some limitation to the exercise of Christian freedom in this respect. Care must be taken that in so doing, a weaker brother shall not be offended; for an action perfectly harmless in itself, ceases to be a matter of indifference when the doing of it offers violence to the feelings or prejudices of a tender, over-scrupulous conscience.

To the second, the writer replies in the negative, because every Christian who is present at the idol feasts, makes himself virtually a partaker of the idolatrous worship, and is so far a heathen. 'Ye cannot drink the cup of the Lord and the cup of devils: ye cannot be partakers of the Lord's table, and of the table of devils.'

In regard to the third particular, the apostle states, that every Christian might be present without scruple, at a private entertainment given by a heathen, and eat whatever should be set before him, without asking any questions about the origin of the food provided. But if any scrupulous guest should say, when a particular dish was brought forward; 'this meat has been offered in sacrifice to an idol,' the Christian is exhorted, in that case, to abstain from the food, not on account of his own conscience, but out of regard to the conscience of the other.

We do not intimate our belief, that the inquiry addressed to the apostle, assumed the preceding form, or that it alluded to the various points embraced in the reply, for the writer was accustomed to look at subjects connected with Christianity in a comprehensive aspect, without being confined to the exact point brought under his notice.

This topic was intimately connected with the relation between the Pauline and Petrine parties. The former, boasting of their freedom of knowledge, and entertaining correct conceptions of the Christian's privileges, *applied* their principles improperly. They joined, without scruple, in festive entertainments, where the flesh left after the sacrifices was presented; and looked upon the uneasiness of the Jewish Christians as a narrow-minded prejudice deserving of ridicule. Thus the great law of love was forgotten in its modifying influence on the social relations. Extravagant ideas of their advancement in knowledge and faith, engendered pride and presumption. An overweening estimate of themselves turned away their attention from others whom they should have also regarded. The Petrine Christians, on the other hand, allowed their minds to be harassed with anxiety, where there was no ground for it. Their scruples of conscience rendered them timid and feeble. They were entangled with unnecessary and slavish prejudices. How wisely and admirably does the apostle deal with the question, when he lays down the doctrine regarding it, that the believer, in the case of practices innocent in themselves, is bound by the law of love to act in such a manner as to promote the conversion of souls, the spiritual prosperity of those who are not so enlightened as himself, and the glory of God. Thus particular circumstances affect things in themselves indifferent.

3. Another subject referred to the apostle, was the demeanour of females in the public meetings. In consequence of a misunderstanding of Christian liberty, females appeared unveiled among a congregation of worshippers composed of both sexes. This practice had been adopted in imitation of the men, who appeared with uncovered heads according to the Grecian custom. A false liberalism had induced them to overstep the bounds of propriety in asserting their privileges under the new religion. The gospel, it is true, broke down the slavish restraints imposed upon the sex in heathen countries, restoring woman to her rightful elevation and dignity. But some had been led to make an improper application of their freedom, as if it placed them upon a perfect equality with the other sex; for they appeared unveiled in the public assemblies, and undertook to pray and to prophesy, assuming the office of teachers. Accordingly the apostle condemns the custom of removing the veil in the promiscuous meetings of the worshippers. as well as that of praying and prophesying in public; although he reserves his denunciation of the latter practice to a subsequent occasion (xiii. 34). He reminds the women of their subordination to the men, and shews the true position which each occupies relatively to the other and to Christ. He deems it improper that woman should appear in the bold openness proper to man, representing the uncovering of her head in the assemblies as unsuited to her modesty and *subordinate* position. The *tendency* of the custom is indicated to be immoral. Some think that Paul also denounces the opposite practice in the men of the Corinthian church, viz. that of keeping the head covered in the public assemblies; but there is no good ground for concluding that the males had fallen into this unseemly habit.

4. The Corinthian church seems to have had a large measure of spiritual gifts. All the forms and manifestations of miraculous power enjoyed by the early Christians appeared in lively action within that society. Powerful excitement was produced among them by the wonderful operation of the Spirit on their susceptible minds. They had great zeal for the cultivation of the spiritual gifts pertaining to public and oral instruction. But these divine impulses were diverted from their legitimate scope by the infirmities of the persons on whom they were bestowed. From deficiency of mature holiness in their possessors, such tokens of inspiration were affected by unworthy motives and desires which were often allowed to obtain undue ascendency. The remains of depravity did not permit the supernaturally

elevated powers to put forth their exercise in an *orderly* and *edifying* exhibition. It is singular that those on whom the ability of speaking in foreign languages was conferred, should have been permitted to pervert it by making a shew of it to their own exaltation. And it is still more inexplicable, that the power should have been *continued* to the men who habitually misapplied it. The *application* of the charismata bestowed on the Corinthians gave rise to numerous abuses. The more striking and dazzling were over-valued, particularly the gift of tongues; because the manifestations of that gift were adapted to fill the people with wonder. Those who possessed it looked down upon others not equally favoured with themselves; while the latter envied the former.

In order to correct this improper use of charismata, and at the same time to point out their right use and object, the apostle enters minutely into a consideration of the subject. It is obvious that speaking in other languages and prophesying were the gifts which he intended especially to notice, inasmuch as these related to *public* speaking, and were therefore most valued. But he treats of the character, value, and object, of spiritual gifts *generally*, for the sake of shewing the proper relation which the gift of tongues bears to other kindred manifestations of supernatural influence. Here he introduces a metaphor taken from the human body, to prove that as all the members form one united organism, none superfluous, none contemptible; so also the different gifts of the Spirit constitute one spiritual organism, each working harmoniously for the good of the whole. After this, he describes the manner in which love should regulate all the gifts, because from it they receive their true value. In the last place, he comes to the main part of the subject, viz., the use of two gifts in the public assemblies—viz. speaking in foreign languages and prophesying. The latter, as tending to the edifying of the church, is preferred to the former.

Eichhorn supposes, that the letter sent by the Corinthians to Paul did not mention the present topic. But we have followed Billroth and De Wette, who think that the apostle's counsel had been asked on this point as well as others. The expressions in which it is introduced intimate that he had been consulted: 'now concerning spiritual gifts, brethren, I would not have you ignorant.' (comp. x. 1.)

5. The last question of the Corinthian church related to the collection for the poor saints at Jerusalem. Respecting the mode of collecting and conveying this contribution, the writer gives some directions.

Art. II—*Antonio Perez and Philip II.* By M. Mignet, member of the Institute of France, Perpetual Secretary of the Academy of Moral and Political Sciences, and translated, with the approbation of the author, by C. Cocks, B.L., Professor of the living Languages in the Royal Colleges of France. London: Longman, and Co.

M. Mignet, like M. Thiers, entered the literary career, twenty years ago, as historian of the French revolution, and, in July, 1830, was, with his competitor and friend, launched into political existence as a councillor of state. The history of the French revolution by M. Mignet, though much shorter than that of M. Thiers, is greatly superior; and exhibited the young author as a more acute observer, a more laborious investigator of events and of their causes, a more faithful adherent to truth, and a more sincere advocate of the great principles, the establishment of which, as the basis of government, was the object of the revolution. In Thiers's history, a miserable compilation, written under the inspiration of the ex-terrorists of 1793 and 1794, and of the ex-censors and *head-spies* of the imperial police, who had amalgamated in the *Constitutionnel*, every one easily discovers the contempt for truth, the barefaced corruption and base servility, which the historian afterwards displayed as a statesman. M. Mignet's work, on the contrary, evinced an earnestness of principles and opinions, and a dignity of character, which completely unfitted him for acting a principal part under the present government. This explains why, with so many physical and mental advantages over the 'monkey' of M. Lammenais, M. Mignet is nothing more, at the present time, than he was in August, 1830—a councillor of state, and *archiviste* of the ministry for foreign affairs; whilst the other has been—in turn, minister of almost every state department.

M. Mignet has no cause to regret the comparative obscurity to which he has sentenced himself; and we are sure that he finds, in his literary pursuits, a gratification much more enviable than that resulting from the enjoyment of ministerial power. Let him persist in his laborious studies, and profit of the opportunity which his present situation offers, to prepare a conscientious and true history of the Consulate, of the Empire, and of the Restoration, which are still wanting, notwithstanding the pretensions of Thiers. This it is which we expect and claim from M. Mignet, instead of his contributions to the heavy, stupid *Journal des Savants*, the fit burial-ground for the philosophical nonsense of Cousin and the historical falsehoods of the doctrinaires.

Let not our readers, however, suppose that in these last observations we intend to throw blame on the subject of the book before us, or on its composition. Far from it. We unhesitatingly declare, that we never met in the *Journal des Savants*, with anything equal to the articles now collected in this volume; that we approve of their exhumation by the author, for real publication; and that Messrs. Longman are entitled to the gratitude of the public, for this translation, which is the best we have seen of any French book.

Although, apparently or purposely, written to elucidate some few historical points, the matter is handled in such a manner as to give to the elucidation all the interest that could be found in a novel; and people of fashion who read nothing but for pleasure, may take this volume without fear of being disappointed. This, however, if it were its only or its principal merit, would not have induced us to recommend it. Our praise even would be much restricted, if, to the advantage of being an entertaining book, it added no other than that of being at the same time an erudite book; but there is something more in it than mere erudition and style. It evinces a moral purpose, which, we have no doubt, the author had in view, when he determined to exhibit, in the middle of the nineteenth century, some of the events which marked the end of the sixteenth. People well acquainted with the present state of France cannot help thinking, on reading this volume, that, in most parts, it is an allusion to the political characters who, to the disgrace of the country, are now eminent in France. It is apparent, that the picture of the wily successor of the great Emperor and King, Charles V., bears a great likeness to the *Napoleon of Peace* and that in the delineation of the characters of the ministers of Philip II., the author had in view some of the ministers of Louis Philippe. We all recognise Antonio Perez.

The theories of Italian policy which were, by the way, but too conformable to the practice usually followed, had given him a perversity of mind which his own disposition had not over well withstood. Being of a quick understanding, an insinuating character, and a devotedness which knew neither bounds nor scruples, full of expedients, a nervous and elegant writer, and expeditious in business, he had gained the favour of Philip II., who had gradually given him almost his entire confidence. By his agreeable manners he tempered and disguised much of the disgust which people felt at the king's shallow and sordid parsimony. Philip imparted to him his most secret designs, initiated him into his private thoughts. Such high favour had intoxicated him. He affected even towards the Duke of Alva, (qy. Dalmatic?) when they met in the king's apartments, a silence and a haughtiness which revealed at once the arrogance of enmity and the infatuation of fortune. So little moderation in prosperity, coupled with the most luxurious habits, a passion for gaming, a craving appetite for pleasures and excessive expenses, which reduced him to receive from every hand, excited against him both envy and animosity in the austere and factious court of Philip II., and, on the first opportunity, inevitably prepared his downfall. This event, too, he himself hastened, by serving too well the distrustful passions of Philip, and, perhaps, even by exciting them beyond measure against two men of his own party, Don Juan of Austria, (the king's brother,) and his secretary Escovedo. (pp. 11 and 12.)

The primordial fact is the assassination of Escovedo, by order of the King. What part did Perez take in the perpetration of that murder? Was he the mere instrument of the suspicious policy of Philip, or did he advise him to rid himself of this secretary, the confidant and agent of his brother? If he urged him by his counsels to this extremity, was he guided by reasons of state, or by private interest? Did he not persuade him to get rid of Escovedo, because the latter exalted the ambitious imagination of Don Juan, and entertained him with dangerous projects? or, did he make use of this pretence, by deceiving Philip, to rid himself of a man who constrained and blamed his amours with the Princess of Eboly, the widow of Ruy Gomez de Silva, whose creatures they both were? Have these amours any foundation; and did they, as has always been believed, cause a rivalry between the king and the minister? Ought the disgrace of Perez, managed with skilful dissimulation, and pursued with implacable rigour, to be attributed to the policy of Philip, who sacrificed Perez, bearing the whole responsibility of the murder of Escovedo? or, ought we also to seek its cause in the vindictive jealousy of the prince, who showed himself inexorable, as soon as he knew that Perez had deceived him? Such are the questions examined and solved in M. Mignet's work.

The trial of Perez, in Madrid; the torture inflicted on him, to obtain the avowal of his treachery; his escape from his dungeon, through the devotedness of his wife; his appeal to the sovereign tribunal of Arragon, where he had taken refuge; the interference of the Inquisition, to take possession of his person, and to deliver him back to the vengeance of Philip; the supreme tribunal yielding to the commands of the inquisitors; Perez saved by a popular insurrection, at the very moment when he was given up to be led to the prison of the Inquisition, and succeeding in escaping into France; Philip sending an army into Arragon, chastising the Arragonese with his customary cruelty, and abolishing their constitutional *fueros*;—finally, the long exile of Perez, passed in a multitude of political intrigues, and his death;—such are the events which are related, with praiseworthy accuracy, and in a most instructive manner.

Art. III.—1. *The Expedition to Borneo of H. M. S. Dido, for the Suppression of Piracy:* with Extracts from the Journal of James Brooke, Esq., of Saráwak, now Agent for the British Government in Borneo. By Capt. the Hon. Henry Keppel, R. N. In two Volumes, 8vo. London: Chapman and Hall, 1846.

2. *Trade and Travel in the Far East;* or, Recollections of one-and-twenty years passed in Java, Singapore, Australia, and China. By G. H. Davidson. 12mo. London: Madden and Malcolm, 1846.

3. *Enterprise in Tropical Australia.* By G. Windsor Earl, M. R. A. S., Linguist to the North Australian Expedition, and Commissioner of Crown Lands for Port Essington. 12mo. London: Madden and Malcoln, 1846.

Our knowledge of the vast region distinguished by the general name of the Indian Archipelago, dates from a period as recent as the discovery of America. To the enterprise of the early Portuguese navigators, and of their successors in maritime discovery and colonization, the Dutch, we were long indebted for an acquaintance with the largest groupe of islands on the globe, occupied by an aboriginal race so different from the other families of nations, in physical type and language, as to form a distinct class of the human species in physiology. Upon this aboriginal population, in times comparatively modern, has been grafted the Malayan stock, imparting, to a great extent, their peculiar character and higher civilization to the Polynesian tribes with whom they have intermingled. The various islands differ, indeed, very remarkably, in their climate, productions, and social condition. The whole Archipelago is situated within the tropics, the equinoctial line running nearly through its centre; but their geographical position, geological formation, and varying fertility combine to produce a very marked diversity; and Mr. Crawford, to whom we are indebted for the best general account of this region, points out five natural divisions. In the very centre, partaking in its vast extent of the climate and character of three of these divisions, lies Borneo, the largest island, if we exclude from that description the Australian continent, in the world; being about nine hundred miles in its extreme length, and seven hundred and twenty miles across at its greatest breadth. A high chain of mountains intersecting it longitudinally, accounts for the diversity of the climate of its eastern and western portions. About two-thirds of the western portion resemble, in physical character, productions, and civilization, the islands which form the western boundary of the Archipelago, together with the Malayan Peninsula; that is to say, Sumatra, Java, Bali, and Lombok, sometimes included under the general name of the Sunda Islands. The whole eastern coast of Borneo, up to about the parallel of 3° N., classes with the large island of Celebes, and the chain of smaller ones between the meridians of 116° and 124° E. The north-eastern angle of Borneo comes within the same natural division as the island of Mindanawi, or Mindanao, and the Sooloo groupe, in which the clove and the nutmeg are indigenous, but of inferior quality. To the north of these, the groupe of the Philippines, lying within the region of hurricanes, forms a distinct and peculiar division. In the opposite direction, between the parallels of 2° N. and 10° S., and extending eastward to longitude 130° E., lie the Molucca and Spice Islands, the strange productions of which, both in the animal and the vegetable kingdoms, are not indigenous to any other parts of the globe.

The Portuguese had extended their maritime conquests and commerce to the Indian Archipelago a century before any other European nation followed in their wake. Diego Lopez de Sequeira, the commander of a royal squadron of four ships, first reached Sumatra and Malacca in 1507; ten years after Vasco de Gama had doubled the Cape. In 1511, Albuquerque, the viceroy of the Indies, effected the conquest of Malacca; and, in the same year, he despatched a squadron to the Moluccas, which touched at Amboyna only, and returned with a cargo of spices. Ten years afterwards, a Portuguese squadron was sent to take possession of the Spice Islands in the name of the King of Portugal; and the commander, by a combination of perfidy and violence which characterized the whole course of the proceedings of the Portuguese in those seas, succeeded in establishing himself in the island of Ternate. Europe, Mr. Crawford remarks, gained no advantage from the discoveries of the Portuguese in the Indian seas. 'By their wars in the Moluccas, the production of spices was diminished, the ancient carriers of the trade were plundered, and the Persian Gulf and Red Sea, the avenues by which the commodities of India reached Europe, were either seized or blockaded by them. The consequence of all this was, that the commodities of India were sold dearer than before the discovery of the new route. The industry of Europe received no new impulse, for no new market was created for her commodities.'*

De Britto, the Portuguese commander of the squadron sent to take possession of the Moluccas, met there, to his astonishment, the companions of Magellan, who had reached them from the eastward in the course of the first voyage round the world. The great navigator himself had been killed in an affray with the natives of one of the Philippines. One of his two ships had been forced back into the Moluccas, in distress. De Britto seized it, and sent the crew prisoners to Portugal. In 1526, the Spaniards made their first attempt to establish themselves in the Moluccas; but, three years afterwards, they consented to renounce their claim for a pecuniary consideration of 350,000 ducats. In 1565, the Spaniards took nominal possession of the Philippine Islands; some years however elapsed before they had established themselves by the conquest of Manilla.

In 1578, nearly seventy years after the discovery of the maritime route, the English, under Sir Francis Drake, first made their appearance in the Indian Archipelago. Drake touched at Java and Ternate, and was followed by Thomas Cavendish, who, in his circumnavigation of the globe, touched at Java in passing through the strait between that island and Bali. In 1596, the first Dutch expedition to the Indies reached Java, where the new adventurers soon embroiled themselves with the natives, and became involved in hostilities with the Spaniards. In 1611, just a century after the establishment of the Portuguese authority at Malacca, the first Dutch governor-general laid the foundation of the future capital at Jacatra. The most flourishing period of their commercial greatness in these seas, was from 1629 to 1675.

Meantime, the English had, in 1603, opened a commerce with Acheen and Bantam; and within fifteen years from their first appearance in the seas of the Archipelago, they had established factories at Patani in the Malayan peninsula, at Acheen, Ticoa, and Jambi in Sumatra, at Bantam and Jacatra in Java, at Sakadana and Banjar-massing in Borneo, in the Banda Isles, at Macassar in Celebes, in Siam, and in Japan. The British settlement at Bencoolen in Sumatra, was established in 1685, and removed to Fort Marlborough in 1714. In 1763, it was erected into an independent presidency; and it was not till 1802, that it was annexed, by act of Parliament, to the presidency of Bengal.† In 1825, it was transfered to the Dutch in

* Crawford's Indian Archipelago, v. iii. p. 216.

† 'The transfer of this settlement to the Dutch, in exchange for Malacca, in 1825,' says Mr. Davidson, 'was a severe blow and great

exchange for Malacca. The first English settlement on Pulo Penang, to which was given the absurd name of Prince of Wales Island, dates from 1785. Malacca was captured by the British in 1795. In 1811, Java, Celebes, and the other Dutch possessions were surrendered by capitulation on the part of the French governor-general, to the British authorities. The British government of Java, under the enlightened administration of Sir Stamford Raffles, lasted only from 1813 to 1816, when, by an act of the most ignorant impolicy, the finest island in the world, in which the commercial, fiscal, and judicial reforms introduced by the British governor were just beginning to exert the most beneficial effort, was abandoned to its old oppressors, the Dutch, together with Malacca, Celebes, and the Spice Islands; and but for the spirited and patriotic conduct of Sir Stamford Raffles, our traders would have been altogether excluded from the Indian Seas.

The very first act of the Dutch, on regaining possession of Java and its dependencies, was, to impose restrictions upon British commerce; this they were enabled to enforce, by having the command of the straits of Sunda and Malacca, which form the western entrance to the Chinese and Java seas; and it at length became evident, that, unless some strong and decisive steps were taken, to which the British Government shewed an unaccountable reluctance, nothing but actual force could obtain for our traders ingress to the thousand isles of the Archipelago. With some difficulty, after having for a long time maintained, single-handed, a contest with the Dutch Colonial authorities on one part, and with those of the East India Company on the other, Sir Stamford Raffles obtained, in a personal interview with the Marquess of Hastings, the sanction of the Bengal

disappointment to all the natives, both high and low. At a meeting of chiefs held at the Government House, at which the English and Dutch authorities were both present, for the purpose of completing the transfer, the Senior Rajah rose to address the assembly, and spoke to the following effect:—'Against this transfer of my country I protest. Who is there possessed of authority to hand me and my countrymen, like so many cattle, over to the Dutch, or to any other power? If the English are tired of us, let them go away; but I deny their right to hand us over to the Dutch. When the English first came here, they asked for and got a piece of land to build warehouses and dwelling-houses upon. That piece of land is still defined by its original stone wall, and is all they (the English) ever got from us. We were never conquered; and I now tell the English and Dutch gentlemen here assembled, that, had I the power, as I have the will, I would resist this transfer to the knife. I am, however, a poor man, have no soldiers to cope with yours, and must submit. God's will be done.' The speaker was an old man, with whose power and will for mischief in former days, the British had good cause to be acquainted.'—'*Trade and Travel*,' pp. 81, 2.

Government to the splendid enterprise of hoisting the British flag at Singapore. In his own words, he wanted neither people nor territory: all he asked was, permission to anchor a line of battle-ship at the mouth either of the straits of Sunda or of those of Malacca, and the trade of England would be secured, the monopoly of the Dutch broken. Thither, accordingly, he proceeded in person, in the discharge of his delicate commission, and, in spite of the protest and opposition of the Government of Penang and the exclusive pretensions of the Dutch authorities, hoisted the British flag, on the 20th of February, 1819, on the island which, he had penetration enough to see, might become in the East, 'that Malta is in the West.' Still, he had reason to fear that the Home Government, directed by the evil genius of the Castlereagh-Bathurst policy, might a second time destroy all the results of his patriotic exertions, and be 'weak enough to sacrifice him, honour, and the Eastern Archipelago to the outrageous pretensions of the Dutch.' For some time, the British Government, in complaisance, deferred to their remonstrances so far as to decline having any thing to do with Singapore, throwing the whole responsibility upon Sir Stamford; and it was not till the settlement had been established for three years, that Singapore was recognized by Great Britain. Meantime, within the first two years and a half after its establishment, no fewer than 2889 vessels had entered and cleared from its port, of which, 383 were owned and commanded by Europeans, and 2506 by natives, their aggregate tonnage amounting to 161,000 tons. Such was the result of the bold step of declaring Singapore a free port, open to ships and vessels of every nation, free of duty; in which, Sir Stamford shewed himself to be far in advance of the narrow commercial policy that had hitherto governed our Eastern affairs.

Until within the last three years, the trade of Singapore has gone on increasing, its harbour being visited regularly by native vessels from all the neighbouring islands, as well as from the Indian Continent. Mr. Davidson gives his reason for thinking, that its trade has now reached its *maximum*. The recent establishment of the British Colony of Hong-Kong, and the opening of the Northern ports on the coast of China, will tend, he fears, to lessen the Chinese-junk trade. On the other hand, the merchants of Singapore are themselves embarking with spirit in the China trade; and even if the settlement should not advance in prosperity at the same rapid rate that has hitherto marked its progress, its advantageous position, delightful and salubrious climate, picturesque beauty, and fertile soil, must always render it at once a valuable possession and the emporium of a considerable trade. Its present aggregate imports and exports are estimated by Mr. Davidson at three millions sterling; and its revenue is more than sufficient to pay its expenses.

It has been in consequence of the decrease of its trade with China, that the merchants of Singapore, and their connexions in Java, have been led to turn their attention to the aggressions made by the Dutch on our commerce with the ports of the Archipelago, and to transmit to the Home Government those urgent appeals which have at length had the effect of directing attention to one of the fairest fields of British mercantile enterprise. In no quarter have our commercial interests suffered so much from deplorable and unaccountable neglect. 'Pirates,' remarks Mr. Earl (in 1837), 'have been allowed to swarm in the immediate neighbourhood of the only settlement which we possess in these seas; and a rival European power has been suffered to commit aggressions on our commerce with impunity; so that, had not the strong desire to obtain British manufactures, displayed by the natives themselves, induced them to overcome the obstacles which have been thrown in their way, an intercourse with the Eastern islands must, ere this, have totally ceased.' How long this disgraceful state of things might have been suffered to continue, so far as the British Government is concerned, it is impossible to say; but the whole merit of awaking the slumbering spirit of philanthropy with regard to these islands, of leading the way to new fields of commercial enterprise, and of overcoming every political obstacle to the carrying out of Sir Stamford Raffles's views over the whole Archipelago, is due to the extraordinary individual whose romantic adventures are detailed in the 'Expedition to Borneo.'

Before we proceed to give an account of what Mr. Brooke has accomplished, it may be a suitable introduction, to advert to the sagacious views expressed by Sir Stamford Raffles, in a letter to Lord Minto, with regard to the importance of a settlement in Borneo, so far back as 1811, and to the valuable information comprised in that letter, respecting the political condition and relations of the several groupes of islands. It does not appear that any of them, taken separately, can pretend to the rank of a powerful or independent state. At no very distant date, the sovereign of Menangkabu, the ancient capital of Sumatra, was acknowledged over the whole of that large island; and its influence extended to many of the neighbouring islands. The respect still paid to its princes by all ranks, Sir Stamford Raffles speaks of as amounting almost to veneration. Borneo, or, as the natives call it, Pulo Kalamantan, appears, on the other hand, to have been, from the earliest times, divided into three distinct kingdoms. That of Borneo (Bruni) properly so called, included the whole northern part of the island, from Cape Datu, in latitude 3° 15′ N. to Kanunkungan Point, in the Straits of Macassar, 1° 15′. The kingdom of Sakadana extended from Cape Datu to Cape Sambar; and the remainder of the island, from Cape Sambar to Kanukungan Point, to that of Banjar-massing. The kingdom of Sakadana was ceded by the rajah of Bantam to the Dutch East India Company; and they had, at one time, the military possession of that of Banjar-massing, their sovereignty actually or virtually extending over the whole island, except Borneo Proper. Sakadana, once the most celebrated city in Borneo, and a great emporium, was destroyed by the Dutch, at the suggestion of the rajah or sultan of Pontiana, almost the only native chieftain in the island whose power has been created, and is still supported, by commerce. His capital is situated in latitude 4° N. The present representative of the sultans of Sakadana is the independent rajah of Matan; one of the most valuable districts of Borneo.

Sir Stamford Raffles enumerates the various groupes of states as under:

1. The states of the Malayan Peninsula.
2. The states of the Island of Sumatra.
3. The states of the Island of Borneo.
4. The states of the Sunda Isles, extending from the straits of Sunda to Timor and Celebes.
5. The states of Java.
6. The states of Celebes.
7. The states of Sooloo and Mindanawi.
8. The states of the Moluccas, comprehending Ceram and Banda.
9. The states of Jelolo, or Little Celebes.
10. The Black Papua states of New Guinea and the Papua Islands.

Borneo, Celebes, Sooloo, the Moluccas, and the islands of the straits of Sunda and Banka, compose what has been denominated the Malayan groupe; and the Malays dwelling on the shores of these and other islands, may with certainty be classed as belonging to the same race. 'In ancient times,' says Sir Stamford Raffles, 'the Malay chiefs, though possessing the title of sultan or rajah, and in full possession of authority within their own domains, yet all held of a superior or suzerain, who was king of the ancient and powerful state of Majopahit, on the island of Java, and who had the title of *Bitara*. Malacca was one of the first states that shook off this allegiance, and became, in the end, so powerful, as to hold a great part of the Malayan peninsula and of the opposite coast of Sumatra, in a similar dependence, although the sovereigns of these states still retained their titles, and exercised their independent authority within their own dominions.*

Malacca itself was founded by a Malayan colony from Sumatra, previously to the introduction of Mohammedism in the thirteenth century; and according to Mr. Crawford, the country of Menangkabu, in Sumatra, is, beyond dispute, the parent country of the Malay race. Previously to their adopting the Mohammedan faith, the religion and civilization of the Malayan tribes were Hindoo. As we advance eastward, the traces both of the earlier Hindoo, and of the later Mohammedan civilization become less marked. In the island of Celebes, that of Hindooism appears to have made very small progress; and it was not till the close of the sixteenth century, that the religion of Mohammed was generally adopted there. Everything concurs to shew, that the civilization of the Indian archipelago has proceeded from the west; although there is equally strong reason to conclude that its islands were originally peopled from the opposite direction. The interior is uniformly found inhabited by various tribes differing from the Malays and from each other, and exhibiting different gradations of early civilization, the greater part of whom are pagans. Sir Stamford Raffles describes the two great tribes into which the more civilized portion of the inhabitants of Celebes are divided—the Macassars and the Bugis,† as the most bold, adventurous, and enterprising of all the eastern nations, and extremely addicted to a military life. 'They are equally celebrated for their fidelity and their courage, and for this reason, they have long been employed, as the Swiss in Europe, not only in the armies of Siam, Kambodia, and other countries, but also as the guards of their princes. They can be recruited with facility, and easily submit to military discipline.' The same remark applies, with nearly equal force, to the inhabitants of Jelolo or Halamahera, situated between the Moluccas and the Papua islands. The Sooloos, who inhabit the groupe to the north of Borneo, between that island and the Philippines, are described as a bold and enterprising race, 'of the mixed Malay and Philippine breed.' They have had frequent wars with the Spaniards of Manilla, and have never acknowledged their authority. They have generally adopted the religion of Islam, and, though active and enter-

* Memoir of Sir Stamford Raffles, vol. i. p. 78.

† About the period of the first arrival of Europeans in the East, the Macassar and Bugis tribes were among the principal dealers in spices; and the island of Celebes was nearly under the authority of a single sovereign. On the breaking down of this great empire, several smaller states rose from its ruins.

prising, are extremely vicious, treacherous, and sanguinary. Sir Stamford Raffles estimates the inhabitants of the Sooloo islands, in their most flourishing state, at not more than sixty thousand souls, or, including their dependencies, at about one hundred thousand. Between eighty and ninety years ago, they were much devoted to commerce; and about the period of the first British settlement in the island of Balambangan, off the coast of Borneo, we had for some time a commercial resident in Sooloo; but the government being too weak to afford any efficient protection, he was withdrawn; and the breaking down of the government has covered the Sooloo seas with fleets of formidable pirates.

The great island of Mindanawi, between the Moluccas and the Philippines, is the original country of the Lanuns, the most formidable of all the Eastern pirates. Its northern coast is under a precarious subjection to the Spaniards; but the great Lanun bight is occupied by a number of small chieftains, who have, from time immemorial, been addicted to piracy. The most powerful state on the island is that of Mindanawi, the sultan of which is a Mohammedan, although the great mass of his subjects are pagans, in almost every respect similar to the Dyaks or aboriginal inhabitants of Borneo.

Numerous and various are the tribes of the Eastern isles which have not embraced the religion of Islam to this day; they are consequently reckoned infidels; and cruises against the infidels are sure to receive the approbation of all the Arab teachers settled in the Malay countries. Hence, piracy has always been regarded by them as an honourable occupation; and the Malay romances and traditions constantly refer to piratical achievements. From considerations of policy, and in conformity to instructions from home, the Dutch colonists, as well as the Portuguese, have promoted the profession of Christianity among the eastern islands. Several small islands in the Malayan archipelago, according to Sir Stamford Raffles, are inhabited almost entirely by 'Christians of the Catholic persuasion;' as the islands of Sanggir and Siauk, between Jelolo and Mindanawi. In many other islands, 'the Protestant persuasion has made considerable progress; and, in the flourishing times of the Batavian regency, teachers were dispersed over all the low chain of islands which extend from Bali and Lambok, to the great island of Timor.' The islands in which the Christian faith has been most extensively diffused, according to the same authority, are, the great island Ende or Manggerai, the isles of Solor, Salerang, Lomblim, and Ombai, the great island Timor, and the several small islands in its vicinity, as Savo, Roti, and Samba.

'Amboyna, Kissa, and Rotti,' says Mr. Earl, 'are the head-quarters of Christianity in the Indian Archipelago; and as the natives are an intelligent people, I look upon them as being likely to prove highly useful to any future settlement on the northern coasts of Australia. They acquire the English language with considerable facility, and many are sufficiently educated to read and write Malayan in the Roman character.'—*Earl's 'Enterprise,' &c.*, p. 122.

In many of these islands, the natives, having no written character of their own, have been instructed in the Roman character, and taught to read Malay and other dialects in it. Various religious formularies have been printed for their use; and translations have been executed for the use of these Christians in some of their languages, which have little or no affinity to the Malay. Mr. Crawford remarks, that 'the Christian religion, as a prevailing worship, can be said to exist only in the Spice islands and the Philippines. In the latter, the converted natives are *nominally* catholics, and, in the former, *nominally* protestants.' 'Both the Portuguese and the Dutch supported schools in the Moluccas for religious instruction; and an allowance of rice was given to the students, which appears to have been the great inducement to frequent them; whence the Dutch often ludicrously denominate the native converts, *'rice Christians.''* † Yet, to even this nominal and mongrel Christianity, a beneficial influence is ascribed. 'The natives of Amboyna who are Christians,' says Crawford, 'are much superior, both in morals and in intelligence, to their countrymen who are Mohammedans: and, notwithstanding all the oppression they have endured, are a peaceable and inoffensive race of men. In the Dutch armies, they ranked above all the other Asiatic troops, and were paid, equipped, and considered on this scale of merit.' The natives of the Philippines also, who have embraced the Romish superstition, are described as possessing a share of energy and intelligence superior not only to that of their Pagan and Mohammedan countrymen, but also to that of all the western inhabitants of the Archipelago,—to that of the very people who, at a former period, bestowed upon them laws, language, and civilization. 'In the inter-colonial navigation of all the nations of Europe in the Indies, the natives of Manilla are almost universally employed as gunners and steersmen; that is, in those offices in which it is necessary to combine skill and firmness with mere physical labour and agility.' In this case, however, it may be suspected, that physical causes of superiority have combined with the influence of Christian civilization; and

* Crawford's 'Ind. Archipelago,' vol. ii. p. 274.

that there has taken place a considerable intermixture of races.*

The Philippine Islands, and a portion of the coast of Mindanawi (or Mindanao), are the only possessions of Spain in the Archipelago; and the Portuguese retain only part of the great island of Timor and the eastern extremity of that of Flores. The southern portion of Timor, and the adjacent islands, the Moluccas, the Carimon Isles, Java, Banca, and portions of Sumatra, Borneo, and Celebes, belong to the Dutch. They have, also, very recently taken possession of the Island of Bali. The British have hitherto had no settlement or harbour between Port Essington, on the northern coast of the Australian Continent, and Singapore; nor, previously to Mr. Brooke's establishing himself on the coast of Borneo, between Singapore and Hong-Kong.

By the treaty between Great Britain and the Netherlands 'respecting territory and commerce in the East Indies,' signed at London in March 1824, mutual freedom of trade is guaranteed, *with the exception of the Molucca Islands,* and especially Amboyna, Banda, Ternate, and their immediate dependencies, including Ceram; the Moluccas being defined to be, that cluster which has Celebes to the westward, New Guinea to the eastward, and Timor to the southward; these three islands *not* being included in the exception. His Britannic Majesty engaged, however, in that treaty, that no British settlement should be formed on the island of Sumatra, nor any treaty concluded by British authority with any native prince, chief, or state therein. Also, that no British establishment should be made on the Carimon Isles, or on the islands of Battam, Bintang, Lingin, or any of the islands *south* of the straits of Singapore, nor any treaty concluded by British authority with the chiefs of those islands. Borneo is not referred to in the treaty; nor was it necessary: of course it follows the rule of Celebes, in *not* being excepted.

The vast importance of this magnificent island had not escaped the comprehensive mind of Sir Stamford Raffles, who commences the letter to Lord Minto, already referred to, with adverting to it as one of the most fertile countries in the world, as well as one of the most productive in gold and diamonds. The camphor which it produces, is the finest in the world; and it is thought, that it is capable of growing every species of

* Mr. Earl remarks, that the mixed descendants of the Dutch at Macassar, in Celebes, 'are an enterprising race, possessing the commercial spirit of their Asiatic forefathers, guided by the superior intelligence of the European.'—p. 123.

spice. The interior has never been explored by Europeans; and this ignorance of the actual state of the country, it is remarked, is probably one of the principal causes that no European settlement has hitherto proved advantageous, but has generally been abandoned after a short trial. The following observations, though made five and thirty years ago, have lost none of their interest and importance.

'The only exception to this observation (the speedy abandonment of the settlements) is the Dutch settlement of Banjar Massing, which continued from 1747 to nearly three years ago, when it was abandoned by Marshal Daendals to the Rajah, by agreement, for the sum of fifty thousand dollars. The Rajah soon after sent an embassy to the government of Penang, *inviting the English to settle in their place*; but, this application not being attended to, *they applied to me*, on my coming down to Malacca last December. During the continuance of the Dutch settlement at Banjar Massing, the expense and revenue were always supposed to be very equally balanced; and the abandonment of the settlement was strongly opposed by many of the Dutch.

'The only other territory to which the Dutch have any claim on the Island of Borneo, is the coast from Sacadana to Mampawa; Pontiana, which lies about twelve miles up the river; and Landa, which lies about seventy miles up the river of that name, navigable by large boats. This territory, they acquired in virtue of a cession from the Sultan of Bantam in 1778; they destroyed Sacadana, and established factories at Pontiana and Mampawa, which they abandoned as unproductive after a trial of fourteen years.

'No other part of the island of Borneo has been settled by Europeans. The English, in 1772, intended to establish a factory at Passir, but abandoned the design on some commotions taking place in that state. Its object was, to make Passir a depot for opium and Indian piece goods, and for the contraband trade in spices. In 1774, a short time after the first settling of Balambangan, Mr. Jesse was deputed as Resident to Borneo Proper, with which state he concluded a treaty, by which the settlement of Balambangan acquired the exclusive trade in pepper; *stipulating, in return, to protect Borneo from the piratical incursions of the Sulu and Mindanawi men*. Neither of the parties, however, fulfilled their agreements, though the Residency at Borneo was continued for some years after the first breaking up of the Balambangan settlement in 1775. On the north-east of Borneo Proper lies a very considerable territory, the sovereignty of which has long been claimed by the Sulu government, and a very considerable part of which, together with the islands of the coast, has been for upwards of forty years regularly ceded to the English by the Sulus, and has, also, at different periods been occupied by the English, without any objection on the part of the government of Borneo Proper. This ceded district, which extends from the river Kiomanis on the north-west, which forms the boundary of Borneo Proper, to the great bay of Towsan Abia on the north-east is undoubtedly a rich and fertile country, though in a rude and uncultivated state; and it is admirably situated for commerce, though the different failures of Balambangan may seem to indicate the contrary. . . . . From the inquiries which I have taken every opportunity of making respecting the island of Borneo, I feel perfectly satisfied that no settlement is likely to succeed in that quarter, which is founded on a commercial, instead of a territorial basis. We have already acquired territorial rights; and the only question seems to be, whether these can be turned to advantage, either by cultivation or by commerce. To this I should have no hesitation whatever in answering, yes; finding the Dayak, or original inhabitants of Borneo, not only industrious in their habits, but particularly devoted to agriculture, and so manageable that a handful of Malays have, in numerous places, reduced many thousands of them to the condition of peaceful cultivators of the ground. Indeed, nothing seems wanting to effect this on a great scale, but a strong government, which can afford efficient protection to property and safety to individuals; and in the case of the Dayak, I regard it as an advantage that they have not hitherto adopted the religion of Islam, and would be ready, from the first, to regard us as their friends and protectors. Another great advantage which attends the formation of settlements in Borneo, is, that there are no territorial claims upon it from any European nation but ourselves.'—*Memoir of Sir Stamford Raffles*, vol. i. pp. 54—58.

The accomplished writer did not survive long enough to see his enlightened suggestions realized; but, like seed sown on the waters, they have at length, after many days, fructified. The spirit of philanthropy which glowed in his bosom, has communicated itself to one who seems in a very special and extraordinary manner fitted and destined to execute his benevolent plan.

James Brooke, the only surviving son of the late Thomas Brooke, Esq., of the East India Company's civil service, was born, April 29, 1803. He went out to India as a cadet, and distinguished himself by his gallantry in the Burmese war, during which he was shot through the body in an action with the Burmese. Having received the thanks of the Government, he obtained leave to return to England for the recovery of his prostrated strength. He resumed his station, but, shortly afterwards, relinquished the service; and, in 1830, left Calcutta for China in search of health and amusement. In this voyage, he saw for the first time the islands of the Asiatic Archipelago, and was struck with their vast importance and picturesque beauty. He inquired, and read, and became convinced, that Borneo and the Eastern Isles afforded an open field for enterprise.

'To carry to the Malay races, so long the terror of the European merchant vessel, the blessings of civilization; to suppress piracy, and extirpate the slave-trade, became his humane and generous objects; and from that hour, the energies of his powerful mind were devoted to this one pursuit. Often foiled, often disappointed, with a perseverance and enthusiasm which defied all obstacles, he was not till 1838 enabled to set sail from England on his darling project. The intervening years had been devoted to preparation and inquiry. A year spent in the Mediterranean had tested his vessel, the Royalist, and his crew; and so completely had he studied his subject, and calculated on contingencies, that the least sanguine of his friends felt, as he left the shore, hazardous and unusual as the enterprise seemed to be, that he had omitted nothing to ensure a successful issue. 'I go,' said he, 'to awake the spirit of slumbering philanthropy with regard to those islands; to carry Sir Stamford Raffles's views in Java over the whole Archipelago. Fortune and life I give freely; and if I fail in the attempt, I shall not have lived wholly in vain.'"—*Expedition to Borneo,* vol. i. pp. 3, 4.

The prospectus of the undertaking was published in the Geographical Journal (vol. viii. part 3), in 1838, when Mr. Brooke's preparations for sea were nearly complete. In his own journal, he expresses his firm conviction of its beneficial tendency, 'in adding to knowledge, increasing trade, and *spreading Christianity.'* On the 27th of October, the Royalist, a schooner of one hundred and forty-two tons, with a picked crew of twenty men, left the river, and, after a succession of heavy gales, quitted the land on the 16th of December. They touched at Rio, and at the Cape, where they were detained a fortnight; and at length, on the 1st of June, reached Singapore. Various causes delayed their sailing again till the 27th of July; and on the 1st of August, the Royalist anchored off the coast of Borneo, the *pirate coast;* for that part has been the harbour for pirates of every description. It had been represented, moreover, as abounding in shoals and reefs, perilous to the navigator. The bay between Points Api and Datu was found, however, free from danger; and nothing could be more majestic than the scenery,—the bay lined with a feathery row of beautiful casuarinas, behind these a tangled jungle, backed by a mountain some two thousand feet in height. On Sunday, August 4th, Mr. Brooke 'performed divine service;' and it is curious enough to find one who had braved danger in every shape, in field and on flood, taking credit to himself for 'manfully overcoming the horror which he has to the sound of his own voice before an audience.' After spending some days in examining the coast, and taking observations, the Royalist entered the Sarawak river, which discharges itself at the eastern corner of the bay; and on the 15th, anchored abreast of the 'town of that name, the residence of the Rajah Muda Hassim, about twenty miles up the river. It is described as a collection of mud huts, erected on piles: the residences of the Rajah and his fourteen brothers occupied the greater part, and the majority of the population, amounting to about fifteen hundred persons, consisted of their followers. The strangers were extremely well received; and permission was readily obtained from the Rajah, to make excursions into the country, but with the intimation that, if they went too far up the rivers, he could not be answerable for their safety, owing to the disturbed state of the interior. The extracts given from Mr. Brooke's journal describe the exploratory trips made up several rivers, which brought him in contact with the Dyak tribes, of whom he gives a very favourable account. In one of these excursions, an interesting discovery was made,—the wild nutmeg-tree in full flower, growing to the height of between twenty and thirty feet; the nutmegs lying in plenty under the trees. 'While the East Indian Company were sending Captain Forest from their settlement of Balambangan as far as New Guinea in search of this plant, how little they dreamed of its flourishing so near them in the island of Borneo!' Mr. Brooke spent about ten weeks in this his first visit to the island of Borneo; and the information he collected was both interesting and satisfactory, so that he left the coast for Singapore 'with an excellent prospect for the coming year.'

Mr. Brooke's next trip was, attended by a Bugis native, to the island of Celebes; and an entertaining account is given of an excursion into the hill-region of the district of Bonthian, which presented the perfection of woodland, combined with the picturesque characteristics of mountain scenery. The party reached the summit of Lumpu Balong, 'never before reached by European.' The Dutch officers stated, that three successive Residents of Bonthian had attempted it, and failed. The chief production of the country is coffee, which is grown in great quantities on the hills, and exported by the Bugis merchants. On his return to Singapore, Mr. Brooke was detained for several months by ill health; but he availed himself of the opportunity to re-copper and re-fit the Royalist; and by the end of August 1840, he again found himself at Sarawak. There, with some reluctance, he was induced to offer his aid to the Rajah in suppressing a rebellion; and he succeeded in bringing the affair to a happy issue by the submission of the insurgents, after a protracted warfare, of which the ludicrous is quite as prominent a feature as the horrible. On his return to Sarawak, he had an opportunity of making the acquaintance of a band of pirates from the island of Gilolo, who came to pay their respects to the Rajah. He returned to Singapore in February 1841, his principal object being to procure a vessel to trade between that place and Sarawak; and early in April, he sailed with a schooner of ninety tons, laden with a suitable cargo, in company with the Royalist, for the seat of his future government;—for the Rajah had made him an offer, which Mr. Brooke had accepted, of the lordship of the Sarawak territory, in return for his services in the war, and upon his engaging to bring down trade to the place. We must pass over the narrative (taken from Mr. Brooke's journal) of the vexatious delays and trying difficulties by which his patience, courage, and strength of purpose were put to a severe test. At issue with the well-meaning, but weak-minded Rajah, beset by intrigues, and surrounded with a fierce and lawless people, Mr. Brooke had the singular courage to despatch both his vessels; one to Borneo, on a mission of humanity, to inquire respecting the fate of the crew of an English vessel, reported to have been shipwrecked, the other to Singapore with a cargo; thus placing himself, with only three companions, at the mercy of circumstances, 'relying on the over-ruling Providence in which he trusted, to bring him safely through all his difficulties and perils.' When, at length, on the 24th of September 1841, the Rajah signed the agreement by which Mr. Brooke became the governor of Sarawak, he had still to contend against a secret conspiracy; while the state of his little dominion, ravaged by war, and torn by dissension, presented difficulties which seem at times almost to have overwhelmed him. His reflections upon commencing a new year (Jan. 1, 1842), though not intended, we presume, for the public eye, are so characteristic that we shall transcribe them.

'This is a year which to me must be eventful; for, at its close, I shall be able to judge whether I can maintain myself against all the circumstances and difficulties which beset me, or whether I must retreat, broken in fortune, to some retirement in my native land. I look with calmness on the alternative; and God knows, no selfish motives weigh on me; and if I fail, my chief regret will be for the natives of this unhappy country. . . . . If the sum of human misery can be alleviated—if these suffering people can be raised in the scale of civilization and happiness,—it is a cause in which I could suffer; it is a cause in which I *have* suffered and *do suffer*: hemmed in, beset, anxious, perplexed, and the good intent marred by false agents, surrounded by weakness, treachery, falsehood, and folly, is suffering enough; and to feel myself on the threshold of success, and only withheld by the want of adequate means, increases this suffering.'—Vol. i. pp. 261, 2.

Six months having elapsed, we find him writing in a more cheerful strain.

'The internal state of the country is decidedly improving and flourishing, and bears the aspect of gradually increasing prosperity. Justice has been strictly administered. Robberies, which, a few months ago, were of nightly occurrence, are now rarely heard of; and that vile intriguing to make poor people slaves, from debt or false claims, is entirely stopped. . . . So far, indeed, nothing can be better than our internal state; there is peace, there is plenty; the poor are not harassed; and justice is done to all. The Dyaks of the interior are improving and content, and gaining courage daily to complain of any wrong that may be offered them.'—Vol. i. p.p. 295, 6.

In July, Mr. Brooke proceeded in person to Bruni, the capital of Borneo Proper, for the purpose of accomplishing three important objects; to effect a reconciliation between the Sultan and his uncle Muda Hassim, in order to pave the way for the return of the latter to Borneo; to obtain the Sultan's approval and ratification of his own instalment in the government of Sarawak; and to procure the release of the *Kleeses* (Hindoostanees) of two shipwrecked vessels. The first object was gained at once; the third was also readily conceded; and on the 1st of August, 1842, in pursuance of a resolution adopted in a conclave of *Pangerans* (Malay nobles), the second was consummated by the signing and sealing of the contract constituting him Rajah of the country of Sarawak. The year 1843 opened under favourable auspices; and in February, Mr. Brooke deemed the affairs of his government in so safe and prosperous a state as to allow of his paying a visit to Singapore. There he met with Captain the Hon. Henry Keppel, who had been ordered by the British Admiral to proceed with his vessel, the Dido, to the Straits, with a view to the protection of trade, and the suppression of piracy. Mr. Brooke gladly availed himself of the offer made him to return to Sarawak in the Dido, in the following May; and the appearance of this ship of war, the largest the natives had yet seen, anchored almost in the centre of their town, struck awe into the Rajah himself, and was regarded by Mr. Brooke as the consummation of his enterprise. 'The Dido was the first square-rigged vessel that had ever entered those waters.'

Captain Keppel's object in visiting Borneo, was, to attack the pirates in their strong-holds; and he commenced with an expedition against those of the Sarebus river. The details of this 'the grandest expedition that had ever been known in the annals of Malayan history,' are narrated by the gallant Captain in a *naïve* and spirited style; and, to many readers, the description of this novel warfare will be the most entertaining portion of the work. The destruction of their strongly fortified places astonished the whole country. In June, the Dido was recalled to China; but, in July of the following year, Captain Keppel, having been ordered to return to the straits, found letters at Singapore from Mr. Brooke, which determined him to proceed at once to Borneo, with the Dido and Phlegethon, and resume operations against the pirates, by whom Sarawak itself was threatened. On the 5th of August, 1844, the expedition proceeded against the Sakarran pirates, whose strong-holds were in like manner destroyed; and this was followed up with a second blow, by which the province was cleared of the worst pirates upon this part of the coast. In September, having achieved this important service, Captain Keppel sailed for Singapore, where he found orders for England. On his return home, he 'had the gratification to learn that Mr. Brooke had been appointed agent for the British Government in Borneo, and that Captain Bethune had been despatched on a special service to that island;' events which he could not but consider as 'of great importance to the best interests of humanity, and to the extension of British commerce throughout the Malayan Archipelago.'

The sequel is supplied from Mr. Brooke's own journal. Captain Bethune, and an enterprising friend of Mr. Brooke's, to whom he acknowledges himself greatly indebted for his present position and success, arrived at Sarawak in Her Majesty's steamer Driver, on the 18th of February, 1845. They brought a letter from Lord Aberdeen, notifying to Mr. Brooke his appointment, and directing him to proceed to Borneo with a letter addressed to the Sultan and the Rajah Muda Hassim. Captain Bethune was, moreover, commissioned to report on the best locality for a settlement or station on the north-west coast. Mr. Brooke and 'the letter' were received at Borneo with due honours. The Sultan was profuse in his kind expressions, and inquired of the interpreter when the English would come to Labuan; adding, 'I want to have the Europeans near me.' Labuan was examined and found to present many advantages as a refuge for shipwrecked vessels, and a windward port relative to China, and as affording abundance of coal for steamers. In the latter respect, and in point of salubrity, it is very superior to the abandoned station of Balambangan to the northward. From Mr. Brooke's brief notes we gather, that he returned to Singapore in the Driver, and, towards the end of May, came back to Borneo; that, after a short stay, he again visited Singapore and Malacca; and on the 8th of August, found himself anchored off Borneo Proper with seven vessels, an eighth being hourly expected. The British Admiral, Sir Thomas Cochrane, had come in person to demand reparation of the Sultan and Rajah for the detention and confinement of two British subjects subsequently to their agreement with our Government. They threw the blame of the outrage upon Pangeran Usop, whom they were unable to control or punish. As this worthy proved contumacious, he was dealt with accordingly; his house was speedily rendered tenantless, but the delinquent escaped by flight. The treaty was thus enforced, and our supremacy maintained. The fleet then proceeded to Malludu bay, notorious as a harbour of pirates; and on the 19th of August was fought 'the celebrated battle of Malludu.' The piratical seriff and his followers made a desperate resistance, and some valuable lives were lost on the side of the victors; but this strong-hold was completely destroyed. Mr. Brooke returned to Bruni on the 31st, and early in September found himself once more *at home* at Sarawak. And the last notice in the journal, after referring to a five days excursion among the Dyak tribes, with Captain Bethune and a party, concludes thus:—

'The progress is ended; to-morrow, I shall be left in the solitude and the quiet of the jungle; but, after witnessing the happiness, the plenty, the growing prosperity of the Dyak tribes, I can scarcely believe that I could devote my life to a better purpose; and I dread that a removal might destroy what I have already done.'—Vol. ii. p. 161.

The remainder of the second volume is occupied with a general description of the Island of Borneo, and an account of the Dyak tribes; 'Mr. Brooke's Memorandum on the Piracy of the Malayan Archipelago,' written after the first blow struck at the pirate communities by Captain Keppel, but prior to the operations of the squadron under Admiral Sir Thomas Cochrane; 'Remarks by Mr. Crawford, late Governor of Singapore, on the advantages of a settlement on the north-west coast of Borneo, and the occupation of the island of Labuan; and an Appendix of Official Documents.'

Among these is a very valuable sketch of Borneo, by J. Hunt, Esq., communicated to Sir Thomas Stamford Raffles, when Lieutenant-Governor of Java, in 1812, which contains the fullest and most complete account of the topographical divisions and natural productions of the island that has appeared. It cannot have been for want of information, that British merchants have neglected this tempting field for enterprise. That the English were not always insensible to the value and importance of the once valuable commerce of Borneo, Mr. Hunt remarks, may be inferred, not only from the number of the Honourable Company's ships annually despatched to its ports prior to the year 1760, but from the efforts they have repeatedly made to establish themselves on its shores. We have seen an old chart of the Borneo river, in which is inserted a reference to the British factory, the remains of which may still exist at Borneo. The failure of those successive attempts, as well as the exclusion of other European powers from the ports of Borneo, is to be attributed principally to the sordid jealousy and intrigues of the Dutch.

'By their intrigues at Banjarmassing, the British attempts at a settlement twice failed; and Forrest, in his Voyage to New Guinea, says, that the Sulos were, by Dutch instigation, induced to cut off the infant establishment of Balambangan in 1775. They frustrated the attempts of the Bridgewater at Passir; and even the massacre of the garrison of Pulo Condore was effected by Javanese soldiers supplied by the Governor of Batavia.'—Vol. ii. Appendix ii. xxv.

Both Balambangan and Pulo Condore were ill-chosen and most unhealthy spots; and Mr. Hunt remarks, that, 'if a capital harbour, a navigable and majestic river, a productive country, a healthy site, population ready formed, and a commerce all-sufficient to pay the expenses of an establishment are required, the East India Company ought to have pitched upon Borneo Proper, which was once a flourishing country; and a very short period under British auspices would render it the first mart in the East for China-Malayan commerce.'

'In looking over the map of the world, it is a melancholy reflection, to view so large a portion of the habitable globe as all Borneo, abandoned to barbarism and desolation; that, with all her productive wealth and advantages of physical situation, her valuable and interesting shores should have been overlooked by all Europeans; that neither the Dutch nor the Portuguese, with centuries of uncontrolled power in these seas, should have shed a ray of civilization on shores bordering upon their principal settlements; that her ports and rivers, instead of affording a shelter to the extensive commerce of China, should, at this enlighted period of the world, hold out only terror and dismay to the mariner; and that all that she should have acquired from the deadly vicinage and withering grasp of Dutch power and dominion has been, the art of more speedily destroying each other, and rendering themselves obnoxious to the rest of mankind.'

But this is not the whole case against the European powers who have abused their maritime ascendancy in these seas for the purposes of a selfish and narrow monopoly. By destroying the direct trade between Borneo and China, Mr. Hunt shows, the Portuguese and Dutch have compelled the Rajahs to have recourse to piratical practices. Formerly, the numbers of Chinese settled on its shores was immense; and they kept up the prosperity of the country by the tillage of the ground, as well as by the commerce of its ports. By degrees, the old Chinese settlers deserted these shores; and to supply the defalcation in their revenues, arising from the decay of commerce and the consequent depopulation, the Rajahs were tempted to turn their views to predatory warfare. In the same manner, slave-hunting is had recourse to by the African chiefs for the purpose of revenue, not in preference to legitimate commerce, but, in many cases, from the want of it. The only effective way to extirpate both piracy and slave-hunting is, by extending adequate protection to both the native cultivator and the native trader. To have suffered piratical hordes to carry on their predatory warfare in these seas for so many years, in defiance of the British flag, and almost to blockade our eastern ports, reflects great dishonour upon our Government. The chastisement inflicted upon the Borneo pirates by the expedition under Captain Keppel, and still more by Admiral Sir Thomas Cochrane's squadron, will no doubt have given a check to piracy for a time; but, unless a just and conciliatory policy, such as that adopted by Mr. Brooke at Sarawak, towards the native goverments, shall inspire them with confidence, and they are guaranteed by the British flag against hostile incursions, we can hardly expect the benefit to be permanent. At present, almost every thing seems to depend upon the frail and invaluable life of an individual. The moral influence of Mr. Brooke's character is working wonders. According to the latest intelligence, all the native tribes in that part of the island were abandoning their feuds and petty warfare, and repairing to Sarawak, as the seat of justice, for the settlement of their disputes. Yet, up to this time, Mr. Brooke has not even a gun-boat, (except his own,) at his command, to protect his little state against any piratical incursion. His confidence in the Divine protection will, we have no doubt, be rewarded; but it is of the utmost importance, that what he has accomplished should not be placed in jeopardy by either the supineness, timidity, or wretched economy of the Home Government. By the convention of 1824, both Great Britain and the Netherlands Government are bound to use their best endeavours for the suppression of piracy. How well the Dutch have fulfilled their part of the engagement, is sufficiently notorious. The truth is, that they would rather connive at any practices that might check or injure our commerce in these seas. Their policy has undergone no change, except such as has been forced upon them by circumstances. They view the settlement made by Mr. Brooke, and the intended occupation of the island of Labuan with more than jealousy, and have even been extravagant enough to remonstrate with our Government against these proceedings.

No time ought to be lost in occupying Labuan as a naval port and commercial depôt. Now that steam communication has been established between Calcutta and Hong-Kong *viâ* Singapore, the importance of the coal-mines discovered in that island renders this step the more imperative. Labuan lies nearly in the direct track both of steam and of sailing navigation between India and China, during the north-east monsoon, being 707 miles from Singapore, and 1000 from Hong-Kong.* Its mines would also serve to keep the Hong-Kong, Singapore, and Penang stations supplied with fuel for steam vessels carrying the mails between Hong-Kong and Suez direct. At present, between Singapore and Hong-Kong, there is no British harbour, no accessible port of refuge; nor is there any other available supply of coal, that of Bengal and Australia excepted, to be found in the wide limits which extend east of the continents of Europe and America. As soon as the British flag shall be erected there, a large influx of settlers, especially of Chinese, may be with certainty reckoned upon. Chinese trade and immigration will come together; and Labuan, as a free port, will become the seat of a larger trade with China than Borneo ever possessed. The existence of a British settlement there would tend more than any thing else to the suppression of piracy. At the same time, the regular visits of British ships of war to the different ports of Borneo and the Archipelago, twice or thrice a-year, would be of incalculable advantage for the protection of British merchants, and for the repression of any attempt to revive piratical operations. All these considerations have been pressed upon the attention of the Home Government, by whom, we believe, their importance is fully recognized; but we are anxious that the British public should be led to take a more lively interest in the providential opening which is thus presented, both for the extension of our commerce, and for effecting a beneficent revolution in the physical and moral condition of the hitherto neglected millions of this fertile and beautiful region. 'Among the numerous visions which open to us, while reflecting on the new prospects of this vast island,' remarks Captain Keppel, 'so little known, yet known to possess almost unbounded means to invite and reward commercial activity, is the contemplation of the field it opens to *missionary labours*.

'When we read Mr. Brooke's description of the aboriginal Dyaks, and observe what he has himself done in one locality, within the space of four or five years, what may we not expect to be accom-

* Sarawak is distant from Singapore, 427 miles; from Labuan, 304; from Hong-Kong, 1199. Singapore may be reached, from Sarawak, by steam, in forty-eight hours.

plished by the zeal of Christian missionaries, judiciously directed, to reclaim such a people from barbarism! There are here no prejudices of caste, as in India, to impede the missionaries' progress.'—Vol. ii., p. 226.

Had Sarawak been occupied for five years by a handful of French, Spanish, or Portuguese settlers, there would already have been a Roman Catholic mission established there. We trust that, ere long, a Protestant Malay mission will have entered upon this interesting field of exertion, with the view of extending the knowledge of a purer faith to this branch of the great Polynesian family.

Before we close this extended article, we must in justice say a few words upon the two other works before us. Mr. Davidson, of some of whose sensible observations we have availed ourselves, has contrived to turn his wanderings and adventures to excellent account for the amusement and information of others, whatever may have been the result to himself. He has crossed the Ocean, he tells us, in forty different square-rigged vessels,—has trod the plains of Hindostan, the wilds of Sumatra, and the mountains of Java,—has strolled among the beautiful hills and dales of Singapore and Penang,—has had many a gallop amid the forests and plains of Australia,—has threaded the reefy labyrinth of Torres' Straits, and visited the shores of the so-called Celestial Empire. His earlier recollections carry the reader back to Java, under the Dutch government of 1823; and he speaks both of the island and of the state of society at Batavia, at that time, in terms of warm eulogy. To Singapore, his recollections seem also to cling with a strong partiality, though its society is, he says, no longer so agreeable as it was ten or fifteen years ago. He has furnished some very pleasing sketches and valuable information relating to the Archipelago; but the most useful, if not the most entertaining portion of the volume, is that which gives an account of his residence and experience as a farmer in New South Wales. His free strictures upon the causes of the recent depression in our Australian colonies, and his remarks upon emigration, appear to us highly deserving of attention; and there are also some excellent practical suggestions relating to the openings for trade in the Far East, the commerce with China, and the new settlement of Hong-Kong. We have rarely met with a volume more entirely free from pretence of every kind, while conveying in a straight-forward, unaffected style, the results of so varied and extensive an experience, both as trader and as settler, in different climes, and where society presents such different aspects.

Mr. Earl's volume relates to *tropical* Australia, containing an interesting narrative of the Port Essington expedition, and an account of the settlement at that extreme point of the northern coast, where it runs out towards the great island of Timor, in the track from Europe to China, from October to March, and the track from Sydney to India, from March to October. The importance of this settlement for checking piracy, seems scarcely inferior to that of Labuan, at the other extremity of the Archipelago.

'Previously to the occupation of Port Essington,' says Mr. Earl, 'every English vessel that had resorted to the islands lying between Timor and New Guinea had been attacked, and, when successfully, the crew murdered; so that the names of many of the larger islands were associated with outrages committed on our countrymen. The Essington schooner, the first vessel sent out to the islands, was saved only by an accidental occurrence. But no sooner had it become known that the British possessed a settlement in the neighbourhood, than these aggressions suddenly and totally ceased. Indeed, I speak advisedly when I say, that small vessels may now traverse the adjacent seas with greater safety than they can coast the island of Java, the oldest established of the European colonies in the Indian Archipelago. The western coasts of New Guinea were never visited by our merchant-ships for purposes of trade previously to our establishment in these seas; but an intercourse has now been opened, which bids fair to become a thriving and profitable branch of commerce. The Timor Laut groupe, again, the nearest to Port Essington of the islands of the Archipelago, were so notorious, previously to our arrival, that even the native traders of the eastern islands dared not visit it. Vessel after vessel, whether English, Dutch, Chinese, or Macassar, was cut off and plundered. But the spirit of peace has now extended itself to this important groupe, and it has become a favorite resort for traders; an intercourse having been established with ports, especially on the southern part of Timor Laut, which were never before frequented.'—*Earl*, pp. 68-9.

The voyage from Sydney to Port Essington usually occupies from fifteen to twenty-five days. The colonists are bent upon opening, if practicable, an overland route from the present frontier of the province of New South Wales to the shores of the Indian Ocean, with a view to secure the advantage of the Indian overland mail. Mr. Davidson thinks, that, during the north-west monsoon, the navigation of Torres' Straits from west to east would be found practicable for steamers, and that the mail might be better transmitted by sea. By this route, 'the passenger for Sydney would find himself at his journey's end in sixty-three or sixty-five days from Southampton, while the mail, *viâ* Marseilles, would be of four days' shorter date.' Such are the wondrous facilities afforded by the application of steam to navigation, for the rapid interchange of mercantile communications, the strengthening of social ties, and the diffusion of the benefits of civilization by means of commerce over all the regions of the earth. The marvellous regularity and certainty of the intercourse thus established between this country and the chain of colonies which encircle the globe, are not less striking and important than the shortening, in point of time, of geographical distance. No settler in any British colony, however remote, can now feel himself a hopeless exile cut off from the means of hearing of friends at home, except at distant and uncertain intervals. In Dr. Morrison's journal, we find the following affecting entry, under the date of July 18, 1834:—'Two hundred and twenty days are now nearly completed since you left. Surely in twenty days more, if the Lord spare my life, I shall hear of your safe arrival in England.' At the end of those twenty days, the letters arrived, but the heart so deeply interested in their contents had ceased to beat! Mrs. Morrison had arrived in England on the 6th of April, after a favorable voyage of nearly four months. Her lamented husband died on the 1st of August, without having heard of her arrival. This was not quite twelve years ago. Now, London letters by the overland mail reach Calcutta in less than forty days, and Hong-Kong or Canton in about forty more. Thus, in less than twelve weeks, intelligence from London will reach China by this route; and the time is probably not very distant, when, by means of more perfect arrangements, answers to letters from Calcutta to London may be obtained in seventy days; and answers to letters from Hong-Kong to London, in one hundred and forty, instead of two hundred and forty days. China is not merely 'opened,' but half the intervening distance is annihilated, while India is brought nearer to us than the further shores of the Atlantic used to be.

Art. IV.—*Debates, Reports of Committees, Petitions, Papers and Notices of Motions in Parliament in* 1845 *and* 1846, *respecting a Change in our Colonial Policy, and in favour of Improvements in the Administration of Affairs in the Colonies, in India and China.*

A FULL catalogue of the documents of which this title is a summary, would be far too long for the heading of an article in a review.

But these documents are deeply interesting. They relate to almost every branch of our colonial affairs; they are the fruits of bitter experience, to which influential members of the legislature thus bear practical testimony; and they indicate, (more especially *the notices of motions,*) that at length the time is really come for changes and for reforms, without which our vast Colonial Government must continue to be no less a disgrace to ourselves than a scourge to the millions whom it oppresses.

The objects of the parliamentary motions to which we refer, and the names of the movers, will sufficiently explain the character of the reforms, of which we now anticipate the early accomplishment; and the *variety* of the inquiries which these motions have in view, proves satisfactorily, that a principle of the greatest importance is likely to prevail throughout this work.

That principle was vindicated in the last century by Edmund Burke, who would have saved America to Great Britain, had his counsels been listened to; and who insisted earnestly upon the necessity of studying the *diversity* of the countries we govern, in order to apply our laws wisely to their respective circumstances.

'I was never wild enough,' said Burke, 'to conceive that one method would serve for the whole of this mighty and strangely diversified Empire—that the natives of Hindostan, and those of Virginia could be ordered in the same manner, or that the Cutchery courts and the grand jury of Salem could be regulated on a similar plan.'*

Carefully keeping this great principle in view, we here accompany a brief sketch of the existing parliamentary proceedings † in favour of what seems to be fast approaching—a thorough colonial reform, with some observations upon its leading objects.

The general subject of such reform is opened by Mr. Hume,‡ in a motion for the production of a code for the administration of colonial affairs, issued by Charles II., in the year 1670. At that period, much practical knowledge of colonization had been gained in an experience of one hundred and seventy years, from the days of Sebastian Cabot, its great leader in the sixteenth century, so ably followed by the settlers of Virginia and Maryland, the pilgrims of New England, and the planters of the West India Islands; and the document in question, con-

* Burke's letter to the Sheriffs of Bristol, 1777. Works, vol. iii. p. 182.

† The various motions referred to in the text were made in 1845 and 1846 by Sir R. Peel, Mr. Hume, Mr. Haw s, Mr. Buller, Mr. Ewart, Mr. O'Connell, Mr. Tuffnell, Mr. Forster, Mr. Trelawny, Mr. Aglionby, Dr. Bowring, Mr. P. M. Stewart, Mr. M. Gibson, and Mr. Masterman. In addition to the proceedings urged by these members, the New Zealand debates contain remarkable speeches on principles of colonial government by Mr. Ellice, Mr. Colquhoun, Lord Howick (now Earl Grey,) Lord John Russell, and fourteen other members of the House of Commons.

‡ H. of C. votes, 3rd of April, 1846. One MS. copy of this document is in the Brit. Mus.—Harl. MSS. No. 6394.

taining the instructions given to the plantations' committee by King Charles must have proceeded from the labours of the Earl of Clarendon, who is known to have deeply studied colonial affairs.* This document contains *a system* of colonial administration at home; and it forms an extensive basis of what ought to be the practice of the colonial office in Downing-street; of which it is really the forgotten law. It is the more valuable, as it is universal in its objects and equal in its scheme—not severing whites from blacks, or colonists from aborigines; but aiming at the good of all, as an amalgamated body, and by adherence to the rules of *justice*,—according to the degree in which various classes of men were, in those days, held to be entitled to it; for it recognises the right of having *slaves*. Its main principle was that our administrators should obtain knowledge of colonial facts.

The next important parliamentary document is last year's report of a committee on colonial accounts, in support of which comes this year a string of motions by Mr. Hume for the production of public colonial defaulters' papers. Dr. Bowring, the chairman of this committee, has given notice of a motion for the further examination of the subject.

Another motion applicable to *all* the colonies was made last year by Mr. Hawes, in respect of *official appointments*. This is a subject of some delicacy. Prosecuted with prudence, the inquiry might advantageously give fresh vigour to the good old law of Richard the Second, against seeking public posts by favour. It must lead also to a proper system of supervision and protection of public officers. At present they either act without any responsibility themselves, or they are subject to the despotism of their superiors without appeal. Mr. Hawes may pursue this topic with great effect. Let the wrong motives for appointing inefficient men to colonial offices be fully exposed; and the worse motives for excluding efficient men from colonial employments be fairly stated; and such a case of mal-administration for many years past, will be brought home to the colonial office, as must compel reform.

Mr. Forster has given notice of an important motion for the establishment of a better *system* for the internal government of our settlements in West Africa; and for their more suitable intercourse with the neighbouring tribes. He has also obtained papers respecting the members of the colonial legislatures, in colonies where there is no elective popular assembly, whilst Mr. O'Connell has obtained papers on New South Wales; and Mr. Tuffnell others on Ceylon.

Mr. Trelawny has moved for a return of the names of the

* Lord Clarendon's own report of the Barbadoes case, in the Privy Council, is most valuable.

agents of the *Crown* colonies, their emoluments, and duties; details already laid before a commission on colonial affairs, which made several valuable reports fifteen years ago.

The motions of Mr. Ewart and Mr. C. Buller, respecting convict transportation can hardly fail of exciting deep interest. A more cruel act of legislation was never passed than that which founded a convict colony in 1786; and the efforts of these gentlemen will deserve all honour if they stop the new project of extending the fatal establishment of European crime in *the neighbourhood* of the populous islands of the East. On this occasion it should not be forgotten, that the intervention of the House of Commons in 1784, stopped a similar frightful blunder in the dispersal of convicts in Western Africa.

The late melancholy wreck in Bass's Straits has led to the production of papers, on the motion of Mr. Hume, respecting *light-houses* on those coasts; — a subject calling loudly for serious attention in regard to all the dangerous shores frequented by our shipping, as shown by the Light-House Committee of 1845; and Sir Robert Peel has opened another great maritime question by moving for papers against a tax proposed for colonial built ships.

These propositions of 1845, and 1846, had intelligible precursors; of which Sir Robert Peel's declaration of 1844, that the colonies must be henceforth dealt with as *integral* parts of the empire was received with delight in its remotest regions. More specific prospects of realizing that principle were distinctly traced in the determination of Sir George Murray, in 1829, to *revive* annual colonial budgets for the House of Commons; — in Mr. Ward's colonial crown-lands committee of 1836;—in Mr. Buxton's aborigines committee of 1835, 1836, and 1837;—in Sir William Molesworth's transportation inquiry;—and in the series of annual motions of Mr. Smith O'Brien upon grants of land in the colonies. In the same spirit of reform, the late Lord Bathurst sent commissioners of inquiry to the eastern colonies, to the West Indies, and to Western Africa; and about the same time the late Sir R. Wilmot Horton originated parliamentary proceedings of great importance respecting emigration, followed up with unequal success by Mr. Baring's excellent bill of 1838, and by Mr. Wakefield's extraordinary efforts,—marred by his powerful party having trusted the Colonial Office in 1840.

Mr. Hume has made the most strenuous efforts to urge the realization of Sir R. Peel's just principle; more especially by claiming *free trade and self-government* for the colonists.

In the House of Lords, also, the subject has not been neglected. The Duke of Wellington, and the Marquis of Lansdowne, have strongly urged the need of a *system* to regulate our new colonial and commercial intercourse with China; the want of which must have occasioned disasters but for Sir Henry Pottinger's admirable conduct.

The unsatisfactory state of the Privy Council, the great court of colonial appeals, has often been complained of in the House of Lords, during the last twenty-four years; and their Lordships now possess in Earl Grey, one who by his frank avowal of our error in colonial policy, and by his acute perception of its cause, has shewn some qualities calculated to correct that great error by a radical change in the present practice. We allude to the speech of Lord Howick, now Earl Grey, upon the disasters in New Zealand—a subject for the privy council restored to its legitimate jurisdiction.

These proceedings evince a considerable activity in parliament on the subject of our colonies. But it would be a great mistake to suppose that nothing more remains to be done. On the contrary, two topics of paramount importance are not touched upon at all in the motions actually before parliament, namely, the question of a representation of colonists in the House of Commons; and that of a body of delegates in the nature of a colonial council to represent the interests of the colonies in connexion with the Secretary of State. A third topic, which will also demand the gravest consideration, was seriously examined by Mr. Ellice alone, of all the speakers in the New Zealand debate last year, namely, the absolute necessity of introducing free legislative assemblies, on the main principle of self-government, into all our *crown* colonies. This last topic was discussed at some length in a former number of the 'Eclectic Review,'* where the novelty of such *crown* colonies was proved from the uniform tenor of our colonial history.

Much more is wanting—and most urgently wanting, than all this. Earl Grey said truly, that our error in colonial *policy* arises from our ignorance of colonial *facts*. His lordship as truly declared, from his own official experience, that this deplorable ignorance is shared by the ministers of the crown. The proofs of the correctness of these observations are but too flagrant; as can be seen in our very recent experience in regard to one quarter of the world—Africa, the favourite object, for very good reason, alike of popular, of philanthropic, and even of court and ministerial sympathy.

Yet undeniable it is, that the climate of Africa, the productions of Africa, and the warlike capabilities of Africans, have been in these latter days so entirely sealed, even to the Colonial Office, that great calamities have arisen from its ignorance of

* In the article on Franklin's Works, by Mr. J. Sparks, July, 1843.

things which might easily, and certainly ought to have been familiarly known.*

How fatal did our ignorance of the fevers of the Niger prove! Equally productive of injury to the industry and civilization of the natives of western Africa, has our ignorance of their *coffee*† proved; and last year, to our no small disgrace and damage, a combined squadron of English and French ships attacked a town in Madagascar, in ignorance of the existence of its formidable fortifications; and really because both governments, our own as well as the French, have rejected the proffered diplomatic intercourse of the queen of Madagascar. Worse disasters still have been the results of this ignorance in the case of Natal in South Africa; and this is an example, which deserves as careful statement as can be made in a few words.

In December, 1845, the colony of Natal was formally established with its due array of authorities, civil and judicial; when it appeared that the great mass of the *white* population had settled in the interior; and it is believed that many of the whites who remain, will also go thither.—That is to say, thousands of *British subjects* prefer incurring all the casualties of a new African emigration, with the prospect of a probably unhealthy climate, to remaining in a British colony, although cheap and valuable land is abundant; although *its institutions are not unsuited to their habits*; and although the climate is unquestionably good. It is, at the same time, capable almost of demonstration, that an ordinarily prudent management of the affairs of South Africa, would *even now* make these people content with their lot in Natal under British sovereignty.

Already extremely bloody conflicts have taken place between these emigrants, the black natives, and ourselves; the emigrants having, since 1836, lost more than six hundred men, women, and children, by the sword, the blacks more than twelve thousand; and our troops having also suffered in a pitched battle with our own subjects.

These evils may reasonably be attributed to the ignorance of the colonial office; and there has been even an unusual reserve of parliamentary documents on this whole case. From 1837, not a line has been published for parliament upon it, except a few meagre and incorrect incidental notices, in the reports of the land and emigration commissioners, although, at least, one call has been made in the House of Commons (by Colonel Fox) specially for Natal papers. So that a new colony is adopted by

* Five centuries ago, Roger Bacon urged the importance of knowledge of such things: Cognitio locorum mundi valde necessaria est rei publicæ, &c.—*Opus Majus*, 1733—p. 189.

† House of Commons Papers, 1839. No. 528, p. 4.

the crown without the cognizance of parliament, contrary to the express recommendation of the aborigines committee.

The delay in settling the government at Natal, has done enormous mischief; and is solely attributable to the colonial office. At length, when, the other day, this body of 800 English, and 1500 Dutch colonists, with 100,000 natives, were rescued from anarchy, so great had become their despondency, that, says the local newspaper, 'hope deferred had made the hearts of the people sick; and when the news arrived of the landing of the lieutenant governor, many refused to believe, to them, so improbable a fact.' * Yet, three years and a half ago, when a reconciliation was made with the Cape emigrants, the military officer who negotiated with them, solemnly pledged himself, that in *a few months,* as might *have been easily accomplished,* government should be provided for them.

This is one of the cases, indeed, which, for its past bad effects, and *its present extremely dangerous position,* ought to be immediately inquired into by parliament; and such *misfeasance,* and *non*-feasance of official duty be signally punished, unless we mean that the government of the colonies shall continue to be a mockery.

Respecting the Caffre frontier also, a scene of the extremest interest, in hope to the philanthrophist, and in principle to the statesman, not a line has been laid before parliament since 1837, although treaties of great importance were made there in pursuance of the advice of parliament, and although the articles of those treaties have been formally altered, whilst the colonists have lately been deeply agitated with rumours of invasions,—perhaps exaggerated rumours, but certainly most disquieting, from ignorance of preceding facts.

At the present moment a correct view of the whole affairs of South Africa would do more for the civilization of its tribes, and for the advancement of British interests to the tropics, than the most sanguine speculator on the good progress of humanity could venture to state in detail. A vast portion of that whole region is fit for fine-woolled sheep; † now increasing with surprising steadiness and rapidity there; and every problem of philanthropy might easily receive its safe and satisfactory solution under our hands in the same region, if its administration

* *Cape Frontier Times,* 13 January, 1846.

† The increase of fine wool from South Africa stands thus:—in 1843, the export was lbs. 1,700,000; in 1844, it was lbs. 2,270,000; and in 1845, it was lbs. 3,600,000,—*the price having exceeded the price of the best Australian wool.* This is a great triumph to the industrious South Africanders; and it deserves to be recorded that the foundation of this success was laid by a *Dutch native of the colony,* now enjoying his reward in an honoured old age.—This is Michael Breda, a member of council at Cape Town.

were conducted on principles of common sense, and in the way dictated by the constitution.

Another case is also of extreme interest, and the ignorance of the Colonial office on this subject, would be ground of an impeachment, *if so many secretaries of state were not concerned in it*. It involves the question of penitentiary discipline, and that of the administration of a convict colony. In the debate in the House of Lords upon the Van Dieman's Land petition, Lord Stanley, the late Secretary of State for the colonies, founded an apology for the deficiencies of a *new* plan of penal discipline he had devised, upon the distance of the colony from England.

'There was no subject,' said his lordship, 'which had given him more anxiety than this ; no subject to which he had more constantly and systematically directed his attention with a view of finding out some remedy for these acknowledged inconveniences. But it took a long time to establish perfectly a system of convict discipline, where all the arrangements to be carried out were to be made between parties at such a distance from each other, and where such a great lapse of time as twelve months necessarily intervened between a communication and a reply.' *

This is a melancholy instance of the slovenly discharge of its duty by the Colonial Office. By an act of parliament framed upon the most able report of the late Mr. John Thomas Bigge, not an offence of the lightest character can take place in our convict establishments, without such records being kept as mark the precise extent of criminality in the population. Transcripts of those records are sent to the Colonial Office. They were on one occasion, through the zeal of Mr. Briscoe, the then member for Surrey, brought before the House of Commons.

Proper analyses, and digests, of these invaluable records, so wisely provided for by act of parliament, would present such a picture of the morality, or immorality of the people, that the working of every change of system could be judged of with unerring certainty.

The discreditable fact is, that Lord Stanley was unprovided with these materials to enlighten him, or he could not have talked of a *twelve month's* correspondence, and of the aid he received from the attorney general and the secretary of New South Wales, who *happened to be in London*.

It is probable, too, that in the Colonial Office, nothing whatever is known now of this act of parliament—of these records—or of their transcripts.

It is fair to our readers to explain how we speak thus posi-

* Morning Herald, 4th March, 1846—so the Times.

tively on a subject belonging to so remote a colony. The hand that writes this article carried the Act of Parliament to New South Wales in 1823; drew the forms for the records, prescribed by the act; attended to their transmission home; and witnessed their production by Mr. Briscoe to the House of Commons.

The affairs of India do not, in all respects, need the same reforms as the colonies. Nevertheless they would be benefitted by a better system of intelligence on our part as to the views of our Asiatic neighbours; since the peace of India would certainly be promoted by more exact knowledge of us being conveyed among our neighbours. A striking illustration of the latter point may be seen in an interesting narrative of the visit of a French traveller to the Sikh Rajah Ghoolab Singh, at this moment, perhaps, the main instrument by whom peace will be restored to India.

'Ghoolab-Sing,' * said M. Jacquemont, in 1831, 'is a soldier of fortune, a sort of usurper. He is a lion in war—a man of forty, very handsome, with the plainest, mildest, and most elegant manners. He took me to see the salt mines.

'Europe, in the most common details of its civilization, is a wonder to these people. They will listen to you all day, with pleasure, when talking of it.

'Two arm chairs were sent on before us; and if we passed near a shady tree, or when I had bundles of plants to tie up, the Rajah and I sat down. He made his two secretaries dismount, and write down what I said.

'These people, above all things, like to hear the political statistics of Europe. They have no idea of them, of our population, of *the strength of our armies*—of the product of our public revenue—of our civil and criminal laws—and, lastly, of the results of science, applied to the arts.

'In the mines I taught Ghoolab Singh a little geology.'†

The lessons of the lively traveller were not the only opportunities which the Sikh chief has had of judging correctly of our

* This is the same chief of whom the Governor-General of India in his despatch of the 19th February, says:—

'I told the Rajah, thus I recognised the wisdom, prudence, and good feeling evinced by him in having kept himself separated from the unjustifiable hostilities of the Sikhs, and I was prepared to mark my sense of that conduct in the proceedings which now must be carried through. I stated, in the most marked manner and words, my satisfaction that he who had not participated in the offence, and whose wisdom and good feeling towards the British Government were well known, has been the person chosen to negotiate the means of atonement; and the terms on which the Sikh Government might be rescued from impending destruction, by a return to amicable relations with the British Government.

† Jacquemont's Letters from India, vol. ii. p. 3.

power; and proper means may be devised for the general indulgence of this inquisitiveness, which is really a mark of capacity for higher civilization. So that whilst our tranquil relations with this people may be secured through their knowledge of our superiority, their progress will be promoted by a more intimate acquaintance with our means of attaining wealth and with our superior general resources.

Other illustrations of good colonial government may be found in the history of Indian legislation. For example:—

'The case of the various Hill people of India refutes the opinion that savages cannot be improved. A single document, of so old a date as 1822, will conveniently open that case. It is entitled "A REGULATION * for exempting the Garrow mountaineers and other rude Tribes on the North-eastern Frontier of Rungpore from the operation of the existing Regulations; and for establishing a special system of Government for the tract of country occupied by them, or bordering on their possessions." It states the case as follows:— "There exist in different parts of the territories subordinate to the Presidency of Fort William, races of people entirely distinct from the ordinary population, and to whose circumstances, therefore, the system of government established by the general regulations is wholly inapplicable. Such were the mountaineers of Bhaugulpore, for the reclaiming of whom to the arts of civilized life special arrangements were made by Government with the chiefs, some time before the introduction of the present system. These arrangements still subsist, having been incorporated into the code by the provisions of Regulation I. 1796, under which an entirely distinct system has been established for the administration of justice amongst the inhabitants of that mountainous tract. Savage tribes, in some respects similar, exist on the north-east frontier of Rungpore, of which the race denominated Garrows, and occupying the hills called after them, are the principal. *As yet little has been done to reclaim or civilize these people.* The reciprocal animosity which subsists between them and the inhabitants of the cultivated country, prevents any extensive intercourse of a specific nature; while, on the contrary, their mutual injuries have produced feuds leading frequently to disturbance and bloodshed. The zemindars of the frontier have, there is reason to believe, usually been the aggressors, by encroaching on the independent territory of the Garrows and similar rude tribes, until, *despairing of other resource, the latter are driven to seize occasions of private revenge and retaliation.* These encroachments having been of long standing, several zemindars were, at the time of the perpetual settlement, in the receipt of incomes derived from cesses of various kinds levied from the tribes, and hence a portion of the tract of country occupied by them has been considered to lie within the operation of the general regulations, as forming part of the zemindarees. This, however, instead of conducing to reclaim the tribes to civilized

* House of Commons papers for 1824, No. 114.

habits, has rather had a contrary effect, the system being totally inapplicable to their savage and secluded condition, and being calculated to leave them at the mercy of the zemindars, rather than to offer any substantial means of redress. *The condition of the Garrow mountaineers and of the other rude tribes on that frontier has, for some time past, attracted much of the attention of the Governor-general in council*, and *the circumstances which have conduced to check the progress of civilization amongst them have been fully investigated and ascertained*. With a view, therefore, to promote the desirable object of reclaiming these races to the habits of civilized life, it seems necessary that *a special plan for the administration of justice, of a kind adapted to their peculiar customs and prejudices*, SHOULD BE ARRANGED AND CONCERTED WITH THE HEAD MEN, and that measures should at the same time be taken for freeing them from any dependence on the zemindars of the British provinces; *compensation* being of course made to the latter for any just pecuniary claims they may have over them.'

'This narrative, (which is only one of several) displays the views entertained for many years by the Indian government on the subject. With a large experience, that government concludes, that the savage *may be civilized* by a system of justice and conciliation; and it is to be expected that the new spirit shown by the House of Commons in the late debates, will lead to *a full inquiry as to the fittest way to introduce such a system universally*;' * SINCE EXPERIENCE HAS PROVED ITS VALUE.

Indian history has, also, just added a *second* example of British magnanimity in refusing to appropriate a country won by the fortune of war. In the first case, that of Caffreland, in South Africa, in 1836, the distinguished general, Sir Harry Smith, saw the dawn of a new system of humane policy, of which he may, perhaps, be destined to witness the complete developement in every part of the British world—a policy that will permit the unlimited peaceful extension of our dominions, provided it violates no rights, nor outrages the common sentiments of national independence.

In order to realize so large a view of colonial greatness, it would be necessary to enter deeply into every separate head of colonial affairs; and into the affairs of every colony separately.

At present the case of New Zealand is, perhaps, the grand source of the interest taken in favour of colonial reform.

In fact, in June and July last, a revolution was begun in British colonial policy, upon the occasion of the affairs of New Zealand being examined by the House of Commons; when, for the first time since the Canada debate of 1791, or even since the old American war, serious attention was given in parlia-

* Introduction to the 'Classical Sources of British History,' by S. Bannister, formerly Attorney General of New South Wales, p. 105.

ment to great colonial topics; and the character of the change is seen in the analogous movement making in the far wider field of our domestic and commercial policy at large, as affected by the corn-laws. In the New Zealand case, almost forgotten in the greater interests which now absorb attention, Sir R. Peel set Lord Stanley and the Colonial Office aside, because he perceived that public opinion condemned them both, and would speedily compel parliament to condemn them; as in the case of the corn-laws, he has now set Lord Stanley, and his friends the ultra-conservatives, aside, because he again sees that their views, in regard to those greater interests, are opposed to the peremptory demands of the age.

The New Zealand case is important in itself, in whichever of its several lights it is looked at; whether in reference to the rights of the natives, whom the wretched system of our Colonial Office has brought into a fearful conflict;—or, in reference to the extensive success of the missionaries, who, if not corrupted by being made political instruments, may still contribute largely to the rescue of the natives;—or, in reference to British interests and British honour, both deeply concerned in the establishment of a system of government capable of conciliating our colonization of New Zealand with the natives' rights. But in reference to the opening of a new policy for all our colonies, which the result of the debates of June and July clearly promised, their importance cannot be exaggerated. They were distinguished, too, by several memorable circumstances. In the first place, they were in no sense whatever *party* debates. The most earnest arguments in favour of a new system, and the severest condemnation of the present practice, proceeded from firm friends of the ministers. Again, the various topics incident to the case were discussed in unusual detail by several groups of speakers, as if their respective parts had been carefully *cast* in concert; although it was plain, that the whole was unpremeditated. All the members, with perhaps the natural exception of the mover, Mr. Charles Buller, obviously spoke unprepared, and all without exception from honest conviction. In some instances, indeed, as in those of Mr. Roebuck, and Sir R. Peel himself, the knowledge of the subject was remarkably small, and the conclusions hasty to rashness. Taken, however, as a whole, these debates form an excellent point of departure for the consideration of the great change, which is indispensable in this branch of our public affairs.

Three of the speakers fully explained the causes of our colonial misfortunes in a very few words; and satisfactory remedies may be suggested for the evils, the sources of which were thus clearly pointed out.

Mr. Milnes said he had found the subject of colonies *odious* to all parties, even to those statesmen to whom is entrusted the duty of administering them. He himself had to struggle against a strong prejudice in resolving to support the proposed inquiry, notwithstanding the fatal and shameful indifference of more experienced men.

Lord Howick (now Earl Grey), said, that our present colonial policy is essentially erroneous, and that the error arises from IGNORANCE.* Having once filled a post in the Colonial Office, his lordship founded this double reproach upon personal experience.

Mr. Barkly gave, if possible, severer testimony against the practices of that office; and his testimony was that of one who frankly acknowledged the courtesies he had himself received in it, but who reluctantly declared its practice to be opposed to all sound principle, and guided solely by a degrading expediency; and by what is called a *see-saw*, between contending parties.

The chain is complete. *Indifference* to colonial affairs charged by Mr. Milnes upon the eminent leaders of all parties, then crowded about him in the House of Commons, necessarily produces the *ignorance* which Lord Howick admitted himself to have shared; and indifference and ignorance together, as necessarily generate the *error* which his lordship, last summer, warmly and successfully appealed to Parliament to renounce; whilst such indifference, ignorance, and error, could not fail in their turn to carry the government headlong into the system of tergiversation and shuffling, reproved by Mr. Barkly.

Sir Robert Peel deserves the credit of seeing the force of the combination thus formed against Lord Stanley from every shade of party; and he wisely gave way before an overwhelming resistance to the Government, without even pretending to understand the subject under discussion. His speeches were striking examples of that ignorance of facts, to which Lord Howick correctly attributed a great error in our colonial policy; and of that violation of correct constitutional principles, which is one of the most dangerous results of that error. Sir R. Peel even assumed against all authority, as good colonial law, that the *discovery* of a savage country by British subjects entitles the Crown to the sovereignty of that country, *without the consent of the natives*. He went further, adding that the true way of settling difficulties in New Zealand from the first was to have acted upon this title; and he even regretted that such a course had not been pursued. Seeing, then, that we have faith in the sincerity of his declaration in Exeter

* This ignorance in colonial affairs is not new: Lord Macartney attributed the loss of America to it.—*Burke's Correspondence*, vol. iii., p. 27.

Hall several years ago,—that he was a true, although a recent philanthropist,—we are entitled to call upon him to reconsider positions opposed as much to our old law, as to the dictates of philanthropy;—and which are sanctioned only by a modern practice, that becomes destructive according as the British nation becomes more enlightened and powerful.

Positive authority of a peculiar character, is not wanting in favour of the humane view of native rights on this head; for the instructions to Captain Cook, on his third voyage, issued in compliance with the strongly expressed sentiments of the times,* required the *consent* of the natives as the condition precedent to the occupation of their country by British authority; and our Indian law, cited above, recognised the principle.

The instructions here alluded to, were introduced in Cook's last voyage, in compliance with public opinion. The period was that in which Granville Sharp (the real originator of our modern philanthropy, and the precursor of Clarkson and Wilberforce, Macaulay and Buxton,) began his marvellous efforts in favour of slaves and free aborigines. Afterwards the latter were neglected in our exclusive vindication of negroes. That is to say, at a period when the extension of our colonies in the South Seas was looked upon as a proper object of British policy, the ministers held it to be their duty to insert in the document originating our acquisition of new countries there, a substantial acknowledgment of the right of the rudest savage to independence. The history of our old colonies is consistent with this solemn act of authority. The rule was afterwards disregarded, at a period when almost every other incident to safe colonization was renounced. Despotic governments were established in all the new colonies on various grounds. Convict settlements were formed at first to the exclusion of free colonists, and at last to the neglect of every good principle of colonization. Missionaries were long discountenanced; and the natives were everywhere more or less oppressed and often exterminated.

The result was, that colonies fell into great public disfavour. The jobbing, and enormous waste of money which they caused, induced some economists, such as those of the Parnell school, to call for the abandonment of colonies, instead of insisting loudly upon the reform of their abuses. The philanthropists, also, instead of demanding colonial reform, as a means of protecting the natives, had long † leaned to the opinion, that

* Dr. Johnson and Adam Smith joined warmly in the public reproval of the massacres of natives in Captain Cook's first voyage. Dr. Hawkesworth lost the post of historiographer to the subsequent voyages for inserting an apology for these massacres in his first book.

† The Jesuits acted on this opinion in Paraguay. Eliot did so in New

their only protection was to *stop* colonization, utterly regardless of the impossibility of doing so. At the same time a sense of incapacity to govern extending colonies, led successive ministries to make the same vain attempt.

In the mean time, old colonists required fresh lands for their increasing families and flocks; and a new emigrating population from home after the general peace, of course required fresh fields of enterprize. From both causes, arose an immense extension of our colonial territory in all quarters, in spite of the resistance of the government, which indeed, after many struggles, adopted vast regions it had refused to acquire upon a rational and humane system. That refusal constituted the *error* confessed by Lord Grey.

Our colonial office in Downing-street is governed by principles, and it pursues practices, which must inevitably, from the nature of things, bring disaster upon all within their range. They oppress private men; they destroy public prosperity; and by a just reaction they expose, degrade, and ultimately ruin those by whom official authority is thus abused.

This is the effect of a picture drawn of those principles and practices by one of the subordinate members of the colonial office itself; who writes, he says, from experience, not from theory. We quote his charge, word for word; and leave the topic to the reader's indignant reflections:

'By evading decisions where they can be evaded; by shifting them on other departments, where by any possibility they can be shifted; by giving decisions upon superficial examinations; by conciliating loud and energetic individuals at the expence of such public interests as are dumb, or do not attract attention; by sacrificing what is feeble and obscure to what is influential and cognizable, by such means and shifts as these the *Secretary of State* may reduce his business within his power, and obtain the reputation of a safe man without any other reproach than that which belongs to men placing themselves in a way to have their understandings abused and debased, their sense of justice corrupted, their public spirit and appreciation of public objects undermined.'—*The Statesman*, 1836, p. 152.

Hence an intriguer in the Colonial Office, taking advantage of single points, is enabled to ruin honourable men, if their general good conduct is no protection.

England. John Newton and Wilberforce agreed, before New South Wales was founded, that no colonization *at all* ought to be begun in New Holland, when they should have joined the party which opposed the wretched colonization of convicts there. The philanthropists are at length changing their views. Lord Ashley seconded Mr. C. Buller's motion for a new system of colonization; and Mr. Gurney and Sir Edward Buxton supported that new system.

Sir Robert Peel has recently put this point strongly, in reference to the case of the Governor General of India:—

'*I will say,*' he declared, '*that it will be destructive of the character of the nation*, it must be a fatal check upon the energies of public men, if you once establish the precedent that you will not allow the general conduct and services of a public man, who may be acting at a distance of five thousand miles, to be pleaded against a single act of indiscretion.' *

But what if the facts as to an alleged indiscretion are disputed, and if in the colonial office a hearing be refused, and the secretary of state prevents the Queen referring claims to the privy council, to decide the dispute upon good evidence and just principles? Then, indeed, we may say, that Bentham was right when he declared that 'abominable intrigue must blind ministers;' and if the system does not make them base, as Mr. Taylor asserts it does, it renders them subservient to others who are base, which is worse. Such a denial of a hearing is directly against the constitution.

The practice of great injustice accompanies and leads to great national calamities. Our colonial empire stands upon the ruins of three which have fallen; and most remarkable it is, that in all three—those of Portugal, Holland, and France—signal injustice marked and preceded their decay.

Camoens says of Portuguese India, that it had become 'the step-mother of honest men, but a nursing parent to villains.'

Tavernier says of Dutch India, that once the Dutch government most scrupulously heard appeals against their distant governors; but in his time the protection of great men only could secure a hearing to the best cause. And another French writer has drawn a picture of the practice of that government, whose hideous features have to the minutest line been reproduced in our days in England.

'The Dutch establishments in India,' says Raynal, 'were now in the extremest bad order; but their reform was the more difficult, since things were as bad at home as abroad. The ministers for the Dutch colonies, instead of being men of business and colonial experience, were usually taken from powerful families which monopolised the great offices. These families were busy, some with their political and party intrigues, some with the more general concerns of the state; and they looked to colonial affairs either to advance the power of their party, or to get places for their connexions; or from worse motives of pecuniary interest. The real business of the colonies, its details, discussions on all points, and with all the men actually engaged in them, and the greatest enterprizes were turned over to a

* House of Commons, 9th Feb. 1843.

secretary, who, under the title of counsel to the office, got everything into his own hands. The ministers came only occasionally to the office, especially during the intervals of the more pressing public calls of business; so that they lost sight of its connecting links. Consequently they were compelled to trust implicitly to the counsel. It was his business to read all the dispatches from the colonies, and to frame all the replies to them. He was generally acute—often corrupt—always dangerous as a guide. Sometimes he was known to lead his superiors into terrible difficulties of his own contriving; and at other times to leave them in scrapes created by their own errors.' —Raynal. Histoire Philosophique, &c., &c., Vol. I. p. 466.

This extremely striking passage furnishes a warning to us. This system of administration is ours almost to the letter; and, as Lord Shelburne said, it lost us *old* America. The Dutch would not abandon corruptions, which hastened their fall. It remains to be seen, whether some attempt cannot be made to add to the stability of our *new* colonial empire, by the timely reform, *which our better popular elements admit of.*

In France it took twenty years before Lally Tollendal could obtain the acknowledgment of the innocence of his murdered father. The fall of French India, if owing to our superiority, was at least attended by the notorious injustice which enfeebles integrity, and invigorates every mischievous passion.* We are now pursuing this last career, of refusing to be just: and if the vigour of the national character arising from other influences, goes far to counteract the effect of this canker, it is not to be doubted that it paralyzes the vigour which would ensure public prosperity.

The cure is—to open the Privy Council *of right* to all Appellants within its jurisdiction.

There are remedies indeed for all colonial evils; and surely we are not so base a people as willingly to sit down in despair under corruptions that admit of cure. The monuments of art springing up all about us, and the astonishing results of our mercantile industry and mechanical ingenuity, and the heroism of our seamen and soldiers, are not the only wonders which are to do honour to our time. Our civil triumphs may and must be extended to our laws and administration abroad and at home. The debates of last year on New Zealand, proved that we have statesmen among us aware of existing evils; and the wise way to Colonial Reform now taken by Mr. Hume through the examination of our Colonial History, justifies a sanguine hope that a future is coming to us in which the lessons of that history, by its warnings so frightfully neglected, will produce for us and for all who are under our influence, peaceful and prosperous days.

* Lord Mahon's History, Vol. IV. p. 543.

Such happy results, however, cannot be secured without a searching inquiry into all that concerns our colonial administration; without securing to the home authorities a complete knowledge of colonial facts; nor, finally, without resorting to the good old English plan of calling into that administration, as legislators, those who are affected by public measures—in one word, without establishing *self-government* for our colonists; to the very utmost extent to which it can be carried, whilst colonies are connected with the mother country.

That great principle of *self government* abroad, introduced with its necessary limitations, is consistent with an institution for which we are now ripe at home;—namely, an institution to be formed, of colonial, Indian, and home members of high rank and extensive experience, analogous to a combination of the old plantation committees of the privy council; of the present colonial agents, and colonial associations; and of the French colonial delegates sitting in Paris. It would exceed the proper limits of this article to set forth the entire composition and attributes of this body; but if it were duly established, simultaneously with elective assemblies in *all* the colonies; and with the admission of a few colonial members into the House of Commons, it would go far to settle all colonial difficulties, and to place this country in the position it ought to occupy.

The scheme of such a colonial council in London, is ably described by Mr. Porter, in the *Progress of the Nation*, vol. iii. p. 317.

The arguments in favour of colonial members in the House of Commons, were originally stated by Baron Maseres, in 1776. They have lately been forcibly urged in a pamphlet by Mr. Thomas Bannister, of the Temple.

Measures like these, will make our colonies one with us; and call forth from the whole empire, its best strength for the general good. They will also save us from new losses, such as those of the thirteen American colonies, seventy years ago—from the mortification of being expelled from Canada, or excluded from Oregon by the superiority of our neighbours in a great art of statesmanship—colonization. They would extinguish such bloody migrations as those of South Africa in the last twelve years, such wars as those of West Africa, and that of New Zealand,—and the more disgraceful, unceasing massacres throughout the Australias,—all attributable to what Sir Thomas Fowell Buxton too mildly stigmatised as the *'Chapter of Accidents,'* of the colonial office.

What this vast colonial empire really is, may be seen to some extent from a paper printed last year by the House of Commons on the motion of Mr. Hume,* which shews our forty-one colonies to have a population of four million, six hundred and seventy-four thousand, three hundred and thirty-three souls; to have exports and imports worth £27,400,000 sterling; and to employ 5865 ships, of 1,171,762 tons burthen, being *double that of all France.*

These figures do not include India or China,—nor do they extend to the millions of coloured people, who are really dependent on our policy in every quarter of the globe.

The army, navy, and ordnance estimates, shew the distribution of our soldiers and sailors throughout the colonies. The papers of the Geographical Society trace the progress of our science; whilst the wider and more important influence of Christian civilization is marked by the missionary stations.

On the head of geography, very much remains to be done for the colonies. Such maps as the excellent *Colonial* Chart, and the still more useful collection of missionary maps, published by Mr. Wyld, of Charing Cross, ought to be distributed largely by the government throughout all the colonies, and at home, as *school books.* Great efforts are making by particular individuals to advance the means of geographical knowledge; but they must fail, if not supported vigorously by government. The ancients placed maps on a vast scale upon the walls of their temples and colleges, to teach the people, and especially the young. A map of the old world, five feet in diameter, was exposed for centuries as an altar-piece of the cathedral at Hereford. A map, by the famous Cabot's own hand, was long to be seen on the walls of the old palace at Whitehall.

The elements of such *instruction by the eye* are most abundantly at our command. Not to mention Cook's South-Sea treasures in the British Museum, and similar treasures in all Missionary and United Service Museums, we have had recent proof of the extent of such resources, in the invaluable collections of Dr. Andrew Smith, for South Africa; of Mr. Catlin, for the Indians of North American; of Mr. Dunn, for China; and of Mr. Angas, for New Zealand and Australia, now exhibiting at the Egyptian Hall in Piccadilly; and well deserving the attention of all classes. The frequenting of these exhibitions is a good sign of the interest taken by the public in the subject of them,—the savage whom we are fast destroying. It may be hoped that means will one day be devised for preserving them at national institutions, after they have ceased to gratify more curiosity.

* House of Commons Papers, 1845.—No. 49.

Art. V.—*The Age of Pitt and Fox.* By the Author of 'Ireland and its Rulers.' In 3 volumes. Vol. I. 8vo. London: T. C. Newby, 1846.

Few periods of our history are more interesting or instructive than that embraced in the work before us. It is sufficiently distant for us to judge of its actors and events with a good degree of impartiality, and yet near enough to engage our sympathies, and to exercise the influence of present and living interests. Some other periods are invested with deeper importance, and present specimens of our common nature, of a higher and nobler mould. This is pre-eminently the case with the times of the Long Parliament and the Commonwealth; but that era stands apart from all others in our history, having qualities of its own which eschew comparison, and for the most part stand out in contrast, with all which preceded or have followed. The age of Pitt and Fox has a distinctive interest, which is greatly derived from the character of its chief actors, and the crisis it constituted in the history of parties. Their talents were singularly varied, yet of the highest order, and their personal history had few points in common. The son of the Earl of Chatham, ending his career as the idol of the Tories and the sworn enemy of reform; Charles James Fox ejected from the North administration, and becoming the eloquent champion of popular rights; whilst Edmund Burke, in some respects superior to both, renouncing his earlier position and friendships, entered into alliances as hostile to his reputation as they were injurious to the progress of liberty throughout Europe. In the contests of that day, however, the highest element of statesmanship is wanted. It is but occasionally that we meet with the nobler spirit which so frequently appeared in the Long Parliament, where the personal was merged in the public, the partisan in the patriot, where an honest consecration to the welfare of the many became the rule, and constituted the end of senatorial labours. Personal ambition, or party feuds, make up for the most part the history. It is a gladiatorial scene which we witness,—the struggles of faction rather than of principle, the vehemence and passion of selfish combatants, rather than the cooperation of enlightened intellects to work out the salvation of nations.

No illusion can be more perfect than that which has been practised on the young intellect of England. To dispel it is no grateful task, but to do so is absolutely needful in order that the true lesson of history should be learnt. We have been accustomed to connect great names with immortal principles, and our admiration of the latter has been associated, by a natural law, with the former. There was little, however, in the spirit and inward purposes of the men to warrant this. They were of the earth, earthy, with views as secular and selfish as the other politicians by whom they were surrounded. Burke was probably one of the purest of his class, but his passions were too vehement, and his judgments too treacherous and hasty, to allow of his being regarded with the confiding admiration which is inspired by the highest class of statesmen. Whilst we listen to the splendid oratory of Fox, unrivalled in his powers of debate, we unconsciously worship the speaker as the anointed oracle of truth. But a moment's reflection and our worship ceases. There is nothing to sustain our faith. The evidences of deep earnestness are wanting, even the ordinary and outward marks of consistency are absent. The actor is more visible than the man. The party leader rather than the self-sacrificing patriot is the image which remains before the mind. The elements of moral greatness were wanting, and his life, therefore, notwithstanding his splendid powers, failed to accomplish its proper vocation. A gambler and a debauchee, he failed to carry along with him the confiding trust of the popular mind, by which alone he could hope to make way against the stolid obstinacy of the king, and the violent prejudices of an ignorant and besotted squirearchy. Thus it has ever been in English history, and though in particular cases we may regret the result, we do not, on the whole, wish it were otherwise. Despotic ministers may work out their designs whatever be their character, but the advocates of popular freedom can triumph only by transparent integrity and deep earnestness. These are the elements of their power, without which they will be like Samson shorn of his strength. It would be easy to name living senators of liberal views, and of more than average talent, who yet fail to make any impression on the country, because there is no faith in the deep seriousness of their advocacy. It was so with Fox and his associates, though the fascination of his manners, the splendour of his gifts, and the fearful tragedies which marked the period of his public life, gave him, probably, greater power than was ever possessed by any other popular statesman similarly constituted. What might have been the result had he associated the elements of moral with those of intellectual greatness, it is not for us to say. We have our opinion on this point, and when occasion requires shall be free to express it.

The work which has given occasion to these remarks—of which the first volume only has yet appeared—is the production of a clever man, completely acquainted with the times described. It is somewhat too sketchy for our taste, and is deficient in what, for want of a better name, we will term the philosophy of the subject. The standard of public morality applied is, moreover, in some cases exceedingly lax, and the style is loose and inaccurate. Yet, notwithstanding these drawbacks, the work is both attractive and useful. It may be read with advantage by all classes, and may serve as a good introduction to the history of the last quarter of the eighteenth century. The period embraced is that which intervened between the close of the American and the commencement of the Peninsular war; and the objects kept in view throughout, and which it is designed to illustrate, are; the nature of the English government, in practice, as distinguished from the technical constitution of law books; the characters and principles of the illustrious men who presided over English affairs; the influence of the French Revolution; and the legislative independence of Ireland. The present volume embraces only a very brief period, and commences with the fall of Lord North's administration in March, 1782. The immediate occasion of this event was the disasters of the American war, which had gradually increased the Whig minorities, until they became too powerful to allow the court favourite longer to retain office. From the year 1775, upwards of one hundred millions had been expended, thirteen colonies, besides several West India and other islands had been lost, and an exhausting war with America, France, Spain, and Holland, was being waged. It was, therefore, obviously quite time, that the obstinacy of the king should be overruled by the popular branch of the legislature, and the minister who had servilely lent himself to the crown should be driven from office.

The party which succeeded was that of the Whigs, and no slight difficulty was experienced in inducing the monarch to recall them to his councils. Nothing but the necessity of the case overcame his reluctance, and, as we shall presently see, he retained them no longer than that necessity lasted. The part acted by the Whigs in 1688 had placed them in a commanding position, and given them a long tenure of office; occasionally, indeed, interrupted in its earlier period, but ultimately settling down to something like a monopoly of civil trusts and emoluments. A knowledge of this fact is essential to an accurate estimate of English history from the period of the Revolution to the accession of George III. The following extract will aid the intelligent reader, in tracing out the threads of a narrative, which exhibits both the glory and the weakness of Whiggism.

'The Whig party had acquired great historical lustre by their overthrow of the Stuarts in the seventeenth century. They had originated the Revolution of 1688: their schemes were sanctioned by the Tories, and that great historical event had been accomplished by the union of both parties. But the burthen of maintaining the Revolution was thrown upon the Whigs. The adherents of the exiled family were formidable in number and influence, and down to the period of 1748, it was not impossible for enterprising statesmen to have effected a counter-revolution. Many of the Tories aided the Jacobites, and the fear of 'Popery' alone deterred a large portion of the nation from championing the ancient Dynasty. In addition to the difficulty of supporting a new family upon the throne, the Whigs were embarrassed by the characters of the two first Georges. They had no qualities of insinuation, and were in many respects unsuited for England; they were formal and pedantic in their notions, and did not properly feel their glory as British kings. On the other hand, the rashness and incapacity of the Stuart Pretenders dispirited the Tories, and nullified their schemes. And from the landing of King William at Torbay, in 1688, down to the Treaty of Aix-la-Chapelle, in 1748, the success of the Revolution wavered, and the great cause of rational and constitutional liberty would have been lost, but for the skill and happy sagacity of Sir Robert Walpole. Thus the services which the Whigs had rendered to the monarchy, gave them a claim to the respect and confidence of the king; but like all political parties they stretched their claims too far, and they evidently thought that the Revolution of 1688 had destroyed the prerogative of the sovereign to rule without responsible advisers, but had also created a privilege for the Whigs to advise the crown in perpetuity.'—vol. i. pp. 7, 8.

Such was the political state of this party when George III. ascended the throne in 1760. The young king, then in his twenty-third year, determined to break through the restraints under which his predecessors had been held, and to assert for the crown, the right reserved to it by the constitution, of choosing its own advisers. His early associates had been opposed to the interests of the Whigs, whose haughty bearing and neglect of the genius and business capacity of 'new men' contributed much to the success of his policy. 'The great revolution families' were astonished at the temerity of the monarch. Their long possession of office had engendered the notion of its being their right. They constituted an oligarchy, popular in their theory, but despotic and corrupt in their rule; overshadowing the throne only to divide amongst themselves the spoils of the state. To their dictation the young monarch refused to submit, and on this point he was clearly right. The great mass of the community felt with him, and had his subsequent selection been wise, had the ministers chosen been men of large capacity and patriotic views, intent on the wise conduct of national affairs and the true interests of both king and people,

George III. would have been entitled to the lasting gratitude of his subjects. That this was not the case we need scarcely remark. Sufficient proof of the fact is furnished by the downfall of the North administration, under circumstances of peculiar ignominy, in 1782.

The cabinet which succeeded took its name from the Marquis of Rockingham, its nominal head. It was composed of two divisions, known as the Rockingham and the Shelburne Whigs, and all its chief offices, excepting the chancellorship, which the king insisted on Lord Thurlow retaining, were distributed amongst the aristocratic members of the party. The following sketch of the two sections which composed this administration, furnishes the secret of its short-lived existence. A house so divided was not likely to stand long against the determined hostility of the king.

'Lord Rockingham's followers were what might be called the family compact Whigs—representing the principles of prescriptive Whiggery. Lord Shelburne's faction had originally been formed by Lord Chatham, and affected to act independently of party ties—they were Whigs of progression, and stoutly combated the leading article of the Rockingham creed—'that the great Revolution families should govern England.' One party was an oligarchy with a historical fame, and confederated under hereditary leaders;—its Russells—Cavendishes—and Bentincks, and a swarm of minor Whig families being all bound together by ancient recollections—habitual intercourse—and family alliances. They formed a vast junto, of great ambition and prodigious power. Their politics had been elaborately digested into a system by the genius of Burke, who gave them a political code, and who furnished them with a variety of maxims, and general principles so happily expressed as to seem suited for the Rockingham creed alone. They were ready to defend the theory of monarchy, and were desirous of keeping the sovereign their creature. They were eager to espouse the popular cause, provided the people were ready to remain their clients. They wished to introduce into political life, new men of genius, who were to exhibit their talents, adorn the party, but should not aspire to sitting in the Cabinet.

'The Shelburne party, on the other hand, cherished the tenets of Whiggery, but it applied them after a different fashion from the Rockingham school. They thought that England should be governed by a much larger and even more formidable junto than the great Revolution families; they cordially acknowledged the existence of a power, which was only superciliously recognized by the Rockingham Whigs; in short, the Shelburne party thought that the true idea of the Revolution of 1688, was that the English public should govern, and not a collection of great families. The supporters of the Shelburne system distinguished between a public and a populace, as they discriminated between a Whig party, and a faction of families. Laughing at the divine right of kings, they spurned the principle that the Dukes of Bedford and Devonshire should parcel out the empire between them. They thought that the king had a right to choose his ministers from the host of public men in parliament, and they boldly claimed the right of men of commanding talent to sit in the cabinet, even though fortune had not given them ancestors, 'who (in the graceful catchwords of the Rockinghams) had bled with Hampden in the field, or died with Sydney on the scaffold.' They went to the king's closet, as his ministers; they did not comport themselves as his masters, or demean themselves (like Lord North and his colleagues) as if they were his servants. A manly sovereign would not be thrown upon his metal by the Shelburne system of politics, nor would a despotic monarch select his tools from men bred in that school. To both king and people their conduct was more truly respectful than that of the Rockingham party.'—*Ib.* pp. 21—23.

Charles James Fox, then 'in the flush of his popularity, and political fame,' was one of the secretaries of state, whilst Edmund Burke, infinitely his superior in morals, and inferior to none of his contemporaries in the gigantic splendours of his intellect, was assigned only the subordinate office of paymaster of the forces. The one was the son of Lord Holland, the other an Irish gentleman of slender means and of no family influence, and in this fact the secret of their disproportionate reward is found.

'Were a man in this country,' remarks the most recent biographer of Burke, 'of great capacity and attainments, though of little influence or fortune, such for instance as Mr. Burke himself was, deliberately to choose his side in politics as he would a profession—that is, for the advantages it is likely to bring—he would, probably, not be a Whig. That numerous and powerful body is believed to be too tenacious of official consequence to part with it to talents alone, and too prone to consider high rank, leading influence, and great family connexion, rather than abilities of humble birth, as of right entitled to the first offices of government. They are willing, indeed, to grant emolument, but not to grant power, to any other than lawyers, who do not materially interfere with their views on the chief departments of government; an opinion which, notwithstanding the profession of popular principles, is believed to have made them sometimes unpopular in the great market of public talent, and to have driven many useful allies into the ranks of the Tories.*

Both Fox and Burke belonged to the Rockingham faction, and the *Correspondence* of the latter, recently published, clearly reveals the want of harmony and consequent lack of cou-

* Prior, p. 233.

fidence, amongst the leaders of the administration. The death of Lord Rockingham, which occurred in the following July, led to the premiership of Lord Shelburne, under whom both Fox and Burke declined to serve. Several members, however, of the former cabinet remained in office, and considerable business talent was secured in the adhesion of William Pitt, who held the chancellorship of the exchequer, and was loud in his profession of reform principles. It will be remembered that Lord Shelburne's was the most popular section of the Whig party. They were in fact the movement party of their day, the Whig-radical division of the liberal host. Yet to this party did the second William Pitt belong, the man whose name was speedily to become the terror of the friends of liberty, and the confidence and hope of despotism, throughout Europe. Such are the changes which we witness in the course of human affairs—

Tempora mutantur
Et nos cum illis mutamur.

In this respect the future prime minister of George III., who was to lead the crusade against European freedom, was greatly in advance of Burke, by whose timely conversion his nefarious designs were to be so powerfully aided. The reformers of the period before us, like those of most other days, were of two kinds, of whom Lord Shelburne and John Wilkes may be taken as types. The former headed the party which represented the views of Lord Chatham, who, in moving an address to the king, in 1770, expressed the opinion that 'an additional number of knights of the shire ought to be added as a balance against the weight of several corrupt and venal boroughs, which, perhaps,' he remarked, 'could not be lopped off entirely without the hazard of a public convulsion!' Wilkes, on the other hand, felt no scruple, and observed no limits. Headstrong, selfish, and venal, he viewed everything in reference to his own base interests, acting the bully, or the hypocrite, just as he deemed it most likely to advance his sinister designs. The blunders of his enemies gave him great advantage by which he was not slow to profit, but the fame and the influence of the demagogue is necessarily brief, and Wilkes lived to inherit the contempt and neglect which he so well merited. Our author has gone out of his way to indulge in much loose declamation—we might use a more significant term—purporting to be a description of the Radical Reform Class of the past fifty years. There is an irritability and want of discrimination in his allusions to this class for which it would be difficult to account, were it not customary with writers who can palliate the dishonesty of Charles James Fox, in signing, as is alleged, his name in favour of vote by ballot, annual parliaments, and other sweeping changes, 'merely from a careless desire of humouring the popular party,' to throw suspicion on the motives and to impeach the conduct of the more upright and consistent friends of liberty. We give the following as a sample, simply cautioning our readers against estimating the writer's impartiality, or judgment, by it. The good taste it evinces is on a par with its discrimination.

'To the exertions of Wilkes and Tooke, aided by the licence of the London rabble, is to be traced the birth of that spirit of false democracy, which under various names duped thousands; and disturbed English society for the succeeding sixty years. One picture of the tribunes of that licentious party answers for their character and purposes at all periods of their history. What knaves! what slanderers of England and its institutions! and side by side with the charlatans and adventurers, what vain and futile theorists, imbecile in devising good, influential in aggravating evils! The aristocratic gambler, driven to politics from his craving for excitement; the notorious profligate, declaiming in favour of political purity; the vain dreamer, the fantastic schemer, the puerile theorist, seeking food for their vanity in public notoriety, or hoping by popular connexions to impart strength to their weak abilities: such are the leaders who periodically return for the disturbance and delusion of the untaught and neglected masses, who smoulder in the purlieus of our great towns. With them are mixed, perchance, some antiquarian dotard, who sees perfection in the parchment constitutions of former ages. His honest folly contrasts with the coarse ambition of the bloated aldermen seeking to buy popular applause at so much *per* shout. And hearken to yon briefless barrister, advertising his fluency of vituperation, while 'hear hims' are cried by the quack, who has risen into bad eminence by calumniating the faculty, or by the clergyman, whose vices have deprived him of his parish! Such are the prominent figures of that grovelling school of reform, founded by Wilkes and Horne Tooke, and continued to later generations, by their equally vicious, but far more contemptible successors. For in truth the polluted characters of the tribunes of the British populace did more for half a century to retard the growth of a true public spirit, and to confirm the power of an oligarchy, than the government of Mr. Pitt, or the eloquence of Mr. Canning, to strengthen and uphold the borough system. It was the lives of the leaders, and not the purposes of their party, which for so many years made Radical a synonyme for rascal. And of all the deceivers of the multitude, none were more worthy of grave censure than the aristocratic libertines, who laughed in their orgies over the success of their efforts in popular delusion.'—*Ib.* p. 72—74.

That there were bad men then, as now, we doubt not—men who traded in patriotism and laughed at the confidence they inspired; but that this was the case with the majority, or even with a large proportion, of those who thought or acted for the people, at the eventful period referred to, we unhesitatingly deny. In private morals, even the worst of this class scarcely sunk below Fox and Sheridan, whilst the great body of them were infinitely their superiors. But so it has ever been. The vices of the great are glossed over and forgotten, whilst those of the people are magnified and repeated *ad nauseam*. The only effectual cure for this is in the people having writers of their own. History has hitherto been in the hands of the aristocracy, and it has told only a one-sided tale. Let us have fair play, and we shrink not from the comparison. We can scarcely refrain from smiling when we read such rigmarole as the following. A man must have large confidence in the ignorance, or gullibility of his readers, to have penned it.

'But though the representative system required reform, its evils were exaggerated. This was found to be the case when men began to reason about the remedy. A large park—a small mound of earth—a castle in ruins—were severally represented by a pair of members, but large towns had no spokesmen in the House of Commons. That was the evil; yet what was to be the remedy? Was England to be placed under the tyranny of a multitudinous constituency? Was the country to be cut up into rectangular districts, and the number of the population taken as the standard of elective right? To these questions the common sense of the country answered in the negative. Many thought, not unreasonably, that the rotten boroughs had their advantages. Men of talent; lawyers of character and political promise; country gentlemen of public spirit greater than their private fortunes; intelligent merchants, who had no local connexions, and whose probity recoiled from the purchase of a few hundred pauper-electors; men of leisure and refined habits, averse to the electioneering chicane, tumult, and obloquy attendant on large constituencies: these various classes of men were enabled to enter public life through rotten boroughs, and to preserve their mental independence free from degrading bondage to popular fanaticism.'—*Ib.* p. 75.

The same want of discrimination and candour is visible in our author's allusions to the American colonies. A blind and unheeding attachment to things 'as they are,' leads him to misapprehend the character of the colonists, and to attribute to them qualities of which they were wholly destitute. This is the more discreditable as sufficient time for reflection has been allowed, and candid men of all parties are now united in opinion, that if ever a justification of resistance was made out, it existed clearly in the case of the American States. If our author's theory is to be admitted, the loss of our American colonies is another of the obligations conferred upon us by our

Established Church. No forethought, or forbearance, would have sufficed to prevent the catastrophe. The infatuation of successive cabinets was not requisite, nor the palpable violation of guaranteed rights required. The same result must have ensued, though at a period somewhat more remote, from the operation of causes inherent in 'the dissenting and puritanical spirit' prevalent amongst the colonies. The following brief passage explains our author's theory and does discredit to his understanding.

'In losing the American colonies, England had to bear that which was certain to occur. For there were many reasons why the American colonists must, in the course of things, have revolted from the mother country. A dissenting and puritanical spirit swayed their minds, and influenced their manners. They left England sour and discontented, and absence from the mother country did not soften their angry feelings. Their religion and politics were equally adverse to all submission of mind and opinion, and they were not satisfied with merely dissenting, but they were fanatically anxious to force their neighbours into their way of thinking. Their manners partook of their religion. Rigid and severe, they had no community of feeling with the social ideas of the English people. Those things which have drawn forth the love and veneration of the English nation were never regarded by them with attachment and pride. In short, there was no moral union between England and the colonies. Thus their separation was certain to occur, inasmuch as the colonists inherited the energy and perseverance of the Anglo-Saxon race.'—*Ib.* p. 128.

We turn from these exceptionable matters to pursue the course of the history. Lord Shelburne's administration was assailed by the united forces of Lord North and of Mr. Fox. The opposition of the former was natural, that of the latter factious and selfish. The Tory minister was to be calculated on as an opponent, but the hostility of the popular leader served to bring his own sincerity into doubt, and to induce the belief that his public life was swayed by personal ambition and spleen, rather than by an enlightened regard to the national welfare. He had frequently denounced Lord North as an incapable and vicious minister, 'the most infamous of mankind,' 'as the great criminal of the state, whose blood must expiate the calamities he had brought upon his country:' 'a man with whom, if he should ever act, he would be content to be thought for ever infamous.' With such a man, unchanged in spirit and principles, were Fox and his Whig associates content to enter into a league offensive and defensive. Over the base recklessness of the procedure, he attempted to throw the veil of a generous forgiveness.' 'It is neither wise nor noble,' he said in his defence, 'to keep up animosities for ever. It is neither just nor candid to keep up animosity, when the cause of it is no more. It is not my nature to bear malice, or to live in ill-will. My friendships are perpetual, my enmities are not so.' The public, however, were not misled. They saw through the sophism, and, as Mr. Wilberforce remarked, expected from the unnatural coalition 'a progeny stamped with the features of both parents, the violence of the one party, and the corruption of the other.' The coalition which ensued was the great blot on the public reputation of Fox, and did more than any other event to damage, at a subsequent period, his nobler efforts against the military crusade, which the monarch commanded, and William Pitt preached. On the meeting of parliament, in December 1782, it was computed that Fox numbered about ninety followers, Lord North one hundred and twenty, and the minister one hundred and forty, the rest being unattached. In an early division Lord North voted with the ministers, and Mr. Fox was left in a small minority. This lesson was not without its effect, and what followed is thus recorded.

'But in the ensuing January fresh endeavours were made to bring Fox and North together. Some of the partizans of the former were most anxious that such a junction should take place. Seeing that Fox was in a small minority, Burke approved of the junction. So far as he was concerned, there was not very much inconsistency in allying himself with Lord North. They were both opposed to parliamentary reform, and Burke adhered to aristocratic opinions, while Fox avowedly committed himself to popular principles. And in the actual state of the case, Burke thought every attempt should be made to crush Lord Shelburne. He thought that the minister would prove the mere creature of the sovereign, and that a party should be formed for taking the practical management of the public affairs out of the hands of King George and his creatures. He favoured, therefore, the idea of the coalition. Such was not the case with Richard Brinsley Sheridan, who was just at that time rising into political eminence. He strongly disapproved of the idea. Remarkably shrewd, with great common sense, and leading a life which brought him into contact with various classes of society, he was well calculated for a barometer of the political atmosphere. He had great knowledge of effect, and he perceived that the proposed junction would not satisfy the public. He strenuously dissuaded Fox from thinking of it. But Lord John Townshend, one of the wits and ornaments of the Foxite party, took great pains to accomplish it. Lord Loughborough also approved of the proposition. By joining with North, Fox would gain numbers to his standard, and on the elevation of Lord North to the Upper House, upon old Lord Guildford's death, Fox would be the recognized leader of a host of members in the Lower House. On the other hand, by junction with Fox, who was so popular, Lord North would be relieved from the odium under which he laboured. Such was the manner in which the coalitionists reasoned.'—*Ib.* pp. 132—134.

Prior maintains that Burke was a reluctant party to the coalition, strongly objecting to it at first, and yielding eventually only in compliance with the earnest solicitations of Fox. No evidence of this, however, is adduced, and the presumption of the case is opposed to it. In his *Correspondence* it is referred to in the genuine spirit of party tactics, and with a morality of which in other matters he would have been ashamed. Speaking of his party, he says, and this appears to have been deemed a sufficient vindication. 'Without that junction, they could have no chance of coming in at all.' * On the 17th of February, 1783, the two statesmen occupied the same bench, and their followers spoke and voted as one party. The minister was, consequently, left in successive minorities, and immediately resigned. What followed is thus described.

'The king was in great embarrassment. He saw nothing but a prospect of humiliation, and struggled hard against what he looked on as a disgrace. He tried to make a ministry through Earl Gower; and next, he tried with the Duke of Portland and Lord North, on condition that Thurlow should remain Chancellor, to which Fox would not consent; and he then tendered the Treasury to Pitt. Never was a more dazzling offer made to a young man; never was a tempting honour more judiciously declined. Pitt, though naturally elated by the brilliant compliment, thought that he would have to fight the coalition at great disadvantage, from the course pursued by Lord Shelburne in resigning. For it was one thing to resist the confederacy without succumbing, and it was quite another thing to oppose it as a minister after the rapid fall of Shelburne. With wary sagacity he resolved to bide his time.

'Again the king had recourse to Lord North, who at once declared that he could do nothing without his ally. The king disliked Fox more than ever, as he had displayed such audacity in making the coalition. The insulting language with which in former years Fox had spoken of his character, might have been pardoned to the licence of a young orator, but how could a manly sovereign endure such domineering authority as that with which Fox menaced him? The audacity of Fox's purpose, more than the violence of his language, roused King George to make every effort to secure his independence. But it was in vain. Shelburne had not the required firmness to deliver his king; Lord North was pledged to Fox. Again on the 24th of March, the king for the second time implored Pitt to become first minister, but Pitt firmly declined. And thus the king, on the 5th of April, 1783, was compelled to receive the Duke of Portland, the nominee of Charles Fox, as first lord of the treasury.'—*Ib.* pp. 156, 159.

* Burke's Correspondence, iii. 14.

Thus was formed the celebrated coalition ministry, which did more to damage the reputation of public men than any event since the pension and peerage of the elder Pitt. 'From the moment,' says Bishop Watson, 'this coalition was formed, I lost all confidence in public men. In the Foxite Whigs coalescing with the Tories to turn out Lord Shelburne, they destroyed my opinion of their disinterestedness and integrity. I clearly saw, that they sacrificed their public principles to private intrigue, and their honour to ambition.'

But one feeling prevailed throughout the nation. Men of all classes, and of every shade of opinion, were disgusted, and it was not long before the popular leader saw that he had lost his way. His support of Mr. Pitt's annual motion on reform, which was opposed by Lord North, failed to recover his popularity; and when, on the discussions respecting the Indian bill, the personal views of the monarch were used to influence the votes of the Upper House, he failed of the support which alone would have sustained him against the influence of the court. On the 18th of December, the two ministers were dismissed without the ceremony of a personal interview. Their talents and parliamentary strength availed them nothing against the king, for the country acquiesced in their defeat, and did not conceal its satisfaction at the due punishment of their selfish and tortuous policy. An important lesson is taught by this passage of our parliamentary history, and we trust that our own times will bear it in mind. In public, as in private life, 'honesty is the best policy!' An opposite course may answer a temporary purpose, but woe be to the statesman who relies upon it for permanent reputation or profit. Fox never recovered from the injury it inflicted. It revealed the weakness of his character, and was an insuperable barrier to the confidence which he afterwards solicited, and by which he might possibly have defeated the despotic policy of his opponent.

William Pitt was immediately created First Lord of the Treasury, and Chancellor of the Exchequer, and might well have been daunted by the imposing array against him.

'The Foxites could scarcely believe Pitt serious in his intention of encountering them. On the 17th, Fox had delivered a stirring invective against Pitt and his party. 'What man,' cried he, 'who has the feelings, the honour, the spirit, or the heart of a man, would, for any official dignity or emoluments whatever, stoop to such a condition, as that which the honourable gentleman (Pitt) proposes to occupy. Boys, without judgment, experience of the sentiments, suggested by a knowledge of the world, or the amiable decencies of a sound mind, may follow the headlong course of administration thus precipitately, and vault into the seat while the reins of government are placed in other hands, but the minister who can bear to act such a dishonourable part, and the country that suffers it, will be mutual plagues and curses to each other.'—*Ib.* pp. 193, 194.

The young premier, however, was equal to the occasion, and though left in a minority on various divisions, was sustained by the confidence of the king and the nation. To the policy of William Pitt we need not express our hostility. It was founded on apostacy, gathered strength under the shadow of the prerogative, and would probably have succeeded amongst any other people in extinguishing the love of freedom. Inveterately hostile to liberty, it constituted the rallying point and the hope of the whole family of European despots, whilst to our own country it was productive of a thousand evils still bitterly felt amongst us. At first unassuming and moderate, it afterwards proceeded with giant's strides, making fear its rule, and arbitrary power the object of its worship. It would betoken little candour, however, if we did not admit the ability, fortitude, and skill, with which he addressed himself to his mission. His adversary had placed himself in a false position, and was, consequently, exposed without defence, or shelter, to the raking fire directed against him. Hated by the king, and mistrusted by the people, Fox had no hope but in his present parliamentary majority, and that was hourly threatened by the prospect of a dissolution. The feeling of the country—though not probably in its full extent—was known to both Fox and Pitt, and the confidence of the latter in the result of a general election, encouraged him to persevere notwithstanding the successive defeats he encountered. Fourteen divisions occurred between the 12th of January and the 8th of March, the dates and numbers of which were as follows:—

January 12th.	232	to	193	majority	39
—	196	to	142	ditto	54
16th.	205	to	184	ditto	21
23rd.	222	to	214	ditto	8
February 2nd.	223	to	204	ditto	19
3rd.	211	to	187	ditto	24
16th.	186	to	157	ditto	29
18th.	208	to	196	ditto	12
20th.	197	to	177	ditto	20
—	177	to	156	ditto	21
27th.	175	to	168	ditto	7
March 1st.	201	to	189	ditto	12
5th.	171	to	162	ditto	9
8th.	191	to	190	ditto	1

Ib. p. 225.

The last of these divisions was the final victory of the coalition. Parliament was dissolved, and the general election of 1784, gave a large majority to the king.

The events which followed, and the altered phases of party shall be noticed on the appearance of the subsequent volumes of this work. In the mean time, and notwithstanding the exceptions we have taken, we thank the author for his labours, and commend his volume to the candid examination of our readers.

Art. VI.—*Recollections of a Tour. A Summer Ramble in Belgium, Germany, and Switzerland.* By J. W. Massie, D.D., M.R.S.A. London: Snow, 1846.

The long duration of peace between this country and the continent, has been highly beneficial in promoting a kindly interchange of visits. National animosities have subsided, and confidence has been partly restored. Numerous circumstances have concurred to facilitate, and render popular, an intercourse with our continental neighbours. Science has contributed her aid to diminish the time and expense necessary;—literature has imparted the light of her 'guides,'—and fashion has thrown her charm over a continental ramble. Under these circumstances, information has been eagerly sought, by our countrymen, and the supply has grown with the demand. Our author does full justice to his predecessors without servilely following in their track. He marks out for himself, a distinct line, in which his success is highly creditable.

"'I would pursue,' he says 'the path they have trod, while I claim some distinction from them in the principles of our creed, and the moral tendency of our observations. I meant from the first to indicate how the scenes and associations *strike a Christian*. I was also solicitous to accumulate local and historical information, rather than poetical descants, or theological disquisitions. I have therefore corrected, as well as recollected; investigated, as well as surveyed: and collected, as well as recited, the traditions and legends of those famed regions. Yet, had I contemplated enquiries so elaborate and diversified as have followed, I should have shrunk from the task, and doubted the wisdom of such an undertaking.'"—p. vi.

Every reader will respect the manly frankness, with which Dr. Massie, at the beginning of his work, has avowed his principles as *a Christian*. He has throughout the volume maintained a consistent adherence to these principles, particularly in investigating some of the prevalent traditions and legends, and in exposing their absurdity, and the wickedness of using them as the instruments of mercenary and subtle priestcraft. The love of *the truth* is impressed on every page. To confirm the veritable statements of preceding writers, to correct errors which have been believed, and to expose to merited disgrace delusions which have been maintained, are objects constantly kept in view. While many publications which have lately issued from the press, will soon pass into oblivion, the work before us has elements of enduring interest which render it worthy of prolonged remembrance. It is replete with sound information and instruction. By the casual reader it will be approved, and by the student it will be prized. It is a work, apart from all adventitious considerations, possessing much merit, exhibiting in a favourable light the quickness of discrimination, practical judgment, and historical knowledge of the author. He has presented the facts which occurred in the towns and cities, through which he passed, with a vividness of description admirably adapted to make a strong impression on his readers. Of this class is the description of Gheut,—a place of deep interest to the lovers of history, as being the birth-place of Charles the Fifth.

'It stands on the Scheldt, which there receives as tributaries the Lieve, the Lys, and the More; whose connexion is completed by several navigable canals. Twenty-six clustering islands are here united by as many as a hundred bridges, as the locality of one city, occupied by 10,000 houses and 30,000 inhabitants. In the thirteenth century it was one of the largest cities in Europe. The circuit of it was double the dimensions of Bruges, and was, in the opinion of many, the best situated for commerce in the midst of the richest and most beautiful part of Flanders. According to Ludovico Guicciardini, it then contained 35,000 separate houses, and five inhabitants to each dwelling; while its walls embraced a circumference of 45,640 Roman feet—which no doubt included many open spaces, whether for gardens or squares. The magistrates of Ghent were then most minute in their fiscal surveillance, and exacted a revenue from every loom. The number of its weaving population is said at one time to have exceeded 40,000. The incorporation of weavers could then, on an emergency, call into the field 18,000 men as soldiers, whose weapons were always accessible. The impress on the general population of Ghent, I think, may be traced to the influence of this body, and evinced much of what I believe to be the characteristic features of the weaver trade in almost all countries. They were a thinking, reasoning, disputatious, and opiniated people, refusing to let go what they deemed to be advantages to please any, even men of exalted rank and power. A consequence of this tenacious habit was, that they and their fellow-citizens had often broils and squabbles with the petty princes that professed to rule them. It moreover happened, that sometimes this turbulent, self-willed, and imperious spirit precipitated them into conflict with stronger powers than themselves, who, with inexorable revenge, delighted to humble them to the attitude of suppliants, and bring them upon their knees imploring pardon, even with a halter round their necks, to add to the indignity.'—p. 19.

Dr. Massie visited other manufacturing towns; and as the result of his observations, shows the impolitic effects of our *protective* system in producing continental rivalship. One remarkable illustration of this is found at Namur, where the old episcopal palace and its extensive grounds are turned into a vast hardware manufactory, giving to the town a resemblance to our Sheffield.

'Namur is to Belgium what Sheffield is to England: the cutlery of the Netherlands is made there. Seraigne, more like a street for continuousness than a town for architecture, nearly a mile in length, stretches along upon the river Meuse between Namur and Liege. An old episcopal residence, in which the prelatic princes of Liege resided in the times of feudal power and grandeur, was a few years ago turned into the vestibule and front section of a magnificent factory for casting and constructing machinery for almost every mechanical purpose; whether for peaceful arts, or as implements of destruction The palatial gardens—no longer the luxurious retreat of lordly churchmen, but now made the storehouse or depository for crude and manufactured iron, and occupied with heaps of coal—have altogether lost their episcopal aspect; and, while yielding to the darkening and sombre influences of some fifty wide-mouth chimneys, and their issuing flames or smoke, the prelatic dignity of the scene may seem to have disappeared—but a no less intellectual and industrious destiny prevails. Ingenuity and patient labour here preside; while nearly every description of iron-work is fabricated, from the heaviest and most potent engine to the most complicated or refined instrument of utility—from the monumental lion which couches on the field of Waterloo, to the lady's penknife which is deposited in her reticule. The vast pile of buildings forms a town within itself. The establishment possesses a great advantage in being placed over the bed of coal from which its exhaustless supply is dug; and the fuel being raised within the limits of the factory, and close to the furnaces near to which the mineral ore is found, the labour is much diminished compared with many English foundries. The workshops of the craftsmen are situated upon the line of railways on the banks of canals leading to the river. The blast furnaces, puddling furnaces, forges, and rolling mills, are on the opposite bank of the river from the houses of the operatives; but they maintain their intercourse between home and the shop by boats provided for their convenience and at their command.

'John Cockerill, as a prince among mechanics, was in partnership (a strange association, and uncommon for the trader) with the late King of Holland, as an engine-builder and machine-maker, which gave celebrity to this large establishment. There have been, and I presume there are still three thousand persons employed in these works, receiving on an average about £2000 in weekly wages. Cockerill sought to extend his connexions and mechanical fame, especially in regions where manufacturing skill was precious. He died at Warsaw, leaving his wealth to his heirs, and his name on many continental locomotives.'—p. 81.

The state of religion throughout vast tracts of the European continent, deeply affected our author. To a devout mind the moral condition of a people must ever be an object of more absorbing interest than the mechanical arts practised, or the natural beauties of the scenery around them. This was pre-eminently so with Dr. Massie. He mourned over the cities through which he passed, and has given his countrymen an affecting statement of the case, and made this statement the ground of an earnest appeal to their benevolent and generous feelings. He urges the appeal by considerations of consistency and economy. The proximity of the sphere of labour compared with the remoteness of other countries which Christians have sought to evangelize,—the immense population thus near,—and the few efforts British Christians have made for their benefit, are the reasons by which his appeal is sustained. He speaks of continued scenes of 'gross popery,' through which he passed. 'From the borders of Belgium to the further territorial confines of the French and Dutch, the people, with but few exceptions, are left to the forms and observances of the Roman-catholic church.'

'I do not,' he adds, 'expect the overthrow of so baneful a system till Britons, or Christians of other lands, those that feel the truth and love the truth, shall arise and avail themselves of the liberty of teaching and the liberty of association, which we find in Belgium; till Christian associations shall arise and go forth with all the pity that has been expended upon Tahiti and the other islands of the South. Tahiti, with its 10,000 inhabitants, has had twenty times the number of missionaries sent to it, that we have sent to Belgium with its 4,000,000 of people.'

'While we have in Belgium the liberty of teaching and of association, we pass over the ignorant and perishing multitudes that are near, who, when themselves enlightened and converted, might work with us in efforts of Christian benevolence; who might expend and consecrate energies and sanctified resources in promoting the same work, and in diffusing the blessings of Christian fellowship amidst the inhabitants of neighbouring lands. Instead of thus concentrating and accumulating our power to do good, we almost neglect the fields of proximate lands, and range the wide extremes of the world, casting our corn in handfuls on comparatively barren rocks. I would say nothing to disparage missionary work, but I would undertake missionary work at home, as well as abroad; I would undertake missionary work amongst the millions of continental nations, as I would undertake missionary work amongst the hundreds of the islands of the Southern Seas. It is the duty of Christians to seize the best means of extending their religion; and I say, let them extend it amongst the countries that are near them, with zeal and energy proportionate to their efforts amongst the countries that are remote.'—p. 102.

We hope this appeal will be followed by immediate and energetic efforts to send Christian truth, in its purity and simplicity, to the Belgians. For though, in Belgium, liberty for Christian teaching and association may be fully allowed, yet most of the governments of the continent are intolerant and persecuting to every form of religion except the one patronized by the state. And this intolerance has deterred Christians from making the Continent of Europe the sphere of their exertions. Germany, however, has furnished several zealous missionaries to the heathen.

The author evinces a generous sympathy with those who labour amidst privation and suffering, depending on the power of truth, and the zeal of its disciples, for the promotion of religion, rather than on the patronage of the state. There were many such scattered along his route, and he neglects no fair opportunity of doing them honour. In this respect he sets a worthy example, which we shall be glad to find extensively copied. Honourable mention is made of the Rev. Edmund Panchaud, pastor of the congregational church in Brussels, who has been eminently distinguished as an evangelical labourer in this unpromising field, and from whose church 'a body of pious and devoted associates, who love and co-operate with him, have been raised up to embark in the evangelization of Belgium.' It would afford us pleasure to quote extensively from these portions of the volume, but we are necessitated to confine ourselves to the following:—

'There is a little society of fervent and zealous Christians, who call their association the Belgian Evangelical Society; and they endeavour to extend the knowledge of the Gospel by means of missions of their own. They have, I think, as many as ten stations, with fourteen or more agents as preachers and teachers, etc., throughout Belgium; and the missionaries whom they employ are French, or those who can speak French; they have made only feeble attempts among the Walloons. The devoted men who are the chief staff of the Evangelical Society, are either Englishmen, or those that act in connection with an English community. The persons that are employed in the mission of the Evangelical Society for Belgium, have numerous assemblies, who congregate from time to time to hear the exposition of Divine truth. They preach the gospel sometimes in the midst of opposition, but oftener among a favourable audience, with tokens of favour. They have converts from the Roman Catholic community; and these converts are frequently instances of the power and beauty of religion. They are, however, but as a handful of corn on the tops of the mountains: as yet a weak and despised few amongst a dense population.'—p. 42.

A well balanced and discriminating judgment is evinced by Dr. Massie in his estimate of Romanism. He is too liberal and tolerant to join in the 'No popery' cry of our political Protestants, at the same time that he is not afraid of the flippant and disreputable sneers with which some literary journals assail every honest effort to expose the real character of popery. There is much which calls for revision in the state of our periodical literature in this matter, and our author is entitled to praise for having fearlessly exposed the truth, notwithstanding the censure thereby hazarded from latitudinarian critics and temporising politicians. Dr. Massie is no alarmist. Whilst many others predict the rapid growth and gigantic sway of papal dominion, he discovers and clearly points out the traces of decay:—

'I was happy to perceive there was much less of the spirit of blood in the memorials of the Gothic church steeples, the watch-towers and castles of bygone times on this river than on the Rhine; whilst the ruins themselves rather betoken the advancement of society, the progress of mind and of liberty, since the classical associations of Ausonius, than the contests between feudal chiefs, or the aggressions of stronger nations. There is here little to excite the regrets of the tourist or the patriot. The ruins were generally the memorials of a system which is decaying, and passions which, no longer cherished, were often the fruit of superstition and caprice. Feudalism has been engulphed in the vortex of a wider dominion; and popular sympathies no longer respond to its assumptions. The larger sovereignties govern more diversified classes, and must minister to more various interests; and therefore must cultivate a more generic character. Nunneries, and institutions fostering celibacy, and ministering to morbid devotion and consecration, do not now people these banks as they once did, secluding amiable and accomplished womanhood from society, and inflicting a suicidal martyrdom upon the fairest portion of our race; destroying themselves, or absorbing their generous sympathies in dreams, vigils, and plaintive sighings, and depriving mankind of the active discharge of their most virtuous obligations. Many of these sepulchral cells, which had entombed the living victim, and robbed the age or generation of nature's best offerings, have been blown to atoms.

It is also a remarkable fact—I wonder it does not excite the attention of the observant catholic—the glory of papal architecture is *antique;* its most gorgeous fabrics are of *former* times: and while many of them are absolutely mouldering into dust, and others cannot be kept in habitable repair, the prodigal liberality of the devotee is insufficient to rear structures which shall supply the place of those which wax old. The nests and hot-beds, the nurseries and cradles of its most precocious progeny, the nunneries and convents, leave their fragments as mausoleums for the shades of superstition; while abbeys and episcopal principalities, and the territorial power and dominions of electoral and palatine prelates, have been secularised, and transferred to the possession of other bodies. What wise man will mourn, when he looks on the ruins of a conventual establishment? What patriot will grieve to see the cotton-mill, the forge, or the implements of husbandry, occupying the palace of the warlike archbishop, or the plundering chieftain? The reflections thus expressed are but the suggestions of the scenes and recollections of the banks and sloping vineyards, the rich harvest-homes, and the manufactories on the Moselle. Here and there the remains of monastic life are traceable, only as discovering how the passion for it has subsided, and how much more active and diffusive are the habits of modern society, than were the practices of ecclesiastical and papal institutions.'—pp. 239—240.

Nothing that belonged to the religious condition of the people could escape the notice of our author. Alive to the spiritual welfare of mankind, he hailed the symptoms of coming deliverance from their present bondage. The movement, which during the last two years has agitated papal Germany, has more moral material to aid its progress, and secure its success, than its first actors imagined. The Governor of the universe had purposed that a more effective and glorious reformation should be accomplished, than the first agitators had contemplated. He sees the end from the beginning; and agents to effect his gracious purpose will be provided. This appears to be the case in the present politico-religious excitement of Germany. It is evidently in an incipient state of its progress; but its issue will be for the emancipation of human spirits from the thraldom of priestly domination.

Rongé was born at Bischofswald, in 1813. At an early age he kept his father's flock at the foot of the Giant Mountains. While thus engaged, he indulged his inclination to think on religion, a future life, and eternity. His 'Catechism' and his 'Bible History' were his constant companions. During nine years he was a scholar at the high school of Neisse, whence he passed to the university of Breslau. At the close of 1839, being then twenty-six years of age, and during his former life knowing but little of restraint, he became a candidate for the Roman Catholic priesthood. From that period, he felt the authority of his ecclesiastical superiors irksome and oppressive, and whilst groaning under his own burden, he shuddered at the thought of subjecting others to a misery which he found to be almost intolerable. 'I murmured,' said he, 'that I should be myself a slave! Must I also be a tool to work the degradation of my fellow-men?' It cannot be matter of surprize, that a young man, naturally energetic, and of such sentiments, should show some signs of resistance and indignation, when commanded to pray, 'that the Spaniards may return to their old ecclesiastical bondage.' He met this papal injunction with the reply, 'It is, indeed, most necessary that we pray for ourselves and for the Spaniards, but it shall be for the freedom and independence of ourselves and them—in union with which alone can true religion and morality exist—and not for slavery and dependence, which can at best engender dissimulation and hypocrisy.'

In September, 1844, he wrote his letter to Arnoldi, Bishop of Treves, exposing the imposture of the *holy tunic,* and in December following, he received the sentence of his 'degradation and excommunication' from the pale of the Catholic church. By this brief sketch of Rongé's history, it will be evident that his dauntless attack upon the Roman Catholic church, chiefly originated in an abhorrence of the authority it assumed over the civil liberties and consciences of men. But other men, such as Czerski, Theiner, and Wigand, have joined the movement, and imparted the salutary influence which their sound scriptural views and personal piety are calculated to exert.

Like many others, Dr. Massie was at first disposed to take a more favourable view of the *present character* of the movement than its real merits appear to justify. That it will be ultimately overruled for the advancement of truth and liberty, there can scarcely be a doubt; but to suppose that it has in it, the essential elements of the Reformation carried on by Martin Luther and his associates, is not borne out by the facts which have come under our notice. Dr. Massie, in his concluding note, has guarded against being misunderstood.

'By some of my readers,' he says, 'I may be thought to have taken too favourable a view of the *present* religious movement and its leaders in Germany. A more mature discussion of the subject would afford a clearer index of my thoughts and inquiries; and I cannot hesitate to avail myself of a communication from a friend, recently a witness of the work and the labourers. His opinions may be useful to others. He found it difficult to sympathize with the movement on acount of its *Rationalism*. He says, 'With but few exceptions (amongst whom Czerski deserves honourable mention, the more especially as he has left that body, and is tolerably orthodox, considering all things) these 'Reformers' are Neologists. The speculations of 'certain journalists' about the real character of this movement are grievously at fault. The fact is undeniable that

Rongé and Kerbler, at least, deny the inspiration of the Bible, the deity of Christ, and the atonement, as fully as ever Belsham did. There is far more political and theological liberalism in the affair than religion.'

" 'This is sad, indeed; but I have the best evidence of its truth. To compare Rongé's agitation to Luther's is preposterous. It is admitted that both are antagonistic to popery; but so were, likewise the leaders of the French Revolution. 'But the Confessions?' Confessions of faith are worth no more in Germany than at Oxford, nor so much even; for subscription is not obligatory. I have attended an ordination of one of their priests, where the only profession was a series of negations, which any Socinian might have declared.'

'The state and tendency of the German mind differ much in the nineteenth century from what they were in the sixteenth. Perhaps something may be ascribed to these differences in the religious revolutions and developments of the present times.'—p. 548.

The friends of republican protestantism have been alarmed by the aggregation of catholic citizens in the state of Geneva, and the increased influence, if not ascendancy, of the papal sect in the home of Calvin. The connection between the church and the state has *therefore* become to them odious, and the source of apprehension. Good has thus been deduced out of evil. Fear has come in aid of the truth, and preparations are made for the crisis to which, in common with the other states of Christendom, Geneva is doomed. This miniature republic, with its manageable ecclesiastical establishment, has tested the compulsory principle, and it is in a suggestive, rather than a polemical strain, that Dr. Massie brings under review some of the most momentous considerations connected with the subject which is destined to become *the question of questions*, not only in Britain, but throughout the continent. We commend to the special attention of our readers that portion of his volume which commences on the four hundred and thirty-fifth page, and lay aside the work with a pleasing impression of the variety and value of the details it furnishes.

Many of our readers had the pleasure of hearing the substance of the volume from the living voice of the author. We hope that *the book* will be as highly appreciated as were *the lectures*, and that it will find a place in many libraries. It well deserves an extensive circulation.

Art. VII.—*A Bill, intituled, An Act for securing the due Administration of Charitable Trusts in England and Wales. Presented by the Lord Chancellor. Ordered to be printed*, 19*th February*, 1846.

JOHN SINGLETON COPLEY, Baron Lyndhurst,—a name rarely seen in subscription lists,—is unable to repress his solicitude for the due administration of charitable trusts! It reminds us of the traitor apostle's anxiety for the poor. Simply to save expense and to check abuses, has the noble and learned lord introduced this bill into parliament. Let us see how he proposes to achieve these ends; and, in order that we may have some chance of understanding the process, let us endeavour to reduce the confused and cumbrous clauses of the bill into the form of analytical digest.

The bill contains sixty-two clauses. It creates a new court, with extensive powers and few and feeble checks. The pretexts for this proceeding are, first, that in numerous cases property of small amount is held subject to charitable trusts in England and Wales, and it is expedient to provide for the due administration of such property, without incurring the expense of proceedings in courts of equity for that purpose (Clause 1); and, secondly, that, in order the more effectually to check abuses in the administration of property subject to charitable trusts, it is proper that regular accounts should be kept of the receipt and expenditure of such property, and that such accounts should from time to time be inspected and examined (1).

The appointment of numerous officers for the purposes of the proposed act, is provided for in clauses 1, 4, 6, 51. These officers are to consist of three commissioners, a secretary, two inspectors, 'clerks, messengers, and officers,' without limitation, and 'a clerk of each trust,' as we read in the margin. The appointments of commissioners and inspectors are to be gazetted (5). No person, while he holds 'any office or employment' under the proposed act, is to practise as a barrister or as a solicitor or attorney (7).

The three commissioners are to be appointed originally and in continuance by the Lord Chancellor, to be styled 'The Commissioners of Charities,' and to hold their offices during good behaviour (1). Every commissioner is to be a person either holding or having held the office of vice-chancellor or of master in chancery, or having held the office of chief justice of the Supreme Court in Bengal, or a sergeant or barrister-at-law in actual practice, and of not less than twelve years' standing at the bar (2). Resignation of the office of master in chancery is not to disqualify a commissioner (*ibid.*),—a superfluous proviso, by the way, since the clause renders those who are, and those who have been masters, alike eligible. Commissioners are to take oath, that they 'will faithfully, impartially, and honestly, according to the best of their skill and judgment, fulfil all the powers and duties' of their office (5). They are to be salaried officers; such of them as may be or may have been vice-chancellor, master in chancery, or chief justice in Bengal, to receive, in addition to the salary or retiring pension connected with those offices respectively, a further salary under the bill (3).

The jurisdiction of the commissioners is to be partly summary and partly limited. Their summary jurisdiction is specially provided for in clauses 10, 13, 14, 18, 19, 22, 30; their limited jurisdiction, in clauses 20, 21, 22, 28, 27, 53. Their summary jurisdiction is confined to cases in which the clear yearly revenue of the charity does not exceed one hundred pounds (10). Their limited jurisdiction extends to all charitable trusts whatsoever, excepting only the universities of Oxford and Cambridge, and the colleges and halls within the same, which, by clause 59, are specially exempted from the operation of the bill.

The *powers of the commissioners* are stated in clauses 2, 10, 12, 13, 14, 18, 19, 20, 21, 22, 23, 25, 27, 30, 31, 32, 33, 34, 35, 45, 46, 47, 50, 53, 56. They are to 'have the superintendence and control of charitable trusts' (2). The acts of 'any two of the commissioners' are to be valid (8).

With respect to any charity not exceeding a hundred pounds a year, if the commissioners shall, by the petition in writing of any informant, or by the report of any inspector, *or otherwise*, be informed of any neglect, abuse, or breach of trust in the management of such charity, or in the administration of its estate or funds, or of the want of a sufficient scheme for the application of its revenues, they are empowered, after such notice as they shall deem fit, to cite before them the parties accused, or the trustees of the charity in question, and to summon, by precepts under their seal (provided for in clause 8), and examine, any person or persons whomsoever in relation thereto; to hear and determine summarily the matter; to make thereon, at their pleasure, an order for the payment, with or without interest, of any money belonging to the charity, in the hands of any person connected with its administration, or for the payment of interest, with or without rests, on balances improperly retained in hand, or for the future administration of the trust; or to make any other order respecting the property or the objects of the charity; or, with the written consent of the special visiter if any, to establish, at their pleasure, a new scheme for the application of the revenues; every such order to be final and conclusive, and not subject to any review, unless the commissioners themselves shall think fit to rehear; the commissioners, for the purpose (not *purposes*) aforesaid, to hold their sitting at, or as near to the locality of the charity as they shall judge expedient (10). In every case within their summary jurisdiction, in which it shall appear to them that a charity is without trustees legally appointed, or that the property is not duly vested in the persons actually administering it, or that, by reason of the reduced number of the trustees, or of other causes, a valid appointment of new trustees cannot be made without application to the Court of Chancery, they are to be empowered to appoint any person or persons as trustees, either alone or jointly with trustees previously existing (13). In the exercise of their summary jurisdiction, they are to be authorised, upon proof, *to their satisfaction*, of any abuse, breach of trust, or neglect of duty, by any trustee, or in the event of any trustee being incapable of acting or desiring his discharge, to remove such trustees, and thereupon, or on the death of any trustee, to appoint any 'new or other trustees, or trustee;' the written consent of special visiters (if any) being necessary, in order to all such removals and appointments (14). Still within the bounds of their summary jurisdiction, they are to be at liberty (but not without the written concurrence of special visiters, if any), upon proof, *to their satisfaction*, that any schoolmaster or mistress, *or other officer of any charity*, has been negligent in performing his or her duties, or that he or she is unfit or incompetent to discharge them properly, either from immoral conduct, age, or *any other cause whatsoever*, to empower the *trustees* to remove such schoolmaster or mistress, *or other officer*, under such conditions as to them (the commissioners) shall appear proper (18). Again, in cases of summary jurisdiction, whenever it shall *appear to them* that property given or subject to any charitable trust, cannot be applied to the purposes directed by and according to the intention of the donor thereof, they are to have authority, on application from the majority of the trustees, and with the written consent of the special visiters (if any), to settle or approve a scheme for the application of the property to *any* charitable purposes that they (the commissioners) shall think fit (19). In the case of all charities of not more than a hundred pounds yearly value, they are to be at liberty, not merely to inquire into the receipt and application of the revenues, but also to make inquiry, inspection, and examination into the administration of them (22). In like cases, they are to have power, whenever they deem the funds of a charity insufficiently secured from misappropriation or loss, to order the transfer thereof to the account of the accountant-general, for investment, in his name, in bank annuities (30).

With respect to charitable trusts in general, the commissioners are to be invested with the various powers now about to be stated. Upon application from a majority of trustees, they may, with the consent (it is not here said *written*) of the special visiter (if any) direct the sale, mortgage, or exchange of lands, rents, or other hereditaments, or the grant of building or other leases, or the working of mines, or the raising of stone, clay, or gravel, whenever beneficial to the charity; may, at their pleasure, appoint surveyors or other persons to examine such applications; and may connect with the transactions such conditions, restrictions, and directions as they shall deem proper (12). They may sanction, at their pleasure, the definitive compromise of claims in behalf of charities, against any person or corporation, in respect of any neglect, abuse, or breach of trust, or in relation to any property subject or *alleged to be subject* to any charitable trust (20). They may make, rescind, and alter, at their pleasure, regulations, as to the form and manner of the accounts to be kept and rendered, and the returns to be made, by trustees and others, and the transmission and production of accounts and vouchers; provided such regulations be forwarded 'to the clerk, *if any*, of such charitable trust' (21),—(Clause 5 empowering them to make the appointment of a clerk imperative on each trust). Any one or more of them (or the inspectors under their authority) may make inquiry into the receipt and application of the revenues of *any* charitable trust in England and Wales (22); may call for and inspect all books of account, vouchers, and other documents concerning such revenues and the receipt and application thereof; may require the attendance of any person acting as trustee, master, officer, or servant of *any* such charity, or as manager or receiver of any estates or revenues subject to *any* charitable trust, or concerned in the administration thereof, or receiving any salary, emolument, or benefit from *any* charitable trust; and may demand from any such person answers, orally or in writing, to *any* questions, and, generally, all the information possessed by such person in relation thereto, as they may think fit to exact (23). Any one or more of them (or the inspectors under their authority) may examine parties upon oath (25). Stock or money passed, with their approbation, by trustees or others acting in behalf of charities, to the account of the accountant-general, is to be 'in trust to attend the orders of the commissioners' (27). All dividends accruing from such investments are to be 'subject to the order of the commissioners' (29, 31), and no payment is to be legal without an order signed by two of them (32). Stock may be sold and the proceeds re-invested in like manner (33), the secretary certifying the stock to be sold and the person to whom (34, 35). They may, on the petition in writing of not less than ten inhabitant householders, appoint trustees of municipal charities, where no application has been made to the Lord Chancellor for the appointment of trustees under the Municipal Corporations Act (45). They may, on the like application, add to the number of trustees of municipal charities, whenever it shall appear that 'the existing number of such trustees does not secure a fair or impartial administration of the income of such estate or funds according to the true intent of the trust;' and they are to have the 'sole power' of appointing new or additional trustees, in cases under the Municipal Corporations Act, excepting that, whenever trustees are removed by the Court of Chancery, that court is to supply the vacancies (47). The commissioners may, 'if they shall so think fit,' re-consider, within two months, any of their orders or proceedings, every such re-hearing to take place before all the commissioners (50). They are to report what charities have in their opinion ceased to be beneficial or have become injurious, and also to state such as require to be regulated and reformed (53). They may require abstracts, or copies of, or extracts from conveyances and assurances, wills or muniments of title, concerning any charity, to be transmitted to their office (56).

It will be the *duty* of the commissioners to cause the examinations taken before them, and all papers and documents connected therewith, to be transmitted to their office (24), which is to be in London or Westminster (8); and also, 'at successive periods in every three years,' (a somewhat indefinite direction,) to submit to Her Majesty reports of the revenues and expenditure of all charities subject to their control and inspection, distinguishing the revenues applicable to education, the number of masters (and, we suppose, of mistresses also) employed, and the number of scholars educated, in whole or in part, by the several charitable trusts (53).

The commissioners are to have the *privilege* of giving full effect to their appointments of trustees, without any deed of conveyance (15),—an enactment needlessly repeated in clause 46.

The orders of the commissioners are to be subject to some *limitations*. Besides their inability to perform certain acts without the concurrence of special visiters, where such officers exist, (as in clauses 10, 14, 18, 19,) the established church, as well as the universities of Oxford and Cambridge, is exempted from their authority. In the case of 'any charity for the purpose of education in connexion with the united church of England and *Ireland*,' (be it observed, the bill extends only to *England and Wales*,—1,61), or which, in the absence of any sufficient scheme, has, for the last twenty-five years, been deemed to be a charity in connexion with the united church of England and Ireland, and administered as such, if there be not any special visiter, the consent of the bishop of the diocese shall be required in order to the validity of any new scheme, in like manner as though he were a special visiter appointed in the instrument of foundation (10, 19).

But the most remarkable case in which the established church is *favoured* by this bill, is to be found in CLAUSE XLVIII., which it would scarcely be an exaggeration to describe as AN ATTEMPT TO REVIVE THE TEST AND CORPORATION ACTS. We transcribe this infamous clause without abridgment:—

'XLVIII. And be it enacted, That in every Case of a Charitable Trust for the Benefit of Persons being Members of the United Church of England and Ireland, or for educating exclusively Persons being Members thereof, *or for the Establishment, Maintenance, or Support of Religious Education or Religious Worship according to the Principles of such Church, or for any other Purpose connected therewith, no Trustee to be appointed under this Act shall be capable of acting in the Execution of such Trust until he shall have made and signed a Declaration in Writing* before some Judge of one of the Superior Courts at Westminster, or before some Justice of the Peace, which Declaration shall be in the Form and shall be attested in the Manner following; (that is to say,)

'I *A. B.* do declare, That I am *really and bonâ fide a Member of the United Church of England and Ireland as by Law established.*

(Signed) *A. B.*

'Signed and declared this Day of in the
'Year of our Lord at in the County of
' before me *C.D.*, One of the Judges of
'[*or* One of the Justices of the Peace for *, as the*
'*Case may be*].'

And every such Declaration shall be thereupon transmitted by such Judge or Justice of the Peace to the Office of the Clerks of the Petty Bag, who shall forthwith file the same in the High Court of Chancery, and no Fee shall be payable in respect of such filing thereof: Provided always, that *the Concurrence of any such Trustee not making and signing such Declaration with the other Trustees shall not be necessary in order to the Validity of any Act* to be done or Instrument to be executed in the Administration of such Charitable Trust.'

The orders of the commissioners appointing trustees of municipal charities, are to be subject to appeal to the Lord Chancellor on the petition of any five or more inhabitant householders (49).

On the subject of excepted matters, it may be added, that the bill is not to dispense with the admittance of trustees to copyholds, &c., nor to affect the right to heriots, fines, &c. (16); and that, save in cases comprehended under clause 20, it is not to affect proceedings now pending relative to charitable trusts (60).

The clauses relating to the secretary are, 9, 34, 35; to the inspectors, 4, 5, 9, 22—25; to other officers, 9.

The expenses that will be incurred under the bill are provided for in clauses 54, 55. A fund is to be created, entitled, 'The Charity Administration Fund.' To this fund the revenues of every charity within the provisions of the bill, 'except such as shall be specially exempted by any order of the commissioners,' are to pay, annually, 'such sum,—not exceeding, in the case of any charity within the summary jurisdiction of the commissioners, *threepence in the pound*; and, in the case of every other charity not exceeding *one penny halfpenny in the pound*, on the net annual amount of revenue applicable to the purposes of such charity, respectively, *and not exceeding in any case the sum of one hundred pounds*,—as the commissioners shall direct' (54); whatever is deficient to be made up by the lords of the Treasury out of the consolidated fund (55). The said 'Charity Administration Fund' is to be applicable to the payment of the salaries of the commissioners, (which are to be fixed by parliament—3,) and of other officers, (to be fixed by the lords of the Treasury—,9) and of all such expenses of the commissioners and their officers as the lords of the Treasury shall authorize to be paid thereout, and all such expenses of suits and proceedings in relation to charities of small amount in value as the commissioners shall authorize to be paid thereout (54).

The bill contains several *penal clauses*—26, 40—43. Any person who, upon examination before the commissioners or the inspectors, shall wilfully and corruptly give false evidence, is to be subject to the pains and penalties of perjury (26). Any person summoned to appear before one or more of the commissioners, or before an inspector, who shall wilfully omit or refuse to appear, or to be sworn, or to answer fully any lawful question, is to be liable to the payment of such fine as the Court of Queen's Bench or of Exchequer shall think fit to impose (40). Any master, officer, or servant of a charity, or any manager or receiver of charity estates or revenues, or any person receiving any salary, emolument, or benefit, from any charitable trust, who shall prevent or in anywise obstruct any commissioner or inspector, or refuse or neglect to give answers, orally or in writing, to their lawful questions, or neglect or refuse to obey their summons, is to be deemed guilty of misbehaviour in his office, and to be subject to removal, on application to the Court of Chancery, which is to make such order with respect to the application, and to the costs, as it shall deem just (41). All trustees refusing or neglecting to obey the directions of the bill and of the commissioners under it, are to be deemed guilty of a breach of trust, and to be subject to removal, on application to the Court of Chancery, the costs, if the court shall so direct, to be paid by the offending trustees (42). Obedience to the commissioners' orders are to be enforced by the Court of Chancery, at the expense of those who shall refuse or neglect to obey them (43).

To complete the analysis of the bill, it needs only be added, that the poor privileges conceded to the public are contained in clauses 10, 45, 47, 49, 50, 56; that municipal charities are affected by clauses 44—47; that the power and jurisdiction of the Lord Chancellor and the Court of Chancery, are referred to in clauses 1, 2, 37, 41—43, 47, 60; that clauses 8, 11, 17, 24—27, 46, relate to questions of evidence, and clauses 10, 15, 21, 27—39, 52, 58, to matters of account; that in clauses 56 and 57 provision is made for the registry and safe custody of deeds relating to charities; and that in clause 62 the usual power is reserved to alter or amend the bill, should it become an act, in the same session of parliament.

Let trustees, and others connected with the administration of charitable trusts, ponder the proposed enactments of this unconstitutional bill, and judge for themselves whether it does not behove them, out of self-respect, and consideration for the charities with which they are connected, to give to it their prompt, energetic, and uncompromising opposition. It contains no definition whatever of what constitutes a charitable trust. This is, no doubt, purposely omitted, in order that the clauses may allow of the utmost latitude of interpretation and application. So far from any attempt being made to narrow the operation of the bill, and confine it strictly to charities in the proper sense of that word, funds merely '*alleged* to be subject to charitable trusts' are brought in express terms within the sweep of its all-embracing clauses. It appears to comprehend every fund created, whether by endowment, bequest, or subscription, for the benefit of others than the parties so creating it: all charities, thus understood, large and small, ancient and modern, national, municipal, or parochial, secular or religious, for foreign or for domestic purposes. It will affect all hospitals, all universities, colleges, and schools (save those specially exempted), all almshouses and eleemosynary doles, all funds for general education or religious instruction, all literary funds, artists' funds, artists' general benevolent societies, and other professional charities, all religious endowments, all chapels and school-houses settled in trust. Every institution which any one portion of the inhabitants of England and Wales have established or may establish, for the benefit of any other persons, will be subject to it. With all of them it will most annoyingly and vexatiously interfere, and over most exert a complete and irreversible control. It is impossible to calculate the immense amount of property which will be placed at the disposal of this close and absolute tribunal, or even the number of individuals that this unconstitutional triumvirate will have at their mercy. The money may be reckoned by millions, and the men by tens of thousands. Happy the trustees that are shielded by a special visiter, or can flee for refuge to episcopal skirts! But all else may be thrown, by a common informer, or any more infamous agency, into the hands of these commissioners, or their prowling and prying inspectors. These modern inquisitors may summon and examine what witnesses they please, attach what importance to their evidence they think proper, decide as they will, make orders without end, divert and pervert the trusts according to their whim (than which no evil now existing can be worse), and all without appeal, except to themselves, and that only when they think fit to revise their own judgments. The 'sole powers' given them over municipal charities will seriously affect the political independence of many parliamentary boroughs.

No distinction is made between the good and the bad; between those charities for the right government of which no adequate security exists, and those which are governed by parties who have an obvious and a direct interest in their just administration. Indeed, it makes the good pay for the bad, or, rather, makes the alleged mal-administration of certain small charities (taxed, by the bye, in a ratio inverse to their value) serve as an excuse for mulcting charities of larger amount, which it does not even pretend to suspect of mal-administration. Because some rural rector has contrived to divert into his own pocket funds bequeathed for the education of the poor of the parish, therefore these commissioners are to divert into their pockets a hundred pounds of voluntary contributions for special objects. Because the poor in 'Little Pedlington' have been robbed by generations of trustees, the London Missionary Society is to be called upon to pay £100 per annum to the 'Charity Administration Fund.' Talk of robbing Peter to pay Paul! this is Judas robbing both to pay himself.

The bill is inquisitorial, and that most where least defensible and least necessary. In its estimation, a special visiter charity is precisely that sort of charity which 'hideth a multitude of sins;' while the voucher of a bishop warrants the presumption of a purity equal to that of his own lawn; but every charity whose door is not thus guarded, falls a prey to this burglarious bill, and the awe-struck inmates must disclose all their affairs, on pain of—no one knows what. Our great societies publish their annual reports, which satisfies the subscribers; but this new triumvirate of bureaucratic kings will extort a great deal more from them, and make them pay for it in the bargain.

The bill is an intolerable insult to the great body of generous and disinterested trustees, who pay instead of receiving, by supposing them capable of misapplying funds, the particular destination of which has, in numberless cases, originated with themselves, while, in nearly all, they are the largest and most constant contributors. 'I belong,' says a correspondent of the *Times* newspaper, 'to a society or social club of professional persons of upwards of fifty years' duration, one of whose members died a few years back, and left a liberal sum to the club to be disposed of by them in charitable purposes, entirely at their discretion. I need scarcely say, that the services of the parties in charge of the fund are gratuitous; and thus, by its passing into the hands of strangers, who will be paid for their services, its humble funds will be diminished, and the society dispossessed of their right.'—This is but one instance of many hundreds, in which the operation of the bill will be thus unjust and prejudicial. Let there be the least probability of such a measure becoming law, and tens of thousands of trustees will either wind up the affairs with which they are thus connected, or will anticipate the odious interference of these paid commissioners, by withdrawing. Those that have no motive for acting in this capacity but the promotion of a benevolent or other good design, will not submit to the degradation of being under the surveillance of this new police. The very existence of many excellent and important charities will be perilled; for, through disgust at the wolfish scheme of fleecing under pretence of protecting them, funds derived from annual subscriptions will be subject to serious fluctuations, and the directors of such institutions will no longer be able to keep faith with those for whose subsistence they have pledged themselves, in full reliance upon the steady flow of public liberality. For similar reasons, the bill will discourage the reviving habit of making charitable bequests, and will deter prudent managers of institutions mainly dependent upon annual subscribers, from fortifying them against contingencies, by reserving a portion of their income for investment in the funds.

In short, the proceeding is altogether indefensible. If, for example, because some charities have been abused, all institutions that the elastic name can by any stretching be made to cover, are to be taxed and overhauled, official assignees might as well be clothed with authority to examine all men's ledgers, because there are some bankrupts, and those bankrupts' affairs ought to be set right at the expense of solvent traders. In one word, the bill is a job, and the proposed commission may be justly regarded as forming a capacious reservoir, into which tens of thousands of charities are to empty their tributary rills. It is an expensive scheme for curtailing expense,—an unjust mode of doing justice,—an uncharitable way of promoting charity. These are doubtless heavy accusations; but the more the bill is examined, the more evident will be the fact that they are richly merited.

It fails at starting. It does not accomplish the legitimate object, while aiming at objects that are not legitimate. We need not go into the history of the Charity Commission,—that leviathan affair, whose labours consumed twenty years, and whose report fills more than twice as many volumes. It results from those prolonged inquiries, that there are as many as forty thousand charities of less than £100 annual value each, their average value not exceeding £30 a year, seven thousand of them being under £5, and six thousand under £3 a year, and the yearly income of three thousand five hundred of them ranging from twenty shillings to one shilling. The right administration of these forty thousand small charities is the ostensible object of the bill. Doubtless, a process applicable to such cases, less expensive and less tardy than the existing regulations of the Court of Chancery admit of, may be desirable. The question is, whether the bill under review supplies the desideratum. Our belief is, that its exempting clauses defeat its object. No charities which have a special visiter, none which are, or for five-and-twenty years have been *deemed to be* identified with the established church, can be touched, without the consent of the visiter in the one case, or of the bishop of the diocese in the other. We should not be surprised to find, that these provisions exclude from the operation of the measure, at least three-fourths of those charities which have furnished the only plausible plea for its introduction. Besides the low average value of these trusts, they are scattered through almost every parish in England and Wales. How can three gentlemen resident in London, with a couple of inspectors and no matter how many clerks, deal advantageously with such a case? By the bill, the one shilling and the twenty shilling charities must continue to be separately administered. For the future, the administrators will be subject to the commission alone. Their large numbers, scattered over the whole face of the country, would render the surveillance merely nominal. And, at all events, the bill contains not one syllable to make the commissioners responsible for the fulfilment of their duties.

Various remedies have been suggested for the admitted evil, the worst of which is far better than this futile, though mischievous bill. For example, a number of these trivial charities might be consolidated under one management, with provision for due publicity; and the administrators might be made elective. Or, an easy method of redress, by appeal to the ordinary courts, might be afforded to all parties interested in the proper administration of the charities. Or, a bill might be brought in to facilitate and simplify proceedings in equity. Why not, as has been suggested by a professional gentleman who understands the subject well, disallow fees to counsel on the preparation and signature of petitions, render the concurrence of the attorney-general, where now required, unnecessary, only allow one counsel at the hearing, reduce or abolish court fees, reduce the scale of payments in the master's office, or abolish them entirely in cases of a certain limited amount, render a report from the master unnecessary, or, if not, simplify the process, and let the suitor go at once to the court and get his order, and let that order vest the property in the persons approved by the master, and thus obviate the necessity for a conveyance. Some such measure as this would accomplish every desirable object, in relation to the diminution of expense. What is wanted is, an appropriate judicial process, combining cheapness with publicity and responsibility. The Lord Chancellor's bill is the very opposite of all these. It erects a secret court. To that court it gives absolute authority, legislative as well as judicial and administrative, without appeal on the one hand, or responsibility on the other. And, certainly, any thing but cheap.

Threepence in the pound on charities under £100, and three-halfpence in the pound on those of higher value, limited though the tax may be, in the latter case, to £100 each, will yield no trifling amount of money; and yet, that this is deemed insufficient, may be fairly inferred from the clause enacting that any deficit shall be paid out of the consolidated fund. If we consider how many and what sort of salaries will have to be paid, we shall soon see that it must be an expensive affair, and that it was necessary to extend the principle of spoliation as well as of arbitrary interference to the larger charities, in order to raise any thing like enough for the purposes of the job. The amount of the commissioners' salaries is in blank; the House of Lords having no power to fill it up, though, strangely enough, that house has, or assumes power to impose a tax on all charitable trusts,—the more important part of the money matter. We may guess, however, how many figures will ultimately occupy the vacant space. Vice-chancellors and masters in chancery are the class of men made eligible for the commissionerships. Now, the Vice-chancellor of England receives £6,000 a year; the other two vice-chancellors, £5,000 each; and the dozen masters, £2,500 a piece. If any of these gentlemen accepts a commissionership, he is to have something beyond his present salary. Should any of them be appointed, and not resign their present places, it would be a proof that they have not now enough to do,—a contingency which at once suggests the possibility of superseding the bill altogether, by devolving upon them, under some suitable arrangement, the business it involves. If, however, the contrary is the fact, and any of them should accept appointments under the bill, it is not to be supposed that they would make a change disadvantageous to themselves. Indeed, it is rumoured that Master Lynch and Master Brougham are already marked out for the new offices (Sir Edward Ryan being understood to be the lucky ex-chief-justice of Bengal, made eligible by the bill). We may consequently conclude, that the mere salaries of the three commissioners will nearly swallow up £10,000 a year; and the stipends of inspectors, secretary, clerks, managers, and officers, with travelling and other expenses, will go very far towards doubling the amount.

And for what purpose is the public charity to be taxed to the tune of some £20,000 per annum? To facilitate the establishment of a new, secret, absolute, and irresponsible tribunal, from whose decisions there will be no appeal, and which, from the nature of its constitution and functions, can never hope to possess public confidence. Indeed, the whole thing might have been framed for the purpose of provoking opposition. What else can be the result of proposing to compel the most powerful companies, societies, and institutions in the metropolis, in common with all trustees of all other charities, to deposit in the office of the commissioners, at their own expense, attested copies of all the deeds of charities entrusted to their management, and to exact annual accounts of the special application of each? What can be more vexatious or uncalled for? Again, the commissioners will be empowered to compel every land-owner, out of whose estate a rent-charge, or other payment, however small, for a charitable purpose, arises, to proclaim to all the world the state of his title at the passing of the bill; to verify it from the date of the instrument creating the charity, and to register in their office all conveyances, leases, etc., in any way concerning his estate. This, surely, will not help the bill through a landlords' parliament! The manner in which it has been received by the governors of the royal hospitals and some other powerful companies, affords it but little promise of success. It is hardly to be supposed, that a body of gentlemen who have given among them a quarter of a million of money for the purposes of the charities they superintend, will continue this rate of liberality for the pleasure of being ordered from pillar to post by an ex-master in chancery, or a briefless barrister of twelve years' standing.

The most material point, however, is that which relates to

trustees. This bill, we beg them to bear in mind, is for their benefit! Its objects are to give them new facilities, and at less expense! And how is all this to be accomplished? Thus. By rendering them liable to answer on oath to unsworn informations. Ordinary witnesses cannot be compelled to travel more than ten miles, but unhappy trustees must obey the summons of these lords commissioners, though they travel from one end of the kingdom to the other. All their books, vouchers, and documents, must be forthcoming whenever called for. They must not flinch from any question put to them. The penalties of perjury hang over them. An unlimited fine, with the agreeable alternative of imprisonment, awaits the refractory. The Court of Chancery is empowered to enforce the orders of the commissioners at the expense of negligent or disobedient trustees. They must keep a clerk if directed. Their accounts must be according to the commissioners' notions of book-keeping, and liable to examination and audit at their high mightinesses' pleasure. Not only must they furnish the commissioners with copies of their deeds, old and new, to lie open for public inspection; but the deeds themselves must be given up, if required, and copies retained for their own use and at their own expense. To crown all, they are, in a great many instances, wholly at the mercy of the commissioners, removable at their pleasure, and their trusts liable to endless tampering and perversion, as well as to annual taxation. And all this for the benefit of trustees, to afford them fresh facilities, and to diminish their expenses! Why, if any thing like such a bill as this were to become law, a trustee would be the unhappiest man alive.

The fact is, that the only case in which a trust estate can be benefited by the bill is, when a new appointment of trustees becomes necessary,—a case which happens not more than four or five times in a century. Now, what are the facilities? You apply to the commissioners: it must be by petition. The bill does not award trustees the privilege of professional aid when cited before them; but such applications will, in general, be made with legal assistance. An attorney prepares the petition, and there must, as evidence of the deaths of trustees, be certificates of burial, duly verified by affidavit. Thus an expense will be incurred, which, added to the new tax, will probably exceed that of an ordinary appointment by deed. These remarks, be it observed, apply only to the minor class of trusts, in which alone the commissioners will have the power of appointment. The larger class will pay the tax indeed, but not derive the benefit, such as it is: they must proceed as before. It is the fault of trustees themselves, however, if they have to incur in any form the expense of new appointments.

It is certain, that, when the provisions of the bill are well understood, all trustees who apprehend correctly their own interests, will prefer the present mode of administering trust property to the oppressive, inquisitorial, annoying, and expensive mode here proposed. The only clause that is not most offensive towards them, is that which gives them an indemnity for all that they may do under the commissioners' direction.

We desire to call the particular attention of dissenters of all classes to the insulting and injurious aspect which this spoliation bill wears towards them and their interests. The Dissenting Deputies have already pointed out, in their petition to the House of Lords, that, although in a bill, under the same title, introduced into their lordships' house in 1844, provision was made for excluding from its operation, 'any funds applicable to the benefit of Roman Catholics, or of the people called Quakers, or of any person of the Jewish persuasion,' and for leaving such funds 'under the superintendence and control of persons of such persuasions respectively,' and although no petitions have been presented to the legislature from Protestant Dissenters praying for any alteration in the law respecting them; yet the legal operation of this bill will be to include all the chapels of Protestant Dissenters, although the greater part of them are supported by voluntary contributions. This is true enough; but a great deal more than this is true. Not only their chapels, but also their colleges and schools, and all their institutions, are placed in jeopardy. We question whether any minister will be safe in his pulpit should this bill pass. It contains a clause which puts every individual having a beneficial interest in a trust estate completely under the thumb, we had almost written thumbscrew, of the commissioners. Certainly it empowers them to declare existing trusts injurious, and wholly to change their complexion and direction. An orthodox trustee may be displaced to make room for a heterodox one—a good Christian for a rank infidel. The established church is well provided for; but, for dissent and dissenters, there is nothing but pains and penalties. Whatever has, for twenty-five years, been *deemed* to be a church charity, with that no dissenter can have anything to do, any more than if it were, by distinct and positive deed, exclusively a church charity. Here comes in the New Test, quoted above, in all its rigour. No dissenting alderman, town-councillor, or parochial officer, can exercise the rights of citizenship in relation to any of these twenty-five-year-old church charities, much less to those positively such. Far be any dissenter from wishing to intrude into charities really belonging to churchmen as such; but there are numberless municipal and parochial charities notoriously designed to be administered without distinction of religious parties, which, nevertheless, under this bill, the church will be enabled to claim; and with them no dissenter can interfere who is not prepared to forswear himself and his principles, by solemnly declaring that he is 'really and *bonâ fide* a member of the established church.' By a strange anomaly, the commissioners' oath of office requires no religious test from them; and, in point of fact, there is every probability that the three classes of religionists whom the present Government has exclusively favoured in former measures, will be represented in the very first board of charity commissioners. We refer, of course, to the church of England, the church of Rome, and the Unitarians. Thus it will come to pass, that, while three commissioners of these several religious persuasions may turn all sorts of trusts, evangelical dissenting or otherwise, upside down and inside out, *a new test act*, enacted for the purpose, will for ever prevent any conscientious dissenter from so much as touching a single charity to which the clergy of the establishment can set up a specious claim of five-and-twenty years' possession. A more absurd anomaly or a grosser insult was never perpetrated. Will the legislature establish the system of *exclusive dealing* by act of parliament?

We call upon the dissenters to arouse themselves. Our Wesleyan friends, with their usual sagacity, have perceived the threatening danger, and are on the alert. Their petition to the House of Lords elaborately exposes the mischievous and iniquitous character of this abominable bill. Once passed into a law, it would cut up their compact and smooth-working system by the very roots. Their chapels and other trust premises are settled on a uniform plan, and, we need hardly say, are of immense value. By their law, no trustees, however embarrassed, can sell or mortgage without permission of Conference. What they borrow, must be borrowed on their own personal security. This, in individual cases, may seem hard; but the Conference, having the interests of their vast Connexion to consider, is governed by their judgment rather than swayed by their feelings. Now, this bill would completely break in upon their rule; for, in all cases, great and small, it empowers the commissioners to give relief to distressed trustees by directing a sale, mortgage, or exchange of property. This would utterly derange the affairs of the whole Wesleyan church, to the very existence of which it is absolutely necessary that the Conference should reign in undisturbed supremacy. Again, it is their invariable rule to appoint no trustees but such as are members of their own communion; and the Conference obtained a legal constitution for the very purpose of appointing ministers to the chapels in their Connexion. Both these essential parts of its economy would be invaded by the bill, which, under given and very possible circumstances, would transfer both these powers to the commissioners; for, as we have seen, the bill empowers them to authorize trustees, 'for any cause whatever,' to discharge any officer of a charity; which, in the case before us, is to make master and servant change places. In short, no such measure could pass into law, without exposing this large and well-organised community to a ruinous and perhaps a speedy revolution. Well might the Committee of Privileges begin their petition to the Peers against it, with the declaration that they view it with 'considerable apprehension and alarm,' and assert that it is 'calculated to undermine and overthrow some of the most important and vital provisions of their body.' Nor can that apprehension and alarm have been mitigated by the opinion which two eminent chancery lawyers appear to have given, to the effect that their missionary society, their theological institution, their book-room, and all their other funds and institutions, will be subject, not merely to taxation—that, though vexatious and oppressive, is a light matter in comparison—but also to the inquisitorial powers of the commissioners and their inspectors, and, through their office, to the world at large. In short, this bill is more to be dreaded by the Wesleyan body than any bill ever brought into parliament, Lord Sidmouth's itself not excepted.

All classes of Nonconformists, Protestant or Catholic, Wesleyans, Presbyterians, Independents, Baptists, and others, have equal cause to complain of the unjust partiality, as well as of the oppressive character of this bill. Why should Oxford and Cambridge be alone exempt? Why should special visiters and bishops *taboo* church charities from the profane touch of the commissioners? On what principle should such charities be protected, while Nonconformist trusts are exposed to the unrestricted control of this unconstitutional and irresponsible triumvirate? If a declaration of churchmanship is demanded from the trustees of church charities, why should not a declaration of Wesleyanism be required from trustees of Wesleyan chapels—of Independency, from those of Independent chapels, and so on? The Toleration Act, and all similar statutes, are a mockery, a delusion, and a snare, unless as much respect be paid by the legislature to the trust property of all classes of Nonconformists as to that of the established church itself. Add to all, the commissioners may, if they choose, exempt all church charities from the taxing clause of the bill; and, judging from its partial complexion throughout, they probably will.

Happy will it be if the different spirit, in which on this, as on many former occasions, it has been proposed to deal with churchmen and with dissenters, should wake the latter to a due sense of their danger and a due appreciation of their principles. This perpetual meddling with religious interests, carried further at every fresh attempt, can be effectually arrested and put down, only by the entire separation of the church from the state. This bill ought to be resisted by all classes, because of its unconstitutional, jobbing, vexatious, and mischievous character; but it deserves the strenuous opposition of dissenters on account of its atrociously sectarian bias: and yet, so long as exclusive privileges are conferred upon a favoured sect, measures equally bad, if not worse, must be expected, as the natural fruit of such a vicious system of legislation. 'To them that have will be given.' The appetite will grow by that it feeds on; and poor human nature will always delight in adding more privileges to those who already enjoy so many. The union of church and state is the animating principle, the life and soul, of this bill. Let it pass, and it will entail a numerous kindred brood. As infallibly as one triumvirate of commissioners has led to more, will this Charitable Trusts Bill, which lays its sacrilegious hands upon every farthing vested in trust, be followed by other bills pleading the precedent for government interference with popular and voluntary institutions, till at length we shall have no security whatever for doing what we like with our own. Government will utterly consume us: we shall be first worried, and then devoured.

Brief Notices.

Elements of General History, Ancient and Modern, to which are added, a Comparative View of Ancient and Modern Geography, and a Table of Chronology. By Alexander Fraser Tytler; Lord Woodhouslee. A new edition, with additions, and a continuation from 1688 to the present time. Edited by the Rev. Brandon Turner, M.A. London. 12mo. 1846.

THIS respectable manual is decidedly improved in the present edition. But it is proper to remark, that room still exists for more improvement. Admirable as all the summaries of history are, the inaccuracies, and even omissions, are frequent. For example, in a very valuable part of the work—*the comparative view of ancient and modern geography*—ALL the divisions of France into *departments*, are left out, although the page would conveniently have contained them. Then in the list of the old provinces of France, Cambresis and Artois stand opposite to a tribe called by a gross error of the press, the *Artnebates,* instead of the 'Atrebates.' Besides the error, surely neither the author of the manual, nor his respectable editor, can be unaware, that our old connections, the *Morini,* with some half dozen tribes more, belonged, in ancient days, to the modern Cambresis and Artois. In this place it is also a grave mistake to call modern Picardy, Artois, etc., 'Gallia,' as the manual does (p. 243), in contradistinction to ancient Belgium. Again, it seems to be an error to call the Frisii, 'Frisi,' and a more serious one to place the old *Treveri* at 'Namur,' instead of their venerable capital, Tréves. The whole of this chapter requires very careful revision.

A great mistake, of another sort, seems to be committed in the section xli. (p. 171) on Carthage. Generally the work is correctly limited to a perspicuous statement of facts. In this passage an *opinion* is expressed that the Carthaginian principle mentioned by Aristotle, against *one* person holding *several* employments, is censurable, because such plurality is 'both expedient and necessary.' We had thought, with Blackstone, that on the contrary, this principle is good in itself, as it certainly, according to the same high authority, is an English principle, however often infringed. Again, the manual here says, that another Carthaginian principle by which the poor were debarred from all offices of trust, or importance, was wise, 'for in offices of trust poverty offers too powerful an incitement to deviation from duty.' We venture to suggest a reconsideration of this point, and that in a new edition of the manual (which we are sure will be called for), the learned and judicious author and editor prepare a chapter in the History of England on the law of Richard II., c. 12, which expressly enacts that offices of trust be bestowed on the *most worthy,* without one word as to wealth constituting a sign of worth.

An omission of importance occurs in the history of France, viz., as to the *Mississippi Bubble*. Our South Sea bubble is properly mentioned (p. 483). Why is the other left out? Both were equally important events, and intimately connected. Both should be stated in all histories of England and France, for this reason, that whilst the Mississippi bubble helped to lay the foundation of the revolution in France, the South Sea bubble, bad as it was in all other respects, produced no lasting injury to England. The causes of the distinction lie deep in the constitution of the two countries.

With these few friendly censures, we leave the book, with warm recommendations, as one of the most useful to be found for daily reference.

The Native Irish, and their Descendants. By Christopher Anderson. The Third Edition, improved. London: W. Pickering.

A THIRD edition of a very valuable book, carefully revised, and published at half-a-crown only. All who would acquaint themselves with the moral and educational statistics of the Irish people, should give it an attentive perusal.

The Dream of the Lilybell, Tales, and Poems; with translations of the Hymn to Night. From the German of Novalis; and Jean Paul's 'Death of an Angel.' By Henry Morley. 12mo. London: Sherwood.

This is one of the fruits of the taste and industry of a few young men of King's College, London, published some time ago, and added to from the author's after years of study. Perhaps, not a little too dreamy in the choice of his topics, Mr. Morley, nevertheless, proves himself a true votary of the muse; and we trust he will zealously pursue his vocation of vindicator of divine poesy in this utilitarian age. The *Lilybell* and the *Ode* to *beauty*, are charming verses. The author is a true scholar; and he will not say we are hypercritical in remarking, that he should look a little closer to his correction of the press, when quoting Latin. *Meddocra*, in the preface, p. vi., is neither good prose, nor good metre; and it is not the only speck of the kind in a beautifully printed little book.

Lectures on the Pilgrim's Progress, and on the Life and Times of Bunyan. By Rev. George B. Cheever, D.D. London: Thomas Nelson. Glasgow: W. Chalmers.

Two neat and cheap editions of a work, which should have an extensive circulation. The Glasgow reprint is certainly to be preferred, though, in its absence, Mr. Nelson's would be an acquisition. Dr. Cheever's is one of the most fascinating books which we have read for a long time, and cannot fail very deeply to interest every admirer of Bunyan.

A Hand-Book for Lewes, with Notices of the recent discoveries at the Priory. By M. A. Lower, author of 'The Curiosities of Heraldry,' &c. &c. London. 12mo. 1846.

Mr. Lower modestly, but we think incorrectly, sets *Guide-Books* at a very 'humble' standard. His own valuable little work, at least, shews that to the historian, the statist, and the lover of the picturesque, local records and scenes may become attractive when in skilful hands. Forty years ago, we roamed among the scenes described by Mr. Lower, and are grateful to him for having called up by his pen and his pencil, the memory of many spots, which time had begun to obliterate. We hope his next edition will have a good map, with the *foot-paths.*

The Church of Scotland Pulpit. Volume First. pp. 373. London: Simpkin & Marshall. 1845.

This Volume consists of eighteen sermons by clergymen of the Established church of Scotland. Of course it would be impossible to characterize them without specifying the distinctive features of each. Their general character is evangelical and practical—but in them as a whole, we do not discern traces of remarkable talent, learning, or eloquence. As ordinary productions of the pulpit, they are respectable, but we do not deem this enough to justify their publication.

Stories of the Primitive and Early Church. By Sophia Woodrooffe. Edited with an Introduction on the subject by G. S. Faber, B.D. pp. 207. Seeley. 1845.

THESE stories were composed, says the editor, for the better training of the elder children in a sunday-school, and they are now published by Dr. Faber, the uncle of the deceased authoress, with a view to counteract the influence of the *Lives of the English Saints*, which are sent forth by the Romanizing party in the English Church. As to their *original use*, we very much question whether the idea of the fair writer was a good one; and decidedly think, with Dr. Faber, that the style would be *rather* above the comprehension of village children. Looking at them as now presented to the public, we can speak of them in praise. We are sceptical of some things recorded as facts, but rejoice in the sound character of the principles inculcated, and admire the beautiful and classical style, as Dr. Faber justly calls it, in which they are developed. We should say that the editor's contributions to the volume are considerable. He has given an Introduction—many notes—and the last three stories.

The Jesuits: their Origin and Order, Morality and Practices, Suppression and Restoration. By Alexander Duff, D.D Calcutta. pp. 56. Grombridge. 1845.

A VERY comprehensive and vigorously written account of a mighty and mischievous people, who have occupied, and will yet occupy, a prominent position in ecclesiastical and civil affairs. All Protestants ought to understand them thoroughly, and Dr. Duff's pamphlet will be serviceable to those who wish to do so.

Passages from the Life of a Daughter at home. pp. 157. Seeley. 1845.

A TALE, without any incidents of interest, designed to shew the triumph of Christian principle, and the peace of Christian service, in circumstances less noticeable, but far from being less worthy of note, than many which receive much more attention.

Knight's Penny Magazine. Vol. I. London: Charles Knight & Co.

'THE Penny Magazine' has strong claims on the cordial support of the friends of popular literature. For fourteen years it has held steadily on in its honourable course, and has probably done more than any other publication, to diffuse sound and useful knowledge amongst the great body of our people. During the whole of this period it has been under the editorship of Mr. Knight, and we are glad to find that this is to be continued in the new series, now commenced. The connexion of the work with the 'Useful Knowledge' Society has terminated, and the property as well as the editorship has devolved on Mr. Knight. Its form is to be altered, each penny number consisting of sixteen pages instead of eight, with more letter-press on the sheet than formerly, but fewer illustrative wood-cuts. It 'is intended to be for the people of 1846, what the Penny Magazine of the Society for the Diffusion of Useful Knowledge was for the people of 1832.'

We cordially wish success to the undertaking, and strongly advise our readers, especially the younger portion of them, to give orders for this most instructive and interesting periodical to be regularly supplied to them.

Fisher's Gallery of Scripture Engravings, Historical and Landscape. With Descriptions, Historical, Geographical, and Critical. By John Kitto, D.D. Parts I.—V. London: Fisher and Co.

These engravings are already familiar to us, having appeared in other publications of the Messrs. Fisher. Their interest, however, is greatly increased, in the present instance, by the literary illustrations furnished by Dr. Kitto. A wiser selection could not have been made. Dr. Kitto is well known, and his name will be received by the public as an earnest of the able and useful execution of his task. Works of the kind thus furnished at a very reasonable cost, and in handsome style, were until recently the exclusive property of the rich. We rejoice in their more extensive circulation, and shall be glad to promote it. The scenes depicted by the old masters are skilfully combined with landscapes by more modern artists, and the two in connection with Dr. Kitto's labours have left little to be desired. The work is issued in quarto on the 1st and 15th of every month. Each part will contain four highly-finished steel engravings at one shilling each.

The Philosophy of History, in a course of Lectures delivered at Vienna. By Frederick Von Schlegel. Translated from the German, with a *Memoir of the Author*. By James Brown Robertson, Esq. Second Edition. Revised. London: Henry G. Bohn.

Another volume of *The Standard Library*, and well entitled to its place. The readers of history, and our intelligent young men especially, will be glad to avail themselves, through the medium of Mr. Bohn's edition, of the genius and erudition of this distinguished German scholar. The work is now within their means, and may be had at a price which our fathers would have *deemed incredible*.

France Illustrated. Drawings by Thomas Allom, Esq. Descriptions by the Rev. G. N. Wright, M.A. Division IV. London: Fisher and Co.

The fourth division of one of the most beautiful drawing-room volumes which has been on our table, for some time past. It conains ten highly-finished engravings, from drawings by Mr. Allom, and has the additional merit of throwing much light on the tradition, history, customs, architecture, and scenery of our continental neighbours. It is published quarterly, at a low price, and is fully worthy of the patronage it seeks. As a work of light reading, at once instructive and entertaining, richly illustrated, and 'got up' in handsome style, it has been rarely surpassed.

Literary Intelligence.

Just published.

Narrative of the exploring Expedition to the Rocky Mountains, in the year 1842, and to Oregon and North California, in the years 1843—1844. By Brevet-Captain J. C. Fremont, of the Topographical Engineers, under the orders of Colonel J. J. Abert, Chief of the Topographical Bureau, with a Map and Illustrations.

Shakspeare's Dramatic Art, and his relation to Calderon and Goethe. Translated from the German of Dr. Hermann Ulric.

A Doctrinal, Experimental, and Practical Treatise on Effectual Calling. By James Foote, A.M.

A Discourse of Matters pertaining to Religion. By Theodore Parker, Minister of the Second Church in Roxbury, Mass.

The Orthodox Doctrine, regarding the extent of the Atonement, vindicated. By Charles Hodge, D.D. With a recommendatory Preface, by Rev. Dr. Cunningham, Professor McCrie, Dr. Candlish, and Dr. W. Symington.

The Rise and Fall of Papacy. By the Rev. Robert Fleming, Jun. Edited, with a Memoir of the Author, by the Rev. Thomas Thomson.

The School Hand-Book to the Holy Bible. By Rev. Ingram Cobbin, M.A.

The Step-Mother. By J. P. R. James, Esq. 3 vols.

The History of England during the Thirty-years Peace, 1815 to 1845. By Charles Knight. Part II.

Tracts of the British Anti-State Church Association.

Knight's Penny Magazine, Vol. I.

The Modern Orator. Being a Collection of celebrated Speeches of the most distinguished Orators of the United Kingdom. Edmund Burke.

Political Dictionary. Forming a work of Universal Reference both constitutional and legal, and embracing the terms of Civil Administration of Political Economy and Social Relations, and of all the more important Statistical Departments of Finance and Commerce. Part 12—first half.

Notes, Explanatory and Practical, on the Epistles of Paul to the Thessalonians, to Timothy, to Titus, and to Philemon. By Albert Barnes. Reprinted verbatim from the American copy.

The Life of Luther. Written by himself. Collected and arranged by M. Michelet, Member of the Institute, Author of the 'History of France,' &c. Translated by William Hazlitt, Esq.

Historical View of the Literature of the South of Europe. By J. C. L. Simonde De Sismondi. Translated from the original, with Notes, and a Life of the Author, by Thos. Roscoe. Second edition, including all the Notes from the last Paris edition. Two vols.

THE

ECCLECTIC REVIEW

For JUNE, 1846.

Art I.—*Memoirs and Correspondence of the Marquess Wellesley.* By Robert Rouiere Pearce, Esq., in 3 vols. Bentley, 1846.

The able author of these volumes could scarcely have selected a more important period, than the present, for favouring the public with his labours. The victories recently gained, at such tremendous cost, on the banks of the Sutlej, have at least aroused public attention; and the eyes of the world are turning towards Hindostan, to watch the successive developments of British power. In previous articles, we have laid before our readers sketches bearing more or less upon the subject. Our vast oriental empire seems to grow as we gaze! Lord Clive and Warren Hastings were succeeded, in the lapse of years, by a genius greater than themselves. The Marquess Wellesley, with all *their* talents for acquisition or administration, possessed in addition what they had not—an imperial mind. He was the Julius Cæsar of our Prætorian Prefects, yet an admirer of constitutional freedom. His intellect abode in strength, and at the same time was adorned with the charms of eloquence, and the plumage of poetry. With an eye of fire he penetrated and baffled all the intrigues of opponents; he foresaw the day, when England would reign from the Indus to the Irrawaddy, and from the snows of the Himmelaya to Cape Comorin and Ceylon; and his aspirations were, that her sceptre might prove a wand of mercy—not the rod of an oppressor. History will tell his posterity whether these wishes are to be realized.

He was born on the 20th of June 1760, at Dengan Castle in the county of Meath, or according to some, at the residence of the Wellesley family in Grafton Street Dublin. As eldest son of the musical earl of Mornington, his early boyhood found a congenial atmosphere at Eton. Its classical associations never forsook him through life. There he swam and rowed in the waters of the Thames, or pursued 'the flying ball' at cricket along its green margin, and composed Latin and Greek verses, under an intellectual inspiration, which might vie with the sweetest efforts of Gray and Addison. Oxford fanned his love for fame; until the death of his father, on the 22d May 1781, called him from Christchurch to Ireland, rather less than a month before he had attained his majority. Succeeding, like many of our Irish magnates, to ancient honours and embarrassed estates, he voluntarily placed his ancestral property under the management of his mother, to support herself in comfort, and pay off an immense amount of pecuniary obligations contracted by his father. He then directed his care to the education of his brothers and sisters,—William Wellesley Pole, at that time eighteen years old, afterwards Lord Maryborough,—Anne, then aged thirteen, afterwards married to Henry, son of Lord Southampton,—Arthur Wellesley then twelve, the present Duke of Wellington,—Gerald Valerian then ten, now a doctor in divinity, and incumbent of the rich living of Bishops-Wearmouth,—Mary Elizabeth then nine, now Lady Culling Smith,—and Henry, then eight, the present Lord Cowley. Had the only divine of the family been made a bishop, the old Countess of Mornington would have seen all her five sons in the House of Lords at the same time, from the lowest to the highest grade of the peerage; an instance of rare occurrence we believe amongst the annals of our haughty aristocracy. But to return to the hero of these volumes, we cannot forbear noticing, that to him every member of the group was greatly indebted for subsequent advancement in the world.

He entered upon public life, amidst the subsidence of the American war, and the agitations preliminary to the French revolution. It was an age of political giants—of Washington, and Jefferson, and Mirabeau abroad; and at home, of Chatham, Pitt, Fox, Grey, Sheridan, Erskine, Flood, Grattan, Burke, Curran, and Plunket. Great Britain and France were cradling two of the greatest warriors that ever appeared on the battlefields of ancient or modern times. Lord Mornington took his seat in the Irish House of Lords, just after the repeal of Poyning's Law, and just before the patriotic ebullitions attendant upon the Irish volunteers. Always in favour of Catholic emancipation, he nevertheless, as it appears to us, would have disappointed the anticipations of our author, in being prepared to insist, had he been at home on the Union, 'either that Ireland should be completely identified with Great Britain; admitted into the great imperial co-partnership on terms of perfect equality; permitted to participate in all the advantages of our laws, institutions, and customs; or else, that she should be rendered competent to legislate for herself, freely and independently.' Our own ideas are, that he deemed the sister island as a kind of consort to England; claiming a right indeed to great conjugal respect 'as the weaker vessel;' yet still bound to put up with that state of things implied in the proverb—'Where two persons sit upon a horse, one must ride behind!' He strongly advocated economy, and various popular measures, such as the liberty of the press; although this last, as we shall soon perceive, was to be under startling limitations, at least in India and the colonies. He spoke frequently and readily, with some theatrical gesture it was then thought; yet to those who heard him, as we had the pleasure of hearing him, in his maturer years, on the repeal of the Habeas Corpus Act, his animation rarely erred against the rules of good taste. Dublin, in 1785, had been too obscure a theatre for his reputation, so that he procured his return to the English house of commons, first for the borough of Beeralston, then for Saltash, and afterwards for Windsor. William Pitt made him one of his junior lords of the treasury in 1786; after which he spoke on the Rohilla war—on the treaty of commerce with France; besides attacking Lord North, just as the representative for Shrewsbury now does Sir Robert Peel. On the regency question he opposed the pretensions of the Prince of Wales in Ireland, and defended the lord lieutenant. We find him in 1793 a British privy-councillor; in 1796, the custos rotulorum of the county of Meath, and one of the chief remembrancers of the Irish exchequer: whilst, on the 29th of November in 1794, he had married Mademoiselle Roland. As to the iniquitous slave trade, his voice and vote were invariably ranged with those of Wilberforce. He resisted Mr. Dundas's motion for gradual abolition. He moved two amendments successively for its immediate suppression: and denounced the entire traffic as infamous, sanguinary and disgraceful to human nature. His eloquence was ripening into manliness and vigour, with considerable felicity in reply, and much of that classical ornament, which illuminates, even where it fails to astonish or overwhelm. The premier had become rather proud of him. He honoured him with confidence, both public and private. His name was inserted in the grand commission for the affairs of India: and whilst in opposing Mr. Grey's proposition for parliamentary reform, he conciliated his Majesty no less than his minister, his acute intellect struck into the right path for power and human glory. In one word, he was directing his attention to the history and affairs of Hindostan.

In the interim, however, Lord Mornington never failed to watch with deepest interest the development of the tragedies at Paris. His mind had grown nobly capacious, although aristocratic predilections grew with his ambition, and therefore narrowed its range. He might have soared higher than he did, could he but fully have mastered the idea, that crowns and coronets are only motes in the sunbeam, when compared with the emancipation and happiness of millions. On the commencement of the war he threw his influence into the scale of despotism as against liberty. The illusions of an age of chivalry carried captive his excited imagination. Few speeches have produced greater results than that which he delivered in supporting the address to the Crown in January 1794. He reviewed in it the whole French revolution, step by step, holding up sometimes most unfairly, its atrocities, blasphemies, perfidy, violence and cruelty, so as to conceal the genuine sources whence all those originated. The strength of his argument lay in pointing out the spirit of aggression, proselytism, and wanton violation of the rights of other nations on the part of France, although this also had been provoked by the confederacy at Pilnitz, and the proclamations of the Duke of Brunswick. Sheridan replied in one of his most brilliant effusions; as he also did on a subsequent occasion, when Lord Mornington spoke on the Seditious Meetings Bill in 1795. The noble Anti-jacobin was in the mouths of all men. He wrote a copy of Latin verses for the prime minister at Walmer, replete with the most acrimonious denunciations of Gallican politics: but better things were in store for him. Sir John Shore returned home from Calcutta to be created Lord Teignmouth. Mysterious intrigues ensued, which to this hour have never been satisfactorily explained or accounted for. Lord Macartney was passed over, instead of being appointed his successor. The pretensions of Lord Hobart were also happily set aside, although nobody knew how. Lord Cornwallis was at length announced; but as it fell out, quite prematurely: and on the 4th of October 1797, the Earl of Mornington received his nomination to the governor-generalship of India, having been raised also to the rank of a peer of Great Britain, by the title of Baron Wellesley. He sailed from England on the 7th of November following, arriving at the Cape of Good Hope in February 1798; at Madras, on the 26th of April; and on the 17th of May at Fort-William, on the banks of the Hoogley.

India was at that period labouring under a crisis of affairs. The new representative of the sovereign of England approached his capital with pride and admiration. Calcutta, as our author well says, may be described as 'the city of the sun, glittering with palaces, gardens and groves, with branching banian-trees, noble palms of every variety, bright green peepuls, and tall bamboos and flowers of every hue.' But Lord Mornington was not so dazzled by the beautiful, as to overlook the danger. The career of Hyder Ali, and his son Tippoo Saib, had placed British power more than once in eminent jeopardy. France was still gloating over a hope of recovering her lost ground in Hindoostan through her alliance with Tippoo. The sultan of Mysore, at the close of the war in 1784, possessed treasure to the extent of £80,000,000 sterling, besides eight hundred thousand stand of arms, and two thousand pieces of artillery, with military stores in proportion. His regular army of infantry and cavalry mustered upwards of a hundred thousand men; whilst his dominions lay almost in the centre of the peninsula, like the lair of a beast of prey inaccessible to the hunters. In 1791, when hostilities had broken out afresh, the Mysorean forces were menacing the very gates of Madras: nor was it, until Lord Cornwallis was storming Seringapatam in the following year, that the son of Hyder consented to accept moderate conditions. 'By the treaty of peace, he was compelled to cede half his territories to the British, the Nizam, and the Mahrattas,—to pay £3,500,000 sterling as the expenses of the war; to deliver up all the prisoners whom he held in captivity, and to surrender his two sons as hostages.' The object of his conqueror was to establish a balance of power, such as might guarantee a continuance of tranquillity. Before long, however, it had become sufficiently apparent, that all this idea was 'as a dream when one awaketh.' During the administration of Sir John Shore, the Soubahdar of the Deccan had been attacked, and his efficiency nearly annihilated by the Mahrattas. Tippoo merely waited his time for revenging himself upon the British, allying himself with the French, and realizing his ambitious schemes with greater certainty than ever. His capabilities for doing mischief had been augmenting for five years, when the new Governor-General rightly judged that he was a tiger in the jungles of oriental politics, not to be trifled or tampered with, but to be either caged or destroyed! The majority of our civil servants at the presidencies, if not quite intellectual pigmies and caitiffs, were, at all events, made of such wretched materials, that no sooner had his lordship announced intentions of attacking Mysore, than they turned pale as ashes, remonstrated on his rashness, and even gently hinted at impeachment on his return home. Instead of quailing at their predictions and pusillanimity, he demonstrated, with unanswerable arguments, the treachery to which they were trusting; that the enemy had already violated in spirit every article of a pacification of which he was about to denounce even the letter; and that, unless they were prepared to crush Tippoo, the latter within less than a few months would be quite ready to crush them. The sorcery of a strong mind over weak ones immediately appeared. Lord Mornington infused his own energies into the various officials around and below him, from the highest commander on his staff to the humblest writer and subaltern on the coast of Coromandel. He left the court of Mysore under the hallucination that he was blind to the approaching conflict. He laid quietly a thousand trains of policy, each perfectly adapted to its purpose, so as to be ready when requisite for the grand occasion. He baffled native intrigue, and the most secret designs of foreign statesmanship. The Nizam, for instance, had been suffered to take into his pay an enormous French corps, which his Excellency contrived to disband without bloodshed, and substitute British troops in its stead. Napoleon was then meditating his Indian invasion, by way of the Euphrates, as Alexander, Tamerlane, and Nadir Shah had done before him. Persia and Affghanistan were co-operating with him on the one hand, and at the same moment with Tippoo Saib on the other. The last had expressly invited Zemaun Shah, the chieftain of Cabul and Candahar, to fall upon Scinde, and join with the entire anti-British confederacy, from Paris to Seringapatam, in the re-establishment of Islamism. It really does strike us, on a calm review of the past, that under Divine Providence, the existence, not to say the expansion of our oriental sway, turned upon the accession of such a man as Lord Mornington to the helm of Indian government.

As the struggle visibly approached, he removed from Fort William to Madras, that he might be nearer the scene of operations. Here it was his habit to prepare his papers, and dictate his orders, in an avenue of magnificent trees attached to his residence. Whilst thus employed, surrounded with secretaries in the open air, pacing up and down, before the power of the sun had got too intense, it failed not to attract the superstitious notice of the natives, that the Uma, or small Indian eagle, came and built her nest in the branches over his head. This was considered a presage of success, no less by the Hindoo, than the Parsee. Events rapidly justified and illustrated the policy which his Excellency had adopted. Before any open attack commenced, he expostulated with the Sultan by letter; unveiling to him, now that the British were ready, a perfect acquaintance on their part, with his recent conduct, and manifest designs. Tippoo, after various evasions, at length replied, with every conceivable expression of friendship, that he was going on a hunting expedition; which really meant that he was just about to assault the lines of General Stuart at Seedapore. This was five days before General Harris entered the Mysore, so that he was an aggressor from the commencement. The Governor-General now issued his declaration in the name of the British government and their allies. Defeat awaited Tippoo at every turn; and on his final retreat to his fortified capital, the tremendous toils of warfare closed around him. Once and again he hinted at an arrangement of terms, but it was too late. On the 30th of April, 1799, breaching batteries opened a heavy fire against the walls of Seringapatam. Two days afterwards an enormous magazine of rockets blew up in the town with a most fearful explosion, 'spreading death and consternation amongst the inhabitants.' The fiery tempest of shot and shell then raged incessantly around the devoted battlements, within which the cruel, yet gallant despot, conducted himself with unmoved resolution. His veteran garrison consisted of twenty thousand troops, with plenty of provisions, and ample means for defence: so that when the British advanced across the river, he addressed his officers with these words,—'we have arrived at the last stage; what is your determination?' They all replied,—'*To die with you!*' He trusted in the strength of his fortress, which had twice repulsed the English, and in the near approach of the rainy season. On the 4th of May, General Baird, at the head of a storming party of 2500 Europeans and 1800 Sepoys, lay ready in the trenches. At one o'clock the signal was given. Baird, drawing his sword, exclaimed, 'Now, my brave fellows, follow me, and prove yourselves British soldiers!' In ten minutes our colours were waving on the walls!

'The attack was made during the heat of the day, when Asiatics usually take their meridian repast, and resign themselves to a season of repose. When the alarm of the assault reached Tippoo he was sitting at dinner under a covered shed. He instantly washed his hands, seized his arms, and mounted his horse. On his way to the ramparts he was told that his general, Seyd Goffar, was killed. 'Seyd Goffar,' he said, 'never feared death; let Mohammed Cassim take charge of his division.' Tippoo opposed himself in person to the left column of the British, and for a time checked their advance; he then dismounted, and on foot animated his soldiers, by firing with his own hands against his adversaries. He was the last man to quit the traverses, and did not leave his post till the impetuosity of the British soldiers drove every thing before them. Two columns of the 12th regiment, one within, the other outside the gate, now poured in a destructive cross fire. The sultan, who had before received a musket ball in the right side, now received another wound. His horse, which he had remounted, was shot under him, and his turban fell to the ground. Some faithful servants then placed him in his palanquin, but being unable to proceed over the heaps of slain, he again sprang upon his feet, and endeavoured to escape. Several British soldiers, just entering the gate, encountered him. One of them, ignorant of his person, but attracted by his jewels, attempted to pull off his sword-belt; but Tippoo, disdaining to surrender himself a prisoner, or announce his rank, wounded the soldier, in the knee with his sabre. The enraged Englishman pointed his musket at the sultan's head, and Tippoo fell a corpse. The moment that possession was obtained of Seringapatam, a strict search was instituted for him: his body was found under a heap of slain: his eyes were open: and stripped of every ornament but his cherished amulet, he was still warm when Colonel Wellesley, who commanded the reserve, which was not employed in the assault, came up. Thus perished this formidable enemy of the British power in India; and thus perished likewise the hopes of those who aimed at the re-establishment of French influence in Hindostan!'—Vol. i. pp. 299-300.

A secret messenger was forthwith dispatched by General Harris to the Governor-General with the glad tidings enclosed in a sealed quill, on account of the disturbed state of the country. The spoils of the Mysore were immense; and the captors proposed setting apart £100,000 of the prize-money for Lord Mornington, who generously declined the gift. His political arrangements, consequent upon the fall of Tippoo Saib, are universally admitted to have been most masterly. He secured the permanent dominion of the British sceptre. He added twelve lacs of pagodas to the annual revenues of the Company, besides strengthening their frontier by establishing a continuity of territory from sea to sea,—from the coast of Coromandel to that of Malabar. None. however, imitated his disinterestedness with regard to the booty. Grievous stains will ever remain upon the escutcheons of various high parties concerned in these memorable transactions. Meanwhile, his Excellency, having received the thanks of both Houses of Parliament at home, with an advance to an Irish marquisate in the peerage, now turned his attention to other public matters. He had dealt very summarily with the press at Calcutta,* when he deemed its freedom

* This refers to what we have already alluded to. His lordship had ordered in April, 1799, that no paper should be published until it had been submitted to government inspection! One editor was sent back to Europe for an infringement of the censorship. All these, and similar proceedings, were certainly 'more in consonance with Asiatic despotism than the enlightened views formerly advocated by the noble lord in College-green!' Calcutta, however, at that period, was very much in the state of a citadel during siege; and whilst in such circumstances, who was to define the precise limits of the maxim *Necessitas non habet legem!*

likely to become prejudicial to the general welfare; and he now suppressed Sunday newspapers. His augmented influence was also thrown generally into the scale of Christianity. He looked favourably upon missions amongst the heathen; endeavoured to set an example in attending public worship; ordained a day of thanksgiving for the recent successes in the Mysore; and sanctioned with all cordiality the well-known sermon preached by Doctor Claudius Buchanan on that occasion. His conduct on these points must not be explored or estimated by the *present* state of public opinion upon such subjects; but rather, we should call to mind the practical atheism which then widely prevailed at the Presidencies. He was the first eminent Governor-General who dared openly to acknowledge the true God in the face and amidst the murmurs of a hundred millions of pagans. Nor was his interest in the welfare of the Peninsula a mere speculative one, when he had sheathed the sword. Its secular, as well as spiritual and intellectual improvement, lay deeply in his thoughts. He aimed at collecting information as to the character and capabilities of every section of its vast territories; as to the vegetables and mode of cultivation suited to the various soils,—as to machinery for irrigation,—as to the different breeds of cattle, the extent and tenures of farms, the price and nature of labour,—the growth of corn, cotton, pepper, cardamums, and sandal-wood. The whole history of caste occupied him in all its bearings. Commerce and manufactures came in for their full share of his observation. His lordship had become imbued with the liberal notions of Adam Smith to an extent surprising in any member of our aristocracy; and were he now alive, his fine intellect would no doubt shed sunbeams of light in a certain very dark house of incurable monopolists. Even forty years ago he could discern that freedom is the life of trade; and nine-tenths of the acrimonious opposition, afterwards destined to await him, sprung from the soundness of his views, on topics which interfered with official extortion and private rapacity. Hence arose, too, his unmeasured abhorrence of what he describes as 'the ignominious tyranny of Leadenhall-street.' He loved India and detested the India House: although, as he told Lord Castlereagh, 'no outrage, injury, or insult which could issue from its most loathsome den,' should ever be suffered to interfere with his devotedness to the national service.

The Marquess Wellesley always carefully calculated the use that might be made of those tributary sovereigns and chieftains, whose successors have dwindled into political phantoms. He negotiated with the Nizam and the Mahrattas, with the Nabobs of Surat and Nepaul; or rather with the rajah of the last, who had taken refuge at Benares. Even Burmah was not overlooked:

whilst, in a different direction, an embassy was sent into Persia, as well as another to the Imaum of Muscat. His lordship well knew that every spell of orientalism must be watched. With the tyrants of the Carnatic, the governors of Madras had always been in relations of a most delicate, and sometimes dangerous kind, until the fall of Seringapatam unveiled the criminality of their intrigues, and subjugated them under the British sway. At the peace of Amiens there occurred several felicitous delays, which enabled Lord Wellesley to pause before giving back to the French their fortresses and settlements in Hindostan. In fact, this was never done at all, so that Gallican influence gained no opportunity for reinstatement: and when the horrors of war recommenced, the foresight of his Excellency had prepared the means for both defence and assault at every point. Those were not the days for rapid intercommunication: and on one occasion, seven clear months elapsed without a single gleam of intelligence from England. Nevertheless, an expedition set sail from India for the Red Sea, and rendered most important services in that quarter. It was about the same period, also, that the kingdom of Oude had to cede some of its richest territories to the Company, through the admirable management of their representative, but for which he was afterwards more violently condemned than for any other portion of his policy. The following are the remarks of our biographer:—

'In the discussion of this and kindred topics, Mr. Mill has chosen to assume as a fundamental principle, that the British government in India had no right to assert in its negotiations *a superiority over the native powers;* but that we were bound to deal with the sovereigns of India on the same terms of equality as we should be with any of the established monarchs of Europe. It would be the greatest hypocrisy, if we were to affect a concession of any such doctrine. Our whole course in India is directly opposed to it. No British statesman, it may be safely affirmed, would venture to act upon such a figment. *England stands confessedly in India as an ascendant power, invested with supremacy, in virtue of European civilization and Anglo-Saxon energy;* which have committed to England a mission to put an end to the frightful disorders and manifold evils which have afflicted the unhappy natives, under the sway of sanguinary and despotic monarchs, whose right to their thrones has usually been based upon violence, deceit, and blood; and who have existed to scourge and afflict, and not to afford the protection of just government to their subjects. To deal with Asiatic kings, who lived by oppression and every species of misrule, and whose absolute authority was exercised without any reference to the inclinations of the people, on whom they trampled, and the *rights of whose ancestors* were not unfrequently based upon the poinard and poisoned chalice, as if they were constitutional sovereigns, supported by the patriotic sentiments of grateful subjects, would appear to be in the highest degree preposterous. The British government in India had clearly a right to interpose in the affairs of any of the native states, the disorders and misgovernment of which disturbed their own dominions; first, on the natural principle of self-preservation, which justifies every legitimate power in taking security for its safety: secondly, because, wherever the British standard is raised in India, the reign of the assassin and plunderer is suspended, and the protection of British justice is afforded to the native population. To place the personal rights of the native sovereigns of Asia, reigning by brute force, without the assent of their subjects, in opposition to the comprehensive plans of a great statesman for the consolidation of British power in India, and for the amelioration of the condition of the people, (assuming that these plans are calculated to secure such ends), is surely little better than trifling with a serious subject.'—Vol. ii., pp. 132, 3.

That there is fundamental soundness in these observations, perhaps few will dispute; and for that reason we have transcribed them; as also because we fully believe that utility (using that term in its most comprehensive sense) furnishes the only rational plea for our entire policy towards Hindostan. In one word, we maintain that in the counsels of Divine providence, European civilization is destined, for the advantage of all, to supersede and supplant oriental systems: whilst at the same time, the honest view of the Roman must be carried out and realized—*Unum debet esse omnibus propositum, ut eadem sit Utilitas uniuscujusque et universorum, quam si ad se quisque rapiat, dissolvetur omnis humana consortio.* That Lord Wellesley entered into the spirit of Cicero, on such points, can scarcely be doubted; and that he was fretted almost to death, by the narrowness and selfishness of many persons officially connected with him, both at home and abroad, is plain enough. He had formed the magnificent design of founding a college for India, which should disseminate the light of knowledge throughout a benighted land; respecting which, nothing could exceed the consternation occasioned amongst the owls and bats of Leadenhall-street. He demonstrated in vain, that their civil and military servants possessed no other regular course of training or study, to fit them for their arduous and important duties. He appealed in vain to the claims of native millions yet unborn, whom the Company had undertaken to provide for, by the very fact of having resolved to govern them. With sundry exceptions, for which we think liberal allowance may be made, looking at the time and circumstances, the regulations were admirably drawn up. The institution was even permitted to commence its career, and bring forth such first-fruits as none but an East Indian director could doubt or condemn. It was the darling object which lay close to the heart of Lord Wellesley; nor could he ever forgive its extinction, nor disguise his contempt and abhorrence for those who contributed to bring about so calamitous a measure. The venerable names of Buchanan and Carey will for ever be connected with his own; and as the Professor of Sanscrit once told him, on a memorable public occasion, 'No revolution of opinion, nor change of circumstances, could rob him of the solid glory derived from the humane, just, liberal, and magnanimous principles, which were happily embodied in his administration.' The present Haileybury College, near Hertford, formed a tardy tribute to the truthfulness and spirit of the Governor-general; and the time, we trust, will yet arrive, when a real 'University of Calcutta will illustrate the renown, and accomplish the mighty ends, which the founder of Fort William College hoped to have seen achieved in his own day.' His lordship had not merely wished to raise the tone of intellect and ability amongst the Company's servants; but he acted upon a plan of conscientious distribution, with regard to his patronage, which it would have been well if his successors had imitated. In appointing to offices, he was solely guided by the personal respectability and capacity of the candidates for them. No letters of recommendation, no family connexion, no aristocratic influence, had the smallest weight with him. Talent and integrity were the only roads to lucrative employment or professional distinction. Hence it came to pass that he was surrounded by able and sedulous adherents, who conducted every department of the public service, under the fullest impression of a direct and immediate responsibility to an executive always ready to appreciate and reward their honest efforts. Even the natives looked up and admired. They heard, perhaps with some natural mistrust, that eight versions of the sacred scriptures were translated under his auspices, in the new seminary he was attempting to create and support: they were probably somewhat startled at the fact, that to its walls more than one hundred of their learned countrymen had resorted for studying European literature and philosophy: they were positively amazed at his success in suppressing the sacrifice of children and other human victims at Saugor, as also that he contemplated the utter abolition of suttees: but at the same moment, they felt that he desired to be their friend, father, patron, and benefactor; and they gazed upon his new palace at Calcutta as the pledge of his taste and munificence, as well as the emblem of a better era.

He remained in India, after the renewal of hostilities between this kingdom and France, to superintend the settlement of the Mahratta war. The military triumphs at Delhi, Laswaree,

Assaye, and Arghaum, are matters of general history. Suffice it to say, that Lord Wellesley effectually broke the power of Holkar, and secured fresh acquisitions of territory and revenue for those whom he served. His return to England, in January, 1806, occurred during the last days of his old friend the premier. On the death of Mr. Pitt, and after the joint administration of the Fox and Grenville party, the Duke of Portland, as is well known, became the nominal head of a feeble and disreputable ministry, whom Lord Wellesley was requested by his Majesty to join, but which he declined doing. One of his most successful efforts, as an orator, was made in defence of the expedition to Copenhagen; and whatever may be the views of ourselves or readers as to that transaction, there can be but one opinion as to the transcendant ability and elaborate eloquence displayed by him on the painful occasion. Mr. Paull now brought forward his charges against the marquess, in the House of Commons, grounded upon his Indian measures, with regard to Oude,—a course followed up subsequently by Lord Folkestone. Parliament, however, not merely rejected the imputations, but sanctioned Lord Wellesley throughout: nor did Sir Thomas Turton succeed better, when he brought forward the Carnatic question. During the Spanish struggle, which commenced in 1808, Lord Wellesley went out to Seville as our ambassador extraordinary. Here his utmost endeavours in supporting his gallant brother, the present Duke of Wellington, were frustrated. Nothing could exceed the neglect and apathy of the Spanish government, except, indeed, its intolerable arrogance, which would seem not to have abated an iota since the days of Charles v. and Philip II.! The battle of Talavera had been fought in vain, and the British general had declared his resolution to retire into Portugal. Meanwhile, all was in confusion at home and abroad. Supplies were wasted, Wellington was retreating, the people were murmuring, our brave and meritorious soldiers were starving, the French were triumphing, Napoleon had married, two British ministers indulged themselves in a duel, and Lord Wellesley could only solicit his recall to London. Happily, on the death of the Duke of Portland, towards the close of 1809, the marquess entered upon the office of Foreign Secretary. But one opinion prevailed as to the desirableness of this appointment, which enabled him effectually to cooperate in advancing the peninsular war. For two years his whole mind was drawn out in resisting popular clamour, persuaded, as he was, that the victory over Buonaparte was only to be won by defeating his projects upon Madrid and Lisbon. Results certainly demonstrated the depth of his foresight. Nor was the Foreign Office, at that particular juncture, a bed of roses. The Berlin and

Milan decrees had embroiled us with America, and almost exorcised from the shadows of the past that formidable spectre, which had haunted our forefathers, under the banners of an armed neutrality. It required more than an ordinary acquaintance with Vattel and Grotius to combat Messieurs Pinkney and Monroe, as well as the whole force of continental opinion. Never was the web of European policy in a greater tangle. Then ensued the permanent insanity of George III. Both houses recognized the constitutional and democratic doctrines respecting a regency. Lord Wellesley continued in office, despising Mr. Percival, loathing the Prince of Wales, appealing energetically to parliament on behalf of the worthless Ferdinand, and declaring that he would watch the last expiring breath of Spanish patriotism, rather than flinch from its side for a moment. We may, and do regret, that *such* energies should have been expended upon *such* subjects; and yet it must not be forgotten, that when Lord Liverpool put the question to Lord Wellington, 'Would it be desirable to withdraw from the contest?'—his answer was, that '*the war would be then transferred to our own shores!*' The heroic brother of Lord Wellesley returned this response from behind his impregnable lines of Torres Vedras, at the foot of which, Massena's army of eighty thousand soldiers was wasting away like a snow-wreath. The expulsion of the enemy from Portugal at length turned the tide of mob-enthusiasm. To maintain the contest in the Peninsula grew to be just as popular, as some months before it had been the reverse. These realms groaned, in fact, under the tyranny of some of the ignoblest mediocrities of mankind, with the exception of here and there such a mind as that of Lord Wellesley. But he had now resolved to withdraw from the cabinet. How, indeed, could he continue to bend his neck under the yoke of his colleagues. Assassination alone, lamentable as it was, has snatched the name of his wretched premier from infamy. The prejudices of Lord Liverpool lay like a load of lead upon every movement; and so the seals of the Foreign Office were resigned into the hands of the Regent, on the 19th of February, 1812.

Lord Wellesley was amongst the warmest advocates for catholic emancipation. It was trusted, but in vain, that when George III. had ceased to reign, the veto of the crown would no longer be cast into the scale of bigotry and intolerance. The marquess distinguished himself during the animated 'war of eloquence,' all through the session of 1812, by many noble efforts on the side of toleration and justice. He declared that he knew the genuine state of the Irish ecclesiastical establishment; how that 'in a very great degree it consisted of bishops without clergy,—of churches without clergymen, and of clergymen without churches,—of parishes, considerable in extent, without congregations,—of many districts consolidated into one, with a common church too remote to resort to.' His quiet caustic sarcasm told exceedingly at the time. We may still feel a debt of obligation to him for such sentiments as the following:—

'I insist that it is contrary to natural justice to inflict any disability upon any class, and to exclude them from the ordinary advantage of the constitution, unless the security of the state necessarily demand the exclusion. I say it is *primâ facie* a gross injustice, which can be qualified only by the clearest proof of its necessity. It is not only contrary to natural justice, but I contend it is contrary also to the spirit of the Christian religion, to impose disabilities merely on account of religious opinions; and I say that these catholic disabilities are, in reality, merely imposed on that account.'—Vol. iii., p. 293.

The violent death of Mr. Perceval brought about an advance, on the part of the high tories, towards both Mr. Canning and the subject of these memoirs; yet neither would consent to compromise his convictions with regard to the Roman catholics. After the successful motion of the late Lord Wharncliffe, for an address of the lower house, the Marquess Wellesley received an authorization from the Prince of Wales to form a government. All his efforts, however, failed, as he ventured to avow in his place as a peer, 'in consequence of the most dreadful personal animosities, and the most terrible difficulties, arising out of complicated and important questions.' Being called upon to explain what he meant by these expressions, his lordship declared that 'he had used them *advisedly* with reference to the Earl of Liverpool and his colleagues, from whom only the obstacles, to which he had alluded, had arisen.' Through that singular conjuncture of circumstances, which no mortal could have then anticipated, Lord Liverpool became first lord of the Treasury for fifteen years, without any right to, or qualification for so elevated and important a position; excepting that he inherited an earldom, stroked the House of Lords, and was not positively disagreeable to his royal Highness the regent.

After these events, the victories of our gallant soldiers having brought the allies to Paris, the blockades and restrictions upon trade were suspended through the peace of 1814. It is not a little interesting, under present political apprehensions and expectations, to observe the course pursued by Lord Wellesley in the grand corn-law controversy. The average prices of wheat for the previous ten years had been ninety shillings a quarter, which was considered a very fair rate, when the peers appointed their committee, and resolved that the importation of corn should be absolutely prohibited, until the price rose to eighty shillings! Violent commotions ensued in the agricultural, and more particularly the manufacturing districts. The military were called out in London, where the populace surrounded the two houses of parliament, and hooted obnoxious members of the legislature. Even Mr. Wilberforce records in his diary, that three soldiers, and one peace-officer, regularly attended his family prayers. On this iniquitous measure passing through the lords and commons, the Marquess Wellesley, together with Lord Grenville, drew up an able protest against it, setting forth that all public prosperity must be best promoted by leaving the currents of industry uncontrolled,—that no legislature ought to tamper with the sustenance of the people,—that to confine the consumer of corn to the produce of his own country, is to refuse to ourselves the benefit of that provision which Providence has made for equalizing the variations of season and climate,—that it must be impolitic to give a bounty to the grower, by a tax levied upon the consumer,—and that the profits expected would be derived from an unsound, because an artificial system, even if the sanguine anticipations of the landed interest should be at all realized. Events form the fairest commentary upon these sagacious suggestions. The wonder is that, for thirty years, oppression has been able to override justice; and that a juggle should have lasted so long, and been suffered to produce such disastrous results, whilst our thousands have been multiplying into myriads, our villages growing up into towns, our towns swelling into cities, with haggard poverty and gaunt famine perpetually stalking through the land! As already intimated, with respect to his notions on free trade, maintained even in India, Lord Wellesley shone conspicuously amongst his colleagues and contemporaries; so that Great Britain remained without excuse, for the follies to which men then adhered, who might easily have known better, had they not been too selfish to love their country, and too dull to understand their own interests.

His voice indeed was now raised as loudly against our foreign policy, as against our domestic and internal regulations. He denounced the entire conduct of the congress of Vienna, as well as the previous treaty of Fontainebleau. He considered that the Bourbons had been imposed upon France in a manner so humiliating to her feelings, that the escape of Bonaparte from Elba, and the subsequent events of the Hundred Days, were matters not difficult to be accounted for. He struggled strongly, in conjunction with Lord Lansdowne, for a large reduction in our military establishments; and generally, for the application of the pruning-knife to every department of the state. His condemnation of the income tax was clear, from first to last: and whilst he pitied the distress and discontent of the working classes, he nobly opposed the suspension of the Habeas Corpus Act. His whiggism, however, did not prevent his appointment as viceroy of Ireland, in 1821, when that unhappy island was in a state of insurrection, worse than it is now, or has been since, —when neither life nor property were safe,—when 'formidable bodies of armed men, bound together by secret oaths, spread terror and desolation through the country,'—when the mail-coaches were intercepted and plundered,—when the royal troops were, on several occasions, under cover of night, openly encountered by the marauders. With the help of an insurrection act, Lord Wellesley restored, at least, the semblance of external order, and, for several years, amidst the most appalling excitement, his administration held on its way, from the tumults in 1822, about decorating King William's statue, to the celebrated scene at the theatre, when a glass bottle, thrown from the upper galleries, had very nearly conferred the fate of Abimelech upon the head of the conqueror of Tippoo Saib. Orangemen abhorred his liberality in treating the catholics as fellow-subjects with themselves. Catholics conceived that little was effected, so long as emancipation was withheld. Nevertheless, there had never been before a lord-lieutenant to be compared with him. He had imitated, towards contending parties, the decision of Luther at the Reformation: he had thwarted the tyranny of exclusiveness, and the greediness of the clergy. He introduced economy throughout the public expenditure: he achieved the removal of various obnoxious and hateful imposts: he brought about a remission of the Union duties, which acted prejudicially against the commerce of Ireland. Preparations were made for a national system of education. He purified the Augean stable of Irish magistracy and jobbery: establishing petty sessions, appointing assistant barristers, administering impartial justice through unexceptionable judicial appointments, organizing an efficient police, extinguishing, for the time, secret and illegal societies, and mitigating the severity of the atrocious tithe system. He recognized no religious, or political differences, at his public levees: and when, in October 1825, he married a catholic lady, the grand-daughter of a celebrated republican, Carrol of Carrolstown, (who signed the declaration of American independence,) the Castle and Phœnix-park were thronged with all shades of opinion, amidst the pious horror of noblemen, like the Earl of Roden, or journals like the Record newspaper. He resigned on the dissolution of the Canning ministry, or, rather, on the appointment of his brother, the Duke of Wellington as premier.

After the emancipation of the Catholics in 1829, which he had advocated for forty years, he was nominated Lord Steward of the Household to William the Fourth, when that monarch had consigned the helm of affairs to Earl Grey. His views on parliamentary reform had been essentially modified, through lapse of time, since he had opposed the celebrated motion in 1793. In 1833, he resumed the government of Ireland, with Mr. Littleton, his son-in-law, as chief secretary. It is now generally admitted, that he administered the coercion bill 'with firmness, yet with clemency and sound discretion.' His comprehensive plans, however, for the final pacification of the sister kingdom, were suddenly interrupted by the unexpected dismissal of the Whigs in 1834: nor is it any longer a secret, that the famous appropriation clause, which, for an interval of more than five years, substituted Lord Melbourne in the place of Sir Robert Peel, was drawn up by his masterly hand. In 1835, after holding the post of Lord Chamberlain, for one month only, he retired from public life, in his seventy-fifth year, 'to spend the evening of his days in the society of a numerous circle of friends, and in those classical and elegant pursuits, which, at all periods of his life, had been his delight and solace.' His '*Primitiæ et Reliquiæ*,'—a volume of Latin, English, and Greek poems, written, many of them, in his eighty-first year, exhibit 'an astonishing degree of freshness and intellectual beauty.' The inscription to the memory of Miss Brougham will remind the reader of those exquisite lines of Bishop Lowth on the death of his favourite daughter Mary: nor have we ever perused any modern elegy more touching than his lordship's lines on the 'Ruins of Jerusalem.' It is melancholy to reflect, that his pecuniary affairs were inextricably involved in debt and embarrassment; so that even the additional grant of £20,000, besides his annuity of £5000 per annum, from the East India Company scarcely, as we have heard, reached its proper destination. His dispatches were handsomely printed at the cost of the same parties, for wide distribution through the three presidencies: and on the 17th of March, 1841, it was resolved, that a marble statue should be erected to his honour, in the India House. He expired at his residence, Kingston-house, Brompton, on the morning of Monday, the 26th of September, 1842, in the eighty-third year of his age: and was buried in the chapel of Eton College, amidst the sympathies of an enormous throng of illustrious individuals, who manifested, by their tears and lamentations, that no ordinary man had departed from amongst them.

Our empire in India constitutes the mightiest monument to his memory. He added to it, either by arms or negotiation, about one hundred and forty thousand square miles of territory, forty millions of population, and nearly £10,000,000 sterling of annual revenue! 'It was his glorious destiny,' observed one of his admirers, 'to place our power in Hindostan, in a position of honour and safety which it had never before attained. His energetic mind, embracing in one comprehensive view, all the elements of Indian policy, enabled him to combine them for the benefit alike of that country and his own. He selected with unerring and intuitive judgment the instruments best calculated to carry out his magnificent plans; while by the force of that influence, which great minds exercise over their fellow-men, he imbued them with his own spirit, and directed vast, distant, and complicated operations, with a degree of precision, scarcely to be looked for in the most ordinary transactions.' In other words, he united in his own person, the characteristics of a Roman Consul with those of a British statesman. The seven years of his Indian administration surpassed the achievements of Lucullus, and the triumphs of Pompey the Great. He conquered both for the present and the future. His political arrangements became just so many processes for immediate security, and subsequent aggrandisement. He attempted to *Europeanise* orientalism, if we may be permitted to use such a phrase. His grand object was to realize the eastern fable of a sovereign, who wore upon his brow a circlet of diamonds, in whose talismanic lustre were concentrated the existence and prosperity of his realm. As to his Irish Viceroyalty, if it was less splendid in incident and circumstance, it was by no means unimportant as to the welfare of these kingdoms. Had catholic emancipation been conceded in time, had his ideas been acted upon with regard to the annihilation of protestant ascendancy,—had he but been permitted to conciliate, where others only exasperated,—had he not been checked and thwarted by his subordinates and underlings,—the sister island might have presented a far different aspect than that in which it now appears. He was born to govern men, and to lay his fingers upon the main-springs of society. As an ambassador and a minister,—as a nobleman and a courtier, his mien and habits of business were dignified and graceful. His style, as an orator, seemed too often diffuse, yet never wearisome. There was always an invaluable vein of good sense running through his longest speeches: whilst his dispatches are clear and luminous beyond parallel. Yet he acted better than he spoke,—and reasoned better than he wrote. 'His person was small and symmetrical,—his face remarkable for intellectual beauty:' his voice was modulated to his subject: and those who listened were generally charmed! *Qui semel auditor semper amicus erat.* He possessed a host of friends, attracted by his gentle and affectionate disposition, his fine sensibilities, his exquisite taste in literature, his high sense of honour as a man and as a companion, and by his generosity bordering upon profuseness. Indeed, as to the last, there was an undoubted lack of prudence; perhaps with some failure in virtue. His temperament manifested, at one period of his life, a trace of the voluptuary: and to the last, in our humble judgment, had a touch of the sultan about it. There appeared more of the loftiness of aristocratic magnificence, than was quite suited to the emancipator of the catholic and the negro, or the conscientious advocate of free trade. In private life he was happier latterly than formerly. His first wife lived apart from him, after his return from India, until her death in 1816: nor were they ever reconciled. We are not informed as to the precise position of their children: nor is it our wish in these pages to meddle with domestic scandal.

The author of these volumes has acquitted himself well throughout his somewhat arduous labours. There is a manliness of thought and independence of manner about them, which are exceedingly attractive. His own reflections are very little intruded upon the reader, and indeed we think there might now and then have been more of them with advantage. We should have preferred the exclusion of certain lengthy and unnecessary documents: and to have had their space occupied with sketches of personages, and summaries of events, which serve to refresh both the biographer and the reader; and which also enable the former to philosophize, at suitable intervals, for the edification of the latter. The chapters now and then seem mere meagre enlargements of the table of contents; nor is there always that unbroken continuity of narrative, which carries the attention forward through the main series of scenes, whilst subsidiary incidents are made to succeed each other in agreeable perspective, without producing either fatigue or distraction. Occasionally, also, there occur exceedingly common-place observations; with a few, which sadly violate all rules of right feeling and good taste,—such as the comparison for example, of Messrs. O'Connell and Shiel, to Moses and Aaron! The biographer, we know, will pardon our freedom, as amongst the genuine marks of real regard from old friends and honest admirers. The three frontispieces to the volumes are beautiful specimens of art, and we recommend the entire work to the enlightened public.

Art. II.—*Sermons preached at St. Paul's Cathedral, the Foundling Hospital, and several Churches in London; together with Others addressed to a Country Congregation.* By the late Rev. Sydney Smith, Canon Residentiary of St. Paul's Cathedral. Longman and Co.

'Our very priests must become mockers, if they shall encounter such ridiculous subjects as you are.' So old Menenius addressed the tribunes. There may be, then, an apology for a 'mocking priest.' We do not affirm that ridicule is the test of truth, for truth is the only test of the ridiculous. But humour may be healthy and have its use: satire and sarcasm are arrow and javelin of good report and avail; nor do we see how we could live at all amicably and good naturedly in this world if we might not laugh at it. The feeling is uncontrollable. The great thing is to ascertain 'the time to laugh.' Nor ought laughter to be often merry,—jocund,—holding both its sides,—it becomes it to rise into contempt and scorn! The little, the mean, the crooked, the vile, it should meet with no sportive sally, but with that withering irony, that deep abhorrence, which demand a smile for their ensign, and an execration for their outburst.

He who is born with the name of the author has much to do to distinguish it. When 'no Smith was found throughout the land,' then would have been the time to make it renowned and memorable. Perhaps it may be attributed to the numberlessness of the tribe that ambition has inspired so many to exalt themselves. The only hope lies in soubriquet or fame. 'Bobus' Smith can never be forgotten. There are others who prefer great and indefeasible titles to remembrance; they repel all jest. Once was it emblazoned by chivalry and achievement. The breaker of the Temple-prison, the hero of Acre, gave to the name a prefix which seemed to insulate and immortalize it. We doubt, however, whether an English clergyman has not more than divided its honors. His god-fathers and god-mothers gave him the same 'Christian' appellation; and we think that the chance of recognition and identification, in all future, sides with the parson rather than the soldier, with the man of cloth rather than the man of steel.

We really are anxious to do justice to Sydney Smith; we have so long heard his facetiæ, his epigrams, his oracles, that there is danger of confounding him with the mere table-wit. The difficulty is in reconciling him with his profession. We have seen him in the pulpit, and the restraint upon him, his very seriousness, was comedy itself; we thought him out of place; any where we should have preferred him than in that tribune,—

in *bottle* than in *wood*; yet he was serious, sententious, pointed. With burly form and rotund speech,—raising his spectacles to give a popular glance and head-shaking emphasis,—he would grandiloquently remark, no one being so aware of the absurdity of that grandiloquence as himself,—'He who would be respected,'—his stride is now in his hand, and his eye searches the stalls,—'must be respectable!!' His earlier preaching essays (the reader may throw the accent as he will) were feeble and jejune; he did not appear to understand the value of common words; he took for a text, 'Vanity of vanities, all is vanity.' He commenced with unquestioning confidence in his terminology: 'Vanity is that passion of the human breast, &c.' His earlier jokes were puerile and strained. If he argued against any natural connection between modesty and merit, all that he would allow, even of plausible and suppositious alliance, was that both begun with a *m*. The best fortune which ever befel him was the turning upon him of one of his malapert indiscretions. He was a West-end chapel preacher, elegant, courteous, pagan,—a lecturer in Albemarle-street, and Zany to Holland-house:—a *locum tenens* (ecclesiasticè, a warming-pan) was wanted for a Yorkshire living. Unbeneficed, he snatched at it; he designed a 'servant of servants' for it; it was low, and but thinly inhabited; he could draw the income, and still be the man on town. But he not only could mimic his superiors, he had a strong passion for a *concio* wherever he could obtain an auditory. Voice, attitude, articulation, led him to the *ex cathedra* style; he loved the airs of counsel and rebuke; he was somewhat theatric. So it came to pass, that, as the junior rector of a visitational district, he must needs address his arch-prelate (the functionary's fondness for quaint, sly, pleasantry, fully justifies his pre-eminence) and the neighbouring pastors. This was an opportunity he could not forego; he was big with the occasion. What should be his theme? how might he fill that hour of pomp? The Residence Act had just received royal consent; it inspired him for his declamations; he could approve without care or loss. A laudatory descant upon the measure would serve his churchmanship, which, haply, had not been rated most sound or zealous. He preached! the oratory took the Bœotian Trullibers and Chopsticks aback. Nothing had been seen on those flats, or by those flats, like this before. The voice ranged in a register of octaves; the hands, it is feared, sawed the air. He had demonstrated that a clergyman should live on his living; this had been believed before, to be the literal truth; he intended something of the 'whereabout,' tether as well as nosebag. The diocesan seized the earliest opportunity of thanking him aloud before the dining conclave. 'Never had he listened to such cogent, convincing, argument. No cavil could be raised against it'—(more than the M's seemed coming together,—the preacher bowed and blushed!)—'and if his reverend brother did not immediately take up his residence among them, he must renounce the living!' 'O most'—not 'lame and impotent,'—'conclusion!' And there for years he vegetated,—an agrestian,—turning turnips, grazing grasses, pyeing potatoes,—almost forgotten but for his light missile at some clerical anti-popish meeting, or his detected domino in the 'Edinburgh Review.' Basil and Nazianzen never bewailed more poignantly their expatriation. His little coinage, a token-sort, circulated among the surrounding gentry, who admired what he meant; he would have ruined their principles of keeping things as they are if they could have understood him; he was terrible in a magisterial committee, and threw an attractive cheerfulness about a gaol commission. It must not be forgotten that during this twofold state of migration and hybernation, he obtained a sheriff's chaplaincy. In the first assize sermon he tiraded the bar; in the second he lectured the bench!

By this time the vegetative process was threatening him, and he was little more than mandrake. Unless stirring times had come it may be questioned whether he could have left behind him more than arborized remains. The agricultural symptoms were distressingly evolved; but though he moved slow in his portliness, and pensive on his glebe,—sometimes with bill in hand slashing copse and hedge,—another bill aroused him, and to more congenial hewing he set himself. Just previously to the reform-struggle he had been presented with a prebend of Bristol; the stipend was reckoned at almost £10 per annum; it flattered his ambition. 'It is not worth your acceptance,' said a friend.' 'It has made me a happy man for life,' was the reply; 'I shall now never go to prayers but behind a silver poker.' It was not only a conceit,—it opened to him the way of preferment. *Wanted no longer* in the East Riding cure, other prizes fell to his share; his friends were now in power; he paid them service still. The parable of Mrs. Partington with mop and pattens really did them good. But, alas, for the consistency, the onward going, of reformers! There was coming the hour of church pruning and cleansing; the heads of the church led the way; the bench they found to be perfect, except a little underpaid! Deans and chapters offered a nobler beginning. Here was abuse! here was scope for despoliation! He was by this time in Amen Corner; he stood in the point blank range of the fire. Whether he would always have objected to the taking of ministers to task we cannot aver; his conscientious scruples were now violently strong; he considered that this was the last point to be touched; it was the altar. He had felt it a relief if the attack could have been directed to any other quarter above him or below him; right wing or left wing; but this was striking, not at the centre, for that was an accident, but at him who happened to be posted there. He called all arts of rhetoric into his cause; he disdained not his playful alliteration. The poor, starveling, dignitaries,—no more choosing among livings nor pampered upon fines,—were described by him as lying at Dives's gate,—Fulham was intended,—'comforted by crumbs and doctored by dogs.'

Our author certainly rose in worth towards the conclusion of his years. We have read these sermons with a deep interest. They are any thing but what Christian sermons ought to be. They can boast no evangelic vein; but allow them their own character and pretension, and there is power in them. You see that the man has feeling. In representing the flatteries and fascinations with which our present queen would be surrounded on her accession, he exclaims—'What other cure but deep religious feeling for all the arrogance and vanity which her exalted position must engender? for all the soul-corrupting homage with which she is met at every moment of her existence! what other cure than to cast herself down in darkness and solitude before God—to say that she is dust and ashes; and *to call down the pity of the Almighty upon her difficult and dangerous life!*' The italics are ours; the pathos, the truth, is exquisite. There is, indeed, no levity in these compositions—the stamp of a perfect honesty is upon them. They glow with a love of freedom. Sometimes he is careless. He will ascribe to Jeremy Taylor a saying of Benjamin Franklin. He winds up a discourse in a peroration of personal feeling. 'I shall exclaim with the *Psalmist*, 'Lord, now lettest thou thy servant depart in peace,' &c.' He can be bitterly faithful; his farewell sermon at Berkeley Chapel is founded on the seventh command: 'Thou shalt not commit adultery.'

Like most of the old school Whigs, he stumbles at the great principles of religious liberty! 'I have lived to see the immense improvements of the church of England, all its power of persecution destroyed, its monopoly of civil offices expunged from the book of the law, and all its unjust and exclusive immunities levelled to the ground. The church of England is now a rational object of love and admiration—it is perfectly compatible with civil freedom—it is an institution for worshipping God, and not a cover for gratifying secular insolence, and ministering to secular ambition.' We believe him to be sincere. This is the statesmanship of all our liberal standard-bearers. But it might have been written with the spirit which he knew so well to keep, the spirit of quiet, piquant, chuckle and fanfaronade. 'All its powers of persecution destroyed!' 'all its unjust and exclusive immunities levelled to the ground!' Can it be said in earnest? We, who live in its invidious shadow, who feel daily its contempt, whose scholarship it denies because it is not beholden to it, whose religious aims it scoffs, whose vital interests are at all points threatened by it, who are insulted by its veriest toleration, —Can we hear it 'without our special wonder?' Let our village pastors and churches be shown this eulogium, and let them be sworn to it.

Here must be the great contest and division of parties. Politicians cannot understand how there can be persecution, and yet not faggot nor sword. Politicians cannot understand how a government is to be carried on without a religious establishment. We may talk of coalitions, but this is the real and fatal one. We have helped those who have avowed civil liberty; we will help them still—we would not turn sullen, nor fall away from every party. We must have combination, and we must act in combination. But where is the religious freedom party? The abettors of a state-church cannot belong to it. We have no public men on our side; the most keen-sighted on these questions cannot perceive that a favoured church is a snare and a wrong. If they catch a glimpse of what we feel as an inconsistency with liberty, as a violence of partiality, they proffer support to all. Thus only will they adjust the case; they will bribe our silence and entangle our rectitude, but nothing may we expect from them to redress our injury and restore our equality!

It may be recorded of Sydney Smith, that he was politically unsullied. He had never flinched from his principles; they were not of the most lofty and generous order, but *Qualis ab incepto processit et sibi constat*.

In the re-publication of his contributions to the great *Northern Journal*, a fine opportunity was given him of cancelling or extenuating his foolish and profane sneers against Christian missions. He renewed them without apology or misgiving. How had that cause gathered proof and glory from its modern career? how had it silenced and shamed its assailants? how had it mightily prevailed! What evidence it had accumulated to convince him! what success had it won that might have awakened the enthusiasm of his admiration! But his was a cold temperament; his scintillations bore no warmth; the grandeur of Christianity found in him no kindred faculty nor sentiment. Sacrificing the friendly feelings of parting, and to the last conveying his contempt of the cause which necessitated it, he is said to have breathed the simple wish to Bishop Selwyn, 'May you disagree with the cannibal who eats you!'

We are in possession of a few anecdotes which we believe are little known. He was not learned enough to be bishop's chaplain and examiner, but the kind-hearted and right merry prelate under whose crozier his northern benefice placed him, loved his company and sought his visit. He rose in the gradations of the palatial table, and sometimes acted as his croupier. His grace hates from his heart scientific and erudite bores; he knows well the points of a horse, and was once complimented by an old clergyman, who thought in Greek roots more than in English vocables, as the most thorough hypocrite of his day. The courtly suffrage was returned by a smile and a bow. But these 'pestilent fellows' would intrude—an entomologist arrived, full of his minute philosophy. As he sate at the right elbow of his host, he inflicted a whole store of *larvæ, antennæ, tentacula,* upon him, until misery reached its utmost. In vain the master of the banquet protested his ignorance, yawned his impatience, absolutely snored. On the torrent flowed; the humourist at the bottom of the table was generally ready for the rescue, while he delayed it in delight of the annoyance. At last he heard the man of insects observe that the eye of the fly was larger in proportion to its body than in any other creature. Sydney Smith gave the statement the rudest, most cat-o'-th'-mountain, denial. Utterly staggered by such a reply, the observer appealed to visual proof. All were now alive to the controversy. With great formality the respondent pointed out the great sources of all truth, even in bardic measures and in nursery rhymes. There lay the common opinion and knowledge of mankind. 'What then? how does all this bear upon the present case?' In thundering recitative, our hero struck up—'I said the fly, with my *little* eye, I saw him die!' The naturalist was as pinned as any of his beetles, and he, who had suffered most of the bore, might have exclaimed—*Sic me servavit!* On another occasion the late Francis Wrangham was dealing out at the symposium far more learning than seemed to be relished by the chair—the vice was imploringly eyed to interfere; immediately he spoke in a loud undertone, a stage aside—'How he is annoying the worthy archbishop; it is easy to see where he is; as usual he is in the Persian war; yes, now he is at Darius Hystaspes. He has presumed too much; his grace is waking up; 'Darius Hystaspes! I never heard of that horse before; what is its pedigree, sire and dam?' The elegant historian with one stride retreated on the bank of the Granicus!

It is difficult to moralise on such a man. If there be in him much to admire, there is much more to lament. He has left warning behind him rather than instruction. There is an arc, and it tells us the orbit he might have run: the disappointment is the more bitter that it is the poor and only fragment of that conceivable circle!

Art. III.—*History of the Reformation of the Sixteenth Century.* Vol. IV. By J. H. Merle D'Aubigné, D.D. Assisted in the preparation of the English original by H. White. Edinburgh: Oliver and Boyd.

This volume is appropriately published, by the author, in English. Its predecessors were originally issued in French, and thence translated into our tongue; but as their circulation in France hardly exceeded four thousand, while upwards of one hundred and fifty thousand copies were sold in this kingdom and America, M. D'Aubigné has naturally determined to give priority to the English edition of the continuation of his work. He has, moreover, superintended its publication, and has thus contributed greatly to the accurate conveyance of his thoughts to the English reader. 'I did not think it right,' he remarks in his preface, 'to leave to translators, as in the cases of the former volumes, the task of expressing my ideas in English. The best translations are always faulty; and the author alone can have the certainty of conveying his idea, his whole idea, and nothing but his idea. Without overlooking the merit that the several existing translations may possess, even the best of them is not free from inaccuracies, more or less important.' This is as it should be. It was due to the people by whom his work had been so extensively patronized, that they should have it in the most complete and perfect form: and we are glad to learn that the earlier volumes of the work are about to appear, under the immediate superintendence and revision of the author. The appeal which he makes 'to English honour' on behalf of the integrity of his copyright, will not, we hope, be without effect, at the same time that the common sense of mankind will dictate the preference of an original over a translation from a French edition. Much, however, will depend on Messrs. Oliver and Boyd supplying the market, at an early period, with a popular and cheap edition. They will be wise to do so without loss of time, and thus deprive the literary smuggler of all reasonable excuse, and diminish vastly the temptation which high prices furnish. It is with books as with brandy or silks. Where the inducement is sufficiently strong, the contraband is sure to compete with the fair trader, and it will therefore be prudent in Messrs. Oliver and Boyd, to bring out the work at such a cost as will diminish, to the lowest point, the probable success of any competitor,

The first part of the present volume details at considerable length, the circumstances connected with the protest of Spire, and with the confession of Augsburg. These events marked the most important epochs of the German reformation, and are worthy of the serious attention of the ecclesiastical student. The latter part of the volume describes the establishment of the Reformation in most of the Swiss cantons, and 'the instructive and deplorable events that are connected with the catastrophe of Cappel!' We shall confine ourselves to the former, as conveying information more apposite to our own day: at the same time that we recommend an attentive perusal of M. Aubigné's narrative of the Swiss reform.

A rapid change had been taking place in the sentiments of Germany from the first appearance of Luther. Several of the states and cities had given in their adhesion to reform. Men of all ranks, from the prince to the peasant, had responded earnestly to his appeal. They were evidently prepared for his mission. He was not born out of due time. Others had laboured, and he now entered into their labours. The way was prepared before him, and his zeal and simplicity of purpose, his highmindedness and faith, conciliated the attention and confidence of large masses of his countrymen. The intellect of Europe had previously been aroused, and the transmission of truth was consequently rapid. Men were waiting the appearance of such a reformer. They had witnessed the abominations of the papacy, its superstitious worship, the corruption and sensuality of its clergy, and the pride and ambition of its councils. The revival of letters enabled them to estimate these things better than their fathers; and the public sentiment of Europe became in consequence hostile to some of the claims of St. Peter. In many cases, religious conviction prompted this hostility; but in others, political considerations were most potent, and the religious only secondary and indirect. Even where the spiritual supremacy of the pope was regarded with superstition, his political power was frequently denounced. The head of the Roman states was threatened, while the successor of St. Peter was adored. Men assailed the former, while they bowed down and worshipped before the latter. A striking instance of this was afforded in 1527, when the imperial forces under the command of the constable of Bourbon, appeared before 'the eternal city,' in open defiance of the powers of the church. Many of our readers are acquainted with what followed; but the passage is too instructive and its incidents too significant of what was passing in men's minds, for us to omit our author's rapid sketch.

'On the evening of the 5th May, Bourbon arrived under the walls of the capital; and he would have begun the assault at that very moment if he had had ladders. On the morning of the 6th the army, concealed by a thick fog which hid their movements, was put in motion, the Spaniards marching to their station above the gate of the

Holy Ghost, and the Germans below. The constable, wishing to encourage his soldiers, seized a scaling-ladder, mounted the wall, and called on them to follow him. At this moment a ball struck him: he fell, and expired an hour after. Such was the end of this unhappy man, a traitor to his king and to his country, and suspected even by his new friends.

'His death, far from checking, served only to excite the army. Claudius Seidenstucker, grasping his long sword, first cleared the wall; he was followed by Michael Hartmann, and these two reformed Germans exclaimed that God himself marched before them in the clouds. The gates were opened, the army poured in, the suburbs were taken, and the pope, surrounded by thirteen cardinals, fled to the castle of Saint Angelo. The imperialists, at whose head was now the Prince of Orange, offered him peace, on condition of his paying three hundred thousand crowns. But Clement, who thought that the Holy League was on the point of delivering him, and who fancied he already saw their leading horsemen, rejected every proposition. After a few hours' repose, the attack was renewed, and by an hour after sunset the army was master of all the city. It remained under arms and in good order until midnight, the Spaniards in the Piazza Navona, and the Germans in the Campofiore. At last, seeing no demonstrations either of war or of peace, the soldiers disbanded and ran to pillage.

'Then began the famous 'Sack of Rome.' The papacy had for centuries put Christendom in the press. Prebends, annates, jubilees, pilgrimages, ecclesiastical graces,—she had made money of them all. These greedy troops, that for months had lived in wretchedness, determined to make her disgorge. No one was spared, the imperial not more than the ultramontane party, the Ghibellines not more than the Guelfs. Churches, palaces, convents, private houses, basilics, banks, tombs,—every thing was pillaged, even to the golden ring that the corpse of Julius II. still wore on its finger. The Spaniards displayed the greatest skill; they scented out and discovered treasures in the most mysterious hiding-places; but the Neapolitans were still more outrageous. 'On every side were heard,' says Guicciardini, 'the piteous shrieks of the Roman women and of the nuns whom the soldiers dragged away by companies to satiate their lust.'

'At first the Germans found a certain pleasure in making the papists feel the weight of their swords. But ere long, happy at finding food and drink, they were more pacific than their allies. It was upon those things which the Romans called 'holy' that the anger of the Lutherans was especially discharged. They took away the chalices, the pyxes, the silver remontrances, and clothed their servants and camp-boys with the sacerdotal garments. The Campofiore was changed into an immense gambling-house. The soldiers brought thither golden vessels and bags full of crowns, staked them upon one throw of the dice, and after losing them, they went in search of others. A certain Simon Baptista, who had foretold the sack of the city, had been thrown into prison by the pope;

the Germans liberated him, and made him drink with them. But, like Jeremiah, he prophesied against all. 'Rob, plunder,' cried he to his liberators; 'you shall, however, give back all; the money of the soldiers and the gold of the priests will follow the same road.

'Nothing pleased the Germans more than to mock the papal court. 'Many prelates,' says Guicciardini, 'were paraded on asses through all the city of Rome.' After this procession, the bishops paid their ransom; but they fell into the hands of the Spaniards, who made them pay it a second time.

'One day a lansquenet named Guillaume de Sainte Celle, put on the pope's robes, and placed the triple crown upon his head; others, adorning themselves with the red hats and long robes of the cardinals, surrounded him; and all going in procession upon asses through the streets of the city, arrived at last before the castle of Saint Angelo, where Clement VII. had retired. Here the soldier-cardinals alighted, and lifting up the front of their robes, kissed the feet of the pretended pontiff. The latter drank to the health of Clement VII., the cardinals kneeling did the same, and exclaimed that henceforward they would be pious popes and good cardinals, who would have a care not to excite wars, as all their predecessors had done. They then formed a conclave, and the pope having announced to his consistory that it was his intention to resign the papacy, all hands were immediately raised for the election, and they cried out 'Luther is Pope! Luther is Pope!' Never had pontiff been proclaimed with such perfect unanimity. Such were the humours of the Germans.'—pp. 21-25.

We need not express our abhorrence of the atrocities practised on this occasion, whether by Spanish or German soldiers. It is a dark chapter that records them, in which, however, may be discovered some traces—sadly disfigured, it is true—of that emancipation from debased and grovelling superstition which the bold heart of Luther had announced. It was a terrible retribution that was inflicted on Rome; the rebound of insulted and depraved humanity when first released from the thraldom of ages. But enough of this. Having noted 'the sack of Rome' as one of the signs of the times, we recur to the progress of the reformation, as detailed by M. D'Aubigné.

The political changes which led to this catastrophe, secured to the reformers a brief period of repose. Instead of marching against them as he had threatened at Seville, the emperor directed his forces against the pope, to whom he addressed a manifesto full of bitter and reproachful terms. 'Let your highness' said Charles, 'return the sword of St. Peter into the scabbard, and convoke a holy and universal council.' Ferdinand was commanded to suspend the edict of Worms and to conciliate the partisans of Luther, and the discussions which followed in the diet of Spire, elicited in a partial and imperfect form the principle of religious liberty. 'In one place' said the deputies of one of the cities, 'the ancient ceremonies have been preserved; in another they have been abolished; and both think they are right. Let us allow each one to do as he thinks fit, until a council shall re-establish the desired unity by the word of God.' This advice was adopted, and it was ultimately resolved that, until such council assembled 'each state should behave in its own territory in a manner so as to be able to render an account to God and to the emperor.'

'Thus,' says our author, 'they escaped from their difficulty by a middle course; and this time it was really the true one. Each one maintained his rights, while recognising another's The diet of 1526 forms an important epoch in history: an ancient power, that of the middle ages, is shaken; a new power, that of modern times, is advancing; religious liberty boldly takes its stand in front of Romish despotism; a lay spirit prevails over the sacerdotal spirit. In this single step there is a complete victory: the cause of the reform is won.'—p. 15.

From this period to 1529 there was a calm throughout Germany, which enabled the reform to organise and extend itself. The good providence of God was signally conspicuous in securing to his church this interval of repose, 'The wrath of man was made to praise him,' and, as the event showed, the friends of evangelical truth were thus enabled to prepare for the struggle which impended. Philip of Hesse was the first to organise an ecclesiastical constitution for his state, and its general character was popular. Unlike most of his compeers he inclined to the Swiss reform, and the fundamental principle of self-government was recognised throughout the plan framed for the churches of his dominions. Content with having thrown off the yoke of the papacy, he had no ambition, like our own Henry, to place himself in the pontiff's stead, but 'was satisfied with an external superintendence necessary for the maintenance of order.' It would have been well for the reformation had his example been generally followed, but men were not yet prepared fon the full apprehension of truth. The school of adversity—the bitter experience of many generations was needed, before they could be taught the insults and the injury done to religion, by permitting the secular power to regulate its worship, or controul the spiritual functions of its ministry. The following, which are amongst the principal features of the ecclesiastical constitution of Hesse, display, under the circumstances of the case, a remarkable approximation to the truth.

' 'The church can only be taught and governed by the word of its Sovereign Pastor. Whoever has recourse to any other word shall be deposed and excommunicated.

''Every pious man, learned in the word of God, whatever be his condition, may be elected bishop if he desire it, for he is called inwardly of God.

''Let no one believe that by a bishop we understand anything else than a simple minister of the word of God.

''The ministers are servants, and consequently they ought not to be lords, princes, or governors.

''Let the faithful assemble and choose their bishops and deacons. Each church should elect its own pastor.

''Let those who are elected bishops be consecrated to their office by the imposition of the hands of three bishops; and as for the deacons, if there are no ministers present, let them receive the laying on of hands from the elders of the church.

''If a bishop causes any scandal to the church by his effeminacy, or by the splendour of his garments, or by the levity of his conduct, and if, on being warned, he persists, let him be deposed by the church.—p. 34.

The popular element of church government was at first generally recognized. Writing to the Calixtins of Bohemia in 1523, Luther had counselled them, where more regular methods could not be adopted, to seek God by prayer, and then to 'choose in the Lord's name him or them whom you shall have acknowledged to be fitted for this ministry.' Subsequent events, however, led him to modify his theory; or rather, the apparent necessities of the case induced him to sanction a practice inconsistent with it. The German reformation can hardly be said to have begun with the lower classes, and hence the character it assumed. Luther deferred too much to this fact. He would have acted a wiser part, one more in harmony with his religious vocation, and better suited to advance the permanent interests of truth, had he discriminated between things secular and religious, ceding to the magistrate a controul of the former, but asserting for the latter an exemption from his jurisdiction, and an innate power of self-preservation and growth. M. D'Aubigné has fairly stated the circumstances which determined his course, though we cannot admit the necessity which he supposes to have been laid upon him. His words are worthy of being noted, and we transfer them for the instruction of our readers.

'But if the people were indifferent, the princes were not so. They stood in the foremost rank of the battle, and sat on the first bench in the council. The democratic organization was therefore compelled to give way to an organization conformable to the civil government. The church is composed of Christians, and they are taken wherever they are found—high or low. It was particularly in high stations that Luther found them. He admitted the princes as representatives of the people; and henceforward the influence of the state became one of the principal elements in the constitution of the evangelical church.

'In the mind of the reformer, this guardianship of the princes was only to be provisional. The faithful being then in minority, they had need of a guardian; but the era of the church's majority might arrive, and with it would come its emancipation.

'We may admit that this recourse to the civil power was at that time necessary, but we cannot deny that it was also a source of difficulties. We will point out only one. When Protestantism became an affair of governments and nations, it ceased to be universal. The new spirit was capable of creating a new earth. But instead of opening new roads, and of purposing the regeneration of all Christendom, and the conversion of the whole world, the Protestants sought to settle themselves as comfortably as possible in a few German duchies. This timidity, which has been called prudence, did immense injury to the reformation.'—pp. 39, 40.

Melancthon's influence in this matter was injurious. His timid and temporizing character unfitted him for the work of reform. We know and love his excellences, and hold him in grateful remembrance. He frequently tempered the harshness of Luther; gave an air of mildness to his measures, which that superb spirit never could have imparted, and rendered important literary aid to the reformation. But on the other hand—and truth must not be sacrificed to our partialities—he would on different occasions have sacrificed the great work, and made a hollow truce with Rome, if the heroism and faith of Luther had not interposed. In the case before us his influence was conservative, not reforming. The love of peace overcame his sense of obligation to truth. He was frequently more apprehensive of danger than alive to duty,—was more concerned to ward off opposition than to carry out the true spirit and intent of reform. His counsel to one of the inspectors was characteristic, and its influence on the German reformation considerable. 'All the old ceremonies' said he, 'that you can preserve, pray do so.' . . . . Do not innovate much, for every innovation is injurious to the people.' It was well for the truth which Melancthon, notwithstanding this, dearly loved, that there were men of firmer mould by his side. Luther was the presiding spirit of the movement, and his sterner nature checked the timid counsels of his associate.

The firmness of Luther was speedily called into requisition. In March 1529, the emperor summoned a diet at Spire, and the political considerations which had previously led him to tamper with the Protestants having ceased, he lent himself entirely to the policy of the Romanists. Their object was to annul the decree of 1526, by which partial religious liberty had been secured, and to revive the edict of Worms 1521, by which the civil power was required to enforce the dogmas of the papacy. It was ultimately resolved, that in all places where the edict of Worms had been received, it should be strictly enforced; and that in other places innovations should be prohibited, and proselytism be severely repressed. The Anabaptists and Sacramentarians were declared to be without the pale of toleration, and a determination was avowed to reinstate the church in its ancient unity and power. It was a fearful crisis which had arrived. Men's spirits were tested by it, and for a moment the result seemed doubtful. The decree was passed on the 7th of April, and unconditional submission was demanded. 'If it became a law, the reformation could neither be extended into those places where as yet it was unknown, nor be established on solid foundations in those where it already existed. The re-establishment of the Romish hierarchy stipulated in the proposition, would infallibly bring back the ancient abuses; and the least deviation from so vexatious an ordinance would easily furnish the Romanists with a pretext for completing the destruction of a work already so violently shaken.' Under these circumstances the princes and deputies met to consult on their common interest, and their resolution was speedily taken.

''Let us reject this decree,' said the princes. 'In matters of conscience the majority has no power.'—'It is to the decree of 1526,' added the cities, 'that we are indebted for the peace that the empire enjoys: to abolish it would be to fill Germany with troubles and divisions. The diet is incompetent to do more than preserve religious liberty until the council meets.' Such in fact is the grand attribute of the state, and if in our days the Protestant powers should seek to influence the Romish governments, they should strive solely to obtain for the subjects of the latter that religious liberty which the pope confiscates to his own advantage wherever he reigns alone, and by which he profits greatly in every evangelical state. Some of the deputies proposed refusing all assistance against the Turks, hoping thus to force the emperor to interfere in this question of religion. But Sturm called upon them not to mingle political matters with the salvation of souls. They resolved, therefore, to reject the proposition, but without holding out any threats. It was this noble resolution that gained for modern times liberty of thought and independence of faith.''—p. 70.

To their remonstrance Ferdinand, the brother of the Emperor, replied—'It is a settled affair, submission is all that remains.' It was a perilous position which the reformers occupied. The power of the empire was against them. The imperial forces were ready to execute the persecuting decree, and the church already fulminated its thunders. They were denounced as rebels and heretics, and the secular and spiritual powers were prepared to inflict on them the terrors of both worlds. Ordinary men would have trembled, paused, and shrunk back. There was much to give an air of justification to such a course. They had done their best to secure a better issue. All which human forethought and faithfulness could suggest had been attempted, and they now stood alone, exposed to a tempest which had never been successfully withstood, and before which their strength would probably be as perfect weakness. Even honest men might have reasoned thus, and had the elector of Saxony and his associates done so, we might have pitied their weakness and reproached their infidelity, but could not have been surprised. Happily, however, they were men of a higher cast of mind, and the Spirit of the living God was powerful upon them. They appealed from the Diet to the word of God, from the Emperor Charles to the King of the princes of the earth. Rising with the difficulties of the occasion, they drew up the famous *protest*,—from which their name was subsequently drawn,—declaring the decree of the Diet to be both unjust and impious. In this noble document, which marks an important era in the reformation, they distinctly asserted the supremacy of Jesus Christ, the inviolability of conscience, and the personal nature of religious service. The right of a majority to regulate the faith of a minority was repudiated, and their determination to stand in the liberty of the gospel asserted in terms not to be misunderstood.

"'Moreover'—and this is the essential part of the protest—'the new edict declaring the ministers shall preach the gospel, explaining it according to the writings accepted by the holy Christian church; we think that, for this regulation to have any value, we should first agree on what is meant by this true and holy church. Now, seeing that there is great diversity of opinion in this respect; that there is no sure doctrine but such as is conformable to the word of God; that the Lord forbids the teaching of any other doctrine; that each text of the holy scriptures ought to be explained by other and clearer texts; that this holy book is, in all things necessary for the Christian, easy of understanding, and calculated to scatter the darkness: we are resolved, with the grace of God, to maintain the pure and exclusive preaching of his only word, such as it is contained in the biblical books of the Old and New Testament, without adding anything thereto that may be contrary to it. This word is the only truth; it is the sure rule of all doctrine and of all life, and can never fail or deceive us. He who builds on this foundation shall stand against all the powers of hell, whilst all the human vanities that are set up against it shall fall before the face of God.' "—74.

The reading of this protest made a deep impression. It was no longer possible to doubt the living energy which characterised reform. Thoughtful men began to feel that it could not be arrested. The mere politician discovered the element of an enduring and powerful party, whilst all devout men recognised an enfranchised gospel. Honour be to the princes and deputies who signed it. Their names should be held in grateful reverence. They went before us bearing the burden and heat of the day, labouring on our behalf as well as their own, achieving for generations to come a spiritual freedom, of which mankind had been destitute for ages. We need scarcely advert to the essential identity of the principles they avowed, and those which we hold. They are substantially one, and the advocates of civil authority in matters of religion, and those amongst ourselves who discountenance an agitation of the State Church question, will be wise to ponder the facts of the case.

'The principles contained,' says M. D'Aubigné, 'in this celebrated protest of the 19th April, 1529, constitute the very essence of Protestantism. Now this protest opposes two abuses of man in matters of faith: the first is the intrusion of the civil magistrate, and the second is the arbitrary authority of the church. Instead of these two abuses, Protestantism sets up above the magistrate the power of conscience; and above the visible church the authority of the word of God. It declines, in the first place, the civil power in Divine things, and says with the prophets and apostles: *We must obey God rather than man*. In presence of the crown of Charles the Fifth, it uplifts the crown of Jesus Christ. But it goes farther: it lays down the principle, that all human teaching should be subordinate to the oracles of God. Even the primitive church, by recognising the writings of the apostles, had performed an act of submission to this supreme authority, and not an act of authority, as Rome maintains; and the establishment of a tribunal charged with the interpretation of the Bible, had terminated only in slavishly subjecting man to man in that which should be the most unfettered—conscience and faith. In this celebrated act of Spire no doctor appears, and the word of God reigns alone. Never has man exalted himself like the pope; never have men kept in the background like the reformers.'—p. 76.

The Diet of Augsburg was held in the following year, under circumstances most inauspicious to reform: Charles had recently been crowned by the pope, emperor of Germany, and when kissing the white cross embroidered on the slipper of Clement, had exclaimed—'I swear, ever to employ all my strength to defend the pontifical dignity, and the church of Rome.' With that oath fresh upon his lips he repaired to Augsburg, whither he had summoned the states to assemble. The Protestant princes hesitated. They suspected his designs, and were apprehensive of their personal safety. An appeal to arms was proposed, and the elector solicited the advice of Luther. 'Attend,' was the magnanimous reply. 'If the emperor desires to march against us, let no prince undertake our defence. God is faithful: he will not abandon us.' This advice was happily complied with, and the memorable *Confession* drawn up by Melancthon, which the reformers presented to the emperor, is one of the most cheished records of the Christian church. Luther's friends prohibited his appearance in the city, but he earnestly struggled with his brethren, and his prayers on their behalf were incessant. Here was the secret of his power, and we need not wonder therefore that secular men do not understand him.

'Luther, besides his constant reading of the word of God, did not pass a day without devoting three hours at least to prayer, and they were hours selected from those most favourable to study. One day, as Diedrich approached the Reformer's chamber, he heard his voice, and remained motionless, holding his breath, a few steps from the door. Luther was praying, and his prayer (said the secretary) was full of adoration, fear, and hope, as when one speaks to a friend or to a father. 'I know that thou art our Father and our God,' said the Reformer, alone in his chamber, 'and that thou wilt scatter the persecutors of thy children, for thou art thyself endangered with us. All this matter is thine, and it is only by thy constraint that we have put our hands to it. Defend us then, O Father!' The secretary, motionless as a statue, in the long gallery of the castle, lost not one of the words that the clear and resounding voice of Luther bore to his ears. The Reformer was earnest with God, and called upon him with so much unction to accomplish his promises, that Diedrich felt his heart glow within him. 'Oh!' exclaimed he, as he retired, 'How could not these prayers but prevail in the desperate struggle at Augsburg!' '—p. 220.

On hearing of Melancthon's despondency and anguish, he wrote him in a strain of heroic fortitude, which to more timid, or more worldly minds, may savour of extravagant self-confidence: but it was really in his case the fruit of a profound abasement at the footstool of God. This was the salient point of his character, whence its worth was derived, and his power of moral achievement drawn. When others trembled he stood firm. The enemies within shook the foundations of his being, but those without he surveyed with calmness and triumph. The former made him doubt himself, the latter never could induce him to doubt his God. Assured of interest in the divine protection, he laughed to very scorn, the threats and curses of his foes. The following to Melancthon is characteristic:—

' 'Grace and peace in Christ! in Christ, I say, and not in the world, Amen. I hate with exceeding hatred those extremes cares which consume you. If the cause is unjust, abandon it; if the cause is just, why should we belie the promises of Him who commands us to sleep without fea-? Can the devil do more than kill us? Christ will not be wanting to the work of justice and of truth. He lives; he reigns; what fear, then, can we have? God is powerful to upraise his cause if it is overthrown, to make it proceed if it remains motionless, and if we are not worthy of it, he will do it by others.

"'I have received your apology, and I cannot understand what you mean, when you ask what we must concede to the papists. We have already conceded too much. Night and day I meditate on this affair, turning it over and over, perusing all scripture, and the certainty of the truth of our doctrine continually increases in my mind. With the help of God, I will not permit a single letter of all that we have said to be torn from us.

"'The issue of this affair torments you, because you cannot understand it. But if you could, I would not have the least share in it. God has put it in a 'common place,' that you will not find either in your rhetoric or in your philosophy: that place is called Faith. It is that in which subsist all things that we can neither understand nor see. Whoever wishes to touch them, as you do, will have tears for his sole reward.

"'If Christ is not with us, where is he in the whole universe? If we are not the church, where, I pray, is the church? Is it the Dukes of Bavaria, is it Ferdinand, is it the Turk, who is the church? If we have not the word of God, who is it that possesses it?

"'Only we must have faith, lest the cause of faith should be found to be without faith.

"'If we fall, Christ falls with us, that is to say, the Master of the world. I would rather fall with Christ, than remain standing with Cæsar.' "—pp. 223, 224.

We had intended to enter somewhat at large into the history of the Diet of Augsburg, and of the memorable *Confession*, but must defer doing so to another opportunity. Our readers will do well—we need scarcely urge them to it—to give this portion of M. D'Aubigné's volume an attentive perusal. On our own mind it has made a powerful impression, more especially, as it respects the character of Luther. We question whether his equal has existed since the days of the apostles, or whether full justice has been done to his moral magnanimity, and distinctive Christian excellences, even by the warmest of his admirers. Would, that the church were again visited by such a reformer. Let but his faith, and patience, and zeal be brought to bear on the discussions of our day, and the emancipation of the church will be speedily completed.

Art. III.—1. *Reports upon the Proceedings of the Council of the French* Asiatic Society, from* 1840 *to* 1845. By Jules Mohl, Assistant Secretary of the Society.

2.—*Prospectus of the Statutes of the German† Society for disseminating Information concerning the East.* By Messrs. Brockhaus, Fleischer, Pott, Rodiger, Seyffarth, and Tuch.

Two French and German productions are here taken as texts for our notice of the valuable volumes published by the English Oriental Translation Committee, instead of those volumes themselves, not only as the mere titles of the latter are too numerous for our limits, but because the subjects also of many of them are too abstruse or too dry for our present purpose. At the same time, their important political and social learning, which is the chief point to be examined in this article, has not escaped our guide Dr. Mohl, the able reporter of the French Asiatic Society; whilst the scheme set forth in the statutes of the new German Oriental Society, offers a gratifying tribute to the usefulness of the labours of our Oriental Translation committee.‡

That scheme, to which we shall first allude, embraces the whole of what is aimed at by the English committee, besides the additions of other objects, worthily pursued, but with far too little public encouragement, by the English society. In order to carry out its extensive purpose, it is to take a full and continuous account not only of the ancient but also of the modern state of Asia, and of that of *all parts of the world intimately connected with Asia*. This is to be effected, as is declared in the prospectus of the German statutes, 1st by a museum of natu-

* Journal Asiatique. 8vo. Paris, 1840—1845.

† Entwurf zu den Statuten der Deutschen Geselschaft für die Kunde des Morgenlandes. 4to. Halle & Leipzig. 1845.

‡ Of sixty-eight translations already published, six are from the Chinese, two from the Japanese, nineteen from the Persian, sixteen from the Arabic, seven from the Sanscrit, six from the Hindustan and other modern Indian languages; two from the Armenian, one from the Hebrew, six from the Turkish, one from the Abyssinian, one from the Syriac, one from the Malay, and one from the Burmese language.

§ The general title of the objects of the German society points only at the East—'Morgenlandes;' and its founders feel the want of a more comprehensive term. So the French *Asiatic* society extends to Africa, contrary to its title. So in the converse case of the distinction between the Christian world, and the rest of mankind, the term *European* includes the Christian Americans. A more correct language will be formed, when more correct ideas of the classification of the human race shall be familiar to us by the adoption of wiser views upon the best means of spreading civilization every where.

ral and artificial oriental productions, and by a collection of printed books and manuscripts; 2nd by publishing, translating, and distributing oriental literature; 3rd, by publishing a journal; 4th by promoting enterprises for the furtherance of the knowledge of the East: and 5thly, by forming connections with societies, and with learned individuals in Germany, and in other countries, having the same objects.

A beginning has been made in two successive years for acting under this comprehensive scheme, by the new form of literary and scientific associations called *Congresses*. The scheme itself probably arose out of the deep interest long felt in Germany before all other countries in oriental literature; and it will be a happy circumstance in the general study of the East, now fast spreading over the whole civilized world, if the Germans shall worthily revive the spirit of Herder, incomparably their greatest writer upon the subject of the fitting application of oriental learning. The Germans, having no direct interest in oriental conquests, or colonial acquisitions, to mislead their judgments, are especially qualified to form impartial opinions upon all oriental and colonial questions; and if they will consult the almost forgotten pages of their Herder* in regard to such questions, they must be listened to with respect.

The reports of Dr. Mohl, delivered for six years consecutively, upon the proceedings of the French Asiatic Society, do justice to all the topics included within the vast range of those proceedings. The French society is remarkable for the success of its oriental *philological* studies. Pursuing them with zeal, and often unavoidably to the exclusion of the matter which the learned prepare for practical application by the statesman to the improvement of human affairs, its political disquisitions have been few and cautious. It has been felt of late, however, that the time is come for using such accumulated stores. Dr. Mohl has expressed this feeling with force, and his remarks respecting us deserve special attention. In the report of 1844, he says:—

'A surprising activity in favour of oriental studies, prevails throughout the civilized world. But great as that activity is, compared with the proceedings at the commencement of the present century it by no means satisfies the demands of the age in regard to theological, to historical, and to archæological research; and far less

* Herder's philosophy of history was well translated by Thomas Churchill, and two editions of the translation sold forty years ago in London A new edition of that translation with additional matter, onght to be published now. It is incomparably the best work of thousands, upon the progress of civilization.

the daily, and more urgent calls of international policy, and the claims of civilization. None can be blind to the fact, that the power and the enterprise of Europeans are bearing down all resistance in order to find fields for increasing numbers; nor be unobservant of the prospect we have of establishing our religion and our science all over the east. But to rule a country wisely, we ought to know it well. Otherwise our new authority becomes a brutal yoke, and must be soon broken asunder. To introduce new ideas with advantage anywhere, the old ones upon which they are to be constructed, must be thoroughly understood. To revive the sciences, we must perceive precisely where they have decayed. These are principles not to be violated without danger; and no greater act of barbarism can be committed, than to disregard them when the manners of one nation are to be transferred to another nation. Such a mistake was committed when the Sultan attempted to force European usages upon the Turks, in utter ignorance himself of the one, and to the aggravated ruin of the other.'—(*Journal Asiatique*, 1844, p. 62.)

Dr. Mohl, knew well that he might have found illustrations of his judicious remarks nearer home; for this fatal ignorance is far from being confined to the semi-barbarous governments of the East. It is the great merit of the Oriental Translation Committee to have done so much already to remove it.

After addressing in a simple statement of facts, a justly severe reproach to the British government, and the British universities, for neglecting the languages of the vast regions which the one rules, and for which the other educates crowds of young men independently of the East India Company's colleges; Dr. Mohl does us the 'justice' as he says, to add, that the British public makes some compensation for this official sin, by supporting learned societies, and buying books of travels. He insists, that sound policy requires the *State* to provide means of familiarity with 'the language, the laws, the history, the civil condition, and the religious faith of the Asiatics, unless we mean to live in perfect hostility with them.' (Ib. 1843, p. 63.)

The Oriental Translation Committee's collection is, however, only one of several formed in the last twenty years, in France, Russia, and in other countries, which are carefully examined in these reports. Such concurrent efforts to enlighten the European public, must tend to realise the hopes of good and wise men, that our progress is not destined to be ever a career of violence; and it will assist the cause of sober reform, to shew some of the advantages to be obtained in this respect from those efforts. For this purpose we have selected a few historical works from the English collection, without including its poetry, its abstract science, or its theology.

Of these genuine oriental productions, the most interesting

are such as describe the political, and social condition of the natives at the time of the rise of our power in India; for the successful, and truly honourable duration of our rule there, must depend both upon our principles of government being good in themselves, and upon our public acts being in harmony with the feelings and wants of the great body of the people; and a more and more intimate acquaintance with what may be called their political, and social literature, will contribute much towards our forming correct estimates of these feelings and wants.

The particular volumes we have selected as calculated to promote this object, shew the rapid decay of the Great Mogul's enormous empire, a portion of which we have already acquired. They also enable us to trace distinctly the struggles of several states, Mussulman and Hindoo, whose rival attempts to found new dynasties upon the ruins of the Mogul empire, we have stopped throughout the whole of western, southern, and central India; whilst the same books furnish ample explanations of perhaps the chief cause of our Indian successes—a source of good only needing complete development, not only to justify, as well as secure our long possession of that country, but further to lead to an extension of European civilization by our influence throughout the whole of Asia, and to a duration of peaceful improvement unknown in the annals of mankind. This has been nobly proclaimed by the Hindoo, Dwarkananth Tagore, in return for well deserved hospitalities. 'India,' he said, 'had derived the greatest benefit from the British nation. *Their influence had relieved the natives from Mohammedan tyranny.* And they now enjoyed by law the same rights and privileges which Englishmen did in their own country.' Clear accounts of that Mohammedan tyranny, and of the most disastrous anarchy which immediately preceded its extinction in what is now British India, especially if written by eastern pens, well deserve our study.

The works of the class to be now examined, begin with Mir Gholam Hussein Khan's *History of the Mohammedan Power in India*. The first volume, translated by General Briggs, was published in 1832; and the remainder, also translated by him, is announced for early publication. Another English translation of it was produced by an ingenious Frenchman in Calcutta, so long ago as in the time of Warren Hastings. Copies of it are extremely rare, most of the impressions having been lost in the wreck of the ship in which it was dispatched to Europe. A portion of the period, and some of the events comprised in this valuable work, will be illustrated in the Bengali History of the Raja Krishna Chautra, translated by Mr. Haughton, but not yet published.

The next work is *Meer Hussein Ali Khan Kirmani's History of Hyder Naik*, better known to us as 'Hyder Ally;' translated from the Persian by Colonel Miles, and published in 1842, with the history of Tippoo Saib, Hyder's son, also translated by Colonel Miles, and published in 1844.

These works embrace the greatest part of the eighteenth century; when, after a series of conquests of two thousand years' duration, it was *for the first time made a serious question* how the oppression inflicted upon India by new invaders from Britain, could be stayed.

The Earl of Chatham raised that question many years before it became the subject of grave discussion in Parliament, and ultimately the occasion of the impeachment of Warren Hastings. It was strong public indignation, embodied in words by the Earl of Chatham,* not factious and party 'manœuvres, personal vanity, and fanaticism,'† as asserted, with an extraordinary disregard of historical truth, by Lord Brougham,‡ which produced and pursued that impeachment; and the impeachment itself was a part only of the great moral drama, begun with the public abhorrence of the avarice of Clive, and not yet closed.

Deeply corrupted as the people of India were by ages of tyranny, and by false systems of faith and morals, they were not unobservant of the great attempt to vindicate their national rights; and it may be hoped, that some written records of the feelings excited among the natives on the occasion may be produced by the activity of the Oriental Translation Committee. So collections of private letters, and official reports from *news writers*, and emissaries, much employed in the east, must exist, and ought to be translated for similar purposes.

The very curious Arabic production of the pen of Sheikh Jeen-ad-deen, entitled '*An Offering to Warriors who shall fight in defence of religion against infidels*,' is, in some respects, like these works. It describes the settlement of the Mohammedans

* The Correspondence of the Earl of Chatham, 1759, vol. 1, p. 392; *ib.*, 1767, vol. 2, p. 153; and *ib.*, 1773, vol. 4, pp. 275—284. These passages are too long to be quoted; but they well deserve to be read over and over again by all who would contemplate the dawn of the great struggle for 'a reformation, which, if pursued in a pure spirit of justice, might exalt the nation, and endear the English name throughout the world.'—*ib.*

† The *Fanatics* were Pitt, Fox, Burke, Sheridan, Wilberforce, and the numerous majority of the House of Commons, which, with the nation at its back, *fanatically*, as Lord Brougham ventures to say, abolished negro-slavery.

‡ Historical Sketches, third series, pp. 199—208; vindication of Marquess of Wellesley.

in Malabar. The translation, by Mr. Rowlandson, was published in 1833.

The small tract, entitled *The Memoirs of a Malayan Family*, published in 1830, from a translation of the late Mr. Marsden, has at present a peculiar interest, in consequence of the extension of our trade and colonization in the Asiatic Islands. This curious portraiture of private life, and of mercantile habits, presents a favourable view of a race whose generally good dispositions have been misrepresented, partly to palliate the misconduct of Europeans, and partly by the mass of the Malays being confounded with the *comparatively* few who are addicted to piracy. The British public is deeply concerned in a correct view being taken of the true character of a people who were enterprizing seamen for centuries when our ancestors were themselves barbarians; and who, under the influence of wise policy on our part, will attain any degree of civilization. It requires no extraordinary stretch of fancy to anticipate the time when Borneo and the rich Archipelago, from the Straits of Sunda to New Guinea, may, by that wise policy, cease to be alternately the scenes of murders of Europeans* by the natives, and something very like massacres of natives by Europeans.

The Japanese account of Corea, and of several other islands, translated by Klaproth, with Chinese memoirs upon the pirates among the southern islands of China, gives important details concerning numerous bodies of more or less barbarous people, with whom our trading vessels and our whalers are often in contact under circumstances which urgently call for attention.

Our survey of these few selected volumes will close with some short extracts from the travels of Evliya Effendi, translated from the Turkish by Von Hammer. It exhibits in a striking light the numerous public establishments for hospitality, education, medical relief, and trade, which existed in Mohammedan countries long before they were extensively introduced into western Europe,—including even Lunatic asylums worth Lord Ashley's notice.

The great oriental works published by the committee, such as the memoirs of the Mogul emperors, and various Arabian histories and travels, along with auto-biographies, and books of eastern legislation, published by the East India Company, and by private persons, fully explain the sources of Mohammedan power in Hindustan; namely, brilliant qualities in a succession of despots commanding the numerous invading armies; and religious fanaticism. The volumes we have selected for notice, sufficiently account for its fall. A cruel system of con-

* See the accounts of the murder of the Honourable Mr. Murray, and of our revenge by Admiral Cochrane, in 1845.

quest generated hatred and unceasing resistance, on the part of the invaded; whilst the extreme corruption, or the extreme weakness of the emperors of the last century, led necessarily to the confusion of which such enemies from without as Nadir-Shah, and such great vassals from within as the viceroys of the Deccan, would naturally take advantage. The rise of the Rohillas, the Mahrattas, the Sikhs, and the two usurpers of Mysore, Hyder and Tippoo, is seen in these volumes to be the simple fruit of ambition, no longer controlled by the sovereigns who had so nearly acquired universal dominion in India, and Central Asia. The Mogul empire must have fallen in the last century, even without the interference of Europeans. A more melancholy picture was never drawn than that in which the corruptions of the court of Ferokhsiar are described by Mir Gholam Hussein Khan. The great officers of the empire who had aided Aurungzebe in his brilliant career, were ungratefully and unwisely neglected, and even persecuted. Mean and corrupt men were raised to power. Enormous cruelties were practised. The most wretched dissensions paralyzed the administration of affairs in all departments. The most miserable distresses afflicted the people. At length the emperor was himself murdered in his own palace.

These events, and the equally important transactions of subsequent reigns, are told with great spirit by Hussein Khan, whose work abounds in anecdote;—and a vein of elevated philosophy may be fairly said to characterize it.

The following story is a companion to the famous case of Lord Russell's father, to whom James II. applied in his distress, in 1688; and whose mild reply that he once had a son who might have served the king, were he still living, was the bitterest of all reproaches.

In the year 1713 the emperor had caused the son of *Assed Khan* to be treacherously strangled.

'The year 1716, which was marked by so many troubles and feuds, became also memorable by the decease of the venerable Assed Khan, that wise pillar of the state, so long prime minister to Aurungzebe. He died after completing the ninety-fifth year of a life full of merit and virtue. He may be said to have been the last member of the ancient nobility, which had conferred so much honour on the empire. He had every quality that can constitute a character equally eminent in public, and amiable in private life; of a placid temper, and of a benignity of disposition so engaging, that to this day his name is affectionately remembered by all who knew him. Long before this venerable man's death, the emperor, whose misfortune it was never to discern real merit, and who now repented of his harshness (in executing the son), endeavoured to make reparation to that noble family. He sent to Assed Khan, expressing a high opinion of his character, and asking his advice in his own perplexity. The venerable old man, after attentively listening to the message, answered mildly: '*You have committed* a very *great error*. The destiny of my son was fulfilled, and you were yourself under the impulse of fate. But now the day of retribution is at hand; you are full in its way. I much fear, from the general disaffection throughout your kingdom, that ruin sits beneath the columns of the throne of Timur.'"—*Siyar-ul-Mutakkherin*, vol. 1, p. 132.

The frequent parallels in this book to examples in our own history, are not its least interesting parts; and they fully justify the remark of the late Dr. Arnold, that the annals of the east and west throw great light on each other. It is much to be wished, that General Briggs, the editor, will soon complete it. His first volume has a few specks, arising from the haste of composition. Its date is the year 1832. Its respectable translator has taken time enough to complete the work; and great as other calls on his attention are, this is one to which he is especially bound to listen. It will at least be an obligation conferred on all who are interested in Indian history, if he would republish the Calcutta translation of 1789, with notes distinguishing exactly the genuine oriental matter from any interpolations of the French translator employed by Hastings.

The biographies of Hyder Ally and Tippoo Saib, the two able men who fought hard for a share of the spoils of the Mogul empire, seem to us to throw much light upon the important point how we crushed our rivals, the French, in India; and then the vigorous rising state of Mysore, under Tippoo. Both successes seem to turn mainly upon our having organised the *Hindoos* as our soldiery. It has been said, with some truth, that the secret of the victorious career of the Arabs for so many centuries, in all quarters, lay in their appealing to the people everywhere against their oppressors,—the nobles and sovereigns of the world. In India we have used the Hindoos extensively against their Mohammedan masters. The French, on the contrary, took the part of the Mohammedans; and especially whilst Tippoo Saib was for years pursuing a career of merciless conversion by the sword, the French officers seem to have been his ready instruments in every atrocious act against the infidels.

These several volumes throw light upon another very important point not enough examined by writers on India, the extent of voluntary conversion from Hindooism to the faith of Mohammed. Without venturing to decide the point from such materials, we remark that they favour the opinion to which we are inclined, that the voluntary conversions were numerous;

and that they shew the gross impolicy of force in the cause of any religion.

The accounts of the Chinese pirates, and of the uncivilized tribes connected with Japan, translated by the Germans, Neuman and Klaproth, deserve more attention than we can now afford. The former reveals a great danger to the Chinese government; the other shews that the wildest aborigines may be ruled and civilised by kindness and justice.

An extract from the single Malay book, already alluded to, will be usefully introduced by a notice of the important steps taken by the French government in the last few years, to promote the study of the Malay language, and literature. Our direct interest in that study, is beyond all comparison greater than the interest of France in it; and every argument urged successfully by a learned French orientalist, M. Dulaurier, to induce his government to make the inquiries which have now been completed, and to establish the professorship, of which he efficiently discharges the duties, is a tenfold stronger argument for the increase of our efforts in the same direction. Besides our interest as great navigators, great traders, and *new* colonists in the Asiatic Archipelago, the history of its successive systems of civilization, well attested by its literature, its languages, and even by the remains of the ruins of Malay civilization, is recommended by every consideration of rational curiosity; as those ruins of which many may be traced to misguided zeal, form powerful appeals to our philanthropy in favour of the establishment of a wiser system.

Perhaps the most valuable memorials of ancient legislation still remaining in the Malay language, are *the laws of the sea*, of which a new collection has been lately published in Paris, both in the original, and in a French translation. A people, known to be spread over 200 degrees of longitude from Madagascar, west, to beyond Easter Islands eastward; and over 70 degrees of latitude from Siam, and Formosa, north to New Zealand and Tahiti, south,—a race of traders and warriors devoted to maritime adventure, as well as acquainted with letters, and with laws beyond all recorded time,—a race too, which the Phœnicians knew—must have been long familiar with the legislation best suited to seamen; and it is among this race that we, another sea-faring people of far greater pretensions, and perhaps for a nobler end, are planting ourselves with irrresistible power.

The Malays are, therefore, well worth studying deeply. Rich in spices, in tin and gold, and in precious stones, their islands are richer still in facilities for navigation. Their maritime codes are clearly derived in great part from a period far antecedent to the Hindoo and Mohammedan invasions of those islands; but these codes are also partially composed from later legislations and usages. The *piracies*, so commonly looked upon as the natural, and general characteristics of the Malay race, are but exceptions in their social existence, and the results of the decline of its old civilization.

The proceedings of the French in this field, amply justify the sanguine expectations and admirable efforts of Mr. Marsden, and Dr. Leyden, and above all of Sir Stamford Raffles, who, in making the best possible use of the best opportunities, proved that a colonial governor may discharge every duty of routine admirably, and at the same time cultivate with effect all branches of science. His example might relieve us from a reproach which has but too justly been addressed by a competent judge, to our Indian government, on this topic of the oriental languages.*

Sir Stamford Raffles, published a part of this maritime code, which M. Pardessus, and M. Dulaurier, have enlarged. The following specimens of it from the new French work, will support our strong opinion, that it ought to appear immediately in English and Malay, in a popular form for the use of our seamen in the eastern seas. Our missionaries can contribute to the improvement of such a volume; and the immense stores of Malay and Javanese MSS. in our collections in London, so well used by the French, would enable us to produce something of the greatest value in this way.

These codes as now published in Paris, are partly the materials which Sir Stamford Raffles used for his summary of Malay sea laws; partly new matter obtained from our missionaries, and from the Dutch. Of the historical importance of these codes, M. Pardessus says everything in the remark, that they may be traced to at least the thirteenth century, 'a period when the most powerful maritime states of Europe, were governed by customs, vaguely known, and not then written at all.'†

In the preface of the very learned author of this great work, on marine laws—a branch of legislation so important to us—he complains of a want of courtesy on the part of individuals in London, and Singapore, from whom he could not get even answers to his reiterated letters on the subject. His own in-

* We quote this reproach in its original text for very shame. 'La Société de Calcutta continue ses travaux. *Elle a été pendant long-temps seule dans l'Inde* à defendre les intérêts de la science contre l'indifférence des gouverneurs généraux, préoccupés de soins plus pressants, et aveuglés par le désir de substituer l'Anglais, comme langue savante, aux anciennes langues du pays. Annual Report of the French Asiatic Society, by Dr. Mohl. 1845, p. 15.

† Collection de Lois Maritimes. Paris, 4to. 1845. Tom. 6, p. 376.

dustry, and the perseverance and activity of M. Dulaurier, now Malay professor in Paris, at length enabled M. Pardessus, to publish in 1845, at the government press, what he endeavoured in vain to procure in the rich English collections, so early as 1832. One eminent individual, whom M. Pardessus accuses by name, of indifference at least to his requests, is so remarkable for more than urbanity in all matters, and the *Translation Committee*, of which that individual is a respected and distinguished member, has during the last twelve years, been pursuing a course of such rare and confidential intercourse with Paris in oriental studies, that it is probable some mistake exists in the case. But a mistake, which places eminent men ill with each other, in a work destined like M. Pardessus's, to last as long as ships sail in the ocean, should be rectified.

'Seeing that these maritime laws contain many injunctions which differ from those of the Coran, we begin by encouraging the servants of God, and by calming their consciences when they obey them at sea. This we do to secure respect to the authority of the ancient usages composing these laws. None must discuss, or dispute them; nor do violence to their shipmates in defiance of them.

'These laws were collected from the mouths of old men, when the kingdom of Malacca flourished under Mahmoud-schah. When collected, they were approved by the old captains; and so have descended to us.

'The object of these laws is to prevent disputes and quarrels on board; to put a stop to violence and arbitrary conduct; and to guard the people on board against misfortunes.

CVIII.—The sailing master is bound to be acquainted with lands, and seas, with breakers and currents, with the changes of the moon and the stars, with the seasons and monsoons, with bays and coasts, with capes, islands, coral reefs, desert places, mountains, and even hills.

'CXV.—If one of the crew draws his dagger, and pursues another in a quarrel aft beyond the mast, he may be put to death; but if he can be made prisoner, he shall be fined five pieces.

'CXVIII.—This code was framed by Haroun and Elias, by Captain Djenal, Captain Boury, and Captain Ishah; who deliberated upon it with all the captains. After their sittings were closed, they were introduced to the kings, who formally granted their collection as laws, and constituted the captains to be 'Rajahs of the sea;' and three of them were to form a tribunal.

THE CODE OF MALACCA, P. 48.—Whoever fixes a mirror so as to see the captain's wife, shall receive seven blows, and be fined a piece of gold.

. . . . .

'If one of the crew is fishing forward, and his hook floats under the ship aft, so as to let another seize hold of it, and the owner thinks he has caught a fish; but the person aft pulls the hook, and is hurt, he or she shall be at the disposal of the owner.

. . . . .

'If necessity requires the service of *all* the crew at the pumps, every officer, and other person on board, is bound to join.

. . . . .

'When a ship arrives at a port, the captains must ask the Schahbander, to grant leave to trade, paying all customs; and he must submit his cargo to the weight and measures of the port.

. . . . .

''Whatever is found at sea, shall be divided into four parts, of which the captain shall have three, and the crew one.

'If the finder of any thing belong to the captain, his share shall depend on the captain's discretion, i.e., in case any of the crew has found any thing when going ashore for wood, or water; for he is then under orders. Otherwise the thing found must be divided into three portions, of which the finder shall have one, and the captain two. If the finder is a debtor of the captain, he shall have half. If a passenger find any thing, it shall be divided between him and the captain.

'If shipwrecked men are rescued from their danger, and offer themselves as slaves to the captain who saves them, they may be sold by the authorities at the first port reached. But one half only of their value shall be given to the captain. They shall keep the other half. No attention shall be paid to the offer made by the men when in danger of their lives.

Cap. XIV.—'When the crew and two officers called the djouromonde, and djourobaton, are unanimous against the opinion of the captain, on any matter, they shall prevail against him.'

Such laws as these do not indicate a mere population of pirates; and the selections from them do Sir S. Raffles, and the Singapore press, much credit, but, we repeat, they ought to be published as completely as possible.

We cannot close this meagre notice of a great collection without adding a few words of respect for the memory, and of deep regret for the untimely and unhappy death of the individual to whom principally the Oriental Translation Committee owed its origin, and much of its usefulness—we mean the late Earl of Munster. Overcoming, by the efforts of a vigorous understanding, and by great diligence, the defects of a mere military education, and turning his service in India from a scene of military rustication 'to one of enlightened research and of honourable ambition,' he placed himself at the head of a body of men, whose labours we have endeavoured to describe. By his successful efforts to promote those labours, his name is one for ever connected with all that is most hopeful in Anglo-Indian story. Men more learned and more experienced than himself, supported the Earl of Munster in his endeavours to enlighten Europe by facilitating the study of oriental letters; but none surpassed him in zeal, or in the happy art of calling forth from all quarters the talents which are powerless, if chilled by neglect, but which prudent encouragement easily guides and strengthens. It was not permitted him to do much for good government in the East itself, but besides the great preparations made for that object, in this remarkable encouragement of the literature of the east among ourselves, we have reason to know, that his Lordship meditated giving back to India, with ample interest, all the benefits which we have gained from thence. He only wanted in an high employment in India, the means of promoting publications of the highest utility in the languages of the country. Among these the first would have been a complete encyclopædia of European knowledge, which would have familiarized the studious and the active with the theory of our practical arts,* in addition to the best courses of literature, and abstract science. He had also carried very far an extensive inquiry, which ran through the whole of Asiatic history; namely, an inquiry into the art of war through a succession of ages, calculated to attract eager readers of all ranks, and capable of being turned to an

* How much *practical* elementary instruction such as much of what Lord Munster contemplated, is needed in British India, at a time when railroads are planned in every direction there, is obvious from the following remarks, lately published in a letter from Calcutta:—'The great Government examination has been held in Calcutta, and the students and aspirants for honours have passed their ordeals in Locke, Milton, Bacon, Shakspeare, and Whewell, and in the more abstruse discussions of natural philosophy and the like. I would rather see classes for practical information, than for the most brilliant acquaintance with mere literature or mere philosophy. The educated are principally Hindoos, and the study of English literature alone will not turn their minds to active pursuits, but rather, still more induce, as the Sanscrit has done for centuries, those habits of seclusion and study which have kept them as a body from any active participation in or improvement of the affairs of life. I believe them to have as keen, discriminating, intelligent minds as Europeans, but this keenness and intelligence requires to be directed to practical results ere they can rise or be of use. I would fain see civil engineering, ship-building, mining, and the theory and practice of machine-making, (all of which can be learned as easily as Locke and Bacon) drawing and painting, introduced gradually and practically; they cannot but turn to good account. Railways will require under engineers, and I conclude natives could rise as engineers as they are rising as medical men, deputy collectors, and the like. I want to see an education given which shall enable them to turn their own natural talents to account, without official employment, without that absolute dependance on Government for advancement, which appears to be the highest aim at present of 'Young India,' and than which nothing can be more depressing. *I hope some of the essays, or remarks upon, or answers to questions given in the examination, will be published. However imperfect, they will at least be curious and interesting, and will deserve more than a passing notice from the press.*'—*Times, December 6th*, 1845.

excellent moral account. The value of what the Earl of Munster really did is a fair measure of what he would probably have accomplished, had his life been spared; and his example should excite those who enjoy better opportunities not to neglect them.

Art. V.—*Sketches from Life, by the late Laman Blanchard; with a Memoir of the Author.* By Sir Edward Bulwer Lytton, Bart. 3 vols. London: Colburn, 1846.

There is much in the career of the literary man in the present day, to awaken deep and melancholy reflection. This remark may appear strange to those of our readers, who are acquainted only with the few instances of excessive remuneration, which have been so ostentatiously paraded by the advocates of 'cheap literature;' but those who are more in contact with the literary world at large, will allow its severe correctness.

It is true, that the man of letters in the present day is no longer subjected to the neglect—even to the scorn, which the writer of the last century, until he had achieved a standing among the scholarship of the land, had often to endure. It is true, 'the sharper trials of pecuniary circumstance,' the severer privations of those days, are less common; the garret is not now pointed to as the appropriate domicile of the young poet, nor need the rising scholar thankfully receive a dinner, perhaps even a cast-off suit from his bookselling Mæcenas. But, although the station of the man of letters is, by common assent, placed rather higher, and such severe struggles for a mere existence, as those which Chatterton sunk under, but which Johnson triumphantly surmounted, can scarcely occur in the present day, we doubt greatly, whether on the whole his lot is so fortunate.

In past times, the literary aspirant, had indeed to live hard, in the earlier stage of his career; but then he had time allowed him to study hard, and the benefit of this, can never be lightly estimated by any one who has witnessed that 'making of bricks without straw,' which is the miserable resource of so many young writers who are compelled by a transient popularity, to pluck the half-formed buds, which time might have ripened into goodly fruitage. The rewards of literary toil too, in a past age, although tardy, were tolerably sure. The career of the writers of the last two centuries, it has often struck us, as not unlike that pointed out to the master Goodchilds of their era, in the emphatic frontispieces of their school books. Here is the young pilgrim toiling up 'virtue's steep sublime,' encountering indeed, many obstacles in his way, but still there is the sunny mountain top, standing out clear in the distance, and there is the smiling goddess, and the victor wreath.

Alas! for the writer of the present day. The goddess, and the wreath may appear but as just awaiting his approach; but onward and onward he toils, and still like the vanishing glories of the rainbow, the prize, apparently within his grasp, recedes as he draws nigh. He gains a small 'present payment' of money, and fame, but it is at the expense of the final settlement; he is cheered onward by the voices of a few, but he loses the loud acclamation that should welcome his finished career. As Sir Edward Bulwer Lytton forcibly remarks, 'in England, in the present day, the author who would live on his works, can live only by the public; in other words, by the desultory readers of light literature, and hence, the inevitable tendency of our literary youth is towards the composition of works, without learning and forethought. Leisure is impossible to him who must meet the exigencies of the day; much information of a refining and original kind is not for the multitude.' We may add there is that perpetual seeking after variety, or after that, which if not new, must be tricked up in a new form, and adapted to address itself to the fleeting fancies of the day. How injurious is all this, not merely to habits of close and long-continued attention, without which a writer can never hope to rise above the standard of a mere graceful trifler, but to the physical, no less than to the mental constitution. Then too, there is a certain amount of work to be done—done in a given time; and the writer, even if on his sick bed, must be roused up to his task, for 'the public' is a despotic tyrant, and will not be baulked of its expected amusement, even for a day.

This toil, this stern task-work, may be continued for years, — even more than twenty years, — and of this sad picture of 'hope deferred,' the writer of the volumes before us affords a melancholy illustration, — and all the while the man has, indeed, been just gaining a livelihood, but nothing more. He now finds, when health is failing, and premature old age creeping on, that the prize for which he has so long struggled is as far as ever from his grasp,—perhaps farther still,—for the long-jaded mind has lost its freshness, without having had leisure to increase its scope and power; and the scanty stock with which his career commenced is now wholly used up. But still he must go on;—not to fulfil the high aspirations of his youth,—for these pleasant dreams of 'some work which the world will not willingly let die,' have long passed away—but for bread, mere bread, still working the subtle machinery of the mind, as the famished weaver plies the worn-out loom, and alas! with the same feeling of hopeless drudgery.

But this cannot last; the subtle machinery will go on no longer, the slave of the pen drops, and insanity, or death, is his sole reward, with, perhaps, a charitable pittance collected for the family.

The graceful memoir of the late Laman Blanchard by Sir E. Bulwer Lytton, prefixed to these volumes, supplies a forcible illustration of these remarks. In early youth, and fresh from the commendations of his instructors, the young aspirant doubted not that he should attain a high place in the literary world. But, unfortunately, when he found that the circumstances of his family would not allow him to pursue the calling on which his mind was set; and that he was 'transferred to the drudgery of a desk in the office of Mr. Charles Pearson, a proctor in Doctors' Commons,' he quitted his employer and his father's roof to take up the certainly far inferior calling of a strolling player.

There is, we think, more of the fine gentleman, than of the sound thinker, in Sir E. Lytton's lamentation over the 'drudgery' to which young Blanchard was doomed. The muse who visited Burns at the plough, and Ebenezer Elliot at the loom, would not have denied her visits to the desk in Doctors' Commons; and had the young writer endured that discipline, we have little doubt that his mental, no less than his moral, powers, would have been greatly invigorated. It is a wholesome task for the young literary aspirant to contemplate the difficulties, the annoyances, and the disappointments, through which nearly all our great writers have passed. How few have enjoyed that much talked-of boon, —'learned leisure;'—how few have been perfectly free to follow the bent of their genius. Spenser, Milton, Lord Bacon,—not to instance a score beside,—how were they trammelled, not with the mere dull routine task-work of the copying clerk, but with important and laborious official duties.

Young Blanchard, disappointed in his application to the manager of a London theatre, engaged himself to one at Margate; but, 'a week was sufficient to disgust him with the beggary and drudgery of the country player's life,' and he came back on foot with his last shilling in his pocket. His next attempt for a livelihood was more respectable; he became reader in a printing-office. His occasional contributions to periodicals, whilst here, seem, however, to have encouraged him to depend on literature for subsistence; and, consequently, soon after the the age of twenty, throwing himself on periodical writing as his only resource.

His articles in the annuals, in the 'Monthly Magazine,' to which for sometime he was sub-editor, and a subordinate place that he occupied in the staff of 'True Sun' newspaper, introduced him to the notice of the literary world; and as 'his practice in periodical writing became considerable, and his versatility was extreme, he was marked by publishers and editors as a useful contributor. His biographer remarks:—

'The man of letters then was living on his calling; his brain ever active—his time wholly occupied. But was he contented, and was it for this that his boyish ambition had been trained, that his imagination had been cultivated, and his mind been stored? Was he fulfilling the promise of his youth, or realising the dreams for which he had deserted the proctor's desk? Editing *Monthlies* and *Belle Assemblées*—at stern task-work on *True Suns* and *Constitutionals*—was he nearer to or further from the goal, the hopes of which had first incited him to the race? We may venture upon the answer. His mind was less contented with its lot than resigned to its necessities. In 1828, when he was but twenty-five years old, Laman Blanchard had published a small volume of poems, called *Lyric Offerings*. In the year 1832, the writer of this slight Memoir became personally acquainted with the poet, and received from him a copy of these effusions. I was then conducting the *New Monthly Magazine*, and I was so delighted with the promise of these poems, that I reviewed them in terms of praise, which maturer reflection does not induce me to qualify.'

'My criticism drew from the author a letter, in which he laid bare much of his secret ambition. 'I look forward (it said) to some day, which the nature of my inevitable pursuits must render distant, when I may realise the dreams I cherished when my little volume was written, and escape from the hurried compositions intended for the day, into what I may call my inner self, and there meditate something that may verify your belief in the *promise* of my early efforts.''—Vol. i., p. xix., xxii.

Soon after this Mr. Blanchard was engaged in the editorship of the 'Courier,' but a change in the politics and proprietorship of the Journal compelled his retirement.

'His services to the Whigs, then in office, had been sufficient to justify a strong appeal in his behalf for some small appointment. The appeal, though urged with all zeal by one who had himself some claims on the government, was unsuccessful. The fact really is, that governments, at present, have little among their subordinate patronage, to bestow upon men whose abilities are not devoted to a profession. The man of letters is like a stray joint in a boy's puzzle; he fits into no place. Let the partisan but have taken orders—let him but have eaten a sufficient number of dinners at the inns of court—and livings, and chapels, and stalls, and assistant-barristerships, and commissionerships, and colonial appointments, can reward his services and prevent his starving. But for the author there is nothing but his pen, till that and life are worn to the stump: and then, with good fortune, perhaps on his death-bed he receives a pension—and equals, it may be, for a few months, the income of a retired butler!

'And so, on the sudden loss of the situation in which he had frittered away his higher and more delicate genius, in all the drudgery that a party exacts from its defender of the press, Laman Blanchard was thrown again upon the world, to shift as he might and subsist as he could.'—Ib., p. xxiv.

From this period, contributions to the 'New Monthly Magazine' and to 'Ainsworth's Magazine,' together with a situation connected with the 'Examiner,' supplied him with the means of support; and thus he contrived, by constant waste of intellect and strength, to eke out his income, and insinuate, rather than force, his place amongst his contemporary penmen.'

'And uncomplainingly, and with patient industry, he toiled on, seeming farther and farther off from the happy leisure, in which 'the something to verify promise was to be completed.'

'No time had he for profound reading, for lengthened works, for the mature development of the conceptions of a charming fancy. He had given hostages to Fortune. He had a wife and four children, and no income but that which he made from week to week. The grist must be ground, and the wheel revolve.

'All the struggles, all the toils, all the weariness of brain, nerve, and head, which a man undergoes in this career, are imperceptible even to his friends—almost to himself; he has no time to be ill, to be fatigued; his spirit has no holiday; it is all school-work. And thus generally, we find in such men that the break-up of the constitution seems sudden and unlooked for. The causes of disease and decay have been long laid; but they are smothered beneath the lively appearances of constrained industry and forced excitement.

'Laman Blanchard was now past forty. He had been twenty-two years at his vocation; it was evident that a man of letters he must continue to the last. At this time, in February, 1844, his wife,—to whom he remained as tenderly attached as ever, was seized with an attack of paralysis (her illness terminating fatally); was constantly subject to fits, and the mind was weakened with the body. A disease of this kind has something contagious for susceptible temperaments; they grow excitable in the excitement they seek to soothe. Those who saw most of my poor friend began to perceive that a change was at work within him. Naturally of the most cheerful habits, especially with those who knew him best, his spirits now failed him, and were subject to deep depression. His friends, on calling suddenly at his house, have found him giving way to tears and vehement grief, without apparent cause. In mixed society he would strive to rally—sometimes with success—sometimes utterly in vain. He has been obliged to quit the room, to give way to emotions which seemed to rise spontaneously, unexcited by what passed around him, except as it jarred, undetected by others, upon the irritable chords within. In short, the nerves, so long overtasked, were giving way. In the long and gallant struggle with circumstances, the work of toil told when the hour of grief came.

'Still, to the public, he wore the mask—which authors wear unto the grave. Still were his writings as full of pleasant amenity, and quiet and ready grace. Still, for the lovers of light literature, the bloom was as fresh as ever upon the fruits of his jaded fancy and grieving heart.'—Ib. p. xxiv.—xxvi.

But this could not last long. His brain became seriously affected, and the day before his wife's death he was attacked by what he feared was a stroke of paralysis, but which arose from congestion of that organ. Still he attempted to toil on, and was even endeavouring to plan new work for himself, although his nervous affection now attacked his sight.

At length violent hysterics came on, which left him in a state of extreme exhaustion.

'Towards night he thought that he could sleep. He dismissed his family to bed, and bade them affectionately good night. A kind-hearted woman, who had attended Mrs. Blanchard on her last illness, now officiated as nurse to himself. He requested her to remain in the next room, within hearing of his knock on the wall, if he should want her. His youngest boy, since his illness, had slept constantly with him. The nurse had not retired five minutes before she heard his signal. On going to him, he said, 'You had better not leave me; I feel a strong desire to throw myself out of the window.' The poor woman, who had rather consulted her heart than her experience in the office she had undertaken, lost her presence of mind in the alarm which these words occasioned; she hurried out of the room, in order to call up the eldest son. She had scarcely reached the staircase, when she heard a shriek and a heavy fall. Hastening back, she found her master on the floor bathed in blood. In the interval between her quitting the room and her return (scarce a minute) the unhappy sufferer, who had in vain sought a protection against his own delirious impulse, had sprung from his bed, wrested himself from the grasp of his child beside him . . . in the almost total darkness of the room, found his way, with the sleepwalker's or maniac's instinct, to his razor, and was dead when the nurse raised him in her arms. This occurred about one o'clock on the Saturday morning, the 15th of February.

'Thus, at the early age of forty-one, broken in mind and body, perished this industrious, versatile, and distinguished man of letters. And if excuse be needful for dwelling so long upon details of a painful nature, it may be found in the deep interest which science takes in the pathology of such sufferers, and in the warnings they may suggest to the labourers of the brain, when the first ominous symptoms of over-toil come on, and while yet repose is not prescribed too late.' '—Ib. p. xxxiii.—xxxv.

The essays contained in these volumes, and which have been collected chiefly from the 'New Monthly' and 'Ainsworth's

Magazine,' exhibit much pleasing writing. The 'extreme facility,' which his biographer remarks upon, renders them amusing reading, and the thoughts and views, although rarely deep, or original,—indeed, how can the magazine writer in the present day be so?—are marked by much delicacy of taste, graceful humour, and correct feeling.

From the essay entitled 'The Eccentricities of Affectation,' we extract the following passage,—the whole, indeed, is worthy of notice, both for the healthful taste and the sound feeling that pervade it; and it renews our regret that a writer who, had his mind been allowed 'fair play,' would undoubtedly have stood high among our essayists, should have been compelled by the exigencies of his circumstances to write too rapidly.

'The affectation of the unintellectual is as marked, as the pretended lack of moral warmth when there is a good blazing fire within. Observe, for instance, what is so frequently to be seen—that pretended indifference to the beautiful, which, if real, would denote a nature 'without form, and void,' with darkness ever growing thicker upon the face of it. There are plenty of good worldly reasons, grounded upon self-interest, personal vanity, or the desire of pleasing even, for exclaiming aloud, 'How beautiful!" at sight of some object of art, or some combination of the forms of nature, which nevertheless produces no corresponding emotion in the spectator. For playing the hypocrite, by affecting admiration, every hour brings with it some inducement; but is it not strange, that anybody born in a steady, respectable planet, and not in a comet, should ever have been tempted to affect an insensibility to the profound and fascinating influences of beauty!—should pretend to be so very much lower than the angels as to see nothing angelic anywhere?

'Nothing is more natural than that a foolish heavy-eyed plodder among pictures should affect to fall into raptures about Raphael, and boast of a capacity to appreciate all his divine doings. But nothing surely is more unnatural than the affectation of not perceiving anything remarkable in the Cartoons; than the affectation of a want of eye-sight, a want of interest, a want of soul, which if real would be a monstrous and most pitiable defect.

'We know well enough, why, in rambles under summer hedges and along garden-walks, the prettiest 'sentimentalities' are uttered about flowers by persons who have no real taste for those perfumed delicacies; but we do not know so well what people mean by affecting a fine disdain, turning up their noses filled with fragrance, and protesting 'that they can't bear flowers.' Yet we witness both spectacles.

'To do at Rome as the English do, when they go there—see all that is to be seen—denotes, at any rate, a laudable curiosity, and a degree of interest which is rather better than the total absence of it; but on the other hand, what a profound affectation of indifference to grandeur and beauty, of insensibility to the charm which thousands, though not sensibly touched, have yet the grace to pretend to be enslaved by, is conveyed in the answer of the elegant tourist to the inquiry—

'' Did you visit Rome?'

'' I think we stopped there to change horses!'

'Equally deep and exquisite was the affectation of a certain scholar, learned in all languages, who was for the space of a minute in some doubt whether he had ever read a tragedy, entitled 'Macbeth.'

'' Yes, I think I did read it once—I believe I considered its merits to be over-estimated. Yes, I remember it now very well.'

'This pretence to a bad memory ranks of course, under some circumstances, among the more reasonable make-believes; it may be convenient to forget; but it must be included in our category of absurdities, because practised often when it would be more rational to remember. Somebody is questioned about an affair familiar to him as his name—he can recollect nothing—it is all a blank. He thinks it looks large-minded to forget, and assures you with a simper that he has a shocking memory.

'Charles Lamb, in one of his admirable letters to Manning when in China, supposes his friend's memory to be weakened by distance; and accordingly, to the information that 'So-and-so is gone to France,' adds, *'You remember France?'* Some people would have face enough to affect to forget it, if they fancied this would add to the dignity of their littleness, or render their ignorance more impressive.'—ib. p. 165—167.

The longest article in these volumes is 'Confessions of a Key-hole,' a series of short stories and scenes. The idea is good, and it is well worked out; there is much severe truth in the exhibition of the various characters in their out-door and in their truer in-door, garb. But the forte of this unfortunate writer is, after all, the humorous, and as an excellent specimen we quote part of the paper entitled 'Young England,' the truth of which we think our 'Mamma' readers will recognize.

'Of Young Germany we are heartily weary, and with Young France we are horribly stunned. Of the one we have had quite enough, of the other a little too much.

'Let the first of these juveniles continue to wrap himself sublimely and mysteriously in alternate revelry and devilry, and find reason, as well as rhyme, in thinking deep and drinking deep. Let the second still rail and rattle on, equally in his own way; gnashing his teeth while he hums an opera air, profoundly bowing where he longs for a bayonet charge, and eating his own heart in sheer excitement as he fattens upon his frogs.

'All the young blood of the earth belongs not to them.

'Of the disposition and dimensions of Young England, however, one has a rather more distinct and definite idea; and at this very moment, not for once so ill-timed and intolerable, the united voices of those sons of freedom, my landlady's nine lively, spirited, frolicsome, delightful little darlings, convey to my mind the most animated sense of his identity.

'Yes, it is Young England, in his habit as he squalls! As he squalls, falls, calls, and bawls; as he laughs, bellows, shrieks, and squeaks; as he stamps, tumbles, jumps, crashes, and smashes; plying, vigorously and simultaneously, his lungs, heels, toes, and hands; as he clatters at the window, kicks at the door, knocks over the inkstand, tugs off the tablecloth, sweeps down swarms of glasses, breaks headlong through ceilings, tramples on tender toes, pokes out eyes with toasting-forks, flattens noses with family bibles, chokes himself with sixpences, weakly and absurdly presented to the little monster as bribes for quietness; hides in a sly corner some small article of indispensable necessity to his doting attendant; drops out of the window the very thing of all others he was told never to touch; makes his sisters' lives miserable; fills his papa's mind with sad apprehensions for the future, almosts breaks his poor mamma's heart once every day; and is, now and always, the sweetest, dearest, most delightful, charming little duck of a child; a darling little love of an angel, sentenced to be affectionately eaten up at least once an hour, and to have a piece rapturously bitten out of his rosy, round cheek, every five minutes; the pride of its father's soul, and the joy of its mother's fond and nurturing breast; a pretty cherub, a love-bird, and a poppet; lastly, in the expressive language of the nursery, which no language beside has endearing epithets to equal, a ducksy-diddly!

'Yes, this must be Young England! Young England all the land over.

'Hark!—but that is of no use; there is too much noise to admit of listening: and yet, how marvellously the accustomed ear discriminates, and detects the various sounds blended in the hubbub. One of the Young English is on a rocking-horse, and one is blessed with a drum, which must certainly be of orchestral proportions; one is, beyond question, spinning his top; and another is, past all doubt, crying out lustily for it. Most distinctly can the experienced sense discover a young lady, with anything but slippers on, practising her skipping-rope; and as clearly may be heard, amidst the exquisite and perfect confusion, the sharp, shrill, continual notes of two undeafened attendants of the softer sex, engaged in an interminable duet, of which the first part says, 'What a naughty boy!' and the second, 'You little darling!'

'Yes, and now, audibly in the midst of the wild dissonance and uproar, I can catch the mild, pleasing, affectionate twang of the maternal voice; the fond accents of my landlady herself, like the sea-music of the note of Mother Carey calling to her pretty chickens in the storm. What does she say?

''Ah, my sweet babes, so you are all merry-making together; I thought, as I came upstairs, I could *hear your voices!*' Dear young middle aged lady! It was only a mother; and a fond one, too; who could have said that. She could just hear her cherubs fluttering their tiny wings, as she came up! What fine ears a mother's heart has.

'Smash, crash! That was a sound of glass. Master Tom, the top-spinner, has had a mull; and the top itself has flown through a large pane into the street, falling with destructive force upon the large family-pie which the baker, board on head, was just bringing to the door. And now, what a shout lifts up the roof of the house! what peals of ecstacy celebrate the exploit! But the soft voice of my landlady is not quite drowned either:

'''My darling boy,' it says, 'what charming spirits you have! but don't break the windows, in case the draught should give you cold.'

'If young England in general should, in the slightest degree, resemble my landlady's lot in particular, why then I wish the Prince of Wales joy of his future subjects. They will be sure to make a noise in the world; and whoever may be the minister that shall have their 'voices' in his favour, he will be stunned—that's all!'—Vol. ii. pp. 386—396.

As we close these volumes, the melancholy thought arises, how many young writers may there be at this moment who have entered on the career of poor Laman Blanchard, and whose fate may be scarcely less mournful. The busy, driving, anxious spirit of the present day has insinuated itself far too much into the walks of literature; and hasty production is demanded of the mind, as well as of the hands. In this state of things we may look back with regret on those more quiet times when the scholar was allowed years to produce some great work; and when he set about his task—and it was a pleasant one—with a sober earnestness, and proceeded in it with an assured hope that his work would reward his pains. Strange it seems to us, when turning to the biographies of the illustrious scholars of the sixteenth and seventeenth centuries, to find that those great men who ransacked whole libraries, and almost half filled them, studied many more hours daily, than the desultory writers of modern days, and yet *they* numbered their threescore and ten, even their fourscore years, while our contemporaries are dropping around us before they have numbered even fifty.

The causes we have already noticed must certainly be taken into account here, but we think, in addition to these, another may be found, in the absence of periods of strict relaxation. This phrase is, we allow, almost an Irishism; but it best embodies our meaning. Periods of relaxation occur, indeed, to every literary man, but he is indisposed to enjoy them, or he is haunted by the remembrance of the work which *must* be finished by a given time, or deterred by the expense which that relaxation may involve. Now what is the remedy save that which has been so mercifully appointed,—the keeping of the Sabbath.

The illustrious scholars to whom we have just referred, belonging to an age in which religion received, at least, an *outward* homage, were secure of those regularly recurring periods of relaxation, in which they were compelled to relinquish their studies. The mere *repose* of the Sabbath may, indeed, be physically beneficial to the mass, although they forget in their Sunday rambles their loftiest duty, that of worshipping their Maker. But for the toil-worn, perhaps, care-worn, man of letters, what will the mere Sunday holiday do? He may wander in the pleasant fields, he may enjoy the fresh breezes from the river, but amid all, the mind *will* recur to its unfinished task, and the pages, still to be written, will float in between him and the loveliest prospect. But let him be bound to the keeping of the Sabbath by the strong tie of religious affection, and then, however pressed for time, however imperative the task, he will rejoice in an institute which affords appropriate opportunity by addressing himself to higher and better themes.

And who, save a writer, pressed with literary toil through the week, can tell the large, the abundant, reward bestowed, when, after availing himself of the Sabbath's repose, he again resumes his labour with a vigour and a freshness at which he himself wonders. In the keeping of *this* commandment, alas! so fearfully neglected by the mass of our literary men, there is emphatically a present reward. It has been our sad lot to witness more than one instance of the literary man prematurely worn out by continued literary toil; men whom 'methodism,' or 'chapel-going,' might have saved. Would that the rising writers of our day—a day of such fierce and eager competition in literature, as in all other things—would at least take example from our great scholars of a past age in the keeping of the Sabbath. They would thus secure that blessing which alone can render the most earnest exertions successful, and they might trust that He, who hath promised length of days to the righteous, would also bestow an honourable, and a happy old age.

Art. VI.—*The Book of Twelve Minor Prophets translated from the original Hebrew: with a Commentary, Critical, Philological, and Exegetical.* By E. Henderson, D.D. 8vo. London: Hamilton, Adams, & Co.

It is a wise maxim—*In all reasonings settle principles as starting-points before you begin the race.*—No superstructure, however fine, can be safe without an adequate foundation; hence many elaborate specimens of ratiocination break down, or fail of producing conviction, because they ultimately rest on principles which the hearer or reader disputes or doubts. The labour is thrown away, if the work is not built upon a rock. We must, therefore, go back with every opponent to some common ground; and many controversies would be settled, if the preliminaries were more closely examined, and not a step taken in advance till the *terminus* had been fixed.

There is no controversy in which this rule is so important as that between the Romanist and the Protestant; and certainly none in which it has been so much evaded. Could attention, in the first instance, be confined to it, many a bewildered spirit would see its way to an oracle, and would hear no uncertain sound. The wanderers in deserts and in dens would stand each upon his pinnacle of light, and exultingly exclaim—'Our soul is escaped as a bird out of the snare of the fowler.'

Religion is one of the most urgent of human wants. Men are willing to pay such a price for it, and are such bad judges of the commodity, that in their haste to possess it, or at least to think so, they have failed to test it; and consequently have in all ages been dupes of imposture. Now religion, to possess any power to impart consolation, must show itself to be divine. No man can put any hearty confidence in a religion that is obviously human in its invention, or that mystifies and conceals its real origin. Every man has a right, nay, it is every man's duty, to examine carefully and scrupulously the question 'Is this doctrine from heaven or of men?' It is a question that ought to be first settled. The belief that the world is in possession of a divine revelation must precede all discussions respecting its import. Its authority cannot be made available until it has been established. But supposing the conviction of its authority once produced by an appeal to adequate evidence, and the book of revelation opened to our understandings, or our understandings to its dictates, we then possess a clear and immutable foundation for what is called *personal religion*, and for every other form or relation which religion can assume. This is its only genuine and living root; the only heavenly plant that will thrive and shed its fruit in our hearts, and every other plant must be rooted up.

It is as disastrous as strange that attempts should have been so long and so extensively made to graft religion on another stock, surely a wild one. Yet so it has been, and so it is still. Reason and common sense are outraged by what is done in the name of revealed religion—not by religion itself, but by its pretended administrators. Throughout the greatest part both of Christendom and the Christian era a foundation demonstrably false has been introduced, not simply to the neglect, but to the modification, of the only true and sufficient one. It might be asked then—does any sect or church called *Christian* allege any other than a divine foundation, or start from any other point than revelation? We say, no; but what is conceded at the first stage is denied at the next.

A Roman Catholic teacher, if called to reason with a sceptic, would, no doubt, first endeavour to establish the proposition that a divine revelation exists, and that he can produce documents which can be historically shown to possess the *ipsissima verba* of inspiration; and supposing him to have wrought that conviction in the mind of the sceptic, he would then resolutely refuse him the privilege of receiving that divine teaching directly from its own documents. He would interpose a human oracle, through which alone the divine instruction is to be received. At the very moment when the sceptic yielded to conviction and admitted that a divine revelation was proved to exist, when he had felt the bond which such a conviction laid upon conscience, and was about to open the book and consult it for himself, his teacher would interpose and lay a prohibition upon the natural and reasonable use of the very volume which he had just proved to be a revelation from God to man. 'The church,' he says, 'is the keeper and guardian of this book. None else is authorized to interpret its contents. You must not consult it as you would any other volume: it is at the peril of your soul to do so. You might fall into ruinous error. Suffer the church to dictate what you shall believe and practice, and renounce at once and for ever all right to indulge in private or personal interpretations. This is the very term of your salvation: reject it, and I denouce you as still an infidel and a heretic worthy of eternal damnation.'

The converted sceptic might very naturally and logically reply—'I will do as you require, unreasonable as it seems, as soon as I am convinced that your requirement is founded on the book itself which you have convinced me is divine; but you will never induce me to forego the right of studying and understanding for myself the precious words of a divine communication, by the force of your *authority*; because, though I have been convinced by the strength of your argument, yet I see nothing in *your* authority above that of a fellow-inquirer after truth. You have convinced me of a fact—a most important and interesting one—and that very fact it is which now enforces upon my conscience the duty of opening the book, that I may ascertain what the will of my Creator may be. You must yourself admit that I can know nothing of your authority or that of your church till I have consulted the book. I admit its divine authorship upon rational evidence—but as to your authority to prohibit my private perusal and interpretation—it may be so, or it may be otherwise—but let me judge of that question by studying the contents of the volume.' 'No,' says the Romanist, 'not one page shall you unfold till you have agreed to accept the sense which the church has put upon the contents, and abjure your right to form your own views thereon.' Here the parties divide on one of the very first foundations of religion. Which of the litigants has clear reason on his side, which does honour to God and his word,—which destroys the only true foundation of religion, and as illogically as impiously, substitutes a false, a human foundation in its place, on which is to rest the superstructure of our personal religion and our immortal hopes,—all can judge.

The existence of a divine revelation, and the correlative obligation of examining and understanding it for ourselves, being the only first principles requisite or admissible, it might have been fairly and rationally inferred, that no man or set of men would ever presume to interpret or direct, by any limitations or restrictions issuing out of their own *soi-disant* authority, the legitimate effect of those principles upon human nature. The attempt to interpose between the word of the Creator and the intellect of his creatures, not by argument, or explanation, but by absolute command and prohibition, is equally degrading to the creature and insulting to the Creator. It is too serious a matter to be passively acquiesced in. It must either be vindicated by the unquestionable testimony of the inspired book; or, if it cannot, it must be spurned and execrated as an attempt at tyranny the most presumptuous, the most preposterously wicked, both against God and man, that was ever perpetrated under the sun.

Some persons have been absurd and presumptuous enough to think and even say, that they could sugggest vast improvements in the laws and arrangements of the physical universe; but we never heard or read of any one who had proposed to improve the element by which our organs of vision act; or of any inventor of a superior medium through which all eyes should be allowed or compelled by statute to contemplate the face of heaven and earth. Yet for many a long century no divine light was allowed to fall upon human intellects, save that which came to them through the refracting, and, we may add, obscuring, medium of the church; and no spiritual reality was allowed to become visible, even by that medium, but just such as the church approved. Still no one certified the world of the church's honesty, verity, and authority *but the church itself*. Yet all the time it talked of logic, and professed to reason; but it was in this vicious circle.

Of all the enormities which human presumption has ever committed, this is obviously the most monstrous, and the most injurious—that both the determination of the text of inspiration, and the interpretation of that text, should be claimed and usurped by a set of men who can show no more title to such authority than any other set of men. Yet Rome has claimed, and does still claim as tenaciously as ever, the exclusive right to settle both these first principles of religion. Its own Latin vulgate has been made to supersede the original text, and is absolutely isolated from all emendation and correction, while even that is not allowed to explain its own meaning, but is forbidden to be understood in any other sense than that in which the church understands it, upon pain of everlasting damnation. This is the triple crime of which in the name of mankind we accuse the church of Rome—a crime to which all its priests and ecclesiastics are accessories—first, *treachery* to their sacred trust; for they received the lively oracles to give unto us: second, *tyranny* over the intellects of God's human creatures; for they debar us from the rational use of those oracles: and thirdly, *treason* against the Lord of spirits; for they have usurped his supreme and exclusive prerogative over conscience.

If the Protestant reformation had effected nothing for the world beyond these two things—the emancipation of the text of Scripture from the iron bands and brazen clasps of Rome, and the vindication of the right of private judgment from the crushing authority of pretended infallible interpreters, it would have merited the admiration and gratitude of all succeeding generations. For what, we may ask, was the position in which, prior to that event, divine revelation was placed? Were its very words before the world? Was it recognised as the basis of faith? Was not even the version which the church professed to hold as its charter imprisoned in a dead language, and all vernaculars forbidden? Were not the originals, from which the church's vulgate was professedly derived, neglected, and all stimulus to compare and examine the *ipsissima verba* of revelation itself withdrawn? nay, had not the original text absolutely sunk into contempt by the final establishment of the vulgate as the sole authority? Undoubtedly this was the state of the matter; and it accounts for the numerous and serious difficulties of various kinds, with which Christian scholars had to contend, when the reformation began to draw aside the veil which had been interposed, and to recal attention to the original text, and to the right of every man to read and understand it for himself. The effort then put forth aimed a decisive blow both against the foundation and the whole fabric of human inventions in religion. Its tendency was soon perceived at the head quarters of the church; and all possible means and appliances were arrayed against it. Of course it was not possible to deny that there were manuscripts and versions in existence of higher innate authority than the vulgate. Rome itself had nourished and still contained scholars who were perfectly aware of the value of their manuscripts, and of the dependence of their own version upon the originals. But criticism was overlaid by ecclesiastical authority. From an infallible standard there could be no appeal. All collections and collations were superseded. Every question relating to the letter of inspiration was foreclosed; and there could be no reason for debating or opening them, save for the gratification of antiquarian curiosity, or the conviction of the sceptic. The library was closed and the priest kept the key of real knowledge in his pocket. Thus Christianity appeared to rest upon a new and artificial foundation. The priesthood had stepped into the Almighty's throne and usurped his functions. They had virtually forbidden God to speak to his creatures but by their mouth. The consequences of this system of treachery and tyranny were patent enough; for everywhere the people were so estranged from the fact of a divine revelation existing in the world, and existing not in the words which man's wisdom teacheth but which the Holy Ghost teacheth, that no man thought of asking 'what saith the Scripture?' but almost uniformly, 'What says the church?' And while the attempt to push the former question was denounced as heresy, and punished with death, the answer of the latter was deemed the end of all controversy.

For nearly a thousand years, or thereabouts, this state of things had continued. It had grown venerable by antiquity, and had become a hoary and an established fraud. It was no easy matter to break up the enchantment of this living ecclesiastical authority, to step back upon the foundation of ancient manuscripts, to determine their relative values; to trace the genealogy of versions and the purity of their sources. During the long period we have indicated, inquiry after the actual word of God had ceased, and the very desire of beholding and of hearing it had to be created. The very languages in which divine revelation xisted were despised. Some few penetrating minds there had always been, which could not repose in human authority though omprising both church and state. These either traced out for hemselves a firmer foundation of faith, or, secretly falling into nfidelity, regarded the whole affair of the church as a very ingenious, but at the same time a very profitable fraud, in which hey might innocently act their part and share the spoil. There an be no doubt that for long periods, and in high places, large numbers of the clergy had been sceptics at heart; for they had cuteness enough to discern the hollowness of the church's preensions, but were destitute of that historical knowledge which vould have enabled them to repose their faith on a divine oundation.

But the noble conception of recovering and making univerally audible the unadulterated testimony of God to his creaures, the bold idea of appealing to every man's understanding nd conscience as to the claims of that testimony upon his faith nd obedience, prior to any authority in the church, whether ontemplated as the germ of the reformation or as its fruit, constituted then, and constitutes at this day, the very essence and um of the controversy with Rome. These are the principles vhich that church resolutely denies, but upon which manifestly ests the hope of the world, as well as the destined glory of the vorld's Redeemer. It was the strength of this conviction in ndividual minds which first made reformers. A pure and exlted heroism moved them to the conflict against those whom hey could regard in no other light than that of enemies to the vord of God, because they kept it in bondage. Their assertion nd defence of their first principles left them little leisure to nquire into the state of the text, or lay down rules of criticism. t was a work of greater urgency, and they wisely felt it, to give he word of God liberty, by causing it to speak in a few of the ernaculars of Europe. It was honour enough for one race of eformers to have vindicated the liberation of that word and the ight to use it. It was hardly to be expected that they should lo more. They stood very much isolated from each other, and ad little opportunity for concert and co-operation. Calm study nd patient research into learned languages, then very rarely ultivated, and, therefore, but imperfectly known, was out of the uestion. Their ground had to be gained inch by inch from a nost resolute, crafty, unscrupulous, and powerful foe, who fought s for life against the startling novelties.

For a length of time, therefore, a beginning, and only a beginning, was made in the arduous task of collecting and reviewing he original text and its various versions. That they should ave found all these matters in a state of uncertainty and confusion is not surprising, since it had been so long neglected: neither is it matter of complaint that they should have done so little towards placing them in a satisfactory state. The very novelty of the work to be undertaken, the paucity of means and opportunities for effecting it, as well as the difficulties everywhere surrounding it, may excuse all the imperfections and mistakes which their successors have detected. Considering the circumstances in which they were placed, they achieved wonders which have never been surpassed. If learned men in Protestant churches, since the reformation, had emulated the noble examples set them in the infancy of the struggle, to make public the pure word of God, if they had possessed equal skill and manifested equal zeal, the important work would have been much further advanced in our day than it is.

But after the settlement of the Protestant churches in something like political security, and the quiet enjoyment of their recovered privileges, a season of repose and indifference succeeded, and the sublime enterprise which had been only commenced, and which ought to have been still pursued, was, in a great measure, neglected. Privileged versions were made and given to the Protestant world; but little was attempted, and, consequently, little effected to secure a standard text. Here and there an individual of indomitable zeal, of superior learning, and of large resources, undertook Herculean labours, and sometimes accomplished works of incalculable importance and of imperishable renown. The revival of classical learning, while it materially assisted, yet, by engrossing attention, in some measure retarded, the work of biblical revision. Even to this day Protestant scholars and divines have been more ambitious of excelling in classics and the exact sciences, than in studies purely biblical and critical.

Every one knows how deficient our own country was for more than a century preceding the commencement of the present, in the knowledge of Hebrew and its cognates. At our universities it had become unfashionable. Divines and theologians were scarcely expected to read it; and though a few scholars throughout the land cultivated it in private, and attained no mean proficiency, yet it had ceased to be made a requirement for the office of a Christian teacher, and was, therefore, not sought as a needful accomplishment. Among Protestant dissenters, however, the case has been somewhat different; for since they have been permitted to set up academies and colleges of their own, they have not only provided for the teaching of Hebrew, but have frequently added Syriac and Arabic—and, as a consequence, we believe we may affirm, that dissenting ministers generally are much better versed in a knowledge of the Hebrew text than their brethren of the established church.

We will not, however, here indulge in remarks which might be deemed invidious. We prefer to speak of our country and of the state of biblical learning generally among the Protestant churches. It is gratifying to observe various, and, we believe, promising, symptoms of improvement. For many years Germany has taken the lead, and been indeed far in advance. We trust, however, that Great Britain, which was foremost to hold up the beacon of divine light to the nations of Europe, and which has in modern times achieved the unrivalled honour of spreading the word of life in the vernaculars of nearly all the nations of the earth, will not be much longer in the rear. With such means as are possessed by our universities, and such patronage as may be readily commanded by those who pertain to the richest Protestant church in Europe, it would be a national dishonour, if we did not keep pace with poorer and weaker communities, in all the studies which are directed to the integrity and elucidation of the sacred text.

We are happy again to meet Dr. Henderson, the theological professor at Highbury college, in that field of labour wherein already he has won unfading laurels. His travels in earlier life, his labours in the dissemination of the word of God throughout Europe, and his acquaintance with modern languages and literature, crowned by the quiet studies and scholastic habits of his latter years, have eminently qualified him for the critical examination of the text, and illustration of the import of sacred Scripture. Few men have enjoyed superior advantages, and fewer still have turned their advantages to better account. We trust his life and health may still be continued to enable him further to serve the important cause to which so large a portion of his labours and studies have been devoted.

The work which is now before us is a companion to his former volume containing the translation of Isaiah, with a critical, philological, and exegetical commentary. It will now only require two or three similar volumes on the writings of Jeremiah, Daniel, and Ezekiel, to complete the prophetical portion of the Old Testament, which it will greatly delight us to know the learned author is enabled by adequate vigour, and encouraged by public patronage, to undertake.

The plan of the present work is precisely similar to that upon Isaiah. He aims throughout to give his readers the mind of the Spirit as imparted in the sacred text. 'With the view of determining this, he has laid under contribution all the means within his reach, in order to ascertain the original state of the

Hebrew text, and the true and unsophisticated meaning of that text. He has constantly had recourse to the collection of various readings made by Kennecott and De Rossi; he has compared the renderings of the Seventy, the Targums, the Syriac, the Arabic, the Vulgate, and other ancient versions; he has consulted the best critical commentaries; he has availed himself of the results of modern philological research; and he has conducted the whole under the influence of a disposition to place himself in the times of the sacred writers, surrounded by the scenery which they exhibit, and impressed by the different associations, both of a political and a spiritual character, which they embody. In all his investigations he has endeavoured to cherish a deep conviction of the inspired authority of the books which it has been his object to illustrate, and of the heavy responsibility which attaches to all who undertake the interpretation of the oracles of God.'

Besides the brief account of its author, which precedes each of these prophetical books, we have a general preface, containing a summary of all that is known concerning what was anciently denominated *The Book of the Twelve Prophets*,—that they were regarded as forming one collective body of writings. The Rabbins called Isaiah, Jeremiah, Ezekiel, and these twelve, the four latter prophets. Gregory Nanzianzen also, in describing the contents of the sacred volume, speaks of them as one book. The time when they were thus collected cannot be determined with certainty; but their number is recognized, and their memory honoured by Jesus the son of Sirach, in Ecclesiasticus xlix. 10, which dates about two hundred years before the Christian era. The collection of the sacred books, generally, is by learned Jews ascribed to the great synagogue, formed under the direction of Ezra, and continued till within three hundred years of the birth of Christ. It appears to be a well-founded opinion, that Nehemiah also had a hand in completing this collection, as well as in gathering together the other books of the sacred canon. In this work he would no doubt avail himself of the assistance of Malachi, as Dr. Henderson has observed; and thus the seal of an inspired prophet would be set to the entire Jewish canon. The testimony of the second book of Maccabees (chap. ii. ver. 13) gives strength to this opinion; and we know of no reason to doubt the historical accuracy of that statement. It is this:—'*The same things also were reported in the writings and commentaries of Neemias; and how he, founding a library, gathered together the acts of the Kings and the Prophets, and of David, and the epistles of the kings concerning the holy gifts.*' There can be no question that these minor prophets were all contained in the Jewish canon, when the

Greek translation of the *Seventy* was undertaken, which carries us back to within a hundred and fifty years of the date when the canon was thus completed.

The task of translating these prophetical writings, and of producing a commentary which should enable the English reader to enter into their full import, is unquestionably one of the most difficult and arduous which any author could undertake. The peculiarities of style, manner and circumstance; the local, national and historical allusions, the bold and unfamiliar imagery so profusely employed to give effect to prophetic representations, all contribute to perplex the interpreter. It is no light praise to say that Dr. Henderson has accomplished this task with a degree of ability never surpassed in any similar undertaking. He has resolutely adhered to the principle maintained in his former work—that no prophecy contains a double sense. His uniform effort, therefore, is to bring to light that one sense which is intended to be conveyed to the mind of the reader. His interpretation of various passages indicates his opinion that the Jews, as a nation, will be restored to their own country. He considers this an inevitable inference from the prophetic page, interpreted according to his principles. It is a matter on which learned authorities so greatly differ, that we are content simply to state the fact, that such is Dr. Henderson's opinion. The objections to it are not formally answered; nor, so far as we have observed, has it been stated whether he expects their return after or before their adhesion to the gospel of Christ.

It would not be suitable here to enter into minute verbal criticisms, or to weigh the reasons which induced a preference for any particular interpretation. Where we differ from the author, which we sometimes do, we admire his skill and learning. Instead of entertaining our readers, however, with criticisms on Hebrew roots, we will present them with a specimen of the work, taken from that remarkable and much controverted prediction in Zechariah, chap. xiv., with part of the comment on the fourth verse.

1. Behold the day of the Jehovah cometh,
And thy spoil shall be divided in the midst of thee.

2. For I will collect all the nations against Jerusalem to battle,
And the city shall be taken,
And the houses plundered, and the women ravished;
And half the city shall go forth into captivity,
But the rest of the people shall not be cut off from the city.

3. And Jehovah shall go forth,
And fight with those nations,
As in the day when he fought
In the day of battle.

4. And his feet shall stand in that day
On the mount of Olives, which is before Jerusalem on the east;
And the mount of Olives shall be split in its midst,
Toward the east and toward the west,
Into a very great valley;
Half of the mountain shall recede towards the north,
And half of it towards the south.

5. And ye shall flee to the valley of my mountains,
For the valley of the mountains shall reach to Azal;
Yea, ye shall flee as ye fled from the earthquake,
In the days of Uzziah, king of Judah;
For Jehovah my God shall come,
And all the holy ones with thee.

6. And it shall be in that day
That there shall not be the light of the precious orbs,
But condensed darkness.
But there shall be one day,
(It is known to Jehovah,)
When it shall not be day and night;
For at the time of the evening there shall be light.

8. And it shall be in that day
That living waters shall proceed from Jerusalem,
Half of them to the eastern sea,
And half of them to the western sea;
In summer and in winter shall it be.

9. And Jehovah shall become king over all the earth;
In that day Jehovah alone shall be,
And his name alone.

10. And all the earth shall be changed
As it were into the plain from Geba to Rimmon,
South of Jerusalem;
And she shall be exalted,
And be inhabited in her place,
From the gate of Benjamin,
To the place of the former gate,
To the gate of the corners;
And from the tower of Hananeel
To the king's wine-vats.
And they shall dwell in her,
And there shall be no more curse,
And Jerusalem shall dwell in safety.

The note upon verses 4 and 5 will greatly displease the interpreters of the Advent school, who have indulged such extraordinary visions upon this passage. It is as follows: the scene is the destruction of Jerusalem by the Romans:—

'These verses convey, in language of the most beautiful poetical imagery, the assurance of the effectual means of escape that should be provided for the truly pious. We accordingly learn from Eusebius, that on the breaking out of the Jewish war, the Christian church at Jerusalem, in obedience to the warning of our Saviour, Matt. xxiv. 16, fled to Pella, a city beyond Jordan, where they lived in safety. As the Mount of Olives lay in their way, it is represented as cleaving into two halves, in order to make a passage for them.' [*Then follow various verbal criticisms, and the note concludes thus*]—'That a future personal and pre-millennial advent of the Redeemer is here taught, I cannot find.'

In conclusion, we beg to recommend the careful perusal of this elaborate work to all biblical scholars. It is an honour to the age, the country, and the denomination of the author, and will, we doubt not, enhance the reputation he has already acquired. Younger scholars must be upon their guard against typographical errors; for though the volume is beautifully printed, yet it requires a much larger table of *errata* than is given. We trust, however, that the patronage of the public will soon afford the learned author an opportunity of correcting them. We heartily wish the work an extensive sale. It will be an invaluable addition to every minister's library. To poor ministers, their friends could scarcely make a more acceptable and useful present, than this and the former volume on Isaiah. Our readers will pardon the suggestion for the sake of the motive.

Art. VII.—1. *Priests, Women, and Families.* By J. Michelet. Translated from the French by C. Cocks, Bachelier dès Lettres, etc. Sixth Edition. London: Longman and Co., 1846.

2. *The People.* By J. Michelet, translated with the author's especial permission, by C. Cocks, B.L. London: Longman and Co., 1846.

3. *The Jesuits.* By MM. Michelet and Quinet. Translated by C. Cocks. B. L. Longman, & Co.

There is no sign of the lively and jealous feelings excited in the public mind in England, by the eager spirit of popish proselytism so broadly manifested of late years, as the reception of the work of M. Michelet—'Priests, Women, and Families.' One publisher boasts to have sold no less than fifteen thousand copies of a translation of this work; another, no less than twenty thousand. Catholic Churches springing up everywhere amongst us; convents founding; the very clergy of the Established Church quitting their warm fellowships and warmer livings to go over to the Church of Rome, are phenomena which strike the reflecting with wonder. They ask,—

"What! are we running back to dark ages? Is this the fruit of science and of philosophy, that we should quit freedom for slavery, enquiry for non-enquiry, the gospel for tradition, truth in all its noon-day clearness for the imbecile mummery and childish legends of Rome? Can all that our fathers have fought for and suffered to break the iron yoke of spiritual despotism be again surrendered? Shall we once more set up that which set up the rack, the dungeon, and the living pile? Have we won the privilege of unshackled opinion; can we enquire and discuss without its being at the risk of our lives and fortunes; and are we ready to stoop our necks again to the soul-petrifying chain of the arrogant priest? Is it possible, that with all our boasted enlightenment, our researches in the regions, both of history and mind, that we can become saintly drivellers, and the world's bright career terminate in mockery and mental servility?"

These appearances of things might well awake wonder; might well warrant these enquiries—but there is little danger—the sun is not going out—it is only a very partial eclipse. There are two causes sufficient to explain all that has taken place in England—the unconquerable ambition of the Romish hierarchy, and the long and happy absence of Popish intrigue and cruelty from the eyes of the British public. Since we gave a pretty tolerably decisive proof of our determination not to allow of the dominance of Popery in England by the expulsion of James II., we have enjoyed a long reprieve from the public arrogance and domestic nuisance of that creeping pest, the bachelor clergy of Rome. Public opinion has gone forward with erect head and bold heart; in our confidence we have resumed the legal disabilities of those who when in power would permit no freedom of opinion, and not even social, much less political privileges to those who dared to differ from their religious creed. We have been, therefore, somewhat startled of late years, to see the symptoms of aspiration in the popish party to which we have alluded. We see Rome openly elated by the recent working of its old leaven in the Church of England, calculating on recovering the rich sovereignty of these affluent kingdoms, and from time to time putting up the most solemn and public prayers for the return of England to the bosom of the knowing, and as she calls herself, the loving old mother. That day, however, will never more arrive. There are in all countries silly people who do not know when they are well off till they get a pinch for their folly, and idle people, who, for the sake of a little excitement, will adopt any novelty, however absurd. But these do not constitute any great proportion of the British public. The heart of England is sound; her intellect is awake, she knows the past, she enjoys the present, and she will take care of the future. If she has forgotten what popery is in the ease of her happy estate, she has only to look abroad, and there she will see enough to secure her judgment from any temporary delusion. The great movement at present going on in Germany is a sufficient awakener. What has stirred like a tempest the whole ocean of Catholic life over almost every district of that great nation? The horrors resulting from the celibacy of the clergy, against which they have long petitioned the Pope in vain, and the insult to the human understanding in endeavouring, amid all the advance of modern intelligence, to chain it down to the idiotic fables and jugglery of the most brutish of past ages? What has kindled civil war in the cantons of Switzerland? The intrigues of Jesuits? What roused that proverbially Catholic Spain to universal hostility to monkery, and broke up at once that old system of epicurean swinery? The fact that no man found himself safe in his most domestic relations, from the insinuating espionage, and corrupting influence of an unmarried, unmarriageable swarm of sanctified idlers? M. Michelet's book comes now forth to show us the monstrous effects of the confessional and of Jesuitry in comparatively free and excitable France.

In Germany, that religious ferment, which broke out on the protestation of Ronge against the Holy Coat at Treves, has been going on for these twenty years in the public mind. The scandal to public morals, and to private manners, everywhere occasioned by the celibacy of the clergy, and the horrors resulting from that diabolical institution, have been of such a nature as completely to open the eyes of the most simple and stupid, and to occasion loud demands for its removal. According to German policy, every means has been used to suppress the knowledge of the terrible revelations which from time to time were taking place. The press was securely prevented by the censor from ever alluding to them; the police hushed all possible discussion regarding them. Yet, spite of all this, such bloody and tragic facts have oozed through the thick walls of nunneries, and cast a horrible shade on the still roofs of village parsonages, as have thrilled with indignant terror the heart of every hearer. In many parsonages the people have preferred to see a family of children growing up of whose parentage no question could be asked, to risking, even by a single remark, the increase of that feeling by which infanticide was made certain, and fearfully frequent. In many states those religious pilgrimages to the shrines of certain popular saints, which still in Austria and Bavaria are very numerous, in which often as many as ten thousand people will be engaged, making long journeys through solitary forests and over the mountains, encamping in obscure places far from towns by night, and, perhaps, for days, at the end of their journey, around the shrine, in some as lonely a spot, have been obliged to be forbidden by government, from the license and the crimes to which they gave origin, and in which the clergy often figured most mischievously for the interests of religion. In Austria the resort to these shrines is still enormous. In the month of September, alone, the visitants to that of Maria Taferl, near Linz, often amount to one hundred and thirty thousand, and all summer the people are streaming from Vienna, and numberless other places, to that of the Black Virgin at Mariazell in Styria. To what miseries and crimes the shameless cupidity and trading blasphemy of Rome have given rise in every part of the world! To what a miserable necessity has it reduced itself by its doctrine of infallibility, for, having once sanctioned these follies, it cannot now condemn or abolish them. It is obliged to maintain them in the face of all Europe, while civilization and science are every day pouring a more intolerable flood of light upon them. It is by this very doctrine of infallibility that Providence has nailed the Mother of Abominations to the tree of destruction. There is no fear of her ever again resuming her sway over the Christian world. The governments of the most Catholic states are compelled to curb that license which she allows, and to put down those atrocities which have received the patronage and the blessings of the most celebrated pontiffs. The very clergy, themselves, writhe and groan under the bondage into which the decree of Gregory VII. has thrown them. A decree which has condemned them to a living death, and made them, where they should be the fountains of holiness, the most prolific fountains of crime and scandal. In vain have they implored the Pope to reconsider and abolish this unnatural decree; its abolition now would bring down the whole papal fabric. They are fast knit together in the doctrine of infallibility, and must stand and fall together. The friends of truth may rejoice that to whichever horn of the dilemma the Romish church may turn, it can there only see destruction. Retain celibacy, and the very clergy will cover the church with disgrace, and finally desert it, as now in Germany; abolish it, and the whole hocus-pocus of papal infallibility explodes. In the Black Songs of Benedict Dalei, purporting to be the poetic autobiography of a Catholic priest, the whole terrible mystery of iniquity, the purgatory and lonely wretchedness of a priest's life are depicted with a feeling that makes you shrink with horror from the contemplation. It is this terrible reality, acting alike on priests and people in Catholic countries, making the priest's life a true misery, converting him into a spy and a tool, compelling him who has vowed before God to proclaim the truth, into a studied and inevitable supporter of the most infamous frauds, a corrupter of the minds of the young, and a tyrant where he should be the friend; it is because the confessional has become the soul-trap of Satan, and the well of all spiritual pollutions, that the popular mind has revolted from the system throughout Germany, and will revolt from it, finally, everywhere. In England we have had these horrors removed from our observation, and, therefore, Catholicism is tolerable and even piquant to the imagination—let M. Michelet say what it is in France.

As might have been expected, M. Michelet, in dealing with Catholic priests comes chiefly in contact with the Jesuits, the most active, able, intriguing, and indomitable of all. Mr. O'Connell, a few weeks ago, in the House of Commons, boasted that there was not a charge against the Jesuits which he could not undertake to refute. It was a vain boast. Mr. O'Connell's word is not of that weight that it will be accepted against all history; and the history of the Jesuits is the same in every nation. In every Christian, and some pagan nations, they have excited the same feeling towards them—that of indignation and distrust. They have been expelled from every country into which they have found their way, and out of Rome itself. Yet Mr. O'Connell will undertake to defend their innocence against all the world, the common sense of all mankind, and the very infallibility of the pope. Mr. O'Connell must himself be a Jesuit, whose doctrine it is that a man may say anything, because the end sanctifies the means. M. Michelet regards the policy of the Jesuits in all ages and in all purposes, even the most bloody, as most effectually served by their influence over women. To this he traces the most horrible wars and massacres which they have stirred up.

'The weak minds of women, after the corruption of the sixteenth century, spoiled beyond all remedy, full of passion, fear, and wicked desires, mingled with remorse, seized greedily on the means of sinning conscientiously, of expiating without either amendment, amelioration, or return towards God. They thought themselves happy to receive in the confessional, by way of penance, some little political commission, or the management of some intrigue. They transferred to this singular manner of expiating their faults the very violence of the guilty passions, for which the atonement was to be made; and, in order to remain sinful, they were often obliged to commit crimes.

'The passion of woman, inconstant in everything else, was in this case sustained by thevigorous obstinacy of the mysterious and invisible hand that urged her forwards. Under this impulse, at once gentle and strong, ardent and persevering, firm as iron, and dissolving as fire, characters and even interests gave way.

'Some examples will help us to understand this better. In France, old Lesdiguières was, politically, much interested in remaining a protestant; as such he was the head man of the party. The king, rather than the governor of Dauphiné, he assisted the Swiss, and protected the populations of Vaud and Romand against the house of Savoy. But the old man's daughter was gained over by Father Cotton. She set to work upon her father with patience and address, and succeeded in inducing him to quit his high position for an empty title, and change his religion for the title of constable.

'In Germany, the character of Ferdinand I., his interest, and the part he had to play, would have induced him to remain moderate, and not become the vassel of his nephew, Philip II. With violence and fanaticism he had no choice left, but to accept a secondary place. The emperor's daughters, however, intrigued so well, that the house of Austria became united by marriage to the houses of Lorraine and Bavaria. The children of these families being educated by the Jesuits, the latter repaired in Germany the broken thread of the destinies of the Guises, and had even better fortunes than the Guises themselves; for they made for their own use certain blind instruments, agents in diplomacy and tactics—skilful workmen, certainly, but still mere workmen. I speak of that hardy and devout generation, of Ferdinand II. of Austria, of Tilly, and Maximilian of Bavaria, those conscientious executors of the great works of Rome, who, under the direction of their teachers, carried on for so long a time, throughout Europe, a warfare which was at once barbarous and skilful, merciless and methodical. The Jesuits launched them into it, and then carefully watched over them; and whenever Tilly, on his charger, was seen dashing over the smoking ruins of cities, or the battle-field, covered with the slain, the Jesuit, trotting on his mule, was not far off.

'This vile war, the most loathsome in history, appears the more horrible, by the almost total absence of free inspiration and spontaneous impulse. It was, from its very beginning, both artificial and mechanical—like a war of mockeries and phantoms. These strange beings, created only to fight, march with a look as void of martial ardour, as their heart is of affection. How could they be reasoned with? What language could be used towards them? What pity could be expected from them? In our wars of religion, in those of the revolution, they were each men who fought, each died for the sake of his idea, and, when he fell on the battle-field, he shrouded himself in his faith. Whereas the partizans of the Thirty Years' War have no individual life—no idea of their own; their very breath is but the inspiration of the evil genius who urges them on. These automatons, who grow blinder every day, are not the less obstinate and bloody.

No history would lead us to understand this abominable phenomenon, if there did not remain some delineation of them in the hellish pictures of that diabolical, *damned*, Salvator Rosa.

'Behold then this fruit of mildness, benignity, and paternity; see how, after having, by indulgence and connivance, exterminated morality, seized on the family by surprise, fascinated the mother, and conquered the child, and by the devil's own art raised the *man-machine*, they are found to have created a monster, whose whole idea, life and action, were *murder*, nothing more.

'Wise politicians, amiable men, good fathers, who, with so much mildness have skilfully arranged from afar the Thirty Years' War, seducing Aquaviva, the learned Canisius, and the good Possevino, the friend of St. Francis de Sales, who will not admire the flexibility of your genius? At the very time you were organizing this terrible intrigue of this second and prolonged Bartholomew, you were mildly discussing with the good saint the difference that ought to be observed between those who 'died in love, and those who died for love.'—pp. 26—28.

Michelet might have added that Ferdinand the II., who, while he sate and told his beads, accomplished the extermination of TEN MILLIONS OF MEN, died, thinking he had done God service.

The atrocities committed in this war have scarcely any parallel. The Jesuit order had arisen as the army of the church to exterminate the heresy of Luther, and they actually did succeed in rooting out Protestantism and almost every living soul from Bohemia, to say nothing of different parts of Germany. The German historians calculate that two-thirds of the whole population of Germany perished. In Saxony alone, within two years, nine hundred thousand men were destroyed. Augsburgh, which before had eighty thousand inhabitants, had, at the end of the war, only eighteen thousand. In Berlin, there were only three hundred burghers left; and the same proportion held in all Germany. The grand triumph, however, of Tilly and the Jesuits, was in the massacre of Magdeburgh. The soldiers amused themselves as a relaxation from their wholesale horrors practised on the adults, with perpetrating tortures on children. One man boasted that he had tossed twenty babes on his spear. Others they roasted alive in ovens; and others they pinioned down in various modes of agony, and pleased themselves with their cries as they sat and ate. Writers of the time describe thousands dying of exhaustion; numbers creeping naked into corners and cellars, in the madness of famine falling upon, tearing to pieces, and devouring each other; children being devoured by parents and parents by children; many tearing up bodies from the graves, or seeking the pits where horse killers threw their carcases, for the carrion, and even breaking the bones for the marrow, after they were full of worms! Thousands of villages lay in ashes; and after the war, a person might, in many parts of Germany, go fifty miles in almost any direction without meeting a single man, a head of cattle, or a sparrow; while in another, in some ruined hamlet, you might see a single old man and a child, or a couple of old women. 'Oh God,' says an old chronicler, 'in what a miserable condition stand our cities! Where before were thousands of streets there are now not hundreds. The citizens by thousands had been chased into the water, hunted to death in the woods, cut open, and their hearts torn out, their ears, noses, and tongues cut off, the soles of their feet opened, straps cut out of their backs; women, children, and men so shamefully and barbarously used that it is not to be conceived. How miserable stand the little towns, the open hamlets! There they lie burnt, destroyed, so that neither roof, beam, door, nor window is to be seen. The churches? they have been burnt, the bells carried away, and the most holy places made stables, market-houses, some of the very altars being purposely defiled with filth of all kinds.'

Whole villages were filled with dead bodies of men, women, and children, destroyed by plague and hunger, with quantities of cattle,—which had been preyed on by dogs, wolves, and vultures, because there had been no one to mourn or to bury them. Whole districts which had been highly cultivated were again grown over with wood; families who had fled, in returning after the war, found trees growing on their hearths; and even now, it is said, foundations of villages are in some places discovered in the forests, and traces of ploughed lands. It is the fixed opinion, that to this day Germany, in point of political freedom, and the progress of public wealth and art, feels the disastrous consequences of this war.

Here is one of the first exploits of the Jesuits after they were organized into the army of the church under their general, Loyola, to extirpate the heresy of Luther. Before Mr. O'Connell proceeds any further, let him justify that deed, if he can or dare. The horrible Tilly, inspired with the most demoniacal fanaticism of Jesuitism amid the smoking ruins of Magdeburg, spoken of above, wrote to the Emperor of Austria, declaring that the destruction of that fine city and the atrocities committed were the finest thing that had been seen since the destruction of Jerusalem, and regretting only the emperor's daughters had not seen it!

M. Michelet traces the progress of priestcraft from 1600 to to the present hour. He gives us the spiritual loves of St. Francis de Sales and Madame Chantal, of Fenelon and Lady

Guyon, Fenelon and Madame de la Maisonfort, of Bossuet and Sister Cornuau, the crimes of Mother Agueda, the loves of Father La Colombière and Marie Alacoque, the history of Quietism, the history of the Sacred Heart, and the condition of the interior of nunneries. It is to the effect of the priestly influence in families in France at the present moment that we shall chiefly direct the attention of our readers. One or two points only stop us a moment by the way. The story of Mother Agueda is an episode of that nature, which, as we have hinted above, might be paralleled in whole volumes from the Catholic secret history of Southern Germany.

'There was amongst the Carmelites of Lerma a holy woman, Mother Agueda, esteemed as a saint. People went to her from all the neighbouring provinces to get her to cure the sick. A convent was founded on the spot which had been so fortunate as to give her birth. There, in the church, they adored her portrait placed within the choir; and there she cured those who were brought to her, by applying to them certain miraculous stones which she brought forth, as they said, with pains similar to those of childbirth. This miracle lasted twenty years. At last the report spread that those confinements were but too true, and that she was really delivered. The Inquisition of Logrono having made a visit to the convent, arrested Mother Agueda, and questioned the other nuns, among whom was the young niece of the saint, Donna Vincenta. The latter confessed, without any prevarication, the commerce that her aunt, herself, and the others had with the provincial of the Carmelites, the prior of Lerma, and the priors of the first rank. The saint had been confined five times, and her niece showed the place where the children had been killed and buried, the moment they were born. They found the skeletons.

'What is not less horrible is, that this young nun, only nine years of age, a dutiful child, immured by her aunt for this strange life, and having no other education, firmly believed that this was really the devout life, perfection, and sanctity, and followed this path in full confidence upon the faith of her confessors.

'The grand doctor of these nuns was the provincial of the Carmelites, Juan de la Vega. He had written the life of the saint, and arranged her miracles; and he it was who had had the skill to have her glorified, and her festival observed, though she was still alive. He himself was considered almost a saint by the vulgar. The monks said everywhere that, since the blessed Juan de la Croix, Spain had not seen a man so austere and penitent. According to their custom of designating illustrious doctors by a titular name, such as angelic, seraphic, etc., he was called the ecstatic. Being much stronger than the saint, he resisted the torture, whereas she died in it: he confessed nothing, except that he had received the money for eleven thousand eight hundred masses that he had not said; and he got off with being banished to the convent of Duruelo.'—pp. 86—7.

M. Michelet considers that the Catholic clergy of the present day are far inferior to those of the early times of the Jesuits. The sons of peasants, not half educated, are chiefly what supply the priestly ranks, and that they endeavour to hide, by an assumed sanctity, their deficiencies, in an age when the laity, on the contrary, are every day becoming better and better informed. He shows, too, that the treatment of the nuns in the convents has much degenerated since the middle ages, and is now most barbarous. Then they were allowed to relieve the *ennui* of their existence by cultivating flowers, and by transcribing manuscripts, and painting in them many of those exquisite miniatures which so completely betray the love and patience of a female hand. At a time when our young ladies in England again begin to take the strange fancy for imprisoning themselves for life, and we have seen in London, that on such a day a nun is going to take the veil, it will be well for every one to read Michelet's account of what that life is now in France. He says:—

'Fifteen years ago I occupied, in a very solitary part of the town, a house, the garden of which was adjacent to that of a convent of women. Though my windows overlooked the greatest part of their garden, I had never seen my sad neighbours. In the month of May, on Rogation-Day, I heard numerous weak, very weak voices, chanting prayers, as the procession passed through the convent garden. The singing was sad, dry, unpleasant; their voices false, as if spoiled by suffering. I thought for a moment they were chanting prayers for the dead; but listening more attentively, I distinguished, on the contrary, '*Te rogamus, audi nos;* the song of hope which invokes the benediction of the God of life upon fruitful nature. This May-song, chanted by these lifeless nuns, offered to me a bitter contrast. To see these pale girls crawling along on the flowery verdant turf, these poor girls, who never will bloom again!—The thought of the middle ages, which had at first flashed across my mind, soon died away: for then, monastic life was connected with a thousand other things; but in our modern harmony, what is this but a barbarous contradiction, a false, harsh, grating note? What I then beheld before me, was to be defended neither by nature, nor by history. I shut my window again, and sadly returned to my book. This sight had been painful to me, as it was softened or atoned for by no poetical sentiment. It reminded me much less of chastity than of sterile widowhood, a state of emptiness, inaction, disgust—of an intellectual and moral fast, the state in which these unfortunate creatures are kept by their absolute rules.'—pp. 126—7.

Such is a peep at the exterior life of a convent; it is a fitting prelude to the dreary interior:—

'Do you believe that this poor nun is tranquil in this life so monotonous? How many sad, but, alas! too true confessions I could relate here, that have been communicated to me by tender female riends who had gone and received their tears in their bosom, and eturned pierced to the heart to weep with me.

'What we most wish for the prisoner is, that her heart, and lmost her body, may die. If she be not shattered and crushed into state of self oblivion, she will find in the convent the united sufferngs of solitude and of the world. Alone, without being able to be lone! Forlorn, yet all her actions watched! The preliminary conession of the nuns to the superior, easily acceded to in the first fit of enthusiasm, soon becomes an intolerable vexation.

'Forlorn! This nun, still young, yet already old through abstinence and grief, was yesterday a boarder, a novice whom they caessed. The friendship of the young girls, the maternal flattery of he old, her attachment for this nun, or that confessor, everything leceived her, and enticed her onwards to eternal confinement. We lmost always fancy ourselves called to God, when we follow an miable enchanting person, one who, with that same smiling, capivating devotion, delights in this sort of spiritual conquest. As soon as one is gained, she goes to another: but the poor girl who followed her, in the belief that she was loved, is no longer cared for.

'Alone, in a solitude without tranquility of mind, and without repose. How sweet, in comparison with this, would be the solitude of the woods! The trees would still have compassion; they are not so insensible as they seem; they hear and they listen.

'A woman's heart, that unconquerable maternal instinct, the basis of a woman's character, tries to deceive itself. She will soon find out some young friend, some lively companion, a favourite pupil. Alas! she will be taken from her. The jealous ones, to find favour with the superiors, never fail to accuse the purest attachments. The devil is jealous in the interest of God—he makes his objections for the sake of God alone.

'What wonder, then, if this woman is sad, sadder every day, frequenting the most melancholy-looking avenues, and no longer speaks?. Then her solitude becomes a crime. Now she is pointed out as suspected: they all observe and watch her. In the day time! It is not enough. The spy system lasts all night: they watch her sleeping, listen to her when she dreams, and take down her words.

'The dreadful feeling of being thus watched night and day, must strangely trouble all the powers of the soul. The darkest hallucinations come over her, and all those wicked dreams that her poor reason, when on the point of leaving her, can make, in broad daylight, and wide awake. You know the visions that Piranesi has engraved: vast subterranean prisons, deep pits without air, staircases that you ascend for ever without reaching the top, bridges that lead to an abyss, low vaults, narrow passages of catacombs, growing closer and closer. In these dreadful prisons, which are punishments, you may perceive, moreover, instruments of torture, wheels, iron collars, whips.

'In what, I should like to know, do convents of our time differ from houses of correction, and mad-houses? Many convents seem to unite the three characters. I know but one difference between them; whilst the houses of correction are inspected by law, and the mad-houses by the police, both stop at the convent doors; the law is afraid, and dares not pass the threshold. The inspection of convents, and the precise designation of their character, are, however, so much more indispensable in these days, as they differ in a very serious point from the convents of the old régime. Those of the last century were properly asylums, where (for a donation once paid,) every noble family, whether living as nobles or rich citizens, placed one or more daughters to make a rich son. Once shut up there, they might live or die, as they pleased; they were no longer cared for. But now, *nuns inherit*, they become an object to be gained, a prey for a hundred thousand snares—an easy prey in their state of captivity and dependence. A superior, zealous to enrich her community, has infallible means to force the nun to give up her wealth; she can, a hundred times a day, under pretence of devotion and penitence, humble, vex, and even ill-treat her, till she reduces her to despair. Who can tell where asceticism finishes and captation begins, that '*compelle entrare*' applied to fortune? A financial and administrative spirit prevails to such a degree in our convents, that this sort of talent is what they require in a superior before every other. Many of these ladies are excellent managers. One of them is known in Paris by the notaries and lawyers, as able to give them lessons in matters of donations, successions, and wills. Paris need no longer envy Bologna, that learned female jurisconsult, who, occasionally wrapped in a veil, professed in the chair of her father.

'Our modern laws, which date from the Revolution, and which, in their equity, have determined, that the daughter and younger son shall not be without their inheritance, work powerfully in this respect in favour of the counter-revolution; and that explains the rapid and unheard-of increase of religious houses. Lyons, that in 1789 had only forty convents, has now sixty-three. Nothing stops the monastic recruiters in their zeal for the salvation of rich souls. You may see them fluttering about heirs and heiresses. What a premium for the young peasants who people our seminaries, is this prospect of power! once priest, they may direct fortunes as well as consciences! Caption, so suspicious in the busy world, is not so in the convents; though it is here still more dangerous, being exercised over persons immured and dependent. There it reigns unbridled, and is formidable with impunity. For who can know it? Who dares enter here? No one. Strange! There are houses in France that are estranged to France. The street is still France; but pass yonder threshold, and you are in a foreign country which laughs at your laws.

'What then are their laws? We are ignorant upon the subject. But we know for certain—for no pains are taken to disguise it—that the barbarous discipline of the middle ages is preserved in full force. Cruel contradiction! This system that speaks so much of the distinction of the soul and body, and believes it, since it boldly exposes he confessor to carnal temptations! Well! this very same system eaches us that the body, distinct from the soul, modifies it by its uffering; that the soul improves and becomes more pure under the ash. It preaches spiritualism to meet valiantly the seduction of the lesh, and materialism when required to annihilate the will!

'What! when the law prohibits to strike even our galley-slaves, who are thieves, murderers, the most ferocious of men—you men of grace, who speak only of charity, *the good holy Virgin and the gentle Jesus*—you strike women!—nay girls, even children—who, after all, are only guilty of some trifling weakness!

'How are these chastisements administered? This is a question, perhaps, still more serious. What sort of terms of composition may not be extorted by fear? At what price does authority sell its ndulgence? Who regulates the number of stripes? Is it you, my Lady Abbess? or you, Father Superior? What must be the capricious partial decision of one woman against another, if the latter displeases her: an ugly woman against a handsome one, or an old one against a young girl! We shudder to think.

'A strange struggle often happens between the superior nun and the director. The latter, however hardened he may be, is still a man; it is very difficult for him at last not to be affected for the poor girl, who tells him everything, and obeys him implicitly. Female art perceives it instantly, observes him, and follows him closely. He sees his penitent but little, very little, but it is always thought too much. The confession shall last only so many minutes, they wait for him, watch in hand. It would last too long, nay prove, that without this precaution, to the poor recluse, who received from every one else only insult and ill-treatment, a compassionate confessor is still a welcome refuge.

'We have known superiors demand, and obtain several times from their bishops a change of confessors, without finding any sufficiently austere. There is ever a wide difference between the harshness of a man and the cruelty of a woman! What is, in your opinion, the most faithful incarnation of the devil in this world? Some inquisitor? Some Jesuit or other? No, a female Jesuit, some great lady who has been converted, and believes herself born to rule, who among this flock of trembling females acts the Bonaparte, and who, more absolute than the most absolute tyrant, uses the rage of her badly cured passions to torment her unfortunate defenceless sisters.'—pp. 129—133.

Such are the fruits of catholicism in convents. Who would not dread to see their spirit amongst us? How misguided by education, unfortunate from circumstances must that young woman be, who can voluntarily condemn herself for life to one of those dens of despotism, those hells of lascerated and lascerating passion. But according to M. Michelet, it is not to converts and religious houses that the plague of catholicism confines itself. It enters every house, and lays waste every domestic hearth where it gains the ascendency; it is in *the family* that he traces out, and most energetically denounces its desolating presence. The priest and confessor is omnipotent. The confessional puts him in possession of the dearest, deepest secrets of woman, and once possessed of them, he is their tyrant and master. By woman he then rules everything. Husband, son, daughter, all are within his reach, and he sways and embitters the existence of all. We may select a portion of a single chapter which will give us a comprehensive insight into the working of the whole.

'If you enter a house in the evening, and sit down at the family table, one thing will almost always strike you; the mother and daughters are together, of one and the same opinion, on one side, while the father is on the other, and alone. What does this mean? It means that there is some one more at this table whom you do not see, to contradict and give the lie to whatever the father may utter. He returns fatigued with the cares of the day, and full of those which are to come; but he finds at home, instead of repose and comfort for the mind, only the struggle with the past.'

'We must not be surprised at it. By whom are our wives and daughters brought up? We must repeat the expression—by our enemies, the enemies of the revolution, and of the future. Do not cry out here, nor quote me this or that sermon you have preached. What do I care for the democratical parade which you make in the pulpit, if everything beneath us, and behind us, all your little pamphlets which issue by thousands and millions, your ill-disguised system of instruction, your confessional, the spirit of which now transpires, show us altogether what you are—the enemies of liberty? You, subjects of a sovereign prince; you, who deny the French church, how dare you speak of France?'

'Six hundred and twenty thousand girls are brought up by nuns under the direction of the priests. These girls will soon be women and mothers, who, in their turn, will hand over to the priests, as far as they are able, both their sons and their daughters. The mother has already succeeded as far as concerns her daughter; by her persevering importunity, she has, at length, overcome the father's repugnance. A man, who, every evening, after the troubles of business, and the warfare of the world, finds strife also at home, may certainly resist for a time, but he must necessarily give in at last, or he will be allowed neither time, cessation, rest, or refuge. His own house becomes uninhabitable. His wife having nothing to expect at the confessional but harsh treatment, as long as she does not succeed, will wage against him every day and every hour the war they wage against her; a gentle one, perhaps, politely bitter, implacable, and obstinate. She grumbles at the fireside, is low-spirited at table, and never opens her mouth, either to speak or to eat; then at bed time, the inevitable repetition of the lesson she has learned, even on the pillow. The same sound of the same bell for ever and ever; who could withstand it? What is to be done? Give in, or become mad!' pp. 148—50.

And thus the slavery is perpetuated. Thus are the thoughts, the concerns, the most secret, the most domestic, the most vital to the honour, safety and interest of every man put at the mercy of the black emissaries of a foreign prince, who has the names even of all school-girls who distinguish themselves for ability regularly sent to Rome to be registered there for future use, that is, to make tools of them when necessary against their husbands, brothers, fathers, and country. Let us thank God that this pestilence has not yet regained its hideous ascendency in this country, and for the hope that it never will. That our domestic hearths are yet free from this most intolerable of curses; that we can repose the dearest secrets of our bosoms in those of our wives, without a fear that some cowled master of the black art may steal into our dwelling in our absence, to draw them thence, aye, by threats of eternal damnation, if necessary, to grin over in fiendish mockery, or to employ them to our ruin. Yet it is for this end that the ceaseless and most strenuous efforts of the whole catholic world, of the whole army of Jesuits are daily directed against England, that wealthiest of nations, that prize so desirable for the poor exchequer of Rome.

M. Michelet having made this masterly *exposé* of the priestcraft of France, takes a more comprehensive subject —The People. This work, as dealing with the French people, must be very interesting to us, because, though the circumstances of France and England are different, we find, on following M. Michelet's details, that the same political and social causes in both countries go on producing the same effects. He finds a decided tendency to centralization and aristocratic absorption of property. The lands which at the Revolution were rent away from the old noblesse and distributed amongst the people, notwithstanding the extreme attachment of the small proprietors to their little possessions gradually, by loans of money, and then by sales, returning to the hands of a few. He traces, what he calls the bondage of the different classes—of the artizan to machinery, the ordinary workman to his habits and ambition of rising out of his class, of the manufacturer to the intense competition with England and other nations; the tradesman, again, by competition which drives him to adulterate and deceive; the official to the same cause, competition for all sorts of offices, and hence low salaries and the temptation to bribery. France, according to Michelet, is ill at ease in her social condition. 'Bondage!' he exclaims, 'heavy bondage! I find it among the high and the low in every degree, crushing the most worthy, the most humble, the most deserving! I do not speak of another kind, of an oblique, indirect dependency, which, beginning high, descends low, weighs heavily, penetrates, enters into details, inquiries, and wants to tyrannize even over the very soul.' In what then does this bondage consist? In a universal ambition to be more than circumstances allow. That same feverish ambition of wealth and station, and distinction which is just as rife on this side of the channel—the fatal disease of aristocratic rivalry engendered by a false condition of things springing up between great possessions and glittering titles, and the acquisition of fortunes which may give those. Europe has yet to pass through this fermentation of a spurious emulation till it finds how empty and joyless it is, and the wise set the example of a return to simplicity, nature, and content. How exactly is the condition of both countries alike in this respect :—

'The more wealthy class become more and more distant; they pass some time in the country, but do not settle there; their home is in town. They leave the field open to the village banker and the lawyer, the secret confessor of all, who preys on all. 'I will no longer have any dealings with these people,' says the proprietor; 'the notary shall arrange every thing; I leave it with him; he shall settle with me, and give out and divide the rent as he pleases.' The notary, in many places, thus becomes the sole farmer, the only medium between the rich proprietor and the labourer. A great misfortune for the peasant. To escape from the thraldom of the proprietor, who would generally wait, and was long satisfied with promises—he has taken for his master the lawyer, the monied man, who knows only when a bill is due.'—p. 39.

Is it better with the manufacturing population?

'We must enter the manufactory while it is working, and then we understand how that silence, that captivity during long hours, enjoin at their exit, noise, cries, and movement, for the re-establishment of the vital equilibrium. That is especially true of the great spinning and weaving workshop—that real hell of *ennui*. *Ever, ever, ever*, is the unvarying sound thundering in your ears from the automatic rumbling of wheels shaking the very floor. Never can one get habituated to it. At the end of twenty years, as on the first day, the *ennui*, the giddiness, and the nausea, are the same. Does the heart beat in that crowd? Very little; its action is as if suspended; it seems during those long hours, as if another heart, common to all, has taken its place—a metallic, indifferent, pitiless heart;—and that this loud rumbling noise, deafening in its regularity, is only its beating. The solitary task of the weaver was far less painful. Why? Because he could muse. Machinery allows no reverie, no musing.'—p. 57.

Of all the officials, the worst paid, according to M. Michelet, is the schoolmaster. The government system of education does not answer in France.

'A baker's boy, in Paris, earns more than two custom-house officers; more than a lieutenant of infantry; more than many a magistrate; more than the majority of professors; *he earns as much as six parish schoolmasters!*

'Shame! shame! the nation that pays the least to those that instruct the people—let us blush to confess it—is France. I speak of the France of these days. On the contrary, the true France, that of the Revolution, declared that teaching was a holy office, that the schoolmaster was equal to the priest. It laid down the principle that the first expense of the state was instruction. The Convention, in its terrible penury, wished to give fifty-four millions of francs to primary instruction, and would certainly have done so, had it lasted longer. A singular age, when men called themselves materialists, but which was, in reality, the apotheosis of the mind, the reign of the spirit.

'I do not conceal it; of all the miseries of the present day, there is not one that grieves me more. The most deserving, the most miserable, the most neglected man in France is the parish schoolmaster. M. Lorain, in his 'Tableau de l'Instruction Primaire,' an official work of the highest importance, in which he gives a summary of the reports of four hundred and ninety inspectors, who visited all the schools in 1833, cannot find expressions strong enough to describe the state of misery and abjectness in which he found our teachers. He declares that some get altogether but one hundred francs, some sixty, others fifty,—two pounds a-year! Moreover, they have to wait a long time for payment, which often is not forth-coming! They are not paid in money; every family sets apart the worst of the crop for the schoolmaster, *who goes on Sunday to beg at every door* with a sack *on his back*: he is not welcome when he claims his small lot of potatoes, *they find he is robbing the pigs!* &c. Since these official reports new schools have been erected, but the fate of the old masters has not improved. Let us hope that the Chamber of Deputies will grant this year the increase of a hundred francs, which last year was demanded in vain.'—p. 100.

M. Michelet complains that the *bourgeoisie,* the middle class, is a failure in France, a spurious mongrel class, aping a nobility, and despising the people out of which it is sprung.

'It is not we who say so, but itself. The most melancholy confessions escape it about its own rapid decline, and that of France, whom it drags down with it.'—p. 107.

'We have seen this man of to-day decrease at every step that seemed to exalt him. When a peasant, he had austere morals, sobriety, and economy; when a workman he was a good companion and a great help to his family; when a manufacturer, he was active, energetic, and had his manufacturing patriotism, which struggled against foreign industry. He has left all that on the road, and nothing has taken its place: his house is filled; his coffer is full, his soul is—empty.'—p. 114.

M. Michelet complains that the old agricultural associations of France are falling into decay; he has no faith in communism;

'As to communism, one word will suffice. The last country in which property will be abolished, will be precisely France. If, as some one of that school said, 'Property is nothing but a theft,' we have here twenty-five millions of thieves, who will not refund in a day.' p. 111.

To what, then, does M. Michelet look for the salvation of society in his country? First to war, a French fascination, but unworthy of the generally humane spirit and enlightened views of our author, and most inconsistent with his other remedies—Nature and Love. Nature and Love! beautiful words and soon spoken, not so soon brought into general operation. We must look for a remedy in another medium, or at least in love producing another means of renovation—the general, sound, and Christian education of the people. It is only in proportion as the mass of the people advances in true knowledge, so as to perceive the advantages of union, and to feel the beauty of moral principle, that they will assert their own rights with that deliberate strength and justice which are omnipotent. As they approach nearer and nearer to this condition, they will more and more exert a salutary influence on society at large. They will claim and secure a more equal share of the fruits of their industry. Thus putting a check on the present inordinate tendency of capital to run into enormous masses, so leaving enormous masses of destitution in other quarters of society! Contented, as they always show themselves, with their due share of prosperity, the charms of reading and of domestic life will place them in a position not to envy, but to look down upon the frivolous pleasures of the luxurious classes. This is the only radical cure for the present evils of society—enlighten, moralize, and make happy. We are glad that M. Michelet, born and educated amongst them, bears such ample testimony to the sound heart and many virtues of the working and peasant classes of France. It is our own experience of the same classes in this country, and affords the most encouraging ground to the unwearying efforts of the schoolmaster and the philanthropist. When we have a good, sound soil to work in, what may we not do? If the crop which is raised from it be not good, it will be the fault of sowing bad seed and tending it badly in its growth. M. Michelet denies the correctness of the common pictures of French society drawn by their novelists. He declares them monstrosities and exceptions. Above all, he relies, in the highest degree, on the moral power of rightly-instructed woman—on the enlightened mother. 'She will tell her child the three revelations she has received. How Rome taught her the Just, Greece the Beautiful, and Judea the Holy. She will connect ier last lesson with the first—the one taught him *God*, the other will teach him the dogma of love,—*God in man*—Christianity.'

With many French characteristics, some vapouring, a great deal of jealousy of England, and the sad crotchet of the benefits of war, M. Michelet still displays a fine and generous mind; the spirit of the philosophy of love; the spirit of popular advance; in a word, he is a writer whom all should read, and whom no one can read without being the better for it.

Of the third work in our list, 'The Jesuits,' we need only say that it is worthy of its title and of its united authors, M. M. Michelet and Quinet.

Art. VIII.—*A Harmony of the Four Gospels, in Greek, according to the text of Hahn, newly arranged, with explanatory notes.* By Edward Robinson, D.D., L.L.D. Professor of Biblical Literature in the Union Theological Seminary, New York, &c. &c. Boston: Crocker and Brewster; London, Wiley and Putnam. 1845.

We have fallen in with no work of recent date, which has more forcibly reminded us than this has, of the old proverb: 'Good wine needs no bush.' A brief inspection of it will satisfy every competent inquirer, that it is a volume of extraordinary merit. Dr. Robinson has not only taken most elaborate pains to arrange the matter of the several gospels as nearly in chronological order as the known chronological vestiges admit, but he has furnished an appendix of instructive valuable notes, in which the reasons which have guided his judgment in cases of difficulty are very satisfactorily elucidated. From these notes it is evident that the same unwearied patience which he had previously, for a series of years, exercised in clearing up the *dubia vexata* of sacred geography, has been applied to this more recent subject of his studies; and when we add, that there really seems to be no recent work upon the Gospels which has escaped his notice, those of our readers who are acquainted with the interest which during the last ten years the Gospel history has attracted in Germany, will at once perceive that he has undertaken a herculean labour, with herculean industry and perseverance. Various questions have suggested themselves to our minds while perusing his notes, which have strongly urged us to defer our review of the work till we could enter more comprehensively and completely into the illustration of its merits, but since the future is always an uncertainty, and we know from experience that future leisure is well nigh the greatest of all uncertainties, we feel that we act more justly towards the work itself, and better consult the interests of Biblical students, by an immediate, though necessarily, a brief and somewhat perfunctory notice.

Our readers are probably not ignorant of the different systems on which harmonies have been arranged, or of the different data which have been made the basis of arrangement. Some, as Andrew Osiander, and in more recent times, Macknight, have assumed that each of the evangelists has followed the order of time in his narrative, and have arranged accordingly. Others, too numerous to mention, have with far greater probability—a probability indeed all but demonstrative—affirmed that similarity of subject has frequently caused facts or discourses to be connected, or consecutively narrated in the gospels, which had no such connexion in reality. Some, again, as Clement of Alexandria and Origen in ancient times, and Priestley among the moderns, supposed that our Lord's ministry continued little more than twelve months, while others, with greater perspicuity in detecting and interpreting the indexes of times and seasons, have extended it to a period of nearly four years. But we need not dilate on these differences, which are discussed or touched upon in various elementary books.* The basis of Dr. Robinson's arrangement is stated, in our opinion, very satisfactorily in his introductory note:

'The gospels of Matthew, Mark and Luke, along with many diversities, have nevertheless a striking affinity with each other in their general features of time and place. But, when compared with John's gospel, there is seen to be a diversity no less striking between them and the latter, not only in respect to chronology, but likewise as to the part of the country where our Lord's discourses and mighty works mainly occurred. The three speak only of one passover, that at which Jesus suffered; and from this it would follow, that our Lord's ministry continued at most only about six months. John expressly enumerates three passovers, and more probably four, during Christ's ministry; which therefore must have had a duration of at least two-and-a-half years, and more probably of three-and-a-half. Again, Matthew, Mark, and Luke, place the scene of Jesus's public ministrations chiefly in Galilee; whence he goes up to Jerusalem only just before his death. John, on the other hand, narrates the miracles and discourses of our Lord, as occurring principally at Jerusalem, on various former occasions as well as at his last visit.

'The first difference is at once set aside by the remark, that although the three evangelists do expressly mention only one passover, yet they do not any where, nor in any way, affirm, or even imply, that

* The late Dr. Lant Carpenter, in particular, has in a small 12mo. volume, on the Geography of the New Testament, which has passed through several editions, given outlines of our Lord's history, in accordance both with the shorter term contended for by Priestley and the usual longer computation.

there were no more; while the testimony of John is express and definite. And further, the incident narrated by all the three writers, of the disciples plucking ripe ears of grain as they went through the fields, necessarily pre-supposes the recent occurrence of a passover during our Lord's ministry, different from the one at which he suffered; and this is further confirmed by Luke's mention of the σάββατον δευτερόπρωτον in the same connection. See Matthew xii. 1. Mark ii. 23. Luke vi. 1. See also notes on sections 35, 37.

'This difference being thus satisfactorily explained, the existence of the second difference is of course accounted for. If John is right in enumerating several passovers, he is right in narrating what took place at Jerusalem on those occasions. But more than this, we find in the other evangelists several things in which they too seem to allude to earlier visits and labours of Jesus in the holy city. So the language in which our Lord laments over Jerusalem, as having rejected his offers, Matthew xxiii. 37; Luke xiii. 34. So too, the mention of Scribes and Pharisees from Jerusalem, who seek to catch him in his words, Matthew iv. 25, xv. 1; and further, his intimate relations with the family of Lazarus, Luke x. 38, 39; compare John xi. 1, 2. See, generally, Neander's Leben Jesu, p. 384, sq. 3te. Ausg.

'For these reasons, I do not hesitate to follow, with most other commentators, the chronology of John's gospel, and assign to our Lord's ministry four passovers, at a duration of three and a half years. The second of these passovers, which is less certain than the rest, and depends on the interpretation of John v. 1, will be considered in its place. See note, on section 36.

'The gospels, and especially the first three, can in no sense be regarded as methodical annals. It is therefore difficult, and perhaps impossible, so to harmonise them, in respect to time, as in all cases to arrive at results which shall be entirely certain and satisfactory.

'There is often no definite note of time, and then we can proceed only upon conjecture, founded on a careful comparison of all the circumstances. In such cases, the decision must depend very much upon the judgment and taste of the harmonist; and what to one person may appear probable and appropriate, may seem less so to another.

'It is the aim of the present work, not so much to ascertain and fix the true and precise chronological order, (although this object is not neglected,) as to place side by side the different narratives of the same events, in an order which may be regarded as at least a probable one. In so doing I may hope to exhibit the legitimate uses of a harmony, and accomplish a threefold purpose, viz. to make the evangelists their own best interpreters; to show how wonderfully they are supplemental to each other in minute as well as important particulars, and in this way to bring out fully and clearly, the fundamental characteristic of their testimony, UNITY IN DIVERSITY.' *pp.* 179, 180.

The careful student of the gospel history will accordingly find in this work a worthy companion to the harmonies of Griesbach,

De Wette and Lücke, Kaiser, Clausen, and Greswell. It possesses in our judgment some advantages over all of them. Though. not like the various editions of Griesbach's harmony, (the best of which is that edited by the late Maurice Rödiger in 1829,) accompanied with any selection of various readings, or printed, like that of Greswell, with a view to the exact comparison of the words and phrases employed by the several evangelists, these disadvantages are more than compensated by the illustrative notes to which we have referred, and which perhaps as much excel the dissertations of Greswell in judgment, as they fall short of them in extent. So lucid however is the arrangement, and so clear the press-work of the present volume, that it is rarely more difficult to compare the phraseology of the several evangelists, when using it, than when using Mr. Greswell's remarkably perspicuous and elegant volume. It has also a marked advantage over the harmonies of Griesbach, and De Wette and Lücke, that it includes all the gospels. Theirs, by incorporating mere selections from John's gospel, have evaded some of the principal difficulties of the gospel history, as *e. g.* the conciliation of Luke, ix. 51 ; xviii. 4, with John, vii. 10.

Dr. Robinson has distributed the matter of the gospels under nine general parts. These are :—

PART I.—'Events connected with the birth and childhood of our Lord.' TIME : *about thirteen and a-half years.*

PART II.—'Announcement and introduction of our Lord's public ministry.' TIME : *about one year.*

PART III.—'Our Lord's first passover, and the subsequent transactions until the second,' TIME : *one year.*

PART IV.—'Our Lord's second passover, and the subsequent transactions until the third.' TIME : *one year.*

PART V.—'From our Lord's third passover, until his final departure from Gallilee at the festival of tabernacles.' TIME : *six months.*

PART VI.—'The festival of tabernacles and the subsequent transactions until our Lord's arrival at Bethany, six days before the fourth passover.' TIME : *six months less one week.*

PART VII.—'Our Lord's public entry into Jerusalem, and the subsequent transactions before the fourth passover.' TIME : *five days.*

PART VIII.—'The fourth passover ; our Lord's passion ; and the accompanying events until the end of the Jewish sabbath.' TIME : *Two days.*

PART IX.—'Our Lord's resurrection ; his subsequent appearances, and his ascension.' TIME : *forty days.*

These nine parts are again subdivided into 173 sections, under each of which, as might be expected from Dr. Robinson's known predilection for geography, the place where the several events occurred is distinctly noted. In the number of sections our harmonist very nearly coincides with De Wette and Lücke, who have 171, under six parts. Griesbach, (Rödiger) has but 150, under six parts. Clausen makes 147, without any general distribution of time. Kaiser increases them to 199.

Among the principal subjects elucidated in Dr. Robinson's notes, and on some of which he has thrown much light, may be named—our Lord's genealogies, pp. 183-187, his baptism and temptation, p. 187 ; the cleansing of the temple, pp. 188, 189 ; the festival spoken of in John, v. 1. (whether it was the passover) pp. 190-192 ; the Sermon on the Mount, pp. 192-3 ; the Demoniacs of Gadara, p. 195 ; the difficulties which attend the harmonizing of John, vii. 10, with Luke, ix. 51—xviii. 14, pp. 198, 202 ; the blind man at Jericho, p. 204 ; our Lord's arrival at Bethany, p. 206 ; the discourse on the mount of Olives, pp. 208, 9 ; the supper at Bethany, p. 210 ; the first day of unleavened bread, p. 211 ; the passover, (a very elaborate note) pp. 211, 224; and Peter's denials, pp. 225, 6. We must own some surprise that the difficult question respecting Judas's participation of the Lord's supper, should have been left unnoticed.

Our readers will obtain some idea of the manner in which these several matters are discussed, from section 144, which relates to the place and circumstances of Peter's denials.

' An oriental house is usually built around a quadrangular interior court ; into which there is a passage (sometimes arched) through the front part of the house, closed next the street by a heavy folding gate, with a smaller wicket for single persons, kept by a porter. In the text, the interior court, often paved or flagged, and open to the sky, is the αὐλή, where the attendants made a fire, and the passage beneath the front of the house, from the street to this court, is the προαύλιον or πυλών. The place where Jesus stood before the high priest, may have been an open room, or place of audience on the ground floor, in the rear at one side of the court ; such rooms, open in front, being customary. It was close upon the court ; for Jesus heard all that was going on around the fire ; and turned and looked upon Peter ; Luke, xxii. 61.

' Peter's *first* denial took place at the fire in the middle of the court, on his being questioned by the female porter. Peter then, according to Matthew and Mark, retreats into the passage leading to the street (πυλών, προαύλιον,) where he is again questioned, and makes his *second* denial. Luke and John do not specify the place. The evangelists differ in their statements here, as to the person who now questioned him. Mark says the same maid, ἡ παιδίσκη, saw him again (πάλιν) and began to question him, v. 69 ; Matthew has ἄλλη, another maid, v. 71 ; Luke writes ἕτερος, another person or another man, ἄνθρωπος, v. 58 ; while John uses the indefinite form εἶπον, *they said*. As, according to Matthew, (v. 71), and Mark, (v. 69), there were several persons present, Peter may have been interrogated by several. The *third* denial took place an hour after, probably near the fire, or at least within the court, where our Lord and Peter could see each other. Luke, xxii. 61. Here Matthew and Mark speak of several interrogators. Luke has ἄλλος τις, and John specifies the servant of the high priest.

'The three denials are here placed together for convenience, although during the intervals between them the examination of Jesus was going on before the high priest; the progress of which is given in section 145.

'Mark relates that the cock crowed *twice*, v. 68, 72; the others speak only of his crowing *once*. This accords also with their respective accounts of our Lord's prophecy; see section 136. The cock often crows irregularly about midnight, or not long after, and again, always and regularly about the third hour, or day-break. When therefore the 'cock-crowing' is spoken of alone, this last is always meant. Hence, the name ἀλεκτοροφωνία, *cock-crowing*, for the third watch of the night, which ended at the third hour after midnight; Mark, xiii. 35. Mark therefore here relates more definitively; the others more generally,' pp. 225, 226.

It is well known that some of the greatest difficulties which the gospel history presents, relate to the narratives respecting our Lord's resurrection. Dr. Robinson truly states, that these difficulties have their cause in the fact that each evangelist 'here follows an *eclectic* method, and records only what appertained to his own particular purpose or experience. Thus, many of the minor and connecting facts have not been preserved; and the data are therefore wanting to make out a full and complete harmony of all the accounts, without an occasional resort to something of hypothesis.' On this subject, the great point of attack with many infidels, on which J. D. Michaelis wrote a considerable volume, and which some of our own countrymen, (among whom we may with advantage specify Gilbert West, and Dr. Townson), have discussed, with marked ability as well as pains, it will not be without interest if we append a portion, for we cannot give the whole, of Dr. Robinson's summary, in section 159.

'The resurrection took place at or before early dawn on the first day of the week; when there was an earthquake, and an angel descended and rolled away the stone from the sepulchre, and sat upon it; so that the keepers became as dead men from terror. At early dawn the same morning, the women who had attended on Jesus, viz. Mary Magdalene, Mary, the mother of James, Joanna, Salome and others, went out with spices to the sepulchre, in order further to embalm the Lord's body. They enquire among themselves who should remove for them the stone which closed the sepulchre. On their arri-

'al they find the stone already taken away. The Lord had risen. The women, knowing nothing of all that had taken place, were amazed; they enter the tomb, and find not the body of the Lord, and are greatly perplexed. At this time Mary Magdalene, impressed with the idea that the body had been stolen away, leaves the sepulchre and the other women, and runs to the city to tell Peter and John.

'The other women remain still in the tomb; and immediately two angels appear who announce unto them that Jesus is risen from the dead, and give them a charge in his name for the apostles. They go out quickly from the sepulchre, and proceed in haste to the city to make this known to the disciples; on the way Jesus meets them, permits them to embrace his feet, and renews the same charge to the apostles. The women relate these things to the disciples; but their words seem to them as idle tales, and they believe them not.

'Meantime, Peter and John had run to the sepulchre, and entering in, had found it empty. But the orderly arrangement of the grave-clothes, and of the napkin, convinced John that the body had not been removed either by violence or by friends; and the germ of a belief sprung up in his mind that the Lord had risen. The two returned to the city. Mary Magdalene, who had again followed them to the sepulchre, remained standing and weeping before it: and looking in, she saw two angels sitting. Turning around, she sees Jesus, who gives to her also a solemn charge for his disciples.

'The further sequence of events, consisting chiefly of our Lord's appearances, presents comparatively few difficulties.' . . . . pp. 228, 9.

The preceding extracts, though they convey a very imperfect idea of the value of this harmony and its elucidations, will yet, we trust, suffice to show that it is not unworthy of Dr. Robinson, and that the peculiar and minute discernment of the author is well put forth and exemplified in it. We need not say that the work has our heartiest recommendation. To biblical students it will be an exceedingly valuable acquisition. Before laying down our pen, we would also take the opportunity, as we have mentioned Rödiger's reprint of Griesbach, to say that it is enriched with a very useful preface of 22 pages, illustrative of the principles of the harmony and the various readings, and an appendix, partly critical and partly elucidatory of the labours of other modern harmonists. Clausen's 'Quatuor Evangeliorum Tabulæ Synopticæ,' Copenhagen, 1829, is also well adapted both to stimulate and reward the student's industry.

Art. IX.—*Narrative of the Exploring Expedition to the Rocky Mountains, in the Year* 1842, *and to Oregon and North California, in the Years* 1843—44. By Brevet Captain J. C. Fremont. 8vo. London: Wiley and Putnam.

The immense region west of the Rocky Mountains extending to the Pacific Ocean, and bounded by the Russian frontier on the north, and by California on the south, is now associated with such important political interests, as to attract general attention, and to increase greatly the importance of correct knowledge. Several exploring tours of the western portion of the American continent, have taken place during the present century. Little, however, has been known in this country, of the region which is now matter of dispute between the States and our own government; and we, therefore, cordially welcome every contribution, on the veracity of which reliance may be placed. On this account we are gratified by the republication of Captain Fremont's 'Narrative,' and hasten to introduce it to the favourable notice of our readers. His volume contains, in a condensed form, a narrative of two expeditions conducted under the sanction and at the expense of the American government. The first embraced the country lying between the Missouri River and the Rocky Mountains, on the line of the Kansas and Great Platte Rivers, and occupied from the 2d of May to the 29th of October, 1842. The second expedition was directed to Oregon and North California, and was designed to connect the *reconnoissance* of 1842 with the surveys which had been made on the coast of the Pacific Ocean, so as to secure a connected view of the interior of the American continent. It was commenced early in the spring of 1843, and brought to a close about the end of summer in the following year. The information supplied throughout the two narratives, though not satisfying all the enquiries we are disposed to make, is yet valuable, and in many respects interesting. It could, indeed, scarcely be otherwise, considering the regions traversed. Nature was found in her wildest and most untramelled form, without any memorials of a former age, save vast forests, and the interminable feuds of Indian tribes. The expedition required much physical strength, great courage, and no common skill, in meeting the contingencies which daily arose. These were pre-eminently possessed by Captain Fremont, in happy combination with the knowledge which enabled him to bring from the comparatively unknown region he visited, important contributions to the sciences of astronomy, geography, botany, and geology.

The party consisted principally of Creole and Canadian *voyageurs*, who had been familiarized to prairie life in the service of various fur companies. They were between twenty and thirty in number, and, with the exception of eight, who conducted the cars containing stores and scientific instruments, were all well armed and mounted. The order of procedure was regulated by the circumstances of the case, and in general was as follows :—

'During our journey, it was the customary practice to encamp an hour or two before sunset, when the carts were disposed so as to form a sort of barricade around a circle some eighty yards in diameter. The tents were pitched, and the horses hobbled and turned loose to graze; and but a few minutes elapsed before the cooks of the messes, of which there were but four, were busily engaged in preparing the evening meal. At nightfall, the horses, mules, and oxen, were driven in and picketed—that is, secured by a halter, of which one end was tied to a small steel-shod picket, and driven into the ground; the halter being twenty or thirty feet long, which enabled them to obtain a little food during the night. When we had reached a part of the country where such a precaution became necessary, the carts being regularly arranged for defending the camp, guard was mounted at eight o'clock, consisting of three men, who were relieved every two hours; the morning watch being horse-guard for the day. At daybreak, the camp was roused, the animals turned loose to graze, and breakfast generally over between six and seven o'clock, when we resumed our march, making regularly a halt at noon for one or two hours.' pp. 6—7.

By the middle of June the party had arrived at the Indian country, and it became necessary to prepare against the chances of the wilderness. This was done with considerable skill and the happiest results. Though surrounded by hostile tribes, who regarded their appearance with mistrust, they advanced without serious casualty, and completed their mission without any of those sanguinary encounters which were to be apprehended. We should have been glad of more definite information respecting the Indian nations visited,—their numbers, habits, and prospects, the history of the past and the probabilities of the future. But such enquiries were beside the object of our traveller's mission, and we must, therefore, be content, on these points, with the incidental notices furnished. It were both unwise and ungrateful to disparage what is communicated, on account of the absence of something else not contemplated in the instructions under which he acted. The monotony of their camp was frequently broken up by false alarms, which, however amusing afterwards, kept them, for the time, in a state of feverish suspense. An instance of this occurred in the early part of their journey, and is given on page 13, but we prefer transcribing the following, as throwing more light on Indian habits.

'Journeying along,' says our author, 'we came suddenly upon a place where the ground was covered with horses' tracks, which had been made since the rain, and indicated the immediate presence of Indians in our neighbourhood. The buffalo, too, which the day before had been so numerous, were nowhere in sight—another sure indication that there were people near. Riding on, we discovered the carcase of a buffalo recently killed—perhaps the day before. We scanned the horizon carefully with the glass, but no living object was to be seen. For the next mile or two, the ground was dotted with buffalo carcases, which showed that the Indians had made a surround here, and were in considerable force. We went on quickly and cautiously, keeping the river bottom, and carefully avoiding the hills: but we met with no interruption, and began to grow careless again. We had already lost one of our horses, and here Basil's mule showed symptoms of giving out, and finally refused to advance, being what the Canadians call *resté*. He therefore dismounted, and drove her along before him; but this was a very slow way of travelling. We had inadvertently got about half a mile in advance, but our Cheyennes, who were generally a mile or two in the rear, remained with him. There were some dark-looking objects among the hills, about two miles to the left, here low and undulating, which we had seen for a little time, and supposed to be buffalo coming in to water; but, happening to look behind, Maxwell saw the Cheyennes whipping up furiously, and another glance at the dark objects showed them at once to be Indians coming up at full speed.

'Had we been well mounted, and disencumbered of instruments, we might have set them at defiance; but as it was, we were fairly caught. It was too late to rejoin our friends, and we endeavoured to gain a clump of timber about half-a-mile ahead; but the instruments, and the tired state of our horses, did not allow us to go faster than a steady canter, and they were gaining on us fast. At first, they did not appear to be more than fifteen or twenty in number, but group after group darted into view at the top of the hills, until all the little eminences seemed in motion, and, in a few minutes from the time they were first discovered, two hundred to three hundred, naked to the breech cloth, were sweeping across the prairie. In a few hundred yards we discovered that the timber we were endeavouring to make was on the opposite side of the river; and before we could reach the bank, down came the Indians upon us.

'I am inclined to think that in a few seconds more the leading man, and perhaps some of his companions, would have rolled in the dust; for we had jerked the covers from our guns, and our fingers were on the triggers. Men in such cases generally act from instinct, and a charge from three hundred naked savages is a circumstance not well calculated to promote a cool exercise of judgment. Just as he was bout to fire, Maxwell recognised the leading Indian, and shouted to im in the Indian language, 'Your'e a fool, G— damn you, don't ou know me?' The sound of his own language seemed to shock the avage, and, swerving his horse a little, he passed us like an arrow. He wheeled, as I rode out toward him, and gave me his hand, striking is breast and exclaiming 'Arapahó!' They proved to be a village of that nation, among whom Maxwell had resided as a trader a year or two previously, and recognized him accordingly. We were soon n the midst of the band, answering as well as we could a multitude of questions; of which the very first was, of what tribe were our Indian companions who were coming in the rear. They seemed disappointed to know that they were Cheyennes, for they had fully anicipated a grand dance around a Pawnee scalp at night.'—pp.26—28.

Occasionally they met with a party of emigrants or of trappers, and in the interchange of kind offices, and the communication of news respecting the opposite points from which they were proceeding, renewed their intercourse with civilized life, and learned something of the dangers, or of the excitements, which awaited them. On the 28th of June, they fell in with a party of this kind, fifteen in number, whose 'forlorn and vagabond appearance' excited their laughter, and from whom they received the welcome intelligence that the buffalo were abundant some two days' march in advance. This intelligence was soon verified. At a considerable distance 'a dull and confused murmuring' was heard, and when the caravan came in sight of the dark masses, 'there was not,' says Captain Fremont, 'one among us who did not feel his heart beat quicker. Indians and buffalo make the poetry and life of the prairie, and our camp was full of their exhilaration.' We need scarcely say, that the promptings of hunger were not requisite to stimulate to the chase. The resolution of attacking the herd was soon taken, and the following sketch gives the idea of much less danger than some popular writers have associated with similar adventures.

'As we were riding quietly along the bank, a grand herd of buffalo, some seven or eight hundred in number, came crowding up from the river, where they had been to drink, and commenced crossing the plain slowly, eating as they went. The wind was favourable; the coolness of the morning invited to exercise; the ground was apparently good, and the distance across the prairie (two or three miles) gave us a fine opportunity to charge them before they could get among the river hills. It was too fine a prospect for a chase to be lost: and, halting for a few moments, the hunters were brought up and saddled, and Kit Carson, Maxwell, and I, started together. They were now somewhat less than half-a-mile distant, and we rode easily along until within about three hundred yards, when a sudden agitation, a wavering in the band, and a galloping to and fro of some which were scattered along the skirts, gave us the intimation that we were discovered. We started together at a hand gallop, riding steadily abreast of each other, and here the interest of the chase became so engrossingly intense, that we were sensible to nothing else. We were now closing upon them rapidly, and the front of the mass was already in rapid motion for the hills, and in a few seconds the movement had communicated itself to the whole herd.

'A crowd of bulls, as usual, brought up the rear, and every now and then some of them faced about, and then dashed on after the band a short distance, and turned and looked again, as if more than half inclined to stand and fight. In a few moments, however, during which we had been quickening our pace, the rout was universal, and we were going over the ground like a hurricane. When at about thirty yards, we gave the usual shout (the hunter's *pas de charge*), and broke into the herd. We entered on the side, the mass giving way in every direction in their heedless course. Many of the bulls, less active and less fleet than the cows, paying no attention to the ground, and occupied solely with the hunter, were precipitated to the earth with great force, rolling over and over with the violence of the shock, and hardly distinguishable in the dust. We separated on entering, each singling out his game.

'My horse was a trained hunter, famous in the west under the name of Proveau, and, with his eyes flashing, and the foam flying from his mouth, sprang on after the cow like a tiger. In a few moments he brought me alongside of her, and, rising in the stirrups, I fired at the distance of a yard, the ball entering at the termination of the long hair, and passing near the heart. She fell headlong at the report of the gun, and, checking my horse, I looked around for my companions. At a little distance Kit was on the ground, engaged in tying his horse to the horns of a cow which he was preparing to cut up. Among the scattered bands, at some distance below, I caught a glimpse of Maxwell; and, while I was looking, a light wreath of white smoke curled away from his gun, from which I was too far to hear the report. Nearer, and between me and the hills, towards which they were directing their course, was the body of the herd, and, giving my horse the rein, we dashed after them. A thick cloud of dust hung upon their rear, which filled my mouth and eyes, and nearly smothered me. In the midst of this I could see nothing, and the buffalo were not distinguishable until within thirty feet. They crowded together more densely still as I came upon them, and rushed along in such a compact body, that I could not obtain an entrance—the horse almost leaping upon them. In a few moments the mass divided to the right and left, the horns clattering with a noise heard above everything else, and my horse darted into the opening. Five or six bulls charged on us as we dashed along the line, but were left far behind; and, singling out a cow, I gave her my fire, but struck too high. She gave a tremendous leap, and scoured on swifter than before. I reined up my horse, and the band swept on like a torrent, and left the place quiet and clear. Our chase had led us into dangerous ground.'—pp. 17—19.

Troops of wolves hung on the skirts of the buffalo herd, and were seen in the morning at a short distance from the camp, waiting the departure of their human foes. They calculated on the refuse of the victims of the former days' hunt, and, probably, were not disappointed. Even the animal creation knows enough of man, to be assured of what follows when he comes in contact with the denizen of the forest or of the plain. His powers of destruction are appreciated, and the inferior tribes await his retirement from the scene of slaughter, in expectation of being gorged by the remains of his feast.

On the 13th of July, the party arrived at Fort Laramie, one of the posts of the American Fur Company, and the account given of the barter trade carried on with the Indians, affords a painful confirmation of the reports which had previously reached us. The use of intoxicating liquors is represented as general, and the passion of the natives for it most intense and inordinate. 'A keg of it,' says Captain Fremont, 'will purchase from an Indian everything that he possesses—his furs, his lodge, his horses, and even his wife and children.' This state of things affords great facilities to the pedlar, and renders it exceedingly difficult for the fur company to discountenance, as our author represents them as desirous of doing, the consumption of alcohol. We know not that the existence of such a passion amongst a people like the American Indians need awaken surprise. The excitement of intoxication furnishes the stimulus they need, and enables them, for a moment at least, to rekindle the enthusiasm and hopes formerly cherished. Living on the borders of civilization, without any of its more virtuous tastes and habits, they eagerly avail themselves of the false stimulus which its vices engender. These vices are unhappily fostered by their more criminal visitors. Hundreds and thousands live upon their ruin, careless alike of the social discomfort and personal degradation induced, so that their gains are but advanced. Secure from the observation of the more virtuous members of their own community, they trade on the misery and vices of the untutored savage. During their stay at Fort Laramie, Captain Fremont employed himself in astronomical calculations, and had many opportunities, as the following brief extract shows, of acquainting himself with the habits of the Indians.

'So far as the frequent interruption of the Indians would allow, we occupied ourselves in making some astronomical calculations, and bringing up the general map to this stage of our journey; but the tent was generally occupied by a succession of our ceremonious visitors. Some came for presents, and others for information of our object in coming to the country, now and then, one would dart up to the tent on horseback, jerk off his trappings, and stand silently at the door, holding his horse by the halter, signifying his desire to trade. Occasionally a savage would stalk in with an invitation to a feast of honour, a dog feast, and deliberately sit down and wait quietly until I was ready to accompany him. I went to one; the women and children were sitting outside the lodge, and we took our seats on buffalo robes spread around. The dog was in a large pot over the fire, in the middle of the lodge, and immediately on our arrival was dished up in large wooden bowls, one of which was handed to each. The flesh appeared very glutinous, with something of the flavour and appearance of mutton. Feeling something move behind me, I looked round, and found that I had taken my seat among a litter of fat young puppies. Had I been nice in such matters, the prejudices of civilization might have interfered with my tranquility; but, fortunately, I am not of delicate nerves, and continued quietly to empty my platter.'— p. 45.

From this point of the journey their contact with the Indians became more frequent and alarming. Several parties were out, the Gross Ventre Indians having united with the Oglallahs and Cheyennes, in order to attack the Snake and Crow tribes. Perpetual vigilance was therefore required, and great presence of mind was needful to bear up amidst the discouragements daily encountered. It is no wonder that the Indians regarded the appearance of white men with mistrust, and did all in their power to prevent their advance. The past was too full of warning to permit them to regard the mission of their visitors with complacency. At Forte Platte, 'a number of chiefs, several of them powerful fine-looking men,' presented to Captain Fremont a written remonstrance against his advancing further, alleging, that their young warriors were out, and would not fail to attack his camp. The remonstrance, however, was disregarded, and although a scarcity of water and of grass was subsequently experienced, the adventurous party continued its route. The ascent of the highest peak of the Wind River Mountains was not devoid of interest, though, as in other cases, the narrative given is too bare and skeleton-like to stimulate the imagination. This is a pervading fault of the work, and arises, in some measure, from its character as an official report.

The second 'Narrative' contained in this volume—and to which we can do little more than refer—was by far the most formidable and dangerous. The party was therefore more numerous, and the time occupied much longer than on the prior occasion. Whatever political results may flow from the information obtained, it is quite clear, that a military occupation of the country by the American people, is almost, if not quite, impossible. The vast distance of the region from the seat of government, and the immense obstacles which present themselves to the conveyance of men and stores, will make a thoughtful people deliberate before they incur the expense and hazard of war for such a prize. The Indians encountered by our travellers on this occasion, were more numerous and warlike than on their former expedition, whilst the severity of the climate added greatly to the difficulties of the mission. Snow fell heavily around them, and marauding parties were on their trail, with a vigilance and perseverance of which an Indian only is capable. 'We had to move all day,' says our author in this part of his journal, 'in a state of watch, and prepared for combat, scouts and flankers out, a front and rear division of our men, and baggage animals in the centre. At night, camp duty was severe. Those who had toiled all day had to guard, by turns, the camp and the horses all night. Frequently one-third of the whole party were on guard at once, and nothing but this vigilance saved us from attack. We were constantly dogged by bands, and even whole tribes of the marauders; and, although Tabeau was killed, and our camp infested and insulted by some, while swarms of them remained on the hills and mountain sides, there was manifestly a consultation and calculation going on to decide the question of attacking us.'

The buffalo, like the Indian, is rapidly disappearing from the country over which he formerly roamed in safety. The American and European trader find their profit in his destruction, and many thousands are in consequence annually slain. Our author furnishes some interesting information on this point, from which we can find room only for the following extract :—

'A great portion of the region inhabited by this nation (the Shoshonee) fomerly abounded in game ; the buffalo ranging about in herds, as we had found them on the eastern waters, and the plains dotted with scattered bands of antelope : but so rapidly have they disappeared within a few years, that now, as we journeyed along, an occasional buffalo skull and a few wild antelope were all that remained of the abundance which had covered the country with animal life.

'The extraordinary rapidity with which the buffalo is disappearing from our territories will not appear surprising when we remember the great scale on which their destruction is yearly carried on. With inconsiderable exceptions, the business of the American trading boats is carried on in their skins; every year the Indian villages make new lodges, for which the skin of the buffalo furnishes the material; and in that portion of the country where they are still found, the Indians derive their entire support from them, and slaughter them with a thoughtless and abominable extravagance. Like the

Indians themselves, they have been a characteristic of the Great West; and as, like them, they are visibly diminishing, it will be interesting to throw a glance backward through the last twenty years, and give some account of their former distribution through the country, and the limit of their western range.

'The information is derived principally from Mr. Fitzpatrick, supported by my own personal knowledge and acquaintance with the country. Our knowledge does not go further back than the spring of 1824, at which time the buffalo were spread in immense numbers over the Green river and Bear river valleys, and through all the country lying between the Colorado, or Green river of the gulf of California, and Lewis's fork of the Columbia river; the meridian of Fort Hall then forming the western limit of their range. The buffalo then remained for many years in that country, and frequently moved down the valley of the Columbia, on both sides of the river, as far as the *Fishing Falls.* Below this point they never descended in any numbers. About the year 1834 or 1835 they began to diminish very rapidly, and continued to decrease until 1838 to 1840, when, with the country we have just described, they entirely abandoned all the waters of the Pacific, north of Lewis's fork of the Columbia. At that time, the Flathead Indians were in the habit of finding their buffalo on the heads of Salmon river, and other streams of the Columbia; but now they never meet with tham farther west than the three forks of the Missouri or the plains of the Yellowstone river.

'In the course of our journey it will be remarked that the buffalo have not so entirely abandoned the waters of the Pacific, in the Rocky Mountain region south of the Sweet Water, as in the country north of the Great Pass. This partial distribution can only be accounted for in the great pastoral beauty of that country, which bears marks of having long been one of their favourite haunts, and by the fact that the white hunters have more frequented the northern than the southern region—it being north of the South Pass that the hunters, trappers, and traders, have had their rendezvous for many years past; and from that section also the greater portion of the beaver and rich furs were taken, although always the most dangerous as well as the most profitable hunting ground.' pp. 139—141.

This tribe is represented as suffering severely from the loss of their ordinary food. The buffalo was their staple article of food, and, in its absence, they are said to be 'miserably poor,' and their figures to be 'lean and bony.' Of the Snake Indians a different and more pleasing sketch is given :—

'Our encampment was about one mile below the *Fishing Falls,* a series of cataracts with very inclined planes, which are probably so named because they form a barrier to the ascent of the salmon; and the greater fisheries, from which the inhabitants of this barren region almost entirely derive a subsistence, commence at this place. These ppeared to be unusually gay savages, fond of loud laughter; and in heir apparent good nature and merry character, struck me as being ntirely different from the Indians we had been accustomed to see. From several who visited our camp in the evening, we purchased, n exchange for goods, dried salmon. At this season they are not ery fat, but we were easily pleased. The Indians made us comprehend, that when the salmon came up the river in the spring, they re so abundant that they merely throw in the spears at random, certain of bring out a fish.

'These poor people are but slightly provided with winter clothing; here is but little game to furnish skins for the purpose; and of a little animal which seemed to be the most numerous, it required twenty skins to make a covering to the knees. But they are still a joyous alkative race, who grow fat and become poor with the salmon, which at least never fail them—the dried being used in the absence of the fresh. We are encamped immediately on the river bank, and with the salmon jumping up out of the water, and Indians paddling about in boats made of rushes, or laughing around the fires, the camp to-night has quite a lively appearance.' p. 170.

The following must close our citations. We give it with reluctance, as it painfully illustrates the false morality which is prevalent amongst American citizens, even of the better class. Few of their number can be trusted where an Indian or a negro is concerned. For the narrative, to be understood, it is necessary to say, that two Mexicans, a man and a boy, suddenly entered the camp, having with difficulty escaped from a party of Indians, who had slain four of their number, and possessed themselves of several horses which were under their charge. Captain Fremont received them kindly, and promised them aid, and on the following day, two of his men, with the Mexican, named Fuentes, were sent in pursuit. Fuentes returned at night, his horse having failed, but the other two continued the search. And now for our traveller's narrative and comment:—

'In the afternoon of the next day, a war-whoop was heard, such as Indians make when returning from a victorious enterprise; and soon Carson and Godey appeared, driving before them a band of horses, recognized by Fuentes to be part of those they had lost. Two bloody scalps, dangling from the end of Godey's gun, announced that they had overtaken the Indians as well as the horses. They informed us, that after Fuentes left them, from the failure of his horse, they continued the pursuit alone, and towards nightfall entered the mountains, into which the trail led. After sunset the moon gave light, and they followed the trail by moonshine until late in the night, when it entered a narrow defile, and was difficult to follow. Afraid of losing it in the darkness of the defile, they tied up their horses, struck no fire, and lay down to sleep in silence and in darkness. Here they lay from midnight till morning. At daylight they resumed the pursuit, and about sunrise discovered the horses; and, immediately dismounting and tying up their own, they crept cautiously to a rising ground which intervened, from the crest of which they perceived the encampment of four lodges close by. They proceeded quietly, and had got within thirty or forty yards of their object, when a movement among the horses discovered them to the Indians; giving the war shout, they instantly charged into the camp, regardless of the number which the *four* lodges would imply. The Indians received them with a flight of arrows shot from their long bows, one of which passed through Godey's shirt collar, barely missing the neck; our men fired their rifles upon a steady aim, and rushed in. Two Indians were streched on the ground, fatally pierced with bullets; the rest fled, except a lad that was captured. The scalps of the fallen were instantly stripped off; but in the process, one of them, who had two balls through his body, sprung to his feet, the blood streaming from his skinned head, and uttering a hideous howl. An old squaw, possibly his mother, stopped and looked back from the mountain side she was climbing, threatening and lamenting. The frightful spectacle appalled the stout hearts of our men; but they did what humanity required, and quickly terminated the agonies of the gory savage. They were now masters of the camp, which was a pretty little recess in the mountain, with a fine spring, and apparently safe from all invasion. Great preparations had been made to feast a large party, for it was a very proper place for a rendezvous, and for the celebration of such orgies as robbers of the desert would delight in. Several of the best horses had been killed, skinned, and cut up; for the Indians, living in mountains, and only coming into the plains to rob and murder, make no other use of horses than to eat them. Large earthen vessels were on the fire, boiling and stewing the horse beef; and several baskets, containing fifty or sixty pairs of moccasins, indicated the presence or expectation, of a considerable party. They released the boy, who had given strong evidence of the stoicism, or something else, of the savage character, in commencing his breakfast upon a horse's head as soon as he found he was not be killed, but only tied as a prisoner. Their object accomplished, our men gathered up all the surviving horses, fifteen in number, returned upon their trail, and rejoined us at our camp in the afternoon of the same day. They had rode about one hundred miles in the pursuit and return, and all in thirty hours. The time, place, object, and numbers, considered, this expedition of Carson and Godey may be considered among the boldest and most disinterested which the annals of western adventure, so full of daring deeds, can present. Two men, in a savage desert, pursue day and night an unknown body of Indians into the defiles of an unknown mountain—attack them on sight, without counting numbers—and defeat them in an instant—and for what? To punish the robbers of the desert, and to avenge the wrongs of Mexicans whom they did not know. I repeat: it was Carson and Godey who did this—the former an *American*, born in the Booneslick county of Missouri; the latter a Frenchman, born in St. Louis—and both trained to western enterprise from early life.' pp. 285—287.

We need scarcely remark on the commendation here expressed. Our circumstances happily exempt us from the perverting influences to which, on this subject, the American mind is exposed, and we consequently condemn as murder, marked by circumstances of atrocious cruelty, what an officer of the Republic can admire as an act of disinterested and noble daring. When will the conventionalities of a low-minded and barbarian morality, give place to the higher and purer rules of God's holy law?

We need not describe Captain Fremont's volume. The extracts given will enable our readers to judge of it for themselves, and our purpose will be answered if their attention be drawn to a region hitherto little known, and to the condition of a people who are rapidly disappearing before a civilization which ought to convey to them the elements of a higher and nobler life.

Art. X.—*Case of Gathercole* v. *Miall.* Morning Chronicle, April 24, 1846.

Among the subjects which must be brought under revision in the great shaking-up of abuses which the destruction of one grand abuse is bringing in its train, is clearly the law of libel. Men thought it dead like the giant Pagan; or at all events reduced so low, as, like his brother Pope, to be able to do little more than grin at pilgrims as they passed, and hold out intimations of what *would* have been done to them in the good old times. But a spirit of forethought has seized on the rheumatic ogre, and he puts in his claim, by a nimbler grip than was expected of him, not to be forgotten in the day when the people reckon up their enemies.

There is always a law for society, and a law to be executed in spite of society, or for the benefit of society's foes. The degree in which these genera are co-existent, depends upon the progress which society has made: and the proportion between them, it is the business of law-makers continually to reduce. That one man should not unrighteously, vexatiously, or maliciously, put another to discomfort by printing or writing, is the law society is willing to support. That a thief shall never be discomforted by being caught, and that cause of action shall exist against all who, by speech or doing, assist to point out or catch him, is the parallel to the law which says no man (thieves included) shall be made uncomfortable. For to this amounts the oral dictum of the sages of the law courts, standing out duly as a proof how easy it is to say by word of mouth what none would dare to write advisedly in a statute.

Society holds together, by making the immoral and dishonest 'exceedingly uncomfortable.' The verdict of a coroner's jury is one of the most discomforting sounds on earth, to many that could be pointed out. Just such chivalry as would put down this, with nice fence about what might, or might not, be done in the way of giving publicity to it by print or otherwise, is the zeal which would strengthen evil-doers at large by making it penal to make them uneasy. What the judge-made law directs itself against, it is true, is not so much the verdict of a jury, as the outcry of a pursuer. It is the preliminary rather than the conclusive act, which it would try to stop. If every thief may have remedy against whoever lifts up his voice with warning shout, thiefdom is the only place benefited, and thieves' interests are all that are promoted. Granted, that once in a way the cry is raised against an honest man, on his way home to carry his wages to his wife and family; but the thing is of comparatively easy remedy, and is a small evil when weighed against the results of punishing systematically the man who cries.

Bad laws are not to cured by leaving the decision to bad juries. And it is of the nature of juries to be bad, or at all events to be worse than they might, when law, or what they hear of it, has run in the course of encouraging them to do amiss. Jurymen have the *moles peccati* in them like other men; and are not slow at coming to a tacit understanding, on the unpleasantness of being attacked when in the course of indulging some cherished scheme of what a man cannot quite defend. If laws make one hole, juries will make another; and the object of laws should be, to direct men's thoughts entirely the other way.

How respectable, for instance, would be the law which should instil, that no man had his claim to a verdict as for libel, except on proof that the libel (or *little book*, for that is all it intrinsically means,) was, in the first place, false, and in the next, malicious. The right of civil action for proveable losses caused, might be left open after all. For juries reason coolly on a mere speculation of damages, who would be carried away in a flood of zeal to whichever side it might happen, by the mere name of libel. For example, if a careless man has printed that Mr. Solomon the respectable orange-merchant in the Minories, is no other than the celebrated 'Ikey' returned from transportation, this might be just matter of verdict for libel, if proved to be first false, secondly malicious. But if the defendant can establish, that though confessedly a mistake, it was entirely an involuntary one, arising, for instance, out of communications sent to him in the way of his business, and warning him against a certain Solomon who had buzzed for awhile about the Minories, but had finally settled in Whitechapel; it would be ground for relieving him from the punishment of libel, though if the upright Mr. Solomon could prove that he had lost a valuable partnership by it, he would appear to have as good a claim to civil action for losses, as if defendant's horse had carried him in spite of his teeth through plaintiff's bow-window.

Another ground which wise men take note of, but which is entirely lost sight of in the existing law or in its modern resuscitation, is, that a plaintiff has not a claim for sufferings for ink-blows, where himself has given the provocation. A man is not to rush into the street and jostle against every one he meets, and then run to a magistrate and complain of the libellous pushes and uncomfortable dabs of hostile matter that may have been discharged upon him in his course. The law is for the clean-handed; and if men, under the impulse of human frailty, engage in mutual quarrel, they are not to appeal to the *hautes œuvres* of the libel law, which, if carried into execution at all, must hang up both at once.

This to the general question. But the particular case which has led to its revival now, has also its important bearings.

The case which has brought the law of libel before the public eye, is less remarkable from its own circumstances, than from the exhibition of judicial bearings and opinions which has been founded on them. That a member of a state church should be overbearing and violent, is no phenomenon to shake a nation from its propriety, or to invite it to any marked course which it would not have taken without. But when this member of a state church succeeds in finding a man to answer him with a Roland for his Oliver, and the leaders of the law, or an effective portion of them, come forward to declare, that in all pulling of caps the state scold has an immunity,—that she is a privileged virago whom ducking-stools have no hold upon, and may insult her betters, either in the open air or under cover, without remedy,—the right of pigeon-cote which was one of the causes of the French Revolution, was nothing to it. The church, like the French aristocracy, is founded on anything but a rock. Many a bitter feeling has been crushed and wrought into its walls. It is at best but a tolerated injustice; the toleration resulting from an estimate of the difficulty of removal. The strength of the church, and of the aristocracy, arose out of the way in which they were connected with the interests of many, though not of all; interests, perhaps, not always thoroughly or well understood, but still felt sufficiently to be effective. Some of these interests came by marriage and family connexions; a point on which the living hierarchy of England has vastly the advantage over that which has passed away. Some rose out of gratitude for past gains, and still more out of that kind of it which has been defined as a lively consciousness of benefits to come. A circumstance in favour of both church and aristocracy, was the opportunity which wealth and power give to all but the actively malevolent, of acquiring a reputation for polished and agreeable manners; in short, the strength of the church denominated of England, lay in its being thought a gentlemanly church, as the strength of an aristocracy everywhere lies, to a great extent, in its being supposed to possess some similar quality which other men admire and aspire to copy. But this was a fund to be discreetly drawn upon, and not to be managed by clergymen engaging in unhandsome feud with men as good as themselves and as well able to resist an injury. Still less was it to be improved by having it declared as 'judges quest law,' that a clergyman had right of impudence;—that to be saucy was his fee simple, in which nobody could control him;—and that to comment upon his public acts, 'or say whether they were good or bad,' was beyond the scope of the citizen. A new light broke out, even while the dictum was in progress. A bill brought into the Upper House by the Lord Chancellor opened the dark lantern on the fact, that these very acts of the state-paid clergyman which were declared to be his ox, his ass, his privacy, his snuggery within which none might interfere, were performances for non-attendance on which one part of the community were punishable by law, and the other part if they attended anywhere else. Why has not a Queen's Speech the same immunity; or rather, if the other be law, can there be any doubt that it has? There is as much reason in representing the one to be an act of sacred privacy, as the other. A general's order to his army, might it not be very convenient to maintain, that *as long as he did not put it into print*, it was safe from the comments of the public critic? The thing is absurd, by all the rules that regulate human judgment in parallel cases. If a man is to be paid, let him do the work he is paid for, whether the payment comes out of other people's pockets against their consent or not. But do not add the folly, with a view to increasing his magnificence, of maintaining that it shall be an actionable offence, to say whether his doings are good or bad, whether they keep within the pale for which the appropriation of other people's property is defended when it *is* defended, or wander abroad into interminable feud and a right of squabble protected by the power of law. What would be the result if dissenting teachers everywhere, walked abroad in their doublet and hose, and threw off the outer garment of moderation and civil harmony? Yet this is what the sages of the law have encouraged every whipper-snapper on whom a bishop has laid unadvised hands, to provoke to the extent of his ability. Bring forth the giant, for whose personal gratification the church and the law have incurred all this unpopularity and danger. Ask, who is benefited by the execution of his ill-humours; or which of 'our peculiar institutions' as an American would call them, is rendered more stable by his sending an execution by surprise into the domicile of his opponent. Take care that holy church never finds herself under obligation for forbearance in a more important matter. Offences will come, and human disputes will be fought out in one way or another, according to the relative degrees of civilization of the ages and the combatants. But woe to them who make them come for the mere indulgence of ill-temper, and peril a plethoric hierarchy that a parish-priest may be lifted up in the eyes of the virgins who make coats and garments for the orthodox poor. Truly these people have a new reading of many an ancient story. Where would the good Samaritan have been, if he had prefaced his work with a discussion upon thirty-nine articles? And what stronger contrast in nature, than between Him who went about doing good, and the shepherd who sits down to make all the mischief in his power within the limits of a parish?

Brief Notices.

On the Scripture Doctrine of Future Punishment: an Argument. In two Parts. By H. H. Dobney. Second Edition. London: Ward and Co.

In a second edition of his work on Future Punishment, Mr. Dobney has done us the honour, not only of acknowledging the candour of our notice of his work, but of replying, at great length, to our observations. We thank him for the terms in which he has referred to us, and most readily give him credit for sincerity in his avowal of non-conviction from our arguments. What he has now written, we have read, not only as befits us, with the gravity of judges, but, as we hope, and as befits us no less, with the impartiality of lovers of truth; but our views remain unchanged. If our arguments have failed to convince him, his have equally failed to convince us. Our conviction, indeed, is, that his remarks constitute a rejoinder, but not an answer. We have no intention, however, of adverting to them in detail; there is one point only on which we feel it necessary to say a few words.

Insisting, as it is quite necessary he should (p. 187), that the word life, in the scriptural phrase, *eternal life*, should be understood as conveying two ideas; first, that of existence, and then that of happiness, he encounters an objection that this is understanding the word both literally and metaphorically at the same time, and is therefore inadmissible. To this he offers two replies. One of them is, that writers on the other side have done the same thing, which could be nothing but an *argumentum ad hominem*, even if examples of it could be cited from our own pages. The other is couched in the following terms: 'I reply by denying the soundness of the principle, *which almost seems made for the occasion*.' The expression which we have marked in italics, is merely a slip of the author's pen. It is, at all events, a deviation—and we are happy to say, a solitary deviation, so far as we have noticed, from the courtesy elsewhere studiously observed towards us.

Mr. Dobney denies the soundness of the principle that a word must not be understood both literally and metaphorically at the same time, and complains somewhat that we laid it down as 'though it was an indisputable axiom.' We must confess that we thought it so, and that we still think it so. It is, to our mind, inherent in the very nature of a metaphor. For what is a metaphor? Turning to the first authority at hand (the Oxford Encyclopædia), we find the following definition of it. 'Metaphor, in rhetoric, a trope or figure, whereby a word is transferred from its proper signification to another different from it, by reason of some similitude between them.' This definition, in which we believe all authorities agree, is decisive to our purpose; for if, in metaphorical use, a word is transferred from its proper signification, to another different from it, it is plainly inadmissible to understand it both literally and metaphorically at the same time. The metaphorical use involves, of necessity, the dropping of the literal meaning.

Examples are not less decisive to this point than definition. We call a blooming child a rose-bud, a courageous man a lion, and youth the morning of life. Here is a metaphorical use of the words rose-bud, lion, and morning, ut in every case the literal meaning is dropped, since no one means to say hat a blooming child is really a rose-bud, or a courageous man really a lion, r youth really the morning. The result will be the same by whatever umber or variety of examples the rule may be tested. And it is the ame with scriptural metaphors as with others; as when we are told, or example, that God is our sun and shield, that our days are a and-breadth, that our life is a vapour. To these illustrations we may dd, that the reason of the rule is obvious, from the manner in which metaphor is formed. It is founded, we are told, 'on some similitude' etween two objects; and hence it is said to be an abridged simile, or a omparison reduced to a single word. The early part of life is, in some espects, like the early part of the day, and this resemblance may be ither drawn out at length into a simile, as by saying youth is like the norning, or condensed into a metaphor, as in calling youth the morning f life. Now the likeness between two objects thus brought into comarison, being never entire, but only partial, it is plain that, in the metahorical use of a term, we must get an idea so far different from the riginal one, that the same things cannot be predicated of both, and it would, consequently, be false to consider both of them as conveyed by it. We call a brave man a lion because in a certain respect he resembles a ion; and as we go on to speak of him in terms in no way appropriate o a real lion, it would be delusive and absurd to hold that we retain the riginal idea of the term, and mean by it a lion and a brave man too. The very notion, indeed, of retaining the original idea of a term used metaphorically involves a fallacy. A metaphor is nothing but an abridged comparison; only let it be spread out into a comparison, and it will be seen that there is, in truth, no original idea to be retained, as when we say, our life is like a vapour, there are simply two objects, the one compared with the other; and in a metaphor, properly understood, there is nothing more.

To apply these familiar distinctions (which we feel ashamed to have to bring out so elaborately on such an occasion) to the case before us. The word life, literally denoting existence, is sometimes employed in scripture to denote happiness, of which it is needless to cite examples, as it is an admitted point; it is also admitted by Mr. Dobney, that this is a metaphorical use of the term life: consequently we affirm, in accordance with the rule laid down, that, when the term life is used to denote happiness, it cannot be held to retain its original idea, or to mean existence and happiness too.

It is in vain for the author to cite the authority of Tholuck, or any other authority, even though it were our own, against this position. It is unquestionably an important principle of interpretation, from the violation of which much mischief has arisen, and nothing but mischief can arise. The disregard of it in his own case has given rise to much of the inconclusiveness discernible in his argument, and has supplied him with his chief facilities for avoiding the force of ours.

The History of British India, from 1805 *to* 1835. By Horace Hayman Wilson, M.A. F.R.S. Vol. II. London: Madden and Malcolm.

THE former volume of Professor Wilson's work was noticed at length in our journal for July last, and we have no inclination, after examining the volume now before us, to modify the high opinion we then expressed. As a continuation of Mill, it is without a rival, and by its own qualities is worthy the honourable relation in which it stands. There are few historical works of modern times with which a judicious man would less desire to have his productions brought into comparison, and it is, therefore, no mean praise to say that our author's *Continuation*, is worthy of the work to which it forms a supplement. As remarked in our former notice, 'His volume is a worthy successor to the labours of the immortal Mill. The mantle of that philosophical historian has fallen upon a congenial mind. His style is lucid and convincing, free from all meretricious ornament,—yet by no means deficient in power.' The present volume is occupied with the period which intervened between the renewal of the East India Company's charter in 1813, and the close of the administration of the Marquis of Hastings in 1823. The events which it records are of deep and permanent value, and the views advocated are, for the most part, of a large and healthful order. To some of the opinions advanced we are compelled to take exception, and we regret to name amongst these, a charge of schism and sectarian zeal, advanced on page 575, against those Christian missionaries, who sought to benefit their countrymen in India, by reclaiming them from the immorality and heathenism by which they were surrounded. If such labours be open to such a charge, may we be liable to it in a tenfold degree. We respectfully submit to Professor Wilson the propriety of modifying this paragraph in the event—by no means improbable—of a second edition of his work.

History of the Reformation of the Sixteenth Century. Vol. I. 12mo. By J. H. Merle D'Aubigné, D.D. Translated by H. White, Edinburgh: Oliver and Boyd.

WE are glad to find that Messrs. Oliver and Boyd have acted so promptly in accordance with the views expressed (page 667) in our notice of the *continuation* of M. D.'Aubigné's work. The volume before us has come to hand since that article was in type, and the edition of which it forms part cannot fail to supersede all others. It is published under the immediate revision of the author, and contains several additions of which the admirers of his History would not willingly be deprived. Whatever, therefore, may be done by the purchasers of other editions of the first three volumes, it is quite clear, that no man of common sense will henceforth buy any other than the edition before us. It were sheer folly to do otherwise, the voluntary preference of an inferior article, when the superior one is equally accessible. The volume is printed in a superior style, and the whole work, including the four volumes published, is announced at the low price of fourteen shillings. We heartily commend this edition to our readers, and advise each of them immediately to possess himself of it.

---

1. *The Life and Pontificate of Leo the Tenth.* By William Roscoe. Vol. II. London: David Bogue.
2. *The Literary History of the Middle Ages: comprehending an account of the state of Learning, from the close of the reign of Augustus, to its revival in the Fifteenth Century.* By the Rev. Joseph Berington. London: David Bogue.

THE first of these volumes completes Mr. Bogue's edition of 'The Life and Pontificate of Leo the Tenth,' and reflects great credit on the enterprise and taste of the publisher. We regret the contemporaneous appearance of two editions of the same work, as involving in considerable uncertainty the profit of the enterprise, and shall be glad to find that there is a remunerative demand for each.

Mr. Berington's *Literary History of the Middle Ages* is not so well known as it deserves. It was originally published in 1814, and, as Mr. Hazlitt justly remarks, 'has been on all hands admitted to be the best account extant, of the important subject to which it refers.' The author was a catholic priest, educated at St. Omer, who having officiated, for some years, in France, as a minister of the Catholic church, returned to England, in the latter part of the last century, and devoted himself to literature. His classical scholarship, like most of the men of his day, exceeded his acquaintance with our national literature, and gave, in consequence, a tinge of ancient times and of foreign associations to his views. It was, however, extensive and liberal, and the work, now happily reprinted in an elegant and cheap form, is therefore adapted to enlarge and improve the mind, by shedding on it the accumulated lights of many generations.

We hope *The European Library* will receive that support which will enable and encourage its projector to carry out his original design of forming 'a complete collection of standard works, in all branches of literature, English, and foreign.'

The Grievances of the Working Classes; and the Pauperism and Crime of Glasgow; with their Causes, Extent and Remedies. By J. Smith, M.A. Glasgow: Alexander Smith.

THIS is an admirable little volume, the wide circulation of which we shall be glad to promote. It is conceived in the best possible spirit, and is executed with skill and diligence. It beautifully illustrates that 'deference to humble life,' which the author notes as 'one of the chief excellencies of our modern literature,' and sets an example which the philanthropists of other towns will do well to imitate. Much time must have been devoted by Mr. Smith to his adopted work, and we trust that he will have the highest and purest reward which a benevolent mind can receive, in the alleviation of human sorrows, and the increase of its virtue and happiness.

Historical View of the Literature of the South of Europe. By J. C. L. Simonde De Sismondi. Translated from the original, with Notes, and a Life of the Author, by Thomas Roscoe. Second edition, including all the Notes from the last Paris edition. Two vols. London: Henry G. Bohn.

THESE volumes belong to '*Bohn's Standard Library,*' and form a perfect marvel in book-making. They contain upwards of twelve hundred pages, are printed in a handsome style, and are published at the incredibly low price of seven shillings. Of the work itself we need say little. It has a European reputation, and is worthy of its celebrity. Hitherto it has been inaccessible to the mass of our countrymen, but it is now within the reach of all who are likely to feel interested in the researches it prosecutes. It had its origin in a course of lectures, which the author delivered in Geneva, his native city, and which he afterwards revised, and published in Paris in 1813. Its influence was powerful throughout the literary circles of the Continent, where it greatly contributed to the study of national literature, and secured for its author a vast accession to his popularity. Italy occupies, of course, the larger portion of the work, and we strongly recommend its attentive perusal, especially to the better educated portions of our young men. Such works are admirably suited to enlarge the mind, to purify the taste, and to give to the literary aspirations of the young a fresh and healthful tone.

The Modern Orator, being a collection of celebrated Speeches of the most distinguished Orators of the united Kingdom. Edmund Burke. Parts, I.—III. London: Aylott and Jones.

The Modern Orator, we are glad to report, proceeds satisfactorily. Sheridan, Chatham, and Erskine, have already been popularised through its medium, and Edmund Burke, one of the most profound and splendid of those geniuses which adorned our parliamentary history at the close of the last century, is now introduced. The speeches are introduced by a brief sketch of Mr. Burke's political career, and are illustrated by notes explanatory of the circumstances under which they were delivered, and of the allusions they supply. We retain the opinion already expressed, that, *The Modern Orator*, is one of the best and most useful publications of the day, and repeat our strong recommendation of it to all classes of intelligent Englishmen.

The Morals of Popular Elections. By Ebenezer Morley. 24mo. Jackson and Walford. 1846.

A SEASONABLE pamphlet at all times, and one which we should be glad to see distributed, as a cheap tract, among all classes of our people, in the prospect of a general election.

The Sabbath-Day Book; or Scriptural Meditations for Every Lord's Day in the Year. By J. Leifchild, D.D. London: Religious Tract Society.

This volume has been prepared with a special design for 'the benefit of those whose circumstances compel them to spend the whole, or a portion of the Lord's-day in their own abode.' The subjects furnish great variety, and are of a devotional, experimental, and practical character. An air of catholicity,—a perfect freedom from sectarian peculiarities, pervades the volume, which is distinguished throughout by a forcible style, sound divinity, experimental piety, and most cogent and faithful appeals. On a Sabbath afternoon, it will be estimated by many as invaluable.

British Female Biography, being Select Memoirs of Pious Ladies, in Various Ranks of Public and Private Life; including Queens, Princesses, Martyrs, Scholars, Instructors, Poetesses, Philanthropists, and *Ministers' Wives.* By the Rev. Thomas Timpson. London: Aylott and Jones.

Mr. Timpson has done good service to the young, by rendering so large a portion of British Female Biography accessible to them. His work is the result of industrious perseverance. It contains fifty abbreviated memoirs, within the small compass of less than four hundred pagas, and well deserves to be extensively circulated.

A Minister's Meditations: Principally designed as a Help for the tried followers of the Lamb. By William Burd. London Houlston and Stoneman.

A pocket volume of about one hundred pages, containing homely and devout observations on Spiritual Topics, addressed by an afflicted and faithful minister, to various classes of characters in his congregation. He divides his hearers into the unconverted, the babe, the young man, and the old disciple in Christ; and the addresses to each class, are appropriate, faithful, and adapted for usefulness.

The Pastor's Office, and People's Duty: A discourse delivered in the Independent Chapel, Atherstone, on occasion of the death of the Rev. R. M. Miller, &c. By John Sibree. London: Ward, 1845.

A funeral Sermon, from Heb. xiii. 7, 8, with a Biographical sketch of the laborious and faithful minister of Christ, at whose death it was preached; and an estimate of his character as a man, Christian, minister, preacher, non-conformist, and author. To it is appended a brief history of the rise and progress of the Independent Dissenters at Atherstone. The whole forms a pleasing memorial, which cannot fail to be valuable to those interested in the locality and circumstances to which it relates.

A Family History of Christ's Universal Church. By the Rev. Henry Stebbing, D. D. Virtue, London.

We rejoice that persons of all classes, are increasingly anxious to become acquainted with the events in the history of the Church of Christ, which followed the age of the Apostles. Many of the most momentous controversies of the day can be decided by this knowledge. In Mr. Stebbing's History copious illustrations are given from the writings of the early defenders of the Gospel, the general progress of the Church is traced, and the labours and struggles of those holy men are described, whose characters are considered by him as affording the best demonstration of the power of the Christian faith. There is too high an estimate in some instances entertained of the value of many of those heterogeneous materials, which the muddy stream of ecclesiastical history has brought down to us, and too ready a credit given to the reported signs and wonders of the martyr age. Nor do we concur with Mr. Stebbing in our view of many events, to which he refers with satisfaction, or believe that the splendour and pomp which followed the professed conversion of Constantine, occasioned a deeper sense of spiritual life!

Surely it was becoming that the historian for Christian families, should leave on record his protest against that act, by which an unconverted monarch, according to Mr. Stebbing's opinion, became high priest and sovereign ruler in the spiritual church of God. We regret that no such protest is recorded. With much that is valuable and excellent, alike in the spirit of Catholic charity and in adherence to principles known as Protestant, the author's volume presents in the judgments and sentiments which it publishes, numerous proofs of having been prepared by a member of our national religious establishment.

Five parts constitute this first volume, which carries on the narrative to the age of Constantine, and may be considered complete in itself. Mr. Stebbing proposes, at his leisure, to complete the history to the period of the Reformation. We shall be glad to observe his future progress, and congratulate him on having presented to a large class of readers an instructive and useful book.

Immanuel. Lectures with notes, on the Divinity of the Son of God, and on Socinianism. By Robert Grace. London: Dyer.

Mr. Grace is the successor in the pastoral office at Battle, Sussex, of Mr. Vidler, to whom Andrew Fuller wrote his letters on Universalism. The sentiments so powerfully attacked by Mr. Fuller, have not become extinct in that locality, and during the last summer our author delivered to his people a course of lectures, on the subject announced in his title-page. His book consists of a compilation of the spiritual arguments for the Deity of Christ, and while the im and desire of the writer are to be commended, it cannot be ronounced otherwise than creditable to his industry and judgment. Ve submit to him, that in a second edition, it might be improved y the division of sentences, many clauses of which are strung togeher by the use of copulative conjunctions; by condensing rather than y expanding, and in some instances, overcrowding his argument; nd by the omission of the various topics which are introduced into is notes. These serve in several instances to divert the attention, nd bewilder the mind of the reader, rather than to elucidate the ubject. In places where opinions unhappily prevail which are erogatory to the honour of the Redeemer, Mr. Grace's compenium cannot fail to be highly serviceable.

Abstract Principles of Revealed Religion. By Henry Drummond, Esq. London: Murray, 1845.

THE substance of this octavo volume, is contained in its preface of ix pages. That preface tells us, there is but one church; as circumcision defined the Jews, so does baptism define the Christians. This church has an organisation as fixed and definite as a human ody, consisting of the bishop and his assistant ministers, nd the apostles and prophets over the dioceses, that withut priesthood there can be no sacraments, and without sacraments o spiritual life; that all the parts of worship, forms of buildings, ites, furniture, vestments, hours of celebration are definite, and the ct which constitutes Christian worship, is literally eating and rinking in the Lord's supper, the body and blood of Christ. These n the main are the abstract principles of Mr. Drummond's religion, nd any of our readers who desire further explanation of them, are eferred to his three hundred and fifty pages.

On National Education; with Remarks on Education in General By Colonel J. K. Jackson. pp. 44 Second Edition. Bailliere, Regent-street, 1845.

A PAMPHLET on a very important subject, which it treats in a superior style. The author is a man of cleverness—but we cannot approve all his positions—and utterly reject his doctrine of '*compulsory universal education.*' We maintain that it is condemned, while he asserts that it is demanded, by 'every principle of sound policy, every dictum of common sense, every sentiment of patriotism, every feeling of affection towards our children, and of humanity to the whole human race.'

The Character and Influence of Satan. By James Hall Wilson, Birmingham. pp. 84. Aylott and Jones. 1845.

WE quite agree with Mr. Wilson that the doctrine of Satanic influence appears to be overlooked by the great bulk of professing Christians, and that it is more than time that they took up the subject If the doctrine be true, it must be worthy of the profoundest investigation, and have practical bearings of immense importance. Any wise effort to vindicate and apply it, deserves well of the church of God. Our Author has brought together a considerable number of sensible observations to illustrate the developement of Satan's character and influence in the cases of temptation recorded in the scriptures; and the designations which they apply to him. Mr. Wilson is not one of those who explain away the doctrine he undertakes to discuss: on the contrary, he sometimes carries his principles further than we should feel disposed to do. Yet if wrong here, his error is in the right direction, and we gladly welcome his intelligent, though brief, remarks on a great truth, as well calculated to check, in some measure, what we cannot but regard as a dangerous tendency of the times.

Theological Study; and the Spirit in which it ought to be pursued. The Lecture delivered at the opening of the United Secession Hall, Session 1845. By John Eadie, L.L.D., Professor of Biblical Literature to the United Secession Church. pp. 31. Edinburgh: William Oliphant and Sons. 1845.

THIS is an excellent address. Its sentiments and tone are of the right kind. After some general remarks on the exposition of Scripture as the 'great business' of the Christian Minister, Dr. Eadie proceeds to impress upon his students 'the necessity of pursuing theological study in a religious spirit, a spirit of prayerful dependence on the enlightening and sustaining influence of the Holy Ghost,' which he does in a manner eminently adapted to secure his object. We have a strong conviction of the need which exists for such a treatment of the subject, and should esteem it a sign of most blessed promise to the churches of Christ, if all who have the preparation of holy men for the work of the ministry possessed as high an estimate of the spiritual principle as Dr. Eadie, and were as able and anxious to promote it in those committed to their care. Amid the increased zeal for intellectual culture, it is of the first importance that the heart should be kept right with God. Nothing can compensate for the want of eminent godliness in those who have to save souls; learning and accomplishments, without it, will only be like the earthly furniture of a temple from which the glory has departed.

The Love of Liberty; a Text-Book for all classes of Reformers. pp. 40. Effingham Wilson. 1844.

A SELECTION of wise and pungent maxims, 'from the best authors, ancient and modern, in behalf of the great principles of civil and religious liberty.'

A Narrative of a Visit to the Mauritius and South Africa. By James Backhouse. Illustrated by two Maps, sixteen Etchings, and twenty-eight Wood cuts. pp. 648. London: C. Gilpin.

The author of this large and well-filled volume, needs no introduction to our readers. We had occasion to speak favourably of the records of his visit to Tasmania and Australia. He has been since removed from this world, having been suddenly summoned away while preparing to engage in a fresh work of love and faith. None, acquainted with his character and labours, can hesitate as to his present state.

The object of the visit to the Mauritius and to South Africa, was, like that of the preceding one, 'purely the discharge of a religious duty,' although, in passing along, attention was alive to a variety of secondary objects, which appeared worthy of notice.' All the towns within the colonies, and all the missionary stations of South Africa were visited.

We can assure our readers that Mr. Backhouse's journal has provided a rich variety of entertainment and instruction. In reading his books, there is no ground for distrust or doubt. The mind may repose implicit confidence in his representations. It is not every one that is competent even to state facts and describe scenes; it is not every one that will take the trouble to ascertain the truth respecting them. Mr. Backhouse was a careful observer, and a faithful recorder. He had a good judgment, and a scrupulous conscience. His description of persons and things we have reason to know to be wonderfully accurate. He is one of the few travellers who do not extenuate or exaggerate.

We most cordially sympathise with the sentiments expressed in the concluding sentence of the Introduction—'the writer trusts, that the perusal of this volume will increase the feeling of Christian interest for all classes of the inhabitants of the countries described; and he especially hopes, that it may promote the feeling of sympathy for the devoted individuals who are labouring amidst many privations, to spread the Redeemer's kingdom.' This hope can scarcely fail of fulfilment to the extent to which the volume is read and pondered.

The Zoology of the British Poets, corrected by the Writings of Modern Naturalists. By Robert Hasill Newell, B.D. pp. 160. Longman, and Co. 1845.

We do not care so much for the mistakes of poets as Mr. Newell appears to do. They are allowed large licence; it is enough for them that popular opinion sustains their figures and allusions. The fable of the Phœnix is constantly employed for the purpose of illustration. At the same time, Mr. Newell has made a very interesting book. A good deal of pleasant instruction on some well-known Insects, Birds, Reptiles, and Mammalia, is connected with many beautiful extracts from eminent poets.

Letters on the Unhealthy Condition of the Lower Class of Dwellings, especially in Large Towns. By the Rev. Charles Girdlestone, A.M., Rector of Alderley, Cheshire. pp. 92. Longman. 1845.

These letters contain the pith of several official documents bearing on the subject discussed. They furnish many distressing facts which ought to be universally known, and many practical suggestions that might, and should, be vigorously adopted.

History of the Reformation in Switzerland. By Abraham Ruchat, Minister of the Gospel, and Professor of Belles Lettres, in the Academy of Lausanne. Abridged from the French by the Rev. J. Collinson, M.A., Rector of Boldon, and Hon. Canon of Durham Cathedral. pp. 328. W. E. Painter. 1845.

Ruchat needs no introduction to those conversant with the history of the Reformation. His work is marked by learning and fidelity, and has maintained its position for upwards of a hundred years.

Mr. Collinson has abridged it, and added the Essay on the Life and Writings of Ruchat annexed to his works in the edition published at Nyon, Switzerland, in 1838.

A Manual, for the Religious and Moral Instruction of Young Children in the Nursery and Infant School. By Samuel Wilderspin, and T. J. Farrington. pp. 112. Hamilton, Adams, & Co. 1845.

This manual consists of 'Remarks on the Religious Instruction of Children,' thirty-five 'Hymns,' forty 'Moral Songs,' eleven 'Practical Religious Lessons,' and forty 'Tunes.' It is unnecessary to say that the sentiments are evangelical, and the tendency of all is highly moral. We doubt, however, whether the style of the prose is well adapted to convey instruction to very young minds, and also whether it is wise to accustom them to the doggrel rhymes that frequently occur in the hymns and songs. The best poetry may be as simple as the worst, and children are quite as able to understand it.

The Words of a Believer. By the Abbé De La Mennais. Translated from the French by Edward Smith Pryce, A.B. pp. 119. Aylott and Jones, 1845.

This work has had a very large sale on the continent, and has been once published in England. The sentiments are generally sound, sometimes rather strong, and the mode of expression and illustration occasionally most apt and happy. But the highly figurative character of a considerable portion of its matter will, we imagine, prevent its being as popular as it would otherwise be.

he Scriptural Argument against Apostolical Succession. In Four Lectures. By Thomas Stratten. pp. 244. Snow, 1845.

'HIS is not the first time that Mr. Stratten has engaged in eccle-iastical controversy. The works he published some years ago on 'ithes, and the Priesthood, proved his possession of a calm and agacious mind, and excited expectations of no common order in eference to the volume before us. Those expectations have been ully realized. Mr. Stratten has succeeded in doing a difficult thing; ie has invested an old subject with fresh interest. Regarding our-elves as pretty well acquainted with the theme he handles, we have een struck with the novelty with which he treats some portions of t. The first lecture is, in our judgment, perfectly conclusive against he claim of a regular succession. We have never seen, within the ame compass, a more thorough demonstration of its rottenness. It s decidedly the best in the book. The second lecture points out in clear and comprehensive manner the fabulousness of Peter's supre-naoy, displaying the contrast between his case and that of Aaron. The third lecture reduces the permanent orders of the Christian Ministry to their scriptural standard—their dual number. The fourth ecture expounds the doctrine of 'laying on of hands,' traces its scriptural history, and advocates a more frequent use of the rite on various occasions. We do not remember to have seen this subject so plainly and fully laid open before, and while we would not be un-lerstood as approving of all Mr. Stratten's recommendations, we hink that Christian churches would do well to consider his remarks.

The chief fault we find with Mr. Stratten relates to the diffusiveness, which occasionally marks his style. He does not always know when o say 'this thought is done,' and weakens the impression by seeking strengthen it. There are several descriptions in his volume which, however good in themselves, are not so good in a treatise of this kind. They interrupt the argument, and stand in the way of the author's ultimate design. But the book is a good one, and we sin-cerely and warmly recommend its perusal to our readers.

The Romish and Prelatical Rite of Confirmation Examined. By Thomas Smyth, D.D. With an Appendix, on the Duty of Requiring a Public Profession of Religion. pp. 198. Edinburgh: W. P. Kennedy. London: Hamilton, Adams, & Co. 1845.

AN able and a learned refutation of the pretensions of churchmen on the subject discussed.

Literary Intelligence.

In the Press.

Memoirs of the Life and Ministry, including Select Literary Remains of the late Rev. Christmas Evans. By D. Rhys Stephen.

Just published.

The Pictorial Gallery of Arts. Charles Knight and Co., Part 16.

Remarks upon Medical Organization and Reform (Foreign and English.) By Edwin Lee. With an Appendix.

The Life and Letters of St. Paul during his second and third Apostolical Journeys. Arranged for use in the Collegiate Schools, Liverpool.

The Literary History of the Middle Ages. Comprehending an Account of the state of Learning from the Close of the Reign of Augustus to its Revival, in the Fifteenth Century. By the Rev. Joseph Berington.

Vital Christianity, Essays and Discourses on the Religion of Man and the Religion of God. By Alexander Vinet, D.D., Professor of Theology in Lausanne, Switzerland. Translated, with an Introduction, by Robert Turnbull.

Clark's Foreign Theological Library. Vol. 2. Hengstenberg's Commentary on the Psalms. Vol. 2.

The History of England, during the Thirty Years Peace, 1815 to 1845. Part 3rd. 1st. half.

Political Dictionary; forming a Work of Universal Reference, both constitutional and legal, and embracing the terms of Civic Administration, of Political Economy and Social Relations, and of all the more important Statistical departments of Finance and Commerce. Part 12. Second half.

Memoir of the Rev. Samuel Dyer, sixteen years missionary to the Chinese. By Evan Davies, Author of China, and her Spiritual Claims.

Life in Christ. Four Discourses upon the Scripture Doctrine that Immortality is the peculiar privilege of the Regenerate. Being the substance of Lectures delivered at Hereford, in the year 1845. By Edward White.

Philip and Theodore, or a Dialogue on the Evangelical Alliance.

Address of the Literary Association of the Friends of Poland, to the People of Great Britain and Ireland.

Hogg's Weekly Instructor. Part 14.

Nelson's British Library of Tracts for the People. Part I.

A Letter to the Dissenters of Bristol on the Anti-state Church Question By one of themselves.

The People's Dictionary of the Bible. Part 9.

The Voluntary, and Anti-state Churchman. New Series. No. 5.

Gesenius's Hebrew and Chaldee Lexicon to the Old Testament Scriptures. Translated, with Additions and Corrections, from the Author's Thesaurus, and other works. By Samuel Prideaux Tregelles.

Gesenius's Hebrew Grammar. From the fourteenth German Edition. Enlarged and Improved by E. Rodeger, Ph. D., D.D., Professor of Oriental Literature in the University of Halle. Translated by Benjamin Davies, Dr. in Philosophy of the University of Leipzic. With a Hebrew Reading Book, prepared by the Translator.

The History of British India, from 1805 to 1835. By Horace Hayman Wilson, M.A., F.R.S. Vol. 2nd.

Glendearg Cottage. A Tale, concerning Church Principles. By Miss Christmas. With a Preface, by the Rev. Henry Christmas, M.A., etc. etc.

On the Speculative Difficulties of Professing Christians.

The Elevation of the People, Moral, Instructional, and Social. By the tev. Thomas Milner, M.A.

The Mission of the German Catholics. By G. G. Gervinus, Professor of listory in the University of Heidelberg. Translated from the German.

Letters on Puritanism and Nonconformity. By Sir John Bickerton Villiams, Knt., LL.D. F.S.A. The second Series.

Edward, the Black Prince. A Tragedy. By Sir Coutts Lindsay, Bart., uthor of 'Alfred.'

A Commentary on the Book of Leviticus, Expository and Practical, with 'ritical Notes. By the Rev. Andrew A. Bonar, Author of 'Memoirs of tev. Robert McCheyne,' 'Narrative of a Mission of Inquiry to the Jews,' tc. etc.

The Supremacy of the Scriptures the Divine Rule of Religion. By the tev. James Davies. With a Recommendatory Letter. By the Rev. J. 'ye Smith, D.D.

Bells and Pomegranates. No. 8, and last. Luria, and a Soul's Tragedy. 3y Robert Browning, Author of 'Paracelsus.'

The Jesuits. By Rev. W. Overbury.

Observations on the Books of Genesis and Exodus, and Sermons. By the ate Robert Forsyth, Esq. To which is prefixed, a Memoir of the Author.

A Year and a Day in the East, or Wanderings over Land and Sea. By Ars. Eliot Montaban.

A Guide to the Anglo-Saxon Tongue. A Grammar, after Erasmus Rask. Extracts in Prose and Verse, with Notes, etc., for the Use of Learners, and n Appendix. By Edward Johnstone Vernon, B.A., Magdalene Hall.

Lectures on the Pilgrim's Progress, and on the Life and Times of John Bunyan. By the Rev. George Cheever, D.D. Collins's edition.

An Introduction to the Critical Study and Knowledge of the Holy Scripures. By Thomas Hartwell Horne, B.D. Ninth Edition, Corrected and Enlarged. Five volumes.

Sermons Preached at St. Paul's Cathedral, the Foundling Hospital, and several Churches in London; together with others addressed to a Country Congregation. By the late Rev. Sydney Smith. 8vo.

Pen and Ink Sketches of Poets, Preachers, and Politicians.

The Modern British Plutarch; or Lives of Men distinguished in the recent history of our country for their talents, virtues, or achievements. By W. C. Taylor, LL.D.

The Punjaub; being a Brief Account of the Country of the Sikhs; its extent, history, commerce, productions, government, manufactures, etc. By Lieut-Colonel Steinbach.

The Eternal; or the Attributes of Jehovah, as 'the God of our Fathers,' contemplated in Christ and Creation. By Robert Philip.

The English Hexapla, consisting of the six important Vernacular English Translations. Part IX.

Pericles. A Tale of Athens in the eighty-third Olympiad. By the Author of 'a Brief Sketch of Greek Philosophy. 2 vols.

The Grievances of the Working Classes; and the Pauperism and Crime of Glasgow; with their Causes, Extent, and Remedies. By J. Smith, M.A.

The Scripture Doctrine of Future Punishment; an Argument, in two parts. Second Edition. By the Rev. H. H. Dobney.

Select Works of the Rev. and learned David Clarkson, B.D. Edited for the Wycliffe Society. By the Rev. Basil H. Cooper, B.A. With Historical Notices of the Life and Writings of the Author. By the Rev. John Blackburn.

INDEX.

VOL. XIX.—NEW SERIES.

END OF VOL. XIX.

London: Printed by G. H. Ward, & Co., 16, Bear Alley, Farringdon Street.

CPSIA information can be obtained
at www.ICGtesting.com
Printed in the USA
BVHW060552280819
556854BV00001B/85/P

9 780371 029305